KT-196-853

High Minds

Simon Heffer was born in 1960. He read English at Cambridge and took a PhD in modern history at that University. His previous books include: *Moral Desperado: A Life of Thomas Carlyle*, *Like the Roman: The Life of Enoch Powell*, *Nor Shall My Sword: The Reinvention of England*, *Vaughan Williams*, *Strictly English* and *A Short History of Power*. In a career of nearly thirty years in Fleet Street, he has written columns for and held senior positions on the *Daily Mail*, the *Daily Telegraph* and the *Spectator*.

Praise for *High Minds*

'*High Minds* is worthy to the task: serious, scholarly, grand and determined . . . an excellent guide to the aesthetics of the age.'
New Statesman

'*High Minds* is partly social history, partly a history of ideas. It is the personalities involved that contribute such liveliness to this assured and magisterial narrative.'
Sunday Telegraph

'A book Heffer's heroes would have loved – and perhaps there no higher compliment than that.'
Sunday Times

000000744335

ALSO BY SIMON HEFFER

High Minds

The Victorians and the Birth of Modern Britain

SIMON HEFFER

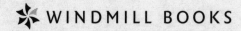 WINDMILL BOOKS

Published by Windmill Books 2014

2 4 6 8 10 9 7 5 3 1

Copyright © Simon Heffer 2013

Simon Heffer has asserted his right under the Copyright, Designs and
Patents Act, 1988, to be identified as the author of this work.

This book is sold subject to the condition that it shall not, by way of trade
or otherwise, be lent, resold, hired out, or otherwise circulated without
the publisher's prior consent in any form of binding or cover other than
that in which it is published and without a similar condition, including
this condition, being imposed on the subsequent purchaser.

First published in Great Britain in 2013 by Random House Books

Windmill Books
The Random House Group Limited
20 Vauxhall Bridge Road, London SW1V 2SA

Addresses for companies within The Random House Group Limited can be
found at: www.randomhouse.co.uk/offices.htm

The Random House Group Limited Reg. No. 954009

www.randomhouse.co.uk

A CIP catalogue record for this book
is available from the British Library

ISBN 9780099558477

The Random House Group Limited supports the Forest Stewardship
Council® (FSC®), the leading international forest-certification organisation.
Our books carrying the FSC label are printed on FSC®-certified paper.
FSC is the only forest-certification scheme supported by the leading
environmental organisations, including Greenpeace. Our paper procurement
policy can be found at:
www.randomhouse.co.uk/environment

Typeset in Dante MT by Palimpsest Book Production Ltd,
Falkirk, Stirlingshire
Printed and bound by CPI Group (UK) Ltd, Croydon, CR0 4YY

To Mark Jones, in admiration and with gratitude

DUDLEY LIBRARIES	
000000744335	
Askews & Holts	26-Jan-2015
	£12.99
CRA	

Estote ergo vos perfecti!

> Matthew 5:48, quoted from the Vulgate
> by Matthew Arnold, *Culture and Anarchy*

Fired with the great spirit of the nineteenth century – at least with that one which is vulgarly considered its especial glory – he resolved to make haste to be rich.

> Charles Kingsley, *Alton Locke* (p. 112)

But is it indeed an error to suppose mankind capable of great improvement? And is it really a mark of wisdom to deride all grand schemes of human amelioration as visionary?

> J. S. Mill, speech on perfectibility, 2 May 1828

Do you mean to build as Christians or as infidels?

> John Ruskin, *The Crown of Wild Olive* (p. 88)

In a progressive country change is constant: and the great question is not whether you should resist change which is inevitable, but whether that change should be carried out in deference to the manners, the customs, the laws, and the traditions of a people, or whether it should be carried out in deference to abstract principles, and arbitrary and general doctrines. The one is a national system; the other, to give it an epithet, a noble epithet – which it may perhaps deserve – is a philosophic system.

> Benjamin Disraeli, speech at Edinburgh, November 1867

This question is no longer a religious question, it has become a political one. It is indeed the question of questions; it has become paramount to every other question that has been brought before us. From the moment that you intrust the masses with power their education becomes an absolute necessity.

Robert Lowe, speech on the Third Reading
of the Reform Bill, House of Commons, 15 July 1867

Quand on fait des omelettes il faut croquer des oeufs.
Samuel Butler, unused epigraph for *The Way of All Flesh*

And not by eastern windows only,
When daylight comes, comes in the light;
In front the sun climbs slow, how slowly,
But westward, look, the land is bright.
Arthur Hugh Clough, 'Say Not, the Struggle Naught Availeth'

CONTENTS

ACKNOWLEDGEMENTS

Extracts from the papers of Prince Albert, the Prince Consort, in the Royal Archives have been used by gracious permission of Her Majesty the Queen. I am also indebted to Miss Pamela Clark of the Royal Archives, and her colleagues, for their help. Dr Owen Walton was also extremely helpful in pointing me to certain key areas of research. I am grateful to the staff of the British Library for access to a number of manuscript collections there, notably the papers of W. E. Gladstone, Sir Robert Peel and Florence Nightingale, among many others. Mr Frank Bowles and Mr John Wells in the Manuscript Department of the Cambridge University Library also gave great assistance, as did other of their colleagues. I am particularly grateful to Matheson and Co for permission to quote matter relating to Sir James Fitzjames Stephen from the Parkes papers in the Cambridge University Library. Reproductions of paintings by Samuel Butler, and quotations from the Samuel Butler Collection, appear by kind permission of the Master and Fellows of St John's College, Cambridge. I should particularly like to thank Mrs Kathryn McKee and Miss Rebecca Watts for their help in using the Collections at St John's. Royal Holloway, University of London, gave me access to the papers of Thomas Holloway and to material concerning the foundation of Bedford College, and I am grateful to the college and to Vicky Holmes for the help she gave me with those collections. I must thank Imperial College, University of London, for access to the archive of the 1851 Commission, and to Angela Kenny for facilitating it. Jacky Cowdrey guided me through the archives of the Royal Albert Hall, for which I thank her. Sue Sturrock helped me with an enquiry at the Royal College of Music, and I am also most grateful to Miss Laura Ponsonby for allowing me to see the archive of Sir C. Hubert H. Parry, and for her hospitality when I visited it.

Modern authors owe a considerable debt to those who have ensured that many primary sources are now available online. Millbank Systems, who have made more than 200 years of Hansard available, merit my particular gratitude.

Mrs Pat Ventre and Mr Gavin Fuller helped find some material for me, for which I thank them. I am also grateful to Mr Murdoch MacLennan, Chief Executive of Telegraph Media Group, for granting me the sabbatical from my duties on that newspaper during which I began the research for this book, and to the Master and Fellows of Corpus Christi College, Cambridge, for allowing me to lodge with them for the year in which that work started.

Dr Frank Prochaska gave me much useful advice and pointed me towards much useful material about the mid-nineteenth century. The Revd Mark Jones, the Revd John Witheridge and Dr Karina Urbach all did me the inestimable service of reading the manuscript, for which I thank them profusely. I am grateful to Mr Fergus Shanahan for reading the proofs at a late stage.

I was guided towards returning to the subject of the Victorians by my agent, Georgina Capel, whose support throughout this process, from conception to birth, has been magnificent. I am deeply grateful to my publisher at Random House, Nigel Wilcockson, not just for his tolerance and forbearance during the production of this book, and his insightful suggestions about its structure, but also for his intelligence and expertise on its subject matter which made my job as author far easier than it might otherwise have been. The book was superbly copy-edited by Mary Chamberlain and indexed by Kate Faulkner.

My wife, Diana, read the proofs at a late stage and applied an invaluable, and sharp, pair of eyes as well as a keen intelligence to the book. But my real and greatest debt is to her for her constant support, understanding and companionship throughout the three years this book was in the making. My sons, Fred and Johnnie, also played their part, and I thank them all profoundly for their considerable roles in making this book possible.

Simon Heffer
Great Leighs
3 June 2013

PREFACE

In the four decades between the rise of political consciousness that manifested itself in Chartism, and the return of William Ewart Gladstone to Downing Street in 1880 after his Midlothian Campaign, when he sought to prove the depravity of Lord Beaconsfield's administration by illustrating its failings in foreign policy, British life changed almost beyond recognition. Although poverty, disease, ignorance, squalor and injustice were far from eliminated, they were beaten back more in those forty or so years than at any previous time in the history of Britain. This was despite, and because of, a population growing faster than at any previous time in the country's history. A nation that might have been overwhelmed by industrial change, rapid expansion and social upheaval instead saw the challenges of modernisation and embraced them.

This book is partly the social history, partly the intellectual history, and partly the political history of those years. It is not strictly a linear account of events between 1838 and 1880: it takes the great themes of that period and seeks to use them as the illustration of a spirit, or cast of mind, that transformed a wealthy country of widespread inhumanity, primitiveness and barbarism into one containing the germs, and in some measure the evidence, of widespread civilisation and democracy. A sense of earnest, disinterested moral purpose distinguished many politicians, intellectuals and citizens of mid-nineteenth-century Britain, and drove them to seek to improve the condition of the whole of society. A constant theme in the writings of one of the period's greatest intellectuals, Matthew Arnold, and a notion shared by many educated people of the time, pervades this book. It is that even if a state of human perfection was unattainable, its pursuit was perhaps the noblest enterprise a

Christian soul (and, in some cases, non-Christian ones) could undertake. If that pursuit did not finish at the goal, it at least made everything better.

The mid-nineteenth century was an era of declining religious observance, but one in which religion still underpinned almost all the great institutions of the nation, dominated education and coloured intellectual discourse. It was one of rigid class distinctions, through which those with talent and good fortune could move if they applied themselves to the task of doing so: and eventually the State extended to many men in the working class the privileges of democracy. It was an era that prized education, but which took a lamentably long time to ensure that most people in England and Wales received one – Scotland was far ahead in that respect – and to see that the teaching offered by the great public and grammar schools was equal to the demands of a modern industrial nation. It encouraged private philanthropy, yet laid the first foundations of a welfare state. It looked fervently to the future, but its vernacular architecture was of the feudal, medieval past. Landed and rich families controlled its ruling class, yet reformed great institutions such as the Army and the Civil Service to create promotion by merit. It was a society that systematically rejected the notion of political, legal and property rights for women, and deplored their attempts to have an education, yet had a Queen as head of state who from time to time behaved in an autocratic manner far from the notion of the constitutional monarchy expounded at the time.

This book omits two aspects of the British experience in the nineteenth century, both of which would be books in themselves: empire and foreign affairs – though the terms were almost synonymous for much of the period – and the unrest in Ireland, save for the effect of the Potato Famine on the repeal of the Corn Laws. The new ideas it describes and discusses prevailed throughout the United Kingdom, though certain currents on which this book concentrates – such as the wave of religious doubt caused by questioning of the 39 Articles of the Church of England, and the drive to provide education to the masses – were necessarily played out in an English context, since the Scottish Kirk was a different animal and that nation had, since the seventeenth century, set an example of extending education to all. Scotland had also pioneered divorce, something on which it took England and Wales until the 1850s to catch up. In its exploration of British social, intellectual and political life the book relies heavily on the diaries, letters and speeches of the men and women who either inspired, influenced or executed change. It shows people as the main actors of the period, and not government, though government passed laws that enabled people of drive and energy to make the changes a civilised and contented society required. Three times in the decades covered by this book – 1842, 1848 and 1866–7 – political instability in Britain was so serious that it seemed to some to be threatening revolution. That it was avoided – and was, each time, less of a threat than before – was not least because of the measures enlightened government took to break the stranglehold of a narrow governing class on the country, and to find ways of engaging, economically and politically, with those who would otherwise be revolutionaries. Enlightenment came throughout the period from a cadre of intellectuals, thinkers and writers whose freedom of speech and thought slowly changed attitudes, greatly to the country's benefit.

When Queen Victoria ascended the throne in June 1837 Britain was a country of rising prosperity, with a growing empire, and a burgeoning middle class made more affluent by industrialism. However, it was also beset by terrible, and destabilising, social problems. There was little or no attempt to regulate public health. Cholera outbreaks were frequent because of the failure to treat sewage, and because no one knew cholera was a water-borne disease. Hospitals and housing for the poor were primitive and squalid. Food was unnecessarily expensive because of import tariffs, and often adulterated or diseased; and water unsafe to drink. Cities teemed with prostitutes, the girls driven to vice by the threat of starvation. Boys and men often lapsed into crime, and were punished with a savagery little diminished from medieval times.

The destitute lived in workhouses where families were broken up. Extreme poverty had been, to all intents and purposes, criminalised by the 1834 Poor Law Act. The mentally ill were still treated cruelly. Women were the property of their husbands. Only a small proportion of adult men could vote. For the minority with the suffrage, there was no secret ballot. Entry to the Civil Service and promotion for officers in the Army could, and usually had to, be bought. There was little in the way of formal local government to provide or oversee basic services, and no sense of municipal or civic pride in many of the cities expanded by the Industrial Revolution. Travel was slow and so expensive that most people never strayed more than a few miles from home. Even communication by letter (for those who could write) was erratic and expensive, until the introduction of the penny post in May 1840. With minor exceptions, in England and Wales only rich males could attend school, and only a small proportion of them went on to a university. Many poor people were illiterate and without means to improve themselves. There were scarcely any libraries, museums or art galleries to which they could gain admission. Workers in the factories that comprised Britain's manufacturing might were only just beginning to have their labour regulated: children as young as eight were working twelve-hour days. Matters were even worse in the mines, where women and girls worked in bestial conditions with men and boys to provide the coal to stoke Britain's furnaces. Taxation restricted the availability of newspapers and therefore freedom of speech, and with that the growth of opposition to the established order. Writers and commentators attacked the misgovernment of the country – what Thomas Carlyle, the age's foremost polemicist, called 'the condition of England question'. The Chartist movement, with its six-point reform plan for Britain, seemed to promise revolution if its demands were not met.

Yet industrialisation created wealth, stimulated innovation, encouraged education and, above all, pricked the consciences of those enriched by it. An intellectual elite sought to liberate minds from the doctrines of religion, and to drive movements for reform in education, housing, public health, the law and the constitution. The educated classes sought to bring a growing number of the uneducated inside the pale of a common civilisation, one rooted in an understanding of the classical world and, in a more contemporary sense, the benefits of an evolving democracy. Between the censuses of 1841 and 1881 the population of Great Britain and Ireland rose from 27 million to 35 million, despite falling by 3 million in Ireland following the great emigration after the Potato Famine. By 1880 most men had the vote, women were no longer their husbands' chattels, and school places were provided for all children. Britain was the world's leading power, and had developed a formidable and distinct contemporary culture along with its prosperity.

But the greatest transformation in those forty or so years was visible all over Britain: whole suburbs of housing, town halls, museums, concert halls, art galleries, schools, colleges, hospitals, libraries, railway stations, market halls and Gothic Revival churches spoke of a country that had with determination, and a sense of common direction, put its new-found wealth to use in improving the lives, the minds and the souls of its people. The pursuit of perfection might have been idealistic, but it did not fail to bring its own, plentiful, harvest. This book will describe this awesome transformation, and will celebrate the men and women who undertook it.

DR ARNOLD OF RUGBY

―――――◆―――――

I

A climate of prejudice about the Victorians still lingers. It began with a mild moral rebellion in the 1890s, before the old Queen was in her tomb at Frogmore. It was active until the 1960s, when the era was passing out of living memory; and those unborn at the time decided to stop wrecking the legacy of the nineteenth century. The saving of the Midland Hotel at St Pancras Station in London from demolition in 1967 signalled the change of mood. Buildings had been one of the most significant representations of Victorian attitudes and purpose, which was not least why some wished to destroy them. However, as the importance of preserving the visible symbols of an era was recognised, so a new perspective on the intellectual and psychological achievement of the Victorians became necessary. After all, without a sense of moral purpose, and moral leadership, the affluence of the few might well have been destroyed by the revolution of the masses, brought about by a sense of injustice not unlike that felt in France in the 1780s. As it was, a social movement from the 1830s to the 1870s helped manage the final trans-formation of a feudal nation into an industrial, democratic one: and it did so not least because of the sense of mission many in the upper and upper-middle classes had towards bringing light into the lives of those whom seismic social upheaval had driven towards darkness.

A prevailing theme behind change in the nineteenth century is a religious, or more specifically Christian, motivation of those who inspired, enabled and undertook it. This ethos was promoted most assiduously by the public schools, almost all of whose headmasters were divines. Many took their cue from one man: Dr Thomas Arnold, head-master of Rugby School from 1828 to 1842. Arnold was savaged by Lytton Strachey in *Eminent Victorians* for his piety, his perceived priggishness and his earnestness: that Strachey felt he had to attack a man who died only five years into Victoria's reign as part of his assault on the values of the age betrays what a towering and enduring influence Arnold was. Since Strachey, others have sought to belittle and diminish Arnold. However, in his liberal belief in the expansion of education and his quest for the moral improvement of society, his influence set the tone of the reforming classes of Victorian Britain. He helped renew the idea of a principle of duty by which more fortunate Christians strove to improve the lives of less fortunate ones. His view of life as a constant struggle between good and evil came to be shared by many Victorians, with a conviction that good must triumph.

Although his direct influence was only on his family, the boys he taught and his colleagues, his ethos came to suffuse the public-school system, and went beyond it, for the rest of the nineteenth century. One of his twentieth-century biographers, T. W. Bamford, argued that 'he is said to have reformed the public schools whereas in fact there is precious little evidence of it'.[1] Although he hardly diversified the curriculum at Rugby, he sought to teach the narrow range of subjects more imagin-atively. He also established a relationship with his assistant masters like that between university dons, and tried to alter the products of his school: which, in time, changed the products of most leading public schools.

Arnold also played a significant part in changing the climate of the age that followed him, through his high-minded moralism in the collected editions of his sermons and his writings. He was a born journalist, unafraid to disseminate his views – much, on occasion, to the annoyance of Rugby's governors. His son Matthew inherited this trait. Some he influenced may have been hypocrites, but they were inspired by Arnold's tone (if not always by his example) to make life better, nobler and less mean. He advanced godliness in a society that would gradually become more secular: but this secularisation came amid vigorous religious debate and dispute, against a backdrop of aggressive church-building – and of taking the Established Church and dissenting congregations into new communities in expanding towns all over Britain.

Arnold's example did not merely transform public schools, and the grammar schools that imitated them, but inspired others – notably Matthew, and his pupils Arthur Hugh Clough and Arthur Penrhyn Stanley – to seek to raise the moral tone of Britain and make people more Christian: and to cause them to devote themselves to improving the lives of others and the society in which they lived. This was not only about making people more godly and pious, as Dr Arnold had intended: it was about extending the intellectual and material aspects of civilisation. Only if the determination to make life better was rooted in faith, they felt, could improvement be possible. Matthew Arnold argued for the extension of civilisation most powerfully in his 1867 polemic *Culture and Anarchy*. Its superscription summed up his mood: '*Estote ergo vos perfecti!*', 'Be ye perfect!' The intense commitment by the mid-Victorians to give life a greater nobility of purpose, founded upon a sense of duty, and to pursue perfection can be traced back to Dr Arnold. Inevitably, this mood also gave rise to incidents of extreme hypocrisy – such as when Arnold's pupil Charles Vaughan resigned as headmaster of Harrow in 1859 because of his homosexual affair with a pupil: but even Vaughan went on to help found University College, Cardiff. The Arnoldian message was never entirely lost on him.

II

Stanley, in writing the life of Arnold, his recently deceased and much-loved mentor, claimed that 'it will be felt that, not so much amongst his own pupils, nor in the scene of his actual labours, as in every Public School throughout England, is to be sought the chief and enduring monument of Dr Arnold's head-mastership of Rugby.'[2] Almost a century and a half later Stefan Collini wrote that 'He [Arnold] transformed what had been a fair specimen of the debauched and riotous establishments known as public schools into the character-building, God-fearing, scholarship-winning model for the reform in the 1840s and 1850s of other schools of its type. He thereby had an incalculable influence on world history, indirectly staffing an empire, and helping to shape, perhaps to stifle, the emotional development of a governing class for several generations.'[3] These are powerful claims, and given what they imply for Victorian society, require investigation.

Arnold was an early meritocrat. His father was postmaster and customs officer for the Isle of Wight, but died in 1801, when Tom was only six. So tight was money that Tom's mother took over as postmaster to keep the family solvent. Tom was sent to Warminster School in Wiltshire: which, although not well known, was a high-achieving school academically. However, when Tom was twelve he moved to Winchester. He had shown ability, and his mother wished him to go to university: but so difficult were things financially that that required Tom to attend a school with well-funded university scholarships.

At Winchester he became an accomplished classicist. He also developed a precocious interest in history. He had a strong character and left his mark on any group of which he was a part. He had just the right combination of force of personality and intellect to be a successful headmaster. With this manner came streaks of anger, impatience and determination.

He won a scholarship to Corpus Christi College, Oxford. Here, as at school, he was bookish. He became something of a poet, a trait that would be more successfully developed by his eldest son, Matthew. He had hoped to enter the Church, but the period from his graduation as a Master of Arts at Oxford in 1817 until the mid-1820s was one of serious religious doubt for him: although he became a deacon in 1818, he struggled with the Athanasian Creed, the nature of the Trinity and aspects of the Thirty-nine Articles. This doubt was not about the existence of God, or with the nature of Christianity, but was a theological problem with the established interpretation of the tenets of Anglicanism. The Articles had defined Anglicanism after the Reformation as distinct from Roman Catholicism. They had in some respects a doctrinaire medievalism that many modern scholars, including Arnold, struggled with. The rise of Nonconformism, notably Methodism, in the eighteenth century had been largely as a reaction to the prescriptive and inflexible nature of the doctrine contained in the Articles, and this had its effect on a generation of Anglicans determined to analyse and reflect upon what they had been taught. Doubt delayed Arnold's entry to the priesthood. Instead, he became the partner of John Buckland, his sister's husband, in a private school at Laleham in Middlesex. He married in 1820, and the first of the Arnolds' eleven children (nine of whom lived to adulthood) was born the following year.

An expanding family and the low earnings of a schoolmaster caused Arnold to work on literary projects in his spare time, notably ancient history. For all the privations, he enjoyed teaching older boys and brought favoured pupils into his family circle. This would set the tone for Rugby. He sought a more lucrative appointment, and applied to become professor of modern history at the University of London; however, he was offered the headmastership of Rugby School in Warwickshire. Arnold was high-minded; but before that notion about him becomes too distracting, it should be noted that he chose Rugby not because he felt a stronger vocation to teach boys rather than men: it was because it was better paid.

His chances when he submitted his name for consideration were felt not to be high, since others had been in the field longer. He was unknown to most of the twelve trustees – noblemen and gentlemen of Warwickshire – even by name, and he had applied late. However, all his references spoke highly of his suitability and qualifications as a schoolmaster; and one, from the Reverend Edward Hawkins (who within weeks would be elected as a famously obstinate Provost of Oriel) 'predicted that, if Mr Arnold were elected to the head-mastership of Rugby, he would change the face of education all through the public schools of England.'⁴ Arnold was elected in December 1827 without even having to submit to an interview, so powerful were the recommendations in his testimonials. He had, nevertheless, felt reluctant to choose Rugby. His religious difficulties had not been entirely resolved, and he felt he would want to take holy orders to be able to administer communion in chapel. However, a way was found for him to interpret the Thirty-nine Articles that removed his problem with them: his ordination followed rapidly. By the time he arrived at the school in August 1828 he was the Reverend Mr Arnold, and his doctorate of divinity came in November.

A second cause for hesitation was that he understood the school to be a moral sink. Lytton Strachey, in his essay on Arnold, famously described the public-school system at the time as 'anarchy tempered by despotism'.⁵ Some boys Arnold could bring into line with a birch rod, and neither he nor the school governors had any qualms about his doing so. But he also wished to expel particularly recalcitrant elements, which might affect the school's reputation and finances; and, also, to remove boys who showed no aptitude for his rigorous teaching methods because of a lack of intellectual curiosity. He was encouraged in this too.

Arnold was conscious that he was assuming a prominent position in a business that had generally sunk in regard and achievement. Many schools were dens of buggery and bullying, with youths out of control.

John Bowdler, nephew of the sanitiser of Gibbon and Shakespeare and a comrade of Arnold's in various theological battles, proclaimed: 'the public schools are the very seats and nurseries of vice.'[6] Arnold himself observed that 'that is properly a nursery of vice, where a boy unlearns the pure and honest principles which he may have received at home, and gets, in their stead, others which are utterly low, and base, and mischievous; where he loses his modesty, his respect for truth, and his affectionateness, and becomes coarse, and false, and unfeeling.'[7]

He distinguished between two forms of removal. The first was meant as a public disgrace and was conducted as such; the second was more discreet, with no shame, but merely (as it was argued to the boys concerned and their parents) in their best interests. It was said of Arnold himself that 'he wakes every morning with an impression that everything is an open question', and he expected his pupils and his staff to take a similar view.[8] Once, after expelling some boys for moral turpitude, Arnold stood before the assembled school and said: 'It is *not* necessary that this should be a school of three hundred, or one hundred, or of fifty boys; but it *is* necessary that it should be a school of Christian gentlemen.'[9] He also said: 'Sending away boys is a necessary and regular part of a good system, not as a punishment to one, but as a protection to others. Undoubtedly it would be a better system if there was no evil; but evil being unavoidable we are not a gaol to keep it in, but a place of education where we must cast it out, to prevent its taint from spreading.'[10]

This was the sort of 'evil' he was determined to vanquish. Sunday after Sunday he would rail against it, each new generation of boys prone to the same pollution, his battle never won. As pupils, Stanley and Charles Vaughan would 'nudge each other with delight' when Arnold entered the pulpit to preach: a reaction probably untypical of boys, and indicative of the priggishness Arnold risked inspiring.[11] 'Evil' was not a term he bandied about casually. He had identified it, and indeed categorised it. He told his boys, in a notable sermon, that there were six sorts of evil, and he listed them: profligacy (or 'direct sensual wickedness', of which he gave the example of drunkenness – sexual impropriety was the great unmentionable and, in all his sermons, unmentioned), systematic falsehood, cruelty and bullying, active disobedience, idleness, and the bond of evil, or the way in which boys feel tied to one another by ties of wickedness rather than by ties of good.[12] 'Let these six things exist together,' Arnold proclaimed, 'and the profanation of the temple is complete.' He set a high standard, and very few boys would be equal to it. He also made it clear that it was not just he who was judging and, if necessary, punishing them. God, too, was taking notes.

Yet Arnold was optimistic: 'Every boy brings some good with him, at least, from home, as well as some evil; and yet you see how very much more catching the evil is than the good, or else you would make one another better by mixing together; and if any single boy did anything wrong, it would be condemned by the general opinion of all the school, just as some wrong things, such as stealing money, for example, are condemned at present.'[13] He was ever confronted by boys of whom 'some are losing their child's innocence, but none, or very few, are gaining a man's virtue'.[14] His aim was to create a sense of 'Christian manliness' in his charges, urgently.[15]

The standard of educational provision and of conduct elsewhere was not high. In other schools discipline was savage but arbitrary. Sanitary conditions were often disgusting. Not the least of the schools' problems was that the teaching was so bad. Arnold tolerated none of these things: and it was his ferocity in fighting against them and setting a standard of reforms that helped begin a revolution in education. This revolution spread not least because he sent out men from Rugby to other schools, and other institutions, who took the Arnoldian message of Christianity (developed by the next generation, with its growing interest in sport and team games, into muscular Christianity) with them and who transformed the attitude of the upper and upper-middle classes. He was motivated by disinterest, a quality his eldest son would make a touchstone of successful criticism, and which would motivate many reformers. 'His consciousness of his own integrity, and his contempt for worldly advantage, sometimes led him to require from others more than might be reasonably expected from them,' Stanley claimed.[16]

It was this fanatical (though Dr Arnold would have repudiated such an adjective) determination to make his charges see life as a battleground between good and evil that made him a figure of fun, or obloquy, to critics. A sympathiser, H. F. Lowry, referring to the famous novel by Thomas Hughes, one of Arnold's pupils, described the caricature: 'To them [his detractors] he will never be more than the pious Englishman who turned Tom Brown's fellows into first-rate prigs and made little boys grow old before their years . . . he was, even in his own time, the embodiment of Duty waiting with a birch in hand, haunting their doubtful dreams like a Hebrew prophet, and summoning on their guilty heads the fiery wrath of God.'[17]

His assistant masters were chosen for their moral and intellectual calibre, and were paid better than previously. Arnold expected complete commitment – too many masters had been clergymen with parishes, sometimes far-flung – and evidence of continued interest in learning. Some of these men became housemasters as Arnold ended the practice of boys lodging at dames' houses in the town. Those masters who were laymen he urged to become ordained, and came to an arrangement with the diocesan Bishop to facilitate this. In appointing staff, he said that 'what I want is a man who is a Christian and a gentleman, an active man, and one who has common sense, and understands boys . . . I prefer activity of mind and an interest in his work to high scholarship.'[18] On a man's appointment to the staff, Arnold would write to him that 'he should be public spirited, liberal, and entering heartily into the interest, honour, and general respectability and distinction of the society which he has joined.'

III

While the Classics were the heart of the curriculum – and, as the Clarendon commission would find in the early 1860s, they were still almost all that was taught in many public schools – Arnold raised the standards of subjects such as modern languages and mathematics, and modern history assumed an increased importance. He introduced the study of geology, something many clergymen regarded as heretical because of what it seemed to say about the Creation. Other physical sciences were not attempted, something for which Strachey mocked him: but his detractor admits Arnold avoided these subjects because he did not believe they could be taught properly, and because the time needed would have had to be taken from other subjects Arnold regarded as more important. He favoured the teaching of physical science, though only if morals were taught alongside it. Strachey, mocking Arnold from the security of the secular world, quotes him as saying: 'Rather than have physical science the principal thing in my son's mind I would gladly have him think that the sun went round the earth, and that the stars were so many spangles set in the bright blue firmament. Surely the one thing needful for a Christian and an Englishman to study is Christian and moral political philosophy.'[19]

Arnold was opposed to the utilitarian notion that saw education as a cramming of the mind with facts, but sought to make it a process that encouraged boys to find out answers to any problem that might confront them. Ironically, it was those of a utilitarian cast of mind who most readily praised his improvements to the curriculum. He brought in mathematics, some Shakespeare (whom he felt grossly inferior to Homer), and also Dante and Goethe. The Greek mathematicians were of natural interest to him, especially Euclid. Despite his belief in teaching modern history he struggled to get past the ancients: 'The history of Greece and of Rome is not an idle inquiry about remote ages and forgotten institutions, but a living picture of things present, fitted not so much for the curiosity of the scholar, as for the instruction of the statesman and the citizen.'[20] Sciences in any depth he believed necessary only for the class of person who would go into industry: in that he helped foster and influence a prejudice among the upper classes against the new source of Britain's wealth, which would handicap the country. As another biographer, Michael McCrum, has written: 'His view was that vocational training did not cultivate the mind and inspire the moral sense.'[21]

Stanley wrote of education at the time of Arnold's translation to Rugby: 'The range of classical reading, in itself confined, and with no admixture of other information, had been subject to vehement attacks from the Liberal party generally, on the grounds of its alleged narrowness and inutility.'[22] He added that 'it was not knowledge, but the means of gaining knowledge that he had to teach; as well as by his increasing sense of the value of the ancient authors, as belonging really to a period of modern civilisation like our own.' He proceeded with his pupils by the Socratic method, of questioning them to elicit knowledge and stimulating them to think about the quality of the answers they gave. 'His whole method,' Stanley wrote, 'was founded on the principle of awakening the intellect of every individual boy.'[23]

Arnold had one profound blind spot, which appears to have been an almost entire absence of the aesthetic sense. Fine art meant little or nothing to him. The notebooks of his foreign travels, reproduced by Stanley, show little regard for some of the cultural wonders of France and Italy. That his example to the products of his school, and to other schools of Christian gentlemen, was so deficient in this respect may explain some of the restrictions in Victorian taste.

He was no tyrant. Stanley writes that 'every three weeks a council was held [for the masters], in which all school matters were discussed, and in which every one was free to express his opinion, or propose any measure not in contradiction to any fundamental principle of school administration, and in which it would not infrequently happen that he himself [Arnold] was opposed and outvoted.'[24] In his dealings with the boys he sought to bring the older ones into line 'by kindness and encouragement attracting the noble feelings of those with whom he had to deal.'[25] He retained flogging 'as fitly answering to and marking the naturally inferior state of boyhood, and therefore as conveying no peculiar degradation to persons in such a state' but, according to Stanley, 'it was confined to moral offences, such as lying, drinking and habitual idleness.' His end was not retribution or the establishment of a reign of fear: 'What I want to see in the school, and what I cannot find, is an abhorrence of evil.'[26] He had moments of intense despair when 'evil' manifested itself too greatly, or when his trust in a boy turned out to be misplaced.

A month into his tenure, on 28 September 1828, he wrote to a friend and fellow clergyman, F. C. Blackstone, to say that 'there has been no flogging yet, (and I hope that there will be none,) and surprisingly few irregularities. I chastise, at first, by very gentle impositions, which are raised for a repetition of offences – flogging will be only my *ratio ultima* – and *talking* I shall try to the utmost. I believe that boys may be governed a great deal by gentle methods and kindness, and appealing to their better feelings, if you show that you are not afraid of them; I have seen great boys, six feet high, shed tears when I have sent for them up into my room and spoken to them quietly, in private, for not knowing their lesson, and I found that this treatment produced its effects afterwards, in making them do better.'[27] Yet the iron hand was in the velvet glove: 'But, of course, deeds must second words when needful, or words will soon be laughed at.'

Arnold was not in the mould of nineteenth-century flagellomaniac headmasters: his contemporary at Eton, John Keate, flogged eighty boys in a day in 1832, a far from unusual occurrence in a regime Strachey described as 'a life in which licensed barbarism was mingled with the daily and hourly study of the niceties of Ovidian verse.'[28] Nevertheless,

Arnold was cursed by a hot temper, and once savagely thrashed in front of a whole class a boy he thought had lied to him. The boy had had a hernia since infancy and needed two days in bed to recover. Arnold thought he was malingering and gave him extra work as a punishment. When it turned out the boy had not lied, Arnold not only apologised to him, but to the whole school. His parents removed the boy and demanded a written apology. Were that not humiliation enough for Arnold, the press – in those days usually deferential – got hold of the story. It was a serious dent in his reputation, and his behaviour suggests a degree of mental instability.

A system of fagging, in which the fag would be made aware of the decency and fairness of the fagmaster, was central to his system of rule. If that was an ambitious ideal, Arnold would reinforce it in his regular pep talks to the sixth formers in whom he would vest such authority: 'I wish you to see fully how many and great are the opportunities offered to you here of doing good – good, too, of lasting benefit to yourselves as well as to others . . . what we must look for here is, first, religious and moral principles; secondly, gentlemanly conduct; thirdly, intellectual ability.'[29] He told his sixth formers that, were they to betray his trust in them, 'you should feel like officers in the army or navy, whose want of moral courage would, indeed, be thought cowardice.' The critic and jurist Fitzjames Stephen, who felt Arnold to have been something of a humbug, nonetheless conceded in 1859 that he had created 'the leaders of every day English life, what we may call the non-commissioned officers of English society – the clergy, the lawyers, the doctors, the country squires, the junior partners in banks and merchants' offices, men who are in every sense of the word gentlemen though no one would class them with the aristocracy.'[30]

IV

Arnold's Christianity was defined specifically by his reverence for Christ and his example. His purpose was to make Rugby a school consonant with his idea of evangelical Christianity. 'The boys were still treated as schoolboys, but as schoolboys who must grow up to be Christian men', Stanley wrote; 'whose age did not prevent their faults from being sins, or their excellences from being noble and Christian virtues.'[31] For Arnold, God was everywhere, and his charges were told that their every act was discharged in the presence of God. Stanley writes of his 'desire of carrying out his favourite ideas of uniting things secular with things spiritual'.[32] In addition to the prayers all boys had in the morning he introduced a separate prayer in the Sixth Form, because he felt their school work was not 'sufficiently sanctified to God's glory'.[33] However, when defending his corner, he was not above a disingenuousness that sits ill with his piety. He was, to say the least, slippery in 1838 when taken to task for running down the lower school – boys younger than thirteen, whom he did not wish to have at Rugby – against the wishes of the founder. McCrum makes much of this: Stanley, as McCrum points out, almost ignores it.[34]

He was the school's chaplain as well as its headmaster from 1831, and his weekly sermons were explicit instructions to his boys in the nature of the Christian life. His charges sat and heard him in silence and, in some cases, reverence: it was a far cry from the experience of his fellow doctor of divinity, Keate, who was routinely shouted down in the chapel at Eton. Strachey raises the idea of the chapel being 'the centre of Dr Arnold's system of education' only to deprecate it.[35] He conjures up the image of Rugby chapel as a place where 'the Doctor himself appeared in the plenitude of his dignity and his enthusiasm . . . rapt in devotion or vibrant with exhortation'. Much of what Strachey writes, as well as being motivated by militant secularism, is sheer supposition. The ultimate condemnation comes in his note of the publication of Arnold's sermons in (he says) five (there were in fact six) volumes that were 'received with admiration by a wide circle of pious readers. Queen Victoria herself possessed a copy, in which several passages were marked in pencil, by the royal hand.'[36]

Arnold also sought to reform his boys by forging a partnership with his prefects, or praepostors, who helped run the institution. A generation before *The Origin of Species*, Arnold instilled an almost Darwinian process into Rugby: it was the fittest who survived, because the morally and intellectually defective were simply thrown out. To those who stayed the course he was an inspirational, if occasionally terrifying, figure. One of the gravest offences, in his view, was lying to a master. Junior boys were flogged for it, senior ones expelled. Arnold would always take a boy's word, because he worked on the assumption that others were inevitably truthful. Stanley says that 'there grew up in consequence a general feeling that 'it was a shame to tell Arnold a lie – he always believes one.'[37]

As well as seeing God everywhere, Arnold saw evil everywhere too. 'At the very sight', wrote Stanley, 'of a knot of vicious or careless boys gathered together round the great school-house fire, "It makes me think", he would say, "that I see the Devil in the midst of them." From first to last it was the great subject to which all his anxiety converged.'[38] This notion entertains Strachey more than almost any other: 'The daily sight of so many young creatures in the hands of the Evil One filled him with agitated grief.'[39] However upright the example he and his masters set, there could be no improvement 'unless there were something to counteract it constantly amongst the boys themselves.' This was why he gave authority to the most senior boys in the school, hoping that their example would make more of an impression on those below them than anything done by the masters would.

Strachey reserved special ridicule for this system – 'the boys were to work out their own salvation, like the human race' while Arnold 'involved in awful grandeur, ruled remotely, through his chosen instruments, from an inaccessible heaven'.[40] Strachey himself was bullied at school, and so may have had particular reasons for disliking systems in which boys ruled other boys, anticipating *Lord of the Flies*. Deploring Arnold's decision to allow the Sixth Form to punish junior boys, Strachey drifts into mockery: 'The younger children, scourged both by Dr Arnold and by the elder children, were given every opportunity of acquiring the simplicity, sobriety, and humbleness of mind, which are the best ornaments of youth.'[41]

Stanley categorises Arnold as a Whig – a man who believed fundamentally in progress and improvement – though argues that 'Liberal principles were not merely the expression of his adherence to a Whig ministry, but of his belief in the constant necessity of applying those principles of advance and reform, which, in their most perfect development, he conceived to be identical with Christianity itself.'[42] Arnold's writings are filled with disobliging references to Conservatism, which he regards as an extreme form of Toryism. 'I think Conservatism far worse than Toryism', he wrote to his friend Mr Justice Coleridge on 16 December 1835, 'if by Toryism be meant a fondness for monarchical or even despotic government; for despotism may often further the advance of a nation, and a good dictatorship may be a very excellent thing. . . . but Conservatism always looks backwards, and therefore, under whatever form of government, I think it the enemy of all good.'[43] For all the assertions of Arnold's liberalism, however, he had some remarkably illiberal ideas. He wanted Jews barred from the universities and from becoming British subjects. He also believed that criminality was genetic and that the immediate descendants of those transported to Australia, to the third generation, should be forbidden from holding any public positions there.

Strachey asserts that 'he had become convinced of the duty of sympathising with the lower orders ever since he had made a serious study of the Epistle of St James [which reinforces the importance of observing Christian duties]; but he perceived clearly that the lower orders fell into two classes, and that it was necessary to distinguish between them. There were the "good poor" – and there were the others.'[44] Strachey seeks to paint Arnold as a hypocrite for making this distinction, which is not quite identical to that made by many of his contemporaries between the deserving and the undeserving. The good poor were those who did not join trades unions or engage in Chartist plotting; a view held by many others at the time, not least Disraeli, who depicts the folly of seeking to subvert the law in Sybil.

Like Gladstone, he would regard the religious impulse as implicit in politics, just as in all else. He wanted a complete identity of Church and State. So did Gladstone, who saw religion as inseparable from a sense of nationality, at least in England, and who wrote a book on the subject in 1839. Gladstone though wanted a marriage between Anglo-Catholicism and the State: Arnold by contrast wanted evangelism to guide national political life, emphasising the importance of converting to Christianity those who did not believe. Gladstone would by 1841 realise the impracticabilities of his idea, not least as the Oxford Movement – which had since 1833 advocated the catholicising of the Anglican Church – went in a direction he had feared to contemplate, with people (including his own sister, Helen) becoming Roman Catholics. Even Arnold, by the end of his life, appears to have started to realise the difficulties of such a thing: and, as Strachey delights in pointing out, would have forced the exclusion of certain groups from the community thus created. 'Jews, for instance, were decidedly outside the pale; while Dissenters – so Dr Arnold argued – were as decidedly within it. But what was the position of the Unitarians? Were they, or were they not, Members of the Church of Christ? This was one of those puzzling questions which deepened the frown upon the Doctor's forehead and intensified the pursing of his lips.'[45] Arnold had had his own problems with the Athanasian Creed, and believed if it could be dispensed with Unitarians would happily join in with their fellow Christians and make his ideal possible. His inability to reconcile this point with reality gives Strachey much pleasure.

V

Arnold was an early advocate of what we would now call 'social justice'. He had supported the Reform Bill of 1832, which widened the political franchise beyond its traditionally very narrow limits, and was so moved by the political currents of the times that he set up a newspaper to advocate his views and those of Christian gentlemen like him: it lasted only a few issues. He had a compulsion to express his opinions: shortly before Christmas 1830 he wrote to his sister Susannah saying that 'the paramount interest of public affairs outweighs with me even the school itself. . . . I must write a pamphlet in the holidays, or I shall burst.'[46] Through a series of letters written to the *Sheffield Courant* in 1831-2 he had set out and analysed the social problems facing the country, notably in the recently industrialised districts of the north. Such writings caused discomfort among the school governors, who felt he should not seek such a profile, and at least once he came close to resignation. In the end the force of his character, that tool used to shape so many boys, helped him prevail. As Stanley put it, 'he governed the school precisely on the same principles as he would have governed a great empire'.[47] Such was his self-belief that he refused to enter into a public debate when criticisms were levelled at him and his methods. He told a colleague: 'I will not condescend to justify the school against attacks, when I believe that it is going on not only not ill, but positively well.'[48]

He believed education should extend beyond the privileged classes, to widen the civilising process and to improve the condition of the poor; and that the poor who went to schools should receive an education, rather than simply enduring rote-learning. 'Many persons confound reading and writing with education: they consider themselves as having been engaged in educating the poor; and then, when they see that their labours have produced little fruit, they are half bewildered when they hear it said that this is plain proof that to educate the poor can do no good. . . . I never knew any poor man who could properly be said to be educated.'[49] This would become a great mission for reformers. Arnold

drew a distinction between a man's 'professional' education, which taught
him his line of business, and his 'liberal' education, which trained him
for 'his general calling, which he has in common with all his neighbours,
namely, the calling of a citizen and a man'.[50] He observed that a man
deficient in the first would be swiftly found out, whereas one deficient
in the second would not, 'because there are so many who share in it'.[51]
As a result, a society had been created which, through ignorance, 'it is
every man's business to meddle in, but no man's to learn.' As a result,
'false notions are entertained and acted upon; prejudices and passions
multiply; abuses become manifold; difficulty and distress at last press on
the whole community.' He also expressed, in 1834, a belief that would
resonate during debates about education over the next half-century: 'If
ever the question of National Education comes definitely before the
Government, I am very desirous of their not centralising too much.'[52]

He wished to stop lower-middle-class boys being taken away from
school 'half-educated' to go into a trade or profession, not least because
he welcomed the prospect of further parliamentary reform after 1832.
However, he wrote, 'I do not see that we are likely to grow much wiser,
or that though political power may pass into different hands, that it will
be exercised more purely or sensibly than it has been.'[53] He was, by the
standards of his times, an extreme democrat: 'The true and only way
to make civil society really deserving of its name, is to give its members
an active and not merely a passive part in the management of its
concerns.'[54] He articulated a view held, silently, by many of the educated
classes: reform would come. Many feared this because they feared
those in whose hands power would then rest. Arnold did not, because
he believed society would by then have educated the new masters. The
thirty years from Victoria's accession until the second Reform Act would
test such assumptions to the limit, because in that time there was no
advance in educational opportunities for the masses who would have
the vote.

He sympathised with the attempts of men to obtain education once
in work; but in a lecture to the Rugby Mechanics Institute in 1838 he
crushed any notion they had that the process they were embarking upon
could be called 'education'. 'It is idle to call Mechanics' Institutes places
of adult education. Physical science alone can never make a man
educated; even the formal sciences, invaluable as they are with respect
to the discipline of the reasoning powers, cannot instruct the judgment;

it is only moral and religious knowledge which can accomplish this.'[55] In 1834, with his mind again on the importance of the civilising process, he had told Chevalier Bunsen, a biblical scholar who became Prussian ambassador, that 'education is wanted to improve the physical condition of the people, and yet this physical condition must be improved before they can be susceptible to education.'[56]

When criticised for engaging in journalism, Arnold simply wrote another screed on the importance of a headmaster such as him having complete independence of action. As we shall see, his son Matthew took rather the same attitude in attacking successive governments for the implementation of the revised code for schools after 1862, even though he was in their employment as a schools inspector. Once Chartist agitation started in 1838, to secure the implementation of a 'People's Charter' of civil rights, Arnold kept a close eye on organised labour, which he distrusted. He wrote sympathetically about the poor, but not about the Chartists, who he felt, because of the violence of their language, were 'slaves of the most degraded sort: and made such not by others, but by themselves.'[57] The theme constant in his writings about the poor is that they were freemen being allowed 'to sink more and more into the state of slaves'.[58] Such a person would end up hating 'the rich as enemies', and anarchy would ensue. He wanted such people to have the benefits of education not least to raise them nearer the levels of those whom they might otherwise seek to attack and overthrow.

For all his idealism about the poor, there is occasionally a sense that it is balanced with a certain pragmatism. 'Has the world ever yet seen a population so dangerous in every respect as to the society in which it existed as the manufacturing population of Great Britain?' he asked in December 1838.[59] He outlined reasons for his concern that would find echoes in Matthew's writings thirty years later: the operatives were 'not restrained by close connexion with other classes of society' and were 'not softened by knowledge', but were 'crowded together in most formidable masses, well aware of the force of organisation'. There was, as he saw it, a central dilemma that made matters so lethal: 'If they were slaves, they might be kept down by force: if they were what citizens ought to be, they would be peaceable alike from interest and from duty; but as they are neither the one nor the other, what is to be done?'

He repudiated the notion, popular in England since the eighteenth century, that 'civil society ought to leave its members alone'. He felt the

poor required serious State intervention, and that it was the duty of the
State 'to provide for the common good of all, by restraining the power
of the strong and protecting the helplessness of the weak.'[60] As the
population grew, and labour became a less scarce (and therefore less
well paid) commodity, these problems, and the need for intervention,
could only increase, making 'an evil of the first magnitude'.[61] Anticipating
Carlyle's strictures on the 'cash nexus', Arnold argued that the relations
between master and man should be the State's business, because 'that
the relation between the rich and the poor in so large a part of the
kingdom is purely commercial, is in itself most mischievous; because a
purely commercial relation not only arises out of nothing better than
self-interest, but it goes on to nothing better; it neither springs from nor
leads to any feelings of admiration, confidence, reverence, or love, which
are the true ties between man and man.' Just as there was an element
of idealism in Arnold's regard for the working man, so too did he dislike
what his son Matthew would term the 'philistinism' of the manufacturing
classes who increasingly employed such men.

This argument would drive some to wish a return to a fantasy, pre-
industrial world. That man had become a commodity and ceased to be
a human being was profoundly shocking, and denigrated capitalism in
the eyes of many who were not natural revolutionaries. As Arnold put
it, 'they are regarded as hands – not as heads, hearts, or souls.' He felt
the nature of the tie these men had to their employer, and therefore
to the place where they lived, as merely 'transient': and that in itself
created a sense of rootlessness, and a lack of loyalty, that could only
corrode society further.[62] He cited the gangs of men shifting around the
country to build the railways, then in the first flower of growth. Such
men wanted 'to become members of a society more varied in its elements
and more wholesome in its character than their own clubs and unions.
Unless these wants can be supplied, they will in some of the most
important points resemble slaves rather than citizens.' But because they
were not chained together like slaves, they had the potential to be 'a
hundred times more dangerous'.

Arnold hoped the Church might provide the sense of community and
permanence he craved on behalf of these people: but to do this would
require a union of Church and State, or indeed of the Christian churches
themselves in the first instance, that was highly unlikely. He exhorted
the Church Building Society – which was attempting, in the late 1830s

and early 1840s, to provide more places of worship to assist the salvation of the lower orders – instead to 'build up living churches – not dead ones of brick and stone. That was a true and living Church which met for prayer and praise in the subterranean quarries without the walls of Rome; and such Churches would better serve our purposes than all the splendour of St Peter's.'[63] He added: 'The money which is given for building places of worship should be given to provide ministers. Those ministers should each have their deacons . . . under the names of visitors of the poor.' Thus the old paternalism of the countryside would be brought, in Arnold's idealistic vision, into the manufacturing towns. 'All that I have been urging was actually the system of our Saxon forefathers. They were fully aware how important it was in society that every man should know every man; they went even farther, and made every man answerable for every man'.[64] Arnold knew society had changed and tried to appear progressive in embracing that change: but he did not see just how much it changed, not least because of the speed at which it had grown in the first forty years of the nineteenth century. Organising the disorganised mass of an industrial society was simply not feasible: at least, not by the Church.

VI

By the mid-1830s Arnold's pupils were winning scholarships to Oxford (notably Balliol) and Cambridge (notably Trinity); he turned out men such as Stanley, who would be Dean of Westminster as well as his biographer, Arthur Hugh Clough and his own son Matthew, who came to Rugby after two unsatisfactory years at Winchester and flourished despite being weighed down by the burden of his father's expectations. Another success was Vaughan, whose brilliant career at Cambridge was a prelude to his becoming headmaster of Harrow, an appointment that ended unfortunately. Through Stanley, Arnold also exercised a posthumous influence over Benjamin Jowett, one of the most influential academics of the nineteenth century, with whom Stanley became close friends. Jowett became professor of Greek and Master of Balliol; when he died in 1893 his pall-bearers were seven heads of house and the Provost of Eton, all former pupils of his.

Arnold worked ferociously hard, setting a system of examinations for the whole school; and he contributed his own money to scholarship funds to give greater incentives to his boys to study, presumably for the benefit of those for whom the glory of God was not enough. He maintained a strong interest in his former pupils once they had left school, particularly in those who, like Stanley, would have careers shaping minds and hearts either through the Church or as schoolmasters. Whatever other criticism may be thrown at Arnold, his vocation was palpable; he would help prepare former pupils for their university examinations, and would sometimes make them presents of books if their circumstances were hard.

By 1841 his stock was high and his achievement widely recognised; he had set a template for the public schools that many would follow in the succeeding thirty or forty years, notably after the Clarendon Commission. Even Strachey, however baleful he might have found it, and however much it demanded his sarcastic inventions, had to concede Arnold's influence: 'Succeeding generations of favourite pupils began to spread his fame through the Universities. At Oxford especially men were profoundly impressed by the pious aims of the boys from Rugby. It was a new thing to see undergraduates going to Chapel more often than they were obliged, and visiting the good poor.'[65] In what appears to be a statement of fact rather than of sarcasm, Strachey adds: 'He became a celebrity; he became at last a great man.' Arnold had also guided his boys towards careers that might be socially useful. The Army and the Navy he regarded as dens of iniquity and profanity. He told his boys they were already soldiers of Christ, and could want no better regiment. Those who, in a civilian occupation, took the message of Christianity and the ethos of Rugby to the corners of the globe were far more highly regarded, as discharging some degree of moral duty. He admired those who studied law and medicine, but found the practice of both repellent: he felt the lawyer had the worst of it, since 'moral nastiness, in which a lawyer lives and breathes, is far worse than objects physically repulsive'. Worse still, 'the lawyer meddles with moral evil rather to aggravate it than to mend.'[66]

The Arnolds took favoured pupils into their family, and they stayed there long after they left Rugby. Arnold's wife, Mary, endorsed this. Writing in 1840 to Richard Congreve – a former pupil who would return to Rugby as a master and then, in 1867, found the London Positivist Society – about a mutual friend's trepidation at examinations, she echoed her husband's voice uncannily: 'We expect . . . that under all circumstances the examination will shew them what university competition is, and the good earnest work which must be required to meet it.'[67] When later that year Congreve himself took a first and Arnold wrote to congratulate him, he observed: 'I quite understand your feeling of not knowing which way to turn in the wide garden of knowledge, now that your path is no longer so strictly defined for you. But the very sense of the Power to turn with effect this way or that way is the best tribute to the goodness of our English System of Education, and shows that it has done its proper work.'[68]

Arnold was appointed Regius professor of modern history at Oxford in 1841, and made a great success. George Moberly, the headmaster of Winchester when Stanley was writing his *Life* (and who, after his retirement, was summoned by Gladstone to be Bishop of Salisbury), observed that in the pre-Arnoldian era 'a religious undergraduate was very rare, very much laughed at when he appeared; and I think I may confidently say, hardly to be found among public-school men.'[69] But of late there had been a 'singular and striking' change and, Moberly asserted, 'this change is undoubtedly part of a general improvement of our generation in respect of piety and reverence, but I am sure that to Dr Arnold's personal earnest simplicity of purpose, strength of character, power of influence and piety, which none who never came near him could mistake or question, the carrying of this improvement into our schools is mainly attributable. He was the first.'

Arnold's death had a neatness at odds with the often turbulent and emotional character of his life. It also had a drama that would feed his posthumous legend. He had for the last academic year at Rugby combined his headmastership with his Oxford chair. The school year was divided into two unequal halves at Rugby, the second running from late January to early June. In June 1842 Arnold was preparing for his summer break at Fox How, his house in the Lake District. He gave his farewell sermon; he gave his farewell dinner to his sixth formers; he settled accounts with his servants, but on the eve of his forty-seventh birthday, just after dawn broke on 12 June 1842, he awoke with the pains of angina in his chest. His condition deteriorated rapidly; a physician was called, but Arnold was dead before eight o'clock, at a similar age to his father and, like him, of heart failure. Stanley describes in almost biblical tones not just the death, but the sense of shock that passed around the school as word was broadcast. In a letter to Clough written immediately afterwards, Stanley spoke with a studied lack of understate-ment of 'the almost royal majesty of his death' and made the immediate judgement that Arnold had been 'one of the greatest and holiest men whom this generation has produced.'[70] The Doctor had died, but his legend was about to be propelled to glory.

Arnold had three stabs at immortality. The first was Stanley's *Life*, which quickly became one of his monuments; the second a novel written by one of his pupils, Thomas Hughes, *Tom Brown's Schooldays*, which put him into legend; and, more than seventy-five years after his death, the cynical deconstruction of him by Strachey in *Eminent Victorians*. The suddenness of his death and the shock it occasioned led to exaggerations about the wonder of Arnold, and the extent of his achievement. These are abundant in Stanley (who writes of 'the almost filial relation in which I stood towards him'), and in Hughes's novel, which ends with Brown, by now at Oxford, coming back to Rugby after Arnold's death and seeking to come to terms with the immensity of his grief. Strachey's was but the first corrective to this view: other less flamboyant revisionist texts appeared after him.[71] However – and this was not apparent when Stanley wrote – Arnold's influence spread as his assistant masters and his pupils went out in the world. His essentially liberal ideals were seldom better or more influ-entially disseminated than through his son Matthew.

Hughes's fictional representation of Arnold is, it seems, accurate. Arnold is spoken of long before he appears, and is a God-like figure: not just in his piety and in his attempt to shape the lives of his charges in a way that will have them do God's will, but in the awesome power of love and punishment that he exerts over his community. Rugbeians, despite Arnold's influence, are just as vile as any boys of that age: while Arnold is with them in chapel one is busy etching his name on the back of the stall in front of him, and 'the general atmosphere was by no means devotional'.[72] However, there then 'came that great event in his [Brown's], as in every Rugby boy's life of that day – the first sermon from the Doctor.' He describes 'the tall gallant form, the kindling eye, the voice, now soft as the low notes of a flute, now clear and stirring as the call of the light infantry bugle, of him who stood there Sunday after Sunday, witnessing and pleading for his Lord, the King of right-eousness and love and glory, with whose spirit he was filled, and in whose power he spoke.' He was, Hughes added, one who 'brought home to the young boy, for the first time, the meaning of his life . . . a battle-field ordained from of old . . . and the stakes are life and death.'[73]

The Doctor, in Hughes's depiction, has his Old Testament moments. He will lose his temper and box a boy's ears; there are frequent floggings. For these and other reasons he inspires fear: but when Brown and his friends come in late from hare and hounds, and are sent up to the Doctor, his response is not to thrash them, but to ensure they are not hurt, tell them to ask the housekeeper for tea, and warn them that they must not do long runs until they are bigger and stronger. After a career of getting into scrapes; being reckless, thoughtless and careless, Tom, inevitably, becomes an upright, responsible, God-fearing youth, captain of the Eleven. At the end, he and his friends reflect on 'the way that all the Doctor's reforms have been carried out when he has been left to himself – quietly and naturally, putting a good thing in the place of a bad, and letting the bad die out; no wavering and no hurry – the best thing that could be done for the time being, and patience for the rest.'[74] It is a metaphor for how change would be accomplished in wider society.

Strachey was having none of this. He set the tone in discussing Arnold's childhood: 'It is true that, as a schoolboy, a certain pompousness in the style of his letters home suggested to the more clear-sighted among his relatives the possibility that young Thomas might grow up into a prig; but, after all, what else could be expected from a child who, at the age of three, had been presented by his father, as a reward for proficiency in his studies, with the twenty-four volumes of Smollett's *History of England*?'[75] The gulf that separated the England of 1918, when Strachey wrote his essay, from that of 1842, when his subject died, contained two seismic events. The first was secularisation, which made Arnold's almost theatrical devotion appear absurd. Strachey quotes, from Stanley, Arnold's dictum that 'nowhere is Satan's work more evidently manifest than in turning holy things to ridicule.'[76]

The second was the Great War, which destroyed the credibility of values such as Arnold propagated. The products of the Victorian and Edwardian public-school systems of which he was the father were buried, in sickeningly large numbers, in the cemeteries of the Western Front: killed in a conflict in which Strachey's own physical feebleness prevented him from participating – his exemption from military service on grounds of health prevented him from the satisfaction of registering as a conscientious objector. He uses psychological inquiry in his writings to present

new perspectives on his subjects, an approach diametrically at odds with
the Arnoldian. Strachey's could be an entirely destructive intelligence
and, in *Eminent Victorians*, largely was.

However, while Strachey notes that Arnold did little to improve
the intellectual attainment of English public schoolboys (an unfair
assertion, given the numbers of scholarships his pupils won to universities), he does concede that 'by introducing morals and religion into his
scheme of education he altered the whole atmosphere of Public School
life. Henceforward the old rough-and-tumble, typified by the regime of
Keate at Eton, became impossible. After Dr Arnold, no public school
could venture to ignore the virtues of respectability.'[77]

After being widowed Mary Arnold wrote to Congreve of her husband's
legacy: 'the happy thoughts that you are and will be one of those active
influences for good by which I feel that my adored husband still lives
even here. And it is in the thought of this double life – his own life with
God and his . . . life in the hearts and lives of those he has left, that I
find my best consolation.'[78] She added, with reference to the inheritor
of the mantle, 'with dearest Matt, the present is a most critical and
important period and I have been greatly encouraged and have felt how
gratified his beloved father would have been by symptoms of growing
thoughtfulness.'

Arnold typifies the Victorian high mind. He exemplifies what Matthew,
in a notable letter to Arthur Hugh Clough, called 'great natures'.[79] One
of his twentieth-century defenders, Basil Willey, described Arnold as
having that characteristic of 'leading men' of his era, that he was
'conscious of a destiny and a duty, whose fulfilment, whether conceived
as an obligation to God or to one's fellow-creatures, would make life
significant and satisfying'.[80] Such men felt that life had 'momentous
meaning', and it was their job to realise it. The march of secularism
required such militant foes as Arnold, but his effects would be limited.

Those, like Strachey, minded to mock have formidable scope to do
so. But Arnold concerned himself in his professional, and much of his
private, life only with the great questions: good and evil, Church and
State, the moral and the immoral. A whole governing class would be
shaped in a variation of his image. His own children and pupils
consciously expanded his legacy; as did their pupils, their congregations,
those who read their writings and those over whom, in all walks of life,
they exerted influence. Arnold had been conscious that he was training

boys to be men, and leaders of men. He was not alone in setting the tone for the decades to come: but few set it so much as Thomas Arnold.

VII

Many of Arnold's pupils, such as Clough, Stanley and Matthew Arnold, went on to play formidable parts in shaping society: though Clough became almost stunted during his short life by the overwhelming religious sense that Arnold had instilled in him. Arnold's direct influence on education was enormous, at a time when the public schools were expanding to cope with the demand created by new prosperity, and reforming to deal with the new challenges of an industrial age. Arnold's name and example were cited during the Clarendon Commission, twenty years after his death, when the political establishment realised the great public schools had to leave the eighteenth century. Many who had neither studied nor taught at Rugby felt inspired by what they knew of Arnold's achievement to reform and improve their own schools, not least because they saw that, with sufficiently strong leadership, such a thing was possible. But his disciples led the transmission of his example. A. O. J. Cockshut, in his study of Stanley's biography, wrote that Arnold 'was not a Victorian. But he trained Victorians. . . . His pupils changed the face of education.'[81]

James Prince Lee, one of Arnold's assistant masters, became headmaster of King Edward's, Birmingham, in 1838. George Cotton, the model for the 'young master' in *Tom Brown's Schooldays*, was one of Arnold's housemasters. He became headmaster of Marlborough in 1852, and introduced organised games to sap the excess energies of boys who might otherwise cause trouble. Cotton became Bishop of Calcutta in 1858, but died after slipping off a plank by which he was boarding a boat, falling into the Ganges and being swept away, never to be seen again. George Bradley succeeded him at Marlborough and served until 1872. Bradley had been a pupil of Arnold, and a master at Rugby, and later succeeded Stanley (his tutor at Oxford, and for whom he felt the sort of reverence Stanley felt for Arnold) as Dean of Westminster. In 1859, Henry Walford, a contemporary of Hughes, became Head Master of Lancing.

One of those instrumental in turning Repton round in the late 1840s and 1850s was G. S. Messiter, a boy under Arnold at Rugby; the headmaster of Repton with whom he worked closely, Stuart Pears, had been a housemaster at Harrow under another of Arnold's products, Vaughan. Henry Highton, who came to the school as a boy the year after Arnold, in 1829, subsequently served as a master there, and in 1859 became Principal of Cheltenham College. His exact contemporary, A. H. Wratislaw, became headmaster of Felsted, where he served from 1852 to 1856. J. D. Collis was headmaster of Bromsgrove School from 1843 to 1867. Later on Edward White Benson, who served as a master at Rugby in the 1850s – after Arnold's time but where he would have acquired the Arnoldian ethos – became the first Master of Wellington College, from 1859 to 1872: and was later Archbishop of Canterbury. John Percival, at Rugby as a master in the early 1860s, became the first headmaster of Clifton in 1862, serving until 1879: and was later headmaster of Rugby from 1887 to 1895. These last two men demonstrate the ease with which Arnold's influence seeped into the foundations of the mid-Victorian age; there were numerous others who felt it indirectly.

The most notable of Arnold's protégés is, however, also the most notorious: Charles Vaughan, headmaster of Harrow from 1844 to 1859. Vaughan was one of Arnold's favourites. He was also Stanley's brother-in-law, exemplifying the closed and almost incestuous society that was one of Arnold's legacies. He was born in 1816, the son of a clergyman, and joined Rugby the year after Arnold, in 1829. A superb classicist, he became a fellow of Trinity College, Cambridge, and applied unsuccessfully for the headmastership of Rugby in succession to Arnold, despite being just twenty-five. His consolation was to have the same parish in Leicester, St Martin's, as his father had had, and then, still only twenty-seven, to gain the appointment at Harrow. As Arnold had, he became a doctor of divinity soon after taking up his post.

Harrow was a shambles when Vaughan took it over: he was warned 'not to throw himself away' on it.[82] However, he was soon credited with transforming it: though this seems as much to have been a victory of propaganda as of fact. The school grew from seventy boys on Vaughan's arrival to 460 on his departure, so he certainly created a momentum. He imposed Arnold's monitorial system on the school and backed his monitors to the hilt, even when in 1853 one of them thrashed a boy so severely as to cause him serious injury and provoke a minor scandal. God was at the centre of Vaughan's world, as in Arnold's, and he ensured the chapel was rebuilt not least to give him a decent pulpit in which he could emulate Arnold's methods of extending influence and building morale by sermonising.

All was not, however, what it seemed: though it would be more than 100 years after Vaughan's sudden retirement from Harrow in 1859, aged just forty-two, before the world knew precisely what a hypocrite he was. One of his boys, from 1854 to 1858, was John Addington Symonds, later a celebrated aesthete and homosexual. Symonds wrote his memoirs just before his death in 1893, but refused to have them published: and his literary executor, who died in 1926, gave the manuscript to the London Library with the instructions that they were not to be published until fifty years after his own death. However, the Library made the manuscript available to scholars in the 1950s. It was used as a basis for Phyllis Grosskurth's life of Symonds, published in 1964, before she published an edition of the memoirs in 1984.

It was in the biography, with Symonds and Vaughan both in their graves for seventy years or so (Vaughan had died in 1897) that the most scandalous story of Victorian public-school life at last came out. In a chapter in his memoirs entitled 'Painful circumstances connected with the last year of my life at Harrow', Symonds begins with the observation: 'One thing at Harrow very soon arrested my attention. It was the moral state of the school.'[83]

He continues: 'Every boy of good looks had a female name, and was recognised either as a public prostitute or as some bigger fellow's "bitch". Bitch was the word in common usage to indicate a boy who yielded his person to a lover. The talk in the dormitories and studies was incredibly obscene. Here and there one could not avoid seeing acts of onanism, mutual masturbation, the sports of naked boys together in bed. There was no refinement, no sentiment, no passion; nothing but animal lust in these occurrences. They filled me with disgust and loathing.'

What Symonds describes (and he depicts various boy-on-boy activities with an alarming degree of detail) was probably common currency in more schools than just Harrow: and to judge from the public-school memoirs of the later Victorian era and the early twentieth century, would be familiar to generations then unborn. That Vaughan failed to police this depravity suggests he lacked Arnold's rigour. Eventually he acquired a note passed from one boy to another, requesting an assignation, in which some of these activities became apparent. He summoned the whole school together, without any other master present, and read the letter out. He condemned the use of female names. He ordered one of the boys to be flogged and the other – whose only crime was being pursued – to write some lines. Symonds calls this a 'very inadequate form of punishment' that failed to recognise 'how widespread was the evil in our school'.[84] It was then that the thunderbolt came.

In January 1858 a friend of Symonds, Alfred Pretor, wrote to him to say that Vaughan had started a 'love affair' with him.[85] Symonds thought Pretor was lying, an impression dismissed rapidly when Pretor showed him 'a series of passionate letters' written to him by Vaughan. If Vaughan was mad to start an affair with Pretor, putting his feelings in writing was, given his position, beyond insanity. The revelation troubled Symonds in more ways than one: it was not merely that Vaughan was 'a man holding the highest position of responsibility, consecrated by the Church . . . a man who had recently prepared me for confirmation, from whose hands, kneeling by the side of Alfred Pretor, I received the sacrament, and whom I had been accustomed to regard as the pattern of my conduct'; it was also that Symonds himself was homosexual, but had imagined such feelings would die out in adulthood. Vaughan's behaviour showed that was not the case. Despite his disgust for Vaughan, he also felt 'a dumb persistent sympathy' for him.

Pretor kept Symonds up to date with the affair, showing him new letters as Vaughan sent them. Symonds found the matter alternately amusing and disgusting: but after a while, wondered whether he ought not to tell his father. He hesitated, but urged Pretor to end the affair. Pretor would not be persuaded. Symonds considered confronting Vaughan about it, in 'the study, which was the scene of his clandestine pleasures' with Pretor.[86] Before summoning the courage to do this Symonds was one day with the headmaster, discussing Greek iambics, when 'he began softly to stroke my right leg from the knee to the thigh'. This was the turning point. 'I never liked the man; he did not possess the intellectual qualities I admired. Now I began positively to dislike him.' Symonds found the moral clarity he sought by a close reading of Plato. He spent his last term at Harrow in what he described as a state of indifference: but on reaching Balliol in the autumn of 1858 started to put a distance between himself and his school. By the following summer he told an Oxford friend what had happened: and the friend told him, unequivocally, to tell his father.

Dr Symonds believed his son's story, and wrote at once to Vaughan.

He said he would not expose him, provided he resigned his post at Harrow immediately, and that he sought no preferment in the Church: it was almost de rigueur at the time for headmasters from great public schools, being usually clergymen, to become bishops. Vaughan's instinct on receiving Dr Symonds's letter was to confront his accuser, and he went at once to Bristol, to the Symondses' house at Clifton, to see what proof of his misconduct could be offered. Shown a letter from Pretor discussing it, he did as he was told: but not before Mrs Vaughan – Stanley's sister – had come to Clifton too, and literally thrown herself on Dr Symonds's mercy. She 'flung herself at my father's knees. "Would Dr Symonds not withhold the execution of his sentence? Her husband was subject to this weakness, but it had not interfered with his usefulness in the direction of the school at Harrow."'[87]

However, Dr Symonds was having none of it. 'My father remained obdurate though he told me he suffered keenly at the sight of this unhappy woman – a Stanley – prostrate on the ground before him. He judged it would be wrong to hush up such a matter of such grave importance to a great public school.' In this, according to Symonds, his father had the support of none other than Stanley himself, brother of the prostrate woman. So Vaughan extricated himself suddenly but skilfully from Harrow, claiming no man could survive more than fifteen years at the helm of a great public school; and, as Symonds puts it, 'the public acclaimed this act of resignation with enthusiasm'.[88]

The government, of course, knew nothing of the true reasons for Vaughan's departure, and therefore made him the apparently compulsory offer of a bishopric – Worcester. Vaughan, with equal compulsion, turned it down. A few months later Palmerston, who was not merely Prime Minister but also chairman of the governors at Harrow, offered him another – Rochester. This time Vaughan accepted, imagining, no doubt, that the wrath of Dr Symonds had been appeased by his resignation from Harrow. He was wrong. The moment word reached Clifton, Dr Symonds sent a telegram to Vaughan instructing him to withdraw, or face the consequences. To the bemusement of his patrons, Vaughan changed his mind. Again, Stanley reinforced him in the view that this was the only correct course, in the interests of the reputation of the Church. As Symonds recalls in his memoirs, suspicions were aroused by Vaughan's resignation and his subsequent refusal of two bishoprics, but no word of the truth leaked out.

Such was the paradox that caused many then, and many more since (led by Strachey) to regard the Victorian era as a period in the history of British morality distinguished by hypocrisy. Yet it also shows how the highest minds, even when corrupted into the lowest behaviour, had a habit of regenerating themselves. Vaughan had to settle for the relatively lowly vicarage at Doncaster, where he spent most of the 1860s and enjoyed great success. He revived the town's grammar school, gave distinguished leadership to his flock during a cholera epidemic, and was regarded with universal admiration for his work in both the spiritual and temporal spheres. While there he also trained 120 young men for ordination: by the end of his life he had more than 450 to his credit, including Randall Davidson, who in 1903 would become Archbishop of Canterbury. There is no suggestion of any further sexual irregularities, with any of them or with anyone else. In 1869 he became Master of the Temple and in 1879 Dean of Llandaff.

Writing of the early 1820s Samuel Butler, who had little truck with Arnoldian approaches to Christianity and to life, said it was an age when 'Dr Arnold had not yet sown that crop of earnest thinkers which we are now harvesting, and men did not see why they should not have their own way if no evil consequences to themselves seemed likely to follow upon their doing so.'[89] John Stuart Mill, in 1867, put it less bluntly. He thought of Arnold as a 'practical reformer' because 'I think that it was in practice rather than in theory that his work and his influence were most beneficial. I look upon the example he set of friendly inter-course between master and scholars, and of effort on the part of the teacher to arouse moral ambition in his pupils, as of great practical value; and if generally followed, sure to produce (as I think it has already produced) a considerable reform in the whole method and results of school teaching.'[90] And, as a result of that reformed school teaching, it reformed the outlook, tone and intentions of much of society: and made, directly or indirectly, many of the men who applied their high minds to the improvement of people, the world in which they lived, and the institutions that ruled them. This was as well, for the challenges were fearsome.

PART I

THE CONDITION OF ENGLAND

CHAPTER I

THE ANGRY FORTIES: POVERTY, AGITATION AND RIOT

I

At quarter-past six in the evening of Monday 30 May 1842, as Queen Victoria and her husband, Prince Albert, drove down Constitution Hill in a barouche and four from her afternoon ride in Hyde Park, a man pulled out a pistol as if to take aim at the Sovereign. 'The powder was observed to flash in the pan, and in another instant, before the miscreant could have time to put fresh priming, a soldier of the 2d battalion of the Scotch Fusilier Guards . . . "pinned" him – that is, laid hold of both his arms at once. In this position he hurried the young man towards the Palace, and two or three other soldiers coming to his assistance, in less than two minutes from the time of the attempt he was housed in the Palace, being taken into the lodge.'[1] There were others keen to claim that it had, in fact, been they who had seized the would-be assassin. One account had it that a policeman, Constable Tanner, who had been watching him loiter suspiciously, had 'pinned' him before the Guardsman did.

The failed assassin was twenty-year-old John Francis, just three years younger than the Queen, 'his height five feet five inches [and] his person somewhat corpulent'. It was, in fact, Francis's second attempt to murder the Queen in two days. On Sunday 29 May he had been seen to draw a pistol as she passed on her way back from the Chapel Royal. Prince Albert had been alarmed, and sent for Sir Robert Peel, the Prime Minister, to discuss what could be done to prevent such an outrage on his wife. As a result the royal party had gone out the following afternoon surrounded by soldiers and policemen. It had made no difference: the

Queen's life was saved not by bodyguards, but by Francis's poor aim. The news of the attempt, and of the Queen's escape, was promulgated around London. To reach a large audience quickly, details were sent to West End theatres. Stage managers told shocked and relieved patrons the news of the 'fiendish attempt' on the Sovereign's life, and there was much singing of the national anthem. The next day Parliament gave thanks for the Queen's deliverance.

Two years earlier, on 10 June 1840, a man called Edward Oxford had tried to shoot the Queen at the same place on Constitution Hill. He had been tried for high treason but acquitted by reason of insanity, and was now in Bethlem Hospital. The Queen and her husband were keen an example should be made of her assailant. Oxford's acquittal had, they felt, encouraged the disaffected to take pot shots at her. When she read in her newspaper on 1 June that a warrant charged 'John Francis with shooting at our sovereign Lady Victoria the Queen, with a pistol loaded with powder and <u>ball</u>' she fired off an immediate letter to Peel to say that 'the <u>crime</u> was <u>shooting</u> at the Queen, and not whether it was with <u>Ball</u> or anything else': her point being that if the offending ball could not be found it would prejudice the case.[2] Within a month Francis was tried for high treason too, convicted, and sentenced to death. The sentence was commuted to transportation for life, not entirely to the royal couple's satisfaction. They seemed to have a point. Two days later, on 3 July 1842, another aggrieved subject, John Bean, shot at the Queen. His pistol seems to have been loaded with tobacco, and he received just eighteen months in prison.

It appears that mental instability, or attention-seeking, or simply a quest for celebrity were behind the first three of Victoria's potential assassins (there would be four more). Yet the attempts of 1842 seem in retrospect emblematic, coming as they did at a time of grave civil unrest in a Britain ravaged by poverty. Rapid industrialisation over the preceding half-century, and the appeal of the higher wages paid by manufacturing, had lured hundreds of thousands of agricultural workers to the towns. A collapse in demand in the early 1840s saw many of these people – and their families – thrown out of work, without the feudal structures of rural society to rescue them. The basic institutions designed to alleviate industrial poverty – notably the workhouses, established under the 1834 Poor Law – were being proved inadequate. Millions in the industrial districts were hungry, angry and agitating. There were fears the whole social order could break down, and trying to kill the Queen, shocking though that was, seemed in tune with the mood of many of her subjects.

Peel recommended to the Queen, via Prince Albert, that the death sentence on Francis be 'commuted into a sentence of transportation for life to the most penal settlement'.[3] The Queen agreed: but Albert was 'very anxious' to see Peel about the implications for the law of high treason, which judges deemed unsatisfactory for a case such as this. He told Peel he considered 'the life of the Sovereign is the most valuable and important in the community . . . is more exposed than the life of any other individual . . . that that liability to be injured is increased, when the Sovereign is a female' and that 'the increase of democratical and republican notions, with the licentiousness of the Press in our days must render people more prone to crimes of that kind.'[4] Judges had said it was not treason unless Francis had intended to kill, but the powder in his pistol had been inadequate for that task. 'I cannot say that the present statute affords that protection to the person of the Sovereign which my acknowledged premises require', Albert concluded.

Peel sent a memorandum to the Cabinet advising that the law of treason be revised to protect the Queen more – assault, when directed at 'the person of the Sovereign' should carry 'heavier penalties than at present'.[5] However, Sir James Graham, the Home Secretary and normally a hard man, warned him to calm things down. He felt transportation already seemed 'disproportionate to the crime' and that anything stronger for such a minor assault 'would violate public opinion'.[6] Having consulted the Cabinet, Peel wrote to Albert to say that a bill would go through Parliament proposing transportation for seven years 'with the alternative of fine and imprisonment with or without hard labour and with or without corporal punishment at the discretion of the court' for an assault against the Sovereign or an attempt to wound her.[7]

Albert was grateful, but split hairs over the word 'wound', wondering whether it was 'comprehensive enough for all the possible injuries and their moral and physical consequences, which may arise out of attempts made upon the Sovereign's person?'[8] He also argued that 'temporary transportation or imprisonment etc etc are calculated to exasperate the feelings of the miscreant and that he will soon be at liberty, considering the Sovereign the cause of his past suffering' and 'seek revenge upon her person.' This thinly disguised plea for severe retribution was rejected by Peel, who wrote back to the Prince on 12 July to point out that any measures should not 'run counter to the public feeling and temper of the times in respect to penal inflictions. If the law were in public opinion one of undue severity it would have less effect in deterring from the commission of the crime against which it was directed than if it had the moral weight and authority of that opinion in favour.'[9] A week earlier Thomas Carlyle had written to his mother of this indication of 'strange times': 'The people are sick of their misgovernment, and the blackguards among them shoot at the poor Queen . . . all men are becoming alarmed at the state of the country – as I think they well may.'[10]

II

The Establishment was alert to the problem of civil unrest, not least because of the constant fear that rioting operatives would wreck property and foment revolution. On 7 May 1842 Peel had convened a meeting with the Archbishop of Canterbury, the Bishop of London and Sir James Graham, to discuss 'the destitute condition of the labouring classes in some districts of the country, particularly in the neighbourhood of Paisley, and in some of the manufacturing towns and villages in Lancashire.' Peel wrote that 'the privations and suffering in these parts of the country have been during the winter and continue very great – the patience and submission with which they have been weathered have been exemplary in the highest sense. The local funds for the charitable support of the sufferers are in some cases nearly exhausted, and great apprehension is entertained by the magistrates and others as to the consequences of a complete exhaustion of these funds.'[11] He advised the Queen to write a public letter to her prelates, to be displayed in churches around Britain, soliciting contributions for the destitute. 'This was done on former occasions in the case of distress in Ireland, and also in the case of distress in the manufacturing districts of Britain.' He concluded by lauding in anticipation 'the moral effect of a demonstration of general sympathy with the distressed and of approval of their peaceable conduct and submission to the law' as 'advantageous'. On 20 May he further told the Queen that 'it appears advisable to YM [Your Majesty's] servants to open a subscription in aid of the distressed manufacturers in certain districts of Scotland and the North of England, the proceeds of which subscription to be applied for their relief together with the sum which may be raised in consequence of the issue of YM letter to the Archbishops and Bishops.'[12]

Such was the urgency, however, that Peel decided that 'in order to provide immediate relief, to give a certain sum from the Treasury without delay, such sum to be repaid from the produce of further subscriptions.' He suggested £500 from the Royal Bounty to go at the head of the subscription. Carlyle had travelled through the north earlier that month and told his friend Thomas Story Spedding that, on arrival at Manchester, 'the most tragic circumstance I noted there was the want of smoke; Manchester was never in my time third part as clear'.[13] There was no smoke because so many factories were closed. Shortly afterwards there were riots in Manchester, whipped up by the Anti-Corn Law League, the movement agitating for the removal of tariffs on imported corn, with the consequent lowering of the price of bread. The Poor Law system was breaking down under the strain in areas as diverse as Leeds, London, Scotland and the Potteries.[14]

In Paisley alone 17,000 people had thrown themselves on the Poor Law in February 1842, and money had run out. The previous month there had been £510 weekly available for what were then 14,817 unemployed, which worked out at eightpence-farthing each. The town produced almost only one commodity, a mixture of cotton and silk. Its main export market was America, where demand had collapsed. Banks in Scotland had then called in loans, leading to bankruptcies. Carlyle had been told that 'two thousand men and women assembled the other Saturday night before the provost's door in Paisley, and stood, without tumult, indeed almost in silence: when questioned as to their purposes, they said they had no money, no food nor fuel, they were Fathers and Mothers, working men and women, and had come out there to see whether they could not be saved alive.'[15] There was no violence, but soldiers were nearby to deter a riot.

A petition from Paisley was presented to the House of Lords on 30 June, signed by 6,000 inhabitants, complaining about how funds for the relief of the poor had been distributed. They had originally been given money-tickets, a form of legal tender usable at any shop in the town, but now were being paid in kind – which meant just bread, meal and potatoes. To make matters worse, this was more expensive than the previous system.[16] The petitioners claimed the local Poor Law commissioner had deliberately decided to distribute relief in kind 'to render the position of the labourers as disagreeable as possible, in order to induce them to emigrate to other parts of the country.' Graham, the Home Secretary, repudiated this suggestion forcefully.[17]

The people wanted relief distributed by magistrates or ministers, trusted members of their own community; and wanted, rather than charity, something done to improve the market for their goods, so they could live by their own labours. The weaving on which Paisley had built its prosperity had been a cottage industry until the 1820s, when the process became industrialised, attracting many more into the locality: a slump in demand had therefore had a catastrophic and concentrated effect. A complacent reply by the Duke of Wellington, on behalf of the government, when the petition was submitted created the belief in Paisley that the government had 'shuffled out' of taking responsibility and that for want of a 'great effort' to find enough provisions 'Parliament will be adjourned, and they will be allowed to starve and die'.[18] Each individual was given an allowance of 1s 2d a week, or, as Robert Wallace, the MP for Greenock put it, 'less than one-half of the allowances being given to common felons in prison.'[19]

In Leeds money had run out too, and only an appeal that raised £6,000 had kept people fed the previous winter. The number of families helped by the Workhouse Board had doubled since 1838; it was estimated that in the first quarter of 1842 one-fifth of the total population of 80,000 was dependent on the workhouse, with the cost of outdoor relief 23 per cent higher than a year earlier. Meanwhile, links between the Anti-Corn Law League and the Chartists – political agitators seeking the implementation of a six-point People's Charter of democratic rights – became ever closer, and the government began to fear a coalition of the lower and middle classes against aristocratic rule. Middle-class establishment figures in depressed towns, notably several mayors, were league members and were pressing the administration to accede to demands for reform. By early June 12,000 people in Glasgow were in receipt of relief because of a slump in trade, and there were rations of food for only about 4,250 people daily.[20] The police were breaking up gatherings of the unemployed in the city, for fear of what they might lead to. The Liberals, led by Lord John Russell, joined in demands for the repeal of the Corn Laws. Peel said there had been prosperity at times when there was no free import of corn.[21] This ignored a fact Peel himself would see within four years, that when times were not prosperous alleviation could be given by scrapping the duty.

III

The 1840s should have been a time of great social improvement. The coming of the railways improved mobility of labour, opened up new markets, and brought a wave of prosperity to Britain. However, the country contained seething discontents and vast inequalities, economic and political. One of the roots of the problem was the rapid rise in population in the first three decades of the nineteenth century. In England it had climbed from 8,308,000 in 1801 to 12,993,000 in 1831, according to the official censuses, growing as much in thirty years as in the previous two hundred. People had migrated from the countryside to towns in search of a better standard of living and for a time they found one. Children could go out to work not very long after they had learned to walk, and were for many families a commercial property; hence the growth in the size of those families. Although this caused overcrowding and sanitary problems, life was just about sustainable so long as the economy was doing well. If order books became empty, as they did after the downturn of the early 1840s, disaster beckoned.

Such periods of high unemployment made it imperative for the government to have a successful strategy for managing the poor at such times. The first Poor Law had been enacted at the end of the reign of Elizabeth I and placed an obligation on the pauper's parish to provide basic support for him and his family. By the 1830s this system was breaking down because of the high concentrations of people who had now moved in to previously nearly empty areas and who threw themselves on the charity of the parish, funded by a local poor rate that was entirely inadequate to the new levels of demand. The Poor Law Act of 1834 was designed to rectify this problem, but outraged not merely those whom it strove to protect but also the educated classes. The idea behind the 1834 Act was that the most obvious means was to deter people from becoming paupers by making pauperism dreadful. It operated on the utilitarian precept that there would be idleness if it was remunerated, and therefore relief should be contingent upon work. The environment in workhouses was made more unpleasant than that outside them, as a deterrent. As well as inmates having to do long hours of soul-destroying, menial tasks, such as breaking stones, crushing bones or picking oakum, families were separated. The inmates were made to wear uniforms of coarse material, and a single gate was guarded to regulate the comings and goings. They were like prisons, and poverty appeared to have been criminalised. Carlyle called workhouses 'Poor-Law Bastilles'.[22] *Oliver Twist*, written by Charles Dickens in 1837, was a propaganda exercise against the Act, and gave a relatively accurate depiction of pauperism.

In 1843 John Walter, proprietor of *The Times* and an MP, listed the humiliations, indignities and degradations inflicted on those who threw themselves on the parish, and the effect of these in destroying their fitness for work. He quoted a correspondent who visited workhouses regularly and who had told him that

> it is a demoralising system, tending to connect poverty with licen-tiousness, and to generate pauperism and crime. I only state to you what I know to be literally true, when I say that in union houses supposed to be administered as well as the system will permit, the work of demoralisation has been going on in every ward except those of sickness and old age. Among the poor unhappy children, among the adults of either sex, among the able-bodied, this propagation of evil has gone on. To particularise and classify its forms would be a revolting task. It would comprehend the recital of some of the most disgusting practices of licentiousness and many acts of crime. Persons well known to me have avowed, that many as were the temptations to sin without these walls, those within were far more mischievous and dangerous.[23]

So successful was the deterrent aspect of the Act in rural areas, where the agricultural way of life was increasingly depressed and uncertain, that it drove agricultural labourers and their families to urban areas where there was more chance of finding manual work and, they thought, of avoiding the workhouse. The commissioners behind the legislation intended this; and it had been accepted by a Whig majority in the first House of Commons to sit after the 1832 Reform Act, in which middle-class utilitarian principles began to assert themselves more than the old feudal paternalism of the aristocracy.

However, a population that had struggled to make a living in the countryside found that in moving to the towns it had exchanged the unpleasantness of the state's rural workhouse for that of capitalism's urban one. In a downturn, the workhouse was sometimes the only option to avoid starvation. The urban parishes to which distressed rural workers migrated found their poor rates rising steeply, to help bear the new burdens. The working class, as it encountered long-term hardship and sank into disappointment, had every incentive to join in the growing political agitation of the 1830s. The economy, at the start of Queen Victoria's reign in June 1837, was undergoing a fundamental restructuring, and one that the exponential growth of railways in the following decade would make almost revolutionary. As with all such restructurings, there were casualties; the effects of poverty shocked the concerned middle classes, provoking a philanthropic social movement to campaign for their alleviation.

Inspired by Carlyle, middle-class writers sought to alert their peers to the plight of the poor through what became known as the 'Condition of England' novel. Elizabeth Gaskell described the squalor of working-class life in *Mary Barton*, published in 1848. 'As they passed, women from their doors tossed household slops of *every* description into the gutter; they ran into the next pool, which overflowed and stagnated. Heaps of ashes were the stepping-stones, on which the passer-by, who cared in the least for cleanliness, took care not to put his foot. . . . you went down one step even from the foul area into the cellar in which a family of human beings lived.'[24] Charles Kingsley, a clergyman, novelist and Christian Socialist, writing a few years later, picked up the theme. 'Foul vapours rose from cowsheds and slaughter houses, and the doorways of undrained alleys, where the inhabitants carried the filth out on their shoes from the back-yard into the court, and from the court up into the main street; while above, hanging like cliffs over the streets – those narrow, brawling torrents of filth, and poverty, and sin, the houses with their teeming load of life were piled up into the dingy, choking night.'[25] Charles Dickens, the pre-eminent novelist of the age, described London in *Little Dorrit* as a city of darkness, misery and squalor. 'Melancholy streets in a penitential garb of soot, steeped the souls of the people who were condemned to look at them out of windows in dire despondency.'[26]

IV

By mid-July 1842 sporadic disturbances were breaking out in Staffordshire and elsewhere, and Graham sent in the militia. There was an unsuccessful attempt by radical MPs to shorten the parliamentary recess, forcing the Lords and Commons to sit in October. This was not so much to deal with the riots, as to make provision for the winter and avoid 'calamities' that bad weather would heap on top of poverty.[27] The government refused to consider this, or to pledge that if things worsened Parliament would be recalled: Graham said such a promise would be 'unconstitutional'.[28] There was talk in the north of revolution: part of this was rabble-rousing by agitators from the Anti-Corn Law League and by Chartists, but part was simple statement of fact. On 15 July the council of the League prepared a declaration stating that 'the country was on the eve of a revolution, and that the wheels of Government should be arrested', which would be among the pronouncements that would later cause its opponents to accuse it of 'treasonable' activity.[29]

At the Chartist Convention Council in Manchester one of the leaders, Dr Peter McDouall, a surgeon from south London, formally called for a general strike. McDouall repeated the call on 26 July at Deptford, and was arrested after speaking for fifteen minutes in the middle of Deptford Broadway. The police dispersed the meeting, which outraged the radicals. The policeman told him that 'you are holding an unlawful and illegal meeting, and using exciting language.' He had referred to 'the tyrant aristocracy of the country, who are trampling on the rights of the poor'. McDouall had form: he had been arrested for sedition in 1839, and was still on recognisance of £500.

By August 'long-continued unemployment had driven many of the men to leave their homes and go round the countryside in large bands, ostensibly begging for charity but overawing the neighbourhoods through which they passed by their mere appearance and numbers.'[30] Many men were on short time, or on strike. Eventually, calls for a general strike until the Charter was enforced became widespread. In Lancashire, Cheshire and Staffordshire pits, mills and factories were besieged and closed down by huge bands of men; and the unrest soon spread. It was not merely the unemployed. Those still in work had had their wages reduced.

Charles Greville, a courtier and diarist, wrote that the riots were 'sufficiently alarming but for the railroads, which enabled the Government to pour troops into the disturbed districts, and extinguish the conflagration at once.' Greville wrote a month after the uprisings: and reflected that 'the immediate danger is over, but those who are best informed look with great anxiety and apprehension to the future, and only consider what has recently happened as the beginning of a series of disorders.'[31] Much of the agitation had nothing to do with Chartist attempts to coordinate political action: but Peel and Graham saw lethal danger if the two forces met and fed off each other.

Fearing a riot on 16 August, on the anniversary of Peterloo – when in 1819 a cavalry charge on a reform demonstration in Manchester killed fifteen people and injured at least 400 others – Peel sent a battalion of Guards to Manchester and issued a Royal Proclamation warning people not to attend potentially violent public meetings. The railways delivered reinforcements to the north quickly: order was soon restored. In London, attempts to hold Chartist meetings were thwarted by swift action by the police and soldiery: Graham sent out orders to arrest the ringleaders and disperse the crowd. As things turned ugly in Staffordshire, Peel sent arms and ammunition for the defence of Drayton Manor, his country seat there. The preparations for class war, or possibly for the resistance against revolution, were in place.

Greville wrote on 2 November 1842 that he had met Lord Wharncliffe, the Lord Privy Seal, and James Kay-Shuttleworth, the Permanent Secretary of the Education Office of the Privy Council, 'who are both come from the north, [and] have given me an account of the state of the country and of the people which is perfectly appalling.'[32] He continued: 'There is an immense and continually increasing population, deep distress and privation, no adequate demand for labour, no demand for anything, no confidence, but a universal alarm, disquietude and discontent . . . Kay says that nobody can conceive the state of demoralisation of the people, of the masses, and that the only thing that restrains them from acts of violence against property is a sort of instinctive consciousness that, bad as things are, their own existence depends upon the security of property *in the long run.*' Although Greville seems typical of his class in apparently having little clue what to do about this, he also, typically, shares its fear and despair at the situation.

I have never seen, in the course of my life, so serious a state of things as that which now stares us in the face; and this after thirty years of uninterrupted peace, and the most ample scope afforded for the development of all our resources, when we have been altering, amending, and improving, wherever we could find anything to work upon, and being, according to our own ideas, not only the most free and powerful, but the most moral and the wisest people in the world . . . One remarkable feature in the present condition of affairs is that nobody can account for it, and nobody pretends to be able to point out any remedy; for those who clamour for the repeal of the Corn Laws, at least those who know anything of the matter, do not really believe that repeal would supply a cure for our distempers. It is certainly a very dismal matter for reflexion, and well worthy the consideration of the profoundest political philosophers, that the possession of such a Constitution, all our wealth, industry, ingenuity, peace, and that superiority in wisdom and virtue which we so confidently claim, are not sufficient to prevent the existence of a huge mountain of human misery, of one stratum in society in the most deplorable state, both moral and physical, to which mankind can be reduced, and that all our advantages to not secure us against occurrence of evils and mischiefs so great as to threaten a mighty social and political convulsion.[33]

In December 1842 the Quarterly Review devoted much space to a review by John Wilson Croker of 'a few specimens of the ephemeral spawn of incendiary tracts, advertisements, and placards with which the Anti-Corn-Law Associations inundate the country' (it added 'they scarcely deserve to be considered as literature').[34] Croker, a former MP for Dublin University and close friend of Wellington, was famed for his animosities and hatreds and also for his adherence to lost causes. He had left the Commons in 1832, pledging never to sit in a reformed parliament. He had contributed to the Quarterly since its foundation, and his approach to any issue relied on abuse of its partisans rather than on evidence-based argument. He was the model for the slimy and scruple-free placeman Rigby in Benjamin Disraeli's novel Coningsby, a comparison that does him no favours. In this article the tone of his strictures moves from the simply aggressively partisan towards the hysterical and irrational. The publications of the League, he said, brought 'to the tribunal of public opinion the foulest, the most selfish, and altogether perhaps the most dangerous combination of recent times', worse even than the Jacobin of the French Revolution, who 'avowed his real designs, and was therefore more easily dealt with than these hypocritical associations, which "grown, like Satan, wiser than of yore", assume more cautious forms and more plausible pretences in pursuit of the same ultimate object.'

He said that the 'war cry' of 'cheap bread' had replaced that of the 'rights of man', but was 'equally deceptive'. He claimed that the up-risings of the previous summer had shocked even the League, whose members (he asserted) had hoped the rioters would do their dirty work for them: but the rioters had felt no great common cause with them. What really upset Croker was the determination by the League to raise another £50,000 to continue its 'lawless crusade' that 'pollutes and perverts the most sacred topics into incentives to pillage and bloodshed.' He thought that raising money 'for the avowed purpose of forcing the legislature to alter the law of the land' was, if not 'criminally punish-able', then 'illegal and in the highest degree unconstitutional'. Anyone who gave money to this cause, he added, would effectively be an accessory to evil; and he ridiculed the claim, made strongly by the League, that protectionism encouraged violence such as had been seen all over northern England a few months earlier.

Croker accused the late Whig ministry in general, and Lord John Russell in particular, of having engineered in industrial towns the appointment of magistrates sympathetic to its policy of repeal, who would then go easy on agitation and agitators. These were, he said, magistrates who 'had many positive disqualifications – who were unfit from station and character for any such trust – who were factious and turbulent when they should have been quiet, and were pusillan-imous or torpid when they should have been active.'[35] There is a tone of *de haut en bas* outrage in the article, not just that a government not run by Tories should have appointed its own placemen to the magistracy – something no Tory would, of course, have ever done – but that the opponents of protection should be upset at what they called '*the unjust refusal of the House of Commons* to hear evidence at the bar of Parliament', or at the '*misgovernment of a rich and powerful aristocracy*'.

He was yet more disgusted that some elements of the aristocracy had lent their names to the activities of the League. The Countess of Ducie and the Countess of Radnor were among its patronesses. He mocked the League for not knowing how to refer correctly to a pair of earl's daughters who had also lent their names, and thundered a rebuke to those who 'should have chosen to exhibit their wives and daughters in the character of political agitators', as if those women were private property.[36]

By the time Croker's *Quarterly* article appeared, with its scaremongering about insurrection and revolution, and its dire predictions of the consequences of conspiracy between Leaguers and Chartists, prosecutions of agitators had wrong-footed the latter group and, to an extent, the former. However, the Provost of Paisley told Peel that the relief operation there had run out of money and that 10,000 people faced a choice between starvation and crime.[37] This same Provost, taken perfectly seriously by Peel, was derided by Croker for having publicly stated his refusal to order troops to fire on rioters if an insurrection broke out.[38] Croker refused to accept the desperate conditions in the industrial districts, and showed contempt for those who described them. Given the article's lack of direct observation it is worthless as journalism, but valuable in what it shows of a cast of mind that, had it been more widespread, would have precipitated the very revolution it savaged the agitators for discussing.

Croker exaggerated the menace to public order: but mocked a claim made by the League in June 1842 about 'public peace in danger from starvation in Manchester', which turned out to be rather nearer the truth than Croker (who made no mention of having visited the distressed districts) would have conceded.[39] It was easy for him, with the varied mass of League propaganda at his disposal, to find extremists among the Leaguers: to find mavericks talking of assassinating Peel, or claiming that 'a callous-hearted aristocracy were determined to goad the people to rebellion, in order to govern by the sword'.[40] He also regarded as seditious the calls for strikes, mocking the notion of 'a fair day's wages for a fair day's work'. His underlying motivation is, by the end, however, quite clear; fear that the League was gaining support; fear that supporters were in some cases donating large amounts of money; fear that some of the well-to-do and the aristocracy were being seduced by the League; and fear, in the end, that the arguments the League advanced, especially when advocated by the likes of Richard Cobden, the radical MP and leader of the League – 'the spoiled child of agitation' – would prevail in the end.[41] Croker's largely ad hominem attack on Cobden reveals no understanding of the man, or of his motivations.

The government was still at a loss to know how to solve the problems that had, during 1842, brought the country to the verge of anarchy. Once the new session of Parliament opened in February 1843 there was a five-day debate in the Commons that reflected the agitation of the political class at what was perceived by Lord Howick, who opened the debate, to be the lack of government action. 'The absence of all announcement of remedial measures', Howick observed, should cause the House 'to consider whether things can be safely left in this situation . . . I believe the situation of the country to be one of the most serious danger.'[42] As well as describing the shocking condition of the industrial districts, he also outlined the suffering of the agricultural worker, as a lack of disposable income had driven down demand for food and therefore for his labour. He said the coal trade would be retaining fewer men on lower wages. The same was true for shipbuilders and shipping companies. The knock-on effects were already serious: forty or fifty shops in Sunderland's High Street were unoccupied. The national excise revenue was down by a quarter; the cost of the workhouse in Sunderland had more than doubled in five years. He feared a new insurrection: 'I cannot help reminding the House that it has already had a warning upon this subject in the disturbances of last summer.'[43]

His suggested remedy caused uproar on the Tory benches: the dropping of tariffs and the application of the principles of free trade, to stimulate industry. He told them they had nothing to fear: 'a large increase in your imports would be attended by a great increase in your exports, and in your manufacturing industry.'[44] To Peel's distress William Ewart Gladstone, the vice-president of the Board of Trade, sought to calm matters by calling the Corn Laws 'temporary'. This unnerved Peel and upset many Tories, but by 20 December 1843 Gladstone was noting in his diary that 'Sir R. Peel expressed *obiter* a strong opinion that the next change in the Corn Laws would be total repeal.'[45] Richard Cobden, who would lead the fight for repeal, was prompted to observe that 'an aristocracy cannot maintain its station on wealth moistened with the orphans' and the widows' tears, and taken from the crust of the peasant.'[46] In a prophetic passage that looked forward to the realignment of the parties three years later, he added that 'it is time, then, to give up bandying the terms Whig and Tory about from one side of the House to the other, and engage in a serious inquiry into the present condition of the country.'[47]

The despair of the ruling class was exacerbated by their perception that the problem of poverty was growing unchecked. Lord Ripon, the

President of the Board of Trade, had said that 'the name of pauper by no means implies, as seems to have been supposed, a man unable or unwilling to work—one whose infirmity or whose idleness would disqualify him from becoming an useful settler. On the contrary, the whole of the married labourers in many of the parishes of the south of England may be correctly described as paupers, inasmuch as the want of employment has depressed wages to a rate at which it is impossible for a man, however industrious, to maintain a family without receiving parochial relief.'[48] However, Sir James Graham, Ripon's Cabinet colleague, maintained a hard line that ensured the concerns of the more liberal-minded went unanswered. He believed that 'the whole policy of the Poor-law has been improved by the alterations effected by the measure which passed in 1834; and if its Christianity be looked at, I say that the great precepts of Christianity—namely, to clothe the naked, to feed the hungry, to visit the sick—are practically carried into effect under the operation of this measure . . . In no Christian community in the civilized world is there a law which provides so humanely, so charitably, so largely, for the sick, the needy and the destitute, in their hours of affliction and suffering.'[49]

This was nonsense, not least because of the failure of the law that Graham praised to make the vital Victorian distinction between the deserving and the undeserving poor. His caustic and haughty personality and his perceived heartlessness had already made him unpopular in the Commons, and interventions such as this made him more so. Since joining the Tories in 1835 he had become attached to social conservatism in a way that would have made him comfortable in Liverpool's government. Peel and he became close; and Peel invited him to be Home Secretary on taking office in 1841. The rank and file of the party continued to dislike him. His complete absence of sympathy with radicalism and the aspirations of the working classes made him a problematical man to have as Home Secretary during the era of Chartism. Those seeking further reform soon cast him as a hate-figure. When Lord Ashley, who would become the noted philanthropist Lord Shaftesbury, wrote to Peel on 20 November 1842 to thank him for meeting representatives of the operatives, he said that 'the delegations from the factory districts were <u>much pleased</u> by their conferences with <u>you</u>; they entertain, I think unjustly, very different feelings towards Sir James Graham.'[50]

General Johnson, a Tory MP, argued that

no one could deny—nay, not even its supporters—that the law was extremely harsh and cruel in its operation. The boards of guardians themselves in many instances were so convinced of its cruelty that they gave alms themselves from their own pockets to those to whom they were not permitted to afford out-door relief . . . It was impossible that a Christian feeling could consent to throw the whole of the poor into one mass, without distinguishing between the bad and the deserving, without drawing a line between those reduced to poverty by their own intemperance and those who were afflicted by the visitation of the Almighty. Could that law be Christian which would subject those two classes to the same treatment? . . . The principle of the present act made poverty a crime, whilst the law of Elizabeth did no such thing.[51]

After 1842, the government was badly on the defensive: with intelligent men such as Peel and Gladstone increasingly aware that upholding the status quo in both the Poor Law and the Corn Laws would simply risk insurrection, it was not a matter of whether the ruling class would act, but when. Those with a vision of change were about to have the upper hand.

CHAPTER 2

NOBLESSE OBLIGE: POLITICS AND THE ARISTOCRACY

I

Dr Arnold, in his contempt for the Tories' opposition to reform, and his despair that the newly prosperous middle classes would ever see the evil of their exploitation of the working classes, had written to a brother clergyman in September 1836 that 'vulgar minds can never understand the duty of reform till it is impressed on them by the *argumentum ad ventrem*; and the mass of mankind, whether in good coats or in bad, will always be vulgar-minded.'[1] Arnold had seen clearly how even well-meaning attempts at improving the condition of the working classes could misfire: he saw the Poor Law Act as 'a measure in itself wise and just, but which, standing alone, and unaccompanied by others of a milder and more positively improving tendency, wears an air of harshness and will, I fear, embitter the feelings of the poorer classes still more.'[2]

He shared these opinions, to an extent, with a man who was fast becoming the most prominent commentator of the day: Thomas Carlyle. Carlyle was an exact contemporary of Arnold, being born in 1795: but outlived the Doctor by almost forty years. Like Arnold, he was a serious scholar, a man of immense learning and deep and wide reading. Unlike him, he was the son of an Annandale peasant who, through his family's industry and sacrifice, was sent to Edinburgh University, often walking there and back at the beginning and end of terms to conserve money. Eventually Carlyle found patrons and broke into the business of writing for reviews. He had also married above his station to the well-to-do Jane Welsh, whose family laughed at Carlyle's lack of breeding but conceded his astonishing talent.

After several years of subsistence living in the Scottish lowlands, the Carlyles moved to London in 1834. In his love of the sound of his own voice and his almost wilful obscurity, Carlyle seems to have had a version of autism: yet he (and more to the point his wife, with whom he had difficult relations that may well have included the non-consummation of their marriage) became a supreme networker, befriending early on John Stuart Mill, with whose liberal philosophy he would come violently to disagree, and then Dickens. Fame came in 1837 with his *History of the French Revolution*, a work of scholarship and research, which (not least thanks to Carlyle's unusual, apostrophising style) at times reads like a screenplay. But for astonishing resolution on Carlyle's part, the work might never have appeared: for he gave the first volume of the manuscript to Mill to read, and Mill's housemaid lit the fire with it. Mill compensated Carlyle financially, and Carlyle wrote the book again. Mill also gave Carlyle part of his own collection of works on the revolution to help his research.

Carlyle's main interest, however, was political rather than historical. He was deeply concerned about how societies worked, or did not work: he saw their coherence as crucial. He had imbibed from history a belief in the rule of an aristocracy, which in return for its status and privileges cared for those over whom it ruled. This attachment to feudalism was romantic in an industrialised society undergoing an explosion in population: but Carlyle would not let such considerations impede him, and he found followers for what even at the time seemed a far-fetched idea.

The social ferment after the 1832 Reform Act electrified Carlyle. He felt he understood why the Act had not solved the problem of social unrest: and he saw the Chartist agitation from 1838 onwards as proof that without a reversion to benign aristocratic rule, and the replacement of the capitalist system, there would be nothing but misery and, in the end, revolution. The Act had extended the franchise, but insufficiently. It retained a too small political class, and excluded many men of intelligence and, more dangerously, political motivation. Carlyle wrote to Mill in the winter of 1838, some months before he began his extended essay called *Chartism*, to voice his pessimism at what could be done for the social conditions of the people in the face of overwhelming odds. 'It is a bitter mockery to talk of "improvement" to the men I have known! Ebenezer Elliot is with me; Machinery, and Population increasing 1200 a day, are with me.'[3]

Writing a year later, on 15 April 1839, to his brother, Carlyle noted how the rest of England looked from his haven in Chelsea: 'The distress indeed I believe to be great and universal in this land at present; and some are beginning to predict now a second year of dearth, so bleak is our spring hitherto. Many thousands of operatives in the North are getting pikes and pistols – poor wretches, their heart is bitter, their case is hard and hopeless . . . people ought to bundle that can; and leave a Country where blood and confusion seem inevitable before very long.'[4]

Carlyle saw Chartism as the inevitable result of the abandonment of the responsibilities of the moneyed classes: a view consequent upon his romantic belief in feudalism. Chartism was 'revenge begotten of ignorance and hunger . . . the material of it exists I believe in the hearts of all our working population.'[5] He made these comments in the summer of 1839, after the wave of riots in the industrial north and midlands (Newcastle, Liverpool, Birmingham and Chester) but also in towns such as Devizes, Welshpool and Warwick. 'Unless gentry, clergy and all manner of washed articulate-speaking men will learn that their position towards the unwashed is contrary to the Law of God, and change it soon, the Law of Man, one has reason to discern, will change it before long, and in no soft manner.'[6] He uttered a remarkably accurate prophecy in the same letter, to Thomas Story Spedding, a Cumberland landowner and scholar: 'The fever-fit of Chartism will pass, and other fever-fits; but the thing it means will not pass, till whatsoever of truth and justice lies in the heart of it has been fulfilled, it cannot pass till *then* – a long date, I fear.'

Mill and Carlyle would take wildly different views of politics and of the answer to the Condition of England question, and drift apart. In October 1840 Carlyle indicated the direction their quarrel would take. 'And now when will you write', he asked Mill, 'of the New Aristocracy we have to look for? That seems to me the question; all Democracy a mere transitionary preparation for that.'[7] Carlyle hoped the newly enfranchised would restore a benign feudalism; Mill, more realistic about industrial progress, the breaking of old communities and social ties, and the growth of prosperity knew democracy was the only bulwark against revolution, and, once installed, would be removed only by force.

Carlyle had Mill to thank for the publication of *Chartism*. After the

Quarterly Review declined to run it, Mill's own *Westminster Review* published it at the very end of 1839. Its first chapter is entitled 'Condition of England Question' – a phrase that would resonate for decades – and began with the understatement that 'a feeling very generally exists that the condition and disposition of the Working Classes is a rather ominous matter at present'.[8] He derided the notion, put out in the establishment newspapers, that the government had seen off the Chartists: he saw no reason why the agitation should end or, indeed, why it should not get worse. He saw the problem as 'weighty, deep-rooted, far-extending'.[9] He felt the reformed parliament incapable of grasping the difficulty, thinking it obsessed with low politics and questions of personal advancement.

'The struggle that divides the upper and lower in society over Europe, and more painfully and notably in England than elsewhere . . . will end and adjust itself as all other struggles do and have done, by making the right clear and the might clear,' he wrote.[10] In other words (and Carlyle is not always direct) a strong leader, using coercive force – perhaps such as his hero Cromwell – would be needed to restore order. However, that was but part of it.

Dr Arnold might have made a case for the Poor Law, but Carlyle savaged it. That it was said to be the 'chief glory' of the administration 'betokens, one would imagine, rather a scarcity of glory there.' He continues: 'To say to the poor, Ye shall eat the bread of affliction and drink the water of affliction, and be very miserable while here, required not so much a stretch of heroic faculty in any sense, as due toughness of bowels.'[11] The poor were like rats who find granaries sealed. They must work or starve: 'The New Poor-Law is an announcement, sufficiently distinct, that whosoever will not work ought not to live.'[12]

Carlyle believed men wanted to work: who in feudal times (before the invention of machinery which, he fails to acknowledge, cannot be uninvented) would have been found work. However, in the industrial society, ruled by laissez-faire and the law of supply and demand, there was not always a job to be done. This required more active government – 'a government of the under classes by the upper on a principle of *Let-alone* is no longer possible in England in these days . . . The Working Classes cannot any longer go on without government; without being *actually* guided and governed.'[13] Yet neither the Church nor the State seemed to want to educate, or to guide, in this manner, and seemed careless of the sufferings of the lower classes.

He doubted Chartism had the answer. 'What are all popular commotions and maddest bellowings, from Peterloo to the Place-de-Grève [the square in Paris used for public executions during the revolution] itself? Bellowings, inarticulate cries as of a dumb creature in rage and pain; to the ear of wisdom they are inarticulate prayers: "Guide me, govern me! I am mad and miserable, and cannot guide myself!" Surely of all "rights of man", this right of the ignorant man to be guided by the wiser, to be, gently or forcibly, held in the true course by him, is the indisputablest.'[14] This would be rejected not just by Chartists, whose argument was that they had had enough of being controlled, but also by a hapless governing class, for whom a return to feudalism was impossible. He did, though, inspire some to act more paternalistically, and as such would influence Disraeli, as novelist and politician, and his fellow members of Young England.

Carlyle would find more support in his assertion – and this was Arnold's point – that instead of a relationship built on governance of the foolish by the wise, the relationship between men was now money. He wrote that in 'the most perfect feudal time . . . Cash Payment had not then grown to be the universal sole nexus of man to man; it was something other than money that the high then expected from the low, and could not live without getting from the low. Not as buyer and seller alone, of land or what else it might be, but in many senses still as soldier and captain, as clansman and head, as loyal subject and guiding king, was the low related to the high. With the supreme triumph of Cash, a changed time has entered; there must a changed aristocracy enter'.[15] But it would not: the landed classes were too busy 'preserving their Game'.[16]

II

Three and a half years after *Chartism* Carlyle published possibly his most rational, compelling and influential work: *Past and Present*. He wrote it in less than two months, while collecting the letters and speeches of Oliver Cromwell, inspired by something he had witnessed in the late summer of 1842 when riding around Huntingdonshire, Cromwell's county. As he passed the workhouse at St Ives on 7 September he saw 'sitting on wooden benches, in front of their Bastille and within their ring-wall and its railings, some half-hundred or more of these men. Tall robust figures, young mostly or of middle age; of honest countenance, many of them thoughtful or even intelligent-looking men. They sat there, near by one another; but in a kind of torpor, especially in a silence, which was very striking . . . there was something that reminded me of Dante's Hell in the look of all this; and I rode swiftly away.'[17]

He was outraged by this waste of potential; this denial, because of capitalism's workings, of the ability of a man to fulfil himself through labour. He cast aside his work on Cromwell and proceeded to attack the system. Many of the arguments, and some of the language, are familiar from *Chartism*. Going beyond that work, however, Carlyle presents his evidence of 'the most perfect feudal times': he quotes extensively from the chronicles of Jocelin de Brakelond, a twelfth-century monk from Bury St Edmunds, whose writings had recently been published by the Camden Society. Jocelin described how a medieval society based upon the abbey at Bury provided work and sustenance for the local people. The message is not so much 'return to this' as 'imitate this': he asks whether some modern equivalent could not be contemplated.

The work is laced with black humour, starting with the grim superscription from Schiller: *Ernst ist das Leben*, life is earnest. He quotes newspaper accounts of the trials of parents charged with killing their children because they could not feed them, and asks how this could happen in what appeared to him to be a land of plenty. He felt the lower classes were asking their betters: 'what is it you mean to do with us?' and hearing no coherent reply.[18] They sought 'a fair day's wages for a fair day's work', which he described as 'the everlasting right of man', and one that 'Midas-eared Mammonisms' had pushed to one side. He had not changed his tune since *Chartism*: an aristocracy, doing its job properly, was needed to rescue the helpless. However, perhaps it was a subtly different type of aristocracy: 'We must have more Wisdom to govern us, we must be governed by the Wisest, we must have an Aristocracy of Talent!'[19] However, he registered his despair at finding it: for so few people, measuring as they did everything by pounds, shillings and pence, did not know what real talent was. 'Supply-and-demand, Cash-payment the one nexus of man to man: Free trade, Competition, and Devil take the hindmost,

our latest Gospel yet preached,' as he also put it.[20] It was, for good
measure, 'the Gospel of Despair'.[21]

If men who were workless were desperate, the fate of those with
work was little better. Carlyle saw them as dehumanised, their work
a 'tragic spectacle. Men in the rapidest motion and self-motion; restless, with convulsive energy, as if driven by Galvanism, as if possessed
by a Devil.'[22] He also gave his opinions on liberty, a decade and a half
before Mill would write his. There was no consonance of view.
'Liberty? The true liberty of a man, you would say, consisted in his
finding out, or being forced to find out the right path, and to walk
thereon. To learn, or to be taught, what work he actually was able
for; and then by permission, persuasion, and even compulsion, to set
about doing of the same.'[23] Democracy was not the answer to
England's problems: 'Democracy, which means despair of finding any
Heroes to govern you, and contented putting-up with the want of
them.'[24]

Carlyle's remedy was that the State, just as it had fighting services,
should have other services that both provided work and sought to reassert order. For a man who would be derided posthumously as a fascist,
he pre-empted much socialism. His state is not run by commissars,
however, but by the old ruling class. He feared society would collapse
unless the traditional order began to function again: 'A High Class
without duties to do is like a tree planted on precipices; from the roots
of which all the earth has been crumbling.' As things stood, nobility
was becoming a meaningless concept.[25] 'The Working Aristocracy: Mill-
owners, Manufacturers, Commanders of Working Men . . . must strike
into a new path; must understand that money alone is not the representative either of man's success in the world, or of man's duties to
man; and reform their own selves from top to bottom, if they wish
England reformed. England will not be habitable long, unreformed.'[26]

Carlyle was not a lone voice. In the early 1840s a group of young
aristocrats and politicians, which came to be known as the Young England
movement, was influenced by Carlyle's highly unrealistic longing for a
pre-industrial society. They also venerated a fantasy medievalism of the
type advanced by Sir Walter Scott, and pursued a romantic idea of
feudalism. The group was led by Lord John Manners, a younger son
of the Duke of Rutland, George Smythe, the son of Lord Strangford,
and Alexander Baillie Cochrane, son of an admiral of the fleet. Unlike

Carlyle, they were rooted in a sentimental view of the past: for Carlyle the romance of feudalism was precisely because of what he believed to be its practical application to the creation of a happy, ordered society, and sentiment did not come into it. Benjamin Disraeli, dandy and novelist turned Tory politician, evoked the mood in his writings of the early 1840s, such as in his description of the young Coningsby (based on Smythe), having sent his luggage on ahead, walking through the Vale of Belvoir in the summer of 1837 on his way to Beaumanoir – in reality Belvoir Castle, seat of the Mannerses. 'It was a fragment of one of those vast sylvan tracts wherein Norman kings once hunted and Saxon outlaws plundered . . . sometimes the green earth was thickly studded with groves of huge and vigorous oaks, intersected with those smooth and sunny glades that seem as if they must be cut for dames and knights to saunter in.'[27]

Lord Blake, in his life of Disraeli, speculated that he espoused this cause purely to keep in with a constituency of glamorous young men in the Commons who comprised the group; and quotes Manners, as wondering whether Disraeli actually believed what he said. He would not be the last Tory to ask that question. Blake himself is not sure.[28] The Duke of Rutland regarded Disraeli as a corrupting influence on his son, as did Lord Strangford on his. Rutland stigmatised Disraeli as 'a designing person', a view that proved accurate when Disraeli dropped the Young Englanders as soon as they were of no further use to him.[29] Disraeli was not from the aristocracy; but he adopted their views and outlook and affected to speak for them in his writings.

Disraeli's novels have little literary merit, though so distinguished a critic as John Holloway wrote that they had 'a colourful, irresponsible brilliance'.[30] They have acquired a currency in political circles because of their espousal by generations of earnest, and not especially analytical, Conservatives, duped by Disraeli just as many of his contemporaries and younger protégés were. He has become a purveyor of metaphors, notably when he sought to describe the divisions of the country in *Sybil*, published in 1845, in terms that would echo down generations of Tory politicians:

'Well, society may be in its infancy,' said Egremont slightly smiling; 'but, say what you like, our Queen reigns over the greatest nation that ever existed.'

'Which nation?' asked the younger stranger, 'for she reigns over two.'

The stranger paused; Egremont was silent, but looked inquiringly.

'Yes,' resumed the younger stranger after a moment's interval. 'Two nations; between whom there is no intercourse and no sympathy; who are as ignorant of each other's habits, thoughts, and feelings, as if they were dwellers in different zones, or inhabitants of different planets; who are formed by a different breeding, are fed by a different food, are ordered by different manners, and are not governed by the same laws.'

'You speak of –' said Egremont, hesitatingly.

'THE RICH AND THE POOR.'[31]

Disraeli, like others in Young England, may have been influenced by *Past and Present*: though no proof can be found that he ever read a word of Carlyle. When Egremont, younger son of a dissolute noble family, meets some strangers in the ruins of Marney Abbey, on his brother's estates, and enters into a discussion with one of them, he is lectured on the superiority of the age when the Abbots of Marney controlled the land compared with the era of the secular, aristocratic landlord. This echoes Carlyle's interpretation of Jocelin de Brakelond exactly, and Jocelin's account of the regulation of society by the Abbey of St Edmundsbury. Such is the discontent of the local peasantry with Lord Marney, Egremont's hard and selfish elder brother, that they have started burning his hayricks.

The stranger tells Egremont:

'The Monastics could possess no private property; they could save no money; they could bequeath nothing. They lived, received, and expended in common. The monastery too was a proprietor that never died and never wasted. The farmer had a deathless landlord then; not a harsh guardian, or a grinding mortgagee, or a dilatory master in chancery, all was certain; the manor had not to dread a change of lords, or the oaks to tremble at the axe of the squandering heir . . . The monks were in short in every district a point of refuge for all who needed succour, counsel, and protection; a body of individuals having no cares of their own, with wisdom to guide the inexperienced, with wealth to relieve the suffering, and often with power to protect the oppressed.'[32]

The key point of comparison with the contemporary aristocracy, however, is:

'The monks were never non-resident. They expended their revenue among those whose labour had produced it. These holy men too built and planted as they did everything else for posterity: their churches were cathedrals; their schools colleges; their halls and libraries the muniment rooms of kingdoms; their woods and waters, their farms and gardens, were laid out and disposed on a scale and in a spirit that are now extinct: they made the country beautiful, and the people proud of their country.'[33]

Disraeli's novel is better as a work of propaganda than of literature. Its plot is absurdly contrived, despite its link to fact and its use of characters based on people Disraeli knew. They vary from the shallow to the incredible, with stereotypes of aristocrats whose haughtiness and lack of feeling verge upon the sociopathic, and of the industrial classes who range from the brutish to a domesticated version of the noble savage. Set pieces make the point by portraying extremes: aristocrats slaughtering game by hundreds of head, and the next day sitting on magistrates' benches imprisoning men for poaching to feed their families. Cobbett, a couple of decades earlier, had made the same point.[34] Though Disraeli, by the time of *Sybil*, was about to break with Young England for reasons of political expediency, homage is still paid to the group's romantic attitude to the past, when the nobility had yet to become degenerate. The only aristocrat who instinctively shows true regard for the poor (unlike Egremont himself, brought to learn it through his devotion to Sybil) is St Lys, the vicar of the industrial town of Mowbray; but then his antecedents came over with the Conqueror, rather than having bought and wheedled their way into the aristocracy in later times. Sybil herself has a concealed aristocratic lineage, a familiar feature of what Gillian Beer has called 'wishful Victorian literature': in other words, when anyone turns up who seems to be from the lower classes and starts to do good, they must (whether we know it or not) be nobility, for blood will out.[35] Professor Beer suggests everything changed with Darwin, when everyone realised we all started from the same point.

Disraeli echoes Carlyle's point that philanthropists should address problems at home before seeking to right the wrongs of the rest of the world. Speaking of how the very poor would be deliberately careless with their children in the hope that they would die and relieve the parents of a burden, he notes that 'infanticide is practised as extensively and as legally in England, as it is on the banks of the Ganges; a circumstance which apparently has not yet engaged the attention of the Society for the Propagation of the Gospel in Foreign Parts.'[36] Later, he has a character ask: 'could they not spare one missionary from Tahiti for their fellow-countrymen at Wodgate?'[37] He draws attention to the rapid increases in population, cited by one of the aristocrats as a reason to stop creating employment, as it only encourages breeding. As one character puts it, 'what are your invasions of the barbarous nations, your Goths and Visigoths, your Lombards and Huns, to our population returns?'[38] Census figures show that the population of England rose from 13.8 million in 1831 to 18 million in 1851. In fact, the population would have grown even faster but for the Potato Famine and outbreaks of cholera in 1831 and 1847. The climax of *Sybil* is the rioting in the north of England in the summer of 1842, an event that allows the martyrdom of Gerard and the demise – 'literally stoned to death' – of Lord Marney.[39] Marney, who felt his people were well off on 7s a week, had his counterparts in reality.

III

While Peel was trying to hold a line between romantic feudalists such as Disraeli and hard-nosed reactionaries such as Graham, Lord Ashley became the leading advocate for improving the working and social conditions of the lower classes. He was heir to the earldom of Shaftesbury, and a Tory MP. Ashley had become a devout evangelical in the 1830s and had the high mind that went with such a persuasion. He supported missionary societies and movements, not those who took the Gospel to the natives of the colonies, but those who took it to the natives of British slums. He also worked for the conversion of the Jews, and regarded those who wished to introduce Catholic doctrine and practice into the Church of England as profoundly sinister. He attributed his religious devotion not to his parents, whom he seems to have loathed, but to a maidservant in their house. His father, the sixth earl, was so vile that Ashley spent much of his adult life estranged from him and barred from his house. One of Ashley's friends at Oxford,

Henry Fox, described old Lord Shaftesbury as 'disgusting, and meaner than any wretch in the world.'[40] Ashley did not have it so badly as his eldest sister, Charlotte, on whom (as he reported) his father poured 'malignity and horror' until his children were old enough to answer him back.[41]

Ashley was clever – with a first from Christ Church, like Peel and Gladstone. He was well connected with the Whigs, and always on the whiggish, or progressive, end of the Tory spectrum. His uncle, the Duke of Marlborough, got him into parliament for Woodstock in 1826, when he was just twenty-five. His philanthropic urges he attributed to seeing a pauper's funeral while a Harrow schoolboy, and his motivation was religious, as he demonstrated in the House of Commons in February 1843 when making the case for educating the poor: 'I know not where to search for these things but in the lessons and practice of the Gospel: true Christianity is essentially favourable to freedom of institutions in Church and State, because it imparts a judgment of your own and another's rights, a sense of public and private duty, an enlarged philanthropy and self-restraint, unknown to those democracies of former times, which are called, and only called, the polished nations of antiquity.'[42] Throughout his life he demonstrated a strong sense of paternalism, and, as with other reformers, one sometimes detects an anxiety in his words and writing about the possible dire consequences of the State not taking measures to improve the lot of the poor.

Rather like Gladstone, the firmness of his cast of mind made him difficult for his political associates to handle. From his earliest days he was driven by a sense of social obligation, yet was a man of certain paradoxes. He profoundly opposed the 1832 Reform Bill and, later, would be a diehard opponent of the secret ballot. Yet among his wide range of good causes he helped drive legislation to protect the mentally ill, and in 1833 became chairman of the Metropolitan Commission in Lunacy. However, during the 1840s his political life would be dedicated to seeking to improve the conditions that industrialisation had created for the urban poor. He was pressed to take on the leadership in the Commons of the campaign to improve conditions in factories and shorten the hours worked there. His desire to limit by law work in factories to ten hours a day became a central cause of his political life. He succeeded in 1833 in influencing the Factory Act, but it fell short of what he and his followers wanted, notably in securing the ten-hour day. It had, though, excluded children under nine from factories, and limited those under thirteen to working nine hours a day. It introduced a regime of inspection, an important ideological step in allowing the State to regulate relations between masters and men.

In April 1840 Ashley backed a law to regulate child chimney-sweeps. There was a widespread view that the 'climbing boys' were 'poor little creatures who had nobody to protect them', and their exploitation would 'deserve the reprobation of the country'.[43] Kingsley described the life of such boys in the opening paragraphs of *The Water-Babies*, published in 1863:

> He could not read nor write, and did not care to do either; and he never washed himself, for there was no water up the court where he lived. He had never been taught to say his prayers. He had never heard of God, or of Christ, except in words which you never have heard, and which it would have been well if he had never heard . . . He cried when he had to climb the dark flues, rubbing his poor knees and elbows raw; and when the soot got into his eyes, which it did every day in the week; and when his master beat him, which he did every day in the week; and when he had not enough to eat, which he did every day in the week likewise.[44]

Ashley felt that 'the condition of [factory] children, was tenfold better than that of the chimney sweepers', and yet Parliament had striven to improve the lot of the former, but done nothing for the latter. Ashley said the use of small boys for this purpose 'had led to more misery and more degradation than prevailed in any other Christian country.'[45] He argued that all but one in 2,000 chimneys could be swept mechanically. He told the Commons in June 1840 that he knew of one case where a boy of four-and-a-half, and another where a boy of six, were climbing up chimneys: and 'the fact, also, that twenty-three climbing boys were now confined for various offences in Newgate, was sufficient to prove the bad moral effects of the system.'[46]

The trade was regulated, but in certain cities the regulations were ignored, and suffering continued for another twenty or thirty years until the practice was outlawed effectively. Reforming factory practices in the teeth of the vested interests of the new middle classes who owned them would be a different matter. He vividly outlined their abuses in an article in the *Quarterly Review* of December 1840 on the subject of infant labour, noting a pamphlet written by Leonard Horner, the Inspector of Factories, and the minutes of evidence given to the Select Committee on the regulation of mills and factories. Horner had commented that the 1833 Factory Act had achieved certain ends, but there was room for improvement, and the law was defective and required amendment to improve it. It was argued that further regulation would not be commercially damaging, since the restrictions placed by the Act had not caused a single mill to go slow or shut for so much as a day for want of hands. Ashley was as concerned, though, about the condition in which children lived when not working in squalid factories or mills. He called 'the crowded lanes and courts of the larger towns', with their 'damp and unhealthy substrata', their lack of drainage and their 'frail tenements' the 'charnel-houses of our race' and 'lairs of filth and disorder'.[47]

These conditions destroyed souls as well as bodies. After toiling for sixteen or seventeen hours a day, teenagers would emerge 'enfeebled in health, and exasperated in spirit', made by the State 'pigmies in strength, and heathens in religion'. He listed the heavy work they did in factories, forges, foundries and mills. What especially angered him was that children so often worked providing luxuries, not necessities – or as he put it, 'on show, on feasts, and a multiplied wardrobe.' The factory inspectorate had found lace factories in Nottingham where the working day was twenty hours, from 4 a.m. until midnight. Some children aged between ten and fifteen worked through the night, being allowed to leave between 8 p.m. and 10 p.m. the next day. Mills closed early, at 8 p.m., on Saturdays by working through the night on Fridays. Some mills had a shift system, so children only had to work ten hours at a time, but two or three times a week they would work the whole twenty. And as the 1833 Act did not apply to lace mills, the law could not prevent this. An inspector, questioned by the Select Committee, admitted the regime was 'injurious to health and morals'.[48] Ashley was contemptuous of this: 'All this for that indispensable demand of our shivering nature – a cheap lace trimming!'[49]

Things were as bad in silk works. 'Ten hours of labour, in each day, are assigned to children of tender years, of eight, seven and even of six – *mostly girls* – and so small, as we learn from the inspectors, that they are not unfrequently placed on stools before they can reach their work.'

This was, in his view, a 'system of domestic slavery'. Prussia, he noted, had banned children under sixteen from working more than ten hours a day. Would England follow? It was important, he stressed, that paternalism, imposed by Parliament, regulated the matter: for 'the two great demons in morals and politics, Socialism and Chartism, are stalking through the land; yet they are but symptoms of an universal disease, spread throughout vast masses of the people, who, so far from concurring in the status quo, suppose that anything must be better than their present condition.'[50]

He continued: 'Our system begets the vast and inflammable mass which lies waiting, day by day, for the spark to explode it into mischief.' It was a system where men would 'exact the maximum of toil for the minimum of wages . . . No wonder that thousands of hearts should be against a system which establishes the relations, without calling forth the mutual sympathies, of master and servant, landlord and tenant, employer and employed.'[51] The human relations that had held society together had been corrupted and were almost destroyed. Whatever the political implications of the treatment of the poor, it was an offence against God and the scriptures, which this evangelical concluded by quoting: 'Break off our sins by righteousness, and our iniquities by showing mercy to the poor, if it may be a lengthening of our tranquillity.'

Ashley's relations with Peel and Graham, as leaders of his party, can partly be explained by class differences, as can his strong dislike of the industrialists' attitude to their workers and the misery he felt they were causing. That class viewed him with equal incomprehension and distaste, and they fought each other bitterly. Peel and Graham were almost, but not quite, two peas from the same pod. Peel's father, the first baronet, was a Lancashire calico manufacturer who bought land and became an MP. Graham, four years younger than Peel, was also the son of a first baronet from the north-west who, like Peel's father, had been an adherent of the Duke of Portland. As a Whig until 1835 he had helped with the drafting of the Reform Bill, but entertained great fears about social upheaval. From then on he became a quite hard-bitten reactionary, taking the side of the ruling class in all its arguments against organised labour and the poor.

It was hardly surprising, therefore, that Ashley's commitment to the ten-hours principle ensured he never held office again. Peel wanted him to join his ministry in August 1841 in a junior post in the Royal Household: Ashley, however, said he could not unless Peel would promise to support all his proposals on factory reform. He had already written, in June 1841, to operatives in the West Riding promising to refuse office that would limit his activities on their behalf, something Norman Gash, Peel's biographer, calls 'emotional and irrational'.[52] It was, however, a view hardened by a tour he had made, days before Peel's offer, of factories in Manchester, Bolton, Ashton, Huddersfield and Leeds. Some cotton masters then announced that they would on principle oppose any measure that Ashley sought to introduce, which forced his hand about taking office: he felt sure Peel would submit to the wishes of the capitalist interest, and that therefore his conscience would drive him out of office within months.

In offering him office, Peel told Ashley that his moral standing was what recommended him. Ashley replied that if he swallowed his principles on the Ten Hours' Bill, his moral standing would be impaired. His religious views had hardened as he became older: by the 1840s he was convinced there would be a second coming, a belief that underpinned the fanaticism and occasional apparent absence of rationality that characterised his political activity. His refusal of office, which he made known to the Leeds operatives (and his motivation for doing so may only be surmised), enhanced his standing in the labour movement.

He wrote to Peel in January 1842 asking him 'whether you have made up your mind to insist or concede the prayer of the operatives for the further limitation of the Hours of Labour between the ages 13 and 21.'[53] Ashley said the time had come for Peel to 'remove the suspense' concerning his policy. Peel replied on 22 January that 'I am not prepared to pledge myself or other members of the Government to the support of a Bill limiting the hours of labour to ten for all persons between the ages of 13 and 21.'[54] He added that Graham had a bill under consideration affecting the education of factory children 'and I am confident that he will, if you will allow him, be glad to have an opportunity of conferring with you.' Ashley told Peel that he would do his 'duty' of talking to Graham; he termed it so because 'various feelers' had already been 'put out' to him 'to ascertain whether I would abate any part of what I require for the benefit of the factory-people. I steadfastly refused.'[55]

Peel wrote back, angered, protesting that 'I was putting out no feeler as you suppose others to have done.'[56] He added: 'I had not the remotest wish, in referring to communications with you on that subject, to impose the slightest restraint either on your opinions or your practical course of proceeding.' Ashley, complaining that Peel had 'misunderstood the word <u>feeler</u>', and assuming the government would, as he had feared, oppose a Ten Hours measure, broke with the Tories.[57] He was not a natural party man: Gash calls him 'an exasperating and unpredictable individualist'.[58] No vestige of party loyalty would stand in the way of Ashley's principles. He wrote to his supporters in the factory districts on 2 February 1842 announcing Peel's refusal to support him, saying that 'I shall persevere to my last hour and so must you; we must exploit every legitimate means that the Constitution affords in petition of parliament, in public meetings, in friendly conferences with your employers; but you must infringe no law and offend no proprietors. We must all work together as responsible men, who will one day give an account of their motives and actions.'[59] Showing his flair for publicity, he sent a copy of the letter to *The Times*. The Tory-supporting *Morning Post* denounced it as 'peevish' and his tone as 'sanctimonious'.[60]

He spoke in the Commons on 7 June 1842 on the report of the Commission into conditions for women and children in the mines. He had been in low spirits since February, though he and Peel had resumed cordial relations. The report gave him an opportunity to show he was motivated by an aristocrat's desire to improve the lot of the people, and not by naked political consideration. In a speech that lasted two hours he said that 'it is not possible for any man, whatever be his station, if he have but a heart within his bosom, to read the details of this awful document without a combined feeling of shame, terror, and indignation.'[61]

He shared with the House details of how 'the extent to which the employment of females prevails varies very much in different districts', but how in most coalfields there were children as young as seven, and quite often as young as five, at work. 'Near Oldham, children are worked as low "as four years old, and in the small collieries towards the hills some are so young they are brought to work in their bed-gowns".'[62] He spoke of small, naked boys dragging carts while crawling on their hands and knees, injuring themselves and being thrashed if they complained. They would routinely work sixteen-hour days. Worse still was what happened to girls. 'The girls are of all ages, from seven to twenty-one.

They commonly work quite naked down to the waist, and are dressed — as far as they are dressed at all — in a loose pair of trousers. These are seldom whole on either sex. In many of the collieries the adult colliers, whom these girls serve, work perfectly naked . . . Any sight more disgustingly indecent or revolting can scarcely be imagined than these girls at work. No brothel can beat it.'[63]

Ashley capped this with the observation that 'if this is bad for children and young persons, the case is far worse for pregnant women. For them it is horrible.'[64] He quoted: 'A woman has gone home, taken to her bed, been delivered of a child, and gone to work again under the week.' He believed that 'every principle of religion' dictated the removal of women from mines.[65] Many men were disabled by forty, and dead at fifty. There were also frequent instances of sheer brutality by men towards children. In one case a boy was regularly hit with a pickaxe, including, once, on his head. Mutilation was routine. One woman had said: 'My boy, ten years old, was at work: about half a year since his toe was cut off by the bind falling; notwithstanding this, the loader made him work until the end of the day, although in the greatest pain.' A boy said: 'Boys are pulled up and down by the ears. I have seen them beaten till the blood has flowed out of their sides. They are often punished until they can scarcely stand.' Ashley claimed that 'about Halifax girls are beaten as severely as boys. They strike them in the face and knock them down.'

The debate that followed is worth pursuing in detail, because it reveals so much about the very different stances that Ashley's upper-class contemporaries adopted. Some were broadly sympathetic; some were self-interestedly dismissive; some noted that reform might stop abuses but would also threaten employment among families who desperately needed every penny; some were suffused with a long-standing commitment to laissez-faire – believing it was wrong to interfere and that the best systems regulated themselves. At one extreme was Hedworth Lambton, the MP for Durham, younger brother of the Earl of Durham, and a mine-owner, who denied that females worked in the mines in his county or in Northumberland. Lambton said he employed no boys under eight; if such children went into the mines it was the fault of their parents 'cupidity'.[66] Nevertheless, he added: 'In the Lambton collieries there is established, and is establishing, at the expense of the coal-owner, three great schools. An able schoolmaster is carefully selected for each. He is allowed £40 a year, a house and fuel; and his school house is found. One of these schools is in full operation; and he (Mr. Lambton) had taken great pains to make it as effective as possible, by framing the regulations according to the best and most approved methods of teaching.'

However, children would not attend, because their parents sent them underground. 'Now', he continued, 'if you will pass a law to prevent the child from going down so very young, you will do an infinity of good in promoting the education of that population. Education is the great instrument and engine by which you must strike at the root of this evil; and I hope and trust that, before long, there will be no colliery establishment where the coal-owner will not have established effective schools at his own expense. It is a duty he owes to his God and his country so to do.[67] However, in saying that, and in calling for legislation, Lambton urged that the House proceed 'cautiously', and be not affected by 'some exaggeration' on the part of the compiler of the report.

Graham said he was 'delighted' by the unanimity in the House towards what had been said, and that he had found Ashley's arguments 'convincing'.[68] He agreed females should not be employed in mines, for to do so was 'degrading to the country', and 'an employment which, if persevered in, would invoke a great moral retribution – which would have a prejudicial effect on the manly bearing of the people, and be attended with great ultimate degradation and loss of national character.' However, Graham stressed Lambton's point about children, and blamed not the largely Tory-voting mine-owners for this abuse, but parents; and, although a believer in the 'sacred' principle of 'non-interference with parental control' he felt that in instances such as those so shockingly outlined by Ashley 'the intervention of the Legislature was indispensable'. He assured Ashley that 'Her Majesty's Government would render him every assistance in carrying on the measure'.[69]

Peel congratulated Ashley for his work against the 'mining abominations'.[70] He told him that 'I admire equally the good feeling and the ability – the qualities of head and heart with which you have forced this matter upon public notice.' Not everyone was convinced. In the Lords on 24 June 1842 the Marquess of Londonderry presented a petition from mine-owners in Northumberland and County Durham protesting about the 'exaggerated impressions' of the commissioners' report Ashley had quoted.[71] He 'denied that such inhuman practices as had been stated prevailed', at least in his area. He urged the Lords, before legislating, to root out 'exaggeration'; and think, instead, of the damage they might do to the coal industry – including, one must suppose, to Lord Londonderry – if they were to legislate 'injuriously'. He claimed the commissioners had come straight from inspecting factories 'with all the prejudices which that commission was likely to excite' and had been looking for 'similar oppressions' among the miners as they had found among the manufacturing classes. They had communicated with 'artful boys and ignorant young girls' and asked them leading questions to elicit the desired answers. Londonderry also claimed there were numerous charities working in the coalfields, and dismissed the need for education, saying that working in collieries was the only employment available to most youths there. He then read a letter that he said illustrated 'the superior advantages of a practical education in collieries to a reading education'.[72]

He refuted claims that any child under eight worked in a colliery in the north-east, except some taken into them 'clandestinely' by their parents.[73] He denied the virtual enslavement of apprentices through the system known as 'binding', under which they were forced to work for years at low pay and at tasks for which they, as boys, had insufficient strength. He claimed most of the young 'trappers' worked only ten hours a day, though conceded some worked more; and they spent much of their time 'generally cheerful and contented' and were found often to be 'occupied with some childish amusement – as cutting sticks, making models of windmills, waggons etc'. This roseate picture of life in the mines was complemented in the Commons on the same day by Lambton, who intervened when Ashley moved the report stage of the Mine and Collieries Bill to say that the mine-owners of his (and Londonderry's) district had nothing to fear from the bill, given the superiority of their practices.

That view was not unanimous: Peter Ainsworth, the MP for Bolton, said he would object to clauses restricting the labour of boys, given the 'great misery' they would cause in Lancashire and Yorkshire coalfields because of the 'discharge of great numbers of persons'.[74] Ainsworth had a point: this was the summer of serious civil unrest in the north, and any measure that restricted the earning potential of families could have serious consequences. When, the following week, petitions were presented to the Lords about the need to relieve distress in the manufacturing districts, Londonderry said the Mines and Collieries Bill would, if enacted, make all this worse.

Ashley feared the failure to ban women from mines altogether, rather than just stop them working in them, would open up loopholes: 'any number of female children may be introduced, and the supply of female labour may thus be kept up', helped by the fact that 'the transactions are all under ground'.[75] Peel said the original wording, amended in the Lords, was (according to the advice of the Attorney-General) too restrictive and would, for example, punish mine-owners for allowing a woman to bring a meal to the pit for her husband. Also, 'suppose a man employed should have a serious accident, preventing his removal from a pit. Would it not be hard to prevent by law the access of his wife and daughter to him?'[76] These objections were rubbished, it being pointed out that it was almost unheard of for a woman to go '200 or 300 fathoms below the surface of the earth' to deliver her husband's food, or tend him if he was injured.[77]

The pressure continued for the bill to be diluted. Ainsworth presented 'fifteen or sixteen petitions' to the Commons on 5 July 1842 'from the working classes of the neighbourhood of Bradford' on the removal of restrictions on boys working in mines.[78] He even said that, while he had no objection to the removal of women from mines, he did think it would add to distress; but the removal of boys would cause 'hundreds of children' in the Bradford area to 'be thrown out of employment, and hundreds of families would be driven into workhouses'. He said Ashley's proposals about restricting hours were 'wholly impracticable', which also compromised the educational proposals. He dismissed the notion that the children had been in poor health because of their work, or had been poorly fed. He described their state as far superior to that of the 'factory children'.[79] In the Lords, Londonderry abandoned any pretence to the contrary, and on 14 July made it clear that the issue was the protection of 'property to the amount of £10,000,000'.[80] When Londonderry tried to have the bill postponed for six months no one would second him.

Graham then decided to take out the educational clauses. Ashley objected, saying Graham's interpretation of the effects were 'incorrect, nay, I think, unfair.'[81] He added: 'surely you cannot withdraw the Bill now on the table – such a step would be a departure from

what is due to the House, to the operatives, and, I may say, to myself.'
He felt Graham had broken faith; and told Peel: 'I cannot believe that
you will allow such a wanton abuse of power, for such it would be.'
Ashley admitted that 'I have no following in the House', but still
hoped 'that some consideration will be shown, not to myself, but to
those wretched people.'

Peel felt there would be 'no advantage to the cause of religious
education in trusting to the co-operation of the Dissenting Body in the
measure we proposed – and that our abandoning it is preferable to
failure after religious strife and contention.'[82] When the Lords amended
the bill in July – Londonderry in particular was bitterly opposed to it
– Ashley wrote an emotional letter to Peel announcing that 'few things
in public life have ever given me more pain.'[83] A note in Peel's papers
quotes Ashley as having said: 'I have thought for some years that Peel
and John Russell are the most criminal of mankind' and that
Graham was 'so thoroughly odious that I cannot find one human being
who will speak a word on his behalf.'[84]

When the bill came back to the Commons, on 6 August 1842, Ashley
said the amendments had 'invalidated the principle of the Bill and made
it inoperative'.[85] Women and young children could still be admitted into
pits, and it would be hard to safeguard against their being employed;
the apprentice system remained in place, with no alternative educational
provisions. Ashley was outraged not least because he was able to produce
letters from mine-owners in support of what he had tried to do.
Palmerston spoke from the Opposition benches in support of Ashley;
Graham contended that the 'great principles' for which Ashley had
fought still stood, and that he personally supported the original bill
'reserving his judgment as to a few details'.[86] The bill was enacted without
its educational clauses; even then, there was an unsuccessful attempt by
Scottish mine-owners in the following session to gain exemption, so bad
had been the effect on their business of the restrictions on child labour.
However, while it remained unthinkable for the State to intervene to
supplement the incomes of families in mining districts, or to ensure
there was schooling for young children, some of the objections raised
to the bill held some force. Stopping a child from working in a mine
was also taking bread from his – or her – family's mouths.

The business of factory conditions remained unfinished, surfacing
again throughout the 1840s. When Parliament debated it again in 1844

Ashley noted he found Graham's opposition to a cut in hours – based on the loss of earnings to industrialists and to the country – 'mean, false and hard hearted beyond himself'.[87] Graham told Peel he 'pledged himself to resign if the 10 hours are carried' because it would reduce output, profits and wages.[88] There were other issues at stake: Graham also told his Cabinet colleagues that 'he did not think [the Corn Laws] would survive it [the ten-hour amendment] 12 months'.[89] So serious did the government's predicament appear that informal discussions were opened between intermediaries of both parties to see whether Ashley might compromise. Ashley replied that he could not have cared less about the Corn Laws, but cared very much about being painted as a hypocrite. During the debate on this new attempt to cut the hours, Ashley had a scrap with John Bright, the incarnation of the type of middle-class industrialist he most despised. Bright saw the limitation on working hours as a limitation on the earning power of the operatives (not to mention the profit margins of his employer). He also stuck to the classical liberal view that the State had no right to interfere in the bargain struck between master and man. He and Ashley also quarrelled about the case of a Bolton mill operative named Dodd, who had lost his hand in an industrial accident. For Ashley, it was indicative of the horrors of industrial life. For Bright, it was an example of what our century would call 'media manipulation'.[90]

The 1844 bill was eventually withdrawn, but Ashley was defiant. He told the Commons: 'I declare, for myself, no earthly consideration shall turn me from the course I have endeavoured to pursue; and, so far as I am concerned, I care not what personal consequences may fall on my own head.'[91] Graham introduced a new measure limiting the hours of children under twelve working in silk mills, and those under fourteen working elsewhere, to six-and-a-half hours. Gash says that Peel's hard line was not anti-humanitarian, but because he saw Ashley's proposal 'as a threat to the economic recovery of the country with a further probability that the working classes themselves would be the first to suffer.'[92] There were rallies and protests in the north against the failure to pass the bill, but fears that unrest on the scale seen in 1842 would be repeated came to nothing. Eventually Ashley and his supporters would have what they wanted, as the ruling class and the owners of capital were shamed into action, but it would take decades.

IV

Ashley argued for the improvement of other features of urban life, not merely the number of hours spent at work. The increasing levels of drunkenness, the rise in crime and the proliferation of brothels he understood to be consequences of a moral problem to do with the lack of cohesion – especially religious cohesion – in the new urban communities. He campaigned about the abysmal levels of sanitation too, which brought him back to the abdication of responsibility on the part of employers and government. Ashley was shocked to read findings by Edwin Chadwick, secretary of the Poor Law Commission, who had reported on the sanitary conditions of the poor. He had noted that 'the formation of all habits of cleanliness is obstructed by defective supplies of water; that the annual loss of life from filth and bad ventilation is greater than the loss from death or wounds in any wars in which the country has been engaged in modern times; that of the 43,000 cases of widowhood, and 112,000 cases of destitute orphanage, relieved from the poor's-rate in England alone, it appears that the greatest proportions of deaths of the heads of families occurred from the above specified and other removable causes.'[93] Carlyle, too, had been shocked by Chadwick's statistics showing the short span of life enjoyed by industrial workers. 'It is one of the most hideous facts I ever fell in with in the history of *Mammon-Worship* and *Laissez-Faire*. The Govt will actually have to attend to all that shortly, or prepare itself for being kicked to the Devil. We *cannot* go on in that way, and will not!'[94] Chadwick had found that in Bethnal Green and Shoreditch the average lifespan of the working classes was sixteen years, thanks to high infant mortality, smallpox and the meanest poverty: a third of the span that 'gentlemen and professional people and their families' could expect.[95] For all their poverty, however, Londoners spent £3 million a year on gin.

Distracted though Ashley was by such considerations, one question, linked to factory conditions, came to dominate his thinking. When children were working in factories they were not being educated. In February 1843 he had made the case in the Commons for the education of the poor, following the publication on 30 January of the second Report of the Children's Employment Commission. It dealt with children working in branches of industry not covered by the Factory Act, describing long working hours in trades such as calico printing, hosiery and metalworking. He conceded that the voluntary bodies, including the dissenters, had done all they could to educate poor people, but 'a great and terrible wilderness' still remained: and the scale of the problem was growing. The population of England and Wales had risen to 15,906,829 at the 1841 census. Ashley calculated that 1,858,819 of these had to be educated at the public expense (excluding 50,000 children in workhouses). He outlined figures for Manchester and Birmingham that showed a correlation between illiteracy and crime, and the incidence of brothels, beer houses and public houses. He cited evidence from the police of the corruption of the morals of young children in these areas, not least as a result of their having little or no work, but instead time to roam the streets unsupervised. Boys as young as nine were found in beer shops, and there was a high incidence of illegitimacy.

Ashley quoted a clergyman as saying: 'The condition of the lower classes is daily becoming worse in regard to education; and it is telling every day upon the moral and economic condition of the adult population.' Another said that the condition of children was 'utterly disgraceful to the character of a Christian country'. One of the children replied to a question put to him: 'I never heard of France; I never heard of Scotland or Ireland; I do not know what America is.' James Taylor, a boy aged eleven, said that he 'has never heard of Jesus Christ; has never heard of God, but has heard the men in the pit say "God damn them"; never heard of London.'[96] It had been estimated that the loss through theft and robbery in Liverpool alone in one year stood at £700,000.[97]

Ashley also addressed the notion that a society could imprison, flog or hang those who became degenerate or criminal as a result of ignorance, and somehow establish order. He attacked 'the utter inefficiency of our penal code' and told the House:

> The country is wearied with pamphlets and speeches on gaol-discipline, model-prisons, and corrective processes; meanwhile crime advances at a rapid pace; many are discharged because they cannot be punished, and many become worse by the very punishment they undergo—punishment is disarmed of a large part of its terrors, because it no longer can appeal to any sense of shame—and all this, because we will obstinately persist in setting our own wilfulness against the experience of mankind and the wisdom of revelation, and believe that we can regenerate the hardened man while we utterly neglect his pliant childhood.[98]

Graham did not doubt what Ashley had said: indeed, he quoted figures from the London City Mission concerning two districts in Holborn. In one, there were 103 families comprising 391 persons, 280 of whom were over the age of six and illiterate. Of those over the age of twenty, 119 could not read. In a contiguous district 102 of 158 heads of families were illiterate.[99] He said the Education Committee of the Privy Council would continue to make grants to bodies that wished to establish schools. The Anglican National Society also began a fund to set up schools in manufacturing and mining districts, and within three weeks it had raised £32,000. The Queen, Peel, the Duke of Portland and the Duke of Northumberland all contributed.[100] Politicians worried about what one called the 'defective education' of schoolmasters, a larger number of whom would be needed.[101] The search for obstacles was always easier than the search for solutions.

When in 1844 the government had limited the working day for children to six-and-a-half hours, it allowed them time to go to school as well.[102] No child would be employed unless he could produce a certificate of attendance at a school. The minimum age for working was raised from eight to nine. Graham expressed the hope that teaching in these part-time factory schools might improve, and that instruction might be based more rigidly on the 'sound principles of religion.'[103] Some suggested education be made compulsory for all children, not merely those in factories or mills. This general lack of schooling was a 'primary evil', as the MP Joseph Hume put it.[104] Graham's difficulty in understanding the importance of educating the lower orders was well expressed, by himself, in a debate in May 1845. He said: 'I contend that no education will be of any advantage to the people, unless it be accompanied with some endeavours to better their circumstances.'[105] Others believed better education constituted an improvement in circumstances and would lead to more such.

V

Ashley resigned his rural seat in 1846 because he felt unable to oppose repeal of the Corn Laws; so was out of the House when the ten-hours measure was finally passed, in 1847. His philanthropy continued from outside Parliament. He had from its inception chaired the Committee of the Society for the Improvement of the Condition of the Labouring

Classes. This organisation, founded in 1844, had grown out of the Labourers' Friends Society of the 1830s, whose main purpose had been to provide the lower classes with allotments on which they could grow food. The Queen and Queen Adelaide, widow of William IV, were its patrons; Prince Albert its president; its vice-presidents (of which Ashley was one) were headed by the Duke of Manchester and the Marquess of Bristol. Its committee comprised clergymen and industrialists. The Society met at Exeter Hall, that place of do-gooding reviled by Carlyle. It sought to build good homes for the poor, alleviating the physical and moral conditions in which many lived. Also, it set up friendly societies to lend money for better housing. The work was 'undertaken on Christian principles for the attainment of Christian ends.'[106] Ashley and the Society were determined that Chadwick's principles of sanitation should be observed in all model dwellings and lodgings for the poor. However, the return on their investment offered to speculative builders to build on behalf of the Society – 4 per cent – was roughly half what Prince Albert himself thought would be needed to persuade builders to join the scheme.

Even more notably, from 1844 Ashley presided over the Ragged School Union, which set up schools run by volunteers for children in the poorest parts of cities. He funded one such institution out of his own pocket. In December 1846 he wrote in the *Quarterly Review* about the schools, and about the children found in them, on the grounds that few of his class would know anything about either. 'Their appearance is wild,' he wrote. 'The matted hair, the disgusting filth that renders necessary a closer inspection, before the flesh can be discerned from the rags which hang about it; and the barbarian freedom from all superintendence and restraint, fill the mind of a novice in these things with perplexity and dismay.'[107] He wrote of the smell of their habitat – 'regions of filth and darkness' – during the summer and the spectacle of 'hundreds shivering in apparel that would be scanty in the tropics' during the winter. He took heart that 'moral and physical degradations have not yet broken every spring of their youthful energies': these children were salvageable.

Yet soon it would be too late. Stagnant pools harbouring a 'mephitic mass' were everywhere in their 'depositories of death'.[108] The older inhabitants were 'living skeletons', reduced to such by a force 'hostile to every physical and moral improvement of the human race'. 'Dampness, dirt and foul air' characterised the interior of these dwellings. There was little furniture, and, Ashley noted with particular horror, 'some few have a common bed for *all ages and all sexes*'. Yet these were 'beings like ourselves' who had 'long subsisted within a walk of our own dwellings' and whose numbers had expanded with the metropolis.[109] People of humble origins had founded the Ragged School movement. City missionaries helped maintain the project. However, it now behoved those of wealth and station to sustain it.

Although the cheapest possible rooms in these unsavoury districts had been hired for teaching, and the teachers themselves worked free of charge, money was continually required. The schools had started in what Ashley termed 'noise, confusion and violence', and neighbours had objected to such concentrations of the lowest classes on their doorsteps.[110] However, once each school was established, order was restored. 'You cannot have a ragged school without its preliminaries; but persevere as others have done, and you will soon overcome the tumult; and those who have the least hankering after better things, will remain and obey you.' Gangs of urchins had been known to enter the rooms by force and occupy them. 'But patience and principle have conquered them all; and now we may see, on each evening of the week, hundreds of these young maniacs engaged in diligent study, clothed and in their right mind.'

As with all of Ashley's causes, this was God's work. 'Simple and fervent piety' guided volunteers 'in the genuine spirit of Christian charity, without the hope of recompense, of money, or of fame'. Many surrendered the Sabbath, their only day of rest, to work in the schools. Their work was made harder by the 'unsettled and lawless habits' of their pupils' elders and the 'physical and moral filthiness of their lives'.[111] Ashley reflected that the teachers 'have attained for themselves by immoveable endurance and pious hope, as much consolation as they have bestowed, rivalling martyrs and ascetics in all the energies of charity and patience.'[112]

The pupils were nothing like 'poor but peaceful children'. The ragged schools were there precisely to accommodate those 'excluded from superior schools by the rules and regulations indispensable to their discipline'. He continued: 'The decent apparel, the washed face, the orderly behaviour, the attendance by day, the penny a week, amount to an interdict on their admission, were they even so disposed, to the

National and British Schools; and, over and above the regulations, the dignity of the parents of the "respectable" pupils – such is the term – would prompt them to withdraw their children from schools where an intermixture like this was allowed.'

Of 1,600 children passing through fifteen Ragged Schools, Ashley had found that a tenth – 162 – had been in prison; 116 had run away from home; 170 slept in lodging houses ('the chief sinks of iniquity in the metropolis'); 253 lived by begging; 216 had no shoes or stockings; 249 never slept in beds; 68 were the children of convicts; 125 had stepmothers; 306 had lost one or both parents, a large proportion being double orphans.[113] The itinerant nature of many children meant attendance was often sporadic; no system of fines could be imagined; the beatings and expulsions used in ordinary schools to maintain order would not work here; coaxing, not coercion, was the way forward. The most reliable attendances were in winter, and bad weather,

Ashley hoped that, if the circumstances of children improved, their passage through the Ragged Schools need only be temporary; but the schools would remain for those who remained ragged. The problem of delinquency – one of the things these schools hoped to ameliorate – was outlined in figures Ashley had obtained from the Metropolitan Police. In 1845 it was recorded that 14,887 persons under the age of twenty were taken into custody. A substantial proportion were female – 1,191 of 3,519 aged between fifteen and twenty dealt with by magistrates, and 257 of 1,139 in the same age group committed for trial. Ashley realised that far more offences went unreported or criminals uncaught. Of those brought to justice their crimes were mainly stealing, or handling stolen goods, and assaults and drunkenness, wilful damage and vagrancy.

He pointed to the lack of moral training that had caused this, though also rebuked the shopkeepers, stallholders and people of London for putting so much temptation in the way of the morally and economically destitute. Children would disappear from the schools for weeks on end while serving prison sentences, then return; the days between their evenings at school would be spent stealing and cheating. Moral progress was slow; but Ashley told how one urchin had robbed a city missionary, not recognising him in an unusual coat: but on realising his error had given him back his handkerchief. He sought to show that acts of sympathy and kindness towards the lower orders had an effect, though the greatest evidence of improvement was among girls. The high moral tone Ashley wanted in the schools would be enforced by religious instruction and observance, something that irritated another prominent supporter of the movement, Charles Dickens. He characterised one teacher who had come under this influence as 'always blowing a shrill set of spiritual Pan's pipes'.[114]

The Ragged Schools, according to the most recent report, numbered twenty-six, with around 2,600 pupils and 250 teachers. Four more schools had just been opened, lifting the enrolment to about 3,000. Enough money had been raised for some paid masters, who ran schools five evenings a week. Only two or three of the schools were open during the day; those that opened on Sunday taught only religion. In the week, the schools began and finished with religious instruction, in between which were reading, writing and arithmetic. In one school, on the fifth day girls were taught needlework and boys tailoring and shoemaking by a master tailor and a master shoemaker, whose wages the charity met. Pupils were admitted only if they had attended on the other four days, as a reward. The school was open each evening from 6 p.m. until 9.30 p.m.; and on the last evening for which Ashley had figures there had been sixty-three girls and forty-two boys present.

The Ragged School Union was ambitious. Ashley hoped an industrial day school could be founded 'in the worst locality in the metropolis, and appropriated to the reception of the most vagabond and destitute boys', to attempt to give those who would otherwise face a life of crime an opportunity to find a trade by which they could live honestly.[115] He saw these children as a metaphor not just for what was wrong with the country, but for what might be put right. 'We must entertain higher thoughts for them and for England – and with a just appreciation of their rights, and our own duties, not only help them, by God's blessing, from these depths of degradation; but raise them to a level on which they may run the course that is set before them, as citizens of the British Empire, and heirs of a glorious immortality.'[116]

Ashley continued to chair the Commission on Lunacy, in which capacity he sought to have decent asylums built at the public expense in every country, and to have lunacy treated humanely and in its early stages. He also led schemes to assist the emigration of young people to countries where their prospects might be better. In 1851 he succeeded his father in the Shaftesbury earldom, and gained a platform in the House of Lords. He did so at a time when the aristocracy's traditional relationship with the lower orders was undergoing radical change; and, just as challenging, when the middle classes were seeking to engage in public life on equal terms with their betters. Holding such a society together would take either supreme statesmanship, or a miracle.

CHAPTER 3

THE ASCENT OF THE BOURGEOISIE: RADICALISM AND THE END OF THE CORN LAWS

I

The new middle class that burgeoned during the mid-Victorian period distressed some elements of the old gentry. It used its money to buy houses and land that had previously been their preserve; it sent its children to the gentry's schools and sometimes even its universities; it sought to move on the fringes of its society, and sometimes more deeply than that; it did so with imperfect manners and taste, which it sought precipitately to improve; it sometimes attempted, successfully, to marry above its station. It did all these things thanks to having made fortunes in trade, and having better liquidity than some of its social superiors. The real blow to the wealth of the landed gentry would come with the introduction of death duties in 1894; but from the repeal of the Corn Laws onwards some fortunes dwindled. It is no wonder there were enmities. In George Eliot's novel *Felix Holt* the rector, the Reverend Mr Lingon, has a decidedly unchristian view of the (admittedly ghastly) attorney Jermyn, whom he sums up as 'a fat-handed, glib-tongued fellow, with a scented cambric handkerchief; one of your educated low-bred fellows; a foundling who got his Latin for nothing at Christ's Hospital; one of your middle-class upstarts who want to run with gentlemen, and think they'll do it with kid gloves and new furniture.'[1] Later on, when Jermyn has buttonholed the local squire, Harold Transome, in an inn, he is told by the baronet Sir Maximus Debarry in a voice of 'imperious scorn': 'Leave the room, sir! This is a meeting of gentlemen!'[2]

In the class war fought in weekly fiction magazines in mid-Victorian

England, the new owners of capital are depicted as despised by their betters and schemed against by their inferiors. Industrialisation had created a powerful new middle class, who paid the price for their new influence by being sneered at for their vulgarity by an aristocracy that, within two or three generations, many of them would join. Some of the fictional mercantilists, however, have a shred of decency. Mr Millbank in *Coningsby* may be a Liberal, and may have strict views about his beautiful daughter marrying above her to the grandson of a marquess, but he is an enlightened mill-owner. His clerk at his mill 'detailed to Coningsby the plans which Mr Millbank had pursued both for the moral and physical well-being of his people; how he had built churches, and schools, and institutes; houses and cottages on a new system of ventilation; how he had allotted gardens; established singing classes.'[3] Mr Thornton in Mrs Gaskell's *North and South* is more utilitarian: though he has some softness in his heart, and gives work to a man who has helped lead a strike. Gaskell showed how class prejudice cut both ways. Margaret Hale, daughter of a clergyman and granddaughter of landed gentry, is 'glad we don't visit' a family who 'made their fortunes in trade'. 'I don't like shoppy people,' she adds. 'I think we are far better off, knowing only cottagers and labourers, and people without pretence.'[4]

When Margaret's father, assailed by religious doubts, moves to a manufacturing town in Darkshire – Lancashire – to work as a private tutor, his daughter asks, with incredulity: 'What in the world do manufacturers want with the classics, or literature, or the accomplishments of a gentleman?'[5] Margaret finds it hard to comprehend that a manufacturer – who has made his own pile – can possibly be a gentleman: all such a man can do is engage in 'pretence'. She has imbibed such doctrine from her mother, who wonders why, if her husband wishes to be a tutor, he could not go back to Oxford 'and be a tutor to gentlemen'.[6] Faced with Milton – Gaskell's fictional representation of Manchester – Mrs Hale is aghast. 'Fancy living in the middle of factories, and factory people!'[7]

Margaret is put in her place once she gets to Milton. She asks Thornton, of another, 'he cannot be a gentleman – is he?'[8] Thornton, a former shop assistant, replies that 'I am not quite the person to decide on another's gentlemanliness . . . I don't quite understand your application of the word.' (Kingsley would instruct him in *The Water-Babies*, in which he characterises the salmon as the gentleman of the fish world.

'Like true gentlemen, they look noble and proud enough, and yet, like true gentlemen, they never harm or quarrel with anyone, but go about their own business, and leave rough fellows to themselves.'[9]) Later on, when Thornton behaves towards Margaret in a way that he thinks gracious but she regards as offensive, she accuses him of doing so because, not being a gentleman, he cannot see his fault.[10] (Again, Kingsley could help: 'Salmon, like other true gentlemen, always choose their lady, and love her, and are true to her, and take care of her, and work for her, and fight for her, as every true gentleman ought; and are not like vulgar chub or roach or pike, who have no high feelings, and take no care of their wives.'[11]) The Hales have not just gone from South to North, but to another planet.

The economic transition was something few in the upper classes could grasp. Their wealth was rooted in land, as agricultural proprietors, but in some districts as mine-owners. In both cases, snobbery about trade was ill-placed. Without a trade in agricultural products or in coal, there was no income for them. The only distinction between their sources of wealth and that of the newly affluent was that the latter had owned their means of income-generation for years rather than centuries. Once the Corn Laws were repealed the value of agricultural land fell; whereas manufacturing would, for most of the nineteenth century, earn its proprietors and shareholders a handsome income. The contribution this made to the wealth of the country would be reflected in the extensions of the franchise, though not always in the attitudes of those with old money.

North and South presents this new reality. Thornton, who made his own money, tries to tell his workforce that if orders dry up, so does the demand for their labour; that striking will simply imperil their livelihoods more; and that the need to invest in machinery soaks up profits, leaving the mill-owner with little room to meet wage demands that cannot be funded by productivity. Thornton's mother regards the strikers as having another, almost Marxist agenda: 'the mastership and ownership of other people's property'.[12] The workforce, in her view, comprised 'a people who are always owing their betters a grudge'.[13]

One of the workers contemplates leaving industrial life and returning to the land, until Margaret Hale acquaints him with the realities of that existence: 'You could not stand it. You would have to be out in all weathers. It would kill you with rheumatism. There mere bodily work at your time of life would break you down.'[14] She goes on: 'It would eat

you away like rust. Those that have lived there all their lives are used
to soaking in the stagnant waters. They labour on, from day to day, in
the great solitude of steaming fields, never speaking or lifting up their
poor, bent, downcast heads. The hard spadework robs their brain of life;
the sameness of their toil deadens their imagination . . . they go home
brutishly tired, poor creatures! Caring for nothing but food and rest.'[15]
The only people from the lower orders with something approaching a
happy existence are domestic servants: for the masses, life was uniformly
a struggle. Gaskell's description of life on the land explains why so many
tens of thousands of families chose to forsake it in the first half of the
nineteenth century, and take their chances in the dark, satanic mills
instead.

Nor, however, was it just the operative class who failed to understand
the new capitalism. Mr Hale, with his feudal instincts, cannot either,
and tackles Thornton about the hardship being passed on to the workers.
Thornton strives to explain to Hale that 'as trade was conducted, there
must always be a waxing and waning of commercial prosperity; and
that in the waning a certain number of masters, as well as of men, must
go down into ruin'.[16] Gaskell notes that 'he spoke as if this consequence
was so entirely logical, that neither employers nor employed had any
right to complain if it became their fate.' Such utilitarian sentiments
shock the Hales: but they show the foundations of Victorian capitalism,
and Victorian commercial success.

II

A middle-class visitor from Germany, twenty-three-year-old Friedrich
Engels, catalogued the conditions endured by the working class in industrial towns. Engels's father was a Prussian industrialist with an interest
in a mill in Manchester. In 1842 he sent his son there in the hope that
seeing the glories of capitalism would cure him of his socialist leanings.
Instead, Engels drew on a brief acquaintance with Karl Marx to develop
those opinions further. He also met a woman of radicalism equal to his
own, Mary Burns, who introduced him to the most appalling sights that
Manchester and industrial Lancashire could offer. The first fruits of these
explorations were three articles on the condition of England published
by Marx in Paris. A longer series of articles, also published by Marx,
formed the basis of a book Engels published in German in 1845 entitled

Die Lage der arbeitenden Klasse in England, which was not published in English (as *The Condition of the Working-Class in England in 1844*) until 1892.

Urban Manchester and Salford horrified Engels. He described the working-class accommodation in those towns as 'cattle-sheds for human beings'. In 1843 in Parliament Street 380 people shared a single privy.[17] The hovels had been erected to make money for speculative builders, and expense had been spared. The inhabitants matched their surroundings. 'A horde of ragged women and children swarm about here, as filthy as the swine that thrive upon the garbage heaps and in the puddles,' he wrote.[18] It was a 'hateful and repulsive spectacle'. He added: 'In such dwellings only a physically degenerate race, robbed of all humanity, degraded, reduced morally and physically to bestiality, could feel comfortable and at home.'[19] Such areas were prone to disease, notably cholera. 'When the epidemic was approaching, a universal terror seized the bourgeoisie of the city,' Engels notes, disgusted at the hypocrisy that caused those same people to have a Health Commission appointed to inspect the 'unwholesome dwellings of the poor': not to protect the poor, but to protect the bourgeoisie.[20] The poor, prone to illness, were also prey to charlatans and quacks who claimed they could cure them, at a price much less than the high fees commanded by doctors, though still barely affordable. Engels wrote that 'vast quantities of patent medicines are sold, for all conceivable ailments: Morrison's Pills, Parr's Life Pills, Dr Mainwaring's Pills, and a thousand other pills, essences and balsams, all of which have the property of curing all the ills that flesh is heir to.'[21] He estimated that between 20,000 and 25,000 boxes of Parr's Life Pills were sold each week: 'And they are taken for constipation by this one, for diarrhoea by that one, for fever, weakness and all possible ailments.'

He savaged a beverage called Godfrey's Cordial, which was full of laudanum, and which women poured down their children to pacify them 'until they die': 'the less susceptible the child's system to the action of the opium, the greater the quantities administered.' The children who didn't die were instead 'pale, feeble, wilted and usually die before completing the second year.'[22] It was yet another contribution to the 'general enfeeblement of the frame in the working-class'. Elsewhere, he found evidence that factory conditions delayed puberty in young girls and caused skeletal problems in all children, as well as the long hours wrecking the nervous system and creating perfect conditions for disease. On top of this, he was shocked to see that most of the food that the poor could afford was adulterated, not merely nutritionally deficient but also in some cases positively harmful.

Apart from the high levels of prostitution, and the enforced intimacy between men and children that overcrowded living conditions created, Engels reported sexual aggression by mill-owners among their female operatives, a *jus primae noctis* of the Industrial Revolution. He quoted from the Factory Inquiry Commission's report a witness from Leicester saying that factories there were 'the gates of hell' for young girls, and that most of the town's whores had started in the mills there.[23] In Manchester, a witness said, three-quarters aged between fourteen and twenty employed in factories were 'unchaste'. As for importuning by masters, Engels asserted that 'the threat of discharge suffices to overcome all resistance in nine cases out of ten, if not in ninety-nine out of a hundred, in girls who, in any case, have no strong inducements to chastity.'[24] Such a claim, lacking supporting fact, smacks of propaganda, but a grain of truth was probably there.

The propaganda message is quite clear. 'The proletariat was called into existence by the introduction of machinery,' Engels wrote.[25] The owners of that machinery had reduced its operatives to a state of such misery. The competition between workers was, he said, 'the sharpest weapon against the proletariat in the hands of the bourgeoisie'.[26] This was why so many employers were against trades unions. Engels felt that the freedom an individual worker had to bargain with his employer was worthless: the employer could always dictate terms. He quoted an east London clergyman describing the hordes of men at the docks each morning, many of whom went away again without work or money, 'cast down by disappointed hope'.[27]

Engels expressed a hatred of the middle class – a subset of which is the manufacturing class – because it was 'enriched directly by means of the poverty of the workers' and 'persists in ignoring that poverty'. This spirit is at odds with what novelists of the time suggest, which is that there was not much active class hatred in England. There was, though, much class ignorance and prejudice. Engels does seem to harbour a blanket prejudice himself. He cannot avoid reckless generalisation: he admits the 'utter ignorance', but says it is of the 'whole' middle class of 'everything' that concerns the workers. This delusion

– a delusion proved by 'middle-class' writers such as Gaskell in her descriptions of working-class life – provokes Engels into announcing that 'before too long' there 'must break out a Revolution in comparison with which the French Revolution, and the year 1794, will prove to have been child's play.'[28] The sheer wrong-headedness of this should cause the reader to discount Engels's assertions, though his facts are plain enough.

A revolution in England had changed the country every bit as the events of 1789 had changed France, he argued. However, the Industrial Revolution raised a question about the people it had displaced from agricultural England, and their descendants who had multiplied in the preceding forty or fifty years: 'What is to become of those destitute millions, who consume today what they earned yesterday; who have created the greatness of England by their inventions and their toil; who become with every passing day more conscious of their might, and demand, with daily increasing urgency, their share of the advantages of society?'[29]

There is an inflammatory, polemical tone to Engels's rhetoric perhaps inevitable in a young man of conviction, angered by the squalor he had witnessed, and fired by his determination to right wrongs through political change. He was angry that the workless operatives did not overthrow a system that he believed turned human beings into commodities, but instead went out and begged. For those in work and whom he perceived to be exploited, he favoured the weapon of the strike. 'If all proletarians announced their determination to starve rather than work for the bourgeoisie, the latter would have to surrender its monopoly.'[30] He felt the new working class, robbed of the protection that had existed to an extent in the more feudal societies of rural England, had far less security in their lives than slaves. 'The bourgeoisie . . . is far better off under the present arrangement than under the old slave system; it can dismiss its employees at discretion without sacrificing invested capital, and gets its work done much more cheaply than is possible with slave labour, as Adam Smith comfortably pointed out.'[31]

There is an element of exaggeration and idealism in his rhetoric, though not in his descriptions of how life was. Much of his evidence is from submissions to the Factories Inquiry Commission, whose report he had studied and from which he quoted extensively. His tone is consonant with propaganda: but if it was his aim to incite a rising of the proletariat in industrial England, it was defeated by not publishing his book in English until much later. Engels had an estimate of the English industrial class based on continental precepts. The disturbances of 1842 might have encouraged him in that belief: the failure of Chartism in 1848 would dash it.

He cites a clergyman from Bethnal Green in east London, who had written that 12,000 people lived in 1,400 houses there.[32] He quotes a coroner's report on the death in 1843 of a forty-five-year-old Bermondsey woman who had no bedstead. When she died she was found lying 'almost naked' on a heap of feathers she had shared with her nineteen-year-old son. 'The feathers stuck so fast over the whole body that the physician could not examine the corpse until it was cleansed, and then found it starved and scarred from the bites of vermin. Part of the floor of the room was torn up, and the hole used by the family as a privy.'[33] The provinces had their own squalor. In Edinburgh the excrement of 50,000 people was cast into the gutters each night and, despite efforts to sweep it away, the smell and the danger of disease lingered. A fifth of the population of Liverpool – 45,000 people – lived in cellars. In Nottingham between 7,000 and 8,000 houses had been built back to back, with inadequate ventilation, several houses having to use one privy. Birmingham had courts full of filth. Its lodging-houses were 'nearly all disgustingly filthy and ill-smelling, the refuge of beggars, thieves, tramps and prostitutes.'[34] Bradford and Huddersfield had streets full of dung-heaps. Leeds, according to the radical newspaper the *Artisan* from which Engels quotes, had areas full of 'miasmatic vapours' caused by ineffective or non-existent sewers.[35] Some streets were a foot deep in mud. And, as Ashley had frequently argued, there were moral sinks as well. 'In Leeds we found brothers and sisters, and lodgers of both sexes, sharing the parents' sleeping-room, whence arise consequences at the contemplation of which human feeling shudders.'

III

That Engels's view of the middle classes was so prejudiced could be seen by the efforts that so many of them made to alleviate the condition of the poor. The great cause behind which they rallied was the repeal of the Corn Laws, the system of tariffs introduced by Parliament in the depression immediately after the Napoleonic Wars to protect the landed interest in Britain by increasing the price of imported cereals. The Tory party, being the party of the landed interest, favoured protection because it safeguarded their incomes. The Whig aristocracy, personified by Lord John Russell, a younger son of the Duke of Bedford, were also land-owners, and therefore hesitant to join any calls for its repeal. With food taking a much higher proportion of the income of low-paid people compared with the rich, the Corn Laws badly harmed the working classes. The liberal wing that was being grafted on to the Whig party in the 1840s – especially the Manchester liberals, personified by John Bright and whose apostolic leader was Richard Cobden – was heavily influenced in its approach to free trade by the classical economics of Adam Smith, who seventy years earlier had argued that free markets were the fastest route to the maximisation of scarce resources and therefore to prosperity.

The Manchester liberals wanted the principles they applied to the price of corn to apply to all traded commodities. A protectionist regime could only harm any industry it affected, or which suffered from it in any protectionist retaliation by other trading partners. So although it was the very poorest who suffered most from the high price of food, the movement to make it cheaper was led by the middle classes, whose further prosperity depended on the widespread acceptance of the economic principle of free trade. It is no wonder that the activities of those who agitated against the Corn Laws aggrieved the landed interest. However, they also excited the suspicion of many in the working classes who feared that all the benefits of free trade would accrue to the manu-facturers and not to those they employed. Landowners exploited this suspicion, arguing that some manufacturers backed repeal because if their operatives' food cost less, they could be paid less. Some working-class activists in the Chartist movement believed them, which led to a mistrust between the two groups at a time when they ought to have been united against the Tories and the landowners.

The Anti-Corn Law League grew out of an earlier Anti-Corn Law Association, formed in Manchester in September 1838 by seven middle-class men. Finding that some of their fellows in the Anti-Corn Law Association were less militant than they were, some of the men took over the town council, then the mayoralty, and finally the chamber of commerce. The purpose was to put pressure on MPs to have them agitate in the Commons for reform. To this end, the Anti-Corn Law League was formed in March 1839, resolving to become a national, and not merely a Mancunian, campaign. The League's eventual success would realign British politics for all time. This would be the most far-reaching consequence of the campaign, even above the freedom of trade that would secure Britain's prosperity until the economic downturn of the mid-1870s. By making the country richer it would provide the resources to fund massive social improvement during the middle of the century, notably in the funding of municipalities such as Manchester, Leeds and Birmingham that helped provide schools, libraries and basic public health.

Its two leading lights, Richard Cobden and John Bright, were both successful industrialists. Cobden, who was born in 1804 and one of eleven children, was a Sussex farmer's son. His father suffered difficulties typical of many in the economic upheavals of the Napoleonic Wars. First his farm failed, then a shop he opened. Richard worked as a clerk and then a commercial traveller for his uncle's warehousing business after his father's farm had failed. When his uncle's business failed too he joined his uncle's former partner, and they made a successful calico-printing business. By 1836 the business, which had moved to Manchester in 1832, was turning over £150,000 a year with a profit of £23,000. Cobden became rich enough to concentrate on politics – fundamental to which was a belief in free trade and liberal economics, forged not least by a close study of Adam Smith. He was also a campaigner for schools and the spread of education. He was emblematic of the self-reliant but compassionate strand in the middle classes that so many found hard to credit.

Bright had had a similar background. Born in Rochdale in 1811, into a large Quaker family, his father was the bookkeeper to a firm of cotton spinners, but in 1823 set up his own cotton business, which flourished. Bright joined the firm when he left school in 1827 and took over the running of it jointly with his brothers in 1839. By that time he had become immersed in local politics, as well as helping to found a temperance society and the Literary and Philosophical Society in Rochdale. He travelled widely in the 1830s, through much of Europe and as far as Egypt. At home he became committed to the cause of further reform but, of more immediate significance, to the repeal of the Corn Laws. He met Cobden in 1837, at a meeting about the importance of education for the lower classes. Bright's reputation in Rochdale rose further when he led the campaign against dissenters having to pay church rates. The town was a highly politically conscious and active place, and was where in 1844 the Co-operative movement began.

But it was Bright's stand against the Corn Laws that defined his politics during his thirties. He had become treasurer of the Rochdale branch of the Anti-Corn Law League in 1840, and until his wife fell ill with tuberculosis had regularly appeared on platforms calling for repeal. She died in 1841, and he was stricken by grief: Cobden urged him into political campaigning as a means of putting his loss behind him. As Bright told the story, Cobden went to see him after his bereavement and said: 'There are thousands of homes in England at this moment where wives, mothers, and children are dying of hunger. Now, when the first paroxysm of your grief is past, I would advise you to come with me, and we will never rest till the Corn Law is repealed.'[36] Cobden suggested that the best use of the long recess in the autumn of 1841 was agitation, and Bright took him at his word. The two men found themselves caricatured as extremists and wreckers by the Tories and their mouthpieces in the press. As well as arguing for the positive effects on economic growth that repeal would have, Cobden claimed the end of protection would make agriculture more competitive and cause an improvement in agricultural methods. In this he was, as in his economic arguments, prophetic.

Cobden arrived in the House of Commons in 1841 preceded by his reputation as principal spokesman of the Anti-Corn Law League. As conditions in Lancashire and other manufacturing districts had worsened in 1842, a decline directly attributable to the effects of protection, Bright widened his militancy, calling for parliamentary reform and opposing the reintroduction of income tax. He found himself opposed to the violent methods of some of the Chartists, and opposed too to their campaign of strikes, which he argued would end only in destitution for those involved. As an employer, he had his own reasons for arguing against strikes. At the Rochdale meeting in 1839 he had encountered a difficulty that divided the working classes: the crowd who came to hear him turned out to be mainly Chartist, and argued for the adoption of the Charter as an essential prelude to repealing the Corn Laws. It occurred to no one that repeal might come at the initiative of a Tory prime minister.

Bright gave a new dynamism to the League's campaign, not least by attracting to it a large body of dissenters: and he was not interested in the possibilities of defeat. He embodied one of the enduring realities of the campaign: the 'enormous but disorganised mass' of poor people could not hope to campaign successfully for repeal without the leadership of the middle class. That repeal was a largely middle-class movement, and the Chartists felt a suspicion and dislike of the middle class, was a fracture in the opposition that the Tories ruthlessly exploited. In 1843 Bright took the fight into parliament, being elected for the City of Durham in July that year. He had fought the seat in April and lost, but had the victor, Lord Dungannon, unseated for bribery. He quickly made a reputation for launching ad hominem attacks on his opponents, which made him unpopular. His skin was thick, however, thickened by his profound belief in the righteousness of his cause.

Cobden had swung the capitalists of Manchester, then the great manufacturing town in England, behind the League for reasons spelled out by Bright when he addressed a rally in Rochdale in February 1839: 'The Corn Laws have had the effect of crippling the commerce and manufactures of the country, have raised up rival manufactories in foreign countries, have been most injurious and oppressive in their operation with the great bulk of our population, and the working classes have been grievously injured by this monopoly of the landed proprietors.'[37] Feeding the poor was only part of the argument for free trade, but as the economy turned down in the early 1840s it became the main one. The Corn Laws effectively stopped the importation of food: and it had only been the revenues from exporting food that had enabled many European countries to buy British manufactured goods. Hence the aspirational classes, already at odds with the aristocracy after the incomplete enfranchisement of 1832, resented further the landlordism that cut the markets for their goods. For the working classes, already hard pressed, it caused a further drop in the demand for their labour.

In his maiden speech in August 1841, Cobden took issue with part of the received wisdom; namely, that the recent election had not been a test of public opinion 'as to the monopolies that were complained of, that it was merely a question of confidence in the ministry.'[38] That, indeed, had been Peel's opinion. Cobden referred also to the notion that the speech on the address was neither the time nor the place to discuss repeal of the Corn Laws. He said that just because the Tories had, so far, ignored the idea of repeal, he did not see any real need to follow suit.

'What', he asked, 'was this bread tax – this tax upon food and tax upon meat? It was a tax upon the great body of the people; and hon gentlemen opposite, who had such sympathy for the poor, when they had made them paupers, should not refuse to give a calm, a marked, and a prominent consideration to this question, as affecting the working classes.'[39] He said that '20 millions in these realms' depended on wages for their subsistence, and a million poor lived off 'public alms'; he claimed the working classes were paying 40 per cent more for their bread than if there were free trade. A working man's family, if they worked at hand looms, earned on average 10s a week. The family spent an average of 5s on bread, 2s of which was the 'bread tax': 20 per cent of the family's income. The richer a family, the lower the percentage of tax: 10 per cent at 20s a week, 5 per cent at 40s. A millionaire landowner whose income was protected by the Corn Laws, who might make £200,000 a year, paid a halfpenny in every £100 for his bread tax, whereas the hand-loom weaver paid the equivalent of £20 in every £100. If an income tax were introduced at such a rate, he argued, the House would never accept it: so why had it accepted this?

Cobden rebutted the argument that the end of protection would mean lower wages. It would mean more trade, and more demand for British goods; and that would increase the demand for labour, and therefore the price of labour. He referred to a recent meeting in Manchester of ministers of religion of many denominations. They had reported, about the 'condition of the labouring classes', that 'the condition of the great body of her Majesty's labouring population had deteriorated woefully within the last ten years, and more especially within the last three years, and that in proportion as the price of food increased, in the same proportion the comforts of the working classes had diminished.'[40] Cobden said he spoke not in a 'party spirit', not as a Whig or a Tory, but as a 'free trader'.

It would be the first of many such appeals to economic and social reason he would make on this increasingly divisive question over the next five years: and he would be vindicated. What even he might not have realised, however, was that the dire situation to which he had referred would become progressively worse. Men in factories could earn between 16s and £1 a week: but only for a relentless week of fourteen-hour days. Women would earn between 10s and 12s. Hand-loom weavers who worked in their own homes, without the benefit of the latest machinery, toiled even longer for perhaps 8s a week. Agricultural labourers earned between 6s and 9s a week. In 1842 a total of 128,000 emigrated and almost a tenth of the English population – 1,429,089 – were paupers.[41]

Answering a debate in May 1843, Gladstone gave an unequivocal 'no' to the demand for repeal.[42] Yet Peel had been shown the inevitability of repeal by his most ruthless colleague, Sir James Graham. He had written to Peel in December 1842 to say that 'in truth it is a matter of time. The next change in the Corn Laws must be to an open trade; and if our population increase for two or three years at the rate of three hundred thousand per annum, you may throw open the ports and agriculture will not suffer. But the next change must be the last.'[43] The rulers realised the game was up, but Tory MPs and peers remained implacable, some even until 1852 when even Disraeli threw in the towel on protection. However, throughout 1844 both Peel and Gladstone adopted increasingly strong positions in favour of free trade, notably on sugar duties. In March 1844 Bright warned that the Anti-Corn Law League had over £100,000 in its coffers, and meant business.[44] By the time of repeal in 1846, the funds had reached £250,000.

IV

Carlyle, who had argued for repeal for years, had written with his customary perceptiveness to the Anti-Corn Law Leaguer Thomas Ballantyne in January 1840 to speak of his certainty that protection would go, but also – with his customary pessimism – to warn that it would, in his view, give only temporary respite. He felt the cause was of more importance to the 'Middle Classes and manufacturing capitalists' than to the lower classes, since an end to protection would open up more overseas markets for British-made goods.[45] He believed most of the leading agitators for reform had a 'profound insensibility to the condition of the poor, and indeed to the condition of anything but their own interests and self conceit'. This, in turn, made him feel there was 'no hope'.

He affirmed that 'abolition of the Corn-Law is as sure to my mind, as six o'clock is when five has struck out of all the clocks and steeples. Abolition of the Corn-Law will very probably, as I compute, enlarge to a great extent the field of manufacturing industry for England; create, we shall hope, an additional demand for labour, raise the *economic* condition of the labourer – for a certain number of years.' Yet, as always with

Carlyle, lasting happiness would require proper leadership from the classes ordained to provide it: 'That surely, even for the labourer's sake, is most important; *during* that number of years, how much, by a Government, an Aristocracy, *aware* of its task, might be done for the labourer! But by a Government not aware of its task nothing will be done.' He echoed these views in *Past and Present*, in which he also warned the government about the effect of the laws: 'Do you count what treasuries of bitter indignation they are laying up for you in every just English heart?'[46] He did not reflect in any detail on them: 'We write no Chapter on the Corn-Laws, in this place; the Corn-Laws are too mad to have a Chapter . . . the Corn-Laws will go, and even soon go: would we were all as sure of the Millennium as they are of going!'[47]

Some in the governing class were aware of at least the preliminaries of this argument. A call for abolition was debated in the House again in June 1844, with the proposer, Charles Villiers, the MP for Wolverhampton, claiming the rapid rise in the population and the restriction on the supply of corn meant that 'a large proportion of Her Majesty's subjects are insufficiently provided with the first necessaries of life'.[48] It again fell to Gladstone to urge the House to reject the proposal, which it did.

But a gulf opened up between Peel and Gladstone on another, more abstruse matter: the increase of a government grant to the Maynooth Catholic seminary near Dublin from £9,000 to £26,000 a year. Peel championed the increase to placate the Irish; but an England in which Protestantism was still dominant and in which Catholic emancipation had been established for just sixteen years was reluctant to increase the grant. Gladstone took this view. He voted for the grant but then resigned from the government, leaving Peel confused. 'I really have great difficulty sometimes in exactly comprehending what Gladstone means,' he wrote to Graham in January 1845.[49] With the Church of England at this time riven by doctrinal controversy between evangelicals and Anglo-Catholics, this was another example of the scope internecine conflict between Christians had to inflict difficulties on the body politic, which had so many more practical problems to deal with.

Cobden had been absent from Parliament for much of 1844, travelling the country preaching repeal. Like Bright, he concentrated especially on swaying opinion in the agricultural districts, seeking to persuade agricultural labourers that they were being cheated and their prosperity undermined just as much as any manufacturer or operative was. Even when agricultural workers began to see the point of the League they counted for little, since they lacked the industrial muscle of operatives in mills and factories.

Cobden introduced a motion in the Commons in 1845 arguing that if the purpose of the Corn Laws was to protect farmers it was failing. He claimed that half of the smaller farmers in Devon were insolvent, and that many in Norfolk were paying their rents out of capital rather than income.[50] The tone of the debate became angrier each time, with Cobden accusing landlords of perpetuating a fraud on their tenants by exacting such high rents, given the commercial climate they had conspired to create. The Commons debated the Corn Laws again in June 1845, and the motion to repeal was defeated by 254 votes to 122, with Peel arguing that to repeal would be to throw many agricultural labourers out of work, as cheap corn would flood Britain. But these arguments, in defence of the landed interest, were threadbare.

The country was in deep crisis. It was by no means the first Peel had faced, and he did not lack the wit or resolve to deal with it. He was a man of immense personal distinction. At Harrow he had befriended Byron and was accomplished at his lessons. He took a double first at Oxford and, thanks to his father's clout as an immensely wealthy textile manufacturer and Tory MP, found a seat in the Commons – the Irish rotten borough of Cashel – shortly after his twenty-first birthday in 1809. Within a few months Lord Liverpool, the Secretary of State for War and the Colonies, had Peel appointed his under-secretary; and since Liverpool sat in the Lords, Peel answered for the War and Colonial offices in the Commons. By his mid-twenties he was, rather like Pitt the Younger before him, seen as a political force. He was made Chief Secretary for Ireland at the age of twenty-four, holding the post for six years. Peel's career was distinguished by two profound, and equally courageous, changes of mind. The most famous was on the question of the Corn Laws; but scarcely less significant was his conversion to Catholic emancipation by 1829, following his recognition that the Protestant ascendancy could not control Ireland. As an Irish MP and Irish Secretary he lectured often on the impossibility of Catholics having political rights, since they had a loyalty to a foreign power. Inevitably, he became known as 'Orange Peel'. When he left Ireland in 1818 he left office, despite entreaties from Liverpool (by then Prime Minister) to join the Cabinet. Eventually he relented, and became Home Secretary in 1822, a post he held (with one short break in 1827-8) until 1830. His great achievement was the creation of a police force: but he also rationalised and consolidated the criminal law of England and Wales. Peel had opposed the Reform Act of 1832 but accepted the outcome; and in the aftermath founded a new Conservative party that included moderate Whigs. In 1834 his Tamworth Manifesto – named after the town near which he held his estate and that he represented in parliament – enshrined his relatively progressive outlook by promising institutional reform and the redress of grievances. He was well aware of the horrors concealed within industrial England: he once conceded to Ashley that colliery apprenticeships were 'slavery disguised'.[51]

It was in such a spirit of humanity that he had finally decided that for the improved condition of the people, and for the sake of trade, the Corn Laws had to go. He had already grasped this when news came from Ireland of the poor potato crop in 1845, with the previous year's yield of nearly 15,000 tons dropping to 10,000 because of an unusual form of blight. This disaster – given the heavy dependence of people and livestock on the crop – would become a catastrophe in 1846, when the yield collapsed to 3,000 tons. It provided the perfect opportunity for free traders, who argued that in order to feed the Irish the price of bread had to be made to fall. There was also a poor harvest in England in 1845. Lord Heytesbury, the Lord Lieutenant of Ireland, wrote to Peel in November 1845 to describe in detail the extent of the problem, and the failure thus far of 'men of science' to do much about it. 'Neither the extent of the Calamity nor the period of the year when the pressure may become urgent can be foreseen with certainty,' he wrote.[52] The new, failed crop was all there was to feed most of the Irish for the next year. 'If this provision be exhausted or destroyed prematurely', Heytesbury continued, 'scarcity and even famine are inevitable.'

He said that Europe and even America were being scoured for extra supplies of seed potatoes, but this was not proving successful. 'In these circumstances,' he concluded, 'it is prudent to make timely arrangements, that we may be prepared to meet and to mitigate as much as possible this great calamity.' In Peel's mind, and increasingly over the next few weeks in the minds of more of his colleagues, that could mean only one thing: removing the duties on imported corn so that there would be enough bread to feed the Irish. Professor John Lindley, a leading botanist, told Peel the condition of the potatoes being dug up was so poor that he doubted they would keep through the winter.[53] Peel was preparing for the worst and anything but complacent; not least because the news from Ireland was increasingly grave.

What Peel heard – and he had been aware of the intensity of the problem since August – was common knowledge around London. Charles Greville wrote in his diary on 16 November 1845 that 'the evil of the potato failure' meant that 'every man is watching with intense anxiety the progress of events, and enquiring whether the Corn Laws will break down under this pressure or not.'[54] Greville also noted that the crisis had caused such a loss of confidence in the economy that it had halted railway speculation. Peel received a message from the Queen, who was at Osborne, on 28 November, to say that 'the Queen thinks the time is come when a removal of the restrictions upon the importation of food cannot be successfully resisted. Should this be Sir Robert's own opinion, the Queen very much hopes that none of his colleagues will prevent him from doing what it is right to do.'

Throughout the autumn, after the failure of the Irish potato crop and the dismal harvest in England, Cobden and Bright stormed the country at meetings of the League. Not being taken into Peel's confidence, they nonetheless knew the Corn Laws were almost defunct: just one more heave was required. It soon became apparent to Peel and Graham, at least, that any attempt to maintain the Corn Laws in the face of possible starvation was politically impossible. The reception Cobden and Bright had been getting around the country proved that. It was not merely a Manchester phenomenon now: all the industrial cities of the north cried out for an end to protection. A key development that autumn, however, was Lord John Russell's announcement that he was committed to repeal: he had been wrestling with his intellect for years. He admitted he had changed his mind, and admitted too the political impossibility of holding any other view except repeal. Other high Whigs were horrified, notably Palmerston: but even they understood the country, and the consequences of seeking to overturn Russell's coup. Bright told Russell, who had announced his conversion in a public letter: 'Your letter has now made the total and immediate repeal of the Corn Law inevitable; nothing can save it.'[55]

In late November and early December the Cabinet met almost daily. Showing that manipulation of the press is not a modern phenomenon, the news was leaked to *The Times* for its 4 December edition that the Corn Laws would be repealed when Parliament met in January. 'Sir Robert Peel in one house, and the Duke of Wellington in the other, will, we are told, be prepared to give immediate effect to the recommendation thus conveyed.'[56] The paper rejoiced in the decision, further marginalising Tory opinion. 'It is enough for the merchant and capitalist to know that by the end of January at the latest, the produce of all countries will enter the British market on an absolute equality with our own,' it wrote. As for Peel's potential enemies, it predicted they would stay their hand: 'the British aristocracy feels no such injurious and suicidal ambition'. It seemed to discount the savagery with which diehards in his own party would attack him. It announced: 'The truth is that it must be done. Necessity knows no laws. The sliding scale cannot, and will not, stand. Protection cannot be maintained. The country cannot be kept in a state of civil war, with the most fearful jealousies daily ripening and coming to a head. The thing must be done, and it is Sir Robert Peel's common-sense and convenient view of the case that he is the actual Premier, and therefore bound to do it.'

Two days later Gladstone noted that, when asked by Lord Lincoln, the First Commissioner of Works and a Cabinet minister, for his views on the Corn Laws, he had replied that 'the old law was a delusion'.[57] Lincoln, who would after the repeal of the Corn Laws be a committed Peelite like Gladstone, had agreed the law was not working well; it had driven up the price and reduced the level of imports, both disastrous given the potato problem. Lincoln was heir to the dukedom of Newcastle: his view that it was 'especially desirable to disengage the Corn Laws if possible from the general interests of the aristocracy' carried clout with Peel and Graham, not least when he argued that the aristocracy was 'seriously compromised' by the status quo. Gladstone left his dinner with Lincoln believing that 'something is in the wind – & something serious.' The Duke of Newcastle reviled his son for supporting repeal, and would shortly have his revenge on Gladstone, whose patron at Newark he was.

However, there was no agreement in the Cabinet about suspending the Corn Laws. Peel thought it would be cowardly of him to resign and leave a mess in Ireland and in England for others to clear up. He then became aware that he had no choice, because of divisions in the Cabinet: though he managed to secure Wellington's support, which was crucial.

He asked the Queen to accept his resignation on 5 December 1845, and she sent for Russell. This was kept secret for several days. However, Russell could not fulfil the Queen's commission, even though she conveyed to him a promise from Peel that he would have the support of the last prime minister in repealing the Corn Laws.

However, Russell did not trust Peel to support the wholesale measure the Whigs would have in mind. He decided to accept the invitation to be Prime Minister: but there were objections among his potential Cabinet to Palmerston's becoming Foreign Secretary. Palmerston was deemed essential, and would take no other post. So after a few days of deliberations by Russell, Peel found himself back in power. As he told Heytesbury, to whom he had a week earlier written a letter of fond, official farewell, 'you will be as much bewildered as I have been by recent events'.[58] Greville observed on 20 December that 'no novel or play ever presented such vicissitudes and events as this political drama'.[59]

Peel told him how Russell had sent for various politicians (among them Cobden, who had refused Russell's offer to become vice-president of the Board of Trade) and then 'they sat about ten days in consultation – some for accepting office, some against. I believe on the tenth day they divided 10 to 5 for acceptance.' Peel disclosed that he had given Russell his assurance that he would support him in repealing the Corn Laws, and that Graham, Herbert and Lincoln would do likewise. However, the night before Peel was to take his final farewell of the Queen he received a letter from Prince Albert, telling of his 'astonishment' that Russell no longer felt, after all, that he could form a government, 'and begging that I might go to Windsor on Saturday at a later hour than eleven. I went at three. On entering the Queen's apartment, she said to me – you are come to take leave of me – but I am without a Minister and without a Government.'

'I replied – I require not a moment's consideration. I will be Your Majesty's Minister and will pledge myself to meet Parliament as your Minister, whatever may happen in the interval.' Peel returned to London and told his shocked colleagues that he had 'resumed office'. He added: 'The question was – not of Corn Laws, but of Government. There was no choice between Lord Grey and Mr Cobden and myself. The Duke of Wellington said he was <u>delighted</u> with the answer I had given the Queen.' He told Heytesbury of the changes he was making, notably that Gladstone would return that day – 23 December 1845 – as Secretary of State for the Colonies. ('Peel was most kind, nay fatherly,' Gladstone recorded in his diary. 'We held hands instinctively & I could not but reciprocate with emphasis his "God bless you".'[60]) Gladstone's restoration to the Cabinet gave Peel more intellectual heft in the highest counsels. However, it robbed him of Gladstone's power in the Commons. He had, under the requirements of the time, to resign and fight a by-election at Newark on his appointment to office. He had the misfortune to have had as a patron the Duke of Newcastle, who withdrew his support: so Gladstone was out of parliament throughout the climax of the debate over the Corn Laws, until returned for Oxford University in 1847.

Peel told Heytesbury: 'Considering that no-one would form a Government on the Protection Principle – that Lord John Russell had failed to form one – had thrown up the task on which he entered for no better reason than that one intemperate and headstrong man [Grey] objected to another Gentleman [Palmerston] having one particular office [the Foreign Office] (for that is the real cause of failure) – considering that there had been an interval of suspense and uncertainty for nearly a fortnight – that the Country was without a Government – a hostile message from the United States impending – I think you and Fremantle will approve at least of one thing – that I instantly resolved to resume office.'

V

Peel, having made his decision, began to explain his reasoning, and to seek the necessary political support for repeal. He used every weapon at his disposal – such as circulating medical reports from Ireland about the terrible state of health of the population there.[61] 'I foresee that these reports will fully demonstrate our Case – that they will cover with confusion those who have been denying the existence of famine in any part of Ireland and have been charging us with exaggeration,' he wrote to Heytesbury on 14 March 1846. Peel was afraid, though, that the opposite case would be made against him, of negligence: and ordered an emergency fund of £50,000 for Ireland to relieve urgent cases of starvation and illness. The tendency in England to disbelieve how bad things were in Ireland was persistent and outlived Peel's administration. Richard Whately, the Archbishop of Dublin, would write to Arthur Hugh Clough in December 1846 to say that 'the distress in this country is real and great. I do not wonder that every report should be distrusted in England, coming from a land so infested with falsehood; and that many should be so sick of the subject as to resolve to believe nothing but what is agreeable. But when you consider that there are about 3 millions who have almost wholly subsisted on the potato, and that this has almost entirely failed, you may guess the consequences.'[62]

The Queen's Speech stated that her government would continue policies 'calculated to extend Commerce, and to stimulate domestic Skill and Industry by the repeal of prohibitory and the Relaxation of protective duties.'[63] In a debate on 26 January 1846 Peel specified that he was not proposing to put any measure of repeal to a vote, but merely wished to give the House an opportunity to voice a contrary opinion, if it still wished to do so given the changed circumstances after the Potato Famine. He also specified that he wished the principle of protection in general to be discussed, and not just as it applied to the landed interest. He said he was considering reducing the tariff on manufactured goods, such as woollens and cotton, too. Lancashire and the West Riding would be called upon to make a sacrifice as well as the corn barons. Leather goods, straw hats and even carriages would have their import duties reduced. 'I am disposed', he told the House, 'to act fairly and impartially in respect to the application of this principle of the reduction of protective duties.'[64]

Having shown that all trade would be free, he then reached agriculture. He wished to lay 'the foundation for a decided and ultimate settlement of the question by a total repeal', so corn could be imported duty free.[65] There would be a phased programme, starting at once and finishing by February 1849, to remove all tariffs. Peel also proposed to modernise the road system, explaining that the existing reliance on 16,000 separate parishes to run it put enormous expense on ratepayers because of the absence of economies of scale, pushing up prices and making it harder for manufacturers or farmers to compete on price. Legislation allowed the voluntary union of parishes for this purpose. Peel proposed to make union compulsory, replacing the 16,000 with 600 local authorities, and doing away with much local bureaucracy and expense.

In a speech that covered making the Poor Law more humane, dealing with medical relief, taking the cost of running prisons off local authorities and beginning changes to the tax system, Peel was sweetening the pill of tariff reform by holding out savings and improvements to, it seemed, the whole population. He was enabled to do this by the three years of greater prosperity, and successive good harvests that pushed down the price of corn, after the locust year of 1842; but the signs in the last quarter of 1845 were that demand in the wider economy had slumped, and only a programme of reforms such as he was outlining would stimulate it and avoid another social disaster such as in the early 1840s. Everything was aggravated by the failure of the potato crop in Ireland. He implored the Commons to consider carefully what he had told them, and the House agreed to debate the proposals, leading to a vote, a week later.

The debate lasted twelve days, and Peel spoke for the last half of the fifth day. Prince Albert was in the gallery for the opening speeches, marking the Court's support for Peel's measures. For the five years of Peel's administration Albert became progressively closer to him, acting as liaison officer between him and the Queen. Greville records in his diary of 16 December 1845 that when Lansdowne and Russell went to Windsor for an audience of the Queen during the crisis that almost caused the Whigs to take office

> the first novelty that struck them was the manner of their reception; all is changed since they went out of office. Formerly the Queen received her ministers alone; with her alone they communicated, though of course Prince Albert knew everything; but now the Queen and Prince were together, received Lord Lansdowne and John Russell together, and both of them always said *We* – 'We think, or wish, to do, so and so; what had *we* better do, &c.' The Prince is become so identified with the Queen that they are one person, and as he likes business, it is obvious that while she has the title he is really discharging the functions of the Sovereign. He is King to all intents and purposes.[66]

Greville observed: 'I am not surprised at this, but certainly was not aware that it had taken such a definite shape.' The situation was manageable so long as confined within the Privy Council. When evidence of Albert's role without the normal confines of the British constitution became apparent outside the charmed circle, which it did when he attended the Corn Laws debate, there was trouble. Albert made a grave error by being present, given what was suspected by political insiders to be his closeness to Peel. His presence was interpreted as applying pressure for repeal, a dangerous constitutional move given the Queen's role above politics.

Much of the debate concentrated on the effect repeal would have on the party system, not least as expressed by aggrieved Tories. Peel argued that party considerations were little compared with 'the measures by which an imminent public calamity shall be mitigated, and the principles by which the commercial policy of a great empire shall for the future be governed'.[67] He outlined what had happened the previous December, when he had sought to resign; and he emphasised that the alternative to what he now proposed to do was 'calamity', a word he repeated several times. There were those who by long-held belief were better placed to repeal the Corn Laws than he was; but they had, when given the opportunity, failed to form a government.

He accepted that those who normally backed him might wish to withhold their support, and feel he had gone against the main precepts of party: but he asked them to believe that in taking this course he was motivated by 'public duty'.[68] He elaborated:

> What were the facts which came under the cognisance of my right hon Friend the Secretary of State for the Home Department, charged with the responsibility of providing for the public peace, and rescuing millions from the calamity of starvation? We were assured in one part of this Empire there are 4,000,000 of the Queen's subjects dependent on a certain article of food for subsistence. We knew that on that article of food no reliance could be placed . . . We saw, in the distance, the gaunt forms of famine, and of disease following in the train of famine. Was it not our duty to the country, ay, our duty to the party that supported us, to avert the odious charge of indifference and neglect of timely precautions? It is absolutely necessary, before you come to a final decision on this question, that you should understand this Irish case. You must do so.[69]

Only 'calamity' had changed the situation. It had not, however, by any means changed the minds of all Peel's party. He had noted the asperity with which some Tories had dealt with his arguments. Faction was rife, and Greville, in his diaries, first talks of 'Peelites' on 22 January 1846, describing the term as by then current.[70] The most extreme example of this, a cross between theatre and stand-up comedy, came late on the eighth night, when Disraeli entered the debate.

If Peel perfectly exhibited the Victorian high mind, Disraeli showed characteristics that were the polar opposite. His position was based on prejudice and not on reason. If he had an intellect – and originality of thought, as opposed to the occasional bout of tactical cunning, was never his strong suit at any stage of his career – he did not apply it in this debate. He was a client of the family of the Duke of Portland and, although a heavily indebted counter-jumper, spoke and acted for the landed interest that funded him. There is no incidence of exercise of integrity in any of his contributions to the Corn Law debates, least of all in the cynical outpouring that followed the statesmanlike remarks of Peel.

He began his two-and-a-half-hour speech by ridiculing some who had defended Peel, and mocking the government's volte-face. He then announced: 'I shall endeavour to show that the system of protection is not that odious system which it has so long been assumed to be,' a view no Conservative would argue in public when the party next held office, briefly, in 1852 – including Disraeli, who would be Chancellor of the Exchequer.[71] He argued that parties existed as expressions of public opinion, and that the public opinion that had elevated Peel to be the Queen's First Minister in 1841 was not behind his policy.

His argument was couched in sarcasm; but he also attempted to repudiate a link between import tariffs on goods and a lack of demand for them. He cited sugar and cotton as examples, which missed the point that neither was a basic foodstuff useful for staving off starvation. He branded the Cabinet 'the children of panic'.[72] He said that Turkish adherence to free trade had destroyed that country's manufacturing industry. He mocked the idea that the condition of the English 'peasantry' was attributable to the evils of protection. In his peroration he argued that favouring agriculture over manufacturing in Britain was right because the nation had 'a territorial constitution', with land the basis of the political settlement.[73]

He contrasted this with the new 'thraldom of capital' in which wealth, rather than intelligence, was everything, and which were the very interests to which he believed Peel was surrendering.[74] Whereas Peel, when he had spoken, had bombarded the House with detail, Disraeli chose instead to hose it with assertion. Even with tariffs, the amount of flour exported from Britain to Ireland had risen from 839,567 hundredweights in 1844 to 1,422,379 in 1845, such was the gravity of the Potato Famine.[75]

On the twelfth and final day of the debate Lord George Bentinck, from the floor of the House of Commons, humiliatingly rebuked Albert in his absence for his attendance. He did not rise until midnight on the final evening, and spoke for three hours, making a statistical case for protection. In tones that would outrage the Queen he said, at the very end of his speech, that he wanted to make a statement 'with regard to our limited monarchy'.[76] The Commons was already impatient: not only had he gone on for three hours, but he had not risen until very late, and his speech had, according to Greville, been 'intolerably tiresome'.[77] His attack on Albert had the merit, at least, of being almost the only interesting part of his oration.

In a seemingly interminable sentence that extended even beyond the following quotation, he said:

'If so humble an individual as myself might be permitted to whisper a word in the ear of that illustrious and royal personage, who, as he stands nearest, so is he justly dearest, to Her who sits upon the throne, I would take leave to say, that I cannot but think he listened to ill advice, when, on the first night of this great discussion, he allowed himself to be seduced by the First Minister of the Crown to come down in this House to usher in, to give éclat, and, as it were, by reflection from the Queen, to give the semblance of the personal sanction of Her Majesty to a measure which, be it for good or for evil, a great majority at least of the landed aristocracy of England, of Scotland, and of Ireland, imagine will be fraught with deep injury, if not ruin, to them'.

Some elements in the press picked up the criticism and amplified it: Bentinck was, after all, brother of the Duke of Portland. Albert lay low, concentrating on building Osborne, and other less controversial projects.

The motion to overturn protection was carried by 337 votes to 240, the victory assisted by Bentinck. Even before him, Greville had described the momentous debate as 'the dullest on record'.[78] The Tory party was devastated by the victory of the notionally Tory Prime Minister: only 112 voted for him, and 231 against. The vote was taken on 27 February. On the next sitting day, 2 March, Charles Villiers, a long-standing free-trader, moved a motion for the total and immediate repeal of the Corn

Laws, rather than waiting until 1 February 1849. Colonel Sibthorp, one
of the Tory party's most boneheaded reactionaries, led the opposition.
He said Peel had 'insulted the country by bringing forward these measures in a deceitful manner', whereas at least Villiers was being 'bold,
manly and independent'.[79] He accused Peel of having changed his mind,
which was fair comment, but he also accused him of lacking 'moral
courage', which was far from the mark. In his peroration he accused
Peel of having 'deceived and betrayed' his party and of 'sowing the seeds
of a revolution': although Sibthorp was an extreme case, it was indicative of how high emotions were running in his party.[80] Greville (a Whig
and a free-trader) described his Tory friends as feeling 'disgust and
indignation' towards their leader.[81] Another dismayed by the calibre of
the Tory protectionists was Prince Albert. He felt that 'they have no
leader and one of their chief members admitted the other day . . . that
they were quite divided and very jealous of each other. There is a host
of young men, who have never in their life paid any attention to public
business, whose chief employment has been hunting and who now come
down to the House of Commons as great statesmen, cheering each
other and rendering it almost impossible for any business to be carried
on.'[82]

Bright warned that the agitation of the League would continue until
repeal was total: so there was nothing to be gained from the delay. Peel
followed him and explained, quite candidly, that the government had
settled on the delay because it had feared that was the best way in which
it could secure the support of the House; and the calamity in Ireland
required immediate attention. He did not wish to alter the government's
plans, and was supported by Russell, for the Opposition. The proposal
was defeated, in the interests of securing eventual repeal. The Whigs
and Liberals feared that to press for immediate repeal would alienate
Tories who, reluctantly, were supporting Peel and providing a parliamentary majority.

VI

When, later in March, the legislation had its second reading, it passed
by eighty-eight votes – nine fewer than in the great debate of February.
Not only was what support Peel had in his own party drifting away, it
was also clear that his party was determined to be rid of him. When

he rose to speak in the second reading debate he was howled down for five minutes by protectionists on his own side who wished to hear one of their own, the Marquis of Granby, heir to the Duke of Rutland, who had deliberately risen at the same time. Eventually order was restored and the Speaker saw that Peel was heard. However, when he observed, matter-of-factly, that he knew the protectionists could, if they wished, turn him out, they cheered 'savagely', according to Greville, who was present.[83]

The diarist continued: 'At present, however, Peel holds office for the sole purpose of carrying the Bill. The Whigs are guarding him, while he is doing this work, ready to turn against him the moment he has done it, and then, this great contest over, the Protectionists will either join the Whigs in their first onset, or leave him to his fate.' A sign that the Whigs were preparing for office was that Palmerston had been to Paris to meet the King of France, his leading courtiers and ministers. The Whigs desired good relations with France. Palmerston was regarded there with fear and loathing. He would have to be Foreign Secretary in any Whig administration. The Queen and his party worried about what effect this would have on Anglo-French relations. Therefore, Palmerston was on what the twentieth century would call a charm offensive.

The moment, and the opportunity, for bringing an end to the divided government came on 25 June 1846. On the same night that the House of Lords gave the third reading to the bill to repeal the Corn Laws, the government lost the Irish Coercion Bill (which would have allowed rule by force in Ireland in times of civil unrest) in the House of Commons by 292 votes to 219. Peel called a Cabinet the next day – 'the shortest cabinet I ever knew', according to Gladstone – and it was agreed the government would resign rather than seek a dissolution.[84] On 29 June Peel told the House he and the ministry had resigned. He began by saying what a relief it was that he had been able to give up his post, and then justified his advice not to ask the Queen for a dissolution – 'the power of dissolution is a great instrument in the hands of the Crown; and it would have a tendency to blunt the instrument if it were employed without grave necessity.'[85] Peel's conscience was manifestly clear: 'During the five years for which power has been committed to our hands, neither the interests nor the honour of this country have been compromised.'[86]

Thus far Peel's valedictory remarks were what would be expected of a prime minister relinquishing office. However, he chose not to leave without rubbing the noses of his former supporters into the dirt. He delivered an encomium about Cobden, the great architect of repeal. 'The name which ought to be associated with the success of those measures [repeal] is not the name of the noble Lord [John Russell] . . . nor is it mine. The name which ought to be, and will be, associated with the success of those measures, is the name of one who, acting, I believe, from pure and disinterested motives, has, with untiring energy, made appeals to our reason, and has enforced those appeals with an eloquence the more to be admired because it was unaffected and unadorned: the name which ought to be chiefly associated with the success of those measures, is the name of Richard Cobden.'[87]

When one recalls the obloquy that Tories, and their stooges such as Croker, had heaped on Cobden – one of the most serious intellectuals of the radical movement and a man, as Peel had affirmed, not in the least motivated by self-interest – one can imagine the effect these words had on Peel's former adherents. Peel himself had had the rough end of Cobden's tongue, notably after the murder of his private secretary, Edward Drummond, in 1843: Drummond was killed by a man who mistook him for Peel, and Cobden hinted that the desire to assassinate the Prime Minister indicated the depth of misery in the country. But Cobden had been the driving force behind the League, and had sacrificed his lucrative business (which had almost gone bust) and his health to a cause in which he passionately believed. Russell, already an admirer, endorsed what he heard Peel say to the extent that he renewed his offer of office to Cobden, this time a place in the Cabinet: but Cobden again declined. He was worried about financial ruin: only a testimonial organised by supporters of the League, which raised almost £77,000, allowed him to pay his debts and establish himself once more on a sound footing. Gladstone noted that 'much comment is made upon Peel's declaration about Cobden last night. My objection to it is that it did not do full justice. For if his power of discussion has been great and his end good, his tone has been most harsh, & the imputation of bad and vile motives to honourable men incessant.'[88]

Having praised Cobden, Peel referred to himself. 'I shall leave a name execrated by every monopolist who, from less honourable motives, clamours for protection because it conduces to his own individual benefit; but it may be that I shall leave a name sometimes remembered with expressions of good will in the abodes of those whose lot it is to labour, and to earn their daily bread by the sweat of the brow, when they shall recruit their exhausted strength with abundant and untaxed food, the sweeter because it is no longer leavened by a sense of injustice.'[89] In a rare break with precedent, those remarks were followed by cheering. However traumatic the event was for Peel, it was incomprehensible to Wellington. He had never seen the necessity of repeal, but with a soldier's tones said to another of like mind 'it is a damned mess, but I must look to the peace of the country and the Queen.'[90] Peel told Bright he 'had no conception of the intense feeling of hatred with which the Corn Law had been regarded.'[91] He had, nonetheless, undertaken one of the great acts of moral courage in British history.

The repeal of the Corn Laws marked another step – some would argue, along with the 1832 Reform Act, the crucial step – in the growth and advance of the middle classes and their power. Cobden identified himself entirely with the middle-class interest against the landed one. Bright was the embodiment of the middle-class advance. The aristocracy would have its incomes reduced by the end of protectionism. An era of lower prices and cheaper food materially increased the prosperity of all who did not draw their incomes from the land. If the landed aristocracy felt they had endured the hardest blow in 1832, that of 1846 was of equal, if not greater, force. Their political power had already been put on the slide: their economic power would now go with it. Those great families who owned coal, or had diversified into shipyards or other forms of heavy industry, would be protected for decades yet: but the land would never again be so remunerative.

Party, as we understand the term, did not exist in the first twenty years of Victoria's reign. Parliament housed Whigs, Liberals and Radicals, Tories, Conservatives and, after 1846, Peelites. It was not until 1859 that the leading Whig, Palmerston, and the leading Liberal, Russell, came together to form a Liberal ministry that also, crucially, included Peelites such as Gladstone. An attempt to unite these factions was made by Aberdeen after 1852, but it foundered on the conduct of the Crimean War. Once the Peelites had welded themselves on to the Liberals, and the Tories had abandoned protectionism, the way was clear to make the modern Conservative party.

Disraeli was an important factor in this realignment, for he was so intensely unpopular with the Peelites and with some Liberals (Whigs such as Palmerston found him amusing) that he became a common enemy and a unifying force. As Lord Blake wrote: 'One sometimes wonders whether Disraeli has a claim not only to be the architect of the Conservative party, but the unconscious founder of the Liberal party, too.'[92] As he would show twenty years later in the arguments over the second Reform Act, he was a man of the most flexible principle, and no sentiment could be allowed to stand in the way of his movement up the greasy pole, or his survival once at the top. Within months he was telling landed proprietors that the game was up with protection: he turned his coat and moved on without ever looking back, which made a retrospective mockery of the intensity of his opposition before 1846.

The argument over the Corn Laws effected a long-term realignment in British politics. It also, potentially, saved the country from severe civil unrest. Once the ports opened, it was estimated that a substantial proportion of Britons became dependent upon 'foreign bread': perhaps 5 or 6 million of the 21,185,000 counted in the census of 1851, according to Board of Trade figures.[93] Peel himself knew that he had led the party to a point of no return – at least so long as he was in charge. He told his last Cabinet meeting that 'he was convinced that the formation of a Conservative party was impossible while he continued in office'.[94] For the next twenty years, with various changes of sides, the realignment would continue: until, by the second Reform Act, the Peelites were all in what was by then known as the Liberal Party, and one was preparing to lead it.

CHAPTER 4

CHARTISM: THE RISE OF WORKING-CLASS POLITICS

I

The working class in the first half of the nineteenth century was a varied coalition of those who principally had in common that they owned little or no capital or land. At the bottom end were manual labourers, whether agricultural or urban, and miners. A cut above them were operatives who had the skills to work machinery in mills, collieries and factories. For the most part, these lowest two classes were uneducated. Then were artisans and craftsmen, some of them sole traders and on the cusp of the lower-middle class, and mostly literate and numerate. For those in the lower categories, the basic problem in life was survival and being able to provide for themselves and their families. For those nearer the top, who had the resources to take subsistence for granted, their attention turned to the question of obtaining civil and political rights. It was as this increasingly politically aware class grew, and was radicalised, that the pressure for more reform became unstoppable.

The story of the working class – and of how other classes interact with them – is the stuff of novels about the 'Condition of England Question'. They, or their parents, had moved to the towns in increasing numbers from the Napoleonic Wars onwards. When trade was good money rewarded their exceptionally hard work; but they endured squalid working conditions, and what Carlyle called 'cheap and nasty' housing. When trade was bad they could be pushed, as we have seen, to the point of starvation. As the population increased and became more concentrated in cities, so squalor increased too. Between 1810 and 1840 consumption of gin rose from a gallon per head per year to a gallon and a half.[1] In England in 1823 duty was paid on 1,976,000 gallons of spirits. In 1837 it was paid on 6,620,000 gallons.[2] It was a sign of greater prosperity, but also an indicator of greater unhappiness. Friedrich Engels wrote that 'competition is the completest expression of the battle of all against all which rules in modern civil society.'[3] He also reported the Sheriff of Glasgow saying that 30,000 working men got drunk in his city every Saturday night. He said that there were 40,000 prostitutes in London in 1844 living 'upon the virtuous bourgeoisie'. Crime had risen sevenfold in England and Wales between 1805 and 1842, despite savage punishments. The principal victims were the lower classes.[4] Engels, quoting the Children's Employment Commission Report, says that half of all criminals were under fifteen. In addition, 'unbridled sexual intercourse seems, according to the opinion of the commissioner almost universal, and that at a very early age.'[5]

The 'Condition of England' novels were designed to alert the literate and leisured classes to the plight of their inferiors. They were also designed to reduce class prejudice. In his preface to *Alton Locke*, Kingsley analysed the origin of what he called 'the hateful severance between the classes' that had been 'unknown to old England.' He continued:

From the middle ages, up to the latter years of the French war, the relation between the English gentry and the labourers seems to have been more cordial and wholesome than in any other country of Europe. But with the French Revolution came a change for the worse. The Revolution terrified too many of the upper, and excited too many of the lower classes; and the stern Tory system of repression, with its bad habit of talking and acting as if 'the Government' and 'the people' were necessarily in antagonism, caused ever-increasing bad blood. Besides, the old feudal ties between class and class, employer and employed, had been severed. Large masses of working people had gathered in the manufacturing districts in savage independence. The agricultural labourers had been debased by the abuses of the old Poor Law into a condition upon which one looks back now with half-incredulous horror. Meanwhile, the distress of the labourers became more and more severe.[6]

There were some enlightened employers. However, the public believed most mill-, mine- and factory-owners had embraced a capitalism red in

tooth and claw, and saw people simply as commodities. Kingsley put
this in the uncompromising language of a Christian socialist:

> We shall become the slaves, often the bodily prisoners, of Jews,
> middlemen, and sweaters, who draw their livelihood out of our
> starvation. We shall have to face, as the rest have, ever decreasing
> prices of labour, ever increasing profits made out of that labour
> by the contractors who will employ us – arbitrary fines, inflicted
> at the caprice of hirelings – the competition of women, and
> children, and starving Irish – our hours of work will increase one-
> third, our actual pay decrease to less than one-half; and in all this
> we shall have no hope, no chance of improvement in wages, but
> ever more penury, slavery, misery . . . You know there will be no
> hope for us. There is no use appealing to government or parliament.[7]

Although most capitalists were gentiles, the Jews were targets not only
for Kingsley's vilification, but also for Dickens's in *Oliver Twist* and in
the writings of Carlyle. Alton Locke is told by his Chartist mentor
Crossthwaite: 'Look at Shechem Isaacs, that sold penknives in the street
six months ago, now a-riding in his own carriage, all along of turning
sweater.'[8]

The economic difficulties experienced by capitalism's army of operatives might have been more easily borne had that class had a formal
political voice: but it had almost none. The 1832 Reform Act had left
five out of six working men without a vote. The rise of the bourgeois
– a new middle class made by the creation of wealth after the first wave
of industrialisation in the late eighteenth and early nineteenth centuries
– had changed the political settlement. An articulate, and increasingly
organised, working class sought to change it further. It was confronted
by a middle class determined to entrench its new-found privileges – a
determination it would adhere to until the defences crumbled in 1867,
and another Reform Bill was passed – and by an aristocracy largely
paralysed with fear at the prospect of an assault on its property and
status, and an uprising by the working class. There was talk not just of
establishing a form of socialism, but also of using violent means to
achieve the working class's aims, as in France half a century earlier.

Not all radicalism was potentially violent: George Eliot's novel *Felix
Holt, the Radical*, written at the time of the second Reform Act about
the climate after the passing of the first, is partly about a man who

determines to secure change peacefully. However, his very definition of his beliefs would be taken as a threat by most of the moneyed classes, even without the promise of force. 'I'm a Radical myself,' Holt announces, 'and mean to work all my life long against privilege, monopoly and oppression.'[9] Mrs Gaskell, in a passage of commentary in *Mary Barton*, reveals her perception of the early 1840s, of the suffering of the industrial workers, and the inevitable political results of that suffering. 'For three years past trade had been getting worse and worse, and the price of provisions higher and higher. This disparity between the amount of the earnings of the working classes and the price of their food, occasioned, in more cases than could well be imagined, disease and death. Whole families went through a gradual starvation. They only wanted a Dante to record their sufferings.'[10]

Mary Barton reflects the widespread fear of violence, and the breakdown of Christian values among masters and men, that was experienced at the lowest point of the early 1840s. It shows men driven by starvation to punish their employer by killing his son; it also shows one throwing acid in the face of another driven by the plight of his own family to break a strike; and the carelessness of the moneyed classes towards the suffering of their workers. Mrs Gaskell was the wife of a clergyman, and her message is that adherence to Christian values by both masters and men would see society through. This meant masters using their resources to support those driven from work by the collapse of demand, and men giving loyalty to the social order in return. Carlyle liked the book, perhaps because it seemed to advocate a variant of his own beloved feudalism.

Mrs Gaskell wrote from profound personal experience of Manchester. Geraldine Jewsbury wrote to Arthur Hugh Clough in January 1849 to say she knew 'the authoress of Mary Barton'. She added: 'She is a very nice woman and was much admired before any of us suspected her of writing a book. It has however raised a great clamour, for it is said to be dreadfully one sided, and from my own knowledge I don't think the masters of the present day deserve such a bad character; it is however a most powerful book.'[11] When Clough, a little later, met Mrs Gaskell he said she was 'neither young (past 30), nor beautiful; very retiring, but quite capable of talking when she likes – a good deal of the clergyman's wife about her.'[12]

She writes that 'the differences between the employers and the employed' are 'an eternal subject for agitation in the manufacturing districts'.[13] John Barton, the father of the eponymous heroine, is a Manchester weaver and Chartist. His wife dies in childbirth. He is on the front line of Disraeli's two nations, and smoulders with anger. We see the gulf between the affluence of the mill-owners, even in times of low demand, and the abject poverty of their employees on short time, or who had been laid off. Mrs Gaskell caricatured the impression only to say that 'I know that this is not really the case . . . but what I wish to impress is what the workman feels and thinks'.[14]

II

Immediately after the Reform Act there were attempts to unionise labour, and these had sometimes been severely repressed: most famously in the transportation to Australia of six agricultural labourers from Tolpuddle in Dorset in 1834 for administering illegal oaths to fellow members of a trades union. When the government refused to overturn the sentences there was a widespread outcry. A huge petition was presented to Parliament, setting a trend for the expression of the discontent of the populace for their rulers that would be further exploited in the years ahead. In 1836 the labourers were pardoned and brought home, and set up with their own farms. The first blood was to the working class. For the moment, at least for those unskilled workers who formed the majority of those unrepresented at Westminster, trades unionism became their collective voice, and almost a challenge to the supremacy of Parliament itself. While the artisan class, with the help of middle-class radicals, drove Chartism, the unskilled used the union movement to seek to achieve something even more fundamental than manhood suffrage – a living wage and the avoidance of starvation.

Allowing workers to form combinations was a big concession: but those who articulated their feelings (or claimed to) had a longer agenda. One was William Lovett, a Cornish cabinetmaker who settled in London in the 1820s. Lovett had a thirst for knowledge, but only a meagre education, which he supplemented by attending public lectures and mutual improvement societies. He came under the influence of the socialist thinking of Robert Owen, who had built the factory town of New Lanark near Glasgow on the principles that if his workers lived in good conditions they would be happier and more productive.

Lovett joined various groups, notably the Radical Reform Association, and at the time of the 1830 revolution in France professed support for a violent uprising in Britain. He made high-profile public protests, such as refusing to serve in the militia unless given the vote, and lobbying for the end of stamp duty on newspapers. He became an early campaigner for the greater provision of education for the working classes; and in 1836 was appointed founder secretary of the London Working Men's Association. Out of this group Chartism was born.

The LWMA held a public meeting at the Crown and Anchor in the Strand in February 1837 to design a petition supporting six demands for reform. These demands, or six points, became the People's Charter, largely drafted by Lovett and Francis Place, a middle-class advocate of reform. They called for a secret ballot; annual parliaments; salaried MPs; equal-sized constituencies; universal male suffrage; and the end of the property qualification for MPs. It was published on 8 May 1838. The point of annual elections was to make bribery impracticable, the secret ballot would help prevent the coercion of workers by their masters, and universal suffrage would allow the working classes to participate in the running of the country. Salaried MPs who did not have to be house-holders or landowners could, equally, come from the working class.

All demands except annual parliaments were acceded to within eighty years. Because of the differences between various gradations of the working class, the entire movement did not, however, immediately accept them. Although Birmingham, with its larger artisan population, did, Manchester and the north – where less-skilled workers predominated – felt them insufficient, and a split opened up. The divisions were obvious at the first meeting of delegates to a National Convention in London in February 1839, a gathering limited to fifty men because of a law forbidding larger meetings. It immediately became apparent that the main division was between those who advocated violence, if necessary, to achieve their ends, and those who did not.

A petition the Chartists presented to the House of Commons noted a painful paradox. Skilled workers produced fine goods that sold all over the world, from a country that had good infrastructure and harbours, and whose agriculture benefited from rich soil and a temperate climate: and yet the ordinary people were 'overwhelmed with public and private suffering. We are bowed down under a load of taxes; our traders are trembling on the verge of bankruptcy; our workmen are starving; capital brings no profit and labour no remuneration; the home of the artificer is desolate, and the warehouse of the pawnbroker is full; the workhouse is crowded and the manufactory is deserted.'[15] The petitioners knew who was responsible: 'The foolishness of our rulers has made the goodness of God of none effect.'

Agitation spread across the manufacturing districts as the weather improved in the spring and early summer of 1839; and in July that year the petition in favour of the Charter, signed by 1.25 million people, was presented to Parliament. This was the Chartists' first failure: they had boasted they would collect 3 million signatures. It was presented by Thomas Attwood, the MP for Birmingham who, as one of the founders of the Birmingham Political Union, had been a motive force behind the 1832 Reform Act. Attwood detailed the consequences of ignoring the claims of the poor. He reminded the House of 'the situation of Louis XVI in 1787 and 1789. When Louis was asleep ruin was stalking through the land. In 1787 an individual who travelled through Burgundy and Champagne found almost every gentleman's house burned to the ground, and their owners murdered. Two years afterwards the Bastille fell. Charles X was hunting in the wood of Fontainebleau when the Revolution [of 1830] took place, and the crown dropped from his head. The crown of James II was shaken from his head. What is the position of the Queen of England at this hour?'[16]

Attwood rejected armed or physical force to achieve the working classes' aims. However, Lord John Russell reminded him – and the House of Commons – that the people whom he was championing 'have been found going through the country, from town to town, and from place to place, exhorting the people in the most violent and revolutionary language – language not exceeded in violence and atrocity in the worst times of the French Revolution – to subvert the laws by force of arms.'[17] Russell and others also mocked the idea that universal suffrage would guarantee widespread prosperity. In this he was supported by a Tory backbencher, Benjamin Disraeli, though Disraeli – who had been in the Commons barely two years – firmly believed some measure of additional civil rights should be accorded to the lower classes. He believed there was an 'intimate connexion' between the New Poor Law and Chartism.[18] He thought that if the national, centralised character of poor relief were persisted in, rather than returning to a local, more humane and comprehensible system, it would 'endanger not only the national character, but also the national throne.'[19]

The Commons threw the motion out by 235 votes to 46, with Disraeli voting against: the Charter was too simplistic, and the call for annual parliaments deemed impracticable even by supporters. If the Commons defeat was a challenge to the Convention to inspire an uprising, the Convention failed to rise to it. For a time Chartism had little or no national cohesion, but existed through local committees. As Parliament rejected the idea, Lovett was arrested for seditious libel, for criticising how a cohort of the Metropolitan Police, sent to Birmingham to put down a riot in the Bull Ring, had acted against demonstrators. He was imprisoned for a year in Warwick jail. His influence dwindled.

Continual, and often violent, disturbances blew up through the summer of 1839. There were riots in Birmingham. A general strike was announced for 12 August. It was the next blow to the movement's cred-ibility that nobody came out. Some of the worst disturbances were at Newcastle-upon-Tyne at the end of July, at which the police and a number of freshly sworn special constables ended up in hand-to-hand fighting with the rioters. The Mayor, John Fife, had issued a proclamation warning that those who were 'calling themselves members, and acting as members of a society or societies of an illegal character,' and were 'inducing others to become members of such society or societies, and to hold intercourse with the same, and by contributions of money and otherwise to aid and support the same' were 'guilty of a combination and confederacy, and, on conviction, are liable to a penalty of £20, or commitment to the House of Correction for three calendar months'.[20]

This had no effect at all. The riot took hold on the evening of 31 July, after Fife had refused a petition from the Chartists to hold a public meeting, because of the effect he and the magistrates feared it would have on the 'preservation of peace'. Word went round during the after-noon of the 31st that a meeting would be held in any case. Fife hoped the swearing in of more special constables would, in itself, deter the Chartists. However, this tactic failed. At 6 p.m. a crowd of forty or fifty men with banners marched through the town: as they went about Newcastle and Gateshead they were soon augmented by other groups of similar size and appearance. 'And so alarming had the aspect become by 10 o'clock, that the mayor, who for a considerable time had been riding about the different streets endeavouring both by persuasion, and eventually by threats, to induce the misguided men to return peaceably and quietly to their homes, was compelled to send for the assistance of the military.'[21] The shops were shut up; the general population barred itself indoors. The leaders of the protest began addressing their followers: Fife ordered the police to seize the banners of the protestors. However, the moment they engaged with them 'brickbats, stones, and other instruments of civic warfare, were to be seen flying about in unusual abundance'. It was reported that one protestor was 'stabbed near the groin' by a policeman. Then the soldiery arrived and 'scoured the main streets'. Forty arrests were made: the foot soldiers and the cavalry patrolled the streets until 4 a.m. If the Chartists wanted a fight, they could have one.

In November there was a small uprising in Newport, in Monmouthshire. A local draper, John Frost, got it into his head that if he started a rebellion in rural Wales, revolution would start in the industrial heartland of northern England. When Chartist leaders in the north heard of his scheme they did all they could to talk him out of it. They failed. Frost led his followers into a rain of fire by the local militia, who killed fourteen of them and wounded ten others. Frost's death sentence was commuted to transportation for life. He was pardoned and allowed to return to England in 1854.

III

By 1842, as the Anti-Corn Law League failed to make any headway, it was drawn towards an alliance with the Chartists, the community of view exemplified by men such as Cobden. On 2 May 1842 a great petition, 6 miles long, was presented to the Commons with a two-mile-long procession behind it. It called for equal representation for all. It said the government had created 'an unbearable despotism' and a state of 'degrading slavery'.[22] It called for resistance to taxation unless electoral reform was granted: of the 26 million in the total population only 900,000 had the vote, and Guildford, with a population of 3,290, returned to Parliament the same number of MPs as Tower Hamlets, which had 300,000 people.

Hansard describes the spectacle: 'A Petition from the working classes throughout the kingdom, of the presentation of which Mr. Thomas Duncombe had previously given notice, was brought down to the House, by a procession consisting of a vast multitude. Its bulk was so great, that the doors were not wide enough to admit it, and it was necessary to unroll it, to carry it into the House. When unrolled, it spread over a great part of the floor, and rose above the level of the Table.'[23] Duncombe, the MP for Finsbury, introducing the petition, said that it had been signed by '3,315,752 of the industrious classes of this country'. He quoted their plea to be heard at the bar of the House, and explained why they felt it necessary:

> That they cannot within the limits of this their petition, set forth even a tithe of the many grievances of which they may justly complain; but should your honourable House be pleased to grant your petitioners a hearing, by representatives at the Bar of your honourable House, your petitioners will be enabled to unfold a tale of wrong and suffering—of intolerable injustice—which will create utter astonishment in the minds of all benevolent and good men, that the people of Great Britain and Ireland, have so long quietly endured their wretched condition, brought upon them, as it has been, by unjust exclusion from political authority, and by the manifold corruptions of class legislation.[24]

Apart from London and its suburbs, which had provided 200,000 signatures, the most names had come from Manchester (99,680) and Newcastle (92,000).

The petition also stated:

> that in England, Ireland, Scotland, and Wales, thousands of people are dying from actual want; and your petitioners, whilst sensible that poverty is the great exciting cause of crime, view with mingled astonishment and alarm the ill provision made for the poor, the aged, and infirm; and likewise perceive, with feelings of indignation, the determination of your honourable House to continue the Poor Law Bill in operation, notwithstanding the many proofs which have been afforded by sad experience of the unconstitutional principal of that bill, of its unchristian character, and of the cruel and murderous effects produced upon the wages of working men, and the lives of the subjects of this realm.[25]

The lack of deference to the Royal Family was apparent from two claims in the petition: 'whilst your petitioners have learned that her

Majesty receives daily for her private use the sum of £164 17s 10d, they have also ascertained that many thousands of the families of the labourers are only in the receipt of 3¾d per head per day;' and 'that your petitioners have also learned that his royal Highness Prince Albert receives each day the sum of £104 2s, whilst thousands have to exist upon 3d per head per day.'

Nor was it just the royal house that had a shot across its bows, four weeks before John Francis would try to kill the Queen: the Church was in the petitioners' sights as well.

Upwards of nine millions of pounds per annum are unjustly abstracted . . . to maintain a church establishment, from which they principally dissent; and beg to call the attention of your honourable House to the fact, that this enormous sum is equal to, if it does not exceed, the cost of upholding Christianity in all parts of the world beside. Your petitioners complain that it is unjust, and not in accordance with the Christian religion, to enforce compulsory support of religious creeds, and expensive church establishments, with which the people do not agree . . . Your petitioners believe all men have a right to worship God as may appear best to their consciences, and that no legislative enactments should interfere between man and his Creator . . . your petitioners direct the attention of your honourable House to the enormous revenue annually swallowed up by the bishops and the clergy, and entreat you to contrast their deeds with the conduct of the founder of the Christian religion, who denounced worshippers of Mammon, and taught charity, meekness, and brotherly love.[26]

The tone of class warfare in this was understandable. Earlier in the year the Duke of Norfolk had suggested, in trying to be helpful, that the working classes should take an occasional glass of water with a pinch of curry powder in it to ward off feelings of hunger. It provided an ideal example for Chartist and Anti-Corn Law Leaguers to use from their public platforms, and increased the discomfort of the government in a land where trade was already on its knees.

The House debated the petition the next day. Duncombe claimed the Chartists were not wild revolutionaries, but merely advocating measures that had been suggested before by 'many eminent men, both of this House and of the other House of parliament'[27]. He cited examples of distress from several parts of the Kingdom, starting with Sheffield, 27,200 of whose people had signed the petition. 'The number of inmates in Sheffield poor-house alone up to April 23 numbered 574 . . . For the last five weeks the number of new applicants for relief have averaged 200 weekly . . . it is said that the trades societies are about to break up, unable longer to keep up their funds: if this should be the case, hundreds, perhaps thousands, will be added to the ranks of the pauperised and destitute. Sheffield is tranquil at present; that it will remain so for any length of time, with starvation and misery increasing daily, is very doubtful.'[28]

Talking of the West Midlands, he said that 'The whole of this district is in an alarming state of agitation. Chartism is rapidly progressing. Towns and villages, where even the name of Chartism a short time ago was unknown, now have their Chartist association; and, unless some effective measures are speedily adopted for the removal of the present alarming distresses of the toiling sons of industry, the consequences are likely to be most serious.' A correspondent in Burnley had told him: 'All are in a feverish state of excitement. I never, in the course of my life, saw this part of Lancashire in such a state . . . Meetings—large meetings—consisting of thousands, are being held almost daily.' He continued: 'Yesterday, on Marsden-height, there was another, of at least 7,000. Today 10,000 have met at Colne, and at each of these meetings there is but one opinion, and that is, that the Charter must become the law of this land before any permanent good can be effected for the working-classes.'[29]

Sir James Graham opposed the petitioners being heard; for while everyone accepted there was distress, the Chartists' pleas were revolutionary. However, conscious of the state of feeling, he admitted that 'the distress was great' and the complaints were 'founded in fact'.[30] However, he was convinced that 'the subversion of all our great institutions must inevitably result from the granting of the prayer of the petition—a result which he thought would in itself tend more directly to lead to the increase of the sufferings of the people than any other cause.'[31] Macaulay followed him, attacking universal suffrage, and showing precisely the want of sympathy with the petitioners that Graham, on behalf of the government, had sought to avoid. Lord John Russell, by contrast, said he was 'expressing my respect for the petitioners, and at the same time, declaring my abhorrence of the doctrines set forth in the petition.'[32] This, he explained, was because he believed that to grant their wishes would be to 'shake property', and to 'unhinge that constitution of society which, complicated and intricate as it is, has produced so many blessings to this country.'[33] Peel deplored the 'most invidious comparison between the expenses of the Sovereign and those of a labourer'.[34] Like Russell, he believed the whole basis of the constitution was threatened. He did not believe constitutional monarchy could survive universal suffrage.[35]

The motion to accept the petition was defeated by 287 votes to 49. It was Chartism's latest failure: the temper of the people remained against revolution, helped perhaps by the lengths to which the State was going to provide basic poor relief, supplemented by private charity. Yet the evidence of massive decay was clear. In Stockport, represented by Cobden, thirty-seven spinning firms had closed in the previous six years; 3,000 dwellings were closed up and 70,000 people were in receipt of relief. It was even worse in Manchester, where 116 mills were idle, 681 shops and offices without tenants, 5,492 homes closed up, and the numbers in prison doubled. This was the damage done by protection and the absence of free trade.

Nevertheless, during 1844 and 1845 the heat had gone out of the problem of the condition of the poor. Railway mania was at its height, and a capital outlay of around an extra £10 million a year provided work for many more labourers, notably emigrants from Ireland. Funds used under the Poor Law for relief fell by 20 per cent in 1844 compared with 1843. The fall in the crime figures also suggested an improvement in the conditions of the poor. Graham told the Commons in May 1845 that between 1842, at the height of the distress, and 1844 commitments for trial had fallen from 31,309 to 26,542, or 15.25 per cent. In 1843 the courts had sentenced 97 people to death, and 4,813 to transportation. In 1844 those numbers had fallen to 57 and 3,320 respectively, declines of 26 and 23 per cent.[36] Emigration to the colonies had been 128,344 in 1842, but only 70,686 in 1844. The figures for the first quarter of 1845 were considerably lower, running at an annualised rate of 54,000.[37]

In 1848, a year of Europe-wide uprisings, the Chartists resolved to remind the government that their grievances remained unanswered. They asked their sympathisers to gather on Kennington Common, a short walk from Westminster, on Monday 10 April. Both sides viewed the event with a mixture of fear, panic and determination. The prospect of perhaps hundreds of thousands of agitators marching on London was worrying enough: that the crowds might cross Westminster Bridge and besiege Parliament terrified the ruling class. There had been a rash of disturbances in northern England during the late winter, and in early March several days of rioting in Glasgow, put down by soldiers and police. No one underestimated the possibility of trouble.

However, the aristocracy, gentry and middle classes met the threat with a solidarity of which Marx would have been proud. Russell, by then Prime Minister, ordered 8,000 soldiers to be in the capital, and 150,000 special constables. Greville, in his diary on the eve of the demonstration, described the precautions as 'so much that it is either very sublime or very ridiculous.'[38] He wrote how all the government service clerks were pressed as special constables, constituting themselves into garrisons. 'We are to take a warlike attitude,' he noted. 'Every gentleman in London is become a constable, and there is an organisation of some sort in every district.'[39] When the day came the protest was a damp squib. The press mocked a claim that 300,000 attended, putting numbers at between 20,000 and 50,000. Although Chartist publications would appear for some years, and in some places Chartist meetings and associations would be considered with suspicion well into the 1850s, the failure of the protest of 1848 began the end of the movement.

That the fires of revolution did not spread to England was not merely a result of the 1832 Reform Act: it was also a sign that the worst of the hungry forties had passed, and prosperity was slowly returning. The Left of British politics did not disappear: but their aspirations became more focused upon the radical movement, and upon the nascent trades union movement in particular, which stepped up its efforts to recruit working men. Both movements abjured the threat of violence that had accompanied Chartism, and had given it a revolutionary aspect. It would be against this background that those minded to improve the British people, and to enhance what passed for their civilisation, would have some conspicuous success over the following quarter-century.

IV

Because of the paternalism still inherent in much of the aristocracy there were plenty from the upper reaches of society who sympathised with what the Chartists sought to do to improve the rights and conditions of working people, though not with their methods, which they saw as a threat to the established order. We have seen how Ashley led the charge on this question; but the man who would become most significant in leading the ruling class's campaign to improve the lot of the lower orders and to extend the boundaries of civilisation was Prince Albert, the Queen's husband. Albert lacked Ashley's evangelical motivation to do good works among the poor, but appears to have been motivated by three things: his genuinely princely sense of *noblesse oblige*, which caused him to want to help improve the poor; his restless intellectual curiosity; and his search for a role.

However, before Albert could embark upon his cultural and educational campaign to transform and elevate Britain, and to engage all classes in that transformation, the sting had to be taken out of the Chartist scorpion. Albert remained, in private, finely tuned to politics, and notably to the renewed agitation by the Chartists after the repeal of the Corn Laws. His concern about working-class agitation, and the nature of his response to it, are unusual only in that he was the Queen's husband; otherwise he shared many of the feelings and thoughts of the enlightened, and sometimes frightened, aristocracy. His own file in the Royal Archives about the troubles of 1848 includes in its title a reference to the 'Chartist conspiracies'.[40] He followed it closely, making clippings from *The Times* of parliamentary debates on the issue. He corresponded with Wellington, the Commander-in-Chief, about the problem. Wellington also advised Russell and the Cabinet, causing Russell to write to the Prince on the eve of the Kennington demonstration to assert that 'If . . . the Chartists fire and draw their swords and use their daggers the Military are to be called out. I have no doubt of their easy triumph over a London mob.'[41]

On the morning of 10 April Albert told Russell that 'today the strength of the Chartists and all evil disposed people in the country will be brought to the test against the force of the law, the Govt and the good sense of the country.'[42] He suggested the solution was 'work for the suffering and unemployed, maintenance of order by police arrangements, and prosecution of the agitators.'[43] He lamented the recent growth in the numbers of unemployed, which he felt were the result of the Commons' demand to save money on public works. He regretted, specifically, that work had been suspended on building Battersea Park – 'surely this is not the moment for the tax payers to economise upon the working classes!' He reminded Russell that he felt 'the Govt is bound, to do what it can, to help the working classes over the present moment of distress'.

The Queen headed for Osborne two days before Kennington, with Albert and her children. This flight provoked gossip in London, in aristocratic drawing rooms and elsewhere, but unfairly. She had given birth just three weeks earlier to Princess Louise, her sixth child in eight years, and was still recovering from a very unpleasant confinement. On 10 April she received a telegraphic message, relayed via HMS *Victory* in Portsmouth Harbour, saying that 'the meeting at Kennington Common has dispersed quietly – the procession has been given up – the petition will be brought to the House of Commons without any display. No disturbance of any kind has taken place and not a soldier has been seen – The Government have taken possession of the electric telegraph to prevent false reports spreading in the country.'[44]

As Russell told the Queen, the meeting was 'a complete failure'.[45] He added: 'the mob was in good humour'. Matthew Arnold, who was in Westminster, told Arthur Hugh Clough that 'the Chartists gave up at once in the greatest fright at seeing the preparations: braggarts as they are.'[46] London was soon 'perfectly quiet', as another signal sent from Buckingham Palace later in the day by Colonel Charles Grey, the Queen's equerry, via *Victory* told the Queen.[47] The disappointing turnout, and the sight of the great petition being delivered to Westminster in three cabs – and bearing 'signatures' of luminaries including the Queen herself, various of her ministers, and even Colonel Sibthorp, the most reactionary man in the Commons – made the event a subject for the English sense of humour.

There had been demonstrations and disturbances in the provinces, but Sir George Grey, the Home Secretary, wrote to Albert at Osborne on 13 April to say that 'accounts received from all parts of the country are satisfactory'.[48] Albert's papers include two arresting photographs of the Kennington meeting, reflecting his intense curiosity about the occasion: he had agonised over whether to go to Osborne with the Queen, for it seems he would have wished to be a fly on the wall at the protests. There had not, though, been much to see. Of the smaller than expected numbers, some went home quickly. Greville noted that it all passed off 'with surprising quiet'.[49] He also observed, more to the point, that the massive display of potential force by the authorities, and the determination of the moneyed classes to defend themselves, made an impression: 'The Chartist movement was contemptible; but everybody rejoices that the defensive demonstration was made, for it has given a great and memorable lesson which will not be thrown away, either on the disaffected and mischievous, or the loyal and peaceful.' During May there were minor demonstrations in east and north London, but they passed without incident. In early June five agitators were arrested for sedition. However, as Greville implied, the peace had been settled, and society could advance with the cooperation of all classes.

Soon after Kennington, Ashley wrote to Albert inviting him to address a meeting at Exeter Hall of the Society for the Improvement of the Condition of the Labouring Classes. Albert wanted to do it; but was advised by both Russell and Grey not to in case the floor was hijacked by Chartist militants. Albert told Ashley that 'I sincerely regret it, as it will be difficult to find another becoming opportunity for expressing the sincere interest which the Queen and myself feel for the welfare and comfort of the working classes'.[50] He asked Ashley to pass this on; and suggested a means be found for the working classes to have more responsibility for improving their lot. He became president of the Servants' Provident and Benevolent Society, and took a keen interest in regulating savings banks, to encourage thrift and self-reliance. He had professed his shock at discovering that in London 'the greater part of the inmates of our workhouses are domestic servants'.[51]

Albert then had second thoughts: by late April he wrote to the Prime Minister to protest that 'I conceive that one has moreover a *Duty* to perform among the great mass of the working classes (and particularly at this moment) which will not allow one's yielding to the fear for some possible inconvenience.' This prompted Russell to say that 'if Your Royal Highness feels it to be a duty to preside at the meeting in Exeter Hall I have not a word more to say. I may likewise have taken too unfavourable a view of the present sentiment.'[52] However, he enclosed a pamphlet containing attacks on the Royal Family, giving Albert an idea of what might await him. Albert was unshaken, telling Russell of his conviction that he should not 'neglect doing what one can in showing one's interest and sympathy for the lower orders'.[53] He said he would ask Grey to see Ashley and settle security arrangements with the police; and he discounted the threat from militant Chartists. As for the minatory pamphlet Russell had sent, Albert said it 'rather furnishes me with a reason more for attending the meeting.' He felt more determined than ever to show that the Royal Family cared for 'the poor labourers' and 'are anxious about their welfare and ready to co-operate in any scheme for the amelioration of their condition.' He continued: 'We may possess these feelings and still the mass of the people may be ignorant of it because they have never heard it expressed to them or seen any tangible proof of it.' He concluded: 'I am President of this society and it might be asked: "Why does the President stay away? Is he afraid of meeting us or does he not care for us?"'

Grey met Ashley at the beginning of May 1848. They agreed to have the meeting in a smaller venue, the Freemasons' Hall, and to make it an all-ticket occasion. Ashley wrote to the Prince confirming that the tickets would be available only through 'the most respectable book-sellers'.[54] On the day itself, he continued, 'all the front benches will be occupied by our friends, and we propose to have in the hall, seated in groups, here and there, of two and three, about one hundred stout, hearty fellows, inmates of the Lodging Houses, who will have both an interest, and a desire, and a capability too, to keep the peace.' He added, reassuringly: 'I am sure that no-one will attempt so <u>unpopular</u> a thing, as to disturb Your Royal Highness when engaged in such work.'

Albert's press cuttings show his deep interest in the upheavals on the Continent: but nothing would deter him. He went with officers of the Society to visit the model lodging-houses from which the 'stout, hearty fellows' who would police his meeting would come. On 17 May, the day before it, Russell offered to go with him, but Albert told him that if he wished to he should go on his own, in a personal capacity, and not be seen to be offering the government's endorsement of the occasion.[55]

Albert's presence caused the hall to be 'besieged': 'every seat and standing room in the spacious and magnificent hall was occupied a few moments after access could be obtained, and more than an hour before the proceedings were advertised to commence,' according to the report in *The Times*.[56] The Prince arrived at noon, ushered in by Ashley, the Duke of Argyll, the Marquis of Westminster, Lord John Russell, a brace of earls, five bishops and several MPs. The draft of the speech the Prince proceeded to give is in his own hand.[57]

He said he was speaking up for 'that class of our community which has most of the toil and least of the enjoyments of this world.' He extolled the 'disinterested' influence of the upper classes being brought to bear on these problems: he spoke of the model lodging-houses, the loan funds and the allotments provided by the Society to improve the lives of the lower orders: things that would enrich them all the more when they had an input, such as in the domestic improvements made in the lodging-houses. He described what a sound investment such things were for those with capital; they, and the people who used them, could profit from them. This had been the aim of the Society since its foundation in 1844: not to dole out food and clothes, but to provide the bases for the lower classes to help themselves become more prosperous, and better housed.

Four new lodging-houses had been provided in central London, giving clean and wholesome accommodation to working men: and it was profitable. Lodgings had been provided for poor widows: and the allotment idea had caught on in 2,000 parishes. The notion of self-help was properly established. Existing lodging-houses were often squalid, with beds of straw. Some had another life as brothels. They also exploited their clientele, charging an unnecessarily high rate and ensuring the workmen had little disposable income left to save for their betterment. Men were often trapped in this lifestyle because renting even a humble property was beyond their means. Thanks to Ashley (who became Lord Shaftesbury during the passage of the legislation), an Act was passed in 1851 to allow local authorities to inspect these lodging-houses, and to close them if necessary. In London, where such houses were famously squalid, the Metropolitan Police took over the inspection, and within a few years standards had risen dramatically.

'Depend upon it,' the Prince added, 'that the interests of the often contrasted classes are identical, and it is only ignorance which prevents their uniting to the advantage of each other.' He said the work of the Society served as an example for others to follow: it encouraged 'self-reliance and confidence in each other' among the lower classes. He warned those 'who under the blessing of Divine Providence, enjoy station, wealth, and education' to 'be careful, however, to avoid any dictatorial interference with labour and employment that frightens away capital.' Such interference was, however, bad for a yet more important reason: it 'destroys that liberty of thought and independence of action which must be left to every man if he is to work out his own happiness.' Albert's message was clear: the quality had had a lucky escape on 10

April, and it should do nothing to provoke the working classes in future, but leave it to make its bargains with the mercantile class, and to become slowly more prosperous. It might have been odd coming from the mouth of the husband of the Queen, but was close to an announcement of the beginning of the end of deference.

Many in the upper and upper-middle classes were still shaken by the close shave they felt Britain had had in avoiding widespread disturbances or a revolution, as in continental Europe; and were anxious to find ways of keeping the lower orders sufficiently content to be under control. Albert was not so cynical. His commitment to social reform long pre-dated Kennington. He saw the contentment of the labouring classes as vital to the British constitutional settlement, and because the European ruling class from which he came remembered well the events of 1789 and after in France. Albert's desire to see improvements went far beyond simply making the workers happy. He had an instinctive understanding that the greater success of all sections of society would not merely cause wealth to trickle down from top to bottom, but would also stimulate the philanthropy to enable the spread of education, the improvement of public health and the building of better housing. He also understood that the more successful industry and commerce were, the more the culture of invention and innovation in industry could be developed, and the more the growth of infrastructure would allow communications to be modernised and facilitate trade and other commercial activity.

Russell told the Queen that Albert's speech was 'exactly what it should be, the best principles in the best language – it cannot fail to do good.'[58] *The Times*, in a leading article, paid what it presumably considered to be the highest compliment to the Prince, saying that it was 'thoroughly English in feeling, English in language, and English in sense.'[59] The paper felt Albert 'understands the philosophy of life, the principles of British society, and the several claims of capital and industry, union and independence, as well as any gentleman born and bred in this country.' They contrasted what Albert had said with what had lately happened in France, with what it called communist demands for a 'utopia'. No doubt things were bad in Britain, but revolution was not the way to make things better.

It complained of the amount of stabling in the metropolis, there not for the purposes of business, but of pleasure. 'The back streets of whole districts are for horses, not men . . . the poor of London are most miserably, most discreditably housed.' The only solution, it felt, was for the wealthy to 'interfere', not least by providing more of the model lodging-houses suggested by the Prince. The next day the paper wrote more on the subject, referring to underfunded hospitals and the shortage of bathhouses for working men. Referring to the slowness in completing one particular public baths, the paper noted the Queen and Prince Albert, and the dowager Queen Adelaide, had each donated £100 to the completion fund. Another £3,000 was needed: and *The Times* asked why the metropolitan rich could not find that 'trifling amount' – 'for what is £3,000 to the wealthy of this metropolis?'[60]

Albert kept cuttings of the press's favourable response to his words. *John Bull* noted that 'it has not often fallen to our lot to see a greater amount of sound sense and sound feeling compressed within a few simple, yet forcible, words . . . never could such an expression of the genuine sympathy for the labouring classes which animates Royalty, have come more opportunely than at the moment when, under no ordinary degree of pressure – pressure felt throughout every class of the community – the working classes have united with them who are above them in station but not in true English feeling – in demonstrations of unshaken loyalty.'[61] The *Examiner* said that 'A Royal Personage who has the good sense in these days to come forward and proclaim the identity of his interest with that of the lowest and least fortunate in the state, not wanting the courage to imply that it befits no man in exalted station to be contented while the masses of men beneath him have just cause for discontent, is entitled to a hearing of the most respectful kind.' The *Morning Herald* spoke of Albert's 'sound judgment and practical sense'.[62] However, this was as close to politics as Albert, now more experienced in the ways of the British constitution, felt able to go. Soon he would find a serious project to occupy him, and fulfil his high-minded desire to lead the improvement of his wife's people.

PART II

THE VICTORIAN MIND

CHAPTER 5

THE GODLY MIND: NATIONAL APOSTASY AND THE VICTORIAN CHURCH

I

In the 1840s Britain's institutions were underpinned by Protestantism. The Monarch was Supreme Governor of the Church of England. Fellows of colleges at Oxford and Cambridge had to sign the Thirty-nine Articles when elected. Outside the Established Church there were numerous Nonconformist and dissenting Protestant sects – Methodists, Baptists, Unitarians and sects within those sects. These had grown in strength with industrialisation and the rootlessness it caused. The dominance of Protestantism was linked in the public mind to the success of the country. It also encouraged a sense of anti-Catholicism, and one that flew in the face of the liberties granted to Catholics by the Catholic Relief Act of 1829, which allowed them to sit in parliament and join the professions. Greater rights for Catholics had helped entrench militant Protestant feeling. Catholicism was widely considered unBritish and foreign. Augustus Welby Northmore Pugin, one of the most radical architects of the time and one who had converted to Catholicism, once made the mistake of crossing himself in a railway carriage. A lady who saw him do this cried out: 'you are a Catholic, sir! Guard, guard, let me out – I must get into another carriage!'[1]

But if Protestantism retained a popular hold, the Established Church's influence had been waning since the growth of dissent in the eighteenth century. Secularisation had been implicit in the Reformation and, from the Glorious Revolution onwards, religion had been moved away from the centre of British society by the development of capitalism.

Old communities broke up, and the towns to which thousands moved during the late eighteenth and early nineteenth centuries had few places of worship and no settled parish structure. Fewer people attended church. Those who had once had a recognised place in a social order in which the Church played a key part became anonymous in the great industrial cities. The move from the land broke the last bonds of feudalism, and the working classes formed a relationship instead with the forces of capital, themselves often secularist in nature.

The nineteenth century was a time when the expansion of knowledge fuelled rationalism and changed the terms of trade for religion. One of the finest scholars of secularism, Owen Chadwick, explored whether the idea had taken off because people knew more, or whether for reasons of class and physical upheaval they felt alienated from the Church.

> Orthodox Christianity was proved untrue because miracles became improbable, and Genesis was proved to be a myth by science, and philosophical axioms were transformed by intellectual processes derived from the Enlightenment, and the intellectual revolution passed from universities to newspaper, and from newspaper to drawing-room, and drawing-room to housekeeper's parlour, the newspaper to working-men's clubs – are ideas what move the souls of men? Or did the working man, thrust by economic development into a new and more impersonal class-structure, develop a consciousness of his class, and distrust or hatred of the middle class, and find the churches middle-class institutions, and start to beat them with whatever sticks lay to hand, and found the weapons of atheist pamphleteers and potted handbooks of evolutionary science?[2]

The State fought to maintain religion. Since the Church Building Acts of 1818 and 1824 – a response to the fears of the ruling class about the effect of the absence of organised religion and worship in the newly expanded urban areas – large amounts of government money had been granted for the building of Anglican churches in those areas. Although the Chartist movement to an extent anticipated Christian socialism, atheism began to become more apparent among radicals. As the mood in society towards the rejection of God changed, so prominent thinkers such as John Stuart Mill eventually admitted their scepticism about religion. Works such as *On Liberty* and *The Subjugation of Women* display a cast of mind at odds with traditional doctrine. However, for all that, perceptions remained of Britain as an overwhelmingly Christian country.

Christianity's defenders could be, and were, as militant as those who sought to expose it as a sham. Even to a man so sophisticated in his theology as Gladstone, it became essential not merely for preserving the social order, but for facilitating progress. In a memorandum written in the early 1840s, he outlined what he believed would happen in a state of 'Christianity abolished': '1. Gladiatorial shows. 2. Human sacrifices. 3. Polygamy. 4. Exposure of children. 5. Slavery. 6. Cannibalism.'[3] Also in the 1840s, in another undated memorandum, he noted that 'in the present, as a critical period, it is more especially expedient to scrutinise our state: not external alone with reference to the common enemy, but internally too, for the foe is everywhere, both where effective Christian principle dwells, and where it dwells not.'[4] In another, apparently from the same period, he reflects upon the pressure that the modern world puts on observance of religion. 'It is impossible for me to fulfil (I use the phrase in the restricted sense in which alone it ever could be realised) all the duty of an English Churchman while I continue in political life: or in other words there are kinds and degrees of co-operation which I might be able like others to render, but which cannot be rendered in my present position.'[5]

At least he tried. Even before Mill's rationalism, or Darwin's evolutionary science, it was hard for many to make time for God. 'Pity', he wrote much later, in the early 1880s after reading Froude's life of Carlyle, 'that Carlyle could not substitute a soothing dependence upon God for his usual and assuredly most valiant strain, defiance of the devil.'[6] He had noted that when Carlyle 'writes to his mother he assumes the phraseology of a Christian . . . this is not hypocrisy but it is fiction; it is deception, beginning possibly in self-deception.' With John Henry Newman, the leading Anglo-Catholic (who, going over to Rome in 1845, eventually became a cardinal), he was much more gentle. In an effusive letter to him of 18 February 1866, he wrote that 'the internal condition of the great and ancient Church, which has for its own one half of Christendom, cannot be matter of indifference to Christians beyond its borders . . . we see before us an ever growing actual necessity, in the world of thought, for a new reconciliation of Christianity and mankind.'[7]

The Church militant was in evidence around the Great Exhibition in 1851: the clergy of London made elaborate plans, and raised subscriptions, for the greater availability of places of worship for the 'unprecedented influx of strangers': a measure of which Prince Albert entirely approved.[8] This was, though, a time of relative ease in the Established Church, for all Gladstone's concerns about the receding Sea of Faith. Butler wrote that 'between 1844, when *Vestiges of Creation* appeared, and 1859, when *Essays and Reviews* marked the commencement of that storm which raged until many years afterwards, there was not a single book published in England that caused serious commotion within the bosom of the Church. Perhaps Buckle's *History of Civilisation* and Mill's *Liberty* were the most alarming, but they neither of them reached the substratum of the reading public.'[9]

Because of the obsession among the leading minds with theological questions – notably questions of doctrine – it is easy to forget the simple faith of the average person that still prevailed, and whose prevalence was indicated by the vast programme of church-building in England between the 1840s and the 1870s: and of the building of dissenting chapels too. Secularisation may not have been confined to the educated classes, but the Church tried to temper its impact on the lower orders, when the buttress of religion could help maintain morale, show an alternative to hard materialism, and even create a sense of community.

Nevertheless, faith was ebbing away slowly. In Mrs Gaskell's *North and South*, Mr Hale – having resigned his Anglican ministry because of doubts – finds himself talking to the weaver Higgins, whose daughter has died after her lungs were destroyed by the toxic air inhaled in the mill. Higgins tells the clergyman that his peers, 'real folk', have abandoned religion: 'They don't believe i' the Bible – not they. They may say they do, for form's sake; but Lord, sir, dy'e think their first cry i' the morning is, "What shall I do to get hold on eternal life?" or "What shall I do to fill my purse this blessed day? Where shall I go? What bargains shall I strike?" The purse and the gold and the notes is real things; things as can be felt and touched; them's realities; and eternal life is all a talk . . .'[10] It is hard for Hale to convince Higgins of the existence of God with his daughter lying dead, aged nineteen; nonetheless Hale succeeds in persuading him, before he leaves the house, to kneel with him and his daughter and join in their family prayers, despite his being an 'infidel'. 'It did them no harm,' notes Gaskell.[11] For many working men, however, capitalism had made the old social order, with God at the top of it, incomprehensible.

II

While religion faced new challenges among the people, some theologians chose to complicate what once had been matters of simple faith. There was a growing belief among some Anglicans that their church had, during the eighteenth century and in the early nineteenth, become increasingly worldly, cynical and (not to put too fine a point on it) degenerate. This had happened, it was felt, not least because of the proximity of the State to the Established Church, which was stipulated by the Thirty-nine Articles. It had had a corrupting effect, reducing the Church's independence and encouraging the manipulation of ecclesiastical wealth and patronage. The Oxford Movement, some of whose founders converted to Roman Catholicism, was an attempt to reduce the interference in religion of a State perceived as incapable of taking its religious duties sufficiently seriously, and determined to reduce the power of the Church and enhance the power of the State. The Thirty-nine Articles were in part regarded with disapproval and disdain by the Anglo-Catholics: and not merely the strictures against the Bishop of Rome.

John Henry Newman, possibly the most eminent member of the Movement, decreed it to have begun on 14 July 1833. That day John Keble delivered the Assize Sermon in Oxford subsequently published under the title of *National Apostasy*, which examined the 'apostate mind' of the era and rebuked the State for interfering in the Church of England. Newman had arrived back in England five days earlier, after seven months travelling the Mediterranean with his friend Richard Hurrell Froude and Froude's father, an archdeacon. His theological mind had been turned first by a visit to Corfu, where he had noted similarities between Orthodox and Roman Catholic worship, and Rome, where he felt the conflict of the religious veneration and piety of the people, and the superstitions and venality of their Church.

This combination of circumstances caused an earthquake in Newman's soul. A fortnight later a group of high-churchmen met at the rectory at Hadleigh in Suffolk, home of the Reverend Hugh James Rose, editor of the recently founded high-church *British Magazine*, to discuss a new approach to doctrine. Newman was not present: but he would soon become a guiding spirit of the movement these men would constitute. He started to write prolifically. On 9 September 1833 he published the first of the *Tracts for the Times*, written anonymously, on the subject of the apostolic succession. Later that autumn he contributed a series of papers to the *British Magazine* that would later be published as *The Church of the Fathers*. He gave weekly sermons in his church, St Mary's Oxford, the university church, outlining his view of the revised doctrine the Anglican Church needed. He had in his sights liberals like Dr Arnold, who wanted the Church to dilute its doctrine to allow it to embrace members of dissenting sects. Arnold and Newman would be at odds for the rest of Arnold's life, and indeed after it.

Keble and Edward Pusey, the Regius professor of Hebrew, were also among the authors of the Tracts, which soon provoked acrimonious argument. Pusey had spent time in the 1820s at Göttingen, which would become Bismarck's alma mater, where he imbibed modern German ideas of religion and was accused, for a time, of being a rationalist. However, his aim on returning to England was to reconnect the Church of England, of which he became an ordained priest, with the Catholic underpinnings essential to it even after the Reformation had installed the King of England as head of the Church, but which were lost in the torrent of anti-popery after the Glorious Revolution. Newman had argued in 1834, in response to the contention that he was undermining the Protestant nature of the Church of England, that the Church could both be reformed and remain Catholic – what he termed the *via media*, or middle way, between Protestantism and Catholicism. The Tracts were widely read and circulated, and the movement caught on: young, impressionable minds at Oxford and elsewhere were swept up in it. Elsewhere among Anglicans there was horror, and a sense of being menaced by this attempt to restore Catholicism to England.

The crucial and, as it turned out, final Tract – number XC – was written by Newman and published on 27 February 1841. It argued that Anglicans could adhere to Catholic doctrine, except for recognising the Pope's supremacy, because the Thirty-nine Articles could have a Catholic interpretation. This was a tendentious reading: it meant a wholesale repudiation of the Reformation. Gladstone, who read it on 12 March, used a single word to describe the effect on him: 'ominous'.[12] Newman was censured by the university's vice-chancellor, proctors and heads of house; and was compelled by his bishop to promise not to publish any more Tracts. This drove Newman from Oxford – to Littlemore, 2 miles outside the city, and part of his parish. It caused him to reflect on what he considered the insufficiently religious tone of the Church of England, and what it could offer in the way of spirituality and devotion to young priests. Rome became an ever more attractive prospect.

Tract XC deeply troubled some who read it or encountered its ideas, but revolted others. In the latter category was Charles Kingsley who, upon reading an extensive account of it in the *Edinburgh Review*, wrote that it supported 'pernicious superstition' and observed: 'Whether wilful or self-deceived, these men are Jesuits, taking the oath to the Articles with moral reservations, which allow them to explain them away in senses utterly different from those of their authors – All the worst *doctrinal* features of Popery Mr Newman professes to believe in . . .'[13]

In October 1843 Gladstone noted in his diary that he had read 'with pain and dismay' a letter Newman had sent to Henry Manning talking of how the 'general repudiation' by the Church of Tract XC was driving him out of the Anglican communion, and how he 'justly felt to be a foreign material incapable of assimilating with the Church of England'.[14] Newman felt the Church was becoming 'alien from Catholic principles', and found 'increased difficulty in contending that she is a branch of the Catholic Church – that it is a dream to talk of Catholicity.' Gladstone was relieved Newman was saying this in public, but he could not keep the truth from Manning, to whom he was close. 'He has considerably weakened his powers for good,' Gladstone noted. 'They remain great for mischief: but we may yet trust he will not be abandoned.'

That hope would not be fulfilled. Within days Manning sent Gladstone a second note from Newman, 'who announced that since the summer of 1839 he had had the conviction that the Church of Rome is the Catholic Church, and ours not a branch of the Catholic Church because not in communion with Rome!'[15] The Movement would fragment, notably with Keble being grieved by Newman's decision, in October 1845, to go over to Rome. The split had been coming for years, with some early adherents realising that there was increasingly little difference between Anglo-Catholicism, as advocated by Newman, and Roman Catholicism. This had become apparent when Newman refused in 1839 to subscribe to a monument to be erected in Oxford to Cranmer, Ridley and Latimer, three of the Protestant martyrs of the sixteenth century. He was keen to be provocative: in an early sermon he said that 'I do not shrink from uttering my firm conviction that it would be a gain to the country were it vastly more superstitious, more bigoted, more gloomy, more fierce in its religion than at present it shows itself to be.'[16] His fundamental criticism of the Protestant Church of England, and its dissenting variants, was that they lacked spiritual authority: and he increasingly came to realise that only one Church, in his view, had the authority he sought.

His friend Hurrell Froude, in one of the statements that would make his *Remains* (edited anonymously by Newman and Keble) so toxic to Newman's cause, said that 'we are Catholics without the Popery, and Church-of-England men without the Protestantism', and that religious life was 'cramped by Protestantism', which rather gave the game away.[17] Gladstone had read the first volume of *Remains* in 1838 'with repeated regrets', for he could see where the movement was leading.[18] The editors went on the defensive in their Preface, arguing, unconvincingly, that the letters that comprised the *Remains* 'bear a strong testimony against the actual system of Rome; strong, as coming from one who was disposed to make every fair allowance in the Church's favour; who was looking and longing for some fuller development of Catholic principles than he could easily find, but who was soon obliged to confess, with undissembled mortification and disappointment, that such development was not to be looked for in Rome.'[19]

These statements were made of one who also wrote: 'The reformation was a limb badly set – it must be broken again in order to be righted.'[20] Rome was the destination, years before Newman bought his ticket. Greville, in his diary in August 1841, recalled meeting at dinner 'a smooth, oily and agreeable Priest', Bishop Wiseman, who talked of little other than the Oxford Movement, and (having claimed close acquaintance with Pusey) said that 'the great body of that persuasion, Pusey himself included, are very nearly ripe and ready for reunion with Rome, and he assured us that neither the Pope's supremacy nor Transubstantiation would be obstacles in their way.'[21]

In 1874 John Morley, who was at Oxford in the 1850s, defended the Movement by saying that 'it was at any rate a recognition in a very forcible way of the doctrine that spiritual matters are not to be settled by the dicta of a political council. It acknowledged that a man is answerable at his own peril for having found or lost the truth.'[22] Gladstone, whose biography Morley would write, became increasingly despairing of the Oxford divines. Tract XC was to him 'like a repetition of the publication of Froude's *Remains*, and Newman has again burned his fingers', he told Lord

Lyttelton.[23] He saw Newman had put himself outside the Church of England 'in point of spirit and sympathy'. Oxford became polarised: an election for the professorship of poetry in December 1841 was between candidates who were avowedly 'no popery' and a Puseyite. Pusey himself was forbidden to preach in the university for two years in 1843.

The mood that helped feed Tractarianism (as the Oxford Movement was also known, because of the religious tracts its members regularly published) was the same that fed Young England: a romantic attachment to the Middle Ages and feudalism, of which the old religion was an integral part. To go back to the Middle Ages was to go back to the religion that had prevailed before the Reformation. That sentiment was reflected in the style of the many new churches built to accommodate the expanding population: the Gothic Revival echoed the style of the pre-Reformation era. The notion of Ritualism that became so significant a part of Tractarianism – the close study of ancient liturgies and then of ecclesiology – was brought firmly to bear on much nineteenth-century church building, and at times gave it an exoticism never before seen in this country.

The horrors of the industrialised society were as much to blame for the debate about faith as for the political quarrels of the time. When society undergoes seismic change – as Britain did in the first half of the nineteenth century – retreat to a familiar past is irresistible, if futile. In the case of the Tractarians, and more so the Ritualists, it was a retreat to fantasy past, as anyone who studies their church buildings and those from the medieval age will tell at once: though some of what the Ritualists wanted to do would have been familiar from the medieval church, such as the adornment of chancels, the use of images and the use of pre-Reformation style vestments. Such things caused heated controversy and even litigation. This was the climate of religious disputation at Oxford into which went three of the most important intellectuals of the early and mid-Victorian period, whom we shall meet in the next chapter: Arthur Hugh Clough, Matthew Arnold and James Anthony Froude.

III

While the upper and upper-middle classes battled with the intellectual niceties of modern theology, and the new middle classes were being shaped by the dissenting sects from which they were often sprung, the working class was having a much more straightforward ride. Engels found in 1844 that 'all the writers of the bourgeoisie are unanimous on this point, that the workers are not religious, and do not attend church.'[24] A spiritual dimension was usually absent from the lives of the lower orders. Spirituality had never encountered them, or vice versa. The new communities in which many lived – they were frequently first- or second-generation emigrants from the countryside – were not merely rootless, but were unserviced by the Church of England. The 1851 census found that for the first time in the history of any significant nation more than half the population was urban. In all industrial towns except Leeds more than the half the population were immigrants.[25]

The dissenting chapels often did not want the working classes, regarding them as incapable of conforming with their core clientele. The move from old community to new seemed to break the tradition of regular churchgoing. Methodism in particular was an aspirational religion, encouraging habits of hard work and frugality; there was little evidence that it was interested in helping the non-aspirational. One of the earliest historians of the Methodist movement observed in 1860 that it hardly had a footing in the large towns, but flourished in small ones.[26] Congregationalists had a similar view: 'Our mission is neither to the very rich nor to the very poor, but to the great middle section of the community,' noted the chairman of the sect, Thomas Binney, in 1848.[27] The duty of helping the dispossessed fell upon the Church of England and on the only Church that had increased its numbers of working-class adherents thanks to the Irish Potato Famine, the Roman Catholic.

In 1851 the census asked, for the first time, about religious worship. On the Sunday before census day details of attendance were supplied by 14,077 places belonging to the Established Church, and from 20,390 dissenting chapels.[28] It found that since 1831 the Church had built 2,029 places of worship, to counter what the report of the census's findings called 'spiritual destitution'.[29] The number of churches in Lancashire had risen from 292 to 521, in twenty years when the population had almost doubled. There was a similar story in Middlesex, which had a church for every 4,658 people, against one for every 5,522 in 1831. Nationally, the census estimated that there were 5,317,915 'sittings' in the 14,077 places of worship in the Established Church, and that 2,541,244 of these were occupied on the census Sunday morning; 1,890,764 in the afternoon; and 860,543 in the evening.[30]

Families might attend church three times each Sunday, so these figures do not merit being added together. A similar proportion of sittings was occupied in dissenting chapels during the morning and afternoon, but with the highest attendance during the evenings. Only the Roman Catholic Church, whose places of worship were still being built in the twenty-third year after emancipation, was overcrowded, with many churches holding more than one morning service. Lancashire had the largest Roman Catholic population of any English county, mainly because of its proximity to Ireland, but also for historic reasons as a centre of opposition to Anglicanism. In 1850 the Pope established dioceses in England, to the outrage of militant Protestants. This outbreak of intolerance coincided with the campaign to welcome foreigners to Britain for the Great Exhibition.

The census counted thirty-five Christian churches or sects in England and Wales. It accounted, in terms of non-Christians, only for Jews ('a nation and a Church at once') finding fifty-three synagogues for 8,438 Jews.[31] It was assumed that accommodation for half of England's 18 million people to worship would be 'ample'.[32] This was because 'immaturity or Sunday-school engagements' would mean about 3,000,000 children would 'justifiably' be absent.[33] Also, a million would be 'usually and lawfully away from public worship' on the grounds of 'sickness or debility', with an equal number kept from worship by household duties, or because they were medical practitioners. Some were employed on the Lord's Day in connection with 'public conveyances'.

The 1854 report concluded that 7,500,000 people would have a valid excuse to be elsewhere, and provision would only be needed for 10,427,609. The holding of three services on a Sunday meant that some who could not attend in the morning might do so in the afternoon or evening: and it reassured the potentially over-zealous: 'It will be found that very many persons think their duties as to Sabbath worship adequately discharged by *one* attendance.'[34] Many sittings were, however, to be found in the ancient medieval churches of largely depopulated villages: and it was in growing towns where 'spiritual destitution' was most prevalent. Of the great towns and cities of England, only Bath, Colchester, Exeter, Oxford, Wakefield, Worcester and York had enough sittings. At the other extreme, Lambeth had sittings for only 24.8 per cent of its people; Birmingham for 28.7 per cent, Halifax for 30.3 per cent, Manchester and Bradford for 31.6 per cent.[35] The report called a central drive to build new churches: because the rootlessness in those towns meant an absence of local wealth and interest to provide them.

However, more than half the 10 million sittings were 'appropriated' – belonging to aristocracy, gentry or the new middle classes who paid 'pew rents'. These rents paid the wages of the sexton or pew-opener: but they severely limited accommodation for the masses. Yet the report admitted that 'it is tolerably certain that the 5,288,294 who every Sunday, neglect religious ordinances, do so of their own free choice, and are not compelled to be absent on account of the deficiency of sittings.'[36] Most who went to church paid to do so, suggesting they were almost entirely well-to-do. The empty sittings suggested that there was no need to build churches, except in places of severe overcrowding; and that the working classes, as Engels had noted, had voted with their feet where religion was concerned, and were seeking a different sort of opium. The report suggested, hopefully, that new churches might attract people who would not worship in old ones, with their class divisions and other social rigidities that suggested exclusivity.

The report observed that it had become fashionable for the upper and middle classes to attend worship if they wished to be seen to be entering into 'the recognised proprieties of life'.[37] However, it was also clear in large towns 'how absolutely insignificant a portion of the congregations is composed of artisans'. It likened them to 'the people of a heathen country' and said they were 'thoroughly estranged from our religious institutions'. More shocking, the author of the report, Horace Mann, noted a specific movement designed to degrade religion: 'There is a sect, originated recently, adherents to a system called "Secularism"; the principal tenet being that, as the fact of a future life is (in their view) at all events susceptible of some degree of doubt, while the fact and the necessities of a present life are matters of direct sensation, it is therefore prudent to attend exclusively to the concerns of that existence which is certain and immediate – not wasting energies required for present duties by a preparation for remote, and merely possible, contingencies.' Mann felt the working population and the 'miserable denizens of courts and crowded alleys' had bought into this 'creed' extensively, but unwittingly: he called them 'unconscious Secularists – engrossed by the demands, the trials, or the pleasures of the passing hour, and ignorant and careless of a future'. He concluded: 'the melancholy fact is thus impressed upon our notice that the classes which are most in need of the restraints and consolations of religion are the classes which are most without them.'

Mann said the artisan could not go into a church without having some 'memento of inferiority' impressed upon him: and called for the abolition of the pew system. 'Religion . . . has thus come to be regarded as a purely middle-class propriety or luxury,' he observed.[38] If artisans felt that class barriers, even beyond the pew system, made it difficult or unpleasant for them to attend church, then Mann felt the Church and the dissenting chapels should put on services especially for the working man and his family: he cited the example of 'ragged churches', emulating the Ragged Schools, that had sprung up in several working-class districts.

Mann also felt that a serious obstacle to working-class attendance was the distinctly unchristian behaviour towards them of some of their social superiors whom they encountered at places of worship. He had detected 'insufficient sympathy' for the 'alleviation of their social burdens – poverty, disease and ignorance.' In this remark Mann identified himself, and the part of officialdom for whom he spoke, with the pursuit of perfection; but he also indicated how far the self-interest of many of the well-to-do set itself against such a notion. Although he conceded that the clergy led schemes to help the poor, the nature of much church philanthropy was not, he felt, designed to secure the gratitude of those who received it.

He also touched on the suspicion that many of the poor had of the motives of the university-trained clergy with whom they came into contact, as if the Christian message were for social control rather than the salvation of souls. He asserted that the conditions in which the poor lived, notably the squalor of their housing, were simply too dreadful to create any faith in Christianity. He reflected that 'teeming populations often now surround half empty churches, which would probably remain half empty even if the sittings were all free'.[39] The only solution, he believed, was missionary work: and he cited the example of the Mormons, who had done such a thing with notably good results.

The London City Mission had been founded in 1835, its 300 missionaries being sent out to distribute tracts to the poor in their homes and to talk to them about religion. Sometimes they would hold prayer meetings or Bible classes: but this was an isolated example. In time the missionary call would be taken up: though not in large numbers until a combination of William Booth and his Salvation Army at one end of the spectrum and the universities and the public schools at the other made a concerted effort to spread the word in the 1870s and 1880s. Mann was so convinced of the 'urgency' of the danger from godlessness in urban England that he suggested that 'street-preaching', under proper sanction and control, would not be a too energetic measure for 'the terrible emergency'.[40] For the moment, it was not more churches that were needed, but more curates. The incumbents of many urban parishes could not cope with the workload of the destitute, and urgently needed practical support.

He also called for the greater involvement of laymen; for the development of more Sunday schools; and for the revival of the principle of suffragan bishops. Two new sees – Manchester and Ripon – had been created shortly before King William's death for the expanding populations of Lancashire and the West Riding. All these proposals invited the same question: would the godless lower orders be remotely interested in taking advantage of the new opportunities for worship that it was proposed to offer them? Mann did not choose to speculate on this: he merely advised his masters in government that 'no inconsiderable portion of the secular prosperity and peace of individuals and states depends on the extent to which a pure religion is professed and practically followed.'[41]

This was the orthodoxy: and the reason why the limited State provision for education of the poor was made through the agency of the Church. Mann commended religion as an instrument of the very social control he had earlier said that the lower classes were so suspicious of: 'Christian men become, almost inevitably, temperate, industrious, and provident, as part of their religious duty; and Christian citizens acquire respect for human laws from having learnt to reverence those which are divine.' To Mann and the whole official and political class, indeed, such a notion justified the pursuit of perfection by means of extending godliness.

It was also perceived to be a barrier – though Mann does not explicitly mention it – that the Established Church remained socially exclusive in terms of its clergy. The great majority were Oxford or Cambridge men. Anthony Trollope observed that the alumnus of a theological college, rather than an Oxbridge one, 'who won't drink his glass of wine, and talk of his college, and put off for a few happy hours the sacred stiffness of the profession and become simply an English gentleman – he is the clergyman whom in his heart the archdeacon does not love.'[42] By implication, such a man would not find preferment easy, and his type was not encouraged. Religious tests as a condition of matriculating or taking a bachelor's degree at Oxford and Cambridge were abolished in the two universities in 1854 and 1856 respectively. By 1878, however, 16,297 of the 23,612 English and Welsh clergy were still Oxbridge men.

The 1851 census showed that there were nearly as many Nonconformists attending places of worship as there were Anglicans. The dissenting congregations had been greatly boosted by the repeal in 1828 of the Test and Corporation Acts, which had excluded their members from many areas of public life and from certain schools, from universities and from being beneficiaries of certain charities. Whether Baptists, Methodists, Quakers, Plymouth Brethren or any other dissenting congregations, what united Nonconformity was its regard of State involvement in religion as handicapping freedom of conscience. The Nonconformists held great sway in the new urban communities, where they had colonised much of the new middle class. They were also among the strictest upholders of Protestantism, their literal interpretations of the Bible far exceeding the lax approach of many Anglican clergy that had so offended the Tractarians.

Yet, as we shall see in the next two chapters, the paradox was that at a time of heightened religious consciousness and, in some places, even religious revival, the orthodoxies of religion, and even the idea of religion itself, were starting to be questioned as never before. Some who had been steeped in Anglicanism from the cradle, and who possessed some of the highest minds in mid-nineteenth-century Britain, began to have doubts about their interpretation of their faith, and about the Arnoldian view of the central part that it should play in life and society. Beyond them, however, a movement was growing up that sought to reject and undermine religion altogether.

Karl Marx despised religion precisely because it offered consolation to the poor for their lot, and sought to anaesthetise them against their suffering. This is why he branded it 'the opium of the people'. He also saw it as a justification of a profoundly iniquitous social order. He wanted the proletariat to fight against it; and atheism would be the great ally in that struggle. This, as Chadwick has pointed out, is a different motivation for secularism from what was usual in the nineteenth century: it was irrelevant to Marx whether Christianity was true or not, for all that mattered was that it impeded the dictatorship of the proletariat.

The new middle classes who felt alienated from Anglicanism were natural converts to dissent, and had the leisure and the opportunity – and, more to the point, usually the education – to engage in the philosophical processes that might lead them away from the Church but keep them within Christianity. An Act in 1843 increased funds to the Ecclesiastical Commissioners to create new parishes and build new churches. It had had the strong support of Ashley, who also led private fund-raising drives to match the grants of public money. As Mill would find, professing atheism was a sure way of inviting obloquy, ridicule and character assassination: so the socialist movement took care to stand apart from the minority who happily declared themselves atheists.

For this reason, around 1850, the word 'secularist' entered the language, used by the Birmingham lecturer and radical George Holyoake to describe himself and to avoid 'the imputations of atheism and infidelity'.[43] Holyoake had been imprisoned for six months for blasphemy in 1842, as the result of an answer he had given during a public lecture in Cheltenham, so understood better than most the importance of treading carefully. When T. H. Huxley popularised the use of 'agnostic' in the 1860s, Holyoake adopted that. During the 1850s secular societies sprang up in parts of England, often in a direct line of descent from Chartism, and by way of a final attempt to keep it going. They were most visible in the industrial heartland of Lancashire and the West Riding.

By then, however, the battle was almost won. Men such as Charles Darwin, John Stuart Mill and Samuel Butler ensured the movement would carry heavier metal than its opponents. However, for most working men and their families, the drift to secularism came not after an intellectual battle, or a feeling that the Church was a weapon of social control that they had to fend off, but because of a lack of education and spirituality in their lives. Between 1841 and 1870 a total of 2,859 new and rebuilt Anglican churches were consecrated, nearly three times as many as in the previous thirty years: but this may have been simply as a result of an over-optimistic miscalculation by the Church, and only created an illusion of a godly nation.[44] The religious superstructure could no longer cope, and the threat of damnation was a fairy story.

The nature of Sundays was changing. Sports may not have been encouraged, but other distractions were becoming more frequent. In 1841 a young Baptist carpenter, Thomas Cook, organised the first railway excursion, for a temperance society. Within twenty years a London clergyman would complain about the temptation to people to treat Sunday as a 'holiday' because of the availability of such excursions.[45] Within another decade or two, the bicycle would cut a further swathe through potential church attendance, with the opening of museums, parks, concert halls and galleries on Sunday afternoons playing their part. Among the lower classes in particular, the widespread availability of alcohol also militated against church attendance.

By the 1840s one thing for certain had changed, which was that the Church had flung off its Georgian lassitude, not least as it better understood how these social and philosophical currents were threatening to undermine it. Any notion that the clergy were guilty of neglect of their duties, and preferred a life of ease, was not always supported by the facts. Gladstone, in November 1842, noted a remark made at dinner by Thomas Grenville that 'the most remarkable change he had witnessed in the course of his long life' was 'without doubt the change in the character of the clergy'. Grenville elaborated that 'in his earlier days, the young clergy were almost as a matter of course gentlemen indeed but unconcerned, in any serious sense, about their parishes or their duties: whereas now the rule was completely reversed and they were as a body zealously and devoutly set upon the work of their office.'[46]

CHAPTER 6

THE DOUBTING MIND:
STRUGGLES IN THE SEA OF FAITH

I

The most profound effect of the Oxford Movement was not John
Henry Newman's conversion to Catholicism, predictable from 1833. It
was the crises of faith and the reconsideration of religion it inflicted on
many of those who came into contact with it. This became a widespread
social and cultural phenomenon in the 1840s. As we have seen, it found
its way even into fiction, such as in the case of Mr Hale, the doubt-ridden
clergyman in Mrs Gaskell's *North and South*. Hale seems an extreme,
almost absurd figure, until one realises that his martyrdom had parallels
in real life that were all too serious for those concerned. Hale's experience was, as we shall see, not far removed from that of Arthur Hugh
Clough, for whom it meant he could no longer subscribe to the Thirty-
nine Articles of the Church of England, with their repudiation of the
Catholic Church and the Pope and their insistence on this true form of
Christianity – and, indeed, their assumption of the inevitable superiority
of Christianity itself. Hale is a pathetically weak man – Clough had more
moral fibre – but he had been 'a perfect model of a parish priest'.[1] He
had a beautiful vicarage in a serene Hampshire village where his wife and
daughter lived lives of fruitful ease, doing good works. Then he was
assailed by 'doubts'. 'How I love the holy Church from which I am to
be shut out!' he protested to his bewildered daughter.[2] But, like Clough,
he is unable 'to make a fresh declaration of conformity to the Liturgy
at my institution'.[3] Then, like Clough, he left his familiar surroundings,
in his case for the industrial north, to work as a private tutor to a mill-
owner whose education was neglected but who, in typical Victorian

style, wished to improve himself. Like Clough, the Reverend Mr Hale died before his time, worn out by the consequences of his doubts, and brought misery upon his family. 'I don't think God endued me with over-much wisdom or strength,' Hale confides in his best friend just before his martyrdom.[4]

Other serious intellectuals in the Anglican tradition had their own problems too. For Matthew Arnold it led to a reconsideration of the profoundly religious teaching he had had from his evangelical father. For James Anthony Froude the debate about Christian worship rocked the foundations of his faith, and, once he came under the influence of Carlyle and his brand of Germanic theism, led to his fundamentally questioning Christianity. At Cambridge, away from these influences, Charles Kingsley found his Anglicanism moving into Christian socialism. All these men, in their different ways, proved the continuing power of religion over them, and the need either to reach an accommodation with it, to redefine it, or to adjust to a more secular society. They were but some of the most notable members of a movement that would have a very profound effect upon society. Each may have had his own response to the problem, but the cumulative effect was to start to weaken the grip of religion on Britain, and to advance a culture in which faith no longer played the dominant part.

II

As a Rugbeian Clough was, in the words of Lytton Strachey, 'an exceptional kind of boy, upon whom the high-pitched exhortations of Dr Arnold produced a very different effect' from the effect it had upon most others.[5] He, and others like him, 'fell completely under his [Arnold's] sway, responded like wax to the pressure of his influence, and moulded their whole lives with passionate reverence upon the teaching of their adored master.' Clough was absorbed almost into the Arnold family. The editor of Clough's letters, Frederick Mulhauser, asserts that because of the absence of Clough's family in America, 'Rugby was his real home and [his] real father Dr Arnold.'[6] The Doctor himself would not have disagreed: he wrote to Clough's uncle Alfred, just as Clough was about to go up to Balliol in 1837, to say he regarded Clough 'with an affection and interest hardly less than I should feel for my own son'.[7]

Clough became a praepostor at Rugby, and head of School House – Arnold's own house. Strachey notes that Clough 'thought of nothing but moral good, moral evil, moral influence and moral responsibility.' He becomes the subject of one of Strachey's better jokes. 'Perhaps it was not surprising that a young man brought up in such an atmosphere should have fallen a prey, at Oxford, to the frenzies of religious controversy; that he should have been driven almost out of his wits by the ratiocinations of W. G. Ward; that he should have lost his faith; that he should have spent the rest of his existence lamenting that loss, both in prose and verse; and that he should have eventually succumbed, conscientiously doing up brown paper parcels for Florence Nightingale.'[8] Clough certainly took his role as a moral exemplar seriously. Writing to his sister on 10 October 1835 he noted that 'there is a deal of evil springing up in the School, and it is to be feared that the tares will choke much of the wheat . . . I am trying to show them that good is not necessarily disagreeable, that a Christian may be and is likely to be a gentleman, and that he is surely much more than a gentleman. It is a weary thing to look around and see all the evil, all the sin and wickedness of those with whom one must daily associate . . .'[9]

He won a scholarship to Balliol, undermining his already weak health in the process. His success was a delight, but not a surprise, to Arnold and his school. He was regarded as by far the most brilliant product thus far of Arnold's reign, and a glittering career at Oxford was deemed to be his desert. He was set to be the intellectual leader of his generation: he should have been one of the key forces that shaped Victorian England. Expectations took their toll upon him, however. On his return from Oxford at the end of November 1836, having sat the examinations, he was nursed by Mrs Arnold for several days while he recovered from the mental debilitation.

He was a promising poet when still at school, but at Oxford became obsessed, to judge from his letters, with the religious controversy that would come to amuse Strachey so much: the Protestantism of Arnold being challenged by the Anglo-Catholicism of John Henry Newman. Ward, who was Clough's mathematical tutor, became such an adherent of Newman that he was thrown out of his tutorship after supporting Tract XC. Ward followed Newman to Rome. Later, Ward inculpated himself for Clough's distraction by religious unease, which led to his underachievement as an undergraduate. Eventually it derailed his academic career, quite possibly shortened his life and, in doing so, robbed Victorian Britain of one of its most brilliant men. Ward wrote that 'I must account it the great calamity of his [Clough's] life that he was brought into contact with myself. My whole interest at that time . . . was concentrated on questions which to me seem the most important and interesting that can occupy the mind . . . it was a very different thing to force them prematurely on the attention of a young man just coming up to college, and to drive him, as it were, peremptorily into a decision upon them; to aim at making him as hot a partisan as I was myself.'[10] He felt that 'the power which Mr Newman then wielded throughout the University' compounded the effect of his own questioning. 'The result was not surprising,' he added. 'I had been prematurely forcing Clough's mind, and there came a reaction. His intellectual perplexity for some time preyed heavily upon his spirits; it grievously interfered with his studies; and I take for granted it must have very seriously disturbed his religious practices and habits. I cannot to this day think of all this without a bitter pang of self-reproach.'

Ward was not the only influence upon Clough. He started to read Carlyle, whose essays he found 'very fine'.[11] He obtained a copy of *Chartism* soon after it was published: he was a prime example of the influence the Sage, not least through his highly original use of the language, had on the intelligentsia of the younger generation. His earlier priggishness was dissipating, and he was attracted by Carlyle's wit: he loved Carlyle's description of Parliament as 'the National Palaver'.[12] However, despite his conscious intellectualism, he missed taking a first-class degree, the first of Balliol's scholars ever to do so. He went to Rugby in 1841, after his finals, and told Dr Arnold: 'I have failed'. Arnold's second son, Tom, who recalled the event more than half a century later, noted that 'my father looked gravely and kindly at him, but what he said in reply I do not remember, or whether he said anything.'[13]

Clough failed also to get a fellowship at Balliol, but in 1842 secured one at Oriel, Arnold's old college. By 1844, however, Arnold might well have been turning in his grave beneath Rugby chapel: for Clough was having the most extreme form of doubt. He doubted the power of the Deity; he doubted the special force of Christianity: 'Is Xianity really so much better than Mahometanism, Buddhism . . . or the old Heathen philosophy?' he asked Hawkins, the Provost of Oriel, and an old friend of Dr Arnold.[14] His immersion in the controversy at Oxford had caused him to analyse the foundations of his own religious belief, and the outcome had not been constructive.

At about this time Matthew Arnold lost his belief in the Resurrection: Carlyle, with his own incomprehension of the Christian miracles, is usually blamed for the apostasy of both men. In the autumn of 1843 Clough doubted he could adhere to the Thirty-nine Articles, a require-ment for his proceeding to the degree of Master of Arts and to his Oriel tutorship. He wrote that 'it is not so much from any definite objection to this or that point, as general dislike to subscription, and strong feeling of its being a bondage, and a very heavy one, and one that may cramp and cripple one for life.'[15] He overcame that problem and signed. Yet a year later, in November 1844, he described himself as merely an 'operative' whose role was 'to dress intellectual leather, cut it out to pattern and stitch it and cobble it into boots and shoes for the benefit of the work which is being guided by wiser heads. But this almost cuts me out of having any religion whatever.'[16] He continued:

> If I begin to think about God, there [arise] a thousand questions, and whether the 39 Articles answer them at all or whether I should not answer them in the most diametrically opposite purport is a matter of great doubt . . . I further incline to hold that enquiries are best carried on by turning speculation into practice, and my speculations no doubt in their earlier stages would result in practice considerably at variance with 39 Article Subscription . . . Without the least denying Xtianity, I feel little that I can call its power. Believing myself to be in my unconscious creed in some shape or other adherent to its doctrines I keep within its pale: still whether the Spirit of the Age, whose lacquey and flunkey I submit to be, will prove to be this kind or that kind I can't the least say. Sometimes I have doubt whether it won't turn out to be no Xty at all.

By 1846 he knew it would be impossible to take orders and told Hawkins so: Hawkins was disappointed but did not try to change Clough's mind.

The following year Clough was distressed when Hawkins said that he regarded a Tutor as 'a teacher of the 39 Articles'; for, as Clough explained, 'for such an office I fear I can hardly consider myself quali-fied. I can only offer you the ordinary negative acquiescence of a layman.'[17] He offered to leave Oriel if Hawkins thought it appropriate; Hawkins, although citing a University Statute that required tutors to subscribe to the Articles, wanted Clough to stay, suggesting that another tutor could lecture on the Articles. All Clough would be required to do was to ensure that his pupils attended a lecture on them and knew them before the examinations. He agreed that Clough, although having originally subscribed, could change his mind: 'No-one, I admit, pledges himself by subscription to hold the same opinions for ever,' Hawkins told him. 'His subscription *per se* implies only his assent at the time.'[18]

Clough did not 'feel debarred' by what Hawkins had told him; but was 'doubtful' how long he would be able to continue.[19] In a lengthy correspondence both he and Hawkins danced on the heads of various pins – not that they probably saw the exercise in those terms – and by January 1848 Clough felt he should resign as a tutor: his fellowship expired in any case the following year. Hawkins did not wish this: 'You have no occasion to give a Lecture on the 39 Articles, and I have entire confidence in your not seeking in the interval either to teach anything contrary to them'.[20] The position was untenable, however, given Clough's cast of mind. He saw Ralph Waldo Emerson during the American's visit to England in the winter of 1848, and they spoke much of their mutual friend, Carlyle: but on seeing Emerson off from Liverpool that spring, Clough said to him: 'Think where we are. Carlyle has led us all out into the desert, and he has left us there.'[21] He resigned his fellowship on 8 October 1848, telling Hawkins 'I can have nothing whatever to do with a subscription to the xxxix articles – and deeply repent of having ever submitted to one. I cannot consent to receive any further pecuniary benefit in consideration of such conformity.'[22]

Hawkins did not let Clough go so easily. He wanted them to talk confidentially about his 'religious difficulties', for 'it is possible that I might suggest some view of things which might prevent the necessity of your resigning'.[23] Clough resigned nonetheless, though he and Hawkins spoke on 18 October. In a note Hawkins kept of their talk, Clough told him that 'he could not honestly pursue Truth, whilst under fetters of Subscription to articles.'[24] He added that the only others with whom he had discussed this were Matthew Arnold and Stanley; and he admitted Stanley had been against his resigning. Hawkins proposed discussing it with Stanley, but to no avail. Clough moved into lodgings in Oxford and sought to make a living by taking private pupils: he had hardly any money. He considered emigration; he considered falling in love; he was writing poetry; he told Hawkins he might travel in Europe with a private pupil.

Clough's life from this point takes a course not unlike that of the unfortunate Mr Hale. However, rather than suffer in the industrial north, Clough accepted (after some negotiation about the religious requirements, and 'with a good deal of misgiving') the post of Principal of University Hall, London, an extension of University College.[25] Although funded largely by Unitarians it sought a non-ordained principal, who was not a Unitarian. Hawkins was still unwilling to announce Clough's resignation of his Oriel fellowship. He wondered whether Clough's difficulties were 'still no more than doubts'. He hoped Clough might be 'pursuing [a] serious line of study with a view to probe your difficulties further or to remove them'.[26] At least resignation spared Clough public humiliation: James Anthony Froude resigned his fellowship at Exeter College in February 1849 but, having committed his heresies to paper in his novel *The Nemesis of Faith*, had to endure being preached against in chapel, denounced in hall, and his book burnt publicly in the college by the Rector of Exeter, William Sewell. If anything this was more medieval treatment than received by Ward, who was merely degraded from his degrees.

Clough published a long poem in 1848, *The Bothie of Tober-Na-Vuolich*, that had elicited praise from Emerson, Froude, Thackeray and Kingsley. It was about a love affair between a young Oxford scholar on a walking holiday and the daughter of a crofter: it was considered radical in its treatment of relationships and class, and in its conversational style. In January 1849 he and a friend, Thomas Burbidge, jointly published a book of verse. Arnold, as always, was frank about the quality of his poetry, and submitted constructive criticisms: the most depressing observation, though, was his injunction to Clough to 'reflect . . . as I cannot but do here more and more, in spite of all the nonsense some people talk, how deeply *unpoetical* the age and all one's surroundings are. Not unprofound, not ungrand, not unmoving:- but *unpoetical*.'[27]

When finally writing to Clough on 28 February 1849 to say he had given in and submitted Clough's letter of resignation to the fellowship, Hawkins disclosed that he had read *The Bothie*, and castigated him for it. 'There are parts of it rather indelicate; and I very much regretted to find also that there were frequent allusions to Scripture, or rather parodies of Scripture, which you should not have put forth.' Hawkins added: 'You will never be secure from misbelief, if you allow yourself liberties of this kind.'[28] However, Hawkins was genuinely trying to solve problems such as these. He asked Clough: 'I remember you said in one of your letters that such studies as I recommend would not meet the difficulties of young men in the present day. Will you do me the favour, some time or other, to tell me what class of difficulties, according to your observation, most perplexes young men at present.'

Clough, having stated that 'I do not think I have sinned against morality' in his poem, advised Hawkins to read *The Nemesis of Faith* to grasp the 'difficulties'. He added that 'elsewhere I think there is a general feeling that the Miracles are poor proofs' – a view straight from Carlyle. 'The doctrine must prove them, not they the doctrine.'[29] Young men, he added, 'have no Christian ideal, which they feel sure is really Christian, except the Roman Catholic.' Clough's view of religion appeared to corrode continually. In his notes 'On the Religious Tradition', published in *Prose Remains* and attributed to the last period in his life, he writes that 'whether Christ died upon the Cross, I cannot tell; yet I am prepared to find some spiritual truth in the doctrine of the Atonement, Purgatory is not in the Bible; I do not therefore think it is incredible.'[30]

During the 1840s Clough began to show he had inherited Arnold's Whiggish-Liberal views and, indeed, taken them (as Matthew Arnold did) to a further remove. He had told Burbidge in a letter on 25 June 1844 that he believed 'that capital tyrannizes over labour, and that government is bound to interfere to prevent such bullying; and I do believe too that in the some way [sic] or other the problem now solved by universal competition or the devil take the hindmost may receive a more satisfactory solution.'[31] He began to correspond with Carlyle and with Emerson. He also supported his sister Anne, who had set up a school, in her aim to further the education of girls and women: she would become the first principal of Newnham College, Cambridge.

Clough had all the social concerns of his class and of the faith in which he had been schooled. He helped the local poor by working for the Mendicity Society in Oxford. One night in June 1844 he 'administered relief to about 6 people only', but told Burbidge that 'they used to come by twenties and one night I remember 80. Yet even now the hay harvest is so scanty that many who usually have work are thrown out . . . they get a pint and a half of broth and a piece of bread for supper, and (at present, only) a small piece of bread for breakfast.' Clough also said he approved 'highly and wholly' of Gladstone's bill that compelled railway companies to reduce their fares if their profit margins exceeded 10 per cent, and forcing them to provide seats for the poor.[32] Yet his approach was practical; and he rejected the romantic fantasy of his political contemporaries in Young England. In 1845 he read *Sybil*. 'There is not much merit in it,' he told Burbidge. 'The story is somewhat flimsy, the thoughts obvious where they are good; and where they are original, I should say, very extravagant.'[33]

He was in Paris in the spring of 1848, as Chartist agitation was reaching its climax in England, and observed the Revolution there. 'Ichabod, Ichabod, the glory is departed,' he wrote to Stanley on 19 May, in an apparent pastiche of Carlyle. 'Liberty, Equality, and Fraternity, driven back by shopkeeping bayonet, hides her red cap in dingiest St Antoine.'[34] A few days later he wrote to his sister, who had complained of the paradox and the problem of the population increasing the more wretched it became: 'I suppose the thing wanted in society is to raise the lower classes either in material comforts or morality or both to that state where they will of themselves feel the duty and find the inclination to refrain – as the upper classes, for the most part, do, at present.'[35] He felt unrest in France would 'on the whole accelerate change in England' and would create a 'palingenesy' there: a rebirth of the nation.[36] When he returned to England he saw Arnold, and one of the first things they did was visit Carlyle.

The surviving Arnold–Clough correspondence is one-sided, because only one letter from Clough to Arnold is extant: written in the summer of 1849, on Italian politics. What the editor of their correspondence calls a 'really remarkable letter' comes next in the sequence. Written by Arnold from Switzerland in September 1849, its interest lies in what it reveals to us about Arnold's poetic temperament: but one also needs to weigh up what the sentiments would have meant to the recipient, at a profoundly difficult stage in his life. His Oxford career had been derailed; his first excursion into poetry had been merely a *succès d'estime*; and he was about to embark upon a risky academic venture at University Hall.

In this delicate, lonely and unsure state of mind, the outpouring of discontent from his best friend cannot but have been salutary.

Arnold told Clough he had been 'snuffing after a moral atmosphere to respire in' more 'than ever before in my life. Marvel not that I say unto you, ye must be born again.'[37] He laid out not so much his own feelings – the expression of which was one of the necessities of a poet – as the power of those feelings and, by inference, how the social critic interpreted society. 'What I must tell you is that I have never yet succeeded in any one great occasion in consciously mastering myself: I can go thro the imaginary process of mastering myself and see the whole affair as it would then stand, but at the critical point I am too apt to hoist up the mainsail to the wind and let her drive.'

Arnold's experience of the zeitgeist seems to overwhelm him: of an England in which change has been postponed rather than cancelled; in which a rising class of semi-educated people, manipulated by those who ought to know better, seems to be moving against reason and civilisation to create an unpleasant modernity. 'My dearest Clough these are damned times – everything is against one – the height to which knowledge has come, the spread of luxury, our physical enervation, the absence of great natures, the unavoidable contact with millions of small ones, newspapers, cities, light profligate friends, moral desperadoes like Carlyle, our own selves, and the sickening consciousness of our difficulties'. Carlyle's choler – clear in his unpleasant essay *The Nigger Question* and clearer still the next year in his bilious *Latter-Day Pamphlets* – was starting to grate with his apostles. Clough had already told Emerson they had been abandoned by him in the desert: now Arnold confirmed to Clough that Carlyle offered them no hope at all. All they could do was to avoid fanaticism and follow their rational hearts.

University Hall was slow to start: two years into Clough's tenure he still had just a dozen students, which worried the governors. As Clough's memoir in *Prose Remains* states, unvarnishedly: 'The change [from Oxford] was in many respects painful to him. The step he had taken in resigning his fellowship isolated him greatly; many of his old friends looked coldly on him, and the new acquaintances among whom he was thrown were often uncongenial to him.'[38] Clough saw the writing on the wall, and applied for the classical professorship at the new college opening in Sydney; the post was combined with that of principal, and was entirely secular. He wanted it not just to escape University Hall, his time at which had become (according to his memoir) 'without doubt the dreariest, loneliest period of his life', but also to raise enough money to marry Blanche Smith, with whom he had fallen in love. He sought a testimonial from Hawkins, who gave it on the condition Clough did not teach divinity; and Arnold wrote that 'it is especially in respect of his moral qualities, and of the intimate manner in which his intellectual qualities are affected by them, that he is distinguished from the crowd of well-informed and amiable men who generally offer themselves for public situations.'[39]

Clough doubted he would succeed; and when his governors at University Hall heard he had applied, they asked for his resignation. He was shocked: but it is clear the governors had wanted a reason to be rid of him, and this lack of commitment provided one. Clough was told that his 'resignation would make an opening for a Gentleman whose connexions might perhaps restore this Institution to some prosperity.'[40] So he was out of work and, as predicted, did not obtain Sydney. He looked forward instead to 'unmarried poverty and literary work', a remark he made to Blanche, with whom he was now largely confined to enjoying an epistolary courtship.[41] Arnold had married, and became, inevitably, more distant; which Clough found depressing. It was not merely his wife who distracted him from his old friend, but Arnold's work as a schools inspector.

Clough's life in London nevertheless introduced him to some great figures of the day: the Carlyles, Tennyson, and Richard Monckton Milnes, who was engaged in a futile courtship with the woman who would become Clough's cousin by marriage, Florence Nightingale. He dined with Darwin, whose celebrity (as with Nightingale's) lay before him. Clough took private pupils. With Arnold's help and his connection with Lansdowne he sought a minor post in the Education Department. His former employers, University College, appointed him professor of English language and literature: for which he received £30 a year. By the summer of 1852 he had come to an understanding with Miss Smith to marry her. To achieve this, he wrote to Emerson to ask about securing an academic post in America. Emerson promised to enquire, but was depressed that a man of Clough's talents, hounded by the Thirty-nine Articles, could find no work in England to occupy him satisfactorily.

Arnold became exasperated with Clough for allowing his great talent to atrophy, and for allowing himself to take passivity in the face of events to the point of becoming completely inert. However much Arnold might have disliked his work, it motivated him, and he considered the standards and extent of education in Britain as one of the most important social and political matters of the age. Clough had no such motivation, not even the prospect that a better position would allow him to marry. Arnold could see this and it angered him; not realising that it was perhaps Clough's sense that he had not lived up to Arnold's father's spiritual expectations that was largely the problem. In June 1852 he urged Clough: 'If possible, get something to do before your term at the Hall expires: living on your resources waiting for something to turn up is a bad and dispiriting business.'[42] He implored him to use the good offices of his admirer Lady Ashburton; which Clough eventually did.

But before that, Clough determined to try emigration to America. The dynamic brilliance that had won him his Balliol scholarship fifteen years earlier seemed to have evaporated. Arnold consoled his friend by observing that 'I am more and more convinced that the world tends to become more comfortable for the mass, and more uncomfortable for those of any natural gift or distinction.' It is a short step from Arnold's final exhortation in this letter – 'nothing can absolve us from the duty of doing all we can to keep alive our courage and activity' – to the message of 'Say Not, the Struggle Naught Availeth'.

Clough sailed to America in the autumn of 1852, encouraged by Emerson. He based himself in Cambridge, Massachusetts, and proceeded to seek pupils as a private tutor. Arnold wrote urging him to earn money – 'the object for you is to do well *commercially*' – showing how far the high-minded had moved towards recognising the necessities.[43] The change of government just before the end of the year, when Aberdeen's Peelite ministry replaced Russell's, brought hopes of patronage for Clough. Lady Ashburton, who as well as having a high regard for Clough was also Carlyle's chief admirer, and whose salon of literary men was legendary, interceded to try to find Clough a post. She failed. Lord Granville, her closest contact with power, then tried to get Clough a school inspectorship in the voluntary sector; but organisations who wanted their schools inspected preferred a clergyman to do it, and not one who had cast himself out through doubt. He turned his hand to writing, but found it difficult. His first substantial literary task was translating Plutarch's *Lives*, but he also wrote for the reviews. Money remained a problem, not least because Clough refused to accept any posting at a school or college that might force him to commit to stay in America. By the spring of 1853 his letters are full of longing to get home.

He continued to fret about religion; in his letters to Blanche not least, for she was having difficulties too, but also to his friends. His contemporary J. C. Shairp, a master at Rugby and a future Oxford professor of poetry, rebuked him for sharing his difficulties with him; difficulties that appeared to have multiplied since sharing them with Hawkins. 'To speak of the historical side of Christianity', Shairp wrote on 19 March 1853, 'as untenable because there may be diff[icul]ties about the origin of some books of the N[ew] T[estament] or to put down the NT as a mass of "unauthenticated records" (was that the word?) seems simply absurd.'[44] Shairp admitted Clough had upset him because 'the main facts of Christianity are inextricably interwoven with my inmost feelings and . . . I shall hope to live and die in them and using them as ladders to ascend to the spiritual.' He begged Clough not to write of his feelings again as it would 'cause only pain. Please, No more of this!'

Then came the chance to return home. Granville had found a clerkship in the Privy Council office. It paid just £300 a year but had prospects. Carlyle wrote to Clough to urge him to accept it – 'England is England', he told him, and as for the low pay it 'will teach you noble thrift, and various high Spartan virtues, which are worth more to a man than all the yellow rubbish which so many two-legged swine are grubbing for' (the gold rush continued in California).[45] At Granville's urging Lady Ashburton also wrote to him, beseeching him to 'prefer us to America'.[46] His main concern was that he should earn enough to marry: he feared the clerkship would not allow that. His prospective father-in-law confirmed it: £500 or no marriage.[47] Then, an offer was made by Mr Smith of an allowance to give the young couple a sufficient income; by mid-July Clough was home and at work in the Privy Council office and, a year later, married.

Clough developed a close association with Florence Nightingale, his wife's cousin through both her mother and her father. Milnes, a friend of Clough, had attempted to court her for years but without success; the sister of another close friend, Stanley, was one of Nightingale's intimates. She warmed to Clough once related to him by marriage, and Clough escorted her as far as Calais on her journey to Scutari.[48] Clough's mother-in-law went to Scutari to assist Nightingale when she contracted 'Crimean fever' – something Clough described as 'a dreadful sickness and leaves the head in a state of protracted feebleness'. He quoted Nightingale herself as calling it 'a compound fracture of the intellects'.[49] He wrote to his friends with pride of his cousin-by-marriage's achievements in saving the lives of so many soldiers: he was as attached to and impressed by notions of improvement as any of his generation.

His work at the Education Office was hardly taxing: he did six hours a day and had long holidays. However, his summer holiday of 1857 saw him drafted in by Nightingale as, effectively, her private secretary, and editor of the manuscript of her *Notes on Matters Affecting the Health, Efficiency and Hospital Administration of the British Army*, published the following year. Judging from the traffic of proofs and corrections during July 1857, this became a much more demanding job than Clough's day job. Nightingale was lobbying the government – as she would for decades to come – to improve sanitary conditions for soldiers overseas. Clough's familiarity with Whitehall and with the language of bureaucracy was useful to her.

His assistance continued when he returned to work in the autumn, and if anything became more extensive. He also took out some poetry written nine years earlier – 'my 5 act epistolary tragi-comedy or comi-tragedy' and tried to prepare it for publication.[50] Both Arnold and Tennyson were struggling with the form and Clough observed that 'England seems as unpoetic as [in the age] between Chaucer and Spenser'. He was reading Gladstone's translation of Homer, which he admired, and Froude's latest volumes of his Tudor histories. He knew that Carlyle, in the midst of an almost soul-destroying effort, was about to produce the first two volumes of *Frederick the Great*. Clough appears to have felt under pressure to create, but his work for Nightingale became more and more important. His summer holiday in 1858 was, like its predecessor, devoted to secretarial tasks on her behalf.

He still felt financial pressure, relieved by a salary Nightingale agreed to pay him as secretary of her fund to establish a training school for nurses. He mentioned in October 1858 that 'Froude I believe has earned £1800 by his books. Hallam, if you care for such statistics, told Sir Francis Palgrave the other day that his total earnings by books had amounted, in all his life, to about £20,000.'[51] Clough was preparing his translation of Plutarch for the press, slowed down by the donkey-work of preparing the index. When it came out in 1859 it hardly sold at all because, Clough thought, the price was too high. However, Longman's agreed to publish an abridged, cheaper edition, and asked him to prepare editions of various classical authors. Although Clough's own voice seemed quietened, he at least was able to raise his income. He also secured a promotion, becoming private secretary to Robert Lowe, who as vice-president of the Privy Council had responsibility for education in Palmerston's second ministry.

Nightingale recognised her debt to him. There is in her papers a note of April 1859 that reads: 'I wish that all that comes to me upon my father and mother's death should go to A H Clough – with only the proviso that whatever he has had out of the N[ightingale] Fund should be repaid but with compound interest.'[52] In the autumn of 1860 Clough sent Jowett the manuscript of Nightingale's *Suggestions for Thought*, without disclosing who the author was. He initially described it as a work of 'remarkable metaphysical and diabolical power'.[53] Jowett suggested it should be rewritten – 'they appear to me to be too emphatic, ecstatic and positive in style – too much impression of certainty and not enough "latent power".'[54] However, once he learned the identity of the author his tone softened – 'I hope Miss Nightingale will not overexert herself in the attempt to correct them.'[55] He added: 'With her experience she must be well aware that it is not always safe to exert the mind because it is clean and bright. If her life is spared she will be hereafter able to rewrite the book so as to do justice to the ideas contained in it.'

In 1861 Clough took prolonged leave of absence. He had struggled to recover from scarlet fever; but was also increasingly exploited by Nightingale, who piled work upon him without regard for his physical or mental state. He went with his family to the Isle of Wight for six weeks in February and March, then on his own to Greece and Constantinople. After his return in the summer he became increasingly ill and went abroad again, to southern France, without his wife and children, in a final attempt to recuperate. He felt 'that my health appears to have suffered with the daily rather-hurrying routine of office work', and he left his wife, in his absence, to negotiate a transfer within the Civil Service to something less demanding.[56] He thought of taking an examinership at the Woolwich Military Academy, which

paid just £150 a year, supplementing it with other occasional government work: but Arnold warned him of the precariousness of such an
arrangement, which piled an additional strain on Clough. He had
extended his leave of absence until mid-November: but, realising how
debilitated he was, wrote from France at the end of July 1861 to
request leave until February 1862; with the promise that if he was still
not fit then, he would resign.[57]

His wife was distressed at his being so ill, and alone abroad for so
long. She urged him to come home, but with reservations, given his
inability to stop work, or to stop being put upon by Nightingale,
against whom Blanche nurtured a serious animus: 'I do feel afraid of
your coming back to these places. If you really could come for 10
days and see the children and take me and never go near any of the
Fund or Flo or anything – I think it might be possible, but I am sure
nothing but the greatest strictness would make it safe.'[58] Blanche had
a daughter in early August, making the separation even more painful.
She wrote to her husband to ask what to call the child: he replied,
by return, 'Blanche Athena'.[59] By now in the Pyrenees, he met the
Tennysons, so at least his isolation was over; and he arranged for his
wife to come to France, as soon as she was strong enough. She reached
the Continent and met her husband in Paris on 18 September. They
travelled through Switzerland to Florence; but he weakened steadily,
first with neuralgia, then with a bout of malaria: he also caught a
cold in the Alps that went to his chest. He died on 13 November, a
month before his exact contemporary the Prince Consort and, like
him, aged just forty-two.

Jowett called him 'one of the very best persons I have ever known,
gifted too with a great deal of genius, though not destined to bring
forth its perfect fruit. He had the trials of genius as well as its gifts.'[60]
Perhaps less tactfully, he told Blanche that Clough had been 'a most
noble-looking youth before troubles and cares and false views of religion
came upon him.'[61] With an equal lack of tact F. W. Newman, John
Henry's brother, in his letter of condolence, wrote that 'I hardly know
whether it lessens the pang of his loss, to be told, (as I have been told),
that the fatal weakness of the brain was induced by overwork in the
cause of Florence Nightingale and her benign plans. Alas, we cannot be
satisfied that one martyrdom should thus entail another.'[62]

It cannot be heartening to hear that one's cousin has killed one's

husband by working him into the ground; however, Blanche was far
from stupid, with no illusions about Cousin Flo. She wrote that 'it was
pure overwork which exhausted his brain and left no strength to stand
against the final attack.' She had been touched by the happiness that,
in his last few weeks of life, attempts to write poetry had brought him.
'He had entirely given up writing while he was at work but the rest
seemed to bring back the power and when I saw that, I could not help
desiring that we might still give up all the money-making and working
for F. Nightingale which had worn him out and let him go and rest by
the seaside and follow his own heart.' But she knew he would not have
been persuaded to do that.[63] Blanche buried him in the Protestant ceme-
tery at Florence.

Blanche's conviction that Flo had pushed her husband into an early
grave was not unique to her. Nightingale herself may have shared it,
for there was a delay in her sending condolences. Such was Blanche's
anger that she asked other members of the family not to give Nightingale
details of Clough's last days: and for a time they did not, which may
help explain the delay in the letter of condolence. In it, Nightingale
professed that although it was tardy, the letter should not suggest she
had been anything other than prostrate at the news: she had felt the
loss 'at every waking hour'. Blanche, in her reply, took the gloves off.
'I know that his loss has been to you what it could hardly be to anyone,
and I have truly grieved for you in your great suffering.'[64]

Arnold wrote: 'People were beginning to say about Clough that he
never would do anything now, and, in short, to pass him over. I foresee
that there will now be a change, and attention will be fixed on what
there was of extraordinary promise and interest in him when young,
and of unique and imposing even as he grew older without fulfilling
people's expectations.'[65] He was stricken: 'Few can have received such a
shock in hearing of his death as I did,' he told Blanche.[66] Even to her,
he expressed his puzzlement at Clough's underachievement. Talking of
how much Clough's men friends had admired him, he said that 'with
no one of them was the conviction of his truly great and profound
qualities so entirely independent of any visible success in life which he
might achieve.'

The greatest frustration was that Clough's genius and promise
would remain unfulfilled. As F. W. Newman also said, 'he always
seemed to me to have his voice choked by his own fullness and by his

conscientiousness, besides his too great modesty.' One of his early biographers, J. I. Osborne, wrote of him that 'Clough's sanction increased the value of any idea, because it was the sanction of a superlatively honest man.'[67] Perhaps Clough's commitment to the work of his wife's cousin was a form of atonement for his loss of faith at Oxford, and the decision to derail, on that account, an otherwise promising career as a teacher and shaper of intellects.

III

Matthew Arnold was Clough's closest friend. He was the second of Dr Arnold's nine surviving children, born on Christmas Eve 1822. His father asked Keble to be the boy's godfather, something he would regret when Keble became one of the leaders of the High Church movement that Arnold regarded with contempt. As a child Matthew had a reputation as the idler of the family. In a life packed with achievement as poet, critic, teacher, school inspector and intellectual, Matthew had one towering success: his championing of the critical faculty, central to a desire to lead humanity towards perfection. He admitted this in the superscription to *Culture and Anarchy*: '*Estote ergo vos perfecti!*'. In 'Be ye perfect!' lay the driving force of what Asa Briggs called 'the age of improvement'. Matthew Arnold taught the benefits of evaluating one's surroundings, culture, way of life, and the understanding that, whatever we had, much could be better. He began as a product of his father – deeply religious, defined by Christianity, which until he went to Oxford was the be-all and the end-all of his life. Then, thinking for himself, and imbibing a wider range of thought, he became a different man. He began to observe, more completely, his context and his surroundings, and the thoughts and attitudes of others. As he became more worldly in the 1840s, he passed through a phase of being a superlative poet. Then he began to become the person he would be: the critic, the teacher, the analyst of mid-Victorian England. His is perhaps the greatest mind of the nineteenth century, in its ability to cut to the heart of debate and to identify what the issues of society really were; but before he could become so influential, he had to shake off his father's obsession with Christianity.

One of the many influences upon him as a poet – and one of the strongest – was his family's friendship with Wordsworth, near whom they lived in the Lake District during school and university vacations at Fox How, Dr Arnold's property in Westmorland. Arnold never conformed with his father's rigid educational structure in the way that Stanley or Clough did, and at Oxford contrived to be as unlike him as possible; yet his father's influence on him was powerful, imbibed as it was from the cradle, and in his maturity it manifested itself mightily. Arnold only joined Rugby for the last four years of his education, from 1837, having previously had an unsuccessful episode at his father's alma mater, Winchester. He showed precocity as a poet and in 1841 won a scholarship to Balliol.

For one who would make a career complaining about the lack of original thought among his countrymen, Arnold as a young man rarely showed the required promise. His father, writing to William Lake, a favoured pupil who had already won a scholarship to Balliol, complained in August 1840 that 'Matt does not know what it is to work because he so little knows what it is to think.'[68] Lake was preparing Matt for a Balliol scholarship; and despite his father's reservations, and the belief the boy was incipiently lazy, he later won one of the two available awards out of a field of thirty-three candidates.

His years at Oxford culminated, to his chagrin, in a second-class degree in *literae humaniores*. This was thanks partly to the distraction of his joining the 'fast set' of drunks and dandies, and partly because of his addiction to poetry. Yet Oxford was in other ways immensely significant. He formed a deep friendship with Clough, who had left Rugby just before Arnold joined; he won the Newdigate prize for poetry, which confirmed him in what he considered his vocation; and when tumultuous intellectual currents were swirling around interpretations of Christianity, he began to question his faith. He had trouble with the Athanasian Creed and the anti-papalism of the Thirty-nine Articles, not least because of what he felt was their propensity to divide rather than to unite Christendom.[69] He was not alone in this problem: Charles Kingsley also had it, feeling the creed laced with 'bigotry, cruelty and quibbling'.[70] Kingsley also struggled with the Trinity, and found it hard to trust clergymen, though that was probably to do with his experience of his father, who had entered the Church largely as a means of earning a living rather than out of any deep spiritual conviction.

Clough reached Balliol as Benjamin Jowett became a tutor there, and in the middle of the fight between Keble and Newman on one side and, shortly to arrive as Regius professor of modern history, Dr Arnold on the other. Matthew came under the influence of Archibald Tait, a fellow of Balliol and arch-opponent of Newman: Tait would succeed Dr Arnold as headmaster of Rugby, and become Bishop of London and Archbishop of Canterbury, while having five of his children die of smallpox.

His friendship with Clough intensified after Dr Arnold's death: they both appear to have lost a father, one literally, the other metaphorically. When fellows of Oriel in the 1840s they lived in each other's pockets, and Arnold's letters to Clough contain much intimacy (he writes to Clough as 'My dear Love' in August 1848[71]) and criticism of the latter's poetry ('I doubt your being an ARTIST,' he told Clough in February 1848[72]). They were close also for a time in 1849–51, when both living in London, and would meet for breakfast twice a week. At Oxford, they entered into a phase of writing more poetry, influenced by the Classics but also by the landscape encountered on their regular walks. They started to read vast tracts of Carlyle, reflecting their political engagement. Dr Arnold, who had supported the French Revolution until it became violent, had greatly admired Carlyle's *History*; his son and star pupil now read *Past and Present*. Matthew's Newdigate-winning poem was about Cromwell, restored to intellectual consciousness by Carlyle in his lectures *On Heroes, Hero-Worship and the Heroic in History*. It would not be long, though, before Arnold dismissed Carlyle to Clough as a 'moral desperado'.[73]

He returned to Rugby briefly as a teacher. Then, despite his second, he secured a fellowship at Oriel, joining Clough there and following in the Doctor's footsteps. His dandyism impaired his attempt to pass as an *homme serieux*; he was also exceptionally partial to champagne. While he took a less literal approach to religion than his father he was moved by the cultural aspects of Anglicanism and held his faith; the importance of Christianity as a heritage informed much of his criticism and social commentary. But just as important an influence was France, to which Arnold became quite attached, from the mid-1840s. He used France as an example when advocating reforms in Britain, notably in education. 'In a few years,' he told his mother in 1848, 'people will understand better why the French are the most civilised of European peoples; when they see how fictitious our manners and civility have been.'[74]

In 1847 he became private secretary to Lord Lansdowne, a role that gave him a modest income but allowed time for travel and writing poetry, several volumes of which would appear in the succeeding years. It also forced him to engage with politics, an accomplishment that never left him. His friends, not least Clough, deplored this new worldliness: but through it Arnold acquired a political sense, well concealed at the time, that gave an edge to his notion of criticism and his application of the critical faculty. Writing, as an expression of the creative temperament, was essential to Arnold; but he relieved this tension with prose more than poetry, as his enormous output of pamphlets, articles and books in the last thirty years of his life would show. Like Clough he became excited by the upheavals in Europe in 1848, his friend describing him as 'really heated to a very fervid enthusiasm', before he became 'very cynical' in the aftermath of the revolution preceding the failure of the Second Republic.[75]

Arnold was heavily influenced by Carlyle's account of the earlier revolution, describing aristocratic Frenchmen as 'gig-owners'.[76] In the same letter to Clough he dismisses a leading article in that morning's *Times* (1 March 1848) that had attacked the socialistic economic policies of the new rulers in France, showing the direction in which his political idealism was moving. But what especially moved him was the 'wide and deepspread intelligence' of the French people, which gave them a consciousness about political questions that he felt his fellow-countrymen lacked.[77] 'We neither courageously have thrown ourselves into this movement like the French: nor yet have driven our feet into the solid ground of our individuality as spiritual, poetic, profound *persons*.' It is a clear representation of Arnold's belief that people will be brought to care about their political condition only by deepening their cultural understanding, an argument that would be refined in *Culture and Anarchy*. On 10 April 1848 he went to Kennington to look at the Chartist demonstration and told Clough 'the Chartists gave up at once in the greatest fright at seeing the [police and military] preparations: braggarts as they are'.[78]

'However, I think the poetism goes on favourably,' Clough observed of his friend.[79] Arnold took himself seriously, not just as a poet, and was inclined to broader social thought than Clough, being perhaps less absorbed by himself. Froude complained to Clough in 1849: 'I wish M didn't so utterly want *humour*'.[80] The 'poetism' produced a first volume that year, prompting one of Arnold's sisters to comment that 'it is the moral strength, or, at any rate, the moral consciousness which struck and surprised me so much in the poems. I could have been prepared for any degree of poetical power, for there being a great deal more than I could at all appreciate; but there is something altogether different from this, something which such a man as Clough has, for instance, which I did not expect to find in Matt; but it is there.'[81] In his essay on the poetry of Byron, Arnold indicated the place of poetry in his analysis of and insight into the world. There were, he wrote, poets who were 'supreme masters in whom a profound criticism of life exhibits itself in indissoluble connection with the laws of poetic truth and beauty.'[82] However, he maintained that all literature was 'a criticism of life', qualifying his remark by adding that 'in poetry, however, the criticism of life has to be made conformably to the laws of poetic truth and poetic beauty.' In prose, truth would be enough: 'felicity and perfection of diction and manner' were poetic virtues.

When, in 1851, he sought to marry, his prospective father-in-law, a senior judge, objected to his penury. Thanks to Lansdowne, Arnold secured a post as an inspector of schools, which brought with it more money and security. He did not enter upon it with enthusiasm – 'I think I shall get interested in the schools after a little time', he told his wife.[83] But he saw the importance of what he was doing, and struck a theme that coursed through the rest of his life: 'Their effects on the children are so immense, and their future effects in civilising the next generation of the lower classes, who, as things are going, will have most of the political power of the country in their hands, may be so important.' His marriage was happy and produced six children, four sons and two daughters. Three sons died within four years – two in 1868, the other in 1872 – and this succession of blows struck him exceptionally hard and cast a shadow over his life.

Because of Arnold's engagement with the wider world, he and Clough grew apart; but the former told the latter in February 1853: 'I am and always shall be, whatever I do or say, powerfully attracted towards you, and vitally connected with you: this I am sure of: the period of my development (God forgive me the d----d expression!) coincides with that of my friendship with you so exactly that I am forever linked with you by intellectual bonds'.[84] Later that year he told Clough: 'If one loved what was beautiful and interesting in itself *passionately* enough, one would produce what was excellent without troubling oneself with religious dogmas at all.'[85] It had been Dr Arnold's aim to remove the barrier between religion and everything else, and this was one of the unfortunate results. Arnold withdrew his most successful long poem, *Empedocles on Etna*, almost immediately after it was published in 1852. Only a request from Robert Browning persuaded him to reissue it in 1867. It reveals the sense of conflict, lack of fulfilment, and bleakness with which Arnold viewed his inner life. Empedocles commits suicide by jumping into the volcano, suggesting a deep-seated unhappiness on Arnold's part, and possibly profound religious doubt.

Arnold's power as a thinker and observer was helped by the extent to which he had to travel, something made easier by the railway. His bailiwick as an inspector comprised much of central England, but it was even more significant to the development of his mind, his outlook and his philosophy that he also travelled widely in France. Having a mind of his own, Arnold was regarded by his superiors as troublesome. He was not a natural bureaucrat. Biographers have used this trait to explain why promotion was slow in coming to a man of his talent. He did not become a senior inspector until nearly twenty years into his job, and only became chief inspector in 1884, two years before retirement. However, public recognition came to him in a way it did not to Clough. In 1857 he became professor of poetry at Oxford, a post he held for a decade. In the 1860s he started writing for reviews, using them as a platform to express his political views. These were collected in 1865 as *Essays in Criticism*, and would have enormous influence, not least in the promotion of that most Arnoldian of virtues, disinterested endeavour. It is a mistake to think of Arnold as primarily a literary critic; his criticism was as much social, and, later in life, religious.

The first edition of the *Dictionary of National Biography* described these writings as demonstrating Arnold's vocation as 'detector-general of the intellectual failings of his own nation.'[86] The writer Richard Garnett, who spent almost fifty years in the library of the British Museum and ended up Keeper of Printed Books, noted that in his critical essays 'the intellectual defects [that he identified in others] were characteristically English defects.' His writings show contemporary British culture failing by comparison not just with the Classics, but with France. These made him unpopular in certain circles; but Arnold thrived on such unpopularity. Stefan Collini deprecated his criticism, in his notice of Arnold in the *New Dictionary of National Biography*, as 'backward looking'; not least because Arnold wrote when the novel was at its apogee, yet chose to write almost nothing on it.[87]

His criticism is not exclusively backward looking. *The Function of Criticism at the Present Time* is, as its title suggests, very much contemporary; so is *Culture and Anarchy*, his prose masterpiece, an exploration of how to deal with the resurgence in the late 1860s of the Condition of England Question. Garnett wrote that 'he had become profoundly discontented with English indifference to ideas in literature, in politics, and in religion, and set himself to rouse his countrymen out of what he deemed their intellectual apathy by raillery and satire, objurgation in the manner of a Ruskin or a Carlyle not being at all in his way.'[88] This approach, as Garnett also observed, had its problems. 'Arnold is as one-sided as the objects of his attack, and does not sufficiently perceive that the defects which he satirises are often defects inevitably annexed to great qualities,' he wrote. 'Nor was it possible to lecture his countrymen as he did without assuming the air of the deservedly detested "superior person".' Garnett, writing at the dawn of the twentieth century, conceded that the 'contemporary influence' of Arnold's prose writings 'is a noticeable ingredient in the stream of tendency which has brought the national mind nearer to Arnold's ideal'. However, he asserted that 'these books are not likely to be extensively read in the future', a judgement correct in respect of some of the minor writings, but wildly inaccurate about *Culture and Anarchy* and *Essays in Criticism*. Arnold's significance in the pursuit of perfection would come in the 1860s, once he had overcome the power of religion in his life, and trained his mind instead to deal with social questions.

IV

Arnold was not the only intellectual who, in shaking off the smothering embrace of religious orthodoxy, found a new voice and added a new tone and approach to English letters. So too did James Anthony Froude, remembered today, if at all, for his sensationally honest and deeply controversial biography of Carlyle, whose chief disciple he became. Before that, Froude had carved out a reputation as one of the age's leading historians – but a historian determined to tell the story of Protestant England, and whose work helped feed the suspicion that educated Victorians held for the Catholic Church. But Froude's first act of notoriety, thirty-five years before his life of Carlyle, was to have a confrontation with the authorities at Oxford on a matter of religious

doubt that made Clough's seem tame by comparison. That episode put
Froude on a path of secularised Protestantism that became highly representative of many of his peers, and which came to flavour the second
half of the nineteenth century.

Froude's childhood and upbringing gave him the force of character
required to survive confrontation with authority and controversy. We
know about it in detail because of fragments of autobiography he left
behind and which, fortunately, his daughter preserved contrary to her
father's instructions to destroy them. In the 1920s she allowed them to
be read and copied by Waldo Hilary Dunn, an American scholar
researching Froude's approach to his life of Carlyle. More than thirty
years later Dunn used them, verbatim, as the basis of his life of Froude.

Froude was born at Dartington, in a Devonshire parsonage, in 1818,
the son of Archdeacon Robert Froude who, with his eldest son Hurrell,
had been the travelling companion of John Henry Newman on his
formative trip around the Mediterranean in the winter of 1832-3.
Anthony's mother died when he was two. Before going to school at
Buckfastleigh, where he was a scholar, aged nine, he was regularly
thrashed by his father: 'We were a Spartan family. Whipping was always
resorted to as the prompt consequence of naughtiness.'[89] His aunt, who
took over once his mother had died, decided when he was three that
he needed 'bracing'. Her means of doing this was to have little Anthony
'taken out of bed every morning and dipped in the ice cold water which
ran from a spring into a granite trough in the backyard. I remember
now the horror of the plunge.' With the urbanity that distinguishes his
prose, Froude adds: 'I didn't die of it, but I didn't grow any stronger.'

In case this abuse was insufficient, Anthony also became the victim
of his intensely priggish eldest brother, Hurrell, who as well as being
one of the progenitors of the Oxford Movement appeared to have
inherited his father's interest in sadism. Anthony worshipped Hurrell,
but Hurrell thought his brother 'wanted manliness'.[90] His remedy for
this was simple. 'A small stream ran along the fence which enclosed the
garden, with newts, frogs and other ugly things in it. I remember Hurrell
once when I was very little [Hurrell was fifteen years his senior] taking
me by the heels and stirring the mud at the bottom with my head.' As
Froude notes, 'it had not the least effect which he desired', so instead
Hurrell took him out on a river in a boat and threw him overboard: that
didn't work either, although Froude appears not to have drowned.

At school he had some respite from persecution, noting he was 'very happy' there: 'the boys were generally gentlemen, and the tone among them was honourable and good.'[91] He had a hernia that prevented his taking part in games; and bullying was regarded as a great crime, with convicted bullies flogged. Froude shone as a classical scholar, and had happy memories of the three years there, from nine until twelve. After that, life took an unpleasant turn.

He was moved to Westminster, where he went as a scholar. His uncle, who delivered him there, was warned by the headmaster that life on the foundation was hard, especially for boys so puny and weak as young Anthony, and that boarding him out would be superior: but there was no chance of that. The youngest boys were fourteen or fifteen; he was barely twelve. No master was in the dormitories to supervise them. Relentless bullying by the younger boys, and thrashings by the elder ones for whom he had to fag, soon became the staples of Froude's life. He recounted being woken by having a lighted cigar pressed to his face, and having his legs set fire to in order to make him dance. He was also force-fed brandy to make him drunk. His health broke down, and he was sent to another house to recover.

He was also starved by having food kept from him by the older boys; his clothes were either torn or stolen, and so were his books. Inevitably, as he recalled, 'I learnt nothing'. This 'den of horrors' went on for three-and-a-half-years.[92] Eventually, returning home for the Christmas holidays at the end of 1833, Anthony was told he would not be going back: but Archdeacon Froude was 'irritated', having had copious bad reports from the headmaster, to whom the boy had been a disappointment. Just as Archdeacon Froude felt no sense of responsibility for having sent his son to such a shocking place, neither did Williamson, the headmaster at the time, feel he had anything to be ashamed of in having allowed such a regime. It would get worse after Froude left and, despite reforms in the 1840s, would still shock the Clarendon Commission in 1862 when they examined it as part of their inquiry into the public schools.[93]

The Archdeacon decided Anthony had pawned the missing clothes and books. 'I was severely beaten, my eldest brother standing by and approving.'[94] Hurrell appears to have derived as much happiness as his father from Anthony's suffering. The boy was ordered by Archdeacon Froude to sign a confession about pawning his effects, but Anthony could not lie, despite being promised a second thrashing unless he did 'confess'.

The Archdeacon then handed the question of Anthony's future over to Hurrell, who pronounced the boy stupid, and suggested he be sent either to a 'cheap school in Yorkshire' – which sounds as if it were Dotheboys Hall – or apprenticed to a tanner. 'I do not think that I resented all this,' Froude writes. 'I had so poor an opinion of myself that on the whole I supposed it was all right.'

The boy took comfort in appearing to be going down with tuberculosis, which had swept away various relatives and was beginning to do its work on the odious Hurrell. Anthony's sickness kept him at home for two years, in which he did a mountain of reading – he was given some divines to read and started to look at history for pleasure – but was largely ignored by his father and forbidden any companions. However, his father did note his reading, and let him go up to Oriel College, Oxford. He arranged to go into residence in the summer of 1836. This would bring Anthony back into close contact with Hurrell, who had been ordained and was a fellow there. Hurrell was also a near contemporary of Newman, and a pupil of Keble. He had introduced the two men to each other and had, therefore, played a key role in the Oxford Movement. Hurrell himself had become a committed Tractarian, working closely with Newman on the development of doctrine, and working out his own hatred of the Reformation, not least because of what he considered to be its effect on destroying the medieval feudal society that had become such a cult among his generation.

Anthony had no exposure to Hurrell at Oxford, however. His brother died of tuberculosis at their father's house in Devon in February 1836, just before his thirty-third birthday. The bereavement made Archdeacon Froude yet more taciturn and sour, if that were possible. Newman had met Anthony through Hurrell, and had visited the Dartington parsonage. He soon saw in the younger brother another potential disciple. Anthony was seduced at first. 'The Newmanites have claimed and made good a right to hold all Catholic doctrines except the supremacy of the Pope . . . I was willing to listen to it, and to my sorrow I did.'[95] On Froude's arrival at Oriel Newman went out of his way to be hospitable. Froude, though, resisted: to him Newman's credo had both highlighted the failure of Archdeacon Froude's approach to Christianity, but had also made an extremist of his deceased brother – an extremism made all the more obvious when, two years after Hurrell's death, Newman and Keble published his Remains in two separate tranches of two volumes each, containing his pro-Catholic outpourings in the shape mainly of letters to his confederates, none intended for publication.

Anthony's contrary feelings, not least his admiration for the Reformation, were expressed in his semi-autobiographical epistolary novel, *The Nemesis of Faith*, published in 1849: though Froude never went so far as his fictional creation, Markham Sutherland, in embracing Tractarianism wholeheartedly before casting it off. In 1842 Froude had become a fellow of Exeter, and, through their common interest in German thought and theology, was attracted to the writings of Carlyle. This gave him a common interest with Clough and Arnold.

Froude shared with Sutherland his reluctance to take holy orders. He had had to become a deacon in 1845 in order to retain his fellowship, and it was expected he would be ordained. However, he soon realised he could not; and that he was barred, because of his diaconate, from pursuing any other profession: he had wanted to read medicine. Like Clough, he struggled with an academic career at Oxford while being unsure of his beliefs. 'Some better foundation must be looked for than a corrupt and corrupting Papacy, but what else and where?' By the autumn of 1845 Newman had joined the Catholic Church; Froude could not follow, and could not proceed to full ordination in the Anglican Church, and was forbidden by law, as a clergyman, from becoming a doctor. He almost went to Ireland to seek an academic post, and toyed with emigrating to Tasmania to become a headmaster. Instead he continued in his fellowship, and turned his hand to writing fiction. His first novel, *Shadows of the Clouds* (sometimes known as *The Spirit's Trials*) contained a subtle, and accurate, fictional depiction of his father, which therefore caused his father and other surviving members of his family to send him to Coventry. Undeterred, he worked at his second attempt in the genre, *The Nemesis of Faith*, from the autumn of 1847. He also frequently discussed with Clough their shared difficulties.

The *Nemesis* offended almost every interested party, except radicals such as Frederick Denison Maurice, the leading Christian socialist, who rather approved of it. 'It is a very awful and I think may be a very profitable book,' Maurice wrote to his disciple, Charles Kingsley, on 9 March 1849. 'God would not have permitted it to go forth if He did not mean good to come out of it . . . it brings us to the root of things.'[96] Mainstream Anglicans felt it proved the corrupting and damaging effects of Tractarianism; to those who were part of the Oxford Movement or

sympathetic to its aims it was heretical. One, William Sewell, the senior
tutor of Exeter, saw an undergraduate with a copy of it on 27 February
1849, snatched it and threw it on the fire. Later that day Froude resigned
his fellowship. Age had not mellowed Archdeacon Froude. His son now
too old to suffer his flagellomania, the Archdeacon cut him off without
a penny instead.

It may be wrong to interpret Froude's resignation of his position at
Exeter as a response to Sewell's insult. He received a 'peremptory
demand' from the Rector and the college authorities for his resignation.[97]
He had written to Kingsley on New Year's Day 1849 of his dissatisfaction
with England – he mentioned the Tasmanian notion – and he told him:
'I wish to give up my Fellowship. I hate the Articles. I have said I hate
Chapel to the Rector himself.'[98] He warned Kingsley – a superior novelist,
whose Yeast was recently out – that his own novel was imminent, and
said that 'it is too utterly subjective to please you'. Kingsley, however,
would be almost the only figure of note to come to Froude's aid when
the storm broke.

On the last Sunday in February Froude found himself preached against
in that chapel. He told Clough on 25 February that he hoped to resign
his fellowship the next day – the day before Sewell burnt the book;
though he feared the college would dismiss him 'in true heretic style'
before he had the chance to go of his own volition.[99] Not for the first
time, he told Clough, Froude found that 'I am generally an object of
much abhorrence'.[100] Exeter washed their hands of Froude willingly: and
the Tasmanian prospect vanished, so angry were the elders of Hobart
at Froude's blasphemy.

The Nemesis was, in its time, shocking. It is partly autobiographical,
and where it veers from autobiography becomes melodramatic.
Sutherland, the hero, is bullied into holy orders by his father, though
only finally submits on the recommendation of his friend Arthur, to
whom the letters in the novel are addressed, and who acts as their editor.
He has been under the influence of the Oxford Movement and of
Newman and is tricked into exposing himself by some parishioners. He
resigns his living and goes abroad. There he meets a married woman
who cares deeply about his doubts, which have altered Sutherland's
religious outlook from Anglo-Catholicism to outright scepticism. The
woman has a boorish husband, and she and Sutherland fall in love: but
the woman has a daughter, and will not leave her husband. The little

girl catches a chill and dies, as Victorian children did. Sutherland sees what has happened as divine punishment for his sin (in Froude's compass, one sort of infidelity inevitably led to another) and contemplates suicide, a course he is talked out of by another friend who is said to represent the influence of Newman over him. He heads for a monastery instead; the bereaved mother for a convent. No one lives happily ever after.

Sewell did not burn the book so much because of its tacky storyline, as for its depiction of a clergyman taking orders in a state of doubt and immediately betraying his faith once there. Sutherland is not only a heretic, he also lapses into socialism – 'an ever increasing multitude of miserable beings must drag on their wretched years in toil and suffering that a few may be idle and enjoy,' he tells Arthur.[101] 'If there be no hope for them; if tomorrow must be as today, and they are to live but to labour, and when their strength is spent, are but to languish out an unpensioned old age on a public charity which degrades what it sustains; if this be indeed the lot which, by an irrevocable degree, it has pleased Providence to stamp upon the huge majority of mankind, incomparably the highest privilege which could be given to any one of us is to be allowed to sacrifice himself to them, to teach them to hope for a more just hereafter, and to make their present more endurable by raising their minds to endure it.'

The religious opinions expressed were, however, toxic. 'Before I can be made a clergyman,' Sutherland tells Arthur, 'I must declare that I unfeignedly believe all "the canonical writings of the Old Testament"; and I cannot.'[102] With distaste and disbelief he adds that 'I suppose, we are to believe that all those books were written by men immediately inspired by God to write them, because He taught them good for the education of mankind; that whatever is told in those books as a fact is a real fact, and that the Psalms and Prophecies were composed under the dictation of the Holy Spirit.' As far as Sutherland, and Froude, were concerned, there were 'scientific difficulties and critical difficulties, and, worse than all, metaphysical difficulties' that made such belief impossible. 'I will not, I must not, believe that the all-just, all-merciful, all-good God can be such a being as I find him there described,' he continued. For, in the Old Testament that Sutherland and Froude repudiate, God is instead 'jealous, passionate, capricious, revengeful, punishing children for their fathers' sins, tempting men, or at least permitting them to be tempted into blindness and folly, and then destroying them.' He protests:

'This is not a being to whom I could teach a poor man to look up to out of his sufferings in love and hope.'[103]

Arnold told his mother that he found the *Nemesis* 'unpleasant: but for all this shrieking and cursing at him I have the profoundest contempt.'[104] Ironically, one who attacked Froude was Carlyle, whom he had, like Arnold and Clough, hero-worshipped, and of whom he would write a revolutionary biography thirty years later. 'Froude's book is not – except for wretched people, strangling in white neckcloths, and Semitic thrums – worth its paper and ink,' the Sage wrote on 4 April 1849, five weeks after Sewell had burnt it.[105] 'What on Earth is the use of a wretched mortal's vomiting up all his interior crudities, dubitations, and spiritual agonising belly-aches, into the view of the Public, and howling tragically, "See!" Let him, in the Devil's name, pass them, by the downward or other methods, in his own water-closet, and say nothing whatever!' A master of vituperation, Carlyle resorted to scatological metaphor only rarely, which suggests he was genuinely upset: perhaps it was the fault of Froude's exclamation in the *Nemesis* that 'Carlyle! Carlyle only raises questions he cannot answer, and seems best contented if he can make the rest of us as discontented as himself.'[106] This was alarmingly near the truth, and echoed Clough's famous criticism of the Sage. Perhaps before his explosion against Froude Carlyle had not read so far as page 156, where his disciple writes that 'I shall not in this place attempt to acknowledge all I owe to this very great man'.[107]

Froude decided to try to make the most of being in the desert, and adopted a revisionist attitude to faith that excited the book-burners further. 'Why is it thought so very wicked to be an unbeliever? Rather, why is it assumed that no-one can have difficulties unless he be wicked?' he asked.[108] The answer was inflammatory: 'Because an anathema on unbelief has been appended as a guardian of the creed. It is one way, and doubtless a very politic way, of maintaining the creed, this of anathema. When everything may be lost unless one holds a particular belief, and nothing except vulgar love of truth can induce one into questioning it, common prudence points out the safe course; but really it is but a vulgar evidence, this of anathema.' A little later, in what is cast as a fragment of the ramblings of Sutherland's distressed mind, he even hints that what is understood by 'sin' is something some cannot avoid. 'Actions are governed by motives. The power of motives depends on character, and character on the original faculties and the training which they received from the men or things among which they have been bred. Sin, therefore, as commonly understood, is a chimera.'[109]

As Sutherland describes first the genius of Newman, and how he fell under the spell of his insights – he writes that any member of Newman's congregation would think he was referring in sermons specifically to him, so targeted did the words seem – he also describes how he began to see through Catholicism. He describes the moment of revelation: 'It is a problem heavier than has been yet laid on theologians to make what the world has now grown into square with the theory of Catholicism. And presently as we began to leave the nest, and, though under his [Newman's] eye, fly out and look about for ourselves, some of us began to find it so.'[110] In his autobiographical notes, Froude would say it was his reading of Carlyle that steered him from Tractarianism, and more besides: 'So Carlyle's teaching passed into me, eventually to transform the entire scheme of my thought and displace the beliefs in which I had been bred.'[111]

The assault that follows in the *Nemesis* on the Catholic Church shows an extreme version of the resistance to Newmanism, by a former devotee. Sutherland writes that 'it is not only necessary to talk of hating the Reformation, but one must hate it with a hearty good-will as a rending of the body of Christ.'[112] He asserts that nations that have stayed Catholic have become 'comparatively powerless' while Protestant nations have 'uniformly risen'; that 'the Catholic church since the Reformation has produced no great man of science, no statesman, no philosopher, no poet'; that modern historical methods had invalidated all authorities that professed the doctrine of infallibility.

Moving, it seems, ever more to an extreme, Sutherland announces that 'the personal character of the people in all Roman Catholic countries is poor and mean; that they are untrue in their words, unsteady in their actions, disrespecting themselves in the entire tenor of their life and temper.' This was thanks to the 'moral dependence' in which they had been trained, 'to the conscience being taken out of their own hands and deposited with priests; to the disrespect with which this life is treated by the Catholic theory; the low esteem in which the human will and character are considered; and, generally to the condition of spiritual bondage in which they are held.'[113] Even Sutherland realises he may be pushing it to say all this, so claims merely that even if it cannot be said for certain, it is 'to be believed nevertheless'.

Many Anglican clergy would have agreed with him: Dr Arnold, arch-critic of Newman, would have found little to trouble him. However, Sutherland – and indeed Froude – is pursuing an inevitable course of logic. 'My arguments', he observes, 'told not only against Catholicism, but against Christianity, considered as historical and exclusive.'[114] He felt that the devil was, under Christianity, painted as 'the main director of what seemed greatest and most powerful' in a world that the religion showed to be a place of 'trial and temptation'. He attacked the Bible because it 'everywhere denounced the world as the enemy of God, not as the friend of God'.

Perhaps most toxic, in an age of growing secularism, was his proclamation that 'the hold of Christianity was on the heart, and not on the reason.'[115] Newman had instructed his followers to undertake 'the surrender of reason', not least because 'daily more and more unreasonable appeared to modern eyes so many of the doctrines to which the Church was committed.'[116] He became disputatious with Newman, exposing one of his fundamental flaws: 'Reason could only be surrendered by an act of reason'.

What finally convinced him to break with Newman was hearing his mentor say from the pulpit: 'Scripture says the earth is stationary and the sun moves; science, that the sun is stationary and that the earth moves.' Froude realised that the casuistry with which Newman interpreted the meaning of the Bible destroyed his own faith: and if words were open to all sorts of interpretations, then 'Scripture, instead of a revelation, becomes a huge mysterious combination of one knows not what . . . this is carrying out the renunciation of reason with a vengeance.'[117] He deplored the notion that 'Unbelief was a sin, not a mistake, and deserved not argument, but punishment.'[118] In that phrase Froude sums up the effect on faith of the intellectual advances of the modern world, and the need to cast out the last remnants of medievalism. Sewell's decision to burn his book made the point as eloquently, had Sewell realised it. Froude told Matthew Arnold in the summer of 1853 that 'the *Nemesis* ought never to have been published'.[119] Forty years later, when (shortly before his death) he was making his autobiographical notes, Froude took a different view, and saw what had happened as a catharsis. 'Having thrown the *Nemesis* out of me, I had recovered my mental spirits and I was able to face the future without alarm or misgiving.'[120]

Whereas Clough's life was derailed by resigning his fellowship, Froude's was enhanced and his horizons expanded. He was unshaken, and unshakeable, in his beliefs, and proceeded to build a career as a historian and critic founded on his opposition to religious cant. Within months he had married Charlotte Grenfell, sister of Kingsley's wife. He also at last (thanks to Clough, who made the introduction) met Carlyle, and grew to share his views on religion, politics and even the destruction of the old feudal arrangements by the Industrial Revolution. Yet however far he embraced some of Carlyle's ideas he did not seek to emulate his tone or his style. Froude's great work of the twenty or so years after he left Exeter was his history of the reigns of Henry VIII, Edward VI, Mary I and Elizabeth I, a work that owed little or nothing to *The French Revolution*, a book Froude nonetheless greatly admired.

Froude's *History* is one of the great works of the nineteenth century, though so radical in its approach that Harriet Martineau said it 'disgusts us much, amidst all its cleverness and real interest. He might learn from Macaulay (with all his faults) not to obtrude himself and his sensibilities on the reader.'[121] She did, however, concede that the work was 'a great effort at rehabilitating himself with "the world".' It was originally published in twelve volumes. It ends not with the death of Elizabeth, but with the defeat of the Armada in 1588. This is consistent with the main theme of the work, to display the triumph of the Reformation and the loathsomeness of Catholicism: themes familiar from the *Nemesis*. Although, for its time, high in standards of scholarship, using a wealth of contemporary documents, it is also laced with Froude's profound anti-Catholicism: one only has to read some of his descriptions of Mary Tudor and her works to begin almost to taste the bile.

In pursuing plotters who sought to put Lady Jane Grey on the throne, Mary is said by Froude to have 'the bit between her teeth, and, resisting all efforts to check or guide her, was making her own way with obstinate resolution'.[122] Awaiting the arrival of her bridegroom from Spain she is 'ill with hysterical longings'.[123] When he arrives she is his 'haggard bride, who now, after a life of misery, believed herself at the open gate of paradise.'[124] One reason why Froude was, and still should be, regarded as a master of prose is the ability in so few words to convey his belief that the Catholic Queen was ugly, wretched and stupid. Of her reign he writes, with the feeling of a man who has himself undergone a minor martyrdom: 'The Catholics, therefore, were committed to continue their cruelties till the cup of iniquity was full; till they had taught the educated laity of England to regard them with horror; and till the Romanist superstition had died, amidst the execrations of the people, of its own excess.'[125]

The *History* was widely feted and read; it played an essential role in defining the English nation as a Protestant nation, and in building a more solid idea among the educated and literate English of themselves and their nationhood. Above all, it took the debate about the national culture from the spiritual realm, where it had lingered between 1830 and 1850, and related it to the secular realities of the modern, real world that was the incidental inheritor of the long-running feud over doctrine and faith. The use of history by the Victorians to confirm the Anglican settlement and to politicise religion, thereby enhancing its secular role, was not entirely initiated by Froude: Macaulay had gone there just before him. However, Macaulay had dealt with the second episode of the doctrinal struggle, in writing of the Glorious Revolution, whereas Froude had returned almost to its origins.

V

There was also a strand in the Church of England that was receptive to ideas, happy to regard orthodoxy as being flexible, and that wanted to bring religion to the people and to put it at the service of the people rather than use it as a form of social control. One such churchman, in the intellectual league just below Arnold, Clough and Froude, is their contemporary Charles Kingsley, best remembered now as the clergyman who trumpeted the evils of child labour in *The Water-Babies*. Kingsley, son of the Rector of Chelsea, was, however, a more experienced and shrewd propagandist than that book – no mere work of children's fiction but, as we shall see, remarkable as a clergyman's defence of Darwinism – suggests. Kingsley was fortunate to be a Cambridge man and not at Oxford, avoiding being sucked in to the Tractarian controversy. Instead, he was increasingly absorbed by the relationship between Christianity and politics, and became a disciple of the founder of English Christian socialism, Frederick Denison Maurice. Kingsley was attracted by the analysis made by Christian Socialists that socialism was inherent not just in the teachings of Jesus Christ – notably in his identification with the poor and the dispossessed – but was even to be found in parts of the Old Testament. Two of his novels, *Yeast* and *Alton Locke*, show his strong Christian socialist principles and his sympathy for Chartism. Mill, who did not give praise readily, told Kingsley in 1859 that he was 'a man who is himself one of the good influences of the age, and whose sincerity I cannot doubt'.[126]

Two childhood experiences shaped Kingsley. At Clifton preparatory school in 1831–2 he witnessed the Bristol riots; then, later, he had cholera, which gave him a lifelong interest in that most compelling question for the Victorians, sanitary reform and the prevention of disease. Kingsley had all the earnestness of his generation. 'I am more happy now than I have been for a long time,' he wrote to his mother in an undated letter of around 1835, 'but I do not like to talk about it but to prove it by my conduct. I am keeping a journal of my actions and thoughts and I hope it will be useful to me.'[127] In 1838 he went up to Cambridge. He began to have doubts while there, the product as much of his isolated lifestyle as of his theology. He became a chain-smoker (an addiction that would eventually kill him, in his mid-fifties) as a means of overcoming his pathological shyness and soothing his religious agonies. While still a student he met his future wife, Fanny Grenfell, whose own religious devotion helped mend his. He was ordained as a curate upon graduating in 1842. Fanny had clearly been tempted by news coming out of Oxford, as Kingsley – a hard-line Protestant – disclosed in a letter to his mother in 1841. Having read a review of *Tracts for the Times*, he complained that 'these men are Jesuits, taking the oath to the Articles with moral reservations . . . all the worst doctrinal features of popery that Newman professes to believe in. Help me to wean her [Fanny] from this pernicious superstition.'[128]

It was Maurice who exerted the main influence over Kingsley. Fanny had introduced Kingsley to Maurice's writings before their marriage in 1844; as she had to the works of Carlyle. Maurice had been born a Unitarian but grew up in a family riven with religious disputes. At Cambridge he had moved towards Anglicanism, and had been one of the founders of the Apostles, through which he met Tennyson, of whom he became a close and lifelong friend. After graduating, Maurice went to Oxford for further study, where he met Gladstone, and was baptised there in 1831. He was ordained in January 1834. Until the early 1850s he defended subscription to the Thirty-nine Articles as an open expression of the terms upon which academic life at Oxford and Cambridge would be conducted, which he found preferable to the matter not being openly discussed. He did however find the Tracts 'more unpleasant than I quite like to acknowledge to myself or others,' he wrote in 1837.[129]

He was, from his time as an undergraduate, inspired by the radical political ideas of Samuel Taylor Coleridge, who led him towards Christian socialism. He and Kingsley met when Maurice rented Kingsley's father's rectory in Chelsea, just as Kingsley settled into his own parish at Eversley in Hampshire. Maurice became chaplain of Guy's Hospital in 1836, and professor of English at King's College, London, in 1840. In 1846 he would become professor of theology at King's College, London. A committed educationist – he advocated the Church devoting more money and energy to educating the poor – he would also be a founder of Queen's College in Harley Street when it opened in 1848 as the first higher education institution for women. Through philanthropists and reformers such as Octavia Hill and Emily Davies, who would become disciples, he would have an immense influence on social improvements in Britain throughout the mid-nineteenth century.

He and Kingsley began to correspond on theological questions, with Maurice as teacher and Kingsley as pupil. He taught Kingsley that Christianity required a social as well as a spiritual dimension. Kingsley was by nature receptive. Having taken over his parish aged just twenty-five, and after the incumbency of a dissolute cleric who absconded with the parish funds, Kingsley had imposed his own social dimension on his flock as a means of improving their living conditions and morals. This had included his establishing a lending library and a loan club to further basic education and self-reliance. Maurice became godfather to the Kingsleys' second child, and in 1848 Kingsley, with Maurice's help, became a part-time professor of English at Queen's College.

Kingsley attended the great Chartist meeting at Kennington. He put up a poster addressed to the militants and signed 'A Working Parson'. This resulted in his being banned from preaching in the Diocese of London, even though he had made it clear he opposed force and deplored violence as a means to the Chartists' aims. J. C. Hare, a friend of Kingsley's, wrote to him after his second letter to the Chartists to say how 'pained' he was by part of it, 'so much so that on reading it last Thursday, before the publication of No 4, I wrote to Maurice earnestly entreating him to get the leaflet cancelled, if possible. He said it was too late, and that he did not concur in my objections.'[130]

Hare objected to his claim that the clergy had misrepresented the Bible, and 'have by no means fulfilled their political duties in England'. He was concerned because 'if there be any feeling universal among the Chartists, it is an almost intense dislike and distrust of the clergy . . . your letter will grievously encourage this feeling. The Chartists will say, there is a parson himself confessing that all his brother parsons are cheating and juggling us: and the mischief thus affected will be more than the Politics for the People will remedy in a twelvemonth.' Kingsley and Maurice went much further than Hare could conceive in supporting Chartism, which they were developing into Christian socialism, a creed of which Maurice would be the spiritual leader. By 1850 Maurice accepted the term 'Christian socialist' to describe his movement, in which Kingsley was his vicar on earth and, through his writings, chief propagandist. It spurred him on, he said, 'to the conflict we must engage in sooner or later with the unsocial Christians and the unchristian Socialists.'[131]

Kingsley and Maurice felt capitalism to be fundamentally flawed. They recoiled from the utilitarian doctrines of Jeremy Bentham, which saw man and his labour principally as commodities, and abhorred the exploitation of the working class. In September 1851 Kingsley lectured in London on the importance of getting a trades union organisation into agriculture. He acquired a popular reputation among the more literate working classes agitating for reform. One, W. H. Johnson ('Anthony Collins'), wrote to him in January 1858 to say that 'speaking for the intelligent minority of the working classes I can only say that at any visit to Blackburn you would meet with a suitable reception from the many who read your works with profit and pleasure.'[132] Johnson said he was an atheist who had edited the *London Investigator* ('and other Atheistic journals') and that 'I find it my greatest pleasure of an evening or a Sunday in collecting my young infidel friends at my home and reading to them *Alton Locke*, or *Yeast*, or *Hypatia*.'

Several bouts of illness in the early 1850s limited Kingsley's active radicalism. He was increasingly absorbed in novel-writing, and the propagation of Christianity became more important to him than the propagation of socialism. *Westward Ho!*, published in 1855, is a historical fiction about the Armada, and its propagandising is for Protestantism. Kingsley told Maurice in 1851 that he wished to 'set forth Christianity as the only really democratic creed'.[133] However, Maurice had such influence over Kingsley that the latter addressed the former in letters as 'my dear Master'.[134] Kingsley, referring to Ruskin's articles that would be published as *Unto This Last*, described himself to Maurice as having 'a sound reverence for political economy of John Stuart Mill's school, and have no leaning towards Mr Ruskin's *Cornhill* views' (the word 'ravings' is crossed out).[135]

Writing to Maurice about *The Water-Babies* in May 1863, sending him a copy, Kingsley said: 'I have tried, in all sorts of queer ways, to make children and grown folks understand that there is a quite miraculous and divine element underlying all physical nature; and that nobody knows anything about anything, in the sense in which he may <u>know</u> God in Christ, and right and wrong. And if I have wrapped up my parable in seeming Tom-fooleries, it is because so only could I get the pill swallowed by a generation who are not believing with anything like their whole heart in the Living God.'[136] He added: 'Remember that the Physical science in the book is not nonsense.' He later told Maurice he had been reading T. H. Huxley; as we shall see, he intended the book also as a defence of Darwin against his critics, a cause of which Huxley was leader.[137]

In the last fifteen or so years of his life Kingsley enjoyed royal patronage. This was less because the Queen was impressed with his Chartist sympathies than because the Prince Consort admired his commitment to sanitary reform, to Protestantism and for a sympathy he had betrayed for German culture. In 1859 he became chaplain to the Queen and in the following year, again thanks to Albert (who was Chancellor of the university) Regius professor of history at Cambridge. He lasted nine years at Cambridge and it was not a happy time: his health, undermined by tobacco, was fragile, he found the work too much for him, and he was short of money to educate his children. He also had to endure a long public argument with Newman, whom he accused in a review of Froude's *History of England* in 1864 of having said that truth for its own sake need not be a virtue of Catholic clergy. Newman was outraged, failed to obtain satisfaction, and ended up writing the *Apologia Pro Vita Sua* to justify himself and defend his integrity.

In 1873, again with royal connivance, he moved to a comfortable canonry at Westminster Abbey: but within two years, aged just fifty-five, he was dead, of an inflammation of the lung. Into that short life, however, Kingsley packed an astonishing amount. In his vocation as a parish clergyman he was exemplary and greatly admired. He had a profound effect on the development of Christian socialism. He was a highly regarded novelist and essayist. He was a campaigner for sanitary and health reform. He was also, in such spare time as he had, an amateur of science, a botanist, and a close scrutineer of the works of Darwin. His energy, and the example he set by it, were prodigious. As such, he typified the Victorian way of getting things done, and of seeking progress.

VI

The agonising done by intellectuals about religion in the mid-nineteenth century may have seemed comical to men such as Lytton Strachey, but it was far from comical to those concerned. Nor was the pain confined to deep intellectuals who wrestled with theological niceties. In his long poem *In Memoriam*, begun after the sudden death from a brain haemorrhage of his Trinity friend Arthur Hallam in 1833 but not published until 1850, Alfred Tennyson wrote that 'There lives more faith in honest doubt, believe me, than in half the creeds'.

In Memoriam was written over a period of more than fifteen years, years that coincided with the great crisis of faith among intellectuals in early Victorian England. It was published in the year Tennyson succeeded Wordsworth as Poet Laureate. The poem's original title was *The Way of the Soul*, and its purpose was to help Tennyson cope with his grief at losing Hallam, who had been destined to marry his sister and become his brother-in-law. The poem deals with the religious doubt that severe loss can occasion: but ends with the poet feeling reconciled to his Christian faith, at least at that stage in a life that still had half its course to run. George Eliot, writing about it in 1855, proclaimed that 'the deepest significance of the poem is the sanctification of human love as a religion.'[138] Tennyson's faith may have been simpler than Clough's, Arnold's, Froude's or Kingsley's, but the feelings it occasioned were no less keen.

Queen Victoria saw nothing secular in *In Memoriam*, regarding it next to the Bible as her greatest comfort in her widowhood. Tennyson had an audience of her at Osborne four months after the Consort's death to discuss the work. Albert had liked it, and Tennyson knew his enthusiasm had been partly why he was invited to take the Laureateship. One cannot doubt Tennyson's religious sincerity when he wrote it: but it required a more subtle intellect than the Queen's to understand that the poet regarded what he wrote as a testament to a feeling at a specific juncture in his life, not as a creed to stand for all time. As with much else in the matter of faith, appearances were not quite everything. Tennyson exemplifies, too, the fluid nature of faith in the second half of the nineteenth century and in an age of rapid change, and is typical of many of his contemporaries in so doing.

In Memoriam is a very clear public statement about religion, dealing in part with the struggles of the soul about faith. By contrast, two poems by Clough and Arnold reflect upon the struggles of the intellect about religion that the two men articulated so extensively in prose, notably in their letters. Clough's 'Say Not, the Struggle Naught Availeth', which appears to have been written in Rome in the late spring or early summer of 1849, and Arnold's 'Dover Beach' (written, it is thought, in 1851 but not published until 1867) are among the most intense manifestations of the high Victorian mind in verse. Each says succinctly what Froude, in elegant prose but at almost distressing self-analytical length, says in *The Nemesis of Faith*. *In Memoriam*, which by its scope and subject matter has become the definitive mid-Victorian poem, was completed in 1849 but its genesis pre-dates both these poems.

Clough's was first published in the American art journal *The Crayon* in August 1855. It has had various non-theological interpretations placed upon it: such as being his lament for the failure of liberalising movements in Europe after the upheavals of 1848, which he had witnessed: Rome was still turbulent when he wrote. A draft appears in his notebook facing the opening page of a diary kept in Rome between 16 April and 17 July 1849, at the time of the downfall of Mazzini's Republic. Yet given what we know of Clough's obsession with his theological problems, 'Say Not, the Struggle' seems more probably to reflect the poet's difficulties with faith rather than his sympathies with failed revolutionaries. There are five extant drafts of the poem: the fourth has the title 'In Profundis', which suggests something more spiritual than political.[139]

'Dover Beach' explicitly deals with faith: and both poets use the metaphor of the sea to suggest the ebbs and flows of devotion. Conflict, manifested as 'struggle', is in both poems: a reminder of the upheavals of the mid-nineteenth century and their effect on 'eternal' values. Clough's poem is a regular scheme of quatrains with alternate lines rhyming, and its first effect is musical:

Say not, the struggle naught availeth,
The labour and the wounds are vain,
The enemy faints not, nor faileth,
And as things have been they remain.

If hopes were dupes, fears may be liars;
It may be, in yon smoke concealed,
Your comrades chase e'en now the fliers,
And, but for you, possess the field.

For while the tired waves, vainly breaking,
Seem here no painful inch to gain,
Far back, through creeks and inlets making,
Comes silent, flooding in, the main.

And not by eastern windows only,
When daylight comes, comes in the light;
In front, the sun climbs slow, how slowly,
But westward, look, the land is bright.[140]

Arnold's, by contrast, is free verse, with an irregular rhyme scheme, the sound and meaning of its words accentuated by irregular rhythmical effects, much like the sea it describes, and broadcasting a moral grandeur that, unlike Clough's, is self-conscious:

The sea is calm to-night,
The tide is full, the moon lies fair
Upon the Straits; on the French coast, the light
Gleams, and is gone; the cliffs of England stand,
Glimmering and vast, out in the tranquil bay.
Come to the window, sweet is the night air!
Only, from the long line of spray
Where the ebb meets the moon-blanch'd land,
Listen! you hear the grating roar
Of pebbles which the waves suck back, and fling,
At their return, up the high strand,
Begin, and cease, and then again begin,
With tremulous cadence slow, and bring
The eternal note of sadness in.

Sophocles long ago
Heard it on the Aegean, and it brought
Into his mind the turbid ebb and flow
Of human misery; we
Find also in the sound a thought,
Hearing it by this distant northern sea.

The sea of faith
Was once, too, at the full, and round earth's shore
Lay like the folds of a bright girdle furl'd;
But now I only hear
Its melancholy, long, withdrawing roar,
Retreating to the breath
Of the night-wind down the vast edges drear
And naked shingles of the world.

Ah, love, let us be true
To one another! for the world, which seems
To lie before us like a land of dreams,
So various, so beautiful, so new,
Hath really neither joy, nor love, nor light,
Nor certitude, nor peace, nor help for pain;
And we are here as on a darkling plain
Swept with confused alarms of struggle and flight,
Where ignorant armies clash by night.[141]

Some scholars believe the poems are linked: that Clough's uplifting message is a direct response to Arnold's notion that faith is in permanent retreat. This would suppose 'Say Not, the Struggle' was written after 'Dover Beach', and that Arnold would inevitably have shown Clough his unpublished writings. There is no evidence, in this case, that it was, or that he did. 'Say Not, the Struggle' seems to have been written in 1849, when Clough was troubled after resigning his fellowship. He wrote out his poem for William Allingham on 13 October 1849, and posted it to Thomas Arnold, Matthew's brother, in New Zealand a fortnight later.

'Dover Beach' is a much harder poem to date precisely. One interpretation is that it was the product of Arnold's honeymoon in 1851.[142] The

Arnolds passed through Dover on 1 September 1851, Mrs Arnold telling her mother 'the sea [was] as calm as a mill-pond and the night very warm.'[143] This chronology raises a question that seems not to have occurred to those who claim Clough was answering Arnold: why should not Arnold have been answering Clough? This was a time of tension in their friendship. Arnold was highly critical of Clough's poetry; Clough perceived distance opening between them. Perhaps Arnold was rebuking him magisterially for his assumption that things could only get better. D. A. Robertson, writing in 1951, felt 'that Clough's "main" may be Arnold's "sea of faith" and that Clough's "tired waves" may be those which in Arnold's poem produce the "melancholy, long, withdrawing roar".'[144] Or it could be the other way round, or it could simply be a coincidence. It is clear from the correspondence of Clough and Arnold that they shared theological concerns. And scholars have found that the works of Thucydides and Sophocles both poets studied at Rugby were heavy with marine imagery.[145]

Clough's poem expresses optimism after a dark personal struggle has been resolved: resolved by the dilution of faith. Arnold's depicts the struggle in progress, and is sceptical about the outcome. It is ironic that a man so weak as Clough wrote so strong a poem about the importance of fortitude; while one so strong as Arnold, who overcame his difficulties with faith, should have written one of apparent surrender. Clough's poem is intensely personal: it is about overcoming defeatism, as Clough had to do after the setbacks caused by his religious feelings. Arnold's is more outward looking, and relevant to a society rather than an individual. It moves from light to darkness; from calm to the clashing of armies. Robertson asserts that Arnold's 'love' cannot have been his wife, since he would not have made a 'plea' to her to be true to him.[146] But is it a plea? It could easily be read as an assumption, an exhortation or a simple statement of fact.

Arnold was assailed by contemporary critics for the grandiloquence and self-absorption of his feelings about faith. However, they also grasped the common feelings of the rarefied intellectual about the problems that Arnold, as one such, had sought to articulate. One critic, R. H. Hutton, wrote that 'when I come to ask what Mr Arnold's poetry has done for this generation, the answer must be that no-one has expressed more powerfully and poetically its spiritual weakness, its cravings for a passion it cannot feel, its admiration for a self-mastery it cannot achieve, its desire for a creed that it fails to accept, its sympathy with a faith it will not share, its aspiration for a peace it does not know.'[147] 'Dover Beach' fails to find a proper substitute for faith, as Arnold had always understood it. His 'love' and he, true to each other, are merely consolations, not replacements: they remain on the darkling plain, in turmoil; he turns his attentions to other concerns, as we shall see, while the eternal note continues to sound.

CHAPTER 7

THE RATIONAL MIND: INTELLECTUALS AND THE GROWTH OF SECULARISM

I

Those afflicted by religious doubt were but one group who leant towards secularism. It was also a product of the scepticism that had been a feature of British philosophical thought during the seventeenth and eighteenth centuries, and which in the nineteenth assisted at the birth of the philosophy of utilitarianism. This was a peculiarly British creed: Bertrand Russell wrote how native thinkers 'remained almost completely unaffected by their German contemporaries'.[1] Since these included Kant, Hegel, Schopenhauer and Nietzsche, this was not intended as a compliment. As Christians found themselves under assault, they sought out targets for a counter-offensive. They quickly identified capitalism as an enemy, and attacked utilitarianism as the philosophy that was felt to have fed its fires. Jeremy Bentham, who at the start of the nineteenth century led the radical movement that created the creed, had been profoundly influenced by one foreign philosopher: the Frenchman Helvetius. In the mid-eighteenth century Helvetius had proclaimed that self-interest was at the root of human behaviour. Life, he felt, was a mission to avoid pain and seek pleasure. In Bentham's hands, this influence was mixed with thought from Locke and Hartley, and reshaped as 'the greatest happiness principle'. Bentham sought to create virtuous men: he therefore said that what was good was pleasure or happiness, and what was bad pain. Any circumstance in which pleasure outweighed pain was better than one in which the reverse was true: and the best was where pleasure exceeded pain by the greatest amount.

Bentham did not invent this doctrine – it is in Locke, Priestley and Hutcheson's thought in the seventeenth and eighteenth centuries. Bentham's distinction lay 'in his vigorous application of it to various practical problems'.[2] One was his argument that the State should legislate in the interests of making the good of the individual coincide with the good of the multitude. It led to Bentham's opposing the death penalty for minor crimes (for which it was still used in the early nineteenth century) because juries refused to convict obvious criminals whose offences did not, in the jury's view, merit death. A lesser penalty would have ensured the crime was punished and justice served: so Bentham contended that abolition for lesser offences would serve justice better. Soon, his point of view prevailed.

To some of the newly rich, Benthamism had a self-evident appeal, because to them the idea of the greatest happiness was entirely material. They argued that their employees became, if not rich, then certainly better paid than had they stayed on the land: in this there was some truth. Lacking was a support system for the hands and operatives on short time or laid off when trade declined, as in the Lancashire textile industry in the early 1840s. A philosophy driven by money and devoid of sentiment took no account of the sufferings of the working class. The ethical aspects of utilitarianism – or lack of them – drew its greatest critics, and inspired a branch of literature. And, because of the identification of the value of labour to those who employed it, utilitarianism also gave rise to socialism, early manifestations of which were seen in the Chartist movement and the trades unions.

Bentham's philosophy was based upon reason: everything, it seemed, could be calculated. He was forward thinking in some ways – he was a passionate exponent of equality and democracy, including votes for women – and backward in others, prizing security above liberty. As a rationalist he refused to believe in God, which made him a peculiar figure at the time. His great apostle was James Mill, towards whom Bentham acted also as patron, providing him with a house while he wrote his history of India. Mill brought up his son, John Stuart, in the educational methods advocated by Bentham, which made the young Mill a youth stuffed with knowledge but cursed with a narrow outlook. Fortunately for him, he realised that deficiency early on, and sought to broaden himself. Russell attacks James Mill for the 'poverty of his emotional nature': along with other utilitarians he hated romanticism and sentiment. Young John, when he grew up and wrote on the subject, employed what Russell called a 'softened form of the Benthamite doctrine'.[3] In the 1840s and 1850s, the younger Mill was the prime exponent of a new version of this philosophy, and as such became a target for those who disputed its sense and veracity.

Mill admitted in his *Autobiography* that his atheism had been hereditary, since his father had realised that he could not believe in God, and had transmitted the feeling to his son. Mill denied that his father had been a dogmatic atheist: his atheism was, 'moral, still more than intellectual. He found it impossible to believe that a world so full of evil was the work of an Author combining infinite power with perfect goodness and righteousness.'[4] He told Mill, when the latter was still a boy, that 'the question "who made me?" cannot be answered, because we have no experience or authentic information from which to answer it . . . I am thus one of the very few examples, in this country, of one who has not thrown off religious belief, but never had it.'[5] As for Carlyle, he was avowedly post-Christian, having embraced Goethe's idea of a God immanent in everything, and being incapable of believing in the Christian miracles.

The most famous attack in fiction on the utilitarians is also perhaps the most famous Condition of England novel: *Hard Times*, by Charles Dickens. Written in 1854, when Dickens was at the peak of his fame, it was (ironically) composed for the most utilitarian of reasons. Dickens's weekly magazine *Household Words* had lost circulation, and the master himself wrote a new serial to pull in the crowds. He attacked the notion that a life based on rationalism and stripped of sentiment (Dickens was the pre-eminent sentimentalist of his day) would be miserable. His object lessons in the novel are Tom and Louisa, children of Thomas Gradgrind MP, a manufacturer, of Coketown in Lancashire. They have been reared in an educational 'system' that caricatures James Mill's, with distressing effects. It is set out at the opening of the novel, by Gradgrind himself – 'A man of realities. A man of facts and calculations.'[6] His two younger children, in case any reader was slow to understand what was going on, are named Adam Smith and Malthus.

Gradgrind tells a class at the school of which he is both benefactor and inspiration that 'now, what I want is, Facts. Teach these boys and girls nothing but Facts. Facts alone are wanted in life. Plant nothing else, and root out everything else. You can only form the minds of reasoning animals upon Facts: nothing else will ever be of service to them.'[7] Gradgrind is bitten by the monster he has created. His daughter, apparently incapable of applying a feeling of sentiment to the marriage her father has arranged for her with his ghastly, vulgar and stupid friend Bounderby, has a breakdown and leaves her husband, to live unhappily ever after. Her brother rebels, becomes a wastrel, robs a bank, flees the country, and dies young. When these utilitarian masters treat their wives and children so cruelly, we may hold out no hope for their operatives.

Hard Times becomes the tale of a wronged man – Stephen Blackpool, one such operative, who is not only suspected by the odious Bounderby ('a man perfectly devoid of sentiment', as Dickens describes him) of robbing his bank, but is publicly vilified by him as well when handbills offering a reward for his capture are put around Coketown. Bounderby is too obtuse, and too snobbish, to see he has in fact been robbed by his own brother-in-law, the wastrel. Blackpool inadvertently meets his death because of Bounderby's persecution of him: a persecution that started because of Bounderby's utter incomprehension of why Blackpool had refused to agree to strike, been sent to Coventry by his union, and become an isolated figure in Bounderby's works. Bounderby vilifies his workers as having the 'object in life' of being 'fed on turtle soup and venison with a gold spoon'.[8] But then he also believes that the mind-numbing, lung-wrecking work they do is 'the pleasantest work there is, and it's the lightest work there is, and it's the best paid work there is. More than that, we couldn't improve the mills them-selves, unless we laid down Turkey carpets on the floors. Which we're not going to do.'

This description of the mill-owner as a monster is consistent with Dickens's darkly comic intentions: but it is also typical of the attitudes by the non-industrial population (of whatever class) of the newly moneyed men who were making Britain the workshop of the world. Dickens attributes to Gradgrind the notion that 'the Good Samaritan was a bad economist', which strips him almost completely of humanity (though his humanity will return when he is confronted with the damage done to his children by his 'system').[9] However, Dickens, like Mrs Gaskell and, in the 1860s, George Eliot, shows equal contempt for the trades union movement, with its rabble-rousing determination to crush whatever individuality remains in a man after the masters have tried to wipe it out. When Slackbridge, the agitator, attacks the 'grinding despotism' of the likes of Gradgrind and Bounderby, it is not least because he has his own version of the same iniquity to use instead once the oppressors have been overthrown.[10]

At the book's grim conclusion – with almost Wagnerian levels of misery, death and disappointment – the only happy character is Sissy, a girl who refused to be cowed by Gradgrind's system, but allowed herself individuality, imagination and sentiment. She also brought out the best in Gradgrind – his charitable instinct, when her father deserted her – which is more than anyone else managed. She is the only beneficiary of Dickens's favourite theme, the decent but hard-pressed character on whom fortune, like a fairy godmother or beneficent uncle, shines. All else is wretchedness, which is what sets this short, vivid book apart from the rest of his oeuvre. By the time he wrote it (and he was followed in *Household Words* as a serial by *North and South*, with its less comic, more intense take on a similar theme), the worst for the operative class was over, as prosperity had returned to the cotton-mills of Lancashire and the wool-mills of the West Riding. But, just as Mrs Gaskell did in her novels, and even Kingsley in *The Water-Babies*, Dickens makes his readers conscious of his disdain for a philosophy at odds with the fundamentals of human nature, and the human spirit.

Capitalism could not be allowed free rein. Peel's government realised the importance of regulating business to protect investors and customers, as manufacturing and the railways grew. The 1844 Joint Stock Companies Act formed the basis of company law down to our own times. Before the Act it had required a Royal Charter or a private Act of Parliament to establish a business incorporated in law. Therefore, most new businesses spawned by the industrial and mercantilist revolution were unincorporated, sometimes with thousands of shareholders. Taking legal action against them was nearly impossible. The Act made it possible to register easily as a joint-stock company, giving those who dealt with such businesses easier redress if things went wrong. In 1855 limited liability was introduced, which further encouraged investment and economic growth by reducing unaccountable risks by investors. By the mid-Victorian period capitalists were being brought properly within the reach of the law.

II

Five years after Dickens had taken a sledgehammer to utilitarianism in *Hard Times*, Mill published his most celebrated work of philosophy, an altogether more subtle discourse. *On Liberty* supercharged the debate about the rights of those outside the traditional governing class. It developed Bentham's idea of the greatest happiness principle by showing liberty as essential to that happiness. The following year Mill would publish his essay *On Representative Government*, which would deal with the pressure for democracy in even more specific terms. He wrote to Gladstone on 6 August 1859 that 'in venturing to send you my last publication, I intended a mark of respect to one of the very few political men whose public conduct appears to me to be invariably conscientious, and in whom desire of the public good is an active principle, instead of, at most, a passive restraint.'[11]

On Liberty has been described as 'the first modern exposition of a theory of the secular state'.[12] As well as taking for granted the end of inevitable obeisance to religion, the argument anticipates the end of the deferential society. Both ideas were consistent with the purpose of the treatise, as set out by Mill: 'The object of this Essay is to assert one very simple principle, as entitled to govern absolutely the dealings of society with the individual in the way of compulsion and control, whether the means used be physical force in the form of legal penalties, or the moral coercion of public opinion. That principle is, that the sole end for which mankind are warranted, individually or collectively, in interfering with the liberty of action of any of their number, is self-protection. That the only purpose for which power can be rightfully exercised over any member of a civilised community, against his will, is to prevent harm to others.'[13] Only in those aspects of behaviour that impinged on others was the individual answerable to society. Otherwise, 'over himself, over his own body and mind, the individual is sovereign.' Ruskin, who largely disapproved of Mill, nonetheless saw the force of some of his arguments in *On Liberty*, though he told John Morley: 'The degree of liberty you can rightly grant to a number of men is commonly in the inverse ratio of their desire for it.'[14]

Such ideas would bring him into conflict with his most articulate critic, James Fitzjames Stephen, whose knowledge of human nature as a criminal lawyer had suggested to him that most people lacked the wit to be sovereign, without constituting a threat to society. Mill did, indeed, write that 'despotism is a legitimate mode of government in dealing with barbarians, provided the end be their improvement, and the means justified by actually effecting that end.' However, he believed the British people were not barbarians; Stephen, suffused with Tory pessimism (even though he considered himself in politics to be a Liberal) disagreed.

Mill's desire for a State with free institutions could not be realised without complete intellectual liberty, and part of that was the right for men to shake off an imposed religion, if they felt the compulsion to do so. He protests in *On Liberty* about the Crown bringing a prosecution for blasphemy in 1857 against a man for writing anti-Christian graffiti on a gate in Cornwall, for which he received twenty-one months' imprisonment (subsequently commuted); and about the discrimination against atheists who could not be sworn as jurymen, one of whom was 'grossly insulted' by the judge; and about another denied justice against a thief because he felt unable to give sworn evidence in a court of law.[15] He felt the law as it stood put those exercising their conscience in the position of outlaws. To the still greater outrage of his critics, Mill defined the great hypocrisy of the age: people professing Christian principles but, in only the rarest cases, actually living by them. He claimed to spot a decline in observance over the history of Christianity. Speaking of the earliest Christians, he wrote that 'when their enemies said "see how these Christians love one another" (a remark not likely to be made by anybody now) they assuredly had a much livelier feeling of the meaning of their creed than they have ever had since.'[16]

The Church of England certainly, at that stage, still saw things differently. Christopher Wordsworth, the poet's nephew and shortly to be Bishop of Lincoln, asked a Tory meeting in Reading in February 1865: 'What, gentlemen, is Conservatism? It is the application of Christianity to civil government. And what is English Conservatism? It is the adoption of the principles of the Church of England as the groundwork of legislation. Gentlemen, I say it with reverence, the most Conservative book in the world is the Bible, and the next most Conservative book in the world is the Book of Common Prayer.'[17] This showed how the influence religion had on the State trammelled individual liberty, in Mill's view, and kept the proletariat in its place in Marx's.

The passage of the Reform Act two years after Wordsworth's remarks confirmed a change in perceptions. Archbishop Manning wrote to his Oxford friend Gladstone, by then Prime Minister, in November 1871 to say that 'I see no principle now but the will of the majority; the will of the majority is not either reason or right. My belief is that Society without Christianity is the Commune . . . what hope can you give me?'[18] But the intellectual case for secularisation was being made more and more forcibly: not just by such as Mill and Butler, but also by John Morley, Gladstone's disciple and eventual biographer, who published an assessment of Voltaire, and by the wider understanding among intellectuals of the German philosophers, such as Hegel, who challenged head on the existence of God. As Chadwick has put it, the 1840s were years in which individual intellectuals, such as Clough or Froude, had doubts. By the 1860s 'Britain and France and Germany entered the age of Doubt, in the singular and with a capital D.'[19]

Mill's eminence as a thinker brought him the respect of Gladstone, with whom he frequently corresponded, and who became a conduit of his influence into the higher reaches of government. In January 1864 he sent Gladstone a pamphlet about the American Civil War. Gladstone was disappointed by it (though 'I speak with unfeigned deference to your more competent judgment'[20]) but craved intellectual intercourse with Mill. His letter ends with a reminder 'of my breakfast table on all Thursdays after Easter at ten, and to express the hope that you will sometimes send me a note to say you will give me, if in London, the honour and favour of your company.' Writing to Gladstone on 23 July 1865, to congratulate him on his election in South Lancashire, Mill identified himself and his correspondent with 'the cause of improvement'.[21]

The relationship continued to develop as Gladstone turned his mind to reform: and Mill seems to have sensed the chance of influencing change that a relationship with so senior a politician gave him. Mill told Gladstone in March 1866 that 'there are few things I more value than the opportunity of cultivating the degree of personal acquaintance to which you have done me the honour of admitting me'.[22] Although Mill rarely went out he continued to send Gladstone his publications, and would join his breakfasts some Thursday mornings, with such great men as J. L. Motley, the historian, and the architect George Edmund Street.[23] By such means did Mill help ensure that his views suffused British policy.

III

Mill's ideal of an extension of liberty required, for its success, a level of self-awareness and responsibility on the part of the liberated; and that in turn required more education. For many adult Victorians the development of educational opportunities that would enable them to think better for themselves and take a more sceptical view of religion and politics came too late. Men with brains but with no means of developing them banded together to form working men's institutes, to which public-spirited educated men would give lectures. Radicals such as Engels despised these associations, feeling they simply served as depots in which the working classes could be indoctrinated with bourgeois values. They did, however, improve many who went to them and who – not that Engels could grasp this – sometimes wanted bourgeois values and knowledge.

The leading institution for educating the working classes was founded by F. D. Maurice and others in Red Lion Square in London in 1854, and became known as the Working Men's College. Maurice called on a distinguished range of intellectuals to teach at the College, including Ruskin and Thomas Hughes. John Stuart Mill, Dante Gabriel Rossetti and Charles Kingsley all lent their names and support to the enterprise. Maurice intended the college not merely to provide a route to improvement for men of ability who deserved an education, but to act as a further dissuasion from the temptation to violent protest. He had support from organised labour and the cooperative movement.

Outside the metropolis, where leading intellectuals were not so readily available to lend glamour and gravitas to the education of artisans, attempts at similar projects were more modest. One such was in Leeds. It had started as a meeting in a workman's cottage, between two or three men who resolved to meet in the evenings to exchange knowledge. In the summer, it moved into the garden, and others joined the group. Soon, the numbers became too large for the cottage, and the men sought premises. All they could afford was a room formerly used as a cholera hospital, cheap because it could find no tenants. The men spruced it up, and, their numbers now 100 strong, proceeded to invite speakers. In 1845, one whom they asked was Samuel Smiles.

Smiles was then thirty-two. He was a Scotsman, son of a merchant in Haddington, where he had attended the grammar school. He was apprenticed to doctors before his fourteenth birthday, and by twenty had obtained a medical diploma at Edinburgh University. However, he was diverted from a career as a surgeon. In 1838 he had become editor of a radical newspaper, the *Leeds Times*, after answering an advertisement. Over the next few years he pursued some of the causes advocated by the paper, notably electoral reform and repeal of the Corn Laws. Smiles was, however, on a political journey from radicalism to conservatism. He was heavily influenced by Carlyle, not least in Carlyle's belief in the almost religious quality of work. He came to distrust the Chartists precisely because he preferred, instinctively, the actions of individuals to those of the collective. Thus it was that he chose his topic for the Leeds working men: 'Citing examples of what other men had done, as illustrations of what each might, in a greater or less degree, do for himself; and pointing out that their happiness and well-being in after life must necessarily depend mainly upon themselves – upon their own diligent self-culture, self-discipline and self-control – and above all, on that honest and upright performance of individual duty, which is the glory of individual character.'[24]

The lecture went so well that Smiles was asked to give more. Using illustrations from the lives of the great men of his own and previous generations, he showed how diligence and perseverance had brought success and fortune. A few years later, one of his audience came back to see him and told him that he had prospered in his own business by taking to heart what he had learned from Smiles and acting upon his precepts. Smiles had kept notes of what he had said in his lectures; they formed the basis of a book that would become a bible in tens of thousands of working- and lower-middle-class houses: *Self-Help, with Illustrations of Conduct and Perseverance*, the first edition of which was published in 1859.

Smiles set out his purpose at once: 'Heaven helps those who help themselves' are the opening words of the book.[25] It is a maxim, he adds, that embodies 'the results of vast human experience'. He continues: 'The spirit of self-help is the root of all genuine growth in the individual; and, exhibited in the lives of many, it constitutes the true source of national vigour and strength. Help from without is often enfeebling in its effects, but help from within invariably invigorates.' *Self-Help* is sometimes represented as work that extols selfishness: but Smiles's intention was to marshal the strength and development of individuals for the good of the nation. The great purpose of the improvement of individuals was to improve Britain: to cement its place as the greatest nation in the world, put there by the efforts and ingenuity of its people.

'National progress is the sum of individual industry, energy and uprightness, as national decay is of individual idleness, selfishness, and vice,' he wrote.[26] Hard work and perseverance are not enough: there has to be a moral dimension to self-improvement, which he characterises as 'uprightness'. This is important, because Smiles addresses those lacking the good fortune to be brought up as gentlemen. Indeed, the appeal of his book, and one of the features of it that caused it to sell almost a quarter of a million copies by the end of the century, was Smiles's showing how men of humble origins had risen to high positions in professions and in societies. Shakespeare's father was a butcher and grazier, as was Wolsey's; Captain Cook's a day-labourer; Ben Jonson's a mason; Inigo Jones's a carpenter; Dr Livingstone's a weaver; and Faraday's a blacksmith. Britain was a land of social mobility that had had an aristocracy of talent for longer than it had had an aristocracy: Victorian snobbery about 'trade' was just that.

In fashioning the book's high moral tone Smiles takes his lead from the man he calls 'the great Dr Arnold', who had led the way in Smilesian philosophy by striving 'to teach his pupils to rely on themselves, and to grow in character by effort.' He recounts the story of Arnold upbraiding a boy who was not doing well in his lessons, who looked Arnold in the eye and asked: 'Why do you speak angrily sir? *Indeed*, I am doing the best I can.'[27] Arnold, he says, would tell the story to his children, in praise of the boy and, it seems, in deprecation of himself. Smiles also quotes with great approval a line from Stanley's *Life*, which seems to enlist the Doctor in the higher ranks of the utilitarians: how Arnold communicated to boys when they arrived at Rugby that 'a great and earnest work was going forward' and how thereafter a boy would sense that 'a strange joy came over him on discerning that he had the means of being useful, and thus of being happy.'[28] This, he said, was the product of the force of Arnold's character, not least in how it was rooted in his commitment to truth, and his respect for work.

He also anticipated, in taking issue with its basic thesis, by a decade the work of Arnold's eldest son in *Culture and Anarchy*. In conceding that a measure of 'self-culture' was important to the aspiring man, he warned that society might overestimate the importance of literary culture – 'we are apt to imagine that because we possess many libraries, institutes and museums, we are making great progress'.[29] Having a library meant being learned no more than having money meant one was generous. 'Thus many indulge themselves in the conceit they are cultivating their minds, when they are only employed in the humbler occupation of killing time.' In one of the book's rare jokes, Smiles observes that killing time is something 'of which perhaps the best that can be said is that it keeps them from doing worse things.'

Smiles, like Matthew Arnold, understood the importance of the pursuit of perfection; but advocated a very different route. After all, as he points out, 'there were wise, valiant and true-hearted men bred in England, long before the existence of a reading public.' It depends on what one means by 'perfection': and Smiles and Arnold appear to have had two very different views of that. Where they would seem to have common ground is in Smiles's assertion that 'self-culture may be degraded' if viewed 'too exclusively as a means of "getting on".'[30] Smiles does, eventually, concede that self-culture 'will at all events give one the companionship of elevated thoughts', and with it the reflective mind that breeds a sense of civilisation.

Character – which Smiles called 'the crown and glory of life' – he defined as 'human nature in its best form.'[31] Men of character were the conscience and 'best motive power' of society. It was a short step from this to the Smilesian definition of a gentleman, that particular facet of character that so obsessed the writers of Victorian fiction. 'Truthfulness, integrity, and goodness' were at the heart of the concept.[32] These, together with politeness, were not exclusive to any rank or station, Smiles argued. 'The True Gentleman is one whose nature has been fashioned after the highest models', he rules. The true gentleman had also self-respect, a sense of honour, and high-mindedness. 'He does not shuffle or prevaricate, dodge or skulk; but is honest, upright and straight-forward.'[33] Bravery is implicit in this. Smiles rounds off his paean to the gentleman by recalling what happened in 1852 at the sinking of the *Birkenhead*, where the cry went up of 'women and children first'. 'The examples of such men never die,' Smiles observed as he noted the upright deaths of those who had put the weak (or the supposed weak) first.[34]

Lest Smiles's audience imagine the ruling class led lives of sheer ease, he pointed out, too, the example of strivers such as Sir Robert Peel: 'He possessed in an extraordinary degree the power of continuous intellectual labour, nor did he spare himself.'[35] Palmerston (whose energies were sometimes expended in ways of which the upright Smiles would not have approved), Russell, Disraeli and, of course, Gladstone were also given honourable mentions as leaders of society who showed the lower orders the importance of effort. Smiles counselled those who strove against defeatism if results did not come quickly: he quoted Ruskin in his aid ('patience is the finest and worthiest part of fortitude . . . patience lies at the root of all pleasures, as well as of all power') and proclaimed that 'patient perseverance' was the key to achievement.[36] It was exactly how Peel had become a fine orator, having been set extempore speaking exercises by his father as a boy: 'By steady perseverance the habit of attention became powerful'.[37] He learned to repeat verbatim sermons he had heard in church. He developed thereby 'the extraordinary power of accurate remembrance' that so wrong-footed his parliamentary opponents. Quoting de Maistre, he said this exemplified the notion that 'to know *how to wait* is the great secret of success'.

However, Smiles also insisted that making money was not enough. A man, as he improved financially, had to improve culturally and in terms of his character too. 'Men of business', he writes, 'are accustomed to quote the maxim that Time is money; but it is more; the proper improvement of it is self-culture, self-improvement, and growth of character. An hour wasted daily on trifles or in indolence, would, if devoted to self-improvement, make an ignorant man wise in a few years, and employed in good works, would make his life fruitful, and death a harvest of worthy deeds. Fifteen minutes a day devoted to self-improvement, will be felt at the end of the year.'[38] For the socially ambitious – and the period of prosperity that followed the hungry forties and lasted until the downturn of 1873 was one of conspicuous social ambition – Smiles had this warning: 'The making of a fortune may no doubt enable some people to "enter society", as it is called; but to be esteemed there, they must possess qualities of mind, manners, or heart, else they are merely rich people, nothing more. There are men "in society" now, as rich as Croesus, who have no consideration extended towards them, and elicit no respect. For why? They are but as money-bags; their only power is in their till.'[39]

The Victorians were practised at various hypocrisies – the related issues of sex and religious observance chief among them – and money was one of the other chief difficulties. Smiles is right to emphasise the number of peerages that emanated from trade, not least when one recalls the abundance of snobbish and condescending references in Victorian literature by those who have not had to make their own money to those who have. Perhaps only two or three generations earlier, the grandfather or great-grandfather of the snob himself was on the receiving end of such patronage. Smiles articulates the middle classes' attitude to wealth in his chapter 'Money – Its Use and Abuse'. He begins by saying that the way a man uses money is 'one of the best tests of practical wisdom', and therefore the measure of a man.[40] He continues: 'Although money ought by no means to be regarded as a chief end of man's life, neither is it a trifling matter, to be held in philosophic contempt, representing as it does to large an extent, the means of physical comfort and social well-being.' He attacks the 'selfishness' displayed by 'inordinate lovers of gain'; and contrasts the 'generosity, honesty, justice and self-sacrifice' exhibited by the best of those who have money with the 'thriftlessness, extravagance and improvidence' of the worst.

Above all – and this would have been considered a quite vulgar admission by some snobs – 'comfort in worldly circumstances is a condition which every man is justified in striving to attain by all worthy means.' Yet in what he has already said, Smiles has given the lie to those who accuse him of exhorting selfishness and materialism. He exhorts, rather, self-denial. 'Every man ought so to contrive to live within his means,' he writes. 'The practice is the very essence of honesty. For if a man do not manage honestly to live within his own means, he must necessarily be living dishonestly upon the means of somebody else.'[41]

There was a consciousness among the ruling class that more had to be done for adults who sought learning. Kingsley wrote: 'I cannot forget, any more than the working man, that the Universities were not founded exclusively, or even primarily, for our own class; that the great mass of students in the middle ages were drawn from the lower classes, and that sizarships, scholarships, exhibitions and so forth, were founded for the sake of those classes, rather than of our own.'[42] He also points out that after the Wars of the Roses the younger sons of gentlemen, no longer allowed to fight and not easily set up with their own land and estates, chose to try to become learned instead: and 'by virtue of their superior advantages' beat the poor boys to university places. Therefore he asked: 'Does not the increased civilisation and education of the working classes call on the Universities to consider they may not now try to become, what certainly they were meant to be, places of teaching and training for genius of every rank, and not merely for that of young gentlemen?' Gladstone, when he read *Alton Locke*, noted the importance of 'university foundations for the poor'.[43] Other politicians were keen to enable the provision of cultural institutions to allow those who had left, or had never had, full-time education to continue to enrich their minds. The Museums Act 1845 and the Public Libraries Acts 1850, 1855 and 1866 all contributed to this cause but, as with much other reforming legislation of the era, were only pushed through parliament in the face of opposition. As with the education of children, the education of adults would happen in spite of government action rather than because of it.

IV

The pursuit of knowledge in mid-Victorian Britain, notably in science, laid the foundations of the modern, secular, world. A climate of discovery, inquiry and curiosity fed on itself, and the appetite grew with eating. Rational answers were sought for phenomena that had hitherto been given spiritual or theological explanations. The sensation caused by Darwin's researches accelerated this process, as did the work of T. H. Huxley, who coined the term 'agnostic'. Scientific progress forced thinking people to reconcile what was now understood about the natural sciences with religious teachings. Novelists such as George Eliot and Samuel Butler undermined religion; and the most popular novelist of the era, Charles Dickens, had little to say in any of his works about its benefits. In Butler's case *The Way of All Flesh* aggressively portrayed it as sustaining and validating Victorian hypocrisy, though his work was considered so scandalous it was published posthumously, in 1903, by which point the world had moved on. Doctrinal disputes such as highlighted by the Oxford Movement caused the Church to appear divided and inward looking, helping reduce its relevance to the masses and making it appear the private property of prelates, dons and theologians.

Those who might have brought religion before a new generation chose instead to voice their doubts. By the 1870s, and despite the adherence to the Church of such prominent politicians as Gladstone, Britain had become an increasingly secularised and rationalist state. Scientists such as Huxley and John Tyndall displayed their agnosticism or atheism, their minds altered by scientific fact. What remained was one of the foremost Victorian hypocrisies – or accommodations – that paid public tribute to the place of religion in society, even while that society made rapid intellectual advances without it – often with the explicit approval of Christian intellectuals.

Describing in his masterpiece *The Way of All Flesh* the mood of the 1830s, when his own hated father (pilloried in the novel as Theobald Pontifex) had been ordained, Butler wrote that 'in those days people believed with a simple downrightness which I do not observe among educated men and women now. It had never so much as crossed Theobald's mind to doubt the literal accuracy of any syllable in the Bible. He had never seen any book in which this was disputed, nor met with anyone who doubted it. True, there was just a little scare about geology, but there was nothing in it. If it was said that God made the world in six days, why He did make it in six days, neither in more nor less; if it was said that He put Adam to sleep, took out one of his ribs and made a woman of it, it was so as a matter of course.'[44]

One of the first significant scientific advances in Britain had been in geology. It had startled the largely irrational world of late Georgian science by observing that evidence suggested that the story of the Creation set out in the Scriptures was unlikely to be accurate. The man responsible, Charles Lyell, had acquired an interest in geology as an undergraduate at Oxford. A massive influence upon him in the early 1820s was the work of Karl von Hoff, which he learned German specifically to read, and which inspired him to begin work on his own *Principles of Geology*, the first volume of which was published by John Murray in 1830. In it, Lyell rounded on geologists who believed that the period of the earth's development was within that specified in the Bible. He realised, as a result of his studies, the impossibility of the earth's having reached its present state in a few thousand years. Like Charles Darwin, who was greatly influenced by him, Lyell had published a groundbreaking work of scientific research that most of his fellow scientists attacked as wrong.

Darwin picked up this baton. He was born in 1809, the son of a doctor in Shrewsbury. He was the grandson of Erasmus Darwin, the physician, botanist, natural historian and poet, on his father's side, and Josiah Wedgwood, one of the giants of the Industrial Revolution, on his mother's. Darwin was a clever student, but the curriculum at Shrewsbury, where he was a pupil, bored him. He was taken out of the school at sixteen. When he spent his spare time conducting experiments in his dormitory the headmaster, Samuel Butler – grandfather of the novelist who would become one of Darwin's admirers and, then, one of his critics – rebuked him for wasting his time.

He went to Edinburgh University to train as a doctor, but found surgery revolted him (this was before the invention of anaesthetics). However, he acquired interests in natural history, particularly of bird life and invertebrates from long walks along the coast of the Firth of Forth, and in geology. He was introduced to the work of Jean-Baptiste Lamarck, the French zoologist who believed the origin and primal function of human organs could be explained through studying certain invertebrates. This began a thirty-year odyssey for Darwin towards his most celebrated and important work, *On the Origin of Species*.

His father settled that Charles should take holy orders, blissfully unaware of how he had come under the influence at Edinburgh of men and ideas that challenged the ideas of Creation. Darwin went up to Christ's College, Cambridge in 1828, and managed to maintain his Christian faith. He had a cousin at Cambridge, William Fox, who interested him in beetle-collecting. He soon made a name for himself as an entomologist; and began to confess to doubts that would make a career in the Church impossible. He refined and deepened his knowledge of geology and its crucial role in providing evidence for what came to be called evolution. He was offered a place as resident scientist on the voyage of HMS *Beagle* to Tierra del Fuego and the East Indies, departing in late 1831 not long after his graduation. As Darwin admits in his *Autobiography*, his life was changed by the five-year voyage. He explored inland during the ship's many stops. He read *Principles of Geology*. Everything he saw validated Lyell, and provided evidence of a time frame of the development of the earth that would accommodate a theory of natural selection. He would later describe Lyell's work as one 'which the future historian will recognise as having produced a revolution in natural science'.[45] He also wrote that 'geology plainly proclaims that each land has undergone great physical changes', and thus 'organic beings' must have 'varied under nature'.[46]

Within a month of his return to England in October 1836 he met Lyell. The two became close friends and, in a sense, collaborators. 'Amongst the great scientific men, no one has been nearly so friendly and kind,' he wrote.[47] Darwin spent several years writing up his account of the voyage of the *Beagle*, and found homes for the collections made on the journey. He became prominent in both the scientific and Whig intellectual life of London, but as his thoughts on evolution developed he kept them, for the moment, to himself. He first set eyes on an ape at London Zoo in March 1838, and noted certain common characteristics. He started to believe that what man was had been determined by his ancestors, not by God. The contemporary notion that science should be used to explain the creations of God was turned on its head: science would now be used to prove the Bible could not be taken literally.

By the mid-1840s he had developed his theory of evolution, but felt unequal to promulgating it – such would have been the climate of hostility. He had determined that natural selection took place, and that overpopulation in all species meant that the fittest adapted and survived while the weaklings died. This had taken place, he knew, over hundreds of millions of years, not in the few thousand specified by the Scriptures. He studied barnacles during the 1840s, and determined how they had descended from crab-like forebears. This confirmed his view that all species, over time, were variable. Then he worked on plants, determining that seeds could be dispersed by ocean currents (he proved that salt water did not kill the seeds) or by birds. Seeds could germinate after being in the bellies of rotting dead birds, or in their droppings. It was then that his study of pigeons, highly influential in his work on evolution, became significant. Darwin had long been influenced by the population theory of Thomas Malthus, and saw it being worked out in animal life – not just pigeons, but in other species too.

At the urging of Lyell ('I wish you would publish some small fragment of your data on pigeons if you please and so out with the theory and let it take date – and be cited – and understood'), and after much discourse with T. H. Huxley, Darwin in 1856 began formulating the work that became *On the Origin of Species*.[48] In his researches he compared artificial selection – the deliberate breeding of new species of domesticated animals – with those developed without human intervention, by natural selection. The man who had found dissection and anatomy repellent now dissected pigeons, ducks and even dogs. The bones in the wing of a domesticated duck, he found, weighed less than those of a wild duck; while the leg bones weighed more in the former than in the latter: because the wild duck did more flying and the domesticated one more waddling.[49]

One reason Lyell had urged him to publish was an article by Alfred Russel Wallace in 1855 that seemed close to Darwin's theories. Wallace indeed wrote to Darwin in June 1858 outlining his own theory, which was identical: and enclosing an essay he had written on the subject. Darwin professed himself 'quite upset' that Wallace appeared to have jumped ahead of him, though he did tell Lyell that 'there is nothing in Wallace's sketch which is not written out much fuller in my sketch copied in 1844'.[50] Darwin was anxious to avoid a charge of plagiarism, and told Lyell of two other scientists with whom he had shared his theories. He wondered whether he could now publish 'honourably', having been sent Wallace's findings. He told Lyell: 'I would far rather burn my whole book than that he or any man should think that I had behaved in a paltry spirit.' To avoid difficulties, Darwin and Wallace agreed to present papers outlining their views to the Linnean Society in London on 1 July 1858. This, and not *On the Origin of Species*, was the first pronouncement of the theory of natural selection. Later that summer Darwin started to write a book unlike the intensely detailed academic treatises he had written before, but designed to secure the widest possible audience for his revolutionary views. Lyell persuaded John Murray, his publisher, to issue it, on 24 November 1859. He arranged to print 1,250 copies, which Darwin considered 'rather too large an edition': it sold out almost at once.[51]

The publication of *On the Origin of Species* is widely regarded as the key intellectual event of the era. It advanced rationalism, undermined religion, and radicalised the comprehension of existence. So thorough was Darwin's research that his ideas could not intelligently be dismissed in the way that serious scientific opinion had attacked, fifteen years earlier, the anonymously written *Vestiges of Creation*, which had speculated on how different species had come about. Gertrude Himmelfarb has observed that 'it was *On the Origin of Species* that precipitated the "war of science and religion", a war that was as confused, complicated, and ambiguous – indeed, as unwarlike – as any that has ever been fought.'[52]

There were many common denominators between Lyell and Darwin, but none so significant as this: if what they said was true, the Bible could not be interpreted literally. And, if the Bible could not be interpreted literally, this meant – in the eyes of some clergy – that the whole basis of Christianity and the Christian faith was open to question. Although Darwin had not put this question himself, there were others happy enough to do so: not to humiliate organised religion, but to defend Darwin's work. And none was a more partisan supporter than the man who came to be known as his 'bulldog', Thomas Henry Huxley.

Huxley had had an unconventional upbringing. Born in 1825, he had a brief formal schooling in Ealing, at a school run by his father that went bust. He was thereafter educated at home, where he read all he could find on science. He also read much Carlyle, which exacerbated his instinctive questioning of his parents' evangelical Christianity. His two sisters married surgeons, and at fourteen he was apprenticed to one himself. He briefly attended an anatomy school in London, and in 1842 won a scholarship to the Charing Cross Hospital medical school, which had only recently opened. Lack of money prevented him from finishing his medical degree, so he joined the Navy and became an assistant ship's surgeon specialising in scientific research.

As his ship, HMS *Rattlesnake*, sailed around Africa to Australia, Huxley collected sea-creatures and dissected them, examining them under his microscope. He surveyed the inner passage of the Great Barrier Reef in 1847–8 and wrote learned articles about what he discovered in the sea-life there. When he returned to England late in 1850 he found himself acclaimed, and acquired supporters such as Lyell and Richard Owen, the celebrated anatomist. He also became more radical and dislocated from religion, despising the class system and the deference given to those at its zenith, and angry at the State's inadequate support of scientific research. He finally left the Navy in 1854 and became a lecturer in natural history and palaeontology at the School of Mines. The following year he became Fullerian professor of physiology at the Royal Institution, and also began a series of regular lectures at working men's colleges. Around 1853 he met Darwin and, although the two men did not agree on everything, a friendship was built upon the younger man's respect for the older.

Darwin's thinking strongly influenced Huxley, giving him intellectual support to gainsay the idea of the Creation, which he had come to

see as an obstacle to progress in scientific understanding. Huxley put
the descent of man at the centre of his studies. His first target had
been Richard Owen, who had defined a new subclass for *Homo sapiens*
based on its having a lobe in the brain that Owen had called a
hippocampus minor. Huxley dismissed this at the Royal Institution in
1858. His support was invaluable to Darwin, not least because of
Huxley's growing influence in the academic world, both as a teacher
and an administrator. He had just successfully campaigned for London
University to have a science faculty and to award the BSc degree; later
he would campaign for the introduction of science into the school
curriculum, and for women to be educated to take their place in intellectual society as men did. Also, Huxley and Darwin developed a circle
of friends and fellow scientists who shared their broadly secularist,
research-based view of science, and created an atmosphere in which
Darwin's theories of evolution and natural selection would not be
dismissed out of hand.

Huxley wrote glowing reviews of *On the Origin of Species*, seeing it
as a massive intellectual breakthrough but also as a weapon in the battle
for the cause of liberalism. He was fascinated not just by evolution but
by the pursuit of perfectibility of the species, and of a more metaphysical
definition of perfectibility too. He attended a meeting of the British
Association for the Advancement of Science held in Oxford – appropriately, in the University's Natural History Museum – at the end of June
1860. There was a debate on Darwin's research between Huxley and the
Bishop of Oxford, Samuel Wilberforce. Huxley had already warmed up
in a public attack on Owen, who had reiterated his theory of the
hippocampus minor, which Huxley now saw as a contradiction of
Darwin.

Bishop Wilberforce was the son of the emancipator of the slaves; he
was also known as Soapy Sam, after his saponaceous personality. He
was a Fellow of the Royal Society, and was a vice-president of the British
Association, which existed to popularise the study. He was also an orni-
thologist. He became Bishop of Oxford in 1845, when just forty. As an
undergraduate he had been famed for his debating skills, and was
regarded as one of the most formidable orators of his day. Oratory,
however, relies to an extent for its success on content: and Wilberforce,
though a regular writer for the reviews on scientific and neo-scientific
subjects, had less idea what he was talking about than Huxley. Darwin

was ill and could not attend, but was lucky to have so intelligent and articulate a partisan as Huxley. He had written to Darwin the previous February to describe an argument he had with Wilberforce about *On the Origin of Species*, in which the Bishop had said the book was 'the most unphilosophical he had ever read'.[53]

No transcript exists of the debate: but many accounts were written, and from them it is possible to reconstruct a sense of what went on. The most comprehensive reconstruction was by J. R. Lucas. Wilberforce claimed to be guided by logic. He objected to Darwin's views 'solely on scientific grounds'.[54] He did not, he added, find against Darwin because he believed him 'to contradict what it appears . . . is taught by Revelation.' One report said that he found against Darwin because when his theory was 'tried by the principles of inductive science' it 'broke down'. He told his audience that Darwin had offered a hypothesis, not a theory; and he was glad to know that many scientists felt as he did, and that the theory was 'opposed to the interests of science and humanity'. Darwin had been 'unphilosophical' and had founded his beliefs on 'fancy'.

Wilberforce's key point was that there was no evidence in the geological record of one species mutating into another – rock pigeons, as he said, had always been rock pigeons. According to Lucas, Darwin explained this away by referring to the 'imperfection of the geological record'. At the time, Darwin was modest enough to admit that Wilberforce, in his reading of *On the Origin of Species*, had spotted all his conjectural points, and had made hay with them. Lucas cited a reminiscence written in 1898 in *Macmillan's Magazine*, by one who was present. The writer recalls what became the most celebrated moment of this celebrated battle, when Huxley demolished Wilberforce. The Bishop, 'turning to his antagonist with a smiling insolence, he begged to know, was it through his grandfather or his grandmother that he claimed descent from a monkey? On this Mr Huxley slowly and deliberately arose. A slight tall figure stern and pale, very quiet and very grave, he stood before us, and spoke those tremendous words – words which no-one seems sure of now, nor I think, could remember just after they were spoken, for their meaning took away our breath, though it left us in no doubt as to what it was. He was not ashamed to have a monkey for his ancestor; but he would be ashamed to be connected with a man who used great gifts to obscure the truth.' The writer adds that the effect of this rebuke 'was tremendous'. A woman fainted and had to be carried out. Although Wilberforce still took much of the audience with him, Huxley was later mobbed and acclaimed for what a substantial minority present saw as his triumph. When somebody said to him later that he wished the moment could come again, Huxley answered: 'Once in a lifetime is enough, if not too much.'

Another version has Huxley saying he would rather be descended from an ape than from a bishop; but there is less satisfactory evidence of that. He also apparently turned to his neighbour before answering Wilberforce and pronounced: 'The Lord hath delivered him into my hands.'[55] Some thought that, whatever was said precisely, Huxley's tone had been insolent; but then so did others believe the Bishop's had been, and he was overdue for a comeuppance. Huxley himself denied having been so rude to Wilberforce, and when the Bishop's biography attributed the remark to Huxley some years later, Huxley demanded, and received, a correction. Huxley believed he had said: 'If I had to choose between being descended from an ape or from a man who would use his great powers of rhetoric to crush an argument, I should prefer the former.' He did admit, in September 1860, that he felt Wilberforce had gone at him 'vulgarly' and he had, therefore, 'determined to punish him'. Another observer, Canon Farrar, later told Huxley's son that the Bishop had lowered the spirits of his own supporters who were present, because 'they recognised that the Bishop had forgotten to behave like a gentleman'. Wilberforce, in protesting against the theory of natural selection, was supported by some scientists present, notably Owen and Benjamin Brodie. Huxley's main point against Wilberforce, however, was that Darwin was a starting point in the new theory of evolution – it was a basis upon which a new line of inquiry could proceed. It was not a finished theorem. But it broke sufficient new ground to stimulate further inquiry, and to change, as it were, the direction of travel.

There were other bizarre incidents at this sensational meeting, which attracted 700 people because of the interest that had so quickly blown up around Darwin's work. A don disputed Darwin's evolutionary theory on the grounds that Homer had existed three millennia earlier and yet had never been replicated, let alone improved upon; and a naval officer from the Beagle held up a bible and pleaded that it, and not Darwin, should be the basis of all understanding. This was truly a turning point; though like many such moments in history, its pivotal nature was only more apparent as time passed. It guaranteed Darwin a serious hearing. It threw the Church on the defensive. It boosted Huxley's reputation as a scientist. It did no damage at the time to Wilberforce, and indeed was looked back upon for the rest of the Victorian period as a triumph for him. Given what we now know, from the line of inquiry established by Darwin, what happened in Oxford on 30 June 1860 can be seen with hindsight as the end of the medieval world, whose ideas were so often rooted in blind faith, and the start of the modern, whose ideas were so often rooted in rationalism. Over the next few decades Darwin's conjectures were replaced by facts, not least as the study of geology became more detailed. Huxley, unlike Darwin, remained implacably opposed to clergy, and refused to believe (even, according to Lucas, when confronted with them) that any clergyman could believe in evolution. Huxley felt that science and religion had to contradict each other. Wilberforce seems, oddly, never to have been quite so dogmatic, nor so determined to seek a confrontation between the two forces. That, though, may have been because Soapy Sam was not interested in the possibilities of defeat, and Huxley felt a rational future relied upon Sam and his kind being defeated.

At the end of *On the Origin of Species*, Darwin asks:

Why . . . have all the most eminent living naturalists and geologists rejected this view of the mutability of species? It cannot be asserted that organic beings in a state of nature are subject to no variation; it cannot be proved that the amount of variation in the course of long ages is a limited quantity; no clear distinction has been, or can be, drawn between species and well-marked varieties . . . The belief that species were immutable productions was almost unavoidable as long as the history of the world was thought to be of short duration; and now that we have acquired some idea of the lapse of time, we are too apt to assume, without proof, that the geological record is so perfect that it would have afforded us plain evidence of the mutation of species, if they had undergone mutation.[56]

He compared the trouble he was having in being believed with Lyell's struggle thirty years earlier: 'We are always slow in admitting any great change of which we do not see the intermediate steps . . . the mind cannot possibly grasp the full meaning of the term of a hundred million

years; it cannot add up and perceive the full effects of many slight variations, accumulated during an almost infinite number of generations.'

Darwin had to manage the controversy stimulated by *On the Origin
of Species* for the rest of his life: he died in 1882. He would not publicly
support atheism – even Huxley, younger and more radical, would never
go further than to describe himself as an agnostic, and someone so
philosophically committed as Mill still found it hard to be anything other
than a closet atheist – but he did say to a correspondent in 1880, who
had asked him 'do you believe in the New Testament?' that 'I am sorry
to have to inform you that I do not believe in the Bible as a divine
revelation, and therefore not in Jesus Christ as the Son of God.'[57] When
On the Origin of Species was published Harriet Martineau, the essayist
and bosom friend of Mrs Carlyle, wrote that it overturned the argument
for 'the being of God' by design.[58]

Between 1860 and 1872 there were five more editions of the book,
many of the changes answering specific points raised by Darwin's critics.
The phrase now most associated with him – 'the survival of the fittest'
– first appeared in the fifth edition in 1869. In 1871 he published *The
Descent of Man*, in which he addressed the very point he had been
unwilling to broach in his earlier treatise: that man was descended from
apes. This caused profound shock. The wife of the Bishop of Worcester
reportedly said to him: 'Descended from the apes! My dear, let us hope
that it is not true, but if it is, let us pray that it will not become generally known.'[59] As we shall see, among those who criticised him was
Samuel Butler, in his own way one of the most remarkable men of the
time, and grandson of Darwin's headmaster. Butler was not one of those
opponents who felt God was being mocked by Darwin's theories, for
he mocked God better than almost anyone. Rather, he disputed that
Darwin was breaking new ground.

Huxley was not merely the great defender of Darwin: he was also
the great defender of science, and the man who more than any other
in the 1860s and 1870s used his clout to argue for the better teaching –
indeed, in most cases, simply the teaching – of science in schools, and
of the establishment of scientific departments in universities. By his
efforts he gave practical force to the secular idealism of Mill, ensuring
that those to whom liberty was being extended had the education to
deal with it, and with a world in which technological advance was
replacing religious superstition. His motivation appears at all times to

advance rationalism. The Clarendon Commission on the Public Schools – whose work is discussed in Chapter 12 – criticised the finest schools in the land for hardly bothering to teach science. For Huxley, this was a scandal. One of the great problems, however, was where to find qualified teachers. In time, Huxley would do all he could to alleviate this – not just by encouraging the wider teaching of science in universities, but by offering six-week summer schools for teachers in his laboratories at South Kensington, as soon as they had opened in 1871: and he managed to persuade Gladstone's administration to pay for them.

The most renowned scientists, such as Huxley and Darwin, had been largely self-taught, or had had to conduct research unguided. The clerical domination of the leading schools and the older universities did not allow much for those who would teach science, though the establishment of the Natural Sciences tripos at Cambridge coincided with Huxley's arrival as a lecturer in palaeontology at the School of Mines in Jermyn Street in the mid-1850s. His eventual achievement (in the teeth of opposition from most of the scientific establishment) was to help turn the School of Mines into the Normal School of Science at South Kensington. In time the Normal School would become the Royal College of Science and, finally, Imperial College, the most formidable scientific institution in the country. But that process would require much struggle and advocacy, not least by Huxley.

When the South London Working Men's College was established in 1868 Huxley accepted the role of honorary principal, in which he served until 1880, and where his involvement was far from just ornamental. He was determined to take education, and especially scientific education, to the people. He wished to redefine what was understood by education: he had told an audience at the University of London in 1858 that 'the time is rapidly approaching when no person who is not moderately conversant with scientific matters will be able to take part in ordinary conversation, or to consider himself an educated person.'[60] When Forster's Education Act of 1870 allowed for the formation of school boards, Huxley stood for election to the one in London, and was successful. From this he was further elected to be chairman of the London School Board's Scheme of Education Committee, which established the pattern of infant, junior and senior schools that was copied across the country. In this position, Huxley used his influence to expand the reach of the curriculum, to secure the independence of teachers, to

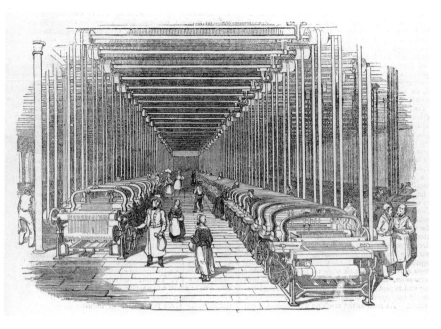

A dark satanic mill: cotton manufacturing in the 1830s.

The romance of Manchester, seen from the Cliff, Higher Broughton.

Anthony Ashley-Cooper, 7th Earl of Shaftesbury, the operative's friend.

Sir Robert Peel, the great repealer.

Sir James Graham, the hard man of Peel's Cabinet.

Chartism's damp squib: the revolution that never was,
Kennington Common, 10 April 1848.

Cobden, the driving force of
Corn Law repeal; his statue at
Mornington Crescent, London.

Peel puts bread in the public's
mouths, 1846.

Family Prayers, by Samuel Butler: the joy of Victorian religious life.

Butterfield's masterpiece: the interior of All Saints, Margaret Street, London.

James Anthony Froude, who made his own nemesis.

Arthur Hugh Clough, for whom the struggle naught availed.

The Revd Charles Kingsley: Christian Socialist, Darwinist, chain-smoker and father of *The Water Babies*.

Frederick Denison Maurice, inventor of Christian Socialism.

Letter from T. H. Huxley to Darwin, 20 July 1868, with
Darwin enthroned as a bishop.

Bishop Wilberforce, or Soapy Sam,
himself descended from apes.

Thomas Henry Huxley, Darwin's bulldog
and one-man Enlightenment.

Samuel Butler, a self-portrait of the artist as a difficult man.

John Stuart Mill, sometimes more logical than practical.

Samuel Smiles, who helped others to help themselves.

Sir James Fitzjames Stephen, the nemesis of Mill.

Benjamin Disraeli, 1st Earl of Beaconsfield, and Carlyle's 'superlative Hebrew Conjuror'.

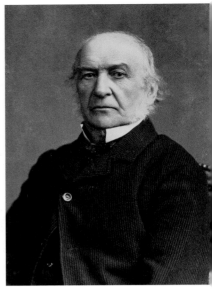

William Ewart Gladstone, the rising hope of those stern and unbending Liberals.

Robert Lowe, a Utilitarian in the Cave of Adullam.

Richard Assheton Cross, driving force of Disraeli's second government.

enforce standards of hygiene the better to preserve health, to institute a regime of physical training, and to discourage and strictly regulate corporal punishment. He also introduced drawing and music, the latter of which he described (showing the breadth of his own mind) as 'one of the most civilising and enlightening influences which a child can be brought under.'

Also, despite his own apparent religious scepticism, and his belief in secularism, he insisted on Bible study being a part of his new curriculum: though this was as much for aesthetic reasons, given what he regarded as the majesty of the Authorised Version, as for any idea that it might inculcate a moral framework into the reader. The condition he expressed was that it be taught 'with rigid exclusion of any further theological teaching than that contained in the Bible itself.' However, he hoped the lives of the children would be 'governed and guided by the love of some ethical ideal'.[61] In saying this he was in tune with prevailing public opinion. He did want morality taught in schools, seeing it as something common to those who argued for 'religious' and 'secular' teaching, and an example of the futility of observing such divisions.

He had the effect of wrenching a primitive and inadequate education system into the modern world, and making it see the realities of that world. He accomplished this in just eighteen months, giving himself a breakdown of health through overwork, but did say that 'I can look back upon that period of my life as perhaps the part of it least wasted.'[62] He was motivated by his belief that the uneducated classes contained an immeasurable resource of ability of which all were unaware, including the people themselves. He wanted those of talent not to have their educational lives cut off at the age of twelve or thirteen when they left elementary schools: not for the utilitarian reason that they might profit themselves and the country by developing themselves further, but because it was their right to be fulfilled and cruel to them to prevent them from expanding their minds.

Huxley wanted social reform outside of education. In 1870, as president of the British Association, he told an audience in Liverpool of his outrage at seeing 'unwashed, unkempt, brutal people side by side with indications of the greatest refinement and the greatest luxury'; and he sympathised with trades unions and socialists in their 'endeavour to put down the savagery of the world.'[63] The way out was 'a great educational ladder, the bottom of which shall be the gutter, and the top of which shall be the University.' On another occasion he observed that 'it is futile to expect a hungry and squalid population to be anything but violent and gross.'[64] Huxley toured the country, noting how even relatively impoverished towns in the north of England managed to find the money, with the help of local businesses, to establish technical institutes. London, by contrast, seemed uninterested in training its working men to be better and to progress. To this end he upbraided wealthy livery companies for not doing more to enhance the skills of artisans in their respective trades. After some prodding, the livery companies funded a technical college in Finsbury that opened in 1883, and the next year opened the City and Guilds College in South Kensington. Although the City provided the money, Huxley provided the expert advice on what should be taught – and how.

V

Huxley thought there could be no accommodation between Christianity and Darwinism. However, to some a synthesis was possible. Charles Kingsley was one such. To generations of children in the late nineteenth and twentieth centuries *The Water-Babies*, a tale he wrote for his son Grenville in 1862, is a fairy-story with a message about the wrongness of mistreating children; from that position it moves effortlessly into a morality tale: 'Those that wish to be clean, clean they will be; and those that wish to be foul, foul they will be.'[65] The book is a description of the life of Tom, a chimney-boy routinely abused by his master, who falls in a river, drowns, and is recreated as an aquatic sprite. In this new existence he comes under the sway of fairies such as Mrs Doasyouwouldbedoneby and Mrs Bedonebyasyoudid, who run a regime in which evil is punished and good is rewarded: the message is clear. However, the book is also a vigorous defence of Darwin's theories and, more to the point, of the importance and necessity of rigorous scientific inquiry; and an assault on the shallowness and prejudice of his critics, by one who as a clergyman might have been expected to count himself among them. He did not feel the theory contradicted his faith. He wrote to Darwin in November 1859 on what Darwin described as 'such notions as mine being *not* opposed to a high conception of the Deity'.[66]

In *The Water-Babies* the author creates a universe based on Christianity: Grimes, the chimney-sweep who abuses Tom, also falls in the river, but he goes to hell. Tom seeks to effect the man's rescue, despite the evil Grimes did to him: and Grimes is duly given an opportunity for redemption. It is the type of world Dr Arnold described to his charges. Kingsley did not doubt the nature and purpose of heaven: the world of the water-babies, which serves as his metaphor for heaven, was filled with

> all the little children whom the good fairies take to, because their cruel mothers and fathers will not; all who are untaught and brought up heathens, and all who come to grief by ill-usage or ignorance or neglect; all the little children who are overlaid, or given gin when they are young, or are let to drink out of hot kettles, or to fall into the fire; all the little children in alleys and courts, and tumbledown cottages, who die by fever, and cholera, and measles, and scarlatina, and nasty complaints which no-one has any business to have, and which no-one will have someday, when folks have common sense; and all the little children who have been killed by cruel masters, and wicked soldiers.[67]

Yet there is another dimension to the book that illustrates Kingsley's radicalism, and his willingness to embrace the intellectual currents that would precipitate the modern world and advance the secularism that challenged Kingsley's most deeply held beliefs. *The Water-Babies* satirises the response to *On the Origin of Species*, a book Kingsley read before its publication, and which he had welcomed. Writing to Darwin in November 1859, days before publication, Kingsley professed he had 'long since, from watching the crossing of domesticated animals and plants, learnt to disbelieve the dogma of the permanence of species.' More to the point, he had 'learnt to see that it is just as noble a conception of Deity, to believe that He created primal forms capable of self development into all forms needful *pro tempore* and *pro loco*, as to believe that He required a fresh act of intervention to supply the lacunas which He Himself had made.'[68]

The Church of England's relationship with science in the nineteenth century and before can be gauged by its refusal, until the late 1820s, to countenance the teaching of geology in the universities. Kingsley uses his invention of the water-baby to highlight the need, in evaluating scientific claims, to rely solely on evidence. In answer to the statement 'but there are no such things as water babies', Kingsley replies: 'How do you know that? Have you been there to see? And if you had been there to see, and had seen none, that would not prove that there were none.'[69] He states: 'Wise men know that their business is to examine what is, and not to settle what is not.'[70] Kingsley was strongly partisan for Darwin, as shown by his ridiculing of Richard Owen's attempt to refute the idea of human evolution from apes. Owen had said the hippocampus minor in men proved they could not be descended from simians. Kingsley said there was a 'hippopotamus test' that showed whether an ancestor could have been an ape: he called the lobe the 'hippopotamus major'.[71]

Evolution is embraced. 'If he says that it is too strange a transformation for a land-baby to turn into a water-baby, ask him if he has ever heard of the transformation of Syllis, or the Distomas, or the common jelly-fish,' Kingsley directs his readers to ask a sceptic.[72] Mrs Bedonebyasyoudid announces that she may have the power 'to make beasts into men, by circumstance, and selection, and competition'.[73] Evolution brings with it a moral consideration: 'Whatever their ancestors were, men they are; and I advise them to behave as such, and act accordingly.' The sanction for not doing so is that Mrs Bedonebyasyoudid would turn a man back into a beast. And for Kingsley, inevitably, there is a further stage in the evolutionary process beyond what happens on earth. Tom 'went downward into the water; but we, I hope, shall go upward to a very different place.'[74] Kingsley tells the tale, but his imagination has been expanded by what Darwin made possible, the clergyman's ultimate tribute to the scientist. As Darwin, quoting Kingsley, noted in the preface to the third edition of On the Origin of Species in 1861, 'a celebrated author and divine has written to me that "he has gradually learnt to see that it is just as noble a conception of the Deity to believe that He created a few original forms capable of self-development into other needful forms, as to believe that He required a fresh act of creation to supply the voids caused by the action of His laws".'[75]

Kingsley was not the only clergyman to support Darwin's views, or to talk of the importance of scientific inquiry. The headmaster of Rugby, Frederick Temple, who would later become Bishop of Exeter and of London, gave a sermon at the June 1860 meeting in Oxford encouraging theologians to celebrate the strengths of scientific research rather than seek out what they saw to be its weaknesses. God was, he reminded his audience, responsible for science just as for the Bible. The journey further into secularism and rationalism had, however, begun. When Darwin published *The Descent of Man* in 1871, and introduced into the evolutionary picture mankind itself, the confrontation would become more intense and open. Adam and Eve would be written out of the script, and replaced, as man's ancestors, by apes. That something such as this would happen was apparent not merely from the publication of *On the Origin of Species*, but from the earlier work of Lyell and Lamarck.

Darwin's works, as they were disseminated among scientists across Europe, spread a message of secularism that it had not been his intention to advance. As Chadwick has put it:

> Not many men would read *The Origin*, or understand it if they read it. The secularising force was not Darwin the author of the book, or of several books. It was Darwin the symbol, Darwin the name which stood for a process, the name which was heard from one side to the other in the polemics of secularist platforms or journals, an imaginary Darwin, a vague Darwin, without the comfortable homely substantial outlines of the real naturalist of a Kentish village, but however imaginary and however vague still bearing a direct relationship to a scientific achievement, which few quite understood, the truth of which many doubted, but which everyone, without knowing quite what it was, knew to be a scientific achievement of the first magnitude.[76]

The battle between theists and atheists would continue into our own times. Himmelfarb reflected that, after the intellectual upheaval caused by Darwin, 'the final irony is to have the old stereotypes, of an enlightened science and a bigoted religion, replaced by new ones: a "scientific naturalism" that was dogmatic, narrow-minded, jealous of its newly-acquired authority, lacking social vision and emotional depth; and a "spiritualism" that was imaginative, open-minded, compassionate, receptive to new forms of consciousness and speculation.'[77] This may well overstate the case: but the role Christianity played in society would hereafter decline further, egged on by Nietzsche. The process had, however, been initiated by Coleridge in his homage to Kant, then continued by Carlyle in his obeisance to Goethe and Schiller. It was developed by disciples of Carlyle, such as Clough, long before Darwin had spoken, and incidentally pursued by freethinkers such as Mill. The stir caused by the Oxford Movement had had its corrosive effect too.

Religion would remain a public doctrine in British society, shored up by an established Church and by a monarch who was supreme governor of that Church. However, its personal applications would become less frequent and more discreet. It would soon be peculiar for a public figure to do what John Bright did in a speech in Birmingham in October 1858, when he returned to the political fray after a long and serious illness. 'In remembrance of all this,' he said, 'is it wrong in me to acknowledge here, in the presence of you all, with reverent and thankful heart, the signal favour which has been extended to me by the great Supreme?'[78] One twentieth-century commentator referred to this display as 'nause-ating', but it is quite likely that Bright said what he did entirely unselfconsciously.[79]

VI

The Christian churches were in some respects their own worst enemies in this era of change. John Ruskin, in his diary on 25 August 1850, showed how his generation were losing patience with methods of worship, in his case after enduring a long and tedious sermon in Edinburgh. 'Really I believe the only good of such sermons is the self-denial exercised in hearing them. How wrong our whole system is . . . . sitting patiently under a piece of dead Talk which would not be endured for one instant if it regarded any real business of life and is only endured because Christianity is not considered business at all. I wonder how St Paul would have liked being shown up into a box and told that he might talk about Christ till lunchtime – if he would do it decorously.'[80]

Some of his illustrious contemporaries, however, retained an unques-tioning and uncomplaining devotion. Florence Nightingale, writing in October 1868 to condole with an acquaintance on the loss of a mutual friend's second child in a short space of time, said:

'Father, thy will be done' – I have had occasion – this year in particular, when I lost the best and dearest of my pupils – to learn how hard it is to say this from the heart. But I have often had cause before. I have survived nearly all my fellow-workers.

But we know that their death is only given to reward the troubles they have suffered for the love of God. The fruit, tho' still in its bloom, was ripe for Him to gather. What cause have we, who loved them truly, to weep as dead those who live with Him in the land of the living? . . . the more we loved them, the more we ought to rejoice . . . to comfort ourselves for their deaths, let us think of our own.[81]

Yet this was the age that caused Owen Chadwick to write that 'contemporaries were agreed that the tone of society in England was more "secular". By that they meant the atmosphere of middle-class conversation; the kind of books which you could find on a drawing-room table, the contents of the magazines to which educated men subscribed whether they were religious or irreligious, the appearance of anti-Christian books on bookstalls at the railway station, the will-ingness of devout men to meet undevout men in society and to honour them for their sincerity instead of condemning them for their lack of faith.'[82]

One educated man who dealt in a matter-of-fact way with his own departure from devotion was James Fitzjames Stephen, who would become an eminent judge via a career as a controversial journalist, writing in the reviews. He had long wrestled with Christian practice and religion. In the 1840s he had disputed for months with his friend George Kitchin (who became Dean of Winchester) about the meaning of baptism. By 1870 he was writing to his brother Leslie that Newman was an 'old idiot', that Stanley was guilty of 'idiocy', and that he felt that 'a curse has descended upon the religious world of all denominations'.[83] Newman 'and his God Almighty' were especially in his sights: 'It is difficult to say whether the man himself, or the creature of his imagin-ation, is the greater fool.'

His father, Sir James Stephen, had had a similar conversation with Carlyle in 1853, after Carlyle had said that 'the Church of England was nothing else than a vast machinery for maintaining religious decorums'.[84] Stephen had been shocked that Carlyle thought they shared a view of religion: and wrote him a long letter saying it was not so. Carlyle had, however, disturbed him, just as he had disturbed other, younger intel-lectuals before him. Stephen admitted he had often felt he had 'difficul-ties', but had 'so seldom avowed them'.[85]

Until his mid-thirties, in the 1860s, Fitzjames Stephen had continued to believe God ordered all things. His belief then declined, as the secular influences on the masses – newspapers and their ability to participate in representative politics – were steering them away from religion too. He wrote to Lady Grant Duff in the spring of 1875 that:

Religious anniversaries . . . I never was taught at any time to attach the least importance to any of them . . . Easter and Christmas never were more than names to me, when I believed most fully in Christianity. As to the balance of good and evil in the Christian religion, which you suggest as a subject for a sermon, I was so much taken with the notion that I actually wrote last Sunday morning some pages of an imaginary sermon on the text 'what think ye of Christ?' I put it in the fire before I had got very far . . . I think in a few words that Christ was made the symbol of the yearning of the people of that age, after an ideal which they perceived was not, and could not be realised in this present world, which never had been realised, which has had its merits and its defects, and has been twisted into a thousand shapes, to suit the temper of the times, and which now I think be dis-onified [obsolete], and left to rest in peace. I come to bury Jesus, not to praise him – might be the motto of such a humour. [86]

He told her how he and his wife brought up their children:

we take them to church, and hold family prayers, which my wife reads. We have always told them that they must believe in God, in duty towards God, and a future state, and as opportunities afford, we have made them understand, and when they became old enough, say at 10 or thereabouts, we have told them – I have told them in the very plainest words – that our object in our religious teaching had been to give them feelings of reverence and a sense of duty to God, that we had taken the only means in our power to do so, but that those means were very imperfect; that a great part of what they heard in church, and read in the Bible, was not true, and that much of the teaching founded upon it by clergymen and others was most immoral and dangerous. I have never let any of my children be confirmed or take the sacrament, and have taken occasion to explain my views when confirmation was suggested to them. I have also made them read books which would show them historically what theology has done.

This diet had included Motley, Froude and Gibbon – 'and I am very much mistaken if after that anyone will ever get much theology in their heads.' He added: 'There is no harm in teaching children what is not true', and set out an Aristotelian creed: 'What is good? I can only say as Aristotle does. Fortitude – temperance – benevolence and justice are good.' By 1879 he was telling the same correspondent that he had just been reading his copy of the *Spectator*, which was 'the nearest approach that I ever make now, except on circuit, to going to church.'[87] The same year he wrote to Lord Lytton that his own disbelief was now profound, but he was concerned that the disease was spreading to those who lacked his own intellectual and moral fortitude and therefore could cope with this difficulty less well than he could. 'I feel much alarmed at the spread of my own opinions. I do not doubt their truth but I greatly doubt the capacity of people in general to bear them.'[88]

He outlined his views on religion more specifically to his children in a long, unfinished letter found and copied out in her neat hand by his wife after his death. It appears to have been written between 1872 and 1876, and so is contemporaneous with his masterpiece, *Liberty, Equality, Fraternity*. He told his children his ideas were meant for them 'as you reach the age at which such matters are apt to press heavily on the minds of all thoughtful persons', and said that 'a great part of my life has been spent in forming them'.[89] That last remark is unquestionably true. This *apologia pro vita sua* is entitled *The Nature of Belief*.[90]

Stephen wrote that 'I do not think it possible to separate a man's opinions on religious questions from the rest of his opinions', a view he had in common with Dr Arnold, though not for the same reasons. After a long disquisition on scepticism and common sense ('there is an important sense of the word sceptical, in which no man can be less sceptical than I') he advised them on the importance of reasoning on probabilities. He commended Mill's system of logic: for all their political differences, they had rationalism in common. 'Memory', he told them, 'therefore enters more or less into all our opinions and beliefs – but of all things memory is the most fallible.'

He talked of the limitations of knowledge, of language, and of the observations of the laws of nature. All this seems to be leading up to a rationalist dismissal of faith, consistent with much in his letters and other writings. However, the letter ends in mid-air. Perhaps he was too busy on the Bench to finish it; perhaps he never had the ruthlessness to impose, even by accident, his views on his children in this way; or perhaps he simply discussed it with them. The least likely explanation is that he had changed his mind and come back into the arms of God.

He discounted the notion that secularism was a mass intellectual movement, since his view was that most people were uneducated and therefore
incapable of participating in such a thing. Instead, there was 'a body of
singers able to drown all discords and to force the vast unmusical mass
to listen to them.'[91] Stephen had to admit defeat in the face of this assault
by the masses: 'To oppose Mr Mill's simple principle about liberty to
such powers as these is like blowing against a hurricane with a pair of
bellows.'[92]

It is ironic Stephen should have ended, on matters theological, in
roughly the same place as his bête noire, Mill. In the years before his
death in 1873 Mill went further than ever to profess scepticism about
religion, if not his atheism. He supported Charles Bradlaugh, the atheist
who, when asked to take the oath as an MP, refused; and he subscribed
to his various campaigns. When a candidate for parliament, Mill found
his enemies used his supposed atheism as a stick with which to beat
him. He expressed in the autumn of 1868 'a determination, on principle,
to answer no questions respecting my religious belief, because I would
not give any encouragement to a practice the effect of which would be
that when no objection could be made to a candidate either on the
ground of character or of political opinions, his opponents would
endeavour to extract from himself materials for raising a religious prejudice against him.'[93] To those who said his support for Bradlaugh proved
the point, he referred them to one of the arguments in *On Liberty*,
namely that 'atheists, as well as the professors of any, even the worst
religions, may be and often are, good men, estimable and valuable in
all the relations of life, and are entitled like all other persons to be judged
by their actions ("By their fruits ye shall know them" are the words of
Christ) and not by their speculative opinions.'[94]

Mill was alert to the potential damage that could be done to a man
in public life who strayed from the social orthodoxy of belief in God.
Somewhat disingenuously, he told another correspondent in November
1868 that 'if anyone again tells you that I am an atheist, I would advise
you to ask him, how he knows and in what page of my numerous writings he finds anything to bear out the assertion.'[95] When defeated at
Westminster in the election that same week he made a point of writing
to Bradlaugh saying that although his support of him might have cost
a few votes, it was not why he lost. 'In any case, it was the right thing
to do and I do not regret it.'[96]

On the Liberal wing of politics, such feelings about God were becoming common. In his 1874 tract *On Compromise*, John Morley – then thirty-six, and a leading intellectual of his generation – wrote that 'religion, whatever destinies may be in store for it, is at least for the present hardly any longer an organic power. It is not that supreme, penetrating, controlling, decisive part of a man's life which it has been and will be again.'[97] The assault on religion had, he felt, been accomplished 'as if by unseen hands': though the reasons for the retreat of the Sea of Faith were clear for all with eyes to see them. 'Those who dwell in the tower of ancient faiths look about them in constant apprehension, misgiving, and wonder, with the hurried uneasy mien of people living amid earthquakes.' Morley blamed the rigidities of the Church for failing to allow it to move with the intellectual spirit of the times. 'While the spirit of man expands in search after new light, and feels energetically for new truth, the spirit of the Church is eternally entombed within the four corners of acts of parliament.' He said this led to a system 'that begins by making mental indolence a virtue and intellectual narrowness a part of sanctity, ends by putting a premium on something too like hypocrisy.' The result was a Church that was 'a political army of obstruction to new ideas'.[98]

Morley had been at Oxford when 'the star of Newman had set, and the sun of Mill had risen in its stead'. His views were more typical by the 1870s. Samuel Butler made a career out of advancing them. But they were increasingly present among more established thinkers. On 2 May 1875 Ruskin noted that Carlyle was 'in an abusive humour; a sorrowful one.'[99] They discussed religion. Carlyle said 'on the whole the right command seems to be the voice of eternal nature.' He attacked Cardinal Manning as 'the most entirely complete representative of humbug we have in the world – "Yon beggarly bag of wind". I saying that I felt greatly minded sometimes to join the Catholics . . . C said "he would desire in such case rather to have me assassinated".' For good measure Carlyle then described the Talmud 'as far as he could learn, an odious rotten dunghill, with jewels scattered in it.' As for 'modern Protestantism', he said that 'you don't feel called on to accelerate by one moment the doom of it, which is legible enough to all men with eyes. They are universally recognizable as people of no sincerity of mind – a puddle of sentimentalities and hypocrisies of all kinds.'[100]

VII

No writer in the second half of the nineteenth century articulates social radicalism better than Samuel Butler; or illustrates better the reaction against early Victorian values. As with Mill in the generation before him – and Bentham in the generation before Mill – he advanced secularisation in the contemporary mind, stripping away religious bigotries, prejudices and superstitions seen as a brake on progress. However, whereas the utilitarians used rationalism to combat God, Butler used a mixture of bitter satire and hostility. His deconstruction and demolition of the Victorian religious mindset was effective, but not entirely rational: which was largely true of other aspects of Butler's life and character. He was deeply cynical, including about himself: 'When I was a boy at school at Shrewsbury,' he recorded in his *Note-Books*, 'old Mrs Brown used to keep a tray of spoiled tarts which she sold cheaper. They most of them looked pretty right till you handled them. We are all spoiled tarts.'[101]

His tone can be blamed upon his father. Butler was born in the rectory at Langar in Nottinghamshire in 1835 under the almost crushing weight of parental expectation. His father was a clergyman in the mould of Archdeacon Froude, and his reward was to become one of the great monsters of Victorian fiction when depicted as the Reverend Mr Pontifex in Butler's semi-autobiographical novel *The Way of All Flesh*. Butler, who in his private expressions as in many of his public ones was unacquainted with understatement, recorded that 'MY MOST IMPLACABLE ENEMY from childhood onward has certainly been my father.'[102] He also observed of family that 'more unhappiness comes from this source than from any other – I mean from the attempt to prolong family connection unduly and to make people hang together artificially who would never naturally do so. The mischief among the lower classes is not so great, but among the middle and upper classes it is killing a large number daily.'[103]

His grandfather, also Samuel Butler, was headmaster of Shrewsbury and then, in 1836, Bishop of Coventry and Lichfield. Butler went to Shrewsbury, in the family tradition, and then similarly to St John's College, Cambridge. Writing to tell his father, in 1853, that he had won a scholarship at John's (one of just five awarded to freshmen), Butler said 'I shall not make any bones about the oaths' that he had to swear in those days of the religious tests.[104] His friend and first biographer, Henry Festing Jones, noted that, when he was at John's, 'Butler had been taught to accept the Christian miracles as self-evident propositions and to believe in a personal anthropomorphic God. He had, at this time, never met any one who entertained a doubt on the matter.'[105]

His single-mindedness was clear as an undergraduate. In notes he made on 31 March 1855 he wrote that 'There are only 10 good men in John's; I am one; reader, calculate your chance of salvation.'[106] He quoted the observation of another Johnian, Bishop Selwyn, made a few months earlier in a series of addresses to the university, that 'the University church is a place too much neglected by the young men up here' and added: 'How far better would it be if each man's own heart was a little University Church, the pericardium a little University churchyard, wherein are buried the lust of the flesh, the pomps and vanities of this wicked world; the veins and arteries, little clergymen and bishops minis-tering therein, and the blood a stream of soberness, temperance and chastity perpetually flowing into it.' A 'Puseyite playing upon an organ' in the College 'playeth his own soul to damnation'. Simeonites he dismissed as 'an acknowledged humbug'.

He graduated twelfth in the first class of the Classical tripos, suffi-ciently high to be considered for a fellowship. He was expected to enter the Church: but it was quickly apparent that his doubts – to use the popular euphemism – would make that unfeasible. He worked for a few months in the slums of the parish of St James's Piccadilly, where he realised that seeking to improve the very poor by spiritual means was a waste of time: they needed money. One of his biographers has summed up Butler's problem with Christianity as being that 'he could not accept a religion that based itself upon the fundamental wickedness of humanity, whose practice was centred on the injunction "Thou shalt not", and whose doctrine pointed to the eternal divide of heaven and hell.'[107] Men such as Canon Froude and Canon Butler certainly took this view of doctrine; it was Butler's misfortune to have been brought up by one of them. 'Is there any religion,' he asked, 'whose followers can be pointed to as distinctly more amiable and trustworthy than those of any other? . . . I find the nicest and best people generally profess no religion at all, but are ready to like the best men of all religions.'

To his father's dismay he abandoned the idea of holy orders. Other ideas for his future vexed his parents. He had to be talked out of growing cotton in Liberia, but finally settled on being an artist even though 'for two or three years I could make no money by it' – as he said he wouldn't,

either, by going into the law, a possibility his father held out to him.[108]
By the late summer of 1859 the Reverend Mr Butler had had enough.
'If you choose to act in utter contradiction of our judgment and wishes
and that before having acquired the slightest knowledge of your powers
which I see you overrate in other points you can of course act as
you like. But I think it's right to tell you that not one sixpence will you
receive from me after your Michaelmas payment till you come to
your senses.'[109] He refused to fund him to go abroad: still angry at his son's
refusal to pursue ordination, he yelled: 'God give you a seeing eye some
day'.

Butler told his mother that 'if I am the pigheaded fool you think me
the best school for me is adversity.'[110] He told his father he would make
his own living. He started to insist that he be allowed to become an
artist. He had some talent for this, but his father was outraged. Father
and son had a negotiation about Samuel's emigrating. Once all other
avenues – diplomacy and the Army were also suggested – were exhausted,
Canon Butler agreed to let his son go and learn sheep-farming in New
Zealand: and to advance him the capital to do so. It was a business
transaction: and Samuel kept his word, making a profit after applying
himself to learn the mechanics of agriculture. His father advanced him
£4,000, a fortune, and Butler sailed from Gravesend in September 1859.
He sat on deck as his ship headed down the Thames. When he went to
bed that evening he failed, for the first time in his life, to say his prayers,
an event so tumultuous that he recorded it in his notebook. In retrospect,
it was more surprising that the ritual had lasted that long. On arrival in
New Zealand, he learned that a ship on which he had originally intended
to sail had sunk with the loss of all on board.

He found some virgin land that would make excellent pasture, and
this was the basis of the commercial success of his venture. This was
not his only enterprise. He also explored the country, and in proper
Victorian fashion sought to improve the cultural climate of the colony
by organising art exhibitions. Perhaps more significantly, he lost what
remained of his faith: he told a friend in 1862 that 'he no longer considered himself a Christian'.[111] He studied the Gospels and was exercised
by their inconsistencies. Since he could find no evidence that Christ died
on the cross, he decided there had been no Resurrection.

He returned to England in 1864, his success having created an investment that would pay him £800 a year, liberating him from his father.

However, some injudicious business decisions in the 1870s made him dependent again, until his father's death in 1886 left him with an inheritance. He was also liberated from his father's doctrines, and made no secret of his own apostasy. This led to a rebuke from his aunt, Anna Russell, who suspected he had been trying to wean her son away from Christianity: she complained about 'the influence you are exerting on other[s], younger, and less skilled in argument than yourself – leading them. It may be, to make the same shipwreck of faith and hope that you have made.'[112] This only provoked Butler to write to her at length about his conception of God, causing more shock and dismay. So settled were his family in their beliefs that to find him so resolute against them – more resolute than they knew, given the anonymity of Butler's writings on the subject at that time – prevented them from grasping his radical course.

He set himself up in London and sought to make a career as a painter, enrolling as a student at several art schools successively over a period of seven years. He was heavily under the influence of Ruskin, having read *The Seven Lamps* at John's. He then read his writings on painting. At this time he painted his best-known and perhaps best picture, *Family Prayers*, a representation of the grim domestic life at Langar that in its suffocating sense of order and closed-mindedness displays his feelings about his family and his upbringing better than words could. At Heatherley's art school in Newman Street he befriended a fellow student, Eliza Savage, who became a muse to him, and urged him to write fiction. Charles Darwin, no less, had congratulated Butler in 1865 on his 'rare powers of writing'.[113] Butler was a man of strong, almost comically polarised, likes and dislikes, and one of the latter was the novel. However, Miss Savage persisted; and when Butler failed to achieve his ambition to become a student at the Royal Academy, he had a change of heart.

He wrote his anonymous novel *Erewhon*, about a utopia based on his experience of New Zealand, and a society in which religion is rejected but in which the Church appears, to be satirised, as a bank. The cult of Ydgrun, a goddess of pragmatism and common sense, has replaced old deities. The truly successful worship her; she is based on Thomas Morton's character Mrs Grundy, a byword for an arbiter of respectability and good sense in society. Butler also undermines parenthood, attacking the notion that parents inevitably know best. *Erewhon* was a critical success when published in 1872. When it was reported that Butler was the author, and word reached Langar, its godlessness shocked his family. His father took his advice not to read it, but word about it caused great unhappiness: so much so that his sister Harriet wrote and ordered him to write a letter of regret, which he did – but later destroyed. His father was forced to admit, in a letter of 12 June 1872, that 'I know that there is a great deal of scepticism in the world'; but he added: 'That unbelief is the badge of the wise and excellent of the earth or of great array of them I totally deny.'[114] To this Butler has added: 'Who ever said it was?' His father professed to be distressed at his son losing the faith that he held so strongly: but the wound went even more deeply. He asked Butler not to visit Langar 'at present' while he and his wife took in the fact that they had a heretic for a son.

Butler had an unconventional approach to novel-writing as he did to everything else, and derided the views of literary society. He wrote to Miss Savage in March 1873: 'I have finished *Middlemarch*. It is very bad indeed.'[115] Nearly two years later, he told her: 'I have been reading a translation of Goethe's *Wilhelm Meister*. Is it good? To me it seems perhaps the very worst book I ever read. No Englishman could have written such a book. I cannot remember a single good page or idea, and the priggishness is the finest of its kind I can call to mind. Is it all a practical joke?'[116] She said she had read it in her teens and found it 'tiresome . . . I shall not read *Wilhelm Meister* again.'[117]

In June 1873 Lord Pembroke sent Gladstone, his godfather, a copy of Butler's next work, *The Fair Haven*, describing the author as 'a modern freethinker of the most thoroughgoing sort, and all the defence of religion and dogma and the refutation of doubt are written in a spirit of carefully concealed irony'.[118] He continued: 'It is a satire of almost repulsive bitterness. Yet its real nature is so cleverly disguised that more than one church paper has treated it to a solemn and favourable review.' He described Butler as being of a school of freethinker 'whose glory and pride is their recklessness of consequences . . . I hope you will forgive me [for sending him the book]. I feel horribly guilty.' Gladstone was duped, but soon corrected himself. 'Dear George, since I wrote to you on Sunday I have learned that the "The Fair Haven" is the work of a writer who does not believe in Christianity. It took me in.'[119] A few days later he added: 'It is rather deplorable that he should bear the name of Butler, but I hope he may grow to be more worthy of it.'[120]

In 1865 Butler had written articles on the Resurrection, which he had sent to Darwin, who had regarded them as 'written with much force, vigour, and clearness'.[121] These developed via a pamphlet entitled, with Butlerian irony, *The Evidence for the Resurrection of Jesus Christ*, into *The Fair Haven*. Miss Savage had been consulted on the manuscript and pronounced it 'wonderful'.[122] When the book was published anonymously in 1873 he sent Darwin a copy. 'It has interested me greatly and is extremely curious . . . it will be a curious problem whether the orthodox will have so good a scent as to detect your heresy.'[123] He told him that 'Leslie Stephen, a regular reviewer, who was lunching here, knew you were the author' and added: 'I have been surprised at the strength of the case which you make for Jesus not having died on the cross.'

The book purports to be a justification of Christian faith, published posthumously with a memoir of the author by his equally fictional brother. Butler felt he had given an intellectual view of the Resurrection in his earlier pamphlet: but he knew such matters had an emotional side, and in this book sought to display that too. When we are told the author died of a brain disease after years of mental indisposition, we should take the hint. The book does indeed purport to be a defence of Christianity: but it is a defence launched by so third-rate a mind that it destroys the very thing it allegedly sought to protect. By taking in various reviewers Butler proved his main point, that the intellectual quality and percipience of many churchmen was deplorably low, and their determination to be convinced in the face of evidence against them was deeply depressing. As the 'author', John Pickard Owen, says, 'Never was there a time when such an exposition [of the foundations of belief] was wanted so much as now. The specious plausibilities of pseudo-science have led hundreds of thousands into error; the misapplication of geology has ensnared a host of victims, and a still greater misapplication of natural history seems likely to devour those whom the perversion of geology has spared.'[124]

Owen goes on, in a bravura display of the very temper Butler was so determined to expose and ridicule: 'Not that I have a word to say against *true* science: true science can never be an enemy of the Bible, which is the text-book of the science of the salvation of human souls as written by the great Creator and Redeemer of the soul itself, but the Enemy of Mankind is never idle, and no sooner does God vouchsafe to us any clearer illumination of His purposes and manner of working than the Evil One sets himself to consider how he can turn the blessing into a curse; and by the all-wise dispensation of Providence he is allowed so much triumph as that he shall sift the wise from the foolish, the faithful from the traitors.'

This blundering attitude permeates the book: had Gladstone not been offended by its mocking of his faith, he would doubtless have been by the extended nature of the single joke upon which the book is based: that proselytisers are so intellectually inept that they inevitably wreck their own case. Tackling those who doubt the Gospels, Owen says that 'if it could be shewn that the belief in Christ's reappearance did not arise until after the death of those who were said to have seen him, when actions and teachings might have been imputed to them that were not theirs, the case would be different; but this cannot be done; there is nothing in history better established than that the men who said that they had seen Christ alive after he had been dead, were themselves the first to lay aside all else in order to maintain their assertion.'[125] To compound his projection of Owen's stupidity, Butler has a friend write to Owen (and the letter is reproduced in the book) begging him to desist from his defence of Christianity, precisely because it is so weak in relying on disregarding the discrepancies in the Gospels. The friend refers him to the weaknesses in Paley's *Natural Theology*, one of the best-selling books of the nineteenth century and a vigorous defence of Christianity, and urges him to expose them: but Owen cannot.

The other necessary element in Owen's idiocy is his lack of understanding of ordinary people in the industrialised, and increasingly secularised, mid-nineteenth century. How wonderful, he surmises, must be the parable of the Labourers in the Vineyard to those who have lost their jobs: 'Few but those who have mixed much with the less educated classes, can have any idea of the priceless comfort which this parable affords daily to those whose lot it has been to remain unemployed when their more fortunate brethren have been in full work.'[126]

Owen is reduced to assertion, as he must be: since there is no proof of the bases of faith. Butler rubs this in. The Resurrection, he says, 'is proved externally by the most solid and irrefragable proofs, such as should appeal even to minds which reject all spiritual evidence, and recognise no canons of investigation but those of the purest reason.'[127] The absence of self-awareness, as well as of intellect, is glaring: 'The fact is, that both we and our opponents are agreed that nothing should be believed unless it can be proved to be true. We repudiate the idea that faith means the accepting of historical facts upon evidence which is insufficient to establish them. We do not call this faith; we call it credulity, and oppose it to the utmost of our power.'[128] The ultimate assertion is when he writes: 'As long as we can be sure that our Lord died and rose from the dead, we may leave it to our opponents to contend about the details of the manner in which each event took place.'[129]

Owen has no doubt, as he has repeatedly told his readers: but nor does he understand that his opponents do not dispute the manner of the Resurrection, but refuse to believe there was a Resurrection at all. The conclusion to his work is similarly absolute, and preposterous: 'In an age when Rationalism has become recognised as the only basis upon which faith can rest securely, I have established the Christian faith upon a rationalistic basis . . . Christianity and Rationalism are not only ceasing to appear antagonistic to one another, but have each become essential to the very existence of the other. May the reader feel this no less strongly than I do, and may he also feel that I have supplied the missing element which could alone cause them to combine. If he asks me what element I allude to, I answer Candour. This is the pilot that has taken us safely into the Fair Haven of universal brotherhood in Christ.'[130] It proved Butler's point that some churchmen, both Anglican and Catholic, felt he made such a good rebuttal of the rationalist arguments against Christianity that they commended the book highly. Miss Savage, indeed, sent the book to religious acquaintances purely to see their response; many were taken in. When people realised they had been duped, Butler was in the doghouse. In his lifetime, his subsequent works sold poorly, and were ignored by all but a small cognoscenti.

When he was plotting the book he wrote to his friend the Reverend F. S. Fleay, on 2 July 1872, telling him frankly of his intention to get 'good useful truth into quarters which it is never otherwise likely to reach: if I could only make an artificial fly with a hook in it so cunningly that the church shd rise at it (and I think I could) I fancy good might come of it.'[131] He promised that 'no rat can be smelt – it is deodorised thoroughly through my method.' He later told Fleay: 'I had written the first chapter in the character of one who had never doubted: I shall write it now in the character of a converted sceptic, it will make my insisting on people's understanding our side less suspicious.' He also made the shocking admission that 'I shall take it [the book] . . . to

Chapman and Hall or Macmillan and give my name and say that I have been converted and have written in consequence – indeed I think I shall let it be known among my friends (except at home – where I shall say nothing) that my opinions are undergoing a change – it will not be published as the author of *Erewhon*, but simply as "by one who has been reconverted" – or something of that sort.'[132]

After publication he told Fleay: 'I am told I have made the satire too quiet, and that it would have been better to have been broader . . . If more open the church papers might have passed it over as they do any serious attack, but now the unwary really go in danger by it. I feel pretty sure that I have taken the course which is most likely to make a row, and that is what I want.'[133] He admitted he still doubted what had happened at the 'resurrection'. 'If any reliance could be placed upon the gospel narratives of the resurrection – then I should think the resuscitation view most probable: but unfortunately we cannot depend upon a single word of them, and so all becomes conjectural. However, the hallucination theory is too great a jump for the average British mind.'

That section of Butler's intellectual energy not devoted to exposing organised religion to ridicule and obloquy was used more and more from the 1860s to the 1880s to attack Darwin. Darwin and Canon Butler had known each other at Shrewsbury and at university. Darwin had stimulated the Canon's lifelong interest in botany on an undergraduate reading holiday in Wales in 1828. Samuel Butler was acquainted with Darwin's children. A copy of *On the Origin of Species* – published while Butler was on his ship to New Zealand – had been sent to Butler. He read it intently. He wrote an article for a Christchurch newspaper about evolution in 1863. He noted at the end of his life that 'The Fair Haven got me into no social disgrace that I have ever been able to discover. I might attack Christianity as much as I chose and nobody cared one straw; but when I attacked Darwin it was a different matter. For many years *Evolution Old and New* and *Unconscious Memory* made a shipwreck of my literary prospects.'[134]

When *Erewhon* appeared Butler, who then was merely sceptical about Darwin rather than hostile to him, conciliated him about his suspicion that it contained a satire on *On the Origin of Species*. He twice visited Darwin at Down, and met other members of the family: relations were cordial. However, the more Butler reflected on Darwin's work, and the more he read elsewhere on the subject, the more his natural perversity drew him into conflict with Darwin. Butler may have been content that he had dealt, by 1877, with the fallaciousness of Christianity. He now decided to deal with the fallaciousness of the cult of Darwin. He did this despite – or, perhaps in his view, because of – his having had no scientific training: and when Darwin's supporters, many infinitely more expert than Butler, turned on him, he bore the wounds as a self-righteous martyr should.

Butler's first serious assault was *Life and Habit*, published in early 1878. He seems to have been motivated to write out of fear that someone would get there before him. 'Charles Darwin is being a good deal discredited,' he reflected, 'and if I do not bring my book out soon it may easily be too late to be effective.'[135] Francis Darwin, the great man's son, was on good terms with Butler, and they corresponded. In November 1877 Butler warned Francis that his imminent book 'has resolved itself into a downright attack upon your father's view of evolution, and a defence of what I conceive to be Lamarck's.'[136] He added, probably not disingenuously: 'I neither intended nor wished this, but was simply driven to it . . . reading your father more closely, and, I may add, more sceptically, the full antagonism between him and Lamarck came for the first time before me.' Butler claimed that 'I have always admitted, and in such way as to leave no sense of *arrière pensée,* the inestimable service which he [Darwin] has conferred upon us by teaching us to believe in evolution; though maintaining that he has led us to believe in it on grounds which I, for my own part, cannot accept.' Butler concluded by observing 'how sorry I was that your father should have been at school under my grandfather, inasmuch as I myself should dislike an attack from a son or grandson of Kennedy's, when I should not care twopence about it from any one else.'[137]

The younger Darwin criticised Butler for arguing that, with the exception of the theory of natural selection, his father had simply lifted all of the *Origin* from Lamarck. 'I went through the earlier part of my book and cut out all support of "natural selection" and made it square with a teleological view – for such I take it Lamarck's is.'[138] Francis replied:

'I confess to feeling lost in astonishment at your saying that you have cut out all support for Natural Selection, and also that you consider it a rope of sand. I suppose from this that you deny any effect to Natural Selection? If so you must find it rather a hard position to hold I should guess. Because of course you have to deny that such a thing as variations occur. For if you allow that variations occur you must allow that heredity is the rule, variations being only occasional lapses in perfect heredity. I suppose I am stereotyped from my education and association, but it does seem to me that if you grant this it is logically impossible to say that natural selection has no effect.[139]

This hit its target, for when Francis read Butler's *Life and Habit* over Christmas 1877 it was 'with great pleasure. I think all the analogy or identity between memory or heredity is very well worked out.'[140] Butler had sent two copies, one of which – if Francis thought it wise – was to be passed on to Darwin. Francis recommended to him the writings of Huxley, notably articles in the *Contemporary Review* entitled 'Animal Automation', in which 'he tried to show that consciousness was something superadded to nervous mechanism, like the striking of a clock is added to the ordinary growing parts.' However, Francis continued that 'I don't think I quite understand what your objection to Natural Selection is'. Darwin's letter came as a 'relief' to Butler, who had been 'afraid you might have considered *Life and Habit* unpardonable'.[141] He continued: 'Pitch into it and into me by all means. You cannot do me a greater service than to bundle me neck and crop out of my present position; this is what I try to do to those from whom I differ, and this is what I wish them to do to me if they think it worthwhile.'

The book had occupied almost two years of Butler's life. He stopped painting and concentrated on literary and intellectual endeavours, spending most mornings in the British Museum reading room. He developed a liking for Disraeli and spent much of 1878 reading his novels, admiring the man 'very heartily'.[142] He found some of the early work 'rather laborious reading' in spite of 'the many brilliant sayings'. Although he discussed some of his ideas with certain friends – notably, and usefully, Francis Darwin – he was seldom up to date on scientific progress. *Life and Habit*, as with other works where Butler tries to undermine Darwin, is a book of debating points rather than serious research. It shows something about the intellectual currents stirred up by Darwinism in the generation after the publication of *On the Origin of Species*. When Francis pointed out elementary mistakes, Butler accepted them and protested that he knew his work would require refinement. This led to three further attempts to outline why Darwin was wrong, none any more successful than the first.

Far from causing him to be taken seriously by Darwin and his supporters, each new work caused them to despair. Butler entirely failed to make them revise their views. By 1880 Darwin was writing that Butler considered him 'a rogue of the deepest dye', though his dismay was confined to his private letters: in public he made no reference to the dispute.[143] Butler could not drop the notion that Darwin was not the great original thinker others claimed: but their dispute (which Butler continued after Darwin's death in 1882) was only about means, not ends. It says much for the bizarre nature of Butler's character, and his almost autistic lack of self-awareness, that he persisted. The more the scientific world ignored him, the more determined he became to make them see how important his voice was.

His next attempt was *Evolution Old and New*, which he started as soon as *Life and Habit* was out of the hands of the reviewers. As well as reheating arguments from the earlier book, the new work introduced a more ad hominem tone: not because Butler wished to insult Darwin, but because his own desire for recognition for the value of his ideas was starting to override normal considerations of good manners. Matters took an even more unpleasant turn, unfortunately, because Butler believed he had discovered plagiarism. He accused Darwin, always the most upright of men, of failing to credit earlier scientists for their contribution to his theory. This entailed him standing up not merely for Lamarck, but for Darwin's own grandfather, Erasmus.

In February 1879, three months before the publication of *Evolution Old and New*, Dr Ernst Krause, a German biologist, published an article on Erasmus Darwin in a German scientific periodical, *Kosmos*. Darwin wrote to Krause in March 1879 proposing to have his article translated, accompanied by an introductory biographical sketch he would write himself. Butler's book was sent to Krause and, he alleged, 'Darwin expressly asked Dr K not to notice it'.[144] Butler's evidence was a letter from Krause to *Nature* on 27 January 1881, in which he said: 'Mr Darwin expressly solicited me to take no notice whatever of Mr Butler's book.' Butler then alleged Krause recast his article before translation using material from *Evolution Old and New*. 'He wound up with an angry attack on Evol O&N leaving the book as a pistol pointed at my head, but never (in consequence no doubt of Ch Darwin's request) mentioning it by name.'

Darwin's work on his grandfather appeared in November 1879. It appeared with what the preface claimed was an accurate translation of Krause, which it was not: this began to stoke Butler's ire. It said Butler's book had appeared after the *Kosmos* piece, but made no mention that it had been rewritten before translation 'with an eye' to *Evolution Old and New*. Darwin said nothing about the article being 'modified into an attack on it'. Butler said he wrote 'very civilly' to Darwin on 2 January 1880 to ask him to explain himself. Darwin immediately conceded the point and said that, when and if a second edition was called for, he would acknowledge what had happened. Butler, however, wanted a letter to *The Times* or the *Athenaeum*.

Darwin was shocked by Butler's vehemence: no wonder he thought himself perceived as a 'rogue of the deepest dye'. Butler – whose obsession seemed to suggest an unbalanced mind – wrote to the *Athenaeum* about Darwin's academic practices. 'I was so angry', he said, making an interesting comparison, 'at finding Darwin treat me exactly as he had treated Erasmus Darwin, Buffon, Lamarck and the Vestiges, that I wrote to *The Athenaeum* at once and stated the facts.' Unfortunately for all concerned, the magazine published it. Darwin – who had made a genuine mistake – was outraged and wished to repudiate Butler equally publicly. Huxley warned him against it, as it could only give credit to a man the scientific establishment regarded as something between a joke and a charlatan. Francis Darwin thought Huxley wrong: Darwin's intellectual force could have crushed Butler once and for all had he chosen to do so. Butler's own notes on the affair record that 'there was no reply from any one, which I took to mean no reply was possible.' As a result, yet another book was written. 'Knowing that C Darwin did not care about a newspaper letter, I wrote my book *Unconscious Memory* and stated the facts in full. It appeared November 1880.'

It prompted 'a savage attack in the *St James's Gazette*' (which pointed out, quite fairly, the lack of scientific research underpinning Butler's effusions), followed quickly by a 'coarsely vituperative' one by George Romanes, the evolutionary biologist and disciple of Darwin, in *Nature*. Romanes began: 'Mr Butler is already known to the public as the author of two or three books which display a certain amount of literary ability. So long therefore as he aimed only at entertaining his readers by such works as "Erewhon", or "Life and Habit", he was acting in a suitable sphere.'[145]

Romanes deplored Butler's attempts to write about 'philosophical discussion'. He continued: 'To this arena, however, he is in no way adapted, either by mental stature or mental equipment; and therefore makes so sorry an exhibition that Mr Darwin may well be glad that his enemy has written a book. But while we may smile at the vanity which has induced so incapable and ill-informed a man gravely to pose before the world as a philosopher, we should not on this account have deemed "Unconscious Memory" worth reviewing.' In the torrent of abuse, one of the gems was 'the only good thing in it is the writer's own opinion of himself.' Romanes admitted it was the 'vile and abusive attack upon the personal character of a man in the position of Mr Darwin', actuated, he thought, by 'petty malice', that had spurred him to have Darwin's revenge for him. Butler did himself no favours by writing to *Nature* to justify himself, referring to the remark about a 'vile and abusive attack' as being, he supposed, 'Mr Romanes' way of saying that I had made a vile and abusive personal attack on Mr Darwin himself.'[146]

Butler's notes were made in the late 1880s, for they include a reference to the grudging (and in Butler's view, plainly inadequate) clarification in the second edition of *Erasmus Darwin*, published in 1887 and edited by Francis Darwin. The wound would not heal. Darwin told Huxley that 'the affair has annoyed and pained me to a silly extent; but it would be disagreeable to anyone to be publicly called in fact a liar. He seems to hint that I interpolated sentences in Krause's MS, but he could hardly have really thought so. Until quite recently he expressed great friendship for me, and said he had learnt all he knew about evolution from my books, and I have no idea what has made him so bitter against me.'[147] Bitterness seems to have been in Butler's DNA, and was not diluted by poor Darwin apologising, as he did in a letter to Butler, for having caused such offence.

Festing Jones contended that 'one of the objects of this book was to show that the idea of descent with modification did not originate with Charles Darwin; and another was to restore mind to the universe, for Butler thought that the tendency of Charles Darwin's writings was to give too much prominence to accident at the expense of design in the theory of evolution.'[148] Butler, wounded by the lack of serious response to *Life and Habit*, was now even more upset, and lashing out. *Unconscious Memory* was the final nail in his coffin as a serious thinker about science. His last book on the subject, *Luck or Cunning?*, was an extended act of score-settling. It appeared in 1886. Darwin was dead, but his adherents remained to be abused and reviled, and to hold Butler in contempt. Butler went to his grave believing he had made a distinguished contribution to the theory of evolution.[149] However, in a remark that gives us the measure of the man, he also said that 'I am the enfant terrible of literature and science. If I cannot, and I know I cannot, get the literary and scientific big-wigs to give me a shilling, I can, and I know I can, heave bricks into the middle of them.'[150]

Perhaps Butler concentrated on scientific matters because he doubted his worth in the debate on Christianity. Sending an acquaintance 'one of the many unsold copies' of The Fair Haven in 1877, he said it was 'what is called the 1st edition, i.e. without the preface, because it is better without it, the preface being written without due thought and in fact a mistake'. He wrote his assaults on Darwin while developing other aspects of a considerable artistic talent: having done with painting, he took up photography, and worked on translations of the Iliad and the Odyssey and on travel writing. However, his crowning achievement was another work he wrote at Miss Savage's instigation, but could not bring himself to publish in his father's lifetime and then, after Canon Butler died in 1886, his own: The Way of All Flesh.

Butler wrote it from 1873 until 1884, contemporarily with his writing on evolution. At the start he spent his days painting, and wrote in the evenings, instead of practising the piano. He knew the offence the novel would cause his family. A discarded title-page, found in his papers after his death, bears the motto: 'Quand on fait des ommelettes [sic] il faut croquer des oeufs'.[151] Miss Savage, who read it as Butler wrote it, told him early on, in August 1873, that 'I read the novel two more times – once to find fault and once for complete enjoyment. As far as it goes it is perfect (at least it is to my mind) and if you go on as you have begun (and I daresay you will) it will be a beautiful book.'[152] In July 1878 he was still sending her the latest instalments of 'Ernest Pontifex'. He told her: 'It is so much less readable than I yet see my way to making it – and it is full of little contradictions.'[153] She loved it and longed for further instalments.

He revised the manuscript continually, though after Miss Savage's death in 1885 hardly touched it again, so important was her critical eye to him: she is immortalised in the book as Ernest's kindly and beautiful aunt, Alethea. As it turned out this great, revolutionary, destructive, modern Victorian novel was not published until 1903, the year after Butler died. He had been right about the outrage it would provoke, not least because the Reverend Theobald Pontifex, the father of the hero of the book, is within a few pages dripping with cant and hypocrisy; and his wife, Christina, is not far behind. Ernest, their son, is said in the narrative to have been born in 1835, as was Butler; and Ernest is the son of a clergyman of the same age as Butler's father.

Theobald is a self-regarding, self-pitying sociopath, sadist, bully, hypocrite and prig. His wife is a vacuous, trivial, oppressed fantasist, compliant towards and conniving in the many beastlinesses of her vile husband. When Christina dies, Butler writes of Theobald that 'he buried his face in his handkerchief to conceal his want of emotion.'[154] Butler's two sisters were horrified. It is no wonder, but it hardly speaks well of them. As well as there being something of Archdeacon Froude in Theobald, there is something of a poor man's Dr Arnold in Ernest's headmaster Dr Skinner (although Butler went to Shrewsbury, he clearly understood the type).

As well as undermining the concept of family life, the book also attacks the foundation for it, religion. 'If you begin with the Bible', the odious Pryer tells Ernest, 'you are three parts gone on the road to infidelity, and will go the other part before you know where you are. The Bible is not without its value to us the clergy, but for the laity it is a stumbling block which cannot be taken out of their way too soon or too completely . . . a more unreliable book was never put upon paper.'[155] That, though, is only one of the related hypocrisies it attacks. 'In his eagerness to regenerate the Church of England (and through this the universe) by the means which Pryer had suggested to him, it occurred to him to try to familiarise himself with the habits and thoughts of the poor by going and living among them. I think he got this notion from Kingsley's *Alton Locke*, which, High Churchman though he for the nonce was, he had devoured as he had devoured Stanley's *Life of Arnold*, Dickens's novels, and whatever other literary garbage of the day was most likely to do him harm.'[156] The higher classes are, in their way, far more disgusting than the lower, whom they so effortlessly patronise. When Ernest is sent to prison, his louche friend Towneley squares the press not to write anything. 'He was successful as regards all the higher-class papers. There was only one journal, and that of the lowest class, which was incorruptible.'[157]

When Ernest suddenly realises, in prison, that Christianity has 'humbugged' him – how Butler felt during his work in the slums in 1858

– it is because he knows that 'the greater part of the ills which had afflicted him were due, indirectly, in chief measure to the influence of Christian teaching'. He wishes to save others from 'years of waste and misery as he had had to pass himself. If there was no truth in the miraculous accounts of Christ's Death and resurrection, the whole of the religion founded upon the historic truth of those events tumbled to the ground. "Why," he exclaimed, with all the arrogance of youth, "they put a gipsy or fortune teller into prison for getting money out of silly people who think they have supernatural power; why should they not put a clergyman in prison for pretending that he can absolve sins, or turn bread and wine into the flesh and blood of One who died two thousand years ago?"'[158]

Festing Jones described his friend's autobiographical novel as 'like the Book of Job and the *Odyssey*, that of the good man passing through trials and coming out triumphant in the end.'[159] This does not take into account what must be jettisoned and destroyed before attaining that triumph. The review in *The Times* was typical. Referring to Ernest's childhood, the reviewer noted: 'We cannot believe it; we are convinced he exaggerates . . . all this part of the book is painful to the last degree, and fills an ordinarily kind-hearted reader with maddening wrath. Exaggerated or not, we treat children very differently; and the Rev Theobald and his wife would hear of the SPCC.'[160] The reviewer went on to castigate Butler for his 'bitter irony', and for expounding a philosophy that was 'wholly negative'. Butler had told Fleay in 1873, when the work was in its early stages, that it was 'getting positively awful as to satire, every time I rewrite the first 3 chapters they come out more bitter and more bitter: yet I imagine – though I hardly dare say so – that the bitterness is not likely to hurt anyone who does not richly deserve it – and these won't be hurt by it.'[161]

He did, however, admit that connoisseurs of humour would not be disappointed. The review ended with the pay-off: 'We admire Mr Butler almost more in this book than in anything else he did; but we liked him better when he was using his intellect and knowledge to prove that the *Odyssey* was written by a woman.' It was probably more of a compliment than that paid by the reviewer in the *Sunday Sun*, who described the work as 'not a great novel, but it is unquestionably a deeply interesting book' with a 'rather foolish title'.

Butler was on the provisional wing of nineteenth-century secularisers.

For all his pretensions, he had no weight of scientific knowledge or discovery to place behind the movement. He was, however, equipped with the courage and the originality of mind to challenge received social and theological wisdom, and he saw humbug with a clarity possessed by hardly any of his peers. He was emblematic of the Victorian determination to construct a new world view, on foundations they themselves had made.

CHAPTER 8

THE POLITICAL MIND: HIGH PRINCIPLE AND LOW AMBITION

I

Politicians in the mid-nineteenth century were just as vulnerable to the tide of social and intellectual change as writers or thinkers were. An extreme example of this new attitude came later in the century when Charles Bradlaugh, an atheist who had been elected an MP, refused to take the Christian oath and therefore could not take his seat. However, Protestant orthodoxy had already retreated at the time of Catholic emancipation in 1829, and Christianity generally soon found itself challenged in the political sphere by the demand to allow Jews to sit in Parliament. As with Catholic emancipation, this entailed a huge challenge to deep-rooted convictions and prejudices.

The long-running debate on Jewish disabilities from the 1830s to the 1850s showed the political milieu of the time at its best and worst. The best was that minds were now open enough to discuss this question; the worst was that a profound strain of anti-Semitism lingered in British political life, partly racialist in nature, partly based on a religious bigotry that still saw the Jews as requiring to be punished for their part in killing Christ. The ability to participate in politics also defined membership of society, and three increasingly important groups found themselves still excluded, their status as outsiders posing an increasing threat to the stability of civil society. They were the working classes, women, and Jews. Catholics had been enabled to sit in Parliament in 1829 by the Emancipation Act. Jews remained barred, but the relief given to Catholics inspired a new wave of lobbying to secure Jewish rights as well. A bill was presented in the year after the emancipation, and Thomas Babington

Macaulay, elected for the first time that year, made his name by supporting it, and attacking the injustice of Jewish exclusion. The bill was defeated in the Commons, but was annually reintroduced. By 1833 the reformed Commons passed it, only to have it defeated by the Lords. The Tory party was opposed, as was King William, on the grounds that Jews were held to have a higher allegiance outside Britain. Huge petitions were presented to Parliament demanding Jews be accorded these rights, but to no avail.

The Jewish lobby turned its attention to securing admission to positions in local government. Such a bill was finally passed in July 1845. Part of the reason for its success was the determination of certain Jews to become High Sheriffs and Aldermen, and those aiming for the admission of Jews to Parliament realised they would need candidates prepared to sit there. The most notable Jew in political life at this time was Disraeli, who had converted to Christianity at the age of twelve. Now one who had not converted put himself forward: Lionel de Rothschild, from the banking family, who stood for the City of London in 1847, and was elected. There had been nothing to prevent his standing: but he could not take his seat. A bill to enable him, and other Jewish MPs, to do so was introduced into the Commons shortly after his election, to allow the will of his constituents to prevail. Opinion had started to soften on the question. F. D. Maurice told Charles Kingsley in November 1847 that 'the feeling that the Jews are aliens used to be decisive with me, till I perceived that it ought only to be decisive as to my own conduct, and is no foundation for a law to deprive the aliens of their ordinary privilege.'[1]

The Lords rejected the bill in the summer of 1848, albeit by the relatively small margin of 163 to 128. Rothschild could not take his seat. However, in 1851 the banker David Salomons, who had led the fight for Jews to be allowed to hold municipal offices, was elected for Greenwich, and insisted on taking his seat in the Commons. He asked to swear the oath on the Old Testament, which the Speaker permitted: however, he omitted the phrase in the Oath of Abjuration 'on the true faith of a Christian'. The Speaker asked him to withdraw, but he went to sit on the government side of the House. He was again asked to withdraw, and did, but his friends in the Commons warned he would be seeking legal redress: which panicked the senior minister present, Charles Wood, the Chancellor of the Exchequer, who sought to delay further discussion until the following week, to allow legal opinion to be consulted. There were demands for a new writ to be issued for a by-election in Greenwich, since Salomons was disqualified from taking his seat. This move was headed off, but the House reconvened the following Monday to discuss what to do.

At the start of the discussion about his position Salomons not only came into the chamber but, to great uproar, sat on the ministerial bench. A motion was immediately proposed that he could take his seat; an amendment was immediately proposed that he should not. The uproar continued. One member stood up and challenged the legality of the Oath of Abjuration, which Salomons had refused to take. The Speaker quoted the precedent of Rothschild's being denied permission to take his seat. An Irish MP, Thomas Anstey, argued that the Oath of Abjuration had been aimed at descendants of James II, not at the Jews; and argued further that the oath had ceased to be legal since the death of George III – it had 'expired' since the demise of the last Stuart pretender. The purpose of the oath was not to affirm the Christian faith, but to affirm that Queen Victoria was the lawful sovereign. Salomons had done that: but in the view of the Attorney-General, Sir Alexander Cockburn, an oath was an oath, and if it was not taken in its prescribed form, it was not taken at all. Cockburn did not quibble over the Old Testament: it was the absence of the words 'on the true faith of a Christian' that caused him problems. However, another member pointed out that the former Attorney, Sir Frederic Thesiger, had said that even an oath including those words would be illegal if not sworn on the New Testament.

The Prime Minister, Russell, said the Commons had to set an example to the people, who generally obeyed the law, and expected their leaders to do so as well. However, even this bromide was unsuccessful, since MPs then disputed whether it would be illegal for Salomons, who had taken an oath to uphold the Queen as sovereign, to take his seat. Just as Quakers had since 1696 been allowed to sit in the Commons simply by affirmation, so should Jews be: this point was also made by John Bright, a Quaker MP.

Richard Bethell, who would become Solicitor-General, argued that:

> by the very Act of this House, in permitting the hon Members to take the oath on the Old Testament, they had expressed their opinion that they had authority to alter the form—that they were

bound to administer the oath in the form that was binding on the hon Member's conscience; and yet; after making that concession, they mocked the hon Member—they mocked the law—they violated the principle of the law by telling him that though they conceded the principle so far—though they gave him the Old Testament on which to be sworn, and by that very Act rendered it incumbent on themselves to obliterate the words, 'on the true faith of a Christian,' yet they refused to obliterate them. He said again they mocked the law, and they mocked common sense by insisting on such a course.[2]

Once the House had conceded the point that a man could swear on the Old Testament, they were, Bethell claimed, 'under a moral obligation to follow that up by omitting the words "on the true faith of a Christian".'

It was agreed that the withdrawal of Salomons should be put to the vote. After several speakers, one of whom had said that Salomons, who was in the House, would 'weaken his own case' if he did not say something about how he intended to proceed, Salomons rose. There were several cries of 'Withdraw!', but many more indicated they wished him to be heard, and the Speaker did not prevent him. He said that:

having been returned to this House by a large constituency, and believing that I labour under no disability whatever, and that I am in a position to fulfil all the requirements of the law, I thought I should not be doing justice to my own position as an Englishman and a gentleman did I not adopt the course which I thought right and proper of maintaining my right to appear on this floor— without thereby meaning any disrespect to you, Sir. I thought I was bound to take this course in defence of my own rights and privileges, and of the rights and privileges of the constituents who have sent me here. In saying this, Sir, I shall state to you that whatever the decision of this House may be, I shall willingly abide by it, provided that just sufficient force be used to make me feel that I am acting under coercion.[3]

He pointed to the 'doubtful' state of the law, and warned the House that the very confusion was reason enough not to override the rights of his constituents.

The House voted by 231 to 81 to have Salomons withdraw. As he had indicated he would, he waited until the Serjeant-at-Arms placed his hand on his shoulder, and then went quietly. The next day Russell moved a motion expressly forbidding Salomons to vote or sit in the House until he took the Oath of Abjuration. He conceded that Quakers could affirm, but the law allowed them to do that: no such law specified that Jews could, and Russell conceded that 'I complain of the state of the law. I think it a very great hardship upon the Jews.'[4]

The question of why that should not be rectified remained. Cockburn, who spoke later in the debate, professed himself to be 'one of those who had all along supported the removal of Jewish disabilities', but said that on this occasion he had to 'act judicially'.[5] The oath may have had its origins in the desire to keep 'Popish recusants' from power, and been worded so as to avoid its being 'evaded': and there was no provision for it to be altered for Jews. He said he was 'sorry' to conclude that Salomons could not take his seat: but the law left him no choice.[6] However, the construction others put on Cockburn's remarks was that the Oath of Abjuration had come to apply to Jews not by design, but by accident.

George Thompson, the Liberal MP for Tower Hamlets, was the first to come close to a question so far undiscussed: how far the reluctance to alter the law to allow Salomons and, indeed, Rothschild, to sit in the House was a question of anti-Semitism, active or passive. His constituency to the east of the City of London included the main Jewish community in Britain, and he asserted that he represented 'the majority of the Hebrew community in the United Kingdom'.[7] He was jeered when he said this, and observed that the 'derisive and insolent' response had given away the true feelings of many MPs about the Jews in Britain. He said that 'they looked at the law in this case not as men caring for the law, but colouring the law to suit their prejudices.' The choice was 'religious liberty' against 'religious intolerance'. Russell said he would do everything in his power to bring forward a bill to abolish the restrictions on Jews.

The electors of Greenwich petitioned to be heard in person at the Bar of the House. So, in the cause of Rothschild, did electors from the City of London. The House still, at the end of a second day of debate, voted to exclude Salomons. For good measure, he was fined £500 for each of the three occasions he had voted, improperly, in divisions in the House. He and those who supported him now awaited the legislation to alter the oath. Bills were brought forward in 1853, 1856 and 1857, but were thrown out by the Lords. In 1853 it had been Aberdeen, by then Prime Minister, who had sought to remove the disabilities, and who in a speech in the Lords on 29 April had attacked the 'remnant of that prejudice' against the Jews that had existed in much of Christendom because the Jews had been 'under the obloquy of a crime of inconceivable magnitude'.[8] Aberdeen continued: 'Vengeance was not ours . . . it was not for us to "repay".' It was unacceptable that 'the Jew, in this country, is the only person who is excluded from full civil and political rights in consequence of his religious belief.'[9] He said that since Parliament imposed the burdens of Englishmen upon Jews, it should confer the rights of Englishmen upon them too.

Aberdeen was countered, however, by Shaftesbury, the most liberal of Tories and the friend of the oppressed. He doubted the Prime Minister's assertion that the public mood was for repeal of these restrictions. He was also, however, unhappy at the logic of a measure that would allow Jews to sit in Parliament, but forbid them from becoming Regent, Lord Chancellor, Keeper of the Great Seal, from presenting to benefices, or 'advising the Crown in reference to the established church'.[10] Shaftesbury maintained that 'if they have a constitutional right to seats in parliament, they also have a constitutional right to all the privileges and consequences of seats.' He was unhappy, too, that the admission of Jews would lead to them making laws that bound the Established Church of which they had no part.[11] The Protestant settlement was embedded deeply in political and constitutional life, and this made the Jewish debate about far more than casual anti-Semitism.

Shaftesbury claimed that:

> to bestow on the Jew privilege and power to exercise an influence and give a vote on laws affecting directly the Church of England, and indirectly perhaps the whole Church of Christ—to allow him to riot and revel legislatively in the indulgence of that peculiar antipathy which is the character and distinction of his name and nation—we are summoned to suppress all mention of that Name which is our glory, our safeguard, and our strength. Well, my Lords, whose freedom is there concerned? I say it is ours. We are called upon to retreat before a man who tells you that his religion solely exists by the denial of yours; and that he must and will have a seat in Parliament, to possess at least the privilege of asserting that religion, and of making laws which will have an effect upon that religion which is the opprobrium of his race.

He mocked the Commons for being 'good enough' to offer an alternative oath, and condemned as 'irreverent' the idea that politicians should 'twist and turn these solemn attestations to suit our political convenience'. He thundered: 'In affirming that Parliament should not be exclusively Christian, it is desirable to weigh fairly and deliberately the effect we shall produce on the nation at large. But admitting, for the sake of argument, the possibility of political benefits, by the large inclusion, and consequent satisfaction, of many discontented and restless spirits, are there no moral mischiefs to make us pause . . .? I confess, my Lords, this seems to me to be a very novel way of conferring a privilege.'[12] He feared, he said, the destruction of the existence of religion in Great Britain. The hysterical mien that Shaftesbury had displayed to Sir Robert Peel had not diminished with time.

Other peers endorsed Shaftesbury's view. However, one with, perhaps, a more detached view of Christianity was the Archbishop of Dublin, who suggested that not to allow Jews in the Commons was an insult to those who had elected them. In what appeared to be a veiled rebuke to Shaftesbury he observed that the measure's opponents 'were altogether in a false position when they proclaimed it would unchristianise the legislature by removing these disabilities, and yet said it did not unprotestantise the legislature to admit Roman Catholics, and that it did not unchurch the legislature to admit dissenters to parliament.'[13] The Bishop of Salisbury disagreed with him, on the grounds of admitting blasphemers into the Commons; and he in turn was attacked by the Bishop of St David's. After a final blast from Lord Colchester about the false analogy between Quakers and Jews – 'at the time that the Quaker was relieved from disability . . . he professed Christianity' – the vote was taken, and the bill thrown out by 164 to 115.

These arguments were rehearsed again for the Oaths Bill in 1854, and the Oath of Abjuration Bill in 1856, and the Oaths Bill in 1857. The denouement came, at last, in 1858. A new Oaths Bill went through the Commons, only to have the clause applying to Jews thrown out in the House of Lords. The Lords objected to two (as they saw it) separate matters being considered in the bill: one to alter oaths generally, the other to address the specific issue facing Jews. The campaign against the bill was led by Lord Chelmsford, the Lord Chancellor, the former Sir Frederick Thesiger. Chelmsford told the Lords that he had always opposed admission of the Jews to Parliament, and intended to be consistent. Aware of the dangers of being thought prejudiced, he noted that another peer had referred to the 'most perfect fairness and good feeling' with which he had conducted his opposition to the relief of Jewish disabilities.[14] He then proceeded to hint that while this question was always discussed in 'tacit reference to one or two individuals who are distinguished members of the Jewish persuasion, who are regarded as types of the whole Jewish people', perhaps not all Jews were like this (he might have observed that not all Protestants were like Lord Derby, the Prime Minister, but chose not to sow confusion in that way). To base the argument on 'gentlemen of the highest character and respectability . . . who live in social intercourse with their Christian fellow-subjects, and who possess none of that exclusive spirit which is considered to be characteristic of the religion which they profess' was a dangerous substitution of personal considerations for a general principle. Chelmsford did not say he feared an influx of moneylenders, old clothes sellers and others from Houndsditch, but then he did not need to.

When even a writer considered to be so humane as Dickens could use Fagin as a representative of British Jewry, anti-Semitism was a grave problem. Yet it was also beginning to be regarded as an ugly prejudice, which would explain Chelmsford's determination to laud himself for his fairness in the matter of the rights of Jews. However, he did not regard the term 'civil rights' as including 'a claim to be admitted to political office or to parliament . . . I contend, my Lords, that no such rights exist indiscriminately for all citizens.'[15] He had no sympathy for the disfranchised electors of the City of London who kept returning Rothschild to Parliament, for they knew the law when they did so. Like Shaftesbury, he protested that 'the legislature, as a legislature, would cease to be Christian' if Jews were admitted to it 'because no test of Christianity would be exacted from its members.'[16]

Chelmsford was politely countered by Lord Lyndhurst, who noted the numbers of prelates who had over the years supported Jews joining Parliament, without expecting the country to be dechristianised by the experience. Jews sat in parliaments in Canada, Australia and New Zealand, whose constitutions had been passed through the House of Lords: these countries had not become unchristian, and nor had their parliaments. 'What, then, becomes of your principle – your high principle?' he asked. 'You throw it to the wind – you think that British subjects in the colonies are not worthy of its protection.'[17] He reminded the House that when

Catholic emancipation was being discussed the arguments against it were that the Catholics looked up to a foreign sovereign, and sought converts. Nonetheless, the Catholics were emancipated. The Jews, by contrast, looked up to no foreign sovereign, and did not proselytise.

The Dukes of Rutland and Marlborough both spoke against, fearing the dechristianising of Britain. The Bishop of Cashel did too, despite protesting that 'I am actuated by no unkind feeling towards them. I love them.'[18] However, he felt moved to remind his peers that the Jews were 'the children of Abraham, but they are degenerate children who walk not in the steps of their father'. It had been they who had cried out 'Crucify him! Crucify him!' Moreover, 'the Jews of the present day show themselves the true children of their fallen fathers, by blaspheming that holy name and speaking evil of Him whom Christians love.' It had only been a matter of time before someone adduced this argument.

The Commons refused to accept this amendment. Russell, as Leader of the Opposition, moved on 10 May 1858 that the House should disagree with the Lords: his main line of argument being that the oaths objected to had been framed to counter the ambitions of seditious Roman Catholics, not Jews. It was decided to appoint a committee to examine the bill again. After a vote was passed by 251 to 196, it appointed to the committee – as it was legally entitled to do – Rothschild, who was still the Member for the City of London even though unable to take his seat. The Lords saw its hand had been forced. On 18 May 1858 a conference was convened in the Painted Chamber of the Palace of Westminster between the two Houses, to discuss the proposition that either House might admit Jews by resolution, with their taking an oath omitting the vexatious words 'on the true faith of a Christian'.

The conference agreed nothing, except that the peers nominated to attend it would report to their House the arguments of the Commons. Earl Stanhope, supporting the Commons's view in a Lords debate a fortnight later, said the majority in the Commons in favour of admitting Jews had trebled in two years – from 49 to 153 – and the Lords could not sensibly go on ignoring this weight of opinion in the elected House. The alternative was a collision with the Commons, which would have widespread constitutional ramifications. There remained some diehard opponents: Lord de Ros, in the most unreconstructed contribution to the debate, asked 'whether on any great emergencies the Jews had ever appeared in arms for the defence of this country? Why, when England was menaced with invasion, did not the Jews imitate the example of the lawyers and other professions and establish volunteer or fencible corps among themselves? Why were they not to be found in Her Majesty's ships and in her army? The fact was that the Jew always looked upon himself as an alien in the country in which he dwelt, and that was a good reason why he should not be admitted to parliament.'[19]

Matters were then delayed by Derby's falling ill. He returned to the Lords on 1 July, at the height of the public health disaster known as the Great Stink, when the Thames was awash with sewage in a heatwave, and shocked peers by saying he had changed his mind and that, to avoid a showdown with the Commons, the Lords should agree that Jews should be admitted to Parliament. His admission of defeat was pure pragmatism: 'I take the course which I have adopted from no other feeling than a desire to see an amicable settlement between the two Houses with regard to a question of grave interest, and with respect to which I see no other solution.'[20] Those who knew Derby doubted the sincerity of his conversion. 'It is difficult to believe that he himself ever cared a straw about the Jew question, or that his opposition had any motive except that of pleasing the bigoted and narrow-minded of his party,' Greville wrote in his diary.[21]

The compromise – that Jews could come to take the oath, object to the phrase about Christianity, and be offered a different form of words – was put by Lord Lucan, the Crimean War commander who had ordered his brother-in-law Lord Cardigan to lead the charge of the Light Brigade. Lucan's compromise stands out in a career of one blunder after another. His callous behaviour as Lord Lieutenant of Mayo in the 1840s during the Potato Famine had made him a hate figure to the Irish, and his role in the Crimea earned him a censure (which he strongly disputed) in dispatches. The bill he had introduced to effect this device had a second reading, despite the usual clamour from those who felt the Jews remained insufficiently punished for their support for the death of Jesus Christ.

When the bill went into committee even the diehards saw the game was up. Some claimed the Lords was being treated unconstitutionally, a synonym for being forced to accept reality. However, the bill went through without amendment at the committee stage, and received a third reading in the Lords with the sole amendment, moved by the Duke of Marlborough, that no Jew be allowed to present to an ecclesiastical benefice. The minority of opponents in the Commons tried but failed to derail the measure there. Samuel Warren, the MP for Midhurst, expressed his 'unconquerable repugnance' at Lucan's bill at its third reading on 21 July, but by now such voices were very much in the minority. Thomas Duncombe, the MP for Finsbury, referred to the absurd position the Lords – a repository of 'bigotry, prejudice and intolerance' – had found itself in when Rothschild was put on the committee to negotiate with them, even though he could not take his seat in the chamber.[22] He argued that the long struggle for Jewish equality in politics was about to end, and he was right. The third reading passed by 129 votes to 55.

Rothschild came to the House on 26 July 1858, determined to use the new law to take his seat. Warren tried to interrupt as he was being sworn, but was told to sit down by the Speaker. Rothschild had formally to object to the oath administered to him so that the House could resolve to offer him an acceptable form of words. Warren intervened again, and this time was deemed not to be out of order. He said the House had arrived at 'a very grave crisis in its constitutional history and that of the country, and a sense of duty will not allow me to remain silent.'[23] He praised the 'spotlessness of character' of Rothschild and protested that 'I have not in my heart one particle of animosity against the Jewish race', but that what the Commons was about to do was 'dangerous'.[24] One or two other Members registered their disagreement with what was happening, prompting others to reflect on the unfortunate prejudice against the Jews. Those so attacked then denied any prejudice, but referred instead to their Christian convictions. The motion was put to allow Rothschild to take the oath.

He then did so, on the Old Testament, with his hat on, and at last took his seat. A by-election was arranged in Greenwich, at which Salomons (who had been Lord Mayor of London in 1855) was victorious, and he took his seat in 1859. Nathaniel de Rothschild became the first Jewish peer, in 1885. Another bastion of prejudice had been breached.

II

The Jewish debate represented a move to a new order, one that was more secular and the result of more pragmatic attitudes. Those who drove it through required an intelligent flexibility of mind that appreciated what was best for the national interest. William Ewart Gladstone was the most principled of men, but would sometimes adapt his beliefs when circumstances changed. His move from protectionism to free trade was perhaps the most significant example of this, creating as it did a cast of mind that forced him to change party altogether. He avoided accusations of hypocrisy, or of putting personal ambition ahead of all else, because it was so transparent that strong moral and religious principles underpinned his conduct. Yet he was a man of great inner turbulence, troubled by sexual repression and a close interest in the erotic.

By the early 1840s Gladstone had established himself as the leader of the next generation of politicians after Peel. Carlyle, who was not disposed to praise others, in 1842 described him as 'a most methodic, fair-spoken, purified, clear-starched, *sincere-looking* man.'[25] Carlyle's acquaintance with him had begun by his reading *The State in its Relations with the Church*, which the Sage – no more easily pleased by intellectual questions than by personalities – had found impressive in its thoughtfulness and scholarship. Gladstone published this in 1838, and a second work of theology, *Church Principles Considered in their Results,* in 1841. The power of Gladstone's intellect and the force of his religious principles made his life a struggle. The earlier book expressed Gladstone's view that the State had a moral role to play as well as a political one; the latter reasserted the primacy of Anglicanism, as the doctrine of the Established Church, within the State. He would strive to uphold these doctrines: they were the foundation of his political creed and the driving force behind his implementation of policy in a period of change and improvement. He was friendly with most of the leading lights of the Oxford Movement. He shared an Arnoldian wish for a completely religious society, but the practicality that encroached upon him in his life as a politician forced him to realise the impossibility of such a thing. He took a close interest in theological questions all his life, and as a minister paid close attention to the politics and patronage of the Established Church.

Gladstone would be a constant presence in British life until his death in 1898. For much of that time he was in high office. He sat on the commission of the 1851 Exhibition; he was a trustee of the British Museum; he was consulted about the contents of the National Gallery and about great architectural projects; he translated Homer; he influenced intense theological questions within the Church of England and within Parliament; he influenced the reform of Oxford University; he stimulated an inquiry that led to reform of the great public schools; he assembled a library of 32,000 books; he resigned and refused office regularly on points of high principle; he developed the hobby of chopping down trees; and he saved fallen women, taking them home and praying for them with Mrs Gladstone. He was learned, brilliant, intensely serious, a moral juggernaut. His was perhaps the highest mind of an age densely populated with them: he embodied the drive to pursue perfection, to advance civilisation and to improve the lives of the British people.

To do this, in a time of rapid social and technological change, entailed making accommodations. Gladstone's success rested not least in his knack of maintaining a high standard of integrity and honesty while making profound changes of position on great questions. He was driven, in doing so, by his intellect, which presented to him on occasion the inevitable difficulties of persisting with certain lines of policy or thought. He was a high churchman who saw the need to disestablish the Irish Church. He was wedded to the Tory landed interest and yet went against them in his support for repeal of the Corn Laws. He found the idea of divorce an abomination, yet devoted much of his charitable work to women familiar with the lowest forms of sexual depravity. He was an imperialist who saw the inevitability of giving Ireland home rule. Most important, he was a Tory who became a Liberal.

He was born in 1809, the fourth and youngest son of a Liverpool merchant, Sir John Gladstone, the first baronet. The Gladstones were Scottish, part of a distinct community in Liverpool. Both William's parents were devoutly religious and evangelical, and he was baptised an Anglican. While at Eton he began to keep the diary that is his greatest monument, and which he kept up for over seventy years. He went up to Christ Church, Oxford, distinguished himself academically as Peel had done there twenty years before, and became president of the Oxford Union. However, his fellows regarded him as a legendary prig, not least because of his religious zealotry. He seriously considered taking holy orders, until his father talked him out of it.

At Oxford he acquired a deep-seated interest in politics. At the Union he passed a motion of no confidence in Wellington's administration. Gladstone was at this stage a supporter of the faction in the Tory party led by George Canning, which favoured Catholic emancipation and a relaxation of tariffs on trade. Gladstone deplored the Whig reform measures that would extend the franchise into the middle classes in 1832, and abolish rotten boroughs in which patronage and not voters controlled an MP's election. However, he deplored even more Wellington's blinkered repudiation of the Whig proposals and his unwillingness to negotiate a less seismic measure. Gladstone's Oxford speech caused him to be noticed at Westminster, and in 1832 the Duke of Newcastle offered him the seat at Newark. Gladstone fought it in the December 1832 election that immediately followed the Reform Act, and took his seat in Parliament the following month. When Peel formed his short administration in 1834 Gladstone was a whip, and then Under-secretary for War and the Colonies. As when Peel held the post, Gladstone's Secretary of State – the Earl of Aberdeen – was in the Lords, so he gained experience, aged just twenty-five, leading for the department in the Commons.

Macaulay, reviewing *The State in its Relations with the Church* in the *Edinburgh Review* in April 1839, famously described its author as 'the rising hope of those stern and unbending Tories'.[26] Even those who, like Peel, had the intellects to digest what Gladstone was saying found the thesis expressed problematical, and Gladstone more unfathomable. However, one of the keys to Gladstone's personality was that for all the ferocity with which he embraced certain positions, he had a flexibility of mind Macaulay could not envisage; when the facts no longer supported the position he had taken, he took a new one.

When Peel offered Gladstone the vice-presidency of the Board of Trade in September 1841 the offer was met with 'protestations of ignorance and unfitness'.[27] Gladstone engaged in a spectacular circumlocution, eventually over several sides of writing paper, about his lack of worthiness. This sentence sums up the tone: 'It is presumptuous, I fear, on my part, to contemplate in any form the notion that I might hereafter be deemed fit for official advancement; I do it only because you yourself were pleased to allude to the present appointment as one which might furnish a proper discipline and an advantageous introduction to others at a future, probably a distant, period; those other employments, as I have been led to infer, (and that inference forms the only ground of the explanation I now offer) being likewise connected with the trade or the finance of this country.' After several hundred more such words he accepted the post, however. Almost immediately, Gladstone was corresponding with Peel about intelligence sent by his brother from Liverpool about agitation there for repeal of the Corn Laws.[28]

By the 1850s Gladstone had become a leader of a sect of Tories – the Peelites, who had followed their former leader on the matter of free trade – and British politics had become increasingly concerned with foreign affairs: the Crimean War, the troubles in India that led to the Mutiny in 1857, and the government takeover of the subcontinent from the East India Company thereafter. It was also the decade when Gladstone carved out a leading reputation as a statesman, and as one clearly heading for the top of what Disraeli would call 'the greasy pole'. He did this as much in his time as an Opposition frontbencher between 1855 and 1859 as he did as Chancellor from 1852 to 1855 (and he would hold that office again from 1859 to 1866). Although ridiculed by Disraeli, who considered him desiccated and priggish, and regarded with a mixture of awe and curiosity by many others, Gladstone had depths to his character at odds with his public persona.

There was far more to him than even the most observant political colleague would ever discern. He had a tumultuous and intense inner life, something he held in common with his sister Helen, who as well as converting to Catholicism had also become a laudanum addict. In his diary he recorded the basics of his life, and sometimes far more than that. His main inner problems were carnal, and are hardly approached even in a document so intimate as the diaries. He endured long separations from his wife. He had an advanced interest in pornography, though what entertained him was quite unlike what is understood by the contemporary definition of the term: the editor of his *Diaries*, Colin Matthew, described his interests as encompassing 'Restoration poems, classical authors such as Petronius, and fabliaux (French verse fables, some of them extremely bawdy).'[29] Some have linked his work rescuing prostitutes to this, but in fact it came through his membership from 1845 onwards of a group of well-heeled Tractarians, who together decided to perform regular charity work. Gladstone started off working in Soho with the destitute of both sexes, but by 1848 found this work too time-consuming.

He seems to have begun combing the streets for prostitutes to rescue some time in 1848, and first mentions the activity in his diary on 25 May 1849. By the summer of 1850, in a period of heightened feeling for him when he, and all the other Peelites, were affected by the sudden death of their leader – thrown from his horse in Rotten Row – Gladstone began to be more systematic about this work. Although he seemed to do it most when Mrs Gladstone was away, she was kept fully informed. The women were brought to the Gladstones' house, where Catherine Gladstone would talk to them. Gladstone would arrange for the women to undergo rehabilitation at the House of Mercy at Clewer near Windsor, after which they were encouraged either to find regular work or a husband, or to emigrate.

He devoted much time to making arrangements for the women but was not especially successful. He recorded on 20 January 1854 that he had spoken to between eighty and ninety prostitutes, but could think of only one who, thanks to his influence, had mended her ways. Another prostitute who failed to graduate from the House of Mercy told him in 1854 that 'I have no doubt that you wished to do me some service, but I did not fancy being shut up in such a place as that for perhaps twelve months. I should have committed suicide.'[30] As Matthew puts it, 'for Gladstone rescue work became not merely a duty but a craving; it was an exposure to sexual stimulation which Gladstone felt he must both undergo and overcome.' The way in which he 'courted evil' became a test, to prove to himself that he could deal with temptation.

Even in an age before mass media and a tabloid press such an association as this risked political disaster, but he seemed oblivious to it. When William Wilson, a Scotsman, tried to blackmail him in 1853, when he was Chancellor of the Exchequer, he went straight to the police. He felt he was undertaking a Christian mission and had nothing to be ashamed of. Of his discussions with prostitutes he noted in his diary: 'These talkings of mine are certainly not within the rules of worldly prudence: I am not sure that Christian prudence sanctions them for such an one as me; but my aim & intention did not warrant the charge wh[ich] doubtless has been sent to teach me wisdom & which I therefore welcome.'[31] Wilson was tried at the Old Bailey in June that year, pleaded guilty, and was given a year's hard labour.

In 1849 Gladstone had started whipping himself after reading pornography. In 1851 he started doing it after meeting prostitutes, if he felt he had become unduly excited. He did find some of the women beautiful, and would describe that aspect in his diaries, in Italian. The *Diaries* provide no evidence of whether he ever slept with them: it seems highly unlikely he did, given the lengths to which he goes to record his resistance to temptation, and the spiritual catastrophe that would have occurred – and which would have found some way to manifest itself

– if he had succumbed. In 1896 he told his son Stephen, in a sealed letter not to be opened until after his death, that contrary to rumours he knew had circulated he had never 'been guilty of the act which is known as that of infidelity to the marriage bed'.[32]

The self-flagellation seemed to follow a pattern. He would have emotionally intense meetings with prostitutes when some other crisis had occurred in his life, perhaps as a means of taking his mind off it – such as when under political pressure, or if some spiritual problem had occurred, such as when two of his closest friends (including Henry Manning, the future Cardinal) left for the Roman Catholic Church in 1851, or when he had read Froude's *Nemesis of Faith*. The group of Tractarians to which he belonged – a secret society known as 'the engagement' – had indicated self-flagellation as a penance in times of such necessity and when in breach of their rules of devotion. It seems likely that it was that, rather than any pornographic association, that caused Gladstone to whip himself. Unlike other Tractarians he never sought spiritual guidance when in these torments. There is no sense that his wife knew of his internal struggle. He went to church two or three times every Sunday, once on most other days of the week, and prayed morning and night. It adds to the astonishing nature of Gladstone the man that at the height of these troubles in himself he was running Her Majesty's Treasury, and with conspicuous success. Later in the 1850s, as a means of working off his surplus energies, he took up the hobby of cutting down trees on his estate at Hawarden in Flintshire.

III

The man who until death in 1881 would from the early 1850s become Gladstone's long-term rival, Benjamin Disraeli, could hardly have been more different from him. He was frivolous, opportunistic, unscrupulous and consumed by personal ambition. In an era of high minds, when those in public life for the most part sought to serve the cause of society's improvement, Disraeli stands as a reminder that some are only ever in it for what they can get out of it for themselves. When, as we shall see, he eventually led a great reforming government in the 1870s, the main reforms (many of whose effects are still felt today) were the initiatives of colleagues. When he reached the top of the greasy pole, what he most wanted to do was enjoy power and patronage, and revel in his place in society. Such things could hardly have mattered less to Gladstone.

He had a less steady climb to the front bench than his rival, ironically profiting from his shabby part in the political assassination of Robert Peel. Disraeli overcame – to an extent – the suspicions of his colleagues (and the fact that he had been on the wrong side of the intellectual argument over the Corn Laws) to get to Downing Street just before Gladstone did. The two men exemplify the Victorian political mind at its best and worst: Gladstone the man of principle, even if he had to engage in occasional contortions to try to remain principled; and Disraeli the opportunist, craving power for its own sake and not because of any great strategy to transform Britain and, as we shall see at the time of the second Reform Act in 1867, willing to throw away any principle in order to stay in office. Although there were many shades and gradations of the political mind in the mid-nineteenth century, these two men represented its poles.

It was perhaps inevitable that, for one whose career was rooted in opportunism, Benjamin Disraeli should have had the most unconventional path to the First Lordship of the Treasury of any nineteenth-century prime minister. The man who would become the literary muse of the ultra-aristocratic Young England movement would, but for an unintended consequence of an action of his father's, have been disqualified by birth. He had been born a Jew in 1804, the eldest son of Isaac D'Israeli (young Ben doctored the surname at an early age, one of many amendments made to his past). Isaac D'Israeli had his four children convert to Christianity in 1817. This was not because, at a time when Jews were barred from the House of Commons, he intended one to become Prime Minister, but because he wished to break with the Bevis Marks synagogue in London, which was demanding money from him.

Disraeli was twenty-one when his first novel, *Vivian Grey*, was published, to some acclaim. This was as well, because he had manufactured a lifestyle that far exceeded any income he might have from his father, and the royalties were useful. So was the minor celebrity he acquired. He made the best of what talent he had and was an assiduous networker in a high society of which he was otherwise a complete outsider. Critics of his art occasionally savaged him. One was Richard Monckton Milnes, who loathed Disraeli from the start (they were near contemporaries in the Commons), and who wrote a lengthy critique of

him as a novelist after the fall of Peel. In it, Disraeli is teased for liking
to make his characters dukes, and for having so little imagination.
Another critic was Anthony Trollope who, in his autobiography, damned
his novels as having 'all had the same flavour of paint and unreality'.[33]
He felt the novels were aimed at turning the heads of the impressionable young; they were certainly written to keep Disraeli in with Young
England, for by that stage he realised that ingratiation with the rich and
influential was an essential tool in his career progress. 'He has struck
them with astonishment and aroused in their imagination ideas of a
world more glorious, more rich, more witty, more enterprising, than
their own. But the glory has been the glory of pasteboard, and the
wealth has been a wealth of tinsel. The wit has been the wit of hair-
dressers, and the enterprise has been the enterprise of mountebanks.'

His novels were used as a weapon against Tory orthodoxy: Coningsby
less so than Sybil, which directly attacks the Tamworth Manifesto and
the conduct of office of Peel. The motivation appears to be personal
ambition rather than principle. Some have detected in Disraeli a dislike
of utilitarianism; which, ironically, would prevail even more when Lord
John Russell took the Liberals into office in 1846, after Disraeli had helped
destroy Peel's administration. However, Disraeli's dislike of this, while
genuine no doubt, seems ramped up for opportunistic effect, as was
much else he said and did after his disappointment of 1841 when he had
unsuccessfully sought office. He never seemed to have a coherent
programme to offer instead; no sign of where the romantic Toryism of
Young England would lead in terms of policy. Neither did Carlyle: but
Carlyle was a professional controversialist and polemicist, while Disraeli
was supposed to be aspiring to the role of statesman.

Politics for Disraeli was about keeping up appearances. Lord George
Bentinck, a leading protectionist and younger son of the Duke of
Portland, became his patron; and he decided to bankroll Disraeli as
spokesman for the aristocracy's landed interest. He and his two brothers
set Disraeli up on a 750-acre estate at Hughenden in Buckinghamshire,
so he could have some of the attributes of a great Tory figure and could
represent the county in Parliament, which he did from 1847. However,
as the deal was going through, Bentinck dropped dead from a heart
attack. Desperate negotiations with the other brothers followed, and the
Portland fortune eventually found the £25,000 needed to set Disraeli up.
This elaborate, almost preposterous exercise in aggrandisement came

when Disraeli was still heavily indebted elsewhere, despite his wife's having come to his aid several times.

Once Disraeli conceived political ambitions – which he appears to have done as a means both of acquiring some social respectability and because of a childlike delight in the 'game' – his need for money became more desperate. He was badly, and chronically, in debt. He entered Parliament at the election of 1837 occasioned by the death of William IV, as one of the two Tory Members returned for Maidstone. It was a stroke of luck for him that his fellow incumbent, Wyndham Lewis, died shortly afterwards, leaving a well-provided-for widow, Mary Anne. Disraeli, though a dozen years the lady's junior, married her. His origins were still mocked by the crowd at the poll in 1837, who assailed him with cries of 'ou' clo'' (the cry of 'old clothes' as popularly uttered by Jewish dealers in that commodity) and 'Shylock'. However, as his biographer Lord Blake points out, England was not a nursery of anti-Semitism at this time, and Disraeli does not appear to have let this unpleasantness defeat him. The same cannot be said for his florid maiden speech, which was popularly accounted a disaster, and which culminated in his yelling above a baying House: 'I will sit down now, but the time will come when you will hear me.'[34]

Despite marrying as well as, or even possibly better than, he might have expected, his financial straits were by now dire. He struggled to pay his election expenses, and such relief as his creditors did get was with Isaac's help. Isaac frequently bailed him out; but this did not prevent him, by the time his party returned to power under Peel in 1841, having debts estimated at £20,000, an awesome sum for the times and equivalent perhaps to £1.7 million today. He continued to write novels, though these struggled to make him much money; and he continued to live extravagantly to keep up with the society that he had decided should be his natural place. His biographer alludes to two arresting facts about him in this early phase in politics: that his wife (who eventually bailed him out to the tune of £13,000) probably knew little, for a long time, about the scale of his indebtedness; and that he was not always truthful on political matters, denying he had said or written things that he had certainly said or written.[35]

His most serious lie – to the Commons, when he was forty-two years of age and had sat in it for nearly nine years (so he cannot be excused an indiscretion of youth or inexperience) – was uttered on 15 May 1846, in the third reading debate on the Corn Importation Bill. He had spoken for the best part of three hours in attacking Peel. Peel rarely bothered to acknowledge Disraeli, whose brilliance as an orator had developed since his first humiliation, but on this occasion he made an exception. Disraeli, having accused Peel of deceiving his party and of adopting 'Machiavellian manoeuvres', had gone on to say that Peel 'has traded on the ideas and intelligence of others. His life has been one great appropriation clause. He is a burglar of others' intellect. Search the Index of Beatson, from the days of the Conqueror to the termination of the last reign, there is no statesman who has committed political petty larceny on so great a scale.'[36]

This was strong stuff for a backbencher to offer the leader of his party, even given the open hostility against Peel. He had then concluded with a peroration of grandstanding quality – 'I have faith in the primitive and enduring elements of the English character . . . when their spirit is softened by misfortune, they will recur to those principles that made England great . . . then, too, perchance they may remember, not with unkindness, those who, betrayed and deserted, were neither ashamed nor afraid to struggle for the "good old cause" – the cause with which are associated principles the most popular, sentiments the most entirely national – the cause of labour – the cause of the people – the cause of England.'[37] Greville was not taken in, finding the speech 'very clever, in which he hacked and mangled Peel with the most unsparing severity, and positively tortured his victim. It was a miserable and degrading spectacle. The whole mass of Protectionists cheered him with a vociferous delight, making the roof ring again.'[38] It was the sort of performance that made Ashley say of him that he was 'without principle, without feeling, without regard to anything, human or divine, beyond his own personal ambition. He has dragged, and will continue to drag everything that is good, safe, venerable, and solid through the dust and dirt of his own objects.'[39]

Disraeli was followed by Russell, in support of the bill, and then Peel rose ('they screamed and hooted at him in the most brutal manner,' Greville noted). His conduct of the question, since he had decided upon repeal, had been marked by its earnestness. He departed from that, outraged by Disraeli's remarks. 'I foresaw that the course which I have taken from a sense of public duty would expose me to serious sacrifices,' he said. 'I foresaw as its inevitable result, that I must forfeit friendships which I most highly valued—that I must interrupt political relations in which I felt a sincere pride; but the smallest of all the penalties which I anticipated were the continued venomous attacks of the Member for Shrewsbury.'[40] He then alluded to Disraeli's having asked him for a job in 1841, expressing his surprise that he should have wanted 'to unite his fortunes with mine in office', given he was guilty of such 'larcenies' as Disraeli had alleged he was.

After a long and, after that, earnest speech, Peel sat down and Disraeli rose once more to correct the 'insinuation' the Prime Minister had made against him of being 'disappointed of office'. 'I can assure the House nothing of the kind ever occurred, I never shall – it is totally foreign to my nature – make an application for any place.'[41] This was the great lie. Peel had the letter requesting a place and others, at that juncture, had seen it. Peel chose not to expose Disraeli, but told the House Disraeli had misinterpreted him. Had he exposed him, Disraeli's political career might have ended there. Perhaps Peel felt it would be stooping to Disraeli's level: and he did not, morally, rate Disraeli highly. As Lord Blake, in his peerless biography, notes: 'It is not an episode on which his admirers care to dwell.'[42] Greville was disgusted, saying that 'to see the Prime Minister and leader in the House of Commons thus beaten and degraded, treated with contumely by three-fourths of the party he had been used to lead, is a sorry sight, and very prejudicial to the public weal.'[43]

Disraeli positioned himself on what would now be called the left of the Tory party, opposing harsh treatment to the leaders of the Chartist movement. His irregularities, inconsistencies, financial instability and simple lack of clout had caused Peel to overlook him when forming his ministry in September 1841, causing in turn Disraeli to write him a letter that describes the open wound the author felt he had sustained to his esteem: 'I have tried to struggle against a storm of political hate and malice which few men have ever experienced . . . I have only been sustained under these trials by the conviction that the day would come when the foremost man of the country would publicly testify that he had some respect for my ability and my character. I confess to be unrecognised at this moment by you appears to me to be overwhelming, and I appeal to your own heart – to that justice and magnanimity which I feel are your characteristics – to save me from an intolerable humiliation.'[44] Peel was unmoved. The letter, which could have done such damage had Peel aired it in 1846, is but one proof of what a political figure before his time Disraeli was: the tone of the aggrieved career politician of the late twentieth or early twenty-first century is apparent in his words. From the moment Peel spurned him, his vendetta against Peel was launched. Disraeli started to feel like an outsider in his own party.

IV

Gladstone, as one of Peel's most devoted admirers, gained the measure of Disraeli by witnessing this scandalous behaviour. When Disraeli became Chancellor in February 1852 his main concern was to find measures that would keep Lord Derby's first administration in power. When Gladstone succeeded him in December of that year it was an opportunity for him to exercise his obsession with the scrupulous use of public money. Fundamental to that was reducing taxation as far as possible, and limiting the operations of the State. He wrote to John Ward of the Inland Revenue on 18 February 1853, before his first budget, on the options open to him. 'One of course would be the immediate abandonment of the Income Tax: and I wish for the best advice upon the question what are the means which we possess of supplying it's [sic] place by a collection of substitutes reaching in all to the same or nearly the same amount of product? Firstly, can this be done at all? Secondly, if at all, how can it be done? It is clearly in the Department of Inland Revenue, if anywhere, that the solution lies.'[45] He suggested a 2.5 per cent land tax and a tax on 'steam boat receipts'.

This was the period of the development of the feud between Gladstone and Disraeli. Gladstone had been the model for the character Oswald Millbank in *Coningsby*, published in 1844 when both men were notionally still Tories. It is ironic that the author, educated at a small private school in Walthamstow, should have represented the Old Etonian Gladstone as someone who only just made it to above the salt in 1830s Eton. Millbank comes from Manchester and his people are in trade; and we first hear Coningsby's view of him when the hero rebukes a friend for asking Millbank to a breakfast party. '"Well," said Coningsby, as if sullenly resigned, "never mind; but why you should ask an infernal manufacturer!"'[46] It is one of those passages that shows Disraeli's uncannily tin ear for dialogue. As well as depicting Millbank as socially inferior, Disraeli compounds the insult by disclosing that 'the secret of Millbank's life was a passionate admiration and affection for Coningsby.'[47] Gladstone was, nonetheless, occasionally charitable about Disraeli's literary attempts. In his papers are rough notes he made on having read *Sybil*, mainly quoting phrases from the book, but also terming one of them 'a capital passage'.[48]

The beginning of the great parliamentary rivalry between the two men is usually dated to the early hours of 17 December 1852. It was the end of the debate on the Budget, the first delivered by Disraeli at what turned out to be the denouement of Derby's 'Who? Who?' ministry (so named because each time one of its nonentities rose to speak in the Lords, the deaf and almost dead Duke of Wellington bellowed at Derby 'Who? Who?' as he had heard of none of them). Disraeli did not want to be Chancellor but, being ambitious, could not refuse the position when offered it. His Budget speech had been applauded, perhaps as much because of the physical achievement of delivering one of such length (about five hours) as because of what it contained. Disraeli had no feel for economics (as his personal finances showed), no understanding of detail, and had to be led by his officials. His Budget was quickly pulled apart, notably for its decision to cut the malt tax and increase the house tax. Gladstone, strong in every department in which Disraeli was weak, chose the last possible opportunity in the debate to savage the proposals. He did so clinically and by analysis, and without the recourse to sarcasm and invective that characterised Disraeli's speeches.

He spoke directly after the Chancellor, rising in a packed, poorly lit House of Commons at one o'clock in the morning. Disraeli realised the difficulties, and in the closing moments of his own speech had warned against the coalition of opinion being raised against him – by Peelites and Whigs – in uttering his notable remark that 'England does not love coalitions'.[49] He was jeered by Derby's supporters, partly because they would have hoped to be getting home to bed, partly because Gladstone was, like them, still notionally a Conservative, and was attacking one of his 'own' side in a way that, it soon became apparent, would kill rather than just wound. He began with a form of moral rebuke for Disraeli, for having used the *argumentum ad hominem* rather too often in his speech: Gladstone intimated he would stick to facts.

He demonstrated the regressive nature of the taxation Disraeli was introducing. He illustrated the hypocrisies of the man who had brought down Peel – the administration of nonentities, after all, had survived in office only so long as it had because of its decision to abandon all ideas of protection, yet much Peelite doctrine in the matter of commercial reform was in the government's programme. He questioned Disraeli's figures. He deplored his implication that the income tax would be permanent, when Peel had always intended it to be temporary. He said that by voting against the Budget one would be upholding Conservative principles, not by supporting it. He spoke for two-and-a-half hours. His speech preceded the vote, in which the government was defeated, and Derby had no option but to resign.

The change of government brought Gladstone and Disraeli into conflict, but on the most ridiculous of matters. For all the height of his mind, Gladstone was not above pettiness when dealing with his rival, and Disraeli, as might have been expected, returned the compliment wholesale. Gladstone agreed to serve in Aberdeen's essentially Peelite ministry, and succeeded Disraeli. Acrimony between the past and present Chancellor was immediate. The furniture in the official residence had hitherto been the Chancellor's private property, and a fee was agreed between chancellors at the change of incumbent to ensure no one went out of pocket. It had been decided that this arrangement was cumbersome, and that the furniture should be sold to the Office of Works, becoming their property in perpetuity. Therefore, at the end of January 1853 Gladstone wrote to Disraeli and said that the Office of Works would be reimbursing him; and he also asked: 'There is, I believe, a robe which passed down under some law of exchange from one Chancellor of the Exchequer to another, and I shall be very happy to retrieve it from you on the ordinary footing, whatever that may be.'[50]

Disraeli, however, wrote to Gladstone to ask him to pay £307 16s for the costs of the furniture. He had paid the Office of Works £787 12s 6d when he succeeded Sir Charles Wood, but having expressed his 'dissatisfaction' at having to take 'many things which I did not require' he was out of pocket. The Office of Works had reimbursed Disraeli £479 16s for furniture it agreed was 'in rooms of public reception' and Gladstone was asked to pay the rest on assuming his new role.[51] He said nothing of the robe. This garment had belonged to Pitt the Younger and Disraeli simply intended to keep it, another interesting mark of his probity.

Gladstone replied that the Office of Works would handle the financial settlement, and reminded Disraeli that he had not mentioned the robe.[52]

Disraeli did not want to try to extract the money from the government, but decided to badger Gladstone for it. He sent a curt note in the third person a week later, the aggressiveness of which may or may not have been a cover for his determination to avoid discussion of the robe: 'Mr Disraeli regrets very much, that he is obliged to say that Mr Gladstone's letter repudiating his obligation to pay for the furniture of the official residence is not satisfactory.'[53] He accused Gladstone of having breached the regulations 'between gentlemen' that had existed in changes of chancellor 'which his predecessors had recognised'. He continued: 'He was bound to act towards Mr Disraeli as Mr D had acted towards Sir Chas Wood.' The note ended: 'As Mr Gladstone appears to be in perplexity on this subject, Mr Disraeli recommends him to consult Sir Charles Wood, who is a man of the world.'

Gladstone replied, also in the third person, that he 'has read with regret and pain the note which he received last night from Mr Disraeli. He has endeavoured in this correspondence to observe towards Mr Disraeli the courtesy which was his due [the words 'he thought' have been crossed out after 'which'] 'and he is not aware of having said or done anything to justify the tone which Mr Disraeli has thought proper to adopt.'[54] Gladstone suggested an independent valuation of what was left, to try to close the matter down; and he concluded: 'It is highly unpleasant for Mr W. E. Gladstone to address Mr Disraeli without the usual terms of courtesy; but he abstains from them only because he perceives they are unwelcome.' Disraeli's biographers – Monypenny and Buckle, and Blake – agree that Gladstone should have paid up (which in the end he did) and not have expected the new rule about the owner-ship by the Office of Works to be made retrospective; but they also agree that Disraeli behaved badly about the robe, which remained in his family, and is still on display at Hughenden.

Unlike Disraeli, Gladstone saw no personal benefit in power. He wrote to John Bright on 22 February 1858, saying that 'The opinions, such as they are, that I hold on many questions of Government and admin-istration, are strongly held; and although I set a value, a high value, upon the power which office gives, I earnestly hope never to be tempted by its exterior allurements, unless they are accompanied with the reason-able prospect of giving effect to some at least of those opinions, and with some adequate opening for public good.'[55] However, Gladstone – still at this stage a Peelite, and therefore notionally a Tory – was regarded as a prize by Derby and his supporters, including Disraeli. Their hopes of establishing a stable ministry once they took office again in February 1858 seemed to rest upon Gladstone's agreeing to be a part of it, and bringing other Peelites with him. Despite – or, perhaps, because of – the rancour between them, Disraeli was sent with the olive branch.

In May 1858 he sent a note to Gladstone marked 'confidential'.[56] It began, without any salutation:

> I think it of real paramount importance to the public interests, that you should assume at this time a commanding position in the administration of affairs, that I feel it a solemn duty to lay before you some facts, that you may not decide under a misapprehension.
>
> Our mutual relations have formed the great difficulty in accomplishing a result, wh I have always anxiously denied.
>
> Listen, without prejudice to this brief narrative.

There follows a self-justificatory account of Disraeli's public life since 1850, when he said he had through Lord Londonderry 'endeavoured . . . for some time and without hope to induce Sir James Graham to accept the post of Leader of the Conservative Party, which, I thought, would remove all difficulties.' He continued: 'When he finally declined this office I endeavoured to throw the game into your hands.' However, Gladstone had not sought it. Then, in 1855, Palmerston had become leader of the Commons and Prime Minister. Earlier in 1858 Disraeli had once more sought to persuade Graham to take over the leadership of the party 'to allow both of us to serve under him.' Graham had replied that 'his course was run'. He added:

> Thus you can see, for more than eight years, instead of thrusting myself to the forward place, I have been at all times actively preparing to make every sacrifice of self for the public good, wh I have ever thought identical with your accepting office in a Conservative government.
>
> Don't you think the time has come, when you might deign to be magnanimous?
>
> Mr Canning was superior to Ld Castlereagh in capacity, in acquirements and in eloquence but he joined Lord C when Lord C was Ld Liverpool's lieutenant and when the state of the party rendered it necessary . . . to be inactive now is, on your part, a real

responsibility. If you join Ld Derby's cabinet, you will meet there some warm personal friends; all its members are your admirers. You may place me in neither category but in that, I assure you, you have ever been most mistaken. The vacant post is, at this season, the most commanding in the commonwealth; if it were not, whatever office you filled, your shining qualities would always render you supreme; and if . . . necessities retain me formally in the chief post . . .

Gladstone replied on 25 May to 'my dear Sir' and said that 'the letter you have been so kind as to address to me will enable me I trust to remove from your mind some impressions with which you will not be sorry to part.'[57]

He observed that Disraeli had given him a narrative of his role as leader of his party, and said that he had 'never thought your retention of that office matter of reproach to you' and that he 'acknowledged . . . the handsomeness of your conduct in offering to resign it to Sir James Graham.' But he continued: 'You consider that the relations between yourself and me have proved the main difficulty in the way of certain political arrangements – will you allow me to assure you that I have never in my life taken a decision which turned upon those relations.'

He warmed to his theme. 'You assure me that I have ever been mistaken in failing to place you among my friends or admirers. Again I pray you to let me say that I have never known you penurious in admiration towards anyone who had the slightest claim to it, and that at no period of my life, not even during the limited one where we were in sharp political conflict, have I either felt any enmity towards you or believed that you felt any towards me.' Gladstone talked to Derby, but told Disraeli that 'the difficulties which he [Derby] wishes me to find means of overcoming are broader than you may have supposed . . . you have yourself reminded me that there is a Power beyond us that disposes of what we will do, and I find the limits of choice in public life to be very narrow.' From that moment, the old enmities reasserted themselves.

V

It was sometimes the case in the political class that good and bad were mixed up in the same character – Gladstonian principle and Disraelian expediency coming together in the same person. This could give rise to the charge of hypocrisy for which the Victorians were so noted. Even Gladstone has been victim of this charge, because of doubts – unsupported by evidence – about the nature of his interest in prostitutes. However, in others, not all public service was what it seemed.

Some, such as the now forgotten figure of Sir Edwin Pearson, did their Christian duty of good works for the poor and for society in general with a distinct view towards social advancement: and of course there were those in high politics, such as Disraeli, who set them a very good example in such full-blooded hypocrisy. A memo in Gladstone's papers from Pearson, dated January 1872, states that: 'In July 1845 the Westminster Improvement Commission [which Pearson chaired] was incorporated for the purpose of removing the most wretched and unwholesome district of Westminster, and of constructing on its site, a new thoroughfare, 80 feet in width between the Houses of Parliament and Buckingham Palace'.[58] This work was completed, at a cost of £50,000, and the new road opened on 1 August 1851. Five lateral streets were also constructed, and 9,300 feet of sewers laid underneath, with more than 12,000 feet of pavement.

'The social and sanitary results of this important improvement', the memo continues, 'have fully corresponded with the extent and character of the works themselves: and this district, which was formerly the most depraved and sickly, is now well ordered, and has become one of the healthiest portions of the Metropolis.' The memo quotes observations by the Dean of St Paul's, H. H. Milman, who had been Canon of Westminster and Rector of St Margaret's.

Nothing could be more deplorable than the state of Westminster before the Westminster Improvement Commissioners began their labours. From the first period of my Ministry as Rector of St Margaret's, I made up my mind that nothing could be done for the moral change (to speak of the spiritual condition would be a mockery) of the dense and swarming population, without a most extensive demolition of the wretched buildings which they inhabited.

There was a considerable area covered with houses, in which to have lived was to forfeit all character, and to be set down as thief or prostitute. These houses were old, worn-out, not worth repair. [This included houses owned by the Dean and Chapter of the

Abbey, on short leases.] These could only be underlet to persons who gave high rents and remunerated themselves by reletting them for the worst of purposes . . . no moral or religious influences could approach those places with any possibility of success. Some years before I came to Westminster they were hardly safe, not indeed till the establishment of the new Police . . . and though neither myself nor my curates met with insult, it was generally said, that no-one but the Parson and the Doctor could enter them without danger. I speak of the moral state rather than as regards sanitary questions, yet even on this account it was absolutely necessary for the public good to sweep away an immense number of these miserable hovels, the established, recognised, irreclaimable haunts of rogues of every description, and women of the lowest profligacy.

Their wholesale demolition delighted the Dean. Pearson also set in train the construction of new dwellings for the poor and the 'industrial inhabitants' of Westminster. He sought to ensure there would be no repeat of the cholera epidemic of 1832, which killed a number of parishioners, and it was he who obtained an Act of Parliament for the improvement works. In 1844 an inquiry had found the area 'without any common sewers at all; or where they existed were from dilapidation or other causes inefficient to the extent. All endeavours of the Inhabitants to keep their vicinity clean and wholesome were frustrated for want of drainage.' All this information and more is contained in a specially printed collection of written testimonials to Pearson: who sent them to Gladstone seeking a government job, possibly a financial reward, and hinting at an honour higher than his knighthood.

This bid failed. So Pearson wrote again to Gladstone in April 1873 with a new specially printed memorandum modestly entitled *Correspondence . . . on the subject of Sir Edwin Pearson's Claim on her Majesty's Government for some substantial recognition of his Public Services*.[59] It included letters from various grandees and public officials, among them Gladstone himself, on the wonder of Sir E. Pearson. It again referred to events many years earlier, such as a note of congratulation from the Earl of Carlisle – the First Commissioner of Works under whom the Westminster improvement had been conducted – to Pearson on his achievements, dated 10 April 1851. There follows several thousand words of Sir Edwin's egomania. One can only begin to imagine the effect this had on so self-effacing a man as Gladstone. The same Lord Carlisle, for example, 'with an honourable appreciation of the injustice done to Sir Edwin Pearson, who, notwithstanding the great services he had rendered, still remained neglected and unnoticed by the Government' had lobbied Palmerston in 1855 for something for Pearson. Thereafter the Duke of Argyll ('I am sure that any mark of Royal favour which may have been usual on such occasions, will be more than usually well-deserved in your case') and various bishops and judges were quoted on the marvels of Sir Edwin.

Pearson persuaded Lord Hatherley, the Lord Chancellor, to advance his case to Gladstone; which he did in April 1870. Gladstone replied that 'I cannot doubt the claim of Sir Edwin Pearson; I can readily promise to consider it, if occasion offer, but I know not when that would be. I have had no office yet to which he could have been appointed; and would advise him to have other strings to his bow.' When Pearson had heard nothing after a few weeks he importuned other Cabinet ministers of his acquaintance, including Cardwell, Hatherley, Argyll and the Attorney General, Sir John Coleridge. They could do nothing for him: so he continued to nag Gladstone directly, asking him outright for a baronetcy. He cited the precedent of Sir James Lawrence, 'having lately [been] recommended for the honour of a Baronetcy in consideration of the Metropolitan Improvements completed under his mayoralty.' Pearson asserted that all such men had baronetcies 'and *there is no instance on record where this rule has been departed from, except my own* . . . I feel a boldness, therefore, in submitting my claims to you, which I do, not as a matter merely of favour, but as one of precedent and right.'

Gladstone was losing patience. He had his secretary reply in January 1872 that 'he is unable to give you any promise to bring your name before Her Majesty for a Baronetcy'. Pearson asked again, with the same result. He then claimed that Gladstone had promised him a baronetcy through the Lord Chancellor, which prompted the curt statement: 'Mr Gladstone is aware of no such promise as you allude to, and he trusts that you will not impose upon him the task of again correcting such misapprehensions as those you appear to be labouring under.' Pearson's rhinoceros skin was astonishing: not least that he should print all these rebuffs in his next submission to Gladstone. He then started splitting hairs about what had been meant by Gladstone's letter to Hatherley of April 1870 – the meaning of which was clear to all but Pearson who 'began to apprehend, for the first time, that Mr Gladstone did not seem to attach the same meaning to his letter to the Lord Chancellor as Sir Edwin Pearson and his friends had done.' This astonishing document concluded by asserting that Pearson's interpretation of the letter to Hatherley was more accurate than Gladstone's; and that it was Gladstone's duty and not his privilege to recommend him to the Queen for a Baronetcy, reinforcing his recommendation by informing the Queen of Hatherley's strong opinion of Pearson's merits. Gladstone's office kept up an iron defence, that he had 'nothing to add' to his former letters.

For a moment it seemed that Pearson had gone away: but on 6 August 1873, on, as he put it, 'the anniversary of the opening of Victoria Street', he wrote again asserting his 'claims'.[60] A line scribbled on the back of the letter observes: 'He has behaved rather badly'. He wrote again on 29 September 'as I have not had the honour to receive any answer to my letter written to you last month' and hoping, somewhat in vain, that 'I shall not appear importunate'.[61] The blackmail continued. 'I am informed by several persons who are intimate with you, that you never failed to do what you had promised to do; and that I may confidently rely upon the fulfilment of any matter about which you had made a promise,' he wrote.

He insisted Gladstone had made a 'promise' to have him honoured. This was too much for Gladstone, the tone of whose marginalia about Sir Edwin had now risen to 'he seems a most troublesome fellow'.[62] Gladstone had his secretary reply, speaking of his 'regret that he must decline to prolong the correspondence, from which he fears no benefit can be derived.' He continued: 'I am directed to add, with reference to your allusion to Mr Gladstone's promise, that if you refer to his engagement to consider your claims, he is able to assure you that it has been fulfilled, although the results have been (he regrets to say) unfavourable. Mr Gladstone is really unable to admit of the existence of any other pledge.'

Pearson was determined to have the last word: so he wrote, on 7 October, to 'ask your indulgence, once more, to allow me to set myself right with regard to the interpretation of your letter to the late Lord Chancellor [Hatherley], on the subject of my claim to some acknowledgment for my public services'.[63] There followed much analysis of Gladstone's earlier words, Pearson becoming excited by the phrases 'I cannot doubt the claim of Sir Edwin Pearson' and 'I can readily promise to consider it if occasion offer – I have no office yet to which he could have been appointed.' He took this to mean that Gladstone saw he merited an honour: the only question was what and when. He made this point, he said 'humbly', 'because I am anxious to vindicate myself from the least appearance of having put a forced interpretation upon the words of your letter.' Scrawled on an adjoining note is the phrase: 'Seems to require no answer'.[64] Sir Edwin's reward for improving the lot of the poor was, no doubt, in heaven.

CHAPTER 9

THE PROGRESSIVE MIND:
THE GREAT EXHIBITION AND
ITS LEGACY

I

The Great Exhibition of 1851 showcased British innovation, engineering and design. It was one of the turning points of the Victorian age, and one of the events that confirmed Britain's status as the world's foremost power. It raised the ambition of Victorian England to an unprecedented height. However, it also confirmed the great Victorian traits of determination and achievement; the aims were high, but they were accomplished thanks to the clear vision and energy of those who undertook them. Snobbery about manufacturing and trade was diluted by the wider recognition of the international respect paid to Britain on account of its achievements in those areas, and the prosperity that resulted from them. As well as obtaining greater international influence for Britain by means other than war, and giving a country so recently riven by conflict and civil disturbance something of which all could be proud, the Exhibition would present the triumph of free trade, and its supremacy over protectionism: something Albert and the Queen had felt strongly for years, and which had driven them to support repeal of the Corn Laws. It was a microcosm of two prime Victorian traits: ambition, and the ability to do great things relatively quickly. The fulfilment of the ambition required leadership, and the Queen's husband provided it. Prince Albert's enduring significance in British history rests in his determination to create the Exhibition. It has become synonymous with his memory: as has the estate of museums and other cultural and educational institutions in South Kensington, which became known as

Albertopolis, and which were partly funded by the £213,000 profit made from the Exhibition.

Albert never intended his legacy to be confined to a few acres of west London. The Exhibition was designed to stimulate a nationwide interest in science and the arts, the former reflecting Albert's very German idea of the importance of technological advancement. Thanks to his leadership, people from the highest circles in the land were motivated to commit themselves to endorsing and financially supporting social reform. It took a German, from a society unencumbered by snobbery about trade, to harness the force of commerce to the glory of his adopted country. He did so, perhaps appropriately, with the help of pushing, ambitious men on the make who were also typical of the new order that social and economic change was creating. The lasting result, ironically, was institutions that became part of the national focus of cultural life, and that underpinned the civilising goal of the pursuit of perfection.

That Albert was able to bring such a radically different, and un-English, cast of mind to bear on the potential for the society over which his wife reigned was down to quirks of his upbringing. He was the second son of the Duke of Saxe-Coburg-Gotha, born near Coburg in August 1819, making him a few weeks younger than his wife. His father was a womaniser and his much younger wife – Albert's mother – had her revenge by having affairs with various courtiers. They divorced when Albert was seven, and his mother died of cancer when he was twelve. Albert roundly disliked his father and had a miserable childhood. It was enriched, however, by his tutor Christoph Florschütz, who devised a rigorous programme of education in a range of subjects far broader than anything an English public schoolboy of the era would have experienced.

This, and his sense of isolation (though he was educated with his brother), caused him to develop into a serious, earnest, high-minded youth, but also one of some talent. Among other accomplishments he wrote, composed music, designed clothes and was largely responsible for the design of Osborne House, the royal couple's private retreat on the Isle of Wight. Early on matchmakers marked him out as a suitable husband for his cousin Princess Victoria of Kent, who seemed likely to become Queen of England. Albert continued his education at the University of Bonn, starting in the autumn of 1837, months after his cousin ascended the throne. He came increasingly under the influence of Baron Stockmar, physician to his uncle King Leopold of the Belgians, who would become his chief adviser. He and Victoria were engaged in August 1839 and married in February 1840; the first of their nine children, a daughter who would become the Kaiserin, was born the following November, and their first son, who became Edward VII, a year after that. Public opinion in Britain had lamented the possible influence a foreigner might have over their Queen, who was not yet twenty-one. The government did all it could to put Albert in his place: it refused him a peerage, granted him a comparatively small allowance (£30,000 a year against the £50,000 Leopold had had when he married the ill-fated Princess Charlotte of Wales in 1816), and imposed various people on his household. Albert began married life feeling humiliated, and soon became frustrated too as he searched for a role that the British constitution could not provide for him.

Yet Albert soon began to start changing the monarchy. The Royal Household was overmanned, poorly structured and woefully inefficient. Albert spotted this quickly and set about overseeing its reform along lines of Teutonic efficiency. His stern, almost puritanical morality was a cold blast after the loucheness and venality of the later Hanoverians. He began to help his wife with her constitutional responsibilities, not least because of her frequent indispositions during her pregnancies. A Regency Act confirmed he would take charge if she died while the heir was a minor. He made formal studies of English constitutional law and history, to help ensure he was not out of his depth.

His big break came with the departure of Melbourne and the succession of Peel in 1841. He quickly befriended Albert and suggested the Prince become head of the Royal Commission on Fine Arts, the main purpose of which was to encourage the arts in Britain. Peel had suggested his name to the Queen on 26 September, linking it to the subject 'of the promotion of the Fine Arts in connection with the Building of the New Houses of Parliament.'[1] He said that if the Queen thought a Royal Commission appropriate for dealing with this subject, perhaps 'YM would deem it desirable that the Prince should be invited in the name of YM to place himself at the head of this Commission, and to give to it the authority and influence of his high name, and the advantage of his Taste and Knowledge.'

This was not pure sycophancy: Albert was an aesthete. 'When you were last here,' begins a letter to Peel from him on 3 October 1841, 'our conversation turned upon the *Niebelungen Lied* . . . I thought it would amuse you to see a very fine edition of the work which has lately appeared, and therefore I send it to you.'[2] Albert went on to appraise the merit of the illustrations in the edition, and then discussed the Royal Commission with Peel, saying how 'glad' he was that Peel's announcement of it 'was so well received in the House of Commons'. He asked that 'there had better be no artist by profession in the Commission. The benefit of an artist's opinion could be <u>equally</u> obtained by taking it upon examination and evidence. And even better, as it would enable the Commission to procure the different opinions of a greater number of artists.'

He said this with humility: 'I only give you my crude views and have no wish whatever to press them against the experience of others.' Peel, nonetheless, replied that he found the Prince's view 'perfectly put'.[3] Peel had the Commission composed almost entirely of Lords and Commons.[4] Albert found this 'an admirable selection, and I can only rejoice that party distinctions should have been excluded from this <u>national</u> undertaking.'[5] When in October 1841 the artist Cornelius came to England he was consulted by Peel and the Prince on his ideas for 'decoration' of the new parliamentary building. 'I can quite enter into Cornelius's opinion,' Albert wrote to Peel, 'respecting the fitness of the English school for historical composition, for I can understand that he may be disgusted with its mistaken tendency: to obtain <u>mere effect</u> and to bribe the senses and acquire applause by rich colouring and the representation of voluptuous forms overlooking at the same time its deficiency in real poetical imagination and invention and the importance of Correct Drawing.'[6] Albert regretted that 'the taste of the public is not now what it ought to be' and indeed that the taste of the artists themselves could do with refinement through further 'study'. After a sizeable disquisition on the benefits of the fresco, he concluded: 'If some were sent to study at Munic [sic], Florence and Rome, I have not the slightest doubt, they would produce works fully equal to the present school of the Germans.'

Albert was courteous and helpful with the Household appointments; and Peel also formed a good relationship with his secretary, George Anson. Conscious of the difficulties Peel was having getting Ashley to serve in the administration, Anson asked Ashley on 7 September 1841 whether he might wish to be Lord-in-Waiting to the Prince, a post declined by Lord Lyttelton: 'Do you think Lord Ashley could be persuaded to take this place about the Prince? The same objections need not apply to his entering the Prince's service as applied to a place offered by the Minister and it would not prevent his being transferred to other office when the factory question was disposed of.'[7] Ashley did not waver.

Albert used his moral force and intellectual energy to transform the Royal Family. His notion of family life, and of his role as paterfamilias, saw the elevation of family values almost to a cult. Whatever an aristocracy that continued to set its own rules thought of this, the expanding middle class strove to emulate it. The self-discipline and self-reliance it preached would over the rest of the nineteenth century make the middle class the true power in the land, not least because its aspirational nature made that class more numerous, more wealthy and more influential. The model Albert set for it was perceptively described, six years after his death, by Walter Bagehot as that of 'a *family* on the throne'.[8] But it was his typically German earnestness as much as his status that ensured the Exhibition would be a success.

II

The Great Exhibition marked a junction of a period of strife and darkness with one of prosperity and light. The French had been in the habit of holding exhibitions to promote their country and its business since the era of Napoleon Bonaparte. In the early 1840s Francis Whishaw, secretary of the Society of Arts, investigated the practicalities of holding such an event in London. Albert was president of the Society, and present at a meeting in 1845 where Whishaw mentioned the notion. The Society had been founded in 1754 and had endured a long period of decline. Albert and the council resolved to reactivate it, and an exhibition seemed a superb means of doing so. It would take a man of extraordinary drive and vision to manage the day-to-day organisation of such a project. Fortunately, such a man was on hand in the shape of a middle-ranking government official named Henry Cole.

Cole would become one of the most important public servants of the era, in some respects the most important. Born in 1808, he had left Christ's Hospital School at fifteen to work in a lowly capacity at the Record Commission, a body whose job was to attempt to assemble and catalogue the nation's public records, which were in an uncodified and shambolic state. Cole was a prime example of the aspirational middle class, the lives of whose members would benefit so much by the range of projects to which he would apply himself during his long and varied career. He also set them a fine example by his push, and by his knack of being deferential only when it furthered his own agenda. After a decade in the department Cole realised it needed radical reform, being even more corrupt and based on jobbery and nepotism than most of the rest of the Civil Service. He took on the role of whistleblower, and was dismissed in 1835 for writing two articles in the *Examiner* exposing the practices of the department. Unfortunately for Cole he wrote these not only because of a principled disagreement about how the Record Commission was run, but after a disagreement about his salary: his motives were open to question.

However, so forceful had been the criticisms that a parliamentary inquiry was set up, as a result of which Cole was exonerated and given his job back. The Record Commission was reformed, and Cole appointed one of the four senior assistant keepers there: but a bad odour lingered. It would not be the last time Cole would use the force of his personality to get what he wanted, or that what he deemed in the best interests of the country would be remarkably similar to what he wanted.

By the time he came to Albert's attention Cole had done considerably more than reform the Record Commission. He had been Rowland Hill's right-hand man in establishing the penny post, which was launched on 6 May 1840 and at a stroke established a communications infrastructure accessible to the entire population as well as to all officialdom: it was a leading tool in the modernisation of Britain under the Victorians. Aided by the existence of this service, Cole also invented the Christmas card in 1843. He lent his considerable weight both as an official and as an accomplished journalist to the establishment of the standard-gauge railway track. There being no limit to his talents, he designed in 1846 a tea service that won a Society of Arts prize and went into mass production. His enthusiasm for a national exhibition came after this triumph, which occurred at the 1847 exhibition of manufacturing that the Society put on of its own accord. After further small, but successful, exhibitions in the two succeeding years, Cole persuaded the Society to petition Parliament to launch a national event, to give a showcase for British manufacturing at a time when markets were reviving around the world and Britain's command of the oceans and growing imperial reach made penetration of those markets relatively easy.

He became a member of the council of the Society in 1847 and by 1850 he was its chairman, a post in which, according to Sir Henry Trueman Wood, a later secretary of the Society, he exerted 'the strongest personal influence over the Society', amounting, in the early years of his reign, to 'total control'.[9] This control was hardly surprising, because Cole was by this time known to have the ear and confidence of the president, Prince Albert, to whom in his role as chairman he answered directly. Cole also made sure that he wrote the petition to Parliament himself. For all his asperities Cole knew how to play the courtier, and Albert placed complete reliance upon him. He teamed up with two others who became driving forces behind the idea: John Scott Russell, secretary of the Society of Arts, and Francis Fuller, an expert on agriculture. These three went to Paris in June 1849 with Matthew Digby Wyatt, the artist and writer, to get the measure of how the French mounted their exhibitions.

Fuller had an important conversation with Thomas Cubitt, the architect and builder, who had been Prince Albert's partner in the design and construction of Osborne, and with whom, returning from Paris, he travelled back from Southampton after Cubitt had been working at the house. Fuller recorded in his diary that, having seen how the French did things, he told Cubitt that 'we could do a much grander work in London by inviting contributions from every nation'. He observed that 'if Prince Albert would take the lead in such a work he would become a leading light among nations'.[10] Fuller seemed to have found for Albert the role he had been seeking that would not drag him into political difficulties: though he may have been rehearsing a view already expressed by Cole, who knew the Prince even by that stage well enough to make intelligent assumptions about what might appeal to his sense of duty – and his sense of frustration.

Cubitt returned to Osborne on business two days after his meeting with Fuller, and told Albert what had been said. Albert trusted him and was swayed by his enthusiasm, deciding it had to be taken further. Knowing Scott Russell and Cole well through his association with the Society of Arts, Albert had informal discussions with them over the next couple of days, and gave Cole an audience on 29 June, where he let it be known that an international rather than a national exhibition would be his ambition. The next day the three Paris trippers and Cubitt were summoned to Buckingham Palace, to discuss a plan. Important ideas were raised at this meeting that would have a direct bearing on the event: such as what the exhibition would consist of and where it would be held. The former would be 'Raw Materials of Manufactures – British Colonial and Foreign, Machinery and Mechanical Inventions, Manufactures, Sculptors and Plastic Art generally'.[11] It was, it seems, the Prince who came up with the idea of an exhibition hall built on the south side of Hyde Park, after such improbable locations as Somerset House and Leicester Square were rejected. Albert also realised that money should be raised: he thought about £100,000, and that the Society of Arts should hold the fund.

The day after the Buckingham Palace meeting Cole took his wife and children to Kensington to inspect the suggested location, and then went to see Henry Labouchere, the President of the Board of Trade, to brief him on the plan, about which he should shortly be hearing from Albert himself. On 9 July Albert wrote to Labouchere saying: 'I should like to have some conversation with you on the subject of a great national and even international Exhibition which the Society of Arts have been anxious to invite for the year 1851.'[12] Albert stressed 'the highest importance' of the project and how it would need to be approached 'in harmony with and under the guidance of the Govt'. Part of the conversation would be about the appointment of a Royal Commission to oversee the exhibition and all the arrangements, and to determine prizes for exhibitors. These would be funded by the Society for Arts. The first prize would be £5,000, a sum deemed large enough to entice even the most hostile manufacturer to take part. Albert suggested the following members of the Commission: the Duke of Buccleuch, the Earl of Ellesmere, Lord Stanley, Lord John Russell, Peel, Sir R. Lane, Sir H. de la Beche and Messrs Labouchere, Gladstone, Cobden, Fuller and Scott Russell.[13]

Cole immediately wrote to Colonel Charles Phipps, Albert's private secretary, urging dispatch in getting the commission formally appointed. When it was, the impartial selection of its members pleased *The Times*, which was also glad to see the manufacturing and mercantile interest so well represented by such as Cobden. Charles Barry, the architect of the new Houses of Parliament, and William Cubitt, president of the Institution of Civil Engineers (no relation to Thomas) were applauded too.[14] The urgent matter was to find a builder who would enter into the scheme on a speculative basis, to be paid a percentage out of the revenues from the exhibition itself, a cost estimated by Cubitt (who was not willing to shoulder the burden himself) at around £50,000. Fuller, through his father-in-law, found such a builder: James Munday, and his nephew George, who on 23 August 1849 signed a contract to build the exhibition hall. The Mundays made it clear that it was Albert's name at the head of the enterprise that persuaded them to take the risk.[15] When the news was broadcast, manufacturers from outside London, annoyed perhaps that they had not been offered a share of these spoils, complained at the speculative nature of the enterprise, and at Albert's association with it. They argued that if the project were destined to be such a success, a public subscription would have paid for the building. The sting was taken out of this complaint when the names of the commissioners were published, and it was clear from it that these were high-minded, disinterested men and not commercial adventurers.

Albert gave formal authority to Cole, Fuller and Scott Russell to visit manufacturing districts to urge participation in the event.[16] Cole had similar high powers vested in him by the Society of Arts, which appointed an executive committee to manage its involvement with the exhibition. He, Fuller and Scott Russell quickly found that, as Albert himself put it, 'the manufacturers generally are very favourably disposed towards the plan'.[17] The substantial prize money had clearly done its work, but so too had Albert's patronage. It was important to gather evidence of a strong desire to participate so it could be presented to Parliament after its return from the long recess, which in those days lasted from August until late January: also, those driving the scheme saw the benefits of advising the Cabinet as quickly as possible of the likely success of the venture. Cole's tour of the British Isles – which included a hugely successful meeting in Dublin – ended with a rousing gathering at the Mansion House in London on 17 October 1849 at which Cole effectively challenged the money men of Great Britain to subscribe to build better and more impressive works than any of their European competitors could.

He told them what he had learned on his travels around England, and about how 'one gentleman only, out of some 600 or 700 whom we have consulted' was in favour of restricting the exhibition to British goods only, rather than those from all over the world.[18] Interestingly, people did not see the event as one solely for Britain to boast about itself or to make money: a clergyman from Dover whom Cole met said it might contribute to world peace, hastening the time when swords would be beaten into ploughshares and spears into pruning-hooks – a quotation met by cries of 'hear, hear' from the meeting. This was very much Albert's view. But Cole also sought to impress and create a sense of awe by outlining what he envisaged would be in the exhibition: 'We shall probably have enormous elephants' tusks from Africa and Asia; leather from Morocco and Russia; Beaver from Baffin's Bay; the wools of Australia, Yorkshire and Thibet; silk from Asia and from Europe; and furs from the Esquimaux.' Perhaps even more exciting, 'the Court of Directors of the East India Company intend to exhibit the best of every-thing that India can produce.' For good measure there would be gold from California and silver from Mexico – and from Cornwall. He also promised displays by the latest machinery: not just the most sophisticated looms, but even such printing presses as could now turn out 10,000 copies of *The Times* each hour.

Cole also explained, to great enthusiasm, why the Prince had chosen the Kensington site. 'High and low, rich and poor, would have equally good access (hear, hear) . . . those who rode down in omnibuses, and those who went in their private carriages, would have equal facilities of approach. (Cheers.)' His peroration was tub-thumping. 'I think we may expect some hundred thousand people to come flowing into London from all parts of the world, by railways and steamboats, to see this great exhibition. I think we may calculate on the advent of foreign merchants who may want to buy, pleasure-seekers in abundance, and men of science anxious to see what has been done. In short, London will act the part of host to all the world at an intellectual festival of peaceful industry suggested by the consort of our beloved Queen, and seconded by your-selves – a festival such as the world never before has seen.' *The Times* report concluded with the information that 'Mr Cole resumed his seat amidst much cheering from all parts of the hall.' Various resolutions about proceeding with the exhibition were then put to the meeting and passed unanimously: the full mercantile wealth of the City of London was now behind the plan.

When deputations from the manufacturing districts sought audiences of Albert via Russell, the Prime Minister, to discuss the project, the Prince was urged to meet them. Stafford Northcote told Grey (who had by this time been promoted from equerry to Albert's private secretary, in succession to Phipps) on 9 January 1850 that Labouchere thought 'the reception of the Manchester deputation by the Prince in person would have a most excellent effect, and would probably ensure the cordial co-operation of the town, which appears to have taken alarm at some of the proceedings of the Society of Arts.'[19] Albert duly met them. The Lord Mayor of London, and his counterparts in Birmingham and Glasgow, quickly attested to the enthusiasm of their constituencies, and asserted that 'money will not be wanted'.[20] Enthusiasm brought its own problems, however, as Grey noted, namely 'the selection of articles to be exhibited'.

The commissioners met for the first time on 11 January 1850, at Westminster, with Albert in the chair. One of the first decisions was that the Mundays should be bought out of their speculative deal and a loan from the government should fund the building of what became the Crystal Palace, so that the only business relationship in the management of the exhibition was between the Commission and the Society of Arts. This created the additional burden on the Commission of finding funds to guarantee the Treasury loan, which would be repaid out of the proceeds of the event. The Commission also assumed some of what had been the duties of the Society; which, as the person of Cole was prominent in both, was easily done.

Cole was seconded from his work at the Record Office to work full-time, and sought Albert's approval for a salary of £1,200 a year. Mundays offered to pay it, but Albert insisted that Cole be on the payroll of the Commission.[21] This netted him only £800 a year, and Cole was always to be financially pressed, having a large family dependent upon him. Albert also had the role of visionary, though one with an eye to the smallest detail; but he sanctioned Cole to communicate with the other commissioners as he saw fit and to push the plan on.[22]

Scott Russell and Stafford Northcote, who had been Gladstone's private secretary, were appointed secretaries to the Commission. Northcote swiftly resigned because of his father's illness – he soon succeeded to his baronetcy – and was replaced by Edgar Bowring, an official from the Board of Trade. Cole, always ambitious, had hoped to be secretary, but ended up with no formal senior role at all, and at a distance from the Prince, who dealt only with the *nomenklatura*. Cole was sent to propitiate prospective members of the Commission, most of whom readily agreed to serve. He remained a member of the executive committee of the Society of Arts, which now had an entirely subordinate function to the Commission. He was frustrated by this, and felt slighted. An appeal to Albert for the committee to be allowed in to the Commission's meetings was rejected: because, it seems, Albert thought that if these men of ideas were allowed in, the commissioners, chosen for their public standing and for the most part with no ideas at all, would begin to feel surplus to requirements.

The Commission met more or less every week. Albert attended meetings assiduously. The project upon which they were working soon acquired the official title of the Great Exhibition of the Works of Industry of all Nations. Albert's patronage ensured the idea caught on quickly among the highest in the land: in February 1850 Wellington wrote to him asking for his name to be entered on the list of subscribers to the project.[23] The task of finding guarantors for the cost of the building continued. Barry, consulted about the work, thought that £190,000 would be taken on the door, but that the sale of 'old material' afterwards and the proceeds of refreshments would raise another £45,000 and £10,000 respectively, and that these sums would more than cover the costs. Cole, less ambitious, thought the takings would be £50,000: in truth, everyone was in the dark. Grey noted that he had read in *The Times* that 27,000 people had visited the British Museum in one day: so anything was possible.[24]

Cole quickly acquired a reputation for being difficult, thanks to his annoyance at being kept from the main decision-making body. Northcote agreed the Commission was 'unfit for executive functions', but that Cole and his committee were not of the calibre to command public confidence if they took them over.[25] However, he also noted, as he told Grey, that the knowledge men such as Cole had made them indispensable to the success of the enterprise. However, on 8 February 1850 he and his colleague Wentworth Dilke resigned, having heard it was intended to appoint over them Lieutenant Colonel William Reid, ex-Governor of Barbados, to act as link man with the Commission. Cole made it clear to Grey that, given his involvement with the scheme from its earliest times, he resigned with great reluctance: but had no choice because of the slight.[26]

'If I were weak enough to consent the Commissioners would despise me,' Cole noted.[27] Grey said the changes to the arrangements proposed had been designed not to disoblige Cole but to make his job easier; but he also warned him that, if he resigned, 'following immediately on Col Reid's appointment as Chairman, it would have the appearance of being dictated by jealousy of him, or an unwillingness to act under him', something he said the public, given Reid's reputation, would not find 'intelligible'.[28] Added to this was the small matter of 'HRH' who 'would regret your resignation very much'. Grey concluded: 'I should consider your leaving the Executive Committee under present circumstances injurious both to the proposed exhibition and to yourself.' After brooding for a couple of days, Cole wrote to Granville, who had become a main patron of his, to say he felt it his 'duty' to stay in his post.[29] He was reluctant to abandon all links with his brainchild, or to admit defeat: he seems to have been a victim of snobbery, and was perhaps aware of it. His middle-class *amour propre* seems to have been incomprehensible to the royalties, nobles and notables drafted in to run the show.

The executive inability of the Commission, however, remained a problem. In March 1850 Peel, a commissioner, complained to Granville about the lack of dynamism among his colleagues, and of Reid's inertia. Meanwhile, Cole was daily recording in his diary his frustration, while Reid waited for orders that never came. Reid was not quite what had been expected, and Scott Russell, the secretary of the Commission, had made things worse by proving 'disagreeable' and 'insolent'.[30] By May 1850 there were signs only of sluggish activity from potential exhibitors. Cole wanted to send a circular to potential exhibitors but Reid, absurdly, was nervous about drawing too much attention to the enterprise in case it became a focus for working-class agitation. Unfortunately, Granville agreed with him. Once more Cole considered resignation; once more, he was talked out of it.

III

Albert devoted enormous amounts of time to the project and engaged with its every aspect: so much so that, for the first time, the Queen began to register concern about his health. He evangelised for the exhibition, notably at a banquet at the Mansion House on 21 March 1850, given by the Lord Mayor of London, to which 'nearly all the mayors or other chief municipal officers of the corporate towns of the united kingdom were all assembled, and in their robes of office surrounded the chief magistrate of London', as *The Times* put it.[31] The paper also noted that it was not least because of the modernity and progress advocated by the Prince, and for which the exhibition was deemed to be a showcase, that such a gathering was possible: it was one of the 'triumphs of modern engineering skill in regard to rapid and convenient transit.' Also present were ambassadors, the commissioners, various courtiers, nobles and bishops, and Gladstone. The event was the culmination of a campaign to maintain enthusiasm for the project in the provinces that had been entrusted to Lyon Playfair, a professor of chemistry at the London School of Mines, whose appointment Peel had secured precisely because he feared that outside London enthusiasm was waning.

When the Prince arrived he was 'loudly and heartily cheered in the street'. He entered a hall decorated with paintings of the produce of the various counties, and of ships discharging their cargoes in the Pool of London for exhibition. Once the notables had dined off turtle soup, turbot in lobster sauce, baron of beef, chicken fillets, sweetbreads, veal, capons, lobster salads, pigeons stuffed with mushrooms, trifles, cabinet puddings, tarts, ices and Savoy cakes (to name but a selection of what was on offer), Albert spoke. He said he was gratified that 'a suggestion which I had thrown out, of appearing to me of importance at this time, should have met with such universal concurrence and approbation.' He proclaimed that 'we are living at a period of most wonderful transition, which tends rapidly to accomplish that great end – to which all history points – the realisation of the unity of mankind.' In that phrase Albert showed either his familiarity with Macaulay, or his instinctively Whiggish outlook.

Once the 'great cheering' that greeted this announcement had died down, he talked of what a small world it was becoming: not just because modern transport could shrink distances, but also because scholarship had made almost all languages intelligible, and means of communication were revolutionised too. Knowledge, above all, was being transmitted as never before. He proposed a unity of his three great interests: science, industry and art. 'Science discovers these laws of power, motion and transformation; industry applies them to the raw matter which the earth yields us in abundance, but which becomes valuable only by knowledge; art teaches us the immutable laws of beauty and symmetry, and gives to our production forms in accordance with them.' This brought him to his main argument: 'The exhibition of 1851 is to give us a true test and a living picture of the point of development at which the whole of mankind has arrived in this great task, and a new starting point from which all nations will be able to direct their further exertions.'

He concluded with a tactful appeal for funds, that the enterprise might be seen to be the work of the whole nation. He sat down to 'enthusiastic cheering, several times renewed.' The French Ambassador, Russell, Stanley and Peel were among those who made short speeches to endorse what Albert had said. If the passion of the evening were a guide, drawing in financial support would not be difficult. At Granville's suggestion, Cole drafted and published a leaflet about the wonders of the exhibition, designed as propaganda to drum up support. It emphasised the improving nature, both moral and practical, of the exercise: not just more about spears into pruning-hooks, but also the 'dignity of labour asserted' and the 'promotion of universal peace'.[32] However, there was still no universal enthusiasm outside the circle of those who had been present at the creation of the idea.

Apart from funding, the other priorities were to settle upon a site and a design for an exhibition building. For the former, the Commission soon settled on the southern fringe of Hyde Park. For the latter, submissions from architects were invited, to be considered by a subcommittee under the Duke of Buccleuch. Within four weeks 245 designs had been sent in, including thirty-eight from overseas.[33] The two most favoured by the Commission were glazed iron-framed buildings, one by a French architect, Hector Horeau, and the other by an Irish firm, Richard and Thomas Turner of Dublin. As soon as they were shown to the public and, more to the point, the architectural press, the chorus of execration began. Indeed, the building committee soon admitted it found none of the designs suitable. It included architects and engineers, such as Isambard Kingdom Brunel, the country's greatest engineer, and Charles Barry. They had their own idea, which was soon also the subject of ridicule: a cathedral-like edifice 'calculated to require between thirteen and nineteen million bricks'.[34]

Once the public – notably the public within shouting distance of Hyde Park – saw the plans of that building their outrage grew about the effect such a monstrosity would have on the park. The *Illustrated London News* published a drawing of the proposed hall on 22 June 1850, which sparked a clamour. Although the Commission had said that any building would be temporary, few believed such a monumental construction would be pulled down at the end of the year, but would blight the landscape indefinitely. There were also some who felt sure the project would end in disaster, and the taxpayer would have to rescue it to save Britain from international humiliation. Even Cole had some moments of pessimism, not least because days and weeks continued to pass without the executive committee being asked by the Commission to execute anything at all.

A movement grew up to have the exhibition relocated to Battersea Park, partly because no one of any quality lived nearby who could be disrupted, and partly because – it was argued – there would be greater ease in bringing all the exhibits in by the river. The Times, which had resigned itself to the exhibition happening but not to its happening in Hyde Park – which was surrounded by a heartland of its readers – wrote on 27 June 1850 that 'the case against the appropriation of Hyde Park . . . becomes stronger as the plans of the projectors are developed. We are not to have a "booth", nor a mere timber shed, but a solid, substantial edifice of brick, and iron, and stone, calculated to endure the wear and tear of the next hundred years.'[35] The paper recoiled from the notion of a dome bigger than St Paul's, and a bill for £100,000 for the edifice. 'By the stroke of a pen our pleasant Park – nearly the only spot where Londoners can get a breath of fresh air – is to be turned into something between Wolverhampton and Greenwich Fair.'

It can be deduced that those two last-named places did not harbour a large number of Times readers, or at least would not do so for much longer. The venting of the editorial spleen continued: 'The project looks so like insanity that, even with the evidence we have before us, we can scarcely bring ourselves to believe that the advisers of the PRINCE have dared to connect his name with such an outrage to the feelings and wishes of the inhabitants of the metropolis.' Worse even than the horrible aspect of this building was the fear that it might never be removed. Hyde Park would undergo a 'permanent mutilation', and the area around it would be choked by traffic during the construction, and during the stocking of the place with exhibits. It added its voice to the call for a site accessible by water, and for Battersea.

The Times lamented further, the next day, that hardly any English architects had put forward a plan deemed acceptable. 'Are we really so far behind the rest of the world in an important branch of the fine as well as the useful arts as this?' it asked.[36] It also attacked the building committee's plan for being so at odds with guidelines it had issued before inviting submissions from architects, and said the proposed huge dome on the building, designed by Brunel, 'dwarfed the rest of the building to absurdity', would necessitate a still bigger edifice beneath it, and would become permanent. The Commission quickly realised the urgency of giving a solemn and binding undertaking that the exhibition would close on 1 November 1851, and the building would be dismantled.

Some local residents, in the summer of 1850, sought leave to obtain an injunction to have the event stopped, because of the damage to their property; but permission was refused by the Attorney General. This caused an outcry in the Commons: Sir Frederick Thesiger, a former holder of that office and a future Lord Chancellor, told the House on 26 July that twenty of the 'most ornamental' acres of the park were about to be blighted.[37] He spoke of mature trees that had already been felled, and of many more facing the same fate. He presented a petition on behalf of local residents and demanded justice for them; and later that afternoon the redoubtable Colonel Charles de Laet Waldo Sibthorp, the MP for Lincoln, moved an emergency debate.

Sibthorp was a devout sceptic in the matter of Prince Albert. He had moved the motion in the Commons in 1840 to ensure the taxpayer did not remunerate the Prince too generously. Now, he saw the prospect of an exhibition in Hyde Park as little other than an assault on the rights of the English people. He had already, three weeks earlier, berated the government for allowing the exhibition to proceed because of the trees that had had to be felled, and because it would make Hyde Park a magnet for criminals. 'The right of enjoyment of our parks was vested in the people of this country, and had been recognised in the reigns of the Charleses, of William III, of George II, of William IV, and in the reign of the present Sovereign,' Hansard records him as saying. It continues: 'He believed Her Majesty to be one of the last persons who would desire to do anything or to sanction anything hostile to the feelings of Her subjects, or which could interfere with their rights and enjoyments.'[38] Sibthorp had, however, a wider agenda than just the rights of people to have a Sunday promenade.

He felt the exhibition to be little more than a means to undermine the works and devastate the morale of all decent Englishmen, not least by exposing them to malign foreign influences, and quite possibly flooding the country with foreign rubbish that the British people would be bamboozled into buying. He roared that:

Hyde Park was emphatically the park of the people, and it was now proposed to be devoted to purposes which he must hold to be prejudicial to the people in a moral, religious, and social point of view. It was sought to appropriate it to the encouragement of—what? To the encouragement of everything calculated to be prejudicial to the interests of the people. An exhibition of the industry of all nations, forsooth! An exhibition of the trumpery and trash of foreign countries, to the detriment of our own already too much oppressed manufacturers. The Commissioners of Woods and Forests, as trustees of the public, were bound to protect their rights, and not permit them to be robbed and spoliated.[39]

The Attorney, ignoring fears about the park becoming a den of thieves, robbers and prostitutes, swatted Sibthorp aside: Hyde Park was Crown land, and the Crown could do what it liked there so long as it stayed within statute law. In the Lords at the same time Lord Brougham, a lawyer of long experience who had been on record from the earliest days of the planned exhibition as opposing its being held in Hyde Park, tried to succeed where Sibthorp had failed; but the government was resolute in not giving way. Albert had told his mentor, Baron Stockmar: 'If we are driven out of the park, the work is done for!'[40] He was playing for high stakes.

There were elements in the Commons that wished Parliament, and the government, to take a strong hand in the running of the exhibition. However, Labouchere, who was both a commissioner and President of the Board of Trade, stressed he did not intend either Parliament or the government to have any hand in the events at all.[41] He emphasised, too, that there would be no call for public money to subsidise the project. This was Albert's particular horse, and he was to be allowed a free rein with it. Albert was also able to use the project not only to further his aims for the development of the arts and sciences, but also to continue his work for the improvement of the condition of the labouring classes. He was determined to arrange a model lodging-house at the exhibition, which he paid for himself; and sought Wellington's approval, as commander-in-chief, to have it placed by the Hyde Park Barracks.[42]

The attempt by some politicians to stop the exhibition was fruitless, not least because it gravely misjudged public opinion. All over Britain, and not just in the manufacturing districts, groups met to discuss how they could contribute to the success of the event. It had captured the public imagination, and presented a unifying goal towards which all classes could work. The notion that the event was a way of asserting British excellence above that of other nations without seeking to make war with them was also attractive. Lord Portman, the local landowner and magnate, chaired one such meeting, in Marylebone on 2 May 1850. He announced, to applause from the 200-strong crowd, that the exhibition was designed 'to cheer the sons of toil and to promote the happiness and comfort of every man who dwelt upon the earth.'[43] Even *The Times* was forced to admit there was now 'general acquiescence' in the plan, and that the whole undertaking was 'very creditable' to Albert.[44]

The matter of the building was soon resolved, thanks to a decisive intervention by the part-time architect Prince Albert. The Queen and he had visited the Duke of Devonshire at Chatsworth a few years earlier, not long after his magnificent new greenhouses, built by Joseph Paxton, had been finished. Albert in particular marvelled at them, and was instrumental in Paxton's being commissioned to design and build the exhibition hall itself. Typically, Paxton had in June signified to Cole his interest in designing the building, and Cole got him in to see Albert. The Commission, under Albert's influence, liked the idea of an iron and glass structure, and urged it on the buildings committee, even though the deadline for submissions had passed. This put the committee in the invidious position of having to reject its own plans, but it did so in mid-July, and agreed to recommend that Paxton be commissioned.

Paxton had started out as the Duke's head gardener – the Queen would refer to him as 'a common gardener's boy' – but had soon become something approaching his agent, handling his financial affairs and also dealing with the design and erection of buildings on the estate.[45] He built up a small architectural practice that put up buildings elsewhere too. Using 4,500 tons of iron as the framework for 293,655 panes of glass, the building was over a third of a mile long, covered 18 acres of Hyde Park and enclosed a number of mature trees, to avoid further controversies about felling them. It also had 24 miles of guttering. The finished product was designed to be a magnification of the Chatsworth greenhouses: and despite claims by its detractors that it would either fall down or be blown down if there was a gale, the building was one of the great and (until it burnt down in 1936) enduring legacies of the Great Exhibition.

It was not all straightforward with the architect, however. Paxton wrote to *The Times* on 20 January 1851 criticising Scott Russell, which left Albert 'a good deal annoyed'. 'He thinks', wrote Grey, 'you would hardly have taken such a step had you given more consideration to the inconvenience which your doing so might occasion.'[46] As architect, Paxton was now in the Prince's view part of the collective responsibility for the exhibition: and any criticisms should be addressed privately to commissioners and not to the press. Granville told Grey that 'Paxton's head has been turned by the events of the last six months, and it is not surprising that they should have had that effect upon a self-educated man.'[47] Seeing which side his bread was buttered, Paxton wrote back to Grey expressing 'sincere regret'.[48] It was enough to get him a knighthood at the end of the year, along with William Cubitt, who chaired the building committee.

Money remained an issue, despite the public enthusiasm. By the summer of 1850, and despite the efforts of the Prince, there was simply not enough. Reid, still fearful that the lower orders would use the exhibition as a rallying point towards revolution, had put an almost blanket ban on publicity, which did not help. Cole, going freelance, started to call in favours from his friends and contacts. A particularly useful one was Samuel Morton Peto, one of the country's leading railway contractors. Cole met him at the Reform Club on 12 July and, as a result of their talk, Peto wrote to Albert saying that in place of a guarantee he had already given for £20,000 he would now guarantee, or advance, £50,000.

Albert was delighted. The guarantee, worth perhaps £4.5 million in today's money, was never called in, thanks to the success of the exhibition: but it was instrumental in its happening at all. Cole's achievement did not go unnoticed by Albert. He had said in Cole's presence that all that was missing from the exhibition was a key man to arrange the exhibits and lay out the building; Cole suggested to Grey that he was that man. Grey made Albert see the sense of this. Cole had, at last, found the job for which he had been searching for months. Reid took the appointment badly: and even Granville had reservations because of Cole's ability to make himself unpopular, though he was in no doubt about Cole's talents.

News of the guarantee was brought to the commissioners on the day they agreed to ask Paxton to build the hall. The first iron column went up on 26 September 1850. Soon 1,500 men were at work, rising to 2,000 by December and January.[49] In December the Commission met in the building, an event marked by Albert's giving the workforce 250 gallons of beer.[50] The final result was a palace of awesome magnificence that captured the public imagination and remained much loved and admired until its destruction. However, when it was moved out of Hyde Park to Sydenham, John Ruskin, a native of those parts, derided it as 'possessing no more sublimity than a cucumber frame between two chimneys', and a building that encouraged the suburbanisation of what had once been bucolic Kent. In the second assertion at least, he was right.[51]

IV

Albert continued to concern himself with every aspect of the exhibition. The archive of the 1851 Commission bulges with letters from Grey, giving royal approval for everything from extra space for the Swiss exhibitors to extra money to provide a dedicated police force for the building. However, the former were told they could not make an exhibition of cheeses, and for the latter there might have to be an allowance for over-time.[52] Albert was conscious of the diplomatic importance of the exhibition, and questioned a suggestion by Lyon Playfair that there should be some sort of official report of the exhibits: 'England,' wrote Grey, echoing his master 'as the hosting nation, must be very careful not to make what might appear like a disparaging report of the exhibits of other countries.'[53] France, Austria and Prussia were particular causes of concern.

A network of local committees, set up on Cole's initiative, helped recruit exhibitors from around the British Isles. The Colonial Office did a similar job around the British Empire. The Foreign Office used its network of ambassadors, consuls and other representatives to bring in participants from the rest of the world. Albert's prestige as the Queen's husband was vital in this, and the Commission inspired the establishment of national committees in many countries to serve a purpose similar to that of the local committees in Britain, and find potential exhibitors.

The King of Prussia was more concerned about other matters. Rather like Reid, he was convinced the exhibition, which his son the Prince of Prussia and his grandson were planning to attend, would act as a cover for revolutionaries. 'Countless hordes of desperate proletarians, well organised and under the leadership of blood-red criminals, are on their way to London now,' he wrote to Albert on 8 April 1851.[54] The King feared insurrection at home; but feared attacks on his family abroad too, not least thanks to the 'liberal laws' of England. He put the matter in Albert's and the Queen's hands, asking them to decide whether it would be safe for the two princes to come, or whether they would meet their doom at the hands of people Friedrich Wilhelm variously described as 'the offspring of monsters' and 'gangs and rabble'.

Albert, who had acquired the national sense of humour in his eleven years in England, would not be deflected. He replied to the King that:

> mathematicians have calculated that the Crystal Palace will blow down in the first strong gale, Engineers that the galleries would crash in and destroy the visitors, Political Economists have proph-esied a scarcity of food in London owing to the vast concourse of people; Doctors that owing to so many races coming into contact with each other the Black Death of the Middle ages would make its appearance as it did after the Crusades; Moralists that England would be infected by all the scourges of the civilised and uncivilised world; Theologians that this second Tower of Babel would draw upon it the vengeance of an offended God. I can give no guarantee against these perils, nor am I in a position to assume responsibility for the possibly menaced lives of your Royal relatives.[55]

When the time to open the exhibition neared there was distress and disappointment that the Queen would not perform the opening cere-mony. She did not much like crowds, perhaps because of the attempts on her life. Granville tried to talk her in to opening the event. Russell did 'not think that the Queen would meet with any risk or discomfort in the building'.[56] He proposed talking it over with Albert; and Granville suggested the Queen should perform the ceremony accompanied by selected people: however, Granville wrote to Phipps, who had become Keeper of the Privy Purse, that 'the list of persons to accompany the Queen should be very carefully considered – I am afraid in the present mood of the public, the wider the line is made of privileged persons, the more dissatisfied persons there will be.'

Also, many who had bought season tickets had done so precisely to see the opening ceremony and the Queen; and if there was to be no ceremony, or one from which they were excluded, anger would mount. Eventually, the Queen, in the words of her Consort, 'signified her inten-tion to comply with a very generally expressed wish on the part of the public to be present at an opening ceremony on the 1st of May, if the commissioners can make the necessary arrangements for it' (this was written on 20 April).[57] Albert also started hurriedly roping in other dignitaries, notably the Archbishop of Canterbury to give 'the blessing of Almighty God . . . upon the undertaking.'[58]

In the four days after the Queen's announcement the number of season tickets sold went up from 7,000 to nearly 12,000.[59] *The Times* advised that a considerable number of season-ticket holders should be allowed into the main aisle with a decent view of the Sovereign, rather than 'banish' them to 'remote galleries'. The next day it reported that 5,000 seats would be placed in the aisle, which it imagined would be 'occupied by ladies, and will thus form a graceful and effectual barrier to the crowds of the male sex collected in close column behind them.'[60] The paper gave extensive previews of the contents of the exhibition, such as the wide range of minerals from all over the British Isles, and the processes used to turn them into products.

As more reports appeared of items being delivered into the building from docks and railway stations, excitement took off, fed not just by the press, but also by word of mouth. The North Western Railway carried an extra 5,000 passengers into London on 30 April, the day before the opening. The Great Western brought an extra 3,000. Other lines reported similar increases, and cross-channel steamers were packed. *The Times* estimated that, altogether, 50,000 people arrived in the capital on the 30th.[61] Tourism, roughly as we now know it, had begun.

By 1 May most problems had been ironed out – though there were ruffled feathers in the *corps diplomatique* about whether or not one of their number would present an address to the Queen. Labourers worked through the last night before the opening to finish making the arena fit for a Queen. The 'State Opening', as it was called, took on a holy significance: the public were to be admitted, but only in parts of the building that were not 'railed off in the Nave and Transept'.[62] *The Times* called the Crystal Palace 'a cathedral, its long avenues stretching from east to west being intersected midway by a transept'. Instead of being handed a bible, the Queen would be handed a catalogue of exhibits; but then, after the Archbishop had delivered God's blessing, a choir would sing the 'Hallelujah Chorus'. Those who approached the entrance did so between two long files of policemen reinforced by Life Guards: the streets were choked with traffic for hundreds of yards around. Men and boys shinned up trees to get a view of the pageant. The Queen was hailed 'again and again with hearty cheers', a salute she returned by 'bowing kindly and graciously'.[63]

She and her retinue processed into the building: and once she had mounted the dais to the throne the National Anthem was struck up on the organ. Albert read an address to his wife on behalf of the commissioners, announcing they had fulfilled the commission given them by her. He also announced that the total of donations to the project was now £65,000, with the name at the head of the list of donors being the Queen's. He reported that there were about 15,000 exhibitors, half of them British. The rest represented forty foreign countries.

The Queen, who was doing her best not to burst with pride, replied briefly to speak of the 'sincere gratification' she felt 'to witness the successful result of your judicious and unremitting exertions in the splendid spectacle by which I am this day surrounded.' The mood was of exultation: a Chinese Mandarin in the crowd 'unable any longer to control his feelings, made his way through foreign diplomatists, Ministers of State, and the distinguished circle with which Court etiquette had surrounded the throne, and, advancing close to Her Majesty, saluted her by a grand salaam, which she most graciously acknowledged.'[64] She then went on a short progress around the new cathedral, together with ambassadors, the commissioners (including such notables, therefore, as Gladstone, Cobden and Russell), a brace of field marshals – Wellington and the Marquess of Anglesey – the Archbishop of Canterbury, and much of the already extending Royal Family, including Albert.

The Times's reporter noted that 'His Royal Highness appeared less composed than Her Majesty, and his emotion was visible when the ceremony and the procession had been happily conducted to its close. It was natural that he should feel strongly the termination of a spectacle, the grandest perhaps that the world ever saw, and with which his name and reputation are henceforth inseparably associated.'

Russell accounted the whole performance a 'triumphant success': though he was writing to the Queen when he did.[65] Her Majesty, writing to Lady Lyttelton in response to another letter of congratulation, admitted that the ceremony had happened on 'the proudest and happiest day of, as you truly call it, my "happy life".'[66] She spoke of her joy 'to see this great conception of my beloved husband's great and good mind, which is always labouring for the good of others'. *The Times* praised Albert for his vision, which it proclaimed had been achieved and fulfilled.[67] It was a moment of supreme triumph for him. *The Times*'s conclusion was that 'republicans and anarchists may be made monarchical by such influences as the ceremony of yesterday exerts, but there seems little prospect of any political movement in the opposite direction.'

Charles Greville, whose high connections could have secured him a place inside the Crystal Palace for the opening, instead thought 'it more interesting and curious to see the masses and their behaviour. It was a wonderful spectacle to see the countless multitudes, streaming along in every direction, and congregated upon each bank of the Serpentine down to the water's edge; no soldiers, hardly any policemen to be seen, yet all so orderly and good-humoured.' After years in which the appearance of any sort of crowd in London signified trouble, this was progress indeed. Writing ten days after the opening, he noted that 'since that day all the world has been flocking to the Crystal Palace, and we hear nothing but expressions of wonder and admiration. The *frondeurs* are all come round, and those who abused it most vehemently now praise it as much.'[68]

Placards were put all over London about the wickedness of the visiting Hohenzollerns: but no attempts were made on their lives. The police were zealous in keeping trouble away, indeed too zealous. One official had to have a word with the Superintendent of Police, in accordance with Albert's wishes, 'to arrange for a more extensive admission of the working classes to the model houses in the park', so that they could benefit from the exhibition too.[69] Albert did, however, resist pressure in the newspapers to lower the price of admission to below a shilling.[70] As it was, even at the higher admission price, the crowds poured in from the first day, and season-ticket sales continued to be strong.

The Queen herself went back with Albert and some of their children on 3 May, two days after the opening, to look mainly at gold, silversmiths and jewellery displays. Once they left, the building was opened again to the public, and for the rest of the day it was packed: that remained the case for most of the duration. The Queen went again four days later, this time to look at the Tunisian, Chinese and Indian collections. There were many more visits, sometimes with her bringing foreign royalty to show off Albert's achievement to them, such as when she took her uncle Leopold, the King of the Belgians, in June. On 5 May the price of entry dropped, not to below 1s, but from £1 to 5s. As a result, money taken at the door rose from around £500 to £1,500 or £1,600. It became clear the event would not just make money, but a lot of money.

When visitors entered the Crystal Palace they discovered it was split into four sections of exhibits, according to a scheme designed by Lyon Playfair, who had become one of Albert's chief scientific advisers. The sections were raw materials, machinery, manufactures and fine arts. As Asa Briggs has written:

> Machinery was in the ascendant, but handicrafts were not yet in general eclipse. Alongside a sewing machine from the United States and cotton machines from Oldham there was fine black lace from Barcelona and pottery from Sèvres . . . the Machinery Court was the noisiest and most popular spectacle inside the Crystal Palace. Crowds of farmers in smocks could be seen admiring the agricultural implements, which included a pioneer reaping machine from the United States; mechanics from Leeds and Birmingham gathered round the Jacquard loom and De la Rue's envelope machine; the Queen herself was specially interested in a medal-making machine, which produced fifty million medals a week. She marvelled, too, at the electric telegraph and sent appropriate messages to her loyal subjects in Edinburgh and Manchester.[71]

In a later book, Briggs pointed out how the exhibition also set the fashion for the Victorian mania of assembling collections: indeed, collections, whether of fossils, stamps, coins or even pictures, were to become one of the measures of respectability for the new Victorian middle class.[72]

As host nation, Britain occupied half the floor space. While some of the main exhibits were of industrial machinery, others were more domestic, and aimed at enhancing the comfort of the rising Victorian middle class. There were numerous sorts of steam engine, a steam hammer, a massive hydraulic press and a printing press that could produce 5,000 copies an hour of the *Illustrated London News*, and various designs of carriages. But there were also Axminster carpets, richly ornamented pianos, and stained glass, all of which helped create the idea of high Victorian art that later became so reviled, and which was predominantly utilitarian. Yet what was most revealed about the Victorian mind was its ingenuity: rubber tubes connected pews to a pulpit so that the deaf could hear; there was a 'defensive umbrella' with a stiletto at the end of it, for use against footpads; and some velocipedes, the first bicycles.

The exhibition was not merely a diversion. To businessmen who attended it was an eye-opener, and provided inspiration to improve their own and the country's fortunes. One example will suffice, but it was replicated numerous times. A man called Sloane came from America, prepared to sell the British patent rights to his new wood-screw. Hitherto, all screws had had blunt ends, which meant that holes had to be bored for them using a gimlet. Sloane's idea had been to make his screws with their own pointed end, thereby having their own gimlet. He had also developed a way of making the screws more quickly and cheaply, using machinery far less labour-intensive than existed already. An industrialist from Birmingham, John Sutton Nettlefold, manufactured screws. On his visit to the Crystal Palace he at once saw the potential of Sloane's inventions for his own business.

To buy the machinery and the idea of the pointed screw required a capital investment of the then gigantic sum of £30,000: but Nettlefold feared that if he did not buy the rights one of his competitors would, and that would be the end of his business. For more than two years he negotiated with Sloane and finally, in 1854, acquired the rights. This would have implications for more than just British manufacturing. Unable to command so large a sum of money himself, he asked his brother-in-law, Joseph Chamberlain, to come into business with him. Chamberlain ran the family shoemaking business in London and was a leading Cordwainer: his was a very different line of business from his brother-in-law's. After much thought, he saw the potential of Nettlefold's idea, but determined to have his own man in the business in Birmingham to oversee his investment. His son Joseph, later widely known as Joe, then just eighteen, was sent to Birmingham to train as a manager in his uncle's business. Once Joe Chamberlain met Birmingham one of the great political careers of the Victorian era would be launched.[73] It was estimated that when young Joe went into the family firm the whole of England was turning out 70,000 gross of screws a week. By 1865 Birmingham alone was making 130,000 gross, and Nettlefold & Chamberlain 90,000 gross of those.

Engineering had ensured that the great Crystal Palace would not be uncomfortable when packed with visitors at the height of summer. Many of the 20-foot sashes could be removed on hot days to improve ventilation; great panels enclosed cotton cloth that would reduce the heat from the sun; and a system of largely concealed wooden guttering, cleverly designed by Paxton, drained away through hollow iron supports the inevitable condensation to avoid it either damaging anything or dripping on the clientele. The building could hold 40,000 visitors at any one time – 25,000 were at the opening ceremony – and had 10 miles of frontage for exhibition space.

Nothing like it had been seen in Britain before, or indeed in the world. And it was Albert's triumph. His hopes for world peace and amity growing up as a result of the internationalism of his concept may not have amounted to anything: but the spectacle he created was world historic, and one that resonates to this day. It came at a cost to his health, for he was naturally fragile: and the effort he put in, not just for the exhibition, but in securing its legacy in the decade of life that remained to him after the doors closed, took its toll. He wrote to his grandmother in Coburg on 15 April, a fortnight before the opening, that 'I am more dead than alive from overwork. The opponents of the Exhibition work with might and main to throw all the old women into panic and drive myself crazy. The strangers, they give out, are certain to commence a thorough revolution here, to murder Victoria and myself, and to proclaim the Red Republic in England; the plague is certain to ensue from the confluence of such vast multitudes, and to swallow up those whom the increased price of everything has not already swept away. For all this I am to be responsible, and against all this I have to make efficient provision.'[74] Yet from the perspective of the twenty-first century, what Albert achieved by these exertions and trials was a quantum leap in the modernising of Britain.

V

Two days after the exhibition opened Albert was guest of honour at the annual Royal Academy dinner: and the success of his venture was already so palpable, with scores of thousands of people queuing up for admission each day, that he was given an ecstatic ovation. The success continued. By mid-August 1851 it was clear that all the estimates of revenue had been extremely pessimistic. When the exhibition closed and the totting-up was done the figures were staggering.[75] There were a total of 6,039,195 admissions. In the final week alone there had been 518,277.

This additional traffic benefited other tourist attractions. Windsor Castle had had 129,400 visitors in 1851 compared with 31,228 in 1850; the British Museum's numbers had risen from 720,643 to 2,230,242. Even Deptford Dockyard had seen an increase from 3,313 to 4,465. The exhibition itself had taken £506,100 6s 11d (of which £74,349 15s 3d was for refreshments) and spent £292,794 11s 3d (including a bill of £22,357 for the Metropolitan Police), leaving a surplus of £213,305 15s 8d.

Those who had participated in the success had their rewards. Cole was presented with a special gold medal and made a Companion of the Order of the Bath; Richard Mayne, the Commissioner of the Metropolitan Police, was made a Knight Commander of the Order of the Bath. Paxton was knighted, as was William Cubitt. Dilke was offered a knighthood but turned it down, thinking he should have had a baronetcy; he eventually had one when he acted as a commissioner for the 1862 exhibition. Scott Russell was the only officer not to be honoured, and complained vociferously. The main players were also offered money out of the profits. Dilke, Playfair and Cole were all offered £3,000, though Dilke told Granville he would not take the money and Granville suspected he really would turn it down. He did. Cole happily accepted it. Paxton was given £1,000 and many smaller sums were dished out to others.[76]

On 10 August, while the event had almost three months to run, Albert wrote a memorandum noting that there was likely to be a surplus of £150,000–£200,000. 'The question arises: what is to be done with this surplus?'[77] He was not convinced the money should be used to maintain the Crystal Palace as a 'winter garden': he wanted to examine the objects of the exhibition, and to use the money to further them. He understood those objects to have been 'the promotion of every branch of human industry by means of comparison of their processes and results as carried on and obtained by all the Nations of the Earth, and the promotion of kindly feelings of all the Nations towards each other by the practical illustration of the advantages which may be derived by each from the labours and achievements of the others.'

This would be his guide; and it led him towards the belief that the purchase of the Crystal Palace as a 'lounging place' was not commensurate with those objects. He felt the connection with the building itself was 'incidental': it had been merely 'a covering to our Collection' whose purpose had come to an end. In any case, the commissioners were legally bound to have it removed by the end of October. What he proposed was using around £50,000 to purchase 25 to 30 acres of land on the other side of the Kensington road, 'called Kensington Gore'. He wrote: 'I would buy that ground and place on it four institutions, corresponding to the four great sections of the exhibition – Raw Material, Machinery, Manufactures and Plastic Art. I would devote these Institutions to the furtherance of the industrial pursuits of all Nations in these four divisions.' He was determined that the legacy of the exhibition should be the continuing enhancement of education and knowledge.

He felt each of these institutions should include a library and rooms for study; lecture rooms; an acre of glass covering for the purposes of the exhibition; and 'rooms for Conversations, Discussions and commercial meetings'. The surplus space might be 'laid out as gardens for public enjoyment, and so as to admit of the future erection of public Monuments there, according to a well-arranged plan.' If desired, there could be a public conservatory. Albert mused that there existed many learned societies in England that pursued the aims and disciplines covered by his four headings: and he asked whether they could not be 'united', with a collection of their relevant materials, and 'open and common to all Nations' so they would 'soon spread their ramifications into all countries'. This, he felt, would perpetuate the aims of the exhibition, bringing 'the different industrial pursuits of mankind, arts and sciences' into a new mainstream rather than in their previous 'state of comparative isolation from each other.' He also noted the locality had already been recommended as a possible site for a new National Gallery, and that would fit well into his general plan. 'I am perfectly aware that this is but a very crude scheme requiring mature consideration and practical tests in its details, but I thought it my duty towards the Commission to lay it before them at as early a moment as possible, in order that the remaining weeks of the Exhibition might be employed in investigating it, or that we might be led by that investigation to the discovery of a more feasible plan.'

At the end of September Albert put the question to a meeting of the Commissioners. This prompted a letter from one of them, Gladstone, on 4 October. He found the plan 'thoroughly congenial to the concentrated aim and character of the Exhibition'.[78] Parliament had long recognised the social benefits of establishing museums, and not just in the metropolis. William Ewart, the MP for Dumfries, had brought in a bill in 1844 to enable town councils to start museums and art galleries in the new manufacturing centres. It was said that the great result of such an enterprise would be that, as experience in London had shown, 'the people had deserted the public houses, preferring to visit places where they could improve their minds, and refresh and strengthen their bodies'.[79] Montagu Gore, the MP for Barnstaple, had backed the policy as one 'improving the morals and purifying the spirits of the people, to extend the basis on which rested the foundation of peace, security and national prosperity.'[80]

The capital would always be called upon to give the lead. As such, Cole had the idea of touring the exhibition before it closed and offering to buy up exhibits that could form the basis of a collection. His notion was that they would serve as teaching examples for students at the Schools of Design. Thanks to Granville, Cole secured £5,000 from the Board of Trade for the exercise. Cole had come to an arrangement with Granville, who had been vice-chairman of the Commission, to become General Superintendent of the Schools of Design, which could be part of the new estate at South Kensington. The Schools became a sub-department of the Board of Trade, which paid Cole a salary of £1,000 a year. He formed a committee to help decide what ought to be purchased, and included Pugin, then in the middle of designing the interiors of the new Houses of Parliament, but also in the last months of his life. Cole also set about establishing a network of provincial art schools under the Schools' auspices.

The Schools of Design already had a substantial collection, which the objects from the Great Exhibition swelled further. Cole secured from Albert the use of Marlborough House in the Mall as a temporary showcase for this augmented collection, but knew it would have to be removed in 1859 when the house became the Prince of Wales's on his eighteenth birthday. Over the next twenty or so years until his retirement in 1873, Cole would engage in a classic exercise of empire building – for the good of the country. The collection, he determined, required a permanent home as part of the estate of learned institutions celebrating science and art that would become the legacy of 1851. Edgar Bowring, who had previously been at the Board of Trade, was then appointed Acting Secretary of the Royal Commission, in which post he undertook the laborious job of buying up the parcels of land that would form what would come to be called Albertopolis. Once the land was secured, Cole could go to work devising what to put on it. The collections of the Schools of Design formed the nucleus of the Victoria and Albert Museum. This project would be the start of the process that would bring a series of museums and educational institutions to South Kensington, the land for them bought with the profits of the exhibition.

Over the next few years Cole, with help from expert antiquaries, toured various royal and government buildings searching out beautiful items shut away in cupboards or simply not used, and either borrowed or bought them for his new collection. He also collected what he called a 'chamber of horrors', items he felt failed the aesthetic test, and displayed these too, explaining their purpose in the museum: as well as becoming a pre-eminent fixer, Cole was making himself an arbiter of taste.[81] By late in 1852 the collection had expanded greatly on the nucleus made up of material from the exhibition. The Queen had lent some Sèvres porcelain, which Cole, in an act that highlighted why the more fastidious of his colleagues found him vulgar and unlikeable, milked for all the publicity it was worth.

VI

Albert had the Office of Works make investigations about land purchase during the winter of 1851–2, and it found that a meaningful-sized plot could be as large as 120 acres, and cost anything up to £400,000. At this stage the question was partly one of the level of the collective ambition, and partly of the indulgence of the government, since the surplus was nothing like that much. Thomas Cubitt had been consulted and said that the price of £3,000 an acre being sought by local landlords was 'much too high'.[82] The government had already considered the land south of Kensington Gore as a possible site for a new, expanded National Gallery.

There was also, at this intensely busy time for Albert and his men, the question of what to do with the Crystal Palace itself. 'Nothing can be worse managed than the present movement to keep the Crystal Palace,' Cole wrote to Grey on 20 April 1852.[83] Cole himself wanted the building retained in Hyde Park: not purely to avoid a public row, but as a permanent exhibition space for central London. However, there was the small matter of the solemn undertaking given to the Office of Woods and Forests that it would be taken down, not that Cole himself would have had scruples about that. The Office itself was demanding compliance. Paxton was lobbying, not especially discreetly, to have the building kept where it was. A current of public feeling said that it should be retained as a great conservatory for London.

Parliament voted in April not to keep it in Hyde Park – enthusing that 'the new Palace will be very splendid, if carried out according to the present elevations and plans.'[84] Sibthorp had not, despite the success of the exhibition, come round to the idea of it, or embraced its civilising mission. He had not, on a point of principle, been to see it 'stuffed with fancy foreign rubbish'. He said of the 'so-called Crystal Palace' that 'if anybody offered him a thousand guineas' he would not enter it as 'the very sight of it almost sickened him'.[85] If it stayed where it was it would simply rob the poor of more of their shillings in the name of 'recreation'. It was 'a transparent humbug'. Once it was settled that the building would not stay in Hyde Park the chairman of the Brighton Railway bought it for £70,000, the money paid on the spot, and proposed to move it to Sydenham, in Kent, to which the Brighton Railway would run a service.[86] It stayed there, as a great tourist attraction, until destroyed by fire in 1936.

During his short chancellorship in 1852 Disraeli, keen to ingratiate himself with the royal house, was helpful in obtaining additional government funds for the building of Albertopolis. He told Albert he had seen 'at once the necessity of securing as large a space of ground as possible. If therefore the commissioners should expend £140,000 in the purchase of property, he thought the Govt should be prepared to lay out £150,000 more.'[87] Albert replied on 10 June 1852 to say how 'very much pleased' he was that the scheme could go ahead.[88] The total purchases he intended cost £250,000; the other £140,000 would come from the surplus.[89] A group of rich men – led by Albert – had clubbed together to give a guarantee to the Bank of England for a total of £150,000 against the loan sought to buy the land in Kensington. Albert was good for £10,000, as was the Duke of Bedford; Samuel Morton Peto promised £50,000. Some other well-known names promised smaller amounts: the Dukes of Buccleuch and Devonshire £5,000 each, Paxton £2,500, Cobden £1,000. There was a great enthusiasm to be associated with a project on which Albert had given such a visible lead.[90]

Cole soon began sending Albert proposals for museums that could be built on the site.[91] Albert was also keen on the government's idea of the National Gallery's being relocated there, and corresponded with Derby on this subject in early August.[92] The School of Mines had been in touch about a geology museum; and there had also been an approach about a School of Practical Art. Not all potential inhabitants were so enamoured of the idea; Derby wrote to Albert in December 1852 warning him that the Royal Society had already raised an objection, since it wished to relocate to near Carlton Mews, and he intimated that other learned societies might have a similar view.[93] When the Queen opened Parliament on 11 November 1852, the intention to proceed with the scheme was proclaimed. 'The Advancement of the Fine Arts and of Practical Science will be readily recognised by you as worthy of the Attention of a great and enlightened Nation', the Queen said from the Throne. 'I have directed that a comprehensive Scheme shall be laid before you, having in view the Promotion of these Objects, towards which I invite your Aid and Co-operation.'[94]

Alert to the need for influential allies, Albert sought to have Disraeli elected to the Commission, which was still run by Granville. He had just ceased to be Chancellor, with the defeat of Derby's administration on the Budget of December 1852. Albert told Disraeli that in his view 'it would be of the greatest importance that you should become a member of our body.'[95] Albert was keen to see established a 'department of practical science' within government to complement what he hoped would be achieved by educational institutions in Kensington, with a minister in charge of it.[96] The Privy Council Office took responsibility for the State's involvement in education, but Gladstone, who had succeeded Disraeli, persuaded the Prince that were such a post to be created it should be within the Board of Trade: not least to avoid the inevitable struggles over religious questions whenever the Privy Council disbursed an educational grant. Edward Cardwell, the Peelite President of the Board of Trade, was charged, in January 1853, with doing this as soon as possible.

Cardwell's leg-man was none other than Cole. He wanted the government to have as little to do with the plans at Kensington as possible for, as he told Phipps on 6 September 1853, 'the more I try to realise the proceedings under Government, the greater the difficulties appear and I feel increased confidence that if the Public are invited to do the work themselves, instead of entertaining jealousies, they would welcome any suggestions from the Prince and be ready to acknowledge him as the

leader in the plans and carry out his views.'[97] Phipps replied that Albert
had read Cole's memorandum 'very carefully' and 'agreed in the main
with the principle which you have therein laid down that works of great
magnitude are more likely to be carried out with grandeur and complete
efficiency by the agency of private enterprise than under the control of
Govt and by means of grants to be made by Parliament.'[98] Albert was
heavily influenced by Cole's arguments, and wished the conduct of the
enterprise to proceed as he suggested. Cole then proceeded to draw up
a paper outlining, as far as it could be told, the plan.

VII

There was constant nervousness about the state of public opinion
towards Albertopolis, or what was still then called 'the Surplus scheme'.
'It has been indispensably necessary to bring as large an amount of
influence as possible to bear upon it by means of discussion in the press,
and thus set the ball rolling,' Bowring wrote to Grey on 4 January 1853.[99]
Suggestions poured in for what museums might be founded on the site:
including a patent museum and an animal products museum.[100] The
Royal Academy of Music applied direct to Albert for a building, in April
1853, causing Grey to comment that 'the result is that another wheel is
added to the machinery which is slowly propelling us towards
Kensington.'[101]

One difficulty in achieving Albert's vision was that his standing with
the public rose and fell. In January 1854 Gladstone wrote in a private
memorandum: 'Twelve months ago, nothing could be more brilliant
than the popularity of the Prince Consort. At the present moment it
seems, so far as the public journals afford a criticism, to be overcast.
Was the view right then, and is it wrong now? Or right both then and
now?'[102] The new unpopularity was based on misconceptions, passed on
by rumour: that Albert 'is commonly present when the ministers have
audience of Her Majesty' and that 'the Prince occupies a seat at the
Council table'. This was compounded by the fact that 'he is by birth a
foreigner and that he has relations abroad with whom he corresponds'.
Albert did attend council meetings when the Queen was present – 'but
not . . . cabinet ministers and the Prince alone'. Gladstone defended this:
senior members of the Royal Household were Privy Councillors and so
attended such meetings, and 'it does not seem wholly irrational that if

the relation of a chamberlain or vice-chamberlain to the Queen's person is such as to bring these functionaries into the Council Chamber, the Queen's husband should likewise be found there.' However, Gladstone attested that Albert took no part in the deliberations, but merely observed.

The public view was different. Arthur Hugh Clough, then a junior employee in the Privy Council Office, wrote to his American friend Charles Eliot Norton at the end of January 1854 to say that the Queen was, after all, going to open the new session of Parliament in person, even though 'it was said [she] was afraid her loyal subjects might pelt her husband'. He added that 'many people do you know really believed Prince Albert was actually sent to the Tower, and some repair being in operation on one of the turrets, a large number of people collected to look on, in the belief that apartments were to be fitted up for HRH.'[103] Describing the actual ceremony, Clough later told Norton that he had seen the procession to Westminster from his window in Whitehall 'and heard the occasional hisses of some members of the assembled town-democracy against Prince Albert'.[104] It was also believed, as Britain went to war with Russia in the Crimea in October 1854, that Albert had pro-Russian sentiments, which did not help.

By April 1853 a steering committee was meeting to discuss the establishment of a 'Museum of Inventions', and was told that 'there appears to be no difficulty about obtaining a good collection of models'.[105] However, such things grew like topsy: the committee also told Albert that 'a Collection of Models would be without vitality if disconnected from a library and the printed specifications.' The committee agreed that to create even a temporary structure for such a collection would cost £10,000. Disraeli warned them that the idea of funding this from patent fees was 'not practicable', and his colleagues on the committee feared that trying to raise a subscription for such an enterprise at that time would not be useful.

Not all the members of the 1851 Commission backed this great concentration of learned societies and museums. Barry, who deeply opposed the idea of the National Gallery moving there, felt Kensington 'is far too much to the west for the general convenience of the Metropolis, particularly for the industrial community and the working classes at the eastern and central portion of the town'.[106] He proposed that the area around the British Museum in Bloomsbury be used instead for this centre of Arts and Sciences: but it was to no avail. The Prince sent his prolix missive on to Granville, who noted that 'it is certainly to be regretted that we shall have Sir Charles Barry against us; but besides the self-contradictions in his memorandum and the distrust of him by the public, he is altogether too late in the field.'[107] He was indeed. Albert had sent a comprehensive memorandum to his fellow commissioners from Osborne on 20 August 1853 suggesting a general plan for the whole site.[108] The new National Gallery would be on a site now occupied by the Royal College of Music, open to the park in front. Behind it, roughly on the site of the Imperial College, the Science and Natural History Museums, would have been two long oblong buildings, either side of a square of gardens and monuments, housing the museums of industrial art and patented inventions and of trade, and with the site entered at the south (at the present entrance to the Natural History Museum) through a triumphal arch. Either side of where the Albert Hall now stands would be buildings housing colleges of arts and sciences; and around the periphery there was scope for smaller elegant buildings housing learned societies and other such institutions. An Academy of Music, or concert hall, was planned, but nowhere near where they ended up; rather on the south side of the main road opposite what is now the Victoria and Albert Museum. Albert's ambition was limitless: if more frontage to Hyde Park could be purchased then the proposed schools could be extended, forming beautiful courts in front of the proposed National Gallery.

VIII

Albert was distressed by a rumour in early January 1855 that Cole had resigned from the Commission. 'If it is the case,' asked Grey, 'what is the _real_ motive for such a step? I can hardly think he wd have taken it without _some_ communication to HRH.'[109] It was not true. Albert was constantly on edge about plots to derail his scheme. When in July 1855 a vote approached in the House of Commons for money to buy more land, Albert wrote to Palmerston, by then Prime Minister, urging him to ensure it passed. It was not just that 'Mr Disraeli, Mr Gladstone and Mr Cobden are personally pledged to support the vote' but that 'departmental jealousy in subordinate ranks in the Treasury is trying to defeat this plan.'[110] Palmerston replied at once that he would table a vote and put the government's weight behind it.[111] On 2 August Albert got his money, £15,000, thanks to support from a combination of Gladstone and Disraeli.

Meanwhile, by late 1854 work was well advanced on the roads on the site and through its centre, with sewers being laid underneath them. Albert decided on the names of the roads in April 1855: one was to be Exhibition Road, another Prince Albert's Road, and the one to the south Cromwell Road.[112] It had been decided to move the Museum of Manufactures, as it had become known, from Marlborough House, to Albertopolis in 1857, when the Queen formally opened what had been renamed the South Kensington Museum. It was now situated in an iron building designed by a Royal Engineer, Captain Francis Fowke, one of Cole's team whose role in Albertopolis would become wider yet. She would reopen it in 1899 in a grand new building as the Victoria and Albert Museum. It soon commanded 40,000 visitors a month, displaying the public's growing hunger for culture. It was central to Albert's conception of this hub of civilisation to have both the National Gallery and learned societies in Albertopolis. There was even a suggestion in 1858 that the Education Department of the Privy Council Office should move to Kensington, and this centre of enlightenment; though this intrusion of government was met with coolness at the Palace.[113] Parliament was, though, reluctant to find money to move the National Gallery, Gladstone's concern for the public purse trumping all other considerations.

Unfortunately for Albert, he had made the relocation of the National Gallery the linchpin of the whole project: and as obstacles arose, his confidence in what could be achieved, and in the vision itself, was undermined. *The Times* suggested that if a new National Gallery were needed there were three Royal Palaces not doing very much, one of which could be used for that purpose: Kensington Palace, St James's Palace or Marlborough House. This outraged the Queen, who wrote to Palmerston that she was 'indignant with the unfair and mischievous article in the *Times* of today and trusts that the Govt will not allow itself to be beaten upon the National Gallery question by a knot of persons who seem to delight in nothing but making mischief and showing their own importance. Really nothing worthy of the Country can be ever produced if the repeated decisions of Royal Commissioners, committees of the House of Commons, Govts etc etc are thus to be everlastingly set aside and all progress and preparation made to be lost labour.'[114] The suggestion that one of her palaces should be used was 'really too bad'. Understanding the exigencies of the situation, Palmerston replied at once that the notion was 'objectionable and absurd'.[115] The problem did not arise, because Parliament flatly refused to vote the money.

The Times's influence was largely blamed for this setback. Granville wrote to Albert on 5 July 1856 comparing the newspaper to 'the King of Naples who is hated, but is feared and obeyed in his own country. I do not know whether anything could be done without affecting Your Royal Highness's dignity to put a stop to these attacks.'[116] He told the Prince of the 'two most important persons' on the paper, John Walter, the proprietor, and John Delane, his editor. 'The first I am told is all powerful when he interferes. I do not know him at all, but I am informed that he is narrowminded and violent, rather a morbid but not a bad man.' As for the editor, 'Delane is vulgar, without much appearance of ability, but must understand his own Trade. He seems very open to personal civility.'

A leading historian of the project, Hermione Hobhouse, has described the 'schizophrenia' present in the development of Albertopolis because of 'the uneasy coexistence of the grandeur of the Prince's original concept with the Commissioners' ability to put it into practice.'[117] She adds, plausibly, that such a project required a '*roi soleil*' who, as well as having a vision, had the absolutist powers to enforce it. The traditional suspicion of the English towards authority, a culture shock to Albert when he left Coburg, would not brook any such attitude. Private property was sacrosanct and interference in it by the State an abomination. For all his influence Albert, in the end, lacked power. Rather than being able to command a grand project, he would have to have Albertopolis built piecemeal; and he would not live long enough to see it built in that fashion largely by Henry Cole.

Vanity Fair would later speak of Cole, his fingers in so many pies, as having had a 'peculiar mission of reviving the artistic sense among his countrymen . . . His great aim and object has been to provide artistic instruction, and to that end he has founded art schools . . . He it is who has been the soul and intellect of all those undertakings which have made South Kensington famous.'[118] Cole achieved all these things

– including, later, his being a motive force behind the museums and the Albert Hall – despite being increasingly unpopular because of his sometimes scheming, sometimes dictatorial methods, and because of his rampant personal ambition.

In May 1858 Bowring suggested to Albert that the commissioners buy out the government's interest in the site, except for £60,000 representing the site of the Science and Art department. Albert thought the suggestion 'very good'.[119] In 1859 Parliament passed the Kensington Estate Bill, guaranteeing the future of the site for the purposes Albert intended. Thwarted on his gallery, Albert conceived instead grand horticultural gardens for the site. He started to draw up plans even before the Horticultural Society had responded to an invitation to become partners, on land roughly where the Royal College of Music and Imperial College now stand. He recruited Fowke to help plan the gardens: Fowke would benefit from his patronage in various schemes in South Kensington – not least the Albert Hall. The Horticultural Society was offered 20 acres and undertook the work with the help of a £50,000 grant from the Commission, which paid for 'a highly decorated Italian Arcade and certain costly earthworks required as the foundation of a garden.'[120] Albert opened the gardens, which were highly acclaimed, in June 1861, and they eventually included a monument to him as a memorial to the Great Exhibition of 1851.

It was also at this time that another inadvertent effect of the Great Exhibition came into being: a business calling itself 'The Great Northern Palace Company' issued a prospectus for its 'Palace of the People, Muswell Hill' to complement the Crystal Palace, now at Sydenham and enjoying huge popularity – 1,384,163 persons visited it during 1859. There was clearly scope for something accessible to those living north of the metropolis. That the prospectus appears in Albert's papers shows how interested he was in this unintended consequence of his big idea.[121] Its proposed devotion to 'general instruction and amusement' would be complemented by 30 of its 450 acres 'of the finest land in the county of Middlesex' being set aside for 'Benevolent Institutions connected with Art, Science, Literature, Music, Horticulture and Railway Interest'. It would have an 'educational department', but this was not merely a philanthropic but also a speculative venture, some of the land being set aside for 'the erection of Suburban Villas'. The main actors were also directors of the Great Northern and other railway companies, whose fortunes would be made by ferrying people to and from this palace of varieties. A number of members of both Houses of Parliament, led by Lord Brougham and Lord Albemarle, were listed as patrons.

In May 1860 plans for the schools of General Education and of Art were sufficiently advanced for Cole to ask Grey whether Albert and the Prince of Wales would be available to lay their foundation stones the following month. It was proposed to hold another exhibition in 1862 under the auspices of the Society of Arts and to use temporary buildings in Kensington to house it. Cole would have his fingers in this pie too. It was also around this time that a possibility arose for a new cultural establishment in Albertopolis: the first suggestion of an 'International Concert Room' was made in June 1861. Albert approved the notion in August.[122]

IX

Almost a decade after the Great Exhibition Albert, egged on by Cole, was still conceiving ambitious projects, and Cole in particular – for all his weaknesses – was still showing he could see them through, before coming back to suggest more. On 23 January 1860 a letter from Gladstone brought the prospect of yet another project, for what would become the Natural History Museum: 'On Saturday the Trustees of the British Museum accepted by a majority of nine to eight a motion of Lord Palmerston's to the effect that it is desirable under existing circumstances that the Collections of Natural History should be removed to another site.'[123] The Trustees had originally wanted the new accommodation to be contiguous with the existing museum in Bloomsbury. The first request to separate the natural history collection from everything else had in fact come five years earlier, from Professor Richard Owen, superintendent of that department. Owen had much in common with Cole: a man of great ability, but also with a gift for unpopularity. T. H. Huxley had written of him in 1851: 'It is astonishing with what an intense feeling of hatred Owen is regarded by the majority of his contemporaries. The truth is, he is the superior of most, and does not conceal that he knows it, and it must be confessed that he does some very ill-natured tricks now and then.'[124]

A Treasury Minute of 23 October 1861 that Gladstone wrote precipitated the foundation of the Natural History Museum. On 21 October

Owen had shown Gladstone round the cramped collections in Bloomsbury, and had not needed to impress upon him how overflowing, and inadequate, the space there was. Gladstone could see this for himself. He sent his minute to the Prince Consort on 14 November 1861, a month before his death. Gladstone's main concern was financial, and in advocating the course to be adopted he identified a saving of between £350,000 and £415,000 if buying land in Kensington rather than Bloomsbury.[125] Fowke laid before the Commons Committee on the South Kensington Museum a plan for laying out the Science and Art Department at a cost of £214,000. The elevations on the south and west sides would be 'suitable for a public building worthy of the nation.' The Committee said it would be 'unwise to commit the country to a heavy expense in anticipation of its wants', but agreed to some limited development. In fact, by 1865 a total of £519,070 had been spent on the site, well over twice Fowke's estimate.

In May 1862 Gladstone explained to the Commons that 'a large majority of the trustees have arrived at the conclusion that it is necessary to separate the collections of the British Museum': and that the best destination for the natural history collection would be South Kensington.[126] He justified the location on the grounds of moderate cost and room for expansion. It would be expensive: 'But the Government think it would be absurd,' he continued, 'to propose to this House any half-measure.'[127] The total saving of Kensington over Bloomsbury would be £300,000, satisfying the Chancellor's iron financial discipline. In the museum in Bloomsbury, Owen had 50,000 square feet of exhibition space. The museum he had planned would have 485,100 square feet. He was not interested in simply attracting serious scientists. He wanted to popularise natural history, and open it up to the middle classes and the autodidact – 'the local collector of birds, birds-eggs, shells, insects, fossils etc – the intelligent wageman, tradesman or professional man, whose tastes may lead him to devote his modicum of leisure to the pursuit of a particular branch of natural history'.[128]

When the matter of funding was discussed in the Commons, Richard Monckton Milnes reflected that:

> If you are to have a great first-rate museum of natural history, you must not have any strict limitation for want of space; you must allow the exhibition to be commensurate with the present state of science. The old idea of a museum of natural history was the

exhibition of a whale, a tiger, and a few birds of Paradise, what are called specimens interesting to the public in general. Such an exhibition could not now be passed off as a museum. Every day science is becoming more and more clearly defined; every day distinctions, imperceptible to the public and even to well-informed men, open to the minds of men of science new regions of discovery and new realms of thought. Look at that great work, the publication of which last year formed the commencement of a new era of science in England—Mr Darwin's work upon the Origin of Species. It is clear that a museum, to be complete, must include many specimens which, although of the greatest importance to the man of science, are of no interest to the mere visitors to the institution.[129]

This was a minority view: the intellectual revolution in science, and its consequences, were beyond the comprehension of many of Milnes's fellow parliamentarians. He used a forceful analogy: that London wanted something as eminent as the Jardin des Plantes in Paris: which no one thought of combining with the Louvre. A serious scientific institution was necessary to the nation and to the cause of science; but it would be expensive, wherever it was built. The House decided the economic question, not the intellectual one. It defeated the motion by 163 to 71. The Queen was 'greatly annoyed' by the outcome, 'knowing as she does the interest the Prince took in the question.'[130] She felt it was a deliberate attempt to thwart Albert's vision, and took it as a personal insult. Grey, her private secretary, was shocked by the defeat, telling Bowring that 'had I had the least idea that it was likely, I wd have tried to keep some of the Opposition Leaders straight.' Disraeli and Northcote had voted against, which had caused particular grief. Gladstone admitted to the Queen that a 'mistake' had been made in seeking so large a sum, and the matter would be considered again.[131]

Rather than find another Royal Engineer to execute Fowke's plan after his sudden death in 1865 – as happened at the Albert Hall, for which he also won the commission – a new architect was recruited: Alfred Waterhouse, one of the towering men of his profession in the generation after George Gilbert Scott, but then only in his mid-thirties, and little known. Waterhouse was a Gothicist and, like Scott and Ruskin, had formed his ideas of the Gothic from extensive European travel. He had had his own practice in Manchester since 1854, when he was twenty-four, and had made his name with the new Assize Courts in the city. He moved to London in 1865, hoping – in vain, as it turned out – that he might win the competition to design the Law Courts in the Strand. He came to the attention of the Establishment via the First Commissioner of Works, William Cowper, an aesthete, friend of Ruskin, and patron of some of the leading architects and designers of the day. It was Cowper who asked Waterhouse to take on the Natural History Museum.

In 1865 Gladstone said that the case for having a larger museum at South Kensington than the British Museum was 'slenderly and scantily shown'. A revised plan was submitted, and it was agreed that the £195,000 required would be spread over six years.[132] However, things again went out of control. Another £463,000 was sought to complete the scheme, way above Fowke's original, modest proposal. Administrative costs for the Science and Art Department were running at around £275,000 a year and rising. The Department claimed it had to perform the functions of a university, schoolmaster, museum, circulating exhibition, storekeeper, producer, architect, builder, decorator, referee, revenue department, public office and department of control: which was why it was so expensive.

It was said that 'the Scientific Men of the Metropolis' opposed relocation. This was untrue, and prompted a memorial to be sent to Gladstone, as Chancellor, signed by Darwin, Huxley and Fellows of the Royal, Linnean, Geological and Zoological Societies, backing the move.[133] They claimed it was 'of fundamental importance to the progress of the Natural Science in this country, that the administration of the National Natural History Collections should be separated from that of the Library and Art Collections, and placed under one Officer, who should be immediately responsible to the Queen's Ministers. We regard the exact locality of the National Museum of Natural History as a question of comparatively minor importance, provided that it be conveniently accessible within the Metropolitan district.'

It had been intended that Waterhouse would execute Fowke's plan. However, the plan was put on hold during the Conservative administration of Derby and Disraeli, between 1866 and 1868, and when it was revived shortly before the election of 1868 Waterhouse was told he could, if he wished, revise Fowke's ideas. His new blueprint was dismissed as too expensive. When Gladstone came to office in 1868 enthusiasm for

the museum came with him, and with Henry Layard, a renowned antiquarian and aesthete, when he became First Commissioner of Works.
Layard was reminded by P. L. Sclater, a zoologist who had signed the
1866 memorial, of the strength of professional opinion behind opening
a separate museum.

In Layard's papers is an estimate by Waterhouse, made in March 1869,
for £1,895,000 for the cost of the Natural History Museum alone.[134]
Waterhouse wrote shortly afterwards: 'I always intended to propose the
use of brick and terracotta and my estimate was based on the assumption that these materials would be employed.'[135] By this stage the debate
on relocation had been going for well over a decade, slowed by the
absence of an Albert-style figure to force the issue. The commissioners
had told successive governments that they would make land available,
and at a very reasonable price; but governments, sensing the likelihood
of massive demands on the public purse, had been sluggish in their
response. In June 1869 Gladstone complicated matters by authorising
Layard to consider 'placing the Natural History Collections on the
Embankment.'[136] Layard's office discussed this with Waterhouse, who
wrote on 16 July 1869: 'I do not like naming a sum which I am not
tolerably sure the building can be done for; but I should like Mr Layard
to understand that if it had been anywhere else than on the Embankment
my estimate would hardly have exceeded the £500,000. The site seems
to me to demand a magnificent building. If, however, the Historical
Commission are willing to forego magnificence and be content with a
respectable building I think I might venture to promise that the accommodation described could all be secured for the half million.'[137]

It was not until Acton Smee Ayrton succeeded Layard that the decision
to proceed as planned, at South Kensington, was taken. Ayrton was the
polar opposite to Layard, lacking in aesthetic sense and obsessed with
not spending public money. Luckily for Waterhouse, Ayrton was also
preoccupied with the construction of the Law Courts, and with making
the life of George Edmund Street, their architect, a complete misery:
so he had relatively little time and energy to interfere with Waterhouse.
However, he cut the budget from £500,000 to £330,000: so Waterhouse
redesigned his building, constructing enough to house much of the
museum, but leaving space for side and rear ranges to be built when
funds allowed. They never did. Parliament then delayed building for two
years during which costs rose. Waterhouse had to make further

economies, shortening the height of the entrance towers and reducing the ornamentation.

He was guided by a plan made by Owen in 1859. The exterior was Romanesque, a variance from Fowke's original idea, which had been Italian Renaissance. It was, however, more in keeping with Waterhouse's pedigree as a Gothicist, being the style from which the Gothic had developed. The great concession Waterhouse made to the Renaissance was the symmetry of the building, a trait found in other works of his (such as Manchester Town Hall) but not admired by other Gothicists. The effect of the regularity of the 680-feet-long facade, with its rows of round-arch windows, is mesmerising: of the Gothic, but not quite Gothic.

The terracotta Waterhouse required was for models of flora and fauna to adorn the exterior; these were designs by Owen himself. It became increasingly hard to obtain these materials in the quantities required, which caused the contractors to go bankrupt in the summer of 1879.[138] The building was not finished until 1881, but the delay had its advantages. The Disraeli administration allowed the towers to be built to their planned height, in order to accommodate water tanks for hoses in case of fire. When opened to the public in April 1881, the museum at last gave Albertopolis the world-class scientific institution of which the Prince Consort had always dreamed, and a public increasingly interested in education, inquiry and self-improvement had a peerless resource.

X

The Albert Memorial in Kensington Gardens – whose tortuous conception and birth are described in the next chapter – was only one part of the capital's remembrance of the Prince Consort. It was strongly felt that the achievement of his other vision, the much-discussed Central Hall of Science and Art, would be the ultimate tribute. It was driven, like the memorial, from the Queen and the Court, and like the rest of Albertopolis was the result of an initiative by Cole, who saw another opportunity to extend his empire. Cole had first suggested a massive concert hall, built by subscription, in 1857. He had hoped it could be built as part of the infrastructure for a Great Exhibition of 1861, to be held to mark the tenth anniversary of the original, and had asked Fowke to come up with something. The exhibition had to be postponed from 1861 to 1862 because of the Franco-Austrian War of 1859, and there was insufficient money to build such a hall.

The land directly south of the Albert Memorial and north of the Horticultural Gardens, considered as the site of the National Gallery, was the obvious place if the money could be found. Sir Charles Eastlake formally suggested a memorial hall to the 1851 commissioners in June 1862. At the same time, at the height of the Queen's grief and of her determination to have Albert commemorated as spectacularly as possible, Cole had secured an interview with her at Windsor where she gave her approval to a hall, provided it was built in conjunction with, and not instead of, a separate memorial. However, money was again the obstacle. Having had to subsidise the memorial, the government was unwilling to part with more public money for this extravagance, particularly so long as Gladstone was Chancellor.

Cole would not be thwarted. He drafted a prospectus in late 1863 inviting public subscriptions for a great hall. He said it would be 'the finest in Europe for hearing, seeing and convenience', and it would accommodate 12,000 people.[139] He sought £200,000, which he proposed to raise by selling 500 'perpetual free admissions' at £100 each, 500 'life admissions' for £50 each, and corporate arrangements for use of the hall on what we would now call a time-share basis. However, the commissioners saw no reason to grant land for this purpose. Their fear seemed to be that sufficient finance would not be forthcoming, and the plan would have to be aborted, or finished with State funds granted reluctantly, if at all.

So Cole tried to find a way out of the impasse. Having enlisted both Fowke, who had scaled down earlier plans for a 30,000-seater hall, and General Grey, they decided to target the cream of society (comprising people of rank or wealth, and in many cases both) to subscribe. It was hoped this would convince the commissioners that the project could not fail. Cole had one more trump, which was to persuade the Prince of Wales to become the hall's president. This would encourage society to invest but would also put huge pressure on the commissioners to give in to Cole's entreaties. Grey, shrewdly, advised the Queen to ask the Prince to take on the role, an offer he could not refuse.

Travelling the Continent for the purpose of acquiring objects for the South Kensington Museum, Cole also inspected concert halls: though it was a visit with Fowke to the Roman amphitheatre at Nîmes in 1864 that most profoundly affected the Albert Hall's development. The proposed building would, however, be more than just a musical venue: the great learned societies so revered by Albert, and whose presence in South Kensington he had always believed vital, could hold their meetings or conventions in it. It could also house future exhibitions: the Crystal Palace, after all, had long been in Sydenham, and the widely execrated building for the 1862 exhibition was already on the way out.

Cole sent Grey a plan of action in the summer of 1864. Grey saw one obstacle in particular – Cole's personal unpopularity – but also realised that his success in South Kensington required his concert hall project to be taken seriously. Derby, then Leader of the Opposition but also a key member of the memorial committee, was prevailed upon by Grey to see Cole and discuss the idea. Derby thought the plan 'visionary', but lacked enthusiasm to push it through. That changed miraculously when the Queen, at Grey's prompting, intimated that she wished such a project to proceed.[140]

A prospectus described how the building would be funded. Cole went through his address book and started to round up big names as vice-presidents. Unpopular he may have been, but he had enlisted fifty by the end of 1864, helped by the Prince of Wales's patronage. And although Scott, as architect of the memorial, was considered the natural candidate to build the hall, and had submitted plans for it, Cole and Fowke understood each other. Cole was unimpressed with Scott as an architect and, as no stranger to jealousy, may have felt he had had quite enough success by securing the commission for the memorial.

Cole took a model of the hall, made by Fowke, to Osborne to show the Prince of Wales on 29 January 1865, at the first meeting of a steering committee to run the project. It comprised the Prince, Phipps, and Grey. Cole and a colleague 'attended by command of His Royal Highness'. The committee saw Fowke's plans from 1859, and the rival submission by Scott. Cole also produced a list of over seventy notables willing to be vice-presidents. He reported enthusiasm among potential subscribers, which meant the Prince could make the following pronouncement: 'His Royal Highness expressed his desire to see the erection of the Hall carried into effect, as a work recommended by the Prince Consort, for its great public utility, and as a necessary part of the Commission's comprehensive plan for the promotion of Science and Art.'[141] The plan was approved – though the capacity had shrunk again, to 6,000.

On 29 May the commissioners, led by Derby, agreed to grant not just the land, on a 999-year lease at an annual rental of 1s, but also £50,000 in cash, with the proviso that the rest be raised within eighteen months. They also asked whether the hall might be reduced in size, but the Queen was having none of that. A meeting of the 'Promoters of the Central Hall of Arts and Sciences' took place at Marlborough House on 6 July: present was a slice of the highest aristocracy of the land, including six dukes, two marquesses, eight earls and three prelates, the last group led by the Archbishop of Canterbury.[142] The Prince spoke of his mother's deep interest in the project, and of her agreement to become its patron. There was unanimous support at the meeting for the project and the terms under which it would proceed. The Prince explained how the surplus from the exhibition had been exhausted in building the memorial, and therefore a public subscription for the hall had been necessary: and he justified the building as something 'the want of which for various purposes connected with Science and Art has long been felt'.[143]

The list of vice-patrons was topped by two royal highnesses (Prince Alfred and the Duke of Cambridge), a serene highness from Saxe-Weimar, a brace of archbishops and seven other dukes. Below them came two marquesses, thirteen earls, four viscounts and nine bishops. Disraeli was among the clutch of MPs on the list, as were the officials of numerous learned societies and most of those who had been associated with the development of the exhibition and Albertopolis – Northcote, Bowring, Dilke, Layard, Owen, Tite and, of course, Cole. He and Bowring joined the provisional committee, led by the Prince of Wales and his brother Prince Alfred, but also including Derby, Granville, Robert Lowe, a leading Liberal, and Grey.

The statement by the Provisional Committee said the movement for a great central institution in Albertopolis had been 'arrested' by the death of the Prince; but the time had come 'to revive a portion of his project, and to seek the means of erecting a Hall on a scale commensurate with the wants of the Country.'[144] The Hall would be available for congresses, *conversaziones* and exhibitions connected with science and art, and indeed 'any other purpose connected with Science and Art'; there could be 'Agricultural and Horticultural Exhibitions'; but, most of all, 'Performances of Music, both choral and instrumental, including performances on the Organ similar to those now given in various large provincial towns, such as Liverpool and Birmingham.' The potential

utility of the Hall was emphasised by the fact that the area was about
to be connected to the Metropolitan Railway.

By 13 July 1865 the sum of £100,200 had been subscribed by a select
group in 'important official positions' and among the committee. It was
then agreed to offer debentures to a wider public.[145] The grant of land
on a 999-year lease at a nominal rent was equivalent to a contribution
of £60,000; but the cost of the actual building, including internal and
external decoration, was estimated at £200,000. The commissioners
promised to guarantee a quarter of this sum and to advance £2,000 for
preliminary expenses. The rest had to be raised by subscription; and the
grant of land would only be made if, by 1 May 1867, sufficient had been
pledged to the hall by the public. It was to be funded by selling debentures: £1,000 for a private box on the first tier that would seat ten, £500
for a box in the second tier seating five, or £100 for a seat in the amphitheatre. The seats bought would be 'practically perpetual' – they would
last as long as the 999-year lease.[146] It was now planned that the hall
would seat 5,600 people. The seats for sale would raise £250,000, the
surplus to be invested for the maintenance of the hall; the other seats
would be offered for sale at each event. The interest in a box or seat
could be sold on, bequeathed or sublet. The committee did not doubt
these seats would be a 'remunerative investment'.[147]

There was one complication. Fowke, who was only forty-two, died
suddenly in December 1865 of a burst blood vessel: just before he expired,
sitting in a chair, he announced: 'This is the end.'[148] Fowke, as an engineer rather than as just an architect, had started to specialise in buildings
with vast floor spaces: he had also just won the competition to build
the Natural History Museum. He had been unwell for months, a condition brought on by overwork in seeking to finish the plans for the
museum. Long rests in Switzerland and Eastbourne had not helped.
Cole visited him in the latter and 'found him very weak with expectora-
tion'.[149] What to do with the Albert Hall was the more pressing problem
than the museum. It was wondered whether to change architects: but
a foreigner was considered out of the question and Scott, the obvious
alternative, considered too expensive in his love of elaborate decoration.
Instead, and mainly for reasons of economy, Fowke's plan was persisted
with where possible, the work being taken over by another of Cole's
cronies, Colonel Henry Scott.

The following April it was agreed to proceed with Fowke's design for the exterior as well as for the interior. Cole drove this decision, despite intensive lobbying from George Gilbert Scott. Cole trusted the Royal Engineers not to be profligate. Colonel Scott did not have too much to do in terms of design: a more convenient siting of the cloakrooms, the provision of crush rooms, better lighting in the corridors and on the stairs, and the stairs to reach each level outside, rather than inside, the corridors. The biggest change was that the floor of the arena would be sunk, but it was understood Fowke himself had contemplated this.[150]

Fowke's vision of his building in red brick and terracotta would be realised. The decision to appoint Lucas Brothers as builders was taken in July 1866; the firm had built Liverpool Street Station and the Royal Albert Docks. The estimate was agreed at £199,748 (to include £27,000 for 'terra cotta ornamentations' and £8,000 for the organ).[151] The other modification was to make the hall more of an oval and less of an oblong.[152] As Henry Scott told his fellow architects at RIBA in January 1872, he had interfered only reluctantly with Fowke's plan: 'Whilst I have always considered that my late brother officer and friend was naturally gifted with unusual architectural and constructive ability, I have not had equal confidence in my own.'[153] The exterior was 272 feet long by 238 feet wide, and built from 6 million bricks and 80,000 blocks of terracotta.

The Queen laid the foundation stone on 20 May 1867, assisted by the Prince of Wales and the committee. A huge marquee was erected over the arena, to accommodate 7,000 guests. The Prince made a speech; Derby, by now Prime Minister, handed the Queen some coins and Granville handed her a glass vessel in which she placed them; the Queen placed it in a recess in the stone, with the aid of a trowel, handed to her by Mr Lucas, the builder. One of Albert's compositions, the 'Invocazione all'Armonia', was then played.[154] It was announced simultaneously that the building would hereafter be known as 'The Royal Albert Hall', by the Queen's command.[155] As well as the crowd of subscribers and dignitaries, there was a large gathering of the public, taking a rare opportunity to see the reclusive Sovereign.

The hall's charter of incorporation set out the purposes for which it might be used: national and international congresses for the furtherance of science or art; concerts; prize-givings by public bodies and societies; and various sorts of exhibition, including agricultural, industrial, artistic and scientific and 'generally any other purposes connected with

Science and Art'.[156] Mrs Henry Cole laid the first brick in November 1867. Work proceeded quickly, and subscribers were invited, on any of the Saturdays in June 1868, to visit and inspect progress. The construction of the roof began on 6 May 1869. The contract specified the hall was to be finished by Christmas Day 1870. A programme of concerts, organ recitals and other musical events was planned for the summer and autumn of 1871. One of the mosaic friezes around the outside of the building stated the purpose of the enterprise: 'The Hall was erected for the advancement of the Arts and Sciences and the work of industry of all nations in fulfilment of the intention of Albert, Prince Consort.'

The Queen visited the almost-finished hall in December 1870, sitting in the Royal Box and elsewhere in the higher parts of the auditorium while musicians performed for her. She liked what she heard, and saw: as she left she observed: 'It looks like the British Constitution.'[157] The State opening was on 29 March 1871. The hall was full. Many of the Queen's ministers were present; she had a guard of beefeaters; and a vast orchestra assembled on the stage. She, inevitably dressed in black, was so overcome that her son had to complete her speech, made in response to his own. It was he who said: 'The Queen declares this hall now open.'[158] The Sovereign was conducted to the Royal Box to hear 'a Cantata, with words from the Bible, composed expressly by Sir Michael Costa', with full orchestra and chorus; she then left, before 'a miscellaneous concert'.[159] There had been a variance of Fowke's final plan: it had been adjusted to accommodate 7,100 people rather than 5,600. At £206,716 11s 3d it came in 3.4 per cent over the estimate. There was plenty of money: the debenture scheme had been so successful that it had had to be limited. New ideas grew out of the hall, according to the 1872 report of the committee responsible – such as for 'a series of cheap concerts for the people' and 'a national training school for music'.[160] The second of those would come in a little over a decade, with the establishment of the Royal College of Music. The first would take another seventy years, when the bombing of the Queen's Hall in Langham Place caused the shift of the Henry Wood Promenade Concerts to the Albert Hall.

XI

The training school for music was perhaps one of the more necessary institutions for a country that considered itself to be advancing civilisation. The Germans called Britain *das Land ohne Musik* – the land without music. Since Purcell's death in 1695 there had not been a single native-born accredited genius in British music. Handel had come over with George I. Arne, Boyce and Sterndale Bennett had done what they could to keep English music alive in the late eighteenth and early nineteenth centuries, but were light years behind Mozart, Haydn, Beethoven, Berlioz and Wagner.

Cole, as always, had a view. In his role at the Society of Arts he had commissioned a report in 1861 on the status and performance of the Royal Academy of Music, founded in 1822 and in cramped premises off Hanover Square. Albert had always hoped to have a conservatoire in South Kensington, and Cole could see that moving the RAM out of Mayfair would help fulfil that vision and solve the institution's accommodation problem. However, when Cole approached the 1851 Commission in 1865 about helping fund such a move they rejected his proposal outright, for reasons of funding. Once the Albert Hall was up and running Cole and the Society of Arts thought again, and decided to propose a National Training School for Music as a separate institution from the RAM, but in Albertopolis. Cole had two advantages in 1873, when he made his new proposals, that he had lacked in 1865. The first was royal patronage – the Duke of Edinburgh, genuinely interested in and knowledgeable about music, agreed to head the committee to drive the project. The second was that a well-known South Kensington property developer, Charles Freake, had agreed to fund the costs of building such an institution, on account of his wife's deep interest in music.

All Cole had to do was persuade the Commission to provide a site for Freake to build on: which, obligingly, it did. It leased Freake some land to the west of the Albert Hall at £80 per annum on a 99-year lease. The building was designed by yet another Royal Engineer and Cole protégé: his own son. The Duke of Edinburgh laid the foundation stone in December 1873 and the building opened in May 1876. The National Training School for Music was ambitious: it set itself up to be a conservatoire on a par with the finest in Europe. Its first principal was a man who would soon be the best-known writer of music in Britain, Arthur Sullivan. However, it quickly ran into financial difficulties: and the commissioners saw no more reason to fund it than they had seen to fund the RAM, had it moved.

The commissioners suggested that the RAM and the NTSM might merge: but the matter would become more complicated yet. In July 1878 it was announced that a College of Music would be established under the patronage of the Prince of Wales: a Royal Charter was obtained for the institution, which opened in 1882. As it opened, the NTSM closed, and the Royal College of Music moved into its premises, staying there until 1894 when the grand building, by Blomfield, that it now inhabits on the south side of Prince Consort Road opened. The RCM was a different matter altogether. It had as its first director Sir George Grove, a remarkable man best remembered today for the dictionary of music that bears his name.

Grove had been a distinguished engineer. He had, inevitably, been an associate of Cole, as an official for the Society of Arts, and had managed the Crystal Palace at Sydenham. He raised funds prodigiously for the RCM, helped not least by having the Prince of Wales's name to bandy about. The Prince used his brother the Duke of Edinburgh's love of music to enlist him to help the fund-raising drive: and by the time the RCM was formally opened by the Prince in May 1883 it had funds of over £110,000. In 1887 Freake gave the RCM the building, picking up a baronetcy in return. Grove persuaded the first two great composers of the English musical renaissance – Charles Hubert Hastings Parry and Charles Villiers Stanford – to join him as senior professors. From then on success was secured: fifty years later the RCM had trained most of the great composers of the early twentieth century, such as Vaughan Williams, Holst, Howells, Bliss, Britten and Ireland. It was exactly what Albert had envisaged. However, the fulfilment of his belief that there should be scientific institutions in Albertopolis would take until the end of the century and beyond.

XII

The Albert Hall, the Natural History Museum and what would become the Victoria and Albert Museum were Cole's direct legacy: the rest of the estate, which now includes the Science Museum, the Royal College of Music and Imperial College, is also indebted to his drive and vision. Predictably, his departure from his official role with the Commission and the government came after he decided to pick a fight. It was with Robert Lowe, Chancellor of the Exchequer in Gladstone's first administration, and a man with many of Cole's characteristics but an even more lethal turn of phrase and a piercing intellect. Colonel Henry Ponsonby, one of the commissioners, told the Queen in 1873 – when the fight with Lowe occurred – that Cole had exercised 'despotic power' in South Kensington.[161] It was decided to split Cole's many functions between several officials, and to persuade him to retire.

Although his caustic and bullying manner was well known to the commissioners, they believed that the Queen should honour him for his work. Gladstone had persuaded her that so numerous and vitriolic were Cole's enemies that to knight him in the Order of the Bath – the accolade normally given to senior and accomplished civil servants – would be a public-relations disaster. Disraeli was scarcely more impressed, but managed to persuade the Queen to knight Cole in 1875. Any hopes that this would buy Cole's silence were short-lived. His house adjoined the estate, in Thurloe Square, and he spent his declining years writing letters and pamphlets complaining to the commissioners and the wider world about the administration of his empire after his abdication. The last trump he had to play – certainly, he would have hoped, in the eyes of the Queen – was that the wishes of the late lamented Prince were no longer being discharged by the commissioners: and therefore the 1851 Commission, he argued in 1876, should be dissolved, and the estate passed to the government. He was ignored. Cole died in 1882, militating to the end.

For all his faults, however, Cole symbolises the can-do attitude that made not just Albertopolis possible, but also many of the achievements of Victorian Britain that still stand today. In cities other than London there are museums, concert halls, learned establishments, libraries and great town halls that are the product of the same mindset that Cole, taking his lead from his master Prince Albert, exemplified; one of ambition, and of a determination to create institutions of a grandeur and permanence that would project not just the names of their creators, but the advances made by Victorian civilisation, for ever.

CHAPTER 10

THE HEROIC MIND: ALBERT AND THE CULT OF THE GREAT MAN

———————

I

From the moment when Carlyle stood up in May 1840 to give his first public lecture in his series *On Heroes, Hero-Worship and the Heroic in History*, the idea of the Great Man pervaded much Victorian thought. It was a natural development for a society that was beginning to question, and even to repudiate, Christianity. Whereas examples of moral conduct had hitherto been drawn from religious teaching, now they were drawn from the lives of men. What also drove Carlyle to celebrate greatness was his contempt for democracy, for he felt great social change and improvement could come only through significant individual acts of leadership of which only great men (women did not enter into his consideration) would be capable. His edition of Cromwell's letters and speeches, followed by his eight-volume life of Frederick the Great, were his leading contributions to this genre.

Following Carlyle's example, much subsequent Victorian narrative history is told through great men – though in the majestic work by his disciple, Froude, on the Tudors, Queen Mary I and Queen Elizabeth I are used to embody, respectively, the wickedness of Catholicism and the virtues of Protestantism. Macaulay's history of the Glorious Revolution is told not least through the characters who made it, notably William of Orange himself. It was also the great age of biography: Stanley's life of Arnold was an early example, then George Gleig's life of Wellington (he also wrote on Clive of India) and later John Forster's life of Dickens.

Once this cult of the great man embedded itself in the Victorian mind it fed, quite naturally, into a subsidiary cult of death, in which the life of the departed great man was commemorated and celebrated out of reverence to him, and by way of example to others. It was seen notably in the funeral of the Duke of Wellington in 1852. On the day after his death in September that year the *Illustrated London News* demanded 'a public funeral, such as was never before seen or imagined in any other country'.[1] They were not disappointed. Thousands of soldiers in full dress uniform, many of them mounted, with military bands playing appropriately mournful marches, followed the massive bronze funeral car – which resembled a small steam locomotive, drawn by twelve horses – from Hyde Park Corner to St Paul's Cathedral. In it, a coffin of scarlet and gold stood on a black and gold pall and rested under an ornate canopy. Greville thought the proceedings 'all well done', except the car, which was 'tawdry, cumbrous and vulgar'.[2] He claimed the design had been directed by Albert, which was 'no proof of his good taste'.[3] Carlyle felt the car 'more like one of the street-carts that hawk door-mats than a bier for a hero'.[4] The public, however, lapped it all up, as they did Tennyson's ode on the subject: 'Let us bury the Great Duke / To the noise of the mourning of a mighty nation . . . the last great Englishman is low.'

Death became an important part of Victorian culture. A nation increasingly conscious of its stature, and of its history, felt that marking the passing of great men in an ostentatious and indulgent way was de rigueur. It validated the average Briton's idea of himself as much as the standing of the deceased. As the secularism that fed the worship of great men advanced, it fed the elevation of death into a cult of its own. Committed Christians sought to emphasise the Resurrection to eternal life, and those of weaker or no faith sought alternatives to the comforts of religion. Although life expectancy increased considerably during the nineteenth century, it remained common for children not to reach adulthood, for women to die in childbirth and for men to be scythed down in their thirties or forties. Elaborate mourning rituals were established not so much to honour the dead, as to honour the cult of the dead. The higher classes wrote letters on black-edged paper for a number of months after a bereavement (the time depending on the closeness of their relation to the dead person). Social engagements were forgone. Black was worn. The lower classes closed their shutters or curtains when a funeral passed through the neighbourhood, and men in the streets removed their hats. Women especially were expected to endure a period of prostration, real or metaphorical. Culture absorbed and reflected the cult: Tennyson's popularity, as we have seen, rested not least on his triumph with *In Memoriam*, which became almost the theme music of the cult, deeply beloved by Queen Victoria herself.

The ritual of the funeral became extensive. Funerary monuments became elaborate – the zenith, or nadir, of this aspect of the cult being reached in the tomb in St George's Chapel, Windsor, of the Queen's grandson Prince Eddy, who died in 1892. A vocabulary of euphemism about 'the departed' and his joining 'the heavenly choir' evolved to allow Victorians to discuss this most compelling of subjects without having to use any unduly stark terms. An even more unsavoury obsession grew up with ghosts, spiritualism and the afterlife, capitalised upon by the growing number of charlatans who posed as mediums and held seances: though their exploitative trade would not really take off until after the holocaust of the Great War.

With one death in particular the cult reached its apotheosis. The awe of death, the exhibition of grief and the sanctification of memory experienced by many Victorians were never engaged in with such reverence, hyperbole, excess and histrionics as practised by the Sovereign herself. Her desire to see her late husband commemorated in the most spectacular fashion led to one of the most distinctive projects of the whole Albertopolis scheme. It drew, once more, on the can-do attitude of the Victorians. Despite the sensitivity of the subject, it provided yet another stage for the clash of egos of those who felt they were making Victorian Britain. It sparked a debate about an appropriate artistic and aesthetic approach to the commemoration of death, and the idea of contemporary style. It cemented the cult of Albert at the heart of the cult of the dead, making him the model for the expression of high Victorian grief. It provided a cultural template for the handling of death that lasted well into the twentieth century.

II

Establishing the habit of a lifetime, Albert Edward, Prince of Wales, still just short of his twentieth birthday, had some illicit sexual encounters with an Irish actress called Nellie Clifden in Dublin in the autumn of 1861, while attached to a regiment at the Curragh. Miss Clifden was an early practitioner of the 'kiss and tell' stratagem, and soon the news was all over Dublin society. Word inevitably sped back to Windsor and outraged the Queen and Prince Albert. They feared the Heir to the Throne might, inadvertently, have set about securing his own line. On 25 November 1861 Albert went to Madingley Hall, just west of Cambridge, where his son was staying while engaging in what purported to be study at the university, to admonish him. They walked outside on a cold, damp day and sat up late into the night while Albert lectured his son about the inevitable decay if he kept on this trajectory, and also about how scandal could undermine the monarchy.

It was not this exacting day on the Fens that killed him: though it weakened his health coincidentally to his contracting either typhoid or Crohn's disease, an inflammation of the bowel, one of which did. Albert had been exhausted all autumn, however, and during the Royal Family's holiday at Balmoral in October 1861 had had several soakings while out tramping through the heather.[5] Not the least preposterous aspect of his widow's hysterical – and there is no other adjective for it – grief was her decision to blame her eldest son for the death of his father. In truth, it had far more to do with that curse of the nineteenth century that technology and investment would soon overcome, poor sanitation. Albert died of the drains at Windsor Castle. There was also a misdiagnosis at the earliest stage of his illness, shortly after he returned from Cambridge, by Dr Jenner, the royal surgeon, who thought Albert had a heavy cold and nervous exhaustion. The Queen told her uncle Leopold on 4 December that Albert had the flu. However, over the next few days his fever intensified and his condition deteriorated. It was not until 12 December that his doctors realised this was more than influenza; but even at this stage it was not clear that they realised it was typhoid. He died two days later, and Victoria's long wallow in widowhood began.

Scarcely was Albert in his tomb than discussions began about a great memorial to him, and to his greatness. Quick off the mark, predictably, was Henry Cole, who had an open letter published in the press calling for the creation of an Albert University. This stimulated no reaction at all, but Cole had signified that should a movement start up to commemorate the life and works of the late Consort, he would (whether anyone else liked it or not) be a significant part of it. The City of London made a more corporate, and determined, effort to launch a memorial appeal. A public meeting took place on 14 January 1862 chaired by the Lord Mayor, William Cubitt, brother and partner of Thomas, the builder 'to consider the propriety of inviting Contributions, for the purpose of erecting a lasting Memorial to His late Royal Highness the PRINCE CONSORT, and to adopt such measures for carrying out the object, as may then be decided upon.'[6] The Bishop of London moved a motion 'deeply deploring the irreparable loss the country has sustained' of the Prince, not least because of his long service 'unceasingly devoted to improving the condition of the humbler classes, and to the development and extension of Science and Art.'[7]

The motion also called for the constitution of a committee of noblemen and gentlemen to see the project of the memorial through. Palmerston, Derby and Disraeli were among the past, present and future prime ministers who sought to serve on the committee. Grey wrote to Clarendon to say the Queen especially wanted him to serve, along with Sir Charles Eastlake, the director of the National Gallery, to give 'advice in the selection of artists' for a memorial and 'the direction of its execution'.[8] Derby, who would chair the committee, raised the question in the Lords on 7 February, stating that £27,000 had already been subscribed, and only uncertainty about how the memorial fund would be managed and disbursed had prevented more from pouring in.[9] The following week Granville announced that as the desire to have a memorial had arisen spontaneously, the government would not dream of seeking to control what would happen. The final decision would be the Queen's. Meanwhile a rash of provincial towns, led by Liverpool and Glasgow, proceeded to make plans for their own memorials.

A Prince Consort Memorial Committee was formally established, comprising Derby, Clarendon, Cubitt and Eastlake, who as the president of the Royal Academy acted as its secretary. It met for the first time at the Royal Academy on 1 March 1862. The Queen had intimated little, in her grief, other than that she expected something of an appropriate scale, and liked the idea of an obelisk.[10] Charles Dickens had heard from a lady-in-waiting that 'she applies herself to all sorts of details appertaining to the Memorial, all the morning, and cries all the rest of the day.'[11] Dickens, who reserved his sentimentality for his novels, observed that Albert 'was neither a phaenomenon, nor the Saviour of England; and England will do exactly without him as it did with him.'

It was clear from the press that 'a large proportion of the public appeared to be desirous of connecting the intended monument with some Institution intimately associated with the Prince's name.' The

Committee, therefore, decided a two-phase memorial would be appropriate, with the institution being devoted to the promotion of the Arts and Sciences, as Albert would have wished. It would also, the Committee felt, reflect his wish – expressed at the opening of the Garden of the Horticultural Society in June 1861 – that those gardens would 'at no distant day, form the inner court of a vast quadrangle of public buildings'.[12] A great hall – something Cole had first envisaged in the late 1850s – would be perfect for that purpose and would 'harmonise with every kind of institution'. So great would be the hall that the monument would need to stand opposite in Hyde Park, not merely being near the site of the Great Exhibition itself, but sufficiently far away from the hall not to be overwhelmed by it.

The immediate consensus was to play safe and support the Queen's idea of an obelisk, preferably of red, but if necessary of grey, granite. Eastlake and other members of the Committee were bombarded with letters from architects, aesthetes, stonemasons and members of the public suggesting how the memorial should be executed. Although obelisks were very much the fashion, and the Queen herself wanted such a memorial, there were doubts whether such an object could be made sufficiently interesting, or sufficiently tall, from a single piece of stone. In April 1862 the Committee wrote to the Queen to make these reservations, and General Grey (upon whom she had immediately come to lean in her bereavement) replied that she had reluctantly acceded to those views.[13] She asked that the foremost architects should be consulted.

Albert's period of unpopularity was fresh in the memory and there was nervousness that a plan might backfire, causing an already hysterical Queen to pitch into even deeper misery. Yet the enthusiasm for the idea seemed to give the lie to fears that it would come to nothing. Grey wrote to Bowring on 31 March about a subscription raised to fund the monument; and he was sceptical. 'Certainly a subscription from 4,500 individuals out of a population exceeding 30 millions does not constitute a *National* Memorial.'[14] The following month Grey suggested, also to Bowring, that an institution might be dedicated to Albert's memory – 'call the building to be erected a College, or Gallery, or what you will' – and that the idea 'deserves consideration'.[15] 'But what chance of getting the necessary funds? The Queen cannot announce such a wish in the chance of having to give it up for want of means – I fear they are sanguine who think the announcement of such a plan would run the subscriptions up to a quarter of a million.' He felt an institution was 'the only satisfactory form that any useful project could, in my opinion, take'. He foresaw that Parliament would be asked to vote £100,000 to ensure that 'the nation's tribute to the Prince's memory' was executed appropriately' and was doubtful that would happen. He asked Bowring to think about it and discuss the matter with him when he had.

A letter of 9 May 1862, written by Sir Charles Phipps to Palmerston five months after Albert's death, raised the question of a 'National Memorial'. The Queen was holed up at Balmoral, prostrate with grief. Everyone around her was in a state of tension. Phipps told Palmerston that if the question were discussed in Parliament it was vital 'to avoid not only all opposition, but all adverse discussion'.[16] The possibility of removing, after all, the National Gallery to Kensington was not to be mentioned (though it resurfaced within a year or two), that having been a great wound to both the Queen and the Prince, and one it was dreaded being revisited, since the Queen felt the decision had been made to keep it in Trafalgar Square out of 'personal opposition to the Prince'. However, there had been a 'change of public feeling' about the Prince: and Kensington would be the obvious place for a memorial, if there were to be one.

Any sort of building, Phipps warned, would require 'a managing body, must be kept in repair, lighted and attended to, and that these expenses would have to be provided for either by endowment, which would require a considerable sum of money, or by an annual vote of parliament, unless the institution were self-supporting, which could hardly be ensured.' Also, 'on account of the distress in Lancashire', where the cotton industry was in a desperate state because of the American Civil War, a vote for any money for a memorial ought, the Queen and her advisers had thought, to be postponed until the following session of Parliament. Phipps reluctantly requested to see Palmerston to discuss the matter: something had to be done.

Cole, writing to Sir Charles Eastlake on 29 May 1862, went to a whole new level of ambition, 'that of connecting <u>all</u> the South Kensington institutions with the Prince's memory. There would be Horticultural Gardens – buildings for the International Exhibitions, South Kensington Museum, Central Hall for Scientific Societies and examinations, and the

Personal Monument on the Highest Ground in Hyde Park.'[17] With his record of success, with no one to challenge his vision, and with the Queen's mood very much set on the creation of the grandest and most extensive memorial possible for her late husband, a crucial phase in Cole's empire building would soon begin.

Another man keen to make his voice heard was George Gilbert Scott, one of the architects consulted. He made a point of writing separately to Eastlake to share his own specific views, and to emphasise that 'I cannot help giving a somewhat large share of my thoughts to it'.[18] Scott would have to go through some hoops before securing the commission: Eastlake wrote to many architects including him, Charles Barry the younger, Philip Hardwick, Matthew Digby Wyatt and Sydney Smirke, inviting them to submit designs. Scott replied that to build something in line with 'public expectations' would cost up to twice the amount suggested in the prospectus.[19] The project at this stage included the central hall as well as the monument, and Scott warned that if an architect who had not foreseen the problem were commissioned – that is, anyone but Scott himself – then the problem would quickly become apparent, and vast modifications would be necessary.

Scott was one of the period's greatest architects, and one of its greatest egos. He was the son of a clergyman, from a clerical family, and had an almost Ruskinian conception of a link between the divine and the Gothic. A family peppered with clergy ensured that when, in the early 1840s, he set about restoring churches that were deemed, in the Victorian estimate, to require improvement, or building new churches in the newly favoured Gothic Revival style, there was plenty of scope for patronage. As a boy Scott had acquired a love of sketching medieval buildings, and in 1827, when he was sixteen, his father had him articled to a firm of London architects.

The boy's genius was not recognised, and his penchant for the medieval was actively discouraged. Scott plodded along until his father died in 1835, at which point he set up his own practice. He hired William Moffatt, with whom he had worked a few years earlier, and they secured a number of commissions to build workhouses required by the passing of the Poor Law Act in 1834. Scott married his cousin in 1838 and had five children with her. She also, after a few years of nagging her husband to do it, sacked Moffatt, who had become Scott's partner shortly before their marriage, and in this she was astute. Moffatt lost money in railway speculation in the 1840s, was rude to Scott's clients and lived beyond his means. When he was eventually imprisoned for debt Scott helped him out.

In the early 1840s Scott moved on from workhouses to churches, strongly influenced by Pugin, most celebrated at that epoch for joining Sir Charles Barry in the design of the new Houses of Parliament. Scott brought to the task his own devout Anglicanism: his style of Gothic frightened no horses. However, his first meeting with Prince Albert had been in 1843, at the opening of one of his humbler buildings, the Wandsworth Infant Orphan Asylum. In 1844 he set out his artistic influences: 'From a very careful consideration of the ancient churches of Germany, France and England, the author . . . has been led to the end of the thirteenth century, viz from 1270 to 1300 AD, as the period at which the most perfect ecclesiastical architecture is to be found: very fine specimens are certainly to be met with both earlier and later than these dates, but still within these limits appear to be comprised the period of the fullest development of the style.'[20] He argued that the architectures of the three countries he had specified had reached a common style by this point 'by coincidence', only to diverge again thereafter. Each 'departed from the simple principles of taste and introduced into their architecture those fantastic and corrupted details, which at length led to the extinction of the style, and a return to the architecture of ancient Rome.'[21]

By the 1850s he had moved on to competing for great public commissions, was writing widely on his art, and was a force to be reckoned with. At the time of the competition for the Albert Memorial he had just started to build the chapel at St John's College, Cambridge – which is by way of a small cathedral, or large town parish church – and was recovering from the controversy, described later, over the new government buildings in Whitehall. In these years, as well as continuing to restore churches (including Westminster Abbey) and cathedrals (including Chichester, St Albans, Salisbury, Lichfield, Chester, Exeter, Rochester and Ely, some of which stand today only because of Scott's work in shoring them up) he would also build the Midland Hotel at St Pancras Station, Leeds Infirmary, Preston Town Hall and parts of Glasgow University. He had around thirty people working for him, and some of the other great names of the period, such as Bodley and Street, passed through. He was very much at the top of his profession: and the memorial to the late Prince Consort was a prize indeed for such a man, with the eyes of the nation upon it.

Eastlake reported to Bowring at the 1851 Commission – upon whose land the memorial would sit – on 10 June 1862 that a group of architects including Scott, Smirke and Tite had investigated the matter, and made the following proposals, which Eastlake now forwarded: 'A monument in Hyde Park, between Rotten Row and the public road; and a Central Hall, south of the public road, in a direct line between the Monument and the centre of the Conservatory.'[22] The idea of a separate monument, free-standing at the south side of Hyde Park, was advanced because of the uncertainty over the future of the rest of the site. This would ensure that, however long it took to construct the rest of Albertopolis, Albert himself would not have to wait too long for his memorial. South Kensington was the overwhelming, but by no means unanimous, choice of site: a long, anonymous letter to the *Morning Advertiser*, under the *nom de guerre* 'ex-MP', said it was yet another example of the 'jobbery' that had gone on about Kensington ever since the exhibition.[23] He wanted the memorial at Burlington House on Piccadilly: his argument died swiftly.

The architects had considered various sorts of memorial. A monolith was out because no single stone of suitable size could be sourced. So too was an obelisk, as one 'built up in several stones would only show an inferiority to the ancients'.[24] A column topped by a statue was ruled out because the statue would not be visible enough. A 'Memorial composed of one or several groups of Sculpture, surmounted by a Statue of the Prince' was a possibility; but bronze, the material of choice, 'soon acquires a dark tone, injurious to the effect of a work of art'. The architects proposed a mixture of metals that 'would acquire an agreeable permanent colour'. Also, it had to be 'upon a very large scale to be effective'. The architects recommended a separate hall because 'we have nothing in London for such an object [meetings connected with the arts and sciences] like the great halls of Liverpool, Leeds and Manchester.'[25]

Derby, who now led the Commission, agreed to reserve land for the hall; and on 12 June Grey wrote to Bowring to confirm the proposal that would be made to the Queen: 'That the personal monument to the Prince shall be connected with a Hall, to form the centre of buildings to be hereafter erected between the Horticultural Garden and Hyde Park for educational purposes as regards Science and Art in their application to productive industry . . . the shape that such an Educational Institute shall take must necessarily be left open for the present.'[26] Fortunately the panel of architects, the commissioners and, most important of all, the Queen all agreed. Grey reported to Eastlake in June 1862 that 'I cannot tell you too strongly how much the Queen is pleased with the shape the proposal for the national monument is now taking.'[27]

In what appears to be the first use of the term, Grey added that 'the "Albert Hall" must be so designed as to form a fitting centre for whatever buildings may, in fullness of time, grow up to the right and left of it.' A marble statue of the Prince was, Grey stipulated, to be 'a principal feature in the interior of the Hall'. By this stage Grey was more positive about the plan to commemorate Albert: he felt that if the plans for the Hall were 'well drawn up, I have little doubt that the whole movement will become so popular as not only to give a fresh impetus to the subscriptions during the present year, both to enable the Government in another session to propose a handsome vote to Parlt for the purpose of giving effect to the scheme, which will receive the ready sanction of the H of Commons.' Consideration of an architect would need to be given carefully – 'rightly or wrongly there is much jealousy of Fowke by the architects generally – and the public would not be disposed in his favour – not understanding that the extension of the Exhibition Building is yet unfinished.'

The Committee invited architects to submit proposals for the monument and the hall in July 1862. It was emphasised that the Queen 'will at all times be consulted' and that the scale would be considerable.[28] The Queen's views, as set out by Grey, were shared with the prospective architects. She had taken quite well the rejection of her idea of an obelisk, not least because of the institution that would now complement the monument. 'Few things could now make the Queen more happy,' Grey told Eastlake on 18 July, 'than to be allowed to witness the realization of some of her beloved husband's noble plans for the benefit of mankind'.[29] She wanted this to be done by the people, by a manifestation of public support, rather than by Parliament. Grey also observed that 'for such an institution, some appropriate title, connected with the Prince's name, will doubtless hereafter be found.' Scott, Sydney Smirke and William Tite were all asked to submit proposals; as were James Pennethorne, Philip Hardwick, Thomas Donaldson, Matthew Digby

Wyatt, Charles and Edward Barry. Designs were required by 4 December 1862, but a short extension was later given, at Charles Barry's request. Tite and Smirke both declined the invitation on grounds of age. The committee also received numerous unsolicited submissions of varying degrees of competence, which it did the artists concerned the courtesy of considering.

However, this optimism was dispelled by an attack on the proposals in *The Times* on 2 August 1862, which Grey found 'most unaccountable – and most unfair.'[30] *The Times* could countenance a personal monument, but not a hall as that monument. Grey noted that the money already subscribed was enough for the personal monument, and suggested that work should proceed on that for the time being 'disregarding all the malignant attacks and absurd suggestions of *The Times*'s correspondents'. He was prophetic to conclude that 'I feel sure that by patience and perseverance the idea of one great institution and entrance to the whole of the estate, bearing the Prince's renowned name, will be, in time, successfully developed.' The *Morning Post* also weighed in with criticisms, which stung because of the paper's alleged proximity to Palmerston. The Committee were not, however, deterred about the idea of a hall. Derby wrote to Clarendon on 14 August to say that the plan had the support of the Prince of Wales, who had promised £2,000.

Scott, ever on the lookout for intrigue, then wrote to Eastlake in December complaining that Tite was making malicious remarks about him. He tarred Smirke with this brush too.[31] He warned Eastlake that because he was the only Gothicist competing others would seek to denigrate him: and added that 'it would be the most miserable weakness on my part not to express my objection'. He and the other architects sent in their plans at the end of January 1863.

The drawings were taken to Windsor in February for the Queen to inspect them. She came to a decision quickly, and on 27 February Grey wrote to Eastlake that, even before the Committee made its formal recommendation to her, 'HM has come to the conclusion that it will be better on the whole to adopt Mr Scott's design for a Gothic Cross – and to abandon the idea of erecting, at the present moment, a Hall in connection with it. Substituting the Gothic cross for an Obelisk, this will in fact be but a recurrence to HM's original suggestion.'[32] The 'Gothic Cross' was by way of an open shrine enclosing a statue of the Prince: influenced perhaps by the memorial to Sir Walter Scott in

Edinburgh, but more recently by Thomas Worthington's design for the Albert memorial in Manchester. Scott himself claimed to have been affected by the design of the original Eleanor Crosses, all of which he had sketched by the time he was out of his teens. The Manchester memorial was in a fourteenth-century style that the aesthete Stephen Bayley described as being perhaps 'ahead of popular taste' at the time.[33]

Scott, in his submission, said he wanted his structure to have 'the character of a vast *shrine*, enriching it with all the arts by which the character of *preciousness* can be imparted to an architectural design, and by which it can be made to express the value attached to the object which it protects.'[34] Scott would come to regard the shrine as his 'most prominent work', and the result of his 'highest and most enthusiastic efforts.'[35] As with another of his great projects, the building of government offices in Whitehall outlined in Chapter 18, it would not be accomplished without much tribulation.

The Queen told Grey that she wanted the memorial to be 'the finest thing of the sort that has yet been seen', and specified the kinds of statuary she wished to see about the base. There seemed only to be one other concern – 'whether Mr Scott's design can be executed for the money is another question'.[36] He had said £90,000, but others had thought it would run to £150,000. Scott himself raised his estimate to £110,000 in a letter to Eastlake of 28 February.[37] The search now began for sculptors of the statuary, and of the effigy of Albert himself. And, although Scott had been told the commission was his, nobody thought to tell the other competitors that they had lost, which prompted a squeal of indignation from Charles Barry (who had submitted a truly monumental design in the Italianate style, a great domed marble edifice sheltering a statue on a high plinth), who wrote to Eastlake when he heard about it by reading in *The Times* a reference Scott himself had made to it.[38]

III

In March 1863 Palmerston, as Prime Minister, agreed to ask Parliament for its support – moral as well as financial – for the memorial. Grey was, nonetheless, nervous about the outcome, fearing that the memory of the 'immense services' of the Prince was fading: he asked Bowring 'pray, influence everyone you can'.[39] Palmerston, who had his own views about Scott, had also found nothing to impress him in the designs – he recorded afterwards that he 'certainly cannot say that any of them appeared to him to be suitable.'[40] He disliked the 'multitude of complicated details' in the plan, because they seemed to obscure the life being commemorated and also to be expensive. He suggested instead 'an open Grecian Temple placed between Rotten Row and the Carriage Drive'.

More thoughtful and detailed in his own criticisms was Cole, who wrote at length to Grey about them on 10 March. Cole claimed that the execution of the idea that he had in mind was, he felt 'certain', 'one which the Prince himself would have approved.'[41] Given Cole's closeness to the late and sainted Prince, this represented the playing of a trump card early on in the game. He recommended that the Queen should retain control, and not Scott, whose reputation had preceded him with Cole. 'The Queen will be able at all times to obtain the best advice possible.' Cole did, however, praise Scott's design. He said it was 'distinguished above all the other designs by its being strictly that of a Memorial character. This character is also pre-eminently English in sentiment; is sanctioned by National associations extending through many centuries when the Fine Arts in England were equal to those in any part of Europe.'[42]

Palmerston, on 23 April in his appeal to the Commons for money, used the Disraelian method of laying on with the trowel his expressions of the size of the loss sustained by the death of the Prince Consort. 'The event struck a gloom into every household – it inspired with deep grief the heart of every subject of Her Majesty,' he said.[43] When Disraeli himself later replied for the Opposition, he seemed to enter into some sort of competition of ingratiation: Albert's death had been a 'great calamity', and he had been 'the peerless husband, the perfect father, the master whose yoke was gentleness'.[44]

The Prime Minister reported on the progress of the submissions by architects, and announced where the memorial would be sited. It would, he said, 'stand as an example to future generations, to stimulate them to emulate those virtues and high qualities which were possessed by the person in whose honour the memorials are erected.'[45] He told the House the memorial would be a worthy object for it to endorse: and that it would be quite in order to vote to make good the difference between the estimated cost of the memorial – put at £110,000 – and the £60,000 or so already subscribed by the public. The Commons gave its support, and a grant of £50,000. The motion to grant the funds was passed *nem.*

con. It was stated that the Queen, not Parliament, would make the final decision about the form of the memorial. Cole and Scott were in the gallery of the Commons to witness Palmerston's achievement. What the Commons could not know was that the Queen was already annoyed that Parliament had not done this sooner: she had told her daughter, the Princess Royal, now the Crown Princess of Prussia, in May 1862 that 'the Government have bungled and been shabby' in respect of a memorial 'and the House of Commons are most difficult people to have anything to do with.'[46]

Cole reported back to Grey the next day that, although cheered by the outcome, Scott had been annoyed by a reference by William Coningham, the MP for Brighton, to a 'monstrous Eleanor Cross' 300 feet high that he was supposed to be building.[47] He told Cole that the monument would be 'a shrine', even if, unlike most shrines, the effigy itself would be open to the elements.[48] In any case, Coningham had been put right on the spot – the memorial would be no more than 150 feet high, and the decision about its exact form had yet to be taken by the Queen.

Derby felt that he and his Committee had done what they best could by advising on the choice of architect: but Grey told him that the Queen wanted to hold them to their original brief of superintending the execution, which Derby knew could take years and would be a thankless task. The Committee managed to persuade the Queen to retain John Kelk to act as its agent as well as the contractor, and keep an eye on progress. Scott, ever on the alert for slights, resented this appointment as an intrusion upon his role as architect, and protested. Derby knew Scott well enough to expect problems. The decision to appoint Kelk was 'given without any reference to his opinion'. Derby remained anxious about the role of the Committee. 'I anticipate no end of embarrassments if we are compelled to act, nominally, as advisers. Every point will practically be decided by others, and we, without the power of imposing any effectual check, shall be held responsible for every blunder, and, above all, for the expenditure of the money.'[49]

He also had Cole to reckon with, as he was making all sorts of enquiries of experts into the durability of some of the materials being proposed for the memorial and the sculpture, and was seeking to know aspects of Scott's business better than Scott did. Cole had also decided he greatly objected to the idea of an open shrine, and sent Grey a long paper explaining why on 4 May 1863, arguing once more for an 'Eleanor Cross'. 'It may be doubted', he wrote, 'if a *single instance can be adduced of a Decorative Shrine ever erected in the open air in this country*. Is an experiment now for the first time to be made with such a memorial as that of the Prince Consort?'[50] Cole kept hammering away at the idea that the statue of the Prince Consort should be exposed to the London weather, even passing on to Grey the suggestion that it should be 'built under one of the Glass Domes of the Exhibition building.'[51] He suggested that a committee be formed to consider the matter, something the Household wisely decided not to gum up the proceedings by acting upon. He also sent Grey a lengthy selection of evidence about Eleanor crosses, distinguished by the exceptional pedantry that had helped make Cole so toxic a personality among those who knew him.

Scott, profoundly irritated, replied in a predictably combative way, dismissing Cole's suggestions. '*The Statue of the Prince Consort himself* . . . should be *the* object which should, at the first glance, strike the eye and explain the whole idea of the monument,' he wrote in a printed memorandum circulated to Grey and others in May 1863.[52] 'To have this concealed in an apartment invisible to the spectator from without, is to destroy the whole ideal of the monument which would become unintelligible except by the verbal explanation that the lower storey contains a room or cell in which the statue is enclosed to protect it from being soiled or injured. This seems to me highly objectionable; indeed, almost destructive to the effect which such a monument should produce.' Scott said he was open to persuasion about materials; but the design was not negotiable. Cole quickly saw he had lost, and surrendered. The decisive moment came at Osborne on 11 May 1863, when Sir Charles Phipps effectively told him to mind his own business, and enlisted the Queen's name to say that such decisions as had been made on grounds of taste were hers, and the matter was closed. It was settled that the monument would be built as Scott wanted: and it was. Meanwhile, Cole considered other means by which he could influence the commemoration of his late patron.

At the end of May Grey wrote to Disraeli, a commissioner as well as Leader of the Opposition in the Commons – to ensure he was on message, and was assured he was. Grey admitted he had felt reluctant to approach other Conservatives, with the exception of Lord Elcho, in case it did more harm than good, but asked Bowring if he could do it, as well as talking to some 'Radicals'.[53] Grey professed himself *'very anxious'* about what Bowring found; fear of further emotional damage to the Queen was clearly at the forefront of his considerations. Later in the summer, when the costs became widely known, there were protests about the extravagance, with one correspondent to *The Times* suggesting that the money be, instead, sent to the north of England for the relief of the poor there.[54]

IV

The Queen gave her permission by the Sign Manual on 6 April 1864 for land in Hyde Park to be used for the memorial. However, the proposal to purchase land on the other side of Kensington Gore for a memorial building was defeated in the Commons the following month. Grey was incandescent, and told Bowring on 19 May that 'I always believed that the main object of those who defeated the proposal to purchase the building was to throw obstacles in the way of the general Kensington scheme with respect to Scientific Institutions etc.' He remained convinced that if such a building were put up some great institution would wish to make it its temporary, and then permanent, home. The problem at this stage seems to have been the Court's determination that the National Gallery, or National Portrait Gallery, should inhabit such a building, which neither wished to do. The idea eventually evolved into a concert and exhibition hall, under Cole's aegis, being the second part of the explicit commemoration of Albert's name, and a consolation to Cole for the removal of the Crystal Palace to Sydenham. It also associated Albert explicitly with the advance of civilisation. However, the idea that memorialising Albert was a universally popular occupation was gainsaid by a remark Dickens made to a friend in Whitby in September 1864: 'If you should meet with an inaccessible Cave anywhere in that neighbourhood, to which a hermit could retire from the memory of Prince Albert and testimonials to the same, pray let me know of it. We have nothing solitary and deep enough in this part of England.'[55]

Eastlake, in his initial discussions with Bowring in 1862, had suggested that there should be a seated statue of Albert in the hall, to distinguish it from the standing one that would be on the monument.[56] However, this was not to be: Albert was to be seated on his memorial. This would cause the most profound problems.

The Queen expressed a preference for Baron Carlo Marochetti as the sculptor of the colossal statue. Marochetti had made some busts of the royal couple in the 1850s that had given much pleasure to them, and had as a result been asked to cast the recumbent figures of Albert and Victoria on Albert's tomb in the mausoleum at Frogmore, in Windsor Great Park. The Queen seems to have decided that Marochetti was the only artist who could capture her late husband as she would wish. Marochetti was a Sardinian noble, but born in Turin in 1805 and brought up in Paris, where his father had been a lawyer, and where he later studied as a sculptor at the École des Beaux-Arts. He was of the Romantic school, and touted himself around Europe from the 1830s onwards seeking, and quite often finding, commissions, specialising in equestrian statues of supposedly great European leaders and soldiers. He impressed the Queen on their first meeting in 1849 with his courtly manners, and soon won the commission for the equestrian statue of Richard the Lionheart that originally stood outside the western entrance to the Crystal Palace at the Great Exhibition. Thanks to an intervention by Albert this statue, popular with the public, was moved permanently to outside Westminster Hall. By the early 1860s, Marochetti was one of the most sought-after sculptors in Britain.

In the early summer of 1864 he was asked to submit an estimate for the cost of building 'the colossal statue'.[57] The reaction ought to have been a warning signal, but so committed was the Queen to the prospect of Marochetti sculpting her late husband that it is unlikely that any warning, however clear, would have been heeded. The Baron asked for £10,000, cash on the nail, roughly twice what Scott had considered likely. He was given £3,000 as an advance, and accepted it, but soon fell out with the Household. Phipps wrote to him in the early summer of 1865, saying he would lose the commission unless he was more cooperative: the Baron backed down, and a new agreement between him and the Palace was concluded in July 1865.

Other sculptors – MacDowell, Calder-Marshall, Thornycroft, Lawlor, Foley, Weekes, Theed and Bell, a cast that would change slightly over the coming years – were then chosen for the allegorical sculptures representing the four corners of the globe and different branches of economic activity, that would be placed around the pedestal. At the bottom would be friezes of 169 sculptures that, in keeping with the cult of the great man, would represent artists such as poets, musicians, architects (of whom Scott, at the Queen's command, would be one) and indeed sculptors themselves, and which, after the Greek example, was called the Frieze of Parnassus. This would be made by two sculptors especially favoured by Scott, Henry Hugh Armstead and John Birnie Philip. The Queen had made the choice of sculptors: she was guided in it by Eastlake, however, since one or two whom the Queen favoured were not considered up to the mark, and needed tactfully to be advised of this. Keeping control of this selection of artists, notably Marochetti himself, would prove a problem, and helped put the completion of the memorial years behind schedule. Poetry, painting, architecture and sculpture would also be the subjects of the four mosaics in the different elevations of the canopy above the shrine, and these were designed by Clayton and Bell.

The supervision of this detail would have been Eastlake's responsibility, but he died in late 1865. After much consideration, it was decided to offer his place as representing the 'art element' on the Memorial Committee, to Austen Henry Layard, a Liberal MP, aesthete, classicist and renowned archaeologist, who in the 1840s had discovered Nineveh.[58] The idea was Grey's and Phipps's, and they reached it not least in the consideration that 'his connection with the Govt might be useful in communicating with them.' Grey wrote to Layard on the Queen's command on 15 January 1866 asking him to take the role. 'I do not think', Grey wrote to him, 'it likely that your acceptance of this charge will entail any great trouble upon you.'[59] Layard, 'very sensible of the honour which the Queen has been pleased to confer upon me', believed him, and accepted by return of post.[60]

Layard, who was born in 1817, had had an unconventional upbringing. His father had served in the Ceylonese civil service but had been an asthmatic, and the family settled in Florence because of the climate. Young Henry had a Filippino Lippi altarpiece over the bed in his nursery and immersed himself in the fine arts. After a failed attempt to become a solicitor in his uncle's London practice, he went exploring in the Middle East, an experience he was lucky to survive. He nearly died of malaria in Constantinople and, seeking to see Petra and the Dead Sea, was robbed and beaten almost to death by unfriendly natives. He learned Arabic and was appointed an attaché by Sir Stratford Canning, the British Ambassador to the Sublime Porte. He persuaded Canning to fund archaeological work on some mounds near Mosul in what is now Iraq, and uncovered three Assyrian palaces there; some of the discoveries were sent to the British Museum, who provided more funding. Layard, after reading further, realised one of the palaces he had discovered was Nineveh.

Excavations continued there until 1851, by which point Layard had become famous for his achievements, and for his combination of scholarship and intrepid exploration. He decided to move into politics, and in 1852 became Liberal MP for Aylesbury. With his deep knowledge of the region he became a fierce critic of Aberdeen's conduct of the Crimean War; and once Russell became Foreign Secretary in Palmerston's administration he had Layard as under-secretary. Layard had become a great connoisseur, notably in Italian art, and had been offered the directorship of the National Gallery, which he refused. He was also, in July 1865, approached by Henry Cole to succeed Panizzi at the British Museum – 'there being a general opinion that you ought to be [a candidate]. Can you tell me if you think you will come forward?'[61] Layard did not: the political urge remained strong.

He could not, however, refuse his Sovereign. He began almost at once touring the studios of the sculptors working on the memorial, though he had to make time first to read the minute-book of the committee he had joined and various files of correspondence.[62] He went on regular visits to the studios of the mosaic sculptors as well, sometimes with Scott, and reported progress to Grey. Buckingham Palace chose to disburse funds to the artists only when Layard told Doyne Bell in the Privy Purse Office that the progress merited it. He also had to ascertain from them what metal would be required to cast 'the colossal statue of the Prince Consort – 'old gun metal', 23 tons of it.[63] The metal would cost £2,000 and the casting another £600.[64] On 19 February Layard for the first time visited the studios of Baron Marochetti. In the main body of his report to Grey he passed no comment on the quality of the work, but observed that the Queen ought soon to go to see it. There was, however, a worrying postscript. 'I may mention', Layard noted, 'that Baron Marochetti has departed in several instances from the small sketch model which had been submitted to Her Majesty.'

The Queen visited Marochetti's studio later in 1866 and advised him on 'likeness and costume'. She also dropped in on Armstead, and relayed back to him her satisfaction with his work. He asked Layard to retail to her his assurance 'that I shall endeavour to justify, in the

progress of the work, the opinion she is pleased to entertain of it.'[65]
She also approved all the sketches of the mosaics sent to her by Scott
before they were executed. Scott and Layard had gone at the end of
February to the studios of Armstead and Philip, where they had noticed
work that was 'susceptible of improvement'.[66] He had alerted Scott to
what he perceived was a 'meanness and stinginess' in some of the
designs, and had left it to Scott to deal with these matters. Layard was
not nit-picking. As he told Grey, the mosaics would be easily scrutinised, and possibly criticised, because they were at eye level, and therefore needed to create nothing but the finest impression. 'It seems to
be highly desirable that they should be executed in the most satisfactory
manner possible.'[67]

Using his skill and knowledge as an antiquarian, Layard wrote to
Philip and referred him to Roman sculptures in the British Museum that
might serve as an example of excellence.[68] He sent Grey a copy of his
letter, and Grey remarked that the sculptor ought to be 'eternally
grateful' to Layard for his trouble.[69] In September 1866 Doyne Bell visited
all the sculptors and reported back on their progress, which he found
satisfactory.[70] During the following winter, however, alarm bells started
to ring at the Palace, notably in Grey's office, about the expense of the
preparations of the mosaics by the engraver, Clayton ('is it absolutely
necessary to make such elaborate oil paintings as Mr Clayton speaks
of?' he asked Layard on 19 February 1867) and also because 'time is really
a very important consideration.'[71] However, the following week Clayton
wrote to Layard to ask whether there was 'any proposal that the period
allowed for the preparation and delivery of the cartoons for the mosaics
of the Prince Consort Memorial be extended – as fairly due to an undertaking of such importance – to eighteen months from the 1st instant – I
would suggest the following details as the basis for a contract . . .'[72]

The new schedule meant that the last mosaic – that of 'Architecture'
– would not be delivered until 31 July 1868. Grey, with resignation and
after consultation with his colleague Sir Thomas Biddulph, the Keeper
of the Privy Purse, conceded to Layard on 4 March that 'we both agree
that there is nothing for it but to accept Mr Clayton's proposal – and
also that it will be desirable to have a written agreement.'[73] He said the
Queen was about to go on another tour of the artists' studios, no doubt
to give inspiration and encouragement. Meanwhile, Layard wrote to
Clayton and told him he would have to sign a binding contract: 'I need

scarcely press upon you the importance of strictly adhering to the terms mentioned by you for the delivery of the cartoons, and I trust that nothing will now stand in the way of their completion.'[74]

The statue of Albert became Layard's main worry. At the end of December 1866 Biddulph had asked him to go to Marochetti's studio 'and report for the Queen's information what the state of his work is.'[75] Layard went within a week. He was unable to appraise the statue properly as it was confined to a small room. The lions for Trafalgar Square were being cast in the same studio, and once they were moved the Prince Consort's statue would be shifted to the great space they were occupying, where Layard said he would get a better view of it. Grey asked Layard to take Scott to see the sculpture; which, within a few days, he did.

On 7 March 1867 he and Scott visited Marochetti's studio, where he found the life-size plaster model of Albert 'almost finished. It only requires some slight alterations in the head and the addition of some details in the drapery.'[76] He remained nervous, however: 'Mr Scott and I think it desirable that the Queen should not see the statue yet. Anything but a favourable impression can be derived from so large a mass in pure white plaster, seen from a very short distance – and without sufficient light and shade to give the proper effect to the modelling of the more delicate parts.' Indeed, Marochetti himself suggested the model should be gilded 'before Her Majesty visits his studio', and Layard thought that the small cost of this process was worthwhile to stave off grief.

He also told Grey of Scott's suggestion that the completed model 'should be placed on a pedestal in the Park' so the effect of the statue could be judged by the Committee before it was cast. Layard supported this, but warned Grey that 'great care must be taken that it should not be seen except by the Queen and those who are immediately concerned with the Memorial – as any premature criticism in the public prints might be prejudicial to the ultimate success of the monument'. The Queen agreed: but Marochetti went to see Layard on 11 March, seeming 'uncomfortable as to the impression that the model has made upon Mr Scott, and is agreed that he may be required to make considerable alterations in it.'[77] Marochetti was telling Scott, however, that 'he has no doubt about its effect and his experience must give him every means of judging, but to others it would be satisfactory to see with their own eyes.'[78] Layard advised Marochetti in late March 1867 to start casting the plinth for the statue, which would 'in no way interfere with any alterations that may hereafter be considered necessary in the statue itself,' a statement betraying Layard's cast of mind.[79]

In early April Marochetti saw Biddulph, and Stanhope reported to Layard that 'the interview was of a much more satisfactory and amicable character than might have been expected'.[80] Marochetti needed an extra £1,000 for the costs of erecting the model. On 6 April Layard told Marochetti that Grey had advised him that the Queen would be ready to go and see the model in the park before the end of the month, and asked him to organise its positioning with Scott.[81] Scott arranged for everything to be in place for 29 April 1867, though Marochetti was reluctant to the last to do this.[82] On 23 April, a few days before the Queen's visit, Scott wrote to Layard to say Marochetti 'has been on the ground and finds things in a state which he thinks so unsuitable for putting up the figure that he wants to delay it till after the Queen's return [from Osborne].'[83] The strain was becoming enormous. 'He wishes to see me this afternoon,' Scott continued, 'but I do not like the responsibility of being a party to the alteration.' He sought Layard's advice, and also wrote to Grey. Marochetti, unnerved, wrote to Biddulph assuring him that all would soon be well.[84]

Scott wrote again on 29 April saying that having seen Marochetti's figure, and having consulted others who had, 'some very decided change is necessary'.[85] He listed the problems: 'The first impression seems to be that of <u>prodigious size</u> and the next one of want of refinement; indeed in plain terms of an ungainly clumsiness. One opinion went so far as to describe this by the term "ugliness", or something stronger.' Scott had seen it three times and had become 'rather accustomed to it . . . when I saw it first in the studio it gave me a severe shock.' He continued: 'It strikes me that, when a statue is to be magnified to so colossal a size, it needs to be refined, its proportions a little lightened, and the folds of the drapery reduced, or it becomes offensive just as a man would if viewed through a gigantic magnifying glass. I had hoped that the distance and height would have modified this, but they fail to do so.' This was not all: the body seemed to have been shortened and the legs 'look unnaturally developed'.

The Queen's visit was postponed, in accordance with Marochetti's wishes: he met Layard on 1 May and they spent two hours on-site discussing the problems, with the model on its pedestal above them, screened off from public view.[86] The sculptor said the problem was that the Prince was sitting down. An equestrian statue would have been easier. But 'Mr Scott objected to an equestrian statue on principle,' Layard told Grey, 'considering that it would be inconsistent with the general design . . . of the monument.' So Marochetti was asked to make the modifications suggested by Scott, though not with much enthusiasm. Meanwhile, hostilities opened on another front: Armstead and Philip told Layard in May that 'they could not possibly finish the podium sculptures within the period specified'.[87] Layard told Grey that they had asked for an additional fifteen months 'at least'. This, too, would have to be referred to Buckingham Palace.

Then Marochetti renewed his demands for an equestrian statue, which upset Scott. 'I am most alarmed at Baron Marochetti's movement in favour of an equestrian statue,' he told Layard on 24 June 1867, 'instead of the enthroned or quasi-enthroned statue for which the monument was designed.'[88] To make matters worse Sir Edwin Landseer, designer of the Trafalgar Square lions, had, gratuitously, offered his own view, taken seriously by some at Court and not least by Grey, that an equestrian statue would be right.[89] Doyne Bell took the opposite view, saying that 'of course, as Baron Marochetti is to do his best to satisfy the Queen, it is only fair that he should be permitted to try every experiment – but the true results of such experiments can *only* be tested on the pedestal in Hyde Park.'[90] The pedestal would not accommodate a horsed Prince Consort.

Scott added: 'I did not feel, when the model was placed in position, that the difficulties arising from the sitting position were the main cause of the defects which we perceived to exist.' He said Marochetti had a poor grasp of perspective – he had not seen 'the well-known necessity of raising a figure upon its seat and thus giving additional slope to the knees'. But the insistence on a 'too great scale', which was not Marochetti's fault, was at the root of the problem. It had been agreed to reduce the scale by one-tenth, and Scott felt it was 'impossible to conceive that an artist of Baron Marochetti's eminence' could not eliminate the difficulties without changing the nature of the statue. Scott told Layard that if Albert were horsed, then 'in the front view the body and the head of the figure of the Prince would be entirely eclipsed by the head of the horse, while from the only position from which the figure of the Prince could then be seen – the side view – the head and tail of the horse would be liable to be cut off from view by the pillars'.

Scott added that 'had I been designing a monument of which the principal figure was to be Equestrian, I should certainly have treated it very differently – and should probably have omitted the canopy and shrine altogether. The whole design is framed for a <u>sitting</u> figure.' Scott had further weapons to deploy, with respect to the mosaics being designed for the faces of the memorial: 'One can hardly conceive of any congruity between a military statue and the symbols of art and science with which the entire monument is exclusively adorned.' The monument was, after all, supposed to commemorate 'the great promoter of art, science and of social virtues in our country', and not a cavalry officer. Scott's arguments were placed before the Queen, who immediately decreed that 'in the face of such a strong expression of opinion from Mr Scott, an Equestrian Statue must not be thought of.'[91] It also helped that Layard had signalled to Grey his entire agreement with Scott, whose arguments he said were 'very weighty'.[92] Cole, who could not bear to keep his finger out of this particular pie, also argued for an equestrian statue: how far he did this because he believed it, and how far because he liked antagonising Scott, is a matter for speculation. Grey bore the bad news to the Baron, telling him that 'that idea must be at once excluded from further consideration.'[93]

By early July one of Clayton's cartoons was ready. This, too, troubled Scott, who asked Layard to come and see it in place on the memorial. 'It looks very fine so far as general design goes but I differ much from Clayton as to the question of tone. As it stands it is very gay, pronounced and prominent, whereas I think it should have a quiet, rich and somber [sic] tone rather like an old painting: rather giving the idea of retiring as the quietest part of the composition than of thrusting itself forward and challenging public gaze.'[94] If Layard shared his view, he said, a little extra time spent rectifying the matter would be well spent.

V

The Queen, now it seems sharing the anxiety of her courtiers on the matter, asked at the end of July for a report on what Marochetti was doing. Scott saw him at the Royal Academy a couple of evenings later and the Baron told him he had made certain changes and 'if it would not do now, nothing would make it do, and that the sitting figure must be given up.'[95] This did not sound promising, and indeed was not. 'I expected from this to find that a strong effort had been made to meet the difficulty supposed to exist, but was disappointed at finding myself mistaken, and that all which had been done was to make a mechanical reproduction, to a scale one-tenth smaller, of the former figure (in the nude).' The Baron proposed to drape this 'lightly', and 'so as to show the outline of the limbs and body which I have no doubt is wise'. However, Scott continued: 'Beyond this, it seems worse than useless to offer the smallest suggestion for, whatever is suggested the Baron not only pronounces, almost before he knows what one is saying, to be wholly inadmissible, but seems rather determined to do just the reverse.' Then came the killer blow: 'My own conclusion is that he has no wish for it to succeed, but by a determined refusal to correct all defects arising from the difficulty of this position to drive us to the adoption of an equestrian figure or to shift the blame for failure from himself to me. I am myself convinced that if he had any real desire to make the figure successful he would have no difficulty in effecting it, but I simply despair of inducing him to make even the smallest effort.'

Scott went on, at length, to describe Marochetti's disdain for him and his opinions, and to create the distinct impression that the end of a road was being reached. 'I would beg you,' he advised Layard, 'before you leave [on holiday] to take the matter seriously in hand, for it is utterly useless for me to say another word about it.' Scott thought Layard might be able to persuade the Baron to be reasonable and stop maintaining that a sitting figure was 'impossible'. 'The only hope', he said, 'lies in your influence'. He made a number of technical suggestions for Layard to suggest to Marochetti in what was clearly going to be a sticky interview: lengthening here, shortening there, lifting up here and there. 'Then, again,' wrote Scott in exasperation, 'I would reduce the <u>chair</u>, but the Baron says <u>no</u>.' What had really aggrieved Scott was that the Baron had told him that all his life he had acceded to the suggestions of others, but could not do so to Scott because of 'the radical error included in my suggestions' on the question of perspective; and this, as Scott rather woundedly added, after 'I was all gentleness and courtesy to him'. He signed off 'leaving the matter to your better management'.

Layard communicated this to Grey, who rightly adduced at once that there was going to be 'a great deal of trouble'.[96] First, Marochetti had just written to Biddulph to ask for £1,000 on account, claiming that all the alterations that had to be made would incur him considerable extra expense – as if the necessity for those alterations was nothing to do with him. Grey worried that, if this demand were met, it would seriously reduce the money available for a new commission. Second, and more to the point, 'the Baron was selected by HM herself to execute the statue – and the agreement with him was only a verbal one.' Marochetti also 'claimed that the Queen had approved of the models'. He feared all the Committee could do at that point was 'to express their decided opinion' that Marochetti had no claim to be paid for unsatisfactory work, but also that 'the alternative he himself suggested to Mr Scott may yet have to be adopted, or another sculptor substituted.' Grey passed the buck back to Layard, asking him to find a way of telling Marochetti that if his work could not be made satisfactory he would not be paid.

Layard replied that he hoped he could persuade Marochetti to 'produce a work which will be worthy of his reputation'.[97] The alternative was stark: 'To take the commission away from him now would be a very serious step, and one most damaging to his fame as a sculptor.' Layard agreed that the demand for £1,000 should not be met, until and unless the work was satisfactory. His papers include a number of drawings of seated classical statues, presumably to pass on to Marochetti. There was by now general pessimism at Court about whether Marochetti could do what was required. Bell wrote in October 1867 that he was 'apprehensive' of the prospect. He regarded Marochetti's remarks about the model as 'singularly wanting in artistic knowledge.'[98] Marochetti had said he could not do any better; this did not bode well for the modifications he was making. However worried the Committee became, it was, in the end, a matter between the Sovereign and the Baron. Marochetti had had a long summer holiday, the latest example of his titanic caprice, and wrote to Grey from France on 22 October to say he would shortly be on his way back to resume battle with the seated figure.[99]

VI

Grey received a letter from Marochetti's son, however, dated 31 December 1867, to say his father had died suddenly in Paris on the 29th.[100] As Scott wrote to Layard on 2 January 1868, after months of waiting to see how much of Layard's counsel the Baron had taken, 'I have heard today with deep concern and surprise the startling intelligence of the death of

Baron Marochetti! I saw him only on the 18th ult in the most perfect health, and he told me that some time during the present month he would have his new model sufficiently forward to be examined. In what a strange position has this so unexpected event placed us in reference to the statue of the Prince!'[101] Struggling to contain himself within the bounds of taste, Scott added in a fine circumlocution: 'I fear that, great as is my interest in the subject, there is some danger of presumption in expressing any opinion as to the course which may be followed. If, however, I dare offer a remark, I would say that we have only one man suited to the work and that that man is Foley.'

Joseph Foley was working on one of the mosaics, and Scott agreed that 'the obvious objection is that he is backward with his group': but Scott felt it could soon be finished. 'Our great statue is of the utmost importance and of great difficulty. I have not seen what Baron Marochetti has been doing, but I would suggest that the new artist ought not to have his ideas cramped by being asked to work with any reference to these merely tentative models but that he should start again on his own thoughts.' Layard knew Foley's work well and had regularly corresponded with him. Also, he and Scott could both pull rank on Foley in a way that was impossible with the Baron: but Scott's main point was that he was 'a man whose artistic force and power is [sic] universally admitted, and whose work will command approval rather than tempt criticism however undeserved.' Scott wrote in a similar vein to Grey, to pull him alongside in this difficult moment. Less tactful was Scott's business partner Arthur Thompson, who wrote imploringly to Bell to do all he could to 'save us' from the Baron's son, and who a few days later reported to the same man that Marochetti's staff were working 'day and night' to get the revised model finished.[102]

Biddulph wrote to Layard on 18 January to say that Marochetti's son had arrived in England and was preparing to make a cast of the model left by his father, something he had indicated he would do in the letter he had sent to Grey announcing his father's death. 'The serious question will arise as to its merits and if it is considered that they are sufficient to incline the Queen to adopt it, in what manner is the work to be completed?'[103] Biddulph suggested appointing a group of 'three gentlemen' – 'it is not settled who the three should be' – whose 'opinions would command respect' to have a look at the cast and take a view. The Queen had thought these might be Lord Stanhope, Lord Taunton and a Mr

Newton from the British Museum. He asked Layard to agree to this, which he did, though asked to be one of the three, supplanting Lord Taunton.

Layard interviewed Marochetti's son in early March 1868; a few days before, on the 18th, the three wise men had been to Marochetti's studio. They sent their report to the Queen who, thanking them for it, decided to go and see for herself, and to meet her three advisers there when she did. The report said unequivocally that they regarded the statue as 'not satisfactory', and added that they did not think 'that any other artist of high reputation would willingly undertake the responsibility of making alterations in it.'[104]

After some rumination the Queen had Biddulph write to Layard on 22 April to say that 'I think the Queen will ask you to sound Mr Foley about executing the Colossal Statue for Hyde Park'.[105] Stanhope and Newton had both agreed to recommend Foley 'in preference to any other sculptor', and so the Baron's masterpiece was not to be. The formal invitation for Foley came on 24 April, with Layard asked to deliver it and find out 'the length of time required, and the amount which he would expect to be paid.'[106] If Foley would not do the casting himself then he was to produce a model, seated, in the robes of the Garter 'but Her Majesty does not wish to bind the sculptor to an over-accurate representation of those robes.' Marochetti's excessive 'drapery' was not to be repeated.

Foley wrote on 11 May with an estimate for the total cost of the work: £10,000 'including charges for gilding and completing it in every respect.'[107] He said he could finish it in two years, but 'I need scarcely tell you I should be compelled to postpone the completion of several works which I am at present commissioned to execute.' The sum shocked Biddulph, who appears not to have noticed that he was being quoted all-in for a finished product. 'I fear Mr Foley misunderstands what is wanted, which I consider to be a model to size of the statue. Surely he will execute that for a far lower sum than £10,000?'[108] When Foley was asked to quote just for a model from which the finished object could be cast, he replied that such a procedure would be 'impracticable. My experience has impressed upon me the imperative necessity for the author of the model to have entire control over the bronze founders and all others engaged upon his work.'[109] The cost would be reduced because the base gunmetal out of which the statue would be cast was already in the possession of the Committee, who would make it available to Foley.[110] Francis Palgrave, the poet, critic and anthologist, wrote to Layard to express relief that the Marochetti model was being dispensed with, his statue of Peel being dismissed by Palgrave as 'wretched'.[111]

Scott told Layard on 16 May that he had spoken to Foley at a dinner, and what Foley had told him confirmed the architect's view that he would cast a statue with proper regard for perspective and 'drapery'.[112] Foley and Layard finally agreed terms on 30 May 1868, his fee being £10,000 less the value of the metal. On 5 August Layard wrote to Biddulph that 'Mr Foley has sent his sketches for the statue of the Prince Consort. They are both very great improvements upon Baron Marochetti's design, and one especially promises to be a very fine work.'[113] Layard was shown alternative designs, 'the Prince seated in his own chair, in the other upon a stool. I much prefer the latter – as the arms of a chair always produce an unpleasant and confined appearance. I have suggested a modification of the stool by changing it into a Gothic chair with a low back and without arms.' Foley made new sketches and Layard and Scott went to his studio to see them on 6 November: both were delighted with what they saw, as Layard told Biddulph that day, with the Prince's 'dignity' and 'character' coming through clearly.[114] He urged Biddulph to get the Queen's approval of the design so that a large model could be made without delay: a small model would be made for her to see within ten days, at the same time as inspecting some of the mosaics. It was fixed that the Queen would visit the site in Hyde Park on 27 November, with Layard summoned to the Palace afterwards to discuss Foley's plans. The sculptor himself was summoned to Windsor in early December with the final sketch where the Queen and the Princess of Prussia 'expressed their approval of it.'[115]

The troubles, though, were not yet over. Scott wrote to Layard in the spring of 1869 about the Albert Memorial – the sculptures around the base were 'costing the sculptors more money than they reckoned'.[116] Kelk wrote to Scott expressing his worries that, as well as the cost, the work was only half finished and was already four months late. The contractor employing the sculptors, Kelk, had written to Scott to express his commitment 'that I can have but one object, and that is to do my duty to my employers, and get the work done, and save the whole thing from becoming a public scandal'.[117] Scott replied that he knew one of the sculptors, Armstead, was 'a man of an excitable nervous system . . . he is personally, I feel convinced, exerting himself to the utmost.' Armstead had said something to Kelk about it taking three more years to finish, and that 'contracts were made to be broken'; Scott hosed Kelk down, though the contractor considered Armstead to have insulted the authority vested in him by the Queen, and therefore the Queen herself.[118] Scott gently rebuked Armstead for having 'offended' Kelk in this way.[119] 'The fact is you did enter into a contract as to time,' he reminded the sculptor, 'and that it proved to be one impossible to act up to; but this is rather a subject for expression of regret than of scornful impatience at any expression of the same feeling on the part of the other party to your contract; especially when that party acts as agent for the Queen herself.' He consoled Armstead by pointing out that he was chivvying another sculptor, Philip, even more. This was true: Scott told the other sculptor that 'the feeling of impatience I mentioned to you has taken a very strong form, and that every exertion on your part is needed to evince your anxiety to meet the views of employers. I shall be <u>very much obliged to you</u> if you will act upon this view.'[120]

Armstead replied that 'anyone who has the slightest acquaintance with me must know that joking is my habit'.[121] However, he added that 'for the last four years my life has passed entirely in work. I rise in the morning to work on, or at, the Memorial, and I reach home of a night so tired that I have not been able the whole of that time to keep up the slightest social intercourse.' Given that the whole of the east centre had been remodelled in the previous year – '34 feet of figures life size' – he said that 'when Mr Kelk called I confess I did not think him serious when he spoke of my not getting on.' Armstead said he had 'modelled and cast and chased in bronze' the figure of Chemistry; that Rhetoric was 'nearly ready for casting' and that he had in the previous year 'carved . . . some 14 heads at the Memorial.' He added: 'I believe that the amount of work mentioned above proves that as far as deeds are concerned I have not been wanting in effort to do all that flesh and blood could do to fulfil the contract on time, although from the first I said that six years would not be too long a time for the work.'

He repeated: 'I am sorry that Mr Kelk should have been annoyed by my jest' but that 'it would be well if I could be left quietly at my work. I have gone through years of high pressure, and my nerves and head are not now strong. If I once wake at night I never sleep again.' He concluded his epistle to Scott with a cautionary postscript further to prove his point. 'As to my nerves, my foreman came to me the other day, whilst I was hard at work carving at the Memorial and said "Mr Kelk is here". I was drilling the sight of an eye at the time – my hand shook, the drill slipped, scratched the marble, and I had to lower the whole of the face.' Both Armstead and Philip had signed fixed-price contracts, and the work was taking them far longer than they had imagined: anyone who visits the memorial and sees the crowd of statues around the base, all made to a high specification, will see why. However, shortage of funds lowered both men's morale, and when the Palace refused to supplement the agreed price, there was little they could do but grin and bear it.

The main effigy of Albert himself, being sculpted by Foley, was proceeding more smoothly. Layard visited Foley and saw his finished second model in early July 1869. 'As far as I could judge, seeing the model thus isolated, there is every reason to hope that Mr F will justify the confidence wh the Queen has placed in him, and will produce a work wh will meet with the approval of HM and of the public. The second model is in many respects an improvement on the first sketch.'[122]

In July 1869 the Queen approved the wording: 'Queen Victoria and her people / To the memory of Albert, Prince Consort / As a tribute of their gratitude / For a life devoted to the public good.'[123] In November Layard, with the Queen's greatest regret, left Britain to become Minister in Madrid, his work with the memorial over, but that enterprise at last on a steady course. Foley was slow in completing his statue, but there were no reservations about it. A model was put on the pedestal of the memorial in 1870 and stayed there until the spring of 1871. It was then cast in bronze from thirty-seven old guns. By the end of 1873 the head had been cast, and the arms and legs were being moulded. In the end, the finished effigy would have 1,500 parts that would need to be welded together: it was not known as the colossal statue for nothing.

The memorial was opened in August 1872, after the Queen had inspected it for the first time the previous month. She found it 'really magnificent'.[124] However, there were still three more years to wait before the colossal statue itself would grace it. The elaborate friezes that had taken so long to sculpt were, at least, well received by the general public. Scott was offered, and accepted, a knighthood: Kelk turned his down, since it was offered by Gladstone, and he expected something better – a

baronetcy – from Disraeli, of whom he was a supporter. He was disappointed. Foley did not live to see his central work put in place, since he
died of pleurisy in 1874: but by then it was possible for his assistant,
Thomas Brock, to complete the job from his model. This was done by
October 1875. In the finished statue, Albert is robed as a Knight of the
Garter, and holds a catalogue of the Great Exhibition. The statue then
had to be gilded, at which point the job was finished. The edifice was
176 feet high on completion, topped by a large golden cross. It had taken
more than a decade and had cost £120,000.

The memorial, which Scott saw as his most prominent work, became
the incarnation of high Victorian Gothic architecture, and the centre-
piece of the cult of death. The subjects of the friezes and allegorical
sculptures, and the determination to commemorate Albert for his
commitment to art, science and the dissemination of knowledge, show
the will of that age to be associated with improvement. Scott's design,
and indeed the Queen's choice of him to execute it in that style, show
the conviction that the Gothic was deemed to be the medium through
which this commitment to high culture would be best expressed. In
terms of the pursuit of perfection, it was, at that moment – the mid-
1860s, when it was conceived and commissioned – the ideal combination
of form and subject.

However, because of its style, and what that style came to represent, the memorial was soon an object of disregard and even of
obloquy. The cult of the great man passed out of fashion, as did high
Victorian taste. When, early in the twentieth century and for much
of the next three-quarters of it, Victorian Gothic came to be regarded
as overblown, tasteless, arrogant and vulgar, Scott's memorial was
deemed one of the most comical symbols of the genre. At the same
time his magnificent Midland Hotel at St Pancras Station, now restored
and considered one of the architectural wonders of Britain, was threatened with destruction. The latest edition of *The Buildings of England*
compares Fowke's Albert Hall favourably with the adjacent shrine,
contrasting it with 'the verbosity of the Albert Memorial opposite'.[125]
When considering the memorial itself, however, the editors do concede
that it is 'rich, solid, a little pompous, a little vulgar, but full of faith
and self-confidence.' Its recent restoration, with the colossal statue
itself gilded once more after the gilt was removed during the Great
War for salvage, makes it again a breathtaking spectacle. The earnest

ideas of the Prince Consort had fallen so far out of favour by the time of his wife's death that they made appreciation of his monument impossible for all but those who could make a leap of the imagination. The new regard in which this masterpiece of Scott's is once more held is nothing to do with the cult of death, but suggests we are, at last, beginning to understand Albert's sincere and beneficent motivation to make Britain better.

PART III

THE TRANSFORMATION OF BRITAIN

CHAPTER II

THE LEAP IN THE DARK:
REFORM AND THE COMING
OF DEMOCRACY

I

Just as educated Victorians had been prevailed upon to take a more enlightened view of the criminal underclass, so too were they asked to engage with the question of what to do to enhance the rights in society of honest and respectable members of the lower orders. As a result of the debate on this question, the quarter-century from 1850 to 1875 saw greater engagement between intellectuals of opposing doctrines than at any time since the 1640s. Carlyle and Mill broadly led the main camps. Carlyle inspired a coterie of reactionaries who (taking their cue from *Past and Present*) looked back at feudal times as the perfect model for society. He led the charge against the 1867 Reform Act and ridiculed the failed attempt by the Liberals in 1866 to pass such a measure. Mill, by contrast, championed the greater liberty of the individual and, especially, the emancipation of women: and engaged with Gladstone and other leading Liberal politicians on the subject. Among Carlyle's supporters, men such as Ruskin (in *Time and Tide*) and James Fitzjames Stephen (in *Liberty, Equality, Fraternity*) argued that only when the working classes had been educated could they be entrusted with the vote. Stephen started out as an admirer of Mill: but when forced to examine the application of the doctrines of *On Liberty* to reality he began to feel it harboured a utopian impossibility, and posed dangers to society.

However, the reactionaries were increasingly confronted by evidence of the squalor in which the poor were forced to live, either in factual accounts by reformers such as Henry Mayhew, the journalist whose research into the London poor shocked the middle classes, or in a new wave of 'Condition of England' novels by writers such as Charles Kingsley in *Yeast* and *Alton Locke*. It also became harder to ignore the increasingly angry, organised and large protests of those who wanted the vote. By the time of Carlyle's death in 1881 the forces of reaction were largely burnt out. Reformers had captured the ear of politicians of both main parties, with much of their programme put into law, or their aspirations enabled by law. The desire for reform seemed unquenchable; and the British constitution, codified unofficially in the late 1860s by Walter Bagehot, was a matter of passionate debate. Meanwhile, attempts to define a coherent national identity as a means of unifying society continued among historians, notably in J. R. Green's *Short History of England* and Froude's *History of the Tudors*. This was a golden age of history as propaganda – a style developed not just by Macaulay, but by Carlyle too. As education and literacy became more widespread, the effect of the propaganda on the national consciousness became more pronounced. Men – and women – wished to be full participants in the new Britain, not just spectators upon it. Literate Victorians were increasingly given an uplifting idea of themselves, which raised their expectations: not least of the perfectibility of men and society.

II

Between the 1831 census and that of 1861 the population rose from 13.9 million to 20.1 million, the majority of whom now lived in urban areas. By 1861, because of the growth of the cotton trade, 12 per cent of the population lived in Lancashire. Nationally, there had been a disproportionate rise in the number of householders paying £10 or more rent a year, a sign of Britain's growing prosperity. In 1850 there had been a million paupers, with 110,000 in workhouses. Yet by 1864 the conditions of the urban proletariat appear to have improved markedly. The governor of the Hull Workhouse, John Fountain, writing to Gladstone's private secretary John Lambert, noted that 'a workman of the present day in Hull generally resides in a small house outside the Docks, instead of hiring rooms in a large house, as was the case some thirty years ago. This is not altogether a matter of choice, many of the large houses so let off having been pulled down for public improvements'.[1]

Fountain continued: 'Families live in a better style than formerly, they keep more company thus causing an increase in the quantity and in most cases a superior quality of provisions is consumed. Respecting dress I may state that a man receiving £90 a year his family dresses much more expensively than formerly [sic], this may be caused partly by his taking excursions and seeing more of the world.' Fountain set out a table illustrating how the cost of living had risen over thirty years for a man on £90 a year, saying that his rent would have risen from £10 to £15, fuel from £5 to £6, provisions from £40 to £45 and clothing from £15 to £23, leaving precisely £1 a year to play with.[2]

Such conditions, in an advanced society, could in part be blamed upon the absence of representation in Parliament of the classes that were so used and exploited. By the 1860s there were millions of politically aware men who lacked the vote because they lived in property of insufficient value to qualify them for it. Most freeholders had the vote, if the annual value of the property was above a certain level. Tenants or copyholders – a feudal form of leaseholder – usually did not. There were also areas of the country that had become densely populated during industrialisation but that had scant representation in the Commons, because so few men who lived there qualified for the vote. Reform would also require a redistribution of parliamentary seats, from rural to urban Britain, which would disoblige the landed interest and its influence in the legislature.

It was increasingly hoped that the economic changes over the previous twenty or thirty years had helped persuade those who had previously resisted reform to see the necessity of extending the franchise. After referring, in his preface to Alton Locke, to the Luddites, Captain Swing, Peterloo, rick-burning and riots, Kingsley exclaimed: 'How changed, thank God! is all this now. Before the influence of religion, both Evangelical and Anglican; before the spread of those liberal principles, founded on common humanity and justice, the triumph of which we owe to the courage and practical good sense of the Whig party; before the example of a Court, virtuous, humane and beneficent; the attitude of the British upper classes has undergone a noble change. There is no aristocracy in the world, and there never has been one, as far as I know, which has so honourably repented, and brought forth fruits meet for repentance; which has so cheerfully asked what its duty was, that it might do it.'[3] This was written in 1854, and was a mite optimistic even then. The aristocracy had far to go before conforming with Kingsley's ideal. So too did those in the middle classes, enfranchised in 1832, who allied their own interests with their betters to the extent of wishing to pull up the ladder behind them. By the mid-1860s, as a result, a confrontation loomed.

There had been four abortive attempts since 1851 to extend the franchise, but none succeeded. Reform's main proponents were radical thinkers such as Mill, who felt social justice required more men (and, in his case, women) to have the vote, and members of the Liberal middle classes such as John Bright who saw the newly enfranchised as being natural Liberal supporters. There was also an element in the old Whig aristocracy that feared the consequences for the stability of society if the franchise were not extended. Liberal support for Gladstone was more logical, as demonstrated in a speech on his Reform Bill in the Commons in 1866 by Mill, elected for Westminster the previous July. 'While so many classes, comparatively insignificant in numbers, and not supposed to be freer from class partialities or interests than their neighbours, are represented, some of them, I venture to say, greatly over-represented in this House, there is a class, more numerous than all the others, and therefore, as a mere matter of human feeling, entitled to more consideration—weak as yet, and therefore needing representation the more, but daily becoming stronger, and more capable of making its claims good—and this class is not represented. We claim, then, a large and liberal representation of the working classes, on the Conservative theory of the Constitution.'[4]

Yet it was not just an idea of justice that Mill used to advocate support for reform. He claimed that, as a result of it, after 'very few years of a real working class representation . . . there would be in every parish a school rate, and the school doors freely open to all the world; and in one generation from that time England would be an educated nation. Will it ever become so by your present plan, which gives to him that hath, and only to him that hath?'[5] That the Liberal (and liberal) ideal of education as part of the pursuit of perfection could be achieved by extension of the franchise was lost on many Conservatives: the one who followed Mill in that Commons debate, Henry Liddell, who would succeed to the earldom of Ravensworth, paid him the backhanded compliment of having delivered 'the subtle speech of the able logician' in favour of an 'insidious Bill'.

Meanwhile, those nervous about reform sought other ways to placate the lower orders. In December 1863 the Marquess Townshend, a Norfolk aristocrat, founded the Universal League for the Material Elevation of the Industrious Classes. Its main purpose was to lower working hours and promote the education of the working classes. However, once Gladstone appeared to be leading the Palmerston administration towards reform – though Palmerston himself remained bitterly opposed – the Universal League threw itself wholly behind that idea. Lord Townshend was alarmed by the rapidity with which the climate had changed, and protested: his followers in the Universal League split from him in February 1865. They founded the Reform League and it was from then that momentum for change really grew.

The first chairman of the League was Edmond Beales, an Old Etonian barrister, radical and peace campaigner. He enlisted a few of his like-minded, well-heeled friends, which lent the movement the respectability for which the Chartists had striven in vain. It also brought in funds. The League not only included politically active members of the working class who had come across from the Universal League, but also members of a radical middle-class group known as the Propagandists, led by John Bedford Leno, a former prominent Chartist and member of the socialist First International, formed by extreme radicals at the time of the Europe-wide upheavals of 1848. The League grew rapidly, through local branches, and thanks to an advertising campaign run by an efficient central organisation. Its programme was helped by three factors in 1865: the return at the election of that year of Liberal MPs committed to its cause; the death of Palmerston; and the readiness of Gladstone, as Leader in the Commons, to take the matter forward (though Gladstone confessed that the news of Palmerston's demise on 18 October 1865 'made me giddy'). Radical support in the Commons for mainstream Liberalism was maintained only by promises to legislate on reform, however much this dismayed some of the old Whigs. By the time Russell, Palmerston's successor, and Gladstone introduced their Reform Bill in March 1866 a nationwide movement demanded an extension of the franchise.[6] Conservative attempts to pretend otherwise were ridiculed by mass demonstrations across the country – Manchester, Birmingham, Edinburgh, Leeds, Liverpool and Rochdale, notably – where resolutions of support for Gladstone and his policy were passed.

The great fear of the ruling class – and this sentiment was by no means confined to the Conservative party – was that it would be suicidal

for the country and its institutions to extend the vote to people insufficiently educated to know how to use it wisely. It was not merely the
supposed stupidity of the working classes that was a problem: it was
also their contingent (or so it was imagined) moral failings, notably how
their lack of money would render them susceptible to bribery. There
was, after all, no secret ballot until 1872. The Liberal party harboured a
group of Whiggish anti-reform MPs whom John Bright named 'the Cave
of Adullam', after the Old Testament fortress where David, anointed as
the successor of Saul, sought refuge from him. They were led by Robert
Lowe, whose intellect and rhetorical power would make him a much
more difficult opponent for the Russell ministry than any Conservative.
He based his opposition not on self-interest, as many Conservatives did,
but on the view that government by the uneducated must be worse
than government by those who knew what they were doing.

Gladstone, however, took a different view. In an undated memorandum he declared: 'It was an invidious doctrine, that political franchise
should not descend to the lowest class of people, with no other incapacity
than idiocy, pauperism or crime.'[7] He said reform 'must be antecedent
to and not contingent upon the general reformation of the human race.'[8]
He noted that:

> this want of substance and of what is popularly called a stake in
> the country is far less applicable to the agricultural classes, when
> well governed: because they migrate less; have more immediate
> and more stable and more kindly connections with the middle and
> again with the higher order; are not so subject to sudden reverses
> in their condition; not so open to that contagious excitement which
> acts upon large and agglomerated masses . . . But in the case of
> our manufacturing districts and large towns, where there is much
> more of a merely pecuniary relation between different classes,
> where the softening and cementing influences of time are scarcely
> felt, where hostile combinations among masters or men are not
> infrequent, where the range of variation in wages, and of conse-
> quent elevation and depression of the physical state of the people,
> is so much greater: in reference to them we are in reason compelled
> very much to fall back upon considerations of interest and exact
> as a pledge for the state the possession of some real substance on
> the part of those who are to elect.[9]

It soon become clear that some ministers (including Gladstone himself) were opposed to an immediate redistribution of seats, which would reduce the number of MPs in depopulated rural shires in order to increase those sitting for seats in urban Britain. They preferred to wait until the Reform Bill had passed, in the hope of not complicating that.[10] This would cause enormous opposition from both sides, as MPs feared a hidden agenda and a redistribution whose radical scope would become apparent only when it was inevitable. Russell and Gladstone proposed a £7 householder franchise, which the government calculated would require an income of 26s a week. This would enfranchise the upper end of the artisan class, who could afford to rent such a property. These proposals would add 400,000 men to the electorate.

The principle was discussed in the Commons in March 1866, its announcement by Gladstone having been 'very coldly received'.[11] The first debate saw a pyrotechnic battle between Lowe and John Bright. Lowe had made a cool but caustic speech about the dangers of giving power to the ignorant. He could not resist goading Bright, who had spoken at Bradford in 1859 about a Reform Bill requiring a redistribution of seats: such as was not in the bill that, nonetheless, had Bright's support. Bright was taken aback and had forgotten what he had said. Lowe retorted: 'He has made so many speeches that it is not always easy to distinguish which.'[12] He turned on Gladstone and said that 'if my rt hon friend does succeed in carrying this measure through Parliament, when the passions and interests of the day are gone by I do not envy him his retrospect. I covet not a single leaf of the laurels that may encircle his brow. I do not envy him his triumph. His be the glory of carrying it; mine of having to the utmost of my poor ability resisted it.'[13]

Bright, for his part, quoted back to Lowe a speech he too had made in 1859, promising if elected to support Palmerston's drive for a Reform Bill. He said Lowe either had a very short memory, or was trifling with the House. Bright then minted the phrase about the Liberals who opposed reform having 'retired into what may be called [their] political Cave of Adullam'.[14] Lowe, the main Adullamite, sat for Calne in Wiltshire, one of the nearest things left to a pocket borough, in the control of the Marquis of Lansdowne. Bright, by contrast, had been returned on a large franchise in Birmingham. He ridiculed Lowe for having been elected for 'a village somewhere in the west of England', and added: 'The right hon Gentleman found on the list of electors of Calne about 174 names, of whom, according to the Blue Book, about seven were working men . . . but the real constituent of the right hon Gentleman is a Member of the other House of Parliament, and could send in his butler or his groom, instead of the right hon Gentleman, to represent the borough.'[15] The mood of deep unpleasantness was unequivocally set.

Gladstone moved the second reading of the bill on 12 April 1866, and professed at once that the government wished to avoid giving the measure 'the character of a party conflict', or the 'still more serious mischief' of a 'conflict between class and class'.[16] On the first Gladstone would be partly right. The bill split the Liberals, a split led by Lowe and his associates. Lowe had already told the House that 'if you want venality, if you want ignorance, if you want drunkenness, and facility for being intimidated, impulsive, unreflecting and violent people, where do you look for them in the constituencies? Do you go to the top or to the bottom?'[17] At another time he had said that 'nothing can be more manifest, looking to the peculiar nature of the working classes, than in passing a Bill such as is now proposed, you take away the principal power from property and intellect, and give it to the multitude who live on weekly wages.'[18] During a riot at an election at Kidderminster in 1857, Lowe received a bad blow on the head from a stone thrown at him. It cut him and fractured his skull, but also shaped his feelings towards the lower classes. He saw little good in them after that.

Gladstone tried to keep his party together, because with its majority the bill would pass through the Commons if discipline were maintained. To avoid any charge that the irresponsible were being given the vote, Gladstone stressed how 'there is not a call that has been made upon the self-improving powers of the working community which has not been fully answered.'[19] He cited working men's free libraries and institutes, which had grown up throughout the country, the high take-up of the services of the Post Office Savings Bank, which he himself had introduced in 1861 in the interests of thrift, and which now had 650,000 depositors. 'Parliament has been striving to make the working classes progressively fitter and fitter for the franchise,' he said, taunting his opponents; 'and can anything be more unwise, not to say more senseless, than to persevere from year to year in this plan, and then blindly to refuse to recognize its legitimate upshot—namely, the increased fitness of the working classes; for the exercise of political power? The proper exercise of that power depends upon the fitness of those who are to receive it. That fitness you increase from day to day, and yet you decline, when the growing fitness is admitted, to give the power.'[20]

Gladstone claimed that five-twelfths of the national income belonged to the working classes: and argued that if this disconnection between economic and political power was to continue, the burden of taxation should be shifted radically on to landed property. He also dismissed the notion that if the working classes were enfranchised they would vote as a class, reading out a letter from a self-professed working-class Tory who was bemused not to have the vote, and to be denied it by those he notionally supported.

There were already eight seats where a majority of voters were members of the working classes. Between them they returned five Liberal and nine Conservative MPs. Gladstone observed, ironically, that this 'revolutionary character' was 'the result, as far as our narrow experience goes, of having the working classes in the majority.'[21] With his customary pragmatism, Gladstone ruled out a great transfer of power from the shires to the towns: an assurance aimed at gaining parliamentary support that further dismayed the League, who saw such a shift as democratically right and proper, given the greatly depopulated nature of the countryside.

Henry Layard typified the moderate Liberal view, saying that, as Member for Southwark, he probably had more registered working-class voters than any other MP. It was self-evident that the working classes were not adequately represented, and discussion of matters affecting them would be far better informed and more useful if they were. On their supposed moral unfitness he suggested – in an obvious reference to Lowe – that those who dismissed the lower orders as susceptible to venality should admit that 'until this House is prepared, until society itself is prepared, to condemn and punish him who corrupts, it has no right to condemn and punish him who is corrupted.'[22] He concluded that if the franchise were extended the working classes 'will give you even greater proofs than they have hitherto given of the love they bear to the Throne, the institutions, and the greatness of their country.'[23]

Thornton Hunt of the *Daily Telegraph* – then the leading Liberal newspaper – wrote to Layard praising him for this speech, but echoed the residual fears of the educated classes:

I cannot tell you how strong a sympathy I feel for the direct and earnest manner in which you speak out for our unenfranchised countrymen. I regard that voluntary fulfilment of the 'patron's' duty, on behalf of the still excluded portion of the plebs, as an invaluable service to this country; not only expediting the day when the claimants shall be admitted, but sparing us the chance of violence, and possibly of bloodshed . . . there is no country in the world where every class can speak its mind and exercise its influence so openly and earnestly as in England; no country where there is so little practicable separation between the several classes, who are all dovetailed together by blood, marriage, and business connexions; none where the freedom of the individual is so absolutely secured; and none where social rank and personal influence enjoy a stronger sway over every class.[24]

Lowe remained unaffected by such arguments. He said that what was proposed was 'the government of the rich by the poor,' which he found 'utterly subversive'.[25] He attacked Mill, prominent in his support of Gladstone, by quoting back a line of Mill's from his *Political Economy* of 1852 about the 'unprepared state of mankind in general, and of the labouring classes in particular; their extreme unfitness at present for any order of things which would make any considerable demand on either their intellect or their virtue.'[26] He conceded that Mill might have changed his mind in the intervening fourteen years, but not that the labouring classes might have shown by example that they were more suited to responsibility. However, he quoted from *On Representative Government*, written just five years earlier, in which Mill had said that 'I regard it as wholly inadmissible that any person should participate in the suffrage without being able to read, write and, I will add, perform the common operations of arithmetic. Universal teaching must precede universal enfranchisement.'

Lowe feared that the organisation now to be found for industrial purposes among the trades union movement would be used for political purposes: as, indeed, it one day would. He made a powerful argument about unions being a weapon against capital, and a coercive force against those who exercised an individual right not to join them. This was not, however, so much an argument against extending the franchise as against the dangers of allowing unions to have unfettered powers, or what Lowe called a 'system of terrorism that lurks behind these trades unions'.[27] Talking of the sort of people the working class would be likely to send to Parliament to represent them, he adduced the example of

America, then recovering from its ruinous Civil War. 'We see in America, where the people have undisputed power, that they do not send honest, hardworking men to represent them in Congress, but traffickers in office, bankrupts, men who have lost their character and been driven from every respectable way of life, and who take up politics as a last resource.'[28] He recalled that when France tried universal suffrage in 1848, the consequent administration had been overthrown in a *coup d'état* after three years. 'Uncoerced by any external force, not borne down by any internal calamity, but in the full plethora of our wealth and the surfeit of our too exuberant prosperity, with our own rash and inconsiderate hands, we are about to pluck down on our own heads the venerable temple of our liberty and our glory. History may tell of other acts as signally disastrous, but of none more wanton, none more disgraceful.'[29]

Disraeli was careful not to express outright hostility to reform. Such opposition would have done incalculable damage to his party and left him with no room for manoeuvre, room he would subsequently need. Instead, he criticised the speed with which the legislation had been brought forward, its poor draughtsmanship, the unknown quantity of the redistribution bill. 'The course they are going to pursue is most unjust and injurious to the landed interest—that is to say, to England, because I say the legitimate interest of the land is the interest of England.'[30] He uttered phrases that would return to haunt him within a year or so, when he pushed through his own measures. Some showed an unbroken thread of thought going back to Young England.

The moment you have universal suffrage it always happens that the man who elects despises the elected. He says, 'I am as good as he is, and although I sent him to Parliament, I have not a better opinion of him than I have of myself.' Then, when the House of Commons is entirely without command over the Executive, it will fall into the case of those Continental popular assemblies which we have seen rise up and disappear in our own days. There will be no charm of tradition; no prescriptive spell; no families of historic lineage; none of those great estates round which men rally when liberty is assailed; no statesmanship, no eloquence, no learning, no genius. Instead of these, you will have a horde of selfish and obscure mediocrities, incapable of anything but mischief, and that mischief devised and regulated by the raging demagogue of the hour.[31]

The result would be a rebuilding of the constitution 'on the American model'.[32]

Disraeli, as always, was most concerned with his own place and his own prospects. Gladstone's views were, by contrast, suffused with a sense of history and of destiny. 'We are now about the process what is called "making History". We are now laying the foundations of much that is to come. This occasion is a starting-point from which I presume to think the career we have to run as individuals and parties will in many respects take its character and colour.'[33] He continued: 'Let us try and raise our views above the fears, the suspicions, the jealousies, the reproaches, and the recriminations of this place and this occasion. Let us look onward to the time of our children and of our children's children. Let us know what preparation it behoves us should be made for that coming time. Is there or is there not, I ask, a steady movement of the labouring classes, and is or is not that movement a movement onwards, and upwards? . . . from day to day, from hour to hour, the heaving forces are at work, and after a season we discern from actual experience that things are not as they were.'[34]

His peroration, quoting a provocative line from the *Aeneid*, represented not only his finest oratory, but also a sense of destiny that, whatever the present tribulations, would be fulfilled.

> Perhaps the great division of to-night is not the last that must take place in the struggle. At some point of the contest you may possibly succeed. You may drive us from our seats. You may bury the Bill that we have introduced, but we will write upon its gravestone for an epitaph this line, with certain confidence in its fulfilment—*Exoriare aliquis nostris ex ossibus ultor* [May you arise from our bones, you unknown avenger]. You cannot fight against the future. Time is on our side. The great social forces which move onwards in their might and majesty, and which the tumult of our debates does not for a moment impede or disturb—those great social forces are against you; they are marshalled on our side; and the banner which we now carry in this fight, though perhaps at some moment it may droop over our sinking heads, yet it soon again will float in the eye of heaven, and it will be borne by the firm hands of the united people of the three kingdoms, perhaps not to an easy, but to a certain and to a not distant victory.[35]

The bill had its second reading by five votes: 318 to 313. Lowe persuaded thirty-one other Liberals to vote with him, and so almost defeat the government. He regarded this as a great triumph. At four o'clock in the morning Gladstone had tea with colleagues in the Commons' dining room, wrote to the Queen, and had three hours' sleep. With such a narrow margin, he and Russell now had no choice but to consider a compromise.

III

After his sleep Gladstone wrote some letters, did some reading, and saw some people, including Hunt of the *Telegraph*. At 1.30 p.m. there was a three-hour Cabinet meeting, at which it was discussed whether the ministry should resign: it had expected victory by fifteen votes. However, Russell and Gladstone hoped the opposition was 'disjointed', and could be divided further.[36] On 7 May Gladstone brought in a bill to propose a redistribution of seats. It passed its second reading without a vote, though provoked bickering about where the new seats were going. The Reform Bill went into committee on 28 May, and the government was defeated on an amendment to restrict bribery and corruption. Gladstone argued against the amendment because he felt it complicated the principle of reform, and should be taken separately. The defeat, by 248 votes to 238, he described as the culmination of 'an ominous evening'.[37] The committee spent several days on the redistribution of seats, a debate that included another mordant speech by Lowe that seemed further to demoralise his party. On the third day in committee – 1 June – Gladstone indicated that the session of Parliament would, if necessary, be extended into the autumn so long as it took to get the bill enacted: he feared the Adullamites and the Conservatives planned to talk it out.

The denouement came in the early hours of 19 June, when the government was defeated on a technical motion by the Adullamite Lord Dunkellin. Gladstone warned that an adverse vote would mean the government would have to resign. It lost by 315 votes to 304, 42 Liberals voting with the Opposition. Gladstone was not impressed by the spectacle: 'With the cheering of the adversary there was shouting, violent flourishing hats, and other manifestations which I think novel and inappropriate.'[38] Next morning, having written to the Queen, he found solace in the works of Cobden, which he read for a while. The Cabinet met at 3 p.m. and decided to resign, even though the Queen, to whom this course had been intimated, telegraphed from Balmoral asking them not to. She refused to leave Scotland in the hope that Russell would carry on. The House was adjourned pending more communication with the Sovereign. The Cabinet had included a minority (notably Russell and Gladstone) who wanted a dissolution, which would mean the matter would be put to the country. A larger faction wanted resignation, to hand the problem to Derby and Disraeli, to see what they made of it. This was the better plan, since it would force a reform measure of a sort uncontemplated by the Liberals in its radicalism, and help assure the election of the first Gladstone ministry in 1868.

The Queen returned to Windsor, and saw Russell and Gladstone there on 26 June. Gladstone admitted that 'I have had a great weight on me in these last days and am glad the matter draws near its close.'[39] When the audiences occurred – he and Russell had them jointly and separately – he found the Sovereign 'showed every quality required by her station and the time'. At Gladstone's audience there occurred the sort of episode that made the Queen loathe him. She was unhappy that the government, which she wished to continue, had not withdrawn the bill, or postponed the matter 'to another year' (which year exactly she did not specify).[40] 'I reminded HM', Gladstone wrote, 'that She had early expressed to me her hope that if we resumed the subject of the Reform of Parliament we should prosecute it to its completion.' The Queen did not like being reminded of her caprice or inconsistency, whereas Gladstone's ultra-logical mind could not help but do so.

She asked both men to go to London, meet the Cabinet, and see whether some course other than resignation might be practicable. They followed her command, but the Cabinet felt it had no alternative. A telegram was sent to the Queen, and Gladstone made a statement to the Commons. A crowd thronged around Westminster, and Gladstone was hailed as the champion of the ordinary man. He explained to the House the impossibility of having a rating rather than a rental franchise, saying that in five boroughs it would have meant enfranchising people with less than a £4 rateable value, for the government to enfranchise the numbers it had intended. Then, able to relax at last, Gladstone went to dinner, looked in at a ball, and ended the day with rescue work of two prostitutes.[41]

IV

Derby accepted the Queen's commission to form a government on 27 June 1866, with Disraeli leading in the Commons. The latter had hoped to be Foreign Secretary, but Derby gave that post to his son, Lord Stanley. Clarendon, the outgoing incumbent, was relieved. Stanley was 'an immeasurably better man than Disraeli, who coveted this office in the exact ratio of his unfitness for it.'[42] There had been a brief dalliance with the Adullamites over a formal coalition, until it became clear they wished to choose both the Prime Minister (Clarendon) and the Leader of the Commons (Stanley); at which point Derby, with Disraeli's full support, bade them farewell. The Queen wanted some Whigs to serve, and Derby sought to indulge her. However, Clarendon refused the Foreign Office, and Lowe declined a place in the Cabinet, and soon it was clear no Adullamite would serve.

The new ministry was formed against a background of widespread unrest. The League organised demonstrations, the most important of which was in London, and culminated in a riot in Hyde Park. On 29 June, while Derby was trying to form his ministry, 10,000 people marched from Trafalgar Square to the Carlton Club, to hoot at those who had killed Gladstone's bill. The previous evening a crowd had assembled outside his house in Carlton House Terrace to cheer him and Mrs Gladstone. The London Working Men's Association unanimously invited him to address a meeting they intended to hold, thanking him for 'his manly and generous defence of the working classes from the calumnies heaped upon them during the Reform debate . . . by members of the Tory party and apostate Liberals'.[43]

Fearing a breakdown of public order, the police tried to ban the Hyde Park meeting. On 18 July, five days before it, Sir Richard Mayne, Commissioner of the Metropolitan Police, told Beales that it 'cannot be permitted'.[44] He acted on Derby's authority.[45] Mayne trusted that Beales, whose name was mentioned in the posters advertising the rally, 'will exert his influence to prevent any attempt to hold this meeting'. Beales replied, thanking Mayne for his 'courtesy', but told him that 'I am unable at present to recognise your power or right to issue any such notice, or to take upon yourself to declare that the meeting cannot be permitted.' He demanded Mayne show him 'under what statute or law, or principle of law, you are acting, for I am at present ignorant of any law or statute empowering or authorising you thus to attempt to prohibit the people from exercising one of their most important and most constitutional rights.'

Mayne's initiative caused outrage. Bright told the League that 'if a public meeting in a public park is denied you, and if millions of intelligent and honest men are denied the franchise, on what foundation does our liberty rest; or is there in the country any liberty but the toleration of the ruling class?'[46] Spencer Walpole, the Home Secretary, said: 'I had hoped that those who had proposed to convene that meeting would have forborne from calling it together. Should they still persevere in their intention, which I trust they will not, I have no other course left open to me but to desire the police to act on the notice issued by Sir Richard Mayne.' The League told Walpole they had a legal right to hold the meeting; and they would hold it. If the police stopped them entering the park, they would march four deep past Parliament and up Whitehall to Trafalgar Square. They urged their followers to stay within the law.

By five o'clock on the evening of the rally groups of protestors met at points around the capital. The Times report said that by early evening there were 'vast crowds' near the park, but also between 1,600 and 1,800 policemen, mounted and on foot.[47] Also at five o'clock, the gates were closed, despite there being large numbers already inside, waiting to meet the groups marching there. The quality stood on the balconies of houses in Park Lane to get a perfect view; every approach to the park was thronged with people. Beales and his lieutenants arrived at Marble Arch at 7 p.m., having led a march from Clerkenwell (though they did not march, but rode in a fleet of hansom cabs). As he went to talk to the line of police blocking his entrance, 'the crowd immediately closed in, and endeavoured by an "ugly rush" to effect admission.' The police started lashing out with staves, and both Beales and his confederate Colonel Dickson were hit. They made a tactical retreat, and pointed the fleet of hansoms towards Trafalgar Square. However, the blood of those less mature in years and less well bred than Beales and the Colonel was up. They decided to forget Trafalgar Square. Disregarding the gates, which were barricaded, they charged and broke down the railings. This was an image that flew around England in the succeeding days, signalling anarchy.

The Times wrote: 'The police, indeed, hastened to every point that was attacked, and for a short time kept the multitude at bay; but their numbers were utterly insufficient to guard so long a line of frontier, and breach after breach was made, the stonework, together with the railings, yielding easily to the pressure of the crowd. The first opening was made in the Bayswater-road . . . the police brought their truncheons into active use, and a number of the "roughs" were severely handled.' St George's Hospital at Hyde Park Corner received both civilian and police casualties. One youth, aged seventeen, was found dead in the park, crushed between two carriages. Mayne had stones thrown at him, and was hooted. Charles Bradlaugh, the atheist, was among leaders of the League who sought to restore calm. For his pains he was accused of being a government spy. As darkness fell the crowd dispersed, but not until speeches had been made calling for Derby's resignation and deploring 'the attempt to rule the country by force'. A gang of 'ruffians' broke windows in Great Cumberland Street until after one o'clock in the morning, and left half a mile of broken park railings and ruined flower beds behind them.[48] This loss of control, and potential for anarchy, seems to have terrified Beales and his well-to-do friends. Lord John Manners saw Beales shortly after the event and told his brother that the League's leaders were 'more frightened than those they had frightened'.[49] Mill, who saw Beales and Dickson too, felt the same.[50]

Next day forty or so demonstrators were before the magistrates at Marlborough Street, charged with a variety of offences from throwing stones to assaulting police officers. 'The prisoners', wrote *The Times*, 'generally were of the class known as "roughs". About half a dozen might be considered as belonging to the better order of the working classes.'[51] There was no exemplary act of official retribution: most were given fines or short terms of imprisonment, seldom more than a month. Over the next few days a steady procession went through the courts. There were many claims of mistaken identity: the police estimate after the event was that 10,000 had been present. *The Times*, as the voice of the Establishment, railed against the damage done by a 'ruthless mob, who appear for the most part to comprise the lowest scum of the London population', but all the Establishment could now do was roar: power was shifting.[52]

It was not only Tories who were shocked: so were some of the old Whigs, who with the departure of Russell had lost the last Whig prime minister. Emily Eden, a friend of Clarendon and with old Whig blood, was livid at the spectacle, and at the support given to it by some Liberals. 'I do not see how we are to die peacefully in our beds without having exterminated that wretched coward Bright,' she wrote. She also went for Layard. 'Did you like that man when he was your under-secretary?' she asked Clarendon. 'Or did you only put up with him? . . . I could forgive Layard for having discovered Nineveh . . . I could not forgive Nineveh for having discovered Layard.'[53]

The riots, and the size of the protest, convinced the government that the mood had changed, and menacingly so. Ministers were attacked in the Commons and in the press for the stupidity of closing the park gates against so large a crowd. Acton Smee Ayrton, the future Commissioner of Works, castigated the government for allowing the Commissioner to impose the ban: and warned that 'it is a very dangerous doctrine for the Government to act upon, that the army is a machine to be used against the people'.[54] It seemed that in more ways than one battle lines were being drawn up, and such talk only inflamed the idea of insurrection. Layard called Walpole's measures 'most injudicious and foolish'.[55]

Mill said that 'noble Lords and right hon Gentlemen opposite may be congratulated on having done a job of work last night which will require wiser men than they are many years to efface the consequences of.'[56] Beales kept his high profile, demanding the right to stage further meetings in Hyde Park, and issuing a veiled threat of the consequences if the League were to be denied that right. He warned that 'the Duke of Wellington granted Catholic Emancipation rather than risk civil war in Ireland. It might seem as if it were better to concede the holding of a meeting for an hour or two in Hyde Park than risk further sanguinary conflicts between the people and the police.'[57] The Conservative party realised that if it were not to be rendered incredible for another twenty years – as, effectively, it had been by being on the wrong side of the Corn Laws debate – it had better follow public opinion on the franchise. The party line had been to claim that working men were indifferent to reform: no one could pretend that now. Branches of the League held meetings around the country in the days after the riot, and showed they were prepared to continue to demonstrate their commitment to their cause. The message was clear.

Disraeli was shaken by the riot, and for him at least the message hit home. Ever prepared to change course to preserve his own power, he proposed to Derby that there should be an immediate Reform Bill.

Whereas the Liberal bill had been based upon rental value, Disraeli's would give the vote to men in urban boroughs whose property had a £6 rateable value, and to men in rural county constituencies whose property's rateable value was £20. This would enfranchise slightly fewer men than the Liberal measure would have done. New constituencies would be created in the northern boroughs. Derby remained cautious.[58] To use Gladstone's phrase, he had time on his side. Parliament would rise on 10 August and would not return until 5 February 1867, allowing the government time to think. There was none of the acute hardship that in the early 1840s had given impetus to the Chartists; but Bright spent his autumn touring the country, addressing great gatherings in Birmingham at the end of August (where 150,000 people turned up), Manchester the following month and Glasgow in October. The momentum from the working-class movement remained strong. However, Bright's rhetoric was deemed to have terrified many on the centre ground, who might, it was thought, now be in favour of such moderate change as the Conservatives contemplated. Even Mill, never at his best in appreciating those who might be considered uncouth, had long considered Bright 'the mere demagogue and courtier of the majority'.[59]

In September 1866 Derby saw the Queen at Balmoral, and found her trembling at the prospect of renewed civil unrest: she wanted the matter resolved quickly. However, Disraeli was rattled by Cabinet disunity, and tried to persuade Derby to delay discussion until well into the parliamentary term. Derby, however, resolved to proceed. Days before the Queen's Speech the Cabinet agreed to mention reform in it. Derby got *The Times* onside, and the paper started to call for a resolution of the problem. The Queen's Speech said attention 'will again be called to the State of the Representation of the People in Parliament; and I trust that your Deliberations, conducted in a Spirit of Moderation and mutual Forbearance, may lead to the Adoption of Measures which, without unduly disturbing the Balance of political Power, shall freely extend the Elective Franchise.'[60]

Disraeli told the Commons on 11 February 1867 what was meant by those words: it was Her Majesty's wish that the Commons should 'divest themselves of that party spirit' that was normally 'legitimate', but which was now, clearly, dangerous.[61] This, he said, was necessary because of the polarisation of views in the country. Gladstone regarded this approach as 'altogether novel', which was not meant as a compliment.[62] He was dismayed that the Speech from the Throne had engaged in 'instructing this House as to the temper in which it was to deal with this subject', a ploy, he said with some understatement, that was 'not very commonly found' in such speeches. However, all that was feasible was engineering a vote of confidence to remove the Conservatives from power: Russell, at a meeting at Gladstone's house the day after Disraeli had spoken to the Commons, argued for just that. Gladstone, better understanding the poisoned chalice this would present, was more cautious.

Derby realised a bill would have to be brought forward sooner rather than later. Getting Cabinet agreement was not easy. An attempt was made at a meeting on 16 February. Cranborne, the Secretary of State for India, objected to Disraeli's initial proposal of awarding the franchise according to rateable value. This in turn upset General Jonathan Peel, the Secretary of State for War, and younger brother of the late prime minister. Peel was leant on by the Queen and did not resign. Gladstone promised support for a Conservative proposal if it satisfied his principles. The Cave of Adullam wanted household suffrage to forestall further agitation. Since this would create a large number of borough electors, Derby ruled that household suffrage on the basis of rateable value would form the core of the bill, since it should bring in support both from the Cave and from Liberals.

However, Cranborne claimed that many small boroughs would be thrown 'into the hands of the voter whose qualification is less than £10'.[63] This meant enfranchising unskilled and semi-skilled men below the artisan class. He told Derby he would have to resign if it were proposed. His leading role in bringing down Gladstone's bill – which he considered far less damaging than Disraeli's – was fresh in the memory: he was not a man to seek a charge of hypocrisy. 'If I consent to this scheme now that I know what its effect will be I could not look in the face those whom last year I urged to resist Mr Gladstone,' he wrote to Derby on 24 February. 'I am convinced that it will, if passed, be the ruin of the Conservative party.'[64]

Carnarvon, the Secretary of State for the Colonies, felt similarly; and Peel became restive again. Carnarvon, who had been at Oxford with Cranborne, told him their mistake had been to imagine Disraeli was acting in good faith: he had played a game, instead, of divide and rule.[65]

When Derby was told of the resignation threats he wrote to Disraeli, exclaiming: 'Utter ruin! What on earth are we to do?'[66] He summoned a Cabinet on 25 February, just two hours before a gathering of Tory MPs would debate the matter. The cabinet meeting was 'of a most unpleasant character', Derby told the Queen, and almost the whole time was taken up with vitriolic argument.[67] It was agreed to proceed on the basis of rateable value.

There was scarcely more enthusiasm in the Conservative party for the proposals than in Cabinet; but it was agreed to support Derby. Disraeli went straight to the Commons to outline the new plan. This was a disaster. He was thinking on his feet, so new was the plan, and even his skills of rhetoric were not equal to his being convincing. He was ridiculed by Lowe, who urged him to stop prevaricating and bring in a bill: though Lowe suggested that the meetings of the working-class movement had not captured the imagination of the country, and that there was, therefore, no urgency. Lowe suspected – and he was largely right – that the main motive driving Tory plans was fear. Bright said, with great percipience, that 'I do not believe that among the ranks opposite me there is a single Member of the Treasury Bench who really believes that the course that has been taken by the Government is a wise one, or ought to be persisted in.'[68] Gladstone continued the attack, and Disraeli, battered, asked for a delay of three days before considering matters further. However, after hearing that the Opposition was organising against the government, he came back the next day and said that by the following Thursday week at the latest he would present a Reform Bill. Some feared insurrection, although with the exception of the occasional outburst there was none of the seditious rhetoric used by the Chartists before the 1848 damp squib. The numbers protesting were, however, unquestionably greater, and the Reform League mobilised people all over the country. Disraeli now took the initiative, to the point that when the bill eventually came into committee he would accept amendments of a far-reaching nature without even asking Derby first, let alone the rest of the Cabinet.

After this shambles, Derby reverted to a policy of offering the vote to every householder, and sought on 2 March to persuade the Cabinet of the sense of this. Cranborne, Peel and Carnarvon all resigned, Derby thought the Tory party was 'ruined', but Disraeli took the opportunity to have three of his friends promoted to the Cabinet, securing his power

base when Derby finally left office. When Disraeli announced the resignations to the Commons on 4 March he announced, too, that the bill
would now be introduced a fortnight later. It was not until during the
week before the first reading that the Cabinet finally agreed on what
would be in it. All men resident in a borough who had lived there for
two years or more and had paid poor rates – the tax on property that
paid for the upkeep of the parish workhouse – would get the vote. It
was also agreed to allow plural voting – to give a second vote to those
who paid 20s in direct taxes as well as the poor rate. This decisive act
by Derby pulled his party behind him, with the faction led by Cranborne
in the wilderness. Derby's health had, though, been wrecked by the
strain. The inevitable legacy was bitterness. When, a few evenings after
Cranborne's resignation, Derby saw Lady Cranborne on the stairs of a
grand party, he asked her cuttingly, in a reference to Cranborne's
agonising about the numbers who would be enfranchised: 'Is Robert
still doing his sums?' Lady Cranborne brilliantly replied: 'Yes – and he
has reached rather a curious result. Take three from 15 [the number of
members of the Cabinet] and nothing remains.'[69]

Disraeli introduced the bill on 18 March, only to have Gladstone assail
him because of its inconsistencies and bureaucratic difficulties, and
notably on plural voting, which Gladstone called 'a gigantic engine of
fraud' because of the corrupt ways in which one could engineer liability
for the taxes that qualified one to vote and, worse, 'a proclamation of
a war of classes'. Gladstone was reading Walter Bagehot's new book,
The English Constitution, and it stimulated him: 'the author of this dual
vote is the man who strikes at the British constitution.'[70] Gladstone
refused to commit himself against the bill *in toto*: but said he would in
no circumstances support dual voting.

The Tories became angry at the extent to which they were being
forced to contradict themselves. A process of rapid and confusing amendment began. Clarendon told Gladstone on 22 March that 'the Govt are
expecting amendments in a radical sense on going into Committee and
are thinking that this will unite their party'.[71] He reported that
'Cranbourne [sic] deeply regrets the determination [of the Liberals] not
to oppose the 2nd reading, but he hopes that Mr G will be able to
arrange for simple rejection of the proposal and go into Committee.
He does not think on consideration that any amendment cd be so framed
as to make it easy for Mr G's party and the Conservative Cave to unite.'

The Duke of Buccleuch spoke for the Tory grandees when, after the heavily amended bill had been enacted, he quipped that the only word in it that remained unaltered was the first one, 'whereas'.[72] Disraeli had created a suspicion among his opponents in the Tory party, and especially among the three resigned ministers and their adherents, that would take years to dispel. Cranborne, writing to Carnarvon on 1 April, observed the impossibility of getting Disraeli to tell the truth about his intentions. 'Privately they assure the Radicals that they mean to give up everything, and the Tories that they meant to give up nothing except duality.'[73]

Disraeli and Derby's successful management of the bill and of their party undermined Gladstone. His attempt to amend the bill to remove the rating qualification for household suffrage, so all householders could vote, was defeated with the help of fifty-two Liberal and Radical MPs, despite his having colluded with Cranborne to try to defeat the government. Success is the great unifier of parties, and Gladstone withdrew from the front line of opposition to the bill. Lord Houghton, formerly Richard Monckton Milnes, met Gladstone at breakfast a few days later and described him as having been 'quite awed with the diabolical cleverness of Dizzy, who, he says, is gradually driving all ideas of political honour out of the House, and accustoming it to the most revolting cynicism.'[74]

The Conservative proposals were insufficient for the League, however, which considered it to be 'trammelling the principle of household suffrage'. It chose to renew its campaign of protest.[75] A small meeting, of only 'a few hundred respectably dressed working men' took place in the park on 19 April, organised by the Working Men's Rights Association.[76] They marched under the red flag while the police circled on horseback and on foot. The main speaker was a Mr Henwood, of the Fitzroy Branch of the Reform League. He told the crowd that 'the people did not want revolution, but the Tory government were driving them to it.' On 24 April Beales and his lieutenants agreed to hold a mass meeting in Hyde Park on 6 May: this shocked the political establishment, and had those who lived near the park writing to the newspapers to demand that, following the previous year's 'disgraceful scenes', it be banned.[77]

Cardwell wrote to Gladstone on 30 April, with this intelligence: 'I have reason to think that a Proclamation is contemplated forbidding the proposed meeting in Hyde Park'.[78] Petitions were delivered to Parliament to ban the rally. On 1 May Walpole, unshaken by the difficulties of the previous year, tried to oblige, issuing a proclamation that 'the use of the Park for the purpose of holding such meeting is not permitted, and interferes with the object for which Her Majesty has been pleased to open the Park for the general enjoyment of her people'.[79] People were 'warned and admonished to abstain from attending'. The police served copies of Walpole's notice on leaders of the League when they met their rank and file in Bouverie Street that evening. Beales ignored it, and made his own statement imploring the working men of England to 'come as loyal, peaceful and orderly citizens, enemies of all riot and tumult, but unalterably fixed and resolved in demanding and insisting upon what you are entitled to'. Bradlaugh, who was also present, made the same point only more colourfully, threatening that 'if violence were used he would be among the first to meet that violence.'

Walpole's proclamation was posted all over London, and torn down almost immediately. Leaguers put up a statement by Beales in its place. A retreat began. The government announced it had been wrong to close the gates in 1866: but those who went into the park on Monday 6 May did so at their own risk. The police were told to discriminate between those who attended to 'look on' and those 'roughs' who wished to cause trouble. However, it was also announced that anyone who continued to address the crowd after being warned to stop would be arrested and removed from the park. Mayne said he would be taking 5,000 police to the park, and that force would be used if necessary. The Household Division, in nearby barracks, would be on standby, and extra troops were ordered to the metropolis. That was the situation on the Saturday before the protest; but on the Monday morning The Times reported that 'the public will hear with surprise, and perhaps, also, with no little discontent, that the Government has at the last moment resolved to permit the Hyde Park demonstration, and, as long as peace is preserved, not to interfere with any of the speakers, the processions, or the crowds that may enter the enclosure.'[80] It had, the paper continued, been discovered that the protest was 'perfectly legal, and that the authorities had no right to interfere'. There had also promised to be an almighty confrontation if Walpole had not backed down. Although the League had many thousands of followers, there were signs that many Londoners were ready to come out and support the government, which it was widely believed was doing its best to secure change. People had been sworn in as special constables on the Saturday, before the ban was rescinded, and an estimated 12–15,000 were to be sworn in on the Monday, all armed with staves. Cavalry had also been brought up to London. Before executing his U-turn on the Saturday, Walpole had gratefully received a petition signed by 16,000 Londoners, deploring the League's plan to go ahead with the meeting.

'The credit,' *The Times* wrote, 'of standing firmly to their purpose certainly remains with the reform league. How Mr Walpole will account to the country for having caused so much agitation, and even alarm – for having persevered in his resolution up to the last moment, and only at the last moment found out that he was acting illegally, is a matter for himself to consider. That his whole policy in the matter will cause deep disgust can scarcely be doubted.' Walpole took the hint and, humiliated and mentally fragile, resigned as Home Secretary, though not before the Commons passed a Royal Parks Bill to make it legal to ban such meetings as the League's. Derby wanted him to remain as Home Secretary, but Walpole's wife insisted he resign, for the sake of his mental health.[81] He became minister without portfolio, his career terminally damaged. The protest 'passed off with the quietness and good order of a temperance meeting'.[82] It was, said *The Times*'s correspondent, like 'a great fair' with 'acrobats, cardsharpers, ballad singers without number, who howled forth such mongrel verses about Reform and Walpole as made one wish more ardently than ever for a settlement of this tedious question.' Five people were arrested, three for picking pockets and two for gambling: but the government had had a warning.

Gladstone might have removed himself temporarily from the fray, but other Liberals, sensing the government's vulnerability, proposed amendments. So determined was Disraeli to get the bill through that he accepted them. One was a lodger franchise; another the reduction of the county franchise to a £12 rental qualification, and to all those owning property worth just £5 a year. Disraeli abandoned 'fancy franchises' that would have given extra votes to university graduates and professional men, which had been an attempt to appease hard-line Tories. The residential qualification was reduced from two years to one. One of the most contentious matters – the 'compound franchise', which would allow the vote to those who had their rates paid for them by landlords out of their rents – was also granted. This enfranchised another half-million tenants in urban Britain. Disraeli, conscious his party was in a minority, had done superbly to get his bill through: but only because of the enormous sacrifices of principle, and the reverses of position, he had chosen to make. The electorate was doubled. In the boroughs the working-class vote was five times larger than it had been, and comprised more than half of the electorate in those places.[83]

Eight boroughs in the industrial north were given an MP; as was Gravesend, in Kent. By the end of the process, all who paid rates in person in boroughs were given the vote, as Gladstone had wished. He had become a temporarily divisive figure among Liberals, and knew it. He told his diary on 15 July that he had decided 'at the last moment' not to speak on the third reading of the Reform Bill 'for fear of doing mischief on our own side'.[84] Derby then had to warn Conservative peers – who formed a majority in the Lords – of the dangers of their not passing it. One, Earl Grey, had given notice he would seek further amendments, which had terrified Derby. He warned his peers that not only would he be forced to resign, but the party would be back where it had been after the Corn Laws debacle: out of touch and irrelevant. His colleagues heeded him, and he steered the bill to a second reading, unamended. There were only minor changes during the committee stage, made in Derby's absence while he was sick. However he returned, ill with gout and rheumatism, to take the third reading – the last step before the Royal Assent – on 6 August.

This was a momentous occasion, and Derby's speech reflected it. The background against which he spoke – though he did not explicitly say so – was troubled. A quarter of a million men, many considered by parliamentarians of all parties to be uneducated and unfit for the franchise, were about to be given the vote. The country had witnessed great unrest; the Queen was unpopular, with stirrings of republicanism evident because of her refusal to engage in public duties except on rare occasions, while receiving vast sums from the Civil List. Derby said he hoped that 'in the adoption of this Bill we may find the means of putting a stop to the continued agitation of a question which, as long as it remained unsettled, only stood in the way of all useful legislation.'[85]

Then, in a borrowed phrase that has passed into legend (it had been used several times in the debates in 1866, notably by some of the Adullamites) he ruminated that 'no doubt we are making a great experiment and "taking a leap in the dark", but I have the greatest confidence in the sound sense of my fellow countrymen, and I entertain a strong hope that the extended franchise which we are now conferring upon them will be the means of placing the institutions of this country on a firmer basis, and that the passing of this measure will tend to increase the loyalty and contentment of a great portion of Her Majesty's subjects.' Benjamin Jowett had written from Oxford to a friend, just before the passing of the bill, to anticipate 'the exultation of the Jew, who has revenged all his personal wrongs, triumphed over the virtue of Gladstone, made himself an historical name, and really done a great service (not taking into account the means). He has got his pound of flesh out of these Tory magnates, who have scoffed at him.'[86]

They scoffed no more. In November, three months after the bill had passed and eight months after the Cabinet resignations, Cardwell had Cranborne and his wife to stay. He reported that 'he and Lady C are as bitter against Dizzy as you or I could be. He is desirous to see the formation of a Government, in which the strong Liberals shall be included, that the proper weight of responsibility might be thrown upon them; thinks it will be our business to raise the question of further redistribution; and does not intend for his own part to interfere any more in Reform discussions.'[87] By that time Cranborne had written an article in the *Quarterly Review* setting out, with candour, his feelings: it was entitled 'The Conservative Surrender'. Disraeli knew Cranborne's clout in the party, and when he succeeded Derby as Prime Minister in February 1868 – 'a proud thing for a man "risen from the people" to have obtained!' the Queen told her daughter, the Crown Princess of Prussia – he asked Northcote to sound him out about rejoining the Cabinet.[88] Cranborne advised Northcote: 'I told him I had the greatest respect for every member of the Government except one – but that I did not think my honour was safe in the hands of that one.'[89] The bitterness between the Conservative party's new Prime Minister and the man who would eventually succeed him had years yet to run.

Disraeli began consciously to identify the Conservative party not with a sectional interest such as had characterised the old Tories, but with progress.[90] The progressive policies that would transform Britain after 1874 did not just continue those of the Gladstone administration; Gladstone's followed on from Disraeli's in his short administration of 1868, after he had succeeded Derby as Prime Minister and 'climbed to the top of the greasy pole'.[91] As well as the Reform Act the Conservatives passed the Corrupt Practices Bill, the legislation pursuant to the Clarendon Commission, reform of the railways, the effective nationalisation of the telegraph services under the Post Office, and the abolition of public executions. Disraeli also established the Royal Commission on the Sanitary Laws.

This descent into liberalism outraged Cranborne, now Marquess of Salisbury having succeeded his father earlier in 1868. He wrote to a former constituent shortly after succeeding to his title that the main purpose of the Conservative party at that time seemed to be to keep Disraeli as Prime Minister. 'If I had a firm confidence in his principles or his honesty, or even if he were identified by birth or property with the Conservative classes in the country – I might in the absence of any definite professions work to maintain him in power. But he is an adventurer: & as I have too good cause to know, he is without principles and honesty.' Salisbury was right to identify Disraeli's 'singular power of intrigue' as the key to his mastery of the party; and to observe that 'in an age of singularly reckless statesmen he is I think beyond question the one who is least restrained by fear or scruple.'[92]

V

The insistence that men cast their votes in public was a relic of the age before 1832. It meant that landlords, employers and others to whom a man might feel he owed either his livelihood or his duty were able to see whom that man voted for. Fear of economic reprisals therefore often meant someone could not vote according to his conscience. The corruption this caused was most famously depicted in *The Pickwick Papers* in 1836, Dickens recycling what he had seen with his own eyes in Sudbury in Suffolk in 1834 as the fictional borough of Eatanswill. The nature, and dangers, of an election before the ballot were also well illustrated in the riot that is the key event in *Felix Holt*. It was not merely that intimidation was rife, but that it was intimidation fuelled by 'treating'. Even before working men had the franchise, armies of them could be recruited to act as intimidators on behalf of a candidate through the liberal supply of free alcohol in public houses. In *Felix Holt*, the coming of the election is signified as 'the time, they say, when a man can get beer for nothing!'[93] Even Mr Lyon, the pious dissenting minister, finds something to be said for not having the ballot: 'To any impartial mind, duly furnished with the principles of public and private rectitude . . . the ballot would be pernicious, and . . . if it were not pernicious it would still be futile.' He believed it would not stop bribery, and would be 'shutting the door against those influences whereby the soul of a man and the character of a citizen are duly educated for their great functions.'[94]

In 1869 a private member's motion to introduce the ballot – cast in the privacy of a polling booth – was thwarted by the government's refusal to make time for it. Sir George Grey, the Home Secretary, told the Commons he and the government accepted the case for the ballot: but they were unsure what would be 'the best means . . . for securing tranquillity, freedom, and purity at our municipal and Parliamentary elections.'[95] Gladstone reinforced this point. The government accepted the moment had come for secrecy, but felt it needed time to handle the transition to it, because of the anger it would cause to landlords and employers who felt they had a right to know how their tenants and employees voted. An element still considered that, far from preventing bribery and coercion, the ballot would conceal it: and that it was 'un-English' for a member of the (recently expanded) electorate not to proclaim for whom he was voting. Richard Cross, who would become one of the century's great reformers, reflected that 'I have always myself strongly opposed the ballot, believing that the right to vote was a trust to be exercised openly.'[96]

Another opponent of the ballot, Lord Claud Hamilton, offered an alternative: 'Let it be announced publicly that any man guilty of bribery shall be excluded from the pale of society as though he were a swindler or a thief, and they would hear little more upon the subject. Instead of doing this they [the House of Commons] listened with complacency, and perhaps, enjoyment, to the tales of the successful dodges by which bribery had been perpetrated with impunity. As long as they admitted men having the moral stain of corruption into their society, he did not believe in the sincerity of their wish to put down bribery.'[97]

Another attempt was made in 1870. Edward Leatham, the Liberal MP for Huddersfield who introduced the measure to bring in the ballot, gave numerous examples of intimidation practised across the country by both parties. This took various forms: mobs threatening voters at the poll itself or, slightly more subtly, landlords refusing to renew tenancies for men who did not vote as instructed. Lord Lothian was cited as an example of such a landlord; and, when asked about it, had expressed astonishment that anyone should have expected him to do differently – 'nor do I see anything which is otherwise than honourable in the course which I have taken.'[98] However, the extension of the franchise had created other, more novel opportunities to influence voters. Leatham referred to a report that 'out of 154 voters employed at the railway works and station at Carlisle, 136 plumped for an eminent railway director, who was a candidate for the city of Carlisle at the last election, and since the political leaning of most of the men was known to be the other way, the inference was drawn that this unanimity of their part was due to the exercise of pressure.' Publicly, the men denied coercion: privately, they admitted they had defied their principles to keep their jobs. Fear of reprisals was why those who scrutinised polls could find no evidence of intimidation, and why the case for the ballot was so hard to prove.

In Ashton-under-Lyme 242 people lost their jobs because they voted Conservative rather than Liberal. In Gravesend a Liberal mob had run through the town on polling day smashing the windows of Conservatives. In Ireland things were even worse: hired and armed mobs were a feature at every election in Limerick, and at Sligo the mob was deemed so important that it was organised fifteen months before the election. The law appeared impotent in the face of bribery, and in the face of 'treating' – buying drinks for voters, or even giving them huge banquets. However, as Hartington, for the government, said, the deliberations of a select committee (of which Hartington happened to be the chairman), appointed after the previous failed attempt at a Ballot Act, had not been completed. Until they were, the government could not in good faith support a bill with which many ministers had great sympathy. It was agreed to postpone further consideration until May – six weeks later – and promised that, when it was considered, Gladstone would be present.

Hartington, in May, introduced a bill to tackle corrupt practices at elections, and proposed the ballot. He felt, after consideration by his committee, that the ballot would not encourage bribery or personation. This was not a view shared widely. Many MPs believed the inability to detect who had voted for whom was an open invitation to electoral malpractice. It was also argued that if the bill were passed it should be with a clause exempting the universities from the ballot, since there could be no question of any corrupt behaviour among so rarefied an electorate. The bill had its first reading: and at its second a few weeks later Gladstone argued, in the triumph of hope over experience, that the question need not be a party political matter. The government's

Achilles heel, now and in future years, was that the question had not been put to the country at the 1868 election, and there was no proof of a popular mandate for it. The bill went no further.

Resistance continued to be ferocious in 1871, for the reason expressed by Colonel Sir Walter Barttelot, the Tory MP for West Sussex,: why ever couldn't men 'be trusted to give their votes freely and independently like Englishmen?'[99] Gladstone respected such convictions, but hoped the bill would be considered on its merits rather than on the basis of the imaginary fears of its opponents. The bill went into committee: where Henry James, who in 1873 would become Attorney General, announced that 'he approached the subject with mingled and varied feeling, for, to his mind, when the Ballot became the law of the land, it would be a day of humiliation, and bitter humiliation to the whole nation; not because there was anything humiliating in recording a vote in secret, but because, by adopting this measure, they as a people, confessed that from causes and conduct which ought to be within their control they were compelled to drive the electors of this country into secrecy, and were unable to permit them to record their votes in an open and public manner.'[100] Michael Hicks-Beach, who would twice serve as Chancellor of the Exchequer in Conservative governments, warned that the ballot would facilitate the creation of 'an organised system of fraud'.[101] He feared mass personation, and he was not sure there were sufficient safeguards against corrupt returning officers. Other MPs feared the ballot would result in most of the MPs returned from Ireland being national-ists: unwittingly making the point that the ballot encouraged genuine democracy. However, William Forster, who piloted the bill through, argued that the logical extension of giving so many more men the vote in 1867 was to give them a free vote.

The bill spent all of July and part of August 1871 in committee. On 24 July the Cabinet, who could see it running out of time, wondered whether to postpone or truncate it, or to suggest an autumn session to complete it. At the third reading on 8 August Disraeli blamed it for holding up other vital legislation, an act of hypocrisy extreme even by his standards. The bill had its third reading unopposed – a vote would have exposed Disraeli's problems with his own party – and went to the Lords, where Shaftesbury tried to derail it. He said he would not argue against the principle of the measure, but against trying to discuss it properly when the House was about to go into recess and, indeed, when many peers had already left London for the Riviera or were on their way to the grouse moor – it was 10 August. The bill was thrown out by a two-to-one majority. The lesson for Gladstone was that if he wanted the measure to stand a chance, it had to reach the Lords well before August to be debated properly. The next bill to introduce the ballot was considered in the Commons two days after the state opening in February 1872.

Shaftesbury had written to Gladstone on 7 December 1871 to say that 'as to the Ballot itself, I regard it with the deepest alarm – my feelings on it are as strong as yours were.'[102] He said it was 'the duty of the Lords – a patriotic duty, I maintain – to throw back, for further deliberation, any Bill that they deem to be dangerous or simply hurtful to the real interests of the country.' Shaftesbury's party was still divided on the issue, which made things easier for Gladstone – though that was not how Disraeli saw it. He personally decided to remain silent as the measure went through, and not to expose the reactionary views of much of his party and provide an excuse for Gladstone to seek a dissolution, go to the country, and quite probably win an election that would end Disraeli's career.

By 1872 the demand for the ballot had become so strong that any attempt by Parliament to ignore it would have had serious consequences. John Bright, in particular, was arguing that many of the newly enfranchised would be afraid to vote in a way disapproved of by their landlord or employer. Forster again took the bill through the Commons. It took the same form as the previous year. The Lords debated it on 10 June. Shaftesbury, the friend of the oppressed, rubbished the notion that men were being intimidated. 'There may', he said, 'be a case of intimidation here and there, but the cases are so few they are not worth recording, to the extent, I mean, of founding on them a new legislative action. Is it not a fact—will any man gainsay it—that the people are too enlightened, the employers are too prudent, and public opinion is too strong for the continued exercise of such an abuse? All testimony is against it.'[103] Shaftesbury's naivety was almost charming, as when he accurately predicted the emergence of the Labour party and modern canvassing if the ballot was introduced: 'If the Ballot should be established agitators would go round to every house in the country and persuade the people to vote for special candidates, by saying that if they got into Parliament not only that the taxes and rates should be reduced—that argument is

legitimate enough—but hinting also, that by a little legislative arrangement there might be a better and a fairer distribution of all kinds of
property.'[104]

He also feared the ballot would hasten the end of the monarchy. In
such remarks we come close to the real reason why so many old Tories
loathed the idea. He concluded on an appropriately hysterical note: 'In
the present aspect of affairs I am prepared for the overthrow of many
of our institutions. I am prepared to see the dissolution of the Church
of England, torn as it is by internal dissension; I am prepared to see a
vital attack made upon the House of Lords, hateful on account of its
hereditary privileges; and I am prepared to tremble for the Monarchy
itself, stripped as it is of its true supporters; but I am not prepared for
an immoral people; I am not prepared to see the people exercising their
highest rights and privileges in secret, refusing to come to the light
"because their deeds are evil".'[105] Despite several other blood-curdling
speeches from the Tory benches, the government got its second reading.

At the committee stage Salisbury complained the bill had only got so
far as it had because of the government's handsome majority in the
Commons. He was acutely sensitive to the amount of ground that
Conservatives had given to Liberalism since 1868 – and, indeed, since
1867 – and was determined not to shift on points of principle until the
last ditch. In 1870, when the Tories were in a stand-off on the Irish Land
Bill, he had told Carnarvon 'that if we make any substantial retreat from
the very moderate position that we have taken up, our future position
in the Constitution will be purely decorative.'[106] On the Ballot Bill, he
told Carnarvon: 'If we listen to the Liberals we should accept all
important Bills which had passed the House of Commons by a large
majority. But that in effect would be to efface the House of Lords.'[107]

Many Conservatives in the Commons disagreed with him. Disraeli's
secret weapon – or so he thought – in keeping his party together during
this difficult passage was making the ballot optional. The Commons
ridiculed this, much to Disraeli's chagrin. It was, however, something
taken seriously by the Lords. Liberals argued that where secrecy was
optional the usual suspects would intimidate voters into waiving their
right to it. Salisbury claimed that even if there were total secrecy voters
could still be intimidated into not voting at all, if it were feared they
would otherwise vote the wrong way. His view swayed the tribunal: the
Lords amended the bill to allow optional secrecy.

The government was having none of this, and used its majority to throw the amendment out in the Commons. It also rejected one to allow the marking of ballot papers to trace who had cast them. Forster said that if the amendment stood it would make the bill 'useless, or worse than useless'.[108] Disraeli said secrecy should be used only in areas with a proven record of intimidation and corruption: he said the measure should be kept in reserve, like the Riot Act. A confrontation was thereby set up with the Lords, who threatened to hold fast in the face of the strongly expressed views of the elected House.

Gladstone was so perturbed by this that he wrote to George Moberly, the former headmaster of Winchester and now, by Gladstone's appointment, Bishop of Salisbury, to seek his help when the measure came back to the Lords in July 1872 'in preventing the very serious evil of a collision between the two Houses with the consequences it might entail.'[109] He sent a similar entreaty to 'Soapy Sam' Wilberforce. Gladstone said it would be 'very dangerous to mistake the general sentiments of the people on this subject': but optional secrecy was an absurdity and had to be killed. He also urged George Glyn, the Liberal Chief Whip, to alert the press to the Lords' determination to defeat the Commons, with a view to newspapers stirring up public feeling by 'pointing to the extreme gravity of the consequences'.[110]

Gladstone was determined not to be worsted by the Lords. The Cabinet met on 6 July and discussed options if the amendment were passed. It ruled out immediate resignation, accepting the amendment, trying again in 1873 or creating peers to vote the measure through as Gladstone wished it. It was decided that if the bill were lost there would be an autumn session and it would be reintroduced. If that failed, Gladstone would seek a dissolution in November. Glyn told him the Liberals would win the ensuing election, though probably with a much reduced majority.

The Lords dealt with the rejection of their amendments two days later. Ripon, who led for the government, warned that if the House insisted on the optional ballot, the bill would be pointless. Peers were reminded that the idea had been thrown out in the Commons by large majorities. The Tories in the upper House were split: the Duke of Richmond insisted on the optional ballot, and the Duke of Northumberland wished he would not. An attempt was made to claim that those Tory MPs recently returned at by-elections who supported the ballot would also support the optional ballot: that was treated with derision. The amendment was not insisted upon: the Tories were reduced to squabbling about the inconvenience that would be inflicted on elementary schools when they were closed to be used as polling stations – another consequence of the measure. The ballot was on the statute book, and the last vestiges of Eatanswill and the pre-reform era were swept away by it.

Both the 1867 Reform Act and the Ballot were steps towards a mature democracy that began from the high-minded impulse of those who wished to involve the lower classes in the political process, and to allow them to engage in it according to their consciences. That said, if they were conceived in idealism they were, in the end, born in pragmatism, because of the fear by the ruling class of what would happen if these civil rights continued to be denied. Disraeli's behaviour in 1866–7 was in that respect far more unprincipled than the conduct of which he had accused Peel in 1845–6, when he had sought to save the poorest in Britain and Ireland from starvation. Once more, hypocrisy oiled the wheels of Victorian progress, but progress, nonetheless, it was.

CHAPTER 12

BROADENING MINDS:
THE BATTLE FOR EDUCATION

———————◆———————

I

Robert Lowe, among others, had foreseen the main social consequence of the Reform Act: the urgent need to educate the people who would now have the vote. Speaking on the third reading of the Reform Bill on 15 July 1867, Lowe had said:

> I shrink from the notion of forcing education on people. It seemed more in accordance with our institutions to allow the thing to work and freely to supplement the system. That whole question has now completely changed. All the opinions I held on that subject are scattered to the winds by this measure of the Government. Sir, it appears to me that before we had entrusted the masses—the great bulk of whom are uneducated—with the whole power of this country we should have taught them a little more how to use it, and not having done so, this rash and abrupt measure having been forced upon them, the only thing we can do is as far as possible to remedy the evil by the most universal measures of education that can be devised. I believe it will be absolutely necessary that you should prevail on our future masters to learn their letters.

He had changed his mind on centralisation, on an education rate and inspection.

> This question is no longer a religious question, it has become a political one. It is indeed the question of questions; it has become paramount to every other question that has been brought before us. From the moment that you entrust the masses with power their

education becomes an absolute necessity, and our system of education, which—though not perfect, is far superior to the much-
vaunted system that prevails in America or any nation on the
Continent, as one system can be to another—must give way to a
national system . . . You must take education up as the very first
question, and you must press it on without delay for the peace of
the country.[1]

It should be noted, though, that when Lowe talked about a national
approach to education, it was very much England and Wales that he
was thinking about. Scottish education in Victorian times was a very
different matter. Inspired by a post-Reformation wish to create a Godly
people, Acts of Parliament in Scotland in the seventeenth century had
imposed the duty upon parishes to set up schools for the education of
the people, and had taxed local gentry to pay for them. Universities,
similarly, offered places to those who wished to attend them, but awarded
no qualifications. Carlyle, aged 15, would walk to Edinburgh from
Dumfriesshire – a journey of almost 80 miles – to study at the university
there, and walk back again at the end of term, living in mean lodgings
and subsisting on a meagre diet. The old English universities, though
more rigorous in their training, offered no such access. As for elementary
schools, England was some 250 years behind Scotland.

In a lecture to the Philosophical Institution of Edinburgh on 1
November 1867, Lowe admitted a moral failure in having opposed education for the masses, but now advanced a utilitarian consideration: 'It was
a great evil that we did so before – it was an evil and a reproach, a moral
stigma upon us. But now it is a question of self-preservation – it is a
question of existence, even of the existence of our Constitution, and
upon those who shall obstruct or prevent such a measure passing will
rest a responsibility the heaviest that mortal man can possibly lie under.'[2]

Lowe's was one of the sharpest and most relentless minds of his
generation. He had been born in 1811, like Samuel Butler the son of a
Nottinghamshire parson. He was an albino with eyes that could hardly
bear the light. He expected to go blind, which he did in old age. He
distinguished himself academically at Winchester (where he had been
bullied and miserable) and Oxford, which he left with a reputation
for brilliance. He regarded Adam Smith's *The Wealth of Nations* as of
near biblical significance, and became an ardent utilitarian, heavily
influenced by Benthamism. He was a radical free-trader of great personal

ambition, with a knack for upsetting people: and Gladstone would make him Chancellor in his first ministry. Lowe was advised to go to the Antipodes in the 1840s, where he worked in the government of New South Wales, to see whether the light would improve his sight. The light being much stronger there, it made it worse.

In 1859 Palmerston sent Lowe to the Privy Council Office, as vice-president with responsibility for education. Lowe was committed to reform, not least because the utilitarian in him saw, like Smith, that education was a sound investment. If a government invested in schools it would improve the life-chances of individuals, help them to be prosperous and to increase the prosperity of society, and remove burdens that would otherwise fall upon private charity and the parish. Lowe was ultra-utilitarian about the curriculum. He told a dinner of civil engineers in 1867 that study of the Classics (in which he had excelled) was merely 'a minute analysis of the forms of expression and the modes of thought which were used by people many thousand years ago, and concerning which there was much controversy and no certainty would be arrived at.'[3] Again, he took his cue from Smith, who had regarded proficiency in reading, writing and arithmetic as vital to the country. Lowe's philosophy, expressed in an article in *The Times* attacking John Bright, was that 'a man must be the architect of his own fortune and rise by his own energy. All Government can do is to remove obstacles from his path.'[4] The devil would take the hindmost.

This view was common across the parties. C. B. Adderley, Lowe's predecessor, had told the Commons in July 1859 that 'the education of children was naturally a parental function and was not the proper duty of the Government, which only interfered where its interposition was absolutely necessary.'[5] Only the most high-minded, such as Matthew Arnold, trumpeted the value of learning for its own sake: it either had a utilitarian function, as men like Lowe would see it, or it had no function at all. Access to schools was controlled by the Anglican Church and by the dissenters, to whom the government made a grant of £20,000 a year (increased to £30,000 in 1839).[6] However, also in 1839, the government voted £70,000 for the construction of new royal stables, which shows how priorities worked.

By the mid-nineteenth century, whether or not they had had a formal education, more people were becoming literate, and therefore able to participate in rather than simply observe the development of society.

That partly explained the rise of political activism from the 1830s through to the 1860s, but there had been other factors. The introduction of the penny post in 1840 had caused an exponential rise in communication. There was a substantial growth in the numbers of periodicals and books published, reflecting the expansion of the middle classes, their literacy and their leisure time. Newspapers also flourished: stamp duty was abolished in 1855, and in September of that year the *Daily Telegraph* was founded. Gladstone, who was Chancellor at the time, was well aware of the revenue raised by the tax: but was concerned about the perception that the government, by imposing this tax on a population growing in literacy and political awareness but still short of money, was restricting the availability of information about its own activities. He had told the Commons in April 1853 that it was not government policy to continue to 'restrain the circulation of intelligence'.[7]

Popular novelists, notably Dickens and Trollope, were serialised in periodicals: within five weeks of Dickens's launching *All the Year Round* in 1859 it was selling 120,000 copies a week.[8] Britain had become a nation of readers, and the pursuit of literacy was a national ideal. Because of this, and the desire for self-improvement, the foundation of libraries became widespread in smaller as well as in larger towns. When the Free Library opened in Manchester on 2 September 1852 the event was attended by 1,000 people. Dickens, who was one, described the enterprise as 'such a noble effort, so wisely and modestly made; so wonderfully calculated to keep one part of that awful machine, a great working town, in harmony with the other.'[9] Such was the significance of the opening that as well as Dickens a number of other notables came from London for it: Thackeray, Shaftesbury, Bulwer Lytton, Sir James Stephen and Richard Monckton Milnes among them.

Philanthropists steadily became more interested in schools as well as in libraries. Shaftesbury led the Ragged School movement for thirty-nine years from 1844, assisted by supporters such as Dickens: 300,000 children in London alone went through these schools between 1844 and 1881. The Education Act of 1870 set up board schools, but these were neither free nor compulsory. Disraeli's ministry of 1874–80 sought to widen provision, with Sandon's Act of 1876 allowing local committees to pay for children whose families had no money. It was not until the next Gladstone ministry that Mundella's Act of 1881 compelled attendance for children aged between five and ten and forced payment of 3d a week.

The Fee Grant Act of 1891, passed by a Conservative government under Lord Salisbury, finally made education for children free of charge.

However, in the middle of the century religion still restricted educational opportunity. By 1851 there were nearly as many Nonconformists in England as Anglicans: but it was not until the University Test Act of 1871 that the bar against non-Anglicans holding fellowships or senior university positions at Oxbridge was removed. The supposedly best schools were also restricted other than by money, until the Clarendon Commission led to the Public Schools Act 1868, which took the nine leading schools in England out of the hands of either the government or the Church and made them independent. Breaking the Church's control allowed a broadening of the curriculum away from the Classics, which helped create a new generation of broader thinkers and innovators more in tune with a world that was changing technologically and socially. The slow, gradual and incomplete separation of religious institutions from educational ones was both driven by the march of secularisation, and drove that march. In parallel with the movement to extend education was a movement to question the hold religion had had on society, and to force religion to confront rationalism. By the 1880s this broadening of minds would initiate a profound change in society, though it did not happen without a fight.

II

The work of Churches to provide education to the lower classes was supplemented by steadily increasing government grants: but it was not enough to provide a decent basic education to all who needed it, and not enough to supply the needs of a fast-growing country whose industrial expansion demanded a larger pool of skilled labourers and literate, numerate clerical workers. Advocates of the extension of education made much of the fact that Prussia had introduced State education, and it was now a right for Prussians to have their children sent to school and be paid for by the State.

In 1848 petitioners from Manchester – where there was plenty of wealth unevenly distributed – had sought parliamentary permission to levy a local tax to pay for schools. Parliament refused. By 1855 both Lord John Russell and Sir John Pakington, a former Colonial Secretary, proposed bills to allow local public subsidy of education. The problem with establishing a system of publicly funded schools, or schools partly funded by the public, was not merely financial: it was also religious, in that dissenters did not wish to pay taxes to support Church of England schools. In fact, in the first full year after the Liberals returned to office in 1859 education accounted for one-fifth of the State's entire expenditure: something that could be ill-afforded after the Crimean War.[10] A grant system had grown since 1839, when Russell invented it, under the aegis of Sir James Kay-Shuttleworth, to cost over £750,000. This was because of the growth in population, the multiplying of schools and the expense of training teachers. Even Russell and Matthew Arnold, respectively the instigator and most fervent supporter of Kay-Shuttleworth's system, felt it required better control.

William Fox, the MP for Oldham, told the Commons on 11 June 1855 that although one child in eight was at school according to the most recent figures – compared with one in seventeen in 1818 – because of population rises 'there were now in Great Britain more children who should be at school, and who were not at school – more by many, many scores of thousands – than there ever were before.'[11] He estimated the number at 2 million. He said that only two in a hundred Prussians aged twenty-one could not read; whereas only one in five 'of our common soldiers, who had enjoyed the advantage of regimental schools' could; and in every two marriages, one party on average signed his or her name with a mark.[12] Pakington also showed that crime rates were far higher in Britain than in Holland and Denmark, where there was universal education.

He tried in 1858 to have a Royal Commission appointed, but 'he was told the information he sought was not required; that all the facts the friends of education could desire could be obtained from the annual reports of the inspectors employed by the Privy Council. He was told that all was going on well; that there was no need of a change; that the progress of education in England was greater during the present century than it had ever been in any other country during the same period of time.'[13] Pakington, and Russell, knew this was complacent rubbish: 'Large masses of the people of this country were in a state of the most deplorable ignorance,' Pakington said. He knew the centrally administered attempt at regulating education was failing, and that some local administration was essential; in large areas of Britain there were either only bad schools, or no schools at all.

At the change of government in 1858 he secured his Royal Commission on the education of the poorer classes. Derby appointed it. He delegated the matter to the second Marquess of Salisbury, who chose the Duke of Newcastle to lead it. Newcastle was a Peelite. He had been Secretary of State for War in Aberdeen's administration and would be Colonial Secretary in Palmerston's from 1859 until his premature death, just before his fifty-third birthday, in 1864. The Commission began in the inauspicious circumstances of the reduction by Gladstone, Palmerston's Chancellor, of the grant for education by over £30,000, for the first time since 1834; this was despite the number of children increasing rapidly.

Newcastle was told 'to consider and report what measures, if any, are required for the extension of sound and cheap elementary instruction to all classes of people.'[14] He drew on the twenty-seven volumes of school inspection reports published since 1839: but 'the Inspectors are Inspectors of Schools, not of education', Newcastle said. Their expertise on the better sort of elementary schools was unrivalled: but there were many more schools, many uninspected. The work was massive: assistant commissioners had to be appointed to visit schools all over the country. They concentrated on two main agricultural districts, in the West Country and in East Anglia and Lincolnshire; on the main manufacturing areas in Lancashire, Yorkshire and around Birmingham and the Potteries; on mining areas in the north-east and in South Wales; in ports such as Bristol, Hull, Yarmouth and Liverpool; and metropolitan London.

Newcastle looked at Catholic schools, dissenting schools, schools run by the National Society for the Education of the Poor in the principles of the Established Church, and other charitable schools such as those of the London Ragged School Union. No government had sought to promote education before 1832, when it was agreed to vote £20,000 a year to the National Society and the British and Foreign Schools Society to erect buildings. The Committee of the Privy Council for Education was formed in 1839, and the annual grant was increased to £30,000. The grant had risen steadily, and had begun to be paid to Roman Catholic schools after 1847. By 1860 it was £798,167 per annum. In 1846 the pupil-teacher system had been set up, under which the State paid the salaries of apprentice teachers for five years while they learned their profession.

Although some assistant commissioners found parents insisting on sending their children only to schools of their own denomination, in other districts nobody seemed to care at all, reflecting the advance of secularisation. Mr Hare, assistant commissioner in the East Coast ports, said that 'everywhere I have found Jews in Christian, and Roman Catholics in Protestant schools, and Church children in British or positively dissenting schools.'[15] Even in Hull, where Protestant feeling was strong, he found Protestants 'in schools managed by Roman Catholic priests and sisters of mercy'. Mr Foster, who covered Cumberland and County Durham, said that 'parents will send their children to whichever they deem the best school, quite irrespective of religious peculiarities.'[16]

It had been hoped that evening schools would allow children who worked in factories or on the land to get an education; but the failure of this system was apparent to Newcastle, and this finding would lead to the eventual compulsory attendance, until the age of twelve, of children at day-schools. A clergyman from Lynn who was the secretary of the local board of education said that children in that agricultural district might attend on winter evenings; but once the days were longer they would more likely be at work. A schoolmaster from Yeovil said of the evening schools he had seen that 'they are, for the most part, failures; indeed, nearly all the elements requisite to ensure success are wanting, viz, apparatus, good teachers, especially a competent superintendent, funds, interest, and support. They are often undertaken by inexperienced, untrained, and badly educated men. The order is that of Bedlam; little or no progress is made; and shortly the number, large at first, becomes reduced to a few, and the scheme is abandoned.'[17] Sunday schools had a better report, largely because of the zeal of those who taught in them, but what they did was almost exclusively confined to religious instruction.

Fees, the Commission found, provided between a quarter and three-fifths of schools' income. Charitable societies levied fees according to the means of the parents. Where fees were 1d a week only 16 per cent of children in Yorkshire were felt able to pay them, and only 23 per cent of those in Lancashire. In an agricultural district such as Cambridgeshire the figure rose to 61 per cent and in the West Country to over 66 per cent.[18] It cost £1 10s a year to educate a child, but even if a family was paying 3d a week (as many were asked to do) this would bring in under 12s a year; 8d a week was needed to cover costs. One of Newcastle's recommendations was that all those who could afford 8d a week should pay it.

Much of the rest of the money came in subscriptions from land-owners, clergymen and householders. In the manufacturing districts many businesses had founded and then funded schools, as part of their obligations to their workforce. Horner, a factory inspector who had visited factory schools found the 'great majority' had failed to educate children even to a basic standard.[19] He described the law that demanded education for factory children as 'delusive'. 'It provides nothing more than that the children shall on certain days of the week, and for a certain number of hours in each day, be enclosed within the four walls of a place called a school, and that the employer of the child shall receive weekly a certificate to that effect signed by a person designated by the subscriber as a schoolmaster or schoolmistress. Not a word is said as to what the instruction shall be, and the lowest possible quali-fications that could be applied for teaching the rudiments of infantine training are declared to be sufficient for the granter of the certificate.'[20] However, from 1 July 1861 no boy under twelve could be employed in any mine or colliery unless it was certified by a 'competent school-master' that he could read or write, and he had to attend school for a certain number of hours each month. This law, like the Act that banned boys under ten from working in collieries, was widely flouted; the Commission estimated that in the Durham coalfield 9 per cent of the boys were under ten.[21]

The 1851 census, the most recent to which Newcastle had access, showed 1,549,312 scholars in 22,647 schools, which included Sunday and evening schools. In 1860 it was found that 917,255 children were in schools to which the Privy Council Committee made a grant; 860,304 were in private schools. Some of these private schools were described as 'very bad indeed'.[22] The better schools, though, were good, and the assistant commissioners found many cases of children coming 2, 3 or even 5½ miles to them. The teachers too were variable. Mr Hare, from the East Coast, said that 'most private schoolmasters are men who have failed in other pursuits, and . . . many of them eke out a subsistence by doing whatever odd jobs chance may throw in their way. One witness specifies quondam barbers, sailors, soldiers and millers as turning to school-keeping, and present schoolmasters as being also interested in ship-owning or engaged in rate-collecting.'[23] In Plymouth Mr Cumin, an assistant commissioner, found one schoolmaster had been a blacksmith, another a journeyman tanner, another a dockyard labourer.

The dregs were found in London: Dr Hodgson, Newcastle's man there, found that 'none are too old, too poor, too ignorant, too feeble, too sickly, too unqualified in every way, to regard themselves, and to be regarded by others, as unfit for school-keeping.'[24] He continued: 'The profession, as such, hardly exists . . . it is a mere refuge for the destitute, and enumerates grocers, tobacconists, linendrapers, tailors, attorneys, painters, German, Polish and Italian refugees, bakers, widows or daughters of clergymen, barristers and surgeons, housekeepers, ladies' maids, and dressmakers, as being found among the teachers of private schools.' Inevitably, many could not spell, and one or two could not even write.

The commissioners also estimated there were 1,248,691 children who derived no benefit from the annual grant.[25] It was estimated that between 5 or 10 per cent of children received no education at all, not even of the useless and disorganised type supplied by evening schools.[26] Even the pupil-teacher scheme, which had been supposed to improve the number of trained people entering teaching, was failing, because it paid so badly; some schools in the more affluent parts of the country found that only by their managers offering an extra £5 a year above what the government would pay would anyone be tempted to take up such a post.[27] Pupil-teachers began at fourteen on 3s 10d a week, rising to 7s 8d at eighteen; but this was no attraction when a boy could earn 10s a week in a factory in Sheffield, or 11s a week as a telegraph clerk on the railways. The work was exceptionally hard, especially, it was found, on young women; the training was 'mechanical' and boring and did nothing 'to elevate the tone of their minds'.[28]

The teacher training colleges were of a higher standard but had their imperfections. A man when fully trained could earn £97 a year; the Commission at least conceded that such men had 'proved beyond all doubt' that they were 'greatly superior to the untrained teachers.'[29] However, even without compulsory education, the growth in population required more teachers. The growth in prosperity – and therefore in expectations of parents paying even modest fees – would further boost demand. There was a grave shortage of teachers in infant schools, with only one training college, run by the Home and Colonial Society, producing them.[30] Newcastle demanded a 'powerful' intervention by the Privy Council Committee if this was to be rectified.[31]

The Commission knew that for some school was about more than learning. 'To very poor children the school is a substitute for a home;

they frequently have no other experience of domestic comfort and decency, and the teacher and those who take an active interest in the school are the only persons of tolerably cultivated minds with whom they are brought into anything approaching an intimate relation.'[32] The moral effect of a school was important, an achievement of Dr Arnold's influence in the public schools: 'A set of good schools civilises a whole neighbourhood.'[33]

Matthew Arnold had been appointed an assistant commissioner to report on education in France. One of his suggestions, as an experienced inspector, was that no prior warnings of inspections should be announced, as schools could prepare and dress themselves up. The Commission ignored his advice, saying inspectors should make allowances for such behaviour. Arnold had seen this in France, but the Commission thought it would not be practicable in England. Arnold was concerned about the dismal standards in British schools: notably of illiteracy, or of children who could read but with no understanding of what they were reading. It was noted that the books with which children were taught to read were packed with examples designed not to interest them, but to give them moral lectures instead. In even the best schools inspected, only about a quarter of boys were deemed 'successfully educated'.[34] The Commission decided 'distinct inducements' should be offered to masters in all schools to teach better and 'to bring their individual scholars, junior as well as senior, to a certain mark.'[35] These unfavourable comparisons with France were meant to prompt improvements, and to an extent they did. But they also irritated those not of Arnold's cast of mind, notably James Fitzjames Stephen, who ridiculed his 'self-imposed mission to give good advice to the English as to their manifold faults'.[36]

The Commission reserved its strongest language to condemn the education of pauper children in workhouses. It wanted to end, by law, contact with adult paupers, which caused a child to lose 'all desire to earn its own living'.[37] The Commission wanted them in separate schools, far from the workhouse, and from the 'injurious' influence of their feckless and often depraved parents. Children from orphanages so often, the report claimed, turned out better than those with parents in work-houses.[38] Otherwise they would turn into 'thieves, or paupers, or pros-titutes'. Boards of guardians were beyond understanding this. Newcastle was unequivocal. 'Pauperism is hereditary . . . children born and bred as members of that class furnish the great mass of the pauper and criminal population . . . the best prospect of a permanent diminution of pauperism and crime is to be found in the proper education of such children.'[39] Schools outside the workhouse would 'emancipate them from pauperism', because workhouse schools were dismally funded and would never attract decent teachers.

A final class of children was that for whom crime was already a way of life, and in reformatories, or industrial schools. The Commission quoted, with approval, an assistant commissioner's report about these places. It was regarded as far superior to the 'closeness, dirt and disorderly freedom of the common lodging houses' where they mostly lived.[40] In an industrial school they had 'airy' dormitories and separate beds, regular meals, exercise and fresh air. They were kept busy and taught trades and skills, such as brick-making and stock-keeping. Above all, 'the Scripture regulation [is] in full force – if a man will not work, neither should he eat.' This prevented the places becoming 'seductive' to the inmates. They were given much religious instruction; they had some wider education.

Some boys ended up on naval training ships in the Thames estuary, 'the most effectual remedies for the enfeebled constitutions and scrofulous tendencies that their parents' vices or their own early destitutions and wretchedness have entailed upon so many of them.'[41] Such boys might indeed end up in the Navy, or the Army, whose last commander-in-chief had once said his men were the scum of the earth. 'The boy who has been for two or three years under steady regulation and instruction in a reformatory is likely indeed to be superior both in intelligence and personal habits to the common lads taken directly from the streets and alleys of our large cities.' The report concluded that 'none of the institutions connected with education appear to be in a more satisfactory condition than the reformatories.'[42] It said education of criminal children must be 'compulsory', for the good of society, and that those under 'special temptations to crime' should attend improved industrial schools.[43]

When the report was discussed in Parliament, on 11 July 1861, Lowe said the lower education spending had been settled before the government had read Newcastle's conclusions.[44] He admitted centralisation was inefficient and expensive, and conceded that the limited funds would be spent better if administered locally. He also conceded that the criticisms of the poor quality of teaching and teachers were 'well founded'.[45] The system, he admitted, was complicated. However, that was because private individuals and institutions – landowners, clergymen, religious groups – had generously paid for different sorts of schools in different places: and Lowe confirmed that the government had no intention of interfering with that system. Despite secularisation, the teaching of religion in schools, and the religious nature of many foundations that ran schools, were still of the highest importance. However, Lowe had a hidden agenda of reducing the religious influence in order to extend the availability of teaching, so that non-Anglicans could attend Church schools. This would, in time, be achieved by the State's refusal to pay specific grants for religious instruction.

Yet while Lowe admitted many of the faults the Commission had found, he did not feel the general recommendation made to rectify them was politically feasible: namely, to maintain the existing system, but to supplement its funding by levying a local rate. He proposed instead to make the payment of a capitation fee to schools contingent on proof that the child on whose behalf the fee was being paid had reached a certain standard in the core subjects. As for some of the worst schools in the country, Lowe said they received no government money because they chose not to be under government control: otherwise, they might be better. The view that all the State would succeed in doing with education would be to make a mess of it was widespread and, indeed, the orthodoxy. Edward Baines, the MP for Leeds, speaking later in the debate, asserted that 'in a country like this, freedom would ultimately produce higher education and higher national character than any system which placed education under Government support and control.'[46]

Since the recommendations were so controversial, Lowe suggested change be pursued by means of a departmental minute, and not via legislation. Granville, his chief, agreed and asked Lowe to frame a new policy. Lowe feared relinquishing central control to county authorities. His experience in New South Wales in the 1840s, where he had tried to establish an education system, had shown the danger of the centre abdicating responsibility. He sought the advice of Henry Cole and Ralph Lingen, Kay-Shuttleworth's successor, and Lingen drafted a minute that, with feline timing, was issued as Parliament was prorogued in 1861. This 'Revised Code' was, as Lowe's biographer puts it, 'deliberately unconciliatory'.[47]

It stated that the grant would be paid according to the number of children who attended a school for a prescribed number of days. It said inspectors would gauge children not according to levels of attainment, but to what they had attained for their age. Each child would be tested in reading, writing and arithmetic; and failure would cause the school to lose one-third of that child's capitation grant. Money would also be docked for shortages of trained teachers and poor facilities or equipment. Lowe described these changes in terms of his own philosophy: 'Hitherto we have been living under a system of bounties and protection; now we propose to have a little free trade.'[48]

The proposals were met with almost uniform outrage from headmasters and clergy. Authorities on education also railed against it: notably Huxley, who believed the code assisted in 'the development of every description of sham teaching' as pedagogues sought to cram children to pass examinations and not to expand their minds. Most aggrieved of all were the inspectors, almost all of whom for different reasons felt the code to be unworkable. Arnold caricatured it: 'A lame man walks ill and to make him walk better, you break his crutches.'[49] Lowe countered by expressing his lack of confidence in the inspectors, and by accusing Anglican prelates of 'extortion' for their determination to extract as much as possible for their schools without using it to improve standards.[50] He believed attack was the best form of defence, and went to these lengths to avoid accusations that the reform was a money-saving exercise. However, it was an exercise Lowe believed could be carried out while simultaneously raising standards.

Arnold also argued that each school had its own social context that made it impossible to apply centralised rules to it. Schools were penalised if the children – now empowered as 'earners' of the capitation grant – did not turn up for the annual examination. This took no account of bad weather, of harvests in rural areas, the needs of parents, or any of a thousand other things outside the school's control. The inspectorate mocked the idea that a child should inevitably have attained a certain standard by a certain age; for they had seen the effects of a shifting population and family breakdown in urban areas. Lowe, ever the ideologue, took no account of this. Such was the outcry that Palmerston ordered the minute be not implemented until Parliament had debated the matter. The measures had, however, acquired the powerful support of Gladstone, who was attracted by the economising aspect.

However, the Revised Code was revised again, with less emphasis on payment by results, though two-thirds of the grant would still depend on the outcome of examinations: and, especially painful to Lowe, children would not be examined by age but by what their teachers considered their levels of attainment. With these compromises, the twice-revised code was passed. Lowe remained angry, however, and through his friend the editor of *The Times* fought a proxy war against the clerical conspiracy he regarded as having done him down. The deepening cynicism of Lowe's approach caused Arnold to reflect that the Revised Code was 'the heaviest blow dealt at civilisation and social improvement in my time.' He wanted a minister of education with a broader view of the State's responsibilities, rather than one who sought to enforce more rote-learning. Teachers and inspectors were demoralised by the code, and rote-learning bored the children, who were more frequently punished. Lowe did, however, champion the cause of the certificated teacher, whom he came to regard as the only remaining guardian of proper expenditure of public money.

Fitzjames Stephen had been cleverer than even he knew when describing Arnold's 'mission', for his determination to have people better educated was precisely that. Arnold savaged the 'twice revised code' in an article of that name in *Fraser's Magazine* in March 1862. He had it printed as a pamphlet, and Kay-Shuttleworth had copies sent to every MP and peer. Disraeli used it as his brief for attacking the code. Arnold had read Kay-Shuttleworth's own pamphlet on the subject and felt it 'too copious' for the general reader: and so decided to write his own, shorter, less detailed, but more pungent.[51] He said the revised code would 'reduce considerably the grants at present contributed by the state towards the support of schools for the poor.' Kay-Shuttleworth's estimate of the reduction was £175,000 a year, two-fifths of the existing grant. Arnold mocked Lowe's wishes as being 'to obtain the greatest possible quantity of reading, writing, and arithmetic for the greatest number'. He clearly wished to end the 'extravagant' expenditure incurred when, in the past, 'paying for discipline, for civilisation, for religious and moral training, for a superior instruction for clever and forward children'.[52] And, Arnold mused, it had been shocking that inspectors had spent their time and efforts commenting on the general discipline and tone of schools while 'the indispensable elements, the reading, writing, and arithmetic, were neglected'.

Given the damage Arnold feared the code would do, he regarded the government's claim that it would extend education into the 'waste places' as 'utterly and entirely delusive'.[53] He cited examples of schools in such places – in rural Wiltshire or Nottinghamshire – that would currently receive £30 a year but which, after the code, would have only £10. There might be the supplement of the prize-grant, awarded according to payment by results: but this would take no account of how generally good a school was, and how high its tone, merely of the statistical outcome of the tests in reading, writing and arithmetic. These were 'the sole objects judged worthy of the grants', though Lowe, under protest, had said the teaching of religion would be 'encouraged' in a similar way.[54] Since Arnold could not believe that he and his brother inspectors would see anything in a school that would force them to recommend a cut in its income, he assumed the scheme would be subverted from the start.

Nor did he think the government's standards especially demanding. He felt that only a quarter of those who attended a school could read proficiently. He quoted one inspector who said that in not more than twenty out of 169 schools he had visited could he find a class at the top of the school able to read a newspaper at sight. The government idea that three-fifths of children should be able to read at that standard was nonsense, especially if funding were cut. Arnold believed such proficiency would be taught only as a part of a general education in which an element of culture was placed at the heart of the experience, and not when teaching was merely by rote. 'If for the object you have in view,' he asked, 'good reading, cultivation in other subjects is necessary, why cut off all grants for these subjects in the hope of thereby getting better reading? How are you thus brought one step nearer to the end you have in view? How are you not rather pushed several steps farther back from it?'[55]

Arnold's most vociferous complaint was that the Privy Council Office had not bothered to consult those, such as himself, who were 'practically conversant with schools', and no notice had been given to voluntary bodies that mainly supported the schools.[56] 'Their own inspectors, education-societies, school-managers, are astounded,' he wrote. He was particularly angry at what he saw as the breaking of the link between the State and education. 'The revised code, by destroying – under the specious plea of simplifying, of giving greater liberty of action to managers – this vital connexion, takes the heart out of the old system.'[57] Arnold knew how poor the teaching was in some schools, and regretted that 'all serious guidance, all initiatory direction by the State' would end under the new system. 'It turns the inspectors into a set of registering clerks, with a mass of minute details to tabulate', who would 'necessarily withdraw their attention from the religious and general instruction and from the moral features of the school.' He said it was 'as if the generals of an army – for the inspectors have been the veritable generals of the educational army – were to have their duties limited to inspecting the men's cartouch boxes.'

In response to the outrage, Lowe had withdrawn proposals to test children under six, and had discovered the importance of encouraging schools to retain children after eleven. But he still planned to impose the code. Arnold did not know Lowe, and would not have known certain of his harsh characteristics, such as the class prejudice that he (to his subsequent regret and embarrassment) vented during the reform debates of 1866–7. However, in Arnold's conclusion, he almost seems to have Lowe's personality in his sights, when he condemns 'the selfish vulgar of the upper classes, saying in their hearts that this educational philanthropy is all rubbish, and that the less a poor man learns except his handicraft the better.' Arnold warned that if this cast of mind prevailed 'there will be only one sufferer; *the education of the people*.'[58]

Nor was this his last word. In his General Report as an Inspector for 1863 he wrote that the old system of inspection had effectively been ended – 'I am speaking of the old inspection considered as an agency for testing and promoting the intellectual force of schools, not as an agency for testing and promoting their discipline and their good building, fitting and so on.'[59] Because children were tested according to what it was felt they had attained, rather than in the context of their class, 'the life and power of each class as a whole, the fitness of its composition, its handling by the teacher' were not tested.[60] He argued that if the examination were persisted with it should be disconnected from the inspection, so the latter could be conducted with the most beneficial effects. He also confronted Lowe, with the realities of examining children in an impoverished area: 'When a boy of 11 or 12 years of age is so shy that he cannot open his mouth before a stranger, one may without harshness say that he ought to have been taught better and refuse him his grant; but when a child of seven is in this predicament one can hardly, without harshness, say the same thing.'[61]

Partly because of foreign travel, and partly because of discontent with the system, Arnold did not submit a General Report for the next four years. In his 1867 report he reflected on how things had changed in that time. He detected 'a deadness, a slackness, and a discouragement which are not the signs and accompaniment of progress. If I compare them with the schools on the Continent I find in them a lack of intelligent life much more striking now than it was when I returned from the Continent in 1859.'[62] There had been an 'ardent and animated body' of schoolmasters and pupil-teachers, but 'the school legislation of 1862 struck the heaviest possible blow at them; and the present slack and languid condition of our elementary schools is the inevitable consequence.'[63] The pupil-teacher system was especially hard hit: its numbers fell from 13,849 in 1863 to 10,955 by 1866.[64] The next year an additional grant was introduced for teacher training, for the system risked breaking down and leaving schools without properly qualified staff. Other problems remained. Arnold found the humanities suffering for want of financial incentive to teach them; with the decline of literature, history and geography, so did he record a further decline in the intellectual life of schools. He would complain about this for the rest of his career – he retired in 1886 – but it was not until the 1890s, after his death, that the system was finally changed.

The effects of the revised code would, in certain areas, be stark. Thomas Guthrie, chairman of a charity running a Ragged School in Edinburgh, wrote to Gladstone on 22 November 1864 to say that 'since the Educational Department of Govt reduced our allowances to a comparatively small sum we are thrown almost entirely on the good will of the people – I regret we ever trusted to anything else.'[65] He said the continued solvency of the Edinburgh school depended on a big public fund-raising meeting the following month: and he implored Gladstone to come and chair it, to attract a crowd. 'We all feel that could we get you persuaded to come north and preside over us, it would be hundreds to our coffers, and so some children saved from inevitable ruin.'

Lowe has been vilified by generations of educationists, following Arnold, for what one of his rare defenders, D. W. Sylvester, calls 'impoverishing the curriculum'.[66] However, Sylvester points to a lack of evidence for a broad curriculum before 1862; indeed, Newcastle's witnesses proved the opposite. Apart from the three Rs, a fourth – religious instruction – dominated the curriculum. Other subjects such as geography or history were sometimes taught, but only to the oldest and cleverest pupils. Also, many inspectors after 1862 found no evidence that payment by results had driven the more ornamental subjects out of the curriculum. Lowe's policy ensured the three Rs remained predominant; but it cannot be said to have altered much else.

III

Lowe believed that solving the problem posed by religion in Anglican schools was largely a matter of enforcing a 'conscience clause' so that Nonconformists and Catholics could attend them without being made to participate in worship or religious instruction there. This made Lowe enemies in the Church, who saw him imposing secularisation on a Christian country. However, as a utilitarian he continued to regard much education as useless: he said it 'does not communicate to us knowledge . . . it does not communicate to us the means of obtaining knowledge, and . . . it does not communicate to us the means of communicating knowledge', because of its continued concentration on dead languages.[67] He was especially afraid that the middle classes would seek to imitate the schools of their betters, with their largely ornamental curriculum that Lowe considered unequal to the challenges of modern life. What they needed, he believed, to acquaint them better with that life and to assist the country, were science and mathematics. And, ironically, he now was in no doubt that the only way to ensure a proper education was provided to these people was to enlist the State. Like Gladstone, when Lowe changed his mind, he did so comprehensively.

Lowe had refused to serve on the Newcastle Commission because of what, with typical haughtiness, he regarded as the low calibre of some of the other members. He had, however, appeared as a witness, and argued for reform and the end of imparting 'obsolete' knowledge.[68] As Lowe's biographer has noted, whereas Arnold wanted to civilise the nation Lowe wanted to modernise it. He believed the pursuit of pleasure in all its forms was the main goal of most people: Arnold, lacking this utilitarian cynicism, felt the pursuit of higher ideals, such as the development of taste, was more important. Lowe was also open to the attacks of other cynics: one, a pamphleteer called A. C. Weir, dismissed his arguments that he was seeking to liberate people from ignorance and to allow them to thrive in the modern world. He said, instead, that Lowe sought to use education as a means of social control, to help maintain the status quo against the 'destructive assaults of the untaught'. He claimed education would be a knife turned in the 'hands of the masses against the masses themselves.'[69] There is much in Lowe's own pronouncements, both about education and reform, that supports Weir's view. In his speech in Edinburgh in 1867 he had said:

> Is it not better that gentlemen should know the things which the working men know, only know them infinitely better in their details, so that they may be able, in their intercourse and their commerce with them, to assert the superiority over them which greater intelligence and leisure is sure to give, and to conquer back by means of a wider and more enlightened cultivation some of the influences which they have lost by political change? . . . The lower classes ought to be educated to discharge the duties cast upon them. They should also be educated that they may appreciate and defer to higher cultivation when they meet it; and the higher classes ought to be educated in a very different manner, in order that they may exhibit to the lower classes that higher education to which, if it were shown to them, they would bow down and defer.[70]

Lowe's biographer acquits him of class prejudice; and argues that he was merely paving the way for a meritocracy of the sort that came after 1918. Giving evidence to Taunton, Lowe had contended that some endowment money be used to fund school and university scholarships for the poor.[71]

He put down an amendment to the Public Schools Bill in 1868 to ensure boys in elite schools took an annual test – with the results made public – in subjects such as reading, writing, arithmetic, English history and geography that any child in a National School would have been trained in. This naked utilitarianism caused Arnold to ridicule him as a philistine, in *Friendship's Garland* and *Culture and Anarchy*: however, both agreed that what the middle classes did in education would shape what the working classes would do when given schools; so setting the right example was crucial. Arnold and he also agreed that getting education right should be a prelude to the widening of democracy, not its consequence. However, after 1867, it was too late for that.

IV

Gladstone told Arnold on 30 March 1869, having received *Culture and Anarchy*, that 'I have always thought it one of the great blanks of my life not to have known Dr Arnold . . . my work, like his, was hard, and I little anticipated how soon the door was to be closed against me.'[72] However, twenty-five years after his death, Dr Arnold prepared to exert his greatest influence yet on British education. His daughter Jane had, in 1850, married the Quaker industrialist William Forster; and in 1867 Forster, by then a Liberal MP whose view of education was profoundly shaped by the beliefs of his late father-in-law, made his first, unsuccessful, attempt to introduce a bill advancing elementary education.

Going to Bradford in the 1840s, he had been shocked by the ignorance in which most seemed to live: and believed the State had an obligation to rectify this. He joined a committee of Leeds and Bradford worthies in 1849 to lobby for a national system of education: but many who believed in education felt the State had no place interfering between parents and children. He was greatly informed too by the experience as a schools inspector of his brother-in-law Matthew Arnold. Gladstone appointed Forster vice-president of the Council, with special responsibility to introduce what would now be a government bill to improve the provision of education for the masses.

Forster's father had been a philanthropist and his mother an associate of the prison reformer Elizabeth Fry. He was of the same cast of mind, influenced by Carlyle, whom he had met in his twenties. He went into partnership with William Fison, a wool manufacturer, in Bradford in 1842, and over the next decade the business expanded. In 1852 he and Fison moved to Burley-in-Wharfedale, and became model industrialists. They established a mill school in 1854 and in 1859 a board of health, and built various public buildings at Burley. Forster frequently visited Burley school, and other schools in the district, studying education. He was nominated to the Taunton Commission on 'middle class schools', and served from 1864 until 1867.

In February 1869 Forster introduced a bill to implement some of Taunton's recommendations: notably to allow the inspection of endowed schools, to certificate schoolmasters according to their competence, and to put the funding of the schools on a basis that might allow more poor scholars to attend them. The schools sent some boys to university; but many left at sixteen or seventeen to be articled in the professions, or to become cadets in the services, and some at fourteen to work in family businesses, notably agriculture. These boys were vital to the professions in an age when many educated at the Clarendon schools would have found working for a living unnecessary or undesirable. It was important, therefore, that they had decent teaching.

Taunton had found many schools woefully deficient in teaching reading, writing and arithmetic. The British Medical Association found that many who sought to be trained as doctors had 'highly unsatisfactory' levels of knowledge in scientific subjects.[73] Nearly 40 per cent of young men in the previous decade had failed to pass the London University matriculation examination, thanks to inadequate preparation at school. Forster told the Commons in March 1869 that a total of 2,957 endowed schools had a gross income of £593,281, of which £340,000 was appropriated to education. It was, he said, an income that 'ought to do a great deal': but it did not.[74]

In one school the headmaster was content to live off the £200 endowment. Another, in a school with an endowment of £651, had made his nephew and son the next two masters in the school. The assistant commissioner who inspected it 'found the discipline most inefficient, and the instruction slovenly, immethodical, and unintelligent; there was no one subject in which the boys seemed to take an interest, and which had been taught with average care or success.' Nearby had been another school with thirteen pupils when the endowment would have provided for almost 'the education of the entire neighbourhood.' In an age of ambition this was unacceptable. All over the country, there were schools with hardly any pupils, the endowments acting as a slush fund for the masters, or providing them with a form of indoor relief. Forster also complained that these schools were increasingly patronised by the children of the rich, who did not need the subsidy. He hoped that the sons of indigent professional men, such as clergy, lower-ranking civil servants or schoolmasters, would benefit more from the charity of the schools.

'We need powers to form, if necessary, fresh trusts, and to reform the management of these endowments,' Forster said. 'We must be provided with power to give the schools, in many cases, fresh governing bodies, to enable the governors to see that the masters teach the subjects which the parents want the children to learn—to give the head master authority over his assistant masters—to give girls, whose education is now the worst cared for, that share in the advantages of these schools, which I am sure was the intention of many of the founders that they should have.'[75] He promised 'free admission by merit' to help put a ladder down to the children of the working classes, to help them out of poverty. To avoid the problem of rich parents having their children better prepared for an entrance examination, Forster promised elementary schools a right to a certain number of places.

Such a system had been established by the headmaster of King Edward VI's School, Birmingham, the Reverend Charles Evans. The school sponsored elementary schools as feeders, and Forster took it as a model. He was determined to start a rigorous system of inspections, to ensure schools did not revert to their former inadequacies. He shrank, at this stage, from legislating for towns to levy a rate to build more secondary schools. He hinted that the government would seek such a law in the next two or three sessions, after a wider change in the provision and regulation of elementary schools.

Forster's bill also sought to remove what he called the 'religious difficulty' in the endowed schools: 'All public schools must be open to the public. It is the pride and glory of these Endowed Schools that they are public; that means that they are open to the public; and it is our duty to see that that large portion of the public who are not members of the Church of England are not excluded from them.'[76] He wanted boarding schools with Anglican masters to offer places to day boys of other denominations, who could follow their religious observances at home. Nor did he wish to enforce attendance at Anglican acts of worship.

The Charity Commissioners would be charged to end the improper use of endowment funds. Children would be examined annually and masters issued with certificates of competence – or not, as the case might be. Forster was driven by a modern vision that he allied to the spirit of the age when, as he said, many of the foundations with which he was now dealing were started. 'Now, again, new ideas have power— this new central idea, bringing with it many others, that no special class is to guide the destinies of England—that not the aristocracy, nor the bourgeoisie, no, nor yet the working class, is to govern England—but that England for the future is in truth to be self-governed; all her citizens taking their share, not by class distinction, but by individual worth.'[77]

Forster wished girls to have more educational chances and to have a greater share of the funds. However, he suspected that even if that happened the demand for places by girls would be less than by boys, and boys would be disadvantaged by having such a cut in their funding. Some MPs advocated developing the intellectual culture of girls; one, George Gregory, dismissed it. He said it had been 'too readily assumed that one of the principal things for which women were qualified was teaching. He would remind the House that the great business of their lives lay in the domestic circle, and things which could not be taught in schools.'[78] Northcote asserted that 'nobody wished that women should be educated in precisely the same way as men'.[79]

The Queen's Speech in February 1870 announced that 'a Bill has been prepared for the enlargement, on a comprehensive scale, of the means of National Education.'[80] Mill wrote to Dilke a few days later about the 'struggle' the Education League proposed to have over church schools. 'I myself would rather, and I should think that the intelligent part of the working class would rather, have no National Education Act for the next five years than have one which should comprise the rush to establish schools on the denominational principle . . . all schools founded by the Government, either general or local, should be purely secular.'[81] He said on this he 'would make no compromise'.

Lowe, now Chancellor of the Exchequer, had come under the influence of Jowett, who had told him that, having considered the question with other dons, they had concluded that 'the first step was to have educational districts on which the inspectors could report, and that this would involve divesting the inspectors of their denominational character.'[82] Jowett and his friends were, however, against compelling parents to send their children to school. Where Lowe was ahead of his party – and of Jowett – was in believing in compulsion. This must, he felt as a matter of logic, come from central government, implemented through local boards. Unrepentant about the Revised Code, he wanted these boards to provide incentives for the highest results. The system he desired should be secular in character.

Jowett, who had come to see Lowe as education's brightest hope in the Commons, was alarmed by the rigidity of his new position – Lowe, as a logician, could be little other than rigid – and on one occasion 'ventured to give him a short lecture about being more conciliatory, and the necessity of uniting persons and classes if he means to do anything about education.'[83] Lowe seems not to have listened. He argued two other points that Forster would adopt in the Education Bill of 1870: the end of denominational inspections, as Jowett had wished, and State funding being made available to denominational schools only if they had a conscience clause, to allow pupils to opt out of religious instruction. Lowe then set out a blueprint for the new system, also specified in the bill, whereby all parishes had a duty to have a school, and the Privy Council had a duty to assist it. Although the 1870 Act was Forster's child, Lowe was a parent too.

A memorandum Forster submitted to Gladstone on 21 October included four options for a national system, one of which was lifted from Lowe's Edinburgh speech. One was for a greater voluntary system, which Forster believed would not work; another was for an entirely publicly funded one, which he feared would be cripplingly expensive and would remove all incentives for such a voluntary system as existed to continue. The third plan was to allow local authorities to levy a rate to build schools where no other local means could be found, to avoid 'educational destitution'; but he considered this impracticable because of the threat of conflict with ratepayers who refused to fund denominational schools.[84] So the fourth option was adopted, with educational 'districts' based on the parish set up to provide schooling.

Gladstone, for whom God suffused everything, was alert from the outset to the difficulties of religion in setting up a wider provision of State education. His party was thick with Nonconformists whose differences with the Established Church he had no option but to respect. With his customary pragmatism, he wrote to Lord de Grey, the Lord President of the Council, on 4 November 1869, having read Forster's submission, and asked: 'Why not adopt frankly the principle that the state or the local community should provide the secular teaching, and either leave the option to the ratepayer to go beyond this *sine qua non*, if they think fit, within the limits of the conscience clause, or else simply leave the parties themselves to find Bible and other religious education from voluntary sources?'[85] Prussia had dealt with a similar problem when establishing State provision, and Gladstone asked de Grey to see how it had done so. Unfortunately, the absolutist fashion in which Bismarck dealt with such questions was not easily replicable in Britain.

Mill had in part enunciated the principles upon which the 1870 Elementary Education Act was founded in a letter of January 1868, two years before the bill's introduction. 'All parents should be required to have their children taught certain things, being left free to select the teachers, but the sufficiency of the teaching being ensured by a govern-ment inspection of schools and by a real and searching examination of pupils.'[86] He was firmly opposed to the government's having any direct control over schools, all the governance residing in a local school committee. So Forster's bill of February 1870 was permissive rather than compulsory, and sought to provide an education – for which parents would still have to pay a fee, and which children would not be compelled to avail themselves of – to all between the ages of five and twelve who wanted it. A system of local boards would regulate the schools, as Mill had envisaged, and would have the power to pass a by-law compelling attendance.

As long ago as 1852 Mill had written to the Reverend Henry Carr, a South Shields clergyman, to tell him that 'what the poor as well as the rich require is not to be indoctrinated, is not to be taught other people's opinions, but to be induced and enabled to think for themselves . . . they cannot read too much. Quantity is of more importance than quality, especially all reading which relates to human life and the ways of mankind: geography, voyages and travels, manners and customs, and romances, which must tend to awaken their imagination and give them some of the meaning of self-devotion and heroism, in short, to unbru-talise them.'[87] Others – such as Lowe, before 1867 – seemed keen to keep them brutalised. Mill understood this to be a deficiency in the education of the upper and middle classes, and until that was resolved – as Dr Arnold and his disciples had sought to do – there would be no light for the lower orders.

Forster's bill was debated in the Commons on 17 February 1870. In a 100-minute speech he claimed the children of the lower classes who were getting an education were getting an 'imperfect' one.[88] The govern-ment was not helping 1 million children aged between six and ten, and another half-million between ten and twelve. He conceded that some of these might go to schools that were voluntary aided: but added that 'the schools which do not receive government assistance are, generally speaking, the worst schools, and those least fitted to give a good educa-tion to the children of the working classes.'[89] He conceded there were exceptions: but his assertion would be borne out by the inspectors' reports.

Attendance was especially bad in industrial cities. In Liverpool 20,000 children between the ages of five and thirteen attended no school and another 20,000 attended a bad one. In Manchester a quarter in that age group – 16,000 – were not at school, but had fewer really poor schools. 'Leeds appears to as bad as Liverpool; and so also, I fear, is Birmingham.'[90] This was why a demand came from all over the country for a system of national education. Forster added: 'I believe that the country demands from us that we should at least try to do two things, and that it shall be no fault of ours if we do not succeed in doing them—namely, cover the country with good schools, and get the parents to send their children to those schools. I am aware, indeed, that to hope to arrive at these two results may be thought Utopian; but our only hope of getting over the difficulties before us, is to keep a high ideal before our minds, and to realise to ourselves what it is we are expected to try to do.'[91]

The government's solution would be bureaucratic: the division of the country into districts, and surveys done in each of the availability of education, to ascertain what should be provided. Forster said England was far behind, in municipal organisation, other European countries and America. The State would provide only where essential. He said that inspection, which had hitherto been denominational, would no longer be so: it was discriminatory and inefficient. He said that if the taxpayer was funding education it should not be an education to whose religious nature he would object. A conscience clause would be included, that allowed a child to be withdrawn from any religious instruction of which his parents did not approve. All children would, though, be taught the Bible so as to have a 'Christian training'.[92]

There was no question of the State paying for the education, above and beyond the grant already made. It could not – or rather would not – afford it. The parents of children who had attended school in 1869 had paid £120,000 for the privilege. Some wanted these fees abolished, but Forster feared that the total cost if education were made free for all might be two or three times that figure. And if the working classes had free education, the middle classes would demand it too. 'Why should we relieve the parent from all payments for the education of his child?' he asked.[93] In cases of absolute hardship 'free tickets' would be given to children and those tickets would have 'no stigma of pauperism attached to them'. Education would be funded a third by the parent, a third by taxes and a third from local funds. Where those were inadequate an education rate would be levied. However unpopular this was, Forster argued that it would 'save the prison rate and the pauper rate'.

Forster then dealt with compulsory attendance. 'To leave it alone is to leave the children untaught, and to force the taxpayers and ratepayers to pay for useless schools.'[94] He said he was putting before the House the principle of direct compulsion. It had already been conceded, in that no child could work unless it went to school for part of the day. The Act would therefore place a duty upon a parent to send a child to school, and on the local board to enforce it, using a by-law passed by the board. Parents who shirked this duty without a reasonable excuse – including there not being a school within a mile of where they lived – could be fined up to 5s.

The government's aims were 'to bring elementary education within the reach of every English home, aye, and within the reach of those children who have no homes.'[95] This revolution – for it was nothing less – would require 'enormous labour', but that was the State's duty. He concluded with an argument straight from Lowe:

We must not delay. Upon the speedy provision of elementary education depends our industrial prosperity. It is of no use trying to give technical teaching to our artisans without elementary education; uneducated labourers—and many of our labourers are utterly uneducated—are, for the most part, unskilled labourers, and if we leave our work-folk any longer unskilled, notwithstanding their strong sinews and determined energy, they will become over-matched in the competition of the world. Upon this speedy provision depends also, I fully believe, the good, the safe working of our constitutional system. To its honour, Parliament has lately decided that England shall in future be governed by popular government. I am one of those who would not wait until the people were educated before I would trust them with political power. If we had thus waited we might have waited long for education; but now that we have given them political power we must not wait any longer to give them education.[96]

MPs praised Forster for his measure, and for his courage. However, dissenters did not wish to subsidise Church of England schools – or to be forced to send their children to them, as in some areas they would be the only schools available. For attendance to be compulsory, this had to be overcome. It was feared elections to school boards would become a battleground for sectarianism. Therefore, on 14 March George Dixon, one of three Liberal MPs for Birmingham, moved an amendment to force all schools assisted by the rates to be non-sectarian: and to ensure that in other schools religious instruction could be given at a specified time when children from different denominations could miss it. It could not, the amendment said, be left to local authorities to decide what the religious instruction in their schools would be. Dixon's amendment was consistent with the ideals Joe Chamberlain had drawn up for the Birmingham Education Society in 1867.

Chamberlain was the driving force behind the National Education League and, although he did not yet sit in Parliament and was unknown to the Liberal front bench, it would be he who would shape the debate on education, unseen and unheard. He had, on behalf of the League, sent what he described as an 'inflammatory' circular to all its branches advising Nonconformists to let their MPs know the force of their objections to Forster's proposals.[97] He briefed Dixon, whom he knew well, and arranged for him to lead a deputation of forty-six MPs and more than 400 Nonconformists to Downing Street on 9 March. Chamberlain joined the deputation, and it was the first time he met Gladstone.

He addressed the Prime Minister on behalf of the League, principally on their fear that the bill would hand over education to the Church of England, but also on the importance of the State paying fees for children whose parents could not afford them. Chamberlain also argued that a 'conscience clause' would be inoperable. It was on that point, notably, that the government and the Nonconformists would disagree. William Harcourt, a Liberal, thought the notion of rival sectarians teaching religion out of school hours would be 'nothing but denominationalism run mad.'[98] The government agreed to modify the bill to allow all shades of feeling to be represented: not least because, as Lowe said on 15 March, the State owed a debt to the voluntary system for all it had done before the State had recognised 'the undoubted duty of the Government of England to provide for the education of the people'.[99] The voluntary system did not deserve to be trampled under a desire for uniformity. Forster, however, became irritated by the infighting between various sorts of Liberal and various sorts of clergy. He wrote on 1 April 1870 to Charles Kingsley, a supporter of the National League. 'I still fully believe I shall get my bill through,' he told him, 'but I wish parsons, Church and others would all remember as much as you do that children are growing into savages while they are trying to prevent one another from helping them.'[100]

It took until May for the Cabinet to devise suitable compromises. These included the opting out of religious instruction and the end of inspection of that subject. They also permitted school boards to give money to denominational schools, provided it was used only for secular instruction; and schools subsidised by the rates should offer non-denominational religious instruction. Lowe, however, was the only member of the Cabinet to object: notably to allowing money for 'secular instruction'. He felt opposition to such a proposal was so strong that the bill would be lost.

He suggested to Gladstone that the money come from the Treasury, not local rates. 'Increase the Privy Council Grant by one half and the thing is done and done in the way most agreeable to the recipients. If this were done I should relieve the Board of ratepayers from any connection whatever with schools other than rate-supported schools. You would thus attain a double advantage, i.e. circumscribe the functions of the dreaded local authority and relieve your proposal from the obloquy of a fresh burden on the rates.'[101] Gladstone agreed and within a few hours had persuaded the rest of the Cabinet. Lowe had, by his refusal to accept the original plan, caused the foundation of what came to be known as the 'dual system': the coexistence of board schools and voluntary schools.

Gladstone outlined this to the Commons at the bill's committee stage on 16 June. He was proceeding 'without involving the State in religious controversy, but confining its central function strictly to its work of obtaining beneficial secular results . . . the great and paramount advantage and blessing of elementary education.'[102] Disraeli said his party had been prepared to support the bill as it stood. He was willing to recognise 'the determination of the great majority of the people in this country that "national education" is to be a "religious education".'[103] However, he was 'at a loss' to know how what Gladstone had just proposed would achieve that. He saw instead 'vacillation of purpose'.[104] Not only did he not have a 'precise and clear idea' what would happen to voluntary schools that were unwilling to be supported by school boards, he also believed there were members of the Cabinet who did not.[105] The bill was therefore a sham, and he and his side could not support it. He wanted longer to consider what the government was proposing, not just a few hours.

There remained serious objections to what it was feared would be a monopoly of Church of England schools. Even the promise that schools could be financed out of the rates, with no denominational religious instruction, was felt an inadequate safeguard against the sectarianisation of those schools. It was feared boards would be dragged into local rows with schools, and that many such complaints would end up with the Privy Council, which would not cope. There was no desire to stop teaching religion: it was felt to be especially good for, as one MP put it, 'precisely that class for which a system of primary education was specially intended – namely, the toiling millions of our countrymen, in order to soften the asperity of their lot, and to irradiate the darkness of their present life with the light of a hope that is full of immortality.'[106] Yet to contrive an ecumenical form of instruction backed by all religions and denominations appeared impossible.

Forster wanted basic religious instruction in schools. He doubted it would be so well organised or delivered if provided only out of school, for he also doubted either children or their parents would attend, or ensure attendance at, such instruction in the evenings or on Saturday afternoons. He could not understand why fellow Liberals were prepared to use 'the force of religious and denominational zeal' to prevent the early attack upon 'the mass of ignorance, destitution, misery and crime' that was the lot of the lowest classes.[107] After four days of debate, secularism was rejected by 421 votes to 60. The bill was back on course, but only because of Conservative support, and by dividing the Liberal party between its Anglican and Nonconformist wings. George Trevelyan wrote to Gladstone on 21 June that 'an extension of the grant to denominational schools', having been 'definitely offered and accepted as a main condition of the Education Bill', meant that he would have to resign as a Civil Lord of the Admiralty.[108] 'I cannot compromise my future action in this matter,' he explained.

Some MPs could not understand why, if the lower classes were to be forced to go to school, the middle and upper classes should not be forced too. The government had to handle claims that families in agricultural districts would be severely affected economically if their children were compelled to attend school rather than helping with farm work. Concessions were made on universal compulsion for this reason. The bill was also amended to allow parents, on the grounds of conscience, to withdraw children from school at a specific time when religious instruction alien to their beliefs was being given. One clause – clause 25 – to allow poor children at denominational schools to have their fees paid by the board slipped through without debate. It caused outrage when spotted by Nonconformists after Royal Assent, who feared subsidising children at schools of whose doctrines they disapproved.

The bill had its third reading on 22 July. Its opponents threatened to seek to amend the Act the minute Parliament returned for the 1871 session. There were also concerns that State funding had not been found to ensure that all families could afford to pay the minimal fees. On compulsion and fees, change would come within a few years. The opponents had mainly been Liberal Nonconformists, and they saw the measure would pass not least because of support from the Conservatives: a clear, early sign, in retrospect, of the reforming tenor of Disraeli's ministry from 1874.

It was also the start of a fractiousness in Gladstone's party that would lead to his defeat in 1874. Gladstone admitted the final measure was not 'perfect': but warned his opponents against their 'declaration of war' upon it, intimating that the country would not forgive further rancour just when the people had realised the national and moral importance of getting more children into education. He gave the voluntary schools credit for avoiding a narrowness in their interpretation of Christianity, and expressed the hope that their sense of philanthropy would help them overcome any denominational difficulties. He welcomed the idea that schoolmasters should engage in 'free exposition of the scriptures', and pleaded for those who still disagreed with that not to impede the education of countless young people by carrying their objections further.[109] Once the bill had gone through the Lords, England and Wales had a system of national education within the reach of every child, providing a school place to between a million and a million and a half who previously had no access to one. And in the Lords, Shaftesbury pointed out that the 300 Ragged Schools, with their average attendance of over 32,000 and with teachers of every denomination, had never in the twenty-five years of their existence experienced the slightest problem with religion.[110]

Nonconformists, though, would not let the religious matter go. They protested that the Act was 'inconsistent with the principles of Religious Equality' and especially objected 'to the specific proposal now agitated on the School Boards of the Country to pay the fees of indigent children attending denominational schools'.[111] The Act did allow school boards to establish free schools for indigent children, or to remit fees in schools where they were normally paid, or to pay fees to denominational schools. Forster, however, had told the board in Liverpool that it would not be 'just' if it did not use 'the whole moral weight of the Department against those Members of School Boards who are anxious to avoid using the Education Rate for the maintenance of denominational schools and who wish to provide for the free education of indigent children in schools under the control of the school board and not under the control of private managers.'[112] His party, from top to bottom, was hopelessly divided: and the drive to stop the subsidy of Anglican schools continued to be led by Chamberlain, laying the foundations of his break with the party over Irish Home Rule in 1886. For the rest of the Gladstone ministry there were attempts to repeal the clause allowing the funding of Anglican schools. It succeeded only in highlighting Liberal divisions.

A Liberal politician, barely four years later, would dismiss the Act as 'of the nature of a very small reform'. John Morley claimed that 'no one pretends that it is anything approaching to a final solution of a complex problem. But the government insisted, whether rightly or wrongly, that their Act was as large a measure as public opinion was ready to support or to endure. It was clearly agreed among the government and the whole of the party at their backs, that at some time or other, near or remote, if public instruction was to be made genuinely effective, the private, voluntary or denominational system would have to be replaced by a national system.'[113] However, Morley argued that the government had introduced measures that would strengthen the very system it wanted to replace, thereby making the ultimate aim harder to attain. Nonetheless, an important principle – of State provision – had been established.

V

Even as the government received – and was, it seemed, quite chastened by – the Newcastle report, there was growing outrage about the great public schools, notably by general consent the greatest, and richest, of them all, Eton College. Two large-circulation periodicals ran articles highly critical of the school. Matthew Higgins, an Old Etonian and journalist, wrote three articles between May 1860 and March 1861 in the

Cornhill Magazine, under the pseudonym 'Paterfamilias'; and Henry Sidgwick, then a young Cambridge philosopher of radical views who would later cause the university tests to be scrapped, wrote one in *Macmillan's* in February 1861. Higgins alleged that fellows – governors – of the school were siphoning off funds meant for educating the poor, and Sidgwick put a price on the racket – around £1,000 per fellow per year 'for doing a minimum of work; and it may be doubted whether this minimum might not be most advantageously dispensed with.'[114] He branded this 'sinecurism' and noted that 'few men, suddenly transferred from a sphere of confined drudgery to £1,000 a year, and nothing to do, would be likely to become useful members of society.'[115] Sidgwick also observed that masters at Eton made money not so much from the salaries paid by the foundation – £45 a year – but from taking in more pupils, which could make them between £1,000 and £2,000 a year. Each extra boy meant another £20 a year, so there were incentives to expand the school beyond a point where boys could be satisfactorily taught and accommodated.

As well as being badly governed and mismanaging its endowments, Eton was said to be failing to teach a sufficiently broad curriculum – something that the pace of change elsewhere rendered all the more glaring – and corrupting the morals of its boys. Since it was regarded as the nursery of Britain's statesmen – Gladstone was but one of its old boys – this was regarded as deeply corrosive and of wider significance. Sidgwick wrote that 'we hope that no inopportune reverence for obsolete forms, and the letter of the founder's will, may prevent the utmost being done to make Eton more fit for the glorious work she has undertaken – that of educating the aristocracy of England.'[116] Also, in an age with an ever more vigilant and inquiring press, scandals in public schools could not be ignored or hushed up as they had been a generation earlier. Sidgwick called the school 'a perfect specimen of those "comfortable bodies" which our ruthless reforming age has insisted upon making uncomfortable, where it has not swept them away altogether. They are a useless relic of past ages – a remnant of the monastic life; ideally, a life of self-denying and learned seclusion, actually so often a life of luxurious and unlearned sloth.'

Gladstone urged Palmerston to launch a new inquiry, along the lines of Newcastle's, into the conduct of the great schools. On 18 July 1861 the government announced its decision to appoint a Royal Commission to look not just at King Henry VI's Foundation at Eton, but at eight other leading establishments: Harrow, Charterhouse, Westminster, St Paul's, Winchester, Rugby, Shrewsbury and Merchant Taylors'. Lord Clarendon, the former Foreign Secretary, was made chairman. This was a useful appointment for Palmerston, since Clarendon deeply disagreed with him and Russell, his Foreign Secretary (who within a fortnight would go to the Lords as Earl Russell), over policy towards Italy, which was about to be unified. While they would have liked to dispense with Clarendon altogether, he was much valued by the Queen and Prince Albert, so finding him an important public position that took him away from foreign affairs was the next best option.

Clarendon's objectivity was assisted by his accomplishment – rare for a grandee of his generation – of not having attended a public school, having been privately tutored by a master at Christ's Hospital before entering St John's College, Cambridge, at sixteen. He intensely disapproved of the narrowness of the school curriculum and the exhaustive emphasis on Latin and Greek. His commissioners included an aesthete, a professor from Cambridge and one from Oxford, two other peers and an MP. Public opinion – recalled by M. E. Grant Duff, the Liberal MP for Elgin – was that the education at public schools was 'extremely bad' and 'sadly inadequate' to the requirements of the age.[117]

The universities had begun to modernise in the 1850s, though progress was as slow as it would be for the schools. Prince Albert had been shocked by the limitations of the curriculum at Cambridge when he became chancellor in 1847, and had been enlisted by enlightened dons who sought to expand the subjects studied beyond mathematics and the Classics. William Whewell of Trinity, the professor of philosophy and the most powerful man in the university at the time, had told Albert that he wished study to include 'some of the most valuable portions of modern science and literature'.[118] Whewell and Charles Lyell, the geologist, drew up a paper describing Cambridge's moribund state, which they sent to Albert. The main purpose of the university was to train men for the priesthood. Standards of tuition were low and clergymen held chairs in subjects they were completely unqualified to teach. The humanities were almost completely neglected. Albert compared what was happening at Cambridge with the wide range of learning at universities in his native Germany, and preached the importance and urgency of reform.

Later in 1847 Albert commissioned research into the curriculum and found an examination system, apart from mathematics, based entirely on knowledge of the Classics and the Scriptures. He soon found Whewell trying to obstruct him, his enthusiasm for change being confined to reforms that could be implemented slowly – he suggested no new scientific theories should be taught for 100 years, so their accuracy could be judged. However, Albert found allies in Robert Phelps, the vice-chancellor, and a subsequent incumbent of the post, Henry Philpott. Philpott, aware the university seemed like a great, down-at-heel theological college, had suggested to Albert that it should start teaching natural sciences and history. A tripos, or degree course, would be established for the natural sciences, but also one for the moral sciences, to include history, law, moral philosophy and political economy. Whewell remained resistant, but Albert talked him round. At the end of 1848 the Senate of the University approved the reforms, as well as a new mathematical tripos, and Oxford soon had to modernise or fall behind.

In the 1850s both universities were further regulated and reformed by Acts of Parliament: Oxford in 1854, Cambridge two years later. This compelled both to allow Nonconformists to matriculate and to admit them to degrees in subjects other than theology, but stopped short of allowing them fellowships or senior appointments, since only Anglicans could join a college foundation. A commission had looked into the workings of each university and had been received with almost uniform hostility at both: neither felt the way in which they regulated themselves was any of the government's business, and both vice-chancellors refused to cooperate. Oxford had been heavily criticised for narrowness, despite having founded schools of natural science, law and history in 1850. The following year Cambridge instituted triposes in the natural and moral sciences.

The conduct of these universities mattered because of the near-monopoly Oxford and Cambridge had on English higher education. Scotland had St Andrews, Glasgow, Aberdeen and Edinburgh of ancient foundation (between 1413 and 1583); Trinity College, Dublin had been founded in 1592. Wales had had the college at Lampeter since 1822. Despite the foundations earlier in the nineteenth century of universities in London and at Durham, the rest of England was slow to advance tertiary education, and the standards of teaching and research in England outside the two ancient establishments were hardly exemplary.

The universities were shaking off restrictive practices that defeated the original objects of those foundations. Goldwin Smith, an Oxford don who became secretary of the Commission into his university, wrote in 1894 that 'liberalism soon took the practical shape of an effort to reform and emancipate the University, to strike off the fetters of medieval statutes from it and from its Colleges, set it free from the predominance of ecclesiasticism, recall it to its proper work, and restore it to the nation.'[119] Something similar would happen to the public and, later, the endowed grammar schools. Progressive dons, such as Jowett of Balliol, by then one of the key figures at Oxford, argued for the expansion of 'intellectual aristocracy'. 'It is of the greatest use', he wrote, 'to awaken in people's minds a sense of the necessity of a liberal education for more than the numbers contained in Harrow, Winchester, Eton etc. The abused Grammar-school and Charity foundations supply abundant means.'[120]

Clarendon spent May and June 1862 touring the schools, and started to take evidence that summer, a year after the publication of Newcastle. Clarendon had three principal considerations: the property and income of the foundations, their administration and management and, most significant, 'the system and course of study pursued in them, to the religious and moral training of the boys, their discipline and general education'.[121] As with Newcastle, questionnaires were sent to headmasters and assistant masters; and the commissioners visited each school to see for themselves. They also took evidence from governors, former pupils, and eminent scholars. They found great discrepancies in wealth: Eton's endowment raised £20,000 a year, Harrow's just £1,000. They found that good management led to better results: 'The practice introduced by Dr Arnold at Rugby, of meeting all his assistants for consultation at frequent intervals – a practice which has been continued, with some interruptions, by his successors and is at present maintained by Dr Temple – appears to have had the happiest results.'[122] Eton and Harrow had also adopted this collegiate method, and Clarendon found them to have benefited accordingly. The Commission however deplored schools, including Eton and Winchester, who drew their masters from a narrow slice of academia, either old boys or fellows of certain Oxford and Cambridge colleges, and excluding all others.

What the report calls 'a gentleman's education' had originally been confined to learning the classical languages.[123] This in time broadened

slightly to include ancient history and even geography, the latter presumably in order to give the boys an idea of where the sites of ancient
civilisation were. They observed that time spent on other subjects that
were not examined appeared wasted 'unless attention is stimulated by
the fear of punishment, or by some form of reward'.[124] The Commission
criticised the means of instilling the Classics, which concentrated on
extensive reading, construing and grammar lessons, much repeated.
What it called 'the assiduous practice of repetition' was 'worse than
useless', because the boredom it created made it 'slovenly'.[125] Eton had
broadened its classical curriculum from what one old boy, Sir John
Coleridge, said had once been a diet of 'Homer, Virgil and Horace; we
never ceased doing Homer, Virgil and Horace'. It now did the Greek
testament, the *Odyssey*, Aeschylus, Euripides, Theocritus, Thucydides,
Demosthenes, Virgil's *Georgics*, Lucretius, Horace, Tacitus and Cicero.[126]

However, progress was at hand: some schools were teaching the new-
fangled subjects of arithmetic and mathematics, and even using the
results of examinations in them to influence where a boy was placed in
the school. And in all except Eton two hours a week was now set aside
for learning modern languages: mainly French and German. At Eton
such teaching was available, but only if a boy could be bothered: the
master who taught French said that in such cases the headmaster 'does
not appear to like to interfere'.[127] French had been compulsory at Harrow
since 1851 and maths since 1837. Dr Edward Balston, the headmaster of
Eton, said school existed to teach boys things they could not learn at
home; and 'there are some things which boys will learn of themselves
or at home, and French is one', he said.[128] Questioned on this, Balston
said he thought that if a boy wanted to learn French he should do so
before he came to Eton, where the school would do what it could to
'keep it up', as it did with English. However, when questioned about
that, he said the teaching of English was not satisfactory either.

The Classics, however, which Balston thought 'the basis of all education and mental training' were 'in themselves distasteful to boys' and
acquired only by 'laborious perseverance'. At Winchester, by contrast,
French was taught to the whole school, and attempts by boys to make
life difficult for the Frenchman who taught it would result in their being
reported to the headmaster, at which point their lives became difficult
too.[129] Charterhouse had gone even further, with some boys in the Sixth
Form learning German; and it taught history until 'the reign of George

III'.[130] Harrow had two resident Frenchmen, one of whom taught German. Lord Lyttelton asked Montagu Butler, the headmaster of Harrow, whether 'a boy of 13 may know French fairly well'. Butler answered: 'We have now one boy who speaks French better than English.'[131]

The report quotes one 'experienced and eminent Head Master' as saying 'I wish we could teach more history, but as to teaching it in set lessons I should not know how to do it.'[132] It was a problem at certain of the poorer schools to attract the right teachers: the Commission found they were underpaid, a problem that could be rectified only by making the schools more prosperous. Rugby, whose numbers had risen to over 460 boys thanks to the momentum created by Arnold, could afford good masters, and by the time of Clarendon's investigations was teaching both mathematics and modern languages to a high standard, and encouraging excellence by a system of prizes.

With the exception of Charterhouse, which had a maximum of twenty boys in a form and minimum of nine, the nine schools had what would now be regarded as alarming pupil–teacher ratios. The smallest class at Rugby was twenty-four boys, the largest forty-two. Eton, though, was even worse, with forty-eight boys in the largest division and thirteen in the smallest. It was also the biggest school, with 806 boys against Charterhouse's 116. Eton had, however, improved since the era of Dr Keate in the 1820s, when 200 boys were in a single division. The Commission also commended competition for prizes: but confirmed that they should be of high esteem rather than great in number. Most damning, though, was the evidence from the ancient universities that the standards of undergraduates from these schools were generally poor, and that many struggled in examinations whose calibre was not, they admitted, high. An Oxford examiner testified that of the forty-seven out of 168 candidates who had failed a university examination '43 failed so universally as to show that they were "utterly unfit to undergo any examination whatsoever".'[133] The conclusions the Commission drew were damning: 'Of the time spent at school by the generality of boys, much is absolutely thrown away as regards intellectual progress, either from ineffective teaching, from the continued teaching of subjects in which they cannot advance, or from idleness, or from a combination of these causes.'[134]

One witness said of Eton that 'position and influence in the school, which are the things that a boy most desires, are gained chiefly, and almost exclusively, by excellence in the cricket-field or on the river . . . intellectual distinctions have little weight in this respect . . . a boy has no chance of becoming one of the leading boys in the school by work.'[135] He was none other than Oscar Browning, then teaching Classics, and who would go on after being sacked from Eton for social nonconformity to become a great figure at Cambridge. If a boy went out of bounds and saw a master, his duty was to run away: to not do so was deemed 'disrespectful'. And although drinking in public houses was banned, there were two – the Christopher and Tap – where they did go, and nobody thought to interfere.[136] As for religious observance, boys regarded attendance at chapel on weekday afternoons as 'little more than a roll call'.[137] Browning also played down any idea that Eton was a nursery of intellectuals. He said that he had only known two boys 'of refined minds, and very gentlemanly manners, and fond of literature.'[138]

Clarendon asked him whether he thought the chapel services 'satisfactory'. 'The services do not produce a satisfactory effect on the boys,' he replied.[139] Clarendon then asked: 'And are they not productive of any reverential feeling?' Browning answered: 'I should say not; the boys' object is certainly to get out as soon as they can.' Clarendon later quizzed him on the teaching of modern languages, of which Browning was in favour: but he said it ought to be done by the classical masters. 'Do you think that a French master cannot keep order and discipline in his class?' Clarendon asked him. 'Experience goes to prove that he cannot,' Browning replied. 'That is to say, that such a Frenchman has yet to be found,' Clarendon suggested.[140] Browning said that the present French master was an Englishman: but he was regarded as inferior to his colleagues because he did not teach Classics. There had been a French assistant who, Browning added, 'was a distinguished man, but he did not understand English boys.'

Goodford, the Provost of Eton, admitted he would always prefer an Old Etonian when appointing staff if there were rival candidates of similar quality. He maintained he would 'fearlessly' appoint a non-Etonian if Etonian candidates were 'inferior', 'but still I say I should like first of all a good Eton man.'[141] Many of these Eton men were, like Browning, straight from university – the sister foundation of King's College, Cambridge, which supplied (as Sidgwick had pointedly observed in his *Macmillan's* article) a disproportionate number of the school's masters. 'Do you think it a point of importance in a large school like Eton to have for junior assistant classical masters men who have had experience in school teaching?' Clarendon asked Goodford. 'No,' the Provost replied. He later told Clarendon that it was 'most desirable', in the interests of maintaining the spirit of the school, that the masters should be 'all Eton men'.[142]

In his evidence, Balston had to admit he was not master in his own house. He could do as he pleased in matters affecting the Oppidans – the 750 boys whose parents paid for their education – but had to seek the permission of the Provost to do anything that might affect the seventy boys on the Foundation. Clarendon quizzed him about how differently he ran his school from how Arnold had run Rugby. 'If I may be allowed to express an opinion,' Balston responded, testily, 'I should say that Dr Arnold was not an every-day man; and it does not follow that what he achieved is attainable by all other Head Masters.'[143] Balston, a divine, then twisted the knife. 'I should also be disposed to question the results of his preaching, eminently successful though it is meant to have been. I think the religious character formed by it was not so genuine as it should have been . . . what I have noticed in Eton men has been an absence of all mannerism, if I may so call it, a freedom from ostentation in the conscientious discharge of what they consider their duty as Christian men.'

Since roughly a third of boys from these schools went to Oxford or Cambridge, the quality of those universities was not improved: and a significant proportion went into the Army, where a preliminary course of education, particularly in mathematics, was often required before they could be of any use. Natural sciences were almost non-existent, and the Commission argued that every boy should have a grounding in them. Where an attempt was made to teach them, such as at Winchester, the methods were 'worthless'.[144] Some schools outside the nine, notably Cheltenham College, City of London School and King's College School, London, had all experimented in this way, and were held up as models to the older, grander establishments. It was possible, the Commission argued, to give a good education that was not saturated in the Classics.

The Reverend Dr George Moberly, the headmaster of Winchester, who had been in post since 1835 and would, after his retirement, become Bishop of Salisbury, was asked: 'Are the physical sciences not of value as a discipline of the mind?' He replied: 'I hardly know what their value is. I do think it is very desirable that young people and old people should know these things. I think they are matters of accomplishment and knowledge which every body should have something of. But as a matter of education and training of the mind, which is our particular duty as instructors, I do not feel the value of them.'[145] Another witness told the Commission that 'the existence of the Modern Department at Cheltenham gives far greater perfection to the system of education, and far better scope for the various ability and knowledge of our boys than could be possible if only the classical system prevailed. I feel sure that it gives a true education, and not mere instruction in various subjects.'[146] However, the Commission was proceeding with caution, and decided that the existence of 'modern departments' in schools was not of sufficiently long-standing, and its results insufficiently substantiated, to recommend they be established in the nine schools.

Mens sana in corpore sano was an abiding consideration. The Commission liked not just physical training and games, but also the establishment of cadet corps. These were flourishing at five of the schools – Eton, Winchester, Harrow, Rugby and Shrewsbury – and one had been tried, but had failed, at Westminster. They were volunteer bodies and it was agreed it was best they remain so. However, the Commission observed that the rifle was now the 'national weapon' in the way the longbow had once been, and teaching boys how to use it might be no bad thing.[147] The Commission found the sanitary arrangements at the schools generally acceptable: though there were already moves to relocate some London schools to the country, where they could buy far more land, expand and have extensive playing fields. Charterhouse and Merchant Taylors' took this step; St Paul's left the shadow of the cathedral to go to Hammersmith, which rapidly urbanised. Westminster talked about going, but stayed, and does to this day.

The moral well-being of boys – which had so obsessed Dr Arnold – was important still. In an Arnoldian phrase, the Commissioners accepted the practice of some boys exerting discipline over their fellows, but argued that 'this authority should not be that of mere physical strength, which is tyranny, nor that of mere personal influence, which may be of an inferior kind, but should belong to boys fitted by age, character and position to take the highest place in the school, that it should be attended by an acknowledged responsibility, and controlled by established rules.'[148] The Commission conceded examples of boys abusing their authority, but these were rare: and would remain so provided masters did not simply hand over discipline to the boys, but remained interested and watchful of how it was imposed. It felt the monitor system had helped 'create and keep alive a high and sound tone of feeling and opinion, has promoted independence and manliness of character, and has rendered possible that combination of ample liberty with order and discipline which is among the best characteristics of our great English schools'; which is what Dr Arnold sought to achieve when making praepostors.[149]

Moral problems resulted from older, stupid boys being kept down in classes full of younger ones because of their inability to keep up with lessons higher up the school. 'This admixture of older and backward boys with younger and more forward ones is a fruitful source of evil,' the Commission observed.[150] However, Rugby was singled out by the commissioners for its exemplary 'moral tone': 'A general silence is studiously kept at the moment of private prayer; profane or obscene language is so far disapproved that a Sixth Form boy would, in a very bad case, report it to the Head Master. Smoking is generally condemned as affectation; drinking, as bravado.'[151]

While aspects of fagging were unfortunate – restricting the fag's opportunities to play games, or making him do things that, in the Commission's view, a servant should be hired for – there was no element of 'tyranny' in it, and it was popular with the boys.[152] W. S. Meyrick, removed from Westminster by his father in 1862 after two years in which he had been little more than a domestic servant and had been frequently, and arbitrarily, punished, took a different view. A favourite pastime for older boys was to make a younger one place one leg on a sink while, standing on the other, he was kicked as often as the older boy chose.[153] According to Meyrick's evidence Westminster in the early 1860s was a den of savagery, not just because of the frequent kickings, but also because of the habit of some boys to cut other boys' hands with a paper knife.

It was felt relations between masters and boys were more 'friendly' than in the past. 'The wholesome personal influence which is within the reach of a powerful mind and kindly disposition, and which indeed any man of sense and character may possess over boys in whom he heartily interests himself and whom he accustoms to regard him as a friend without annoying him by importunity or inquisitiveness and without trying to impress his own idiosyncrasy on his pupils, is probably better understood than formerly, and is far more frequently exerted.'

It helped that masters no longer thrashed their charges so often as in the old days. 'Flogging, which twenty or thirty years ago was resorted to as a matter of course for the most trifling offences, is now in general used sparingly, and applied only to serious ones.' Moberly said that though flogging was far less frequent than when he was a boy, he still doled out 'from 10 to 20 floggings in a year, perhaps in some years a few more', but did that in public, to encourage the others.[154] At St Paul's, nobody was flogged at all; and at Westminster, where the boys appeared to have taken responsibility for institutional barbarism, hardly any. At Harrow the head boy could cane a serious offender in front of the whole school – a ceremony known as a 'public whopping'.[155] At Charterhouse the headmaster, Richard Elwyn, was quite birch-happy, a boy on the Foundation there saying that he flogged boys probably two or three times a week: but it was not thought a severe punishment, and nobody dreaded it.[156]

There are, however, well-documented cases of sadists in charge of lesser schools, notably Thomas Hopley, who beat a fifteen-year-old boy to death at his private school in Eastbourne in 1860 using an inch-thick stick with a brass casing on the end, and a skipping rope. After Hopley and his wife tried to cover up the crime and were exposed, he received four years for manslaughter at Lewes assizes: which sent a message that moderation in this particular hobby might be advisable. He had only escaped a charge of murder because, as the boy's schoolmaster, he had been *in loco parentis*, exercising what he considered to be reasonable chastisement. Hopley's lack of contrition or repentance during and after his conviction brought him abundant hate-mail. The public's attitude to children was changing profoundly, even despite Hopley's having obtained the advance permission of the boy's father for the beating he gave him, which had been designed to stop the boy (who, it turned out, was suffering from water on the brain) from being 'obstinate'.[157]

In the higher class of private school, according to Clarendon, 'more attention is paid to religious teaching . . . and more reliance is placed on the sense of duty.' At Winchester boys were supervised saying their prayers; elsewhere there were Bible study classes and prizes for distinction in religious knowledge. This, again, was exactly what Arnold had intended, and the Commission saluted him: 'The principle of governing boys mainly through their own sense of what is right and honourable is undoubtedly the only true principle; but it requires much watchfulness, and a firm, temperate and judicious administration, to keep up the tone and standard of opinion, which are very liable to fluctuate, and the decline of which speedily turns a good school into a bad one . . . it has been eminently successful, and . . . greatly improved during the last 30 or 40 years, partly by causes of a general kind, partly by the personal influence and exertions of Dr Arnold and other great schoolmasters.'[158] The report quoted eminent university men saying how much the moral character of their undergraduates had risen in the preceding years, to confirm the point.

Clarendon urged reform of governing bodies, to make them more accountable and efficient. As well as setting fees and holidays, and having special regard to the welfare of scholars paid for by the foundation, they should have the power to hire and fire a headmaster, to ensure adequate sanitary arrangements, to ensure attendance at divine service, but also to oversee introduction of new branches of study. There were to be rigorous examinations, and boys who could not keep up should be asked to leave. However, the findings were in some respects quite conservative: below the governors, headmasters would retain enormous power over staff, boys and curriculum, and the Classics would remain dominant, even though more maths and science were desirable. Heads were, though, to make annual reports to the governors, which were to be printed.

The commissioners found that, compared with their own schooldays, 'petty tyranny and thoughtless cruelty' had gone. 'The boys are better lodged and cared for, and more attention is paid to their health and comfort.'[159] The aim had to be to ensure schools equipped pupils for a fast-changing world in which a country's prosperity was led not just by manufacturers, but by highly educated men in the professions. Moreover, 'these schools have been the chief nurseries of our statesmen; in them, and in schools modelled after them, men of all the various classes that make up English society, destined for every profession and career, have been brought up on a footing of social equality . . . they have had perhaps the largest share in moulding the character of an English gentleman.'

Clarendon broke the stranglehold of Classics on public-school education. In 1865 a select committee of the House of Lords discussed science teaching. It asked Huxley what should and should not be taught, and how; how it should be examined; and whether it should be made compulsory.[160] Huxley was especially keen on physics and human physiology, but only to teach so much as could be taught thoroughly. And, although a liberal and therefore distrustful of the State, he felt it would be an act of 'wisdom and justice' to force schools to teach science. No such compulsion occurred: but following Rugby, Harrow and the City of London School, Winchester started in the early 1870s. Eton stood out, but in 1879 Huxley was appointed to its governing body. Moves to teach science had, despite massive resistance from masters, begun before then, but Huxley's arrival hastened and completed the process, with new laboratories being built, and old ones re-equipped. He also proselytised for science teaching in the universities, and with similar success: he failed, however, in a campaign to have Greek abolished as a requirement for those wishing to embark upon honours courses at Cambridge. Those studying the expanding range of scientific disciplines would need a small command of the tongue until 1919.

There were recommendations for each school. Even Rugby, which had tried so hard to pursue perfection, received sixty-seven recommendations, many to do with governance, finance and the award of scholarships. When the report was received by Parliament in May 1864 there was dismay that prejudice about the state of the schools had been proved right. MPs seized on the limitations of the curriculum, and the uninspiring and counterproductive way in which the Classics were taught. One of the most damning statements was quoted by Grant Duff: 'We have been unable to resist the conclusion that these schools, in very different degrees, are too indulgent to idleness, or struggle ineffectually with it, and that they consequently send out a large proportion of men with idle habits and empty and uncultivated minds.'[161] This was the cadre from which the leaders of a fast-growing nation, and its empire, would be drawn. Grant Duff also said that the headmasters of seven of the nine schools – the honourable exceptions were Rugby, whose teaching was richly praised, and Shrewsbury – were so concerned by the 'inferior article' that was their average boy that they refused to allow the Commission to interview any of them.[162] Eton came in for particular criticism: notably for how the Provost, Hawtrey, obstructed Goodford, his very experienced headmaster and Balston's predecessor; and for the way in which assistant masters were never consulted on anything. Eton was not, however, the worst offender.

The barbarities of some of the schools caused particular outrage: notably the kicking of boys at Westminster, and other revelations about that establishment, 'reflect the greatest disgrace upon all those who have had any share in its management for some time back'.[163] The Archbishop of Dublin, who as the former Dean of Westminster had some responsibility for the school's governance, was explicitly criticised; and Grant Duff challenged Dean Stanley, his successor, saying that as the biographer of Dr Arnold he could not possibly allow such 'infamies' to continue. It used evidence from the headmaster, Dr Scott, to adduce that the state of scholarship in the school was 'wretchedly, and indeed ludicrously, low'.

Gladstone conceded that the Classics were forced on too many who could not profit by them; but he hoped they would be available, as the core of the curriculum, to those who could. He also made a case – stronger than that made by the report – for the teaching of Italian and German as well as of French, not for utilitarian purposes, but as one who would always 'value cultivation and literature for their own sakes'.[164] While agreeing there was room for improvement, he also referred to Clarendon's criticism of parents who took no trouble to encourage habits of learning and culture at home. He quoted the report exactly: 'Several of the masters whom we have examined have dwelt in strong terms on the ill-prepared and ignorant state in which boys are very frequently sent to school . . . it is clear that there are many boys whose education can hardly be said to have begun till they enter, at the age of twelve or thirteen, or even later, a school containing several hundreds, where there can be comparatively little of that individual teaching which a very backward boy requires.'[165]

Gladstone had his own critique of the decline of a society whose wealth and reach were, paradoxically, expanding:

When we say that the fault lies with the parents, what does this mean? It means that we are living in an age in a great degree pampered in luxury, in which self-indulgence pervades more and more largely the habits of an ever-increasing class of society, the rapid extension of which we may see indicated by the continual addition, not only of large streets, but of whole quarters, in themselves great towns, to this metropolis; and a necessary consequence of that self-indulgence is a growing indisposition to the severe discipline which study and education invariably require . . . in one sense, in our attempts to improve the public schools, we are fighting against the age. The wealthier we become, the more difficult does it grow to apply to our children, or to realise to ourselves, the necessity of a severe self-discipline. I say this not to extenuate the mischief, but to show that the mischief is profound.[166]

It was precisely because of factors outside the schools' control – but to which they would have to adapt if they wished to survive – that Gladstone warned the Commons that there would 'be no violent or precipitate legislation upon the subject'. He advised expansion of the curriculum, saying that there were 'eight or nine' branches of learning that ought to be included in it. Religion was first, and Classics second, of these: 'then come mathematics, natural science, English composition, history, geography, and the alternative of drawing or music.'[167] This was in line with what Clarendon had recommended; but Gladstone recognised that it would not be easy to fit all this in, not least because of the new importance of games: schools had moved into the era of muscular Christianity.

The following year Gladstone asked himself what education meant, and what was required of it: 'What is the true relation between professional education, which aims at excellence in the exercise of a particular calling, and general education, which aims at the highest excellence of the mental powers and aptitudes? What classes would partake of the one or the other, or how in each class their relative spheres would be adjusted, are questions wholly behind the present purpose . . . There is also such a thing as general training, which must be kept alive as a portion at least of the apparatus of civilisation, and which has a purpose and a province of its own.'[168] He asked whether classical studies, which had always been central to achieving 'the divine government of the world', were now enough.

In 1864 Northcote, who had been a commissioner, said the great schools had struggled to move with the times because of the constraints placed upon them by their founders, who had established small grammar schools. Such people could never have envisaged an industrialised world of shrinking distances and growing populations. Northcote hoped these schools would have 'an important bearing on the formation of the national character', saying they should be 'schools for the moral, physical and intellectual training of boys between the important years of twelve and eighteen, and which should make of those boys young men – men in every sense of the word.'[169] This was the complement to Gladstone's idea – and indeed Matthew Arnold's idea – of the 'cultivated' mind: the practical idea that the powerhouse of an empire required a cult of manliness among its leaders if it were to survive.

Clarendon himself amplified the core findings in the Lords a few days later. He proposed a thirty-seven-hour week in the schools: twenty to be devoted to lessons of an hour each, but with ten additional hours for preparation in the Classics, two in modern languages and five in composition. He had been exasperated by some of the attitudes uncovered – 'though a knowledge of the French language was admitted to be requisite for an English gentleman, yet the authorities at Eton obstinately refused to make it any part of the education of the school'.[170] Yet he was most concerned about resistance to teaching natural sciences, something the Germans were particularly assiduous in doing.

He said that 'we believe that its value, as a means of opening the mind and disciplining the faculties, is recognised by all those who have taken the trouble to acquire it, whether men of business or of leisure. It quickens and cultivates directly the faculty of observation, which in very many persons lies almost dormant through life, the power of accurate and rapid generalisation, and the mental habit of method and arrangement; it accustoms young persons to trace the sequence of cause and effect; it familiarises them with a kind of reasoning which interests them, and which they can promptly comprehend.'[171] While expressing his 'sincere respect for the opinions of the eminent schoolmasters who differ from us in this matter', he emphasised that a 'regular course of study' of science was 'desirable': and he added that the committee had preferred the views of eminent scientists, such as the Astronomer Royal, on this subject to those evinced by the pedagogues. The absence of enthusiasm for science was widespread, despite the exciting example of Darwin and others. Sir Benjamin Brodie, President of the Royal Society, had written to Palmerston on 25 January 1861 to say that his council failed to spend all the £1,000 granted to the Society for 'the promotion of scientific investigation' in 1859, leaving them with a surplus, 'in addition to which they have just received the sum of £1,000 granted in 1860. Under these circumstances the Council feel that there will be no occasion for them to avail themselves of the liberality of Parliament during the present year.'[172]

Clarendon presented the Public Schools Bill in the Lords on 30 May 1864. It mainly regulated the appointment of governing bodies, believing such reform would help direct the right sort of changes in the schools. At the second reading on 7 June Lord de Ros, an old boy of Westminster, a general in the Army and the Premier Baron of England, said fagging 'was one of the most useful trials to which boys were exposed'. He added that 'in early days he had the honour of frequently cleaning the shoes of the most rev Prelate at the head of the Bishops' Bench [the Archbishop of Canterbury, Charles Longley], and he had never found himself the worse for it. The most rev Prelate treated him with the kindness and good nature which his Grace had ever since displayed, and had never felt degraded by fagging for him in this way.'[173] De Ros did, though, have a radical element, admitting that it would be 'far better' to substitute French or German for further training in Greek iambics.

VI

There was an abiding sense after Clarendon that, however many Royal Commissions investigated the question, education would not be improved until the government gave a sufficient lead; and it would not be able to give that lead until it had recognised the need for a proper Ministry of Education, under a dedicated minister. The Committee of the Privy Council that currently disbursed grants was composed of men with other jobs. Lowe ran the Board of Health while speaking on behalf of the Committee; the other members were the Lord President, the Chancellor of the Exchequer, the first Lord of the Treasury, the Foreign Secretary, the Lord Privy Seal, the first Lord of the Admiralty and the President of the Poor Law Board.

Such was the workload of these ministers that education, however committed each might be to its cause, could only be an afterthought in their political lives. In 1865 Pakington attempted to have a select committee appointed to discuss whether the time had not come for a better system of overseeing education. He claimed that because of inadequate administration, out of 15,000 parishes in England no fewer than 11,024 received no benefit from the £700,000 or so disbursed as a grant.[174] It had been left to extra-governmental forces – notably the philanthropist Angela Burdett-Coutts – to suggest improvements, such as the grouping of rural parishes under the charge of a certificated teacher – to counteract what Pakington called the relative 'inaction' of the Committee since 1839.

Lowe, who had resigned in 1863 over a perceived slight to his honour, stressed that the government's role should be to assist the voluntary system – though it had a duty to ensure the schools it assisted were good enough to merit the help. He felt that the purpose of Newcastle had been to examine whether the Committee of the Privy Council had been adequate. Members of that Committee had been examined, and re-examined, continually: and Lowe felt they had not been found wanting.[175] He feared that any bureaucracy such as Pakington wanted would use up funds that could otherwise be spent on schools. Others feared the bureaucracy would have to become localised, to provide proper accountability: and that, too, would be expensive. Yet the Commons had to concede that the present arrangements might not have been equal to the demands of the modern State: Pakington got his select committee, and was made chairman.

However, Clarendon's recommendations were not finally legislated upon until 1868. The process also included the establishment and deliberations of a select committee, which included three members of Clarendon's Commission and was chaired by Clarendon himself. He introduced a bill in 1865, but it ran out of parliamentary time. It was reintroduced in a much-amended form in 1866, but was going through at the change of ministry in June 1866. Clarendon, fearing his work would come to nothing, wrote to Gladstone on 8 July to ask him 'will you give the Public Schools Bill the advantage of your protection in the H of C or, if not, will you ask one of our late colleagues to take charge of it? After the delay that has inevitably occurred I should be sorry to have the Bill postponed for another year, and I don't think there will be much opposition to it – though we must endeavour to insert the clause empowering the Executive Commissioner to reform the Governing Bodies which Derby by a majority of one struck out in the H of Lds, although he had agreed to it after much consideration in the Select Committee.'[176]

Another amended bill was introduced in 1867, by the Conservative government and taking, therefore, a less radical line. It, too, was savaged in the summer of 1868 by radical MPs who suspected it did not force sufficient reforms on the finances of Eton and Winchester. It was further amended, though remained the subject of intense criticism, and finally received the Royal Assent in July 1868, the Liberals still complaining that their views had received inadequate consideration. It did, however, start a top-down process of reform of the English secondary education system that not least in terms of curriculum would set an example to the more humble establishments that grew up after Forster's Act in 1870.

VII

Arnold and Gladstone had come to know each other in 1859, when Gladstone read a pamphlet by him on Italy and sent a note of approval to Longman, his publisher. 'It is an honour to be read by you,' Arnold told him, 'a still greater honour to be read by you with sympathy – the greatest honour of all to be read by you with sympathy when one writes of Italy, for which you yourself, by what you have written, have done so much.'[177] He was further grateful in 1864 to Gladstone for sending him a copy of his translation of Homer, and they agreed to meet, not least to discuss the utility of hexameters. Having established this intellectual consonance with so prominent and powerful a politician, Arnold presumed further on their relationship to put into the highest political circles his views on extending high-quality education to the middle classes, and on the need for the State to play a larger role in education than contemporary views would consider acceptable. 'Meanwhile you must allow me to intrude upon you yet once more, by sending you a book on the Popular Education of France, which I am going to publish in a few weeks . . . if you could find time to give a glance at the introduction, and at one or two of the latter chapters, I should be very glad.'[178]

Arnold went to France on behalf of Newcastle for several months in 1859 'enquiring into the working of the French law of public instruction', as he had told Gladstone.[179] 'In the last few months,' he said on 5 August 1859, writing from Dover, 'I have visited nearly every part of France and seen all classes of society from archbishops and prefects to village schoolmasters and peasants.' The result of his travels was *A French Eton*, first published in 1864, which begins with the joke that 'in that famous seat of learning, a vast sum of money was expended on education, and a beggarly account of empty brains was the result'.[180]

He sent a copy to Gladstone on 10 June 1864, calling it 'a little essay upon a subject for which no-one can do so much as yourself – Middle Class Education.'[181] Lowe – Arnold's bête noire – would define the middle classes educationally as those who would never send their children to elementary schools used by the lower classes, but lacked the money to send them to public schools.[182] The findings of the Taunton Commission were largely anticipated by Arnold, and, inevitably, exceeded by him. He knew what a pool of talent resided in the middle classes, and a talent moreover often coupled with a drive and energy not always found in the more languid and privileged upper classes. His work can be read as an attack on the official mind in Britain, which he regarded as lacking in perception and intelligence, and certainly in radicalism. He also saw it as tainted by utilitarianism, and undermined by rote-learning. These suppositions, and Arnold's regular assertions that things were ordered better on the Continent, help explain why he did not enjoy great popularity among the Establishment, and why promotion in the inspectorate was so elusive.

He urged Gladstone to note his suggestions not as Chancellor of the Exchequer, but as MP for Oxford University: 'I have noticed from time to time what you have said against State interference; but, even though it may be true that the perfect end to reach at last is that individuals should do all things well and rightly for themselves, I cannot but think that before reaching that end, and in order that we may reach it, we in this country shall have to use the State's help much more freely than we have hitherto done.' He hoped Gladstone would at least listen to his arguments: and added that 'in a now twelve years' acquaintance with British schools all over the country and with their promoters, I have perhaps had more than common opportunities for studying the English middle class and particularly one of its strongest and most characteristic parts, the Protestant dissenters; this, and the reflexions such a study irresistibly awakened, is my excuse for touching a subject which is certainly social and political rather than literary.'

Arnold doubted Eton could teach 'profound wisdom', but felt it did teach 'her aristocratic pupils virtues which are among the best virtues of an aristocracy – freedom from affectation, manliness, a high spirit, simplicity.'[183] He hoped this would affect the non-aristocratic pupils, but feared unrealistic expectations: 'To convey to Eton the knowledge that the wine of Champagne does not water the whole earth, and that there are incomes which fall below £5,000 a year, would be a kindness towards a large class of British parents, full of proper pride, but not opulent.'[184] Later on, he argued that 'for the class frequenting Eton, the grand aim of education should be to give them these good things which their birth and rearing are least likely to give them: to give them (besides mere book learning) the notion of a sort of republican fellowship, the practice of a plain life in common, the habit of self-help.'[185]

This was what the middle classes needed, but Clarendon would not help them. 'I hope that large class which wants the improvement of secondary instruction in this country – secondary instruction, the great first stage of a liberal education coming between elementary instruction, the instruction in the mother tongue and in the simplest and indispensable branches of knowledge on the one hand, and superior instruction, the instruction given by universities, the second and finishing stage of a liberal education, on the other – will not imagine that the appointment of a Royal Commission to report on nine existing schools can seriously help it to that which it wants.'[186] He regretted that the commissioners had felt unable to look further afield for examples, because he felt France had much to teach Britain.

Arnold had noted how the *lycée* system was organised by the State and funded partly by it and partly by the locality, with small fees paid by the pupils – from £4 8s 4d a year to £7 4s 2d a year. No school could charge even this modest fee without the State inspector's having approved it as equal to the task for which it was charging. Arnold felt, too, that through exercise and healthcare the physical well-being of the youths he had seen was superior to that of their English counterparts. He admired the curriculum too. This brought him to his big question: 'Why cannot we have throughout England – as the French have throughout France, as the Germans have throughout Germany, as the Swiss have throughout Switzerland, as the Dutch have throughout Holland – schools where the children of our middle and professional classes may obtain, at the rate of from £20 to £50 a year, if they are boarders, at the rate of from £5 to £15 a year if they are day-scholars, an education of as good quality, with as good guarantees, social character, and advantages for a future career in the world, as the education which French children of the corresponding class can obtain?'[187] He conceded there was nothing like Eton in France, and that 'the English public school produces the finest boys in the world'. However, he added, 'but then there are only five or six schools in England to produce this specimen-boy; and they cannot produce him cheap. Rugby and Winchester produce him at £120 a year; Eton and Harrow (and the Eton schoolboy is perhaps justly taken as the most perfect type of this highly-extolled class) cannot produce him for much less than £200 a year.' For £30, Arnold mused, one did not get much quality.

The middle classes, he said, 'will not pay for their children's schooling a price quite disproportionate to their means.'[188] He derided establishments that advertised 'educational homes' for boys of this class at £20 or £30 a year, for those who knew about education knew they were rubbish. They lacked proper supervision and public scrutiny, and had no reputation to lose. 'The mass of mankind do not so well know what distinguishes good teaching and training from bad; they do not know what they ought to demand, and, therefore, the demand cannot be relied on to give us the right supply. Even if they knew what they ought to demand, they have no means of testing whether or no this is really supplied to them.'[189]

He said they did things better in France because of the over-arching role of the State there, 'the organisation of a complete system of secondary schools throughout France, the abundant supply of institutions, with at once respectable guarantees and reasonable charges, fixing a general mean of school-cost which even the most successful private school cannot venture much to exceed.'[190] Others – notably Nathaniel Woodard, founder of Lancing and, in time, ten other public schools – had noticed a problem for the middle class: it was more or less the only one for whom some State or charitable provision for education was not made. The destitute had Ragged Schools, the working class church schools; the universities and the great public schools had huge endowments. Woodard had said that 'the lower middle class [Arnold wondered why he had added the word 'lower'], politically a very important one, is dependent to a great extent for its education on private desultory enterprise. This class, in this land of education, gets *nothing* out of the millions given annually for this purpose to every class except themselves.'[191] Arnold mocked Woodard for seeking public subscriptions for new schools, asking how this spared the middle classes the mercies of 'private desultory enterprise'. Only a State system, Arnold felt, would work. Woodard could build schools in Sussex, and good schools they might be: but what could he do for the rest of Britain?

Arnold believed that 'to the middle class, the grand aim of education should be to give largeness of soul and personal dignity; to the lower class, feeling, gentleness, humanity.'[192] Only the State could do this. 'Education is and must be a matter of public establishment. Other countries have replaced the defective public establishment made by the Middle Ages for their education with a new one which provides for the actual condition of things. We in England keep our old public establishment for education . . . we must not forget to provide for the actual condition of things.'[193] He denied having any 'pet scheme to press'. He was, though, resolutely opposed to the learning-by-rote satirised by Dickens in *Hard Times*, in Mr M'Choakumchild's school where Mr Gradgrind's system is in place; and also in *The Water-Babies* by Kingsley, who in a reference to Grimes the sweep's broad Lancashire dialect says it is something 'whereby you may perceive that Mr Grimes had not been to a properly inspected Government National School'.[194] Arnold again voiced his outrage that Lowe's inspection system was precisely calibrated to measure success in teaching 'facts'. Within a few years, however, even Lowe would be advocating a liberal education for the middle classes at least, including the study of English literature, French, German and – to discipline the mind – at least one of the physical sciences.[195]

There was a prejudice that being educated by the State was akin to pauperism. Arnold ridiculed it. 'Humiliated by receiving help for himself as an individual from himself in his corporate and associated capacity! Help to which his own money, as a tax-payer, contributes, and for which, as a result of the joint energy and intelligence of the whole community in employing its powers, he himself deserves some of the praise! He is no more humiliated by being on the foundation of the Charterhouse or of Winchester, or by holding a scholarship or fellowship at Oxford or Cambridge . . . he is no more humiliated than when he crosses London Bridge, or walks down the King's Road, or visits the British Museum.'[196]

This led into a wider discussion of the State: 'The State mars everything which it touches, say some. It attempts to do things for private people, and private people could do them a great deal better for themselves.'[197] He quoted a *Times* editorial saying that 'the State can hardly aid education without cramping and warping its growth, and mischievously interfering with the laws of its natural development.' Arnold argued that the generality of what had to be done required the State to do it; but 'we can make it our agent, not our master'.[198] He said the middle class had done so well precisely because it had kept the State at bay, while securing 'for itself that centre of character and that moral force which are, I have said, the indispensable basis upon which perfection is to be founded.'[199] He would say it again in *Culture and Anarchy*. This class had been swept up in 'a widespread mental movement' indicated by its greater intellectual curiosity and its appetite for reading. 'Will this movement go on and become fruitful: will it conduct the middle class to a high and commanding pitch of culture and intelligence? That depends on the sensibility which the middle class has for *perfection*; that depends on its power to *transform itself*.'[200] That, indeed, would be the message of *Culture and Anarchy*: '*Estote ergo vos perfecti!*'

Arnold had high hopes for the 'transformed' middle class, 'raised to a higher and more genial culture.'[201] He said that 'in that great class, strong by its numbers, its energy, its industry, strong by its freedom from frivolity, not by any law of nature prone to immobility of mind, actually at this moment agitated by a spreading ferment of mind . . . what a power there will be, what an element of new life for England! Then let the middle class rule, then let it affirm its own spirit, when it has perfected itself.' It was up to them to solicit the help of the State for this advancement. The precepts he outlined would underpin the State education system created over the succeeding eighty years.

CHAPTER 13

THE END OF PRIVILEGE: INVENTING THE MERITOCRACY

I

In the mid-nineteenth century Britain was still held back by the system of appointing men – and it was almost exclusively men – to positions of influence according to their social standing, connections, means and religion rather than on merit. This was true in the state sector especially, not least because the two most glaring examples of this were the higher reaches of the Civil Service, and the officer class in the Army. However, England's two old universities were also undermined by a form of discrimination, which meant that academic freedom existed only for members of the Established Church. Those who were not members would find higher degrees and senior college and university posts closed to them. At a time when the country needed to harness its talent as much as possible, that was a severe handicap. A rising middle class – especially if it was Nonconformist, had no private means and lacked social clout – would find Whitehall, the Army and the old universities barred to it.

The main problem with the Civil Service was that men entered it so young that it was often impossible to get an estimate of their ability: and if they were third-rate, it was impossible to be rid of them. The private sector, at least, embraced stiff competition, and if a man was a drain on a business he was usually sacked. However, in the Civil Service many of the young men appointed spent years copying papers and advanced no further beyond that, leaving them bored and depressed. Promotion was based on Buggin's turn. When a really senior post became available there was often no one within the service with the skills to fill it: therefore someone from outside had to be promoted over the heads of long-term civil servants, who were demoralised as a result. Nor were men moved from one department to another, which made them narrow in outlook and restricted their chances of advancement.

The Crimean War was handled disastrously by Whitehall, and made its own case for radical change. But there was also evidence in many of the questions of the day, domestic as well as foreign, of inconsistency and incompetence making things worse. As the population grew, and with them the wealth, reach and influence of the country, and the demands being made to handle that expanding population, the old Civil Service was no longer up to the job. Only gross misconduct could result in a civil servant being sacked, and few seemed to have either the wit or the energy for that. As an official report of 1853 into the Civil Service said, 'The feeling of security tends to encourage indolence, and thereby to depress the character of the Service.'[1]

There was strong resistance to the idea of Civil Service reform, and not merely from nepotists and reactionaries who saw career opportunities for mediocre gentlemen disappearing into the hands of talented men on the make. In 1854 Sir James Stephen, a former under-secretary at the Colonial Office and Regius professor of modern history at Cambridge, had said he felt work in the Civil Service was insufficiently demanding to be given to men of outstanding ability, who would be bored by it. He had found his former colleagues to be of a low calibre, but to have done, nonetheless, what was expected of them. With a senior clerk earning between £700 and £1,000 a year, but junior clerks on between £160 and £300, they were not paid well – nor, in his view, should they be – and he asked 'why expect to attract, by such inducements as these, any man of eminent ability to whom any other path in life is open?'[2] The dull man was suited to it because 'he labours in an obscurity as profound as it is unavoidable', and it was as well he might not understand much that he was asked to do, for if he did he would probably disapprove of it. Also – and displaying the brutal cynicism inherited in such large measure by his distinguished son Fitzjames, whom we shall encounter later – Stephen could not understand why the Civil Service should regulate entrance on merit, since in most of life merit did not come into it. This was not merely for corrupt purposes. 'It is not without some reason that in all other pursuits in life, patronage, exercised in the spirit of nepotism, is made the shelter of the weak and otherwise helpless. Those whom nature and training have made strong can usually help themselves.'[3]

There were also radicals who made their less urbane voices heard every bit as loudly as Sir James Stephen had: such as the Irish journalist Matthew Higgins, who wrote in his *Letter on Administrative Reform* of 1855 that there was an 'upper ten thousand' who had 'hitherto monopolised every post of honour, trust and emolument under the Crown, from the highest to the lowest. They have taken what they wanted for themselves; they have distributed what they did not want among their relations, connexions and dependents. They have all in turn paid their debts of friendship and of gratitude, they have provided for their younger sons and their worn-out servants with appointments in the public service.'[4] Another critic, W. R. Greg, announced that 'every Englishman is proud of his country. No Englishman is proud of his Administration.'[5]

Gladstone shared that view. After becoming Chancellor of the Exchequer in late 1852, he had commissioned a report into Civil Service reform from Sir Charles Trevelyan and Sir Stafford Northcote. Northcote had been Gladstone's private secretary at the Board of Trade – recruited by the meritocratic method of Gladstone's having written to a friend at Eton and asking him to recommend one of his most impressive former pupils. The two men had formed a high estimate of each other. Northcote had been a scholar at Balliol with Clough, whom he got to know only a little because of Clough's incipient shyness.

Succeeding his grandfather in the baronetcy in 1851, he would become an MP in 1855, serve as Disraeli's Chancellor for the whole of the 1874–80 government, and be Foreign Secretary briefly in 1886–7 under Salisbury, dying in office. In the later 1850s, he would steer through legislation to improve reformatories and set up industrial schools, so that young criminals could learn a trade and contribute to society, rather than face a lifetime of crime and an early demise. When Chancellor he would regulate and ease the path of friendly societies, which won him the affections of many of the working class who, especially through the formation of burial societies, had attempted to help themselves in difficult circumstances. Most recently, he had been a highly effective secretary of the 1851 Commission.

Trevelyan was older than Northcote – forty-six to his thirty-five when they began their work – and had been a distinguished colonial civil servant before becoming Assistant Secretary to the Treasury, its most

senior permanent official. He had coordinated relief for the Irish Potato
Famine, for which history has not, with good reason, treated him kindly.
He was strongly influenced by the thought of Thomas Malthus, the
economist, and believed the Famine had been a 'mechanism for reducing
surplus population . . . the judgment of God sent the calamity to teach
the Irish a lesson, that calamity must not be too much mitigated . . .
The real evil with which we have to contend is not the physical evil of
the Famine, but the moral evil of the selfish, perverse and turbulent
character of the people.'[6]

Their report, signed off in November 1853 and published in 1854, was
entitled *The Organisation of the Permanent Civil Service*. A masterpiece of
concision – it runs to just twenty-three pages, a model for public documents on great subjects – it sought to end admission by patronage and
instead admit according to merit proved through competitive examination. 'The great and increasing accumulation of public business' made
reform a necessity: the responsibilities of the State had grown with
prosperity and expansion and the present forces were 'far from perfect'
and unequal to handling them.[7] The supposed ease of the work meant
that there were 'strong inducements to the parents and friends of sickly
youths to endeavour to obtain for them employment in the service of
the Government', and the report commented that the number of civil
servants on sick pay or on pensions drawn early, at the public's expense,
had to be seen to be believed.[8] The authors sought not to damn all civil
servants, but did observe that 'there are probably very few who have
chosen this line of life with a view to raising themselves to public
eminence.'

The key question they asked was in two parts: 'What is the best
method of providing it [the Civil Service] with a supply of good men,
and of making the most of them after they have been admitted?'[9]
Admission by examination, followed by a period of probation, and with
it being understood that advancement would 'depend entirely on the
industry and ability with which they discharge their duties', were all
deemed essential.[10] Some form of examination already took place in
several departments of State, including the Treasury, the War Office,
the Board of Trade and the Colonial Office (the Home and Foreign
Offices were notoriously resistant to anything that might undermine
patronage). This new admissions process had to be centrally administered
(though it should, they argued, be held in regional centres to encourage

wide entrance), held at a fixed time, and not left to individual departments. It also had to be independent, and with a wide range of subjects examined – not merely Latin and Greek, which would favour a narrow group of men. The report stressed 'the importance of establishing a proper distinction between intellectual and mechanical labour'.[11]

Northcote and Trevelyan had made a powerful argument for reform. The report also made a distinction in Civil Service work between high-level policy-making and the simply clerical. This distinction, while sensible, tended to restrict the upper levels of the Civil Service to the aristocratic and well-to-do who could afford a decent public school followed by Oxford or Cambridge. Trevelyan admitted this but defended the proposal on the grounds that those aristocrats who made the grade would at least be 'worthy', rather than being 'the idle, and useless, the fool of the family, the consumptive, the hypochondriac, those who have a tendency to insanity'.[12] Trevelyan intended that the country would 'invite the flower of our youth to the aid of the public service'.

The question of ease of promotion had arisen earlier, according to a letter from Cardwell to Gladstone in January 1854, when the former had some vacancies to fill at the Board of Trade. 'I agree in the wisdom of making broad lines of demarcation, between the different classes: but I doubt the policy of making these lines impassable.'[13] He added: 'If the juniors are not to be gentlemen, they will never in any case be fit for promotion; their powers derived from education and training will not be suitable for superior work. If, on the other hand, you establish hard work, low pay, no claim to promotion, and a probationary year, then I think you will do much to exclude <u>fine</u> gentlemen, while real, hard-working gentlemen will come in, relying on their own powers to free themselves upwards on the ground of superior merit.' Cardwell had also recommended varying the composition of any board of examiners that was set up, and creating 'a greater degree of strictness in the service: and to this the abolition of Patronage would tend – for it is difficult now for the head of a department to dismiss incompetent, or unwilling, men.' Northcote and Trevelyan wanted promotion to depend on ability, hard work and results, a revolutionary concept.

Gladstone drafted a memorandum on Civil Service reform in response to Northcote and Trevelyan, noting that 'candidates for those grades in the Civil Service to which appointment takes place in youth with a view to succession, will be examined in groups: the examinations being open to all qualified persons. A number corresponding with the number of vacancies will be selected by the examiners, according to merit.'[14] Gladstone understood how destabilising this would be to the old hands: 'Nor is it unnatural that the man who has been brought into the service by favour in preference to other men of superior merit should resent the attempt to stop his promotion upon a plan which if good at all should have prevented his admission.'

Trevelyan told Gladstone on 8 July 1854 that an article about Civil Service reform had appeared in the *Westminster Gazette* 'saying that our plan is a great improvement upon the present, but that it is pregnant with danger. No better arrangement is, however, suggested.'[15] Trevelyan kept up the pressure, telling Gladstone in a letter of 17 January 1855: 'It is generally admitted that the incompetent youth of the country gravitate towards the public services. To whatever degree, therefore, a check can be put upon this tendency, the public good will be promoted. At present the object is admitted to be very imperfectly attained by means of departmental examinations. And it is also admitted by all the best authorities that it is desirable to substitute for departmental examinations the superior security of the agency of officers appointed expressly for the purpose and acting according to prescribed rules.'[16]

He conceded a difference of opinion as to the best kind of examination: but urged that whatever it was 'the examinations may be conducted either wholly or partly on the principle of competition'. The Committee of Inquiry into the Organisation of the Permanent Civil Service had recommended that 'a central Board should be constituted for conducting the examination of all candidates for the public service whom it may be thought right to subject to such a test. Such board should be composed of men holding an independent position, and capable of commanding general confidence; it should have at its head an officer of the rank of Privy Councillor.'[17]

Northcote and Trevelyan had said in their original report: 'We are of opinion that this examination should be in all cases a competing literary examination. This ought not to exclude careful previous inquiry into the age, health and moral fitness of the candidates . . . We see no other mode by which (in the case of the inferior no less than of the superior offices) the double object can be attained of selecting the fittest person, and of avoiding the evils of patronage.'[18] They were also keen to ensure that the entry requirements should therefore include physical fitness.

'Nothing is commoner than for young men to be got into the Public Offices expressly on account of their having a weakly inefficient physique,' he told Gladstone on 9 February 1855, 'and this may not always be detected by the single medical examination.'[19] Trevelyan tried to find a chief examiner; but first Benjamin Jowett, at this stage in his career a tutor at Balliol and one who had sat on the Reform Commission, and then Frederick Temple, a school inspector who was a former fellow of Balliol and a future Archbishop of Canterbury, declined. Jowett – probably the country's leading don, with his pupils routinely picking up strings of firsts – strongly supported reform, imagining (correctly, as it turned out) that it would give an enormous boost to university education.

The Commons expected to be consulted, but Gladstone and Trevelyan hoped the changes could be made by Order in Council. In May both the *Westminster* and *North British Review*s praised the reform, which cheered Trevelyan considerably. The reform was debated and on 14 July Trevelyan wrote to Gladstone to thank him for 'your great personal kindness in defending and doing justice to me.'[20] Once the principle took hold in the Home Civil Service pressure was placed on the government to introduce it for entrants into the Indian; and for entrance for potential officers in the artillery and engineers to find young men 'advanced in mathematics'.[21]

Competitive examination got off to an uncertain start in 1855, being used to sift out a pre-selected group of candidates rather than opening the field. In 1857, when he wrote *Little Dorrit*, Dickens satirised the workings of the Civil Service in his account of the Circumlocution Office, staffed in its highest ranks by connections of a self-perpetuating oligarchy. By judicious oiling and greasing to the grandee Lord Decimus Tite Barnacle, using his wife's salon in Harley Street, the fraudster Merdle obtains a position for his stepson. The youth has no merit or qualification whatever, and is in his way as much an impostor as his stepfather; and the purpose of the Circumlocution Office, to achieve nothing, to throw a spanner into all available works, but merely to provide a living for the meretricious, is further served by his appointment. 'In a day or two it was announced to all the town, that Edmund Sparkler, Esquire, son-in-law of the eminent Mr Merdle of world-wide renown, was made one of the Lords of the Circumlocution Office; and proclamation was issued to all true believers, that this admirable appointment was to be hailed as a graceful and gracious mark of homage, rendered by the graceful and gracious Decimus, to that commercial interest which must ever in a great commercial country – and all the rest of it, with blast of trumpet.'[22]

Inevitably, the logic of what Trollope sneeringly called 'the grand modern scheme for competitive examinations' was extended, and not just to those whom the heads of department wished to invite in to take the tests.[23] But before it could be 'destined to revivify, clarify, and render perfect the Civil Service of the country', as Trollope also put it, many old prejudices had to be broken down.[24] This took until 1870, when Gladstone, the godfather of Northcote-Trevelyan, finally decided to bring the system into kilter with modern demands.

The engine for this second tranche of reform was Lowe. His first attempts to bring meritocracy into the public service were in 1853, when he joined the campaign for open competition in the Home Civil Service sparked off by the Northcote-Trevelyan Report. Gladstone, as Chancellor and the sponsoring minister, had had to abandon plans for such reforms because of overwhelming opposition in the Commons and the Lords in the late spring of 1854. A Civil Service Commission was established by an Order in Council in 1855 to approve new civil servants, but open competition was conducted in less than 30 per cent of vacancies between 1855 and 1868. Lowe had a deep-seated conviction that further reform was essential, but there was no support for it in the country, Parliament or in Gladstone's Cabinet. He wrote to Gladstone on 10 November 1869 to say that 'as I have so often tried in vain will you bring the question of the Civil Service before the Cabinet today. Something must be decided. We cannot keep matters in this discreditable state of abeyance. If the Cabinet will not entertain the idea of open competition might we not at any rate require a larger number of competitors for each vacancy, five or seven or ten?'[25]

He forced the issue with Gladstone about his own department, arguing that the Treasury should recruit through open competition. Gladstone conceded that this strategy was 'very likely . . . to be the right one'.[26] He was worried about strong objections from Clarendon and Bright, and wished to avoid resignations. He proposed widespread consultation with other ministers, and the maximum of flexibility. In December 1869 the Cabinet agreed each department of State could decide for itself whether to use open competition: only the Home and Foreign Offices declined to do so. Any department that started to backslide was told by Lowe that the pension entitlements of civil servants not recruited by this method would be refused. This ended the old system of patronage except in the Foreign Office, which did not change until after the Great War: though appointments by nomination were made in the Education Department as late as 1911.

Lowe drew up regulations for the examinations at three different levels of entry. In June 1871 Thomas Farrer, the Permanent Secretary at the Board of Trade, drew his colleagues' attention to implications of the changes in the rules for the organisation of Civil Service departments, according to Lowe's arrangements. He outlined the three classes of civil servant that Lowe proposed:

1. A comparatively small class of established clerks, with high salaries, fixed tenure, and pension selected by open competition of a high class.
2. An intermediate class of established clerks with lower salaries, but with fixed tenure and pension, and also selected by open competition, though of a lower kind.
3. A class of writers with 10d an hour (or 30s per week), selected by the Civil Service Commissioners, but without fixity of tenure, pension or possibility of reward, or prospect of any kind.

Those who enter each of these classes will do so on their first entering the service; they will remain in the class to which they are to belong as long as they remain in the public service, and there is to be no possibility of promotion to a higher class or degradation to an inferior class.[27]

Lowe stipulated that before anyone could compete in classes 1 and 2, he had to take a preliminary test to prove a sound basic level of education. The tests for the top grade included English composition, language and literature; English history (notably constitutional history); Greek and Latin language, literature and history; and the language, literature and history of France, Italy and Germany – though the modern languages carried only half the number of marks of the Classics. Mathematics and natural sciences were also tested, as were the moral sciences, jurisprudence and political economy. Those aiming for the second class were faced with far fewer demands, such as handwriting, indexing and docketing, spelling and arithmetic. Lowe limited his meritocracy to the university-educated: for only they would manage to wrestle with the subjects in the examination for the top grade, and therefore only they would have the chance to progress to the highest levels in the Civil Service. However, he ensured that only the most intelligent and best educated would go to the top. It was then up to society to engineer reforms elsewhere – notably in admissions to the universities from a wider range of schools and therefore backgrounds.

Farrer's point about the impossibility of promotion was well made, but Lowe would have shrugged it off. He understood that in the highest ranks of the public service intellectual ability was important: but so were *savoir faire* and social skills. Those with an education that would allow them to enter the middle grade would almost certainly not have the background to allow them to rub shoulders with the highest in the land with complete ease: so it would be out of the question to promote them. Lowe expressed his views on this to a select committee in 1873: 'The education of public schools and colleges and such things, which gives a sort of freemasonry among men which is not very easy to describe but which everybody feels: I think that is extremely desirable: there are a number of persons in those offices who are brought into contact with the upper classes of this country and they should be of that class in order that they may hold their own on behalf of the Government.' He added: 'Supplementary Clerks might be found wanting in the very things to which I attach great value in the upper class; perhaps he might not pronounce his "h's" or commit some similar solecism, which might be a most serious damage to a department in case of negotiation.'[28]

Farrer said that while competition was sound, other aspects of the new rules 'will make things much worse than they are'. He said the divisions between the grades were 'arbitrary'. He argued that some who passed into the highest grade would 'go back rather than forwards, and they are more likely to do so if they know they cannot be passed by those below them.' As for those further down the chain, 'there are sure to be some men of energy and ability, who have not been able to pass a first-rate examination at the age of twenty, but whose education, ability, and character develop as life goes on. These are, in my experience, some of the most valuable men in the service; but against such men the new scheme shuts every door of promotion and hope.' He condemned the plan for its 'aristocratic or rather plutocratic character.

It selects men by a competitive examination, demanding an expensive education in high subjects in early years, which only the rich can afford.'[29] He accepted that a more fluid promotion scheme would be open to abuse, but something more flexible had to be tried. This, however, was as far as Gladstone could go.

For the 'writer' grade, boys between fourteen and eighteen would be tested on 'Handwriting, orthography and arithmetic (elementary)' and men over eighteen in those subjects too, together with 'copying manuscript' (fiendishly difficult given the illegibility of much contemporary handwriting) and an optional 'Proportion, practice, and Vulgar and Decimal Fractions.'[30] At the other end of the scale, Lowe's reforms provided a new impetus to universities to improve their teaching to a level where their graduates would be able to enter this high-status and well-paid career. It broadened what they normally did, which was to prepare men to be schoolmasters, dons or clergymen: they became more outward-looking, more modern, and more relevant. They, like the schools he had so firmly supported, became the great engines of the meritocracy that would secure Britain's prosperity and success into the twentieth century.

II

The Crimean War was fought between an alliance of Britain, France and the Ottoman Empire against the Russians between 1854 and 1856. France and Russia had fallen out over which of them had the divine right to protect Christians in the Ottoman Empire, which was in steady decline. Britain, at that stage in a strong imperialistic mindset, saw opportunities to secure influence in the Middle East. Its Army was, however, appallingly led, quite often by stubborn and stupid old men who had bought their commands. As a result, some of the fighting had been a debacle, as depicted by Tennyson in 'The Charge of the Light Brigade': his immortal line 'someone had blundered' serves as a useful motto for the entire war. Support was so poorly organised that in the early months, even after Florence Nightingale took control of the medical treatment there, more men died of disease than of wounds. There were 21,097 British dead altogether: 2,755 were killed in action, 2,019 died of wounds and 16,323 died of disease. The war was, as has been mentioned, one of the main causes of reform of the Civil Service. It would also become a main cause of reform of the Army, whose inefficiency and mismanagement it had exposed.

As in the Civil Service, change would not come quickly. Various inquiries after the debacle in the Crimea recommended reforms, but by 1868, a dozen years after the last shot had been fired, none of any depth had been completed. This was thanks to the entrenched resistance of the officer class, whose vested interests were an immoveable obstacle. Army pay was reasonably good, but money was made by selling promotions. When a man wished to be promoted, he bought a place in the next rank up from an officer who was either retiring or moving up himself. When an officer finally retired he could sell his place and, depending upon his seniority, expect to be set up nicely in old age with the proceeds. The smartness of the regiment also affected the price: Lord Cardigan, a commander in the Crimea, bought the colonelcy of the 11th Hussars for £40,000, a vast fortune at the time. Those who retired after twenty-five years did so on half pay; after thirty years, full pay.

A Royal Commission of 1857 had decreed the practice of selling commissions 'repugnant to the public sentiment of the present day, and equally inconsistent with the honour of the military profession'.[31] It had continued that the system gave 'an undue pre-eminence to wealth, discouraging exertion, and depressing merit.' Also, since a man's commission died with him, soldiers went into battle knowing that apart from death they often had to fear the loss of a sizeable asset for their families. In the market for commissions, honour and disinterest were sacrificed to a commercial consideration. Cardwell also echoed the report's belief that some positions in the Army were so important, with the lives of countless men depending on the exercise of sound judgement by a senior officer, that they should be filled only on merit, not on the basis of who could afford them. Palmerston, in 1860, had accepted the burden of these criticisms; but eleven years later nothing had been done, usually because of the cost.

Not the least resistant to change was His Royal Highness Prince George, the Duke of Cambridge, a cousin of the Queen and Commander-in-Chief since 1856. Merit had not really entered into the Duke's military career. A colonel at eighteen, he was a major general by twenty-six. He had commanded a division in the Crimea, though poor health cut short his campaign there. In 1862 he became a field marshal. The Duke regarded the officer class as socially exclusive and intended it to stay that way.

Theoretical questions of warfare or organisation were of no interest to him, and he gave no encouragement to anyone else to pursue them. The idea of a meritocracy in the Army that might improve it was anathematical to him. However, he had been an early advocate of the breech-loading carbine in the late 1850s and early 1860s, and instituted annual manoeuvres to keep the Army on its toes. He supported the creation of the Staff College and the Royal Military School of Music, and he had, before it was limited by law, restricted flogging to habitual offenders.

Gladstone appointed Edward Cardwell to the War Office, and he set about reform. The penal character of the service (with flogging and other brutal punishments) had been alleviated by the outgoing government, whose Mutiny Act abolished flogging except in military prisons after a court martial, putting the punishment on a par with that awarded in civilian courts for violent offences. There had been resistance in the service to this – the Duke of Wellington had been a committed flogger and, although dead since 1852, his model was one adhered to by the Duke of Cambridge and the senior cadre in the service. Cardwell's main target was something even more entrenched: the purchase of commissions. He wanted to ensure that advancement in the Army was by ability and not birth, as was happening in the Civil Service. He did not want this just for its own, egalitarian sake: but because all other structural reform of the service flowed from the establishment of a meritocracy within it.

George Otto Trevelyan, then a young Liberal MP, had written a pamphlet on the subject, which he had also sent to Gladstone in July 1868, advocating the abolition of purchase 'on the ground of public morality quite as much as on that of national defence.'[32] He and Florence Nightingale had corresponded about the inadequacies of the Army. In November 1868 he said he was glad she saw 'the indefensible character of the present army system and the necessity of modifying it, whatever the difficulties may be.'[33] She had complained to him of how 'an enormous amount of confusion, complication and means of jobbing exists in the present system' and how 'this is traceable upwards to the purchase system.' However, she worried whether 'our army can exist without purchase'. Trevelyan said 'the practical effect of purchase is to confine the Army to aristocrats, or persons who wish to take rank as such, and the residuum and waifs and strays of society. The middle class and the

real working class have at present no place in the army, which offers
them neither remunerative wages nor an open career.' He continued,
on the subject of the costs of messing, that 'the only way to reduce
regimental expenses of all kinds is to increase the proportion of officers
who enter the army as a profession and live by it, which can only be
done by the abolition of purchase.'

Nightingale was concerned about the social consequences: and he
reassured her that 'Earls would not have to meet labourers' sons as
fellow-officers, if by labourers' sons [we mean] persons of inferior education and coarse vulgar manners, who are unfit for the society of
gentlemen.' There would, though, be a rule that 'a fixed proportion of
the vacant commissions in each regiment should be given to non-
commissioned officers <u>provided candidates are forthcoming who are in
every way qualified to bear Her Majesty's Commission</u>. Of this the
officers themselves would be the judges, as they are in the highly aristocratic Austrian and Prussian armies where the majority of officers are
promoted from the ranks.'

Trevelyan, however, was sanguine about fluidity in society. 'I cannot
admit that the upper classes in this country shew any indisposition to
associate freely with the lower classes <u>as such</u>. On the contrary, it is the
glory and strength of our aristocracy that they are constantly undergoing
a process of renovation from below, and that they mix without reserve
in Parliament, in private society, in the Church, the Law, the English
and Indian Civil Services, in associations for public and private objects
of every sort, with persons of inferior rank. There is no such thing as
a hard and fast line between our aristocracy and the rest of the community.'[34] He added: 'In spite of the exclusive system upon which our army
is founded, the generous open-hearted manners of English gentlemen
prevail there as everywhere else, and nothing can be more remarkable
than the welcome uniformly given to deserving non-commissioned
officers who are promoted to commissions. This is so even now when
the persons promoted are in large proportion of inferior education and
manners.' Nightingale still feared that abolition of purchase would
imperil the aristocracy, but Trevelyan informed her that 'if there were
no such thing as an army the aristocratic principle would still be strong
in English society. Real equality is impossible in human affairs, and least
of all in this country of increasing personal activity and competition.'

At Cabinet level, the main consideration was what to do about the

Duke of Cambridge: and if he could not be removed, how best he could be circumvented. Gladstone knew that the Duke 'is appointed not for any limited period but during HM's pleasure'.[35] There was always a difficult relationship between him and the Secretary of State. Cardwell submitted to Gladstone in February 1870 that if Army discipline were thought to be unsatisfactory, and 'if there were anything in the conduct of the Commander in Chief, which required the interference of the Secretary of State, the Secretary of State has not only the right, but it is his bounden duty to interfere'.[36] He concluded: 'It will be desirable that you should submit your views upon the subject to the Queen.'

The Duke was touchy. When Trevelyan, in a speech in Hawick early in 1869, said that 'I do maintain that it is not right that a Royal Duke should be placed permanently in such a situation as that of Commander-in-Chief', the Duke and the Queen were outraged.[37] Trevelyan was a Civil Lord of the Admiralty, appointed just a few weeks earlier. Gladstone felt constrained to write to Sir Charles Trevelyan, his father, on what he called this 'embarrassing and grave matter' to try and engineer the required grovelling apology.[38] Cardwell then spent the best part of a fortnight hosing down the Duke and the Queen while the right level of contrition was obtained from young George. His father helped him: as he told Gladstone, with mandarin ambiguity, 'no one can feel more strongly than my son the mistake he made in alluding to His Royal Highness'.[39]

The miscreant himself wrote to Gladstone on 8 January partly blaming the press. The comments were 'copied into the *Pall Mall Gazette*: a form in which those remarks appear even more indiscreet than they in fact were. I enclose a full report: but even in this shape I feel – and felt the moment the words had been spoken – that they were unwise in the highest degree.'[40] However, his main wrath was reserved for 'journalists', since 'the idea of anyone except the Commander-in-Chief being alluded to never seems accordingly to have occurred to them.' However, resuming contrition, he added: 'I have received a lesson I shall never forget,' and offered his resignation. 'Whatever course you consider it best to adopt I shall readily acquiesce in . . . it is for you to judge in what capacity I can do it [the government] the best service and the least damage.'

Gladstone reassured him. He had had 'one of those lapses of tongue to which as I well know we are all liable.'[41] He added that trying to explain what he had meant would only compound his fault. It would be best simply to apologise unreservedly, 'freely, I mean unsparingly, in a letter to me.' He would then have the letter sent on to Osborne. Trevelyan did just that, apologising again to Gladstone for his 'exultation' in the matter of Army reform that had caused this excess of zeal.[42] He was helped by the fact that Gladstone agreed with every word he had said. That was the Queen placated: the Duke was another matter, and Trevelyan and Cardwell had to discuss how to deal with him: Cardwell would, as the senior minister, present Trevelyan's contrition on his behalf.

Cardwell raised the question of Army reform in the spring of 1870. It became far more pressing with the instability of the near Continent, caused by France's declaration of war on Prussia on 19 July that year. On 1 August Gladstone gave Disraeli notice that, as a result of the emergency, he would ask Parliament to approve an extra £2 million for the two Armed Forces, and the recruitment of another 20,000 men for the Army. It was feared Britain might, as would happen in 1914, have to respond to an attack on the neutrality of Belgium, of which it was guarantor. It was also felt that a larger military establishment, with greater demands made on it, could not exist side by side with so antiquated a system as that of purchase regulating commissions and promotions. A Royal Commission that year found that there had been a 'habitual violation of the law by officers of all ranks under that of major-general, supported by long-established custom and unchecked by any authority' in the matter of regulating the prices of commissions.[43]

Gladstone and Cardwell started to discuss details of the abolition of purchase in the autumn. For Gladstone, abolition was necessary not merely to raise the standard of the officer class, but also to remoralise a class that had become indolent and was contributing insufficiently to society. He wrote a lengthy memorandum about this on 13 October 1870, an interesting example of how his mind worked. If one part of the Army's organisation were to be reformed then, he felt, the whole institution should be reformed in a way that was 'complete and definitive'.[44] It was not just the home Army, but the Indian and Colonial Armies and the militia too that required modernisation. Given the crushing success Prussia was having, that state's army was taken very much as the model for what Gladstone desired, especially in the arrangements for officering the Army.

This would be controversial, not least in imposing Gladstone's moral framework on a group of men who did not entirely share it. He was determined there had to be 'an accurate and close adjustment between work, pay and privileges'. This was how things were for NCOs and other ranks; he could not see why it should not be the same for the officer class. The most expensive commissions were, inevitably, those that brought the largest element of sinecure. Together with the abolition of purchase, sinecures should be cut down, and holders who survived should be on reduced rates of pay. 'As this country has a vast leisured and wealthy class,' he wrote, 'and as it derives advantage therefrom in an unpaid magistracy and Parliament, so the same constitution of our society should be borne in mind when we proceed to readjust the system of officering for the army. That description of labour, important as it is, should not be dear but cheap.'

He worried that young men went into the Army too young. 'That portion of our youth who go into the army, are certainly and must be on the whole below the average in avidity for knowledge,' he observed, crushingly. 'Yet they have hitherto when mere boys been separated from their schoolfellows, prematurely installed in the privileges of manhood, and surrounded with all the dangers of idleness.' Happily, Britain attempted to avoid war: 'The greatest difficulty of all in truth is this: to redeem the officer's life from idleness in time of peace . . . this profession is, in time of peace, apt to fall as much below the ordinary standard of need for continuous energetic exertion, as in war it rise above that standard.' To do this Gladstone wanted a European-style cadetship, in which youths would learn the art of soldiering as the ordinary soldier did. This would become the routine at Sandhurst, which had been on the Berkshire/Surrey border since 1813 and trained 'gentlemen cadets' for the cavalry, infantry and Indian Army, and in other officer training schools.

The Prime Minister was under no illusion that this reform would be 'an enormous business', and that a detailed alternative system had to be in place before proceeding.[45] He was also clear that nothing could be done to disturb the equilibrium of the Army until after peace was made between France and Prussia, in case it had to go into action. Lowe, the Chancellor, threw up an obstacle in January 1871, just before Parliament met for the new session. He told Gladstone that the sum required to compensate officers whose commissions represented one of their main assets, but who would no longer be allowed to sell them on, was so huge that the country would need to go into debt to pay it.

Gladstone told Cardwell this news was 'a perfect bombshell', and constituted 'a measure the most destructive to our finance that has been either adopted or suggested in my time.'[46] He continued: 'To have been for near ten years the finance minister of this country, and to end my career with a loan in aid of the annual expenditure for the redemption of Commissions is not possible.' He said it was 'impossible' for him to assent to the proposal as it stood. The next day Cabinet discussed it, and agreed a potential £3 million increase in the Army estimates, so important was it agreed that abolition of purchase had become. In the mid-nineteenth century, to buy the rank of lieutenant colonel in a guards regiment would cost about £7,250: but the officer could sell his majority for £5,350, so he had to find £1,900 to fund his promotion. A major at the time earned £315 a year, rising to £427 as a lieutenant colonel.[47]

Cardwell, summoned to Osborne, asked the Queen on 22 January 1871 to approve in principle the abolition of purchase and changes in the conditions of employment of officers on the reserve: and this necessitated making the office of Military Secretary a public one, removing it from the personal staff of the Duke.[48] He told the Queen that it 'was not possible to defend the absolute exception of his office from the 5 years rule'. The Queen told Cardwell that 'she hopes to be able to give her assent to the proposals' but would write to him about it, presumably after further discussions with the Duke, who would also be expected to move his office from Horse Guards to the War Office, where Cardwell could keep a closer eye on him. The Duke agreed to this last point under duress, according to the Queen, who with the aid of the random and aggressive underlining that characterised her moments of emotion in her letters, said it was 'on condition that it is clearly understood and stated that he does so <u>temporarily</u> to facilitate the transaction of business and that it is <u>intended</u> to build a new War Office in <u>connection</u> with the <u>present Horse Guards</u> <u>as soon</u> as possible and further the Commander in Chief must have a <u>distinct</u> and <u>separate</u> entrance into <u>that portion</u> of building allotted to him in Pall Mall, which must be called 'the Horse Guards'.[49]

The matter came to the Commons on 16 February 1871. The Cabinet had decided that entry to the commissioned ranks of the Army would in future be from: Sandhurst, 'admission to which shall be obtained by competitive examination'; from subalterns in the militia with more than two years' service who had passed an examination and been recommended by their district staff officer; from the ranks of NCOs, by open competition; and from Cadets.[50] Promotion thereafter would be founded upon 'a principle of selection'. Regiments would decide promotions from subaltern to captain, the Army would decide the rest. Control of the militia passed from the Lords Lieutenant to the Secretary of State.

The Army Regulation Bill itself mentioned that the buying and selling of offices had technically been abolished under Edward VI, and again in 1809 under George III, with an exemption for the 'sales or exchanges of any commission in Our Forces'. It proposed now to 'render illegal' all sales.[51] There would be compensation on retirement for those who had bought something they now could not sell on. In the three years 1868–70 the officer class had had 330 new recruits by promotion and 932 by purchase. Of the 330, Sandhurst had provided 268, and sixty-two had come from the ranks, though that number had dropped from thirty-six in 1868 to eight in 1870.[52] A system of gradual retirement would be imposed, so the large sums of money required – possibly £7.5 million to £8.5 million – would not all have to be paid out at once: but there would still be huge objections to it being paid at all. Since first commissions could no longer be bought, Cardwell announced that they would be awarded to men who completed the course at Sandhurst and showed they were fit to be officers; and admission to Sandhurst would be by competitive examination. Thus officers would still be gentlemen; but they would not be able to buy their way to a commission by affording to be educated at Sandhurst and to maintain the dignity of an officer once commissioned. University graduates would be eligible for commissions too, and members of the public could apply for one by competitive examination. Promotion would be on merit, and on the basis of detailed reports of the officer's conduct and abilities.

This statement of intent also opened a hornet's nest in the shape of the continued rule of the Duke of Cambridge; but since the man opening it was George Trevelyan, it did not entirely dismay the Liberal leadership: though having aired the matter Trevelyan was urged by Cardwell not to press the question to a vote. He moved a resolution in the Commons on 21 February that no military reorganisation could be considered complete unless it altered the tenure of the Commander-in-Chief 'in such a manner as to enable the Secretary of State to avail himself freely of the best administrative talent and the most recent military experience from time to time existing in the British Army'.[53] No one could pretend such a definition included the Duke. The joke then got better, for the second part of Trevelyan's resolution urged that 'the consideration of the cost involved in the abolition of the Purchase system urgently calls for the immediate removal of obsolete and antiquated sources of military expenditure.'

The problem was a system of dual government: the Duke running the Army from his desk in Horse Guards, and Cardwell trying to run it too from his desk in the War Office. Trevelyan observed it was impossible to remove the Commander-in-Chief 'without some stigma being inflicted', and claimed the Duke had done nothing in his service to deserve that.[54] However, he suggested the job ought to go to an active senior officer, and be held in rotation among the best in the Army, so that the Secretary of State's principal military adviser would be someone with very recent experience of the sharp end of soldiering. What Trevelyan was suggesting was remarkably similar to how the administration of the service evolved in the twentieth century, with a Chief of the General Staff holding his position usually for three years. Not wishing to insult the Duke of Cambridge too directly, Trevelyan referred instead to the obstinacy of the Duke of Wellington, who until 1852 ran the Army as it had been during the Peninsular Wars, with a regard for obsolete weaponry (the musket being preferred to the rifle), a wilful detestation of all modern advances and practices, and retaining a fanaticism for excessive and savage corporal punishment that made the Army seem more like a prison than a decent fighting force. Permanent tenure for the incumbent of the post was a disaster for the Army, and leaving control of promotion in the hands of the Duke utterly undesirable, given his opposition to selection on merit.

Trevelyan was concerned that, with purchase likely to be abolished, great power would remain vested in the Duke to advance or retard the careers of young officers. Open competition was essential: it had operated in the Civil Service since the Northcote–Trevelyan reforms, it had operated in the public schools since the Clarendon reforms, and there was no reason at all why it should not operate in an institution so vital as the Army. Part of his purpose was to highlight the Duke's resistance to the abolition of purchase: the Commander-in-Chief, manifestly not understanding the government-controlled way in which commissions would be obtained in future, had said abolition would not work because it would be replaced by under-the-counter purchase.

For good measure, he pointed out how, thanks to the Duke's lassitude and indulgence, a number of senior officers received enormous pensions for doing nothing, and a number of serving officers, notably in the Brigade of Guards, did nothing in return for their handsome remunerations either. Trevelyan, on behalf of numerous Liberal MPs, said the time had come for control of the Army to pass from the Court to the elected government. On the other side, as became apparent during the subsequent debate, the Tories still liked the Duke and claimed in their defence that he had the backing of the Army. He also, of course, fulfilled the function when the Liberals were in power of obstructing them in what might be considered the Tory interest. Cardwell attempted to soothe matters. He announced that dual government was over, an Order in Council having settled the Secretary of State's authority over the Army: and, for good measure, as agreed with the Queen, the Duke would be moving into the War Office, to work more closely with Cardwell. He also, perhaps less sincerely, defended the present tenure of the Duke's office by raising the fear that a rotating appointment would become politicised. Nonetheless, Trevelyan forced a vote; and although he lost by 83 to 201, he showed a substantial minority were unhappy with the status quo.

When the Army Regulation Bill had its second reading some former officers in the Commons vigorously defended privilege and assaulted the proposed meritocracy. Although some disclosed their inherent snobbery – the Nightingale point that someone who was not a gentleman might slip through – the principal excuse was the expense of compensating those nearing retirement. Europe was tense because of the Franco-Prussian war and the unification of Germany, which had happened just six weeks earlier: if, one former officer argued, there was all this money (and the figure discussed varied between £8 million and £14 million, an inexactitude seized on by supporters of reform), would it not be better used to defend the nation? The MP concerned, Colonel Charles White, dismissed the advantages of selection on merit. The present system, he said, had 'much to be urged in its favour'.[55] 'Denounce it as hon. Gentlemen may at Birmingham, Manchester, and elsewhere, it has officered our Army for centuries with a class of men who have made the term "an English officer" and "a gentleman" to be synonymous, and to be understood all over the world. It has officered our armies for centuries with a class of men, whom, though you will not believe it—we soldiers know it—the British soldier as at present constituted prefers to obey willingly, to serve cheerfully, and to follow devotedly. The British officer belongs to a class who have led the armies of England—as I very much doubt their successors will lead them—to a class whose memory defies you to dare to detract either from their character or efficiency.'

White ridiculed the notion that selection or promotion on merit could be carried out fairly or satisfactorily, because it would be based on a system of 'secret reporting', which was 'un-English'. It would change officers from what they were then – 'manly, generous and open' – into 'sycophants, fawners, and time-servers.'[56] He pointed to 'the case of a subaltern who got all his hunting leave because he scrupulously supplied his colonel's wife every morning with hot-house flowers'. His final harrumph was to assert that the government was legislating on the whim of one man – a dig at Trevelyan, and an absurd one, given the determination across the Liberal benches to abolish purchase.

The debate lasted five days: and when Cardwell eventually spoke on the fourth he summed up the opposition he was facing in addressing one of his military critics: 'the right time will never come for abolishing purchase when the hon Gentleman does not wish purchase to be abolished at all'.[57] He maintained that 'my impression is that if we pass this Bill into a law, its effect will be to attract to the Army the aristocracy of merit and professional talent, which is after all the true aristocracy.'[58] Gladstone, closing the debate, argued that the abolition of purchase was not 'in itself a great reform', but was 'the removal of what we believe an insurmountable impediment to essential reform'.[59] The bill received its second reading, Disraeli understanding the system could not continue as it was, though promising to offer amendments to the bill when it went into committee: the fight had only really started. In a memo of 8 March 1871 Gladstone had expressed his 'fear that the heavy cost of abolition of purchase would cause many of the liberals to hesitate as to giving it . . . support when they connect it with the large increase in the estimates.'[60] A few days later he noted that 'the expectations which were fostered in the country by members of the present Government previously to their attainment of office are not sustained by the proposals with respect to military expenditure which they have laid before Parliament.'[61]

The committee stage started on 8 May, with Colonel the Hon. Augustus Anson, the son of an earl, describing promotion on merit as 'a system antagonistic to the instincts of a soldier, and consequently hateful to him'.[62] He said the exchange of commissions between officers was vital for the social lives and professional prospects of many soldiers, and the reforms had complete disregard for this. He accused Trevelyan of having misled public opinion, and the government of ignoring how it made money out of selling commissions: sixty-six colonelcies had been sold in the preceding nine years for a total of £276,000, or an average of almost £4,500 each. Yet all the abuse was being directed at the officers who had supposedly been sole beneficiaries of the system, and were now, he claimed, being accused by the Prime Minister of bearing the responsibility for the present difficulties. They had had – he said – enough.

This was too much for Gladstone, who intervened and told Anson that he, and the government, had done nothing of the sort. Anson disputed this, saying Gladstone had described the government's role as being that of 'steward' between one officer and another when transactions took place. Anson also asked what would become of the ensign who had just paid £450 for his commission, and would lose every penny unless he retired at once? And what about the non-purchase officers – of whom there were many in the less smart regiments – who had been told they would be paid the full value of their commissions after twenty years' service? And wasn't it, he suggested, unfair that officers who had purchased seniority above those of the same rank should, if merit were to start to come into it, find their seniority reversed by the promotion of others? 'Infinite jealousies and heart-burnings' would result, he predicted, 'tending to the utter extinction of the existing discipline and morale of the Army.'[63]

Although some senior and progressive Conservatives questioned the bill – Richard Cross, the great reforming force of the Disraeli administration after 1874, conceded it would improve the Army, but at the cost of impoverishing it because of the huge sums required for compensation – it was left to the military old guard to mount the main defence. Cardwell goaded them: he suggested to Anson that he cared not a jot for privates, non-commissioned officers or poor officers, but only for the value of the assets of rich men. On 27/28 May 1871, in the middle of committee stage, Gladstone and Cardwell exchanged letters about the state of play. Gladstone found it hard to understand why a young man of eighteen receiving a commission – whether by purchase or otherwise – should effectively have a job for life, when he might turn out to be a useless officer. 'I suggest that we should attach to commissions of first entry *into* the army a temporary character. A great number of temporary or term-officers you have now, & you must have hereafter. Why are they to be such at their own pleasure only?'[64] He argued that in years to come the admission of new officers on a temporary basis would allow many to be shown the door, and would reinforce the principle of selection on which both he and Cardwell hoped to make the Army proceed.

Cardwell replied the next day: 'The abolition of purchase is a clear gain to both rich and poor. The outcry against it is unreal and as Vivian [a Liberal MP] truly said they are only trying "what more can we get?" But the abolition of the practice of selling exchanges is the exclusion of the indolent and self-indulgent from the service, and the prohibition to the others of a gain which they now enjoy from ministering to the indolence and self-indulgence of men whom the service can very well spare.'[65] He concluded, rousingly, 'In short our principle is that the officers shall be made for the Army. Their principle is that the Army is made for the officers.' The argument about money overrode all others as the discussions wore on, though Cardwell did separately promise that more detailed reports would be made by their superiors on all officers in future, so the Commander-in-Chief could have the most complete understanding of an officer's character and abilities before recommending him for promotion. This, though Cardwell was too tactful to say it, would obviate the problem of the Duke having to judge the merits of a gentleman whom he did not know socially. The diehard Tories against the bill in the Commons, seeing no hope of success there, started to threaten that it might never get through the Lords, where their party commanded a majority and where it had a history of blinkered recalcitrance. They claimed the imposition on taxpayers was too high, even though public opinion, they conceded, supported the abolition of purchase, and even though the numbers of officers who would be allowed to sell out in any one year was to be strictly regulated by law, to avoid breaking the Treasury.

One scandal that emerged during the long debate was over-regulation prices: officers paying more than the set tariff for a particular posting, because of the laws of supply and demand working in the favour of the seller. This was illegal, but had been connived at by the War Office and the Army for years, and by commanders-in-chief such as the Duke of Wellington, who had in the 1830s argued that the emoluments of one officer be increased precisely because he had had to pay over the odds to secure his position. It was alleged that more than £3 million had been paid illegally by serving officers. When they came to be compensated, they would receive only the tariff price, and so were about to be financially punished for having broken the rules. The government did not regard this as its problem.

However, over-purchase was a problem for the Army. It tainted everyone who engaged in it or condoned it, from the Duke downwards. It created an alternative view of an officer class whose honour, decency and selflessness had been paraded around the Commons all through the spring of 1871, and showed officers instead in some instances to be little better than tradesmen. Given what had turned out to be the officer class's obsession with money, Cardwell did some research into how their pay compared with that of officers in the army he most admired, the Prussian. In reforming the Army Cardwell took Prussia very much as his model. He sought to discover, in June 1871, what the comparative rates of pay were between the two armies.[66] It was found that a lieutenant colonel in the infantry was paid £360 4s a year, whereas his Prussian counterpart received £266 8s: however, purchasing power was very different between the two countries, and it was noted 'that money is three times more valuable in Prussia than England'.[67] A better comparison, it was decided, was America, where a lieutenant colonel earned £514 a year, though a War Office official added this note: 'It is worthy of note that the Prussian officers [are] essentially an aristocratic body [and] as a rule practise the utmost frugality.'

Gladstone told the Duke of Cambridge on 9 July, after the bill had cleared the Commons, that as the charging of over-regulation prices was illegal, the purchase question had reached the stage where 'it must go forward in the hands of any Govt whatever, and consequently that the recognition of this necessity cannot constitute a mark of adhesion to any one Govt in particular, or a ground of quarrel or misunderstanding with any other.'[68] To do otherwise would be to condone a system that had, it was now proven, fostered illegality. In case the Duke was still thinking of abstaining when the measure came to the Lords, he was told by Gladstone that this view 'in substance [has] the sanction of HM.' Gladstone also offered to go to see him, and pointed out the precedent of the Duke's predecessor, the Duke of Wellington, supporting government measures. Gladstone followed this up five days later telling the Duke that 'nor is any declaration asked as to purchase on its merits. Purchase is gone. The only question remaining is the mode of abolition; and I learned with pleasure from YRH that as matters now stand you consider the passing of the Bill to be the best mode.'[69] Since the exposure of what had effectively been a racket, support for the status quo had dropped, and the diehards were becoming more marginalised. Cardwell and Gladstone's decision to pursue abolition came to look more and more sensible and inspired by the day.

Yet despite this hopeful observation the Duke, who 'has been making great efforts and holding rather strong language', according to a conversation Gladstone had had at Windsor in early July 1871 with the courtier Sir Thomas Biddulph, remained a big obstacle to change.[70] The Duke let it be known he was minded to tell the Lords to look after the officers; Gladstone wanted him simply to recommend they pass the bill. The Duke had sought to enlist his cousin, the Queen, to bring Gladstone into line, by explaining to him that it was wrong that a royal personage should vote in the Lords (even though the Duke had, on several occasions, done just that): but in one of those exchanges that so endeared the Prime Minister to the Sovereign, he refused to be cowed: 'I said that what the Cabinet had mainly discussed and had in view was the Duke's recommendation to the House which would come in a speech: but I observed that the Duke's own position would be most unsatisfactory, and scarcely worthy, if he advised the House of Lords to take a certain course, and then shrank from taking it himself.' In a separate note to Cardwell, Gladstone went so far as to describe the Duke's prospective position, in a note to his Cabinet, as 'unmanly'.[71]

'I shall be glad to know how this point strikes my colleagues,' Gladstone continued. 'I do not think that we could guarantee the defensibility of the Duke's position if he declines to vote; though some weight might be allowed, under favourable circumstances, to the plea that it is his general rule to abstain from voting.' Lord Hartington, the Irish Secretary, advised Gladstone that 'if the Duke of Cambridge will recommend the House of Lords to pass the Bill on the grounds that purchase will sooner or later be abolished, and that the terms of the present measure are liberal to the officers, I think that he will have done all that can reasonably be asked. If the Duke has usually abstained from voting, I should not think it necessary to insist upon it in this case.'[72] Lord Halifax, the Lord Privy Seal, agreed with him. However, Lord Ripon, the Lord President, agreed with Hartington on the first point, but said he would 'greatly regret for HRH's own sake if he were to abstain from voting after having urged the House of Lords to pass the Bill: such a position does not seem to me to be tenable.'[73] Chichester Fortescue, the President of the Board of Trade, agreed with Ripon.

Cardwell himself asked what the arrangements for the Duke's continued tenure could be if he were unhelpful – not least since Cardwell, who wanted the Duke out, had agreed to his tenure being extended in return for his cooperation. 'It seems to me that this is a very serious question, and that HRH ought distinctly to understand the position in which he will be placed towards the Government and the Government towards him, if he does not fulfil the spirit of the engagement which was made on his behalf.'[74] George Goschen, the First Lord of the Admiralty, agreed. Hatherley, the Lord Chancellor, said the Duke's position would be seen as 'hostile' if he abstained.[75] So did Henry Bruce, the Home Secretary, and Lord Kimberley, the Colonial Secretary. Lowe asserted that:

> the appointment of the Commander in Chief for an indefinite time was justified on the grounds that he ought not to retain office at all if his views were not in accordance with those of the ministry of the day . . . I always regarded this decision as establishing that this was not a staff but a political appointment and would treat it accordingly . . . It is very well known that the Duke has allowed himself great licence of language on this question and that his immediate entourage has assisted in getting up the opposition to our Bill . . . he should be told that he can only retain his place on the condition of voting and speaking without reservation in favour of the Bill and that we should make up our minds to give the fullest effect to what we say – otherwise I do not think you can count on the support of the House in finding the money for War Reform and you will stand convicted of deceit and bad faith. [76]

The Lords tried to prevent a second reading until it had more detail of the new means of granting commissions and allowing promotions.

The bill did not merely abolish purchase: it also sought to put the militia on a more efficient footing and to reorganise it and the regular Army. It was deemed by Tories in the Lords that not enough detail had been provided on these points either. There was talk of a Royal Commission, which would have delayed progress by a year or two: and all this came on top of the obstreperousness of the Duke, and his determination to save as much of the old, Wellingtonian, order as possible. The Cabinet, meeting on 12 July, considered its options. One was to stop proceedings and start afresh the following session: Parliament was due to rise for the long recess in a month. This idea, which would have undermined the government drastically, was not pursued. However, another option – to abolish purchase by means of a Royal Warrant, and let the Lords do what it would with the bill – was. After all the time spent discussing abolition, this coup caused outrage, with peers and MPs asking why it had not been adopted before. Gladstone's excuse was that the illegal activity of over-purchase had now been exposed, and could not be allowed to continue a moment longer. As the illegal activity had been condoned by Royal Warrant in 1809, Royal Warrant could stop it. And it did. The government also protested that Army organisation was not a matter for an Act of Parliament, but for day-to-day management by the administration: but this could not happen efficiently while what Lord Northbrook, who spoke for the War Office in the Lords, called the 'spider's web of vested interests' that was the purchase system remained in place.[77] He gave examples of whole regimental reconstructions thwarted because senior officers would lose money; and stressed the impossibility under a purchase system of moving officers from the regular Army to the militia, and vice versa.

The star turn in the Lords' debate was, inevitably, the Duke of Cambridge, who on 14 July 1871 took the House into his confidence. He was conscious that, if the bill was enacted, 'the serious responsibility of . . . selection, which all admit is difficult, and many declare to be next to impossible' would devolve upon him.[78] He spoke of his devotion to the regimental system, and added that 'It is intended, unless I am greatly mistaken, that after purchase has been put an end to the system shall be one of seniority tempered by selection; for example, if an officer is unfit to command a regiment he will not, by the course of promotion, receive the command of one, and, on the other hand, eminent profes- sional talent will be recognized and encouraged; but care will be taken, as I understand, to preserve the regimental system as far as possible, providing also that purchase does not revive under a new form.'[79]

The Duke admitted the Army had been a shambles when he took it over, and that the Franco-Prussian conflict had concentrated minds, at last, on putting the service 'on a more secure and satisfactory footing'.[80] However, he also stated – principally, one supposes, to his brother officers – that he had no power as Commander-in-Chief to initiate policy, which was the duty of Her Majesty's ministers. Lest this be thought a Pontius Pilate move, the Duke set out his views unequivocally. Purchase, he said 'cannot be defended for a moment'.[81] It should be abolished, even though he had given evidence to the inquiry into the subject stating the opposite. He explained his U-turn. 'I felt it to be absolutely necessary that there should be a flow of promotion in the Army, and because the purchase system maintained such a flow; and the money came out of the pockets of the officers. But now that the country is prepared to make the necessary sacrifice, and is willing to incur a vast expenditure in order to put an end to the system, and is also willing to provide good retirements, the injustice of abolishing and the advantages of retaining purchase have disappeared altogether.' He had simply not believed the Commons would vote such a generous sum, but it had. The Queen persuaded him not to vote against the bill, and he abstained.

The abolition by Royal Warrant had one profound drawback for the privileged class that had opposed it: it gave them none of the compensation the bill had offered. If the bill were enacted, there would be compensation. Suddenly, after much expression of outrage, the Lords passed it, securing the financial rights of their own class. Cardwell and Gladstone could breathe again, but the time devoted to the measure wrecked the rest of the government's legislative programme for that session. Nevertheless, the Army had been given modern foundations, and its officer class forced to live according to the meritocratic principles that Gladstone so admired in the next rank down of society.

Gladstone's difficult relations with Queen Victoria were not eased by his asking her to intervene with her cousin. However, the real problem he had with her was her caprice. The word she used time and again to describe the man who served her four times as Prime Minister was 'incomprehensible'.[82] Writing to her daughter the Crown Princess of Prussia in September 1869, after Gladstone had been at Balmoral, the Queen said that 'I cannot find him very agreeable, and he talks so very much.'[83] This was mild compared with what she would be saying later in his premiership. In February 1872 she asserted that 'Mr Gladstone is a very dangerous Minister – and so wonderfully unsympathetic.'[84] In the former observation she merely repeated something said to her by Palmerston.[85] These opinions, too, were mild compared with how she would regard him after he had left office, and had begun to concern himself with the Eastern question. The Queen regarded his views on that as objectionable, since she felt he wished to hand Constantinople over to the Russians. By 1877 she was referring to him as 'that half-madman'.[86] Within a few weeks he had been promoted, and had become quite simply 'that madman'.[87]

Her daughter, who from the safe distance of Berlin had no day-to-day experience of Gladstone, surmised that 'the government is composed of very clever, talented, eminent, and highly cultivated men – who hold all the principles which seem philosophically to be the undoubtedly right ones for the present day, but they seem to lack that tact and *savoir faire* which is the essence of statesmanship and which does not depend upon knowledge alone, at any rate one has seen it oftenest in the highest – but not in the most highly educated and learned men.' In other words, Gladstone was too intelligent and principled to fawn in the way that some of his predecessors and colleagues had or did, which the Royal Family put down to intellectual arrogance and a lack of breeding. What the Princess called 'modern middle-class government' might have been recognised by her as a necessary reflection of changes in society, but had (to the Royal Family) its disadvantages.

Unfortunately, Gladstone and the Queen needed each other. Although she never admitted it, she needed him to support her at a time when her behaviour had made her deeply unpopular. Public feeling against her was stimulated by her refusal to participate properly in public life, while costing the taxpayer an inordinate sum. George Leaper, the honorary secretary of the Hull Republican club, wrote to Gladstone on 30 July 1873 enclosing a resolution 'unanimously adopted at a large meeting held in Hull last evening in condemnation of any further grant of public money being made to the Duke of Edinburgh on his approaching marriage.'[88] But Gladstone defended her against extravagance. After a pamphlet was published entitled *What does she do with it?* asking where all the money went, Gladstone wrote a rebuttal. It began with the statement: 'no accurate information can be obtained on this subject.'[89] He was a loyal Prime Minister, not least because, at moments such as with the Duke of Cambridge, he needed her.

III

Apart from the Army and the Civil Service the other closed elite the Gladstone ministry resolved to take on, in the interests of meritocracy, were the ancient universities of Oxford and Cambridge. Dominated by the Established Church, they were more like seminaries than places of intellectual development. Though nominally wedded to minimalism in government, the Liberal party wished to make changes to benefit the poor and improve social mobility. When Layard stood for election in Southwark in November 1868, he told his electors: 'I have ever supported such Liberal measures as tend to the amelioration of the condition of the people.'[90] Thus, in 1869 the government decided to compel in the universities 'that amount of religious freedom in regard to all the subjects of the Queen which the House of Commons at least by overwhelming majorities on previous occasions has declared that it thinks just and right.'[91] The latest example of injustice was that the Senior Wrangler at Cambridge had been a Jew, but was not allowed to receive the distinction. The Oxford and Cambridge Universities Acts of 1854 and 1856 respectively had removed the need for those wishing to matriculate at the universities, or to take degrees, to sign the Thirty-nine Articles. However, the pursuit of academic excellence was handicapped by the inability of men who could not sign the Articles from proceeding to the degree of Master of Arts, to doctorates or to fellowships, or to receive university prizes and distinctions: the problem Clough had had twenty years earlier. It was ironic that the administration seeking to remedy this was led by probably the most profoundly Christian Prime Minister of the nineteenth century, and quite possibly in British history.

Although secularisation was perceived to be on the advance, many in the Church of England, especially in Oxford and Cambridge, would not admit it. They also maintained that the State had not contributed to the wealth, endowment or work of Oxford and Cambridge, and therefore had no right to dictate how the universities would regulate themselves. It was also feared the universities would, if allowed to forgo the religious tests, become magnets for Nonconformists, and would be ruined as places for the teaching of religion. However, supporters of the abolition of the Test could not understand why the Church felt so insecure that it wished to continue to deny a fellowship to those who would not sign the Thirty-nine Articles.

After Henry Sidgwick, a distinguished utilitarian philosopher, resigned his fellowship at Trinity College, Cambridge in 1869, because he could no longer subscribe to the Articles and felt he should not hold an appointment that required him to, some in the university decided to seek abolition of the religious tests. However, on 13 January 1870 a memorial was sent to Gladstone, signed by 'the leading Residents, and senior members of the Senate' of the university, deploring the passing of any legislation that would facilitate such a thing. They argued that it would 'seriously imperil the Christian character of the said University and Colleges and their efficiency as places of Religious Education', and added that they 'earnestly deprecate any legislation by which the government and teaching of the Universities of Oxford and Cambridge, or of the Colleges in the same, may be transferred altogether or in part into the hands of persons who are not members of the Established Church.'[92] However, one of those driving the reform was the Master of St John's College, Cambridge, W. H. Bateson, who wrote to Gladstone in February 1870 to say that, following deputations from both universities to Gladstone, further consultations had proved 'extremely satisfactory' to the cause of repeal.[93] He submitted a draft bill drawn up by representatives of both universities. Gladstone was under severe pressure from his own supporters to get the bill through, in the interests of furthering 'the cause of religious liberty'.[94]

A difficulty for the old universities was not just that so many of their fellows were in favour of ending the tests: it was the question of, as Forster put it in a speech in 1869, 'how well the Nonconformist bodies had done without the Universities, giving instances in which they have flourished and advanced in science because they have not had a University education.'[95] Sir John Coleridge, the Solicitor-General, introduced the University Tests Bill in May 1870. It was designed to scrap the tests entirely rather than allow individual colleges to decide whether to administer them or not, as had been intended by an unsuccessful bill the previous year. This was to preserve 'unity of feeling' in the universities; but also to ensure religious teaching and worship could be carried on as before, something it was feared the scrapping of the Act of Uniformity might imperil.[96] Coleridge felt it 'a most highly improbable event' that the educated classes, as represented by fellows of Oxbridge colleges, would ever become estranged from Anglicanism.[97] The Church was so wealthy, and had such a hold over education, that it could not possibly suffer from the scrapping of the tests. Rather, that Act would breathe new life, he believed, into these old institutions.

Spencer Walpole, MP for Cambridge University and the former Home Secretary, said he did not wish to deprive non-Anglicans of an education at the old universities; but he felt the estrangement of the universities from the Church would lead, soon, to disestablishment. He believed the bill gave too much to the Nonconformists, but allowed too few safeguards of the religious character of the universities. He was distressed that the bill prescribed the end of compulsory chapel; and by wording that seemed to encourage Roman Catholics to fill offices intended for Anglican clergy, or to become masters of colleges. Walpole also noticed that the bill promised to repeal a part of the Act of Uniformity that had specified that 'no form of prayer, administration of sacraments, rites and ceremonies, shall be used in any church or chapel, or other public place, in either of the Universities, excepting that which is prescribed by the Book of Common Prayer.'[98] Why, he asked, repeal that? It had not been designed to exclude dissenters, but to give worship in Anglican chapels the protection of Parliament.

Lord Edmond Fitzmaurice, who had recently come down from Cambridge and was the younger son of Lord Lansdowne, ridiculed the fact that Oxford had harboured Jews in the thirteenth century, when they had been thrown out of England, yet a Jewish Senior Wrangler in the nineteenth century could not become a fellow of Trinity. Only twenty years old, Fitzmaurice showed the generational shift in thinking about these matters. Since the Act of Uniformity had pulled the universities into line 'the century and a half after [it] was the darkest and dreariest period in the history of the Universities. They became a by-word, not only in England but on the Continent. They were the home of Jacobite Toryism; they published declarations against civil and religious liberty . . . of educational work there was little or none, and religion showed its presence chiefly by those libations of port wine of which Gibbon preserved so keen a recollection.'[99] Things had only begun to improve when the barriers against dissenters had begun to be relaxed: to pass this bill would complete the process.

Gladstone set out his own creed: that 'it would be wise, if practicable, with safeguards, of what character I know not precisely, to settle this question on the basis of the withdrawal of every religious test which forms a barrier to the free and equal personal enjoyment of all except purely ecclesiastical and spiritual offices by the subjects of Her Majesty, irrespective of religious professions.'[100] This was exactly the view of Jowett, one of the leading campaigners for reform at Oxford.

There was a strongly contrasting view. Charles Newdegate, the Tory MP for North Warwickshire, was thirty years' Fitzmaurice's senior, a landowner and Tory 'ultra' with a consistent record of opposition to the relief of Catholic disabilities and a strong advocate of the Protestant settlement and its privileges. He believed those who agitated against the tests were jealous of the privileges enjoyed by the ancient universities, and their fellows. He felt dissenters behaved in a way 'consistent only with despotic government' in seeking to have the State interfere with the private property rights of an institution such as a collegiate university.[101] Above all, he warned dissenters directly that if they sought to humiliate the Church of England 'retaliation will become a necessity': 'You forget that you are trifling with a great issue. You forget that, in violating with exultation every Protestant feeling in the breasts of members of the Church of England, and in striking down those rights and privileges which are characteristic of their freedom, you are inviting us not to respect your own.'[102] The High Victorian mind remained not just staunchly Anglican, but in its resistance to the interference of the State profoundly eighteenth century.

The bill had its second reading, despite this yell of outrage; and helped by the MP for Tiverton, George Denman, recalling that Dr Whewell, the former Master of Trinity College, Cambridge, had warned him that he would come a cropper if he did not go to chapel one Sunday afternoon. No harm had come to him, and therefore he realised conformity was neither here nor there. It passed serenely through its committee stage but then the Lords rejected it, saying they wished to be satisfied that religious teaching in the universities would not be undermined. An inquiry was promised into this aspect of the problem: and having been satisfactorily completed, the bill was introduced again in 1871, when Gladstone argued the necessity of its now being passed in order to enrich the talent pool in the universities and to improve and widen their teaching.

Some on his side, however, wanted still more. He had to resist the growing demand for men who were not in holy orders to be allowed to hold the headship of and certain fellowships in many of the colleges. He argued, instead, that the bill should be presented to the Lords in the same form as in 1870 in order to maximise its chances of succeeding. It had a second reading unopposed, but an attempt was then made to amend it to widen opportunities for those not in holy orders. 'The object of the Bill', said Fitzmaurice, 'was to completely overthrow religious inequality at the Universities; but how could anyone admit this object would be carried out as long as the holding of certain Fellowships was confined not only to the members of, but actually to the clergy of, a particular sect?'[103] He felt no need to appease the Lords by sending back an identical bill. However, Gladstone – who pleaded that raising the question of fellowships would be a mistake – and his solicitor-general both argued against the amendment, and narrowly won the day.

Lord Kimberley, who piloted the bill through the Lords, told peers that the decision to admit Nonconformists to the universities made it inevitable that the religious tests would become unacceptable. He also claimed there was 'a large body of graduates, both at Oxford and Cambridge, in favour of the Bill', including, at Oxford, 'a majority, I believe, of the tutors in the different colleges.'[104] He felt all that was at stake was privilege, and that that was an obstacle to 'the promotion of sound and useful learning in every branch of knowledge' that universities supposedly existed to perform.[105] Salisbury tried to amend the bill to force university teachers to make a solemn declaration that they would not teach anything contrary to the Bible, claiming freedom of thought at Oxford in particular was getting out of hand. Kimberley rejected this new test that Salisbury had invented, not least on the grounds that it would be impossible to define just what teaching contrary to the Bible was. In his support came the Archbishop of York, who observed that 'if Oxford is, as it is said to be, sunk in infidelity—though I deny the truth of the statement—then that is a strong comment upon the system of tests already existing.'[106] He dismissed Salisbury's proposal as 'useless' and said it would do nothing to protect the teaching of the Church of England. Salisbury, he felt, sought to legislate from 'panic'.[107] After all that had happened in the climate of religious opinion in the preceding thirty years, it was striking that one of the most senior prelates should have owned up to the realities of spiritual life in modern England.

After several bishops had gone against the Archbishop, and highlighted the alleged depravities of Oxford in particular, the amendment was carried by five votes. A further amendment barred Nonconformists from holding certain posts in the universities. What other peers termed 'a collision' with the Commons now seemed inevitable, and Salisbury refused to back down.[108] What he was seeking to prevent was what one of only two renegade Liberal peers, Lord Lyttelton, termed 'open attack on the Bible being made by college tutors'.[109] The bill passed its third reading in the Lords duly amended: the collision was on. On 23 May 1871 the Commons reversed the amendment exempting heads of house from the provisions of the bill. On 13 June, with Salisbury having signalled he would insist on his 'test' for those holding offices in the colleges, the Lords debated whether to press its views on the Commons again. He forced another vote. This time he lost by forty, and, in a rather sour temper, declined to force votes on anything else. The Commons got its bill at last.

It was a defining moment in the history of the old universities, a crucial step not just in their modernisation, but in their ability to capitalise on the opportunities of the modern world. Dean Stanley preached in Oxford just after the Act had received Royal Assent. He spoke of 'the glorious prospect' of Oxford now becoming 'the neutral, the sacred ground, where the healing genius of the place and the equal intercourse of blameless and generous youth shall unite the long estrangements of Judah and of Ephraim, of Jerusalem and Samaria'.[110] More to the point, no one would be prevented from proceeding to the highest academic distinction simply on account of his faith.

The scrapping of tests was, however, viewed by some as another step not only towards secularisation, but to undermining of the Anglican Church. An anonymous pamphlet of 1871 entitled *Shall We Give It Up?*, in which the writer mused on whether there was any longer any point in subscribing to the Conservative party, referred to the end of the tests as a measure of the party's impotence. He wrote that the Oxbridge colleges would now 'exhibit no foolish attachment to the Church of England, or, indeed, for any religion at all, but just to go the way which chance or indifferentism may happen to lead them.'[111]

He added that the passage of the bill was not 'the only slap in the face which the Church of England has received during the last session. The Commons have again passed a bill to enable ministers of all denominations to officiate in churchyards . . . the so-called Conservatives, who would have rallied bravely upon any personal matter between Mr Gladstone and Mr Disraeli, did not think it worth while to make a party fight of it. In that impossible hypothesis of my being a Liberal, possessed with the usual Liberal hatred to the Church of England, I can scarcely conceive a fact more calculated to give me pleasure than the approaching triumph of this measure.' For, the writer asked, would a dissenting minister be made to stand outside the building – notably in bad weather – while a funeral service was being conducted inside the church? He added that what with the clamour for the secret ballot, and Gladstone's apparently hinting that universal suffrage could not be long delayed, 'a faster gallop towards Secularism and Democracy I cannot imagine.'[112]

CHAPTER 14

THE RIGHTS OF WOMEN: DIVORCE, THE VOTE AND EDUCATION

The extension of the meritocratic principle in the Army, Civil Service and universities during the first Gladstone ministry applied only to men. Emancipating women would prove a far more contentious and difficult exercise. John Stuart Mill likened the condition of women – of all classes – in the mid-nineteenth century to slavery, and with reason. 'Women's rights' was an oxymoron: women and any assets they brought into their marriage, or inherited while married, were the property of their husbands. If married, a woman could own no property. She had no right to any earnings she might make. She could not make a will. She had no separate existence in law. She could not conclude contracts or leases with another party. If she attempted to flee her husband, he had the legal right to enter the property of anyone harbouring her, and remove her by force. She could sue for 'cruelty that endangers life or limb', but had she condoned such behaviour before that her suit would fail. She could not sue for divorce, however atrociously her husband behaved. If he sued her for it, which required a hearing in an ecclesiastical court, followed by one for 'criminal conversation' (or adultery) in a common law court, followed by an Act of Parliament, she could not defend herself, or to be represented in the legal arguments. Nor was her husband bound to keep her: he was bound merely to see no one else went to that expense. If a deserted or wronged wife had funds, she was expected to support herself: but before her divorce, her husband could appropriate those funds. That was largely a problem for spirited women of the middle and upper classes. Working-class women had to stay and take it.

On top of their legal disadvantages, women bore the frequently lethal burden of having children. The sharp decline in infant mortality figures during the nineteenth century only partly reflects a decline in women dying in or shortly after childbirth. Even Queen Victoria, not spared the most lavish medical care money could buy, had some difficult and excruciatingly painful births having her nine children. For less privileged women, if they survived, the experience was often hideous.

While an improvement of women's healthcare depended to an extent on scientific advances, the promotion of their liberties relied upon a Parliament that was universally male. The first female MP would not sit until 1919; and although there were a few peeresses in their own right – mostly ancient creations that allowed descent by the female line, but also including contemporary ones such as Baroness Burdett-Coutts, the philanthropist – they were barred from sitting in the House of Lords. With universal female suffrage not being attained until 1928, equal employment rights taking until 1975, and an Equality Act being deemed necessary in 2010, such steps as the Victorians took to empower women were the first on an exceptionally long road. The only woman with complete freedom of manoeuvre was the Queen herself, precisely because she was in these respects without the law.

Other high-born women were small in number. They had lives of ease, but also quite often of stultifying boredom. The difficulty began with their education, if they had one. In the 1860s the parents of Miss Frances Cobbe paid £500 a year for her to attend a school in Brighton whose aim was to produce 'ornaments of society'. She studied mainly music and dancing.[1] The wretched Mrs Transome in *Felix Holt*, a once-beautiful but now desiccated woman, old in her mid-fifties, epitomises the fate of even privileged females in the mid-nineteenth century: 'A little daily embroidery had been a constant element in Mrs Transome's life; that soothing occupation of taking stitches to produce what neither she nor any one else wanted, was then the resource of many a well-born and unhappy woman.'[2]

Since such women were not expected to work, their fathers regarded education as pointless. An exception, as we shall see, was the case of the Nightingale sisters, Parthenope and Florence. However, the part-training of their minds only served to increase their frustration when they could find no useful occupation. Although it drove Florence into nursing, with great social benefits, it also seems to have made her an obsessive: as was her sister, more damagingly as Parthenope had a mental breakdown. The home education the Nightingale sisters had was about the best that could be hoped for: there were relatively few formal establishments for girls and young women. Middle-class women, who might be called upon to earn their living as governesses or teachers, were more fortunate; not least because their fathers had often climbed up the social ladder through education, and saw the value and necessity of it as a means to improvement. There were exceptions, such as the five Brontë sisters, the elder two of whom died in girlhood after being sent to a brutal school for the daughters of the clergy in Lancashire, their plight only eventually occasioning concern in their widowed father. The right for women to work in professions such as medicine or law came slowly – although there were women doctors by the mid-1870s the first woman would not be called to the Bar until 1922. The necessary education was hardly available.

For working-class women, with little or no hope of a serious education, life was relentless drudgery. Those who did not die in childbirth had their lives shortened by the grind of physical labour. Ashley had in 1843 successfully made Parliament prevent women from suffering the degradation of going down coal mines; but they laboured for five and a half long days a week in mills and sweatshops. In 1851 there were 600,000 women operatives in textile factories alone. Working-class women would rely on the social superiors of their sex to secure liberties before them as a necessary prelude to their securing them themselves.

II

If one social injustice above all others emphasised the lack of rights for women it was their inability to escape an unhappy, and in some cases downright cruel, marriage. The most prominent case of a wronged woman seeking, but being unable to obtain, a divorce was that of Caroline Norton, who became the leader of the movement for reform of the law. She was the granddaughter of Richard Brinsley Sheridan, the playwright. Although she was an exotic beauty, the depressed finances of the Sheridan family left her short of prospective husbands. In what seems to have been an act of desperation she married George Norton, brother of Lord Grantley, in 1827, when he was twenty-seven and she was nineteen. Norton was a Tory MP and a barrister but, more significantly, his brother had no children, and he hoped to inherit the family estates.

He physically and psychologically abused Caroline from the start: provoked not least, it seems, by his wife's being cleverer and quicker witted than he was. In using these weapons against him she lacked the deference he expected. She testified later that the violence he had offered her was 'such as is brought before the police-courts'.[3] There were rows about money, and the state of the family finances caused the marriage to take a difficult turn. Caroline had some talent as a writer, and used the proceeds from volumes of verse to supplement the family budget. Between 1829 and 1833 the Nortons had three sons, which stretched the finances further. Norton was idle by disposition and relied on a favour from Lord Melbourne, the Home Secretary, to give him a post as a stipendiary magistrate on a salary of £1,000 a year. It did not improve his temper towards his wife that this favour was called in through her: it was she, not Norton, who knew Melbourne, a Whig with no political or social sympathy with Norton. Soon, Norton felt socially humiliated that his wife's income helped support his family, and this attitude became even more toxic when he became jealous of her celebrity as a writer. She befriended Dickens, Disraeli, Thackeray and Tennyson, adding literary clout to her political salon.

Her engagement with the world of letters deepened the more tiresome and unpleasant Norton became, and so the estrangement from him grew. She started to write novels. These increased her income, which upset him further. Her husband's boorish aristocratic friends and their dull wives found Caroline vulgar and flashy. However, she entranced some men – not least Melbourne, who by 1834 was Prime Minister. He took to visiting the Norton house in Storey's Gate, usually when Norton was not there. Norton found letters from Melbourne in his wife's bureau and argued with her about them.

Rumours abounded: fed not least by Grantley, a Tory who saw the chance to embarrass a Whig Prime Minister. Norton realised that if Melbourne were committing adultery with his wife, he could be sued for damages, leaving a healthy profit for him. The marriage broke down: Caroline was barred from the house and her children were taken away. Norton refused to make a financial settlement on Caroline as part of a separation. He blackmailed her emotionally, offering occasional visiting rights with the children provided she would agree to his not bankrolling her. Finally, he accused Melbourne of having had a 'criminal conversation' with his wife – the technical term for adultery – and sought to sue him for £10,000 damages. Melbourne was allegedly so panicked that he took to his bed, ill.[4]

It is impossible to tell whether Melbourne and Caroline committed adultery. The jury thought they had not, and threw out Norton's suit within hours, regarding the evidence given by his former servants as entirely unreliable, not least because of their bad characters and because they had been bribed by Grantley. Caroline, as wife of the litigant, was barred from testifying. Had Norton won he could have proceeded to sue for divorce: that was now not possible. However, Caroline had plenty of reasons to divorce Norton, not least that he exercised his right to remove her children far away from her – they were sent to Yorkshire – and to raid what was technically his but actually her money. When she left him in 1836 and tried to exist on her royalties, he had her earnings confiscated.

Caroline appears from her writings, and from the testimony of others, to have been manipulative and something of an actress. However, she had one great advantage over her husband, not unknown in people of those qualities, which was popularity. Although some in society shunned her as a scarlet woman, she had enough friends not just to provide moral support, but friends in sufficiently high places to help her develop a campaign for the reform of the divorce law. Her opening salvo was a pamphlet published in 1837, *Observations on the Natural Claim of the Mother to the Custody of her Infant Children; as affected by the Common law Rights of the Father*. Sergeant Talfourd, a prominent judge and Member of Parliament best remembered now for his pioneering work on the law of copyright, was persuaded to introduce a bill in the Commons for the custody of infants, but it failed. Caroline wrote more pamphlets. She even wrote to *The Times* complaining about the injustice being done to her and women such as her.

The stimulus for *The Times* letter was what she called 'a very long, very coarse, and very violent attack' upon her in the *British and Foreign Quarterly Review* that she had read 'with astonishment'.[5] She vigorously denied – with good reason – having written a pamphlet entitled *Statement of the Wrongs of Women*, which the *Review* had attributed to her; she was angry because the work was a feminist tract and, whatever else she was, Caroline was no feminist. 'I believe', she wrote, 'the beauty and devotion of a woman's character mainly to depend on the consciousness of her inferiority to man, and that the greatest suffering a right-minded woman can feel, is [to be] unable to respect and look up to her husband.' Her own pamphlet had celebrated the 'religious duty a woman owes her husband'. The *Review* had also accused her of having co-written *Observations* with the help of Talfourd, something she dismissed as a falsehood too as she did not know him at the time. She was outraged by 'a cunning and plausible attempt . . . to create a prejudice against the [Infant Custody] Bill by mixing up my affairs with its discussion.'

Talfourd tried again: and in 1839, with the aid of Lord Lyndhurst, a former Lord Chancellor, the Infant Custody Act reached the statute book. The burden of legal opinion was very much in favour of it: the *Quarterly Review of Jurisprudence* argued that the existing regulations had been 'shockingly abused'.[6] This was a landmark in women's rights. If a woman had not had adultery proven against her in a court of law, she could have custody of any child under seven. Only one of Caroline's three sons was sufficiently young, and Norton, whose vindictiveness knew no bounds, moved them to Scotland, where the Act did not apply. It was not until her youngest son died of lockjaw in 1842 that she was allowed custody of the other two boys – then aged thirteen and eleven – for half the year. The tragedy was another weapon against Norton: she later wrote that the death, from an infected cut in a riding accident, came 'for want of the commonest care a mother would have given to her household'.[7]

In the 1840s Caroline was the mistress of Sidney Herbert, who would be patron of Florence Nightingale's nursing career. Caroline was, of course, unable to marry him: and when he married in 1846 the affair, which had lasted the best part of five years, ended. As their sons grew up Norton became more financially mean with Caroline. Her inheritance of a small annuity in 1851 prompted a further bout of parsimony from Norton, and reactivated her militancy in the cause of divorce reform. He was entitled not just to the proceeds of her literary work, but also to her legacy, despite their not having lived together for fifteen years.

Caroline tried to play Norton at his own game. The only benefit of her having no legal rights was that her creditors could not sue her, but had to sue him. One did so in 1853, for £49 4s 6d owed for the repair and upkeep of Caroline's brougham. In the consequent disclosure of the details of her financial affairs, it was discovered that on his death in 1848 Melbourne had left her a small legacy. Norton's lawyers used this to smear Caroline again. This time at least she could defend herself, and made a good job it. 'These tradesmen would have been paid if Mr Norton had not performed the greatest breach of faith that was ever accomplished by man.'[8] This referred to Norton's having stopped her allowance. The judge said her onslaught was 'irregular', but she persisted, as the newspaper report put it, 'with determination'. It was her finest performance.

In one of those exposures of private matters that shocked the Victorians so deeply, but which even editors so refined as those at *The Times* knew sold newspapers, Caroline proceeded to air the intimate details of her and her husband's business affairs. 'I believe Mr Norton's income to be about £3,000 a year . . . I was parted from him in 1836, and the following year he offered £500 a year until we could arrange our matters, but made me a compulsory allowance of £400 per annum. He stipulated that I should give up my children, and I said that I would rather starve than lose them.' Norton had stopped her allowance in March 1852. 'My husband can cheat me because I am his wife.' She admitted an allowance was being paid to her, via Lady Palmerston, from Melbourne's estate: in January and July 1852 it amounted to £291 5s on each occasion. She said it was discretionary. 'Lord Melbourne is dead. No one is bound to give me one farthing.'

The court found in Norton's favour. Caroline renewed her career as a *Times* letter-writer, attacking her husband for having his lawyer claim he would pay an allowance to her only if she were not being supported by Melbourne's estate.[9] Since, she argued, Norton's agreement to pay her had been concluded before Melbourne's death, it could not have taken into account bequests she was supposed to be due from him. She said he had lied to save himself paying £500 a year. 'Once and for all,' she wrote, 'I did not part from my husband on Lord Melbourne's account; nor had Lord Melbourne anything whatever to do with our quarrel. I parted from Mr Norton because I persisted in an intention to take my children to my brother's house, where my husband, on account of his own conduct, was not received.'

On 24 August 1853 he wrote to *The Times* 'as a magistrate, an administrator of justice' to seek to sustain his 'public character' – 'my private one is safe in the hands of those who know me.'[10] Norton attacked not just the judge, but even his own solicitor in the opening paragraphs of his complaint. Explaining how his estranged wife had been allowed to vilify him in court, he said: 'Unhappily the judge and every one engaged for or against her in the cause seemed overpowered by Mrs Norton's demeanour, and those who had a turn for the drama (of whom, unfortunately, my own solicitor was one) were suspended in breathless, helpless inaction.'

He admitted he had made it no condition of an allowance that she should have no money from Melbourne: but also claimed that after Melbourne's death his brother had opened a letter from him that asked for an annuity to be provided for Caroline. 'I was surprised and disgusted,' Norton wrote. She denied receiving it at the time, which was true, but within three years it was being paid, as had been established. He had asked their elder son to take the matter up with his mother: she had denied it to him, too, and he had relayed the denial to his father. Norton accused Caroline of lying to both of them, and whined about how much his sons cost him – one in the diplomatic service, the other at Oxford. It appears no one was advising him: the worst damage done to his reputation was by his own hand.

Caroline wrote to the newspaper again on 2 September. It was not so much a letter as a fragment – and a substantial fragment at that – of autobiography. She began with irony, expressing her gratitude that he had put before the public matters her own discretion had kept concealed: but she wished to refute his accusations of extravagance, and of much else besides. 'The charge comes ill from one who owes me £687, and who does not even deny the debt, but merely says he cannot be compelled to pay it, because, as was stated in court, he is not bound in law, but only "as a man of honour".'[11] Her main complaint was that 'twice in my life he has endeavoured, on a false pretence, to rob me of my reputation.' On that front, she washed all the dirty linen in society's newspaper. She spoke of the 'slander' against her and of how she had 'struggled like a drowning person against disgrace'.

During the 1840s there had been attempts at divorce reform. Sir Howard Elphinstone, a Whig MP, had tried to introduce a Marriages and Divorces Bill in 1843. The divorce cases currently heard were in the ecclesiastical provincial courts, and a recent one had cost £1,500, the cost of which had fallen upon the woman: her adulterous husband was insolvent. The existing procedure – a suit at common law, an appeal to the ecclesiastical tribunal and, finally, a bill in Parliament – was, he argued, too complex. He wanted just one divorce court as, he said, 'was the law of every Protestant country but this'.[12] His seconder, William Ewart, said the average cost of a divorce was £800–900; in Scotland, where there were divorce courts, it was £30, which meant that even quite poor people could afford them. The government objected because of opposition from the Church; the measure was defeated, as was another attempt in 1852.

After her public row with her husband, Caroline realised she had to broaden the argument from her own circumstances and deal instead with the plight of English womanhood. She urged several politicians of her acquaintance to speak for the cause in Parliament. The first blast of the new campaign was her pamphlet *English Laws for Women in the Nineteenth Century*, but it received little attention from a public grown weary of her and her case. A wider campaign was already under way for property rights for women, led by Barbara Bodichon, the leading feminist of the 1850s. She and other women supporting her were censorious of Caroline's campaign, feeling her to be motivated unduly by self-interest and not enough by the condition of women generally. Caroline was no more of a feminist in the 1850s than in the 1830s, and found elements of Bodichon's campaign unattractive.

Independent of Caroline's activities, Lord Cranworth, the Lord Chancellor, introduced a bill in the Lords in 1855 to make divorce more widely available. This prompted another pamphlet from Caroline, *A Letter to the Queen on Lord Cranworth's Marriage and Divorce Bill*, which drew on her own experiences and made the case for separated women to have rights to their own property. She wrote to the Queen, as she put it, 'as one who has grievously suffered', striking that note of personal interest that made it increasingly hard for others to assist her.[13] She addressed the Sovereign not because she sought to take her wrongs 'to the foot of the throne' but because the Queen was a married woman with children. Caroline said that 'I desire to point out the grotesque anomaly which ordains that married women shall be 'non-existent' in a country governed by a female Sovereign.'[14] She was also conscious that any reform of the law would require the Queen's assent.

Caroline conceded that 'there are bad, wanton, irreclaimable women, as there are vicious, profligate, tyrannical men: but the difference is this: that to punish and restrain bad wives, there are laws and very severe laws (to say nothing of social condemnation); while to punish or restrain bad husbands, there is, in England, no adequate law whatever.'[15] She claimed the existing law put a premium on infidelity: a woman divorced for her adultery and who subsequently married the man who had cuckolded her husband suffered far less than the wronged wife who did not deserve to suffer at all. She described the cost of divorce as 'an indulgence sacred to the aristocracy of England'.[16] The only recourse to the poor man betrayed by his first wife and seeking a second was, she argued, bigamy, and children who were bastards. None of this, she said, pertained in Scotland, where divorce was possible, where women had a right to have their property protected, and where they could sue for divorce just as their husbands could. South of the border, class and gender justice prevailed.

In English and Welsh divorce cases as the law stood an examination of both parties was conducted in the House of Lords, a practice one peer had denounced in recent years as 'disgusting and demoralising'.[17] Another, Lord St Leonards, had called the state of the law 'a disgrace to the country'. Those who objected to a change in the law to make it equal with Scottish practice – where desertion and adultery were grounds for a woman to sue for divorce – seemed to suggest Scotland was a more immoral country than England. Caroline said she understood the practice in Roman Catholic countries, where marriage was deemed indissoluble: but she could not understand how, in Protestant England, it could be deemed dissoluble by the male party only. In any case, since 1836, when Lord John Russell had sponsored the Act of Parliament that allowed civil weddings, many marriages had nothing to do with the Church. 'Either let men renounce the privilege of divorce,' she wrote, 'and the assertion that marriage is a dissoluble contract, or allow the weaker party that refuge from intolerable wrong, which they claim as a matter of necessity for themselves.'[18]

Much of this was sound: but Caroline could not resist a further assault on Norton. 'Lord Melbourne', she wrote, addressing directly a Queen of whom Melbourne had been almost as great a favourite as of Caroline – 'declared that, so far as Lord Melbourne was concerned, he believed the action to be brought entirely as a means of obtaining money . . .

he considered it was a political plot on the part of a small section of the Tories, to ruin him as Prime Minister. And' – and here came a further sting – 'I know that in this opinion your Majesty's uncle, King William IV, entirely concurred.'[19] She even adduced the heroine status of Florence Nightingale – then in the Crimea – as a reason why women required improved legal rights: though as Nightingale was unmarried, she had her own property rights. Cranworth's bill failed, at the fall of the Aberdeen government, even though he continued as Lord Chancellor under Palmerston. Much of what Caroline had advocated in her pamphlets found its way into this bill, and as such she can be said to have been one of the architects of a reform first advocated more than 200 years earlier by John Milton. Cruelty, desertion, bigamy and incest were to be grounds on which a woman could sue for divorce, but not, as originally proposed, adultery: that was to remain a cause for a man only.

Caroline wrote in January 1857 of the need for a Court of Divorce to be set up, arguing that 'it is precisely because I think such a court would diminish, instead of increase, the number of separations and divorces that I desire to see it established.'[20] She felt that in many cases – including her own – the very existence of a divorce court would lead to compromise between couples in conflict. As it was, the absence of such a court had caused the strife in her own marriage to become chronic and intense, and now she and her husband could not possibly be reconciled.

She sought to calm those men who saw it as an assault on their rights and on the institution of marriage. 'Men are to be the judges; that is surely a great security against the false alarms of multitudinous divorces on the petitions of wives. I never argued for facility of divorce. I believe, even if it existed, it would be the last remedy women in general would seek. Thousands of women (and I am one among thousands), would rather endure any degree of poverty and loneliness than see a stepmother set over their children, if there were no other reason against divorce.' She concluded: 'I hope to see such reform as shall give this power to some distinct legal tribunal in the coming session, and that many a young angry couple, who stood on the brink of the precipice that led to utter disunion, may find from it the benefit, not of divorce, but of a rescued future, so that "peace and possibly sunshine" may settle on their lives long after the stormy light of ours shall have gone down into the darkness of the grave.' The phrase in quotation marks was an ironic usage of words by her own husband, years earlier, and which had come to nothing.

A bill to allow divorces to be granted by a court and without the necessity to prove a criminal conversation was announced in the Queen's Speech on 3 February 1857. Its passage was intensely controversial: the womanising Prime Minister, Palmerston, came under sustained attack from one of his eventual successors, Gladstone, who regarded the proposal as an assault on the authority of the Church. Paradoxically, one of the main supporters of the reform was the Archbishop of Canterbury, despite strong opposition to the bill from thousands of his clergy. The bill was almost identical to one the House had previously passed, and the Lords had rejected, except that it omitted an amendment to allow all parties except adulterers to marry again. Cranworth said he considered the proviso 'most objectionable' as 'it involves a most cruel punishment upon the woman, and I am afraid in nine cases out of ten it will be a great boon to the adulterer.'[21] In other words, men – who were usually the ones acting adulterously – would never be able to follow through and marry the object of their desires, much, it was assumed, to their relief.

There would be but one divorce court, at Westminster. The Bishop of Exeter, another pro-divorce prelate, complained this would not achieve an intention he had for the reform, to help the poor as much as the rich: those living in the north of England, and of limited means, could not hope to use the court. He argued for district courts throughout the country. His brother prelate, the Bishop of Oxford – 'Soapy Sam' Wilberforce – had a more traditional objection. He believed 'it would tend greatly to unhinge men's minds as to the sanctity of marriage, and would lead to no permanent and purifying result'.[22]

A committee in the Lords examined the bill at the end of May. It consisted largely of bishops quoting scripture to each other and arguing over the interpretation of it. This continued at the third reading before the whole House on 23 June, with Wilberforce maintaining that 'there was no doubt that the words of our Lord forbade the adulterous woman remarrying in the lifetime of her husband'.[23] He added that if the bill were passed, those responsible would have 'intentionally and knowingly declared that the law of England should contradict the law of Christ.' Despite Viscount Dungannon, moments before the vote was taken, announcing that the bill was 'one of the most mischievous ever submitted to Parliament' and 'calculated to undermine all the moral principles of society', the third reading was given, signalling the Upper House's final approval.[24] It was now up to the Commons to decide whether to legalise divorce.

Before it even reached the Commons an attempt was made, on 24 July, to prevent its being discussed at all. The MP for Oxfordshire, Joseph Henley, tried to have it thrown out because insufficient time remained to discuss it properly. He noted, too, that a petition signed by 6,000 clergy (and attracting new signatures daily) had been offered against the bill. It was a 'crude, ill-digested and not well-considered measure', he added.[25] Sir George Grey, the Home Secretary, countered him. He said that the existing law on divorce created 'scandals'.[26] This brought Gladstone into the fray.

'I must confess,' he said, 'I scarcely know what those scandals are'. He conceded there were questions concerning a woman's property that were scandalous, but the proposed measure did not cover them. He felt it was a scandal that the rich could obtain a divorce when the poor could not; but that required lengthy discussion: a reason, he felt, not to proceed at that point. He also felt Grey had sought to politicise the question, which annoyed him: 'I frankly own that I entertain no doubt with respect to the main question which is involved in the present measure. I refer to the question of the true interpretation of the Christian law of marriage.'[27] With Parliament set to rise in mid-August, Gladstone was suspicious that the Commons had had to wait until 24 July to start to consider a bill that he called 'hasty and slovenly'.[28] He felt he, and others like him, were being bounced into a profound social change that stood at odds with centuries of Christian teaching.

He displayed his finely analytical mind at its best:

If the Bill gave but two alternatives—one, the indissoluble marriage, to which we have adhered since England was England; the other, dissoluble marriage, well understood, carefully limited, sustained by the clear authority of learned men, and the legislation of other countries—the ground would be much cleared and simplified; but there is not a country which has legislated with a view to make marriage dissoluble which has legislated in the same manner. The proposal is one of a perfectly novel character, not only with respect to the law of England, but also as regards the law of Christendom; it is one which never to this hour in the history of the world has been adopted. It is opposed to the law of the Church; to the law of nature, and to the law of God; and, whether good or bad, was one upon which the wit of man had never been able to hit before. The law of no country has ever made marriage dissoluble but upon principles far wider than those which are now proposed for our adoption.

Despite his objection to the principle, he also felt that if the law were to be changed then it had to be changed equitably. He, too, complained about the centralised nature of the proposed court. He drew parallels with Scotland, saying that it did not really have a divorce court, but that part of it that lay within easy reach of Edinburgh did. As for the rest of Scotland, divorce was largely impossible unless the parties concerned were rich. He argued that, instead, a proper system of local courts should be instituted. If this could not be contemplated, the law should not be altered.[29] There had to be equal rights in the matter of divorce:

It is impossible to do a greater mischief than to begin now, in the middle of the nineteenth century, to undo with regard to womankind that which has already been done on their behalf, by slow degrees, in the preceding eighteen centuries, and to say that the husband shall be authorised to dismiss his wife on grounds for which the wife shall not be authorised to dismiss her husband. If there is one broad and palpable result of Christianity which we ought to regard as precious, it is that it has placed the seal of God Almighty upon the equality of man and woman with respect to everything that relates to these rights, and I will offer the utmost resistance to any attempt to induce this House to adopt a measure which I believe would lead to the degradation of woman.[30]

Gladstone was more of a theologian than many of the bishops, and inevitably his argument moved on to religious matters. Was Parliament 'bound to frame the legislation of this House upon the law of Scripture'? The question was one 'of great solemnity and difficulty; but I will say, it appears to me that by this Bill we are dealing with an unprecedented levity with matters which do not belong to us.'[31] He continued: 'I speak of the religion which we entertain, and I do say it is a matter of the deepest consequence to take care that in our legislation with respect to matrimony we do not offer profanation to that religion by making its sacred rites—designated by apostles themselves with the very highest appellations—the mere creatures of our will, like some turnpike trust or board of health, which we can make to-day and unmake to-morrow.' Referring to Russell's Act of 1836 that introduced civil marriage, he asked whether Parliament proposed to introduce civil divorce and civil remarriage as well: this was another consideration that demanded more time.

Palmerston decided to conclude the debate. He expressed astonishment that a group of MPs should attempt to push the bill into the next session – which meant the procedure would have to start from scratch again, going through the Lords as well – solely because they expected not to have enough time to discuss it now, and to do so before a syllable of debate on it had been uttered in the Commons. He dismissed this as a 'pretence', and a 'shallow' one at that.[32] He goaded those seeking a delay by saying it would have been 'much more honourable' to have argued against it on the second reading rather than to prevent that from happening at all. He mocked Gladstone's objections by claiming his speech had been of such eloquence and intelligence that he was as ready to discuss the shortcomings of the bill then as he would be in twelve months' time. The country knew what the bill contained and was ready for it; yet he asserted that the clergymen who had signed the petition against it were not aware of its provisions. He said he was happy to sit until the middle of September if it meant getting the business through. By 217 votes to 130 the House backed him, and the second reading debate happened a week later.

Sir Richard Bethell, the Attorney General, attempted to soothe opposition by saying the bill would simply transfer to a court of law something that had required the sanction of a legislative assembly after two other court hearings, including 'the most abominable proceeding', the action for criminal conversation, a system that was 'a great reproach to this country'.[33] The acceptance of divorce itself in England dated back to the Reformation: nothing extraordinary was being done, though he did concede that a woman would be given grounds against a husband whose conduct was so shocking that she could not be expected to live with him. Some remained to be convinced. Sir William Heathcote spoke of 'a body of dissolute and depraved men [who] were already exulting over the licence which they expected to receive at the hands of the Legislature'.[34] Henry Drummond argued that the measure would merely 'continue the same tyranny of the male over the helpless female which now exists'.[35] There was much talk of a thin end of the wedge: that if it were agreed now that divorce could be granted for adultery, it would not be long before it could be granted for other reasons.

Gladstone remained implacable. He pointed out, opening the second day of the debate, that after the Attorney General the previous day eight speakers had risen in turn against him: the supporters of the bill had decided not to speak but to hurry through to a division. He said he had letters from all over the Kingdom arguing that even more petitions would be submitted against the bill. From Cornwall, he heard the labouring classes were entirely against it. In Lincolnshire it was 'thoroughly hateful in the eyes of the great mass of the middle classes and the poor'.[36] He had seen evidence that even among the educated classes there was widespread ignorance about the bill's provisions. Gladstone said he considered it 'one of the most degrading doctrines that can be propounded to civilised men' that 'the Legislature has power to absolve a man from spiritual vows taken before God.'[37] Eventually, he reached the question of sexual continence.

He felt the high incidence of this was:

> attributable to the indissolubility of marriage according to the English law . . . The marriage state is a total and absolute change. You pass over a gulf which you know you cannot repass; you enter upon a new state, and you adopt all its obligations; but you are now going to make that gulf which has hitherto been impassable, passable; you are going to say to the woman who has sinned, although she may have sinned under the strongest temptation, 'Your sins shall be unpardoned; you shall be divorced, and nothing shall reconcile you to the man from whom you have been divorced. You may marry again, and you may offend again, *toties quoties*; your sin shall be unpardonable by the person you have offended, though with his whole heart and soul he may be desirous to forgive you.' That to me is a most doubtful state of things as regards the shutting the door to the penitent; but still more doubtful is the shaking the great idea of the marriage contract

in the minds of the English people. Do not let us deal with humankind as if they were creatures of pure intellect, and as if life was governed by conviction. The traditions of past times, and the rules and customs of society, which a man inherits as it were from those who have gone before him, have more perhaps to do with the government of life than any other consideration. The indissolubility of English marriage is an idea which has never been shaken in the mind of England. At no time have the middle and lower classes of the English people known what it was to have marriage, dissoluble. Take care, then, how you damage the character of your countrymen. You know how apt the English nature is to escape from restraint and control; you know what passion dwells in the Englishman; but here is a great feeling of restraint observed among your population, and which has prevailed ever since England was England, that the marriage tie is indissoluble.[38]

His epic and wide ranging two-hour speech – on which his opponents congratulated him – was literally unanswerable. No one present had the wit to engage with him; Grey, who followed him, merely contradicted him. The only person who attempted to engage in theological argument was Spencer Walpole, who was not in Gladstone's league: he bravely concluded that 'the charm, the happiness, and the unspeakable blessing which now surrounds an English home' would be better preserved with a divorce law rather than without one.[39] The government had the numbers, however, and did not need to rely on force of argument: the second reading was given by 208 to 97.

By this stage 10,000 clergy had signed the petition against the bill. The main issue among objectors was that the bill would permit remarriage among guilty parties in a divorce, and clergy might be called upon to marry them, which seemed to have become the sticking point. The petition itself had demanded: 'Remembering also, that it is declared in the Word of God, that marriage with a divorced woman is adulterous, we fervently pray that the Clergy of this realm may never be reduced to the painful necessity of either withholding the obedience which they must always desire to pay to the law of the land, or else of sinning against their own consciences, and violating the law of God by solemnizing such marriages as are condemned as adulterous in His Holy Word.'[40]

A committee of the whole House of Commons considered the bill clause by clause. 'What is to become of society,' asked Samuel Warren, the Tory MP for Midhurst, 'if every man's obedience to the law is to depend on his own notion of its conformity with the law of God?' Warren was in no doubt that the Christian legislature should follow the Bible, and he could find no precedent for divorce there. Instead, there would be a system under which the State would say to proven adulterers, 'Never mind the Church – go and be married under the authority of the State.'[41] There was widespread feeling that only the wronged party should ever be allowed to marry again; and that clergy should quite specifically be exempted from having to marry a divorced person at all.

The new wave of publicity had not merely stimulated more clergymen to object to the bill, but had drummed up more petitions from the public. More than 16,000 women had signed one. Warren argued that the good things the bill did – such as protecting women against 'cruel and profligate' husbands – could be achieved short of condoning divorce. One MP pointed out with shock that in San Francisco, where divorce was allowed, 130 – or one every three days – had been granted the previous year: he trusted matters would never reach such a pass here.

The government's majority swatted aside almost all opposition. Some notions of radicalism were too much, however. An attempt to allow a woman's earnings to be considered separate from her husband's even when they were living together harmoniously was rejected as 'monstrous'.[42] However, the government failed to stop the move to allow local jurisdiction in divorce cases: and a larger problem reared its head in the question of equal remedies for men and women who were the victims of adultery. The view was that while God regarded unchastity as equally repellent whether practised by men or women, it was much more damaging to society when done by a woman. Chastity was the point of honour in women, as one MP put it, but not with men. Adultery in women was 'attended with uncertainty as to the parentage of the offspring'.[43] There was also the contention that 'if the same facility for divorce was extended to the women as was given to the man, a power would be given to a selfish husband, by committing adultery, to drive the wife into the Divorce Court.' She was, it seemed, supposed to grin and bear it.

Gladstone described this point as 'one of the most serious and greatest moral and social questions that can be submitted to discussion'.[44] He remained against reform of the law: but saw it was inevitable, and so amplified his belief that it should operate as equitably as possible. Opponents of equality said that giving a woman the right to sue for adultery would increase the number of divorces. He, however, said that 'I confess when driven to a choice between the mischief of adding somewhat to the number of cases of divorce *a vinculo* on one hand, and the mischief, on the other hand, of writing on the statute book that principle of inequality . . . I make my choice deliberately in favour [of equality].'[45] The greater evil was introducing inequality. 'I take my stand in the first place on this, that if it be assumed that the indissolubility of marriage has been the result of the operation of the Christian religion on earth, still more emphatically I believe it may be assumed that the principle of the equality of the sexes has been the consequence of that religion.'

The Gospels showed many instances of the imperative of treating men and women equally as Christians. He asked: 'if adultery really constitutes in the sight of God that right to release from the marriage tie, and absolutely abolishes the marriage tie, so that those of whom one party has committed adultery are no longer married—if that be so, where do you find your title to withhold from women the remedy which you give to men? Is it to be found in considerations of social expediency? I am ready to dispute and to deny those considerations; but, suppose that it be, what right have you to set them up in bar of the charter which you say is written by God himself?'[46]

By arming women with the power of divorce, their husbands would behave better than otherwise: and it was husbands, whose adulterous leanings were far more evident, who needed the restraint that equality would provide. Women could, under the proposals, divorce for cruelty:

Is not the cruelty of insult just as gross, just as wicked, just as abominable as the cruelty of mere force? And is not that a very common class of case? Is it not too notorious that there exist a multitude of instances in which no remedy has been sought for, or none granted by our law—instances in which the adulteries of the husband have not only been occasional, but continuous; not only continuous, but open; not only open, but committed under his very roof, and in connection with persons placed in the closest relations with the wife? And is not the insult inflicted in these cases one which sends the iron into the soul as deeply, and far more sharply, than any material instrument can send it into the body? On what principle, then, is it that you give a remedy to the wife in a case of bodily cruelty on the part of the husband, while, where the cruelty is directed to the soul, though this may inflict tenfold greater torture, you declare there shall be no remedy at all?[47]

Gladstone argued that if the bill passed without this equal right, men would feel they had tacit permission from Parliament to indulge in profligacy, creating an 'oppressed and helpless wife'.[48] He invited the accusation, however, that husband and wife would collude for the husband to commit adultery – which carried a lower social stigma – to put an end to the marriage: something that did, indeed, become one of the most widespread features of the law once it was passed, and a source of income to prostitutes and private investigators well into the twentieth century. Even Palmerston, who maintained there was no real social requirement for equality, conceded he could not win that argument and would accept the principle: despite this flying in the face of what his own Attorney General had just said.

The Attorney sought a middle way, offering an amendment to allow a woman to sue for divorce if a husband kept his mistress under their own roof: the law in France allowed for this if a man had his 'concubine' in the home. Joseph Henley, President of the Board of Trade in Derby's ministry, rejected this on the grounds that 'in English society it would be hardly possible to find a single man who was sufficiently a villain to outrage all laws so as to bring him within the category'.[49] Henley added: 'A man might commit adultery with the housemaid, the lady's maid, or any sort of maid, but that would not fall within the hon and learned gentleman's category of a mistress kept in the conjugal residence.' Palmerston prevailed, but women still did not have equality. While men could divorce simply for a wife's adultery, adultery was only to be an issue for a woman divorcing her husband if it was supplemented by some other offence – sodomy, bigamy, cruelty or desertion, for example. Not until the 1937 Matrimonial Causes Act would that wrong be righted.

The bill had its third and final reading on 21 August 1857. Thirteen changes of substance had been made to it in committee, ten without a vote – an admission by the government of the imperfection of its measure. The most significant was the concession towards women, and enhanced rights for the custody of children; scarcely less important were the establishment of local tribunals, and what was effectively a conscience clause for clergy. Palmerston puffed and preened with satisfaction that he had seen off Gladstone and those others in the Commons who had determined to stop the bill.

The Lords agreed to consider the amendments, rather than throw the bill out, by a majority of just two. When, on 25 August, the day before the prorogation of Parliament, the Act was finally on the statute book, divorces could be granted on account of the adultery of either spouse: or, in the case of a woman, adultery aggravated by the cruelty of or desertion by her husband for more than two years. There were three divorce cases in 1857, and 300 in 1858, the Act coming into force on 1 January that year.

III

With the extension of the franchise to all men in 1867, it was natural that the more radically minded should turn their attention to the extension of the franchise to women. John Stuart Mill had tried unsuccessfully to push the point by organising petitions to be presented to Parliament in 1866, 1867 and 1868. A bill to effect this was introduced in May 1870 by Jacob Bright, younger brother of John and of Priscilla Bright McLaren, an early campaigner for women's suffrage. Bright's measure would have given votes to women in boroughs 'if they are householders, if their names are on the rate-books, and if they pay their rates.'[50] In the counties women would vote if householders with houses rated at £12 or above, 'or if they should be possessed of any description of property which now entitles men to vote.' This was far from universal suffrage. Bright's research caused him to estimate that in Bath one woman would have the vote for every 3.8 men, but in Walsall it would be one to every 22.9 men. In Bristol and York the ratio was one to seven; in Manchester one to six; in Newcastle one to eight and in Northampton one to thirteen. With an eye on his opponents he said that 'the number of persons we propose to enfranchise by this Bill is so small that no fear need be entertained on the present occasion.'[51] The number of women who would be enfranchised would be too small to cause a social and political revolution.

Bright said he was pursuing this end 'on the grounds of public justice and of practical necessity'. He pointed out that the householder franchise led to men in an astonishing degree of ignorance being allowed to vote. Yet women who paid taxes, and who rendered valuable service to the nation – he invoked the name of Florence Nightingale – were not. The men who had demanded the vote before 1867 had, said Bright, argued that to be denied it was 'tantamount to a declaration of our moral and intellectual inferiority'.[52] He emphasised what he felt should be the link between taxation and representation and, even more radically than demanding votes for women, highlighted the unfairness of their pay: 'There is not a male and female rate of taxation, but there is a male and female rate of wages and earnings. Women everywhere, with a few remarkable exceptions, are getting far less money than men; they have to work much longer for the same money; and they are even paid much less when they are doing precisely the same work. Taxation must, therefore, fall somewhat more heavily upon women than on men.' There were, he protested, 'inferior men in every rank of life' who 'have no objection to degrade women and keep them in degradation.'[53]

The women who would be eligible could already vote in municipal elections: but Parliament deemed them unfit to vote on 'imperial affairs'. Bright's bill would not give the vote to married women, though he made it clear he regretted this expediency, which he considered necessary if his bill were to have any chance of success – 'a married woman, in regard to the rights of property, is in the position of the negro in the Southern States of America before the American Revolution [the Civil War].' The Married Women's Property Bill had three times been passed by the Commons but thrown out by the Lords twice. If the Commons could see the injustice that that bill sought to put right, why should it not see the injustice of denying women of property the vote?

Bright made the obvious point that the Sovereign herself was a woman, and there was an inconsistency between her considerable power and the denial of modest political power to all other Britons of her sex. This was not, he stressed, a point original to him: Disraeli had made it in a speech some time earlier. He referred again to the effect of the

American Civil War: black men had been held in contempt before it, but now 4 million of them had the vote. He referred to the growing organisation of women's groups that had agitated for the introduction of the bill he was proposing, as a testament to the intelligence and political consciousness of women – things denied by their opponents. More than 100,000 of them had signed petitions about the importance of ending the injustice of their treatment. He implored his fellow MPs to think of their own wives, mothers, sisters and daughters, and to admit the interest that many of them took in politics – proved by the number of them who came to watch from the Ladies' Gallery. He concluded by imploring Gladstone, famed for his integrity and sagacity, to support him.

The opposition to Bright was led by John Scourfield, the Tory MP for Pembrokeshire. He carefully avoided discussing the alleged inferiority of women, but concentrated instead on what had been claimed was the lack of 'sufficient evidence that it was the wish of the women of England to have this privilege conferred upon them'. Scourfield claimed he was always asking women whether they wished to have the vote, and they invariably replied that they did not. They did not seek the responsibility that went with the franchise, and they felt it would erode their social position. He found it necessary to quote Dr Johnson's insulting line about a woman preaching being like a dog on its hind legs: 'It is not done well, but you are surprised to find it done at all.' He was quite clear about what their purpose in life was: 'Their vocation was to make life endurable,' he said, and he simply wished them to continue being 'admirable, amiable, and delightful'.[54]

William Fowler, the MP for Cambridge, said that if women were given the vote there was no logical reason why they should not sit in the Commons, and therefore he was profoundly opposed to the bill. Women had duties – of educating their children, of having 'to adorn the sphere in which they live' – that would be impeded by allowing them to become involved in politics. He did not dispute that there were some women who spoke very well in public; but he did not think that 'a natural position for women'.[55] He did think the state of their property rights was an injustice, and he would support any move to rectify that: but giving them the vote was too much, and he said his motive in not supporting Bright was 'to save them [women] from what would be rather an injury than a blessing'.[56]

Sir Charles Dilke, whose own parliamentary career would be undermined by a scandal caused by his being rather too appreciative of women, sprang to their defence, ridiculing the arguments against their having the vote:

There is only one class of the inhabitants of full age except the insane, who are passed over in this Parliamentary franchise. You do not pass over negroes, for there are negro voters in almost every borough in the country; but you pass over one class—the class of women. It is quite clear that you have passed them over on account of some grave incapacity. If that were not clear from the general nature of the case, it would be clear from what Blackstone [the commentaries on the laws of England] says. Blackstone, describing those who are subject to political disability, says that 'No vote can be given by lunatics, idiots, minors, aliens, females, persons convicted of perjury, subornation of perjury, bribery, treating or undue influence, or by those attainted of felony, or outlawed in a criminal suit.' If you exclude aliens—and no country permits the subjects of a foreign Power to exercise the Parliamentary franchise—the disabled people divide themselves into two classes—those convicted of crime and those who are under some incapacity of mind. It is quite clear that no one would propose to rank women among criminals, and it would seem that they are ranked amongst the incapable.[57]

Lyon Playfair took up this point too. 'That women are capable citizens must be admitted from our laws of property, and from their possession of the municipal franchise,' he said.

Their capability is further allowed by the Constitution, which entrusts to them the highest share in government. Female Sovereigns may sit on the Throne, and in past times, as now, adorn their high position. But if they are capable of exercising the highest function of government, they must be fit to perform the lowest functions—that of delegating their interests to a representative who may protect their property against undue taxation, and their persons against the injurious influences of bad legislation. . . . it is assumed that it is not a suitable or becoming thing in wives and mothers to attend to politics, because their function is rather domestic than civic. Well, we do not ask the suffrage for those who are wives and have their interests represented by their husbands. But there are 487,000 widows and 2,110,000 spinsters who have no such natural representatives of their interests. They surely have a right to interest themselves in affairs external to the domestic hearth.[58]

He added: 'The very names of Miss Florence Nightingale, Miss Harriet Martineau, and Miss Burdett Coutts' made the case for the vote. 'I admit that the education of women, as a class, has not been of a character to attract them to political subjects. Whose fault is this? Men have monopolised all the higher schools and Universities for themselves, and have thus lowered the education of women. Grant them the suffrage which we now ask, and I promise you that they will quickly lay claim to a fairer share in the educational resources of this country. Give to women the responsibility of power, and their fitness to exercise it will be developed rapidly enough. This has always been proved by our past history, even when you have lowered the suffrage below the then educational level of the people.'[59]

These arguments were powerful; Bright and his friends triumphed, and the bill passed its second reading. Once it went into committee the trouble began. Edward Pleydell-Bouverie, President of the Poor Law Board in Palmerston's first administration, feared that the grant of the vote to unmarried women would inevitably result in its being granted, in time, to married women. 'The consequence of this will be a dual vote and a dual government in every house. I must protest against such a system of domestic anarchy.'[60] He added: 'The real meaning of this bill is that we are to unsex women altogether. They are the weaker portion of human creation. Nature has ordained that they should be so. Are we to take them down from their pedestal, and make them enter into rough competition with men? Are they to come into this House and to sit on these benches? If so, why should they not sit on the Treasury Bench?'[61] That was not the limit of the potential horror. 'It is avowed that we are to become a nation of Amazons; that we are to have women barristers, attorneys, doctors, and for aught I know, Bishops.'

He rounded off his argument by quoting a feminist who said she hoped women would sit on juries; and was followed by Lord Elcho, who dismissed out of hand the notion that the vote was a 'just right' of women: 'The worst service . . . that they could do to the women of this country was to give them votes.'[62] Eventually Gladstone himself intervened. He explained that the government had not taken a view not because it did not regard the measure as important, but because it did not wish to invade the liberties of independent Members. However, he had to admit that 'it would be a very great mistake to proceed with this Bill.'[63] He explained himself by saying that 'the real matter at issue is much broader, for the question really is whether there is a necessity, nay, even, whether there is a desire or a demand for this measure. I must say I cannot recognize either the one or the other which would justify such an unsettling not to say uprooting, of the old landmarks of society, which are far deeper than any of those political distinctions which sep-arate Gentlemen now on these Benches from those on the other. I am not aware of any such case.'[64] Despite a last minute plea from Bright, that to leave things as they were would exclude from the franchise one-seventh of all the owners and occupiers of property in the kingdom, the bill was thrown out.

IV

Despite such setbacks, the women's suffrage movement gained momentum from the late 1860s onwards. Huxley, a firm believer in equality, raised the question of women's social and political rights in a magazine article of May 1865. He asked his readers, if they accepted 'the alleged defects of women', then 'is it not somewhat absurd to sanc-tion and maintain a system of education which would seem to have been specially contrived to exaggerate all these defects?'[65] He called the existing system of female education 'inherently absurd' and made a plea to 'emancipate girls'. He continued: 'Recognise the fact that they share the senses, perceptions, feelings, reasoning powers, emotions, of boys, and that the mind of the average girl is less different from that of the average boy, than the mind of one boy is from that of another; so that whatever argument justifies a given education for all boys, justifies its application to girls as well.'[66] He saw no reason why they should not become 'merchants, barristers, politicians'; and he felt men had nothing to fear from this. 'The big chests, the massive brains, the vigorous muscles and stout frames of the best men will carry the day, whenever it is worth their while to contest the prizes of life with the best women'. His conclu-sion had no trace of irony: 'The duty of man is to see that not a grain is piled upon that load beyond what Nature imposes; that injustice is not added to inequality.'[67]

Several women who would be prominent in the drive for higher education for their sex – such as Emily Davies and Barbara Bodichon – were active in the suffrage movement. Mill was drawn into it not least through his stepdaughter, Helen Taylor. During the passage of the 1867 Reform Bill he attempted, and failed, to have the bill amended to allow votes for women. A few dozen MPs sympathised with him: but the passage of the bill and the small core of support for votes for women prompted Mill to think the cause was not lost. In July 1867 he ensured Florence Nightingale was invited to join the committee of the London National Society for Women's Suffrage.[68] It already included Misses Cobbe, Hampson, Hare and Lloyd, and Mesdames Fawcett, Lucas and Stansfield. Mill sought to enlist Nightingale in this battle because he understood, having read her *Notes on Nursing*, her belief that 'women should not be excluded by law or usage from the liberty of trying any mode of exertion open to men, at their own risk in case of failure.'[69] They had also corresponded in 1860 on the subject, when Mill had criticised some advocates of women's rights – including, as he supposed, Nightingale – for being 'ready to make what appear to me far too great concessions as to the comparative unfitness of women for some occupations.'[70] Although Nightingale had been reluctant to put her bonnet above the parapet, she had gone so far as to sign Mill's suffrage petitions.

Mill told her he knew 'how fully you appreciate a great many of the evil effects produced upon the character of women (and operating to the destruction of their own and others' happiness) by the existing state of opinion' and said he had pushed her towards the LNSWS since he believed it was 'aimed . . . at the very root of all the evils you deplore and have passed your life in combating.'[71] Replying to him in August 1867 Nightingale said: 'That women should have the suffrage, I think no-one can be more deeply convinced than I. It is so important for a woman, especially a married woman, especially a clever married woman, to be a "person".'[72] However she added, with a note of prophetic realism, 'it will probably be years before you obtain the suffrage for women.' She also asked whether there were not 'evils which press more hardly on women than not having a vote . . . I do not know. I ask the question very humbly and I am afraid you will laugh at me.'[73] She had her own ideas: 'Could not the existing disabilities as to property and influence of women be swept away by the legislature as it stands at present? And equal rights and equal responsibilities be given as they ought to be, to both men and women?' She knew this from having been a matron and had such women work under her. 'Till a married woman can possess property there can be no love and no justice.'[74]

She wrote that 'I have been too busy for the last fourteen years (which have never left me 10 minutes leisure – not even to be ill) to wish for a vote – to want personal political influence. Indeed I have had, during the 11 years I have been in Govt offices, more administrative influence than if I had been a Borough returning two MPs.'[75] She said there was nothing she would not do for Mill, but she was too busy to go on the committee – 'I could not give my name without my work.' She added that she was 'an incurable invalid'. Mill replied four months later, from Avignon on New Year's Eve 1867, saying that 'if you prefer to do your work rather by moving the hidden springs than by allowing yourself to be known to the world as doing what you really do, it is not for me to make any observations on this preference . . . other than to say that I much regret that this preference is so very general among women.'[76] He told her that 'I think that man, and woman too, a heartless coward whose blood does not boil at the thought of what women suffer.'

He tried to make her see that many of the other reforms she sought – such as easier entry of women into the professions, from some of which, like the law, they remained absolutely barred – would be facilitated if women's suffrage were granted. Knowing the power of her name and reputation, he was frustrated and angry that she would not take the lead in this movement. 'Political power', he told her, 'is the only security against every form of oppression . . . at the present day in England it would be easier to attain political rights for such women as have the same claims as enfranchised men, than to obtain any other considerable reform in the position of women.' He concluded with the veiled rebuke: 'While I have seen with much regret that you join in so few movements for the public good, I have never presumed to think you wrong, because I have supposed that your abstinence arose from your devotion to one particular branch of public-spirited work.' Despite his entreaties she held her ground, but eventually sent a guinea to the LNSWS in December 1868.[77]

Mill castigated 'advocates of the "rights of women"' for being 'ready to make what appear to me far too great concessions as to the comparative unfitness of women for some occupations.' Nightingale told him that in America, where women had begun to become doctors, 'the women have made no improvement: they have only tried to be "men" and they have only succeeded in being third rate men.'[78] Lest Mill savage her for this assertion, she added: 'I am only here stating a matter of fact. I am not reasoning, as you suppose.' Mill replied that, given the novelty of women's entry into that profession, 'it is to be expected that they will be pupils at first, and not masters'.[79] He maintained that they had a 'moral right' to enter the profession.

By the 1870s there were more concerted attempts to extend suffrage to women. For radicals such as Mill it now became an issue above party politics. He told George Croom Robertson in November 1872 that 'the time, moreover, is, I think now come when, at parliamentary elections, a Conservative who will vote for women's suffrage should be, in general, preferred to a professed Liberal who will not . . . the bare fact of supporting Mr Gladstone in office, certainly does not now give a man a claim to preference over one who will vote for the most important of all political improvements now under public discussion.'[80]

William Forsyth, the Liberal MP for Marylebone, introduced a bill in April 1875 to allow unmarried women who had the appropriate property qualifications either in boroughs or in counties to have the vote. Forsyth, progressive though he was, remained strongly opposed to married women voting, because to do so would 'introduce discord into married life'.[81] He argued that public opinion strongly supported allowing unmarried women with a property qualification to vote: and that women had shown their active interest in politics and the parliamentary process, by petitioning Parliament in large numbers on the Deceased Wife's Sister's Bill – a perennial measure designed to allow a widower to marry the sister of his dead wife – and the repeal of the Contagious Diseases Act, a highly restrictive and controversial measure designed to keep prostitutes away from barracks and naval dockyards that was intensely degrading to women. Forsyth claimed that both Disraeli and Gladstone had expressed conditional support for female suffrage – in Gladstone's case, in a speech in 1871, through a male proxy. Petitions had been presented in favour of Forsyth's bill signed by some of the most eminent women in the land, including Nightingale.

However, the proponents of women's suffrage were up against some formidably prehistoric arguments. One MP had argued that because women had not stood alongside the barons at Runnymede who forced Magna Carta out of King John, they did not deserve the vote. Another, Henry Chaplin, argued that 'the collective wisdom of the ages, the teaching of all religion in every form and under every guise, and, as I believe, the instincts of the whole human race' were against women having a vote.[82] Women were also 'not great logicians'.[83] It was extensively argued that granting equality in the franchise would bring demands for it in legislative and administrative areas: in other words, it would be the thin end of a wedge that would culminate in allowing women equality in every field of life. Patrick Smollett, the MP for Cambridge, demonstrated the full extent of the hypocrisy of the time towards women. The example of women's 'hysterical crusade against the Contagious Diseases Act' had been an episode in which women 'championed the right of their fallen sisters to spread disease broadcast among the brave defenders of their country in seaport towns and in camps'.[84] When another MP challenged this, calling the Contagious Diseases Act 'grossly unjust, unconstitutional and immoral', he was shouted down.[85] Another statistic aired during the debate suggested one reason why some men resisted more power for women: there was a surplus in the United Kingdom of women over men of 925,764.[86]

The 1864 Contagious Diseases Act was a prime example of the sort of law that could be passed when no woman, other than the Queen, had an input into politics. It was put on the statute book without debate in either House of Parliament. It followed an investigation by a Civil Service committee in 1862 into the high incidence of venereal disease in the armed forces. It empowered police in eleven garrison and dockyard towns in England and Ireland to apply to a magistrate to have medically examined any woman suspected of being a prostitute and carrying a venereal disease. If a woman were found to have a disease she could be detained for up to three months. The 1864 Act was of limited duration and was replaced by a new one in 1866, this time with a cursory debate in the Commons. This enabled women to be medically examined over a period of twelve months, and to be detained for up to six months. In 1868 there were attempts to extend the Acts, and more garrison towns were added to the list.

This savage legislation had widespread support among doctors and clerics: however, those against it included Mill, Nightingale and Harriet Martineau. Mill was angered by the brutal treatment of women by the police, whose 'abuses of power' were not 'accidents which could be prevented. I think them the necessary consequences of any attempt to carry out such a plan thoroughly.'[87] He felt the Acts were a means of oppression that far outweighed any advantages they might bestow on servicemen. Mill also wondered why the soldiery was being kept in 'idleness and vice' and why the country was 'keeping a large army of prostitutes to pander to their vices', a state of affairs he thought 'monstrous'.[88] He was also offended by the 'gross inequality between men and women' that was caused by the Acts, which he felt should be 'swept away . . . in accordance with democratic principles of government'.

The debate raged for years, and caused a new bill to be introduced by Gladstone's Home Secretary, H. A. Bruce, in February 1872, aimed not just at containing contagious diseases but also at protecting women. Bruce's bill would apply to the whole country and not just garrison and dockyard towns; and said that a woman could be arrested for prostitution and, if found after her conviction to be diseased, could be detained for up to nine months after serving her sentence. The bill was never enacted; and the Acts, whose provisions came to be used less and less, were repealed in 1886.

V

Votes for women had almost another half-century of argument ahead of it; another injustice was, as with divorce, rectified more swiftly. The Married Women's Property Bill had its second reading a week after the failure of the Women's Franchise Bill. It proposed to allow a woman to keep any money she earned or inherited as her own, and not have it made the property of her husband. Several attempts had been made to secure a reform for which Parliament had received numerous petitions, and for which a growing number of men, convinced of the injustice of the status quo, were now calling. One particularly iniquitous effect was that 'although a husband might have deserted a wife and be living in adultery, the wife supporting her family, a portion of the property would go to the husband or his creditors.'[89] The Court of Chancery had said that while it should consider the fate of a wife and her children, it should consider that of the wife and children of an estranged husband's creditors too, whose wronged wife, it was stated, would have to be robbed of her money to pay his debts.

Nor was the effect confined to those well-to-do families with a house or land: women shareholders in cooperative societies found their husbands had a claim on the money they made in dividends: however, 'so strong was the public feeling in Rochdale in support of the payment of those profits to the women that none had ventured to enforce their claim.'[90] One other shocking case had been that of Susannah Palmer, a battered wife from London, who had been thrown out of her house by her husband. She had gone out to work and made enough money to rent a room for herself and her children: but no sooner had she done so than her husband, aware of her new circumstances, turned up and claimed her house as his – as he had the legal right to do. Only when her accommodation was put in the name of the Sheriffs of London was she allowed to stay there unmolested. The duty of a husband to provide for his wife and children – even with her money – was limited to a requirement under the Poor Law to see that they did not starve.

There had been several earlier attempts to right these injustices. In 1869, George Jessel, the Liberal MP for Dover, had echoed Mill's doctrine in saying that the present law was a relic of slavery. In addition to denying her property rights, the law also (and Jessel spoke as a lawyer, one of sufficient eminence that he would become Solicitor General) still allowed the husband the right to beat and imprison his wife, as he would a slave. Nor could a woman sue for libel or personal injury: her husband had to do that for her, if he were so minded. These iniquities had only survived so long because 'the laws of this country were made by the rich for the rich'.[91]

However, there remained serious objections to such a law. One who objected to the 1869 bill, Massey Lopes, did so because 'it would go far to impair the confidence that ought to exist between husband and wife, and which was the mainspring of domestic happiness.'[92] In the end it failed not just because the proposal seemed an intrusion of the State into the

private affairs of married couples, but also because of inadequate protection of the interests of children against a mother who, despite being
granted her own property, surrendered it to her husband, or who was
extravagant. The 1870 bill 'proposed to interfere between husband and
wife only when there was a presumptive necessity for such a proceeding.'[93]

The question of the Rochdale cooperative society was raised again.
Russell Gurney, who introduced the measure, said that

> there is in Rochdale a co-operative society with 7,000 members,
> including many married women who hold shares in their own
> name. In some cases the husbands have claimed these shares, to
> which, of course, they have a legal right; but the Committee,
> consisting as it does entirely of working men, have invariably
> resisted the claim, and such is the state of public feeling that in no
> one case has the husband's right been enforced. I have heard of
> another co-operative society where a similar course has been
> pursued. In legislating, therefore, in the way I propose, we shall
> not be running before public feeling, but shall be rendering that
> legal which in these cases is done in defiance of the law. The effect
> of the present state of the law seems to be equally bad on the
> husband and the wife. It makes—as one of the witnesses said—'the
> men idle and the women reckless.'[94]

Henry Raikes, who had moved the rejection of the bill the previous
year on its third reading, had had a change of heart. He saw 'the miserable and scandalous state of the law' and 'the absolute necessity for a
great and speedy change'.[95] On the same day another bill to give women
property rights would have a second reading, proposing an alternative
means of protecting women from bullying or criminal husbands. The
House heard of women whose earnings were taken from them on a
Saturday evening by their brutal husbands, to be spent on drink. The
bill had full government support. A further Act of 1882 would allow a
married woman to keep all her own property, whatever its source.
Despite these reforms, and the progress being made in female education, women were still denied the right to participate in politics.
However, the establishment in law of the principle that women had a
life and property independent of their husbands can be seen as the
opening of the route to full female emancipation that would be achieved
over the succeeding century.

VI

One of the keys to the emancipation of women was educating them: a process for which hardly any means existed at the start of Victoria's reign. By the mid-1840s the desire of women to be properly educated could no longer be ignored. Schools for girls existed largely as establishments to teach deportment and the management of households; or they were rudimentary, harsh, uncivilised institutions such as that attended by the Brontë sisters, which made no pretence of feeding the intellect. Most girls who had an education were taught by governesses, usually, again, to a rudimentary standard, and with no expectation of the education being put to any use − there were no places of higher education for females, and the professions were closed to them. Domesticity was the only prospect for most of them.

Frederick Denison Maurice and his disciple Charles Kingsley steered the movement to effect change. Maurice's interest came through his sister, a governess who had talked to him about the importance of training women such as herself properly for their educational duties. At the same time a Miss Murray, one of the Queen's maids of honour, was raising funds for women's education. The two forces collided, and the result was Queen's College, in Harley Street in London. Maurice, who would also found the Working Men's College and, later, the Working Women's College, became principal on its foundation in 1847. Two of the finest girls' schools were given an impetus by Queen's College: in its first intake of students were Frances Buss, who would found the North London Collegiate School, and Dorothea Beale, who in 1858 would take over, and transform, Cheltenham Ladies' College, the first girls' boarding school in England. Miss Buss and Miss Beale exemplified the aims behind the foundation of Queen's College: to train women to go out and teach girls to a higher standard than ever before, to help women aspire to a place in the world away from hearth and home.

Among intelligent and independent-minded women the foundation of Queen's caused something like a contagion. Henry Crabb Robinson, the diarist, reported in April 1848 that Elizabeth Jesser Reid, whom he had seen at a dinner, was 'all alive to the new female College which has been instituted for the education of Governesses'.[96] Mrs Reid was a unitarian philanthropist. She was famed for the zeal with which she enforced her opinions and was unafraid to pick fights and make enemies. The success of Queen's College inspired her to attempt to replicate it, and supporters of that enterprise endorsed the idea of another establishment to meet the demand from the daughters of the affluent middle classes.

A group of ladies met in the spring of 1849 to resolve to found the college – Mrs Sophia de Morgan, Mrs Scott, Miss Julia Smith, Mrs Rich, Mrs Hensleigh Wedgewood. In an undated letter from that time, Mrs Reid told Mrs de Morgan: 'let our guiding principle be Love and not Fear. Let us make it our object to see our Coll as perfect as we can make it without troubling ourselves about other folk's prejudices.'[97] Already a stalwart of the anti-slavery movement and other Exeter Hall activities, she told Mrs de Morgan how much she liked Maurice's lectures – 'there is a charm in the man's earnest devout spirit'. God was in everything for Mrs Reid: 'I am sure lectures on the Old Testament might be made most delightful and instructive and we don't want a weekday sermon instead: nine churchgoers out of ten have no idea of the connection of what they have been pleased to distinguish as Sacred and Profane History – that they are actually and in reality the same persons in each.' Religious opinions were to be of no account, and no pupil would be required to attend religious instruction. Bedford Square was chosen as a location because it was an affluent neighbourhood housing precisely the clientele the founders sought. Although religion was no object, the 'respectability' of the pupils was, and references would be sought.[98]

Mrs de Morgan warned her of the difficulties of getting such an enterprise started, and of the financial risk to Mrs Reid as the backer. Mrs Reid was resolute. 'I am perfectly happy to take the risk as you term it and feel far too confident of its success to admit of any generosity in the affair.'[99] She was going to lend them the money, and said that if they paid her interest on it she would spend it on the pupils; and if they were at some point able to repay her, the money would be put to a similar philanthropic use.

She found it easy, at first, to get potential pupils and teachers, and settled on 46 Bedford Square for premises. The hunt then began for 'patrons and patronesses', with an emphasis on the latter, with various peeresses of the committee's acquaintance being approached, but also women of distinction in various learned fields, notably Maria

Edgeworth, the novelist and children's writer. Emily Taylor, who ran Queen's College, advised Ann Scott of the committee that, when it came to teaching music, she could not do better than to choose 'a capital female Teacher for the Piano-Forte, leaving the lessons on Harmony to be an after, tho' very important business. If you fix *first* on a celebrated Professor of Harmony, you must allow him to make all the necessary musical arrangements, and, depend upon it, a woman will then never be chosen; but if a Professor recommends, as is very likely, young men for teachers you will have the trouble of providing someone always to be present.'[100] She recommended a Miss Speyer, who had been a pupil of Mendelssohn.

By January 1850 Mrs Reid told Robinson that she 'will give an education to any girl of suitable character and position who wants it.'[101] It was far from easy, not least because many of the families to whom Reid spread the word about the benefits of educating their daughters were entirely uninterested in the notion. Harriet Martineau wrote in May 1851 to console her, saying 'I am a good deal surprised, and very deeply grieved, at what you tell me of the doings and feelings of parents about the education of daughters'.[102] Two years earlier, when Reid had sent her a prospectus, she had questioned the need for it, coming just a year after the foundation of Queen's. 'I don't see why there should be a second college unless the first is overfull. Is it the teaching that is different or the plans? Or is it for the sake of a new neighbourhood?'[103] She had praised her, however, for advancing feminist doctrine and aspirations. Yet by the autumn of 1851 Reid was touting for business, seeking to persuade her friends to spread the word and recruit any eligible young women to come to be educated. Martineau was not very helpful. 'I wish I could help you about your college, but I know no young people, except impracticable ones.'[104]

A problem with recruiting pupils inevitably led to one with recruiting teachers, partly because of a shortage of pupils to teach, and partly because of the resulting lack of funds to pay salaries. Robinson noted on 14 October 1851 that 'Mrs Reid . . . is suffering seriously on account of the difficulty they find in filling the ladies' college with professors, of which she is to a great degree the foundress.'[105] He found learned men to introduce to Reid whom she could seek to persuade to take jobs at her college. The problem then became paying them. She had to spend much of the 1850s soliciting funds to keep it going. She told Robinson in 1858 that 'it is often referred to among us – and with some disappointment and wonder that Mr Carter [a solicitor with a daughter at the College] and you should be the only gentlemen in England who have ever given £50 to promote the higher education of Women.' She added: 'If they could but see and feel, as I do, that we never shall have better Men till men have better Mothers, they would come flocking about us . . . An able, earnest, liberal minded Man or two, or three, is at this moment our great want, not to teach, but to be Members of the council and be ready to advise and assist in private; a man of education experience and leisure.'[106] She had trouble with anti-feminism when seeking male teachers. She told Robinson on 17 June 1856 that 'the difficulty is to find one who is deliberately of the opinion that female education, the improvement of the Moral and mental education of Women is of any importance to society; while all the time the good man may be teased with a very silly and tiresome wife himself, who is spoiling the minds of his children.'[107] She hired a man called Beesly, a friend of Robinson and a professor of history at University College, to teach Latin to her girls: but in October 1861 she had 'taken offence' at him 'for stating as a fact that Woman as such was a *subordinate* to *man*' during a class when he was trying to demonstrate, without much tact, the etymology of the adjective.[108] He had already offended her, and caused her not to appoint him a professor, by mocking the slavery abolitionists: the American Civil War was under way. She tried to hire Maurice, knowing well his pro-feminist credentials, but he refused because of the presence of F. W. Newman on the staff.

Reid routinely badgered her friends for help. On 10 May 1854 Martineau wrote to her in response to a letter describing the financial distress of the college, and asking for suggestions of rich potential benefactors. She named Erasmus Darwin, Lady Shuttleworth and one 'Dr Davis (a niggardly Jew)', whom she approached, one presumes out of desperation, despite her disobliging view of him.[109] Martineau had already lent £500 and had no more. By 16 October 1857, however, Robinson recorded in his diary that he had visited Mrs Reid and the college in Bedford Square 'which she represents to be flourishing'.[110] That December, though, Reid was told by the Duke of Bedford to remove her pupils, as such an establishment was against the terms of her lease. Negotiations ensued, but for a while the relationship was precarious.

Reid feared that her premises drove away the clientele. 'I am sure that the meanness and shabbiness of our interior has cost us many pupils,' she told Robinson in 1856, 'but what can we do? My £1,500 has melted away; could I give another, I would gladly do it, but I can only live on my savings now. You would not advise me to cut up the goose that lays the egg. "It ought to be self supporting", gentlemen say to me. Perhaps it ought, but it is not, and it cannot be for a long time to come. Who can shew me a College for men that has been self supporting while these are of old and ours are [sic] new and in advance of public opinion, more than we were aware of? Nor did we calculate enough on the opposition of the clergy when we began.'[111]

She professed that 'the care of young Girls and helping them on to growing goodness and usefulness, being my vocation [is] my one object in life.'[112] She put this another way in a letter found in her papers after her death, written to her colleagues Jane Martineau and Eliza Ann Bostock: 'the elevation of the moral and intellectual character of Women'.[113] In the same letter she said: 'The condition of women never was quite so good, or by a great deal so hopeful as at this moment – and that the enemy is wide awake and in full activity is corroboration of the truth – nevertheless by untiring efforts and extreme patience we may, with God's blessing, obtain a glorious result in a quiet, unobtrusive, resistless success.'

Reid was greatly inspired by Angela Burdett-Coutts's pamphlet *Daughters of the Middle Classes* in 1858. She felt her pupils could do great work in schools for the poor. She told Robinson in March 1858 that 'I am convinced that a lady is no more unfitted to teach the lowest and meanest by our College, than a clergyman is by going to Oxford; the desire is everything with either. I must add that perhaps half of our Young Ladies rank as such more by good manners and ability than birth and that if you know anyone disposed to place another of this description under Miss Rankin's care for three or four years at an expense of £50 per annum he would be a Patriot indeed!'[114] She had hoped that a charitable foundation would support the college as a place for the education of the daughters of unitarian ministers. Thanks to her efforts, and those of her supporters, her enterprise flourished and, with the growth of the middle classes and the increased under-standing of the value of education for young women brought about by such establishments as Queen's College and Bedford College, its place was soon secure. By 1869 Bedford College was so successful that it was incorporated, and in 1874 it moved to larger premises off Baker Street.

The lack of schooling for girls limited the supply of those equipped for a university education. Reid founded her own girls' school in 1853 as a feeder to Bedford College, but the problem remained acute. In the 1860s the Taunton Commission heavily criticised the shortage of endowed schools for girls, and warned the government that more funds would need to be provided to educate them. After the 1860s, and in spite of the revised code, new opportunities for young women to enter teaching, and therefore a profession and a calling of reasonably high social standing, became more widespread. The great increase in pupil-teachers facilitated by the Forster Act in 1870 largely comprised young women. In 1870 there had been 6,384 males and 8,228 females in training in elementary schools. By 1880 the figures were 10,822 and 21,306 respectively.[115]

VII

The shortage of decent secondary schooling for girls was accentuated when in 1868 Cambridge agreed to admit them as candidates for local examinations. Although these were short of the standard of the university tripos – which women would start to sit within a few years, without being permitted to graduate – most girls were of insufficient standard to be serious candidates even for these. This prompted Arthur Hugh Clough's sister Anne, a campaigner for women's higher education, to suggest what was in effect the beginning of the university extension movement, which would provide lectures in major provincial towns and cities and, indeed, partly as a result of an initiative by Jowett and Oxford, led to a campaign in 1874 to found a university at Bristol, which opened in 1876. It had been difficult enough to launch new institutions to teach young women to degree standard. The next challenge, though, was to breach the walls of the two ancient English universities, and have them accept women. Emily Davies was a pioneer of this movement; and like many of those in the field of women's education, brought with her an entire package of feminist views that followed the idea of education of women to a logical conclusion: women should also have the vote, and they should find none of the professions barred to them.

Davies was born in 1830, the daughter of a clergyman, John Davies, whose intellectual reputation had been sufficient for him to be offered the chair of moral and political economy at London University. He sent his sons to Repton, but his ideas of educating children did not extend to his daughters. They were consigned to a life of assisting with the family needlework and, when old enough, doing good works in Gateshead, Mr Davies's parish. Davies resented this; in her twenties, however, she met two women who inspired her to campaign for women's education and suffrage. One was Elizabeth Garrett, six years her junior, who would become the first female doctor in Britain; the other was Barbara Bodichon, three years her senior.

Bodichon was then known for her campaign to reform women's property rights, but was also one of the most prominent members of the Langham Place circle of feminists, which from 1858 under Bodichon's leadership published the radical *English Woman's Journal*, for which Davies would become a main writer and editor. Bodichon's grandfather had been one of the MPs who supported Wilberforce in the abolition of slavery; her father, Benjamin Smith, was a radical MP. She was a first cousin of Nightingale, whose mother was her father's sister: but Barbara was illegitimate, and much of the family refused to know her. In keeping with his beliefs Smith had Barbara educated by private tutors and at various schools; and when she came of age in 1848 her father gave her shares and property to provide a private income, allowing her the independence to pursue her main career interest (which was to become an artist) and to engage in political campaigning. That activity would lead her into close associations with Mill, through his stepdaughter Helen Taylor, and George Eliot. She regarded her money as 'a power to do good . . . a responsibility we must accept.'[116] She was also what the twenty-first century would call a ferocious networker, and it was not least thanks to her network that she was able to advance her various feminist causes so well as she did.

Davies also had a link to Maurice's circle through her brother Llewellyn, a friend of Maurice and a member of the proto-feminist National Association for the Promotion of Social Science. Visiting London in 1859, she and Garrett attended lectures given by Elizabeth Blackwell, an Englishwoman who had become the first female doctor in the United States, and who inspired Garrett's campaign to allow women into the medical profession in Britain. Blackwell had been urged to come to Britain by Bodichon, to help Garrett's campaign. Davies also joined the Society for the Promotion of the Employment of Women, and on her return to Gateshead founded a branch. This further motivated her to campaign for women's education, and she joined Garrett's drive to have London University award degrees to women. One of her campaigns was to allow girls to take the Cambridge local examinations, in which she had the support of Matthew Arnold, who wanted women teachers to have a recognised qualification.[117] When it succeeded, Davies found eighty-three girls in just six weeks to take the exams, twenty-five from Frances Buss's North London Collegiate School. It was also thanks to one of Davies's campaigns that the Taunton Commission considered the education of middle-class girls as well as of middle-class boys. When she gave evidence to it in 1865 it was the first time a Royal Commission had ever examined a woman.

Her next campaign was to draw up the petition for women's suffrage that Mill presented to the Commons in 1866. For a time she was secretary of a suffrage committee under the auspices of the Kensington Society, a group that also included Barbara Bodichon, Elizabeth Garrett, Miss Buss and Miss Beale. However, Davies feared that her role in this campaign was potentially damaging to her ideal of creating more educational opportunities for women, and so withdrew. In 1866 she set out her aims in her book *The Higher Education of Women*, arguing that university courses and the professions should be opened to females: and she disposed, with cool rationality, of the arguments that women were biologically inferior to men, and therefore could not cope either with the pressure of examination, because of a tendency to hysteria, or with the demands of a serious career.

From her next organisation, the London Schoolmistresses' Association, the idea emerged of founding a women's college that would award degrees. The initial idea was to persuade Queen's College to ask London University to allow its women to take their degrees: but that proved impracticable, and the ambition was conceived to raise funds for a women's college at Cambridge: Oxford was deemed too hostile, whereas several prominent Cambridge dons had indicated their support. A committee met in December 1867, under Davies's direction, to set about raising the £30,000 that would be needed. The committee included some of the academics who had earlier indicated their support, such as J. R. Seeley, the historian; and pillars of society such as Lady

Augusta Stanley, a confidante of the Queen and the wife of the biographer of Dr Arnold. Barbara Bodichon, who had financed a secular coeducational school in London from 1854 to 1863, gave much of her time, and some of her money. She had been an advocate of a women's university education since visiting her brother at Cambridge in the late 1840s. However, Davies initially suppressed her name from the list of supporters because of the strong association Bodichon had with radical feminism.

What Davies sought for her college was markedly different from what another group with similar ambitions hoped to achieve at Cambridge. Henry Sidgwick, whose article on Eton had been one of the causes of the Clarendon Commission and whose resignation as a fellow of Trinity would cause the University Tests to be abolished, had with Anne Clough obtained the university's agreement to establish special examinations for female students: these would not lead to a Cambridge degree, thanks partly to Sidgwick and Clough's belief that the inadequacies of girls' education made such an aspiration unrealistic. Sidgwick and Clough had become friends not least because of his reverence for her brother's poetry: he was also, like the poet, a Rugbeian. When resigning his fellowship in 1869 on the grounds of apostasy, he had identified with Clough's experiences at Oriel twenty years earlier. Trinity promptly appointed him to a lectureship, so he could continue his college teaching without a fellowship, and threw its considerable weight behind the campaign for abolition of the test. The climate had changed radically since Clough's enforced isolation.

Sidgwick wrote that, like Clough before him, 'I can neither adequately rationalise faith, nor reconcile faith with reason, nor suppress reason.'[118] He added: 'I do not feel called or able to preach religion except as far as it is involved in fidelity to one's true self.' Strongly influenced by Mill in his philosophical thought, Sidgwick committed himself to women's education, becoming involved with university extension teaching for the new Higher Local Examination. He and others in Cambridge saw the advantages of founding a college for the purpose not just of lecturing for these examinations, but to bring women up to the level required for the tripos. This commitment, and his Clough-like behaviour at Trinity, caused him to be venerated by Anne Clough.

Davies despaired at what Sidgwick and Clough proposed, considering the diluted examination as 'devised to suit struggling governesses'.[119] She wanted her students to follow the same courses, attend the same lectures, and take the same degrees as men. This refusal to compromise was logically sound but strategically problematical: it cost Davies supporters and funds. Her vision of a women's college was achieved not in the first instance at Cambridge, but in a rented villa in Hitchin in Hertfordshire – something Bodichon deplored because she saw the money spent on rent as a waste but which, being halfway between London and Cambridge, Davies considered to be a prime location, and well away from the distractions of male undergraduates.

Davies took out newspaper advertisements to promote the scheme and ask for money. The shock to the unthinking man was profound: 'Our age has been so prolific of absurdities, that we cannot well be expected to feel any very great surprise at the incubation of one foolish project more,' steamed *The Imperial Review*.[120] It went on to condemn 'this preposterous proposal of a University career for the potential wives of Englishmen', which was 'calculated to unfit women for the performance of the very duties to which . . . women only are intended and adapted.' Davies and her supporters were, inevitably, hardened to their task by such bigotry. Occasionally, there was a sense of the women being carried away. In the autumn of 1868, describing her vision of the college as an integral part of Cambridge University, Davies proclaimed that 'it will aim at no higher position than, say, that of Trinity College.'[121] This attracted the notice of *The Times*, which noted that 'such a degree of humility will not be considered excessive.'[122]

The Education Department of the Privy Council held back from endorsing the project. *The Times* itself, for all its irony, conceded that 'an advance in the system of female education would be of unquestionable benefit'. It admitted that 'we have advanced, indeed, beyond the time when a knowledge of conversational French and "accomplishments" formed the sole acquirements of a "finished" girl.' However, the 'fatal defect', as it saw it, was that 'girls do not generally possess the physical strength which minute and thorough study requires . . . the simple truth is that the intellectual work in which men excel requires not only intellectual capacity, but severe physical labour.' The widespread recognition of this apparently indisputable fact meant teachers would never be so rigorous with girls as with boys, which in turn meant girls were doomed to fail. It could see the benefits of founding a college where women would, in time, be brought up to the level of attainment of the average public schoolboy. It saw no reason why Miss Davies's plan to have women pursue something beyond this should not be tried: but no one should expect it to succeed, nor to serve any useful purpose in a world where women were designed 'to make their husbands happy, and to rear and educate their children,' in a climate in which 'their very virtue is dependence'.

Prospectuses to attract students were sent out to girls' schools in the spring of 1869, and eighteen young women sat an entrance examination at the University of London, under Davies's supervision, in July that year. Thirteen passed: three more sat the examination in October, in Bodichon's house in London, and soon afterwards five women began their studies. Dons came by train from Cambridge to teach them, and Davies wished to build a larger establishment in Hitchin. However, Bodichon and others pressed her to move to Cambridge, and in the autumn of 1871 a site was secured in the village of Girton, a couple of miles north-west of Cambridge. It was not merely that land was more easily available outside the town; it was also that the honour of the young women would, it was felt, be better preserved if they were kept at a distance from male undergraduates.

Davies scaled down her expectations of funding from £30,000 to £10,000, and more than a quarter of that had to be borrowed. George Eliot, who had met Davies and had expressed her support, sent £50 'from the author of *Romola*'.[123] Bodichon promised £1,000 for the building of the college provided that her friend Elizabeth Blackwell was appointed professor of hygiene there; that it was entirely secular; and that it was built in the middle of Cambridge. On each she would be disappointed; but nonetheless she gave the money, chaired the fund-raising committee for further buildings, and joined the executive committee that ran the college. Once it was built she contributed books and furniture. For all these reduced circumstances, Davies could still afford to engage Alfred Waterhouse as her architect, and the original college building is one of his finest early works: and the artistic Bodichon superintended all the details closely. Half of Waterhouse's main block opened in October 1873, with thirteen students admitted and living and studying in what was still a building site. Three women had unofficially sat the tripos examinations earlier in the year, two for Classics and one for mathematics: Davies had not had to dilute standards, but the women were still not permitted to proceed to degrees.

From 1872 women studying in Cambridge were allowed to attend lectures at the discretion of the lecturer; and in 1881 they no longer had to take tripos exams surreptitiously, but could do so openly. In 1880 Miss C. A. Scott of Girton was placed equal to the Eighth Wrangler in the mathematics tripos when examined unofficially. A huge campaign, reported in the newspapers, was launched for the right of women at Cambridge to enter examinations officially and to take degrees. Henry Sidgwick worked to get a recommendation through the Senate that teaching and examination should be put on an equal footing, even if the women could not take degrees at the end of the process. It passed, on 24 February 1881, by 331 to 32, the enemy having retreated.

Davies served as mistress until 1875, and then as secretary of Girton's executive committee until 1904. She oversaw the college's rapid expansion, being determined that as many young women as possible should have the opportunity of an education there: by 1884 Girton had grown substantially in terms of its buildings, with a library and large kitchens, and more accommodation allowing eighty women to be admitted. This caused tensions between Davies and the teachers, who would have preferred such funds as were raised to support their work and research. Davies remained adamant that broadening access should always be Girton's first priority. Bodichon gave the college £5,000 in 1884 and left it another £10,000 in her will on her death in 1891, as well as donating the pictures she had lent it. This generosity secured Girton's finances. Although recognised in 1924 by Royal Charter as an institution for the higher education of women, it did not become a college of Cambridge University until 1948, when its women could at last proceed to Cambridge degrees.

Cambridge's other pioneering women's college, Newnham, had its origins in October 1871 in a house in Cambridge. Whereas Girton was a predominantly feminist-driven enterprise, Newnham came about not least because of the determination of Cambridge dons. Sidgwick played a conspicuous role in its foundation. A committee to raise funds met in the Cambridge drawing room of Millicent Fawcett. She was Elizabeth Garrett's younger sister, and the young wife of Henry Fawcett, the Liberal MP and campaigner for women's rights and, at this stage, professor of political economy at Cambridge. Millicent was already a committed member of the women's suffrage movement, having at an early age come under the spell of Maurice. Sidgwick and others offered their services free of charge while money was raised for teaching: Mill and Helen Taylor offered £40 a year for three years, but the inflow of funds, ironically, raised pressure to find accommodation for students and for teaching.

Raising money for accommodation and sustenance was, as Emily Davies had found, harder. Although a few others made discreet donations, Sidgwick took the initiative. 'Mr Sidgwick, acting on his own account, took and furnished a house for five girls in Regent Street. He gave up his holiday for the purpose. "I have no money," he explained, "the cares of a household being incumbent. As a friend puts it, I am going to have all the fun of being married, without the burden of a wife."'[124] 'Girls' is not an entirely accurate description: one, Ella Bulley, was thirty, and another, Mary Kennedy, daughter of the Regius professor of Greek, twenty-six. The legends of the unprepossessing nature of women students of this era have a rocky basis in fact. Sidgwick was so disturbed by the pulchritude of two – Mary Paley and Mary Kennedy – that he was heard by Mrs Peile, wife of the future Master of Christ's, to mutter in despair: 'It's their appearance, their *unfortunate appearance!*'[125]

Sidgwick and Fawcett invited Clough, who had run a girls' school in the north of England, to come and superintend the house in Regent Street. Following the failure of her father's Liverpool cotton business in 1841, she had set up schools and taught in them to earn a living. Since her brother's death she had lived with her widowed sister-in-law in order to educate his children. One, Blanche Athena, would become her protégée and devote her life to Newnham. Clough had founded the North of England Council for Promoting the Higher Education of Women, with herself as secretary and Josephine Butler, the prominent feminist renowned for work for the welfare of prostitutes, as president. 'It was generally imagined that a severer intellectual training than women had hitherto received would make them unwomanly, hard, unlovely, pedantic and disinclined for domestic duties, while the dangers to physical health were dolorously predicted by medical men.'[126] Mrs Butler's response was 'No! It would not impair the Home; it would extend the best home influences from where they were at present penned up, to humanise the mechanical charities and cold, large institutions of men. It would be a setting-free of feminine powers from narrow and listless lives.' Clough had written for periodicals about the advantages of a school in training the minds of girls, compared with teaching them at home. She made a name for herself with this, and also by her work in having Cambridge academics come to the provinces to give lectures, the beginning of the extension movement.

Davies, who had felt piqued about the rival project, was less impressed with Sidgwick. His willingness to compromise about standards outraged her. He said she had written to him describing him as 'the serpent that was eating out her vitals'.[127] In 1873, as Girton opened, Sidgwick and Clough formally appealed for building funds, with the distant reinforcement, from Oxford, of Jowett. The Ladies Lectures Committee became the Association for Promoting the Higher Education of Women at Cambridge. Sidgwick's first success came in 1874: two women – Mary Paley (later Mrs Alfred Marshall) and Ella Bulley (later Mrs Brooke), unofficially took honours in the moral sciences tripos, invigilated upon by Professor Kennedy.

Demand for places rose steadily and quickly. In 1874 St John's College sold a lease on the land for what became Newnham. Newnham Hall opened in 1875, a healthy three miles from Girton, and by the following year had sixty students. Clough remained principal, though took no salary. Mindful of her late brother's torments over religion, she insisted on Newnham's being non-sectarian; though to avert claims of the college encouraging godlessness, she made a point of asking each student about her place of worship. If anyone under twenty-one answered that she had none, this would be tolerated only after the girl's parents had given consent. In the early years Newnham's facilities, as with Girton's, were rudimentary: no space was set aside for a chapel, and a bathroom had to serve as a laboratory until 1879. That same year the governing bodies of both King's and Christ's agreed that women could attend lectures in their colleges, following the example of several professors who had admitted women to their lectures since the mid-1870s: a breakthrough had been made. Although Newnham was later into the field than Girton, by 1880 it had 258 students against Girton's 113, thanks to the flexibility offered to women who needed more preparation for their courses.

In 1876 Sidgwick married Eleanor Mildred 'Nora' Balfour, sister of the future Prime Minister Arthur James Balfour, and a member of the political and intellectual aristocracy. Her husband had got to know her when he sought support – moral and financial – for Newnham; it is not believed their marriage, which was happy, was consummated. She was well read and deeply religious and became active in the Society for Psychical Research, which her husband had founded. She wrote that the 1860s was an exciting decade for new ideas, which came so abundantly that 'even sluggish minds were caught by the current, and swept into new regions'.[128] Nora was not the humourless old bluestocking her photographs may imply. Her niece, in her memoir of her, recalled how in 1872 she had accompanied her sister and brother-in-law, the future Nobel-prize-winning scientist Lord Rayleigh, to Egypt. Nora had recalled 'at about eighty, being asked if she had ever smoked: "Once I smoked, in a harem".'[129] Nora gave Newnham £500 on its foundation, and founded a scholarship; in the end, her donations totalled £30,000. She was Newnham's treasurer for thirty-nine years, presiding over its constant development and expansion, with her husband negotiating the acquisition of the freehold of the site from St John's. She became vice-principal in 1880.

Gladstone's daughter Helen came to Newnham in 1877, and later became Mrs Sidgwick's secretary. Nora inspired awe in those women who met her. Helena Powell, who came up in 1881, said that 'when I saw the Vice-Principal, very slight and fragile, her smooth fair hair covered with a little lace cap such as young married women used to wear in those days, almost as shy as myself, fear went at once, to be replaced by a wondering awe, which grew and grew as the years went on, as slowly I learnt how all greatness is spiritual.'[130]

Clough remained principal until her death in 1892, when Mrs Sidgwick succeeded her. Until the Great War the college educated women to whatever standard they could comfortably attain, since many were still handicapped by lack of a formal school education. However, by the second decade of the twentieth century an expanding network of girls' schools, staffed and led not least by alumnae of Girton and Newnham, had raised the calibre of the woman undergraduate. Most could take, and succeed in, the examinations taken by men, though they still could not proceed to degrees.

During the 1870s Parliament began to take an active interest in women's education, not least because of a prevailing mood that the country was neglecting this human resource, and would suffer accordingly. Former Liberal minister William Cowper-Temple, in a Commons debate on 12 June 1874, said that:

the chief nations of Europe were in advance of Great Britain in the higher education of women. In the University of Paris 10 female students were to be found at that moment, and Englishwomen went there for medical degrees. Women might take degrees at the Universities of Lyons and Montpellier, at all the Universities of Italy, at Vienna, and Leipzig. At St. Petersburg 250 young women were receiving medical education; some had gone from Russia to the University of Zurich, from whence they were recalled for political reasons, as Zurich was the resort of refugee Poles. The Universities which had taken the lead in this important matter were the University of London, the University of Cambridge, and the University of Edinburgh. [131]

Women had just moved in to Girton, and Newnham was being developed, and at University College, London, about 300 women attended classes specially for them, and about 150 attended mixed classes. London University awarded them certificates of efficiency, but a memorial signed by 500 graduates of University College said degrees ought to be given to women. Oxford followed shortly behind Cambridge. A group of dons and women educationists formed a committee in 1878 to establish a college: but two factions immediately fell out over the question that consistently dogged education: religion. One wanted an Anglican college; the other did not. They went their separate ways, the Anglicans establishing Lady Margaret Hall in 1878, and those who wished education to be free of religious considerations founding what would become Somerville in 1879.

Despite the evidence of women's ability to cope with intellectual rigour, there were still politicians uneasy about academic equality: whether out of fear of what educated women might do to men's privileges, or out of genuine but patronising concern for their welfare, it is hard to tell. In the 1874 Commons debate Lyon Playfair observed that 'it may be that the Universities, which by long experience have been adapted to men, may not in their present form be fitted for women. There is, at least, sufficient doubt on the subject to make us cautious in legislation. So far as American experience of mixed Colleges has gone, it appears, on the ground of intellectual teaching and morality, that the fitness of both sexes is the same—but on the ground of health, it is still doubtful whether women can bear the strain of University studies. This subject is being fully discussed at present by American medical men, and is exciting keen interest in this country.'[132]

However, Playfair was at least willing to countenance a concession to what appeared to be the weaker sex. 'I do not attach much force to the objection, because I think it could be obviated by a postponement of the age at which female students might be matriculated. But I do not think it improbable that a different course of studies ought to be followed for male and female students. We ought to give the women of this country a higher and nobler education, instead of the narrow and trivial education which they now receive. But if our Universities were thrown open tomorrow to women, are there half-a-dozen in any University town who by their school training could follow the courses necessary for one of our degrees?'

This was to an extent a fair point – it was the argument of Sidgwick and Clough, for which the former was reviled by Emily Davies. Although she was unwilling to make any concessions, Playfair felt that without them women would be at a severe disadvantage. 'The degrees in Arts, Law, Divinity, or for Doctor of Medicine, all involve a knowledge of Greek. I know of only two small schools in which that is given as a subject of female education. That which I have given as an illustration in regard to Greek holds also, in a less degree, as to other fundamental studies, such as Latin and mathematics. Therefore you must make female degrees lower than male degrees—that is, you must fundamentally change the educational requirements of graduation, or you must revolutionize the preparatory schools of the country in regard to female education.'

VIII

Cowper-Temple was not interested simply in getting women into universities: he knew the next step was for them to enter the professions. Foremost among these was medicine, not just because numerous women wished to become doctors, but because more women wanted their own sex to care for them when they fell ill. Cowper-Temple described the profession as one 'for which they were by nature most peculiarly suited. A woman was in her best position by the side of the sick bed or in the hospital, and those whom nature had prepared to be nurses, art could easily make into doctors. A Petition had been presented to that House signed by above 16,000 women, declaring that they desired the opportunity of consulting good medical advisers or properly qualified persons of their own sex, and that they thought it a hardship that the laws of this country should lead to regulations that prevented any woman adopting medicine as a profession.'[133]

He knew there was:

a considerable objection to this in the medical profession as represented in the Universities; but he had observed that in cases of alterations or innovations proposed to be made in professions, whether military, naval, or legal, the public could not submit to professional opinion. The members of a profession were often unable to consider without bias innovations relating to themselves; and much as he respected the medical profession, he would still say that Parliament ought not to give undue attention to objections which they might raise in matters relating particularly to their own profession. Let them rather look to the needs and desire of the public at large, and they would see that female medical practitioners in London and Birmingham had met the wants of numerous patients.

Cowper-Temple struggled for support among the reactionaries of the Commons, but was vigorously supported by the scientific and educational establishment. In 1869 Edinburgh University had broken the mould in Britain by accepting a twenty-nine-year-old woman, Sophia Jex-Blake, an alumna of Queen's College and a former mathematics tutor there, to read medicine. Jex-Blake had argued the point Cowper-Temple subsequently made: that many women wanted medical attention from one of their own sex. When Jex-Blake was accepted by Edinburgh she advertised for other like-minded women to join her, and six did. They met serious opposition from elements in the university, being denied the right to attend lectures. They had to raise the money to pay lecturers to teach them separately, but even then Edinburgh would not award them degrees. In 1874 she was a founder of the London School of Medicine for Women, and campaigned for legislation that enabled, but did not compel, examining bodies to treat women medical students just as they treated men. Jex-Blake was not a beneficiary of this law, qualifying at the University of Berne first. The College of Physicians of Ireland was the first in the United Kingdom to admit women to medical degrees: Jex-Blake subsequently took the Licenciate's examination there, which enabled her to be registered with the General Medical Council and to become only the third registered female doctor in the country. She set up a practice in Edinburgh and, in 1886, founded the Edinburgh School of Medicine for Women.

Elizabeth Garrett had been the first on the register. In 1849 her father had been sufficiently enlightened to send her, aged thirteen, to a girls' school in Blackheath run by Robert Browning's step-aunts. The teaching was unimpressive – deportment was on the curriculum – but Elizabeth did pick up a love of reading and, with it, a profound intellectual curiosity. Once her education finished she continued to read, and studied Latin and mathematics more deeply in her own time. She read an article by Elizabeth Blackwell in the *English Woman's Journal*, and conceived the idea of becoming a doctor. Emily Davies attended Blackwell's London lectures with her and supported her. The obstacles were, though, formidable.

Fortunately for Garrett, her father supported her financially. Her training began in the only way it practically could, with her working as a nurse at the Middlesex Hospital. After she had excelled in that vocation, and had been allowed to attend operations, she applied to join the medical school there. 'It appears to me', she wrote to Davies in October 1860, 'that I should not go on receiving instruction as a pupil under the guise of a nurse, and that it will be right to ask the college authorities to allow me to pay the usual fees in these special departments and to have the run of the hospital as at present for medical observation.'[134] Her application was rejected: but the hospital's apothecary gave her private tuition while she continued her nursing duties, in return for a donation to the hospital.

Her father hired her a tutor in anatomy and physiology during her evenings off; and eventually she was allowed to attend chemistry lectures and dissection. However, the last of these raised matters of delicacy, because of what Garrett described as 'the general larkiness of the students'.[135] Her sympathetic teacher, Mr Nunn, the dean of the school, tried to see whether a separate dissection room could be made available for women students: which prompted her and Davies to look for other potential female doctors. This, and her success in her study, caused some of the students to resent her. Sensing what might be about to happen, some men protested against her ever being admitted as a fellow student.

In 1861 she had, therefore, to leave, though not without certificates in chemistry and *materia medica*, and despite having received encouragement from several eminent doctors at the medical school. 'It is', she told Davies, 'very disagreeable, but I suppose one will overlive it somehow.'[136]

She obtained, privately, certificates in anatomy and physiology, while applying to most medical schools in the country and being refused admission. Her father petitioned London University, which was seeking a new charter, to include in it the power to admit women. It failed by a small majority when voted upon in the Senate; a second attempt weeks later was lost only on the casting vote of the chancellor. Davies wrote a paper entitled *Medicine as a Profession for Women* that was delivered at the 1862 annual meeting of the National Association for the Promotion of Social Science, and subsequently published as a pamphlet. Thus a propaganda campaign was instigated, in which the columns of the *English Woman's Journal* formed a main theatre of war.

Huxley opened his South Kensington lectures to women, and admitted Garrett to his classes. In 1865 she sat the examination of the Society of Apothecaries with six other candidates. Three, including Garrett, passed, and she obtained the highest marks: though she admitted to Davies that 'the examination was too easy to feel elated about,' which raises questions about the dismal standards expected of the men who took the course.[137] This made her a Licenciate of the Society and allowed her to practise medicine. The Society marked her achievement by amending its rules to prevent other women doing what she had done: one of the more extreme examples of men trying to put the genie of equality back in its bottle. Five years later, once the Sorbonne in Paris had decided to admit women to medical degrees, Garrett learned French and took the higher qualification there. She then, in 1873, and having married Skelton Anderson, became the first and only female member of the British Medical Association, which promptly followed precedent and banned any other women from joining.

In the interim, barred from any hospital post because of her gender, Garrett had set up her own dispensary for women outpatients in the West End of London. By 1872 her dispensary had become the New Hospital for Women and Children, later the Elizabeth Garrett Anderson Hospital; and she was co-founder with Jex-Blake of the

London School of Medicine for Women in 1876, an institution that had the explicit support of Huxley. She would become dean of the school and hold that post for almost twenty years, the school eventually being incorporated into the medical school of University College, London.

The Hospital for Women included female doctors who had qualified at European medical schools, but who because of restrictions placed on the General Medical Council's acceptance of degrees could not register in Britain. In 1875 Cowper-Temple, one of the MPs behind the formation of the GMC as a means of protecting patients, urged the government to stop this discrimination. The GMC itself had proposed a separate examination for women of equal standard to that taken by men, which would enable a woman to be registered if she passed it. He said that if the government would not support this, he would introduce a private bill to force them to do so. Lord Sandon, who answered him, said that the government had consulted the GMC and was pondering what to do. Russell Gurney, another pro-feminist MP, observed that the GMC, 'after long and anxious consideration, had expressed a decided opinion that women ought no longer to be excluded from the profession. After such a declaration one would hardly imagine that the existing state of things could remain unaltered.'[138] The government took the hint, and another bar to women was soon lifted.

Garrett Anderson sought to blow away the ignorance of male doctors about what were considered to be maladies of women caused by their inherent weakness. Well aware that most women still led sheltered lives of boredom and unfulfilment, she spoke out about the need for women to be allowed to expand their horizons just as men had, rubbishing notions that women could be over-educated to a point where they would suffer nervous and mental disorders. Although not active in the wider world of women's political rights in the manner of her younger sister, Garrett Anderson was a supporter of women's suffrage, regarding the progress she helped women to make in medicine as only one of the battles to be fought.

IX

Florence Nightingale had become a beacon for women's advancement in mid-Victorian Britain, even though her own belief in feminism was ambiguous to say the least. She had returned from the Crimean War as one of the most celebrated women in Britain, but underneath her image lay a mass of contradictions, complexities and hysteria. She came from an affluent family, and her father (who funded several schools around his estates in Hampshire and Derbyshire) had extended his belief in education to include his daughters, unusually for that era. Florence was given a sound education in both modern and classical languages and in other subjects: had there been women at Oxford and Cambridge in the late 1830s, she would have given most men a run for their money.

Her mother kept a salon, and Florence as a teenager met many of the leading men of the day. Fanny Nightingale also had the measure of her daughter early on. Writing when Florence was eighteen, she said that 'Florence is much admired for her beauty and she, too, is reckoned very clever and amusing, but her stately manners keep people at a distance, so I do not expect that love passages will be frequent in her life.'[139] Florence would never marry: but she was a tall, slim, austere beauty with admirers, the most notable of whom was the Whig politician and (among other things) proto-feminist Richard Monckton Milnes. He would have married her, and they had a courtship of sorts over about nine years. However, Florence only seemed to realise this was something she would like when it was too late, and Milnes was in the process of marrying someone else.

Despite – or perhaps because of – her education, Florence became frustrated and depressed. In her writings there is the occasional note of hysterical despair, and of religious mania. Her principal problem was her only sibling, her sister Parthenope, a year older than her and also unmarried. Parthenope – known in the family as 'Pop' – had become obsessed with her sister, to the point where after a separation from her she had a mental breakdown. Florence took Pop's collapse as a salutary warning about what could happen to women with overactive imaginations and native intelligence who were imprisoned in their lives and, in both their cases, still at home past the age of thirty. It seems, however, to have been a factor in Florence's decision not to pursue marriage that she believed that, if she did marry, her chances of doing something great herself would be killed. Her part in the emancipation of women would be conspicuous, but required the sacrifice of her not having a husband and children.

She conceived nursing as a means of escape. She decided God had sent her a message to tend the sick. Like many thinkers of the age just before Darwin she had begun to reject the notion of the Bible as literal truth. She did, however, believe God gave people missions in life to accomplish His work, and she had unquestionably found hers. Her parents disapproved of the direction in which she believed God had sent her, hardly surprising in an age when nursing was deemed a calling followed largely by women of the servant class, and with a reputation for drunkenness and immorality. She went to Kaiserwerth in the Rhineland to see how modern nursing was done, and returned convinced she could devise a superior system. Through connections she became superintendent of the Establishment for Gentlewomen During Illness in Harley Street in 1853, quickly making a name in her new calling. Her decision to take the job was helped by the eventual acquiescence of her father, who made her an allowance of £500 a year, more than enough to support her. She also helped at the Middlesex Hospital when it became overwhelmed during the cholera epidemic of 1854: immensely useful training for the Crimea.

Nightingale had been helped to develop her nursing career by Sidney Herbert, a family friend to whom she was devoted. He had the misfortune to be Secretary of State for War when British troops first went to the Crimea in the autumn of 1854. Word quickly got back to England that the sick and wounded were dying for want of proper nursing, and Herbert arranged for Nightingale to lead thirty-eight nurses to Scutari, where they arrived on 4 November. Nightingale immediately imposed her will and her personality on the situation. When Army doctors and other officers were obstructive, she made no bones about her direct line to the Secretary of State. Her first priority was to improve hygiene, and she succeeded, though not without sacking some of the nurses she had brought with her, whose standards she considered insufficiently high.

Aside from saving the lives of many soldiers, Nightingale's achievements were revolutionary in other respects. Women did not normally take the type of leadership role that she did (the Sovereign being considered something of an exception). A gentlewoman did not get her hands dirty, or go among the common soldiery, as she did. This helped create a legend around her, fed when she felt forced to broaden her remit in the Crimea, and lobby Herbert not just for better medical supplies, but also for better clothing, food and cooking. She even arranged for the head chef at the Reform Club to come out and shake up that side of the operation. The flood of casualties after Balaclava put her under severe stress: she coped, and raised standards not least by her dictatorial methods, but her health went to ruin.

This was when, thanks to a line in *The Times*, she became known as 'the Lady of the Lamp', and her selflessness and heroism in the face of disease and appalling conditions cemented the legend. In thanks for her recovery a fund of £45,000 was raised, though she had no idea what to do with it. When the War ended in March 1856, Nightingale concluded that the alarming death and casualty rates had been largely preventable. One in five of the 94,000 men sent to the Crimea died of disease, only 4,000 of wounds, and another 13,000 were invalided. When John Bright said the Angel of Death was abroad throughout the land, he had omitted to say he was armed with infection, not a rifle.

Arthur Hugh Clough, her cousin by marriage, wrote of the problems Nightingale had had to contend with in the Crimea: and they were not confined to disease and poor sanitation. He noted in a letter of 14 September 1855 to Ralph Waldo Emerson that 'the Nurses in general have been only too faithful to their old metropolitan habits of drinking, thieving and the like – and numerous discharges have been necessary'.[140] It was not least for reasons such as this that on her return to England she was urged to set up the Nightingale Training School for Nurses, using the £45,000 fund. She found the request a bore, and lower on her list of priorities than writing a long report for the government about what was wrong with medical care in the Army, and how it might best be put right.

The woman who returned to England in the summer of 1856 was unrecognisable, in stature and personality, from the one who had left in October 1854. She was invited to Balmoral to share her experiences with the Queen and Prince Albert. She used her contacts with them to demand a Royal Commission into the Army Medical Service and, after much foot-stamping and the threat to publish her own report on the question (which would have embarrassed the administration hideously), one was set up. She wrote, and privately distributed, her own 830-page report, which showed how avoidable so many of the deaths in the Crimea would have been if only the standards of hospitals had been higher. As a result of the commission – and as a result of Nightingale's insistence that there should be one – the AMS was reformed, which provided her with her first great triumph.

The school was eventually set up, not least after the appointment of the devoted Clough as secretary of the fund. Nightingale was soon relied upon by the government to supply nurses of the highest calibre to fill significant posts in the superintendence of public health. Sir John Pakington, the Secretary for War, asked her to find 'an official person to occupy the post now vacant of Superintendent General – and also Matron for Netley Hospital.'[141] She replied that 'I beg to say how glad I shall be to do everything in my power for procuring and training an efficient nursing staff for Her Majesty's Hospitals according to the Secretary of State's desire.' She also found herself consulted on the building of hospitals, and the creation of more voluntary hospitals to care for people who would have languished at home or, worse, in workhouse hospitals where the standards of care were often abysmal.

In the late summer of 1857, after months of relentless overwork writing her report, she went down with what she thought was typhus, but what subsequent medical authorities believe was *Brucella melitensis*, contracted in the Crimea. Her life was at risk but she recovered. All Britain waited on news of her, from the Queen downwards, and with widespread prayers for her. To add to her reputation as Britain's most famous woman after the Queen, she assumed the mantle of Britain's most famous invalid. There is no doubt that she endured agonising and debilitating bouts of illness, but she also became mildly hysterical about it, and seemed sometimes to milk it for all it was worth.

Illness made her a recluse, old before her years. However, from her house off Park Lane (provided by her father) she led a movement to reform not just healthcare, but also the very standards of living among the most vulnerable in Britain. She became obsessional about health statistics, but her methods of interpreting them were soon widely taken up as more accurate and serviceable: one of the by-products of massive change had been the propensity for bureaucrats and private individuals to assemble statistics, and for those who sought evidence to underpin calls for further change to take them seriously, whether in matters of health, sanitary reform or education. Nightingale was consulted by the great and good whenever they sought to establish or modernise a hospital about how to do it, and how to raise standards of nursing there. However, in 1860, aged just forty, she suffered another complete collapse. Again she recovered, but was left feeling sick and depressed, and began another long period as an invalid. Her illness, for which the doctors recommended complete rest, gave her an excuse to leave society and to concentrate on improving healthcare.

She became a ferocious letter-writer: the British Library groans with her correspondence. Refusing to visit anyone because of illness, she used that excuse – and that of her fame – to summon them to her bed or couch-side in Park Lane. This was all part of her dictatorialism: she was enormously effective on any subject of which she had specific knowledge (whether nursing, sanitation or the Army) provided she could be in charge of coordinating the response to any problem on that subject. The Nightingale School of Nursing opened in 1860, and was her next great achievement: but in its early stages she was too ill to have much to do with it, and the men she had appointed as chairman and secretary respectively – Herbert and Clough – were both dead by the end of 1861. Luckily, other prominent members of her extended family took up the reins: her cousin Henry Bonham-Carter succeeded Clough, and her brother-in-law – Pop eventually married in her late thirties – Sir Harry Verney, a Liberal MP, became chairman.

One of her intellectual heroes was Mill, an accolade he bore with gentility and respect, even though he at least could see that theirs was not a meeting of minds. Mill had an extensive correspondence with her, in which she described herself as 'one of your most faithful adherents' and told him 'your "logic" – especially as regards "law", "free will" and "necessity" has been the forming influence of it [an article on religion she had written and sent him] and of "me".'[142] Nightingale wrote a monograph on a form of religious belief that entailed doing God's work without the trappings of conventional worship and faith. Writing about this to Mill in 1860 – they had not met, because of her reclusiveness, but she had been put in touch with him by Edwin Chadwick – Nightingale said that 'Many years ago, I had a large and very curious acquaintance among the artisans of the north of England and of London. I learnt then that they were without any religion whatever, though diligently seeking after one, principally in Comte and his school. Any return to what is called Christianity appeared impossible.'[143] Mill agreed to be consulted on *Suggestions for Thought to*

Searchers after Religious Truth 'since I probably stand as much in need of conversion as those to whom it is addressed.'[144]

Once he had read a substantial extract from what he called her 'treatise', Mill told Nightingale, as tactfully as he could, of his own shortcomings in the matter of religious faith: 'I tried what I could do with that hypothesis many years ago; that a Perfect Being could do everything except make another perfect being – that the next thing to it was to make a perfectible one – and that perfection could only be achieved by a struggle against evil.'[145] He had to admit: 'I confess that no religious theory seems to me consistent with the facts of the universe, except (in some form or other) the old one of the two principles. There are many signs, in the structure of the Universe, of an intelligent Power, wishing well to men and other sentient creatures. I could however shew, not so many perhaps, but quite as decided indications of an intelligent Power or Powers with the contrary perpetuity. But (not to insist on this) the will of the benevolent Power must find, within its own incompleteness, or in some external circumstances, very serious obstacles to the entire fulfilment of the benevolent purpose.'[146] Crucial to his secularism, Mill added that 'another point in which I cannot agree with you, is the opinion that Law, in the sense in which we predicate it of the arrangements of Nature, can only emanate from a Will . . . it is much more natural to the human mind to see a divine will in those events in which it has not yet recognised inflexible constancy of sequence, than in those in which it has.'[147]

Mill made attempts to radicalise Nightingale, telling her in 1867: 'Political power is the only security against every form of oppression'.[148] He also told her, with a view to her becoming involved in the feminist movement, that 'there are a great number of people, particularly women, who from want of the habit of reflecting on politics, are quite incapable of realizing the enormous power of politics, that is to say, of legislation, to confer happiness and also to influence the opinion and the moral nature of the governed.'[149] He continued: 'I am convinced that this power is by far the greatest that it is possible to wield for human happiness, I can neither approve of women who decline the responsibility of wielding it, nor of men who would shut out women from the right to wield it.'

Mill hardly knew how radical she already was. She noted in 1868:

'Labour should be made to pay better than thieving. At present, it pays worse. What is the cause of pauperism in England? Unlimited liberty and the Poor Law.'[150] She wrote a paper on pauperism and sent it to Froude, 'although unable to claim the honour of your acquaintance . . . to ask you whether you can do anything with it.'[151] Froude, whose own solution to pauperism included wanting Canada made part of England for resettlement purposes, found it 'most useful and interesting'.

Nightingale then found a new challenge: sanitary reform in that most insanitary of British possessions, India. Soldiers of the Queen died in peace just as much as in war, usually because of the military authorities' inability, or lack of will, to deal with cholera. She became an expert on India, summoning other authorities to Park Lane to brief her, immersing herself in statistics, and arguing, above all, for a supply of clean water. She befriended viceroys and governors general, all of whom deferred to her expertise on the subject, even though she had never set foot in the country. She began to bombard great men such as Gladstone with entreaties about how better sanitary principles might be applied to the soldiery there and, eventually, the natives ('In Lower Bengal also the people are crying out for an Act to enable the villagers to do their own sanitary work').[152]

In 1864 she wrote to Gladstone, sending him a pamphlet on the sufferings of the cholera-ridden soldiery in India, warning him that what she had written was merely the start: 'I have been prevented [from full disclosure] because these things are contained in private official documents.'[153] Writing to any public figure was a chance for Flo to project herself. Gladstone had made a speech about the travails of the industrial classes, and she wrote to him: 'I have been myself for the last ten years of my life under the sentence of hard labour, quite as much as (or more than) any working man – and with the addition of constant pain and illness, which make the intervals between work and work only one of "unnatural endurance". Few men can sympathise with what you said as I do.'

Nightingale was demanding and exceptionally tiresome, but her demands and tiresomeness were rarely made from self-interest. Her divine mission to heal the sick, or to prevent people from becoming sick, was her life's purpose. Her autocratic style and the imposition of her will on others were exercised in that cause, and in the interests of rectifying a scandalous state of affairs that did not need to exist. During the 1860s more and more nurses were trained in her name, in her school, and in her methods.

Perhaps most significantly, she led a movement to improve workhouse infirmaries, in some of which there were conditions hardly better than those she had found in Scutari. This led to the passing of the Metropolitan Poor Law Act in 1867, legislation on which she was consulted, and the first step towards the creation of district hospitals once a new structure of local government was established in 1888. She also championed and assisted in the training of district nursing to look after the indigent invalid at home. In the twenty years after her return from the Crimea she led a revolution in the healthcare of the lower classes that signalled, for perhaps the first time, that their lives were no less dispensable than those of their superiors.

X

After more than twenty years of serious feminist projects in education, civil rights and the professions, a philosophical underpinning was at last provided for the movement. Mill published *The Subjection of Women* in 1869. He had written it nearly a decade earlier but decided to publish 'at the time when it should seem likely to be most useful'.[154] He now thought the time was right, following the Reform Act and the growth in parliamentary support for universal suffrage, to share his thoughts with the world. His unswerving belief in female equality was informed partly by his rationalist beliefs and partly by the experience of his long association with, and short marriage to, Harriet Taylor. Mrs Taylor, whom he married in 1851 after her husband's death and who herself died in 1858, was an educated woman of strong opinions. Mill claimed that 'all that is most striking and profound' about his tract was down to his wife. His belief in equality preceded his association with Mrs Taylor, and had he said been the result of the application of his logical mind to the question. He also believed that her initial interest in him, two decades before they married, was because of his feminism. What had been so important for Mill in her was that:

> until I knew her, the opinion was in my mind little more than an abstract principle. I saw no more reason why women should be held in legal subjection to other people, than why men should . . .

but that perception of the vast practical bearings of women's disabilities which found expression in the book on the 'Subjection of Women' was acquired mainly through her teaching. But for her rare knowledge of human nature and comprehension of moral and social influences, though I should doubtless have held my present opinions, I should have had a very insufficient perception of the mode in which the consequences of the inferior position of women intertwine themselves with all the evils of existing society and with all the difficulties of human improvement.[155]

Mill viewed the denial of rights to women as an outrage, and his tract compares it frequently with slavery. However, he also had a further, less obvious inspiration: the second part of Nightingale's religious treatise, which he had read in manuscript in 1860. It included a description of the lives of middle-class women in mid-Victorian England that had begun its life as a thinly disguised autobiographical novel. In the work she spoke of how 'the accumulation of nervous energy . . . makes them feel . . . when they go to bed, as if they were going mad.'[156] The family had become an institution for the oppression of women, in her view. This deeply affected Mill, for as he read Nightingale he was working on *The Subjection of Women*, and he was confronted by evidence of precisely the problem he had identified. He paid tribute to Nightingale for the inspiration she had given him about the tyranny of the conventional family over daughters, and mentioned how 'a celebrated woman, in a work which I hope will some day be published, remarks truly that everything a woman does is done at odd times.'[157]

Yet his commitment to what in the twentieth century became known as feminism was prompted not just by humanitarianism, but by utilitarianism. The greatest happiness of the greatest number would, he asserted, be achieved by the liberation of women from their form of slavery; not just because they would enjoy and benefit from their liberation, but because society generally would be improved by it. 'The legal subordination of one sex to another', he wrote, 'is now wrong in itself, and now one of the chief hindrances to human improvement.'[158] He took the specific example of the bar on women sitting in the House of Commons. 'Any limitation in the field of selection deprives society of some chances of being served by the competent, without ever saving it from the incompetent.'[159] He also wrote that allowing women to participate fully in society would double 'the mass of mental faculties available for the higher service of humanity'. Mill had contempt for his fellow man for his active participation in the exploitation of women, and therefore his condoning the retardation of progress, and expressed it in terms that also echoed his cynicism about religion: 'We daily see how their gratitude to Heaven appears to be stimulated by the contemplation of their fellow-creatures to whom God has not been so merciful as he has to themselves.'[160]

Mill, writing four years after the abolition of slavery in America, claimed the condition of women in Britain was 'the primitive state of slavery lasting on'; and while he admitted it had been mitigated and softened, the 'taint of its brutal origin' lived on.[161] He understood that resistance to the idea of women's rights would come from those who described subjection as 'natural', just as until recently slave-owners in the Southern states had regarded what they did as 'natural'.[162] He argued that the position of women was actually worse than that of a slave. 'The wife is the actual bondservant of her husband: no less so, as far as legal obligation goes, than slaves commonly so called. She vows a lifelong obedience to him at the altar, and is held to it all through her life by law. Casuists may say that the obligation of obedience stops short of participation in crime, but it certainly extends to everything else. She can do no act whatever but by his permission, at least tacit. She can acquire no property but for him; the instant it becomes hers, even by inheritance, it becomes *ipso facto* his. In this respect the wife's position under the common law of England is worse than that of slaves in the laws of many countries.'[163]

Even Uncle Tom, Mill argues, had his own life in his cabin: whereas a woman was her husband's chattel. A female slave in Christian societies had the right to refuse her master what Mill euphemistically calls 'the last familiarity': a wife had no such right. Her husband 'can claim from her and enforce the lowest degradation of a human being, that of being made the instrument of an animal function contrary to her inclinations.'[164] And any children who arrived as a result of this bestiality – or even after an act of love – were their father's property, and he alone had rights over them. In the event of the father's death the mother was not even automatically the children's legal guardian, unless such an appointment had been specified in the father's will. This cruelty was similar to that of the near-impossibility of divorce, which Mill also likened to slavery. 'In some slave codes the slave could, under certain circumstances of ill usage, legally compel the master to sell him. But no amount of ill-usage, without adultery superadded, will in England free a wife from her tormentor.'[165]

In a society where men made the rules, those rules discriminated against women: but they did so, Mill argued, without ever understanding or getting an estimate of the true nature of women, because their rules distorted and suppressed that true nature. This could not prevail much longer. As well as wanting the vote, 'the claim of women to be educated as solidly, and in the same branches of knowledge, as men, is urged with growing intensity, and with a great prospect of success; while the demand for their admission into professions and occupations hitherto closed against them, becomes every year more urgent.'[166] Mischievously, he added: 'Women who read, much more women who write, are, in the existing constitution of things, a contradiction and a disturbing element: and it was wrong to bring women up with any acquirements but those of an odalisque, or a domestic servant.'[167] The genie was out of the bottle. Mill urged women to follow the example of their sisters in America, and in parts of continental Europe, and organise themselves to ensure their displeasure was relayed more keenly to the male-dominated authorities.

A new middle class of self-made men was becoming more economically and politically important, and their social mobility was a further impetus to women to improve their standing. Religious disabilities had largely disappeared in the preceding quarter-century. Only an accident of birth now disadvantaged half the human race. This was 'a single relic of an old world of thought and practice exploded in everything else, but retained in the one thing of most universal interest.'[168] It was a force preventing the world from being properly modern, and increasingly at odds with the rise in social mobility. 'The law of servitude in marriage', he wrote, 'is a monstrous contradiction to all the principles of the modern world, and to all the experience through which those principles have been slowly and painfully worked out. It is the sole case, now that negro slavery has been abolished, in which a human being in the pleni-tude of every faculty is delivered up to the tender mercies of another human being, in the hope forsooth that this other will use the power solely for the good of the person subjected to it . . . there remain no legal slaves, except the mistress of every house.'[169] As in the rest of Mill's philosophy, he believed competition between men and women would ensure the best rose to the top. He did not seek what would now be called 'positive discrimination' for women: just for them to have the same rights as men.

Mill knew why so many professions barred women. 'I believe that their disabilities elsewhere are only clung to in order to maintain their subordination in domestic life; because the generality of the male sex cannot yet tolerate the idea of living with an equal. Were it not for that, I think that almost every one, in the existing state of opinion in politics and political economy, would admit the injustice of excluding half the human race from the greater number of lucrative occupations, and from almost all high social functions; ordaining from their birth either that they are not, and cannot by any possibility become, fit for employments which are legally open to the stupidest and basest of the other sex.'[170] Those who connived in this justified themselves as serving the interests of society, 'by which they meant the interests of men'. He added: 'It cannot be inferred to be impossible that a woman should be a Homer, or an Aristotle, or a Michael Angelo, or a Beethoven, because no woman has yet actually produced works comparable to theirs in any of those lines of excellence . . . But it is quite certain that a woman can be a Queen Elizabeth, or a Deborah, or a Joan of Arc.'[171] Men simply could not know what women were like: 'They have always hitherto been kept, as far as regards spontaneous development, in so unnatural a state, that their nature cannot but have been greatly distorted and disguised: and no-one can safely pronounce that if women's nature were left to choose its direction as freely as men's, and if no artificial bent were attempted to be given to it except that required by the conditions of human society, and given to both sexes alike, there would be any material difference, or perhaps any difference at all, in the character and capacities which would unfold themselves.'[172] Those who believed women were intellectually inferior because they had produced no great works of philosophical or scientific thought were wrong, because they had been denied the education to allow them to advance in such fields.

Women's dislike of violence might help avoid war and conflict. Men would cease to be corrupted by the unfair advantage they were otherwise given in life. Women would learn self-respect and the means of self-help. They would also learn how to get on without using their sexuality to exert power over men, but by relying on their intellect and force of reason. 'The love of power and the love of liberty are in eternal antagonism,' he wrote.[173] 'Where there is least liberty, the passion for power is most ardent and unscrupulous.' Otherwise, women were prey to 'mischievous luxury and social immorality' to get their way. 'Any society which is not improving, is deteriorating', he observed.[174] 'The moral regeneration of mankind will only really commence, when the most fundamental of the social relations is placed under the rule of equal justice, and when human beings learn to cultivate their strongest sympathy with an equal in rights and in cultivation.'[175] He proposed, in terms more radical than almost all males could countenance, the most profound means of improvement available. He would not live to see the victory of his ideas, but victorious they would be. On receiving his book Gladstone wrote to him, in June 1869, to say that 'whether I am able or not to adopt your broad proposition I shall derive great profit from the perusal, and everywhere find scattered what will claim my sympathy.'[176] His ministry would take tentative steps towards liberating women, but the process would run into the next century.

Meanwhile, some women suffered brutality from their husbands, which the State by its inaction condoned. In May 1874 Colonel Egerton Leigh, a Conservative MP, begged the government to deal with 'the very insufficient punishment awarded to men for violent attacks on women'.[177] He knew much was said about women's rights, but thought the first duty of Parliament was to redress women's wrongs. The press reported 'outrageous and cowardly attacks upon women by men.' He added: 'Sometimes a woman who has only been married a fortnight appeared before a magistrate with two black eyes . . . sometimes men put their wives on the fire; sometimes they jumped upon them.' Many such women would lie – 'there was no lie a woman was not ready to go through to save these rascals of men from punishment. In one case, where a woman's nose was much injured, she declared that she had bit it herself.' He added that a boy who saw his father beat his mother would do the same to his own wife – 'what the children in some families saw was enough to infernalise a whole generation'.

He had a ready solution. The garotting epidemic of the 1860s had been stopped by the determined and merciless use of the cat-o'-nine-tails. Flogging, in ever larger quantities if the offence were repeated, would presumably bring cruel husbands under control too. 'It might not succeed,' he added. 'But if it did, it would be a great thing to have put an end to a practice which was a disgrace to this country in the eyes of all continental nations, who believed that if the English people could not sell their wives, they could beat them to death almost while they were alive.'[178] As with too much else concerning the rights of women, the State chose not to listen.

PART IV

THE BIRTH OF THE MODERN

CHAPTER 15

THE PURSUIT OF PERFECTION: VICTORIAN INTELLECTUALS AND THE NEW BRITAIN

I

The intellectual climate in which attempts at reform were made in the 1850s and 1860s had been shaped, as far as the Liberal ruling class was concerned, by Thomas Babington Macaulay. In the 1840s and 1850s Macaulay had published his *History of England*, and in it had set a tone of self-confidence for the times that was rooted in what the twentieth century came to call 'the Whig interpretation of history': a story of inexorable progress from darkness to light in a secure, Protestant and increasingly liberal society. No one could have disagreed with this analysis more than Carlyle, and the passing of the Reform Act was his opportunity to say so. He was one of several great thinkers of the period – Mill, Ruskin, Huxley, Arnold and Stephen were the others – who used the earthquake of reform to recast their minds about the new future of Britain. This debate made the period immediately following 1867 one of the most intellectually turbulent of the century: but, unlike other great periods of ferment, this one was sparked by the new secularism and the increasingly democratic society it had helped create, not about the old, theocentric Britain of the era before Chartism.

Carlyle exhibited his rage in *Macmillan's Magazine*, republishing his essay as a pamphlet. Despite the growth of the press, magazines and reviews remained a powerful – perhaps the most powerful – medium for the dissemination of ideas from intellectuals or politicians to a wider, intelligent public. *Shooting Niagara: and After?* was Carlyle's last significant political pronouncement: he was seventy-one, in indifferent health, and, though he would live until 1881, only his *Reminiscences* remained to be written of his serious literary work. He had been widowed the previous year, was engaged in revising *Frederick the Great*, which hung around his neck like the proverbial millstone, and was suffering from dyspepsia. He told his brother John, a doctor, that 'my digestion etc etc has gone quite to chaos'.[1] His pessimism and unhappiness translated into a work that was by his own admission 'very fierce, exaggerative, ragged, unkempt and defective.'

All this combined with Carlyle's loathing of democracy to produce a brutal attack on the political class. He had noted in his journal throughout 1867 his feelings about reform, and one metaphor stands out: 'England getting into the *Niagara rapids* far sooner than I expected.'[2] He was feeling apocalyptic: 'Newspaper editors, in private, I am told, and discerning people of every rank, as is partly apparent to myself, talk of approaching "revolution", "Commonwealth", "Common illth", or whatever it may be, with a singular composure.' Carlyle seemed to represent no view, by this stage, except his own: but when published in pamphlet form once the bill had gone through Parliament it sold 4,000 copies in three weeks. However, Carlyle's influence was waning, something Fitzjames Stephen had noted three years earlier: 'To take Mr Carlyle as a great leader of English thought, to describe him as the representative of a thing called English Idealism, is to misunderstand him altogether. His thought . . . has had singularly little influence upon the world . . . he has exercised hardly any perceptible influence upon English philosophy . . . politics, morals, theology, metaphysics, political economy . . .' He had not, Stephen added, 'materially influenced the main current of thought in this country on important subjects.'[3] Stephen was a committed utilitarian, something Carlyle abhorred and had called 'pig philosophy' in the *Latter Day Pamphlets*.[4] Stephen's rationalism made much of Carlyle's doctrine, with its search for heroes and lamentations of the end of feudalism, quite unpalatable: however, the two men admired each other, so much so that Carlyle made Stephen his executor, and left him his writing-desk.

In *Shooting Niagara*, Carlyle started with the assertion that there had not for a thousand years or 'since the Heptarchy ended' been an epoch in English history when 'the question of utter death or of nobler new life for the poor Country was so uncertain'.[5] He compared 'the Niagara leap of completed democracy' with the resolve of Bismarck in forging

Prussia into a dominant force, implicitly prophesying Britain's subjection to Germany.[6] He feared democracy had made men into a 'swarm', and suggested that after 'manhood suffrage' there would be Horsehood and Doghood suffrage too.[7] He felt no good would come to the slaves emancipated after the Civil War in America; nor, by the same token, would much good come to those formerly unfranchised who would be given the vote in Britain. He snarled: 'Bring in more voting; that will clear away the universal rottenness, and quagmire of mendacities, in which poor England is drowning; let England only vote sufficiently, and all is clean and sweet again. A very singular swarmery this of the Reform movement, I must say.'[8]

He damned the Reform Bill as 'the calling in of new supplies of blockheadism, gullibility, bribeability, amenability to beer and balderdash . . . the intellect of a man who believes in the possibility of "improvement" by such a method is to me a finished-off and shut-up intellect, with which I would not argue: mere waste of wind between us to exchange words on that class of topics.' He had no doubt why this thoughtless pursuit of the Niagara rapids was happening: 'Traitorous Politicians, grasping at votes, even votes from the rabble, have brought it on'.[9] His principal target was 'he they call Dizzy', 'this clever conscious juggler', 'a superlative Hebrew Conjuror, spell-binding all the great Lords, great Parties, great Interests of England, to his hand in this manner, and leading them by the nose, like helpless mesmerised somnambulant cattle, to such issue – did the world ever see a *flebile ludibrium* of such magnitude before?'[10] The Latin means 'a farce to weep at': 'The end of our poor Old England (such an England as we had at last made of it) to be not a tearful Tragedy, but an ignominious Farce as well!'

He derided Edmond Beales, the leader of the Reform League, as having been assisted by 'ragamuffins'; accused Walpole of having been intimidated into appeasement; and suggested the government's behaviour had been of a piece with its treatment of Edward Eyre, the late Governor of Jamaica, who had been recalled and threatened with impeachment for his severity in putting down a rebellion. Carlyle rebuked 'the Majesty's Ministers, who, instead of rewarding their Governor Eyre, throw him out of window to a small loud group, small as now appears, and nothing but a group or knot of rabid Nigger-Philanthropists, barking furiously in the gutter, and threatening one's Reform Bill with loss of certain friends and votes'.[11] He taunted the ministry for its capitulation to Beales: 'Safer to humour the mob than repress them, with the rope about *your* neck.'[12]

The House of Commons was, plainly, an institution of which Carlyle had expected no better. The support of the Lords for the bill he found shocking. 'What are you good for, then?' he yelled at the aristocracy. 'Show us, show us, or else disappear!'[13] Yet he still expressed the hope that the aristocracy, which he saw as retaining many of its old virtues, would come to the rescue; and if it did not, there might be an aristocracy of talent and courage, rather as in Cromwell's time, that would save the country. It was the old call, again, for the Hero to come forward, just as he had uttered nearly thirty years earlier, translated to 'these ballot-boxing, Nigger-emancipating, empty, dirt-eclipsed days'.[14] Yet there was no more prospect of it than in 1840; indeed, much less so. Meanwhile, spurred on by reform, the trades union movement 'with assassin pistol in its hand, will at once urge itself on Reformed Parliament'.[15]

He believed it would take a 'kingly soul' to do what was necessary to improve society, such as by setting up schools: 'Right schools were never more desirable than now. Nor ever more unattainable, by public clamouring and jargoning, than now.'[16] He felt modern education was mostly about teaching people to speak, rather than to think. As always with Carlyle, speech was silvern; silence was golden. The Reform Act would only make things worse. By the end of the essay he is just ranting, roaring with despair at a situation he has decided is irredeemable. He observes that, for good measure, getting everybody to engage in military drill would be no bad idea. 'That of commanding and obeying, were there nothing more, is it not the basis of all human culture?'[17]

His conclusion was typically Carlylean: no proposal, but a dramatic prophesy. There would have to be a 'sheer fight' between Anarchy and Anti-Anarchy: 'nothing short of a duel to the death could ever void that great quarrel'.[18] He believed, however, that 'to Anarchy, however million-headed, there is no victory possible'; because the decent men – those such as had served in the New Model Army under Cromwell – would eventually put themselves to the fight. 'What are Beales and his 50,000 roughs against such; what are the noisiest anarchic Parliaments, in majority of a million to one, against such?' His residual hope was that 'the Aristocracy, as a class, has as yet no thought of giving up the game, or ceasing to be what in the language of flattery is called "Governing Class".'[19] He was right in that the aristocracy would fight for a while yet, until defeated by the 1911 Parliament Act; but even he, in his shouting and bawling, seems to have seen the game was up.

II

Carlyle had been reduced to ranting; a more rational assault on the democratic mood after the second Reform Act was found in James Fitzjames Stephen's *Liberty, Equality, Fraternity*, published in 1873. Stephen, a barrister, enjoyed an enviable reputation as a journalist and had made himself an equally formidable one as an intellectual. He had just returned from two years in India, attempting to codify the laws of that country. Coming from an England in which, as he saw it, the threats and occasional manifestations of a mob had intimidated the ruling class into change, he had been impressed to see how, less than fifteen years after the Mutiny, India was ruled firmly but well without resort to democracy, by a small elite cadre of Oxbridge-educated civil servants.

Stephen was born in 1829 into the intellectual aristocracy, to James Stephen, an eminent jurist and civil servant who in 1849 became professor of modern history at Cambridge. Young Fitz was an outsider despite his Establishment grounding. In the mid-1840s his father took a house at Windsor so that he and his brother Leslie – the father of Virginia Woolf and an architect of the *Dictionary of National Biography* – could be day-boys at Eton. The other boys, swift to pounce on anything smacking of irregularity, proceeded to bully him. Unsurprisingly, this seems to have affected young Fitz's cast of mind in more ways than one. 'I was in the school, but not of it, and was a kind of Pariah,' he recorded in a fragment of his unpublished autobiography.[20]

'It had however the great advantage of keeping me in my father's society, and acquainting me continually more and more with his opinions on all sorts of subjects.' He regarded this as his real education, and talked of how it 'gave me feelings of contempt for the inanity of the Eton masters'. His father's discussions with his children were literary, religious, political and historical, and there were frequent references to the great men of the day and their part in events: great men Stephen knew personally, and tales of whom kept his son enthralled so much that 'I could have listened . . . forever'. He talked of Macaulay, 'infinitely more eloquent and learned' than Stephen himself; and of Carlyle, 'striking and picturesque'. Although young Fitz would come to find

Carlyle shallow, long on rhetoric and short on analysis, he also came to understand in his late forties and early fifties that Carlyle's interpretation of power and the uses of authoritarianism had much to commend it.

Fitz sought to be a writer of such eminence as to have an entry into the salons and literary life of London. His powers of expression and thought were sufficient to find him space in the reviews. He established himself by the 1860s as a formidable critic of politics and society, just as had the historian Carlyle, the art critic Ruskin, or the school inspector Arnold. He made a particular name from the mid-1850s on the *Saturday Review*. He savaged writers so eminent as Dickens and Mrs Gaskell for sentimentality. His writings have the common theme of pursuit of the truth, and that sentimentality is an obstacle to be cleared before the object can be attained. Stephen was a rationalist, and to him the worlds of such novelists had no rationality at all. He deplored the novel as an instrument of propaganda, and lambasted 'the political novelists with their . . . hasty generalisation and false conclusions [who] exercise a very wide and very pernicious political and social influence.'[21]

Although Stephen taunted Dickens and poked Carlyle through the bars of his cage, the great intellectual assault of his literary career would be on Mill. This could not have been predicted, as Stephen – a Benthamite – had admired Mill's logic and his writings. Also, though a late developer intellectually, Stephen had no record of academic achievement to suggest he could take Mill on. His Cambridge career ended with a mere pass degree, though he had been an Apostle. It was unclear whether he had the makings of a man who would seek to shake the accepted currents of thought of the day. Logic was the antithesis of the sentimentalism Stephen so abjured, and Mill's formulation of it deeply attracted him when younger. He saw the framework of logic could be applied to the social sciences – such as history, economics, politics and sociology – and help instill more intellectual rigour and make them, therefore, more credible. His writings contain many reflections upon this necessity, and Mill's system of logic is Stephen's model.

However, in time Stephen came to feel Mill's logic was unequal to some of the realities of life to which Stephen wished to apply it, not least because another of Mill's works – *On Liberty* – seemed to contradict it. These contradictions made Stephen take Mill on, after years of reverence and admiration: he had reviewed *On Liberty* in 1859 and expressed agreement with it. Stephen would, in the 1870s, seek to apply logic to jurisprudence, in a lengthy but futile attempt to codify the criminal law of England: he became one of the most significant and influential thinkers on the common law of the nineteenth century. His relationship with logic is more revealing, however, when applied to his social and political thought, since it exposes tensions between intellectuals about the perfectibility of the human condition and of society. However, as he would later write: 'Mill seems to me to be one of those people whose logical and thinking power is quite out of all proportion to his seeing power. For the purpose of arranging his thoughts and putting them all in proper relation to each other, he is incomparable and unapproachable, but the quality of the thought itself seems to me to be exceedingly poor and thin. His whole concept of human nature appears to me to be a sort of unattractive romance, yet it is the romance of a man who, in some aspects, is very good.'[22]

Once his work as a man of letters had progressed, Stephen had turned to Mill as a mentor. He wrote to Mill in April 1864 to say that 'I have long entertained a sort of notion of writing a book on the fundamental problems of religion and morals. I had the opportunity, though I have no settled scheme as to the form into which I should work it.' He wished to write a book of 'high importance and of permanent value' and asked for 'your candid opinion if whether from what you know of my writing you think it probable that I could produce such a book?'[23] He volunteered to go to Blackheath to discuss ideas with the sage. Mill regarded this as a question 'which it is very difficult, or rather impossible, to answer satisfactorily. There is no-one living of whom I would venture to affirm beforehand that he might be expected to work such a treatise on the fundamental problems of religion and morals that it would be good for him to give up a profession he likes and change his plans of life rather than not write it.'[24] He thought 'it could at the least contain a great deal that is valuable. But it deserves consideration whether even the best book that could be written in our day, on morals and religion generally, would do more good than may be done by the continual illustration and discussion of the leading points of these subjects, in connection with particular speculative or practical questions.' Stephen was set back by this answer; he replied to Mill that 'I think it probable that I shall decide to let matters take their course'.[25]

However, he and Mill continued to have cordial relations: he reviewed Mill's writings favourably, and even asked him to return the compliment in May 1865 by writing him a testimonial for a vacancy for a readership in constitutional law and legal history under the Committee for Legal Education.[26] As late as 1869 Stephen received with delight from his friend a new edition of works by Mill's father, and in the same year urged Mill on in an argument with W. E. H. Lecky, the historian, about utilitarianism.[27] He even wrote to Mill from India in 1871, to discuss points of interest in the codification of the laws of evidence in that country.[28] On the same trip he was dissecting *On Liberty* as a preliminary for writing *Liberty, Equality, Fraternity*. Another incident had coloured Stephen's feelings towards Mill, when the philosopher asked the lawyer for a legal opinion on the case of Governor Edward Eyre. Eyre had put down a rebellion in Jamaica with severity, imposing martial law and ordering 300 executions and many hundreds of floggings. There was outrage among liberals, led by Mill, when word of this reached London in late 1865. The opinion Mill and his fellow members of the Jamaica Committee sought was whether Eyre and General Nelson, the commander of the local garrison, might be tried for murder. Stephen felt they might, arguing that Eyre had behaved in a way that was 'violent, tyrannical and imprudent to a degree which I had hardly imagined possible.'[29]

Stephen succeeded in having Nelson tried for murder, but a jury threw the case out. He failed to persuade a bench of magistrates that Eyre should be tried. Mill, however, refused to take no for an answer, which Stephen found wilful, obstinate and narrow-minded. Stephen started to see that Eyre, however excessive his actions had been, had been under severe pressure in managing a collapse of law and order; a collapse of the sort England might have come close to in the reform disturbances had the mob not been appeased. It vexed Stephen that Mill could not see the other side to the story, and exposed a limitation in his hero.

India changed many of his views. In May 1872 he told his sister-in-law Lady Egerton:

> I returned to my Mill today, and fired more shots into him. It is curious that after being, so to speak, a devoted disciple and partisan of his, up to a certain point, I should have found it at last impossible to go on with him; but his politics and his morals are not mine at all, though I believe in and admire his logic, and his general notion of philosophy. I recollect about three or four years ago, I had a battle royal on these points with my brother Leslie, and we at last came to the conclusion that the real difference between us

was that he thought better of mankind than I do. It is a long story, to show how this difference colours not only one's politics, but one's morals, and one's religion too – but it does, and I am rather taken by the idea of making Mill's later works the peg on which to hang the statement of a variety of doctrines on this subject, which I have been forming for many years. He has certainly given me a good broad mark to fire at.[30]

Writing to her from Cowes on 12 September 1872 he announced that 'the most exclusive bit of journalism I have done is a set of articles which have not yet been, but which soon will be published about Liberty, Equality and Fraternity, falling foul to the best of my ability of John Mill – in his modern and most humane mood – or rather, I should say, in his sentimental mood, which always makes me feel that he is a sort of denier of the proper principles of rigidity and forcity in which he was brought up.'[31] In his correspondence with his sister-in-law he made it clear he would not equivocate: 'the morality of persecution depended on the truth of the doctrines', for example.[32]

You ask, who is to determine what is true? I answer, everyone must determine for himself – and the result will be war and strife, which ought to be modified in its earnestness by the recollections of our fallibility. I do not believe in the possibility of devising a scheme whereby all human affairs can always be conducted harmoniously and well, though the people who conduct them are ignorant, weak and often wicked. You must choose between the evils of conflict and the evils of acquiescence in a bad state of things, and I think that of the two, the first is the smaller evil, if brave, honest and forbearing. Complete tolerance means perfect indifference, complete harmony is probably unattainable even by individuals, though a considerate approach may at times be made to it. All human life lies between the two, and may tend towards either. I had rather try after harmony by agreement as to what is true, than after indifference.

He was sensitive about an apparent remark of Emily Egerton's about his treatment of Pilate, saying that that passage 'was to show how Pilate must have looked upon Christ, not to show how I looked upon him. It is Mill's great illustration of his doctrine about toleration.' He admitted he had enjoyed writing the articles: 'they are a very comprehensive declaration of opinion on many matters, and they have been a good deal noticed in England by various people.' In February 1873 he affirmed to her that the articles 'express, only in an understated form, the strongest convictions I have; convictions not the less strong because they are very vague, and consciously so. The older I grow, the more I realise the extent of our ignorance, the more valuable does the amount of light, if it can be called so, which remains to us, appear to me.'[33] It was quickly decided to republish the articles as a book, and Lady Egerton read the proofs for him. He claimed that where they differed it was 'rather a difference of colour than of substance. I think I am quite as humane and public-spirited as my neighbours.'[34]

The book was not just the product of a close, critical and cynical rereading of *On Liberty*. It was also the result of several years' brooding by Stephen on Britain after the Reform Act: on what the changes had meant not merely for the general public, but for those whom they elected, and therefore for the future direction of the country. His early adult life had been spent in a period of political uncertainty, from 1852 until the events of 1867, with the failed attempts at reform making the unfranchised more militant and aggressive. To a man as wedded to the idea of order as Stephen, this had been disturbing, and had put him, as a Liberal, firmly in the Adullamite camp. As he considered the reform question the contradictions of Mill's position came home to him more and more acutely. This was a man who, as a Benthamite like himself, thought majority rule must be good because it meant the wishes of the greatest number were being executed: but Mill had also described the working classes as 'habitual liars' and in his *Political Economy* had observed: 'As soon as any idea of equality enters the mind of an unedu-cated English working man, his head is turned by it. When he ceases to be servile he becomes insolent.'[35]

Stephen could understand this. In twenty years defending and pros-ecuting criminals, and latterly as a judge (he had sat as a recorder since 1868, and would in 1881 be advanced to the High Court Bench) he had seen human nature at its worst, and considered himself, with much justification, a connoisseur of that section of society in a way Mill could not pretend to be. (Once, however, on the Bench at Liverpool, he brought about astonishment when asking what the Grand National was.) He was not a forgiving man, and believed society drew insufficient distinc-tion between right and wrong, not so much in its support of the former as in its lack of condemnation of the latter. That is why Stephen, in eventually joining the Bench, found his true vocation.

On 8 August 1868 he wrote to his wife that 'I sat yesterday as "My Lord" for the first time in my life, and judged the people for five or six hours. It appears to me the very easiest work I ever did. It just takes all one's attention, and saves one all the trouble of thinking, while one is at it, and it is rather interesting. I had a rare set of scoundrels before me, and had to give some heavy sentences. One old fellow (who had thrown vitriol into a man's face, on account of a quarrel) made such a howling appeal for mercy in such a way that the jury, to my great disgust, let him off altogether, which shows what idiotic things juries will do at times.'[36] He would describe a High Court judge as 'the organ of the moral indignation of mankind', and maintained some men were simply evil and had to be treated as such.[37] His own views on religion were unconventional, but he saw the use of religion as a weapon of social control – though one progressively less effective as secularism took hold. In the absence of theological restraint, he believed a deal had to be made clear to the potential criminal: 'Let him at least be plainly told what are the acts that will stamp him with infamy, hold him up to public execration, and bring him to the gallows, the gaol or the lash.'[38]

In his laudatory review of *On Liberty* Stephen had raised a caveat about Mill's belief in the decay of individualism and the commensurate attraction of collectivism. This had, over the following thirteen or fourteen years, grown greatly in his mind, and formed one of the great themes of *Liberty, Equality, Fraternity*. So too did Stephen's belief in legitimate authority as a bulwark against anarchy, which had seemed imminent at the time of the Hyde Park riots. This owed more to Thomas Hobbes, of whom Stephen was a profound admirer, than to anything in Mill's intellectual compass. A man who revered Hobbes could not revere Mill. As John Morley later wrote, the book was 'the first effective attack on Mill's pontifical authority'.[39] Stephen had a wit and bluntness in deploying it that minced his opponents: such as when he ruminated, in response to Mill's saying that he would rather go to hell than worship a God who punished people by sending them there, on what Mill would say after being there for half an hour.

The book is not merely a shooting-down of Mill. It is an exploration of the three concepts in its title, and of the idea, predominant among liberals, that the perfectibility of the human condition was in sight. It repudiates the pursuit of perfection. In this, too, the former disciple of Mill acknowledges the force of the arguments of Hobbes: his main issue with Mill is that he could ever have harboured such optimistic notions as expressed in *On Liberty* about perfectibility. Ever the rationalist, Stephen saw the concept of authority in a State as based upon where the means to use force lay; a view informed by his belief that a substantial proportion of the population, crude and uneducated, would be compelled to understand the use of force against them as they would be compelled to understand little else.

In the opening paragraphs of *Liberty, Equality, Fraternity* Stephen depicts Mill as of the English school of Comte, and therefore the local spokesman of the creed of positivism. Thus the reader is warned that the optimistic take on human nature is specious, and the pursuit of perfection is a delusion. Stephen identified the cult of 'Liberty, Equality, Fraternity' as a religion, and stated plainly: 'I do not believe it.'[40] He said he was no adherent, either, of 'Slavery, Caste or Hatred'; but felt that those who subscribed to the cult exaggerated its benefits and glossed over its failings. He also doubted whether a society that fully embraced the cult would be one 'which a reasonable man ought to regard with enthusiasm'. Mill had created a philosophy that was 'unsound'. And, although Stephen said he was proud – up to a point – to describe himself as one of Mill's disciples, 'there is a side of his teaching which is as repugnant as the rest of it is attractive to me, and this side has of late years become by far the most prominent.' Mill had promulgated a 'religious dogma' of liberty, and his writings on the subjection of women and utilitarianism had exemplified what Stephen found objectionable about equality and fraternity too.[41]

Stephen considered himself a Liberal in politics, but his view of the human condition is suffused by a deep pessimism about his fellow man typical of the most profound Tory. 'I cannot but think that many persons must share the feeling of disgust with which I for one have often read and listened to expressions of general philanthropy,' he writes.[42] 'I know hardly anything in literature so nauseous as Rousseau's expressions of love for mankind when read in the light of his confessions. "Keep your love to yourself, and do not daub me or mine with it," is the criticism which his books always suggest to me.' Frederic Harrison, the positivist who wrote a savage, and uncomprehending, review of *Liberty, Equality, Fraternity*, felt this confirmed Stephen as 'an egotist and a misanthrope'.[43]

All Stephen saw, however, was the cant of calling the rest of the human race his brothers and sisters, since he was perfectly indifferent to the vast majority and found many others specifically objectionable. Mill's rose-tinted vision of his fellow man granted him potential for improvement, provided he was given sufficient love and liberty – in Stephen's analysis. He could not credit this as having any relationship to reality. 'I further believe that between all classes of men there are and always will be real occasions of enmity and strife, and that even good men may be and often are compelled to treat each other as enemies either by the existence of conflicting interests which bring them into collision, or by their different ways of conceiving goodness.'[44] As he put it elsewhere 'the great defect of Mr Mill's later writings seems to me to be that he had formed too favourable an estimate of human nature.'[45] Some coercion was beneficial to the human spirit: learning to contend with it bred character and resourcefulness.

Stephen's relationship with religion was complicated and almost grudging; but of one thing he was certain. The possibility of eternal damnation exercised some sort of constraint upon those in the lower orders who, faced with constant temptation, chose to resist it. 'Though Christianity expresses the tender and charitable sentiments with passionate ardour, it also has a terrible side. Christian love is only for a time and on condition. It stops short at the gates of hell, and hell is an essential part of the whole Christian scheme.'[46] In this sense the much-vaunted religion relied just as much on coercion to achieve its ends as any authoritarian, temporal, government. He ridiculed Mill for taking the other view: 'A God who punished anyone at all, except for the purpose of protecting others, would, upon his principles, be a tyrant trampling on liberty.'[47] He saw Mill's doctrine as immoral, contending that he thought it would be good on the Day of Judgement to say that 'I pleased myself and hurt nobody else'.

Stephen's view of society is, for all his criticisms of Carlyle, deeply Carlylean. Good is only achieved by coercion, not by laissez-faire. He cites numerous historical precedents for this view, back to the English civil wars and the Reformation. He argues Britain only had something resembling a cohesive society because people had been coerced into it, and had come to accept the value of institutions established by coercion.

This left him at odds with a society shaped by the consequences of the 1867 Reform Act; but in which it amused him to find coercion being carried on, as he saw it, by other means.

'Parliamentary government', he wrote, surveying the *status quo post*, 'is simply a mild and disguised form of compulsion. We agree to try strength by counting heads instead of breaking heads, but the principle is exactly the same.'[48] Echoing Carlyle, consciously or unconsciously, he added that on any question it is not the wisest side that wins, but the one that has shown superior strength by drumming up the most support. 'The minority gives way not because it is convinced that it is wrong, but because it is convinced that it is a minority.' In the past, great men had emerged as leaders because they had the strategic sense to suppress anarchy and unite a polity. He cites Charlemagne as an example but also teases his critics by citing Abraham Lincoln, already a liberal demigod, as another. 'President Lincoln attained his objects by the use of a degree of force which would have crushed Charlemagne and his paladins and peers like so many eggshells.'[49] A civilised society could still use force, but had to be more careful than a rough one in how it did so.

Despite his own reservations about religion Stephen backed laws against freedom of expression, including the punishment of blasphemy, because 'it seems to me that to publish opinions upon morals, politics and religion is an act as important as any which any man can possibly do; that to attack opinions on which the framework of our society rests is a proceeding which both is and ought to be dangerous. I do not say that it ought not to be done in many cases, but it should be done sword in hand, and a man who does it has no more right to be surprised at being fiercely resisted than a soldier who attacks a breach.'[50]

Justifying coercion, Stephen adduced one particular example where it had been used, if not successfully, then in good faith. 'Was Pilate right in crucifying Christ? I reply, Pilate's paramount duty was to preserve the peace in Palestine, to form the best judgment he could as to the means required for that purpose, and to act upon it when it was formed. Therefore, if and in so far as he believed, in good faith and on reasonable grounds, that what he did was necessary for the preservation of the peace of Palestine, he was right. It was his duty to run the risk of being mistaken, notwithstanding Mr Mill's principle as to liberty, and particularly as to liberty in the expression of opinion.'[51] Not being omniscient, Pilate was not to know that something deemed so beneficial as

Christianity would be the result of his judgement: such are the consequences of coercion.

Stephen's society is one in which a class system, its divisions between the educated and the uneducated and the responsible and the irresponsible, is inevitably in place and must be reckoned with. Again, one is reminded of Carlyle's assertion that the one human right worth having was the right of the foolish to be governed by the wise. The responsible must govern the irresponsible, if necessary with a firmness that borders upon harshness, if the society they have made, with its institutions, is to be preserved. For this reason he deplores, in a passage vigorous even by his standards, Mill's attempt to depict certain acts as 'self-regarding' and therefore without the State's competence to restrict or punish. He cites fornication as one such, but muses whether licence should be extended to those who wish to be pimps or run a gambling-house.

Stephen calls this the permission for 'an experiment in living', and is outraged at the very notion. 'How can the State or the public be competent to determine any question whatever if it is not competent to decide that gross vice is a bad thing? I do not think the State ought to stand bandying compliments with pimps.'[52] In Stephen's view, society must have standards, and it is the duty of the educated classes to impose them and to ensure that those most subject to temptation abide by them; something insufficiently appreciated when so many men of the baser sort now had the vote, and when the sense of power that went with it had gone to their heads. Were he to come across such an experimental pimp, Stephen would have said: 'You dirty rascal, it may be a question whether you should be suffered to remain in your native filth untouched, or whether my opinion about you should be printed by the lash on your bare back. That question will be determined without the smallest reference to your wishes and feelings; but as to the nature of my opinion about you, there can be no question at all.'[53] On the purely political question, Stephen noted that 'it is quite true that in these days we have not much titular inequality. It is quite true that we have succeeded in cutting political power into very little bits, which with our usual hymns of triumph we are continually mincing, till it seems not unlikely that many people may come to think that a single man's share of it is not worth having at all.'[54] If parcelling out the franchise had created equality, Stephen listed all those more profound inequalities that continued – wealth, talent, education, sentiment, religious belief and so on.

'Nearly every newspaper, and a very large proportion of modern books of political speculation, regard the progress of democracy, the approaching advent of universal suffrage, with something approaching to religious enthusiasm. To this I for one object.'[55] He dismissed the effects of reform. 'Political power has changed its shape but not its nature. The result of cutting it up into little bits is simply that the man who can sweep the greatest number of them into one heap will govern the rest. The strongest man in some form or other will always rule . . . in a pure democracy the ruling men will be the wirepullers and their friends.' This actually had nothing to do with equality, or with liberty. 'Universal suffrage . . . tends to invert what I should have regarded as the true and natural relation between wisdom and folly. I think that wise and good men ought to rule those who are foolish and bad.'[56]

Through Sir John Coleridge, Gladstone's Attorney General, he helped the Liberal government frame the Evidence Bill in 1873. He stood as a Liberal in a by-election in Dundee in August 1873, lamenting that it cost him £1,000 in expenses 'and I know not what in regard of pay as a judge'.[57] He found himself an agent and a committee, but after some public meetings realised that 'there is no sympathy whatever between them and me. They want a thoroughgoing radical, and I am not one and cannot pretend to be one – it is found out in every possible way, on all occasions.'[58] Within a few days he found that all the 'educated people' were for him, and confided in his wife on 2 August that 'I am by no means sure I shall not win as it is.'[59] But he was out of his depth, 'badgered' by the electorate on subjects about which he knew little or nothing. 'I am sick of the election,' he told his wife on 5 August, 'and all its works'. When he lost he told her: 'I am not really disappointed, though my fall has been a great one.'

His defeat was just as well. He was no admirer of Gladstone, telling Lady Egerton in 1875 how an article he had read of his 'shows for the 20th time what an essentially radically small and weak mind he has. It is, in a roundabout way, to me rather a comfort to see what a fool in matters of speculation a man may be, who in practical politics has played such an exceedingly prominent vigorous part. It seems to show that the fact that I have no turn for parliamentary life does not prove me to be a fool . . . this I am ashamed to say is a comfort to me in my gloomier moments.'[60]

III

In a land whose attitudes were deplored by such as Carlyle and Ruskin, and which no longer automatically deferred to God and the established order, other means had to be found to stabilise society and secure its eventual improvement. Matthew Arnold's *Culture and Anarchy*, written in the autumn of 1867 and published over several numbers of the *Cornhill Magazine*, attempted to suggest a means for this in a fashion that avoided the rhetoric of despair. Carlyle and Stephen had seen the barbarians as beyond redemption; Arnold saw them as barbarians who could be taught. It was, however, vitally important to work out what they should be taught; Arnold did not want utilitarian, middle-class values forced down the throats of those waiting to be educated. He showed he was his father's son, pleading for the extension of education and civilisation as a bulwark against anarchy and the destruction of the social order. He had already stated his desire to encourage the British 'to healing measures and an attractive form of civilisation'. From its title page onwards, *Culture and Anarchy* was devoted to the pursuit of perfection, however unattainable the ideal might seem.

The work in some ways was the fruit of his friendship with Clough, in which from the 1840s onwards the ideas about civilisation and the civilising process that Arnold presents were thrashed out between them. But much, too, comes from Arnold's experience as a schools inspector. Few understood the true nature of what passed for civilisation in England better than he did, or the nature of the relationship between the ordinary individual and society. *Culture and Anarchy* – like much of Arnold's writings – is a remarkable work of extended journalism, and owes much of its effect to the direct and persuasive language Arnold uses in it. However, as he told his mother in a letter of 27 July 1866, he lived in the same square as Mayne, and 'on the Monday night we were on our balcony and saw the crowd break into our square, throw a few stones at Sir R Mayne's windows opposite us, and then be dispersed by police . . . here a man feels that the power which represses him is the Tories, the upper class, the aristocracy, and so on; and with this feeling he can of course never without loss of self-respect accept a formal beating, and so the thing goes on smouldering.'[61] This first-hand witnessing of the violence had a profound effect on Arnold's writing.

Arnold and those who thought like him saw education as having a wider reach: the defeat of philistinism would be accomplished not just by schools and colleges, but by museums, concert halls, art galleries, evening classes and libraries. This was the seed most successfully sown by *Culture and Anarchy* and by Arnold's *Essays in Criticism*, both of which while advocating education for the masses for its own sake also saw that it was, in an increasingly secular society, an insurance policy against unrest and revolution. However, Arnold believed that before civilising the newly enfranchised, the newly enriched bourgeoisie required further training. Arnold's experience in France had shown him that the middle classes were capable of better. Lionel Trilling, in his critical survey of Arnold, deployed T. S. Eliot's metaphor of Arnold trying 'to make the past of Europe march with the future'.[62] In *The Function of Criticism at the Present Time* – the opening essay of *Essays in Criticism* – Arnold had observed that, once man had made himself physically comfortable, 'this progress is likely, though not certain, to lead in the end to an apparition of intellectual life'.[63] Having acquired comfort, man 'may begin to remember that he has a mind, and that the mind may be made the source of great pleasure.' Philistinism – the prejudices of the middle classes, notably utilitarianism – however, intervened: comfort seemed only to have brought 'a self-satisfaction which is retarding and vulgar-ising', whereas the true function of criticism – the disinterested scrutiny of life in pursuit of the truth – was to prevent such vices in a man, and instead 'to lead him towards perfection, by making his mind dwell upon what is excellent in itself, and the absolute beauty and fitness of things.'[64] Unfortunately, the middle classes, who should have been setting a posi-tive example, were wallowing in their smugness, defining 'unrivalled happiness' as their property's being safe, having freedom of speech, and being able to 'walk from one end of England to the other in perfect security.'

Arnold knew that those – usually politicians – who said such things were deluded, or propagandising, or both. He contrasted the self-satisfaction of the 'old Anglo-Saxon race', allegedly the finest in the world, with a story he read in a newspaper about a child murder in Nottingham. He quoted: 'A girl named Wragg left the workhouse there on Saturday morning with her young illegitimate child. The child was soon afterwards found dead on Mapperley Hills, having been strangled. Wragg is in custody.'[65] '*Wragg!*' Arnold exclaimed. The depravity and wretchedness of the story was bad enough; but he also asked: 'If we are to talk of ideal perfection, of "the best in the whole world", has any one reflected what a touch of grossness in our race, what an original shortcoming in the more delicate spiritual perceptions, is shown by the natural growth amongst us of such hideous names – Higginbottom, Stiggins, Bugg!' They were names that reflected the 'dismal' environment in which the girl had lived – 'the gloom, the smoke, the cold, the strangled illegitimate child.'[66]

The newspaper could not even afford Wragg the courtesy of a Christian name. 'There is profit for the spirit in such contrasts as this,' he wrote. 'Criticism serves the cause of perfection by establishing them.' However, the cultivation of the disinterested mind required for such a sensitive process, and for the spread of enlightenment and true progress, was rarely achieved. 'The mass of mankind will never have any ardent zeal for seeing things as they are,' he lamented. 'Very inadequate ideas will always satisfy them.'[67] In the pursuit of perfection, there could be no satisfaction until the final goal was reached. What the politicians, and their clientele in the self-satisfied middle classes, would not see was that 'the British Constitution itself' was 'a colossal machine for the manufacture of Philistines.'[68] It could not hope to produce people of learning and judgement with the critical faculty Arnold deemed essential to the pursuit of perfection, to enable 'a disinterested endeavour to learn and propagate the best that is known and thought in the world.'[69] This sentiment was not universally approved of, even among intellectuals. Stephen disagreed violently: and Samuel Butler may have had Arnold in mind when he observed that 'critics generally come to be critics by reason not of their fitness for this but of their unfitness for anything else.'[70]

A similar argument is in Arnold's earlier essay on Heine. 'Modern times find themselves with an immense system of institutions, established facts, accredited dogmas, customs, rules, which have come to them from times not modern. In this system their life has to be carried forward; yet they have a sense that this system is not of their own creation, that it by no means corresponds exactly with the wants of their actual life, that, for them, it is customary, not rational . . . to remove this want of correspondence is beginning to be the settled endeavour of most persons of good sense.'[71] Change was a challenge: it had to be managed, and people brought along with it, not made to feel they existed in spite of it. The creation of more 'persons of good sense' was essential.

Culture and Anarchy also echoes – and is in some ways an interesting development from – Arnold's essay introducing *The Popular Education of France*, published in 1861. It was his minority report on the Newcastle Commission, published with the Commission's approval. The introduction was republished in 1879 as the essay *Democracy*. As in *A French Eton*, he argued that 'undoubtedly there arrive periods, when, the circumstances and conditions of government having changed, the guiding maxims of government ought to change also.'[72] Britain may not have had a revolution, but industrialisation had changed it profoundly. The effects of those changes had to be dealt with.

He noted in his 1861 essay that Liberals (with a fringe of Radicals) and Conservatives had replaced Whigs and Tories. The old parties had been 'aristocratical', their power rooted in the land or in Court favour. They shared a common culture, 'the feelings and habits of the upper class of the nation'.[73] The aristocracy might not have been intelligent but it had nobility of purpose; and, like the Roman aristocracy, 'they each fostered in the mass of the peoples they governed – peoples of sturdy moral constitution and apt to learn such lessons – a greatness of spirit . . . they made . . . great peoples, peoples *in the grand style*.'[74] However, the notion that the aristocracy were the only natural leaders now had to be discounted. 'The time has arrived,' he wrote, 'when it is becoming impossible for the aristocracy of England to conduct and wield the English nation any longer.' He had learned from France that aristocracies 'inevitably fail' to appreciate, or even to take into their minds, 'the instinct pushing the masses towards expansion and fuller life'; and, as a result, 'they lose their hold over them'.[75] Any Englishman would have seen this happening, in various manifestations, since the Chartist riots of 1839 and 1842 and the unease of 1848. Arnold said this lack of comprehension was the ancient fault of aristocracies, and why they always came unstuck.

Like his father, Arnold supported democracy: not because it was inevitable, but because it was just. However, he believed that 'if the worst mischiefs of democracy ever happen in England, it will be, not because a new condition of things has come upon us unforeseen, but because, though we all foresaw it, our efforts to deal with it were in the wrong direction.'[76] The main obstacle to cultural advancement was not the State, but the proud new middle classes who just wanted to be left alone, and felt they could provide perfectly well for themselves. Yet they lacked the trained minds and experience of culture to create schools that would emulate the best. This, again, echoed his father's argument, that the middle classes tended to leave school to be articled or apprenticed in some calling, lacking time to be taught the rudiments of sweetness and light.

He accepted that the middle classes had been zealots for liberty and paragons of industry: but 'all the liberty and industry in the world will not ensure these two things: a high reason and a fine culture.'[77] Without those, Britain could never be 'more than an independent, an energetic, a successful nation' – it could never be 'a *great* nation'. He felt that the part played by high reason was growing, not diminishing: and a nation that failed to develop reason in its people would fall behind. He felt the French had it – a contention perhaps belied by their tripping into the disastrous war with Prussia in 1870 – and it would never do for England to fall behind the French. A truly glorious people had both character and culture: character without culture was 'something raw, blind and dangerous'.[78] He took the example of ancient Athens, 'the spectacle of the culture of a *people* . . . the middle and lower classes in the highest development of their humanity that these classes have yet reached.' This was an example not just of the heights a society could attain, but evidence that a classical education was not 'an aristocratic impertinence' nor the remains of the ancient world 'so much lumber', which were the views of people he dismissed as 'friends of progress'.

The middle classes had to decide whether to civilise themselves or to surrender the chance to make Britain great. He feared if they rejected the help the State could give in improving schools and their curriculum, 'if they go on exaggerating their spirit of individualism, if they persist in their jealousy of all governmental action, if they cannot learn that the antipathies and shibboleths of a past age are now an anachronism for them', they might get control of their country, but would do little good with it.[79] They would, in his uncomplimentary phrase, 'Americanise' it: separate it from sweetness and light, from true culture, and make it simply a machine. And without culture – and here lay the seed of his great work of later in the decade – 'society is in danger of falling into anarchy'.

His peroration made *Culture and Anarchy* inevitable, for the book is an extended echo of this final paragraph.

Undoubtedly we are drawing on towards great changes; and for every nation the thing most needful is to discern clearly its own condition, in order to know in what particular way it may best meet them. Openness and flexibility of mind are at such a time the first of virtues. *Be ye perfect*, said the Founder of Christianity. *I count not myself to have apprehended*, said its greatest Apostle. Perfection will never be reached; but to recognise a period of transformation when it comes, and to adapt themselves honestly and rationally to its laws, is perhaps the nearest approach to perfection of which men and nations are capable. No habits or attachments should prevent their trying to do this; nor, indeed, in the long run, can they. Human thought, which made all institutions, inevitably saps them, resting only in that which is absolute and eternal.[80]

Where this essay ended – with *estote ergo vos perfecti!* – so, seven years later, *Culture and Anarchy* began.

By 'culture' Arnold means a system of civilisation, a condition in which the people are invested with the full sense of their humanity. Culture embraces truth, morality, reason, faith. To achieve this state is to achieve perfection; it is, though Arnold never says so, impossible. Some of serious purpose might attain something close to it; but for a whole society to do so was utterly unpractical. The book must be read as an exhortation towards an aspiration, written at a time of frightening upheaval. *Culture and Anarchy* marked his move towards social conservatism and away from liberalism. It said that a regard for institutions and the benign State should play a larger part in British life: an important chapter is devoted to attacking the notion of 'doing as one likes', and the cult of the individual. Arnold seems to feel that a dose of authoritarianism was required to put Britain on the right path, a trait he shared with Stephen, who nonetheless continued to criticise him.

He particularly took against the Nonconformists who comprised so much of the new middle class. In his scheme, that class would rescue England from the rule of the ignorant, promulgate sweetness and light, and lead the pursuit of perfection: so it needed to do better. Its members were obsessed with what he called 'machinery', material rather than metaphysical objects. If all reform meant was that more had been liberated to pursue an existence rooted in mediocrity and ignorance, then Arnold, too, would have to consider the vocabulary of despair. He wished 'to recommend culture as the great help out of our present difficulties; culture being a pursuit of our total perfection by means of getting to know, on all the matters which most concern us, the best which has been thought and said in the world; and through this knowledge, turning a stream of fresh and free thought upon our stock notions and habits, which we now follow staunchly but mechanically, vainly imagining that there is a virtue in following them staunchly which makes up for the mischief of following them mechanically.'[81]

Arnold subtitled *Culture and Anarchy* 'an Essay in Social and Political Criticism'. The discerning public was used to him as a poet, and as a literary critic, educationist and theological scholar: all these come together in *Culture and Anarchy*. The book's first chapter, *Sweetness and Light*, was Arnold's outgoing lecture when he vacated the chair of Poetry at Oxford. He saw a society suddenly transformed by the extension of political power, but in need of transformation in its educational, moral and spiritual contexts. He savages various public figures (it is a deeply satirical and humorous book) who have provided leadership in the wrong direction: notably Bright, with his rabble-rousing, and Lowe, whom Arnold the school inspector had not forgiven for the Revised Code. Bright he assailed for using his 'noble oratory' to laud only material improvements:

> And though our pauperism and ignorance, and all the questions which are called social, seem now to be forcing themselves upon his mind, yet he still goes on with his glorifying of the great towns, and the Liberals, and their operations of the last thirty years. It never seems to occur to him that the present troubled state of our social life has anything to do with the thirty years' blind worship of their nostrums by himself and our Liberal friends, or that it throws any doubts on the sufficiency of this worship. But he thinks what is still amiss is due to the stupidity of the Tories, and will be cured by the thoughtfulness and intelligence of the great towns, and by the Liberals going on gloriously with their political operations as before; or that it will cure itself. So we see what Mr Bright means by thoughtfulness and intelligence, and in what manner, according to him, we are to grow in them.[82]

Arnold may be criticised for intellectual snobbery: he cringes at the notion that Manchester, or Rochdale, or Bradford could represent a route to the pursuit of perfection. But his criticism of Bright and those like him is just, and important: by all means make material advances that lift people out of poverty, and that indeed improve whole districts and cities; but do not suppose these are the only advances worth taking seriously. For society to be happy and harmonious there needs to be (and for this Arnold borrows a phrase from Swift) 'sweetness and light': beauty and intelligence. Arnold maintained he had 'traced much of our present discomfort to the want of them'.[83] He specifically blamed the 'provincialism' of the Nonconformists, which it was his aim to 'extirpate'. His language sometimes has the imagery of violence, reflecting his sense that England was at a turning point, and whoever fought hardest would win. The middle classes had to end their betrayal of true culture, forsaking the utilitarianism that poisoned their outlook.

Indeed, Arnold imagines he is still fighting the Civil War, aligning Nonconformity with Puritanism and identifying a shared narrowness.[84] He searches for a new centre of authority – open-minded, benign, intellectually curious and valuing the growth of intelligence. Such leadership would help new voters understand their responsibilities, and exercise their vote with disinterestedness rather than self-interest. 'What is alone and always sacred and binding for man is the making progress towards his total perfection,' he writes.[85] Expanding upon this, he says that 'culture, disinterestedly trying, in its aim at perfection, to see things as they really are, sees how worthy and divine a thing is the religious side in man': which further set him against the narrowness he perceived in Nonconformity, so prevalent in the great provincial towns admired by Bright.[86]

Arnold had been brought up a Liberal and still professed to be one – 'yet I am a Liberal tempered by experience, reflection and renouncement, and I am above all a believer in culture'.[87] This was what sundered him from the Liberal masses. It was not just that some – including Lowe – had disparaged culture as the learning of dead languages, not understanding, or choosing not to understand, the wisdom, history and philosophy to which those languages were the key. Arnold felt they regarded culture as something 'valued either out of sheer vanity and ignorance, or else as an engine of social and class distinction, separating its holder, like a badge or title, from other people who have not got it.'[88] He continued: 'No serious man would call this *culture*, or attach any value to it.' For him, culture did not originate in intellectual curiosity, but 'in the love of perfection; it is the study of perfection. It moves by the force, not merely or primarily of the scientific passion for pure knowledge, but also of the moral and social passion for doing good.'[89] He took a phrase of Montesquieu for his definition – 'to render an intelligent being more intelligent' – and one of Bishop Wilson, an eighteenth-century prelate, whose maxims he had discovered in his father's library, and which Arnold had rather taken to: 'To make reason and the will of God prevail!'

Gladstone, Prime Minister when *Culture and Anarchy* appeared in book form in 1869, grasped Arnold's view of culture. The breakfasts the two men shared demonstrated the politician's regard for the critic, as did Gladstone's assiduous reading of Arnold's work. Gladstone saw that criticism could be applied to society as well as to creative work: and that enabled one 'to see things as they really are'. Arnold also helped influence him to cross one of the Liberal rubicons: his regard for the power of the State as a civilising force, which he had taken from his experience in France, set Arnold apart from most Liberals. They regarded the State as an instrument of the destruction of liberty, and cherished an English ideal of the ordinary man being left alone. The way Gladstone would bring the State into the regulation of education owed much to Arnold's advocacy, and nothing to the Liberal tradition.

All the main writers on the reform crisis – Carlyle, Ruskin and Stephen as well as Arnold – had diverse views of what could, or should, be done. They agreed on the need for reason, a commodity all saw to be in short supply. Arnold believed that spiritual means, rather than temporal force or coercion, could inspire it. Culture was not just the means to see and learn the will of God, but to make it prevail: and at which point 'the moral, social and beneficent character of culture becomes manifest'.[90] For all his doubts, and his gloom about the Sea of Faith, Arnold could not but see religion (by which he meant the Established Church, in the English context) as central to his thesis. He wrote of 'religion, the greatest and most important of the efforts by which the human race has manifested its impulse to perfect itself – religion, that voice of the deepest human experience – does not only enjoin and sanction the aim which is the great aim of culture, the aim of setting ourselves to ascertain what perfection is and to make it prevail.'[91] This is an assault on the secular society: there can be no true culture, in Arnold's view, without faith. Just as the Kingdom of God is within you, culture places 'human perfection in an internal condition, in the growth and predominance of our humanity proper, as distinguished from our animality.' His mission was to rescue England from the savages. He might have struggled against his father's example; he might have entertained doubts and seen his closest friend subsumed under them; but in the end, religion remained the key to civilisation, to reason, to seeing things as they really were.

However, the pursuit of perfection would struggle against the overwhelming force of materialism. 'The idea of perfection as an inward condition of mind and spirit is at variance with the mechanical and material civilisation in esteem with us and nowhere, as I have said, so much in esteem as with us.'[92] The great material triumphs of the last thirty years were not 'ends in themselves', however much that might seem to be the case. Arnold had a word for those who succumbed to this danger: 'The people who believe most that our greatness and welfare are proved by our being very rich, and who most give their lives and thoughts to becoming rich, are just the very people whom we call Philistines.'

These middle-class bêtes noires might have known better had they not been so badly led. 'Culture says: "Consider these people, then, their way of life, their habits, their manners, the very tones of their voice; look at them attentively; observe the literature they read, the things which give them pleasure, the words which come forth out of their mouths, the thoughts which make the furniture of their minds; would any amount of wealth be worth having with the condition that one was to become just like these people by having it?"'[93] Arnold hoped the dissatisfaction with materialism that this understanding might create would save 'the future, as one may hope, from being vulgarised, even if it cannot save the present.'

His enemies – such as Bright, whom he kicks constantly – are enemies not because of their malevolence (even Bright's worst enemy would struggle to accuse him of that) but because of their ignorance. The very notion of the pursuit of perfection, with a recognition of sweetness and light at its core, is a Greek one, and the Greeks attached 'immense spiritual significance' to it.[94] 'And Mr Bright's misconception of culture, as a smattering of Greek and Latin, comes itself, after all, from this wonderful significance of the Greeks having affected the very machinery of our education, and in itself a kind of homage to it.' If one sought proof that the opposite was currently pertaining, one had only to look at 'London, with its unutterable external hideousness, and with its internal canker of *publice egestas, privatim opulentia* . . . unequalled in the world!'[95]

That city harboured a newspaper with the largest circulation in the world – the *Daily Telegraph*, which Arnold reviled. It proved its inhabitants were as far from human perfection as could be measured. It was they for whom Lowe had sought to die in the last ditch, as he manifested 'the hardness and vulgarity of middle-class Liberalism.'[96] Now they had been swept from power by the democratic tide Lowe had resisted, an opportunity arose to make them realise materialism was not everything. At the other extreme of Liberalism, and representing the new democratic masters, was Bright: and Arnold ridiculed him for leading 'his disciples to believe – what the Englishman is always too ready to believe – that the having a vote, like the having a large family, or a large business, or large muscles, has in itself some edifying and perfecting effect upon human nature.'[97] The idea of sweetness and light, Arnold argued, was one the new democracy needed far more 'than the idea of the blessedness of the franchise, or the wonderfulness of its own industrial performances'.[98] 'The pursuit of perfection,' he decreed, 'is the pursuit of sweetness and light.'[99]

Arnold was mocked by those, such as the editor of the *Daily Telegraph*, who accused him of not understanding the realities of life. He countered by saying that if people had been better educated – if someone had taken the trouble to develop their intelligence – then the 'rougher and coarser movements' might be a little less rough, and a little less coarse.[100] Instead, the working class – which Arnold termed the Populace – 'pressed constantly by the hard daily compulsion of material wants, as he realised, had become 'the very centre and stronghold of our national idea, that it is man's ideal right and felicity to do as he likes'.[101]

The decline of deference meant that 'the anarchical tendency of our worship of freedom in and for itself, of our superstitious faith, as I say, in machinery, is becoming very manifest.' Leading on from this was the notion of an Englishman's right 'to march where he likes, meet where he likes, enter where he likes, hoot as he likes, threaten as he likes, smash as he likes. All this, I say, tends to anarchy; and though a number of excellent people, and particularly my friends of the Liberal or progressive party, as they call themselves, are kind enough to reassure us by saying that these are trifles, that a few transient outbreaks of rowdyism signify nothing, that our system of liberty is one which itself cures all the evils which it works, that the educated and intelligent classes stand in overwhelming strength and majestic repose, ready, like our military force in riots, to act at a moment's notice.'[102] Arnold had no truck with such complacency, and in this he was at one with Carlyle, Ruskin and Stephen. He knew that the cast of mind that had broken down the railings in Hyde Park had been appeased, not improved, and remained a threat to civilisation.

The problem, in a society riven by class differences, was that there could be no agreement on where the centre of authority lay. For Carlyle it was in the aristocracy, but that was a fantasy. For Lowe it was in the middle classes, but they had been defeated. For Bright and the Reform League it was the working class, but they were unfit. Arnold asked what constituted the State in post-1867 Britain: what was 'the power most representing the right reason of the nation, and most worthy, therefore, of ruling – of exercising, when circumstances require it, authority over us all?'[103] It was 'culture, with its disinterested pursuit of perfection, culture, simply trying to see things as they are, in order to seize on the best and to make it prevail' that would help one make the best judgement on where the new authority lay.

While Carlyle's aristocrats had sweetness, they were short on light. The Liberal middle class, mocked by Arnold when he refers to their desire to have a man allowed to marry his deceased wife's sister, were too obsessed with the machinery of life, and light was scarce among them too. It had an 'incomparable self-satisfaction' about being sufficiently educated.[104] Its mind would always be narrow; and it was too pliant in the face of the threat of anarchy, too concerned to allow the potential anarchists to do as they liked, to be a safe berth for authority. The philistines had chosen 'some dismal and illiberal existence in preference to light', and were beyond reasoning with.[105]

The working class were 'one in spirit with the industrial middle class', as was only to be expected as they watched the next rung on the ladder.[106] 'It is notorious', Arnold observed 'that our middle-class Liberals have long looked forward to this consummation, when the working class shall join forces with them, aid them heartily to carry forward their great works, go in a body to their tea-meetings, and, in short, enable them to bring about their millennium.' He was alert to the attempt to forge working-class power independently of the Liberals, through the trades union movement: the first Trades Union Congress was held in 1868. This movement was built on self-interest, not disinterestedness, and nothing about it suggested the pursuit of perfection.

Beyond this was 'that vast portion . . . of the working class which, raw and half-developed, has long lain half-hidden amidst its poverty and squalor, and is now issuing from its hiding-place to assert an Englishman's heaven-born privilege of doing as he liked, and is beginning to perplex us by marching where it likes, meeting where it likes, bawling what it likes, breaking what it likes.'[107] This was Arnold's populace, and it plainly horrified him, not least because he struggled to find anyone with the will to keep it in check or the determination to try to improve it. Arnold makes no direct reference to Mill; though the chapter *Doing as one Likes* is a critique of *On Liberty*, and opens up a new debate in the family of liberalism.

He felt that among the barbarians (the aristocracy), the philistines and even the populace there were 'natures' who understood 'the love and pursuit of perfection' and the importance of 'sweetness and light [as] the true character of the pursued perfection'.[108] He added: 'This bent always tends to take them out of their class, and to make their distinguishing characteristic not their Barbarianism or their Philistinism, but their *humanity*.' These were 'aliens', not led by class spirit, but by 'a general humane spirit, by the love of human perfection'.[109] It was in these rare people that the hope for Britain's future lay, if they could emerge from the crush of others doing as they liked and asserting their freedom to be boors. Arnold returns to the classical teaching Bright mocked and Lowe despised as lacking in utility: such as Socrates's 'the best man is he who most tries to perfect himself, and the happiest man is he who most feels that he *is* perfecting himself.'[110] Hellenism is the term Arnold uses for the pursuit of sweetness and light, and he contrasts it with the Hebraism that imbues so much of the theology of the Nonconformists. Hebraism 'manifested itself in Puritanism, and has had a great part in shaping our history for the last two hundred years.'[111]

The enemy of reason now, however – and here Arnold anticipates Stephen's arguments in *Liberty, Equality, Fraternity* – is 'the notion of its being the prime right and happiness, for each of us, to affirm himself, and his ordinary self; to be doing, and to be doing freely and as he likes.'[112] This, he says, lies 'at the bottom of our present unsettled state'. As a result there is a 'disbelief in right reason as a lawful authority'. The long-term effect of Hebraism on British society was that the people 'have been led to regard in themselves, as the one thing needful, *strictness of conscience*, the staunch adherence to some fixed law of doing we have got already, instead of spontaneity of consciousness, which tends continually to enlarge our whole law of doing.' This was why Nonconformity bred narrow-minded provincialism: it took no account of what Arnold saw as the Hellenic half of a person's nature, or the Platonic aspects of intellectual development. As this nature atrophied or was confined, so too did, and was, society. Arnold lauded Greek art and beauty, dismissed by Bright and wilfully closed off from himself by Lowe, as the prime example of the 'impulse to see things as they really are'.[113] Greek art rested on a fidelity to nature, allowing a 'delicate discrimination of what this best nature is'.[114]

Arnold's final substantive chapter is entitled *Our Liberal Practitioners*, and is an assault on the party that had ruled for most of the previous thirty years – and that, as he wrote, would shortly return to power – for its complacency. The new religion of free trade, he observed, had left one in nineteen a pauper: he was unclear why increases in trade and population should be regarded as goods in themselves. He referred to the East End of London, with which he was familiar in his work as a schools inspector. When times were good, all was reasonably well: but when trade slackened off, when the docks were quiet, when demand for the goods from the sweatshops slumped, there was squalor, poverty and misery. That was how the laws of supply and demand worked in an industrial society, which was, as Carlyle had said since the early 1840s, nothing like had used to be the case. The Liberals seemed to have no answer.

However, Arnold knew the pursuit of perfection had to be a mass movement. 'The fewer there are who follow the way to perfection, the harder that way is to find.'[115] He added: 'So all our fellow men, in the East of London and elsewhere, we must take along with us in the progress towards perfection, if we ourselves really, as we profess, want to be perfect; and we must not let the worship of any fetish, any machinery, such as manufactures or population – which are not, like perfection, absolute goods in themselves, though we think them so – create for us such a multitude of miserable, sunken, and ignorant human beings, that to carry them all along with us is impossible, and perforce they must for the most part be left by us in their degradation and wretchedness.'

The continuation of the economic ideology of 'our Liberal practitioners' would create more paupers, and the burden, in all ways, would become unbearable.

Arnold knew the political nature of his message. He sent Disraeli the text in time for the campaign of 1868; could Disraeli begin to grasp the stately prose, or the layered irony? In truth, there was little he could do to quell what Arnold himself saw as the bigotries and prejudices not only of the two political parties, but of the mass of Nonconformity, that in their different ways were impeding disinterestedness. Arnold knew his high-minded view of the one thing needful was never likely to chime with that of the political class, let alone of the masses over whom they ruled. If Disraeli did not comprehend him, Gladstone – a far more subtle intellect, and cut from the same cloth as Arnold – would. But what could Gladstone do, even had he wanted to? Few men alive had done more to support and design the present economic system than he had: and he would not be persuaded so easily that it was failing.

Arnold's conclusion was laced with pragmatism. The Hyde Park riots and working-class unrest had disturbed him. He said of society: 'Whoever administers it, and however we may seek to remove them from their tenure of administration, yet, while they administer, we steadily and with undivided heart support them in repressing anarchy and disorder; because without order there can be no society, and without society there can be no human perfection.'[116] He quoted his father, citing one of his sayings from memory: 'As for rioting, the old Roman way of dealing with that is always the right one; flog the rank and file, and fling the ringleaders from the Tarpeian Rock!' Stanley thought it might have been 'crucify the slaves' rather than flogging, but Arnold was sure he had it right.[117] He endorsed his father (though the family were sufficiently upset by this exhibition of the Doctor's illiberal side that he was prevailed upon to excise the reference from the second edition), mocking the Liberals for finding 'a little rioting . . . useful sometimes to their own interests.' However important it was, when necessary, to show the iron hand, he still refused to believe the notion that 'the world wants fire and strength more than sweetness and light'.[118]

Time was, he feared, running out: soon Bradlaugh and his friend Odger 'will be there with their mission to oust both Barbarians and Philistines, and to get the heritage for the Populace.'[119] And, as its contribution to the fight for culture, sweetness and light, the Liberal party sought to 'abolish the Irish Church by the power of the Nonconformists' antipathy to establishments, or they enable a man to marry his deceased wife's sister.'[120]

'It is so much a counsel of perfection,' wrote Trilling, 'that it becomes a counsel of despair.'[121] Trilling's definition of perfection – entirely reasonably – is 'the conscious effort of each man to come to the realisation of his complete humanity'. He perhaps takes Arnold too much at face value. The social and moral unities Arnold sought had always been unattainable; just as the unity his father, thirty years earlier, had sought between Churches and State was. They required a shift of national consciousness of which a society like Britain's, and especially England's, with its proud record of individualism, could not contemplate. But Arnold would set the course for the establishment of a State-backed education system. He did not deal with the detail of what would be taught in it, or how.

Kingsley told Arnold that *Culture and Anarchy* was 'an exceeding wise and true book: and likely as such, to be little listened to this autumn: but to sink into the ground and die, and bear fruit next spring: when the spring comes.'[122] John Morley said that 'when all is said for and against the worth of his contribution to theology, the debt of Liberalism to Arnold as a general critic of our needs will long deserve grave commemoration.'[123] The non-intellectual view was summed up by Disraeli, who after *Culture and Anarchy* told Arnold he was the only living Englishman to have become a classic in his lifetime. By the time of the second edition, seeking yet more divine guidance, Arnold went to the Vulgate, and from there borrowed for a superscription a phrase from St Matthew's Gospel, in a language some of his detractors would not have understood: '*Estote ergo vos perfecti!*' – Be ye, therefore, perfect.

IV

Huxley ('whom I thoroughly like and admire', Arnold told Kingsley, 'but find very disposed to be tyrannical and unjust'), too, took up these arguments.[124] In his inaugural address to the South London Working Men's College in January 1868 he described educating the working class as 'great work . . . the greatest work of all those which lie ready to a man's hand just at present'.[125] The work of education was being led from the industrial centres because 'nobody outside the agricultural interest now dares to say that education is a bad thing.' It was deemed 'bad' there because education would disrupt the supply of cheap, tied labour that landowners relied upon. The general view was that 'if the country is not shortly to go to the dogs, everybody must be educated.'

Although Huxley was no utilitarian, he saw that Britain would lag behind if it wasted its human resources. He despised those with ulterior motives for extending what he saw as this human right to a large swathe of humanity: 'The politicians tell us, "you must educate the masses because they are going to be master". The clergy join in the cry for education, for they affirm that the people are drifting away from church and chapel into the broadest infidelity. The manufacturers and the capitalists swell the chorus lustily. They declare that ignorance makes bad workmen; that England will soon be unable to turn out cotton goods, or steam engines, cheaper than other people.' Huxley's view was quite different: 'A few voices are lifted up in favour of the doctrine that the masses should be educated because they are men and women with unlimited capacities of being, doing, and suffering, and that it is as true now, as ever it was, that the people perish for lack of knowledge.'

He had contempt for those who stood in the way of alleviating this suffering. 'Compare the average artisan and the average country squire, and it may be doubted if you will find a pin to choose between the two in point of ignorance, class feeling or prejudice.'[126] If there were to be change, then 'why should we be worse off under one regime than under the other?' He savaged the old universities – none of which he had attended – as having a 'posture of half-clerical seminaries, half race-courses, where men are trained to win a senior wranglership, or a double-first, as horses are trained to win a cup, with as little reference to the needs of after-life in the case of the man as in that of the racer.' He argued for compulsory education, if it could be agreed what that education should be; he thought that simply teaching reading, writing and arithmetic was 'very like making a child practise the use of a knife, fork, and spoon, without giving it a particle of meat.'[127] He defined education as 'the instruction of the intellect in the laws of nature, under which name I include not merely things and their forces, but men and their ways; and the fashioning of the affections and of the will into an earnest and loving desire to move in harmony with those laws.'

What passed for the primary education some children received was nothing like this. Despite instruction in reading and writing, few children took pleasure in reading, or were able to write the commonest letter properly. They learned 'a quantity of dogmatic theology, of which the child, nine times out of ten, understands next to nothing'; plus 'a few of the broadest and simplest principles of morality', 'a good deal of Jewish history and Syrian geography' and 'a certain amount of regularity, attentive obedience, respect for others.'[128] He wanted working people taught the connection between moral probity and a stable society; and wanted to end the system whereby 'the child learns absolutely nothing of the history or the political organisation of his own country.'[129]

The danger of educating the lower classes was that they would realise who was really responsible for the conditions in which they had to live; and, when they had the vote, they could act upon that knowledge. Huxley noted that educating the poor would diminish neither 'misery nor crime among the masses of mankind.' He asserted that 'if I am a knave or a fool, teaching me to read and write won't make me less of either one or the other – unless somebody shows me how to put my reading and writing to wise and good purposes.' Wisdom, not rote-learning, was needed: 'Teach a man to read and write, and you have put into his hands the great keys of the wisdom box.' But then he had to open the box; and be guided about how to use what he found in it.

Huxley believed secondary schools were even more shamefully negligent than the primaries. Devoting their time to rote-learning of Euclid, algebra and the catechism, it meant 'modern geography, modern history, modern literature; the English language as a language; the whole circle of the sciences, physical, moral and social, are even more completely ignored in the higher than in the lower schools.'[130] He said that, until Clarendon, 'a boy might have passed through any one of the great public schools with the greatest distinction and credit, and might never so much as heard of one of the subjects I have just mentioned.' He would never have learned the earth went round the sun, that England had a revolution in 1688 and France one in 1789, or that Chaucer, Shakespeare, Milton, Voltaire, Goethe or Schiller ever existed. He feared that 'the time will come when Englishmen will quote it as the stock example of the stolid stupidity of their ancestors in the nineteenth century.'

What most worried Huxley was that the schools for the middle classes – many newly enfranchised – emulated the old public schools in teaching little but Classics, but teaching them badly. He claimed a great sympathy for the Classics – 'a great section of the palaeontology of man' – but wished they could be taught 'not merely as languages, but as illustrations of philological science', and allowing 'a vivid picture of life on the shores of the Mediterranean, two thousand years ago' to be 'imprinted on the minds of scholars.'[131] He wanted boys who learned ancient literature to be impressed with 'the grand simplicity of their statement of the everlasting problems of human life, instead of with their verbal and grammatical peculiarities.'[132] In this, he was completely at odds with Arnold, and seemed to be embracing the very philistinism from which the author of *Culture and Anarchy* wished Britain to be saved. There would have to be a battle over the way forward.

V

John Ruskin, feted as Britain's leading art critic since he began precociously to publish *Modern Painters* in the early 1840s, when barely down from Oxford, turned his considerable intelligence to political and social questions. Like many in his generation – he was the same age as Clough, and three years older than Arnold – he had come under the influence of Carlyle but, unlike Clough and Arnold, had stayed there. He was an odd fish. It is said he failed to consummate his marriage out of shock at the sight of the pubic hair of his wife, Euphemia 'Effie' Gray, who wrote to her father that Ruskin was 'disgusted with my person the first evening': such details had not been accentuated on the classical statues from which he had deduced his anatomical knowledge of women.[133] Their marriage was annulled.

He then, in his late thirties, conceived an affection for ten-year-old Rose La Touche, to whom he later proposed marriage, when he was forty-seven and she eighteen. In her fragment of autobiography Rose, who became a religious maniac, wrote that 'I think it was Mr Ruskin's teaching when I was about twelve years old that made me first take to looking after the poor – at least that made me see it as a thing Right, and a part of Christ's love, and I got easily very fond of them and liked doing it. So I used to take them tracts in a basket (that papa gave me) and used to read the Bible to them, and go to see them when they were ill (and well too) and I suppose enough of childishness mixed with my visits to make them pleasant as well as "profitable". I always liked the poor.'[134] Rose died at twenty-seven, possibly of anorexia. Before then her parents had at various times forbidden Ruskin to communicate with her, not least because of Mrs La Touche's having had a conversation with Effie Gray, now Mrs John Everett Millais. Ruskin was destined to be unhappy, and to make others so.

He is an other-worldly figure in a way the other main intellectuals of the mid-Victorian era are not: perhaps because of his being rooted in the rarefied environment of art and architecture. He also exhibits a far more unquestioning Christian faith than most of his more cerebral contemporaries, most of whom struggled to profess any sort of faith at all. The editors of Ruskin's diaries begin their introduction with the observation: 'It is the solitary man who keeps a diary; and Ruskin, though he never lived and rarely travelled alone, was a man doomed to intellectual and spiritual solitude.'[135] By the time of his death in 1900, after more than a decade of madness, he was revered not just as an art critic, but by many in the nascent Labour movement as one of its leading influences. Few took his views on political economy seriously, but they had an impact because of Ruskin's reputation made elsewhere, and because of his eloquence of expression.

Ruskin was the only child of an intense and unusual family. His parents were first cousins. His father made a small fortune importing sherry, and his mother was the daughter of a publican from Croydon. His paternal grandfather, John Thomas Ruskin, had a history of mental and financial problems. He killed himself in 1817, the year before Ruskin's parents married and two years before his grandson's birth. The family young John grew up in was successful, but the success was founded on hard work, and Ruskin's father took until 1832 to pay off John Thomas's debts. Young John was educated at home and by tutors, the absence of childhood friends contributing to his solitary nature as an adult. It was from his father, a serious collector and a patron of Turner, that he acquired an interest in art, and from him too that he learned to draw and to love the novels of Sir Walter Scott.

From his mother he imbibed a religious intensity that would colour all his works, artistic or political. His mother made him read the Bible every morning, and memorise passages, from the age of three: his literary style, which verges on the magnificent (note, for example, the opening and closing lines of the first volume of *The Stones of Venice*) owes much to this. However, by his early teens his interests in the aesthetic were at the forefront of his intellectual curiosity, and his parents did all they could to stimulate them. By fourteen he had seen most of the fine landscapes and treasures of Britain: he then embarked on tours around Europe, notably France, Italy and Switzerland. He went up to Christ Church, Oxford in January 1837, after a short course of lectures at King's College, London.

Luckily for Ruskin, his father was prepared to subsidise a literary life based upon art criticism; and it was his desire to defend his and his father's friend Turner that was the genesis of *Modern Painters*, a multi-volume work that occupied Ruskin on and off from 1842 until 1860. In that period he continued his European travels and studies in the great galleries and museums of the Continent, eventually without his parents, moving from painting to architecture by the late 1840s. The first fruit of this developing interest was *The Seven Lamps of Architecture*, published in 1849, a crucial work culturally in giving further momentum to the Gothic Revival.

The Seven Lamps was, however, but an hors d'oeuvre to what in many respects is Ruskin's masterpiece, *The Stones of Venice*, published in three volumes in the early 1850s after Ruskin and Effie – they married in 1848 – had spent two winters in the city, staying first at the Danieli and then in private apartments, while Venice was under Austrian occupation. Both books extol the moral aspects of architecture: the pious Gothic is preferred to the depraved baroque. Given this approach to his subject, it was a short trek from there to social and political commentary; a progress aided by Ruskin's having met Carlyle in 1850, and having fallen under the spell of his love of feudalism.

In April 1854, out of the blue – or so it seems – Effie served papers on Ruskin for the annulment of their marriage on the grounds of its non-consummation because of his impotence. Ruskin did not deny the non-consummation – Effie had been medically examined, which removed any doubt in the matter – but did deny he was impotent. The marriage ended while he was with his parents in Chamonix in July 1854, taking the mountain air. Ruskin and Effie had spent large parts of their married life apart, with Ruskin apparently unable to sever the bond with his parents, and Effie's father becoming more and more concerned on her behalf. In July 1855 Effie married John Everett Millais, the pre-Raphaelite painter who had collaborated with Ruskin on the illustrations for *The Stones of Venice*.

Before Ruskin began social and political commentary he had, though only in his mid-thirties, exerted the most profound influence over the next generation of Victorian artists. As well as Millais, Dante Gabriel Rossetti, William Morris and Edward Burne-Jones had all been attracted by his aesthetic criticism. He assembled a collection of Turners for exhibition out of the legacy to the National Gallery, which showed him as a leader of taste. Not least through the Carlyles and their circle, Ruskin met many of the leading literary figures in London: Froude, Tennyson, the Brownings, Coventry Patmore and William Allingham. He also met F. D. Maurice, who enlisted him as part of the intellectual arsenal of his London Working Men's College, where he would give drawing lessons.

By 1860 Ruskin had undergone fundamental changes in character and outlook. His relations with his parents had been strained since the end of his marriage, he underwent a period of religious doubt that put him at a distance from his mother, and his anti-capitalism had become more pronounced, not least since he saw capitalism as a destroyer of beauty. He had also suffered from bouts of depression. This was the background to his four articles on political economy in the *Cornhill Magazine* in 1860, edited by W. M. Thackeray, and republished in 1862 as *Unto This Last*.

Ruskin had chosen the *Cornhill* because of its middle-class readership, but they were so outraged by the anti-utilitarian tone of the first three articles that Thackeray told him the fourth would have to be the last. Indeed, the tone is not merely anti-utilitarian, but can be seen as an attack on capitalism and the mercantile system. For the benefit of those who could not grasp his message the first time, Ruskin used the preface to the reissue of the four essays to spell out a vision for the improvement of society that was, effectively, the establishment of a welfare state, with nationalised industries, of a sort that would take another eighty-five years to be created. He more than hinted that capitalism was not honest, and that 'the acquisition of wealth was finally possible only under certain moral conditions of society': which suggests the high idealism of his thoughts.[136]

His vision was in four sections. The first was that youth training schools should be set up, at the State's cost, and all children permitted ('and, under certain cases, be under penalty required') to pass through them.[137] In them a youth would learn 'the laws of health, and the exercises enjoined by them; habits of gentleness and justice; and the calling by which he is to live.' Second, the government would also set up and regulate factories and workshops, not just for the production but also for the sale 'of every necessary of life', with which private enterprise would be expected to compete.[138] Third, the unemployed would be set to work by the government. If they were insufficiently educated to do a job, they would be trained. If they were too ill, they would be looked after until well. If they simply objected to work, they would be given the most 'painful and degrading' labour, until they mended their ways. Fourth, 'comfort and home' would be provided for the old and destitute. At the high water mark of Liberal individualism and the power of the free market, it is little wonder that this manifesto of Tory paternalism, veering into socialism, should have caused such outrage.

Ruskin's attack on wealth, apart from being other-worldly, also seemed to consist in his resentment at the power that wealth gave a man over his fellow men. He quotes Adam Smith's dictum of needing to 'buy in the cheapest market and sell in the dearest', but questions the morality of that process: the process that had made Victorian Britain as prosperous as it was.[139] Ruskin had reached the stage where he saw wealth as something that could not be measured in money – a view he would confirm in practice when inheriting his father's considerable estate and art collection a few years later, when he proceeded to give much of it away. His attack on the mercantile class – the engine of Victorian prosperity – was unbridled. He described the notion of 'robbing the poor because he is poor' as 'especially the mercantile form of theft, consisting in taking advantage of a man's necessities in order to obtain his labour or property at a reduced price'.[140] He saw the relationship between master and servant as inherently unjust; he saw markets, regarded by Liberals as a meeting place for the exercise of respective free wills, as unjust too, feeling that the power always lay with the rich and never with the poor. He repeated a line he had written in Modern Painters, hoping it would have a wider audience now: 'Government and co-operation are in all things the Laws of Life; Anarchy and competition the Laws of Death.'[141]

Ruskin accused society of having become profoundly unchristian: 'I know no previous instance in history of a nation's establishing a systematic disobedience to the first principles of its professed religion,' he writes at the end of his third article, Qui Judicatis Terram. 'The writings which we (verbally) esteem as divine, not only denounce the love of money as the source of all evil, and as an idolatry abhorred of the Deity, but declare mammon service to be the accurate and irreconcilable opposite of God's service: and, whenever they speak of riches absolute, and poverty absolute, declare woe to the rich, and blessing to the poor.'[142] Given his readership, Thackeray took a risk allowing Ruskin to write a fourth and final broadside against their values. In fact the last essay is a damp squib, a religiose expression of Ruskin's homespun ideas on economics. However, the damage done in the earlier essays by a man of Ruskin's standing against the cult of capitalism was already serious enough.

By 1867, like Carlyle, and for similar reasons, Ruskin doubted reform would bring happiness. He had outlined his views in his letters to Thomas Dixon, a Sunderland cork-cutter, published that autumn as *Time and Tide*. In his preface Ruskin states his intentions in writing the letters: 'The reform you desire may give you more influence in parliament; but your influence there will of course be useless to you – perhaps worse than useless – until you have wisely made up your minds what you wish Parliament to do for you; and when you have made up your minds about that, you will find, not only that you can do it for yourselves without the intervention of Parliament; but that eventually nobody *but* yourselves can do it.'[143] This was *estote ergo vos perfecti!* again, expressed in less erudite terms.

The letters are not so much Ruskin's thoughts on reform as some early workings-through of his view on capitalism, and the relationship between master and servant. Like Arnold, he felt capitalism to have been far from an unbridled good. However, he sought to disentangle the demands for the ballot with those for shorter hours and more wages. Just as Arnold had noted the effects on the East End of an economic downturn, so did Ruskin discern the 'utter grief, which the lower middle classes in England are now suffering'. He likened it to 'as if I were living in one great churchyard, with people all round me clinging feebly to the edges of the open graves, and calling for help, as they fall back into them, out of sight.'[144]

He voiced contempt for the law of supply and demand, destroying families when demand tailed off. He suggested the working class should organise, not to 'make a noise' about laws it did not like, 'nor call meetings in parks about them, in spite of railings and police; but keep them in your thoughts and sights, as objects of patient purpose and future achievement by peaceful strength.'[145] He warned them that revolution would bring poverty, as capital would flee to a safe haven, 'and you would perish in riot and famine'. He recommended honesty, and education, instead; and warned his upper-class readers to recognise the dignity of the labour of those who made their shoes or dug their gardens.

In *The Stones of Venice* he had called for a State education system, advocating a welfarist ideal that was anathema to 'our Liberal practitioners'. He repeated this in *Time and Tide*: 'Finally, I hold it for indisputable, that the first duty of a State is to see that every child born therein shall be well housed, clothed, fed, and educated, till it attain years of discretion. But in order to the effecting this the Government must have an authority over the people of which we now do not so much as dream.'[146] Education was the only way to limit crime; and he saw education as teaching, or developing, 'reverence and compassion'.[147]

He did not doubt that the 'teaching of truth as a habit will be the chief work the master has to do.'[148] Like Arnold, with whom he shared a Christian faith, he believed in the possibilities of perfection; unlike Stephen, and to an extent unlike Carlyle – both of whom struggled with orthodox religion – he took an optimist's view of human nature. He recalled seeing dirty small children in the slums of St Giles's, as he walked to the British Museum: but 'in those worst treated children of the English race, I yet see the making of gentlemen and gentlewomen – not the making of dog-stealers and gin drinkers, such as their parents were; and the child of the average English tradesman or peasant, even at this day, well schooled, will show no innate disposition such as must fetter him for ever to the clod or counter.'[149]

In 1873 Ruskin issued his collection of three lectures given in 1865–6 on aspects of social criticism, *The Crown of Wild Olive*, with the addition of a substantial fourth lecture, *The Future of England*. The lectures touch on ideas already expressed in works such as *Unto this Last* and *Time and Tide*. The preface concentrates on a stretch of once beautiful Surrey countryside ruined by the advance of capitalism; and the pointlessness of fencing off a small piece of land in front of a new public house with elaborate railings so as to create a rubbish dump. Sweetness and light remain absent.

The Future of England was given to an audience of young officers at Woolwich in December 1869. Ruskin again amplified a theme from *Time and Tide*: 'A struggle is approaching between the newly-risen power of democracy and the apparently departing power of feudalism; and another struggle, no less imminent, and far more dangerous, between wealth and pauperism.'[150] He lamented that these two struggles were viewed as identical, when he felt they were distinct. Riches, he believed were adverse to noblesse – great dynasties had always been founded by the poor, and truly chivalric knights never kept treasure for themselves. Also, 'all anarchy is the forerunner of poverty, and all prosperity begins in obedience'.[151]

However, Ruskin conceded that nineteenth-century cynicism about kings and aristocratic rule had some justification – 'the people have been misgoverned', which led them to seek a form of rule without masters.[152] Presciently, he reflected that 'the world may be quite content to endure much suffering with this fresh hope, and retain its faith in anarchy, whatever comes of it, till it can endure no more.' The lower classes were right to think they had done all the hard work, and their masters had taken all the profits of their labour. A result of the development of the mercantile State since Tudor times had been the creation of 'a class among the lower orders which it is now peculiarly difficult to govern' that had 'lost the very capability of reverence, which is the most precious part of the human soul.'[153] He echoed Arnold when he said that there is a 'vast populace' which 'exists only in worship of itself – which can neither see anything beautiful around it, nor conceive anything virtuous above it; which has, towards all goodness and greatness, no other feelings than those of the lowest creatures – fear, hatred and hunger; a populace which has sunk below your appeal in their nature, as it has risen beyond your power in their multitude; whom you can now no more charm than you can the adder, nor discipline, than you can the summer fly.'[154] He said that 'light' – one cannot tell whether the Arnoldian reference was conscious – was now required if the 'darkness' he had outlined were to be lifted. Otherwise, a new gospel would be preached – 'Let the weak do as they can, and the wicked as they will.'[155]

Although some of what Ruskin said smelt of Arnold, he was still under the sway of Carlyle. '"Govern us," they cry with one heart, though many minds. They *can* be governed still, these English; they are men still; not gnats, nor serpents.'[156] Yet his solution is the most idealistic of any, but rooted in his eccentric ideas of political economy. He agreed that to make people governable they must be educated: but did not share Arnold's view of what education was. 'Education does not mean teaching people to know what they do not know. It means teaching them to behave as they do not behave.'[157] He said this was not about learning to read and count, since such talents could be put to nefarious uses: but 'training them into the perfect exercise and kingly continence of their bodies and souls.'[158]

He claimed that as much was spent in England in a year – £800,000 – on training horses as in educating children: and that the cost in the upkeep of paupers and the incarceration of criminals made it counterproductive not to have a compulsory, State-funded education system. 'For every pound that we spend on education we spend twelve either in charity or punishment'.[159] However, his other remedies are implausible: a compulsory national labour system (with no sign of how it would be funded or administered) with those thrown out of work by the advance of machinery put to mending the infrastructure and beautifying the landscape. There is a touch of Luddism in Ruskin, visible from his earliest essays on political economy in the late 1850s and from *Unto This Last*, published in 1862. One senses that when Carlyle laments an unattainable past he knows the game is up: but with Ruskin, defeat is never admitted. He continues to exhort and expect a class enriched by capitalism to make fair shares of their spoils with those put out of work, or kept from prosperity, by the effects of their investments. Ruskin was a *soi-disant* Tory – 'a violent Tory of the old school; – Walter Scott's school, that is to say, and Homer's' – but it is clear from *The Crown of Wild Olive* why he became lauded as a father of English socialism.[160]

The gulf between his – Carlyle's – school and Mill's continued to expand. Ruskin noted in his diaries on 30 October 1874 Carlyle's disdain for Mill, showing the power his mood had over Ruskin. 'We fell away upon Mill's essay on the substitution of patriotism for religion. "Actually the most paltry rag of" – a chain of vituperative contempt too fast to note – "it has fallen to my lot to come in with. Among my acquaintance I have not seen a person talking of a thing he so little understood."' The point of his indignation was Mill's supposing that, if God did not make everybody 'happy', it was because He had no sufficient power – 'was not enough supplied with the article . . . Nothing makes Carlyle more contemptuous than this coveting of "happiness".'[161]

VI

Millicent Garrett Fawcett reviewed *Liberty, Equality, Fraternity* in June 1873, three months after its publication, and republished her remarks in a pamphlet – *Mr Fitzjames Stephen on the Position of Women* – a few weeks later. Of all Stephen's conservative arguments in the book, none has stood the test of time so poorly as his dismissal of women, and his disdain for their 'rights'. Lady Egerton took him to task, but he was having none of it. 'You think K[ate, his daughter] might have been educated into an equal to the boys. I think it would have spoilt her very much to try to make anything but a woman of her – indeed my own enthusiasm about women whom I really care for, is one main reason why I do not want them to be pitted against men. It is like trying the strength of porcelain or glass against . . . brass . . . or like putting a man who works with his brains against a man who works with his limbs in a trial of the strength of the limbs.'[162]

Although *Liberty, Equality, Fraternity* is usually viewed as an assault upon *On Liberty*, it is also in part an attack on *The Subjection of Women*, as part of an attempt to undermine the whole of Mill's system of beliefs. 'All the talk in the world will never shake the proposition that men are stronger than women in every shape,' he asserts.[163] 'They have greater muscular and nervous force, greater intellectual force, greater vigour of character,' he added. This was a 'general truth'. Stephen's views on women, more than perhaps on anything else in his book, are based on assertion rather than deduction: he simply cannot imagine a world in which 'boys and girls [are] educated indiscriminately, and . . . instructed in the same things . . . Are girls to play at cricket, to row, and be drilled like boys? I cannot argue with a person who says Yes.'

It was Stephen's defence of the inferiority of women in marriage that caused most outrage. He said it was important that marriages should be incapable of being dissolved, because otherwise women would be the slaves of their husbands, rather than merely subordinate to them. 'A woman loses the qualities which make her attractive to men much earlier than men lose those which make them attractive to women,' he wrote.[164] Fitz at this stage was forty-four, with the build and aspect of an all-in wrestler, it should be noted; but was also exceptionally happily married. 'The tie between a woman and young children is generally far closer than the tie between them and their father. A woman who is no longer young, and who is the mother of children, would thus be absolutely in her husband's power, in nine cases out of ten, if he might put an end to the marriage when he pleased. He then sets out his view of the marriage contract which he says is 'as clear as that of a proposition in Euclid':

1. Marriage is a contract, one of the principal objects of which is the government of a family.
2. This government must be vested either by law or by contract in the hands of one of the two married persons.
3. If the arrangement is made by contract, the remedy for breach of it must either be by law or by a dissolution of the partnership at the will of the contracting parties.
4. Law could give no remedy in such a case. Therefore the only remedy for breach of the contract would be a dissolution of the marriage.
5. Therefore, if the marriage is to be permanent, the government of the family must be put by law and by morals in the hands of · the husband, for no-one proposes to give it to the wife.[165]

Stephen proclaims that 'Mr Mill is totally unable to meet this argument,' which given how far it rests on assertion and a series of begged questions is hardly to be wondered at. However, it would not be Mill, who died on 8 May 1873, but Mrs Fawcett, who would seek to answer him.

Stephen was not impressed by her attempt. In the second edition of his book, published in 1874, he allowed her a footnote in response to a point she had made about a man who exercised his legal right to the extreme showing himself as acting in 'a very brutal manner'. Stephen observed, with what his editor terms 'brusque impatience', that 'this is as true as it is irrelevant. It is the only remark of Mrs Fawcett's which I think it necessary to notice, and I notice it only as an illustration of what she understands by argument.' We can deduce that what Fitz understood by argument, when he was unequal to someone else's, was to be offensive in return.

Mrs Fawcett derided the book as 'the latest revelation of the Gospel according to St Stephen', and suggested that the motto 'this is the way, walk ye in it' should be printed 'in letters an inch high on the top of every page.'[166] She added that 'the reader feels as he studies these passages that the author is shouting in his ear.' She questioned Stephen's belief in the submission of women, as the weaker sex, to their husbands as a precept of the common law, asking 'is the wife to obey the husband when, in obeying him, she does something she believes to be wrong? If the answer is "yes", the possession of a husband may become the screen of all kinds of iniquity, from murder and robbery downwards. If the answer is "no", everything is conceded that the advocates of equality in marriage demand, for many wives may and do think it wrong to encourage a spirit of despotism in their husbands by invariably allowing the husband's authority to be supreme.'[167]

Mrs Fawcett rejected Stephen's metaphor of the family as a ship, with the husband as captain. She likened it to a government, with husband and wife as two chambers of Parliament, and the children being admitted to the conclave once they were old enough. Decisions would be debated and agreed rather than handed down. 'The law sanctions the ship-captain theory, but the moral sentiment of many persons is superior to the law, and therefore there are many happy marriages.'[168] In unhappy marriages there was no easy escape from abuse of authority. 'The indissolubility of marriage renders all these so-called parallels entirely fallacious,' she wrote, 'and makes it necessary for the protection of the wife that she should not be either actually or legally subjugated to her husband.'[169] She ridiculed Stephen's premise that in return for submission women received protection. 'That is to say, in return for submission married women get the protection of losing all control over their own property; they also have the inestimable advantage of possessing no legal right to the guardianship of their own children even after the death of their husbands.' Twisting the knife, she pointed out that 'in return for the submissiveness of women, little girls of twelve years old are, for the purposes of seduction, legally regarded as women – a most noteworthy instance, this, of the kind of protection the present state of the law affords.'

She noted also that irrespective of what 'protection' men afforded their wives, the legal system seemed to treat with excessive leniency assaults by men upon their wives. She quoted an article in *The Times* from April 1872 – 'every day the reports of our police courts and of our criminal tribunals still repeat the tale of savage and cowardly outrages upon women: and every day we have reason to marvel, not without a mixture of indignation, at the leniency with which some of our judges treat offences of this kind.'[170] The article had concluded, with deep disapproval, that an Englishman, 'within certain limits, may beat his wife as much as he pleases.' Fawcett quoted the same newspaper, four months later, observing that 'recent trials have revealed a prevalent indifference to the maltreatment of women, which is a heinous disgrace to English nature.'[171]

Fawcett noted that in the better classes women had small favours shown them – 'being "seen home" from evening parties, being helped first at dinner, having chairs offered, doors opened, umbrellas carried and the like' – but that they more than returned the compliment 'by sewing on buttons, working slippers, and making puddings for the mankind of their domestic circles.' However, she noted that 'it is a small consolation for Nancy Jones, in Whitechapel, who is kicked and beaten at discretion by her husband, to know that Lady Jones, in Belgravia, is always assisted in and out of her carriage as if she were a cripple. It is a small consolation to a widow whose children are taken from her and handed over to the guardianship of a stranger, to know that a gentleman will never pass out of the room before her, and that she may always take the inner side of the pavement.'[172]

She concluded that:

if women are to understand that the courtesies they now enjoy are simply yielded to them on condition of their legal and actual subjection to men, there are few women who would not at once declare that they were being grossly overcharged for the article, and also that these small privileges become utterly valueless unless they are completely voluntary in their character . . . it is quite an appalling thought to a woman in whom the English virtue of resistance to arbitrary authority is strongly developed, that, although she is ignorant of the fact, she is daily receiving concessions and having a thousand things done for her on condition of a submission which she never intends to give. When the settling day comes, she will have nothing to meet the demands of her creditors.[173]

She conceded, though, that Stephen's case against equality for women was 'one among the many proofs of the growing importance of the movement for the emancipation of women' because he was such 'heavy artillery'. She contrasted his with the weak arguments deployed in debates on female suffrage in the Commons by the Home Secretary, which were so pitiful as to merit no reply.

It was clear by the 1870s that for most educated men – with the exception of the odd hardcore feminist such as Mill or Sidgwick – the duty of their class to stabilise society through measures of reform had been fulfilled by giving all men the vote. Given the extent to which this had alarmed the likes of Carlyle, Stephen and Ruskin, and given the reservations about it felt by Arnold, the final stage of reform

– inviting women into the political process, and ending their role as the chattels of men – would take much more effort yet, as Fawcett seems to have understood. Fortunately for them, there were other crucial areas of life – such as philanthropy, which we shall explore in Chapter 16 – where they could, despite the disabilities inflicted upon them by men, make their mark.

VII

For all the aggressive modernity of mid-nineteenth-century Britain, aspects of medieval life still lingered. Yet this was a period of rapid change and – as would be seen with reform of the franchise, and with women's rights – ancient prejudices and practices could be discarded without so much as a backward glance. Until the 1860s, however, the way in which society dealt with crime and meted out punishments remained atavistic, even though a debate about abolishing public executions had been going on for over twenty years. Richard Monckton Milnes had said in the Commons in 1845 that 'executions in this country formerly were conducted as spectacles for the people. It was supposed that they would work on the public mind, to the prevention of crime.' He doubted this was still so, and claimed that 'the progress of civilization', which had stopped corporal punishments from being conducted in public, demanded the same be done to capital sentences.

He argued that 'the Judge who passed sentence on the prisoner should also be authorised to name the place (within the walls of the prison) of his execution. He proposed that the execution should take place in the presence of the authorities, and also that the reporters of the public press should be admitted.' He added: 'Public executions were defended on the ground that they improved the morals of the people. This could hardly be the case, when they reflected that those who attended executions were the dissolute and the desperate, and they were looked at as a sort of gladiatorial exhibition, and were visited as a kind of barbarous diversion.'[174]

Dickens was prominently associated with the cause of abolishing public executions. On 13 November 1849 he attended the hanging of Frederick and Maria Manning outside Horsemonger Lane gaol in Southwark. The Mannings – he a career criminal, she a Swiss–French domestic servant – had been convicted of the murder of a wealthy friend, Patrick O'Connor, whom they killed after inviting him to dinner, and buried under their kitchen floor. Apprehended with his money, they were soon convicted, and became the first married couple to be hanged for 150 years. Dickens was so appalled by what he saw that he wrote twice to *The Times* about it: 'I believe that a sight so inconceivably awful as the wickedness and levity of the immense crowd collected at that execution could be imagined by no man.'[175] It 'made my blood run cold,' he wrote, not of the hangings themselves, but of the sounds of the crowd of 'thieves, low prostitutes, ruffians and vagabonds of every kind'. The bloodless reaction to the fate of the Mannings was for Dickens as 'if the name of Christ had never been heard in this world.' He called public execution a 'moral evil' to be 'rooted out'. It is not recorded what he thought of what happened to their corpses after they were cut down: a cast was made of their skulls for the purpose of phrenology (the phrenologist found them consistent with the skull shape of other murderers), and a sample taken of their brains.

The Times paid tribute to Dickens as 'a great novelist, whose knowledge of the human heart and its workings under the infinite varieties and accidents of modern life needs not our praise'. However, it warned against his radical prescription: 'It appears to us a matter of necessity that so tremendous an act as a national homicide should be publicly as well as solemnly done. Popular jealousy demands it. Were it otherwise, the mass of the people would never be sure that great offenders were really executed . . . the mystery of the prison walls would be intolerable.' Dickens wrote again five days later to enlarge upon the depravity of the spectacle: Calcraft, the hangman, he said 'should be restrained in his unseemly briskness, in his jokes, his oaths, and his brandy.'[176] He called for a 'witness jury' of twenty-four members of the public, drawn from all classes, to be summoned to executions if held in private, and for prison officials to attend too; and for all the bells of churches in the town to be tolled during the hour while the body hung at the end of the rope, and all the shops to be closed 'that all might be reminded of what was being done'. The arguments made no impact for some years. However, by the 1860s the spectacle seemed at odds with the society the Victorians thought they were creating. The Commons discussed the matter on 23 February 1864 on a motion of John Hibbert, the Liberal MP for Oldham, the day after five foreign brigands had been hanged at Newgate for piracy and murder when attacking a British ship.

Hibbert saw them as a 'disgusting display' that lagged behind the other reforms in the penal system over the preceding half-century.[177]

Dickens had been present too, describing the occasion as 'a diabolical fair'.[178] Public hangings were, Hibbert argued, the relic of a time in which women were burnt for witchcraft and prisoners tortured for refusing to talk. He disputed that the spectacles were a deterrent. 'As to the criminal classes,' he added, 'it was found that they were always largely represented on such occasions, and that the spectacle had very far from a wholesome influence upon them. In the victims themselves, the publicity of the execution tended to produce bravado and hardness of heart.'[179] Most MPs were familiar with the scenes that attended hangings at Newgate. Hibbert recounted the hanging of two murderers at Kirkdale, near Liverpool in 1862, the crowd for which was delivered by special trains, and to which people walked miles from rural Lancashire and Cheshire 'to gratify their depraved appetite'. The railway companies, ever open to a further profit, were always alert to hangings, which further reduced the respect in which they were held by the political class. Hibbert observed that women and children were present, and 'the hours previous to the execution were passed in dissipation and debauchery'. His seconder, George Hadfield, the Liberal MP for Sheffield, radically suggested that as there had been no rise in forgery since it ceased to be a capital crime, the government might look at the point of having a death penalty.

Sir George Grey, the Home Secretary, felt the public hanging of the pirates had been a useful exercise, and disputed that such spectacles were demoralising. The crowds were, he argued, only so large because hangings had become markedly less frequent than they used to be; and crowds of lower class people behaved disgustingly wherever they were to be found, at a hanging or any other spectacle. 'Does that show that the effect of an execution is altogether lost?' he asked.[180] It was perhaps as well that so many criminals were at such events, for 'who can tell in how many instances a deep and lasting impression may be made upon the minds even of some of the most criminal class, which may check them in a career of crime, and, inducing them to abstain from the course to which they are prompted by passion, vicious habits and early association, tend to rescue them from the same ignominious end?'

Lord Henry Lennox had gone to Newgate the previous morning to see whether the accounts of executions that he had read were accurate.

He found they were, and was disgusted. 'Anything more utterly unsuccessful, as an attempt to convey a moral to the people, he had never seen'.[181] He read at length from that morning's *Daily News* about 'the obscene and blasphemous cries of the crew engaged in mocking the preachers, the fierce cheers with which the constant fights were encouraged, the screams and whistling, the hideous groans and indecent songs, which, as an open expression of abandoned depravity and rampant sin, has probably not been exceeded since the world began.' Because hangings were usually held on a Monday, Lennox was angry that the Sabbath was routinely violated by people arriving during Sunday to get a decent view, and engaging in depravity of one sort or another. He asked Grey to move the day of executions, if he insisted on retaining them as a public spectacle.

Some wished to discuss abolishing the death penalty entirely. The range of crimes for which someone could be hanged had been steadily reduced, not least because so few were executed for forgery, burglary, sheep-stealing or other former capital crimes that it acted as an encouragement to commit the offences. William Ewart, the MP for Dumfries, argued that so many now were acquitted of murder because juries did not think they should hang that the capital sentence had been brought into disrepute. Acquittal rates for capital crimes had become so high that someone tried for one was four-and-a-half times more likely to get off than someone being tried for a non-capital one. He quoted a newspaper that said 'punishment for murder has become a lottery'.[182] He alleged that 800 infanticides were committed each year, but there were no prosecutions as the crime carried the death penalty. Grey was against abolition, and believed the country was too: in that he was almost certainly right, at a time when even liberals such as Mill and Dickens felt there were cases when the penalty of death was the only suitable punishment.

The preparations for the execution in front of Newgate, on 14 November 1864, of a German murderer, Franz Müller, reveal the inconvenience of the public execution, never mind its pornographic effect. 'The excitement caused by the near approach of the execution is almost unprecedented,' *The Times* reported on that same morning:[183]

> From 3 o'clock until 5 yesterday afternoon, although the day was wet, a crowd of people had assembled in front of the prison. Most of the crowd were then dispersed by a heavy shower of rain, but

only to collect again on its cessation, and at 8 o'clock last evening the Old Bailey was all but impassable. In the open space opposite the gaol, and, indeed, throughout the whole length of Old Bailey from Ludgate Hill to Newgate Street, formidable barriers have been erected, about 20 feet apart, to lessen the pressure of the crowd, and especially to prevent the fearful surging which takes place on extraordinary occasions of this kind, and to which the weak are liable to succumb.

Similar precautions had been taken in surrounding streets where a view 'however remote' could be obtained. 'The windows of the Court-house in the Old Bailey have been barricaded, as has also the churchyard of St Sepulchre, where loss of life was caused about 30 years ago, on a similar occasion, by the palisading along the top of a dwarf wall surrounding the church, and to which people had clung in great numbers, giving way.'

Müller was hanged 'before such a concourse as we hope may never be again assembled either for the spectacle which they had in view or for the gratification of such lawless ruffianism as yesterday found its scope around the gallows.'[184] They were a 'dismal crowd of dirty vagrants . . . loungers . . . drunken men', and on the night before the hanging they were joined by 'a thick, dark, noisy fringe of men and women [who] settled like bees around the nearest barriers'. There was a party atmosphere: 'well-dressed and ill-dressed, old men and lads, women and girls. Many had jars of beer; at least half were smoking.' The gallows themselves were wheeled out of the Debtor's Door in the early hours, to the cheers of a crowd that by then numbered about 5,000. The police surrounded the scaffold. 'Then, as every minute the day broke more and more clear, the crowd could be seen in all the horrible reality in which it had been heard throughout the long wet night. The women were 'of the lowest and poorest class'. The men were 'such . . . as only such a scene could bring together – sharpers, thieves, gamblers, betting men, the outsiders of the boxing ring, brick-layers' labourers, dock workmen, German artisans and sugar bakers, with a fair sprinkling of what may be almost called as low a grade as any of the worst there met – the rakings of cheap singing-halls and billiard rooms, the fast young "gents" of London.' As *The Times*'s reporter laconically noted, 'there can be only one thing more difficult than describing this crowd, and that is to forget it.' Well-dressed people who made the mistake of attending found their hats knocked off and their pockets picked. 'None but those who looked down upon the awful crowd of yesterday will ever believe in the wholesale, open, broadcast manner in which garotting and highway robbery were carried on.' By the time of the hanging there were an estimated 50,000 people crammed into the streets outside the prison: and as eight o'clock struck and the condemned man was brought out, a cry went up of 'hats off!', and the men in the crowd moved as if one. A prison chaplain, the Reverend Mr Davis, led the way, reading sentences from the Burial Service. Müller, pale of face but rigid of bearing, went up the steps and stood on the trap under the noose.

'Following him close came the common hangman, who at once pulling a white cap over the condemned man's face, fastened his feet with a strap, and shambled off the scaffold amid low hisses.' A Lutheran pastor who had accompanied Müller to the gallows urged him to confess his guilt before the drop; which he did, in German, and then the bolt was pulled. This alone silenced the crowd, which was, for five or ten minutes, 'awed and stilled by this quiet, rapid passage from life to death'. This did not last for long: 'before the slight, slow vibrations of the body had well ended robbery with violence, loud laughing, oaths, fighting, obscene conduct, and still more filthy language reigned round the gallows far and near.' A ballad was written about the execution, and sold 280,000 copies, proving the ability of the spectacle to seize the public imagination.[185]

As the campaign to end public executions continued – given great impetus by every event such as this, which seemed to belong to a Hogarthian London of gin-soaked whores and thieves of a kind contemporary society tried to convince itself it had left behind – the campaign to abolish hanging altogether became stronger. William Tallack, a Quaker in his early thirties, became secretary of the Society for the Abolition of Capital Punishment in 1863, and sought to recruit strong forces to give evidence to a Royal Commission on the subject that was set up the following year. However, abolitionism was an extreme minority interest, even among advanced liberals. Tallack wrote to Mill in January 1865 to solicit his support, only to receive the reply that 'I have a very strong opinion against its total abolition, being persuaded that the liability to it . . . has a greater deterring effect, at a less expense of real suffering, than any other penalty which would be adequate to the worst kind of offence.'

Mill sent his regrets, pleading that if the Commission wished to summon him as a witness, it would not be on the 'right side' from Tallack's point of view.[186] He was, indeed, the very antithesis of the bleeding-heart liberal that he might have been mistaken for. He fully supported flogging for crimes of brutality, and told Florence Nightingale in 1860, when she urged a forgiving aspect on society, that 'with many minds, punishment is the only one of the natural consequences of guilt which is capable of making any impression on them. In such cases, punishment is the sole means available for beginning the reformation of the criminal; and the fear of similar punishment is the only inducement which deters many really no better than himself from doing acts to others which would not only deprive them of their own happiness, but thwart all attempts to do good to themselves and others.'[187]

When the Royal Commission reported in 1866 its recommendations on the abolition of public executions were at last acted upon. Lord Cranworth, the Lord Chancellor, told the House of Lords on 1 May that year that 'most of the theoretical objections to private executions are absurd'.[188] Lord Malmesbury disagreed: the 'fear of disgrace' attendant on being publicly executed being, he thought, an important part in the deterrent effect of the capital sentence.[189] He also felt that 'the English mind' would 'revolt' at the idea of a 'secret' execution: and that the inevitable consequence of making executions private would be the abolition of hanging altogether.[190] Shaftesbury dismissed the point about disgrace, observing urbanely that 'he did not believe that the sense of shame had much influence on that class; indeed, he was convinced that in the great class from which murderers were taken the sense of shame was wholly extinct; and such men often looked forward to the time when they would appear on the scaffold and publicly exhibit their hardened state of mind to a crowd of companions.'[191]

The upheavals over the next two years, as the Reform Bills were considered, led to further delay: but in the spring of 1868 the Capital Punishment Within Prisons Bill was introduced into the Commons, and passed. It received Royal Assent on 29 May 1868, three days after the hangman, William Calcraft, had conducted what would be the last public execution in Britain: hanging the Fenian Michael Barrett at Newgate for his part in a bombing in Clerkenwell the previous December that had killed twelve people and injured another fifty. Capital punishment in

Britain would last for almost another 100 years, but thereafter always away from the eyes of the mob.

In some respects the Victorians humanised the penal system, but in others an Old Testament belief in retribution continued to inform their policy. Throughout the period new prisons, emblematic of the harshness of the system, had been opened, and many survive today: Pentonville had been built in 1842, Dartmoor (originally a prison for Napoleonic prisoners of war) in 1850, Wandsworth in 1851 and Holloway in 1852. Many operated on the 'separate' system, where prisoners were kept apart, and forbidden to talk when engaging in any communal activities, such as on the treadmill or when picking oakum. The separate system required many cells and was so labour intensive for the warders that prisoners had to be drafted in to work in the prisons on tasks that warders would normally have done. Further pressure was put on the jails by the restrictions applied to the sentence of transportation to the colonies by the 1853 Penal Servitude Act, which decreed that no one could be transported for less than fourteen years. Transportation was abolished altogether in 1857. However, punishments sometimes became harsher. The response to an epidemic of garrotting in 1863 was the Garrotters Act, which specified that those convicted of this fashionable offence would be sentenced to the cat-o'-nine-tails as well as a term in prison. This savage punishment had the desired effect: garrotting soon went out of vogue. The Victorians liked to feel they were advancing the cause of humanity, but not at the expense of their personal security.

CHAPTER 16

DOING GOOD: PHILANTHROPISTS AND THE HUMANE IMPULSE

I

It had been clear to Gladstone, and would be made equally so to Disraeli when he regained power in 1874, that great advances in the condition of the people were best kick-started by State intervention. However, the prevailing sentiment – more usual among Liberals than Conservatives, who increasingly believed that paternalism was the duty of the State – was to champion individual responsibility. The poor were expected to do all they could to sustain themselves; and the rich were supposed to be alert to their obligations as Christians to help those less fortunate. The rich paid very low rates of tax, mainly in the form of duties on luxury goods. They therefore had the disposable income to support their pet causes. However, it was apparent to some of the rich that, if they were employers, philanthropy brought additional advantages such the health and loyalty of their staff: a helpful thought in a more secular age in which Christian obligations counted for less than formerly.

Some rich people also realised that the stability of society, from which they derived particular benefit, could in part be bought by charitable work that kept the poor docile and, even more useful, grateful to their betters. The Hyde Park riot of 1866 reminded the ruling class of the monster in their midst. Although there was serious poverty all over Britain, the epicentre was in London, the largest city and one whose population – of poor, notably – was growing rapidly. And the worst part of London was the East End, not only because of the large numbers of destitute and exceptionally poor people who lived in places such as Spitalfields, Limehouse, Wapping, Bethnal Green,

Mile End, Hackney and Stepney, but also because the middle classes, who had built fine houses in those places during the eighteenth century, had all but deserted them, fracturing society in the process and removing any sense of support or example from the lowest classes. In time, the need for middle-class influence in such areas became widely accepted: and many in the middle classes began to understand the moral and social importance of their going back into what had become poor communities.

It was what Beatrice Webb, alluding in her autobiography to a verse from Hebrews, called 'a new consciousness of sin among men of intellect and men of property'.[1] She detected various stages of this consciousness: 'at first philanthropic and practical – [Richard] Oastler [a colleague of Shaftesbury in the movement to pass the Factory Acts], Shaftesbury and Chadwick; then literary and artistic – Dickens, Carlyle, Ruskin and William Morris; and finally analytic, historical and explanatory – in his latter days John Stuart Mill; Karl Marx and his English interpreters.' She had not been talking about personal sin, but about 'a collective or class consciousness; a growing uneasiness, amounting to conviction, that the industrial organization, which had yielded rent, interest and profits on a stupendous scale, had failed to provide a decent livelihood and tolerable conditions for a majority of the inhabitants of Great Britain.'

The Victorians discriminated between the deserving and the undeserving poor. The former found themselves in poverty through no fault of their own – widows, orphans, the sick and maimed, the victims of the caprices of the free market on which the prosperity of Britain was based. Many were poor despite working long hours in menial tasks, often out of doors, desperately trying to find enough money by their labours to afford basic food and the meanest lodgings. The latter were criminals and those who, by a determination not to live by what Riderhood, the malevolent waterman in Charles Dickens's *Our Mutual Friend*, called the sweat of their brows, put themselves on a par with criminals in the eyes of Victorian morality. Work was a duty owed to God: *laborare est orare*. However, some – led by Carlyle – believed it was the duty of the State to provide work for the unemployed. Pauperism brought despair and shame. For most it was a temporary condition, experienced during economic downturns. To a feckless few, mostly drunks, it was a permanent, and inevitably life-shortening, event. In the 1860s and 1870s there were roughly a million paupers in England and

Wales, a rate varying between about forty and fifty per thousand of the population.[2]

Philanthropists helped the poor in two principal ways: they gave their money, or their time. Some who gave money also gave time, though not usually in dispensing soup from soup kitchens, but rather attending committee meetings of boards of trustees. Some who gave time did not simply scour the streets looking for orphans, but engaged in acts of propaganda against the failure of society to improve or alleviate the conditions of the poor: Dickens most notably, but also Kingsley, Ruskin and other writers. There was a predisposition to help the deserving poor, not least because when there was so much poverty and misery it would have been heaping a further injustice on the deserving poor to help the undeserving first: and means were limited.

II

No person of celebrity campaigned for the poor so much as Dickens. He did so not out of religious duty – he had an advanced scepticism about religion – but out of a sense of personal outrage that became politically motivated. Dickens is important to an understanding of mid-Victorian Britain not simply because he was a pre-eminent cultural figure, shaping the minds of his readers by his subtly propagandistic tone; but also because his enduring popularity has ensured that he remains a prism – for many people, indeed, the only prism – through which the period from about 1837 to 1870 is viewed today. His world contains all human life – from the malevolence of Bill Sikes and the sadism of Mr Murdstone to the naivety of Copperfield, Pip and Chuzzlewit and the benevolence of Peggotty, the Cheerybles, Mr Brownlow and Mr Pumblechook; via the repellence of Merdle, Uriah Heep, Squeers and Pecksniff. He shows us the poverty, the rigidities of class, the easy disposition to criminality, the injustices and the hypocrisies that we associate with the period.

Dickens was perhaps the most famous man in England by the 1860s – indeed, given his celebrity in America, perhaps one of the most famous men in the world. He had made his name in the late 1830s with *The Pickwick Papers* and *Oliver Twist*. Capitalising on the expanding literate population, Dickens edited and wrote for two successive publications – *Household Words* and *All the Year Round* – that serialised his novels, and also those by writers such as Elizabeth Gaskell and Wilkie Collins.

Dickens's life is often discussed in the context of his having to work pasting labels on pots in a blacking factory in 1824, at the age of twelve, when his father was imprisoned for debt; and, related to that experience of going down in the world, campaigning for humane treatment of the unfortunate and impoverished.

Before the blacking factory Dickens had had a happy and stimulating childhood spent mainly in Chatham, where his father had worked as a clerk in the Navy pay office. He had been an insatiable reader, and the everyday life of Chatham and Rochester provided him with the types and characters that would populate his novels; but so too did his time in poverty, and his outrage against the fecklessness of his father and his failure to provide for his son and family. When finally Dickens's father was discharged the young Dickens only left the blacking factory because his father had an argument with the proprietor. His mother tried to smooth things over so the boy could return, which caused Dickens to detest her as well.

This connection with life's hardships would become the main inspiration behind much that he wrote. His novels either reminded his readers of whence they too had come, or allowed his more genteel audience to console themselves with the thought that they had avoided such a life altogether. He succeeded, above all, in representing to his readers a life they could all identify with and recognise. The caricatures that are so many of his characters, and the usually inevitable happy endings, are sufficiently well crafted not to provoke what would be a fatal failure to suspend disbelief.

After the blacking factory he resumed his schooling, at an establishment that presaged Dotheboys Hall. It ended permanently at the age of fifteen, after which he became a solicitor's clerk, a vantage point from which he later constructed Jarndyce versus Jarndyce. That soon bored him. He taught himself shorthand and became a parliamentary reporter. In his spare time he devoted himself to self-improvement: often in the reading room of the British Museum, where he devoured such English classics as had escaped him in a childhood of exceptionally wide reading. In his early twenties he began to contribute short stories to periodicals under his pseudonym, Boz, and established himself at the handsome wage of five guineas a week as a reporter on the *Morning Chronicle*. It was from this base that his brilliant career took off.

His first *Pickwick* story appeared at the end of March 1836, two days before he married his wife, Catherine Hogarth. *Pickwick* was the engine of his fame. By the time its monthly serial ended in November 1837 it had a circulation of 40,000. Dickens started to work at a rate that would eventually kill him: he wrote *Oliver Twist* while writing *Pickwick*, and started to write *Nicholas Nickleby* while writing *Oliver Twist*. His first trip to America was in 1842, though Dickens found it, like all his subsequent voyages, utterly exhausting: but as with every experience it provided food for his writing, notably in *Martin Chuzzlewit*. As he made money he continued to champion the needs of the poor. His politics were radical, and when his friend John Forster (who would later be his biographer, and was principal consultant on all Dickens's literary projects) was running the radical newspaper the *Examiner*, Dickens wrote for it, anonymously, on social issues that angered him. When after 1850 he edited *Household Words* he took his polemicising there, both in his novels and in his essays. His serialised *Child's History of England* showed a disregard for deference and hierarchy, and especially for the idle rich.

As Britain grew more prosperous after the early 1840s, he became steadily angrier that the new wealth was not used to alleviate the most scandalous suffering. His assault on the Poor Law had begun in 1837, with *Oliver Twist*. In *Hard Times* in 1854, Mr Bounderby caricatured the heartless and unfeeling attitudes of new money towards those further down the ladder, a contrast to the outlook adopted by the landed gentry and aristocracy, conditioned by centuries of feudalism in the care of their tenantry. Bounderby finds the demand for a fair day's wages for a fair day's work as the equivalent of the poor demanding to be fed on turtle soup and venison with gold spoons. The character of Betty Higden in *Our Mutual Friend*, written in 1864–5, is drawn by Dickens to show the determination an elderly washerwoman has to find a way of earning a living without, in extreme old age, having to throw herself on the parish. In his Postscript to *Our Mutual Friend*, dated 2 September 1865, Dickens wrote that 'I believe there has been in England, since the days of the Stuarts, no law so often infamously administered, no law so often openly violated, no law habitually so ill-supervised. In the majority of the shameful cases of disease and death from destitution that shock the Public and disgrace the country, the illegality is quite equal to the inhumanity – and known language could say no more of their lawlessness.'[3]

He wrote *Hard Times*, he told Carlyle, to 'shake some people'.[4] Its successor, *Little Dorrit*, while widely seen as an attack on the notion of imprisonment for debt, is as much an assault on the unreconstructed institutions of the State, in the incarnation of the Circumlocution Office, that pertained before the Northcote–Trevelyan reforms; and on the dangers of capitalism, depicted not just in the unscrupulous and posturing Merdle, but also in the greedy idiots who are his clients. Trollope trod this path twenty years later in *The Way We Live Now*, less originally and less pungently.

Dickens includes philanthropic characters in many of his novels, not merely to win the affections of his readers but to set an example: Mr Brownlow, the saviour of *Oliver Twist*; the Cheerybles, who by employing Nicholas Nickleby allow him to provide for his family; Mr Garland in *The Old Curiosity Shop*; and the Boffins in *Our Mutual Friend*, whom Dickens seems to depict almost as an ideal of human kindness and decency, whose values had survived the harsh employer to whom they had devoted their lives. They were 'a hopelessly Unfashionable pair' but 'these two ignorant and unpolished people had guided themselves so far on in their journey of life, by a religious sense of duty and desire to do right. Ten thousand weaknesses and absurdities might have been detected in the breasts of both; ten thousand vanities additional, possibly, in the breast of the woman. But the hard wrathful and sordid nature that had wrung as much work out of them as could be got in their best days, for as little money as could be paid to hurry on their worst, had never been so warped but that it knew their moral straightness and respected it.'[5]

III

It took a partnership with the richest woman in Britain for Dickens to achieve his greatest successes in the field of helping the poor. At twenty-three, in 1837, Angela Burdett inherited £1.8 million from the widow of her maternal grandfather, Thomas Coutts, who had with his elder brother been a partner in the bank bearing their name. The newspapers observed that to lay out a line of sovereigns equivalent to this amount would occupy 24 miles. She also had an income of £50,000 a year, the proceeds from her half-share in the bank. Under the conditions of her step-grandmother's will she took her grandfather's name by Royal Licence, becoming Angela Burdett-Coutts. The will also forbade her from marrying a foreigner and from interfering in the running of the bank. Her father, Sir Francis Burdett, had been a Radical MP, and in her parents' house she had met most of the great men of the day, including Gladstone, Disraeli and Charles Dickens.

She had been brought up a devout evangelical, and her faith informed her life. Her main purpose became philanthropy. Despite being bombarded by gold-digging suitors, she did not marry until 1881 – to her twenty-nine-year-old American secretary – partly because to have done so would until the law changed have made her fortune her husband's; and partly because of her devotion to Mrs Brown, her companion and former governess, who lived until 1878. She ignored the advice of the Archbishop of Canterbury that she might adopt her fiancé instead of marrying him; because he was foreign she forfeited a substantial part of her fortune to her sister, but over the preceding forty-four years had already disbursed enough to change the lives of thousands of people. She shocked the Queen, who felt – with justification – that Burdett-Coutts had become unbalanced since the death of Mrs Brown, and risked 'an unsuitable marriage'.[6] The bride was unmoved by the warning. The marriage seemed straight out of a Dickens novel.

The Church was her first priority. By 1840 she knew London now had 1.7 million souls, but church accommodation for only 101,000 of them, and few resources for clergy and volunteers to undertake social work. So she built and endowed churches: the first of which was St Stephen's in her father's old constituency of Westminster, a parish that housed some of the most depressed and dangerous slums in London, despite the presence of Parliament and the Abbey. She funded schools, notably one under the auspices of St Stephen's. She realised there was no point trying to teach poor children anything until they had been taught the practicalities of survival – especially that girls should learn the basics of cookery, laundry and hygiene. She founded the National Society for the Prevention of Cruelty to Children, and was a supporter of the Royal Society for the Prevention of Cruelty to Animals. She became president of its Ladies Committee in 1870, where she advanced her principle that all life, whether human or animal, was sacred; and that 'inhuman treatment of animals should be held to be a wrong and a sin.'[7] She frequently wrote to The Times expressing outrage at any act of cruelty she witnessed towards dogs or horses, the main objects of her concern.

Burdett-Coutts was committed to the idea of improvement, and not

Victoria and Albert in typically upbeat mood.

Henry Cole, inventor of the Christmas card and the dynamo of Albertopolis.

The Albert Memorial, by George Gilbert Scott but a work of many hands.

A symphony in terracotta: Alfred Waterhouse's riot of decoration over the main entrance to the Natural History Museum.

The Hyde Park Riots, July 1866: even the
flower beds were trampled.

The Tory Cabinet of 1867, which brought in reform. Derby
addresses the group from one end of the table, Disraeli
reads a newspaper at the other.

The Foreign Office, Whitehall, as Scott was forced to build it.

George William Frederick Charles, 2nd
Duke of Cambridge, cousin of the Queen
and Commander-in-Chief of her Army.

Edward Cardwell, who by defeating
the Duke in a battle of ideas modernised
the Army.

A Ragged School in Smithfield, London: at the sharp end
of the civilising process.

Matthew Arnold, in pursuit of
perfection.

William Edward Forster, father of universal
education.

Caroline Norton, campaigner
for divorce.

Millicent Garrett Fawcett, pursuing
women's equality.

The ladies of Newnham shortly after its foundation, in
the era of Mrs Sidgwick and Miss Clough.

William Booth, shining a light
in darkest England.

Thomas Holloway and his wife,
in the courtyard of his College.

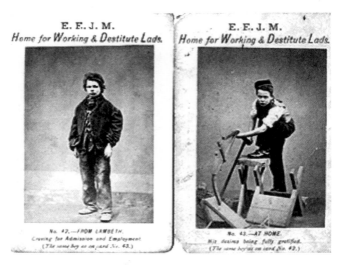

A 'before and after' of a Barnardo's boy, dressed
down for the occasion and depicting the Doctor's
difficult relationship with the truth.

Octavia Hill, who taught the poor
to live respectably.

Angela Burdett-Coutts, Queen of the
Costermongers and much else besides.

One of George Peabody's estates in Blackfriars Road, London,
showing the success of private charity.

Sir George Gilbert Scott, who built not least his own titanic ego.

George Edmund Street, who eventually built the Law Courts.

Scott's masterpiece, the Midland Hotel at St Pancras, London, saved from the wrecking-ball and now a great enduring symbol of Victorian achievement.

just in Britain: she gave money for humanitarian causes and education all over the world, notably in Africa, where (as in other parts of the Empire) she funded missionary work. She endowed bishoprics in South Africa, Australia and Canada for the benefit of emigrants from England, whose new life she hoped would be a Christian one. She also helped pay for those who wished to work, but could find none, to emigrate: the export of surplus labour was one of Victorian Britain's leading commercial activities. She was concerned about children going hungry, and thereby rendering themselves unfit for work: so she founded the Destitute Children's Dinner Society in 1866. She built drinking fountains for dogs, and for people: one, in Victoria Park in Hackney, by her favourite architect H. A. Darbishire, is spectacular, if ridiculously ostentatious. She helped Shaftesbury's Ragged School Union. She paid for hundreds of destitute boys to join Royal and Merchant Navy training ships. She funded the Temperance Society. She also set up the first residential home for art students, in Brunswick Square, in 1879: she was a great patron of struggling artists.

Like her friend Gladstone she was concerned by the descent of women into prostitution, and affected by their ubiquity even in the salubrious part of Piccadilly where she lived. This is where her friendship with Dickens would bear the most philanthropic fruit. In 1847 she put up the money for a hostel for women who wished to escape from vice, called Urania Cottage, at Shepherd's Bush in west London. Her main collaborator was Dickens, who had become her principal adviser in philanthropic matters, diverting more of her largesse away from the Church and its educational work. Dickens had had the idea of saving fallen women, and had written Burdett-Coutts a fourteen-page letter outlining the plan for a 'home' for them, a halfway-house to their full rehabilitation. He was keen to take a strong hand in running it himself. He told her: 'I need not say that I should enter on such a task with my whole heart and soul.'[8] Through two friends who were governors of London prisons – Coldbath Fields and the Middlesex House of Correction in Tothill Fields – he had met some likely candidates for admission, and his urge to help these women drove him to press her to fund the scheme.

Burdett-Coutts had met Dickens at around the time of her inheritance: he had been much admired in the Burdett household, one where *Oliver Twist*, with its philippic against the Poor Law, had had the effect the author desired. In 1839 and 1840 she had frequently asked him to dine with her, and he had frequently refused; he was not especially enchanted by high society. However, he soon warmed to her, so much so that when in May 1841 he decided to kill off Little Nell, she was one of only half a dozen friends alerted before that number of *The Old Curiosity Shop* was published.[9]

By 1843 Dickens and Burdett-Coutts had become exceptionally close. She paid for his son Charley to go to Eton, and it illustrates the dynamic of her relationship with the great author that his wishes for the boy to go to Harrow were overridden by his benefactress. Dickens had been attracted by the Ragged School movement, and mentioned to John Forster that his wealthy friend would be amenable to helping fund such institutions. He had sent her 'a sledge-hammer account of the Ragged Schools', having seen her name high on the list of subscribers to the clergy education fund.[10] He 'took pains to show her that religious mysteries and difficult creeds wouldn't do for such pupils. I told her, too, that it was of immense importance they should be *washed*.' Dickens used his literary skills to outline what he saw on his visits to these schools, where he found masters struggling to make any impact on their charges, and the charges almost beyond help. Burdett-Coutts's first contribution, to a school Dickens told her was roughly in the area of Fagin's den, was to provide public baths and a larger schoolroom. Dickens had had no doubt she would supply whatever he had asked her for, and she did not disappoint. 'She is a most excellent creature, I protest to God, and I have a most perfect affection and respect for her.' Dickens marked the next stage in their relationship by dedicating *Martin Chuzzlewit* to her.

For the moment, their main project would be Urania. Existing refuges for prostitutes came in two forms: they were places of temporary respite that gave women basic board and lodging before putting them back on the streets; or they were nunneries. This would be different. Women would be taught basic skills, such as knitting and sewing, that would help them resist returning to prostitution. They would have some elementary schooling. They would be given a plot of garden to tend – Shepherd's Bush, where Dickens located the ideal house, was still rural. They shared the household chores. They would make soup for distribution to the poor, to make them understand the benefits of service to others. There were prayers morning and night, and church on Sundays. They could either seek work in London, or be equipped to start a new life in one of the colonies. Once the house was secured, on a lease for £60 a year, and with stables that could be converted into a wash house, Dickens romantically imagined the inmates sitting in the garden, singing or tending flowers.

He would later describe the home's purpose as 'replacing young women who had lapsed into guilt in a situation of hope and secondly to save young women who are in danger of falling into like condition.'[11] He had told the benefactress, in his proposal on 26 May 1846: 'I would put it in the power of any Governor of a London Prison to send an unhappy creature of this kind (by her own choice, of course) straight from his prison, when her term expired, to the Asylum. I would put it in the power of any penitent creature to knock at the door, and say For God's sake, take me in.'[12] He envisaged a two-stage process, first of probation, then of entering into 'the Society of the house'.[13]

During the probationary stage, a girl would be told she was there for repentance and reform; and that for all the harm she had done, the most destructive effect had been on herself. She might be degraded and fallen, but was not lost. She would be told that 'the means of Return to Happiness are now about to be put into her own hands, and trusted to her own keeping.'[14] Rather than her being kept on probation for a fixed time, there would be a marks system, and when she had earned sufficient marks by good conduct she could become a full member of the home. Marks could be deducted for bad behaviour – 'ill-temper, disrespect, bad language, any outbreak of any sort or kind'. The object was to prove a woman could be responsible for herself, and could understand that her progress (or lack of it) was entirely within her control. What Dickens admired about this system was that it was a 'preparation . . . for the right performance of duty outside, and for the formation of habits of firmness and self-restraint.'[15]

Dickens said he understood the regime must be 'grounded in religion, most unquestionably'.[16] Yet this must be complemented by a system of training, 'which, while it is steady and firm, is cheerful and hopeful. Order, punctuality, cleanliness, the whole routine of household duties— as washing, mending, cooking—the establishment itself would supply the means of teaching practically, to every one. But then I would have it understood by all—I would have it written up in every room—that they were not going through a monotonous round of occupation and self-denial which began and ended there, but which began, or was resumed, under that roof, and would end, by God's blessing, in happy homes of their own.'

He told Burdett-Coutts:

Such gentlemen as Mr. Chesterton of the Middlesex House of Correction, and Lieutenant Tracey of Cold Bath Fields, Bridewell, (both of whom I know very well) are well acquainted with the good that is in the bottom of the hearts, of many of these poor creatures, and with the whole history of their past lives; and frequently have deplored to me the not having any such place as the proposed establishment, to which to send them—when they are set free from Prison. It is necessary to observe that very many of these unfortunate women are constantly in and out of the Prisons, for no other fault or crime than their original one of having fallen from virtue. Policemen can take them up, almost when they choose, for being of that class, and being in the streets; and the Magistrates commit them to Jail for short terms. When they come out, they can but return to their old occupation, and so come in again . . . Very many of them are good, excellent, steady characters when under restraint—even without the advantage of systematic training, which they would have in this Institution—and are tender nurses to the sick, and are as kind and gentle as the best of women.[17]

Dickens knew exactly how to play Burdett-Coutts, by emphasising the virtuous qualities of women presumed singularly lacking in virtue. He argued that women who absconded should be allowed readmission, subject to the managers of the home feeling they were still capable of reforming, and would not prove a corrupting influence on other inmates. Moral exhortation would be an important part of the regime, and the act of philanthropy would be represented as having consequences for more than just the immediate recipient: 'I would have it impressed upon them, from day to day, that the success of the experiment rested with them, and that on their conduct depended the rescue and salvation, of hundreds and thousands of women yet unborn. In what proportion this experiment would be successful, it is very difficult to predict; but I think that if the Establishment were founded on a well-considered system, and were well managed, one half of the Inmates would be reclaimed from the very beginning, and that after a time the proportion would be very much larger. I believe this estimate to be within very reasonable bounds.' In that, he would be justified.[18]

Burdett-Coutts chose an appropriate chaplain and devised religious instruction for the women. Dickens, having found the house, also found the matron, a Mrs Holdsworth. He found the first inmates in the Middlesex House of Correction. He had read them a mission statement, in which he said that 'there is a lady in this town who from the window of her house has seen such as you going past at night, and has felt her heart bleed at the sight . . . the thought of such fallen women has troubled her in her bed.'[19] Later, he would find girls at Ragged Schools, resident in workhouses, who were suitable candidates. Burdett-Coutts paid around £720 a year for all the outgoings connected with the home, including the costs of emigration for those who stayed the course.[20] Some girls, such was their ignorance, were appalled by the prospect of emigration, which they thought was the same as transportation. 'It is astonishing', Dickens told Burdett-Coutts, 'and horrible to find how little education (worthy of the name in any respect) there has been among the common people.'[21]

Dickens visited the house almost daily during the autumn of 1847, in preparation for its opening. As well as overseeing the alterations to the house he bought, wholesale from a shop in the Tottenham Court Road, the women's uniform dresses, which were 'very neat and modest', and the linen. He also found a piano. He regarded music as part of the civilising process, and an adjunct to the religious life in the home. 'I think it extremely important that the assistant should at least be able to play simple tunes on the Piano; and I am looking about, high and low, for a cheap second-hand one, to stand in Mrs. Holdsworth's room. The fondness for music among these people generally, is most remarkable; and I can imagine nothing more likely to impress or soften a new comer, than finding them with this art among them, and hearing them sing their Evening Hymn before they go to bed.'[22]

His only worry was that Burdett-Coutts's religious aspirations for the home would alienate the inmates. He feared the average cleric would not know where to start with the average prostitute: a problem exemplified by Butler in *The Way of All Flesh*, when Ernest Pontifex comes unstuck with such a woman. However, a chaplain was found who was to everyone's taste. Dickens told Burdett-Coutts:

In proportion as the details of any one of these young lives would be strange and difficult to a good man who had kept away from such knowledge, so the best man in the world could never make his way to the truth of these people, unless he were content to win it very slowly, and with the nicest perception, always present to him, of the results engendered in them by what they have gone through. Wrongly addressed, they are certain to deceive. The greatest anxiety I feel, in connexion with this scheme—it is a greater one than any that arises out of my sense of responsibility to you, though that is not slight—is, that the clergyman with whom I hope I am to act as one confiding in him and perfectly confided in, should be not only a well-intentioned man, as I believe most clergymen would be, but one of the kindest, most considerate, most judicious, and least exacting of his order.[23]

Religion was to cause an immediate problem, but not in the way Dickens had feared. The deputy matron, a Mrs Fisher, of whom he thought highly, was dismissed by Burdett-Coutts for being a dissenter. It was not on that account that she was sacked, but because she had not admitted the fact to Dickens when he interviewed her. He strongly disagreed with her dismissal. The women, at least, were mostly happy: one cried with joy when she saw her bed.[24] Having put up the money, Burdett-Coutts kept at arm's length, visiting from time to time and occasionally attending the monthly meetings of the committee she and Dickens had appointed to oversee it. The day-to-day superintendence fell to Dickens, to whom the matron went when a problem with either the house or the women had to be addressed, and it became his main charitable work for the next decade. There were ups and downs. It was hard to find a matron who took what Dickens and Burdett-Coutts regarded as the right approach to their charges, though it did not help matters that the two principals could not always agree on the purpose of what they were doing. Dickens, who understood the minds of lower-class women better than the benefactress, thought the best aim would be for them to marry. Burdett-Coutts saw no reason why they could not be saved and remain unmarried, apparently disturbed by the prospect that they might seek a husband.

Dickens told Burdett-Coutts on 3 November 1847, as the home opened, 'that their past lives should never be referred to, at the Home, there can be no doubt. I should say that any such reference on the part of the

Superintendent would be an instance of blind mistake that in itself would render her dismissal necessary.'[25] The past was no longer relevant: all Dickens cared about was that the girls and those looking after them should concentrate upon capitalising on the fresh start. Dickens remained a firm believer in exhortation:

> In their living room I have put up two little inscriptions selected from the sermons of Jeremy Taylor and Barrow—both very simple and beautiful in themselves, and remarkably appropriate (as I hope you will think) to the purpose. Also a little inscription of my own, referring to the advantages of order, punctuality, and good temper; and another setting forth the Saviour's exposition of our duty towards God, and our duty towards our neighbour. In each bedroom is another Inscription, admonishing them against ever lying down to rest, without being affectionate and reconciled among themselves. And I am now writing a little address which Mrs Holdsworth shall read to each, alone, when she comes in.[26]

Not all the girls conformed. One, Jemima Hiscock, broke into the beer cellar with knives 'and drank until she was dead drunk', Dickens reported to Burdett-Coutts on 17 April 1850.[27] At that point, 'she used the most horrible language and made a very repulsive exhibition of herself'. She tempted another woman to drink with her. Hiscock was to be expelled: her accomplice kept in disgrace until Dickens had a chance to enquire into the matter. Hiscock was so drunk that Dickens doubted the beer alone could have done it; he suspected she had smuggled spirits in from outside. Two women absconded with the linen, adding insult to injury by taking it after it had been washed and ironed.

Another, Sesina Bollard – herself sounding like a character from a Dickens novel – was so amoral that, in his view, she would 'corrupt a nunnery in a fortnight'.[28] The women expelled from the home often went back to prostitution, to prison and, in some cases, to an early death. One expelled in 1850, Hannah Myers, committed a felony almost immediately, and was back in the Middlesex House of Correction for a year. Two other girls, both aged seventeen, robbed the matron of goods to the value of £7 10s, but gave themselves up: they were sent to jail for six months, having pleaded guilty. However, the redemption of other women offset these failures. Many were launched on new lives in the colonies, where the support networks in the dioceses founded by

Burdett-Coutts in Adelaide or Cape Town ensured they stayed on the straight and narrow. Her emigration project had ramifications beyond the home: Mrs Gaskell, through her association with Dickens, managed to place a fallen girl from Manchester in Cape Town in 1850. However, colonial society was in some respects more moralistic and unforgiving than British. 'Let me caution you about the Cape,' Dickens told Mrs Gaskell, with a view to the intelligence being passed on to the girl. 'She must be profoundly silent there, as to her past history, and so must those who take her out. Miss Coutts and I are just now in the receipt of reliable intelligence from that quarter (we have sent three girls there) which assures me that this caution is imperative, or she will either be miserable or flung back into the gulf whence you have raised her.'[29]

The rehabilitative process, based on compassion and strict discipline, seemed to work: later, other such homes and refuges would emulate it. Dickens told Burdett-Coutts, in 1851, 'imagining backward to what these women were and might have been, and forward to what their children may be, it is impossible to estimate the amount of good you are doing.'[30] All went well until 1858, when Dickens's marriage broke down because of his affair with Ellen Ternan, an actress. In the scandal that followed he felt able no longer to take a role at the home; whether because he felt compromised by the exposure of his own sexual morality, or because he did not wish to bring shame on Burdett-Coutts among the few who knew her role in the enterprise, is a matter for conjecture. It soon became apparent how much Dickens had been the power behind the home: not just in terms of his administrative work and superintendence, but also as a procurer of inmates. By 1862, without him, the home was no more.

Dickens began to perform a role for Burdett-Coutts that echoed what Arthur Hugh Clough was doing for Nightingale. From time to time, with his other responsibilities – his novel-writing, his journalism, and his editorship of Household Words and, later, All the Year Round, he became exhausted by it, as Clough did. He acted as the conduit through which any private appeal went to Burdett-Coutts; he undertook administration for her; and he made suggestions about where her resources might be targeted next. Dickens was at heart a journalist: and his journalistic instincts told him that what Burdett-Coutts was doing was a good story, and ought to be more widely known. She, though, disliked publicity: she did not engage in philanthropy for commercial reasons, or to enhance her reputation or position. Eventually, Dickens persuaded her to allow him to write about Urania in *Household Words*, but only on the express condition that he concealed the identity of the benefactress.

The article, published in 1853, did, however, reveal the relative success of the undertaking: of fifty-six women who had been through the home since 1847, thirty were deemed to have graduated with honours. They had included 'starving women, poor needlewomen who had robbed . . . violent girls imprisoned for committing disturbances in ill-conducted workhouses, poor girls from Ragged Schools, destitute girls who have applied at Police offices for relief, young women from the streets – young women of the same class taken from the prisons after undergoing punishment there as disorderly characters, or for shoplifting, or for thefts from the person: domestic servants who have been seduced, and two young women held to bail for attempting suicide.'[31]

The Urania project had introduced Burdett-Coutts to the realities of poverty, 'the poor' having been an abstract concept to her until then. It prompted her to want to do more to treat the causes of the disease rather than just its symptoms. Dickens encouraged her to become a shareholder in the Metropolitan Association for Improving the Dwellings of the Industrious Classes, where she and others invested in new housing for the deserving poor. Its purpose was to 'provide the labouring man with an increase of the comforts and conveniences of life, with full compensation to the capitalist': a definitive Victorian project.[32] It had completed its first apartment block, for 110 families, in Old St Pancras Road in London in December 1847. The block was regarded as a huge advance in sanitary living. Dickens endorsed the society as 'sensible and really useful', feeling it a cut above Shaftesbury's evangelical Society for Improving the Condition of the Labouring Classes, with which it appeared to be in unofficial competition.

Burdett-Coutts wanted to do more, however, and chose to concentrate on one of the most sordid areas of London's East End, Bethnal Green. Again, Dickens was the influence: Bethnal Green was where Nancy, the prostitute in *Oliver Twist*, had lived. Burdett-Coutts had already put up money for church schools in Stepney, in 1856, in an area described by *The Times* as 'in the centre of the wretched district of St Peter's, Stepney, one of the vilest in the vicinity, and in a hot bed of vice where they are greatly needed.'[33] She wanted to build model dwellings there. Dickens suggested that before she did she should visit some already built to get an idea of what worked, and what was required. Dickens reconnoitred such places for her, and introduced her to his brother-in-law, Henry Austin, an architect and sanitary engineer, who became an adviser. Darbishire was soon engaged as the architect: he would later work for George Peabody, the housing philanthropist.

Dickens argued for mansion blocks rather than streets of conventional housing, to try to contain the sprawl of London. He said it would be easier to provide services such as water, gas and drainage. Columbia Square, as the development was called, was opened in 1862. It was built on the site of one of the worst slums in London. It had also been the setting, in the 1830s, for some of the most notorious body-snatching, so was a place of more than average infamy. Each of the development's four blocks contained forty-five flats, mostly two-room family sets: even in these comparatively luxurious dwellings, whole families would have to sleep together in one room and live together in the other, the bedroom being merely 12 by 8 feet. They were, at least, light and well ventilated, warm and free from damp. Each block had its own laundry with a massive spin-dryer, and rubbish chutes were on every floor. At Burdett-Coutts's insistence, each block had its own reading room. Her example was followed elsewhere in the metropolis, notably by the Corporation of London, which set aside land in Clerkenwell and £120,000 for apartment buildings for the working classes. It was when he saw what she had done the American philanthropist George Peabody, who had set up a business in London and had become enraptured by his new homeland, ordered similar buildings for Spitalfields and Islington.

Later in the 1860s, and to encourage a commercial life among the tenants of Columbia Square, she funded and built the Columbia Road market, an astonishingly fine High Victorian building by Darbishire where local traders could sell their wares and local people could more easily buy fresh and healthy food at reasonable prices, and especially have access to fresh milk, when the poor were vulnerable to adulterated and in some cases toxic food. She had also been concerned about the hygiene implications of refuse from barrows left to rot in the streets, and believed a market building would be easier to keep clean. However, when costermongers were harried by the authorities over their street-trading, she paid for her own solicitor to represent them and secure their right to earn a living: she became known as Queen of the Costermongers. Her love of animals made her acutely aware, too, of the importance to traders of animals. She had stables built near Columbia

Square, and put up drinking troughs there and in other towns around England to water the beasts.

However, the building, a masterpiece demolished after the Second World War, was impossibly grand and impracticable. No swearing was allowed in it, which challenged the habits of a lifetime; nor could it open on a Sunday, a traditional trading day, not least because of the number of Jews in the area. The traders preferred to revert to street barrows and forsake the great Gothic hall: this happened within six months of its opening by the Prince of Wales in April 1869. Burdett-Coutts hatched a new plan: she would have the hall used to trade fish, to break the monopoly of Billingsgate and to provide a source of cheap fish for the locals. This, too, came to nothing, not least because of the restrictive practices of Billingsgate. She gave the building to the City of London, but they could do nothing with it, and returned it to her after a couple of years. She tried various other schemes over the next decade – a meat market, then another attempt to sell fish – but neither succeeded. Eventually, she had it turned into a tobacco factory to provide jobs for local women.

In another declining part of the East End, Spitalfields, she set up a sewing school for women put out of work when the local silk industry contracted, establishing the notion of re-skilling but also, she hoped, deterring them from prostitution. She funded night schools at which working people could acquire new skills or develop existing ones. The schools became centres for the distribution of clothes, food and medical supplies to the destitute, and coordinated nurses to visit those seriously ill at home. She hired an accountant, John Sapsford, as bursar for her relief work in the East End, with a budget that began at £6,000 a year but that rose, in the cholera epidemic of 1867, to £20,000, because of the food parcels sent to the families of the sick, and the nursing staff and sanitary workers deployed at her expense.

Her market building drew attention to all she was doing, and had done for some years, in the East End and elsewhere. Gladstone sent a note to Granville, the Leader of the House of Lords, on 4 May 1871 noting that Burdett-Coutts 'has handed over in trust to the Corporation of London, Columbia Market, which will save expenditure on Billingsgate. Is there any way in which the remarkable services of Miss BC to the public cd be acknd?'[34] Granville agreed there was and, given her three decades of generosity and service to the poor, a peerage would be in order. Gladstone agreed. Although peerages awarded to women were not unprecedented, they were highly unusual, and a woman peer could not sit in the Lords.[35] Burdett-Coutts was touched by the offer, but took days to consider it before a correspondence ensued with Gladstone about her title. Her companion, Mrs Brown, urged her to accept. To the public, however, she acquired another title, and a new realm to add to that of the costermongers: she became known as 'Queen of the Poor'.[36]

She stimulated cancer research by helping fund the Brompton Hospital. She gave an interest-free loan to its founder, William Marsden, so he could build the hospital that now, as the Royal Marsden, bears his name. She laid its foundation stone in 1859 and continued to subscribe £50 a year. Hospital funding was especially precarious, with the sick poor nursed almost entirely at home. Hospitals were treated as businesses rather than charities, which reduced their income because of taxation – something about which Shaftesbury complained bitterly to Gladstone in 1863. He urged on 2 May that year 'the necessity, nay the duty, of withdrawing your proposed tax on the incomes of hospitals for the relief of the sick poor. You will inflict an amount of suffering on the labouring classes that it is fearful to contemplate.'[37] He was worried that, if the proposal went ahead, there would not be sufficient money to pay doctors. His appeal succeeded.

Burdett-Coutts was particularly keen to advance scientific education, and in 1861 endowed scholarships at Oxford in geology and natural science, also donating to the university a rare collection of fossils from Devon. She recognised the importance of vocational education, to equip the working classes with the skills to earn a living and improve themselves. She founded the Westminster Technical College, her greatest success in this respect. Burdett-Coutts also funded a brigade of 'shoe-black boys', uniformed youths who went about London to polish the shoes of gentlemen as they passed. Critics argued that all this did was put out of work boys who had blacked shoes for years, but had had no one to set them up in the business. For the destitute and unemployed she set up soup kitchens; but she also encouraged enterprise among the lower orders. She extended her protection to flower-girls, who were often accosted by men who treated them as prostitutes, providing the money and support to organise them into a brigade like the shoeblacks. Not all her domestic philanthropy was centred upon the metropolis: she also funded a programme of 'ambulatory schoolmasters' in rural Devon

– she wintered in Torquay – to try to raise the standards of the dame schools by having a salaried visiting schoolmaster take them under his wing.[38] Later, she would repeat the process in rural Scotland.

When she died in 1906, aged ninety-two, it was estimated that she had given away between £3 and £4 million. The amount had decreased since her marriage, because of her reduction in income through marrying a foreigner. She never sought recognition, but for the last half-century of her life the public, and especially that section of it that benefited directly from her largesse, paid her tribute and displayed their gratitude. During one of the marches of December 1866 en route to one of the great reform demonstrations, those walking under her window in Piccadilly cheered her for two hours, aware that some in the privileged classes had their interests at heart.

IV

Those with high ideals have an unusual power to shock when they compromise their standards. Gladstone's keen interest in pornography had such an effect, and Dickens was no exception either, falling prey to the sexual hypocrisy that so blighted the age, and leaving his private life at odds with his public persona. His marriage, which had produced ten children, had been in trouble since the early 1850s. In a very frank passage in his biography – he was writing before Froude had revolutionised the genre in his life of Carlyle – Forster observed that by the mid-1850s 'the satisfactions which home should have supplied, and which indeed were essential requirements of his nature, he had failed to find at home.'[39] He had indeed written to Forster to obtain 'the relief of saying a word of what has long been pent up in my mind. Poor Catherine and I are not made for each other, and there is no help for it. It is not only that she makes me uneasy and unhappy, but that I make her so too – and much more so . . . God knows she would have been a thousand times happier if she had married another kind of man, and that her avoidance of this destiny would have been at least equally good for us both. I am often cut to the heart by thinking what a pity it is, for her own sake, that I ever fell in her way.'[40]

What Forster does not mention was that Dickens consoled himself, from 1857, with a nineteen-year-old actress, Ellen Ternan, twenty-six years his junior, and known as Nelly. In 1858 he sought a legal separation from his wife, publishing a statement in *The Times* and in *Household Words* to the effect that rumours about his dalliance with another woman (rumours, it is thought, put around by members of Catherine's family) were untrue. There was nothing amicable about this separation. A letter to a friend hinting that Catherine was mentally unstable ended up in the public prints. Burdett-Coutts sought to act as an honest broker, only for Dickens to tell her that Catherine was causing him 'unspeakable agony of mind' and that he wanted no more to do with her. From that moment on she was the enemy. Until his death twelve years later he sent her only three short letters, all in reply to enquiries from her.

From then on Dickens lived in a decidedly odd ménage. His house at Gad's Hill near Rochester – which, in Smilesian fashion, he had bought decades after admiring it as a small boy, having made something of himself – was run not just by one of his daughters (which was usual for the times) but also by his sister-in-law Georgina Hogarth, sister of his much-maligned wife (which was not). Most of his numerous surviving children took the view that their father, once their mother had gone, could not have cared less about them, and had them out of the family home as early as possible. Meanwhile Dickens bought Nelly a house in north London, where she lived in some style with her mother and two sisters. Just as we know no exact details of the Carlyle marriage, we do not know whether Nelly Ternan was Dickens's mistress or an adopted favourite daughter. Given Dickens's interest in procreation, it may be safer to assume the former.

These upheavals caused Dickens huge expense. He spent much of the last decade or so of his life giving public readings to earn money. A final reading tour of America and of Britain in the winter of 1870 wore him out. Shortly before his death he had an audience of the Queen, in which he complained about class divisions and expressed the hope that they would decline. He had a stroke while working at Gad's Hill on 8 June 1870 and died the next day. Another version of his demise, that he had an apoplexy while visiting Nelly at Peckham, to where she and her mother had removed, and was brought back in secret in a hackney carriage is discounted as 'wild and improbable . . . but not entirely impossible' by Claire Tomalin, his latest biographer.[41] It is profoundly ironic that a man so much of whose philanthropic energy was devoted to fallen women should have had so much havoc in his own personal life. His final wish, to be buried in a graveyard next to Rochester Castle, was ignored: England's most famous man went where her famous men often go, to Westminster Abbey.

V

Thomas Barnardo was another great man with a darker side to his life. He started work among destitute children in London's East End in the late 1860s. Barnardo developed a refreshingly twentieth-century approach to fund-raising: he faked 'before' and 'after' photographs of rescued children to inspire people to give him money for his work, and for a time lied about his qualifications by describing himself as a 'doctor'. As with Dickens, there was something of a contradiction between public intent and private behaviour. The son of a Dublin furrier of Jewish-Prussian origins, Barnardo was lower middle class and of limited means. He represents the other strand of Victorian philanthropy from that exemplified, and led, by Angela Burdett-Coutts. Having all her outrage about the condition of the poor, but lacking her resources, he gave, instead, his time and energy, both to alleviate misery directly, and to encourage others to fund his work.

Barnardo shared with Burdett-Coutts a deep Christian faith. This motivated his philanthropy and how he did his work. He was born in 1845, and under the influence of his mother and elder brother converted to Protestant evangelicalism at sixteen, joining the Open Plymouth Brethren. He came to London in 1866 and enrolled as a medical student at the London Hospital. He was 5 foot 3 inches tall, but made up in pugnacity what he lacked in stature. As he examined the city around him, he was shocked to find children living on the streets, starving and begging, some maimed after industrial accidents. One in five in London's most insanitary districts was dead before its fifth birthday. His first foray into philanthropy was teaching at a Ragged School in Ernest Street in Stepney, through his link with the Plymouth Brethren, during the cholera epidemic of 1867. He also became a street preacher during the worst of the outbreak, on waste ground in Mile End where William Booth, the founder of the Salvation Army, would also preach. An estimated 3,000 people died in the epidemic, including many breadwinners, leaving their families destitute.

Barnardo fell out with others at Ernest Street, not least because of disputes over the use of funds. It was the first, but not the last, time he would court controversy by sharp practice. Never at ease with the authority of others, he raised money to take over two workman's cottages and set up a Ragged School and mission of his own. The new school was around the corner from the old, and those who ran Ernest Street were angry that Barnardo was distracting attention from, and possibly undermining, their work: it was one of many examples of competitive philanthropy that hustlers of the charity world such as Barnardo would sometimes engage in.

In the winter of 1869–70, an orphan called Jim Jarvis took Barnardo around the East End to show him how many children lived: he saw some sleeping on roofs and in gutters. Jarvis had slept the previous night on straw at the haymarket in Whitechapel. They had the option of the workhouse: but the stigma of pauperisation, and the harsh regime of such institutions, deterred many. His witnessing of extreme poverty was life-changing for Barnardo. Hitherto his main concern had been with children's spiritual welfare: now he saw the urgency of catering for their material and practical welfare too. However, he was shocked when Jarvis told him he believed Jesus was 'the Pope o' Rome'.[42] He began raising money to set up a home for destitute boys. In 1870 he started the first of what would become a national network of such homes on Stepney Causeway. His medical studies went into abeyance.

He went into the slums to look for inmates. The home's reputation soon spread, and it filled up. One evening John Somers, an eleven-year-old boy, was turned away because it was full. He was found dead from malnutrition and exposure two days later, having slept in a sugar barrel. After this, a sign was posted at the door that read: 'No Destitute Boy Ever Refused Admission.'[43] Barnardo was determined to equip his children to earn a living. Soon after establishing the home in Stepney he developed the brigade principle that Burdett-Coutts had started, initially with brigades of City messengers and wood-choppers. He also had his own brigade of shoeblacks. When funds permitted, he set up workshops where boys could learn boot-making, brush-making and carpentry. In time there would be emigration programmes and training ships.

At the end of his first year in his East End Juvenile Mission Barnardo reported that he had room for fifty destitute boys and had up to that point accommodated thirty-three. He had managed to raise (in part from rich evangelicals) the prodigious sum of £2,428 5s 4d, considerably more than the £933 16s 7d cost of the mission: he had also raised £53 2s

6d from lodgers – boys who worked and could afford to pay their way.[44] It was at around this time that Shaftesbury heard of Barnardo, and invited him and leaders of other East End missions to discuss the problems they were dealing with. Shaftesbury's reputation in the evangelical world did Barnardo's appeal for funds no harm.

Barnardo, like Booth, saw alcohol as the principal evil, and proselytised for the temperance movement. He computed that 85 per cent of the boys who turned up were destitute because of the effect of drink on their parents or guardians.[45] A foray into a pub to try to spread the word of the possibility of redemption through abstinence resulted in his being beaten up and having two of his ribs broken. In 1872 he bought a pub and music hall of ill repute in Limehouse, the Edinburgh Castle, having appealed for funds to acquire this 'citadel of Satan' for temperance. He converted it into a mission church and coffee house called the British Working Man's Coffee Palace. The music hall became an evangelical mission. Huge meetings that had hitherto been confined to the summers, when they could be held in tents, could now happen all the year around.

The following year he married Syrie Elmslie, whom he had met when addressing a Ragged School in south-west London: their daughter would marry Somerset Maugham. As a wedding present a wealthy supporter gave them a lease on a large house at Barkingside in Essex. The Barnardos wanted to help orphaned girls as well, and their property made this possible. Barnardo had been horrified by the extent of child prostitution. The Barnardos launched an initial, unsatisfactory, experiment of putting sixty girls in the coach-house of their home. They realised that girls needed a conventional home if they were to flourish. Barnardo's vision – which he said came to him in a dream, but which had been tried on the Continent – was to build a 'village' of cottages for smaller numbers of girls to be housed in each, under the supervision of a 'mother'. And, whereas the boys in Barnardo's care were found work outside the home when not doing schoolwork, the girls acted as their own domestic servants.

He held public meetings in 1874–5 to appeal for money for his cottages. He argued that girls needed to be treated differently, not just to domesticate them, but to give them 'everything which can train them to honour their bodies and keep pure the souls God has given them'.[46] He knew the workhouse failed in this respect: and told a story (which may be a fabrication: Barnardo and the truth were, from time to time,

strangers) that of eighty girls from one workhouse all ended up prostitutes. The line worked, and money came in. Thanks to rich evangelicals, Barnardo built thirty cottages, eventually accommodating 1,500
destitute girls in a small village. Lord Aberdeen, another of Barnardo's
aristocratic supporters, laid the foundation stones of the first nine
cottages in June 1875.

The first cottage at the 'Village Homes for Orphan, Neglected and
Destitute Girls' was given in memory of a dead child, as were several
subsequent ones: Lord Cairns, the Lord Chancellor, opened the first
fourteen on 19 July 1876. The slogan was now 'No Destitute Child Ever
Refused Admittance'. *The Times*'s report stated that Barnardo had spent
£4,000 to £5,000 transforming the 'singing saloon known as the Edinburgh
Castle' into a place of worship; and 'upwards of 120 street Arabs are
sheltered from evil influences and brought under the power of Christian
teaching and example' in Stepney.[47] The purpose of the new village,
under Mrs Barnardo's supervision, was to take girls with 'evil associations' and produce 'a band of kitchenmaids, dairymaids, parlourmaids,
housemaids, laundrymaids and cooks, to meet the demand everywhere
existing for cleanly and instructed female servants.' A report of how this
would be achieved was read out during the opening ceremony. 'In a tent
the band of the East-end Juvenile Mission played a succession of joyous
tunes,' *The Times* wrote. 'Lady Cairns declared the laundry open by
setting the machinery in motion.'

When Barnardo set up his homes, he also laid out the principle on
which they would be run. He would take in children without having
them subject to any form of discrimination: by his definition, any child
was part of the deserving poor.

> Before proceeding to detail, it may be well to set in the forefront
> the Religious Principles upon which the Homes are conducted.
> The Homes have from the beginning been conducted on defin-
> itely religious lines. They are Christian institutions, carried on in
> the spirit of the Gospel. They are, of course, Protestant, but no
> creed or party can claim their work exclusively for its own. Every
> candidate, or his or her responsible guardian, is plainly informed,
> at the time of application, that these are Protestant Homes, and
> that no other religious instruction is afforded than such as is in
> accordance with the teaching of the Word of God. As of yore, I
> could not allow any question of sect or creed to close my doors

in the face of a really destitute and homeless child, and admission
is in no single instance with a view to proselytism.

The Homes are conducted on the broadest Christian basis
consistent with loyalty to the truths of the Gospel. They are inter-
denominational Homes in the following very important senses:

1. They receive children of all creeds or of none, without any regard
   to denomination.
2. They are supported by sympathizers in all sections of the Church
   of Christ, irrespective of sect.
3. They are carried on and practically managed by workers who,
   like the subscribers, belong to almost every section of that Church
   Universal, which is made up of all those who love our Lord Jesus
   Christ in sincerity.
4. An earnest endeavour is, therefore, made to bring up each child
   in the Church to which its parents nominally belonged. I am
   bound to add that the chief aim of all associated with me (irrespective of Churches or denominations) is to bring these children
   up, experimentally, in the fear of the Lord, and to draw them in
   faith and love to the feet of our Saviour Christ.[48]

However, he began to attract the envy of less energetic and charis-
matic philanthropists. He dressed up some children in the filthiest rags
better to accentuate the beneficial effects of his work, and raised funds
by selling the notorious 'before' and 'after' photographs. He was accused
of using funds for his own ends, and calling himself 'Dr Barnardo' when
he had no medical qualification. In what became a full-dress attempt to
discredit him, there were also rumours he had had a carnal relationship
with his landlady while a medical student. Some of the rumours about
his private life and his financial integrity seem to have been propagated
by his fellow evangelical Frederick Charrington, of the brewing dynasty,
who resented Barnardo's intrusion on his turf in Mile End. Charrington,
ashamed of how his family had prospered, ran a mission in Tower
Hamlets whose attendance had been depleted after the conversion of
the Edinburgh Castle. The family brewery was in the Mile End Road,
and its proximity to Barnardo's area of operations was more of an affront
than Charrington could take.

The last straw for Charrington was when Barnardo promised to open
a coffee palace, called the Dublin Castle, in the Mile End Road.

Charrington asked Barnado not to; but Barnardo, who seems to have veered between divine inspiration and megalomania, refused to comply, and published a pamphlet defending his right to do so. Charrington took this as a declaration of war. The Charity Organisation Society – whose work is detailed later – secretly helped another of Barnardo's detractors, George Reynolds, a Baptist minister, to publish in 1875 a pamphlet attacking him, entitled *Dr Barnardo's Homes: Startling Revelations*. Reynolds was in league with Charrington. With the matter brought to public attention, the COS could investigate him formally. In 1875, thanks not least to his showmanship, Barnardo raised £23,000. He did so without having trustees, or a treasurer: only he scrutinised how his money was spent. Even if he was entirely honest, the practice was highly irregular. The COS blacklisted Barnardo, which prompted him to slap a writ on Reynolds, whom he unwisely attacked. Even more unwisely, Barnardo produced a document that claimed he had qualified as a doctor at the University of Geissen, which was proved a forgery.

The two sides slugged it out in the press. One newspaper published letters under the pseudonym of a clergyman who claimed to have known Barnardo since childhood, and who would vouch for what a fine fellow he was. Unfortunately, these testimonials – which as well as defending Barnardo's honour also savaged his opponents – were written by Barnardo himself. Even he realised he had gone too far, and compounded the absurdity of his deceit by writing to the newspaper and condemning what he had already, pseudonymously, written.

The way Barnardo ran his charity did not stand up to scrutiny. He recognised this – helped by some supporters, who had conveyed their disenchantment – and the charity was given a new management structure. Barnardo stayed, no longer as proprietor but as director, employed by and answerable to the trustees. The various properties, such as the Edinburgh Castle and the house at Barkingside – from which the Barnardos had moved because of the cost of its upkeep and its distance from Stepney – were put into trust. This should have restored confidence, but donations fell. Barnardo saw he had to play straight if his project were to survive, and (having from around the time of his marriage instructed others to call him 'Dr Barnardo'), went up to Edinburgh to complete his medical education, which he did in four months, qualifying in 1876.

The allegation of improper use of funds was among a number tested at a formal arbitration in 1877, the trustees having ordered Barnardo to withdraw his writ against Reynolds, and having succeeded in persuading Reynolds to accept the arbitration process. Barnardo was also accused of mistreating children and dressing them up to look better cared for than they really were when visitors came. Perhaps most damaging, it was alleged there was inadequate religious instruction in the homes. Lord Cairns organised a defence fund for Barnardo. The COS bankrolled Reynolds, its director, C. S. Loch, having developed a complete lack of confidence in the newly qualified doctor. It also used its resources to investigate Barnardo further, in the hope of finding more dirt to be used against him.

The arbitration seemed to be going Barnardo's way when Charrington admitted having paid for the pamphlets Reynolds had circulated against Barnardo. However, it ended unsatisfactorily because Reynolds withdrew from the process, and because Barnardo refused to admit he had written the pseudonymous attacks on Reynolds in 1875, in his retaliation for the pamphlets. Also, Shaftesbury came out on the side of Charrington (he was president of Charrington's mission in Tower Hamlets) and against Barnardo, which stung him.

The arbitration lasted thirty-eight days. Barnardo's accusers occupied the first twenty, and his own evidence took eighteen. 'This unjustifiable conduct of Dr Barnardo,' said the official report, referring to his refusal to answer questions about his authorship of the attacks on Reynolds, 'and this withdrawal at the latest hour by Mr Reynolds in the face of the Arbitrators' remonstrance, deprived them of the full effect that would have been produced on Dr Barnardo's evidence by its being subjected to cross-examination.'[49] However, Barnardo was cleared of any wrongdoing. Some of the accusations were so extreme that they were easily dismissed. There was no proof, the arbitrators said, that a room in which bad boys were locked 'swarmed with rats' or that 'the boys were nailed up as in a living tomb.' The evidence that boys were dressed up especially was dismissed as 'of the most shadowy kind'. And as for the claim of no proper religious teaching, the court found 'a prominent place given to the moral and religious instruction, while evil habits and bad language and lying are guarded against and corrected.' An additional allegation, that children were riddled with disease because of the appalling diet Barnardo inflicted on them, was described as 'wholly without foundation in fact'.

The court condemned Barnardo, however, for the forged pictures, calling the practice 'morally wrong' and capable of growing 'into a system of deception dangerous to the cause on behalf of which it is practised.' He accepted the impropriety of the pictures, and stopped making and selling them. The arbitrators described his boys' home in Stepney and girls' village at Barkingside as 'real and valuable charities, and worthy of public confidence and support.' That was the finding that mattered.

The COS, however, continued to attempt to discredit him, Loch regarding Barnardo as a charlatan who had had a lucky escape. This was despite the arbitrators having urged both sides to stop their 'defamatory charges' and to adhere to 'the standards of conduct recognised among gentlemen and to the dictates of Christian charity whose obligations are pre-eminently binding upon men professing to take a lead in religious and philanthropic work.' The COS started to attract hostile comment for its vendetta against Barnardo. Questions were asked about its use of scarce resources to this end. However, the publicity it generated made Barnardo's name widely known, yet at a price. He ended the arbitration in serious debt, no longer master in his own house, and the charity poorer than might otherwise have been the case.

The rebuilding of Barnardo's reputation took years. The charity was often in debt because of its all-embracing policy, and Barnardo does seem to have confused his own private means with those of the charity, though not with intent to defraud. He was well served by an intemperate performance by Reynolds in the witness box. The scandal led to Barnardo's leaving the Plymouth Brethren, which caused him grave distress. As well as being dogged by an element of public suspicion he was also, from his early thirties onwards, plagued by ill health, and a sufferer from both mental and physical exhaustion. To cap it all his private investments were disastrous, and he was forced to ask the trustees to pay him a salary in 1883, which they unhesitatingly agreed to do.

Cairns took over the running of the board of trustees. This was a recommendation of the arbitrators, as was ending the practice of solitary confinement as a punishment, and having the homes inspected by government inspectors. Cairns, who was still Lord Chancellor, was a man of the highest probity, and his own reputation lent lustre and credibility to the charity. Without his name it might have collapsed by the late 1870s. As it was, by the late 1880s it had awesome debts of

£200,000, thanks to a national expansion, and it was well into the twentieth century before the finances were regularised: by which time the homes were under royal patronage. Fortunately, the banks did not call in their mortgages.

By his death in 1905 Barnardo had established ninety-six homes all over the country. He had also established boys' and girls' clubs in industrial areas that young people working in factories could attend for wholesome activities, and to receive a moral education of varying degrees of subtlety. It took a memorial fund and several more years after Barnardo's death before the charity was thriving; by which stage the children he had helped could be counted in the tens of thousands, many of whom were established in respectable and self-sufficient lives in Britain and the colonies.

William Booth, the founder of the Salvation Army, worked in a similar milieu to Barnardo. Booth, born in 1829, had started out as a pawnbroker, but had hated his work, for it showed him the extreme poverty in which so many existed and the misery this caused. 'When but a mere child,' he later wrote, 'the degradation and helpless misery of the poor Stockingers of my native town, wandering gaunt and hunger-stricken through the streets, droning out their melancholy ditties, crowding the Union or toiling like galley slaves on relief works for a bare subsistence, kindled in my heart yearnings to help the poor which have continued to this day and which have had a powerful influence on my whole life.'[50] Two years into his apprenticeship he converted to Methodism, prompted by confessing his sins of sharp practice in the pawnbroking business, and began to proselytise for the faith.[51] He also developed Chartist sympathies.

He moved to London and became a lay preacher, but could find few opportunities to preach. So he started to do it outdoors, on Kennington Common, and in the streets. In 1851 he joined the Methodist Reform Church: and on his twenty-third birthday, in April the following year, became a full-time itinerant preacher, based in the church's headquarters in Clapham. Booth had a revolutionary, dramatic style, in which he had been inspired by watching a visiting American revivalist. His message was that eternal punishment awaited those who did not believe in the Gospel and who failed to see the need of repentance from sin. He was preaching in 1865 outside the Blind Beggar pub in the Mile End Road when he was heard by a group of missionaries, who were greatly impressed. They invited him to preach to a series of meetings in Whitechapel, and he held the crowd at one, on 2 July 1865, completely rapt. He realised he had found his true vocation. He formed his own movement, which he called 'The Christian Revival Society', later renamed 'The Christian Mission'. It met in the East End every evening – in a warehouse through whose windows street urchins threw stones and firecrackers – and on Sundays. From his platform Booth urged the derelicts of this community – the thieves, prostitutes and drunks – to repent and find salvation. He also opened soup kitchens, much to the despair of the Charity Organisation Society, which felt they encouraged the poor not to work.

His work was physically hard, and sometimes dangerous. He preached in the poorer parts of London and would return home exhausted and often bloodied, having been pelted. His was one of 500 charitable and religious groups in the East End at the time. He pressed on throughout the 1870s: but it was not until 1878, when he changed the name of his mission to the Salvation Army, that it really took off. Booth was dictating a letter and used the phrase 'we are a volunteer army'. His son Bramwell, deeply involved in the mission, protested he was not a volunteer, but a regular. Booth's secretary was instructed to cross out the word and wrote instead 'we are a salvation army'. The name change was inspired, and the notion of an army fighting against sin to save the poor sinners caught the public imagination, not only in Britain.

Like an army, they marched, had ranks, bands, uniforms and flags. The Salvation Army had a sworn enemy in the drinks industry, which feared it existed largely to stop the lower classes drinking. In the 1880s there were 190,000 public houses in Britain, and 200,000 arrests a year for drunkenness. A group of Booth's opponents, the Skeleton Army, set out to disrupt his meetings, not least by assaulting him and his soldiers. In 1882 a total of 662 soldiers were assaulted, 251 of them women. Thanks to the influence of Booth's wife Catherine, the rescue of prostitutes was undertaken exclusively by women soldiers, which made the Salvation Army an engine of female equality.

Booth had been heavily influenced by Carlyle's strictures against the British for their treatment of the poor, and especially his notion that they were more likely to offer decent treatment to their animals. He compared the poorest people with a cab-horse: if they were underfed, or possibly even overworked as well, they would break down. He also made Carlyle's point that Britain had ended slavery, but had done nothing to liberate its poor. 'This Submerged Tenth – is it, then, beyond the reach of the nine-tenths in the midst of whom they live, and around whose homes they rot and die?'[52]

Like Barnardo, Booth endured accusations of self-interest, peculation and corruption. The Anglican Church was hostile, with Shaftesbury moved to describe Booth as the Antichrist. The General was notoriously unbending, and ruled as an absolute monarch in his domain. However, the idea caught on and spread, not just in Britain but also abroad. When Booth wrote his testament and mission statement, *In Darkest England and the Way Out*, in 1890 the Army had assets in Britain of £377,000, and a worldwide total of £641,000. It had diversified from slum missions to homes for fallen women, brigades to meet released prisoners as they left jail to help place them on the right course, labour exchanges, a shelter for the destitute, a home for drunks, food depots and a factory for the unemployed. It also assisted with and gave advice on emigration, using its network in Australia, Canada, New Zealand, South Africa and America. Booth became so celebrated that in 1902 he was invited to the Coronation. By the time of his death in 1912 his movement had spread to fifty-eight countries.

VI

Some idealists wished to create communities for the lower classes in which the types of problems Burdett-Coutts, Dickens, Barnardo and Booth tried to deal with would simply not exist in the first place. One such was Titus Salt, a woollen manufacturer who built the model town named after him, Saltaire, to the west of Bradford to house his workers and their families. Salt's father was a wool stapler in Bradford, the worsted centre of the world. Titus, born in 1803, had early ambitions to be a doctor. However, he fainted at the sight of blood, and so followed his father into the business. After working for him for ten years he set up his own firm, and cornered the market in fabrics that were a mix of mohair and alpaca wool. This made him astonishingly rich by the 1840s: and he decided to move his operations not merely to build a better factory in which to manufacture his goods, but also to get away from the squalor of Bradford. The population of the town had grown from 13,000 in 1801 to 104,000 in 1851, and it was regarded as the most polluted town in England. By 1851 it had 200 factories pouring out smoke, and its sewage was emptied directly into the River Beck, from which the town obtained its drinking water.

Salt started to build Saltaire in 1851. He wanted to consolidate on one site the work done in five mills he had in Bradford, doing the rounds of which was exhausting him. Salt had, however, already given extensively to charities, and he also seems sincerely to have hoped that by taking his workers out of the miasmatic and debauched lives that so many in the industrial classes had, and giving them what would come to be termed 'sweetness and light', he would be improving his little part of the world. He saw that high productivity and a competitive advantage could be better obtained if the workers were happy, healthy and well educated. He seems to have been influenced by Robert Owen, half a century earlier at New Lanark in Scotland, in associating a high performance by workers with wholesome living and working conditions.

The great mill at Saltaire – at 545 feet long on its south front it was the same length as St Paul's Cathedral, and it was also six storeys high – was opened on Salt's fiftieth birthday, on 20 September 1853: around 3,500 guests, including 2,400 of his workers brought by train from Bradford, sat down at a banquet in the combing-shed to celebrate the opening. They ate 'four hind-quarters of beef, 40 chines of beef, 120 legs of mutton, 100 dishes of lamb, 40 hams, 40 tongues, 50 pigeon pies, 50 dishes of roast chickens, 20 dishes of roast ducks, 30 brace of grouse, 30 brace of partridges, 50 dishes of potted meat of various kinds, 320 plum puddings, 100 dishes of tartlets, 100 dishes of jellies, etc.'[53] This was complemented by half a ton of potatoes, various desserts, and champagne and other wines.

While the government still struggled to legislate in the matter, Salt instituted the maximum ten-hour day for his male operatives. The output was in any case massive: fourteen steam-driven boilers consumed 50 tons of coal a day. The weaving-shed had 1,200 looms producing 30,000 yards, or nearly 18 miles of fabric (mainly alpaca) a day, or enough in a year to stretch from Bradford to Peru, the home of the alpaca. By 1871 his workers and their families gave Saltaire, with its giant and majestic mill on the River Aire, a population of nearly 4,400. The mill, like other buildings in Saltaire, was built in the Italianate style so disliked by Ruskin, of whose writings Salt was an admirer.

The condition of employment and residence was clean living. Drinking was frowned upon – there was no drink in the town, except on special occasions when Salt provided it. Salt was not opposed to alcohol as such, but to pubs as places where men could congregate and talk politics. There were no unions in Saltaire – but also no police. Salt's factory overseers kept an eye on everyone. His other objection to public houses was that, when Bradford had endured a cholera epidemic during his mayoralty in 1848, he had noticed that many of the victims had also been heavy drinkers, which he believed had weakened their constitutions. He also saw a strong connection between drink and crime, and banned pubs out of 'paternal solicitude for the moral and physical health of his people'.[54] His people were, it seemed, grateful: the *Saltaire Monthly Magazine* in March 1871 thanked him 'for his stern exercise of his proprietorial rights, through which he preserved the residents . . . from the annoyance and temptation of public houses and beer shops.'[55]

Salt led by example. As his friend and biographer, the Reverend Robert Balgarnie, wrote, he rose early, worked hard, and was punctual. He was also a man for 'methodical exactness'. Balgarnie continued: 'He was scrupulously exact in the arrangement of his papers, and knew where to lay his hand on any document when required. His letters were always promptly answered. He was exact in his accounts, exact in the words he spoke – which never had the colour of exaggeration about them – exact in his purchases and sales.'[56] In what Balgarnie calls his 'wholeheartedness' he was the very model of a Victorian self-made man.

Salt's spacious, well-lit and well-ventilated mill – the largest of its kind in the world, where all the processes needed to turn alpaca into cloth were under one roof – provided a pleasant workplace, light years ahead of the conditions elsewhere. He installed lavatories, which was unusual, though the urine was carried away especially for use in the dyeing process. Outside the mill, the means of the pursuit of perfection were all around. He built nearly 850 houses, conspicuously not on the unsanitary back-to-back model. As well as a back garden, the average dwelling had three bedrooms, a parlour, kitchen and pantry: there were some boarding houses and some houses for larger families. Salt may have been radical in his approach to industrial conditions, but he had a strict understanding of hierarchy. Houses in Saltaire fell into four categories – large villas for executives, well-appointed terraces for overlookers, the basic workman's cottage described above, and the boarding-houses.[57] The entire cost of the town's construction was £106,562. Salt's philanthropy did not end at Saltaire: he gave money to churches and chapels all over Yorkshire, including York Minister, and in Scarborough, his favourite watering-hole: he gave money to hospitals and asylums in Bradford and also in Lancaster, and to Bradford Grammar School.

The town had shops, a Congregational church (the denomination of which he was a devout member), a Wesleyan chapel, a school for 750 children (which Salt, despite his Nonconformity, decreed should be subject to the State's inspectorate), a club, a working men's institute with reading rooms, baths and a wash house (he had been offended by the sight of washing hanging out to dry, spoiling the beauty of his urban estate), a library, a laboratory, an art school and a gymnasium, almshouses and a huge park in which to play cricket and croquet. Concerts and lectures were a regular feature of the Institute. He also built an infirmary, not least to give rapid treatment to any of his people who suffered an industrial injury. Anyone so badly injured that he or she could do no work would receive a pension for life; the elderly and infirm were accommodated in the almshouses, free of charge. There was a 500,000-gallon reservoir, which collected rainwater off the massive roofs of his buildings, obviating the need to drink polluted water. Gas provided heat and light, and every house had an outside lavatory. The main roads in Saltaire were named after the Queen and her Consort, lesser ones after Salt's family and even after his architects, Lockwood and Mawson.

Salt had a deeply moral attitude, and he hoped – and expected – to encourage a strong morality among his workforce. To codify what Salt expected of them, he drew up a dozen rules. Rule one was 'Throughout the village, cleanliness, cheerfulness and order must reign supreme'. Rule two was 'Only persons who are good, obedient, honest and hard-working will be allocated a house in the village', and rule three 'anyone caught in a state of inebriation will immediately be evicted'. Rules four to seven deal with the importance of maintaining the property, repairing damage, and forbidding the keeping of animals – with the Founder making a periodical inspection to ensure all was in order. Rule eight was an aesthetic consideration, maintaining the founder's sense of equilibrium by forbidding the hanging-out of washing. Other rules prescribe attendance at school up to the age of twelve, forbid subletting, and ban gatherings of more than eight persons in the street. Rule nine is perhaps the most indicative of Salt's rigid paternalism: 'The founder would recommend that all inmates wash themselves every morning, but they shall wash themselves at least twice a week, Monday morning and Thursday morning; any found not washed will be fined 3d for each offence.'[58] The method of inspection is not described.

Salt sat in Parliament as a Liberal for two years from 1859 (though he never spoke, reticence being one of his trademarks, and as such he became the incarnation of a Carlylean hero) and was created a baronet. By his beneficence, he appeared to have eased the clash between labour and capital: if only all employers were like him, the threat of revolution would disappear, many believed. Others found his paternalism oppressive and controlling. Some, notably Ruskin, felt he exerted too much power over his workforce. Ruskin felt Salt had only done what a decent employer should: he would not concede that Salt's benevolence was far in excess of what most employers could afford, or most employees would ever expect. This was typically capricious of Ruskin: Salt was only following Ruskin's prescriptions for enlightened capitalism, after all. He was keen to show his works off as an example to the wider capitalist class. For the first few years visitors came through Saltaire, for whom every facility was provided. Soon, though, Salt found it in his best interests to restrict the procession. It was not simply that they were distracting the operatives: they were also engaging in industrial espionage, taking careful note of Salt's state-of-the-art machinery.

VII

For all the generosity of rich philanthropists, and the devotion of the lives of others to the service of the poor, resources were scarce. Indiscriminate charity offended on two counts: it squandered some resources and provided help to the undeserving, demoralising those who fended for themselves and further preventing the undeserving from mending their ways. The challenge for those who would do good was not just to tackle a problem that, paradoxically, had grown with prosperity, but to tackle it in the most morally productive way. Even such bleeding hearts as Dickens saw that to give help to those who could help themselves, but who refused to do so, was to undermine the foundations of society. This was the beginning of a twentieth-century impulse that believed charity – or welfare, as it became – could only be effective if overseen by a central bureaucracy, which eventually meant the State.

In 1869 a body was formed to bring together, and to an extent to regulate, the charities that sought to do good works: the Charity Organisation Society, an upright and perhaps uptight operation that, as we have seen, crossed swords with such great philanthropists as Barnardo and Booth. Dickens, who had managed to do charity work successfully for the best part of thirty years by the time the COS came along, lampooned it as the 'Haven of Philanthropy' in *The Mystery of Edwin Drood*.[59] To some of its detractors, because of the strictly moralising attitude it was perceived to have towards the indigent classes it purported to serve, its acronym stood for 'cringe or starve'. Its own historian – the grandson of one of its founders – takes a more constructive view, arguing that the COS 'embodied an idea of charity which claimed to reconcile the divisions in society, to remove poverty and to produce a happy, self-reliant community.'[60]

The COS's ideology irritated freelance philanthropists such as Dickens. It was that 'indiscriminate charity only made things worse; it demoralised.'[61] The COS effectively sought to establish a programme of social work by the 'more fortunate classes', a form of friendship that would 'restore a man's self-respect and his ability to support himself and his family.' Motivated by this ideology, a group established to coordinate the work of charities ended up as 'a movement to reform the spirit not only of charities but of society.' It equated indiscriminate charity with socialism. The COS did, however, originate the idea of casework and, with it, founded the idea of the social worker. The social worker was the friend the poor needed to remoralise themselves.

The COS was founded when numerous charities were coming into existence, when the rich were becoming very rich because of the growth of their markets, of the middle class and of consumerism, while the poor, unaided by the State, were being cast ever further adrift from the rising standards of living enjoyed by most workers. The population was growing rapidly, but the infrastructure to support such people barely existed, especially sanitary housing, schools (before 1870), hospitals and remunerative work. For those who lapsed into criminality judicial punishments were severe – even after the abolition of transportation by the 1857 Penal Servitude Act, and the restriction of the death penalty to murder, treason, piracy and arson in Her Majesty's dockyards, sentences of flogging for youths and men and long periods of hard labour for men and women were routinely handed down.

Pauperism decreased in London in the 1860s as a proportion of the population, but rose in absolute terms because of the rapid growth in numbers in the city. One deficiency had been care of the sick, highlighted in the 1867 cholera epidemic in London. The Tory government passed the Metropolitan Poor Act that year, which established a common fund for the whole of the Metropolis for the provision of hospital care and asylums. Each individual parish union contributed to the funds, but they were administered centrally. Care of the mentally handicapped and mentally ill was, by any civilised standards, a disgrace before this Act: but it at least established three asylums for 'idiots, imbeciles and harmless idiots' – the terminology would soon be changed to the 'feeble minded', though those who were a danger to society were designated 'lunatics' – in the London area, a precedent soon followed by the counties.[62] However, the law did not finally draw a distinction between harmless lunatics and dangerous ones until 1889. A committee in 1875 chaired by Sir Charles Trevelyan also argued that the State should support those from the lower-middle and respectable working classes who needed institutional care but could not afford it, to ensure they were not lumped in with the lunatics of the lowest class. Class distinctions were important, even in insanity.

Another widespread problem by the late 1860s was street begging, some by the genuinely destitute, but some just cynical exploitation – such as parents dressing their filthy children in rags and sending them barefoot into the streets to solicit money. Some begging was aggressive, aimed at women and designed to intimidate them into opening their purses. As the middle and upper classes sought to have the laws against vagrancy and begging enforced, so too they began to feel that a more organised form of charitable provision would eliminate the need for such behaviour. It was quite clear that much fraud was taking place, and that money was being diverted from the deserving to the undeserving as a consequence.

In rural areas the gentry would visit their local poor and see that their needs were catered for; and would seek to set an example, and make exhortations of thrift so that occasional hard times could be managed out of savings. But, as Edward Denison, a young MP and son of a bishop had lamented, there was no such moneyed class in the East End of London, merely a sea of destitution, crime and vice. It was Denison's writings on the need to stop indiscriminate charity that brought about the COS in 1869. It would become one of the main roles of the Society to recruit 'friendly visitors' to go among the poor, not perhaps like Lady Bountiful, but to give practical help, advice and support to those who could stand on their own two feet. It would become a principle of the COS that charity was given not out of religious obligation, but out of friendship, and friendship with the best interests of the recipient always at heart.

One of the roots of the COS was in the Society for the Relief of Distress, founded in 1860. It advocated a series of district officers in the poorest areas who would coordinate the charitable work for the locality, and would work closely with the Poor Law guardians. As the number of charities grew, so too did calls for there to be a body that audited their accounts. In the aftermath of the 1867 cholera outbreak so many new charities moved into the East End that some felt the increased relief was encouraging some of the poor to make claims they would never otherwise have attempted.

It was at around this time that the colourful figure of Henry Solly came into the story. Solly was son of a London timber merchant whose financial ruin in 1837 meant his son had to work for a living. Solly disliked commerce, but at the dawn of Victoria's reign had undergone a religious and political radicalisation. He was fortunate to marry into money – his cousin, the daughter of an Essex landowner – and this enabled him to become a Unitarian minister in Somerset. His family had long been dissenters, though Solly soon found he did not much like being a Unitarian. Yeovil, where he was based, had glove factories, and his contact with workers there caused him to engage with Chartism. The Yeovil Unitarians regarded this as rabble-rousing, and he was dismissed from his ministry. For the next decade he operated from various pulpits in Devon, Somerset and Gloucestershire, while his commitment to radical causes expanded beyond the six points of Chartism and into anti-slavery, anti-Corn Law agitation, education reform and the cooperative movement. He found a pulpit at Carter Lane in the City of London in 1852, but considered his work there a failure. He went to Lancaster in 1858 but, after 1862, gave up the ministry.

This decision was, however, the making of Solly as a social reformer. For all his political radicalism he believed in the established order, but was committed to the idea of improvements within it, notably for the lower classes, whose path to respectability he wished to smooth. His big idea to achieve this was the Working Men's Club and Institute Union, of which he was one of the founders in June 1862. The Union also came to Solly's aid: he was without a pulpit and an income, and became the first professional secretary of the Union the following year. His instinct about the clubs was that they should be places of fellowship and recreation but with an alternative focus from the other magnet for the working man, the pub. Solly was a lifelong teetotaller. He worked hard to build the movement, and travelled thousands of miles. A network of clubs was soon all over England: the only difficulty was that the high-minded ideals Solly had for them were at odds with the desires of their members. He left the movement in 1867 after an argument but returned shortly afterwards, only to leave for good in 1873, when the members' desire to buy and drink alcohol in their clubs proved too much for him.

Solly had not done with social reform, however. Determined to help the poor by encouraging hard work and thrift, he was instrumental in founding the London Association for the Prevention of Pauperism and Crime in 1868. He had read a paper that year at a meeting of the Society of Arts that had been entitled *How to deal with the Unemployed Poor of London and with its Roughs and Criminal Classes*. Directors of charities discussed the paradox of pauperism increasing the greater the efforts to alleviate it. The conclusion was that the Poor Law guardians were incapable of assessing the needs of their parishes, and a more formal system of dispensing relief was needed. It was suggested that a body be established, funded by a 1 per cent tax on all the charities, to provide the auditing and regulatory services, inquiring into all applications by the poor for help, that now seemed so badly needed.

The following year the broad group that Solly (another of whose ideas was for industrial villages which, although they did not get off the ground, gave the germ of the idea for the garden city movement) had formed evolved into the Charity Organisation Society, whose aims were to ensure the more responsible and targeted spending of charitable funds. Lord Lichfield found the new society offices in the Adelphi, where it set up home in March 1869. The full title of the body was the Society for Organising Charitable Relief and Repressing Mendicity, which describes the importance to its founders of the aim of driving beggars off the streets either by satisfying their needs through benevolence or, if found to be bogus, driving them into the arms of the police.

From the outset the COS employed an element of social work, giving counselling and advice to the cases it helped, encouraging them to be self-reliant. It formalised the distinction between the deserving and the undeserving poor: the former being those prepared, if given support, to help themselves. So it was that charity was diverted to act as a springboard to personal responsibility, rather than supplanting it or rendering it, in some cases, unnecessary. It also took on the important role of coordinating philanthropy, and ensuring those who established charities were genuinely helping the poor. To ensure its own bona fides was rock solid it recruited vice-presidents and a council of the highest in the land, including dukes, marquesses, archbishops and bishops, MPs, distinguished public servants such as Trevelyan, and Ruskin and Octavia Hill, the last two of whom had their own project to house the poor. The only name missing to begin with was the high priest of Victorian philanthropy, Shaftesbury, but within a couple of years he was added to the list.

The COS's first annual report announced its intention to set up an office in each Poor Law division, managed by a local committee and under the leadership of a professional agent. The effectiveness varied from area to area. The first parts of London to set up such committees were where areas of extreme wealth lay alongside areas of poverty – Kensington, Marylebone, Paddington and St George's, Hanover Square. In areas such as the East End where there were no upper or upper-middle classes – or even middle classes – finding volunteers, and money, was much harder: this was missionary work rather than neighbourliness. The COS, whose purpose was, after all, coordination of philanthropic efforts, sought (with limited success) to have the richer committees help the poorer ones.

The agent's job was to liaise with the local charities, Poor Law officials and others such as clergy who might help look after the needy. It was also his job to examine cases of serious hardship not being dealt with adequately by the existing structure of charity and parish relief; and, where he was satisfied the need was genuine, to help. The poor were given tickets to exchange for food, rather than money that could be spent on drink or tobacco. In its second report, it stated that 'to give material relief, food or money, to everyone who asked for it on the sole conditions of their being what is commonly called deserving and in want, even after the most careful verification of those conditions, would inevitably do more harm than good, though this might not be seen during the first year or two.'[63]

The COS disliked soup kitchens, some of which gave soup and other basic food out free of charge, while others sold it at a subsidised rate. They constituted the 'indiscriminate' charity the COS believed wasted money, encouraged begging and deterred self-sufficiency. Poor people who did not have to buy food had money for other purposes, notably drink. As the COS's history points out, in the early 1870s there were 165 pubs in a square mile of the East End, with a turnover of £450,000 a year. A 2d school fee in the area, which many parents said they could not afford, would raise just £10,053.[64] Many requests for help with the school fee were refused: in its seventh annual report in 1875 the COS recorded that 'but for the thorough system of investigation adopted by the society, relief might often have been given to undeserving and worthless persons whose earnings, if they had not been wasted through intemperate habits, would have enabled them to provide for the wants of their families.'[65]

The government approved the COS's mission: George Goschen, who ran the Poor Law Board in Gladstone's first ministry, published a minute in November 1869 entitled *Relief of the Poor in the Metropolis*. It sought to distinguish between the Poor Law Board, which would help the destitute, and private charity, which could help those who were just very poor – by, for example, supplementing the low earnings of a widow, or helping a man seeking work to buy tools or to have his travelling paid for. The Poor Law could not pay for such things. Goschen also suggested charities should not help those being assisted by the Poor Law Board. Thus there would be cooperation regularly between both sides so each would know what the other was doing. With this encouragement from the government, the COS set about opening divisional offices, and had covered most of the Metropolis by 1871.

However, the COS relied not only on cooperation from the government: it also required cooperation from charities and clergy, and this it did not inevitably receive. In some parts of London the main charities supported the COS and cooperated fully: Octavia Hill's, in Marylebone, was one such, and in the hard winter of 1872–3 the local Poor Law Guardians supplied her with a daily list of applicants for relief from her district. In others, however, there was no such interaction. Yet the Society persisted: and although it never achieved complete coordination of charitable activities in London, it was in all Poor Law Divisions able to establish a committee to adjudicate on who was deserving, and who undeserving; and to further 'the promotion of habits of providence and self-reliance, and of those social and sanitary principles, the observance of which is essential to the well-being of the poor and of the community at large.'[66]

The district offices were staffed by volunteers – usually women – for several hours daily to supplement paid staff: but the volunteers were often at the sharp end, meeting the poor, and drawing up their cases. When a case was taken on, volunteers would visit the family regularly until it was either back on its feet, or so beyond help that the workhouse or some other intervention from the Poor Law Board was the only option. However, the aim of enabling those being helped to help themselves was never abandoned unless absolutely inevitable. The COS would arrange loans, grants for emigration, apprenticeships, places in convalescent homes; and give practical help such as enabling those seeking work to buy clothes, or giving widows a mangle so they could take in washing, or a sewing machine to enable them to make and mend clothes. In extreme cases the COS would arrange small pensions for those respectable elderly who could no longer work: the State would not do this until 1908.

Many applied for medical help, which caused the COS to examine the organisation of provident funds. None suitable for the lower classes existed: but the COS found that, if one did, around half who applied for help – of those giving correct addresses – could have afforded to pay in to one. It established a sub-committee to look into the prospect of establishing one, and did so in 1879 with the launch of the Metropolitan Dispensaries Association: Sir Charles Trevelyan undertook much of the work required for its foundation.

For all the initial difficulties, the COS made a valuable contribution to the relief of poverty in London. It handled 12,506 cases in 1871, its third year of operation. It referred 3,909 of these on to other agencies, including 1,482 to the Poor Law guardians. It directly helped 4,360, including 2,446 by making direct grants, 828 by making loans, and 295 by finding work. It turned down the other 4,237: of those 286 had given false addresses, but the other refusals came into three categories. It decided 818 were 'not requiring relief', in that their income was sufficient for them to survive, provided they showed self-discipline and thrift. Another 1,983 were 'ineligible'; but the last 1,150 were 'undeserving', showing the moral dimension the Society attached to charity.

This hard-line approach may or may not have affected the figures for paupers in London during the 1870s, or there may have been other factors: in 1871 there had been 44.2 paupers per thousand of the London population, but by 1878 the figure had fallen to 23.4 per thousand. Given the economic downturn after 1873, those figures are all the more remarkable.[67] The COS's history outlines some specimen 'undeserving' cases, which show just how hard the line was. A widow with a broken collarbone was unable to work because of her injury, and unable therefore to buy her ten-year-old son some boots for his work. The committee made inquiries and found she was in her local pub every evening, and had broken her collarbone falling over while drunk. A married couple with four children was refused help when the father was unemployed because inquiries showed he was 'very lazy' and he and his wife were both drunks.[68] Such people would be referred to the workhouse where, it was deemed, life would be so unpleasant that they would soon mend their ways. The COS had no qualms about the sins of the parents being visited upon their children. The moral question cut both ways: when a woman with four children came to the COS in distress because her husband had deserted her, the COS had the husband arrested and sent to prison for three months. By the 1880s, the COS had modified its language for fear of being branded unduly judgemental. Those who had been 'undeserving' now became 'not assisted'.[69]

VIII

Octavia Hill would be celebrated for establishing sanitary housing for the poor. However, she began her work among the destitute when her mother decided to befriend poor women from their neighbourhood, and invite them to her house once a week for a sewing evening, accompanied by a conversation. This not only gave the women subtle instruction in how to conduct their lives, but also helped establish a sense of community, and the type of 'friendship' the COS would argue was the best form of philanthropy. It was another attempt to recreate in the urban environment that sense of duty from the better-off towards the poor that continued, to an extent, to exist in the countryside.

Octavia was born in 1838, and was so named because she was the eighth daughter of James Hill, a Cambridgeshire corn merchant and proto-socialist disciple of Robert Owen, the utopian. Her father went bankrupt when she was two, and abandoned his responsibilities for his family. Her mother, his third wife, brought up her five daughters with help from her father, Thomas Southwood Smith, a celebrated doctor, Unitarian, vigorous campaigner against children working in mines and an advocate of slum clearance. Smith worked among the poor in London's East End, was a close friend and collaborator of Ashley, and another stimulus to his granddaughter's sense of philanthropy. She spent most of her formative years in his house at Highgate. She had no formal education.

In 1852, when Hill was fourteen, her mother became manager of the Ladies Guild, a cooperative crafts workshop in Holborn whose aim was to provide an occupation for working-class women, and whose existence had been inspired by the Christian Socialist movement of F. D. Maurice. Another of Maurice's disciples who had done social work in Holborn was Thomas Hughes, who would write *Tom Brown's Schooldays*. Maurice preached in Lincoln's Inn chapel, and the Hills were often in his congregation. Octavia had grown up in a dissenting family, but under Maurice's influence moved to the Church of England, with two of her sisters, and Maurice stood godfather when she was baptised. Octavia became her mother's assistant, and looked after girls from the local Ragged School who made toys in the workshop. She became aware of the dreadful conditions in which the girls lived in the rookeries of Holborn.

Maurice encouraged Hill in social work. However, the greatest influence of her philanthropic career was John Ruskin, whom she met through the Guild, and whose writings she read avidly. In 1856 the Guild failed commercially, and Maurice rescued her by offering her the job of secretary, at 10s a week, to the women's classes at the Working Men's College in Holborn, of which he had been principal since 1854. The vice-principal was Llewelyn Davies, a clergyman and brother of Emily. The classes were never intended for working-class women, and operated in the afternoon when the men were at work: they came in the evening. Ruskin also taught there, and engaged Hill as a copyist, working for him in the Dulwich Art Gallery and the National Gallery, making copies of pictures for him to use as teaching aids. Hill started to teach at the Working Men's College too. Her consciousness of women's disabilities was raised through this work, and in 1856-7 she collected 24,000 signatures for a petition in favour of a married women's property Act. She also volunteered to teach at Barbara Bodichon's secular, coeducational school in Paddington.

Hill longed to provide better housing for the very poor, especially unskilled labourers whom she felt had not been assisted by various Acts and charitable endeavours that looked after more accomplished artisans. However, not only did she lack the means of a Burdett-Coutts or a Peabody, her family had never recovered from her father's bankruptcy and were themselves living only a little above the breadline. Her opportunity came, however, after the death of Ruskin's father in 1864. The following year he used part of his £120,000 inheritance to buy three houses in Paradise Place, Marylebone, for the working classes to live in under Hill's management. 'One day he and Miss Octavia Hill were having a friendly chat,' one of Hill's friends recalled in 1905, 'and he lamented the dreariness of life without an object other than the usual daily round . . . "One longs to do something more satisfying".' Hill agreed, and when Ruskin asked her what she would like to do, she replied: 'something to provide better homes for the poor.' Ruskin 'turning sharp round in his seat' asked: 'How could it be done? Have you a business plan?'[70] Hill quickly gave him a plan. For Ruskin this was a business venture rather than a straight act of philanthropy, something the hard-minded Hill not only understood, but welcomed: he lent the money with the promise of a 5 per cent return through rents on the freehold property, and 3 per cent on the leasehold.

Ruskin described in *Time and Tide* how the plan worked, allowing himself at the same time a swipe at Mill, of whom he had – not least under Carlyle's influence – become an adversary.

The most wretched houses of the poor in London often pay ten or fifteen per cent to the landlord; and I have known an instance of sanitary legislation being hindered, to the loss of many hundreds of lives, in order that the rents of a nobleman, derived from the necessities of the poor, might not be diminished. And it is a curious thing to me to see Mr J S Mill foaming at the mouth, and really afflicted conscientiously, because he supposes one man to have been unjustly hanged, while by his own failure (I believe *wilful* failure) in stating clearly to the public one of the first elementary truths of the science he professes, he is aiding and abetting the commission of the cruellest possible form of murder on many thousands of persons yearly, for the sake simply of putting money into the pockets of the landlords. I felt this evil so strongly that I bought, in the worst part of London, one freehold and one leasehold property, consisting of houses inhabited by the lowest poor; in order to try what change in their comfort and habits I could effect by taking only a just rent, but that firmly.[71]

Hill initially tried to buy some houses around where she lived in Nottingham Place, Marylebone, only to find potential vendors changing their minds when they learned what she intended. She found some squalid ones a short walk away that would, once repaired, serve her purpose. Paradise Place had been built in the 1830s and was home to many working-class families, packed far too many to a room and living in utterly insanitary conditions. The new landlord allocated two rooms to each family rather than one. Hill could see that the women who lived there under the previous regime were forced into such impossible squalor that they had simply given up caring. She hoped that by allowing them to have accommodation of which they could be proud, they would take better care of it, and feel responsibility towards themselves and their families. The houses were redecorated and their drains cleaned out; they were given improved ventilation and put into good repair. 'I have long been wanting to gather near us my friends among the poor,' Hill wrote to a friend, 'in some house arranged for their health and convenience, in fact a small private model lodging-house, where I may know everyone, and do something towards making their lives healthier and happier.'[72]

At the core of her ideology was the idea that the poor had to help themselves as much as possible. She was a devotee of Samuel Smiles, and sought to put his example into practice. Those who broke her rules by not paying their rents, or damaging the property or causing disturbances, were thrown out. She or one of a small, hand-picked and carefully trained group of lady assistants visited weekly to collect rents, and to monitor matters. They continued that 'friendship' with her tenants that gave her landlordism an aspect of social work, and which would put her in tune with the aims and policies of the COS. In particular, Hill and her colleagues could watch the children in her cottages, and see they were set an example and steered towards an education that would help make them responsible and respectable adults. Hill believed the small family unit was the basis of social improvement, not least because of the ability to teach an example and the requirement of the acceptance of responsibility, and the houses in which her families were brought up were ideal for this purpose.

After Paradise Place a network of houses grew up. Hill was de facto landlady and mentor to the tenants, to whom she taught the basics of household management and thrift. Her tenants were usually casual or seasonal workers and therefore ineligible for the new model dwellings – but not necessarily because of problems of character. Part of the social work aspect to her and her assistants' roles was to seek employment for those willing to work, so they could avoid falling behind on rent. Although Hill had little money – she depended on her work at the WMC and from Ruskin to keep solvent – she underestimated the struggle so many of her tenants had to meet their obligations.

She had, in 1869, at the inception of the COS, argued in a paper of the same name 'the importance of aiding the poor without alms-giving'.[73] That was the basis upon which she ran the properties. She also wrote at this time that 'where a man persistently refuses to exert himself, external help is worse than useless.'[74] Her views were strongly influenced in this, as in so much else, by Ruskin, who became a vice-president of the COS. But she also took the idea of friendship, or setting an example, to new lengths. She started singing classes and sewing classes and made playgrounds for the children. She asked children from her Ragged School to befriend and mentor a child from her dwellings. She arranged educational outings for the children, to open their eyes to a world outside their apartments. She made the tenants responsible for the maintenance of the properties and for keeping them clean, paying some to act as cleaners when they could not find work to pay their rents. Once Ruskin had had his 5 per cent return, the tenants could use any surplus to improve their surroundings. They – guided by their landlady – decided how it was spent, increasing their sense of responsibility.

By 1874 Hill had fifteen schemes with 3,000 tenants. The success attracted more investors, which meant more properties could be acquired, and more volunteers could train, effectively, as social workers. Ruskin put more capital up and bought more cottages for Hill. Members of the Royal Family and the aristocracy subscribed, as did businessmen. Some volunteers, such as Beatrice Webb, went on to develop a philanthropic career elsewhere, having learned much by Hill's example. Hill was a superb public speaker and travelled widely, describing to other groups of social reformers and philanthropists her system and how it could be replicated. As, indeed, it was: not just in cities all over Britain, but abroad.

The personal service provided in her schemes, and by her volunteers, would in later years cause her to harden her heart against impersonal, publicly subsidised schemes. Once she had established better homes, she set about making facilities that gave a sense of community, and allowed for the improvement of the lives and minds of its members – rather as Salt had done in Saltaire, but without the focus of a common place of work. She built halls for musical evenings and the production of plays. London was growing rapidly and open space was at a premium: and Hill fought to preserve what was there, not always successfully, though the survival of Parliament Hill Fields was partly down to her. Her belief in preserving nature and beauty was not least what compelled her to take an active role in the formation of the National Trust in the 1890s; in her work in providing better housing for the poor, she sought also to bring a standard of aesthetic pleasure into their lives, instinctively sharing as she did the Arnoldian view that a sight of perfection was possible for everyone.

Such was Hill's reputation that she was, in 1872, offered the position of a Poor Law inspector, a job never before given to a woman. She turned it down, partly because of her determination to remain involved with the lives of her tenants, and partly because of regular bouts of ill health. Her most significant collapse was in 1877, when she was ill for many months. A number of events conspired to bring this about, not least a failed engagement to an MP, Edward Bond, a volunteer with her charity, and the death of a close friend, Jane Nassau Senior, who had become the first female Poor Law inspector.

But Ruskin dealt the hardest blow of all. Those who knew him well (and this included Hill, who was under no illusions) knew he was unstable. His failed marriage to Effie Gray and his bizarre infatuation with Rose La Touche were testament enough to that. He had also engineered, in the 1860s, a ridiculous feud (subsequently made up) with Carlyle; and much of his writing on aesthetics reveals an absolutism, and an intolerance of the opinions of others, that suggest an uneasy relationship with the rest of the world. He had sought to change the basis of his dealings with Hill, by making his stake in the houses over to the St George's Guild, his charitable trust established to do good works in Sheffield, though with the properties still under her management. He chose to announce this in the pages of Letter LXXVI of *Fors Clavigera*, his series of pamphlets and letters addressed to working men, published throughout the 1870s. He explained himself by saying that 'I have already had the value of it back in interest, and have no business now to keep it any more.'[75]

Hill had her doubts about Ruskin's business sense, based on what she had witnessed of his attempts to run a tea-shop in Paddington, staffed by a couple of his mother's maids. It was aimed at providing somewhere civilised for the local poor to meet, and its wares were relatively cheap, being run at his insistence on a non-profit-making basis. However, it also at his insistence sold tea of such a refined taste – and did not sell either sugar or coffee – that the local proletariat hardly went there. Hill feared that a change in the management of his money would put his continued ownership of the properties at risk. Ruskin wanted the Guild to buy farmland and establish a utopian farming system. Hill's father had tried something similar in the 1840s and it had led to his ruin, so she had reason to be nervous that the properties she managed were about to be put into such a venture. Ruskin had wind of her views, and they infuriated him.

He then wrote, in *Fors Clavigera*, that 'for the last three or four years it has been a matter of continually increasing surprise to me that I never received the smallest contribution to St George's Fund from any friend or disciple of Miss Octavia Hill's.' Ruskin felt Hill had an obligation towards the St George's project: but she was not prepared to engage. He described himself as 'utterly disappointed', and continued: 'To my more acute astonishment, because Miss Hill was wont to reply to any more or less direct inquiries on the subject, with epistles proclaiming my faith, charity, and patience, in language so laudatory, that, on the last occasion of my receiving such answer, to a request for a general sketch of the Marylebone work, it became impossible for me, in any human modesty, to print the reply.'[76] He confessed that what had upset him most was that a potential benefactor to the Guild had been dissuaded from giving funds 'by hearing doubts expressed by Miss Hill of my ability to conduct any practical enterprise successfully.'[77] Hill denied the accusation, in a passionate letter to Ruskin: which he then printed in *Fors*, together with an extended correspondence between them that illustrates the mistake Hill made, in her innocence, in seeking to argue with a very sick mind: such as 'I know not a single piece of business I

have ever undertaken, which has failed by the fault of any person chosen
by me to conduct it. Tell me, therefore, of two at least. Then I will
request one or two more things of you; being always, Affectionately
yours, J R.'[78] In an even more hysterical postscript, he added: 'Of all
injuries you could have done — not me — but the cause I have in hand,
the giving the slightest countenance to the vulgar mob's cry of "unpractical" was the fatallest.'

Ruskin should not have published this correspondence: it is a further
sign of his instability that he did. He was months away from his first
full-scale mental collapse, which silenced him for over two years. He
did not attempt to tone down the sentiments when he revised *Fors* in
1888, but did admit that he wished to 'ask forgiveness' for his 'anger and
pride'.[79] Given how much of his fortune, by his own admission, Ruskin
had frittered away through poor investments, gifts and other indulgences,
Hill – who shared the COS's determination to see funds spent to the
maximum moral effect – had a point. Once Hill recovered from her
breakdown she built a cottage in Sussex, where she could rest; and she
acquired a female companion, Harriot Yorke, who shared the administrative burdens with her until Hill's death in 1912.

The breakdown was not the end of Hill's philanthropic work, but she
did move into a different gear. In the 1880s the Church Commissioners
asked her to take over the improvement of many of their urban properties, having discovered the Church had become a slum landlord. It was
too much for volunteers, and a cadre of trained and salaried women
housing officers was established. She gave evidence to a Royal Commission
on Housing in 1885, having been vetoed by Sir William Harcourt, the
Home Secretary, to serve on it; but served on one for three years from
1905 that investigated reform of the Poor Law. Yet it was her pioneering
work in the 1870s that stands out, and which in an age that did not so
readily discount the achievements of women would have had her covered
with the honours and official regard she unquestionably merited.

IX

There was a third reason, beyond doing God's work or seeking to keep
the poor docile, why philanthropy happened: it was a useful means for
humble or even dodgy businessmen to buy respectability and esteem,
something that would set a standard for much twentieth-century practice.

During the mid-Victorian period it was difficult to open a newspaper or periodical without seeing this advertisement, or a version of it:

Holloway's Pills and Ointment
By a steady and searching trial in all parts of the World for upwards of Half a Century
Have earned the reputation of being the
MOST RELIABLE CURES FOR ALL DISEASES
They are particularly recommended in cases of
Liver and Stomach Disorders, Gout, Rheumatism, &c; also for all Complaints of the Throat and Lungs.[80]

It is doubtful whether Thomas Holloway's pills and ointment were of the slightest use, although the former were claimed to ease digestion and any other internal difficulties the mid-nineteenth-century hypochondriac might feel, and the latter professed itself the ideal ameliorative for gout and rheumatism. Although the composition of both apparently remained unchanged throughout the rest of the nineteenth century – scientific developments held no attraction for Holloway – the range of ailments they could conquer continued to expand. Late Victorian advertising claims the pills will deal with 'indigestion, biliousness, sick headache, loss of appetite, nervousness, palpitation, heartburn, sleeplessness, want of energy, languor etc'. As for the ointment, that will also be 'a blessing' for 'lumbago, sciatica, pleurisy, cramp, stiff joints, glandular swellings, bronchitis, asthma, sore throat, quinsy, hoarseness etc', not to mention its indispensability for 'sores, old wounds, bad legs, piles, fistulas, chaps, chilblains, burns, scalds, scurvy and all skin eruptions'.[81] Armed with these products, one required nothing else, it seemed, for the Victorian medicine cabinet. In an early manifestation of the consumer society, many people (especially of the lower-middle and middle classes) suspended (or never encountered) disbelief about the properties of these substances, and bought them in vast quantities. As a result Holloway became immensely rich.

Holloway was born in Devon in 1800, the son of a baker who moved to Cornwall and became a publican. After a basic education in Penzance he assisted his mother in her grocery business until he was twenty-eight, when he left for France to work as a general merchant. He moved to London in 1836 and set himself up as a commercial agent. After meeting a Torinese quack and leech-seller, Felix Albinolo, he sought a partnership with him in his ointment business. He introduced Albinolo to a doctor at St Thomas's Hospital who, examining his ointment, found it was a similar oil and wax mixture to that already used at the hospital. The business opportunity Holloway thought he had sniffed out suddenly seemed less attractive.

However, an idea took root. By the autumn of 1837 Holloway had manufactured his own ointment, in his mother's kitchen, and was advertising it in the London newspapers. 'The first ointment that I made', he recalled in a letter towards the end of his life, 'was in my mother's saucepan, which held about six quarts, an extra jump was in a long fish kettle, and after that her little copper, which would hold about 40lbs.'[82] He endured first a volley of abuse from Albinolo for breaking what had hitherto been his monopoly, and then the threat of legal action for stealing the Italian's formula and using testimonials that Albinolo had believed were his. The two men embarked on an advertising war that bankrupted both of them, and ended with Holloway's being imprisoned for debt in Whitecross Street jail until his mother bailed him out. He made it an iron rule thereafter that he would pay all debts on the day they were incurred.

He began to produce digestive pills too. He sold these – laxatives of castor oil and ginger – from a shop in the Strand, demolished in the late 1860s to make way for Street's Law Courts. He married in 1840 and his wife worked with him, he claimed for eighteen hours a day. They had no children, an influential factor in his philanthropy. He struggled at first: he resorted to sending his brother Henry around shops to ask for the pills and the ointment, and to express shock that the shopkeepers hadn't heard of them. Later in the day Holloway himself would call as a commercial traveller, and sell them his goods.

He rapidly grasped the link between advertising and sales, and ran a substantial advertising budget. His strategy worked, and was not confined just to the domestic press. He researched the press of his overseas markets, and advertised there too, building up a massive export business. He would visit the docks and sell his pills to people about to embark on voyages, and hoped word of them would travel around the world. It did. At home and abroad people became more aware of their aches and pains, and sought remedies. He was spending £5,000 a year on advertising by 1842 and by the end of his life, in 1883, about £50,000. With the money from his patent medicines he became a serious investor in other businesses, and spent much time managing his own portfolio.

By the 1860s he was a millionaire – so rich that in 1871 he offered a loan to the French, rebuilding after their war with Prussia – but lived simply. To be fair to Holloway, he did seem to develop a sense of social obligation that took his philanthropy beyond self-service. He had offered to establish a charitable foundation in Devonport, his birthplace: but the citizens did not want the money of a purveyor of quack medicines. A notice was placed in the *Builder* inviting suggestions for how his philanthropic impulse might be realised. Holloway had started to examine lunatic asylums, visiting twenty in fifteen counties in the winter of 1871. He began to develop the idea of building better and more humane ones. He had once attended a meeting addressed by Shaftesbury about the need for such institutions for the respectable classes. He decided he wanted to spend half a million pounds: and he would rather spend it on one or two grand projects than on many small ones. As was later reported: 'He had been guided by the consideration that rich people so unfortunate as to suffer from cerebral disease needed no monetary assistance, and the poor are already cared for in public asylums.'[83] Holloway became distinct among major Victorian philanthropists in seeking to help the middle rather than the working classes; and rare among them in having absolutely no religious motivation to do so.

Having consulted Shaftesbury, he decided to build on his estate at Egham in Surrey 'The Holloway Sanatorium for Mental Disorders for Males and Females of the Middle Class', which he emphasised would be 'self supporting' and would accommodate 240 patients.[84] Only curable cases would be admitted, and no one would be allowed to stay beyond twelve months. Once opened, people from the upper-middle classes and the aristocracy had to be admitted too, to ensure the finances remained sound, as Holloway had not endowed it. The building cost £300,000, grand in scale not least because of his insistence that every patient should have his or her own room. To avoid delays in building, he bought his own brickworks. Apart from its architectural distinction, the sanatorium also precipitated a revolution in care for the mentally ill by introducing standards that would not be routine in Britain until the mid-twentieth century.

The benefaction brought Holloway's name before the highest in the land. Mrs Gladstone arranged for him to come to meet her and the

Prime Minister on 17 June 1873. As Gladstone recorded in his diary: 'We had a long conversation with Mr Holloway (of the Pills) on his philanthropic plans: wh are of great interest.'[85] Whether Gladstone was responsible for a shift in Holloway's intentions one does not know: but his second great philanthropic plan, to build a big convalescent home and hospital, was not pursued, but supplanted by another, even more ambitious idea. Holloway announced in December 1874 that he intended to build a 'Ladies University' at Egham that would cost more than £200,000 (in the end the bill was nearer £700,000), and which he did not intend to endow.[86] He said there would be rents from some building land on the estate that the university could use to maintain its fabric for the first few years, until money accrued from fees. Those fees would be 'at the lowest scale commensurate with high efficiency'.[87]

He also announced that 'the Clerical influence usually so prominent will be limited to a minimum'. Holloway had a lifelong prejudice against parsons (he had ordered that no chaplain be attached to the sanatorium), lawyers and, unsurprisingly given his line of business, doctors. None was to be allowed on the governing body of his college. He wanted twenty professors for 400 ladies, and had a clear idea of the curriculum: 'Modern Languages, French, German, Italian, Latin, Greek, Algebra, Geometry, Physics, Chemistry, Botany, Music, Drawing, Mill's Logic, Mill's Political Economy, Green's English History, English Composition, Physiology, Natural Science, and such other subjects as may be suggested by Professor Fawcett and other competent advisers'. His Ladies would have to pass the Cambridge examination to get in, after which they would be prepared for the ordinary BA degree. He had the matter of scholarships 'under consideration' when he drew up his initial plan in 1874–5.[88] 'My ambition', he said, 'is to leave it so complete that its equal cannot be found in Europe or America.'

Holloway was keen to ensure his foundation would be in keeping with the grandeur and permanence apparent in so many other Victorian establishments, and of a standard familiar from the older universities. His 'Ladies College' would be constructed 'at a cost and in a manner that may in some measure be worthy [of] the acceptance of the nation to which I intend to dedicate it.'[89] He pledged 'whatever sum may be necessary to accomplish this object' and stated that he wanted it built in the Renaissance style. 'This may be somewhat expensive, but for a public building I do not regret it.' Modestly, he added: 'This building may hereafter serve as a starting point for someone else to do a great deal better.' His architect for the college, as for the sanatorium, was William Henry Crossland, a pupil of Scott and the architect of the town hall at Rochdale. The inspiration for the latter was the Cloth Hall at Ypres, which exhibited the Gothic influence central to Scott's work, and for the former the Chateau de Chambord, on the Loire (which he had visited with Holloway), which did not.

He wanted his ladies to be able 'to obtain either MA or BA or even a Double First'. To advertise his plan and call for support for it he convened a public meeting on 10 February 1875 to which many of the leading women of the day were invited: notably Millicent Fawcett, Elizabeth Garrett Anderson and Emily Davies. Sir James Kay-Shuttleworth and David Chadwick, Holloway's principal friend in politics, were also present. Crossland laid preliminary, outline plans for the institution on the table, that everyone might see the grandeur Holloway intended for his college.

Holloway was ambitious for the institution. He told Chadwick before the public meeting that he hoped it 'could be considered as a sister college say to Cambridge', and hoped Cambridge itself might recognise the quality of the degrees his ladies took and, where they were worthy, confer degrees on them.[90] The Cambridge comparison extended to the architecture. Crossland had told James Beal, Holloway's builder, that 'the founder intends that there shall be nothing like it in Europe.'[91] Holloway and Crossland met Kay-Shuttleworth, who suggested the college be split into four divisions, one a training college for teachers and another a high school where those being trained could try out their skills. This was not Holloway's vision. He told Chadwick that 'he must leave it to some other person who can conveniently part with a quarter of a million to do that, but as for himself, he shall either carry out his plan of making it a college for the Higher Education of women, and in all respects similar to the Universities of Oxford and Cambridge, or do nothing of the kind.'

Holloway expressed the fear to John Morley that unless degrees were conferred by Oxford or Cambridge, women would not feel encouraged to attend.[92] He told Morley: 'To say that a young woman was at college may mean but little – but if she could say she had taken a degree – how many mothers would say to their daughters "now you must endeavour to do the same"? Should he find this plan of his meet with public disfavour, then he would abandon the whole scheme and devote his money to other purposes.'[93]

In keeping with his anti-parsonical prejudice, Holloway wanted a secular institution. 'It shall not either now or hereafter, if my deed can prevent it, be of the religious teaching of the Church of England, and I should therefore wish that this point be settled definitely.'[94] He wanted no church or meeting house built on the land. 'I have provided for a very beautiful chapel where a doctrine that can offend no-one may be preached.' Crossland visited Cambridge with Holloway in April 1875 to look for ideas, and then, on his return to Virginia Water, started to draw up plans. Holloway's brother made an exploratory visit to Vassar College in New York, and reported back.

He took enormous interest in the most minute architectural details and corresponded frequently with Crossland about them, on both the sanatorium and the college. 'Boilers,' he wrote on 11 November 1874. 'Should they be 16 or 18 feet long?'[95] His descriptions of what he wanted Crossland to do often include the adjective 'magnificent'.[96] He had bought the Mount Lee estate at Egham for £25,000, and told Crossland he had a budget of £150,000 to do the job properly. To inspire him, he told Crossland that 'it will be larger than Wellington College and where young Ladies will receive a classical education . . . there will be nothing like it in Europe.'

Holloway called Chadwick 'one of the godfathers or sponsors of the Ladies College, the duties of which you are fulfilling in a manner more like a father than a Godfather'.[97] Holloway made contact with Emily Davies at Girton and asked for advice. She told him not to admit any girl under seventeen, to ensure they passed a stiff examination at the end, and not to bother to teach music. He agreed with all three points. Then the inevitable happened: he wrote to her on 4 June 1875 and asked: 'I presume you could not be tempted hereafter to leave Girton to become the Lady Principal of the "Holloway College"?'[98]

The foundation stone – or rather brick – was laid in September 1879. Gladstone admired what Holloway was doing, referring in a letter to Chadwick in 1881 to his act of 'so much munificence'.[99] He was worried, though, by Holloway's zeal against religion being framed in the charter, since he feared it would end up excluding those of faith. While grasping Holloway's desire for his institution to break the mould of the older universities, he advised against the charter repudiating 'old traditions', without it saying what those 'old traditions' were. Holloway's final act of philanthropy was to spend £83,000 on an art gallery in his college.

A week before Holloway's death *The Times* wrote a respectful article on his college and his sanatorium. 'The mere money expended upon them surpasses in amount anything hitherto done by private means, for upon them considerably more than a million has been spent, including an endowment fund of £300,000 for the college.'[100] 'Both these institutions are especially designed by the founder for the benefit of the middle classes,' the paper explained, and they were designed to be 'self supporting' so they would not have to rely further on charity. The sanatorium was described as 'very large and handsome' with 'all the comforts of home' and 'the ulterior view of forming a valuable and profitable school for the special study of mental ailments.' The sanatorium was due to open the following year: and had 'walls ornamented in compartments with cheerful pictures of rural life, all painted by lady artists' among its other facilities.

It said the college 'is a building much larger than any college in this country, being considerably larger than Trinity College, Cambridge'. It described the facilities: 1,000 rooms, with the 250 students each having a separate study and bedroom – and the 'dining hall, music room, library, museum, chapel and picture gallery all of magnificent proportions'. The founder now waited for the Act of Parliament or Royal Charter that would allow the college to award degrees. The Lady Principal was empowered to arrange whatever religious worship in it might from time to time be deemed necessary, 'but no arrangement shall be made which would identify the college in any way with any particular sect or denomination of Christians.' Finally, there would be a system of Founder's Scholarships.

Dying on Boxing Day 1883, Holloway did not see his college completed and opened by the Queen on 30 June 1886: she proclaimed it 'Royal Holloway College'. *The Times* devoted a leader to him on his death, saying he was 'best known to the world as a manufacturer of patent medicines, and better deserving to be known for other qualifications less frequently and less obtrusively thrust before the public eye.'[101] It added: 'It will be by these princely foundations that Mr Holloway's name will be remembered among generations yet to come. By men of the present day it will be associated chiefly with the manufacture and advertisement and sale of ointments and pills. On the intrinsic merits of these much vaunted drugs we cannot pretend to be informed. If they possessed one-tenth part of the wonderful virtues which have been assigned to them, their discovery may safely be set down as marking an era of no small importance in the progress of the curative art.' The best it could say was that in the many years they had been before the public 'no bad consequences have been proved to follow from their use'.

John Betjeman called Holloway's college and sanatorium 'two of the most amazing buildings in Britain . . . they have to be seen to be believed, and once seen they haunt the mind like a recurring and exalting dream.'[102] The college is the leading physical monument to Victorian philanthropy in Britain: a memorial not only to the scale of one man's generosity, but also to the ambition of an entire era.

CHAPTER 17

THE WAY WE LIVE NOW: THE CREATION OF THE VICTORIAN CITY

I

Some of the challenges presented by the growth of British towns and cities in the mid-nineteenth century were beyond the scope of philanthropists, however generous, and charities, however well organised, to tackle. Matters such as sanitation, public health and the development of infrastructure required a strategic treatment, either by local authorities (which did not exist in anything like their present form until 1888) or, more usually, direction and intervention from central government. A glance at the population statistics illustrates the problem. In 1801 the population of London was 958,863. By 1881 it was 4,776,861, the city having burst at the seams into Essex, Kent, Surrey and Middlesex. Manchester had 75,281 inhabitants in 1801; by 1851 it was 303,382 and by 1881 over half a million. Leeds went from 100,000 in 1801 to 430,000 in 1881, Liverpool from 90,000 to 650,000 and Birmingham from 95,000 to 530,000. These cities needed hospitals, sewerage systems, road and rail links, vast amounts of housing and, in the end, graveyards (cremation was illegal until 1884).

There was a particularly fast expansion of cities in the two decades after the Great Exhibition during a period of economic growth unparalleled in British history, which was ended suddenly by the economic downturn of 1873. Britain at this point truly was the workshop of the world; competition from Europe, notably Germany, and from America, had yet to challenge the supremacy of British goods. Other domestic factors helped: the repeal of the Corn Laws, the extinction of Chartist unrest and the effects of the dramatic spread of the railway network. Although at the Great Exhibition the British won fewer prizes per exhibit than the French, the event inspired British manufacturers and businessmen, and boosted domestic industry. Lyon Playfair wrote to Colonel Grey on 4 June 1852 to report that one potter had told him how 'the nine months subsequent to the Exhibition had done more to advance the Ceramic Art than the ten previous years' and that the practical outcome of this was £2 million in exports.[1] The same improvements were widely reported, and led to a trickling down of prosperity through society. It was even reflected in the Speech from the Throne on 11 November 1852 at the opening of Parliament, when the Queen said: 'It gives me Pleasure, by the Blessing of Providence, to congratulate you on the generally improved Condition of the Country, and especially of the Industrious Classes.'[2]

The demand for labour in industrial centres remained strong for the next couple of decades, attracting more migrants from agricultural districts. The work these migrants did fuelled the building that drove the physical expansion of cities. By 1860 the average per capita income in Britain was £32 12s a year. In Germany, by comparison, it was only £13 6s. British gross national income was estimated to be £523.3 million in 1851. By 1871 it was £916.6 million.[3] Between 1846–50 and 1871–5 money made from exporting rose by 229 per cent.[4] It was a measure, though, of the strength of the economy in the 1850s and 1860s that even the fast-depopulating countryside became more prosperous. The railways enabled farmers to find more and better markets for their produce, and to transport them more cheaply and easily; and the growing industrial and urban population constituted the main, and fastest-growing, market. By 1881, over 70 per cent of the population would be urban. The value of labour, and what it could produce, was being maximised: the country could earn more from manufactured goods than from agricultural produce.

Expansion of towns was driven not just by houses and places of employment, whether factories or offices, but by all the other trappings of civilised living: shops, parks, concert halls, theatres, museums and libraries. The example of Albertopolis was copied around Britain, often financed by local acts of philanthropy. Local charities gradually built new hospitals for these expanded towns, such as George Gilbert Scott's magnificent infirmary at Leeds, opened in 1869. Prosperity brought with it an expectation that communities would ensure there was some sort of provision to care for people from cradle to grave.

British cities were transformed by the influx of money between the 1850s and the 1870s, and greater ease of communication, notably London. With the spread of education many in the working class became lower-middle class, moving from manual into clerical work. Suburbs grew to house them, and the phenomenon of the commuter was born. It was a time of often incomprehensible change. Despite the social improvement of a substantial proportion of the people, what William Booth, founder of the Salvation Army, would call 'the submerged tenth' was still trapped in poverty, beyond the reach of the ladders of social mobility, living in benighted slums, prone to lethal disease, and in or near criminality. Like all periods of rapid transition, it was an age of extremes. The one consolation that society had was that the poor were an ever-diminishing proportion of the population. In 1849 figures showed that 18.9 per cent of the population was in receipt of either indoor or outdoor relief. By 1877 it was 8.7 per cent.[5] However, the demands that growing numbers in all classes made on infrastructure were becoming enormous. The State would have no choice, if chaos were to be avoided, but to change the whole political culture and intervene to regulate the various mechanisms needed to cope with rapid urbanisation and the expansion of the population.

II

Utilitarians had a strong interest in matters of public health. This was partly because of the drain on the economy of dealing with the consequences of poor sanitation, and partly because of a wish to maximise what the twenty-first century calls 'human resources'. Principal among the sanitary reformers of the age was Edwin Chadwick, a Benthamite and criminal barrister who, in 1832, had been offered a place on the Commission of Enquiry into the Poor Law. This gave him a lifelong interest in the conditions of the indigent. As well as being close to Bentham, who left him a lock of his hair, a ring and much of his library of law books, he was a friend of Mill, and partly of his cast of mind. He had helped draft the first Factory Act of 1833, and the Poor Law report of 1834. Chadwick's biographer admits that the Poor Law system that sprang from the report was 'blind and cruel and bitterly unpopular'.[6]

Chadwick himself had seen his proposed system as creating the basic conditions for capitalism: he had also envisaged the workhouses as places of education, refuge and recuperation, not of humiliation and oppression. The Benthamite belief in the perfectibility of society through the exercise of enlightened self-interest caused Chadwick to be committed to education as a means to enlightenment. He saw education as the way to prevent pauper children becoming pauper adults, or criminals. He also thought the Poor Law Board would oversee free movement of labour, but it did nothing of the sort. Therefore Chadwick, one of the system's progenitors, became one of its bitterest critics.

This, and his growing unpopularity with politicians who resented being told by an official where they had made important mistakes, marginalised him on the Poor Law Commission, and caused him to take a greater interest in public health. In 1837 he had urged the establishment of a register for epidemic diseases. He argued that money spent by local Poor Law unions to remove stinking refuse and empty stagnant pools would pay dividends eventually by avoiding the higher costs of treating the casualties of cholera and typhoid, and the economic damage done by such outbreaks. Malaria was also a problem in the London slums, and fever was bred by the proximity of slaughterhouses and other polluting businesses near the source of water – though all 'experts' believed diseases such as cholera and typhoid were not waterborne, but acquired by exposure to 'the miasma'. Chadwick was alarmed by what he discovered from the statistics of poverty. He investigated 27,000 cases of pauperism and found that 14,000 had become paupers because of catching fever. Of those, 13,000 had died. As well as the human cost, the economic cost of disease was vast.

When Chadwick began to disseminate facts about how bad things were he was accused of exaggeration: one aristocrat, Lord Normanby, was taken to Bethnal Green by a colleague of Chadwick's to see for himself and, far from finding things exaggerated, realised the description of the horrors did not go far enough.[7] On 19 August 1839 Bishop Blomfield moved in the House of Lords that a formal inquiry be held into the causes of disease among the labouring classes: two days later Lord John Russell asked the Poor Law Commissioners to launch such an inquiry. The result was Chadwick's *Report on the Sanitary Conditions of the Labouring Population*. The inquiry coincided with the economic depression with which the Poor Law, never mind the conception of public health, simply could not cope. A quarter of Carlisle's population were near death from starvation by 1842. Consumption of provisions in Manchester had fallen by a third between 1836 and 1842. Only 100 people out of 9,000 were in work in Accrington, and families would live for days on boiled nettles. The Poor Rate in Sheffield rose from £142 a quarter in 1836 to £4,253 a quarter in 1842. The contingent effect of this new wave of extreme poverty on health was predictably savage.

By the end of 1841 he had finished his report, the last draft revised for him by Mill, who told him: 'I do not find a single erroneous or questionable position in it, while there is the strength and largeness of practical views which are characteristic of all you do.'[8] Chadwick, who had once believed that the root of all evil was the poor state of individual dwelling houses, now argued that external sanitation and drainage were the keys to improvement. It required not just mains drainage, but a constant, high-pressure water supply. These proposals upset the government and the Poor Law Commission. Therefore, as a compromise, the report was published under Chadwick's own name. As his biographer points out, this not only ensured his name was linked for ever with sanitary reform. It also alerted the British to the fact that, in the new, industrialised world of pollution and growing population, they lived on a dungheap.

Chadwick argued that, just as Britain led the world in industry, so it did in engineering, giving it the means to construct a perfect sanitary system. It was urgent to do this, because the decade from 1831 to 1841 recorded an increase in the average death rates in Leeds, Birmingham, Bristol, Manchester and Liverpool from 20.69 per thousand to 30.8 per thousand.[9] The huge growth of these towns in the first forty years of the nineteenth century had exceeded any administrative or sanitary improvements that would have allowed a strict regime of public health. London, for example, had grown from 958,000 people in 1801 to 1,948,000 in 1841. Water supplies, and the means to dispose of industrial and domestic refuse, were utterly inadequate. Nor were there statutory authorities to manage the problem. Mills had dammed rivers, making them stagnant, and pumped refuse into them, making them like open sewers. Houses had no drains and inadequate ventilation, and in urban areas human excrement would overflow into streets and courts from inadequate cesspools. Water often came from public standpipes whose supply would be contaminated by the lack of sewerage; one lavatory would be shared between thirty houses, which were being built to the lowest specification. To make matters worse, houses for single families ended up accommodating up to a dozen.

Chadwick recommended administrative reform to ensure regulations for housing, industry and waste disposal were devised and enforced. Having consulted engineers, he wanted a system of sewers for urban areas with water of a velocity that would bear away the waste to distant outlets. This would be driven by the key to Chadwick's reforms: hydraulic power. This required a constant supply of water: as Chadwick later said, 'the establishment of the economy and the efficiency of the constant supply will, when fully considered, be found to be a great work – the completion of what I venture to call the venous and arterial system of towns.'[10] What had troubled him most was what to do with the sewage: because ideally there would be an unpolluted river from which the water would come through the taps and into the water closets, and out again into the sewerage system. He decided that this 'liquid manure' should be directed to flow on to outlying fields, where it would encourage the growth of crops. To oversee and regulate this, Chadwick recommended a local drainage authority, and a district medical officer. The Poor Law Act 1847 established better parliamentary control of workhouses in the light of serious criticism of the inhumanity of these institutions, notably their treatment of the sick. Eventually, the Vaccination Acts of 1853 and 1867 made the vaccination of children against certain diseases compulsory.

III

The massive growth of London required new amenities, notably parks. In 1850 Lord Seymour, who had taken over the Office of Woods and Forests, received deputations from the people of Finsbury asking for a park there. He hesitated for a year, then consulted the Treasury, which advised him to make a survey. By the time he had made one, a speculative builder had bought some of the land required, and offered to do a deal with the government – which was refused. The Treasury had in any case declined to commit money until surveys and inquiries were complete. Seymour came to favour the scheme, with the government buying land to sell to builders to fund the park. He told Gladstone this 'desirable object' would cost £60,000.[11] Other English towns and cities followed suit in the 1850s, with local industrialists (such as Titus Salt) often providing substantial sums to buy land that would be earmarked for recreation.

In 1844, as the East End of London expanded, the government set aside 262 acres in Bethnal Green for what became Victoria Park, 179 acres of which had already been in public ownership and administered by the Commissioners of Woods and Forests. The rest would be compulsorily purchased, though the existing landlords, sensing the value of their property, were demanding a high price. The more cities expanded, the more the need for open spaces – for ventilation as much as for recreation – became pressing, but the demands of speculative builders and the growing middle classes meant that green land close to the centre of cities – especially London – was vulnerable to development. A classic example of central government coming to the aid of local was seen in the 1866 Metropolitan Commons Act, which empowered local authorities within the Metropolitan Police District to use the rates to maintain and preserve open spaces. It was the first of a series of Acts passed until 1878, which enabled the preservation of, for example, Clapham Common; a separate Wormwood Scrubs Act secured that stretch of common land in north-west London for the use of its local inhabitants. A similar Act enabled authorities outside London to buy land for parks, though this could cause controversy. The Liverpool Corporation paid £250,000 in 1867 to buy 375 acres from the Earl of Sefton to form the park that still bears his name, because of the urgent need for an open space near the ever-more crowded city. The price caused outrage, even though it was in part defrayed by the building of large villas on the park's perimeter for the quality of the city.

Another equally visible legacy of the Victorians in most British cities are the great suburban cemeteries. By 1845 Parliament was forced to consider an aspect of public health that was being aggravated by the enormous growth of towns: the question of burying the dead. The tradition of doing so within the confines of old towns, in existing churchyards, was becoming unfeasible. Reformers wanted larger cemeteries outside towns, something the government opposed on the grounds of popular sentiment. A committee of medical experts appointed by the Commons recommended ending interments in large towns, and spoke of the 'shocking practices prevalent in the graveyards of the Metropolis'.[12] Typhus, the committee said, had become common because of the 'putrid miasma' and 'effluvia' seeping through the soil of overcrowded burial grounds because of shallow graves.[13] This was also a problem in provincial towns that had had population booms: North and South Shields, Sunderland, Coventry, Chester and York. London was the worst, though. Chadwick had written a report detailing how a court near Drury Lane was a 'mass of corruption', and how at Rotherhithe 'the interments were so numerous that the half-decomposed organic matter was often thrown up to make way for fresh graves, exposing sights disgusting, and emitting foul effluvia'.[14] He also reported that even the burials of the well-to-do under the flagstones of churches, and in good coffins, were problematical: 'Sooner or later every corpse buried in the vault of a church spreads the products of decomposition through the air which is breathed, as readily as if it had never been enclosed.' A leading campaigner for new cemeteries, William MacKinnon, the MP for Lymington and chairman of a select committee on the question, had spoken of his incomprehension at the claim that people were 'still desirous to continue the custom of interring the dead in the midst of the living', for none of his inquiries had revealed any such demand.[15]

Mackinnon read a letter from George Brace, the Principal of St Clement's Inn in London, that outlined an even worse problem than shallow graves: inadequately constructed crypts and vaults. Brace told of an infants' school separated only by a timber floor 'the rafters of which are not even protected with lath and plaster' from a cellar in which, between 1823 and 1840, had been deposited more than 10,000 corpses, 'not one-fiftieth part of which could have been crammed into it in separate coffins, had not a common sewer contiguous to the cellar afforded facility for removal of the old, as new supplies arrived.'[16] The letter continued:

> In the cellar there are now human remains, and the stench which at times issues through the floor is so intolerable as to render it absolutely necessary that the windows in the lantern roof should be kept open. During the summer months a peculiar insect makes its appearance; and in the adjoining very narrow thoroughfare, called St. Clement's Lane, densely inhabited by the poor, I need scarcely inform you, that fever, cholera, and other diseases, have prevailed to a frightful extent. Over the masses of putrefaction to which I have alluded, are children varying in number from one to two hundred, huddled together for hours at a time, and at night

the children are succeeded by persons, who continue dancing over the dead till three and four o'clock in the morning. A band of music is in attendance during the whole night, and cards are played in a room adjoining this chapel-charnel house.

It was clear that moral and religious as well as sanitary considerations were at work.

Another speaker, Joseph Hume, quoted a Dr Reid on the subject 'of the extent of the evil arising from the miasma of graveyards'.[17] The doctor had 'detected deleterious gases escaping from graves 20 feet deep, and stated that he had found the ground in many churchyards perfectly saturated with carbonic acid gas'. Hume said that the philanthropists who 'employed thousands and tens of thousands for the benefit of people in foreign countries whom they knew nothing of, might turn their humane intentions to the position of their fellow countrymen at home.' Graham, whose responsibility this was, however claimed that the British people would rather cling to their customs, and bury their dead among the living. He disputed that the existing graveyards spread ill health – he quoted the proximity of the House of Commons to St Margaret's churchyard, and argued how exceptionally healthy everyone in that part of Westminster appeared to be.

For all his talk of not offending 'social and religious feelings', Graham's opposition suggested other considerations, notably the possibility of great public expense in buying land for cemeteries. He also sought to ridicule Chadwick, who had suggested precisely that policy, with the government taking over responsibility for the safe and sanitary disposal of corpses.[18] Graham could not promise this: it is yet another example of his resisting inevitable change until forced upon him, and another reason why his historical reputation is poor. He was attacked by later speakers for ignoring the overload on some parish churches in urban areas to hold funerals: one spoke of a church where fifteen had been fixed for the same hour.[19]

Lord Lincoln suggested suburban cemeteries would be impossible for the poor to use, because of the 'very burdensome' cost of moving the corpse and transporting the mourners 'from St Giles's to Hampstead or Harrow.'[20] Lincoln also attacked Chadwick, claiming his proposals would 'make the rich pay for the poor', since a tax would have to be raised to pay for new arrangements. Graham returned to the dispatch box, and maintained again that 'the remedy proposed by Mr. Chadwick appeared to him to be entirely inapplicable to the present feelings and wants of society'.[21] He added that out-of-town burials were also 'beset by equal difficulties arising from the objections of Dissenting bodies. To almost every Dissenting chapel there was a burial ground attached, in trust for all who worshipped in that chapel; and not only were their pecuniary interests thus involved, but their feelings also.'

He continued: 'If they determined that Churchmen and Dissenters should not bury in the accustomed places of sepulture, but at a distance from towns, then every poor individual wishing to attend his friend to his long home must forego a day's wages; and in winter he must travel four or five miles from home and back. To attend a funeral would be extremely inconvenient, unless conveyances were provided; and if they were provided, the cost to the poor would be oppressive. There was a desire in the human breast of laying our bones beside those of our departed relatives and friends. This feeling . . . was stronger than reason, and was connected with the best sentiments of human nature.'

IV

Since 1815 it had been permissible for London's domestic waste to be poured into the Thames. Coinciding as this did with a great expansion in the city's population, and the development of industries on the south bank of the river, this could hardly have been a worse policy. Poor people lived in extreme squalor, many to a room, with nothing resembling modern conveniences. Those who either could not afford a cesspit, or to have them emptied, simply dumped waste in the gutters, hoping it would be washed away. Before the internal combustion engine the streets were strewn with horse manure, pushed into gutters by crossing-sweepers (who would be tipped a penny or two for their trouble by the quality as they crossed the road). Horse and human waste was carried out of the city every night, but this barely addressed the problem. It was also estimated that by the 1850s around 1,000 horses a week were being destroyed, presenting the problem of disposing of their rotting carcases.[22] Within a little over thirty years, and not entirely because of the cholera epidemics, it was obvious that London's effluent disposal policy would have to change, or there would be a calamity.

Britain in the 1840s was still susceptible to cholera, because of the foul water recycled for drinking: 52,000 died in the outbreak of 1848–9, an estimated 14,000 of them in London, the capital's problems exacerbated by an order to close all cesspits. The Public Health Act 1848, which made this order, also set up a central board of health, forced towns with a death rate of more than twenty-three per thousand to set up local boards of health, and allowed other towns to set up boards if 10 per cent wanted them. It also set up the Metropolitan Commission of Sewers in London, whose policy was strongly influenced by Edwin Chadwick, who also led it. It set about trying to empty all the cesspits in the capital – it was estimated there were 200,000 of them – and have all the effluent pumped into the Thames. The flush lavatory had been patented by Joseph Bramah in 1778 and by the start of the Victoria's reign was found in most well-to-do households. Its popularity caused the amount of contaminated water to increase greatly, and cesspits routinely overflowed. This was before the physician John Snow argued in 1854 that cholera was waterborne, though others were slow to believe him, preferring instead to think it was airborne, passed on through a 'miasma'.

In 1854 Palmerston had told the Commons that the Commissioner of Sewers (Chadwick had long been relieved of his post because of a bureaucratic shambles at the Commission, and also because of a series of disagreements with the engineers) had made a plan that he 'had thought might probably be adopted for the great arterial drainage of London in parallel lines, or at least in some relation to the course of the Thames, with a view of preventing the sewage of London from falling into the river'.[23] A debate continued about the relative merits of small-bore against large-bore sewers, and Palmerston mentioned that the former, obviously, were cheaper. Henry Drummond, the MP for West Surrey, spoke of how cholera had been an ever-present threat for seven or eight years, and yet no one had done anything about it. There were more flush lavatories in London with each day that passed, and 'the Thames was getting dirtier every day, because the more water that was introduced into the dwellings of the poor the more filth was driven into the Thames.'[24]

Despite the plans to build new main sewers, the cost – a rate of three-farthings in the pound – was deemed too much. There were even plans to defray the cost by making the sewage suitable for agricultural purposes: but the plan in 1854 for the sewers along the Thames did not include ones branching out to take away the effluent from other communities far from the river. So still nothing was done, because the richest nation in the world would not afford the cost. That is not to say that the Commission was entirely inert; from 1849 to 1854 inclusive it laid 163 miles of public sewers and 366 miles of private ones. However, *The Times* reported in July 1855 that 'there are yet urgently required about 400 miles of sewers', and about another 20 miles 'so defective as to require rebuilding'.[25] The cost it estimated at £1,500,000, and it was proposed by the parliamentary committee examining the question that bonds be sold to raise the money, as had happened in Paris for the embanking of the Seine.

Over the next three years this conversation occurred several times in the Commons, with demands routinely being made to set a date after which no sewer would be allowed to be discharged into the Thames. In 1855, following much public and press criticism of the state of the river, the Metropolitan Board of Works was set up by Act of Parliament to undertake the sanitary improvement of the metropolis. All the board lacked was money. 'Londoners were warned years ago that this noble stream was not intended by nature for a sewer,' *The Times* wrote in July 1855, 'and that it was an abominable perversion of the gifts of Providence to use it so'.[26] The paper pointed out the blindingly obvious: the more effectually people removed effluent from their houses, the more effectually they polluted the river, the only receptacle for it now that cesspits had been banned. It expressed its exasperation that, given the requisite engineering science was available (and as Joseph Bazalgette, the eventual engineer of the sewerage system, would point out, had been for half a century), the metropolis did not get on with it, and build the necessary drainage system to distant outfalls. The alternative – reopening the cesspools – was unthinkable, but the river could not go on being 'so very foul, so very fetid, and so thoroughly defiled'. Nor was it only the Thames that was being defiled, but its tributaries as well.

The individual parish councils, or vestries, along the river could not be expected to find the funds to cure this health hazard. It did not merely require sewers: it also required embanking the river on both sides from around Chelsea to the Tower, because the human and animal waste floating in the river would often be cast up, fetid and pungent, on the pebbly foreshore that ran along its course through the cities of London and Westminster. For the moment, Parliament had no inclination to vote funds for the project.

The matter always became more urgent in the summer, especially during heatwaves. This became acute in June 1858, when the Thames and the urban creeks that flowed into it overflowed with sewage. The temperatures were in the 80s Fahrenheit most days, there was no rain to wash away the effluent, and the Thames was by mid-June estimated to be 20 per cent sewage 'and much of it lay spread out over the mud banks, literally boiling in the sun'.[27] Some who had to cross Westminster Bridge required smelling salts to do so. A correspondent wrote to *The Times* on 16 June that 'I took my wife and a country lady up the river from London Bridge to Kew on Saturday last, and . . . the stench from the water was unbearable. Our country friend felt "awful queer" in such an atmosphere.'[28] Another described the Thames as 'a huge sewer' and the smell 'abominable'. Two days later another correspondent, a lawyer resident in the Temple, wrote that 'if I open my windows in rushes the stench, and I imbibe large draughts of the poisonous matter . . . I am quite conscious of the fact that I am being killed by inches.'[29] He was outraged that the government was doing nothing: 'I want to know if they are waiting for a pestilence to break out before they will do any thing; if they think it will be quite time enough to commence their labours when the dead cart shall have begun its rounds.'

On 15 June the shade temperature in London reached 91.2 degrees Fahrenheit. The next day it was 92.6 degrees. It was perhaps as well for the people of London that among the first to be affected by the mephitic smell from the river were members of the legislature. When the Irish MP John Brady said that MPs sitting in the Committee Rooms and in the Library 'were utterly unable to remain there in consequence of the stench which arose of the river', Lord John Manners, the First Commissioner of Works, simply shrugged his shoulders and replied that 'the River Thames was not in his jurisdiction, and therefore not under his control.'[30] This attitude was attacked as 'nonsense' by a *Times* corre-spondent, who wrote that 'if it is not technically their business now, they can easily make it so; parliament is absolute.'[31] A few days later, when the smell had become worse, Manners repeated that the river was nothing to do with him, or with the government, but for the Metropolitan Board of Works that had been set up under an Act of 1855 to coordinate the maintenance of London's infrastructure. The board took a slow approach to the problem, causing one MP to propose putting its members on a river steamer, and sending them up and down the river to see – and presumably smell – the problem.[32] There were warnings that if cholera came to London, with the present state of the river, there would be death on a scale not seen since the plague of 1665. Cartloads of fish were taken out of the Thames daily poisoned to death, whereas within living memory there had been salmon in the river.

The problem was where to put the sewage, and how to get it there. Specialist engineers called in to advise the Board had said London would probably treble in size 'in a few years', so there was no point in half measures in building a new sewerage system. The cost would be £10 million or £11 million. A plan had been drawn up in 1855 for fifty-one sewers on the north side of the river and twenty on the south, to be in place by the end of 1860: but nothing had happened, because of a reluctance to spend money. In the Palace of Westminster canvas blinds inside the open windows were moistened with a mixture of zinc and lime to purify the air. Boatloads of lime were being spread over the mud banks by the river to try to neutralise the smell at source: the lack of efficacy of these measures should, however, have been manifest to anyone inhaling in the Palace.

The smell became still worse. An aggrieved correspondent wrote to *The Times* on 21 June to speculate that 'if the members of both our Houses were to be suddenly seized with English cholera a committee sitting over the vapourous exhalations of the Thames would soon report that the river must be purified, and the fiat, supported by personal considerations, would be carried out notwithstanding all opposing sponsorship.'[33] A week later there was a call for a Royal Commission to embank the Thames and build sewers 'without delay'.[34] The works manager at the Commons had told the Speaker that 'he can no longer be responsible for the health of the House; that the stench has made most rapid advance within two days'. The miasma had also taken over the law courts, then still in Westminster Hall and adjacent to it. A doctor appearing as a witness in a case there had said it was not safe to breathe the air, and not safe for those with business at the courts to remain there: malaria and typhus were an immediate threat. The Lord Chief Baron had pronounced that 'the stench from the river is most offensive, and I think to take public notice of this, that in trying this case we are really sitting in the midst of a stinking nuisance.'[35] There had been cases of cholera, and the smell stretched from Chelsea to Greenwich.

Around 90,000,000 gallons of sewage were discharged into the Thames daily; only four times that amount of pure water flowed down the river, insufficient to dilute it. For £2.5 million the sewage could be carried 10 miles to Barking Creek; or could be taken 20 miles further east, and pumped into the sea – but that would lead to much of it being carried back up the river at flood tide. Sir Joseph Paxton mentioned the plan of Joseph Bazalgette, who had said that for £6 million he could take the sewage down to the German Ocean – the North Sea. 'It was important that the matter should not be done in a niggardly way, and if London was to be drained it should be done effectually'; but he did not believe there was any need to embank the river.[36] He felt it could be done with 'intercepting sewers' – which would intercept existing drains and take all their effluent as far as Barking Creek. Given the urgency, he could not see the point of a formal commission: the job should simply be done.

Yet money remained the great obstacle. The estimate for the sewer laid down when Victoria Street had been built a few years earlier had been £12,000. It had in fact cost £70,000 and the sum was still rising, and some feared it would end up costing £200,000. Committing to two great sewers – one north and the other south of the river – would be a huge commitment of money. MPs realised the government would have to find the money to sanitise what was, after all, the Imperial capital. The works would take years; but would never be finished if they were not started. Meanwhile, *The Times* published a leading article venting the spleen of the upper-middle classes: 'Foreigners have always been disappointed in London, but now-a-days they are astonished, not to say disgusted . . . London proper is becoming more foul and dingy and dilapidated and stinking every day. The Parisian, the Viennese, the New Yorker is surprised at the meanness of the houses, the closeness and smallness of the shops, and the general slovenliness and want of care which meet the eye on every side.'[37]

Two days later a doctor from Bermondsey, John Challice, said that 'I have daily persons consulting me who have been seized with nausea, sickness, and diarrhoea, by them attributed to the effects of the effluvia from the river. Some have complained that the peculiar taste remained on their palate for days.' He warned that the river was becoming daily more poisonous, and that were an epidemic of cholera to occur its effects would be 'unprecedented'.[38] One MP after another piled on the tales of suffering to make the point that the taxpayer would have to fund sewers.[39] However, the *argumentum ad pecuniam* could be applied

in more than one way. George Bentinck, a Norfolk MP, deplored that
the taxpayer should fund the sewers, when London was so wealthy, and
London would be the main beneficiary. Disraeli, as Chancellor, agreed
the government had no legal responsibility to tackle the Great Stink:
but it did, he felt, have a moral one 'to prevent public disaster'. He
declared that 'the time has come when it is absolutely necessary that
action should commence.'[40] He criticised Palmerston for setting up the
Metropolitan Board of Works and then not funding it – it relied on rates
collected from individual vestries, or parishes, in London, and these were
inadequate for serious projects. He would ensure the Board was funded,
and the Great Stink finally tackled. The next day Charles Greville
recorded in his diary that 'the foul state of the Thames . . . has suddenly
assumed vast proportions'.[41]

The deliberations of a parliamentary committee during July ended
in the Commons voting the money for the project, requiring a 3d in the
pound tax for forty years on the inhabitants of London. In 1859
the Metropolitan Board of Works embarked on the massive project. The
main responsibility devolved on the MBW's chief engineer, Joseph
Bazalgette. Despite Snow's strong arguments to the contrary, it was still
believed that it was the 'miasma' from the smell that caused cholera,
rather than the contamination of water by sewage. Bazalgette's plan to
take sewage far downstream before letting it out into the river – so far
downstream that it would not be washed back up to the metropolis –
removed the smell, but also, unintentionally, removed the problem. There
would be one further outbreak of cholera – in 1866, in east London –
but this was because of water from the polluted River Lea entering a
reservoir. Once rectified – further proving Snow's point about cholera
being waterborne – London had no more epidemics.

Bazalgette had cut his teeth on great railway projects in the 1840s,
but had also undertaken land drainage and reclamation projects. He had
joined the Metropolitan Sewers Commission as assistant surveyor in
1849, succeeding to the post of engineer three years later when the
incumbent, Frank Forster, died of stress and overwork. Bazalgette
himself had come to work for the Commission while recovering from
a nervous breakdown because of his exertions during the 'railway mania'.
What he found in his early days at the Commission will not have
improved his mental health. He made unofficial inspections of existing
sewers and found them often in a shocking state of repair and requiring

wholesale replacement. It was during these years that Bazalgette and his colleagues updated a plan by Forster for a London main drainage scheme, a plan that would have to remain a pipe dream for want of funds or, indeed, of political vision.

Another cholera epidemic in 1853 killed 10,738 Londoners. When the Metropolitan Board of Works succeeded the Commission in 1855, on an initiative by Sir Benjamin Hall, Palmerston's First Commissioner of Works, Bazalgette became chief engineer, not least on the recommendation of his friend Isambard Kingdom Brunel. His plan was to build intercepting sewers along the north and south banks of the Thames, not tunnelling to build them, but running them along the contaminated beaches and foreshores and concealing them within new concrete embankments with roadways and public gardens above them. They would link up with his earlier plan for the London main drainage. His was not simply a scheme of sanitary improvement, but a massive infrastructure project that would also come to accommodate the underground railway from Tower Hill to Westminster. It was one of the most modernising projects in London's history.

Bazalgette wanted to build 1,300 miles of sewers to lead into a main network of three sewers north of the Thames, and two to the south, the main sewer network being 82 miles long. What was dumped miles downstream past Barking Creek was by that stage diluted by rainwater but was still untreated – and would remain so for many years – but at least the problem was removed from the seat of population. To assist the passage of the effluent Bazalgette built several pumping stations, at Chelsea, Deptford, in the Lea Valley and on the Erith marshes. His greatest stroke of genius, however, was to build his main sewers to a particularly wide bore. He had already plotted the size to account for a generous personal allowance of daily sewage for Londoners, but he then doubled it. As a result, modern London still uses Bazalgette's infrastructure. He is the personification of the Victorian determination to build to last, and for the future.

As well as a sewer running along the line of the river before diverting north-east near the Tower, another sewer would run from Kensington through the West End to north-east London, where it (like the Thames sewer) would link up in the Lea Valley with a sewer running through the expanding northern metropolis from Hampstead, which would carry on down to the river at Barking. South of the Thames, which was less populated, there would be two sewers, linking at Deptford before proceeding to outfall. The 82 miles of this main system had a capacity of 400 million gallons. Construction proceeded rapidly on all but the most important sewer, along the Thames, because of concerns about the cost and disruption to commercial life that its construction would cause. It was not until 1862 that Parliament agreed to what is now the Embankment being built from Westminster to Blackfriars, whence the sewer would divert up Queen Victoria Street to the City. The MBW was also overseeing road-building in the city, which coincided nicely with laying drains and sewers underneath.

The northern network was functioning by 1868, the southern by 1875. Three major embanking projects were completed, beginning with the Albert in 1868, on the south bank opposite the Palace of Westminster, the Victoria on the north opposite it and leading up to Blackfriars in 1870, and the Chelsea in 1874. Once those tasks were completed Bazalgette oversaw the transfer of Thames bridges from private contractors, who collected tolls to fund their businesses, to the government: this required him not merely to value the bridges, but also design new ones; though his design for Tower Bridge was not built. The process of protecting London from being killed, literally, by its own filth had taken a typically Victorian course: endless wrangling among politicians about whether or not to spend the money, a final recognition of the inevitable caused by massive social change, and a determination to build what was necessary as permanently as possible.

V

The success of sanitary reform in London persuaded Parliament to apply the principle more widely across Britain, and to take a more active interest in the promotion of healthy living. The Sanitary Act 1866 compelled provision of sewers, water and street cleaning, banned overcrowding and set up Sanitary Inspectors. Such a measure was long overdue, and closed a loophole in the 1848 Act that enabled many towns to evade their responsibilities. Francis W. Newman, writing to Kingsley in 1851, described the way the sewers of the time worked: 'Every running sewer has generated evil gas. So notorious is that fact that every sewer has holes which are periodically opened, to let out the gas against the unfortunate houses which happen to be near: did they not do so, the sewers would explode. Thus the sewers are worse than the cesspools, because they have so much greater a surface. The Sanitary Gentlemen say that 'running' sewer water generates no gas, but only odours. I do not yet believe them.'[42] Bazalgette, who had an extensive private practice, was asked by a number of expanding towns to design their main drainage systems.

An Act of 1835 had allowed large towns to become chartered and set up municipal corporations. By 1861 a total of 29 had done so, but the only obligation on a town that had been chartered under the new Act was to set up a constabulary. Like much legislation of the time it merely enabled, rather than compelled, the local authority to undertake certain actions. Even so long as the legislation was permissive it started to have an effect on improving not just quality of life, but also lifespan. The overall death rate in Liverpool fell from an average 31 per thousand between 1850 and 1855 to 25.6 per thousand in 1885. But in the 1850s slums still teemed in most British cities, and so long as they did lethal disease went with them. At this time, for example, the industrial canal in Bradford was so polluted, and giving off such toxic gases, that youths could set fire to it on hot summer days.[43]

However, many of those same cities embarked on improvements, beginning with new municipal headquarters from which to direct the modernisation of the locality. The growing success of industry and the creation of wealth provided the money to start this process, and an idea of civic pride grew up in many newly expanded towns. This led to the building of town halls and other civic institutions. Towns such as Liverpool, Manchester, Leeds, Bradford, Glasgow and Newcastle-upon-Tyne acquired great town halls and other municipal buildings that expressed the status of the community. More than a century and a half later, the image we have of many of those cities even today is rooted in the period of their greatest pomp in the nineteenth century, and tied to the success of the industries to which they were home.

Cities grew in different ways and for different reasons. Manchester was built on the cotton trade, Bradford on wool. Joe Chamberlain's biographer, J. L. Garvin, described the Birmingham of this era as a 'dense, formless creation of the machine age . . . a powerhouse of moral and material energies.'[44] The town was characterised in the early nineteenth century as a place of small manufacturing businesses, where the enterprises rapidly grew. If it became well known for anything it was the gun trade, and prospered abnormally during the Crimean War. But it also specialised in all sorts of metalwork, from the nibs for fountain pens to the screws made by Chamberlain's family. It was a city that flourished on free trade, but which had to ensure it kept ahead of its rivals. Chamberlain's own job, as a young man in the late 1850s, was to ensure that with the valuable patent rights for the new, pointed screws and their manufacture that his uncle and father had obtained from America, the firm could dominate not just the British market but Europe as well.

This, too, was when steam-driven machine-made goods improved the profitability of businesses and the prosperity of the city. Modernisation brought casualties, or at least men who had to adapt. The many small manufacturers of blunt-ended handmade screws whom Nettlefold and Chamberlain put out of business often ended up working in the factory of their nemesis: that was thanks to Joe Chamberlain's success as a salesman, and the new markets he conquered, which managed to provide work for many who had not caught the tide of change. That was not the half of it, however: as Garvin recalls, 'the work-people gained by larger and lighter buildings, better sanitary conditions, more regular employment, shorter hours and higher wages, as well as by the firm's "welfare work", far ahead of general example.'[45] This was the progressive Birmingham that John Bright, having lost his seat in Manchester, would represent in Parliament, and of which Chamberlain would become a radical, and phenomenally successful, mayor.

Bright and Chamberlain were at opposite ends of the Liberal spectrum, but had important things in common. Chamberlain, like Bright, lost his first wife when still young, in his case two days after the birth of the first son, Austen, in 1863. And, like Bright, Chamberlain threw himself into his work to anaesthetise the pain of his bereavement. This was not just at the screw factory. He was a deeply religious man – a Unitarian, whereas Bright was a Quaker – and used much of his spare time doing good works, and teaching in Sunday school. Yet he became a founder member of the Birmingham Liberal Association when it was formed in 1865, and that would become his political power base.

Because of Bright's association with Birmingham the city became a centre of the reform agitation in 1866–7: and it was then that Chamberlain felt himself drawn into politics. In August 1866, after the defeat of Gladstone's Reform Bill, an estimated quarter of a million attended a reform rally just outside the city. Chamberlain was marched to the rally, and that evening heard Bright address a smaller, packed gathering in Birmingham town hall. After reform Chamberlain, like many other middle-class people, worried about the uneducated having the vote. What drew him into local government first and foremost was the need to provide schools for the poor in Birmingham. Around half the children in the city in 1867 received no education at all: and around half of the newly enfranchised were illiterate. Chamberlain was a founder member of the Education Society in the city, which pondered how best to improve matters.

In a campaign reminiscent of Shaftesbury's Ragged School movement, volunteers scoured the streets for children. There was a fund-raising drive to pay the fees of some of them: though the money raised was inadequate to the task. Chamberlain himself was deeply driven. 'It is as much the duty of the State to see that the children are educated as to see that they are fed,' he wrote in 1867, and added that 'the enjoyment of this right ought not to depend on the caprice of charity or the will of parents.'[46] The Society's aims were free education for all those whose parents could not afford it, and an unsectarian education in all new or State-supported schools. His concerns anticipate the debate in 1870 over the Education Bill, but they are significant in his case as the motive force that brought him into politics.

Chamberlain became a councillor in November 1869, not least to find a platform from which to advocate educational reform. His agitation during the passage of the Education Bill in 1870 has already been described. Once it was law, and allowed the subsidising of Anglican schools by dissenters and Nonconformists, he became even more aggressive in his political activity. He threatened to lead a rates strike in Birmingham and, along with numerous others, to have bailiffs come to seize his property rather than give a farthing to the maintenance of a denominational school. It did not come to this, because the Anglicans who controlled the school board in Birmingham lost their majority, and the Liberal-dominated council endorsed Chamberlain's position. His was a powerful example, however, of how the 'new men' were determined to shape the new industrial cities of Britain, and not leave it up to an old Establishment or their representatives to do so instead. And, outside politics, the success of his business resulted in its building new works and setting up its own iron mills. By the early 1870s, for good measure,

Chamberlain had taken over almost the entire Birmingham screw trade, first by buying up his main rivals, and then by crushing the minnows that were left.

By late 1873 he had no rival for the post of Mayor, and determined to bring Birmingham, with a population of around 300,000, completely into the modern world. He determined on a programme of sanitary reform, new street lighting, and numerous architectural improvements. He used his considerable experience in business to find the revenues for the city to do all these things. He persuaded the council to agree to buy the two local gas companies that held the monopoly in the city. Running them like businesses and not, in the manner of twentieth-century nationalised industries, like social services, he turned a profit of £25,000 in the first six months of municipal ownership. As this profitability continued, so was the money found to improve Birmingham.

Having accomplished this, Chamberlain then won approval for the compulsory purchase of the municipal water system, which was largely primitive and still a carrier of disease. The water companies had been less willing to sell than the gas companies. Chamberlain argued that natural monopolies ought not to be in private hands, but should be controlled by the representatives of the people. At least fifty or sixty other large towns now owned their water supplies, and had upgraded them and run them at a profit. Chamberlain did not seek to run the water supply in order to fund more improvements: he sought to run it in order to give everyone in Birmingham a clean, reliable supply, and to reduce the cost of it. This led to a wider improvement in sanitation and a new sewerage system. Then came the greatest health improvements of all: slum clearance, restrictions on the emission of smoke, and the extension of hospitals. He also had 100 miles of pavements renewed and gave a large sum of his own money for the improvement of the Art Gallery. Perhaps most significant of all, he ensured an assize court was established in Birmingham. Previously the perquisite of a medieval town, its establishment showed Birmingham had arrived.

VI

Much of the growth of cities after 1840 was directly attributable to 'Railway Mania'. Not only could goods be moved more cheaply: so could people. For the first time 'mobility of labour' began to mean something.

Nor were the benefits simply economic: minds were opened, and broadened. People who had scarcely strayed beyond the next village went across counties and countries. Some of them saw the country more widely than anyone had ever done: such as Matthew Arnold, whose itinerant life as a schools inspector entailed his spending undue hours in railway-station waiting rooms, but also allowed him to acquire a strong grasp of what England was really like.

Engineers such as Isambard Kingdom Brunel, architect of the Great Western Railway and designer of three great steamships, were synonymous with this movement. Scarcely less of an achievement was that of George Parker Bidder, who as well as helping to build the London to Birmingham railway also built the Victoria Docks in London, and was responsible for the expansion of the electric telegraph along the railway network and under the sea. Britain was expanding, but it and the world were shrinking. This social and industrial revolution was also driven by Robert Stephenson, remembered today for his feats of engineering railway bridges; and by Daniel Gooch, the greatest locomotive engineer of his day.

Early on, governments saw the economic potential of the railways, but also the potential dangers: one prominent politician, William Huskisson, had been killed by Stephenson's Rocket at the opening of the Liverpool to Manchester railway in 1830. Gladstone, as President of the Board of Trade in 1844, had introduced regulations specifying the standards to which railways should be built, to protect the public. In 1845 the average express train on the London and North Western Railway was travelling at an awesome 37 miles per hour, an almost shocking prospect for many.[47]

It was easier to protect passengers' physical safety, however, than to guarantee the financial security of investors. Also in 1844 Gladstone introduced a bill to regulate the commercial activities of railways, which made the provision of cheap travel for the lower classes a condition of running a railway (it became known as the 'parliamentary train'). The law specified that 'each company be required to run over their line on each weekday at least one train conveying third-class passengers in carriages provided with seats and protected from the weather, at a speed of not less than twelve miles an hour, including stoppages, and at a fare not exceeding one penny a mile for adults, children under twelve half price, and under three free, 56lb of luggage to be allowed without charge.'[48] The provision of third-class accommodation was often beyond basic: in some instances simply planks set in a low wagon, which in a notorious accident at Sonning in Berkshire on Christmas Eve 1841 caused people to fall out and break their necks when the train was hit by a landslide; or people were conveyed in what were effectively cattle-trucks, standing up with no possibility of sitting down. Gladstone recognised that the railways would become a national resource, like the highways, and the bill also gave the government the power to buy any railways built subsequent to its enactment after a period of twenty-one years.

Railways were not regarded as an unmixed blessing, even though they shrank distances and supercharged prosperity: the more rapid movement of goods facilitated trade and enhanced choice for consumers, and the greater ease of the movement of people around cities such as London, Manchester and Birmingham caused the development of suburbs. But suburbs eroded countryside, as the population of England and Wales grew by more than 10 per cent between 1851 and 1861. The railways themselves carved through hundreds of linear miles of hitherto untroubled rurality; they altered the cohesion of communities by linking villages to nearby towns; they created noise and, above all, change. They helped broaden horizons and create restlessness and curiosity. More prosaically, many people put their shirts on speculative ventures concerning the railways, and lost them.

An early enemy of this naked progress was John Ruskin, whose name blazed in the cultural world of the 1840s and 1850s. His highly influential treatise about the moral force of buildings, *The Seven Lamps of Architecture*, was published in 1849, more or less at the height of railway mania. In it he wrote that 'another of the strange and evil tendencies of the present day is to the decoration of the railroad station. Now, if there be any place in the world in which people are deprived of that portion of temper and discretion which are necessary to the contemplation of beauty, it is there. It is the very temple of discomfort, and the only charity that the builder can extend to us is to show us, plainly as may be, how soonest to escape from it.'

That was not, however, the limit of his criticism.

The whole system of railroad travelling is addressed to people who, being in a hurry, are therefore, for the time being, miserable. No-one would travel in that manner who could help it – who had time to go leisurely over hills and between hedges, instead of through tunnels and between banks: at least those who would, have no sense of beauty so acute as that we need to consult it at the station. The railroad is in all its relations a matter of earnest business, to be got through as soon as possible. It transmutes a man from a traveller into a living parcel. For the time he has parted with the nobler characteristics of his humanity for the sake of a planetary power of locomotion. Do not ask him to admire anything. You might as well ask the wind.[49]

The problem with these 'miserable things', as Ruskin called them, was not just that they sought improperly to use beauty, but that they destroyed it: the landscape as nature had intended – and Ruskin was a connoisseur of landscape – was violated by the iron road. Something similar was probably said, though not written, by an ancient Briton surveying Roman road-building 1,800 years earlier. And, as he said, the railway was simply about 'business', and business was dehumanising: themes that, as we shall see, Ruskin the social and political commentator would revive militantly in the 1860s. For him, and for others less articulate, the railways represented a destruction of nature by the unnatural demands of capitalism, and would become a talisman of the battle between progress and the ordered, comfortable past. The freedoms and prosperity they offered would usually most directly benefit a class that did not include the likes of Ruskin and his high-minded, aesthetic followers.

In the 1840s Parliament had been overwhelmed with private bills to allow railway-building. Although some landowners had objected, and driven hard bargains, the public were generally in favour, and the social life of the nation was revolutionised. The Board of Trade was criticised for how it had overseen the expansion of the railways, not least in that it appeared to have ended up creating and endorsing monopolies. One or two politicians fought against the railways per se – notably Colonel Sibthorp – but most saw the inevitability of their rise and sought to harness them to the country's good. The imperative was to ensure as much competition as possible within the system so that poorer people, and their goods, could be conveyed as cheaply as possible, in the interests of economic growth. Even Sibthorp, whose loathing of the railways was based on what he considered to be their danger to public safety and their temptation to investors who were then ruined financially, travelled to his election at Lincoln in 1847 by train.[50]

By 1844 Parliament was seeking ways in which bills could be consolidated – passed several at a time – to ease the pressure on the machine; it was said that 248 possible bills might come before the Commons in the foreseeable future.[51] This inevitably meant scrutiny was reduced, and some landlords and localities felt they had suffered injustices. In the 1845 session alone the five MPs on one of the committees considering railway bills had to consider twenty-three new lines; and the total in that year of all railways considered required decisions about £100 million worth of property, and new lines totalling 4,000 miles. In that session, 240 bills were presented to the Commons and 119 of them had received approval from the Board of Trade. Scrutiny could not be complete. Companies often broke agreements about fares and freight charges, to the anger of the public; anger with political consequences, or so many MPs feared. Also, the government wanted the mail to be moved by rail, and to have the railways in times of emergency to move troops and police. The political stakes became high, and shareholders became annoyed at the prospect of State interference. By the end of 1848 12,000 miles of railway had been authorised by Parliament: it was not until the late 1860s, however, that the network actually reached that size.

Meanwhile, some shareholders made a fortune. There were allegations of conflicts of interest for certain MPs who sat on railway boards; and complaints about the fortunes being made by the inevitable beneficiaries of such a massive construction and property development project, the lawyers. The question of MPs having an interest – not just as shareholders, but as landowners – was highly likely, given, for example, that the 186 miles of the proposed railroad from London to York passed through 300 parishes. Speculation could, however, be ruinous, especially if the capital raised for a scheme were expended on the legal and parliamentary preparations for it, and it failed. Lord Brougham told the House of Lords in 1845 about legal actions failing because of the vested interests of jurors, and about a clergyman who had invested £5,000 in railway shares to raise money for his family and, having been promised he would quadruple his money, found his investment plummeting instead.[52] Others had borrowed to buy shares in the expectation of their rising, only to find that they fell, and they could not pay their debts. Sibthorp told the Commons that the inevitable consequences of railway speculation were 'ruin, crime, madness and suicides'.[53]

The railways greatly facilitated, and cheapened, the transport of coal and manufactured goods. They helped cities grow. They also made certain foods available in places where they had been scarce before, and at affordable prices. By 1845 the price of cod in Manchester had fallen to between 1½d and 2d a pound; it had previously been between 8d and 1s a pound, because of the difficulty in transporting sufficient supplies from the east coast while keeping it fresh. There had been a correspondingly beneficent effect on the east coast fishing fleet.[54] The cost of laying railway had also dropped: in the early days it had cost £50,000 a mile to lay the Great Western, but the cost had now dropped to between £10,000 and £12,000 a mile.[55] As the railway extended its range, stagecoach companies collapsed, and the canals, which had previously transported so many goods, went into decline after a brief prosperity.

However, by 1846 Peel felt he had to say to the Commons that 'I think every person in this House witnessed the extent of railway speculation which took place last winter and the preceding autumn with great regret'.[56] He observed that 'we then saw railroads proposed not for any legitimate purpose of speculation, and not for the purpose of constructing works of public utility in the vicinity of those who were engaged in the speculation, but in a fit of one of those speculative fevers, from which the country has in many instances suffered so severely.' There had been a huge transfer of money from capitalists to landowners; the latter, along with lawyers, were the great winners of railway mania. No fewer than 1,400 schemes had been registered by 31 December 1845. When, in the early 1840s, some of the main lines out of London had been built, and had given a handsome return to their investors, the desire to build more took off in a fashion that did not even appear limited by the availability of capital.

By 1846 it was clear to all, except to some investors, that many of the proposed schemes could not come to fruition or, if they did, would never make money. More and more were ruined by subscribing to shares they hoped to sell at a profit before ever having to pay for them, only to find they had to pay before registering their profit – a profit that only rarely came in any case. Sometimes the names of subscribers were fictitious, in order to make a speculative scheme look more attractive than it was. It would ratchet up share prices to where insiders could sell and transfer their gains into sound stocks, leaving those holding railway shares to lose all when the crash came. It should have been obvious to any sensible investor that plans to link for the second or third time two unprepossessing provincial towns could not possibly work, even if Parliament allowed its development.

In August 1845 the Marquess of Clanricarde told the Lords of a case concerning 'two brothers named Guernsey, sons of a charwoman living in a garret, in Angel-court, one of whom had signed for £12,500, and the other for £25,000, the latter being a porter to a wine merchant named Hitchcock.'[57] The two men earned around 'a guinea and a half a week' between them. One, 'Charles Guernsey, stated that he never applied for any shares, but that a stockbroker brought him letters of allotment to the above amount. When he signed the deed, the broker took the scrip, and he never received one farthing; that he was only nineteen years of age, and in the receipt of only 12s a week.' The following May Clanricarde complained that railway speculation had simply fuelled 'the gambling operations of the Stock Exchange'.[58] It was beyond doubt that many whose names had been put down for shares had no means of paying.

This speculative building was only the start of great expansion, which continued throughout the 1850s to the 1880s. After the great boom years of 1845 and 1846 development slowed, but remained steady. In 1846 around 4,540 miles of route were built; in 1847, the bubble having burst, just 1,295 miles.[59] The railway from Doncaster to London was opened in time for the Great Exhibition, with a return fare of 5s. The line from London to Salisbury was finished by 1857: it reached Exeter in 1860. By the 1880s the great main lines to the north and west from London were established, as were the railways to Norwich and the line to Holyhead that took the mail (and British officialdom) to and from Ireland. If rail travel had originally been the preserve of the rich, the railway operators soon saw the benefits of coupling third-class carriages to the end of the train, with fares as little as 1d a mile, above and beyond what Parliament had enforced. Gladstone was determined that such regulation as was necessary did not inhibit the spread of the network. In 1850 a total of 67.4 million passengers were carried. By 1875 the number had reached 490.1 million, with the freight carried trebling over the same period.[60]

One essential regulation was standardising the gauge of the tracks. What had started out as a series of local systems would soon join up and form a national network. This meant, when engineers were making rapid advances developing locomotives to pull the trains, those locomotives might work only on a limited part of that network, and therefore could become obsolete quickly. The lack of uniformity also impeded the railways' economic contribution. Freight had to be unloaded and reloaded where two different gauges met, which increased the cost of the shipment, delayed it, and often caused avoidable damage to the goods. Stephenson had used a gauge of 4 feet 8 ½ inches on the Liverpool and Manchester Railway, and this gauge – which became known as standard gauge – had caught on. It met firm resistance, however, from Brunel, building the Great Western at a gauge of 7 feet 0 ¼ inch. Brunel believed broad gauge trains would be more stable and capable of higher, safer speeds. Brunel's difficulty was that, at the end of 1844, he had only 223 miles of broad gauge line whereas the Stephenson gauge already had 2,013 miles.

The Eastern Counties Railway, begun in 1843, used a gauge of 5 feet exactly. It soon realised the difficulties of an incompatible gauge and changed to Stephenson's within two years. Brunel, however, stood firm, even when a Royal Commission in 1845–6 recommended the universal adoption of Stephenson's gauge. Parliament's will to enforce a standard gauge had been fed by a group of MPs witnessing the performance of unloading and reloading at Gloucester, where goods from Bristol to Birmingham had to change gauges. An Act later in 1846 compelled all new railways to be built to the standard gauge. Brunel held out, and his gauge long survived him: but in 1892 the Great Western at last admitted defeat, and converted to the standard gauge after all.

For all the horror that the Sibthorps felt about progress as represented by the railways, those who built them sought at least to keep them consonant with the highest standards of building of the period. Ruskin's injunction not to waste money or effort making railway stations attractive was widely ignored. As many surviving stations testify, the railway estate contained some of the finest examples of mid-Victorian architecture. The combined work of Scott and Barlow at St Pancras in London remains the best known: but countless provincial and rural stations boasted decorative ironwork, ornate canopies and handsome red brick or stone. Viaducts evoked the aqueducts of ancient Rome; and the largest termini echoed cathedrals. Peace, quiet and isolation might have gone in some places for ever: but the railway system became the prime example of the attempt by the Victorians to combine functionality with craftsmanship and beauty. It was something of a reaction against the great wave of factory building of the

1810s and 1820s which, with certain distinguished exceptions, Blake was justified in describing as 'dark, satanic mills'.

The growth of the railways also allowed the growth of the imagination. The line that became the Great Central Railway, from Manchester across the Pennines to Sheffield and then to London, was intended to carry on to the Kent coast, where it would submerge into a Channel Tunnel and come out in northern France: a vision that took until the early 1990s to realise. A line was, though, opened from London to Dover via Croydon, Tonbridge and Ashford that could speed travellers from the Channel steamer up to the capital, with Dover being reached in 1844. From July 1841 trippers could go to Brighton from London for the day, and during the 1840s the rest of the Sussex coast was brought into easy reach by branch lines.

By the 1860s railway companies owned around a third of the canal system. By 1870 the railways had largely destroyed the turnpike system of roads, and as turnpikes went bankrupt local authorities, financed by hard-pressed ratepayers, had had to take over the upkeep of roads that, for forty or fifty years until the coming of the motor car, would be quiet except for local journeys by pony and trap. Throughout the 1850s and 1860s, however, roads became marked out as the locations of telegraph wires.

Railways, in the 1840s, came to embody the unacceptable face of capitalism. The evils of the doctrine were well depicted by both Trollope – the odious Melmotte in *The Way We Live Now* – and before him Dickens, through Merdle in *Little Dorrit*. The filth of speculation, manifested in real life by the likes of George Hudson, the railway king, is well described in the epitaph Dickens writes for Merdle:

> The late Mr Merdle's complaint had been, simply, Forgery and Robbery. He, the uncouth object of such wide-spread adulation, the sitter at great men's feasts, the roc's egg of great ladies' assemblies, the subduer of exclusiveness, the leveller of pride, the patron of patrons, the bargain-driver with a Minister for Lordships of the Circumlocution Office, the recipient of more acknowledgement within some ten or fifteen years, at most, than had been bestowed in England upon all peaceful public benefactors, and upon all the leaders of all the Arts and Sciences, with all their works to testify for them, during two centuries at least – he, the shining wonder, the new constellation to be followed by the wise men bringing

gifts, until it stopped over certain carrion at the bottom of a bath and disappeared – was simply the greatest Forger and greatest Thief that ever cheated the gallows.[61]

George Hudson himself had a life beyond the imagination of even the finest fiction writer. Born in 1800, he was a farmer's son who left school at fifteen and became apprenticed to a draper in York. He was given a share in the business after his apprenticeship, and then married the daughter of another partner. At twenty-seven he inherited the then massive sum of £30,000 from a great-uncle. Like many rich men since, he felt this entitled him to enter politics. He became a Tory activist and, in 1837, Lord Mayor of York. Four years before that he had made his first investment in railways, in a line linking York with one from Leeds to Selby. He became the largest shareholder and, in 1837, the chairman. His company – the York and North Midland Railway – hired George Stephenson as its engineer.

Hudson built lines elsewhere in Yorkshire, the north and the Midlands. Even at the depths of the depression in 1842 he was still finding money to expand, and doing so with a confidence that betokened better times. By 1844 he had 1,000 miles of railway from Birmingham in the south to Newcastle in the north, and began to be called 'The Railway King': it was not an appellation he resisted. In June 1844 a through train ran from Euston, where it began on the tracks of the London and North Western Railway, moving on to Hudson's track at Rugby and continuing north to Gateshead, covering 303 miles in nine hours twenty-one minutes (eight hours eleven minutes excluding stops, or an average speed of 37 miles an hour). To cover such a stretch of England well within a working day was regarded at the time rather as space travel would be in the 1950s. It was proof, were it needed, that Britain was a small country, and becoming smaller. The following month Hudson opened a railway from Edinburgh to Berwick, and secured an Act of Parliament the following year to link Berwick to his existing track at Newcastle, creating what would become the North British Railway. Thanks to amalgamations he controlled a network that started at Bristol, ran up to Rugby, and thence north to Edinburgh.

He also resisted Gladstone's attempts to regulate the railways. His methods were seldom ethical. He bought land to prevent competitors driving rival lines through them. He tried, unsuccessfully, to derail the Great Northern's attempts to build a line from London to York – a link to London was the jewel missing from the Railway King's crown. Elsewhere his kingdom grew, almost to the size of an empire. As well as going west to Bristol, he owned the Eastern Counties railway that took him into East Anglia. One of his trains took the Queen to Cambridge when Albert was installed as Chancellor of the university in 1847.

Even he, however, lacked the resources to keep his competitors at bay for ever, and he was marginalised by his failure to secure a line from the north to London. He was threatened, and he knew it, by the proposal in 1844 (which won parliamentary support) to run a line from King's Cross to York via Huntingdon and Peterborough, roughly along the line of the Great North Road. On 17 December 1847 the opening of the line between Oxenholme and Carlisle linked Glasgow and Edinburgh with London, the trains coming in to Euston. The Great Northern, which sought to operate the line from King's Cross, was also in dire straits: in the four months from March to July 1848 its revenues were £2,502 19s, yet it had spent £2.5 million.[62] Seeing their distress, and thinking of a way out of his, Hudson did a deal with the GNR to allow it to use his lines north of York. Shareholders in his Midland company were outraged, because the deal with the GNR created a shorter route to the north from London than that via Rugby.

In August 1848 the banks called in £400,000 of Hudson's debt. When word spread his share price fell. Standards of accounting at the time were primitive, and Hudson took full advantage. He took a huge personal dividend out of his enterprises, to buy estates in Yorkshire and a house in Knightsbridge. As shareholders in his various companies smelt something unpleasant, inquiries were launched. It was discovered he had been rigging share prices, to his own benefit, and paying dividends out of capital rather than out of profits. He had lied about almost all his enterprises. It was proved that company money had been diverted into his bank account when it had been intended to pay contractors.

He attempted to defend himself by saying that it was commercially more sensible to do a deal with the GNR than to seek to fight it – which he had long tried to do, with little success. He was forced from the chairmanship of the Midland railway, and the other investigations of the byzantine accounts of his other companies – notably the Eastern Counties – showed he had rigged figures to alter the share price. To make matters worse, it turned out that some of his managers had also been behaving fraudulently and cheating shareholders. Hudson also had the stupidity to sue a newspaper for libel, and lost. By mid-1849 he had been forced to resign all his chairmanships, though he had been elected to Parliament for Sunderland in 1847 and was, indeed, re-elected in 1852 and 1857. This gave him immunity from arrest for debt when Parliament was sitting. When it was not he fled abroad. However, his election also made him a target, for both radicals and for the press, and *Punch* (which had been launched in 1843) started to make him a regular object of caricature. His political prominence had also invited scrutiny of his business dealings, which led to his downfall.

He lost his seat in 1859 and stayed abroad. Although he had acted criminally, it was widely perceived that the loose company law exploited during railway mania had given him the means to do so: the State had woefully failed to protect the public. Eventually, his creditors had him arrested for debt in 1865 when he returned to England to seek election at Whitby. He was jailed for three months before his creditors, recognising they would never get their money, gave up pursuing him. He managed something of a rehabilitation – a feat that says much of his personal charm – and was even elected as chairman of the Smoking Room at the Carlton Club shortly before his death in 1871.

To Carlyle, who always sought new examples of the wickedness of capitalism and the cash nexus, Hudson presented an irresistible target. He was the subject of the seventh of *The Latter Day Pamphlets*, published in July 1850, and written at a time of his life Carlyle later described as one of 'deep gloom and bottomless dubitation'.[63] This may explain the extra ferocity of the attack on Hudson, to whom Carlyle suggested, given his embodiment of the modern British way, someone should erect a statue. It would enable the country to say 'there is one God, you see, in England; and this is his Prophet.'[64] He despised the recent reverence of the 'divine Hudson'. He bellowed that 'Hudson the railway king, if Popular Election be the rule, seems to me by far the most authentic king extant in the world. Hudson has been 'elected by the people' . . . his votes were silent voluntary ones, not liable to be false; he did a thing which men found, in their inarticulate hearts, to be worthy of paying money for; and they paid it. What the desire of every heart was, Hudson had or seemed to have produced: Scrip out of which profit could be made.'[65]

Carlyle's other objection was that the change, and modernisation, that the railways accomplished wrecked for ever the basis of the feudal England to which he had sought a return. No longer were people moored in their communities, a journey of even a few miles being difficult for them. 'Railways are shifting all Towns of Britain into new places; no town will stand where it did, and nobody can tell for a long while yet where it will stand. This is an unexpected, and indeed most disastrous result . . . Reading is coming up to London, Basingstoke is going down to Gosport or Southampton, Dumfries to Liverpool and Glasgow; while at Crewe, and other points, I see new ganglions of human population establishing themselves, and the prophecy of metallurgic cities which were not heard of before.'[66] He felt that towns that had subscribed to have railways built had been 'cutting their own throats. Their business has gone elsewhither'. Shops and houses in those places, he argued, were now 'silently bleeding to death'.

The Industrial Revolution had been nothing compared with the railway revolution. The former had shifted populations and had altered the economic basis of British power: but had not had the true revolutionary impact that comes with mobility. That, in particular, was what had unhinged Carlyle. Much of England was, to him, still recognisable after the Industrial Revolution: now it would be permanently moving, shifting, changing, and disconnecting itself day after day from its historical roots.

For all his crookery, Hudson had a massive ambition that fitted in exactly with the tenor of the age. The Midland and the Great Northern railways flourished until their amalgamations in the London Midland and Scottish Railway and the London and North Eastern Railway respectively in 1923. Meanwhile, King's Cross Station – then the largest in the land – was finished in 1852, the first train out of it to York leaving at dawn on 14 October. The communications system on which the advance of Victorian Britain would be based – the rapid movement over long distances of goods, people and mails – was established.

VII

The railway business, because of its vital strategic importance, remained under political scrutiny long after the initial burst of expansion had finished. The government launched an inquiry in 1865 into the prices being charged by railways for the conveyance of people and goods:

because in many areas they were an effective monopoly, and were restricting economic growth. Gladstone explained that 'the object of the Commission on Railways is to ascertain, by careful inquiry, not only how to meet particular evils or inconveniences now suffered by portions of the public, but how to increase in the greatest degree, of which they may be found susceptible, the already vast advantages which the introduction of railways has conferred upon the subjects of HM', it stated.

'Now that the protective system has been broken down, the great work of the liberation of industry and capital, on which the comfort and material well-being of the people principally depend, can in no way be more effectually promoted, than by improving and cheapening the conveyance both of persons and of commodities from place to place.'[67] Gladstone added that the revenue of the railways now exceeded one-half of the total revenue of the country. It had one-fifteenth of the property of the nation. He wanted the cost of fares to drop by a quarter, to the advantage mainly of the 'labouring classes', but also to help agriculture, by making the shipping of goods cheaper. The commission would have the power to 'enforce the rendering of information' from railway companies, such was the economic importance that Gladstone attached to this.

As a prelude to this Douglas Galton, the secretary of the Railway Department at the Board of Trade and yet another cousin by marriage of Florence Nightingale, had written to Gladstone on 31 December 1864 about 'the difficulty of the Railway question'.[68] He had sounded out various leaders of the railway industry. One, George Bidder, 'civil engineer largely interested in the management of the Great Eastern Railway' and president of the Institution of Civil Engineers was, he said, 'the only one of the railway men who would transfer the railways to the state – the others would mend the present system.' There was one exception, Mr Hawkshaw, another civil engineer who had been communicating with Rowland Hill about the movement of post, who said things would be best left as they were.

Galton said that the provision of railways by the private sector and not by the State had created more permanent way in a shorter time 'than could probably have been obtained under any other system'. This did not mean, however, that this was the best system for the future. Cartelisation and avoidance of competition, to the detriment of the customer, were creeping in. Managers of rival companies were forming agreements 'known only to the officials'. He argued that 'the rapid development of wealth which has taken place in the country during the last few years has been rendered possible principally by the existence of railways – there is coal enough under parts of the country yet untouched to enable that development to continue for generations. This will require a continued extension of the Railways, but the more the railway system approaches to a protected interest the less room will there be for those appeals to competition by new companies which have hitherto aided the progress of the system. A period may arise therefore when the progress of the country may require some new arrangements to prevent the industry of the country from being fettered.'

Galton felt five points especially needed to be addressed: uniformity of fares and rates; the scale of fares and rates 'to be the lowest compatible with a fair profit – third class trains to be cheaper and more numerous'; the obligation on companies to charge passengers travelling through from the lines of other companies the same rates as charged to their own; the development of new classes of traffic; and the co-ordination of timetables to avoid long delays at junctions. The question was, he said, whether the companies would do these things left to themselves, or whether it would have to be taken over and done by the State. Galton himself was not sure: 'Much could be obtained for the public either way.'

The railways had their grievances. They were taxed too much; local rates were too high; and compensation in case of accidents was unlimited and possibly bankrupting. Galton suggested to Gladstone that he try to redress these grievances in return for the companies' cooperation. Galton saw dangers in nationalisation that would be proved right when it happened over eighty years later: 'my experience of a large government executive department is that the universal tendency is to increase the salaries and diminish the work of individuals.' He argued that 'it would be more economical to bring in the aid of private enterprise – and the advantages of further improvements might be obtained for the public by leasing the lines to private companies for limited periods of 7, 10 or 14 years.' Galton said it was clear the system was not yet complete, but also that 'the state could not undertake the construction of new lines without risk of political jobbing.' He concluded that the cartelisation was detrimental to the national interest, and might require intervention. 'Railway companies have come into existence by putting in force the principle that property may be purchased compulsorily when such purchase is for the benefit of the community; they cannot therefore reasonably object to the same principle being applied to them.'

Gladstone wanted 'a good arrangement for allowing new companies to come into the field: and to prevent their being opposed by either future Lessors or Lessees of existing lines.'[69] Galton sent back word later in January 1865 that the railway companies would happily consider lower fares for third-class passengers in return for certain favours, notably lending money to those companies who wished to expand but who had exhausted their capital.[70] There would be no repeat of railway mania, but new lines would be added, faster and more reliable locomotives would be designed, and, for a time, the experience for the passenger would consistently improve. As a symbol of progress and modernity, and indeed of the creation of a whole new sort of society, the railways stood out alone.

CHAPTER 18

A GLIMPSE OF THE GOTHIC: FOUNDING A NATIONAL STYLE

I

The most visible legacy of the Victorians is their architecture, the representation of the ambition to improve, and to make works of art that would endure. Theirs was an era that determined to use its new prosperity to leave its mark upon the world, and to make buildings worthy of the greatest imperial power. In the buildings of the mid-nineteenth century, as in the paintings of the period, are seen the consequences not just of the social and technological changes of the time, but also of the intellectual and spiritual currents. The link with God, and an idea of Christianity, that drove some to build, and others to interpret building in a specific way, infuses much of the period's work. Now, when one looks at Victorian buildings as speaking of an age, it is their solidity and self-conscious mock-medievalism that loom large. Victorians built with an equally self-conscious idea of the divine informing their purpose.

Most Victorians forswore the classicism popular since the era of Inigo Jones more than two centuries earlier and, as in politics and in the Oxford movement, reached back to a Europe before the Reformation. In 1836 Charles Barry had won the competition to rebuild the Palace of Westminster – which had burnt down two years earlier – and was asked to build the Gothic palace that stands on the Thames today. What most of all give the buildings their status as a masterpiece are, however, their interiors, notably the House of Lords, which Barry deputed to the leading Gothic artist of the time, Augustus Welby Northmore Pugin, and the clock tower – housing Big Ben – which was the last thing Pugin designed before he died in 1852. The Middle Ages were Pugin's visiting card. At the Great Exhibition there was, apart from the progressive, forward-looking machines and products, a Medieval Court that he had designed, showing an aesthete's determination to root Britain in a glorious, godly past at a moment when it seemed concerned only about its future. However much the visitors raved about the new machines they could witness in action, and see changing their futures, they still had an urge to dwell in the past.

It was the supposedly glorious past of Carlyle's 'perfect feudal times' and of the Eglinton Tournament and Young England. Pugin had a strong influence on public taste at a time when sudden prosperity, as it so often does, provided a temptation towards ostentation. However, his lessons for other architects cannot be understated, especially upon those such as Butterfield who built ornately decorated churches in keeping with the Anglo-Catholic aesthetic of the Oxford Movement. The Gothic to which they returned had never entirely gone away, and had been revived (as Gothick) in the eighteenth century. The romantic medievalism it evoked was almost a comfort-blanket in a time of rapid change and social upheaval: there is a link here with the mentality that drove Carlyle to embrace and celebrate feudalism. Until his untimely death in 1852 Pugin was designer-in-chief of the feudal fantasy. The Gothic novel was popular at the beginning of Victoria's reign for similar reasons, and antiquarianism of the sort that infuses the writing of Sir Walter Scott was another strong social current. When the florin, or 2-shilling piece, was redesigned in 1851 (it had been introduced just two years earlier as a possible prelude to decimalisation, 2 shillings being one-tenth of a pound) the design and lettering were Gothic. In buildings, literature, culture and even in the coinage, the Gothic seemed to have become the national style.

Great though the early dominance of Pugin was as a guide of taste, it was John Ruskin's idea of the Gothic as the godly way of building that soon became the most hugely influential after Pugin's untimely death. Ruskin had not inspired the Gothic Revival, but his propaganda on behalf of it kept it going far longer than might otherwise have been the case. His voice was so strong, in the 1850s and 1860s, that it shaped taste and began to inform opinion about what a country that wished to consider itself advanced, progressive, civilised and Christian should do when building. While the burden of the argument in *The Stones of Venice* is about the superiority of the Gothic over the Renaissance style also so prevalent in Venice, the path had been made clear in *The Seven Lamps of Architecture*. Both works aimed to foster an aesthetic climate in which the Gothic Revival could prosper, with arguments presented about the moral superiority of the style. A country steeped in the Classics looked back to the Middle Ages not least because the Middle Ages, unlike antiquity and unlike the mid-nineteenth century, were unequivocally Christian.

Ruskin's travels had been extensive and his research diligent, so there were few who had seen or examined so much who could gainsay him. He also, though, spoke with such an egotistical authority that he crushed all except those with an opinion formed out of equal erudition. His casual attack on St Paul's Cathedral in *The Seven Lamps* is typical. Having written at length on the appropriate ornament for Gothic buildings, and on how floral decorations seemed completely unnatural for Renaissance ones, Ruskin asks: 'Who among the crowds that gaze upon the building ever pause to admire the flowerwork of St Paul's? It is as careful and as rich as it can be, yet it adds no delightfulness to the edifice. It is no part of it. It is an ugly excrescence. We always conceive the building without it, and should be happier if our conception were not disturbed by its presence. It makes the rest of the architecture look poverty-stricken, instead of sublime.'[1]

The Seven Lamps advanced the religious view of architecture. It was conceived as an exposition of the moral force of the discipline. The seven lamps are the seven spirits that architecture should embody: Sacrifice, Truth, Power, Beauty, Life, Memory and Obedience. Architects, amateurs of architecture and the art-consuming intelligentsia devoured it in the two or three decades after it was written, when Ruskin's sway was greatest. Ironically, the foremost exponent of the Gothic Revival, George Gilbert Scott, had a cordial detestation for Ruskin of the sort that the man who does often conceives for the man who simply teaches; despite there being a similar religious motivation behind his own buildings, and having at first been influenced by *The Seven Lamps* and *The Stones*. By the time *The Seven Lamps* appeared Scott was a reasonably well-established architect, who had been building Gothic Revival churches across England for several years. Scott's own preference for the Gothic, and his belief that its degeneration had led to the classical becoming so popular, had been his artistic creed since the mid-1840s, and was similar to Ruskin's. Scott's eventual disregard for Ruskin came not least because of an ego every bit as monumental as some of his buildings.

In 'The Lamp of Obedience', Ruskin set out some of what he considered the ground rules for the Gothic Revival. 'The choice of Classical or Gothic . . . may be questionable when it regards some single and considerable public buildings; but I cannot conceive it questionable, for an instant, when it regards modern uses in general: I cannot conceive any architect insane enough to produce the vulgarisation of Greek architecture.'[2] Beyond even that, Ruskin was clear which styles of Gothic were preferable: the Pisan Romanesque, the early Gothic of the Western Italian republics, the Venetian Gothic ('in its purest development') or the English earliest Decorated. 'The most natural, perhaps the safest choice, would be of the last, well-fenced from chance of again stiffening into the perpendicular'. Ruskin also sought to define the moment in the adoption of 'unnatural' window tracery when the Gothic started to decline in the fourteenth century, so could be particular about these things.

Carlyle's reverence for the Middle Ages complemented Ruskin's belief that architecture should exhibit the best moral aspects of a people: architecture had political and philosophical as well as aesthetic roots. Ruskin's and Scott's generation was also affected by Matthew Holbeche Bloxam's *Principles of Gothic Ecclesiastical Architecture*, published in 1829 as a slim volume and revised so extensively during the author's long lifetime that it reached a three-volume edition by its eleventh printing in 1882. Despite – or perhaps because of – the pressures of secularisation, both the Established Church and the dissenting creeds strove to build churches and chapels, and to make them look like medieval institutions. What Bloxam called the 'vestiges of antiquity' to be found in the British Isles were of huge importance to him, and he made them of huge importance to many of his fellow countrymen and women, by whom hitherto the physical manifestations of the past had been taken for granted.[3] As well as instilling a consciousness of the past, Bloxam provided a blueprint of the different types of Gothic. This would have been well known to specialists such as Scott and Ruskin, but not to the clergy, industrialists, politicians and private individuals who would be the patrons of Scott and other architects.

Gothic churches are a familiar Victorian legacy to even small towns, and other Victorian architecture is ubiquitous. The expansion of the population in the second half of the nineteenth century meant many more houses were built, for all classes of the population. Schools, hospitals, courthouses, town halls, shopping streets, universities and colleges, lunatic asylums, libraries, museums, art galleries, market halls, public houses, municipal baths, theatres, concert halls and railway stations remain monuments of the age. The names of the men who designed them resonate too: notably Scott, Butterfield, Street, Pugin, Waterhouse, and Bodley. The abundance of private and public commissions ensured the profession of architect flourished as never before. It would not be until the end of the nineteenth century that the first university courses in architecture were established: Scott (like others) had pupils articled to him for five years, who learned on the job. To judge from the enduring quality of the work, it was no bad training.

II

Ruskin led the battle between Gothicists and classicists. In Bradford in the late 1860s, in a lecture on the occasion of the decision to build a new exchange there, thirty years after he had first joined a society at Oxford to preserve Gothic architecture, he said he had noticed that in the new northern towns 'the churches and schools are almost always Gothic, and the mansions and mills are never Gothic.'[4] He could not understand why. 'When Gothic was invented, houses were Gothic as well as churches; and when the Italian style superseded the Gothic, churches were Italian as well as houses.' He asked why 'you live under one school of architecture, and worship under another'.[5] He worried that if the people regarded Gothic as so sublime that it had to be reserved only for religious buildings (and the schools, then, were usually religious foundations or enterprises) 'it signifies neither more nor less than that you have separated your religion from your life.' The world of commerce – the fruits of which were to build Bradford's new exchange – had become a substitute religion. As he had written in The Stones, 'the Gothic architecture of Venice had arisen out of, and indicated in all its features, a state of pure national faith, and of domestic virtue; and . . . its renaissance architecture had arisen out of, and in all its features indicated, a state of concealed national infidelity, and of domestic corruption.'[6]

To Ruskin and his followers the division between the two schools of architecture had a profound theological significance. The one indicated piety, godliness, the glory of God; the other self-interest and the glory of Mammon, and the advance of secularism. There was something about the Gothic style that spoke of the pursuit of perfection; something about the Renaissance style that spoke of indulgence and self-satisfaction. 'Do you mean', Ruskin asked his audience at Bradford, 'to build as Christians or as infidels?' For, he added, 'in all my past work, my endeavour has been to show that good architecture is essentially religious – the production of a faithful and virtuous, not of an infidel and corrupted people.'

This did not mean good architecture had to be ecclesiastical; it just had to be the work of 'good and believing men'.[7] For, he said, 'every great national architecture has been the result and exponent of a great national religion'.[8] Now, though, Christianity had become the 'nominal religion, to which we pay tithes of property and sevenths of time; but we have also a practical and earnest religion, to which we devote nine-tenths of our property, and six-sevenths of our time . . . the ruling goddess may be best generally described as the "Goddess of Getting-on", or "Britannia of the Market".'[9] Talking of the harbours, warehouses and exchanges that were the temples of this faith, he observed: 'It is quite vain to ask me to tell you how to build to *her*; you know far better than I.'[10]

The Oxford Movement affected ecclesiastical architecture. The pursuit of religious perfection was, its adherents felt, possible only in a Gothic church building. Perhaps most influenced among architects was William Butterfield, the longest lived of the great Victorian builders – he died in 1900 just short of his eighty-sixth birthday. He was the son of a Nonconformist chemist, apprenticed to a Pimlico builder at sixteen. At twenty-four he was articled to Harvey Eginton, a Worcester architect, and set up his own practice in Lincoln's Inn Fields in 1840. Like Scott and Street he travelled widely on the Continent to learn about Gothic buildings, and to absorb their influence. Butterfield joined the Ecclesiological Society – which had been founded at Cambridge in 1839 as the Cambridge Camden Society, devoted to the study and promotion of Gothic architecture – and regularly wrote for, and published designs in, its magazine the *Ecclesiologist*. Then the Oxford Movement shaped him. His religious feelings translated into designs not merely pre-Reformation in their elevations but also in their interior decoration. In endorsing the aims of the Ecclesiological Society he accepted that churches had to be planned as metaphors for the spiritual functions of sacrament and worship. This is why his churches are so different from those built or restored by his very Protestant contemporary, Scott.

To go inside Butterfield's masterpiece, All Saints, Margaret Street, is to be transported: either to somewhere in Italy, or back to the English Middle Ages of lavishly painted walls and Catholic – or rather, Anglo-Catholic – images. The church is a few dozen yards north of the vulgarity of London's Oxford Street, on the site of the eighteenth-century Margaret Chapel, which had by the late 1830s become a centre for Tractarian worship. It has been said that All Saints, designed in 1850 (the year Pusey laid its foundation stone) and completed in 1859, initiated high Victorian Gothic. Pugin might quarrel with that: there are few interiors of which All Saints is more reminiscent than the House of Lords. The tall spire of the church – almost the only part easily visible from a distance, as other buildings enclose it in this crowded part of the West End – is of north German influence, and the use of brick reminiscent of German churches too. Butterfield fiddled with the decoration for the rest of his life – another forty years after its supposed completion – but the exuberant floor tiles and the marble and granite pulpit are from the original plan.

Butterfield's patrons were the Ecclesiological Society, with two of its members in particular taking the closest interest: Sir Stephen Glynne and Alexander Beresford Hope, a Conservative politician who would in 1865 become president of the Institute of British Architects. Beresford Hope was an unrepentant medievalist who paid much of the £70,000 cost. All Saints realises the ideal the Society's members had for Christian worship. It was intended as a 'model' church, with extensive use of polychromy. Outside, its red brick includes courses of black or blue bricks. There was an element of this in Butterfield's original plans, but these were revised extensively during 1849–50. This was at the behest of the patrons as well as of the architect, the use of colour having been influenced by *The Seven Lamps*. There are bands of stone on the spire. Inside, there are courses of marquetry and decorative tiles, and judicious use of marble. It is that, the painted walls and the coloured roof that make it seem Italian. However, the tracery, arches and capitals mimic a style on the cusp of Early English and Decorated. The riot of decoration in the windowless north aisle is the epitome of Italian style, though a modern critic has called it 'dazzling, though in an eminently High

Victorian ostentatiousness of obtrusiveness . . . from everywhere the praise of the Lord is drummed into you. The motifs are without exception big and graceless.'[11] Even the *Ecclesiologist* thought it ugly, though conceded the power and force of its decorations.

Over the next twenty years Butterfield would use polychromy in other notable commissions. Between 1868 and 1876 he built at Rugby School in this style, and Keble College, Oxford. He built a number of other churches and chapels, mainly in the South Country, notably Wiltshire. He also restored many churches, obliterating genuine Gothic features, a vandalism he had in common with Scott.

III

The Gothic may have been the divine style, but many who had to live and work in it loathed it. A battle raged during the late 1850s and 1860s about whether it, or the classical style, should be the predominant style in Britain's public architecture. As with so many other Victorian disputes on high-minded matters, it was frequently conducted in the gutter.

Even before the Palace of Westminster was completed it was intensely unpopular, and not least with Lord Palmerston, Prime Minister from 1855 to 1858 and again from 1859 to 1865. This was the era of 'the Great Stink'. Parliament then sat only outside the shooting season, usually from early February until mid-August. The last two months of the session became unbearable as the temperature rose. It was hot in the building, which had inadequate ventilation, and the windows could not be opened because the smell was too nauseating. Various reasons have been cited for Palmerston's dislike of the Gothic – such as his having had to work in ill-lit buildings as a younger man and not wishing to inflict the experience on anyone else – but his dissatisfaction with the Gothic House of Commons (where, as an Irish peer, he sat as an MP) might also have had something to do with it. He felt the Regency buildings of his youth represented the height of architectural achievement, and thought them more suitable to be used as government offices than something resembling 'a continental cathedral'.[12] Gothic, when it came to public buildings, was an experiment he wished not to be repeated. Palmerston was, in architectural terms, a philistine. When he had extended his estate at Broadlands in Hampshire he had, precisely because they failed to conform with his

Regency prejudices, pulled down an ancient manor house and cottages, much to the fury of local antiquaries.

The Foreign Office, an early Georgian house in Downing Street, was inadequate for a country with a growing empire and a great power in the world. Sir Benjamin Hall, the First Commissioner of Works, and the man after whom the bell in Westminster's clock tower would be named, had instituted the competition not just to build a new Foreign Office, but also a new War Office (the conflict in the Crimea had not long ended; and the government had realised that, in an age of expansion, more wars were possible). There had been numerous submissions by British and European architects; an exhibition of their drawings had been held in Westminster Hall; and judges had been appointed. When Hall explained to the Commons on 10 August 1857 why public money would be spent replacing this inadequate building with something in keeping with mid-Victorian Britain's idea of itself, he found himself under attack for the way in which the competition for the buildings had been conducted.

A committee had the previous summer examined only two witnesses about this huge outlay of public money: the official surveyor of public works, Mr Hunt, who would have known on which side his bread was buttered, and Sir Charles Trevelyan. Trevelyan had sounded a note of caution not about the idea, but about the process – he had recommended that 'before anything was done in the matter of rebuilding the public offices some comprehensive plan should be agreed on, combining administrative efficiency, perfect accommodation, architectural beauty, and that the buildings should be raised gradually, one after another, as necessity called for them.'[13]

Hall had put the question out to competition partly because he disapproved of how the government exercised patronage, and partly because he had a low opinion of James Pennethorne, the government's official architect, who had worked on ideas for the site since 1854. The result of the competition was chaotic. 'A French gentleman got the first prize for the block plan, including both Foreign and War Offices; an Englishman got the prize for the Foreign Office, which was incapable of being worked into the block plan; and another Englishman got the prize for the War Office, which was equally at variance with the block plan and with the Foreign Office.' None of these prize-winners was George Gilbert Scott, whose acquisition of the commission for the offices was, it was alleged, not remotely regular, but the result it seemed of patronage and jobbery. Hall had swiftly dismissed as inadequate the plan the judges had chosen (with some strong dissenting opinion) as the best for the Foreign Office, by the Scottish architects Coe and Hofland. In his despair Hall returned to Pennethorne, which caused further complaints from the profession.[14] One came from Scott, who had come third in the Foreign Office competition, and who had already acquired a reputation for blowing his own trumpet. In his memoirs Scott castigated the judges as men 'who knew amazingly little about their subject' and who 'were not well-disposed towards our style.'[15] Beresford Hope, Butterfield's patron, argued that the whole project should be put on hold while a Royal Commission considered, in depth and without such haste as had already been witnessed, what to do about the whole question of improving Whitehall. He convened a meeting of eminent architects, among them Scott, Barry and Digby Wyatt, to arrange to protest at this affront, and to have the competition reopened.

George Cornewall Lewis, the Chancellor of the Exchequer, a polymath who in his spare time wrote books on linguistics, astronomy, philosophy and law, wanted to proceed without delay; but did not imagine that meant the government should 'seize the occasion offered by the want of new public offices to embellish the metropolis with a series of magnificent palaces'.[16] He was supported by Russell, who noted that the architects 'very naturally gave play to their fancy, and a series of beautiful plans and sketches of buildings, embellished with every costly architectural decoration, had been sent in, of no other use, in my eyes, than to gratify the sight of the public, and to show the comparative ingenuity and ability of the French and English architects.'[17] Russell exhibited the radical antipathy to ostentation, believing his generation did not need to flaunt its power by architectural might. Instead, he said, 'I hope . . . that in future the Government will, in erecting new buildings, consider exactly what is required for the purpose to which the building is to be applied.' He claimed to be articulating the opinions of the Monarch, who had declined when Peel was prime minister, and again under Russell, the offer of building a new palace for her and her family because she 'with her usual thoughtfulness and forbearance, immediately desired that no additional expense should be cast upon her subjects. We have now schemes proposed for the erection of buildings far more like palaces than public offices.'

Hall justified his initiative by claiming, with a little hyperbole, that 'there were no public offices in the world which were so inconvenient or in so ruinous a state as our own'.[18] He certainly had a point about the War Office, which had 'several branches . . . located at different places in the West-end.' He defended himself against the charge of extravagance by saying that the accommodation proposed was requested by Clarendon, the Foreign Secretary, and Panmure, the Secretary for War. And if the elevations were deemed grand then, Hall argued, 'surely it was desirable, if they were to rebuild the public offices, that they should have some design for an elevation which should be really worthy of the country, seeing that the constant complaint was that the public buildings in the Metropolis were such wretched abortions.'[19] However, Hall was chastened: he agreed that for the moment land would be set aside in Downing Street, but building would only start once the Commons had sanctioned it – and agreed to find the money.

That was considerable – £380,000 to purchase and clear the land. William Tite, the MP for Bath, said the cost of building the winning block design would be from £5 million to £10 million – 'no prudent country would embark on such a scheme.'[20] Yet Tite, an architect himself, also raised matters of taste: some of the plans had been Renaissance, or French, or Italianate in style and were one of them adopted it 'would create a great incongruity with Sir Charles Barry's building' – the new Palace of Westminster, which had also overrun in costs. In fact, 'the architectural question' had not been considered: merely 'the question of the propriety of acquiring a site and sufficient land to carry out what might be desirable with reference to public offices'.[21] To have ignored this question ignored also the desire to use these showpiece offices as a display of British stature and, just as worryingly, ignored the factionalism between those who wished to promote the Gothic and those who opposed it. The problems of what to build, in what style, and how extravagantly to build it, had barely begun.

Scott was not one to wait to be told what to do by a team captain: he was his own team, and his own captain. He wrote to *The Times* on 26 August 1857 to dismiss Coe (one of his former pupils) and Hofland's winning effort and that of Banks and Barry (who had come second), but promoted his own on the grounds that 'my design has been placed by the judges at the head of those which were founded upon a develop-ment of our mediaeval architecture, and, which is more to the present purpose, of those which treated the two offices first to be erected as essentially a single and indivisible group.'[22] Combining the Foreign and War Offices, as he had done better than any other, was 'a most essential element to the success of the project'; though heaven forbid anyone should think he was acting 'from any wish to push my own claims'. He was right to say, however, that the decision to hold a competition for separate designs for the two buildings, to be erected on a single plot of ground, risked 'the ruin of this grand architectural scheme by dividing it into unconnected blocks'. The result was merely an architectural competition for which some had won prizes: it contributed nothing to the 'magnificent project for at once beautifying the neighbourhood of the House of Parliament and supplying a great public necessity'. Furthering his own cause, he quoted Tite: 'No man of taste would wish to place a renaissance (and *a fortiori* a classic) structure in proximity to House of Parliament [sic] and Westminster Abbey.' That would, however, be precisely what would happen, and Scott would be the architect.

For a time it looked as though Scott would not only have the commission, but could build as he wished. Palmerston's administration fell in February 1858 and the incoming Tory one had Lord John Manners, son of the Duke of Rutland, in Hall's place. Manners changed the terms: the public offices would be the Foreign Office and the India Office, since India was coming under direct control following the mutiny of the previous year. The India Office would be funded from a separate budget, the revenues for which were raised in India, so the cost to the British taxpayer would fall. Manners, a Gothicist, appointed Scott in November 1858, after a new select committee had deliberated. Helpfully for Scott, its chairman had been none other than Beresford Hope.

When Parliament resumed in February 1859 Tite, who had also been on the committee, attacked Scott, arguing that his design was 'inconvenient and expensive'.[23] Tite's main beef was his belief that Scott's building would not have sash windows and 'every hon Gentleman who had served on Committees of that House would, he thought, agree with him, that the simple method of drawing down the sash of a window was a better mode of ventilating a close room on a hot day than more complicated arrangements, however ingenious.' He had a personal point too: that 'Mr Barry, son of Sir C Barry, but in no other way connected with that eminent man, felt that he had not been quite fairly dealt with.' This was because Barry had finished above Scott in the competition; but even he had not won it. Barry would spend much of the next decade, on this and other matters, protesting that he had been unfairly treated, and was on the way to becoming expert in the injustices of his profession. Scott called Tite's criticism – and Palmerston's support for it – 'as absurd and unfounded as anything could be'.[24]

Manners said the committee had simply advised that one of the successful (that is, ranked) competitors should be appointed. They had also said, in reference to architectural styles, that 'there is no material difference as regards economy, commodiousness, and public utility between the rival styles'.[25] He had been constrained by restrictions on the size of the site, the need to have the new India Office on it, and the need to find an architect who could extract maximum utility from that space, combining the two offices. That man was Scott. 'I am in daily expectation of receiving the drawings and plans, and the course I propose to adopt is one which, if the House should sanction it, will, I think, tend to promote the public convenience, and be consistent with due economy,' he said. 'A Foreign Office will be erected worthy of the country.'

Hall sharply observed that 'if it were to be decided that a Gothic building should be constructed in the midst of buildings that had nothing Gothic about them, no architect could be found who understood that style of architecture better than Mr Gilbert Scott'.[26] He wished to know, however, why it had been decided to appoint a man who came third. Beresford Hope enlightened him. 'On the list of judges of the designs exhibited there was only one professional gentleman . . . and there were two professional assessors,' he observed.[27] The 'professional gentleman' was the architect Burn, who was rebuilding Montagu House at that time for the Duke of Buccleuch, who happened to have been the chairman of the judges. The professionals had put sixth the man the majority of judges had placed first, had put Barry and Banks first for the Foreign Office but nowhere for the War Office, but had put Scott second in both categories. 'According, then, to the award of the professional gentlemen, who must be supposed to know more of the matter than amateurs, however skilful, the sum total of merit in the competition rested with Mr Scott.'

He added that to have done other than select Scott 'would have been a miscarriage of injustice [sic], and a great injury to a most distinguished man.' He said Scott had made modifications to ensure a good flow of air on hot days; and he dismissed, too, notions of incongruity of style, reminding the House that the Gothic of the Palace of Westminster and the Abbey would be in the same locus and that 'all forms of Gothic were but phases of the same style'. His killer point was that Barry *père*, whose views had been prayed in aid by the anti-Scott faction, had 'said that if he were going to erect a great building in close proximity to St Paul's, it would not necessarily lead him to adopt the Italian style; and when he was asked if he would put a large Gothic building in St Paul's Churchyard, he replied that he was not prepared to say he should not.'

Palmerston followed, proclaiming that 'I have never heard a less satisfactory explanation, both as regards the selection of the architect and the choice of style in which the Foreign Office is proposed to be built, than that given by the noble Lord the First Commissioner of Public Works.'[28] He ridiculed Scott's appointment 'on the principle, I suppose, that the two negatives make an affirmative.' He continued: 'It certainly is a new doctrine. What would be said if it were applied to horse-racing, and the horse which ran second in two heats were held to be entitled to the cup?'

It was the Gothic, more than Scott, that upset him. 'We are told that it has been adopted because it is the national style, suited to Teutonic nationalities, and all that sort of thing. If that theory of nationalities is to be carried out in our public buildings, the noble Lord the Secretary for India, in building his new office, should be lodged in a pagoda or a taj-mahal.' That was only the start. 'In my opinion it is going back to the barbarism of the dark ages for a building which ought to belong to the times in which we live,' he said. 'It is said it is the intention to fill up the entire space between Downing Street and Westminster Abbey with buildings, all of which are to be Gothic, and that therefore it is desirable to begin with a Gothic Foreign Office. This is, to my mind, a reason against the proposal . . . instead of being an ornament to London, [it] will create a black spot in the metropolis.' Much of this was misrepresentation and exaggeration. 'We should have to Gothicise the Horse Guards'. He spoke of the 'great mistake' of having made the new Palace of Westminster Gothic. The certainty with which posterity feels the Victorians built was rarely apparent at their buildings' conception, or even after birth.

All Palmerston could do was huff, puff and tell jokes. Scott dismissed his intervention as 'a quantity of poor buffoonery which only Lord Palmerston's age permitted'.[29] However, to Scott's misfortune a general election was called in June 1859 and won by the Liberals, putting the old buffoon back into office: 'My arch-opponent', as Scott rather dramatically put it, 'became once more autocrat of England.'[30] Scott's main hope was that as the Liberal party had absorbed some old Peelites he might, at least, have a friend at court. Gladstone, on whose estate at Hawarden Scott had worked on a church a few years earlier, was Chancellor of the Exchequer. Scott seized his chance. He wrote to him on 19 July 1859 to say he was 'suffering severely from prejudgment or misapprehension on some points' to do with his commission.[31]

It is of the utmost importance to me that my position should be thoroughly understood in all its bearings before any decision, mental or otherwise, is come to – or I feel that there is a danger of a very serious injustice being inadvertently done to me . . . I have definitively and unconditionally been appointed architect to a great and most important public work . . . my name has long since gone forth throughout Europe as the architect appointed to this great work. I think you will see that, after this, to treat me still as a mere competitor and to threaten my position from causes which I had no means of avoiding is a course which I had hardly a right to expect and which is not in accordance with the customary conduct towards professional men.

I have gone into this business with the utmost ardour and enthusiasm, and I do confidently trust that Her Majesty's Government will see that my moral claims under their protection and support are of no ordinary character: and I cannot but feel (though I have hardly a right to an opinion) that the building I propose is such as future ages would think worthy of the government to whose inspection the drawings of it (now ready for actual execution) are now submitted.

He concluded that he was 'earnestly begging your kind aid in this very difficult and painful position.'

Palmerston started playing rough. He appears to have hoped to impose such unreasonable conditions on Scott that the architect would resign the commission: which shows Palmerston did not quite know his man. He wrote to Scott, demanding he submit a new, Italian or classical, design, on 26 July in response to a letter Scott had sent him – 'and I can assure you that I much regret that you should feel the disappointment which that letter expresses'.³² Scott had complained about the waste of his labour, but Palmerston argued that 'the internal arrangements which you have settled for the two offices in question will be equally applicable, whatever may be the style of the external elevation; and when the question to be decided regards a building which is to cost a good deal more than Two Hundred Thousand Pounds, and which for much more than Two Hundred Years is to be an ornament or the Contrary to this Metropolis, Regard for Personal Feelings must give way to Higher Considerations.'

Palmerston blamed Manners – 'it is much to be regretted that the late Board of Works should have encouraged you to go on with your Gothic Plan' given 'the strong expression of opinion elicited from the House of Commons in the Session of Parliament in 1858 against the choice of the Gothic Style.' However, he stressed it was not so much the feeling of the Commons as the feeling of Palmerston that was at issue. 'You say that the Gothic Style is the English and National Style for public Buildings, but I wish to know where in the United Kingdom the public buildings are to be found that are built in that style.' He said the main public buildings he knew were in other styles; and that this was the case 'for public buildings for civil and secular Purposes.'

Scott had told Palmerston that 'the eye of the spectator would not be offended by the Contrast which would be presented by your Gothic Building in the immediate neighbourhood of structures in another style'. However, the Prime Minister asserted, 'if that argument be good it may be turned the other way and the eye would be still less offended by the contrast between an Italian structure in Downing Street and the more remote House of Parliament and Westminster Abbey.' Then the gloves came off: 'I own I could not contemplate without alarm the Idea of filling up with gloomy looking Buildings in the Gothic Style, the whole of the space between Downing Street and Great George Street.' He dealt his final blow: 'I cannot entertain the smallest doubt that an Architect of your known Talent and Ability will find it an easy Task to design an Elevation in the Italian or the Classic Style, the more especially as those styles are simpler than the Gothic, and do not require such minuteness of small Details.' He told Scott he only intended to ask Parliament to vote money for laying the foundations of the building, 'and therefore there is no necessity for hurrying you in the Preparation of the altered Plan, or rather I should say, Elevation.'

The attempt to oust Scott outraged the profession, and damaged Palmerston's reputation. Scott, buoyed by the support of his peers, went to see Gladstone. They met on 2 August. Scott wrote to him later in the day, reviewing their conversation with his usual egotism, saying that 'I felt my consistency, having put myself forward publicly and frequently as a champion of Gothic Architecture, demands that I should state my views on the application of that style to the Government offices in some ostensible manner.'[33] However, he explained that 'the fact is that I am viewed by the very numerous body throughout the country, and still more widely spread, who ardently favour the revival of this style, as one of the leaders of those who take this view; and that it is necessary to my position with them as well as to my personal consistency to lose no proper opportunity, in such matters as this, of stating my individual views – though I trust I do so temperately and with all the consideration and respect due to those who differ from me.'

On 4 August Lord Elcho, a Whig MP, used a debate in the Commons to complain about the delay in proceeding with the project. 'The present Foreign Office was in such a state, that whenever receptions were given by the Foreign Minister it was found necessary to prop it up, and the Foreign Secretary sat in his room writing important despatches, with the chance that at any moment the roof might come down upon his head.'[34] Elcho also put on the record something Palmerston had apparently said at a private meeting a few days earlier, and which had found its way into the press: 'that Mr Scott's design was one of the most monstrous things he had ever seen – that it was more fitted for a monastery than anything else, and that as long as he held office he would never consent to the adoption of Mr Scott's plans.' Henry Bruce, who would briefly in 1868 serve as Home Secretary, urged the importance of allowing Scott to build in the style to which he was accustomed. 'They must take care', he warned the House, 'not to fall into the mistake committed in regard to Sir Christopher Wren who, having great reputation as a Palladian architect had been employed to erect two Gothic towers to Westminster Abbey. Naturally he performed the work in the most unsuccessful manner, and his two cumbrous erections were a great disparagement to the beauty of that noble edifice.'[35] Charles Buxton, who spoke last before the Prime Minister, said that 'Mr Scott's design would form one of the most beautiful buildings in the country' and that 'the Italian style was becoming effete'.[36]

With the House about to go into recess, Palmerston said no final decision would be taken until it met again: a further delay of the best part of six months. He refused to be embarrassed by Elcho's disclosure of his undiplomatically expressed feelings towards Scott's plan. 'The Gothic style might be admirably suited for a monastic building, a monastery, or a Jesuit college, but it was not suited, either internally or externally, for the purpose to which it had now been proposed to apply it.' Nor was he shaken by the effect a change of plan might have on Scott: 'The model which Mr Scott had exhibited was, no doubt, the result of very much labour, and if that labour should be thrown away – it would be very unfortunate for him, but it was no fault of his [Palmerston's].'[37] Then came an observation that, presumably, was intended to force Scott to draft his letter of resignation. 'Nevertheless his opinion was that Mr Scott, like any other clever architect, would be able to construct a different building for the ground plan, and he did not see that there was such a necessary connection between Mr Scott and the Gothic style that the Government should be prevented from inviting him to endeavour to design his elevation on a different plan.'

Manners rounded on Palmerston about the absurdity of this. 'The noble Lord who had said Mr Scott was a monomaniac, now said that he was very eminent in his profession, and he had no doubt could erect a building in the Italian style quite as well as in the Gothic. But if a man had obtained a world-wide reputation for his success in one style of architecture, would anyone in his senses give that man a commission to execute a work in an entirely different style? Would any man in his senses commission Sir Edwin Landseer, who was renowned for his paintings of animals, to execute a picture of the Holy Family?'[38]

On 23 August Scott wrote again to Gladstone. 'A deputation of architects has recently waited upon Lord Palmerston to express their concurrence in his views. It is, of course, a mere truism at a time when an art is divided into two rival branches to say that there are, of course, abundance of its practitioners to express their adherence to either – such expressions have, therefore, little moral value, even if made at a suitable time and with the best motives. In the present matter I strongly hold that the right time for such expression had *long since* gone by, and that the coming forward to give an additional blow to a brother architect in a moment of weakness was anything but a generous act.'[39] Scott felt it was 'more or less directly connected with a wish to displace me and to substitute another architect in my place. This Architect is Sir Charles Barry's son who, although among the first to congratulate me on my appointment and to wish me success has not (I am sorry to say) ceased from that turn to make use of all means in his power for my displacement.'

Scott added that

I felt convinced that advantage would be taken by his advocates of certain expressions made use of by those who spoke in the House of Commons in favour of my design, to the effect that, being a Gothic architect it would be inconsistent to ask me to make a design in another style; and I imagine that such has been the case, for Lord Palmerston, though he had hitherto always said that from knowing that I had been educated in classic architecture he felt no doubt that I could design as well in either style, yesterday told me that he had been considering what Lord John Manners and others had said and felt there was a great deal in it; and that he had consequently been thinking of associating another architect with me to assist me in doing so. On my remonstrating, he consented to postpone such a step and I have since written to him giving my reasons for considering it to be wholly incompatible with my position.

He spoke to Gladstone of the 'utter impossibility' of such an arrangement as Palmerston suggested. 'I was appointed by Lord John Manners in conformity with the report of a select committee', as 'the architect to design and carry out necessary work' and 'it made no mention of the subject of style, though it was, of course, natural that I should follow that of my competing designs.' He added:

Now, I put it simply on the ground of moral right that if this design be disturbed either from a new Government not approving the style or from the House of Commons taking the same view, I have a clear claim to the refusal or acceptance of the commission to make a new design, and that it would be a distinct infringement of this right if a competitor were prescribed to me. . . . It is morally impossible for two artists to work together at the same design unless one is the actual designer and the other quite subordinate to him. . . . The peculiar position which I hold in my profession and the strong opinions I have expressed as to the demand for reformation and 'new blood' in our vernacular architecture will compel me in any new design I may make to claim the right to considerable freedom and originality and prevent my making a design in the ordinary and, as I think, dull and worn-out style which has so long been considered in this country to be what is meant by 'classic' or 'Italian' architecture.

Scott, never the most balanced of men, now found himself 'thoroughly out of health, through the badgering, anxiety, and bitter disappointment which I had gone through'.[40] He took two months off, the first holiday this workaholic had had in years. He steeled himself to call Palmerston's bluff, and to agree to design an Italianate building. He did it not just to spite Palmerston, but to spite fellow architects who had lobbied him (he suspected: and he may well have been right) because they were jealous of Scott's pre-eminence and of his success. 'To resign', he wrote, 'would be to give up a sort of property which Providence had placed in the hands of my family, and would be simply rewarding my professional opponents for their unprecedented attempt to wrest work from the hands of a brother architect.' His design would be 'Byzantine . . . toned into a more modern and usable form, by reference to those examples of the renaissance which had been influenced by the presence of Byzantine works.'[41] For all his reluctance, he claimed to have found it 'both original and pleasing in effect.'

Scott then discovered why Palmerston had suggested he might design the building jointly with another architect. Palmerston had in secret asked Charles Barry Junior to make a design for the Foreign Office. Scott heard this through a friend. 'Lord Palmerston had hoped at first to be able to thrust this gentleman upon me as a colleague; but, failing that, had secretly encouraged him to make a design, that he might have "two strings to his bow".'[42] Palmerston still held out hope of having Barry's design. He asked Scott to 'modernise' his Byzantine plan: he strove to be so unreasonable that eventually Scott would give up. The Office of Works sought to force further changes to Scott's conception of the Italianate. Scott was unhappy, but did it.

The debate leaked into the press. One of Scott's supporters wrote to *The Times* saying that the Gothic was as convenient as the classical, but cheaper. This prompted Matthew Arnold to write that 'the one famous experiment we have before our eyes seems to contradict this assumption: The Houses of Parliament are eminently inconvenient and eminently dear.'[43] After a swipe at Barry – 'not a good Gothic architect' – Arnold also ridiculed the notion that Gothic was 'the national architecture of England. It might be so if there had been no Revival of Letters, no Reformation, no Elizabethan Age, no Revolution of 1688, no French Revolution. As it is, it is not so.' Arnold, a sometime evangelical, could hardly be expected to endorse the feudal-Catholic fantasies of Pugin and Ruskin.

As soon as Parliament went into recess in 1860 Palmerston sent for Scott and told him he could forget any idea of his original Gothic design being used, and that his Italianate one was 'a regular mongrel affair': he would have nothing to do with that either.[44] Palmerston delivered the ultimatum he had been building up to for months: 'He must insist on my making a design in the ordinary Italian, and that, though he had no wish to displace me, he nevertheless, if I refused, must cancel my appointment,' Scott recalled. For good measure he said that the whole configuration of offices would have to be changed, as the India Office, he had decided, would share the St James's Park front of the building with the Foreign Office.

Scott 'came away thunderstruck and in sore perplexity, thinking whether I must resign or swallow the bitter pill.'[45] His friends told him to think of his family, and his reputation, and that it was no bad thing for an architect to be receptive to the views of his clients. Wresting himself out of a 'terrible state of mental perturbation', Scott bought a pile of books on Italianate architecture, bit his lip, and 'set vigorously to work'.[46] His ego drove him: 'I was so determined to show myself not behindhand with the classicists, that I seemed to have more power than usual.' Palmerston approved the design; the Gothic party in the Commons attacked it, egged on, privately, by Scott.

Scott admitted afterwards that he would never have embarked on the process had he known what it would have entailed. He built, as it turned out, one of the most stately of Victorian buildings, but one entirely out of kilter with the spirit of the age, and outside the normal run of his work. 'I was step by step driven into the most annoying position of carrying out my largest work in a style contrary to the direction of my life's labours. My shame and sorrow were for a time extreme, but, to my surprise, the public seemed to understand my position and to feel for it, and I never received any annoying and painful rebuke, and even Mr Ruskin told me I had done quite right.' That he should resort to invoking Ruskin in his support shows exactly how wounded Scott was, and how deeply he felt his reputation and his integrity had been affected.

There is no question that a Gothic palace where Scott's Italianate pile now stands would, as Simon Bradley has put it, 'throw Whitehall out of balance visually'.[47] Bradley also observes how Scott managed to suppress 'his usual leaning towards picturesque variety', though he and other critics have found the grand building picturesque nonetheless, especially the end near St James's Park that once housed the India Office. The asymmetrical tower Scott sneaks into the building here is a hint of the architect's Gothic leanings. Otherwise it is a symmetrical building, and Scott had intended domed towers on each of its four corners, until the expense proved too much. The building exhibits the Renaissance styles of Genoa and Venice, but there are some foliage pier capitals further showing Scott's true colours.

Scott remained a constant irritant to politicians, usually through subtle and not-so-subtle acts of touting for business. He wrote to Gladstone, for example, on 2 January 1872 to say that the restoration of the Chapter House at Westminster – which Scott flatteringly called 'emphatically your own work' – was complete.[48] 'You have seen it when approaching completion, and therefore know the beauty of the building thus recovered by your timely intervention from depredation and ruin.' There was a purpose behind Scott's ingratiation. 'You must, however, have observed one glaring and painful defect; and, had you been there during a sunny day, you would have been the more strongly impressed by it. I allude to the absence of stained glass, which renders the building, with all its dignity and beauty, a mere Greenhouse.' He continued: 'The internal space is surrounded by probably more glass than wall – so that to speak of the building as "restored" while this remains untempered and unadorned, is a misnomer.' He said that stained glass would cost £6,000: 'My object in writing is to entreat you to complete the good work you have begun and carried on so far towards a successful completion, by allowing the funds necessary to this very essential part of it.'

Money was rarely an object in Scott's view. Writing to Gladstone from Rome on 8 December 1873 he said he had heard from Ayrton, the First Commissioner of Works 'informing me that Her Majesty's Government had not entertained favourably my appeal in favour of flanking towers which formed part of my design for the front of new Home and Colonial Offices. May I be excused in saying that the intelligence is a source of bitter disappointment to me, and in <u>entreating</u> you to give the question a more favourable consideration?'[49] He said the towers were an 'inherent part' of the design, which would be 'reduced to an idealess mass by their omission.' He continued:

> As an artist, I beg to enter my firm, though respectful protest against the omission which I view as in every sense as a <u>great and serious mistake</u>. As the author of the design I feel myself bound to use every effort to induce you to allow me to carry it out in its integrity; as well as, failing that (which I earnestly trust will not be the case) to protect my future fame against the [illegible] arising from the abortive character of the design if thus shorn of its leading characteristics. But what is my future reputation compared with the spoiling of a great public building? Were I to lodge in every Academy in Europe drawings of what I intended and protests against its mutilation, it would avail nothing when compared with the fact that a building erected . . . in one of the greatest thoroughfares of the Chief City in the world had been deprived of its most pronounced features!

In 'entreating' Gladstone again to act, Scott urged him to 'avert this severe blow upon the architectural fame of our Country!' Gladstone's private secretary has written 'he must be mad?' on the back of the letter: Gladstone asked 'when and by whom were the cupolas first struck out?' It turned out that in 1870 Lowe, as Chancellor of the Exchequer, had set out to reduce Scott's estimate by a third 'by various alterations', including the cupolas: which Ayrton had disliked from the start. State patronage at a time of British pride was a magnificent boon to the lucky architects: but, in utilitarian times, every penny was counted, and art – Gothic or classical – came second.

It is, as Bradley has put it, a 'persistent legend' that Scott recycled his plans for the Gothic Foreign Office into the building many regard as his masterpiece, the overwhelming and now magnificently restored Midland Hotel at St Pancras Station in London.[50] The building exhibits much of the detail, and evidence of the research and study, that Scott put in to his designs for the government offices. They are what a near-contemporary critic described as reminiscent of 'the Lombardic and Venetian brick Gothic' with 'touches of Milan and other terracotta buildings, interlaced with good reproductions of details from Winchester and Salisbury cathedrals, Westminster Abbey' and even 'the ornaments of Amiens, Caen and other French edifices.'[51] The building is of brick from Nottingham – a station on the railway's route north – dressed with stone from elsewhere in the Midlands. Had Scott had a free hand it would have been a storey higher, with a taller clock tower. So representative did this building become of the high Victorian style that it attracted many twentieth-century critics who wished to demolish it, including its owners, British Railways. What is certainly true is that the experience of designing a great Gothic building was one of the influences brought to bear on the Midland Hotel, which stands today as one of the greatest and most powerful representations of an age when buildings were made not simply to last, but to represent to the future a whole idea of culture.

IV

The battle between the Gothic and the classical was not, however, over. The next great government commission would give the Gothicists the chance to reassert themselves and, albeit with great pain and difficulty, they seized it. In the mid-1860s the government decided there should be new law courts on a site near the Inns of Courts, where the Strand meets Fleet Street in London. In 1861 the government began to issue compulsory purchase orders for properties on the site, most of which were among the most revolting slums in the metropolis. Henry Abraham, a surveyor who worked for the government and had hopes of being asked to design the courts, gave a vivid description of how dreadful life was on the site: 'It is almost impossible to remain for any length of time on some parts, the stench is so dreadful. The condition of the people is, I can use no other word than, terrible; the vice and wretchedness in the young, the decrepitude in those of middle age, and the dreadful condition of those in premature old age is appalling.'[52] During his survey he was attacked by some locals and nearly robbed. Much of the area appeared to be a gigantic brothel, and there was no drainage of any description.

As satirised by Dickens, the law had enormous backlogs, and justice was denied to many litigants who ran out of money. Eventually this was recognised, and in the mid-nineteenth century reforms of legal procedure took place, creating courts of appeal and higher courts in civil cases. Sir John Soane had built some higher courts around

Westminster Hall, but these were now inadequate. In keeping with the physical modernisation of Parliament and Whitehall, it was felt a new palace of justice would symbolise this new era for law in England. The expense, however, would be vast, and Gladstone was horrified by projections made during 1861 and 1862 for likely cost. The conflict between his ambition for the enterprise – he was its most high-profile supporter – and his personal and professional belief in economy was stark, and apparently irreconcilable. In February 1865 he reported the cost would be £892,895.[53] His ideas, shared with those who later submitted designs, were based upon a great hall, off which the courts, offices, retiring rooms and other facilities would be sited, on four floors.

When Gladstone presented a plan in the summer of 1865 it provoked demands to consider a site on the Embankment, then being developed, east of Somerset House but adjacent to the underground railway and road being built along the river. Pennethorne surveyed the site and his estimate of £1 million for the land alone put paid to that discussion – for the moment. The question also arose of what would be done with the 4,175 people it was computed would be evicted from the Carey Street site when their 343 dwellings were compulsorily purchased. It is a measure of what a slum this was that the working-class element was set at 3,082, living in 1,163 rooms in 172 of the houses. In Robin Hood's Court fifty-two people lived in two houses.[54] The numbers in the slum were even greater than these figures, because many buildings were lodging-houses that accommodated even more by night. Despite some Liberal MPs demanding new lodging-houses be built, the government held to the view that the denizens would inevitably find somewhere better than their existing accommodations, and proposed nothing to help them. As with the provision of education, a roof over the head of the poor was not, at the time, considered a matter for the State, but for private charity, if necessary.

A new Royal Commission assembled in the summer of 1865 to decide how to proceed. It decided that even more functions would need to be housed in the new buildings, including those of the Masters in Lunacy and the Judicial Committee of the Privy Council. This required a bigger building, and more land, with an extra cost estimated at £488,620, which shocked Gladstone. There was a strong feeling at Westminster that the design should reflect the great standing of the nation; and that the selection panel – which as well as Gladstone included the Lord Chancellor, the Attorney General and the Commissioner of Works – all had too much else on their plates to make a sensible decision, arrived at after lengthy consideration.

On the original list of six architects invited to compete for the commission was George Edmund Street. Street, born in 1824, had been a pupil of Scott and has been judged by history to be almost equal to him. After an unsuccessful start as a solicitor – his father's profession – Street had been articled to Owen Carter, a provincial architect in Winchester whose masterpiece was the Winchester Corn Exchange. Carter also had a profound interest in the Gothic and built several straightforward Hampshire churches in the style. Street pursued his own studies in Gothic architecture and was well versed by the time he joined Scott's practice in 1844. He had obtained an introduction to Scott through a connection, and was taken on as temporary help. Scott soon realised his qualities and gave him a permanent job. He admired his pupil greatly, both because of his thoughtfulness about architecture but also because of his skill as a draughtsman. His contemporaries in Scott's practice were G. F. Bodley and William White, and together they began to revise the idea of the Gothic away from the purist strain championed by Pugin. Throughout the 1850s and 1860s their view would prevail: this was the school that came to be called high Victorian.

Street spent five years with Scott, and won his first commission to design a church – in Cornwall – in 1847. He set up his own practice in 1849, and made his name designing churches, many in the diocese of Oxford, and in a revival of the thirteenth-century Early English style. Street's conviction about the superiority of the Gothic was rooted in his admiration for the technical supremacy of the arch, its ability to bridge large spaces using small stones, and especially its use in vaulting. As his fame grew he built more secular buildings, and began to write widely. Like Ruskin, he travelled extensively and wrote prolifically about what he had seen, and became a great admirer of his fellow critic: unlike Ruskin, and perhaps because Street had the practical experience of a man whose designs had to be built, he was broad-minded and lacked Ruskin's peculiar other-worldliness. Street became a great teacher of architects whose names would resonate later in the nineteenth century, notably Norman Shaw and William Morris.

By the time of the competition for the Law Courts Street was at the peak of his profession. However, the tension between those who built in the classical style, and those who built in the medieval, had still to be resolved. Scott's defeat by Palmerston suggested the institutional prejudice lay with the former. Street was determined to make high Victorianism a style in which the beauty of the medieval could be seen also to be original, modern and what a later age would call 'state of the art'. As David Brownlee, one of Street's biographers, has observed: 'Street maintained that medievalism could be made modern by extracting these principles from the study of Gothic, by admitting a wider historical and geographical range of precedents than the purists of the forties had allowed, and by permitting a process called 'development' to transform Gothic architecture to meet the needs of the nineteenth century.'[55] Street's high Victorian was not merely a copy of what had gone centuries before, but an advance upon it. 'Copyism' was what Pugin had done.

Designs for the Law Courts had to be submitted by October 1866. When the question was raised in the Commons the previous April, Lord John Manners threw an entirely predictable spanner in the works: he asked 'whether any intimation had been given to the architects who had been invited to compete as to the style of architecture preferred by Her Majesty's Government? The omission to give such an intimation has resulted in a blunder six years ago, and it was therefore desirable to know whether Her Majesty's Government had decided as to the style to be now adopted.' Henry Cowper, the minister responsible, told Manners that the style was an 'open question'.[56]

A plan to invite only six architects to compete was attacked in the Commons on 22 March 1866 by George Bentinck, who complained that a commission of this size should, like the Houses of Parliament thirty years earlier, be open to all comers. The six were Street, Waterhouse, Henry Garling, Thomas Deane, Raphael Brandon and George Somers Clarke. All except Garling were medievalists. Edward Barry, Scott, Hardwick and Wyatt had declined to enter: it was thought because of a condition that the successful architect would not, in the three years it was expected it would take to build the courts, take on any other work without the consent of the Treasury. However, this restriction was not seen as unreasonable, as the fee would be 5 per cent of the cost, or £37,000 over three years: a small fortune. Eventually, the field was expanded to eleven, including, after all, Barry.

The chairman of the judges was William Cowper, Palmerston's stepson and First Commissioner of Works in his administration. Cowper had just chosen Waterhouse to build the Natural History Museum after Fowke's death, so seemed disposed to the Gothic, unlike his stepfather. Roundell Palmer, the Attorney General and future Lord Chancellor, had chosen Waterhouse to build his country house, and was on the panel. Gladstone installed himself as a judge; as Chancellor, he would write the cheques. His affection for the Gothic was well documented. He knew Street, had admired his work at Cuddesdon where Street had built the Theological College, and had read some of his writings. Street, like Scott and Butterfield, was an occasional visitor to Gladstone's Thursday breakfasts.

The Law Courts were to this era what the Houses of Parliament had been to early years of the reign: the single most important building of the period, an institution designed to reflect the new might and sway of an imperial power that led the world and enjoyed the foremost prosperity. In February 1867 the public were invited to scrutinise the drawings. A special pavilion was erected to display them in Lincoln's Inn. It was immediately apparent that all the designs were Gothic, with even the two architects who might have been considered classicists having submitted medieval designs. This was saluted as a triumph by the *Ecclesiologist* but lamented as retrogressive by the *Builder*, which still sought a vernacular that could be called the age's own.

The *Quarterly Review* was even more disdainful. While it conceded that the area to be demolished for the courts was a 'foul blot on London', it felt that what was proposed to replace it would constitute 'an irreparable mistake'.[57] The courts constituted 'the greatest building of modern times', and the *Quarterly* wondered whether the plans addressed 'the first requisites of utility'. What it saw reflected instead was a 'growing taste for material vastness' that had taken root in Britain since the building of the new Houses of Parliament. The Palace of Westminster it regarded as 'a mere mechanical feat', since its accommodations were 'most cheerless and revolting in every sense' – unless one happened to be on the river front, which had improved since the Embankment put an end to the great stinks.

The outcome, the article went on, was to create 'such a strong antipathy to Gothic Architecture . . . a *Palace* was ordered, where there should have been *Houses*; just as now we ask for *Courts of Law*, and they offer us a *Palais de Justice*. Palaces are state residences: not places for public business. They are built not for convenience or comfort; but for pomp and ceremony.' The main complaint was that neither House of Parliament was discernible by looking at the exterior of the new building; and no court of law would be discernible from the exterior of any of the eleven proposed *palais*: just 'a screen, masking the essential parts of the building'.[58] So it was that one man's – or eleven men's – pursuit of perfection was another's aesthetic cul-de-sac. It was also argued that the building would be incongruous in the Strand, 'a street of shops, a long bazaar'.

The *Quarterly* wanted an even bigger site, to make the accommodation less crowded, and to rid London of a few more slums. There was no money for this: and it would mean the eleven architects starting again, so was an entirely pointless, almost mischievous, observation. It argued for a 'noble avenue' to run from St Clement Dane's to the river (which did happen) and a subway from the Law Courts to the underground railway (which did not).[59] Having condemned the designs for making courts of law seem like a palace, it also condemned them for looking ecclesiastical: which brought the *Quarterly*, in denouncing the architects for taking cathedrals as their model, to its fundamental complaint about the designs: that they were Gothic.

It railed against 'Gothic imitations'. It referred to Inigo Jones, observing that 'there were giants on the earth in those days'. It said the architects had 'had to satiate an ignorant and exacting multitude, who have money and who will have show.'[60] It suggested, unfairly (considering the erudition and aesthetic sense of Gladstone, for one), that the committee of judges were there by 'mere wealth and position', and not because of their 'intelligence and culture'. The use of the example of ecclesiastical architecture in the secular would result only in 'degradation'. This litany of abuse ended with the resounding climax: 'The simple sad truth is, that Architecture in England is a dead art.' The 'works of our modern architects are composed in a foreign language; a style as suitable for our Law Courts as if the barristers were to plead in Greek or medieval Latin, or the judgments were to be given, as of old, in Norman French.'

The article's conclusion, in lamenting the modern interpretation of medievalism, made a point that resonates to this day about the effect Victorian Gothicists had on the fabric of many ancient buildings: these architects were merely 'a number of superior mechanics, whose works, whether in wood or metal, are destroying the individual artistic character of every church and cathedral that falls within the scope of the "restoring mania.'"[61] It continued: 'In everything we are too elaborate. A city warehouse in the Gothic style must have the marbles and enrichments of a cathedral presbytery: even a village church is not allowed the dignity of simplicity, and is nothing if not pretty.'[62] It attacked the politicisation of architecture, something inevitable when so many great commissions were State patronage. It might be thought that this, therefore, was an assault on the Gothic: but the article ended by hoping that the necessary style was 'purely English': 'Let us start again from the pure Gothic of the fourteenth century, and let every advance be a genuine and sympathetic development of this, not a mere addition of inconsistent and incoherent forms.' This was disingenuous: it was too late for that, and had been too late for it for 500 years. It enunciated a truth, however, that marks the Victorian epoch in building: 'Buildings are enduring monuments of the character of an age.'[63]

At that time, the zeitgeist was against these strictures, with their implicit support for classicism. It was not only the committee appointed by Gladstone, before the Liberals left office in the summer of 1866, that favoured the Gothic: so too did an informed public whose awareness of architecture was fed by a strong sense of historicism or atavism. The Gothic Revival defined a new, contemporary style. It was about show, and show paid for by a prosperous country (however parsimonious Gladstone might try to be). That was the spirit of the age, which had in many respects, ever since the Great Exhibition, been one of greater ostentation and less restraint. The majority of architects built in that style because of public demand: they would have been short of work had they not.

Street's biographer has described his submissions as the 'ideological ally' of Scott's, with a regularity and developed medievalism typical of high Victorianism, with a low, predictable roofline of a quadrangular building punctuated by the obligatory towers.[64] The style, as with many of Street's earlier buildings, especially his churches, is early French Gothic tempered by English Decorated of the fourteenth century: the interior of the Law Courts as eventually built is entirely fourteenth-century English. As such it was raved about by the *Ecclesiologist*, but dismissed by the *Builder*. His critics said the elevations were monotonous and showed a lack of imagination. His was certainly not nearly so picturesque as the other designs. Nor did his designs redeem themselves by the utility of their interiors: Street's original plan did not allow adequately for the separate circulations of public and lawyers, which the legal profession (consulted at every stage) deemed a most important feature. However, his designs would, if executed, be within the budget allowed; and he did seem to have striven for the *sine qua non* of high Victorianism, classical order and regularity combined with the picturesque of the Gothic.

V

The judges deliberated from February 1867 until July. They wanted Street's elevations and Barry's interiors. This offer of the commission to two incompatible men, whose aesthetics and ways of working were so profoundly different, was at least recognised by one judge – Gladstone – as the worst possible outcome. In June 1868 he lamented that he and his fellow judges 'had so entirely failed in rendering effective aid to the Government' when choosing a design.[65] As soon as the judgement was announced the Treasury tried to declare it invalid, as the rules had decreed the appointment of one architect. The judges were asked to think again. They met in November and announced stalemate: they were still split between Barry and Street. In an attempt to calm matters various of the other architects announced they supported the judges' decision: notably the two winners, who professed they could work together.

Almost no one else agreed with this, including *The Times*, which observed on 19 November that of the designs 'Mr Barry's exhibits the nearest approach to convenience, and Mr Street's is thought the least unsightly, and as no one candidate is found to combine the useful and the ornamental the Commission appears to be of the opinion that these two gentlemen can do it together.'[66] It ridiculed the eleven designs as 'an indistinct recollection of facades, groups of towers, and plans ten times more intricate and incomprehensible than the Labyrinth of Crete.' Understanding the artistic temperament, the leader-writer doubted that a collaboration in which one architect had constantly to consult another, rather than the muse, would work. 'Such works require an incubation, which is a solitary process.' It urged another competition: it said that 'our medieval ancestors made their wants the rule for their edifices, and adapted the outside to the inside.' That was how this should proceed: and the style could follow from that.

On 14 May 1868, the day before the Commons debated the project, the Attorney General decreed that the judges' decision to award a joint commission could not be binding upon the Treasury. After a fortnight's consideration the Chancellor of the Exchequer, George Ward Hunt, announced the Treasury would exercise its right to appoint a sole architect, and he would be Street. There has been much speculation on why they made this choice: Street's best political contact was Gladstone, who was not in power. Theories include the greater expense of Barry's design, the complexity of its network of offices, the inconvenience of its space for keeping records (this was a special gripe of the Probate Department), even Disraeli's affection for medievalism because of his Young England connections. Barry had also just been announced as winner of a competition for a new National Gallery (which was never built), which may or may not have been his consolation for losing the Law Courts. Whatever the reason, Barry was outraged, and began a self-destructive campaign to do down Street, of which the successful architect soon became painfully aware.

Barry wrote to the Treasury – a letter helpfully copied to *The Times* for publication – on 8 June complaining about the decision, and reminding the government that his interiors had been deemed the most satisfactory. He listed the conditions laid down by the judges, and spoke of how he had fulfilled them and Street had not. He said the rules stated that the judges' decision was final, but this had turned out not to be so. He whined that 'I must, in justice to myself, maintain that by the award of the judges my claims were made superior to those of any other single competitor, and no other ought to have been preferred to me.'[67] He urged the government to stick by the original ruling, since the alternative course would be 'a serious loss and injury' to him. He claimed to write 'in no spirit of hostility to my friend Mr Street', but that was not how Street took the publication of this letter, which had made its points clearly enough when it remained private.

Street sent a long, defensive memorandum to the Treasury on 22 June that was copied to Layard. Street told Layard in a covering note that Barry was seeking to undermine him by making 'a very incorrect statement' about the proposed arrangement of rooms, and sought Layard's support at the imminent debate on the Select Committee.[68] A week later he wrote to Gladstone, then Leader of the Opposition. On finishing his book on Gothic architecture in Spain ('on which I have taken a good deal of pains, and as the subject has never been treated of before') he had asked Gladstone whether he would agree to be the dedicatee.[69] 'I do not suspect you, in the midst of all your work, to interest yourself much in such a subject; but I can hardly say how much pleasure it would give me to be able thus to express the extreme respect and admiration which for a very long time I have felt for your character.'

He had been reluctant to presume upon this connection, but now felt the time was right to do so. Street said that he had 'been very careful for the last two years, ever since I was asked to compete for the new Law Courts, to avoid all attempts to see you, feeling a certain delicacy about claiming any acquaintance with one who had so much to do with the decision.'[70] However, Street added that he had been 'strongly advised now by one of your followers in the House of Commons' – possibly Layard – 'that I ought not any longer to let this feeling exist.' He told Gladstone he had been at work 'literally night and day on the plan'. Yet he found himself 'threatened' by a motion put down by Lowe that evening in the Commons which promised 'a re-opening of the whole question.'

Barry had put Lowe up to this. 'I cannot pretend to suppose that as the judges of the design reported my merits and Mr Barry's to be equal, they will now be at all likely to give a different verdict. But you will have seen, no doubt, that Mr Barry maintains that if one architect is to be appointed he ought to be the man. I on the contrary hold that if the award was invalid the Government was entitled to select me.' Then there was the small fact that, once the estimates had been considered, Street's plan was £90,000 cheaper than Barry's. 'I feel it would be a very real injustice to me if after having been appointed architect by the Government my appointment were to be disputed or cancelled,' he concluded, after professing his willingness to make whatever modifications were necessary. 'I can hardly exaggerate the difficulty which I feel as an artist in working with these parliamentary attacks pending.'

He entreated Gladstone: 'I venture to hope therefore that you will lend the great weight of your authority to support my appointment – I venture to say that there never was one made which was more entirely free from personal bias. I have absolutely no speaking acquaintance even with any member of the present government.' He added: 'I did not expect the opposition which I have met from Mr Barry,' since Barry had written to him three weeks earlier complaining that 'I have not been well used at the Law Courts, and then you will hear no more of me in connection with the matter . . . I can fully sympathise with your natural joy in being independent, and I have no doubt of the result being a worthy building.' He mentioned that Waterhouse had written to say that 'our common cause will receive a great stimulus by your work, and it will be a great glory to you'. Clearly pained, Street added: 'I have attempted in this great competition to do nothing which as a gentleman or an artist I could be ashamed of – I have said nothing against the other competitors, and as you no doubt are aware, I competed with my own hands trusting entirely to my own drawings, and not borrowing other men's talents to put an attractive face on my designs.'

Street, conscious of the shortcomings of his earlier work, produced revised plans that strove to be more picturesque. The old Battle of the Styles was, however, reopening, partly because of a new discussion about whether the Carey Street site would be used after all, or whether advantage would be taken of a vacant site by Somerset House on the Embankment, made feasible by Bazalgette's embanking of the river. In 1869 Lowe told Layard, who having become First Commissioner of Works in Gladstone's administration now had some official say in the matter, that in the event of the Embankment site being used the new Law Courts 'must be in some sort of harmony with Somerset House'.[71] He added: 'Consequently we should stop Mr Street in his plans for the erection of a Gothic temple.' Street took this remarkably well, saying that although his layout of courts and offices had been 'pretty nearly decided' they could 'no doubt be transferred to the other plan which I shall be keen to make.' The Inns of Court were consulted and expressed their support for the Embankment site.[72]

The Commons discussed the matter on 20 April 1869. Lowe's idea of the Embankment site was widely supported.[73] The next day Layard told the Chief Baron, Sir Fitzroy Kelly, that 'the Govt will now have to propose a scheme, and the one sketched out by the Ch of the Exch last night offers many very important advantages.'[74] Layard was, it will be recalled, also seeking to have the Natural History Museum on this site, or adjacent to it. He asked Sir Fitzroy on 11 May 1869 to make 'an expression of opinion on the part of yourself and the Common Law Judges on the subject of the Thames Embankment site.'[75] He said this would now be of 'great importance, and would give much support to the Govt in their endeavours to move the Courts from their Carey Street site.' The Law Society objected as soon as Layard introduced his bill

– 'the concentration of the courts and offices will fail to effect the objects in view unless that concentration be carried out in immediate proximity with the chambers of counsel and solicitors . . . this proximity is secured by the Carey Street site, but would be lost on the Embankment.'[76]

Lowe intervened on 18 May. He agreed with Layard that the required buildings could not be put on the Carey Street site. 'It's very hard to fight with the lawyers. My opinion is that their influence will overbear all considerations of taste and of public convenience and that the only chance of beating them is to shew that they are involving us in a great expense, in other words that the buildings and strictly necessary approaches on the Carey Street site cannot be made for anything like the £1,500,000 authorised by Parliament.[77] Layard, however, had already admitted defeat and asked Street to draw up revised plans for Carey Street. Street, at least, was happy. 'I am really delighted with the way in which my plan is working out, and I hope now that it may live through the threatened opposition,' he wrote on 19 May.[78]

Street sent a long memorandum to Layard on 21 June, showing how his plan could be built on the site – though he suggested it might have to be more high-rise in order to fit in all the office space, which he said would 'damage most seriously the convenience and usefulness of my plan'.[79] Also, he was emphatic that there should be no 'reduction in size of all the open courts, areas, open quadrangles, or streets within the building from which light is derived or access obtained for the offices and courts'. Layard was asked whether the government would adhere to the statement he had made in May that the building would be in the style of the 'Gothic employed by the Italians in the early part of the 15th century', and whether Street's building really was of that style.[80] He was also asked, somewhat mischievously, whether the three towers in the design were meant for the storage of documents, or were merely ventilation shafts. He vigorously defended Street, saying 'it was never his good fortune to see a more beautiful and artistic piece of work'; that he had been misquoted about the fifteenth-century Italian, having merely pointed out that the Italians had used Gothic for a similar purpose in the fifteenth century; and that the three towers were merely a sketch, and in time a model of the building would be placed in the Commons for inspection.

When the final designs were published Street was attacked from several quarters, notably in *Macmillan's* in January 1872 by James

Fergusson. Fergusson had written to the *Builder* in August 1871 on the subject, and there had been an extensive correspondence in *The Times*. He had said in the *Builder* that he had 'no hesitation in saying that it is the meanest design for the principal front of so important and pretentious a building which has been proposed in our day'.[81] He called the Central Hall 'useless' and an 'imperforate' and 'gloomy vault'. Street, in a specially printed pamphlet, dismissed the criticism of the front as 'a question of taste'; he went on to attack Fergusson's opinions as 'founded in prejudice, and fortified by an ignorance which it would be hard indeed to account for on any but Mr Fergusson's own explanation, which is that "architecture is not an art to be learned in a day, or practised by amateurs. Long apprenticeship, and severe study are requisite for success, and if architecture ever passes out of professional hands the art will be something one dreads to look forward to." There is no-one to whom these words apply with more singular exactness than they do to Mr Fergusson himself.'[82]

Fergusson had certainly behaved badly. In his *Macmillan's* article he had said that the government had been 'worried and perplexed by the rival claims of the competing architects' and had given Street the commission 'because his design was the worst – a perfectly competent tribunal having awarded him only three marks in the competition, while it had assigned Edward Barry forty-three.' Street described it as 'improbable' that the government would have chosen the worst design or that 'the House of Commons, by a majority of two to one, would have confirmed the selection as it did, when it was challenged by Mr Edward Barry's friends.'[83] The 'two most important' criteria for the competition were the provision of 'ample uninterrupted communication and accommodation for those who have legitimate business in the New Courts' and that 'the comparative cost of carrying out such design will be an important element in determining the competition'.

What seems especially to have annoyed Street, however, was Fergusson's impugning his architectural taste, which suggested that 'the sun of art stood still when Edward III died in 1377, and has not moved forward since that time.'[84] Lawyers, Fergusson said, 'must be content to lounge in vaulted halls, with narrow windows filled with painted glass, and so dark that they cannot see to read or write in them. They must wander through corridors whose gloom recalls the monkish seclusion of the Middle Ages. They must sit on high, straight-backed chairs, and be satisfied with queer-shaped furniture, which it is enough to give one rheumatism to look at.' 'This tirade contains not a word of truth,' Street retorted.

Fergusson accused Street of plagiarising medieval Gothic; which, Street remarked, showed what an ignorance his critic had of that style. 'The ground of my love for Gothic is that it is a real, free, and living style, in which copyism is not necessary or likely to be indulged in by any one who knows his art at all well.'[85] Fergusson had been his heaviest, but not his only, critic. *The Times* had felt the building 'too English and too ecclesiastical.' Another critic had attacked him for not copying. Finally, 'Mr Sydney Smirke complains that my Law Courts are not like the Flavian Amphitheatre, and Mr E W Pugin (if I understand him aright) that they are not modelled on the Granville Hotel, Ramsgate!'[86] But for Street, this argument was not a matter of taste. 'I believe that no one can have read what I have written, or can have followed the attacks on me in *The Times*, without seeing how very much personal animus runs throughout them.'[87] He derided Fergusson for saying he was 'proud to call me his friend'.[88] 'What more or what worse he could have done for me if he had been my enemy, and had the greatest possible contempt for me, I know not!'

It was not until 27 May 1873 that Street finally had the go-ahead to build the Law Courts 'in the way proposed by me'.[89] It is the last great high Victorian building, and it bears the imprimatur of Gladstone upon it. The Prime Minister himself insisted on Street's design, not least because it was a work of architecture that reflected his own views about the high-minded message of the Gothic, and, although a secular building, embodied a style very much to the glory of God. As Barry and Pugin had created the ultimate monument to purist Gothic, so Street would build the ultimate temple of high Victorianism. In so far as a building could manifest an idea of perfection, this, supposedly, was it. It was the climax of the Gothic Revival, and a work of such scope that it would not be completed until 1882, the year after Street's death. It remains one of the most celebrated and conspicuous monuments to the Victorian mind.

CHAPTER 19

THE REFORMING MIND: PARLIAMENT AND THE ADVANCE OF CIVILISATION

I

In the 1840s, before the repeal of the Corn Laws, the intervention of the State in the lives of the public was regarded almost as anathema. By the 1870s attitudes had changed dramatically. It was widely felt that Britain could only be effectively governed – and its prosperity safeguarded – if the State made certain strategic decisions and enforced them through Acts of Parliament. This was not least because of the level of political engagement of those outside the traditional Establishment – formalised by the 1867 Reform Act – and the fear that Establishment had of the consequences of neglecting the masses. Once it was clear how thoroughly that legislation had been accepted, it appeared both possible and necessary to follow electoral reform with social reform.

Government itself became more professional, and modern, after Gladstone's determination to enforce collective ministerial responsibility. A draft Cabinet minute of 21 June 1869 proclaims that: 'The Cabinet desires notice to be taken by all members of the Government . . . [that] much inconvenience will be avoided if the person or persons concerned communicate with the Treasury before making any declaration, or taking any public proceeding, of a nature to commit themselves or the Government, so that the matter may be considered, and a common conclusion arrived at.'[1]

The Liberal ministry also promoted social reform, as we have seen, by measures to advance meritocracy. However, the predominant theme of the dozen years between Gladstone's winning office in 1868 and

Disraeli losing it in 1880 was that of the State seeking improvements in public administration that would enhance the lives of the masses, with continued development of education for the poor chief among them. In addition to the reforms already discussed, Gladstone's first ministry passed the 1872 Public Health Act, which divided the country up into rural and urban sanitary districts; the former under the jurisdiction of the Boards of Guardians, the latter under town councils, improvement commissioners or local boards appointed under the Public Health or Local Government Acts. It also allowed for the appointment of medical officers of health. The Licensing Act of the same year restricted the places and times of the sale of alcohol, restrictions eased under an Act of 1874 passed by the Conservatives, whose supporters in the drinks trade had been badly affected by the new law.

Some great issues, however, were not addressed, because the ministry was losing support. For example, Liberal jurists yearned to codify and thereby modernise the criminal law, which had expanded greatly in the nineteenth century, but which still harboured elements of medieval practice. In 1872, following his successful codification of the criminal law in India, James Fitzjames Stephen advocated doing the same in England, to overcome the complexity of statute law. He said:

> It is a new experience to an English lawyer to see how easy these matters are when they are stripped of mystery. I once had occasion to consult a military officer upon certain matters connected with habitual criminals. He was a man whose life was passed in the saddle, and who hunted down Thugs and Dacoits as if they were game. Upon some remark which I made he pulled out of his pocket a little Code of Criminal Procedure, bound like a memorandum book, turned up the precise section which related to the matter in hand, and pointed out the way in which it worked with perfect precision . . . The only thing which prevents English people from seeing that law is really one of the most interesting and instructive studies in the world, is that English lawyers have thrown it into a shape which can only be described as studiously repulsive.[2]

He cited eleven subjects that could comprise a code: 'Private relations of life (husband and wife, parent and child, guardian and ward); succession to property; landed property; contract; wrong; trust; crime; civil procedure; criminal procedure; evidence; limitation and prescription.

We should then have a code in the – I had almost said transcendental sense which some persons seem to attach to the word – but we should have the working kernel of the law stated in such a shape that, with the necessary amount of sustained industry, any one might acquaint himself with it.'[3] However, the political means for the Liberal government to achieve this were, by 1872, wanting: too much capital had been expended on the other great reforms.

II

Gladstone's high-flown interests, and above all his fascination with theological and theocratic questions in the Anglican Church, put him out of touch with his party. As the editor of his diaries points out, his high mind failed to give him the interest in gossip that might have alerted him to difficulties: and his forbidding, moralising manner deterred others from telling him things that might have been useful to him.[4] Ever since the debate over the Education Bill he had failed to realise how restless the Nonconformist element was, and, indeed, how much it had him in its sights. As party unity was undermined, so too was the ministry. When it was defeated in March 1873 on the Irish University Bill the government resigned, only to have Disraeli refuse to take office. It was a brilliant calculation by Disraeli, who saw that the Liberals had more scope yet to be weakened, and he did not wish to spare them that pleasure before winning a later, and more comprehensive, election victory.

Another difficulty the Liberal party faced was National Education League candidates running against Liberals in by-elections throughout 1872 and 1873. The interlopers made little progress, but did succeed in driving many Liberals away from voting at all. At a by-election in Greenwich in August 1873, caused by the death of the Jewish pioneer Alderman Salomons, six candidates stood, five of them different sorts of Liberal. Gladstone was another MP for the borough, but, inevitably, the Conservative candidate joined him in the Commons. Between 1871 and 1873 the Liberals, and their great reforming government, lost twenty by-elections. Some town councils, including Rochdale and Barrow, refused to pay their education precepts, on the same grounds as Birmingham had. An attempt to amend the 1870 Act by transferring the authority to levy rates from the school board to the local Poor Law guardians was a disaster. It appeared to the Nonconformists to disregard the principle they felt to be at stake and only alienated them further. They also regretted that the government had ignored an opportunity to write compulsory attendance into the law.

Passions were absurdly high. In the summer of 1873 Bright condemned the 1870 Act – now regarded as the landmark change that paved the way for universal, free education – as 'the worst Act passed by a Liberal government since 1832'.[5] However, just when the League thought it had signed up the greatest orator and campaigner of the day on its side, Bright rejoined the Cabinet as Chancellor of the Duchy of Lancaster, rendering himself silent: he had been President of the Board of Trade from 1868, but resigned after two years because of ill health. In this same reshuffle, announced the evening Parliament went into recess, Gladstone appointed himself Chancellor of the Exchequer, and moved Lowe (who had failed to run a sufficiently tight ship at the Treasury) to the Home Office. Gladstone claimed to take the post with extreme reluctance, but at the urging of his colleagues.

It was a nice point whether Gladstone, who was, of course, already Prime Minister, had accepted an office of profit under the Crown and therefore, under the Septennial Act, should resign his seat and fight a by-election to secure the approval of his constituents for his new appointment. Much discussion took place among politicians, constitutionalists and officials during late 1873 about whether it was legally required. He invoked a clause in the 1867 Reform Act in support of his position, since it specified that those who took another office in lieu of an existing one were not deemed to have vacated their seats. This was not, however, quite what had happened. He consulted both his law officers; they supported his contention that having been re-elected on assuming the position of First Lord of the Treasury, he need not be re-elected again. However, by the time the new session of Parliament approached Gladstone had acquired a new Attorney and a new Solicitor General, who were less sure what his course of action should be. It was suspected the matter would be raised as soon as Parliament reassembled, on 5 February 1874. Gladstone was prepared for a long fight.

Days after becoming Chancellor he confided in Cardwell his desire to abolish income tax in 1874, thanks to a surplus that unexpectedly appeared on the Treasury's books. This ambition, which he regarded as essential if his party were to stand a chance of winning the election due by late 1875, forced the sudden dissolution in January 1874. Some in his

Cabinet said the electorate would need to give a mandate for reductions of between £600,000 and £1 million in the Army and Navy estimates that he realised would also be required to execute the plan in a fiscally responsible way. Cardwell, however, felt such economies would be impossible, and was prepared to force the point. An election became inevitable if Gladstone were to proceed with his plan to abolish the income tax.

Most MPs – all indeed except the Cabinet and Gladstone's intimates – only heard of the dissolution when they read of it in their newspapers on Saturday 24 January, after more than five months of recess. 'It was at first believed to be a hoax,' wrote Richard Cross, who was staying at Knowsley with the Earl and Countess of Derby and was brought the news over his breakfast by his hostess.[6] The Duke of Devonshire, who also read it in *The Times*, was furious, believing Gladstone – one of his oldest political friends – should have taken him into his confidence.

The Tories regarded Gladstone's plan to abolish the income tax as a bribe to voters, and one to be paid for by a sacrifice of national security. It seemed especially to bribe the newly enfranchised classes, who had understood hitherto that taxation went with their privilege of representation. However, many radical Liberals saw it as a bribe to the rich who, with tax avoidance then being in its infancy as an art, paid the most income tax. Joe Chamberlain called the proposal 'simply an appeal to the selfishness of the middle classes'.[7] The country had a surprise for Gladstone: he lost the election by forty-eight seats, thanks mainly to the development of a centralised campaigning machine by Disraeli that set the pattern for Conservative organisation for more than a century ahead. His party, which he had instructed to fight on a platform opposing class conflict, won outright for the first time since 1841.

Many Liberal MPs had seen the defeat coming: Gladstone, as usual uninterested in the trivial, human side of politics, appears not to have done. He blamed the 1872 Licensing Act for his defeat. It had restricted the hours during which alcohol could be served, and the notion of a closing time had been especially unpopular with the working classes. It had also restricted which premises could be licensed and created the offence of being drunk in public. However, there is no evidence that Gladstone was the victim of a concerted putsch by brewers and publicans.

The election marked another advance in British democracy. Gladstone, despite the heavy losses, was determined to meet Parliament, until his colleagues talked him out of it. He felt it was the job of Parliament, not electors, to dismiss governments. As with Disraeli in 1868, he should, they said, accept the decision of the people. He saw that times had changed, and did. When Gladstone lost, one who could hardly conceal her delight was, inevitably, the Queen. She crowed to her daughter, the Crown Princess of Prussia: 'Did you ever see such a universal and over-whelming result of a Dissolution against a Minister as there is against Mr Gladstone? It shows how little he is trusted and how unpopular he is! What you used often to say to me about him and his talented colleagues is most true.'[8]

III

Disraeli, however, was deeply unpopular with many Conservatives by halfway through Gladstone's first ministry, his party demoralised by legislation that had diminished religion and advanced democracy. 'When Mr Mill calls us "the stupid party", is he so far wrong?' asked the anony-mous author of *Shall We Give It Up?* in 1871.[9] Having talked of the purposes of Conservatism – 'the projection and development of the Church of England . . . the defence of the Throne, the maintenance of the House of Lords, the integrity of endowments . . . the arrangement of the franchise so as to guard against the tyranny of mere numbers, the preservation of our colonies, the efficiency of our army and navy, the promotion of proper and not cheese-paring economy in the public expenditure, the diminution of pauperism, the improvement of the dwellings of the labouring classes, the gradual amendment and codifica-tion of our laws, and generally, the adoption of a policy at once tolerant of reasonable change, and impervious to restless innovation' – the writer asks his correspondent: 'Can you look me gravely in the face, and tell me that these ends are likely to be advanced, especially those of them that are more distinctly Conservative, by our again putting the author of "Lothair" in the position of Prime Minister?'[10] He added: 'Mr Disraeli's leadership of the Conservatives is a great practical joke . . . That the chief originator of the most democratic measure that ever received the sanction of the English parliament should lead the gentlemen of England against democracy is in itself more remarkable than the wildest combin-ation in his own works of fiction.'

Once Disraeli had become Prime Minister in 1867 traditional forces went to work: Clarendon referred to him as 'the Jew' in two letters of the autumn of 1868 in which he exposed Disraeli's misunderstanding of diplomacy following a gaffe in his Mansion House speech about relations between France and Prussia.[11] Distrust of him, not based entirely on incipient racism, was profound in his own party. When he won the election in February 1874 almost his first priority was to square Salisbury, who had not forgiven 1867, was a leading figure on the Tory benches in the Lords, and had the power to make Disraeli's life a misery. The two were reconciled, but only after a 'severe mental struggle' by Salisbury and the intervention of his stepmother, the Countess of Derby.[12] His view of Disraeli did not improve, at least for the moment. 'D is sublimely ignorant,' Salisbury told his wife on 18 February 1874, just as he accepted office.[13] Four days later he told her: 'We did not discuss policy at all, but my impression is that D's mind is as enterprising as ever and therefore the experiment will be a trying one.'

Disraeli was a prime manipulator. Earlier in his career he had used wit to get others on his side, as is often the way with unpopular boys in any playground. His lavish ingratiation with Queen Victoria was the supreme example of his cynical use of those whose compliance he needed to advance himself. He had got off to a bad start with the Court in the 1840s. Prince Albert had been close to Peel, whose assassin Disraeli in part was. The Queen, under Albert's influence, had been a committed free-trader, and had held Disraeli in suspicion for his opposition to the creed. Disraeli won her round with the elaborate courtesy and chivalry he displayed towards women of a certain age; all the more efficacious in the Queen's case, as no man had ever dared treat her so. He gossiped with her and kept nothing from her. They became, effectively, partners in crime. His greatest achievement, however, was that he was not Gladstone. Before he went to kiss hands in 1874 one of the Queen's ladies-in-waiting had told him that 'my dear Mistress will be very happy to see you again'.[14] There is no record of such a sentiment ever being conveyed to Gladstone.

Her unequivocal support meant he could do what he liked. He even conducted a winsome correspondence with her about his gout, to deepen their intimacy. It had, he told her, 'broken out late in life, but which, now understood, may be conquered with care and diet. What details for a servant of the Crown to place before a too gracious mistress! His cheek burns with shame. It seems almost to amount to petty treason.'[15]

As he told Matthew Arnold shortly before he died, he did this absolutely consciously, to achieve his ends. 'You have heard me accused of being a flatterer. It is true. I am a flatterer. I have found it useful. Every one likes flattery; and when you come to Royalty you should lay it on with a trowel.'[16] He flattered Arnold too, almost as if he could not help it: 'The young men read you; they no longer read me. And you have invented phrases which everyone quotes – such as "Philistinism" and "Sweetness and Light".'[17]

The prelude to Disraeli's administration of 1874 were two speeches he, as Leader of the Opposition, made in 1872, at Manchester and at the Crystal Palace. It was almost four years since his defeat. The Tories had been accused of being bankrupt of policy and, therefore, unable to offer the expanded electorate a real choice. On 3 April Disraeli spoke at the Free Trade Hall in Manchester. With his usual chutzpah he took head-on the claim that he had no ideas. 'Gentlemen, if a political programme is a policy to despoil Churches and plunder landlords, I confess that the Conservative party has no political programme. If a political programme is a policy which attacks or menaces every interest and every institution, every class and every calling in the country, I confess that the Conservative party has no political programme.'[18] He described his creed as 'the same and unchangeable . . . a policy that would maintain the monarchy limited by the co-ordinate authority of the Estates of the Realm'. He insinuated that the recent outbreak of republican sentiment was inspired and fed by the Liberal party.

Disraeli trotted out a defence of the Monarchy culled almost verbatim from Walter Bagehot's The English Constitution, published five years earlier. He pointed out the wisdom of a long-serving Sovereign (the Queen was about to mark thirty-five years on the Throne) and how England being a 'domestic country . . . where home is revered and the hearth is sacred' it would be a country 'properly represented by a family – a Royal Family.'[19] He dismissed the complaints about the Royal Family's expenses with a reference to the 'becoming dignity' that should characterise the institution, and the importance of the Queen's not having a standard of living inferior to that of some of her grandest subjects. The Queen, he said, could live well enough had she not made the Crown estates' revenues over to the Exchequer; and since she had, it was only fair to use part of those revenues to support her and her family adequately.

This was a reasonable point, and it addressed a pressing issue: but it did not constitute a programme for the Conservative party that would have any immediate appeal to the voters; any more than would Disraeli's next remarks, about the importance of maintaining the hereditary House of Lords and the Established Church. However, something more subtle was at play. Disraeli was delineating a country of old and serviceable institutions that worked and were benign, and that provided security and continuity within which consolidations and improvements could take place. This was a land, unlike France, free from repeated revolution; it had an aristocracy 'open to all who deserve to enter it'; it might have a class system, but all were 'equal before the law'.[20]

He contrasted the Manchester he had first seen forty years earlier with the one he saw now; and proclaimed there had been 'immense results' for the working classes in that time. 'Their wages have been raised, and their hours of daily toil have been diminished – the means of leisure, which is the great source of civilisation, have been increased'. And, above all – and thanks to the last Conservative government – political participation by working-class men had been increased. It almost seemed that the pursuit of perfection had been concluded. He praised 'the revolution in locomotion, which has opened the world to the working man, which has enlarged the horizon of his experience, increased his knowledge of nature and of art, and added immensely to the salutary recreation, amusement and pleasure of his existence.'[21]

The cheap postage since 1840 had had 'moral benefits . . . which cannot be exaggerated'. And there was now an 'unshackled press', since the stamp duty had come off newspapers in 1855, 'which has furnished him with endless sources of instruction, information and amusement, and has increased his ideas, elevated his self-respect, and made his life more varied and delightful.' The result was a 'vast increase in the intelligence, happiness, general prosperity and self-respect of the working classes.' Neither of these important reforms had been the work of Tory ministries: but then even in adducing the support of history, Disraeli was a chancer. He also sought to be all things to all men. Sensing his remarks, in that setting, would be interpreted as applying to the industrial working classes, he argued that the agricultural labourer had benefited too: but wages were lower in the countryside, and Britain was on the verge of an agricultural depression because of the growing efficiency of the North American grain producers.

This roseate picture did not prevent Disraeli from saying there was still more that could be done: and his emphasis was on 'sanitary legislation'. He said that 'pure air, pure water, the inspection of unhealthy habitations, the adulteration of food, these and many kindred matters may be legitimately dealt with by the legislature.'[22] He made a joke about it, adapting the Vulgate's *'vanitas vanitatum, omnia vanitas'* to *'sanitas sanitatum, omnia sanitas'* – but did so to emphasise that 'it is impossible to overrate the importance of the subject.' He said that 'the first consideration of a Minister should be the health of the people' because 'if the population every ten years decreases, and the stature of the race every ten years diminishes, the history of that country will soon be the history of the past.'

He had said he had not come to make a party speech: but proceeded to attack the government. Institutions such as he had defended were 'impugned'; he said this was not least because this had been 'the first instance in my knowledge of a British Administration being avowedly formed on a principle of violence'.[23] This was a reference to a laxity of policy in Ireland, which he said had led to 'sedition rampant and treason thinly veiled', with new MPs now being 'pledged to the disruption of the realm'. It was an outrageous claim, for there had been no sign that a Conservative response to the situation in Ireland after the Fenian conspiracy would have been any better at avoiding these consequences than the Liberal one had been.

Disraeli cited as an example of Liberal destruction the Cardwell reforms, which would have far-reaching benefits for the professionalisation of the Army: but he could offer no explicit criticism. 'They took in hand the Army. What have they done? I will not comment on what they have done. I will historically state it, and leave you to draw the inference.' He led up to the joke for which this speech is best remembered. 'As I sat opposite the Treasury Bench, the Ministers reminded me of one of those marine landscapes not very unusual on the coasts of South America. You behold a range of exhausted volcanoes. Not a flame flickers on a single pallid crest. But the situation is still dangerous. There are occasional earthquakes, and ever and anon the deep rumbling of the sea.'[24] This was not only a party speech, but a weak one – it contains little evidence of what he would do with power if he had it, and no disabling proof of the damage supposedly done by the Liberals.

He spoke again, eleven weeks later, on 24 June, at the Crystal Palace

in Sydenham, at a banquet of the National Union of Conservative and
Constitutional Associations. As the second barrel in Disraeli's fusillade
against those who accused him of having no policy, this speech concentrated on the British Empire, and on the Conservative party's support
and defence of it. He reiterated his belief in institutions: and yet seemed
to reinforce the view that the opportunity of power for him, were it to
come again, would be to maintain the status quo. Sanitary reform was
important: but it would not occupy a Parliament of perhaps seven years,
years Disraeli seemed to expect would be distinguished by management
of the Empire and the conduct of foreign affairs generally. That would
be true in some measure: but the newly enfranchised classes would
demand more in domestic improvements and reforms than Disraeli
realised. He would have to be steered in that direction by a wiser and
more practical man: and was fortunate that fate would present him with
one.

IV

Disraeli's most brilliant appointment was that of Richard Assheton Cross
as Home Secretary. Any great initiatives would have to be designed by
the ministers themselves rather than Disraeli, and few were more abundant in ideas than Cross. He wrote, in 1908, of the intense disappointment
he felt when attending his first Cabinet meeting at the 'want of originality' in the Prime Minister, finding Disraeli had hardly any idea of what
to do with the power he had won: 'From all his speeches I had quite
expected that his mind was full of legislative schemes, but such did not
prove to be the case; on the contrary, he had to entirely rely on the
suggestions of his colleagues, and, as they themselves had only just come
into office, and that suddenly, there was some difficulty in framing the
Queen's speech.'[25] Once some platitudes about foreign affairs and the
marriage of the Duke of Edinburgh, the Queen's second son, had been
aired, the speech was, Cross felt, 'not much to boast of'. Only one
measure raised in the speech became law, but it was indicative of Cross's
purpose and of the civilising drift of the administration: it regulated the
sale of alcohol.

Cross had been born in 1823 into the Lancashire gentry: and had been
a pupil of Arnold's at Rugby, taking into his life precisely the inspiration
the Doctor would have liked. He was a notable all-rounder: he was a

top-flight oarsman at university and president of the Cambridge Union. He went into the law and became one of the most successful barristers on the Northern Circuit. He was elected as Conservative MP for Preston in 1857, but left Parliament in 1862 to succeed his father as a partner in a private bank, of which he eventually became chairman. This period in his life was, however, crucial to his success as a politician when he returned to Westminster: for while working both as a banker and as a barrister he became prominent in several Lancashire charities, in his local quarter sessions, board of guardians and highway board. Unlike Disraeli, the man who would be his chief, Cross accumulated extensive first-hand experience of life on the front line in industrial Britain.

His re-entry into Parliament was achieved in a remarkable fashion, as he defeated Gladstone at the 1868 election in the new constituency of south-west Lancashire, a victory attributed to Cross's enormous local popularity. When Disraeli made him Home Secretary it was the first post Cross had held in government. However, Disraeli had – with help from Derby, who knew Cross well through the Lancashire connection – realised Cross's particular experience made him invaluable to the sort of reforming administration he had promised in the Manchester and Crystal Palace speeches, but which he had little idea how to implement. That is why Cross became the commanding figure of the ministry.

Disraeli's election address in 1874 made little mention of the social reform that would characterise his administration, for the very good reason that it had not occurred to him.[26] Over the next few years, however, Cross and his colleagues would find their talents put to work in certain distinct categories of legislation, as they identified problems bedevilling the country that required attention. Acts would be passed to give local authorities the power to improve the lot of the people, such as the Artisans' Dwellings Act. There would be some that compelled change, such as long-overdue legislation to criminalise the use of chimney-boys. Others would address long-running arguments but, because of the continued absence of consensus, would still leave the business unfinished, as, notably, in education. And, because Disraeli's was nothing if not a cynical ministry, there would be laws passed with the chief aim of ensuring his re-election when the time came.

The new Licensing Bill came into that category. It was not the most propitious of starts for a man of high principle such as Cross, as it was designed to get the brewing trade off the Conservative party's back.

Cross felt compelled to admit 'the evil effect of drunkenness . . . the crime, misery, and wretchedness' inflicted on society because of the widespread availability of cheap alcohol.[27] Even with the measures the previous administration had taken, there were still, in 1873, around 182,000 people proceeded against for drunkenness. English consumption had been prodigious; also in 1873, an estimated 63,500,000 bushels of malt, 40,000,000 gallons of spirits and 18,000,000 gallons of wine had been consumed. The population had increased: but between 1853 and 1873 the number of public houses had risen from 87,625 to 97,132.[28] Cross alluded to the growth in real wages as a factor behind the growth in consumption; but also blamed 'the want of a happy home'. He added: 'If you want to go to the bottom of this evil, you must go further. You must improve the education of the people, and try to induce them to learn that there are other enjoyments than the mere sensual enjoyments of the moment, and you will do this if you make their homes happy and comfortable.'[29] This presaged his own plans to improve working-class housing; and he used that as an excuse for liberalising the licensing laws, saying that better housing 'will do more to improve sobriety than any measures you may pass to prevent the sale of intoxicating liquors.' The cart was, however, being placed before the horse.

Cross acknowledged that some wanted to ban alcohol altogether, an idea he called 'impossible' as one could not 'legislate beyond public opinion.' There were also those who wanted no restrictions at all, something that had been tried in Liverpool, where anyone who had asked for a licence had been given one. The result had been endemic drunkenness. So he conceded the need for regulation, notably about opening hours, preferring it to be left to local judgement rather than imposed nationally. This would allow some pubs to remain open longer, the measure most sought after by the brewers. They would be further propitiated by his plans to reduce the penalties on keeping a disorderly house, and to make it easier for people of good character to enter the licensed trade. It was a mark of his subtlety as a politician that this cynical piece of legislation embraced a decent Conservative principle – that of providing powers to local authorities rather than compelling them from the centre to act – and was also presented as paving the way for wider, less partisan reforms.

Once he applied his considerable mind to factory legislation it became clear how far ideas of treatment of the working class had developed since Shaftesbury's battles in the Commons in the 1840s, and how far the question of child labour had now become indivisible from that of education. With the rise of the middle class, and the spread of more progressive values, attitudes had changed sharply over the preceding 30 years. A nation that prided itself on being more civilised found some social abuses so shocking that even a Tory government committed to persuasion rather than compulsion had, in certain instances, literally to lay down the law. The 1874 Factory Act further regulated the work of women and children in textile mills. Liberals continued, with some justification, to argue that the educational provisions successive Acts had made for children in factories had had only a limited effect. The Commons was told that of 963 young women aged from sixteen to twenty-three who had been to a sewing school in Manchester, only 199 could read and write.[30] Before the 1870 Education Act 2,000 children of working age in Stockport who had supposedly had part-time schooling included fewer than 400 who could read. However, better education was not why the Liberals tried to amend Cross's Factory Bill in the Commons: it was the enlightened question of the health of the 574,000 females over the age of thirteen engaged at that time in the textile industry.

Anthony Mundella, a Sheffield MP who would serve in Gladstone's third and fourth administrations, argued that to have girls aged between thirteen and eighteen put to work (and there were many under the age of thirteen, illegally working in the mills too) was to endanger their health at a vulnerable time in their lives. Mundella said the strain on them would result 'in phthisis, in indigestion, in pulmonary diseases of various kinds, and in a great deal of uterine disease'.[31] He added that while maternity could not possibly be a disqualification from working, 'when women, after being delivered of children, return to the mill at the end of three days surely something ought to be done in order to prevent the danger and the indecency of their so doing.' Mundella said, however, that his proposed amendment would mean more work for women and not less, because of raising the lower age limit on child workers.

One theme familiar from the 1840s remained consistent: strong opposition to a reduction in hours from MPs who argued that British competitiveness would suffer in comparison with the Continent, where, it was alleged, the average hours of work were twelve a day.[32] Cross, knowing the cotton districts well, proceeded with caution. The last reports of the Factory Inspectors showed that 4,500,000 people depended, directly or indirectly, on the prosperity of the cotton industry: so government interfered at its peril. There were 2,484 mills in Great Britain, with £87 million of capital tied up in them.[33] A restriction in hours would damage the trade; it would damage the banks that had lent it money; it would lower the wages of operatives. He adduced figures showing a vast increase in the consumption of cotton in continental markets over the preceding thirty or so years, but with British exports only accounting for a small part of that increase. A further anti-competitive move would have dire consequences. Cross was prepared to consider amendments to the Factory Bill, to avoid agitation, but wanted more time to consult. It was a measure of his reasonableness, and the respect in which he was held on both sides of the House, that Mundella's amendment was withdrawn. By the middle of June 1874 Cross was ready with his bill to regulate the work of women in textile factories. Women, children and those under eighteen would be prevented from working more than fifty-six hours a week, over five and a half days, with an extra half-hour allowed at the end of the week for cleaning. No one would be allowed to be in a factory for more than twelve hours a day, with two of those twelve hours set aside for mealtimes and 'recreation'. Cross regarded the 'great safeguard' on the health of women and children that they should not be allowed to work for more than four and a half hours without a meal break.[34] He also proposed to raise from nine to ten the age at which a child might start work part-time in a factory – for some of the time had to be given over to education – and from thirteen to fourteen those who could be employed full-time.

Even these quite mild regulations inspired opposition, led by Henry Fawcett, who would be Postmaster General in Gladstone's second ministry. He wanted to know why the textile manufacturers were deemed so 'peculiarly deficient in independence and wanting in capacity to manage their own affairs' that they required to be legislated against in this way.[35] He claimed that if all the women went home an hour before the men the factories would have to come to a halt, for the jobs done by each were dependent upon the other. He also asserted that medical evidence supplied to the government showed that the dangers to women's health in the mills were often overstated: 163 doctors had been examined by a Royal Commission into the question, and 131 stated that the hours worked by women were not too long.

More to the point, that Commission had itself admitted that three-quarters of women working in textiles were employed in branches of the trade that were 'not prejudicial to health'.[36] He ridiculed Shaftesbury, accusing him of exaggeration, and of always having 'some anonymous bogey or undivulged monster' of a mill-owner 'at hand wherewith to terrify and alarm the timid and the prejudiced.' As with so many other perceived social problems, Fawcett thought the key to better female and child health was better housing, not shorter hours. He cited cases of mill-owners who had built new housing stock for their operatives, and who had seen the beneficial results – one, a Mr Hugh Mason from Manchester, ended up with his area having a lower death rate 'than was to be found in the healthiest rural districts in England.'[37] What was needed was more mains drainage, and fewer cesspools. Fawcett attacked the logic of the government's legislating just for the factories: why not, he asked, for women who work in shops, or women in agricultural areas 'bedraggled in mud and wet up to their middles when weeding a turnip field'?[38]

The latter especially would, of course, affect the landed interest that supported the government. And, in reducing working hours, even a careful government had to start somewhere. Also, as Mundella pointed out, the 1870 Education Act was a 'dead letter' unless the hours children could work were further restricted.[39] He also spoke up for a clause forbidding the return of a woman to her factory for six weeks after her confinement: saying that when such a measure had been introduced in Alsace, the infant mortality rate fell by 80 per cent the following year. Not to protect women in this and other ways would render Britain like Belgium, where there were no restrictions on what a woman could do or for how long she could do it, 'and the result was that while the women in that country were working in the mines the men were drinking in the cabarets.'[40] Cross, winding up, agreed with such contentions: the future of the British people would be improved, and their prosperity with it, if their women were not worn out by work, and their children not weakened as a result. The second reading passed by a handsome majority.

In one respect, and despite attempts to legislate in the past, there was one trade in which children were still being cruelly exploited. Two Acts regulating chimney-sweeps had been introduced in 1834 and 1864 to improve the lives of the boys who worked for them. The first such Act had, indeed, been in 1788. However, in the winter of 1875 a fourteen-year-old boy called George Brewster died in a flue in Cambridge, where his master had sent him. The coroner brought in a verdict of manslaughter against the master. A child of ten had died in 1874 in a chimney in Gateshead, which Shaftesbury, who continued to campaign against such treatment, did not hesitate to call 'murder'.[41] The problem did not exist in big cities: it seemed only to happen in smaller towns. The boy in Cambridge had died of suffocation because of soot in his lungs and windpipe. The problem was, Shaftesbury thought, that some magistrates were using their discretion not to refer the cases to a higher court.

This scandal drew out more information. It turned out that many of chimneys in Limerick were swept by climbing-boys, and the law there was largely evaded. Where such cases of flouting the law arose, the government ordered the local authorities to enforce the existing regulations. Shaftesbury, however, decided the present law was not tight enough, the enforcement inadequate and the penalties insufficient. He introduced his own bill to seek to tighten things up. At its second reading on 11 May 1875 Shaftesbury said the earlier measures had been characterised by 'timidity'.[42] The 1834 Act had banned anyone under the age of twenty-one from climbing a flue, but had been widely evaded. The worst excesses of the old days – parents selling their children of four, five or six years old to climb up chimneys – had not, however, gone after 1834: hence the measure of 1864, an Act initiated by Shaftesbury himself. An inquiry in 1863 had found children as young as four-and-a-half being trained for the job, flouting completely the existing law: and the nature of the training had been horrific.

A Mr Ruff of Nottingham, described as a master sweep, had said: 'No one knows the cruelty which a boy has to undergo in learning. The flesh must be hardened. This must be done by rubbing it, chiefly on the elbows and knees, with the strongest brine, close by a hot fire. You must stand over them with a cane, or coax them by a promise of a halfpenny if they will stand a few more rubs. At first they will come back from their work streaming with blood, and the knees looking as if the caps had been pulled off. Then they must be rubbed with brine again.'[43] There were further tales of small children being whipped, beaten, kicked and stamped upon by nailed boots, and in the process often scarred for life, until they would do exactly what they were told. Another master sweep, a man called Stransfield, had said: 'In learning a child you must use violence. I shudder now when I think of it. I have gone to bed with my knees and elbows scabbed and raw, and the inside of my thighs all scarified.'[44] He added: 'In some boys I have heard the flesh does not harden for years.' Children had their flesh rubbed with a 'lotion' of old urine and hot cinders.

Some boys were sent up flues that were on fire. Since 1840, twenty-three boys had been stifled. However, these were boys employed by sweeps who had not invested in the modern equipment common in big cities such as London, Glasgow, Edinburgh and numerous other towns where no climbing-boy had been found for decades. Where boys were used, magistrates found excuses not to take the crime seriously. They either refused to believe that patently small boys were under the age of twenty-one; or chose to believe that the flue in which a boy had been was in his own house, and he had a perfect right to be up it. Shaftesbury believed that magistrates who refused to enforce the law used the services of such boys themselves.

Shaftesbury wanted the law changed so that no one could carry on the trade of chimney-sweep without being licensed: and with the licence contingent on inspection by a competent authority. His idea was welcomed in the Lords: and the Bishop of London, John Jackson, further suggested that it should be an obligation on the part of householders to ensure their sweep was licensed before they used him, with their being culpable if he was not. Once the bill had been waved through the Lords, Shaftesbury asked Cross to get it through the Commons.[45] Cross had to do relatively little: there was no opposition to the bill, which reached the statute book with ease. Victorian sensibility was at last turning against the exploitation of children.

V

It was one thing not to exploit children, however, but quite another to maintain a laissez-faire approach towards them that would lead to those near the bottom of the ladder remaining there in ignorance and squalor. The provisions of Forster's 1870 Education Act, now quite rightly regarded as a landmark of social reform and of the advancement of the disadvantaged, had not reached all the country's children, and for that reason continued to provoke argument. Because of the absence of compulsion, those who saw education as a necessity inevitably regarded the question as unfinished business. A private bill to try to compel attendance was heavily defeated in 1874. There was great support for such a measure but also widespread cynicism, and not always from the quarters one might expect. As long ago as 1867, in framing his General Report for the year, Matthew Arnold had disclosed that compulsion was 'becoming a familiar idea' in the districts he inspected, but such was the state of schools after the Revised Code that, he wrote, 'the difficult thing would not be to pass a law to make education compulsory; the difficult thing would be to work such a law after he had got it.'[46] Prussia had introduced compulsion with great success, and it was often adduced as an example England should follow. However, as Arnold pointed out, in Prussia 'education is not flourishing because it is compulsory, it is compulsory because it is flourishing.'[47]

He added that 'because people there really prize instruction and culture, and prefer them to other things, therefore they have no difficulty in imposing on themselves the rule to get instruction and culture. In this country people prefer to them politics, station, business, money-making, pleasure and many other things; and till we cease to prefer these things, a law which gives instruction the power to interfere with them, though a sudden impulse may make us establish it, cannot be relied on to hold its ground and to work effectively.' Arnold also raised the question of fees. The Prussian system charged an average of the equivalent of 1d a week. In France it was 4d a week, but many children had free places, and the French were moving towards a system of taxpayer-funded State education. In England compulsion would be difficult unless more of the indigent classes had support to pay for their children to attend.

Another attempt to legislate was made in 1875, by George Dixon, the MP for Birmingham, who had initiated the previous attempt. Dixon envisaged a network of school boards to monitor and enforce attendance. The prospect of this bureaucracy had been a main reason why the bill failed in 1874. The prejudice against compulsory attendance appeared to be dying out: Dixon told the Commons in June 1875 that even in agricultural districts, where parents had wanted their children to help with farm work, a feeling was growing up against ignorance. In Dorset and Somerset, Dixon said, the people were calling for school boards to be set up 'so that the disgrace of so many men and women being unable to read and write, and believing in witchcraft, ghosts, and fairies, may not continue in this so-called Christian country.'[48] In May 1875 a meeting in Birmingham of delegates representing 50,000 agricultural labourers had unanimously passed a resolution in favour of compulsion; shortly beforehand the National Union of Elementary Teachers had also passed a resolution unanimously demanding compulsory education to the age of ten, and that until the age of thirteen the amount of schooling demanded by the Factory Act be required of all children: and children would have to reach a certain standard of education before being given the certificate that allowed them to work in a factory.

London and some other large towns did have school boards. They had caused an increase in attendance of 53 per cent on average: but in Birmingham the increase had been 94 per cent, in Hull 99 per cent and in Sheffield 120 per cent.[49] Dixon wished boards to compel children not in work to go to school, just as those who wished to work were made to do as a condition of being allowed to work. Also, he could not understand why the recognition by towns that education should be more widespread was not shared by the countryside. He conceded that in certain villages a combination of the squire and the parson ensured that an excellent standard of education was provided: but he feared that many MPs, knowing that in their own areas there were such public-spirited men, imagined they were everywhere. Dixon asserted that 'thousands' of villages were 'very backward indeed', and it was on behalf of these 'backward districts' that he urged the Commons to pass the bill.[50] The backward districts were the ones that contained the highest proportion of agricultural labourers; and he argued that only a system of school boards would ensure that parents in those districts sent their children to school. The other advantage that boards, provided they had a modicum of State funding, would have is that they could take over voluntary – mainly Church – schools where those schools were underfunded and failing. The Church itself admitted that in some areas this was so.

Dixon's opponents argued that compulsion should come from government action, not after a private member's bill. It was also felt that ratepayers in areas that did not need school boards would be punished financially. Also, education seemed – if numbers were any guide – to be doing well without compulsion. In the last year before the passing of the 1870 Education Act there had been 7,845 schools, accommodating 1,765,000 pupils, and an average attendance of 1,062,000. In 1874, once the 1870 Act had had time to allow the building of schools in areas short of them, the number had grown to 12,167 and the accommodation provided to 2,871,000, with an average attendance of 1,678,000. However, of this increased number of schools just 838 were run by school boards, offering 245,000 places. Of these only 131,000 on average were taken each day, despite the boards having the power to pass by-laws to enforce compulsion. Hence, it was argued the system did not work.[51]

One opponent, John Scourfield, the MP for Pembrokeshire, described compulsion as 'un-English', and as inflicting a 'heavy cost' upon the public – inspectors were paid between £80 and £100 a year, and there would need to be more. However, the facts continued to suggest that education was failing. It was estimated that 3 million children were of an age when they ought to be in schools, against the 1,678,000 who actually turned up. Switzerland had one-eleventh of the population of England, but twice as many pupils passed the sixth standard examination. Another speaker accused Dixon of 'fanaticism', saying he should be content with the 'experiment' of 1870, which was delivering 'progress' without compulsion.[52] It was also not clear how compulsion would work: though the example of a separate law passed for Scotland in 1872, under which parents had been summonsed for not sending their children to school, had proved successful once parents began to be convicted.

However Viscount Sandon, who as vice-president of the Council was the minister responsible, refused to commit the government, saying the law in Scotland had not been in operation long enough for any sound conclusions to be drawn from it. Nor was he sure the higher attendances in urban areas could be attributed to the boards in those areas, but rather to 'enormous' additional expenditure by the voluntary sector.[53] He also felt denominational schools had an interest in compulsion less connected with the expansion of knowledge but more with raising extra money, since compulsory attendance would result in more parents paying fees. He said that of the 515 boards formed between May 1874 and May 1875, only ten had passed a by-law to enforce compulsion: so the link between boards and compulsion did not seem essential.[54] Compulsion, he said, would also mean those school boards able to regulate education without compulsion would be made to enforce it. He was criticised by Forster, who reiterated Dixon's point that urban children were being directed towards an elementary education, while rural ones were not.

The government itself sought, in part, to address this problem in 1876. Attendances at schools, whether in urban or rural areas, had increased since 1870 but were still poor: of the 614,670 children estimated to live in London, only 288,497 had attended during the previous half-year. Sandon introduced a bill on 18 May 1876 to assist attendance, and suggested – not entirely successfully – that something so important to the working classes and the employers of Britain as improving education should not be a party political matter. Two separate commissions had investigated the work done by children in factories and on the land – the principal causes of non-attendance at school. The government proposed to legislate on the basis of their findings. Sandon asserted that it was 'the determined and final and settled wish of the whole country' that 'no child in the country should hereafter enter on the struggle of life without having those simple tools needed by our present civilization to enable him to work his way hereafter'.[55] He argued that society would no longer tolerate 'gross ignorance' – even the landowners and farmers who benefited so much from the child labour that helped provide their incomes.

The government was now giving £1 million a year for education. A similar amount was raised annually in fees; and £660,000 came from the voluntary sector. As a result, places were provided for 3,150,000 children in elementary schools, and 100,000 in what Sandon called 'private adventure schools', which were of an appallingly low standard and outside State inspection. This meant that 1,450,000 children who ought to be at school still were not attending. If 'all talent and merit should have an opportunity of rising', which Sandon said had been a doctrine of the country since after the Reformation, more had to be done.[56] But even children of no talent required a basic schooling. This, he reminded the House, had been the stated desire of Liberals such as Lowe and Radicals such as Bright.

The half-time system, which applied to factory children between ten and twelve, already enforced an element of compulsion, and Scotland had its legal powers. Children could only work on the land if they could produce a certificate of attendance at school. There was a mass of different regulations depending on the trade in which a child worked, and they neither protected the interests of children nor ensured a decent basic education. Some school boards had enforced compulsion, but this was only in areas with no voluntary schools. Sandon feared universal compulsion enforced by the State would bring an end to the voluntary sector. He proposed instead a certificate of education without which no child could work: and since it was usually in the parents' interest that the child did work, they would be motivated to ensure attendance. There would be certain well-defined exemptions at harvest time.

One reason why the government would still not contemplate direct compulsion was that it feared confrontation with employers, landowners and, perhaps worst of all, Nonconformists. The age at which children could work, and when they would need the certificate, would be ten; and local authorities would enforce this power. Parents who refused to comply would be punished by law: as would those who allowed their 'wastrel' children, over the age of ten, to idle about, neither in school nor in work, robbing orchards and poaching. Such children might be ordered to an industrial school – a forerunner of the approved school, with arduous work and severe discipline. Lyon Playfair attacked that last proposal, saying such action would punish the child when the State ought to be punishing the parent. 'The industrial school', he said, 'was really a prison where children on the verge of crime were detained; and would the interests of education, which people should be led to regard as a good and worthy thing, be served by associating these children with others on the verge of crime?'[57]

Forster congratulated the government on preventing children younger than ten working: but he could not see why children whose parents neglected their education should, for want of the requisite certificate, be forbidden from working between the ages of ten and thirteen, and left in a destructive idleness through no fault of their own. Sandon said that the local authority, whose responsibility it was to detect when children were not attending school, would provide for such victims of neglect: so such cases should not arise. Poor districts would be given extra resources. In the desire to raise school attendance, the State would have to requisition, in some cases, the role of parent.

Liberals welcomed this: but could not see why there could not be clear, centralised, universal compulsion. In a sign of how far the civilising process was moving on, there were requests for better provision for blind, deaf and dumb children. There were still representatives of the landed interest who argued against restricting child labour in the fields, given the concentration of effort required at harvest time. One, Clare Read, the Conservative MP for South Norfolk, said the notion of half-time in factories was one thing: but in agriculture it was, he said, 'simply preposterous and ridiculous'.[58]

At the bill's second reading on 15 June Mundella, who would have Sandon's job when the Liberals returned to power in 1880, launched a demand for universal school boards. He threw back at Sandon his admission that there were 'millions of children in the country who did not attend school at all.'[59] Those children were in areas without school boards – areas where the voluntary sector had, before 1870, supplied enough places for all the local children. School boards, with their powers of compulsion, ensured most children in their districts went to school. The various Labour Acts regulating factory and agricultural work had achieved nothing but confusion: a system of boards would be far preferable. The regulations under the Acts for attendance at school were inadequate, and the standards achieved by children subject to them derisory. The commission that had inspected the factories, and the education of children there, had said there should be education between the ages of five and thirteen, and at least five hours a day, with half-time attendance only allowed to children in permanent employment over the age of ten. The government appeared to be diluting this.

'Why', Mundella asked, 'should the cities and towns of England have a good system of education while the rural districts had a bad one? The opposition to compulsion did not proceed from the artisans or the agricultural labourers.'[60] Education had become 'a great public necessity'. The damage caused by ignorance was everywhere apparent. British workers, through lack of education, were increasingly unable to compete with those from other advanced nations. The country's moral character left much to be desired. The franchise had been extended, and 'in time the agricultural labourer would be in possession of it, and that being so, it became the duty of the State to see that he was so far educated as to understand the value of the right which he possessed.' Liberals such as Mundella were not prepared to quibble about expense. The richest nation in the world contributed relatively little to education compared with other powers, notably America, and much of what was spent came from the Church rather than the taxpayer. The government was happy to spend money on ironclads and new rifles for the Army: it was less enthusiastic about educating, to a basic level, all its children. Mundella might have added that, at the same time, a bill was speeding through Parliament to punish severe cruelty to animals: which seemed to have a higher priority, and provoke more unanimity, than of that to children.

The religious question came back, as always. While the argument
for boards had been forcefully made, some Liberals promised they
would insist, on their party being returned to office, on the establishment of at least one non-sectarian school under every board.
Nonconformists and Roman Catholics would risk, otherwise, having
their children driven into Anglican schools. Towns required compulsion, which was possible under school board by-laws: in the country
things were very different. As so often before, religious bigotries were
going to impede all children, urban or rural, getting the education
they needed.

The problem with the type of bill Sandon had introduced, with its
attempts not to aggrieve religious groups or to upset more than necessary the agricultural interest to which his party was so wedded, was that
the means of achieving all these things was excessively bureaucratic.
There were grave concerns about who would award the certificates to
permit children to work legitimately: if it were left up to schoolmasters,
there was scope for abuse. If it were entrusted to local authorities, it
would simply add to the burdens on them: a burden that could be
avoided by straightforward compulsion. The Workshop Act, the Mines
Act and the Factory Acts all set out how many hours children should
go to school: would this bill override them, or simply conflict with them?
That problem, too, could be solved by straightforward compulsion.
James Kay-Shuttleworth, to whom opinion in the House deferred on
educational questions, lamented the 'weak, half-hearted and inefficient
Bill' before them, rendered so by the attempt not to upset the
Nonconformists and the agricultural landlords.[61]

Despite Sandon's entreaties, the discussion became nakedly partisan.
The Conservatives admitted its defects: but they argued that it was trying
to extend the scope of the 1870 Act, which the Liberals were in no position to criticise because of its own shortcomings. There were concerns
that children who did not qualify for an attendance certificate because
of feckless parents would suffer because they could not work, and
contribute to the family income, and therefore would be half-starved as
a result. Also, as one Irish MP put it, 'compulsory education would in
many instances amount to religious persecution'.[62] It would allow the
Church to spread its doctrines in a way that was improper and unfair.
However, the commissioners who had looked at the problem had recommended direct compulsion: why did Parliament not want to carry out

the recommendation? Compulsion, where it was enforced, was expensive: the court procedures entailed meant it cost 7 guineas to get a child to school, and in areas where there was mass non-attendance, the bureaucracy was unequal to the problem.

Forster himself, who had had to handle the Nonconformists with care in 1870, now from the luxury of opposition said that direct compulsion was essential. Sandon could not agree with him: 'No doubt a great evil was to be met, but to say to every poor man that his children were, under all circumstances, to attend school every day would be a bad and undesirable thing.'[63] This marked out the division between the state of Conservative and the state of Liberal opinion on the question of whether children should be forced to go to school. The Liberals were now, six years after Forster's Act, unequivocal in support of the notion of the State intervening in this way: the Conservatives could only see their way to a form of compulsion by the back door, and by providing an indirect pecuniary incentive to the lower classes to send their children to school, in the alleged interest of encouraging parental responsibility for their children.

A main obstacle to compulsion was the primitive, labour intensiveness of agriculture, hop-picking, fruit-picking and so on. However, there was to the end deep opposition on religious grounds. Henry Richard, the Nonconformist MP for Merthyr Tydfil, described it as 'the worst Bill, the most unjust, the most reactionary, the most tyrannical in spirit, that has been brought before Parliament since Lord Bolingbroke proposed his Schism Bill in the reign of Queen Anne.'[64] He protested that 'the attempt to make national education sectarian is an absurdity and a contradiction in terms, and that it is impossible to have a denominational system imposed upon the people with adequate securities for the rights of conscience.' The offending clause in the 1870 Act – which allowed school boards to pay the fees of poor children, using ratepayers' money – would be repealed, and the payment of fees for the poor handed over to the local boards of guardians. Religious views would not be considered; which was a large part of the problem. Yet again, a bill had failed to separate secular instruction for all from religious instruction to be given elsewhere. Nothing had changed since 1870. The government had, however, succeeded in making it more attractive for parents to send their children to school where they were not already compelled to do so.

VI

Because compulsory attendance at school had still not been agreed, it remained possible for employers to deploy child labour in a fashion that offended the increasingly progressive values of Parliament and the general public. The Factory Act of 1878 sought to address this, by compulsion rather than by permissive legislation, consolidating earlier laws, and acting on recommendations of a Royal Commission of 1876. The programme of regulating industry since 1833 had been piecemeal, with fifteen Acts of Parliament in force by 1878 to deal with various trades – such as agriculture, coal mines, ore mines, textile mills, bleach and dye works, ironworks, paper works and so on. Small manufacturers with fewer than fifty hands came under the Workshops Regulation Act of 1870. The mass of regulation created not just inequalities in the workplace, but a bureaucratic nightmare of enforcement. There were special problems with children, and numerous loopholes that allowed them to be exploited still: the hours a child could work, or should spend at school, would depend on which trade it worked in. A child in the mines could work full-time at twelve; in textiles it was fourteen; in agriculture there was no limit of age. The provisions of the 1876 Education Act addressed some, but not all, anomalies.

There was another, more fundamental problem. Many children could not meet the prescribed educational standard at the age of thirteen; they stopped going to school but could not work full-time, and so were idling. At one of the largest woollen mills in the West Riding 62 per cent of the children were unable to reach the standard that would allow them to work under age: their enforced idleness cost their families an estimated £11 or £12 per child per year. The country was in an economic depression; such loss of earnings was hard for many families. The factory laws were absurd: educational privileges were allowed to people in some trades that were barred in others. Sanitary rules varied from factory to factory. Safety rules were far more stringent in one dangerous trade than in another equally dangerous. The Factory Inspectors knew the arrangements were ridiculous, and urged the government to standardise the regulations across industry. However, the Royal Commission dismissed the need for uniformity, since industry itself did not demand it.

Robert Tennant, the MP for Leeds, wanted the government to go beyond the recommendations. He conceded that conditions for workers were unrecognisably better 'in this present age of enlightenment of public opinion and spread of education' than when the first Factory Act was passed. However, he pleaded that 'so long as labour requires the protection of the State, let that protection be granted equally and universally; and I trust I shall not appeal in vain to the House, not, on the one hand, to subject certain classes of manufacture to invidious restrictions and unfair competition, nor, on the other hand, to withhold from large numbers of operatives those social, educational, and sanitary blessings which should alike be extended to all.'[65] On a more practical level, most parents would not have a clue at what age their children could be legally employed in any given factory.

The bill proposed to put workshops and factories in the same category, at least. But uniformity, as Mundella pointed out, was made difficult precisely because of the different workforces employed from trade to trade. In the textile industries, 76 per cent of workers were women and children; some workshop-based trades were almost entirely men with a handful of boy apprentices. The 1876 Act appeared effective: Mundella reported that in Keighley 400 children had been examined for permission to work and 340 had been rejected as having too little educational attainment. He claimed that 'these facts showed that nothing could better stimulate parents to attend to the education of their children'.[66] But he conceded that without uniformity there was, in areas such as the Midlands where there was a mixed economy, an unfortunate loophole. Children could leave school at ten and work full-time in agriculture without having to prove any educational attainment. They could do that until they were fourteen, at which point they could work in a factory, being old enough to do so without having to present a certificate from school.

The legislation was also widely avoided by two other sorts of child – usually boys – who worked in large numbers on the streets: newspaper sellers and match sellers. Cross argued that the authorities who should clamp down on them were the school boards, which, being largely urban entities, operated where match and newspaper sellers were most typically found. Similarly, he said that Boards of Guardians should seek to prevent abuses in the countryside. He said the bill proposed as much uniformity as was feasible.

However, once the bill went into committee, the calls continued for children working in agriculture not to be deprived of the education that children destined to work in factories now had by law. Thirteen-and-a-half hours of school each week were required before a child aged between ten and thirteen could work part-time, and attendance could be enforced until fourteen if a child had not reached the required level by thirteen. But for children working on the land the State, as one MP put it, 'washed its hands altogether of his education' at ten.[67] Henry Fawcett said that part of the opposition was because an army of inspectors would be required to patrol the countryside ensuring children went to school: but since the State had already resigned itself to having such an army in the industrial regions, he could not see the difficulty. The landed interest, however, did not want children in schools when they should be getting in the harvest, or dealing with ploughing and sowing. An MP said that equality between the two classes of children would simply 'harass one of the greatest industries in the country'.[68] This argument prevailed: while it was accepted that factory law could be made more consistent, there was no mood to bring agricultural workers under the same provisions.

Cross was also keen to ensure that the conditions for adults were brought up to a modern standard too. He ensured that sanitary regulations were standardised, notably to improve ventilation in factories and workshops to try to limit the spread and incidence of disease. Part of the problem was that owners provided the means of ventilation; but the operatives preferred to work in warm conditions, and would not open windows and skylights. However, some diseases were caused by the noxious materials used in manufacturing, such as that known as 'lead paralysis' caused by the paint used to give a gloss to earthenware: and there were calls to ban the use of such substances. The Potteries in particular was a region where lung diseases scythed through the working population. The French had already legislated to prevent such a problem; when would Britain?

The bill also proposed to fence in dangerous machinery to keep operatives from being injured by moving parts, and screening off vats into which they might fall. The cleaning of machinery in motion was also banned, and the length of time for which anyone could work without a break was fixed to four-and-a-half hours: though such rigidities were complained about, since they might interrupt work and processes that were, technically, uninterruptible. It was made quite clear that the employment of children under ten in factories and workshops was absolutely prohibited, as was the employment of women, children and young persons on Sundays: exceptions were allowed for Jews.

It also fixed penalties for employers who failed to allow staff the statutory public holidays – more bank holidays had been introduced by Gladstone in 1871, an acknowledgement of the benefits of recreation – and standardised the certification of children allowed to work because of their educational attainment and their state of health. A network of examining surgeons also had to be established, at considerable expense, to ensure that factory workers were physically equal to the task: the principal way in which Cross had justified this bill was that it was sanitary. It introduced a uniform procedure for the accidents causing death or serious injury. The detail of what would now be termed health and safety legislation was remarkable: alerted, for example, to the dangers of spontaneous combustion in Turkey-red dyeing, Cross ensured that special additional precautions would be taken.

This required a sizeable inspectorate, within easy reach of the main towns and cities. Cross resisted calls to set up offices in those towns, saying instead he would publish the addresses of the inspectors so the public could find them. The expense of offices was not something he could countenance. He also limited the right of inspectors to enter workshops where they were parts of dwelling-houses. This, though, was controversial, as many sweatshops operated in cottages, and it was known that in some of them children were mistreated. Factories and workshops were also instructed to keep their own registers and records, and to display relevant extracts from the Act for their workers to read.

Although much appeared to have moved on since the reports of squalor familiar from the factory debates of the 1840s, in some respects the primitive conditions continued, and this bill was an opportunity to eliminate them. Sir Charles Forster, the MP for Walsall, sought to prevent girls under sixteen from being employed in chain and nail factories. He quoted a report from a Black Country newspaper to substantiate his case. "'I was a stranger come out of curiosity to see the chain-making country." "And a bad place you've come to," said an old woman. "It's the worst country God ever made. The women do all the work, and the men nearly nothing." "But they work sometimes," I ventured to remark. "Yes, they do, sometimes," was the reply, "but they always spend all they earn, and more too."' The report went on to describe a row of some four or five chain-makers' shops in close proximity to some offensive cesspools.

> The fires of these workshops were all going, and none but women were at work. It must not be supposed, however, that the men were absent—not a bit of it. The lords of the creation were there in full force, but they were not working. They were amusing themselves with skylarking, and courting the girls who were hammering away at the chains.
>
> At the bottom of Cradley was a pool close to the high road, where he saw men bathing and running about naked. Chain shops were close at hand, and a small brickyard, with young girls at work there. He would ask what must be the moral condition of a district where such scenes took place?

He added that

> it was impossible to read the Reports on the subject without coming to the conclusion that the health of young females must be seriously jeopardized by this kind of labour. They heard a good deal, in the evidence taken before the Royal Commission, of an instrument called an 'oliver,' used in welding the links of the chain, whose weight was in proportion to the size of the links, some being heavier and more laborious to work than others. The evidence described the 'oliver' as shaking the lower parts of the body, and, therefore, dangerous to women in child-bearing . . . and yet instances were given of these instruments being used by women within a week of their confinement. Was it, then, too much to ask that in trades requiring such an instrument, the labour of young females should be restricted in the manner which he proposed?[69]

Cross sympathised with the argument, but advised that the Royal Commission had heard witnesses who described nail- and small-chain-making as no more injurious than anything else women in the locality did. The Commission itself, however, had not agreed: it felt the labour required to make heavier nails and chains was too hard for a woman. It could not, however, work out where to draw the line between work that was light enough and work that was not. Cross chose to rely on the sense of women not to take on work that was too arduous, rather than seek to legislate. The bill had a third reading unopposed, except for Fawcett complaining that, when British trade was facing stiffer competition than ever, the proposed Act would represent an unwarranted interference in the commercial activities of businessmen.

He was advancing what, after the upheavals of the preceding years, had come to appear a very eighteenth-century view.

> It was all very well to consider an ideal state of society, in which every woman, when she came to a certain age, should be married and be in a comfortable condition of life, the husband working for her and she at home looking after her domestic duties and attending to her children . . . [however] There was no fact which was truer, there was none which was more apparent than that hundreds of thousands, he might almost say millions, of women were not thus provided for by husbands, and they had to earn their own livelihood in the best way they could. If they closed to them the avenue of honest employment, depend upon it, at the same time, they opened wide the portals which led to vice, misery, and ruin.[70]

Fawcett knew the House was against him, and that the country was against him: but the time would come when opinion, which he said was already beginning to shift, would demand the same liberties in the workplace for women as for men. Cross respected his opinion: but also, speaking as a representative from Lancashire, he knew how much the condition of the people had been improved by the Factory Acts throughout the preceding forty years: and he believed this one would improve it further. He acknowledged the liberty of men to work as many hours as they pleased: but he also believed in the duty of the State to protect women against things that might be injurious to their welfare.

When the bill reached the Lords, Shaftesbury, whose own work in labour reform dated back over forty-five years, commended it. He summed up Cross's achievement: he had 'consolidated the whole of the existing Factory Laws—and he was lost in wonder at the amount of toil, of close investigation, and of perseverance, which the Home Secretary must have brought to bear on the preparation of this Bill. The right hon Gentleman had had to deal with 45 Acts, extending over a period of 50 years, and in many cases contradictory of each other, often impossible to understand, and impracticable to be put into operation. By this Bill, the whole of this scattered legislation would be brought into one lucid and harmonious whole.'[71] Shaftesbury alluded to the outrages that went on despite the laws passed since the 1830s: such as children as young as four working in match factories for long hours each day. Where children worked in regulated factories, by contrast, they looked 'hale and stout', their appearance radically different from that of children from a generation or two earlier. He said that 'some two million of people of this country would bless the day when Mr Cross was invited to become the Secretary of State for the Home Department.'[72]

VII

The 1878 Factory Act represented a significant progression in society's treatment of women: but in many respects their lot remained not merely unequal, but downright shocking. Although much had been done since the 1850s to recognise that women had, or should have, legal rights – mostly to protect them from abuses by men – and although the head of steam that would result in the suffragist movement was building only slowly, there was still one respect in which they were treated in a fashion that outraged civilised opinion. The Contagious Diseases Act had been passed in 1864 and extended in 1866 and 1869. It gave the police power, in certain specified districts, to arrest any prostitute (or woman suspected of being a prostitute) and to subject her to a compulsory medical examination for venereal disease. If found to be carrying it, she would be confined in something termed a 'lock hospital', from which she would not be released until 'cured'. The original Act was in response to a supposed epic of VD in the Army and Navy, and only advanced feminists thought to argue that this might be more the fault of the men who contracted it rather than the exploited women who gave it to them. Prostitution was a widespread activity in the 1860s, with police estimating that more than 5,000 such women worked in London, and 30,000 in all of England and Wales.[73]

An attempt was made to repeal the Acts in 1875, though with the MP who introduced the repeal measure, Sir Harcourt Johnstone, apologising for bringing a matter 'so revolting, so loathsome' before the Commons.[74] The law had, he said, become increasingly 'despotic' and 'dangerous to public liberty'.[75] Women whose only offence was to be drunk near a ship or a garrison could be, and had been, taken into custody, with their lives ruined as a result. Nor had those investigating the effects of the

Acts been able to prove that the incidence of venereal disease in the services was any less as a result of the legislation. A commission had inquired into the operation of the Acts, examining eighty witnesses over forty-five days, so the investigation had been thorough.

The commission showed that the number of brothels had declined since the Acts went into operation, and there had been fewer young girls going into the business. There was evidence that women detained under the Act helped drive down the figures of those diseased by receiving treatment. However, the paradox of the Acts was that they had effectively regulated prostitution, and provided an approved class of medically examined woman for the benefit of soldiers and sailors. Those who wanted repeal did so not least for moral reasons. Johnstone said three main considerations motivated him and his friends.

> They hold, in the first place, that it is not the business of the State to provide the means of self-indulgence for the Army, the Navy, or any other class of society in this country or elsewhere; secondly, that it is not the business of the State to connive at the maintenance of houses of ill-fame, but to suppress them, and that, not by a central agency, but by means of the local authorities; and the third great principle they maintain is this—that, so long as they are in this House, they should endeavour to see that no Act of Parliament should be passed that will allow any office or Department, whether the Home Office or any other, to frame and carry out regulations that are inconsistent with the liberty of the people, and with constitutional law.[76]

The residents of ports such as Chatham and Portsmouth were strongly against the Acts because of the entrenchment of prostitution that they caused. It was felt they encouraged very young girls – the age of consent was still only thirteen – into a life of vice. The Acts also displaced prostitution to places outside the operation of the Acts. Women who did not wish to be regulated in Windsor, where because of the garrison the Acts operated, simply went to the village of Datchet a couple of miles away and offered their services there. However, in areas where the limits were geographically greater, the consequences were even more pernicious. 'The moment a woman has been examined and liberated,' Johnstone observed, 'it is just as well known that she has been discharged as fit for the public service.'[77] There was no element of reclamation – or what Gladstone would call 'rescue work' – in the existing laws at all. They did nothing to improve the moral health of the country, and as such were 'injurious to private liberty and public morality, and repulsive alike to Christianity and civilisation.'[78]

Rather as when Cardwell was trying to abolish purchase, those who purported to speak for the Army in the Commons said that the health and welfare of soldiers would be imperilled if this draconian imposition on the liberties of women were to be lifted. One such, Colonel Claud Alexander, said that all the State was saying to prostitutes was that 'if you insist on carrying on your immoral occupation we must take care that you do not communicate horrible disease to our soldiers and sailors. To do this effectually we consider periodical examination necessary, and if you should be found diseased detention in hospital. During that detention you will not be subjected to undue restraint. Chaplains, medical officers, and matrons will minister to your spiritual and temporal necessities. You will be brought under the influence of humanising agencies, and if disposed to reform you will be placed in situations or restored to your friends.'[79]

He added that the examinations were useful for the women: if serious venereal disease was caught in its early stages their treatment would be straightforward. However, if a woman wished to exempt herself from such treatment, her options were clear. He noted that the petitions calling for repeal came almost entirely from areas where the Acts did not operate. Joseph Henley, the octogenarian MP for Oxfordshire, put another view: 'It was no business of the State to provide clean sin for the people'.[80] However, the House went with the evidence of the commission that prostitution and disease had declined since the Acts were enforced: the bill to repeal was thrown out. It would take another eleven years, and a vigorous campaign led by Josephine Butler to expose the hypocrisy and double standards of men, before these humiliating Acts were finally repealed and, incidentally, the age of consent raised.

VIII

Perhaps the most fundamental and abiding problem that blighted urban life in the 1870s as it had in the 1840s was squalid and disease-ridden housing for the lowest classes. A Conservative MP, Ughtred Kay-Shuttleworth, recalled that in the Manchester speech the Prime

Minister had enunciated the motto 'sanitas sanitatum, omnia sanitas'.[81] Kay-Shuttleworth spoke about what he had seen on his walks around the poorer areas of London: narrow courts covered with human excrement, houses poorly built and open to the elements and to vermin; and all of them drastically overcrowded. Yet there was still much derelict land close to the City of London, and he called for compulsory purchase powers to be made available for it to be brought into use for development. The Artisans' Dwellings Act of 1868 was insufficient in this respect: all it enabled was compulsory repair and demolition, not further building, a provision to that end having been taken out by landowners in the House of Lords. As for raising the money for such purchases, Sir Sydney Waterlow, who seconded Kay-Shuttleworth's motion, said a penny-in-the-pound rate levied for forty years on property in London would pay the interest on a £2 million loan to cover the cost of demolishing all those houses in London unfit for human habitation. This would reduce the mortality rate and disease rate, which would have a beneficial economic effect.[82] Waterlow claimed that for every person who died there were two more unfit for work through disease.

Cross had been lobbied by both the Royal College of Physicians and the Charity Organisation Society to stimulate the replacement of housing for the poor. He praised the Peabody Trust for building mansion blocks on what land it had managed to purchase in London: but agreed Parliament must do more. He promised a measure as soon as possible: and the Artisans' and Labourers' Dwellings Improvement Bill followed within weeks. It introduced the principle of compulsory purchase by local authorities for slum clearance, and allowed them to rent out or sell land for the building of homes for the lower classes. It also ensured the newly built areas were policed by public health officials and sanitary inspectors, to see that they did not lapse back into squalor, and encouraged the establishment of more mains drainage. And, to avoid too much urban concentration, Cross also ensured open spaces were maintained near all large towns, following on from the example of the Metropolitan Commons Act. The Public Health Act 1875 further regulated food (which had, since the Food and Drugs Act 1860, been free from adulteration), street lighting and markets, and the notification of diseases.

He introduced the Artisans Dwellings Bill on 8 February 1875. It kept a promise made in the previous session to a backbencher who had asked for the legislative means to clear slums in overcrowded industrial towns.

It would become the latest, but by far the most radical, of a number of measures in the preceding thirty years to relieve the insanitary and decrepit condition of much of the housing of the lower classes: such as the 1866 Housing of the Working Classes Act, which enabled landowners or businesses to borrow from the Public Works Loans Commissioners to buy land to build houses. The government had no intention of providing housing itself – public housing was still decades away. But it was resolved to make it easier for private developers to do so, not least by allowing local authorities to clear the land on which they could build.

Cross emphasised that he proposed a 'facilitating' measure.[83] He admitted that the government had been stirred to action by a report of the Charity Organisation Society, published the previous year, from which he quoted: 'That the dwellings of the poorer classes in various parts of the metropolis are in such a condition, from age, defects of construction, and misuse, as to be deeply injurious to the physical and moral welfare of the inhabitants, and to the well-being of the community at large.'[84] More telling, the government had had representations from the Royal College of Physicians, who told Disraeli 'that over-crowding, especially in unwholesome and ill-constructed habitations, originates disease, leads to drunkenness and immorality, and is likely to produce discontent among the poorer portion of the population.'

The generosity of private philanthropists – Cross singled out the Peabody Trust, which had by then spent £600,000 on buildings in London – had made a start on addressing the problems of the Metropolis. Together with other philanthropists, Peabody had provided housing for around 30,000 people: but London had grown by 40,000 a year for each of the preceding ten years, and 'much more must be done if we wish to reach the root of the evil to be remedied'.[85] The COS had suggested to the government that it constitute public bodies in urban areas with powers of compulsory purchase: something similar had happened in Glasgow, Edinburgh and Liverpool. Cross had an ideological objection to public housing, which he outlined specifically: 'I take it as a starting-point that it is not the duty of the Government to provide any class of citizens with any of the necessaries of life, and among the necessaries of life we must include that which is one of the chief necessaries—good and habitable dwellings. That is not the duty of the State, because if it did so, it would inevitably tend to make that class depend, not on themselves, but upon what was done for them elsewhere, and it would not be possible to teach a worse lesson than this—that "If you do not take care of yourselves, the State will take care of you".[86] He also argued against large charities, such as the Peabody Trust, offering dwellings at rents below the market rate. If supply increased, rents would in any case fall.

He justified his proposals as being within the State's remit because it came under the heading of sanitary reform, which no one disputed was one of government's functions. He argued that health was wealth: that if Britain wished to continue to grow in prosperity and power, it had to ensure the fitness of its people. That required, fundamentally, better housing. He spoke of the wastes of life and strength among the existing population. The death rate was 22.5 per thousand nationally: yet in London it was 24.5, in Manchester 30, and in Liverpool in the previous ten years 38. Parts of Liverpool were hotbeds of disease, and in one district of Manchester the prevalence of fevers had put the death rate up to 67 per thousand. In another Manchester district there were 49.7 deaths of children under five per 100 total deaths.[87] The national mortality rate for this age group was 18 per hundred.

He had seen for himself the squalid courts of London areas such as St Giles, and was categorical that the only thing to be done with them was to demolish them. 'Family after family goes into a house, and it is certain to catch the fever which has killed off the previous occupants,' Cross said. 'And unless you step in and interfere this will go on for ages.'[88] He had also been to Liverpool, Glasgow and Edinburgh, where local Acts of Parliament had allowed compulsory purchases, to see what mistakes had been made, in order to seek to avoid them in the national legislation he was proposing. In Liverpool expense had been higher than necessary because of complications about compensation. Edinburgh had had more extensive clearances, breaking up many dens of crime, and reducing the number of brothels from 204 to twenty in the three years from 1870 to 1873.

The government proposed to confine legislation to London and other large towns. Powers would be vested in the Metropolitan Board of Works in London and in corporations elsewhere. No longer would local authorities need a private bill, and the agreement of their ratepayers, to take over slum properties, clear them and improve them. An arbitrator would be appointed locally to agree the price of the land to be compulsorily purchased. The council would also be given the power to build houses, to ensure that no cleared land remained empty in what Cross considered the unlikely event of no commercial builder being interested in developing an empty site. For that reason, there was also provision for the Public Works Commissioner to lend money to the councils at a certain rate of interest.

Cross said that the measures, if enacted, would have no immediate effect. But he proclaimed:

> The evil we desire to root out has been the work of generations; and though I believe the ratepayers will be more than fully recouped in the long run, yet for a time, at least, the measure must be worked at some expense. Nevertheless, considering the state of the people at the present time, considering how little has been done for them, and considering also the absolute necessity of raising this almost degraded class, who have been brought up in sickness, and who will perpetuate disease, if we do not afford them the means of improving their conditions, I ask you on those dens of wretchedness and misery to cast one ray of hope and happiness; I ask you on those haunts of sickness and of death to breathe, at all events, one breath of health and life; and on those courts and alleys where all is dark with a darkness which not only may be, but is felt—a darkness of mind, body, and soul—I ask you to assist in carrying out one of God's best and earliest laws—"Let there be light".[89]

The Opposition sought to have the provisions extended to towns of only 10,000 inhabitants instead of the proposed limit of 25,000. Cross objected, saying smaller towns tended to have spare land nearer to the centre where new dwellings could be built that was nearer to the centre than was the case in larger ones: and therefore they did not need the same compulsory purchase powers as larger ones to remain properly sanitary. Cross had already made a concession, lowering the limit from 50,000: he was reluctant to extend powers such as compulsory purchase any further, in case the extreme burden it would put on ratepayers made what should be a great reforming measure unpopular. Also, Disraeli had been determined not to make the legislation compulsory in case it was perceived as an attack on landlords, who were predominantly supporters of his party.

As Cross had said, the provisions took time to make a difference. The Artisans' Dwellings Act was designed to begin slum clearance: but Blake observed that by 1881 only ten of the eighty-seven English and Welsh towns to which it applied had begun to implement its provisions. The quality of housing in England was improved by the spread of prosperity, thanks to England's commercial and mercantile successes, which led to the creation of middle-class and lower-middle-class suburbs and a mass of speculative building from 1870 until the Great War. Cross's judgement was that the Act had made a start, but in the nation's capital rather than in the squalid northern industrial towns. 'All the really large old rookeries in London', he wrote in 1903, 'were swept away under this Act.'[90] It was also, however, the measure that enabled Joe Chamberlain to clean up the slums of Birmingham. At a cost of roughly £1.5 million, the council bought nearly 50 acres of slum housing, and the scheme was driven through largely because of the confidence Chamberlain inspired as a municipal leader. His biographer, J. L. Garvin, wrote: 'From that day the centre of Birmingham began to be Haussmannised. Where the jumble of slums had stood Corporation Street rose into being. Twenty-two yards wide, it was; with tall shops, offices and institutions on both sides, creating a new architectural vista.'[91] Behind the street on both sides were built streets of new, improved housing, and the death rate in the area tumbled year upon year. In one street, Bailey Street, there had been 97 deaths per thousand of population in 1873–85. By 1879–81 it was 25.6. 'The children did not perish nor become withered and stunted, as they used. Good lighting, pure water, fresher air, cleansed streets, more space within and without, sanitary measures of strict vigilance – all these benefits were brought into the reconstructed quarter.'

IX

When in June 1876 the Queen learned, through her private secretary, of Disraeli's mounting infirmity – he was seventy-two – she offered him an earldom. 'She knows how valuable he is to herself and the country,' she wrote, making the offer. 'The Queen throws this out, as she feels the immense importance he is to the Throne and country and how – more than ever now – she wishes and hopes his Govt may be long maintained.'[92] The intensity of her feeling was not remotely constitutional, but cannot be explained by her fearing a return of Gladstone, who was no longer leading the Opposition.

Disraeli's instinct was to retire altogether. He was still a martyr to gout, increasingly afflicted by bronchitis, and prone to exhaustion. He claimed not to be interested in a peerage, having no heir. However, the Queen persuaded him to stay as her minister, but in the Lords. He consulted the Duke of Richmond, who led in the Lords (and would be displaced by Disraeli's going there). Richmond told him what he wanted to hear, that it would be 'fatal' to the party for him to retire, and that going to the Lords was the obvious solution. Derby and Salisbury supported him too.[93] The Queen had earlier made his late wife the Viscountess Beaconsfield in her own right; when Disraeli decided to go upstairs he chose the title of Earl of Beaconsfield, which he insisted on being pronounced BEAconsfield, not BECConsfield.

Once it was clear to her that he would continue, the Queen was relieved, telling her daughter the Crown Princess of Prussia that 'his retirement would be a very serious calamity'.[94] He laid it on with an even larger trowel than usual: 'They', he said, talking of his peerages (he had also been created Viscount Hughenden), 'would not be mean distinctions, even for the most exalted, but what enhances them to him beyond all price, is that your Majesty has condescended to express your Majesty's personal gratification in rewarding a servant who, whatever his deficiencies, is, he hopes, from his very heart, devoted to your Majesty.'[95]

Disraeli had prided himself on passing 'permissive legislation'. The Artisans' Dwellings Act was a prime example: legislation that kept the State at one remove, by making it possible for individuals, institutions or local authorities to make improvements instead. Disraeli's line was that such an approach was more appropriate to the democratic mood of the times. In 1875, on a bill to reform agricultural tenancies, he said: 'It may be all very well for hon and right hon Gentlemen to treat with affected contempt the notion that our legislation should be founded on permission, but permissive legislation is the characteristic of a free people. It is easy to adopt compulsory legislation when you have to deal with those who only exist to obey; but in a free country, and especially in a country like England, you must trust to persuasion and example as the two great elements, if you wish to effect any considerable change in the manners and customs of the people.'[96] By the time Beaconsfield's government fell, Cross had successfully 'decontaminated' the Tory brand, and had made it clear to the aristocrats who still ran the party that only by constant attention to the conditions of the poor would they hope to avoid civil unrest. Nonetheless, and for all these great advances, Beaconsfield would find he could not win.

His move to the Lords coincided with a new emphasis in British politics on foreign affairs. The Eastern Question, which would culminate in the Congress of Berlin in 1878, dominated the government's considerations: and Gladstone's condemnation of Britain's foreign policy after the Bulgarian atrocities – the persecution of Christians by the Muslim Ottoman Empire – would inspire not only his Midlothian Campaign before the 1880 election, but also make inevitable his restoration to the leadership of his party and to the position of the Queen's first minister. After forty years of being a country forced by circumstances to manage the massive and urgent social questions that sprang from industrialisation, the spread of wealth, a population explosion and a revolution in communications, Britain now once more looked abroad. Despite a dozen years of governments of both parties delivering profound social reform, the 1880 election would, ironically, be decided on a question of foreign policy.

Gladstone objected that it was immoral for the British government to lend economic support to the Turks, to help maintain the Ottoman Empire as a force against the Russians after the Crimean War. At a time when it was still unusual for senior politicians to make big speeches outside Parliament – though Palmerston had done it, and Disraeli had had conspicuous one-offs such as the Manchester and Crystal Palace speeches – Gladstone caused a sensation by doing so: a sensation intensified by the assault on government policy, the language in which it was couched, and in the way that it repudiated the notion that Gladstone had retired. He had assiduously courted lobby journalists when Chancellor and Prime Minister. He was adept at what we would now call media management. He also saw that by making a sensational speech he would command enormous press coverage. One consequence of the Midlothian campaign was that it changed the nature of the conduct of British politics, with other leading politicians increasingly seeking to secure exposure by the same means. The campaign was an inevitable consequence itself of the extension of the franchise in 1867, and it set the template for the conduct of British politics during the succeeding century.

Over the next three-and-a-half years he became ferocious, and indeed almost messianic, on the immorality of Beaconsfield's foreign policy.

Beaconsfield had never liked Gladstone: now, the attacks on his foreign policy incensed him. Those so high-minded as to believe that politics, particularly foreign affairs, had a moral dimension had, in Beaconsfield's view, no place in public life. He wrote to Derby, his Foreign Secretary, in October 1876 describing Gladstone as an 'unprincipled maniac' who was an 'extraordinary mixture of envy, vindictiveness, hypocrisy and superstition'.[97] A Conservative just held Beaconsfield's former seat of Buckinghamshire at the by-election caused by his elevation; it was clear Gladstone's passionate attacks were already having their effect, and the theme would become louder and clearer for several years.

Other foreign issues besides the Eastern Question dominated the last two-thirds of the administration. There was the possibility of war with Russia, a war in Afghanistan, unrest in Egypt and the Zulu War in southern Africa. However, it was unrest in Ireland, and obstruction in the Commons by Irish Home Rulers, that finally caused an exhausted Beaconsfield to ask the Queen to dissolve Parliament in March 1880. Gladstone had taken his attack on foreign policy around his constituency of Midlothian in Scotland; but as the election neared he spoke all over the country. Thousands attended his rallies; the press reported him widely. Among the messages of support that poured in were some from Florence Nightingale. 'All through this Eastern controversy, the most painful of my life', he wrote to her in January 1879, 'it has been a consolation to learn that I was in sympathy with you.'[98]

The Tories were no match for him. The election was fought on the ground of Gladstone's choosing. Once it was called he broadened his attack, mainly through speeches in his constituency: domestic policy had been neglected, international instability had harmed business, the public finances had gone into deficit. Not just foreign policy, but Beaconsfield's whole conduct of government, became a moral question. This idealism, this infusion of the business of the State by fundamental Christian teaching, was what Dr Arnold had dreamed of. In the 1880 election campaign, the doctrine, for once and once only, held back the tide of secularism, and prevailed. It also, incidentally, established Gladstonism as the preponderant strain in Liberal politics, and ensured his second premiership.

Gladstone's faith, constant since his youth, continued to shape his public life in this increasingly secular society. When he was returned in Midlothian on 5 April he wrote in his diary: 'Wonderful, & nothing less, has been the disposing guiding hand of God in all this matter.'[99] The next day, going back to Hawarden, he wrote: 'travelled all night & had time to ruminate on the great hand of God so evidently displayed.' On 8 April he heard that Samuel Plimsoll, the Liberal MP, and others were planning a rally in London, effectively to demand he be made Prime Minister. 'The triumph grows & grows,' he recorded. 'To God be the praise.'[100] Plimsoll – 'an original and childlike man' – came to see Gladstone the next day, and Gladstone talked him out of the idea of a rally.[101] On 10 April Gladstone had word that Hartington and Granville wanted to see him. 'God will provide,' he observed. Gladstone's whole life had, to an extent, been a religious experience: and this moment appeared to be its climax, a self-justification he portrayed to himself as divine.

Three days later Gladstone made it clear to Lord Wolverton – who had brought the message from the Whig grandees – that there was 'only one form and ground of application' to him that could work, namely that he should become Prime Minister.[102] He recognised he was the dominant figure in his party's politics, and saw no reason to pretend otherwise: and so much of his writing at this time advances his belief that he was in God's hands, doing God's will, on a divine mission to reinforce the moral foundations, and moral purpose, of the nation. As the editor of his diaries, H. C. G. Matthew, has pointed out, this was the era of *The Way We Live Now*, Trollope's novel of 1875 that detailed the corruption apparently inherent in capitalism. Matthew interpreted Gladstone as lamenting 'the failures of moral education to match the progress of capitalism'.[103] The failure of his opponents, including the Queen, to understand this was not all that made them think he was mad, and a demagogue: but for Gladstone it had become the only tone in which he could conduct politics.

The general election was a disaster for Beaconsfield and his party. The Liberals won 352 of the 652 seats in the Commons; the Conservatives lost almost a third of their MPs, returning only 237, one of the worst results in their history. The party machine that had worked so well in 1874 had operated only superficially in 1880. It was Beaconsfield's political death knell: the literal one followed a year later, when he died on 19 April 1881, in his seventy-seventh year. Hartington had led his party since January 1875 and in the election campaign: but no one, inside or outside the party, was in any doubt that it was Gladstone who had given the moral lead. It was he, and not Hartington, who had the authority to lead the country.

The Midlothian campaign had signalled Gladstone's resurrection, and in it he showed himself, finally, not only as the towering politician of the age, but the towering moral force too. His denunciations of the failures of the Conservative government seemed to overwhelm the country with their sense of conviction. Beaconsfield, old, in poor health and demoralised, could fool the public no longer. That was not, of course, how he saw it. Cross described him as being 'mortified' and added that 'he felt that the country had given him a rebuke which he had not deserved'. From the size of the rebuke, the country plainly did not agree.[104]

All through April 1880 there was speculation about what would happen if the Liberals won. Beaconsfield briefed Lord Barrington, a Conservative, that 'the Queen would certainly send for Granville, and he and Hartington would certainly form a Government whether Gladstone liked it or not.'[105] Beaconsfield assumed Gladstone would refuse to serve under Granville, Foreign Secretary from 1868 to 1874, but that he would depose him after a year or so. Gladstone he denounced as having acted like 'an irresponsible demagogue'. Whether or not Beaconsfield had shared these feelings with the Queen she was said to be 'in despair'. She had been 'disgusted' by the 'crude appeal' of the Midlothian campaign, and had not imagined her people would feel any differently.[106] Now, as she told Beaconsfield, 'nothing more than trouble and trial await me. I consider it a great public misfortune.'

In her petulance the Queen found it easy to dismiss facts. She wrote to Beaconsfield on 4 April, when it was already obvious his party was being trounced, to say that she felt sure the Liberals would have 'the very greatest difficulty' forming a government.[107] If she did have to part with her beloved Prime Minister it would, she said with what she hoped was certainty, be 'for a very short time'. Five days later, as the Liberal majority rose, she told him that 'of course I shall not take any notice of . . . Mr Gladstone'.[108] That day she also told Sir Michael Hicks-Beach, the Secretary of State for the Colonies, that she preferred Hartington to Granville, even though the latter was older and more experienced, because Granville 'would be too pliable to Radical influence'.[109] Hicks-Beach warned her that that would create a dangerous position for Gladstone – dangerous to the Queen, that is. He suggested that, with

Hartington as Prime Minister, Gladstone would have power without responsibility.

The Queen felt Gladstone would take nothing but the top job, and she was right: but she also felt from some remarks in his recent speeches that he did not even want that, which was a delusion. Whatever happened, she would not send for Gladstone in the first instance. Nor did she need to; he had resigned the leadership in 1875, had passed the baton to Granville, whom he regarded as his successor, and Liberal MPs had chosen Hartington to lead them in the Commons. Her choice, therefore, was between the leaders of the two houses. Yet, as everyone knew – though she would be the last to admit it – the moral leader of the Liberal party was Gladstone. John Bright went to see him on 16 April, and they spent the day discussing the situation: Bright told his diary that evening that Gladstone would not serve except as Prime Minister.

The Queen was not constitutionally obliged to seek Beaconsfield's advice: but such was her degree of trust in him that, inevitably, she did. They met on 18 April. In a note of their meeting, the Queen wrote that Beaconsfield advised her to send for Hartington. 'He was in his heart a conservative, a gentleman, and very straightforward in his conduct.'[110] Granville, by comparison, was 'less disinterested'; Gladstone 'was only clung to by the Radicals'. Beaconsfield told her that while some 'dreadful people' like Bradlaugh had been elected, many Liberals were old-fashioned Whigs; and were a Whig asked to lead the party, he would have his own people around him. The Queen confirmed to her Prime Minister that on no account would she send for Gladstone: it was 'impossible'.[111] To her he was a cause of mischief who had done all he could to weaken her government in a time of trial. She felt sure, she consoled herself, that in any case he would not wish it. 'This was no ordinary change of government,' she continued. It 'had been brought about by the most unjust and shameful persecution of [i.e. by] Mr Gladstone'. Beaconsfield's advice was prejudiced and factually wrong: Hartington had far fewer supporters in the party than Gladstone.

Gladstone returned to London on 19 April, still in God's hands: 'May He who has of late so wonderfully guided, guide me still in the critical days about to come,' he wrote in his diary.[112] He was in no doubt why the constitutional process had slowed down. 'This blank day is, I think,' he wrote on 20 April, 'probably due to the Queen's hesitation or reluctance, which the Ministers have to find means of covering.' He saw Hartington, Granville and Wolverton for talks, as all the Liberal leadership awaited word from Windsor.

The Queen sent for Hartington on 22 April. After living according to the fantasies of her retiring Prime Minister for the best part of three weeks, she was jolted into reality by her conversation with the Liberal leader. She appeared 'embarrassed' and 'pressed upon him strongly his duty to assist her as a responsible leader of the party now in a large majority.'[113] She emphasised to Hartington that what especially commended him was his 'moderation', a phrase Gladstone noted had often been used about him in recent days in the Daily Telegraph, which had since 1877 become the house journal of Beaconsfieldism. He told her bluntly that no Liberal government could be formed unless Gladstone were a member of it, and the only position he would accept was that of her first minister. He advised her to send for him. The Queen was horrified, and charged Hartington to ask Gladstone directly whether he would serve under him or Granville. Hartington met Gladstone at 7.00 that evening back in London, and Gladstone gave him the expected answer. He would not serve, but would promise not to interfere if they went ahead without him

The following day both Hartington and Granville went to Windsor at lunchtime and told the Queen she must send for Gladstone. Her horror deepened, for she realised she had no choice. She asked Beaconsfield, privately, what she should do. He advised her, outrageously, to send for Gladstone and ask him whether he could form a government, but to make it clear in the audience that she was doing so 'in the spirit of the constitution', not because she had any personal desire to do so.[114] She sent for Gladstone on St George's Day 1880, her message to him conveyed by Granville in the presence of Hartington.

He presented himself at Windsor at 6.30 p.m., having spent the afternoon writing a memorandum on his meeting with Hartington the previous day. The Queen kept him waiting for twenty minutes. She received him 'with perfect courtesy, from which she never deviates.'[115] She justified not having sent for him first, and he agreed with her decision. He accepted her commission. The Queen asked whether he would definitely form a government, or whether he would attempt to do so. He undertook to do the former. She could not resist, or perhaps it was that she could not help, ticking him off. As Gladstone recalled the meeting: 'She said I must be frank with you Mr Gladstone and must fairly say that there have been some expressions, I think she said some little things, which had caused her concern or pain.'

He assured her he was sensible of his responsibility, was grateful for her frankness, and admitted having 'used a mode of speech and language different in some degree from what I should have employed had I been the leader of a party or a candidate for office.' No doubt what cheered her most was Gladstone's assertion that, because of his advanced years – he was seventy – 'I could only look to the short term of active exertion and a personal retirement comparatively early.' The Queen warned him 'with some good-natured archness' that he would have to bear the consequences of his rhetorical excesses. 'All things considered I was much pleased. I ended by kissing HM's hand.'

'He said he accepts all facts,' the Queen told Beaconsfield in a telegram, 'and that bitterness of feeling is past.'[116] Later that day, in a letter, she wailed that 'her trial is great . . . Mr Gladstone looks very ill, very old and haggard and his voice feeble.' With utter impropriety, she maintained a private correspondence with Beaconsfield until his death, confiding in him her feelings about Gladstone, and never ceasing her lamentations that her adored Dizzy was not still her first minister. Hartington, by his refusal to take office, might have caused the Queen distress, but he had forced her to recognise the consequences of democracy. Gladstone's second premiership was, ironically, a dividend of the very 1867 Reform Act he had opposed.

Thus it was that the highest mind of all returned to lead British political life, and to steer the State. In his second ministry, in times radically different from his first, Gladstone would once more bring to bear all the Arnoldian virtues that informed his humanity as a statesman. If *Culture and Anarchy* had been a blueprint for the humane and wise governance and civilisation of a people, Gladstone was the finest imaginable man to implement it. He retained the highest opinion of Arnold: to Arnold's surprise, he had him awarded a civil list pension of £250 a year in 1883, which allowed him to retire in 1886. The pension was not a reward for his services as an inspector: it was offered 'in public recognition of service to the poetry and literature of England'.[117] It may have been prompted by a pamphlet Arnold sent Gladstone in April 1882 about the need to extend copyright for authors' works after their deaths: Arnold was not yet sixty, but had been told he had the same heart defect that had killed his father. His financial position was precarious: yet he had many works in print and a large reading public, and wished his family to benefit from his work after his death, if it came early.[118] The pension would help stave off some of these worries. Gladstone saw that, in the interests of sweetness and light, patronage of literary men and women was as important as any social measures that he might champion.

He had tried to persuade Tennyson to take a baronetcy in March 1873: but Tennyson had written back and said 'not only on account of my feeling for yourself, but also for the sake of that memory which we share, I speak frankly to you, when I say, that I had rather we should remain plain Mr and Mrs, and that, if it were possible, the title should first be assumed by our son at any age it may be thought right to fix upon.'[119] He added: 'But like enough this is against all precedent and could not be managed; and on no account would I have suggested it were there the least chance of the Queen's construing it into a slight of the proffered honour.' He enclosed a second letter accepting the honour, which he instructed Gladstone to act upon if the Queen would be offended otherwise. Gladstone was prepared to negotiate this unprecedented procedure; but then Tennyson wrote to him a fortnight later to say that 'Hallam . . . would not like to wear the honour during my lifetime.'[120]

He offered Harriet Martineau a pension, which she declined. 'The work of my busy years has supplied the needs and desires of a quiet old age. On the former occasions of my declining a pension I was poor . . . now, I have a competence, and there would be no excuse for my touching the public money.'[121] But Gladstone also brought the trained critic's keen appreciation of life to his considerations, as Matthew Arnold would have wanted. After Carlyle died, early in 1881, Gladstone wrote: 'If Carlyle was vain it was not with a vulgar vanity. If he was selfish, if intolerant, or whatever faults they were always idiosyncratic: so powerful an individuality overspread them all. It is this individuality which attracts, even more than genius.'[122] He read Froude's *Life* on publication and annotated it: this set him further thinking about the Sage and, while staying with Lord Rosebery at Durdans, he scribbled down that 'he wanted reverence, resignation, tolerance, patience; he was reckless.'[123]

The cultural world, however, was changing too, as everything else was. A letter of July 1881 – a year into the second ministry – asks: 'Will you do me the honour of accepting my first volume of poems – as a very small token of my deep admiration and loyalty to one who has always loved what is noble and beautiful and true in life and art, and is the mirror of the Greek ideal of a statesman.'[124] It is signed 'Your most obedient servant, Oscar Wilde.'

EPILOGUE

Writing in 1948, Basil Willey, the King Edward VII Professor of English Literature at Cambridge, reflected that 'in our own unpleasant century we are mostly displaced persons, and many feel tempted to take flight into the nineteenth as into a promised land, and settle there like illegal immigrants for the rest of their lives. In that distant mountain country, all that we now lack seems present in abundance: not only peace, prosperity, plenty and freedom, but faith, purpose and buoyancy.' Reflecting during a period of austerity, with two catastrophic world wars in his experience, Willey can be forgiven this burst of nostalgia. There is no doubt he and many others felt this: that the generation that had greedily devoured Strachey and others who sought to mock and undermine the Victorians in the heady period after the Great War now began to realise that they had perhaps been unfair to their predecessors.

Yet there is a rose tint to Willey's spectacles. As we have seen, there may have been international peace (though one should not forget the Crimea, and imperial skirmishes in Africa and on the Indian sub-continent, and the tribulations of Ireland), but prosperity came in interludes between the hungry forties and the great depression of the mid to late seventies. Plenty, as such, was an experience not shared by all; and faith was constantly under assault: for the educated classes, from the Oxford Movement onwards; and for the rest, as a consequence of the upheaval brought by industrialisation.

Purpose, though, the Victorians had in abundance, and it was the key to their achievements. The years between the late 1830s and the early 1880s did not merely include radical change in the abstract; they included radical change of a physical nature. What underpins the revolutionary nature of life in the mid-nineteenth century was the determination by people of intelligence and will not to accept the status quo, and to move society in time with technology. Many more men obtained the vote; women began to obtain something approaching their rights; children were more widely educated and less widely exploited; the tone of human relations had changed. These abstract changes reflected – and were in some measure accelerated by – visible ones. Britain had shrunk because of the railway and the telegraph. Its prosperity, and the political consciousness of its working class, had been supercharged by continued industrialisation. Linear miles of sewers and drains and square miles of sanitary, well ventilated housing improved the health and welfare of the people. A flourishing press, and growing literacy, not only informed the masses about the decisions their rulers took for them, but assisted their participation in that process.

A nation with riches built institutions that reflected its new status: not merely practical edifices such as law courts, government offices, railway stations, schools and colleges, but institutions that suggested the importance of an intellectual and spiritual dimension to the lives of millions: museums, galleries, libraries and churches. Many were in the medieval style fashionable at the time; yet this was an era that cast off many of the surviving relics of the pre-democratic society. By the close of the period the monarch had been forced to take as her First Minister the man the electorate sent her, and not the man she would have liked to choose. Her subjects became more equal before the law, as the laws of contract and conspiracy were reformed. The House of Lords would not until 1911 end its practice of over-ruling the elected House, but it was made increasingly aware of the provocation issued when it did so, and it did so more rarely.

Perhaps most important, the tight hold the Established Church had over many state and private institutions was severely weakened. Schools were no longer its near-monopoly. It lost what had, effectively, been the right to admit to the ancient universities. With the expansion of prosperity it saw philanthropy, albeit often conducted in the name of Christ and His example, taken more into private hands and out of its own. The advance of science placed divines on the defensive. Some medieval practice was unthinkable by the 1880s: no longer would a man suffer having his book burned as a public spectacle for heresy, and no longer would a man have to throw in his livelihood as a university teacher because of his inability to confirm with the rites of the Church of England.

The Britain of 1838 bore only a superficial resemblance to that of 1880. The foundations of the modern nation had been laid. Privilege had not been expelled, but meritocracy was steadily supplanting it. The craving for wealth and status that a patriotic, self-confident and even jingoistic people had by the 1880s was not one that could be satisfied by the existing ruling class, but required a different army of the talented, with different motivations. The framework of a competitive, self-reliant society had been put in place. It was now up to individuals to advance it.

The great politicians of the period had all been propelled towards making improvements for those whom they led: Peel, Gladstone, Cardwell, Disraeli, Cross. Such people as Mill, Arnold, Dickens, Eliot, Ruskin and, grumbling throughout the period like a volcano about to erupt, Carlyle had pointed the way for the statesmen. Most important, the philosophers, propagandists and statesmen exhorted and encouraged numerous individuals who translated idealism into reality: Burdett-Coutts, Peabody, Nightingale, Octavia Hill, Emily Davies, Anne Clough, Holloway, Booth, Barnardo and, another constant presence, Shaftesbury. And the towering example of the age was the man who was part statesman, part philosopher, part man of action: Prince Albert.

The greatness of the age was the product of a conjunction of technological revolution, wealth, energy and high minds. It could have resulted in the construction of the greatest temple of Mammon the world has ever seen, a place for tribute to be paid to the gods of utilitarianism alone. That it became more than that was thanks to the mission of benevolence – the pursuit of perfection – that people as diverse as Gladstone, Arnold, Shaftesbury, Mill, Eliot and Dickens took out into the world at this moment when the tectonic plates of society were shifting as never before. If perfection remained elusive, the greater civilisation that they helped foster did not. The pursuit of perfection, a minority activity in 1838, had become almost an obligation by 1880.

BIBLIOGRAPHY

Manuscript Sources

In the footnotes, the principal archives are identified as follows:

BC: Samuel Butler Collection, St John's College, Cambridge.
BC RF: Bedford College Archive, Royal Holloway College, Egham.
BL: British Library, London.
RA: Royal Archives, Windsor.
RAH: Royal Albert Hall Archive, London.
RC: 1851 Commission Archive, Imperial College, London.
RHC: Royal Holloway College Archive, Egham.
UL: Cambridge University Library.

Some online references are included, notably to the Darwin Project, run by Cambridge University, which is putting online the correspondence of Charles Darwin; the Morgan Museum and Library Collection in New York; and the Barnardo's website, which contains much historical information about Thomas Barnardo. The British Library catalogue is fully searchable online and will identify the particular collections in which papers of the subjects listed below can be traced:

Prince Albert: Royal Archives, Windsor; Imperial College (1851 Commission Archive).
Thomas Barnardo: www.barnardos.org.uk/.
William Booth: British Library.
John Bright: British Library.
Baroness Burdett-Coutts: British Library.
Samuel Butler: British Library; Cambridge University Library; St John's College, Cambridge.
Edward Cardwell: British Library.

Thomas Carlyle: National Library of Scotland, Edinburgh.

Joseph Chamberlain: British Library.

4th Earl of Clarendon: British Library.

Richard Cobden: British Library.

Henry Cole: Imperial College (1851 Commission Archive); Royal Albert Hall Archive.

Richard Cross: British Library.

Charles Darwin: www.darwinproject.ac.uk.

Charles Dickens: British Library; Morgan Museum and Library, New York (online collection, www.themorgan.org/collections/works/dickens/).

George Eliot: British Library.

W. E. Forster: British Library.

James Anthony Froude: National Library of Scotland, Edinburgh.

W. E. Gladstone: British Library.

Sir George Grove: Shulbrede Priory.

Octavia Hill: British Library.

Thomas Holloway: Royal Holloway.

Charles Kingsley: British Library.

Sir A. H. Layard: British Library.

F. D. Maurice: Cambridge University Library; British Library.

Henry Mayhew: British Library.

John Stuart Mill: British Library.

John Henry Newman: British Library.

Florence Nightingale: British Library.

Caroline Norton: British Library; Pierpoint Morgan Library, New York.

Parkes Papers: Cambridge University Library.

Sir C. H. H. Parry: Shulbrede Priory.

Sir Robert Peel: British Library.

Elizabeth Jesser Reid: Royal Holloway.

Sir George Gilbert Scott: British Library.

Henry Sidgwick: Cambridge University Library.

Sir James Fitzjames Stephen: Cambridge University Library, Parkes Papers.

G. E. Street: British Library.

Charles Trevelyan: British Library.

George Otto Trevelyan: British Library.

Printed Sources
Books

The books are listed under the author's abbreviations for them as used in the notes to the text. Some are titles, but most are under the name of the books' authors.

A&C: *The Life and Letters of Benjamin Jowett, MA,* by Evelyn Abbott and Lewis Campbell (John Murray, 2 Vols, 2nd Edition, 1897).

Arnold, C&A: *Culture and Anarchy: An Essay in Social and Political Criticism,* by Matthew Arnold, edited by J. Dover Wilson (CUP, 1950).

Arnold, Essays 1: *Essays in Criticism,* by Matthew Arnold (Macmillan, 1886).

Arnold, Essays 2: *Essays in Criticism, Second Series,* by Matthew Arnold (Macmillan, 1921).

Arnold, Eton: *A French Eton or Middle-Class Education and the State,* by Matthew Arnold (Macmillan, 1892).

Arnold, Letters: *The Letters of Matthew Arnold,* edited by Cecil Y. Lang (University of Virginia Press, 6 Vols, 1996–2001).

Arnold, MW: *The Miscellaneous Works of Thomas Arnold, DD, Collected and Republished* (B. Fellowes, 1845).

Arnold, Poems: *New Poems,* by Matthew Arnold (Macmillan, 1867).

Arnold, Reports: *Reports on Elementary Schools 1852–1882,* by Matthew Arnold, edited by Rt Hon. Sir Francis Sandford (Macmillan, 1889).

Arnold, Sermons: *Sermons,* by Thomas Arnold (Longmans, Green, 6 Vols, 1878).

Bagehot: *The English Constitution,* by Walter Bagehot (Oxford's World's Classics, 1928).

Balgarnie: *Sir Titus Salt, Baronet: His Life and its Lessons,* by Rev. R. Balgarnie (Hodder & Stoughton, 1877).

Bamford: *Thomas Arnold on Education,* edited by T. W. Bamford (CUP, 1970).

Bayley: *The Albert Memorial: the monument in its social and architectural context,* by Stephen Bayley (Scolar Press, 1981).

B&B: *The Great Exhibitor: The Life and Work of Henry Cole,* by Elizabeth Bonython and Anthony Burton (V&A Publications, 2003).

Beer: *Darwin's Plots: Evolutionary Narrative in Darwin, George Eliot and Nineteenth-Century Fiction,* by Gillian Beer (Routledge & Kegan Paul, 1983).

Best: *Mid-Victorian Britain, 1851–75,* by Geoffrey Best (Fontana, 1979).

Bibby, Education: *T. H. Huxley on Education: A Selection from his Writings,* by Cyril Bibby (CUP, 1971).

Bibby, Scientist: *T. H. Huxley: Scientist, Humanist and Educator,* by Cyril Bibby (Watts, 1959).

Biswas: *Arthur Hugh Clough: Towards a Reconsideration,* by R. K. Biswas (OUP, 1972).

Blake: *Disraeli*, by Robert Blake (Eyre & Spottiswoode, 1966).

Bloxam: *The Principles of Gothic Ecclesiastical Architecture*, by Matthew Holbeche Bloxam (W. Kent & Co, 10th Edition, 1859).

Booth: *In Darkest England and the Way Out*, by General Booth (The Salvation Army, 1890).

Bostridge: *Florence Nightingale: The Woman and Her Legend* by Mark Bostridge (Penguin, 2007).

Bradley: *St Pancras Station*, by Simon Bradley (Profile Books, 2007).

Briggs, *Cities*: *Victorian Cities*, by Asa Briggs (Odhams, 1963).

Briggs, *People*: *Victorian People*, by Asa Briggs (Odhams, 1954).

Briggs, *Things*: *Victorian Things*, by Asa Briggs (Batsford, 1988).

Bright: *The Diaries of John Bright*, with a foreword by Philip Bright (Cassell, 1930).

Brown: *Palmerston, a Biography*, by David Brown (Yale, 2010).

Brownlee: *The Law Courts: The Architecture of George Edmund Street*, by David B. Brownlee (Architectural History Foundation, 1984).

Burn: *The Age of Equipoise*, by W. L. Burn (George Allen & Unwin, 1964).

Butler, *Flesh*: *The Way of All Flesh*, by Samuel Butler (Oxford World's Classics, 1936).

Butler, *Haven*: *The Fair Haven*, by Samuel Butler (Watts & Co., 1938).

Butler, *Note-Books*: *The Note-Books of Samuel Butler*, edited by Henry Festing Jones (Fifield, 1912).

Butler, *Savage Letters*: *Letters between Samuel Butler and Miss E. M. A. Savage 1871–1885* (Jonathan Cape, 1935).

Carlyle, *Letters*: *The Collected Letters of Thomas and Jane Welsh Carlyle* (Duke University Press, Duke-Edinburgh Edition, 39 Vols, 1970–2011).

Carlyle, *Reminiscences*: *Reminiscences*, by Thomas Carlyle, edited by C. E. Norton (Dent, 1932).

Carlyle, *Works*: *The Works of Thomas Carlyle* (Chapman & Hall, Centenary Edition, 30 Vols, 1897–1902).

Cate: *The Correspondence of Thomas Carlyle and John Ruskin*, edited by George Allan Cate (Stanford University Press, 1982).

Cecil: *The Life of Robert Marquis of Salisbury*, by Lady Gwendolen Cecil (Hodder & Stoughton, 2 Vols, 1921).

Chadwick: *The Secularization of the European Mind in the Nineteenth Century*, by Owen Chadwick (CUP, 1975).

Chedzoy: *A Scandalous Woman: The Story of Caroline Norton*, by Alan Chedzoy (Allison & Busby, 1992).

Clapham: *An Economic History of Modern Britain: Free Trade and Steel, 1850–1886*, by J. H. Clapham (CUP, 1932).

Clarendon: *Report of Her Majesty's commissioners appointed to inquire into the Revenues and Management of certain Colleges and Schools, with the Studies pursued and Instruction given therein; with an Appendix and Evidence* (HMSO, 4 Vols, 1864).

Clark: *The Royal Albert Hall,* by Ronald W. Clark (Hamish Hamilton, 1958).

Clough, Letters: *Correspondence of Arthur Hugh Clough,* edited by F. Mulhauser (OUP, 2 Vols, 1957).

Clough, Poems: *Poems,* by Arthur Hugh Clough (Macmillan, 1862).

Clough, Remains: *Prose Remains,* by Arthur Hugh Clough (Macmillan, 1888).

Cobbett: *Rural Rides,* by William Cobbett (Dent, 2 Vols, 1912).

Cockshut: *Truth to Life: the Art of Biography in the Nineteenth Century,* by A. O. J. Cockshut (Collins, 1974).

Collini: *Arnold,* by Stephan Collini (OUP, 1988).

Cook: *The Life of John Ruskin,* by E. T. Cook (George Allen, 2 Vols, 1911).

Cowling, 1867: *1867: Disraeli, Gladstone and Revolution, the Passing of the Second Reform Bill,* by Maurice Cowling (CUP, 1967).

Cross: *A Political History,* by Richard Cross (privately printed, 1903).

Curl: *Victorian Architecture: Its Practical Aspects,* by James Stevens Curl (David & Charles, 1873).

Daiches: *Some Late Victorian Attitudes,* by David Daiches (Andre Deutsch, 1969).

Darley: *Octavia Hill: A Life,* by Gillian Darley (Constable, 1990).

Darwin, LL: *The Life and Letters of Charles Darwin, including an Autobiographical Chapter,* edited by Francis Darwin (John Murray, 1887).

Darwin, OS: *On the Origin of Species,* by Charles Darwin (Wordsworth Classics of World Literature, 1998).

Davenport-Hines: *Gothic: Four Hundred Years of Excess, Horror, Evil and Ruin,* by Richard Davenport-Hines (Fourth Estate, 1998).

Davis: *The Great Exhibition,* by John R. Davis (Sutton Publishing, 1999).

Dickens, ED: *The Mystery of Edwin Drood,* by Charles Dickens (Popular Edition of the Complete Works, Chapman & Hall, 1907).

Dickens, HT: *Hard Times,* by Charles Dickens (Popular Edition of the Complete Works, Chapman & Hall, 1907).

Dickens, Letters: *The Letters of Charles Dickens* (Oxford University Press, 12 Vols, 1965–2002).

Dickens, LD: *Little Dorrit,* by Charles Dickens (Popular Edition of the Complete Works, Chapman & Hall, 1907).

Dickens, OMF: *Our Mutual Friend,* by Charles Dickens (Popular Edition of the Complete Works, Chapman & Hall, 1907).

Disraeli, *Coningsby*: *Coningsby*, by Benjamin Disraeli (Dent, 1911).

Disraeli, *Sybil*: *Sybil, or The Two Nations*, by Benjamin Disraeli (Oxford World's Classics, 1925).

D&M: *Victorian Architecture*, by Roger Dixon and Stefan Muthesius (Thames & Hudson, 1978).

Dunn: *James Anthony Froude, A Biography*, by Waldo Hilary Dunn (OUP, 2 Vols, 1961–3).

Eliot, *Holt*: *Felix Holt, the Radical*, by George Eliot (Oxford World's Classics, 1911).

Ellis: *British Railway History 1830–1876*, by Hamilton Ellis (George Allen & Unwin, 1954).

Engels: *The Condition of the Working-Class in England in 1844*, by Frederick Engels (George Allen & Unwin, 1892).

Eyck: *The Prince Consort*, by Frank Eyck (New Portway, 1975).

Ferriday: *Victorian Architecture*, edited by Peter Ferriday (Jonathan Cape, 1963).

Festing Jones: *Samuel Butler, Author of Erewhon (1835–1902): A Memoir*, by Henry Festing Jones (Macmillan & Co., 2 Vols, 1919).

Finer: *The Life and Times of Sir Edwin Chadwick*, by S. E. Finer (Methuen, 1970).

Finlayson: *The Seventh Earl of Shaftesbury*, by Geoffrey B. A. M. Finlayson (Eyre Methuen, 1981).

Flanders: *The Victorian City: Everyday Life in Dickens' London*, by Judith Flanders (Atlantic Books, 2012).

Forster: *The Life of Charles Dickens*, by John Forster (Dent, 2 Vols, 1927).

Froude, *Carlyle*: *Thomas Carlyle, A History of the First Forty Years of his Life* and *Thomas Carlyle, A History of his Life in London*, by J. A. Froude (Longmans, Green & Co., 4 Vols 1882–4).

Froude, *MT*: *The Reign of Mary Tudor*, by James Anthony Froude (Dent, 1910).

Froude, *Nemesis*: *The Nemesis of Faith*, by J. A. Froude (John Chapman, 1849).

Froude, *Remains*: *Remains of the Late Reverend Richard Hurrell Froude, MA* (Rivington, 1838, 2 Vols).

Fulford, *DC*: *Darling Child: Private Correspondence of Queen Victoria and the Crown Princess of Prussia 1871–1878*, edited by Roger Fulford (Evans Brothers, 1976).

Fulford, *DM*: *Dearest Mama: Letters between Queen Victoria and the Crown Princess of Prussia 1861–1864*, edited by Roger Fulford (Evans Brothers, 1968).

Fulford, *YDL*: *Your Dear Letter: Private Correspondence of Queen Victoria and the Crown Princess of Prussia 1865–1871*, edited by Roger Fulford (Evans Brothers, 1971).

Gardiner: *The Life of Sir William Harcourt*, by A. G. Gardiner (Constable, 2 Vols, 1923).

Garvin: *The Life of Joseph Chamberlain* (Vol. 1), by J. L. Garvin (Macmillan, 1935).

Gash: *Sir Robert Peel: the Life of Sir Robert Peel after 1830* by Norman Gash (Longman, 1972).

Gaskell, MB: *Mary Barton*, by Elizabeth Gaskell (Oxford World's Classics, 1906).

Gaskell, N&S: *North and South*, by Elizabeth Gaskell (Oxford World's Classics, 1908).

Girouard: *Alfred Waterhouse and the Natural History Museum*, by Mark Girouard (Yale, 1981).

Gladstone, Diaries: *The Gladstone Diaries*, edited by M. R. D. Foot and H. C. G. Matthew (OUP, 14 Vols, 1968–94).

Gloag: *Victorian Taste: Some Social Aspects of Architecture and Industrial Design from 1820–1900*, by John Gloag (A&C Black, 1962).

Greville: *The Greville Memoirs* (Second Part): *A Journal of the Reign of Queen Victoria*, by Charles C. F. Greville (Longmans, Green & Co., 3 Vols, 1885).

Harrison-Barbet: *Thomas Holloway, Victorian Philanthropist*, by Anthony Harrison-Barbet (Royal Holloway, 1994).

Hartley: *Charles Dickens and the House of Fallen Women*, by Jenny Hartley (Methuen, 2008).

Hawkins: *The Forgotten Prime Minister: The 14th Earl of Derby*, by Angus Hawkins (OUP, 2 Vols, 2007–8).

Healey: *Lady Unknown: The Life of Angela Burdett-Coutts*, by Edna Healey (Sidgwick & Jackson, 1978).

Heffer: *Moral Desperado: A Life of Thomas Carlyle*, by Simon Heffer (Weidenfeld & Nicolson, 1995).

H&I: *Punishment: Rhetoric, Rule and Practice*, by Christopher Harding and Richard W. Ireland (Routledge, 1989).

Himmelfarb: *Marriage and Morals among the Victorians, and other essays*, by Gertrude Himmelfarb (Faber, 1986).

Hobhouse: *The Crystal Palace and the Great Exhibition – Art, Science and Productive Industry: A History of the Royal Commission for the Exhibition of 1851*, by Hermione Hobhouse (Continuum, 2002).

Holloway: *The Victorian Sage: Studies in Argument*, by John Holloway (Macmillan, 1953).

Honan: *Matthew Arnold, A Life*, by Park Honan (Weidenfeld & Nicolson, 1981).

Hughes: *Tom Brown's Schooldays*, by Thomas Hughes (Dent, 1906).

Hutton: *Literary Essays*, by R. H. Hutton (Macmillan, 1888).

Inglis: *Churches and the Working Classes in Victorian England*, by K. S. Inglis (Routledge & Kegan Paul, 1963).

Isba: *Gladstone and Women*, by Anne Isba (Continuum, 2006).

JL&S: *Saltaire: The Making of a Model Town*, by Neil Jackson, Jo Lintonbon and Bryony Staples (Spire Books, 2010).

Kemp: *The Desire of My Eyes: A Life of John Ruskin,* by Wolfgang Kemp, translated by Jan van Heurck (HarperCollins, 1991).

Kincaid: *The Novels of Anthony Trollope,* by James R. Kincaid (Clarendon Press, 1977).

Kingsley, AL: *Alton Locke,* by Charles Kingsley (Macmillan Pocket Edition, 1895).

Kingsley, W-B: *The Water-Babies: A Fairy-Tale for a Land Baby,* by Charles Kingsley (Penguin, 2008).

La Touche: *John Ruskin and Rose La Touche: Her Unpublished Diaries of 1861 and 1867,* introduced and edited by Van Akin Burd (OUP, 1979).

Lang: *Life, Letters and Diaries of Sir Stafford Northcote, First Earl of Iddesleigh,* by Andrew Lang (Blackwood, 2 Vols, 1890).

London 3: *The Buildings of England: London 3: North West,* by Bridget Cherry and Nikolaus Pevsner (Penguin, 1991).

London 4: *The Buildings of England: London 4: North,* by Bridget Cherry and Nikolaus Pevsner (Penguin, 1998).

London 6: *The Buildings of England: London 6: Westminster,* by Simon Bradley and Nikolaus Pevsner (Yale, 2003).

Lowry: *The Letters of Matthew Arnold to Arthur Hugh Clough,* edited by Howard Foster Lowry (OUP, 1932).

Lutyens: *Effie in Venice: Her Picture of Society and Life with John Ruskin 1849–1852,* edited by Mary Lutyens (John Murray, 1965).

Macaulay: *Critical and Historical Essays, Contributed to the Edinburgh Review,* by Lord Macaulay (Longmans, 1899).

Mann: *Census of Great Britain, 1851: Religious Worship in England and Wales,* abridged from the Official Report made by Horace Mann, Esq, to George Graham, Esq, Registrar-General (George Routledge, 1854).

Martin: *The Dust of Combat: A Life of Charles Kingsley,* by R. B. Martin (Faber, 1959).

Martineau: *Autobiography,* by Harriet Martineau (Smith, Elder, 3 Vols, 1877).

Maurice: *The Life of Frederick Denison Maurice, Chiefly Told in his own Letters,* edited by Frederick Maurice (Macmillan, 2nd Edition, 2 Vols, 1884).

Maxwell: *The Life and Letters of George William Frederick, Fourth Earl of Clarendon,* by Sir Herbert Maxwell (Edward Arnold, 2 Vols, 1913).

Mayhew: *London Labour and the London Poor,* by Henry Mayhew; a Selected Edition, edited by Robert Douglas-Fairhurst (OUP, 2010).

M&B: *The Life of Benjamin Disraeli, Earl of Beaconsfield,* by William Flavelle Monypenny and George Earle Buckle (John Murray, 6 Vols, 1910–20).

McCrum: *Thomas Arnold, Head Master,* by Michael McCrum (OUP, 1989).

Milford: *Essays, Mainly on the Nineteenth Century, Presented to Sir Humphrey Milford* (OUP, 1948).

Mill, *Autobiography*: *Autobiography*, by J. S. Mill (Oxford World's Classics, 1924).

Mill, *Later*: *The Later Letters of John Stuart Mill, 1849–1873*, edited by Francis E. Mineka and Dwight N. Lindley (University of Toronto Press, 4 Vols, 1972).

Mill, *Liberty*: *Utilitarianism, Liberty and Representative Government*, by J. S. Mill (Dent, 1910).

Mill, *Subjection*: *The Subjection of Women*, by J. S. Mill (Hackett, 1988).

Mill, *C.W.*: *The Collected Works of John Stuart Mill*, edited by John M. Robson (University of Toronto Press, 33 vols, 1965–96).

Morley, *Compromise*: *On Compromise*, by John Morley (Watts, 1933).

Morley, *Gladstone*: *The Life of William Ewart Gladstone*, by John Morley (Macmillan, New Edition, 2 Vols, 1905).

Morley, *Recollections*: *Recollections*, by John, Viscount Morley (Macmillan, 2 Vols, 1917).

Mowat: *The Charity Organisation Society 1869–1913: Its Ideas and Work*, by Charles Loch Mowat (Methuen, 1961).

Newcastle: *Report of the Commissioners appointed to inquire into the State of Popular Education in England* (HMSO, 19 Vols, 1861).

N-T: *Report of the Organisation of the Permanent Civil Service, together with a Letter from the Rev. B. Jowett* (HMSO, 1854) [The Northcote–Trevelyan report].

Osborne: *Arthur Hugh Clough*, by James Insley Osborne (Constable, 1920).

Parry: *Democracy and Religion: Gladstone and the Liberal Party, 1867–1875*, by J. P. Parry (CUP, 1986).

Porter: *The Thames Embankment: Environment, Technology and Society in Victorian London*, by Dale H. Porter (University of Akron Press, 1998).

R&A: *The Parliamentary Career of Charles de Laet Waldo Sibthorp, 1826–1855*, by Stephen Roberts and Mark Acton (Edwin Mellen Press, 2010).

Raby: *Samuel Butler, a Biography*, by Peter Raby (Hogarth Press, 1991).

Reid: *Life of the Right Honourable William Edward Forster*, by T. Wemyss Reid (Chapman & Hall, 2 Vols, 1888).

Reid, MM: *The Life, Letters and Friendships of Richard Monckton Milnes, First Lord Houghton*, by T. Wemyss Reid (Cassell, 2nd Edition, 2 Vols, 1890).

Rhodes James: *Albert, Prince Consort*, by Robert Rhodes James (Hamish Hamilton, 1983).

RIBA 1871–2: *Papers read at the Royal Institute of British Architects*, session 1871–2.

Ridley: *Lord Palmerston*, by Jasper Ridley (Constable, 1970).

Roberts: *Salisbury: Victorian Titan*, by Andrew Roberts (Weidenfeld & Nicolson, 1999).

Ruskin, *Crown*: *The Crown of Wild Olive: Four Lectures on Industry and War*, by John Ruskin (George Allen, 1902).

Ruskin, *Diaries*: *The Diaries of John Ruskin*, edited by Joan Evans and J. H. Whitehouse (OUP, 3 Vols, 1956–9).

Ruskin, *Fors*: *Fors Clavigera: Letters to the Workmen and Labourers of Great Britain*, by John Ruskin (George Allen, 4 Vols, New Edition, 1896–9).

Ruskin, *Lamps*: *The Seven Lamps of Architecture*, by John Ruskin (Dent, 1907).

Ruskin, *Last*: *Unto This Last, and other Essays on Art and Political Economy*, by John Ruskin (J. M. Dent, 1907).

Ruskin, *Praeterita*: *Praeterita: Outlines of Scenes and Thoughts perhaps worthy of Memory in my past Life*, by John Ruskin (George Allen, 3 Vols, 1896).

Ruskin, *T&T*: *Time and Tide by Weare and Tyne: Twenty-Five Letters to a Working Man of Sunderland on the Laws of Work*, by John Ruskin (George Allen, 1906).

Russell: *History of Western Philosophy: And its connection with Political and Social Circumstances from the Earliest Times to the Present Day*, by Bertrand Russell (George Allen & Unwin, 1946).

Russell, G.: *Collections and Recollections*, by One Who Has Kept a Diary [G. W. E. Russell] (Smith, Elder, New Edition, 1899).

Sanders: *Harriet Martineau: Selected Letters*, edited by Valerie Sanders (Clarendon Press, 1990).

Scott: *Personal and Professional Recollections*, by Sir George Gilbert Scott, edited by Gavin Stamp (Paul Watkins, 1995).

Shannon: *Gladstone: God and Politics*, by Richard Shannon (Hambledon Continuum, 2008).

Shrosbree: *Public Schools and Private Education: The Clarendon Commission 1861–64 and the Public School Acts*, by Colin Shrosbree (Manchester University Press, 1988).

Sidgwick: *Mrs Henry Sidgwick: a Memoir by her Niece Ethel Sidgwick* (Sidgwick & Jackson, 1938).

Silver: *The Family Letters of Samuel Butler 1841–1886: Selected, Edited and Introduced by Arnold Silver* (Jonathan Cape, 1962).

Smiles: *Self Help: with Illustrations of Conduct and Perseverance*, by Samuel Smiles (Institute of Economic Affairs, 1996).

Smith: *James Fitzjames Stephen: Portrait of a Victorian Rationalist*, by K. J. M. Smith (CUP, 1988).

S&S: *Matthew Arnold and the Education of the New Order*, by Peter Smith and Geoffrey Summerfield (CUP, 1969).

Stanley: *Life and Correspondence of Thomas Arnold, DD*, by Arthur Penrhyn Stanley, DD (Ward, Lock & Co., undated single-volume edition).

Stephen: *Liberty, Equality, Fraternity*, by James Fitzjames Stephen, 2nd edition, edited by R. J. White (CUP, 1967).

Stephen, B.: *Emily Davies and Girton College*, by Barbara Stephen (Constable, 1927).

Strachey: *Eminent Victorians*, by Lytton Strachey (Chatto & Windus, New Edition, 1921).

Sutherland: *Faith, Duty and the Power of Mind: The Cloughs and their Circle*, by Gillian Sutherland (CUP, 2006).

Sylvester: *Robert Lowe and Education*, by D. W. Sylvester (CUP, 1974).

Symonds: *The Memoirs of John Addington Symonds*, edited and introduced by Phyllis Grosskurth (Random House, 1984).

Tennyson: *Poetical Works, Including the Plays*, by Lord Tennyson (OUP, 1953).

T&L: *The Poetry of Matthew Arnold: A Commentary*, by C. B. Tinker and H. F. Lowry (OUP, 1940).

Tomalin: *Charles Dickens: A Life*, by Claire Tomalin (Viking, 2011).

Trevelyan: *The Life of John Bright*, by G. M. Trevelyan (Constable, 1913).

Trilling: *Matthew Arnold*, by Lionel Trilling (George Allen & Unwin, 2nd Edition, 1949).

Trollope, *Autobiography*: *An Autobiography*, by Anthony Trollope (Oxford World's Classics, 1923).

Trollope, *TC*: *The Three Clerks*, by Anthony Trollope (Oxford World's Classics, 1907).

Vicnius: *Suffer and be Still: Women in the Victorian Age*, edited by M. Vicnius (Methuen, 1980).

Wagner: *Barnardo*, by Gillian Wagner (Weidenfeld & Nicolson, 1979).

Waller: *The English Marriage*, by Maureen Waller (John Murray, 2009).

Ward: *William George Ward and the Oxford Movement*, by Wilfrid Ward (Macmillan, 1889).

Webb: *My Apprenticeship*, by Beatrice Webb (Longmans, Green, 1926).

Willey: *Nineteenth Century Studies*, by Basil Willey (Penguin, 1964).

Wilson: *The Victorians*, by A. N. Wilson (Hutchinson, 2002).

Winter: *Robert Lowe*, by James Winter (Toronto University Press, 1976).

Woodward: *The Age of Reform*, by Sir Llewellyn Woodward (Oxford University Press, 2nd Edition, 1962).

W&WM: *Life of Carlyle*, by David Alec Wilson and David Wilson MacArthur (6 Vols, Kegan Paul, Trench, Trübner & Co., 1923–34).

Reference Works

The Annual Register, HMSO, various years.

Burke's Peerage, Baronetage and Knightage.

The Dictionary of National Biography [DNB].
Hansard.
The New Dictionary of National Biography.

Pamphlets

Anon.: *Shall We Give It Up? A Political Correspondence* (Robert Hardwicke, 1871).

Disraeli, Manchester: *Speech of the Right Hon. B. Disraeli MP, at the Free Trade Hall, Manchester, April 3, 1872* (National Union of Conservative and Constitutional Associations, 1872).

Fawcett: *Mr Fitzjames Stephen on the Position of Women*, by Millicent Garrett Fawcett (Macmillan, 1873).

Festing Jones, D/B: *Charles Darwin and Samuel Butler: A Step towards Reconciliation*, by Henry Festing Jones (Fifield, 1911).

Norton: *A Letter to the Queen on Lord Chancellor Cranworth's Marriage and Divorce Bill*, by the Hon. Mrs Norton (Longman, Brown, Green & Longmans, 1855).

Street: *The New Courts of Justice: Notes in Reply to Criticisms*, by George Edmund Street, RA (Rivingtons, 1872).

Weir: *Primary Education Considered in Relation to the State* (Edinburgh, 1868).

Newspapers and Periodicals

The Builder
Carlyle Studies Annual
The Edinburgh Review
The London Gazette
Macmillan's Magazine
Nature
The Nineteenth Century
Quarterly Review
Quarterly Review of Jurisprudence
Saturday Review
The Times
Transactions and Proceedings of the Modern Language Association (PMLA)
Victorian Studies
Weekend Telegraph
The Artisan

The Examiner / John Bull / Morning Herald
Westminster Review
Morning Post
Fraser's Magazine
Cornhill Magazine
The Ecclesiologist
The Illustrated London News

NOTES

All abbreviations may be found in the Bibliography on page 821.

Prologue

1. Bamford, p. 5.
2. Stanley, p. 104.
3. Collini, p. 19.
4. Stanley, p. 30.
5. Strachey, p. 180.
6. *Ibid.* p. 181.
7. Arnold, *Sermons*, Vol. II, p. 81.
8. Stanley, p. 58.
9. *Ibid.* p. 66.
10. *Ibid.* p. 74.
11. McCrum, pp. 45–6.
12. Arnold, *Sermons*, Vol. V, p. 66.
13. *Ibid.* p. 35.
14. *Ibid.* Vol. IV, p. 9.
15. *Ibid.* p. 30.
16. Stanley, p. 59.
17. Lowry, p. 3.
18. Stanley, p. 61.
19. Strachey, p. 188.
20. Arnold, *MW*, p. 399.
21. McCrum, p. 65.
22. Stanley, p. 56. 'Liberal party' is an anachronism for the late 1820s.
23. *Ibid.* p. 79.
24. *Ibid.* p. 60.
25. *Ibid.* p. 66.
26. *Ibid.* p. 67.
27. *Ibid.* p. 136.
28. Strachey, p. 180.
29. Stanley, p. 69.
30. *Edinburgh Review*, April 1859, p. 557.
31. Stanley, p. 62.
32. *Ibid.* p. 57.
33. *Ibid.* p. 74.
34. McCrum, pp. 101–3.
35. Strachey, p. 188.
36. *Ibid.* p. 190.
37. Stanley, p. 65.
38. *Ibid.* p. 67.
39. Strachey, p. 199.
40. *Ibid.* p. 183.
41. *Ibid.* p. 186.
42. Stanley, p. 109.
43. *Ibid.* p. 265.
44. Strachey, p. 191.
45. *Ibid.* p. 193.
46. Stanley, p. 161.
47. *Ibid.* p. 58.
48. *Ibid.* p. 73.
49. Arnold, *Sermons*, Vol. II, pp. 264–6.
50. Arnold, *MW*, p. 232.
51. *Ibid.* p. 233.
52. Stanley, p. 223.
53. Arnold, *MW*, p. 234.
54. Stanley, p. 216.
55. Arnold, *MW*, p. 423.
56. Stanley, p. 227.
57. Arnold, *MW*, p. 496.
58. *Ibid.* p. 497.
59. *Ibid.* p. 453.
60. *Ibid.* p. 454.
61. *Ibid.* p. 456.
62. *Ibid.* pp. 459–60.
63. *Ibid.* p. 499.
64. *Ibid.* p. 500.
65. Strachey, p. 202.
66. Stanley, pp. 313–4.

67. BL Add. MS 45241, ff. 8–9.
68. BL Add. MS 45241, f. 10.
69. Stanley, p. 104.
70. Clough, *Letters*, Vol. I, p. 119.
71. Stanley, (Preface), p. ix.
72. Hughes, p. 104.
73. *Ibid.* p. 105.
74. *Ibid.* p. 261.
75. Strachey, p. 178.
76. *Ibid.* p. 185.
77. *Ibid.* p. 206.
78. BL Add. MS 45241, ff. 11–12.
79. Lowry, p. 111.
80. Willey, p. 60.
81. Cockshut, p. 88.
82. Briggs, *People*, p. 142.
83. Symonds, p. 94.
84. *Ibid.* p. 96.
85. *Ibid.* p. 97.
86. *Ibid.* p. 98.
87. *Ibid.* p. 112.
88. *Ibid.* p. 113.
89. Butler, *Flesh*, p. 23.
90. Mill, *Later*, Vol. III, p. 1246.

Part 1: The Condition of England

Chapter 1: The Angry Forties (page 33)

1. *The Times*, 31 May 1842, p. 5.
2. BL Add. MS 40434, ff. 121–2.
3. BL Add. MS 40434, ff. 161–2.
4. BL Add. MS 40434, ff. 163–4.
5. BL Add. MS 40434, f. 174.
6. BL Add. MS 40434, f. 178.
7. BL Add. MS 40434, f. 183.
8. BL Add. MS 40434, ff. 184–5.
9. BL Add. MS 40434, ff. 188–9.
10. Carlyle, *Letters*, Vol. XIV, pp. 215–16.
11. BL Add. MS 40434, ff. 65–6.
12. BL Add. MS 40434, f. 81.
13. Carlyle, *Letters*, Vol. XIV, p. 183.
14. Gash, p. 339.
15. Carlyle, *Letters*, Vol. XIV, p. 183.
16. Hansard, Vol. 64, cols 785–7.
17. *Ibid.* Vol. 64, col. 885.
18. *Ibid.* Vol. 64, col. 867.
19. *Ibid.* Vol. 64, col. 870.
20. *Ibid.* Vol. 64, col. 862.
21. *Ibid.* Vol. 64, cols 920–1.
22. Carlyle, *Works*, Vol. X, p. 169.
23. Hansard, Vol. 66, cols 1168–9.
24. Gaskell, *MB*, p. 66.
25. Kingsley, *AL*, p. 95.
26. Dickens, *LD*, pp. 32–3.
27. Hansard, Vol. 65, col. 412.
28. *Ibid.* Vol. 65, col. 440.
29. *Quarterly Review*, December 1842 (Vol. LXXI), pp. 158–9.
30. Gash, p. 342.
31. Greville, Part II, Vol. II, p. 98.
32. *Ibid.* p. 119.
33. *Ibid.* p. 136.
34. *Quarterly Review*, December 1842 (Vol. LXXI), p. 134.
35. *Ibid.* p. 137.
36. *Ibid.* p. 144.
37. BL Add. MS 40613, f. 53.
38. *Quarterly Review*, December 1842 (Vol. LXXI), p. 156.
39. *Ibid.* p. 153.
40. *Ibid.* p. 154.
41. *Ibid.* p. 171.
42. Hansard, Vol. 66, col. 449.
43. *Ibid.* Vol. 66, col. 463.
44. *Ibid.* Vol. 66, col. 474.
45. BL Add. MS 44777, f. 108.
46. Hansard, Vol. 66, col. 834.
47. *Ibid.* Vol. 66, col. 835.
48. *Ibid.* Vol. 66, col. 1163.
49. *Ibid.* Vol. 66, cols 1179–80.
50. BL Add. MS 40483, f. 37.
51. *Ibid.* Vol. 66, col. 1205.

Chapter 2: Noblesse Oblige (page 50)

1. Stanley, p. 284. The Latin implies that the vulgar will not take notice until they are threatened with going hungry.
2. *Ibid.* p. 293.
3. Carlyle, *Letters*, Vol. X, p. 15. Elliot was 'The Corn Law rhymer'.
4. Carlyle, *Letters*, Vol. XI, pp. 83–4.
5. *Ibid.* p. 160.

6. *Ibid.* p. 161.
7. Carlyle, *Letters*, Vol. XII, pp. 278–9.
8. Carlyle, *Works*, Vol. XXIX, p. 118.
9. *Ibid.* p. 119.
10. *Ibid.* p. 123.
11. *Ibid.* p. 130.
12. *Ibid.* p. 135.
13. *Ibid.* p. 155.
14. *Ibid.* p. 157.
15. *Ibid.* p. 162.
16. *Ibid.* p. 204.
17. Carlyle, *Works*, Vol. X, p. 2.
18. *Ibid.* p. 18.
19. *Ibid.* p. 30.
20. *Ibid.* p. 169.
21. *Ibid.* p. 184.
22. *Ibid.* p. 207.
23. *Ibid.* p. 212.
24. *Ibid.* p. 215.
25. *Ibid.* p. 179.
26. *Ibid.* p. 177.
27. Disraeli, *Coningsby*, p. 91.
28. Blake, p. 175.
29. *Ibid.* p. 184.
30. Holloway, p. 87.
31. Disraeli, *Sybil*, p. 67.
32. *Ibid.* p. 63.
33. *Ibid.* p. 64.
34. See, for example, Cobbett, Vol. II, pp. 151–6.
35. Beer, p. 63.
36. Disraeli, *Sybil*, p. 99.
37. *Ibid.* p. 170.
38. *Ibid.* pp. 127, 140.
39. *Ibid.* p. 423.
40. Finlayson, p. 15.
41. *Ibid.* p. 14.
42. Hansard, Vol. 67, col. 48.
43. *Ibid.* Vol. 53, cols 1092–3.
44. Kingsley, *W-B*, p. 1.
45. Hansard, Vol. 53, col. 1093.
46. *Ibid.* Vol. 55, col. 109.
47. *Quarterly Review*, December 1840 (Vol. LXVII), p. 94.
48. *Ibid.* p. 95.
49. *Ibid.* p. 96.
50. *Ibid.* p. 97.
51. *Ibid.* p. 98.
52. Gash, p. 280.
53. BL Add. MS 40483, ff. 44–5.
54. BL Add. MS 40483, f. 46.
55. BL Add. MS 40483, ff. 47–8.
56. BL Add. MS 40483, ff. 49–50.
57. BL Add. MS 40483, f. 51.
58. Gash, p. 332.
59. BL Add. MS 40483, f. 53.
60. Finlayson, p. 179.
61. Hansard, Vol. 63, col. 1321.
62. *Ibid.* Vol. 63, col. 1322.
63. *Ibid.* Vol. 63, col. 1327.
64. *Ibid.* Vol. 63, col. 1328.
65. *Ibid.* Vol. 63, col. 1337.
66. *Ibid.* Vol. 63, col. 1353.
67. *Ibid.* Vol. 63, col. 1354.
68. *Ibid.* Vol. 63, cols 1357–8.
69. *Ibid.* Vol. 63, col. 1359.
70. BL Add. MS 40483, ff. 68–70.
71. Hansard, Vol. 64, cols 538–9.
72. *Ibid.* Vol. 64, col. 540.
73. *Ibid.* Vol. 64, cols 541–2.
74. *Ibid.* Vol. 64, col. 616.
75. BL Add. MS 40483, f. 79.
76. BL Add. MS 40483, ff. 80–1.
77. Hansard, Vol. 65, col. 1101.
78. *Ibid.* Vol. 64, cols 999–1000.
79. *Ibid.* Vol. 64, col. 1001.
80. *Ibid.* Vol. 65, col. 101.
81. BL Add. MS 40483, ff. 108–9.
82. BL Add. MS 40483, ff. 110–11.
83. BL Add. MS 40483, f. 124.
84. BL Add. MS 40483, f. 192.
85. Hansard, Vol. 65, cols 1094–5.
86. *Ibid.* Vol. 65, col. 1098.
87. Finlayson, p. 212.
88. BL Add. MS 40483, f. 194.
89. BL Add. MS 44777, f. 149.
90. Hansard, Vol. 73, col. 1155.
91. *Ibid.* Vol. 73, col. 1626.
92. Gash, p. 444.
93. Hansard, Vol. 67, col. 70.
94. Carlyle, *Letters*, Vol. XV, p. 3.
95. Finer, p. 9.
96. Hansard, Vol. 67, cols 60–1.
97. *Ibid.* Vol. 67, col. 66.
98. *Ibid.* Vol. 67, col. 71.
99. *Ibid.* Vol. 67, col. 76.
100. Gash, p. 383.
101. Hansard, Vol. 67, col. 106.

102. BL Add. MS 44777, f. 103.

103. Hansard, Vol. 72, cols 280–1.

104. *Ibid*. Vol. 72, col. 281.

105. *Ibid*. Vol. 80, cols 916–7.

106. Finlayson, p. 250.

107. *Quarterly Review*, December 1846 (Vol. LXXIX), p. 128.

108. *Ibid*. p. 129.

109. *Ibid*. p. 130.

110. *Ibid*. p. 131.

111. *Ibid*. p. 132.

112. *Ibid*. p. 137.

113. *Ibid*. p. 136.

114. Dickens, *Letters*, Vol. VI, p. 167.

115. *Quarterly Review*, December 1846 (Vol. LXXIX), p. 140.

116. *Ibid*. p. 141.

Chapter 3: The Ascent of the Bourgeoisie (page 81)

1. Eliot, *Holt*, p. 33.

2. *Ibid*. p. 464.

3. Disraeli, *Coningsby*, p. 136.

4. Gaskell, *N&S*, p. 18.

5. *Ibid*. p. 42.

6. *Ibid*. p. 51.

7. *Ibid*. p. 50.

8. *Ibid*. p. 195.

9. Kingsley, *W-B*, p. 68.

10. Gaskell, *N&S*, p. 233.

11. Kingsley, *W-B*, p. 69.

12. Gaskell, *N&S*, p. 136.

13. *Ibid*. p. 137.

14. *Ibid*. p. 367.

15. *Ibid*. p. 368.

16. *Ibid*. p. 181.

17. Engels, p. 61.

18. *Ibid*. p. 60.

19. *Ibid*. p. 63.

20. *Ibid*. p. 64.

21. *Ibid*. p. 104.

22. *Ibid*. p. 105.

23. *Ibid*. p. 148.

24. *Ibid*. p. 149.

25. *Ibid*. p. 15.

26. *Ibid*. p. 76.

27. *Ibid*. p. 86.

28. *Ibid*. p. 18.

29. *Ibid*. p. 17.

30. *Ibid*. p. 76.

31. *Ibid*. p. 80.

32. *Ibid*. p. 29.

33. *Ibid*. pp. 29–30.

34. *Ibid*. p. 37.

35. *Ibid*. p. 40.

36. Trevelyan, p. 43.

37. *Ibid*. p. 31.

38. Hansard, Vol. 59, col. 233.

39. *Ibid*. Vol. 59, col. 235.

40. *Ibid*. Vol. 59, col. 241.

41. *Ibid*. p. 59.

42. Hansard, Vol. 69, col. 59.

43. Trevelyan, pp. 86–7.

44. Hansard, Vol. 73, col. 944.

45. Carlyle, *Letters*, Vol. XII, p. 23.

46. Carlyle, *Works*, Vol. X, p. 165.

47. *Ibid*. p. 181.

48. Hansard, Vol. 75, col. 1353.

49. Gash, p. 457.

50. Hansard, Vol. 78, col. 785.

51. BL Add. MS 40447, f. 134.

52. BL Add. MS 40479, f. 523.

53. BL Add. MS 40479, ff. 525–6.

54. Greville, Part II, Vol. II, p. 301.

55. Trevelyan, p. 138.

56. *The Times*, 4 December 1845, p. 4.

57. BL Add. MS 44777, f. 233.

58. BL Add. MS 40479, ff. 538–41.

59. Greville, Part II, Vol. II, p. 330.

60. Gladstone, *Diaries*, Vol. III, p. 506.

61. BL Add. MS 40479, f. 555.

62. Clough, *Letters*, Vol. I, pp. 175–6.

63. Hansard, Vol. 83, col. 238.

64. *Ibid*. Vol. 83, col. 252.

65. *Ibid*. Vol. 83, col. 260.

66. Greville, Part II, Vol. II, p. 323.

67. Hansard, Vol. 83, col. 1003.

68. *Ibid*. Vol. 83, col. 1008.

69. *Ibid*. Vol. 83, col. 1009.

70. Greville, Part II, Vol. II, p. 354.

71. Hansard, Vol. 83, col. 1319.

72. *Ibid*. Vol. 83, col. 1335.

73. *Ibid*. Vol. 83, col. 1346.

74. *Ibid*. Vol. 83, col. 1347.

75. *Ibid*. Vol. 84, col. 19.

76. *Ibid*. Vol. 84, col. 348.

77. Greville, Part II, Vol. II, p. 372.

78. *Ibid*. p. 367.

79. Hansard, Vol. 84, col. 431.
80. *Ibid.* Vol. 84, col. 435.
81. Greville, Part II, Vol. II, p. 368.
82. Eyck, p. 37.
83. Greville, Part II, Vol. II, p. 380.
84. BL Add. MS 44777, f. 245.
85. Hansard, Vol. 87, col. 1043.
86. *Ibid.* Vol. 87, col. 1047.
87. *Ibid.* Vol. 87, col. 1054.
88. BL Add. MS 44780, f. 175.
89. Hansard, Vol. 87, col. 1055.
90. Trevelyan, p. 144.
91. *Ibid.* p. 179.
92. Blake, p. 407.
93. Clapham, p. 3.
94. BL Add. MS 44777, f. 245.

Chapter 4: Chartism (page 112)

1. Hansard, Vol. 51, cols 1233–4.
2. Engels, p. 126.
3. *Ibid.* p. 75.
4. *Ibid.* p. 130.
5. *Ibid.* p. 200.
6. Kingsley, *AL*, (Preface), p. lxxxix.
7. *Ibid.* pp. 114–15.
8. *Ibid.* p. 114.
9. Eliot, *Holt*, p. 187.
10. Gaskell, *MB*, pp. 96–7.
11. Clough, *Letters*, Vol. I, p. 234.
12. *Ibid.* p. 238.
13. Gaskell, *MB*, p. 23.
14. *Ibid.* p. 24.
15. Trevelyan, p. 45.
16. Hansard, Vol. 49, col. 231.
17. *Ibid.* Vol. 49, col. 236.
18. *Ibid.* Vol. 49, col. 247.
19. *Ibid.* Vol. 49, col. 252.
20. *The Times*, 31 July 1839, p. 5.
21. *Ibid.* 2 August 1839, p. 5.
22. Hansard, Vol. 62, col. 1376.
23. *Ibid.* Vol. 62, col. 1373.
24. *Ibid.* Vol. 62, cols 1374–5.
25. *Ibid.* Vol. 62, col. 1377.
26. *Ibid.* Vol. 62, cols 1379–80.
27. *Ibid.* Vol. 63, cols 16–17.
28. *Ibid.* Vol. 63, cols 21–2.
29. *Ibid.* Vol. 63, cols 22–3.
30. *Ibid.* Vol. 63, col. 41.
31. *Ibid.* Vol. 63, col. 43.

32. *Ibid.* Vol. 63, col. 71.
33. *Ibid.* Vol. 63, col. 76.
34. *Ibid.* Vol. 63, col. 77.
35. *Ibid.* Vol. 63, cols 77–8.
36. *Ibid.* Vol. 80, col. 913.
37. *Ibid.* Vol. 80, col. 916.
38. Greville, Part II, Vol. III, p. 164.
39. *Ibid.* p. 165.
40. RA/VIC/MAIN/C/56.
41. RA/VIC/MAIN/C/56/14.
42. RA/VIC/MAIN/C/56/12.
43. Eyck, p. 161.
44. RA/VIC/MAIN/C/56/18.
45. RA/VIC/MAIN/C/56/19.
46. Arnold, *Letters*, Vol. I, p. 100.
47. RA/VIC/MAIN/C/56/20.
48. RA/VIC/MAIN/C/56/34.
49. Greville, Part II, Vol. III, p. 165.
50. RA/VIC/MAIN/C/56/50.
51. RA/VIC/MAIN/C/59/18a.
52. RA/VIC/MAIN/C/56/55.
53. RA/VIC/MAIN/C/56/56.
54. RA/VIC/MAIN/C/56/60.
55. RA/VIC/MAIN/C/56/65.
56. *The Times*, 19 May 1848, p. 6.
57. RA/VIC/MAIN/C/56/66.
58. RA/VIC/MAIN/C/56/68.
59. *The Times*, 19 May 1848, p. 4.
60. *Ibid.* 20 May 1848, p. 5.
61. RA/VIC/MAIN/C/56/72.
62. RA/VIC/MAIN/C/56/73.

Part 11: The Victorian Mind

Chapter 5: The Godly Mind (page 135)

1. Davenport-Hines, pp. 223–4.
2. Chadwick, p. 12.
3. BL Add. MS 44792, f. 24.
4. BL Add. MS 44793, f. 133.
5. BL Add. MS 44793, f. 289.
6. BL Add. MS 44766, f. 195.
7. BL Add. MS 44409, f. 207.
8. RA/VIC/MAIN/F/24/59, 63.
9. Butler, *Flesh*, p. 209.
10. Gaskell, *N&S*, p. 270.
11. *Ibid.* p. 279.

12. Gladstone, *Diaries*, Vol. III, p. 89.
13. Martin, p. 47.
14. Gladstone, *Diaries*, Vol. III, p. 321.
15. *Ibid.* p. 322.
16. Willey, p. 85.
17. Froude, *Remains*, Vol. I, p. 404.
18. Morley, *Gladstone*, Vol. I, p. 306.
19. Froude, *Remains*, Vol. I, (Preface), p. xi.
20. *Ibid.* p. 433.
21. Greville, Part II, Vol. II, p. 25.
22. Morley, *Compromise*, p. 56.
23. Morley, *Gladstone*, Vol. I, p. 306.
24. Engels, p. 125.
25. Inglis, p. 3.
26. *Ibid.* p. 12.
27. *Ibid.* p. 15.
28. Mann, (Preface), p. vii.
29. *Ibid.* p. 13.
30. *Ibid.* p. 14.
31. *Ibid.* p. 55.
32. *Ibid.* p. 57.
33. *Ibid.* p. 58.
34. *Ibid.* p. 59.
35. *Ibid.* p. 64.
36. *Ibid.* p. 89.
37. *Ibid.* p. 93.
38. *Ibid.* p. 94.
39. *Ibid.* p. 96.
40. *Ibid.* p. 97.
41. *Ibid.* pp. 102–3.
42. Inglis, p. 41.
43. Chadwick, p. 91.
44. Parry, p. 6.
45. Inglis, p. 75.
46. BL Add. MS 44819, f. 83.

Chapter 6: The Doubting Mind (page 152)

1. Gaskell, *N&S*, p. 13.
2. *Ibid.* p. 36.
3. *Ibid.* p. 38.
4. *Ibid.* p. 420.
5. Strachey, p. 201.
6. Clough, *Letters*, Vol. I, (Preface), p. xvi.
7. *Ibid.* p. 61.
8. Strachey, p. 202.
9. Clough, *Letters*, Vol. I, p. 20.
10. Ward, pp. 109–10.
11. Clough, *Letters*, Vol. I, p. 96.
12. *Ibid.* p. 100.
13. *The Nineteenth Century*, Vol. 43, p. 106.
14. Honan, p. 72.
15. Clough, *Remains*, p. 91.
16. Clough, *Letters*, Vol. I, p. 140.
17. *Ibid.* p. 191.
18. *Ibid.* p. 193.
19. *Ibid.* p. 194.
20. *Ibid.* p. 197.
21. Lowry, p. 47.
22. Clough, *Letters*, Vol. I, p. 219.
23. *Ibid.* p. 220.
24. *Ibid.* p. 221.
25. Clough, *Letters*, Vol. I, p. 242.
26. *Ibid.* p. 237.
27. Lowry, p. 99.
28. Clough, *Letters*, Vol. I, pp. 247–8.
29. *Ibid.* p. 249.
30. Clough, *Remains*, p. 419.
31. Clough, *Letters*, Vol. I, p. 127.
32. *Ibid.* p. 128.
33. *Ibid.* p. 153.
34. *Ibid.* p. 207.
35. *Ibid.* p. 209.
36. *Ibid.* p. 215.
37. Lowry, pp. 109–11.
38. Clough, *Remains*, p. 40.
39. Clough, *Letters*, Vol. I, p. 298.
40. *Ibid.* p. 299.
41. *Ibid.* p. 303.
42. Lowry, pp. 122–3.
43. Lowry, p. 125.
44. Clough, *Letters*, Vol. II, p. 400.
45. *Ibid.* p. 430.
46. *Ibid.* p. 432.
47. *Ibid.* p. 447.
48. *Ibid.* p. 502.
49. *Ibid.* p. 504.
50. *Ibid.* pp. 546–7.
51. *Ibid.* p. 557.
52. BL Add. MS 45795, f. 9.
53. BL Add. MS 45795, f. 19.
54. Clough, *Letters*, Vol. II, p. 579.
55. BL Add. MS 45795, ff. 25–6.
56. Clough, *Letters*, Vol. II, p. 588.

57. *Ibid*. p. 594.
58. *Ibid*. p. 596.
59. *Ibid*. p. 597.
60. *Ibid*. p. 604.
61. *Ibid*. p. 605.
62. *Ibid*. p. 606.
63. *Ibid*. p. 608.
64. Bostridge, p. 384.
65. Lowry, p. 157.
66. *Ibid*. p. 159.
67. Osborne, p. 176.
68. Honan, p. 45.
69. Arnold, *Letters*, Vol. I, p. 37.
70. Martin, p. 44.
71. Arnold, *Letters*, Vol. I, p. 117.
72. *Ibid*. p. 82.
73. Lowry, p. 111.
74. Arnold, *Letters*, Vol. I, p. 91.
75. Clough, *Letters*, Vol. I, p. 215.
76. Lowry, p. 68.
77. *Ibid*. pp. 72–3.
78. *Ibid*. p. 79.
79. Clough, *Letters*, Vol. I, p. 215.
80. *Ibid*. p. 251.
81. Lowry, p. 27.
82. Arnold, *Essays 2*, p. 186.
83. Arnold, *Letters*, Vol. I, p. 227.
84. Lowry, p. 130.
85. *Ibid*. p. 143.
86. *DNB*, Vol. XXII, Supplement, p. 72.
87. See Professor Collini's article on Arnold in the *New Dictionary of National Biography* at http://www.oxforddnb.com/view/article/679.
88. *DNB*, Vol XXII, Supplement, p. 73.
89. Dunn, Vol. I, p. 17.
90. *Ibid*. p. 18.
91. *Ibid*. p. 26.
92. *Ibid*. p. 34.
93. *Vide infra*, Chapter 12.
94. Dunn, Vol. I, p. 39.
95. *Ibid*. p. 75.
96. Maurice, Vol. I, p. 517.
97. Dunn, Vol. I, p. 146.
98. *Ibid*. p. 131.
99. *Ibid*. p. 132.
100. *Ibid*. p. 134.
101. Froude, *Nemesis*, p. 8.

102. *Ibid*. p. 10.
103. *Ibid*. p. 11.
104. Arnold, *Letters*, Vol. I, p. 144.
105. Carlyle, *Letters*, Vol. XXIV, p. 13.
106. Froude, *Nemesis*, p. 35.
107. *Ibid*. p. 156.
108. *Ibid*. p. 84.
109. *Ibid*. p. 92.
110. *Ibid*. p. 144.
111. Dunn, Vol. I, p. 74.
112. Froude, *Nemesis*, pp. 144–5.
113. *Ibid*. pp. 145–6.
114. *Ibid*. p. 147.
115. *Ibid*. p. 148.
116. *Ibid*. p. 157.
117. *Ibid*. p. 158.
118. *Ibid*. p. 148.
119. Lowry, p. 140.
120. Dunn, Vol. I, p. 148.
121. Sanders, p. 139.
122. Froude, *MT*, p. 76.
123. *Ibid*. p. 137.
124. *Ibid*. p. 143.
125. *Ibid*. p. 320.
126. Mill, *Later*, Vol. II, p. 633.
127. BL Add. MS 41298, f. 8.
128. BL Add. MS 41298, f. 16.
129. Maurice, Vol. I, p. 225.
130. BL Add. MS 41299, ff. 7–8.
131. Maurice, Vol. II, p. 35.
132. BL Add. MS 41299, f. 53.
133. BL Add. MS 41297, f. 15.
134. BL Add. MS 41297, f. 23.
135. BL Add. MS 41297, f. 136.
136. BL Add. MS 41297, ff. 147–8.
137. BL Add. MS 41297, f. 154.
138. *Westminster Review*, October 1855.
139. Milford, p. 34.
140. Clough, *Poems*, p. 60.
141. Arnold, *Poems*, pp. 112–14. In later editions 'ebb' in line 8 is replaced by 'sea', accentuating the metaphor, and 'suck' in line 10 by 'draw'.
142. Honan, p. 234.
143. Arnold, *Letters*, Vol. I, p. 214.
144. *PMLA*, Vol. 66, No. 6, December 1951, p. 920.
145. See, for example, T&L, p. 177.

146. *PMLA*, Vol. 66, No. 6, December 1951, p. 924.
147. Hutton, p. 350.

Chapter 7: The Rational Mind (page 197)

1. Russell, p. 801.
2. *Ibid.* p. 803.
3. *Ibid.* p. 804.
4. Mill, *Autobiography*, p. 33.
5. *Ibid.* p. 36.
6. Dickens, *HT*, p. 2.
7. *Ibid.* p. 1.
8. *Ibid.* p. 113.
9. *Ibid.* p. 192.
10. *Ibid.* p. 123.
11. BL Add. MS 44392, f. 115.
12. Chadwick, p. 30.
13. Mill, *Liberty*, pp. 72–3.
14. Morley, *Recollections*, Vol. I, p. 64.
15. *Ibid.* p. 90.
16. *Ibid.* p. 102.
17. Chadwick, p. 108.
18. BL Add. MS 44249, f. 282.
19. Chadwick, p. 184.
20. BL Add. MS 44402, ff. 24–8.
21. BL Add. MS 44407, ff. 91–2.
22. BL Add. MS 44409, f. 242.
23. BL Add. MS 44439, ff. 23, 52.
24. Smiles, (Preface), p. xv.
25. *Ibid.* p. 1.
26. *Ibid.* p. 2.
27. *Ibid.* p. 193.
28. *Ibid.* p. 229.
29. *Ibid.* p. 200.
30. *Ibid.* p. 202.
31. *Ibid.*, p. 234.
32. *Ibid.* p. 236.
33. *Ibid.* p. 244.
34. *Ibid.* p. 249.
35. *Ibid.* p. 13.
36. *Ibid.* p. 41.
37. *Ibid.* p. 59.
38. *Ibid.* p. 167.
39. *Ibid.* p. 191.
40. *Ibid.* p. 176.
41. *Ibid.* p. 181.
42. Kingsley, *AL*, (Preface 'To the Undergraduates of Cambridge'), pp. xcii–xciii.
43. BL Add. MS 44793, f. 170.
44. Butler, *Flesh*, p. 52.
45. Darwin, *OS*, p. 214.
46. *Ibid.* p. 353.
47. http://www.darwinproject.ac.uk/entry-319.
48. http://www.darwinproject.ac.uk/entry-1862.
49. Darwin, *OS*, p. 11.
50. http://www.darwinproject.ac.uk/entry-2294.
51. http://www.darwinproject.ac.uk/entry-2496.
52. Himmelfarb, p. 51.
53. www.darwinproject.ac.uk/entry-2694.
54. J. R. Lucas, Wilberforce and Huxley: A Legendary Encounter, found at http://users.ox.ac.uk/~jrlucas/legend.html.
55. Himmelfarb, p. 52.
56. Darwin, *OS*, p. 362.
57. http://www.darwinproject.ac.uk/entry-12845; http://www.darwinproject.ac.uk/entry-12851.
58. BC RF 103/14/21.
59. Bibby, *Education*, p. 41.
60. *Ibid.* p. 20.
61. *Ibid.* p. 113.
62. *Ibid.* p. 23.
63. *Ibid.* p. 33.
64. *Ibid.* p. 45.
65. Kingsley, *W-B*, p. 8.
66. http://www.darwinproject.ac.uk/entry-2565.
67. Kingsley, *W-B*, p. 109.
68. Darwin, *LL*, p. 287.
69. Kingsley, *W-B*, p. 37.
70. *Ibid.* p. 40.
71. *Ibid.* p. 85.
72. *Ibid.* p. 41.
73. *Ibid.* p. 135.
74. *Ibid.* p. 48.
75. Beer, p. 128.
76. Chadwick, p. 174.
77. Himmelfarb, p. 69.
78. Trevelyan, p. 268.

79. Burn, p. 39.
80. Ruskin, *Diaries*, Vol. II, p. 466.
81. BL Add. MS 45801, ff. 131–2.
82. Chadwick, p. 37.
83. UL Add. 7349 1/9/12a–b.
84. UL Add. 7349 1/6/1.
85. UL Add. 7349 1/6/4.
86. UL Add. 7349 1/13/3.
87. UL Add. 7349 1/13/6.
88. Burn, p. 275.
89. UL Add. 7349 2/21.
90. UL Add. 7349 2/22.
91. Stephen, p. 94.
92. *Ibid.* p. 101.
93. Mill, *Later*, Vol. III, p. 1478.
94. *Ibid.* p. 1479.
95. *Ibid.* p. 1483.
96. *Ibid.* p. 1487.
97. Morley, *Compromise*, p. 15.
98. *Ibid.* p. 17.
99. Ruskin, *Diaries*, Vol. III, p. 843.
100. *Ibid.* p. 844.
101. Butler, *Note-Books*, p. 9.
102. Raby, p. 23.
103. Butler, *Note-Books*, p. 31.
104. BL Add. MS 44027, f. 20.
105. Festing Jones, Vol. I, p. 58.
106. BC VIII/I/3a.
107. Raby, p. 95.
108. BL Add. MS 44027, f. 63.
109. BL Add. MS 44027, f. 67.
110. BL Add. MS 44027, f. 68.
111. Silver, p. 94.
112. *Ibid.* p. 114.
113. BL Add. MS 34486, f. 56.
114. Silver, p. 121.
115. BL Add. MS 44027, f. 240.
116. BL Add. MS 44028, f. 23.
117. BL Add. MS 44028, f. 24.
118. BL Add. MS 44439, f. 48.
119. BL Add. MS 44439, f. 55.
120. BL Add. MS 44439, f. 62.
121. http://www.darwinproject.ac.uk/
     entry-4902.
122. Festing Jones, Vol. I, p. 173.
123. BL Add. MS 44027, f. 239.
124. Butler, *Haven*, pp. 66–7.
125. *Ibid.* pp. 70–71.

126. *Ibid.* p. 207.
127. *Ibid.* p. 142.
128. *Ibid.* p. 148.
129. *Ibid.* p. 211.
130. *Ibid.* pp. 222–3.
131. BC, VIII/38/12.
132. *Ibid.*
133. *Ibid.*
134. Butler, *Savage Letters*, p. 40.
135. BL Add. MS 44028, f. 162.
136. Festing Jones, Vol. I, pp. 257–9.
137. *Ibid.* p. 260.
138. BL Add. MS 34486, f. 69.
139. BL Add. MS 34486, ff. 72–3.
140. BL Add. MS 34486, ff. 74–5.
141. BL Add. MS 34486, f. 77.
142. BC VIII/38/13, letter of 22 July 1878.
143. http://www.darwinproject.ac.uk/
     entry-12545.
144. BC, VIII/4/2.
145. *Nature*, 27 January 1881, p. 285.
146. BL Add. MS 44029, f. 14.
147. Festing Jones, *D/B*, p. 19.
148. *Ibid.* p. 9.
149. Butler, *Note-Books*, p. 66.
150. *Ibid.* p. 183.
151. Festing Jones, Vol. I, (Preface), p. xiv.
152. *Ibid.* p. 203.
153. BL Add. MS 44028, f. 149.
154. Butler, *Flesh*, p. 395.
155. *Ibid.* p. 241.
156. *Ibid.* pp. 245–6.
157. *Ibid.* p. 279.
158. *Ibid.* p. 290.
159. Festing Jones, Vol. II, p. 1.
160. BC VIII/14/1.
161. BC VIII/38/2.

Chapter 8: The Political Mind (page 252)

1. Maurice, Vol. I, p. 445.
2. Hansard, Vol. 118, col. 1187.
3. *Ibid.* Vol. 118, col. 1213.
4. *Ibid.* Vol. 118, col. 1323.
5. *Ibid.* Vol. 118, col. 1332.
6. *Ibid.* Vol. 118, col. 1337.
7. *Ibid.* Vol. 118, col. 1356.
8. *Ibid.* Vol. 126, col. 754.

9. *Ibid.* Vol. 126, col. 755.
10. *Ibid.* Vol. 126, col. 761.
11. *Ibid.* Vol. 126, col. 763.
12. *Ibid.* Vol. 126, col. 765.
13. *Ibid.* Vol. 126, col. 773.
14. *Ibid.* Vol. 149, col. 1758.
15. *Ibid.* Vol. 149, col. 1760.
16. *Ibid.* Vol. 149, col. 1767.
17. *Ibid.* Vol. 149, col. 1776.
18. *Ibid.* Vol. 149, col. 1793.
19. *Ibid.* Vol. 150, col. 1156.
20. *Ibid.* Vol. 151, col. 697.
21. Greville, Part III, Vol. II, p. 204.
22. Hansard, Vol. 151, col. 1894.
23. *Ibid.* Vol. 151, col. 2106.
24. *Ibid.* Vol. 151, col. 2107.
25. Carlyle, *Letters*, Vol. XIV, p. 240.
26. Macaulay, p. 468.
27. BL Add. MS 40469, ff. 6–9.
28. BL Add. MS 40469, ff. 11–14.
29. Gladstone, *Diaries*, Vol. III, (Preface), p. xliv.
30. *Ibid.* (Preface), p. xlv.
31. *Ibid.* Vol. IV, p. 525.
32. *Ibid.* Vol. XIII, p. 428.
33. Trollope, *Autobiography*, p. 236.
34. Blake, p. 149.
35. *Ibid.* pp. 161, 164.
36. Hansard, Vol. 86, cols 674–5.
37. *Ibid.* Vol. 86, col. 677.
38. Greville, Part II, Vol. II, p. 392.
39. Woodward, p. 116.
40. Hansard, Vol. 86, col. 689.
41. *Ibid.* Vol. 86, col. 707.
42. Blake, p. 239.
43. Greville, Part II, Vol. II, p. 392.
44. Blake, p. 164.
45. BL Add. MS 44374, f. 43.
46. Disraeli, *Coningsby*, p. 33.
47. *Ibid.* p. 36.
48. BL Add. MS 44792, ff. 49–50.
49. Hansard, Vol. 123, col. 1666.
50. M&B, Vol. III, p. 477.
51. BL Add. MS 44374, f. 75.
52. M&B, Vol. III, p. 478.
53. BL Add. MS 44374, f. 104.
54. BL Add. MS 44374, f. 106.
55. BL Add. MS 43385, ff. 5–6.
56. BL Add. MS 44389, ff. 225–8.
57. BL Add. MS 44389, ff. 233–5.
58. BL Add. MS 44433, ff. 85–6.
59. BL Add. MS 44438, f. 201.
60. BL Add. MS 44439, f. 271.
61. BL Add. MS 44440, ff. 119–20.
62. BL Add. MS 44440, f. 121.
63. BL Add. MS 44440, f. 173.
64. BL Add. MS 44440, f. 175.

Chapter 9: The Progressive Mind (page 285)

1. BL Add. MS 40432, f. 204.
2. BL Add. MS 40432, f. 218.
3. BL Add. MS 40432, f. 220.
4. BL Add. MS 40432, f. 262.
5. BL Add. MS 40432, f. 268.
6. BL Add. MS 40432, ff. 256–9.
7. BL Add. MS 40432, f. 67.
8. Bagehot, p. 34.
9. Hobhouse, p. 5.
10. *Ibid.* p. 8.
11. *Ibid.* p. 8.
12. RA/VIC/MAIN/F/24/1.
13. RA/VIC/MAIN/F/24/1A.
14. RC/H/1/2/1.
15. Hobhouse, p. 11.
16. RA/VIC/MAIN/F/24/6.
17. RA/VIC/MAIN/F/24/9a.
18. *The Times*, 18 October 1849, p. 6.
19. RA/VIC/MAIN/F/24/17.
20. RA/VIC/MAIN/F/24/30.
21. B&B, p. 123.
22. RA/VIC/MAIN/F/24/14.
23. RA/VIC/MAIN/F/24/20.
24. RA/VIC/MAIN/F/24/33.
25. B&B, p. 126.
26. RC/H/1/2/57.
27. B&B, p. 127.
28. RC/H/1/2/58.
29. RC/H/1/2/66.
30. B&B, p. 129.
31. *The Times*, 22 March 1850, p. 5.
32. B&B, p. 131.
33. Hobhouse, p. 19.
34. *Ibid.* p. 20.
35. *The Times*, 27 June 1850, p. 5.
36. *Ibid.* 28 June 1850, p. 8.

37. Hansard, Vol. 113, col. 334.
38. *Ibid.* Vol. 113, cols 352–3.
39. *Ibid.* Vol. 113, col. 353.
40. Hobhouse, p. 22.
41. Hansard, Vol. 110, col. 1237.
42. RA/VIC/MAIN/F/24/66.
43. *The Times*, 3 May 1850, p. 3.
44. *Ibid.* 6 May 1850, p. 4.
45. Ferriday, p. 163.
46. RA/VIC/MAIN/F/24/67.
47. RA/VIC/MAIN/F/24/72.
48. RA/VIC/MAIN/F/24/73.
49. Hobhouse, p. 34.
50. B&B, p. 139.
51. Ruskin, *Praeterita*, Vol. I, p. 57.
52. RC/H/1/B/6, 10.
53. RC/H/1/B/9.
54. RA/VIC/MAIN/F/24/89.
55. Rhodes James, p. 200.
56. RA/VIC/MAIN/F/24/100.
57. RA/VIC/MAIN/F/24/107.
58. RA/VIC/MAIN/F/24/108.
59. *The Times*, 25 April 1851, p. 5.
60. *Ibid.* 26 April 1851, p. 5.
61. *Ibid.* 1 May 1851, p. 5.
62. RA/VIC/MAIN/F/24/129.
63. *The Times*, 2 May 1851, p. 4.
64. *The Times*, 2 May 1851, p. 5.
65. RA/VIC/MAIN/F/24/130.
66. RA/VIC/MAIN/F/24/144.
67. *The Times*, 2 May 1851, p. 4.
68. Greville, Part II, Vol. III, p. 405.
69. RA/VIC/MAIN/F/24/153.
70. RA/VIC/MAIN/F/24/162.
71. Briggs, *People*, p. 38.
72. Briggs, *Things*, pp. 52–102.
73. Garvin, pp. 51–3.
74. Rhodes James, p. 202.
75. The following figures are taken from RA/VIC/MAIN/F/25/112.
76. Hobhouse, p. 76.
77. RA/VIC/MAIN/F/25/1.
78. RA/VIC/MAIN/F/25/15.
79. Hansard, Vol. 78, col. 387.
80. *Ibid.* Vol. 78, col. 391.
81. B&B, p. 154.
82. RA/VIC/MAIN/F/25/83.
83. RC/H/I/B/26.

84. RC/H/1/B/60.
85. Hansard, Vol. 120, cols 1357–8.
86. RA/VIC/MAIN/F/25/97.
87. RC/H/1/B/45.
88. RA/VIC/MAIN/F/25/102–3.
89. RA/VIC/MAIN/F/25/104.
90. RA/VIC/MAIN/F/25/110.
91. RC/H/1/B/64.
92. RA/VIC/MAIN/F/25/124–5.
93. RA/VIC/MAIN/F/25/131.
94. RA/VIC/MAIN/F/25/127.
95. RA/VIC/MAIN/F/25/146.
96. RA/VIC/MAIN/F/25/137.
97. RA/VIC/MAIN/F/25/170.
98. RA/VIC/MAIN/F/25/171.
99. RC/H/1/B/85.
100. RC/H/1/B/106, 109.
101. RC/H/1/B/110.
102. BL Add. MS 44743, ff. 121–2.
103. Clough, *Letters*, Vol. II, p. 472.
104. *Ibid.* p. 473.
105. RA/VIC/MAIN/F/25/159.
106. RA/VIC/MAIN/F/25/175.
107. RA/VIC/MAIN/F/25/176.
108. RA/VIC/MAIN/F/25/168.
109. RC/H/1/B/168.
110. RA/VIC/MAIN/F/26/19.
111. RA/VIC/MAIN/F/26/20.
112. RC/H/1/B/174.
113. RC/H/1/C/294.
114. RA/VIC/MAIN/F/26/34.
115. RA/VIC/MAIN/F/26/35.
116. RA/VIC/MAIN/F/26/43.
117. Hobhouse, p. 108.
118. *Ibid.* p. 109.
119. RC/H/1/C/297.
120. Hobhouse, p. 115.
121. RA/VIC/MAIN/F/27/24.
122. RC/H/1/D/393.
123. RA/VIC/MAIN/F/27/20.
124. Girouard, p. 7.
125. RA/VIC/MAIN/F/27/114.
126. Hansard, Vol. 166, col. 1903.
127. *Ibid.* Vol. 166, col. 1904.
128. Girouard, p. 13.
129. Hansard, Vol. 166, col. 1915.
130. RC/H/1/D/412.
131. RC/H/1/D/413.

132. BL Add. MS 44617, f. 42.
133. BL Add. MS 38996, f. 114.
134. BL Add. MS 38996, f. 171.
135. BL Add. MS 38996, f. 183.
136. BL Add. MS 38996, f. 274.
137. BL Add. MS 38996, f. 334.
138. Hobhouse, p. 155.
139. Clark, p. 16.
140. *Ibid.* p. 17.
141. RAH Minute Book 1, p. 8.
142. *Ibid.* p. 12.
143. RC/75/1, p. 2.
144. RC/75/1, p. 3.
145. RAH Minute Book 1, p. 48.
146. RC/75/1, p. 4.
147. RC/75/1, p. 5.
148. Clark, p. 29.
149. B&B, p. 223.
150. RAH Minute Book 1, pp. 42–3.
151. *Ibid.* pp. 81–2.
152. RIBA 1871–2, paper by Major General Scott, diagram facing p. 83.
153. *Ibid.* p. 83.
154. RAH Minute Book 1, p. 90.
155. *Ibid.* p. 40.
156. Clark, p. 35.
157. *Ibid.* p. 50.
158. *Ibid.* p. 59.
159. RAH Minute Book 1, p. 153.
160. RC/72/2/4.
161. Hobhouse, p. 172.

Chapter 10: The Heroic Mind
(page 340)

1. *Illustrated London News*, 18 September 1852, p. 214.
2. Greville, Part III, Vol. I, p. 7.
3. *Ibid.* p. 8.
4. Carlyle, *Letters*, Vol. 27, p. 362 (n).
5. Rhodes James, p. 267.
6. Bayley, p. 16.
7. RA/VIC/ADDH/1/1.
8. Maxwell, Vol. II, p. 258.
9. Hansard, Vol. 165, col. 88.
10. RC/75/2/28.
11. Dickens, *Letters*, Vol. X, p. 54.
12. RC/75/2/29.
13. RA/VIC/ADDH/1/211.

14. RC/H/1/D/408.
15. RC/H/1/D/409.
16. RA/VIC/F/27/152.
17. RA/VIC/ADDH/1/353.
18. RA/VIC/ADDH/1/368.
19. RA/VIC/ADDH/1/434.
20. Scott, p. 124.
21. *Ibid.* p. 125.
22. RC/75/2/41.
23. RA/VIC/ADD/1/456–7.
24. RC/75/2/42.
25. RC/75/2/43.
26. RC/H/1/D/414.
27. RC/75/2/35.
28. RC/75/2/26.
29. RC/75/2/25.
30. RC/H/1/D/416.
31. RA/VIC/ADDH/1/480–1.
32. RA/VIC/ADDH/1/574–7.
33. Bayley, p. 24.
34. *Ibid.* p. 40.
35. *London 3*, p. 489.
36. RA/VIC/ADDH/1/574–7.
37. RA/VIC/ADDH/1/580.
38. RA/VIC/ADDH/1/625.
39. RC/H/1/D/424.
40. RA/VIC/ADDH/2/354.
41. RA/VIC/ADDH/2/355.
42. RA/VIC/ADDH/2/356.
43. Hansard, Vol. 170, col. 601.
44. *Ibid.* Vol. 170, col. 608.
45. *Ibid.* col. 604.
46. Fulford, *DM*, p. 65.
47. Hansard, Vol. 170, col. 607.
48. RA/VIC/ADDH/2/469.
49. Maxwell, Vol. II, p. 261.
50. RA/VIC/ADDH/2/515.
51. RA/VIC/ADDH/2/518.
52. RA/VIC/ADDH/2/566.
53. RC/H/1/D/425.
54. RA/VIC/ADDH/2/276.
55. Dickens, *Letters*, Vol. X, p. 425.
56. RC/75/2, f. 38.
57. RA/VIC/ADDH/2/866.
58. RA/VIC/ADDH/2/1333.
59. BL Add. MS 38992, f. 165.
60. RA/VIC/ADDH/2/1356.
61. BL Add. MS 38991, f. 275.

62. BL Add. MS 38993, f. 1; 38992 f. 194.
63. BL Add. MS 38993, f. 11.
64. BL Add. MS 38993, f. 133.
65. BL Add. MS 38993, f. 39.
66. BL Add. MS 38992, f. 244.
67. BL Add. MS 38992, f. 250.
68. BL Add. MS 38992, ff. 268–9.
69. BL Add. MS 38992, f. 271.
70. BL Add. MS 38993, ff. 202–3.
71. BL Add. MS 38993, ff. 322–3.
72. BL Add. MS 38993, f. 340.
73. BL Add. MS 38993, f. 349.
74. BL Add. MS 38993, f. 353.
75. RA/VIC/ADDH/2/2010.
76. BL Add. MS 38993, ff. 356–9.
77. BL Add. MS 38993, f. 379.
78. BL Add. MS 38993, f. 389.
79. RA/VIC/ADDH/2/1778.
80. BL Add. MS 38894, f. 1.
81. BL Add. MS 38894, f. 20.
82. BL Add. MS 38894, ff. 45–6.
83. BL Add. MS 38894, f. 47.
84. RA/VIC/ADDH/2/2028.
85. BL Add. MS 38894, ff. 61–3.
86. BL Add. MS 38994, ff. 69–70.
87. BL Add. MS 38994, f. 81.
88. BL Add. MS 38994, ff. 161–5.
89. RA/VIC/ADDH/2/2043.
90. RA/VIC/ADDH/2/2044.
91. BL Add. MS 38994, f. 174.
92. RA/VIC/ADDH/2/2051.
93. RA/VIC/ADDH/2/2057.
94. BL Add. MS 38994, ff. 202–4.
95. BL Add. MS 38994, ff. 251–7.
96. BL Add. MS 38994, ff. 287–9.
97. BL Add. MS 38994, f. 301.
98. RA/VIC/ADDH/2/2078.
99. RA/VIC/ADDH/2/2079.
100. RA/VIC/ADDH/2/2428.
101. BL Add. MS 38995, ff. 1–4.
102. RA/VIC/ADDH/2/2430, 2436.
103. BL Add. MS 38995, ff. 27–8.
104. RA/VIC/ADDH/2/2462.
105. BL Add. MS 38995, ff. 141–2.
106. BL Add. MS 38995, ff. 145–6.
107. BL Add. MS 38995, f. 156.
108. BL Add. MS 38995, f. 159.
109. BL Add. MS 38995, ff. 163–4.
110. BL Add. MS 38995, f. 165.
111. BL Add. MS 38995, f. 166.
112. BL Add. MS 38995, f. 174.
113. BL Add. MS 38995, ff. 291–2.
114. BL Add. MS 38995, f. 348.
115. BL Add. MS 38995, f. 388.
116. BL Add. MS 38996, f. 81.
117. BL Add. MS 38996, f. 85.
118. BL Add. MS 38996, f. 82.
119. BL Add. MS 38996, f. 86.
120. BL Add. MS 38996, f. 87.
121. BL Add. MS 38996, ff. 87–8.
122. BL Add. MS 38996, f. 321.
123. BL Add. MS 38996, f. 345.
124. Bayley, p. 142.
125. *London 3*, p. 489.

Part III: The Transformation of Britain

Chapter 11: The Leap in the Dark (page 377)

1. BL Add. MS 44402, ff. 53–4.
2. *Ibid*. f. 55.
3. Kingsley, *AL*, (Preface), pp. lxxxix–xc.
4. Hansard, Vol. 182, cols 1255–6.
5. *Ibid*. Vol. 182, col. 1263.
6. Gladstone, *Diaries*, Vol. VI, p. 391.
7. BL Add. MS 44793, f. 125.
8. BL Add. MS 44793, f. 126.
9. BL Add. MS 44793, f. 130.
10. Gladstone, *Diaries*, Vol. VI, p. 414.
11. Lang, Vol. I, p. 246.
12. Hansard, Vol. 182, col. 151.
13. *Ibid*. Vol. 182, col. 164.
14. *Ibid*. Vol. 182, col. 219.
15. *Ibid*. Vol. 182, col. 220.
16. *Ibid*. Vol. 182, col. 1124.
17. *Ibid*. Vol. 182, cols 146–7.
18. Sylvester, p. 27.
19. Hansard, Vol. 182, col. 1132.
20. *Ibid*. Vol. 182, col. 1133.
21. *Ibid*. Vol. 182, col. 1137.
22. *Ibid*. Vol. 182, col. 1445.
23. *Ibid*. Vol. 182, col. 1459.
24. BL Add. MS 38993, ff. 41–2.
25. Hansard, Vol. 182, col. 2095.
26. *Ibid*. Vol. 182, cols 2096–7.

27. *Ibid.* Vol. 182, col. 2103.

28. *Ibid.* Vol. 182, col. 2107.

29. *Ibid.* Vol. 182, col. 2118.

30. *Ibid.* Vol. 183, col. 89.

31. *Ibid.* Vol. 183, col. 93.

32. *Ibid.* Vol. 183, col. 113.

33. *Ibid.* Vol. 183, col. 131.

34. *Ibid.* Vol. 183, col. 148.

35. *Ibid.* Vol. 183, cols 151–2.

36. Gladstone, *Diaries*, Vol. VI, p. 433.

37. *Ibid.* p. 439.

38. *Ibid.* p. 444.

39. *Ibid.* p. 446.

40. *Ibid.* p. 447.

41. *Ibid.* p. 446.

42. Maxwell, Vol. II, p. 322.

43. *The Times*, 29 June 1866, p. 8.

44. *Ibid.* 20 July 1866, p. 12.

45. Cowling, *1867*, p. 131.

46. *The Times*, 23 July 1866, p. 9.

47. *Ibid.* 24 July 1866, p. 9.

48. *Ibid.* 25 July 1866, p. 8.

49. Cowling, *1867*, p. 31.

50. Mill, *Autobiography*, p. 246.

51. *The Times*, 25 July 1866, p. 5.

52. *Ibid.* 26 July 1866, p. 12.

53. Maxwell, Vol. II, p. 321.

54. Hansard, Vol. 184, col. 1390.

55. *Ibid.* Vol. 184, col. 1401.

56. *Ibid.* Vol. 184, col. 1411.

57. *The Times*, 28 July 1866, p. 9.

58. Hawkins, Vol. II, p. 315.

59. Mill, *Later*, Vol. II, p. 655.

60. Hansard, Vol. 185, col. 6.

61. *Ibid.* Vol. 185, col. 215.

62. *Ibid.* Vol. 185, col. 243.

63. Roberts, p. 91.

64. Cecil, Vol. I, pp. 233–4.

65. Roberts, p. 89.

66. Briggs, *People*, p. 272.

67. Hawkins, Vol. II, p. 337.

68. Hansard, Vol. 185, col. 966.

69. Cecil, Vol. I, p. 237.

70. Hansard, Vol. 186, cols 42–3.

71. BL Add. MS 44133, f. 107.

72. Gardiner, Vol. I, p. 177.

73. Cecil, Vol. I, p. 255.

74. Reid, *MM*, Vol. II, pp. 174–5.

75. *The Times*, 2 May 1867, p. 7.

76. *Ibid.* 20 April 1867, p. 9.

77. *Ibid.* 26 April 1867, p. 12.

78. BL Add. MS 44118, f. 229.

79. *The Times*, 2 May 1867, p. 7.

80. *Ibid.* 6 May 1867, p. 9.

81. Cowling, *1867*, p. 42.

82. *The Times*, 7 May 1867, p. 9.

83. Cowling, *1867*, p. 46.

84. Gladstone, *Diaries*, Vol. VI, p. 536.

85. Hansard (Lords), Vol. 189, col. 952.

86. A&C, Vol. I, p. 423.

87. BL Add. MS 44118, f. 234.

88. Fulford, *YDL*, p. 174.

89. Cecil, Vol. I, p. 291.

90. M&B, Vol. IV, p. 557.

91. Blake, p. 487.

92. Blake, pp. 500–501.

93. Eliot, *Holt*, p. 139.

94. *Ibid.* pp. 185–6.

95. Hansard, Vol. 194, col. 1499.

96. Cross, p. 12.

97. Hansard, Vol. 194, col. 1504.

98. *Ibid.* Vol. 200, col. 12.

99. *Ibid.* Vol. 205, col. 1053.

100. *Ibid.* Vol. 207, col. 561.

101. *Ibid.* Vol. 207, col. 774.

102. BL Add. MS 44300, ff. 56–9.

103. Hansard, Vol. 211, col. 1450.

104. *Ibid.* Vol. 211, col. 1455.

105. *Ibid.* Vol. 211, col. 1460.

106. Cecil, Vol. II, p. 25.

107. *Ibid.* p. 26.

108. Hansard, Vol. 212, col. 350.

109. BL Add. MS 44541, f. 147.

110. BL Add. MS 44541, f. 148.

Chapter 12: Broadening Minds (page 412)

1. Hansard, Vol. 188, cols 1548–9.

2. Sylvester, p. 120.

3. Briggs, *People*, p. 256.

4. *The Times*, 24 November 1860, p. 8.

5. Hansard, Vol. 155, col. 329.

6. Gash, p. 228.

7. Hansard, Vol. 125, col. 1148.

8. Shrosbree, p. 45.

9. Dickens, *Letters*, Vol. VI, pp. 752–3.
10. Winter, p. 174.
11. Hansard, Vol. 138, col. 1803.
12. *Ibid.* Vol. 138, col. 1804.
13. *Ibid.* Vol. 164, cols 700–1.
14. Newcastle, Vol. I, p. 7.
15. *Ibid.* p. 36.
16. *Ibid.* p. 37.
17. *Ibid.* p. 45.
18. *Ibid.* p. 72.
19. *Ibid.* p. 204.
20. *Ibid.* p. 205.
21. *Ibid.* pp. 215–6.
22. *Ibid.* p. 91.
23. *Ibid.* p. 93.
24. *Ibid.* p. 93.
25. *Ibid.* pp. 82–3.
26. *Ibid.* p. 85.
27. *Ibid.* p. 101.
28. *Ibid.* p. 107.
29. *Ibid.* p. 149.
30. *Ibid.* p. 165.
31. *Ibid.* p. 169.
32. *Ibid.* p. 89.
33. *Ibid.* p. 273.
34. *Ibid.* p. 273.
35. *Ibid.* p. 274.
36. *Saturday Review*, 3 December 1864, p. 683.
37. Newcastle, Vol. I, p. 356.
38. *Ibid.* pp. 374–5.
39. *Ibid.* p. 384.
40. *Ibid.* pp. 409–10.
41. *Ibid.* p. 411.
42. *Ibid.* p. 413.
43. *Ibid.* p. 414.
44. Hansard, Vol. 164, col. 720.
45. *Ibid.* Vol. 164, col. 722.
46. *Ibid.* Vol 164, col. 753.
47. Winter, p. 176.
48. Hansard, Vol. 164, col. 736.
49. Winter, p. 178.
50. *Ibid.* p. 178.
51. *Fraser's Magazine*, March 1862, p. 347.
52. *Ibid.* p. 348.
53. *Ibid.* p. 349.
54. *Ibid.* p. 351.
55. *Ibid.* p. 354.
56. *Ibid.* p. 358.
57. *Ibid.* p. 360.
58. *Ibid.* p. 365.
59. Arnold, *Reports*, p. 97.
60. *Ibid.* p. 99.
61. *Ibid.* p. 104.
62. *Ibid.* p. 110.
63. *Ibid.* p. 111.
64. Sylvester, p. 100.
65. BL Add. MS 44404, ff. 126–7.
66. Sylvester, p. 91.
67. *Ibid.* p. 161.
68. *Ibid.* p. 164.
69. Weir, [Pamphlet] pp. 5–14.
70. Winter, p. 169.
71. *Ibid.* p. 171.
72. BL Add. MS 44536, f. 137.
73. Hansard, Vol. 194, col. 1359.
74. *Ibid.* Vol. 194, col. 1361.
75. *Ibid.* Vol. 194, col. 1367.
76. *Ibid.* Vol. 194, col. 1373.
77. *Ibid.* Vol. 194, col. 1382.
78. *Ibid.* Vol. 196, col. 1761.
79. *Ibid.* Vol. 196, col. 1763.
80. *Ibid.* Vol. 199, col. 2.
81. BL Add. MS 43897, f. 12.
82. A&C, Vol. I, p. 393.
83. *Ibid.* p. 394.
84. BL Add. MS 44611, ff. 99–102.
85. BL Add. MS 43513, f. 282.
86. Mill, *Later*, Vol. III, p. 1348.
87. *Ibid.* Vol. I, p. 80.
88. Hansard, Vol. 199, col. 440.
89. *Ibid.* Vol. 199, col. 441.
90. *Ibid.* Vol. 199, col. 442.
91. *Ibid.* Vol. 199, col. 443.
92. *Ibid.* Vol. 199, col. 458.
93. *Ibid.* Vol. 199, col. 455.
94. *Ibid.* Vol. 199, col. 459.
95. *Ibid.* Vol. 199, col. 464.
96. *Ibid.* Vol. 199, col. 465.
97. Garvin, p. 109.
98. Gardiner, Vol. I, p. 216.
99. Hansard, Vol. 199, col. 2065.
100. Reid, Vol. I, pp. 490–1.
101. BL Add. MS 44301, f. 146.
102. Hansard, Vol. 202, cols 284–5.
103. *Ibid.* Vol. 202, col. 286.

104. *Ibid*. Vol. 202, col. 287.
105. *Ibid*. Vol. 202, col. 290.
106. *Ibid*. Vol. 202, col. 503.
107. *Ibid*. Vol. 202, col. 595.
108. BL Add. MS 44335, ff. 23–4.
109. Hansard, Vol. 203, col. 749.
110. *Ibid*. Vol. 203, col. 845.
111. BL Add. MS 44617, ff. 14–15.
112. BL Add. MS 44617, ff. 22–3.
113. Morley, *Compromise*, p. 113.
114. *Macmillan's Magazine*, February 1861, p. 294.
115. *Ibid*. p. 298.
116. *Ibid*. p. 299.
117. Hansard, Vol. 175, col. 108.
118. Rhodes James, p. 177.
119. A&C, Vol. I, p. 177.
120. *Ibid*. p. 184.
121. Clarendon, Vol. I, p. 1.
122. *Ibid*. p. 6.
123. *Ibid*. p. 11.
124. *Ibid*. p. 13.
125. *Ibid*. p. 14.
126. *Ibid*. p. 75.
127. *Ibid*. p. 85.
128. *Ibid*. Vol. III, p. 114.
129. *Ibid*. p. 350.
130. *Ibid*. Vol. IV, p. 19.
131. *Ibid*. p. 170.
132. *Ibid*. Vol. I, p. 17.
133. *Ibid*. p. 24.
134. *Ibid*. p. 26.
135. *Ibid*. p. 91.
136. *Ibid*. p. 95.
137. *Ibid*. p. 97.
138. *Ibid*. Vol. III, p. 177.
139. *Ibid*. p. 176.
140. *Ibid*. p. 180.
141. *Ibid*. p. 73.
142. *Ibid*. p. 74.
143. *Ibid*. p. 100.
144. *Ibid*. Vol. I, p. 146.
145. *Ibid*. Vol. III, p. 345.
146. *Ibid*. Vol. I, p. 38.
147. *Ibid*. p. 42.
148. *Ibid*. p. 42.
149. *Ibid*. p. 43.
150. *Ibid*. p. 109.

151. *Ibid*. p. 259.
152. *Ibid*. p. 44.
153. *Ibid*. Vol. III, p. 485.
154. *Ibid*. Vol. I, p. 153.
155. *Ibid*. p. 221.
156. *Ibid*. Vol. IV, p. 64.
157. H&I, p. 189.
158. Clarendon, Vol. I, p. 44.
159. *Ibid*. p. 56.
160. Bibby, *Scientist*, p. 166.
161. Hansard, Vol. 175, col. 107.
162. *Ibid*. Vol. 175, col. 108.
163. *Ibid*. Vol. 175, col. 122.
164. *Ibid*. Vol. 175, col. 129.
165. *Ibid*. Vol. 175, cols 132–3.
166. *Ibid*. Vol. 175, cols 133–4.
167. *Ibid*. Vol. 175, col. 135.
168. BL Add. MS 44754, ff. 162–3.
169. Hansard, Vol. 175, cols 139–40.
170. *Ibid*. Vol. 175, col. 714.
171. *Ibid*. Vol. 175, cols 716–7.
172. BL Add. MS 44395, f. 97.
173. Hansard, Vol. 175, col. 1242.
174. *Ibid*. Vol. 177, col. 856.
175. *Ibid*. Vol. 177, col. 877.
176. BL Add. MS 44133, f. 86.
177. BL Add. MS 44392, ff. 109–10.
178. BL Add. MS 44395, ff. 174–5.
179. BL Add. MS 44392, ff. 109–10.
180. Arnold, *Eton*, p. 1.
181. BL Add. MS 44403, ff. 107–8.
182. Sylvester, p. 173.
183. Arnold, *Eton*, pp. 2–3.
184. *Ibid*. p. 4.
185. *Ibid*. p. 62.
186. *Ibid*. pp. 4–5.
187. *Ibid*. pp. 37–8.
188. *Ibid*. p. 41.
189. *Ibid*. p. 44.
190. *Ibid*. p. 47.
191. *Ibid*. p. 51.
192. *Ibid*. pp. 62–3.
193. *Ibid*. p. 69.
194. Kingsley, *W-B*, p. 4.
195. Sylvester, p. 173.
196. Arnold, *Eton*, pp. 80–81.
197. *Ibid*. p. 83.
198. *Ibid*. p. 99.

199. *Ibid.* p. 108.
200. *Ibid.* p. 114.
201. *Ibid.* p. 126.

Chapter 13: The End of Privilege (page 469)

1. N-T, p. 5.
2. Burn, p. 141.
3. *Ibid.* p. 142.
4. *Ibid.* p. 143.
5. *Ibid.* p. 144.
6. Quoted in a Cork University project at http://multitext.ucc.ie/d/ Charles_Edward_Trevelyan.
7. N-T, p. 3.
8. *Ibid.* p. 4.
9. *Ibid.* p. 8.
10. *Ibid.* p. 9.
11. *Ibid.* p. 17.
12. Briggs, *People*, p. 109.
13. BL Add. MS 44118, ff. 60–61.
14. BL Add. MS 44743, ff. 132–4.
15. BL Add. MS 44334, f. 61.
16. BL Add. MS 44334, f. 181.
17. BL Add. MS 44334, f. 183.
18. N-T, p. 11.
19. BL Add. MS 44334, f. 192–3.
20. BL Add. MS 44334, f. 208.
21. BL Add. MS 44334, f. 213.
22. Dickens, *LD*, p. 541. 'Father-in-law' was the contemporary term for 'stepfather'.
23. Trollope, *TC*, p. 4.
24. *Ibid.* p. 126.
25. BL Add. MS 44301, f. 104.
26. BL Add. MS 44537, f. 149.
27. BL Add. MS 44617, f. 37.
28. Sylvester, p. 202.
29. BL Add. MS 44617, f. 38.
30. BL Add. MS 44617, f. 40.
31. Hansard, Vol. 204, col. 339.
32. BL Add. MS 44334, f. 223.
33. BL Add. MS 45801, ff. 141–4.
34. BL Add. MS 45801, ff. 141–4.
35. BL MS Add. 44119, f. 50.
36. BL MS Add. 44119, ff. 96–7.
37. BL MS Add. 44334, f. 230.
38. BL MS Add. 44334, f. 226.
39. BL MS Add. 44334, f. 230.
40. BL MS Add. 44335, ff. 10–11.
41. BL MS Add. 44335, f. 15.
42. BL MS Add. 44335, ff. 16–17.
43. BL MS Add. 44617, f. 60.
44. BL MS Add. 44759, f. 169.
45. Gladstone, *Diaries*, Vol. VII, p. 376.
46. BL MS Add. 44539, f. 140.
47. http://www.cwreenactors. com/~crimean/purchsys.htm.
48. BL MS Add. 44119, ff. 212–14.
49. BL MS Add. 44119, ff. 224–5.
50. BL MS Add. 44617, f. 67.
51. BL MS Add. 44617, f. 45.
52. BL MS Add. 44617, f. 47.
53. Hansard, Vol. 204, col. 590.
54. *Ibid.* Vol. 204, col. 593.
55. *Ibid.* Vol. 204, col. 1411.
56. *Ibid.* Vol. 204, col. 1412.
57. *Ibid.* Vol. 205, col. 123.
58. *Ibid.* Vol. 205, col. 137.
59. *Ibid.* Vol. 205, col. 254.
60. BL Add. MS 44760, f. 15.
61. BL Add. MS 44760, f. 17.
62. Hansard, Vol. 206, col. 406.
63. *Ibid.* Vol. 206, col. 414.
64. Gladstone, *Diaries*, Vol. VII, p. 501.
65. BL Add. MS 44119, ff. 239–40.
66. BL Add. MS 44617, ff. 1–6.
67. BL Add. MS 44617, f. 7.
68. BL Add. MS 44431, ff. 106–7.
69. BL Add. MS 44431, ff. 132–3.
70. BL Add. MS 44760, ff. 53–4.
71. BL Add. MS 44540, f. 68.
72. BL Add. MS 44760, ff. 55–6.
73. BL Add. MS 44760, f. 56.
74. BL Add. MS 44760, f. 58.
75. BL Add. MS 44760, f. 59.
76. BL Add. MS 44760, ff. 61–2.
77. Hansard, Vol. 207, col. 1550.
78. *Ibid.* Vol. 207, col. 1690.
79. *Ibid.* Vol. 207, col. 1690.
80. *Ibid.* Vol. 207, col. 1693.
81. *Ibid.* Vol. 207, col. 1694.
82. Fulford, *DC*, p. 222, for example.

83. Fulford, *YDL*, p. 248.
84. Fulford, *DC*, p. 29.
85. *Ibid*. p. 162.
86. *Ibid*. p. 242.
87. *Ibid*. p. 251.
88. BL Add. MS 44439, ff. 227–8.
89. BL Add. MS 44617, f. 159.
90. BL Add. MS 38995, f. 371.
91. Hansard, Vol. 194, col. 1042.
92. BL Add. MS 44424, ff. 93–6.
93. BL Add. MS 44424, f. 224.
94. BL Add. MS 44424, f. 247.
95. BL Add. MS 44157, f. 7.
96. Hansard, Vol. 201, col. 1194.
97. *Ibid*. Vol. 201, col. 1195.
98. *Ibid*. Vol. 201, col. 1204.
99. *Ibid*. Vol. 201, col. 1211.
100. *Ibid*. Vol. 201, col. 1234.
101. *Ibid*. Vol. 201, col. 1244.
102. *Ibid*. Vol. 201, col. 1249.
103. *Ibid*. Vol. 204, col. 512.
104. *Ibid*. Vol. 205, col. 41.
105. *Ibid*. Vol. 205, col. 42.
106. *Ibid*. Vol. 206, col. 358.
107. *Ibid*. Vol. 206, col. 360.
108. *Ibid*. Vol. 206, col. 604.
109. *Ibid*. Vol. 206, col. 706.
110. A&C, Vol. II, p. 25.
111. Anon., p. 5.
112. Anon., p. 6.

Chapter 14: The Rights of Women (page 506)

1. Burn, p. 31.
2. Eliot, *Holt*, p. 96.
3. *The Times*, 2 September 1853, p. 8.
4. Chedzoy, p. 119.
5. *The Times*, 29 August 1838, p. 5.
6. *Quarterly Review of Jurisprudence*, Vol. XXI, p. 145.
7. Norton, p. 69.
8. *The Times*, 19 August 1853, p. 10.
9. *Ibid*. 20 August 1853, p. 8.
10. *Ibid*. 24 August 1853, p. 7.
11. *Ibid*. 2 September 1853, p. 8.
12. Hansard, Vol. 68, col. 1244.
13. Norton, p. 3.
14. *Ibid*. p. 4.
15. *Ibid*. p. 13.
16. *Ibid*. p. 14.
17. *Ibid*. p. 17.
18. *Ibid*. p. 59.
19. *Ibid*. p. 65.
20. *The Times*, 28 January 1857, p. 7.
21. Hansard, Vol. 144, col. 1687.
22. *Ibid*. Vol. 144, col. 1707.
23. *Ibid*. Vol. 146, col. 210.
24. *Ibid*. Vol. 146, col. 228.
25. *Ibid*. Vol. 147, col. 380.
26. *Ibid*. Vol. 147, col. 383.
27. *Ibid*. Vol. 147, col. 385.
28. *Ibid*. Vol. 147, col. 389.
29. *Ibid*. Vol. 147, col. 392.
30. *Ibid*. Vol. 147, col. 393.
31. *Ibid*. Vol. 147, col. 394.
32. *Ibid*. Vol. 147, col. 412.
33. *Ibid*. Vol. 147, col. 723.
34. *Ibid*. Vol. 147, col. 742.
35. *Ibid*. Vol. 147, col. 743.
36. *Ibid*. Vol. 147, cols 828–9.
37. *Ibid*. Vol. 147, col. 832.
38. *Ibid*. Vol. 147, cols 853–4.
39. *Ibid*. Vol. 147, cols 885–6.
40. *Ibid*. Vol. 147, col. 1028.
41. *Ibid*. Vol. 147, col. 1031.
42. *Ibid*. Vol. 147, col. 1230.
43. *Ibid*. Vol. 147, col. 1270.
44. *Ibid*. Vol. 147, col. 1271.
45. *Ibid*. Vol. 147, col. 1272.
46. *Ibid*. Vol. 147, col. 1273.
47. *Ibid*. Vol. 147, col. 1276.
48. *Ibid*. Vol. 147, col. 1277.
49. *Ibid*. Vol. 147, col. 1557.
50. *Ibid*. Vol. 201, col. 194.
51. *Ibid*. Vol. 201, col. 195.
52. *Ibid*. Vol. 201, col. 197.
53. *Ibid*. Vol. 201, col. 198.
54. *Ibid*. Vol. 201, cols 211–12.
55. *Ibid*. Vol. 201, col. 213.
56. *Ibid*. Vol. 201, col. 216.
57. *Ibid*. Vol. 201, cols 220–21.
58. *Ibid*. Vol. 201, col. 231.
59. *Ibid*. Vol. 201, col. 232.
60. *Ibid*. Vol. 201, col. 611.
61. *Ibid*. Vol. 201, col. 612.
62. *Ibid*. Vol. 201, col. 614.
63. *Ibid*. Vol. 201, col. 619.

64. *Ibid.* Vol. 201, col. 620.
65. Bibby, *Scientist,* p. 67.
66. *Ibid.* p. 68.
67. *Ibid.* p. 69.
68. BL Add. MS 45787, f. 34.
69. BL Add. MS 45787, f. 2.
70. BL Add. MS 45787, f. 7.
71. BL Add. MS 45787, f. 36.
72. BL Add. MS 45787, f. 38.
73. BL Add. MS 45787, f. 39.
74. BL Add. MS 45787, f. 40.
75. BL Add. MS 45787, f. 41.
76. BL Add. MS 45787, f. 43.
77. BL Add. MS 45801, f. 148.
78. BL Add. MS 45787, f. 11.
79. BL Add. MS 45787, f. 18.
80. Mill, *Later,* Vol. IV, p. 1917.
81. Hansard, Vol. 223, col. 419.
82. *Ibid.* Vol. 223, col. 432.
83. *Ibid.* Vol. 223, col. 437.
84. *Ibid.* Vol. 223, col. 450.
85. *Ibid.* Vol. 223, col. 453.
86. *Ibid.* Vol. 223, col. 460.
87. Mill, *Later,* Vol. IV, p. 1681.
88. *Ibid.* p. 1688.
89. Hansard, Vol. 195, col. 762.
90. *Ibid.* Vol. 195, col. 764.
91. *Ibid.* Vol. 195, col. 771.
92. *Ibid.* Vol. 195, col. 774.
93. *Ibid.* Vol. 199, col. 285.
94. *Ibid.* Vol. 201, col. 882.
95. *Ibid.* Vol. 201, col. 887.
96. BC RF/104/2/21.
97. BC RF/103/3/2.
98. BC RF/103/3/18.
99. BC RF/103/3/4.
100. BC RF/103/3/12.
101. BC RF/104/1/37.
102. BC RF/103/14.
103. BC RF/103/14/7.
104. BC RF/103/14/11.
105. BC RF/104/2/25.
106. BC RF/104/2/41–2.
107. BC RF/104/2/34–6.
108. BC RF/104/1/117.
109. BC RF/103/14/15.
110. BC RF/104/1/90.
111. BC RF 104/2/36–7.
112. BC RF 104/2/41.
113. BC RF 104/2/45.
114. BC RF/104/2/42.
115. Sylvester, p. 101.
116. Stephen, B., p. 34.
117. Arnold, *Letters,* Vol. II, pp. 360 and 387.
118. Sutherland, p. 85.
119. Stephen, B., p. 217.
120. *Ibid.* p. 173.
121. *Ibid.* p. 175.
122. *The Times,* 10 October 1868, p. 8.
123. Stephen, B., p. 173.
124. Sidgwick, pp. 39–40.
125. *Ibid.* p. 63.
126. *Ibid.* pp. 30–31.
127. *Ibid.* p. 40.
128. *Ibid.* p. 22.
129. *Ibid.* p. 33.
130. *Ibid.* p. 76.
131. Hansard, Vol. 219, cols 1526–7.
132. *Ibid.* Vol. 219, col. 1545.
133. *Ibid.* Vol. 219, cols 1535–6.
134. Stephen, B., p. 61.
135. *Ibid.* pp. 63–4.
136. *Ibid.* p. 66.
137. *Ibid.* p. 80.
138. Hansard, Vol. 226, col. 270.
139. Bostridge, p. 66.
140. Clough, *Letters,* Vol. II, p. 506.
141. BL Add. MS 45801, f. 102.
142. BL Add. MS 45787, f. 1.
143. BL Add. MS 45787, f. 2.
144. BL Add. MS 45787, f. 7.
145. BL Add. MS 45787, f. 14.
146. BL Add. MS 45787, f. 14.
147. BL Add. MS 45787, ff. 15–16.
148. BL Add. MS 45787, f. 44.
149. BL Add. MS 45787, ff. 36–7.
150. BL Add. MS 45801, f. 170.
151. BL Add. MS 45801, ff. 191–2.
152. BL Add. MS 45807, f. 229.
153. BL Add. MS 44404, ff. 102–3.
154. Mill, *Autobiography,* p. 225.
155. *Ibid.* p. 207.
156. Bostridge, p. 372.
157. Mill, *Subjection,* ch. 3.
158. *Ibid.* p. 1.
159. *Ibid.* p. 19.
160. *Ibid.* p. 36.

161. *Ibid.* p. 6.
162. *Ibid.* p. 12.
163. *Ibid.* p. 32.
164. *Ibid.* p. 33.
165. *Ibid.* p. 35.
166. *Ibid.* p. 14.
167. *Ibid.* p. 30.
168. *Ibid.* p. 21.
169. *Ibid.* p. 86.
170. *Ibid.* p. 53.
171. *Ibid.* p. 57.
172. *Ibid.* p. 61.
173. *Ibid.* p. 105.
174. *Ibid.* p. 101.
175. *Ibid.* p. 103.
176. BL Add. MS 44536, f. 170.
177. Hansard, Vol. 219, cols 396–7.
178. *Ibid.* Vol. 219, col. 398.

Part iv: The Birth of the Modern

Chapter 15: The Pursuit of Perfection (page 577)

1. Heffer, p. 358.
2. Froude, *Carlyle*, Vol. IV, p. 350.
3. Smith, p. 36.
4. Carlyle, *Works*, Vol. XX, p. 315ff.
5. *Ibid.* Vol. XXX, p. 1.
6. *Ibid.* p. 3.
7. *Ibid.* p. 4.
8. *Ibid.* p. 9.
9. *Ibid.* p. 10.
10. *Ibid.* p. 11.
11. *Ibid.* p. 12.
12. *Ibid.* p. 13.
13. *Ibid.* p. 15.
14. *Ibid.* p. 30.
15. *Ibid.* p. 31.
16. *Ibid.* p. 39.
17. *Ibid.* p. 41.
18. *Ibid.* p. 44.
19. *Ibid.* p. 47.
20. UL Add. 7349 2/19/29.
21. Smith, p. 16.
22. UL Add. 7349 1/8/13.
23. UL Add. 7349 1/11/1.
24. UL Add. 7349 1/11/2.
25. UL Add. 7349 1/11/3.
26. UL Add. 7349 1/11/4.
27. UL Add. 7349 1/11/6–7.
28. UL Add. 7349 1/11/8.
29. Smith, p. 147.
30. UL Add. 7349 1/8/16–17.
31. UL Add. 7349 1/8/57.
32. UL Add. 7349 (c) 1/8/3–5.
33. UL Add. 7349 (c) 1/8/20.
34. UL Add. 7349 (c) 1/8/24.
35. Mill, CW, Vol. XIX, p. 338; *ibid.* Vol. II, p. 146.
36. UL Add. 7349 1/7a/64.
37. Stephen, p. 4.
38. *Ibid.* p. 5.
39. Morley, *Recollections*, Vol. I, p. 55.
40. Stephen, p. 53.
41. *Ibid.* p. 54.
42. *Ibid.* p. 221.
43. *Ibid.* p. 240 (fn).
44. *Ibid.* p. 226.
45. *Ibid.* p. 81.
46. *Ibid.* p. 259.
47. *Ibid.* p. 58.
48. *Ibid.* p. 70.
49. *Ibid.* p. 71.
50. *Ibid.* p. 103.
51. *Ibid.* p. 110.
52. *Ibid.* p. 137.
53. *Ibid.* p. 138.
54. *Ibid.* p. 207.
55. *Ibid.* pp. 210–11.
56. *Ibid.* p. 212.
57. UL Add. 7349 1/7a/80.
58. UL Add. 7349 1/7a/82.
59. UL Add. 7349 1/7a/83.
60. UL Add. 7349 (c) 1/8/36.
61. Arnold, *Letters*, Vol. III, p. 58.
62. Trilling, (Preface), p. xv.
63. Arnold, *Essays 1*, p. 17.
64. *Ibid.* p. 21.
65. *Ibid.* p. 23.
66. *Ibid.* p. 24.
67. *Ibid.* p. 25.
68. *Ibid.* p. 26.
69. *Ibid.* p. 38.
70. Butler, *Note-Books*, p. 107.
71. S&S, p. 4.
72. *Ibid.* pp. 41–2.

73 *Ibid.* p. 43.
74. *Ibid.* p. 45.
75. *Ibid.* p. 51.
76. *Ibid.* p. 61.
77. *Ibid.* p. 68.
78. *Ibid.* p. 69.
79. *Ibid.* pp. 69–70.
80. *Ibid.* pp. 74–5.
81. Arnold, *C&A*, p. 6.
82. *Ibid.* pp. 18–19.
83. *Ibid.* p. 22.
84. *Ibid.* p. 23.
85. *Ibid.* p. 29.
86. *Ibid.* p. 30.
87. *Ibid.* p. 41.
88. *Ibid.* p. 43.
89. *Ibid.* pp. 44–5.
90. *Ibid.* p. 46.
91. *Ibid.* p. 47.
92. *Ibid.* p. 49.
93. *Ibid.* p. 52.
94. *Ibid.* p. 54.
95. *Ibid.* p. 59.
96. *Ibid.* p. 63.
97.·*Ibid.* p. 64.
98. *Ibid.* p. 65.
99. *Ibid.* p. 69
100. *Ibid.* p. 73.
101. *Ibid.* p. 75.
102. *Ibid.* pp. 76–7.
103. *Ibid.* p. 82.
104. *Ibid.* p. 90.
105. *Ibid.* p. 102.
106. *Ibid.* p. 104.
107. *Ibid.* p. 105.
108. *Ibid.* p. 108.
109. *Ibid.* p. 109.
110. *Ibid.* p. 134.
111. *Ibid.* p. 142.
112. *Ibid.* p. 145.
113. *Ibid.* p. 147.
114. *Ibid.* pp. 147–8.
115. *Ibid.* pp. 192–3.
116. *Ibid.* p. 203.
117. Arnold, *Letters*, Vol. III, p. 273.
118. Arnold, *C&A*, p. 205.
119. *Ibid.* p. 210.
120. *Ibid.* p. 212.

121. Trilling, p. 252.
122. Arnold, Letters, Vol. III, p. 448.
123. Morley, *Recollections*, I, p. 131.
124. Arnold, *Letters*, Vol. III, p. 449.
125. *Macmillan's Magazine*, March 1868, p. 367.
126. *Ibid.* p. 368.
127. *Ibid.* p. 369.
128. *Ibid.* p. 371.
129. *Ibid.* p. 372.
130. *Ibid.* p. 373.
131. *Ibid.* p. 374.
132. *Ibid.* p. 375.
133. Lutyens, pp. 20–21.
134. La Touche, p. 159.
135. Ruskin, *Diaries*, Vol. I, p. v.
136. Ruskin, *Last*, p. 110.
137. *Ibid.* p. 111.
138. *Ibid.* p. 112.
139. *Ibid.* p. 142.
140. *Ibid.* p. 146.
141. *Ibid.* p. 160.
142. *Ibid.* p. 161.
143. Ruskin, *T&T*, (Preface), pp. ix–x.
144. *Ibid.* p. 138.
145. *Ibid.* pp. 18–19.
146. *Ibid.* p. 87.
147. *Ibid.* p. 116.
148. *Ibid.* p. 118.
149. *Ibid.* p. 130.
150. Ruskin, *Crown*, p. 173.
151. *Ibid.* p. 174.
152. *Ibid.* p. 175.
153. *Ibid.* p. 177.
154. *Ibid.* p. 178.
155. *Ibid.* p. 181.
156. *Ibid.* p. 182.
157. *Ibid.* p. 185.
158. *Ibid.* p. 186.
159. *Ibid.* p. 188.
160. Ruskin, *Praeterita*, Vol. I, p. 1.
161. Ruskin, *Diaries*, Vol. III, p. 821.
162. UL Add. 7349 (c) 1/8/11.
163. Stephen, p. 194.
164. *Ibid.* p. 195.
165. *Ibid.* p. 196.
166. Fawcett, [Pamphlet] p. 5.
167. *Ibid.* p. 7.

168. *Ibid.* p. 9.
169. *Ibid.* p. 11.
170. *Ibid.* pp. 11–12.
171. *Ibid.* p. 13.
172. *Ibid.* pp. 13–14.
173. *Ibid.* pp. 14–15.
174. Hansard, Vol. 81, cols 1413–14.
175. *The Times*, 14 November 1849, p. 4.
176. *Ibid.* 19 November 1849, p. 5.
177. Hansard, Vol. 173, col. 941.
178. Dickens, *Letters*, Vol. X, p. 361.
179. Hansard, Vol. 173, col. 942.
180. *Ibid.* Vol. 173, col. 948.
181. *Ibid.* Vol. 173, col. 952.
182. *Ibid.* Vol. 174, cols 2056–7.
183. *The Times*, 14 November 1864, p. 10.
184. *Ibid.* 15 November 1864, p. 9.
185. Briggs, *People*, p. 5.
186. Mill, *Later*, Vol. III, p. 987.
187. *Ibid.* Vol. II, p. 713.
188. Hansard (Lords), Vol. 183, col. 241.
189. *Ibid.* Vol. 183, col. 242.
190. *Ibid.* Vol. 183, col. 243.
191. *Ibid.* Vol. 183, col. 257.

Chapter 16: Doing Good (page 632)

1. Webb, p. 155.
2. Mowat, p. 5.
3. Dickens, *OMF*, p. 779.
4. Dickens, *Letters*, Vol. VII, p. 367.
5. Dickens, *OMF*, pp. 95–6.
6. Healey, p. 198.
7. *Ibid.* p. 173.
8. Hartley, p. 25.
9. Healey, p. 66.
10. Forster, Vol. I, p. 282.
11. Healey, p. 116.
12. http://www.themorgan.org/collections/works/dickens/letter?page=7.
13. http://www.themorgan.org/collections/works/dickens/letter?page=8.
14. http://www.themorgan.org/collections/works/dickens/letter?page=9.
15. http://www.themorgan.org/collections/works/dickens/letter?page=10.
16. http://www.themorgan.org/collections/works/dickens/letter?page=11.
17. http://www.themorgan.org/collections/works/dickens/letter?page=12.
18. http://www.themorgan.org/collections/works/dickens/letter?page=14.
19. Healey, p. 98.
20. Hartley, p. 59.
21. Dickens, *Letters*, Vol. VI, p. 83.
22. http://www.themorgan.org/collections/works/dickens/letter?page=30.
23. http://www.themorgan.org/collections/works/dickens/letter?page=30.
24. Healey, p. 99.
25. http://www.themorgan.org/collections/works/dickens/letter?page=22.
26. http://www.themorgan.org/collections/works/dickens/letter?page=28.
27. http://www.themorgan.org/collections/works/dickens/letter?page=32.
28. http://www.themorgan.org/collections/works/dickens/letter?page=36.
29. Dickens, *Letters*, Vol. VI, p. 29.
30. *Ibid.* p. 323.
31. Healey, pp. 117–8.
32. Dickens, *Letters*, Vol. VI, p. 752.
33. *The Times*, 3 January 1857, p. 7.
34. BL Add. MS 44430, f. 179.
35. Healey claims that Burdett-Coutts was the first woman to be recognised in this way, but that is not so. One earlier example from the nineteenth century is the Rayleigh barony, created for the wife of a Member of Parliament by George IV in 1821. Burdett-Coutts was the first to be ennobled for her own, as opposed to her husband's, deeds.
36. Healey, p. 177.
37. BL Add. MS 44300, f. 19.
38. *The Times*, 19 January 1865, p. 6.
39. Forster, Vol. II, p. 193.
40. *Ibid.* p. 198.
41. Tomalin, p. 396.
42. Wagner, p. 33.
43. http://www.barnardos.org.uk/barnardo_s_history.pdf.
44. Wagner, p. 35.
45. *Ibid.* p. 55.
46. *Ibid.* p. 81.
47. *The Times*, 20 July 1876, p. 10.

48. http://www.barnardos.org.uk/
barnardo_s_christian_heritage.pdf.
49. *The Times*, 19 October 1877, p. 6.
50. Booth, (Preface), p. i.
51. See Frank Prochaska's article on
Booth in the *Dictionary of National
Biography*, http://www.oxforddnb.
com/view/article/31968?docPos=4.
52. Booth, p. 23.
53. Balgarnie, p. 98.
54. *Ibid.* p. 174.
55. Curl, p. 102.
56. Balgarnie, pp. 64–5.
57. JL&S, p. 72ff.
58. Taken from 'Rules for Living in
Saltaire Village', available from
Saltaire.
59. Dickens, *ED*, p. 176.
60. Mowat, p. 1.
61. *Ibid.* p. 2.
62. *Ibid.* p. 59.
63. *Ibid.* p. 25.
64. *Ibid.* p. 53.
65. *Ibid.* p. 54.
66. *Ibid.* p. 26.
67. *Ibid.* p. 35.
68. *Ibid.* p. 36.
69. *Ibid.* p. 37.
70. Cook, Vol. II, p. 119.
71. Ruskin, *T&T*, pp. 175–6.
72. Darley, p. 91.
73. Mowat, p. 25.
74. Darley, p. 115.
75. Ruskin, *Fors*, Vol. IV, p. 88.
76. Darley, p. 193. This passage was posthumously excised from *Fors*.
77. Cook, Vol. II, p. 397.
78. The excised correspondence is to be
found in full at http://www.pseudo-
podium.org/repress/
ForsClavigera/86.html.
79. *Ibid.* p. 396.
80. RHC RF/103.
81. See image at http://www.fulltable.
com/vts/h/holl/10.jpg.
82. Harrison-Barbet, p. 22.
83. *Ibid.* p. 44.
84. RHC GB/130/1/77–8.
85. Gladstone, *Diaries*, Vol. VIII, p. 341.

86. RHC GB/130/1/101.
87. RHC GB/130/1/166.
88. RHC GB/130/1/167.
89. RHC GB/131/50/1.
90. RHC GB/130/1/178.
91. Harrison-Barbet, p. 51.
92. RHC GB/130/1/181.
93. RHC GB/130/1/202.
94. RHC GB/130/1/231–2.
95. RHC GB/130/1/48.
96. RHC GB/130/1/18–19.
97. RHC GB/130/1/253.
98. RHC GB/130/1/267.
99. RHC GB/131/4/4.
100. *The Times*, 19 December 1883, p. 3.
101. *Ibid.* 28 December 1883, p. 7.
102. *Weekend Telegraph*, 19 March 1965,
p. 27.

Chapter 17: The Way We Live Now (page 691)

1. RC/H/1/B/43.
2. RA/VIC/MAIN/F/25/127.
3. Best, p. 21.
4. Burn, p. 16.
5. Best, p. 167.
6. Finer, p. 93.
7. *Ibid.* p. 161.
8. *Ibid.* p. 210.
9. *Ibid.* p. 213.
10. *Ibid.* p. 223.
11. BL Add. MS 44374, f. 299.
12. Hansard, Vol. 79, col. 330.
13. *Ibid.* Vol. 79, col. 331.
14. Finer, p. 231.
15. Hansard, Vol. 79, col. 332.
16. *Ibid.* Vol. 79, col. 333.
17. *Ibid.* Vol. 79, cols 336–7.
18. *Ibid.* Vol. 79, col. 341.
19. *Ibid.* Vol. 79, col. 345.
20. *Ibid.* Vol. 79, col. 353.
21. *Ibid.* Vol. 79, cols 357–8.
22. Flanders, p. 138.
23. Hansard, Vol. 131, col. 200.
24. *Ibid.* Vol. 131, col. 197.
25. *The Times*, 16 July 1855, p. 12.
26. *Ibid.* 19 July 1855, p. 8.
27. Porter, p. 71.
28. *The Times*, 16 June 1855, p. 5.

29. *Ibid.* 18 June 1855, p. 12.
30. Hansard, Vol. 150, col. 1921.
31. *The Times*, 18 June 1858, p. 12.
32. *Ibid.* Vol. 151, col. 28.
33. *The Times*, 21 June 1858, p. 6.
34. Hansard, Vol. 151, col. 421.
35. *Ibid.* Vol. 151, col. 423.
36. *Ibid.* Vol. 151, col. 430.
37. *The Times*, 22 June 1858, p. 8.
38. *Ibid.* 25 June 1858, p. 9.
39. Hansard, Vol. 151, col. 436.
40. *Ibid.* Vol. 151, col. 440.
41. Greville, Part III, Vol. II, p. 203.
42. BL Add. MS 41299, ff. 17–18.
43. Porter, p. 52.
44. Garvin, p. 54.
45. *Ibid.* pp. 56–7.
46. *Ibid.* p. 92.
47. Clapham, p. 180.
48. Ellis, p. 129.
49. Ruskin, *Lamps*, p. 122.
50. R&A, p. 20.
51. Hansard, Vol. 77, col. 265.
52. *Ibid.* Vol. 79, col. 228.
53. *Ibid.* Vol. 79, col. 1069.
54. *Ibid.* Vol. 78, col. 1214.
55. *Ibid.* Vol. 78, col. 1215.
56. *Ibid.* Vol. 85, col. 593.
57. *Ibid.* Vol. 82, col. 1421.
58. *Ibid.* Vol. 85, col. 1350.
59. Ellis, p. 163.
60. Best, p. 92.
61. Dickens, *LD*, p. 675.
62. Ellis, p. 172.
63. Carlyle, *Reminiscences*, p. 85.
64. Carlyle, *Works*, Vol. XX, p. 256.
65. *Ibid.* p. 264.
66. *Ibid.* p. 266.
67. BL Add. MS 44754, ff. 61–3.
68. BL Add. MS 44404, ff. 226–32.
69. BL Add. MS 44405, f. 23.
70. BL Add. MS 44405, ff. 53–4.

Chapter 18: A Glimpse of the Gothic (page 728)

1. Ruskin, *Lamps*, p. 115.
2. *Ibid.* p. 213.
3. Bloxam, p. 1.
4. Ruskin, *Crown*, p. 83.
5. *Ibid.* p. 84.
6. *Ibid.* p. 88.
7. *Ibid.* p. 89.
8. *Ibid.* pp. 90–91.
9. *Ibid.* p. 96.
10. *Ibid.* p. 97.
11. *London 3*, p. 598.
12. Ridley, p. 518.
13. Hansard, Vol. 147, cols 1296–7.
14. Porter, p. 8ff.
15. Scott, pp. 179–80.
16. *Ibid.* Vol. 147, col. 1302.
17. *Ibid.* Vol. 147, cols 1302–4.
18. *Ibid.* Vol. 147, col. 1305.
19. *Ibid.* Vol. 147, col. 1306.
20. *Ibid.* Vol. 147, col. 1309.
21. *Ibid.* Vol. 147, col. 1311.
22. *The Times*, 26 August 1857, p. 9.
23. Hansard, Vol. 152, cols 262–3.
24. Scott, p. 182.
25. Hansard, Vol. 152, col. 264.
26. *Ibid.* Vol. 152, cols 266–7.
27. *Ibid.* Vol. 152, cols 267–9.
28. *Ibid.* Vol. 152, cols 270–2.
29. Scott, p. 182.
30. *Ibid.* p. 185.
31. BL Add. MS 44392, ff. 66–7.
32. BL Add. MS 48581, ff. 13–14.
33. BL Add. MS 44392, ff. 103–4.
34. Hansard, Vol. 155, cols 920–3.
35. *Ibid.* Vol. 155, cols 926–7. The architect of the towers was actually Nicholas Hawksmoor.
36. *Ibid.* Vol. 155, cols 929–30.
37. *Ibid.* Vol. 155, col. 934.
38. *Ibid.* Vol. 155, col. 937.
39. BL Add. MS 44392, ff. 139–48.
40. Scott, p. 191.
41. *Ibid.* p. 192.
42. *Ibid.* p. 193.
43. *The Times*, 1 November 1859, p. 10.
44. Scott, p. 197.
45. *Ibid.* pp. 197–8.
46. *Ibid.* p. 199.
47. *London 6*, p. 265.
48. BL Add. MS 44433, ff. 6–8.
49. BL Add. MS 44441, ff. 198–9.
50. Bradley, p. 46.
51. *London 4*, p. 363.

52. Brownlee, p. 69.
53. *Ibid.* p. 74.
54. *Ibid.* p. 76.
55. Brownlee, p. 21.
56. Hansard, Vol. 183, col. 184.
57. *Quarterly Review*, July 1867, pp. 49–50.
58. *Ibid.* p. 51.
59. *Ibid.* p. 55.
60. *Ibid.* p. 56.
61. *Ibid.* p. 60.
62. *Ibid.* p. 61.
63. *Ibid.* p. 62.
64. Brownlee, p. 138.
65. Hansard, Vol. 193, col. 330.
66. *The Times*, 19 November 1867, p. 6.
67. *The Times*, 15 June 1868, p. 5.
68. BL Add. MS 38995, ff. 233–4.
69. BL Add. MS 44404, ff. 172–3.
70. BL Add. MS 44415, ff. 237–40.
71. BL Add. MS 38996, f. 3.
72. BL Add. MS 38996, f. 160.
73. BL Add. MS 38996, ff. 162–3.
74. BL Add. MS 38996, f. 164–5.
75. BL Add. MS 38896, f. 186.
76. BL Add. MS 38996, f. 192.
77. BL Add. MS 38996, f. 200.
78. BL Add. MS 38996, f. 203.
79. BL Add. MS 38996, f. 297.
80. Hansard, Vol. 196, col. 1210.
81. Street, p. 4.
82. *Ibid.* p. 5.
83. *Ibid.* pp. 6–7.
84. *Ibid.* p. 9.
85. *Ibid.* p. 10.
86. *Ibid.* p. 12.
87. *Ibid.* p. 17.
88. *Ibid.* p. 21.
89. BL Add. MS 44438, f. 325.

Chapter 19: The Reforming Mind (page 765)

1. BL Add. MS 44637, f. 73.
2. Parkes 29/4, p. 8.
3. Parkes 29/4 p. 9.
4. Gladstone, *Diaries*, Vol. VIII, (Preface), p. lxxxiii.
5. Garvin, p. 139.
6. Cross, p. 19.

7. Gladstone, *Diaries*, Vol. VII, (Preface), p. lxxxvii.
8. Fulford, *DC*, p. 129.
9. Anon., p. 8.
10. *Ibid.* p. 10.
11. BL Add. MS 44133, ff. 131 and 133.
12. M&B, Vol. V, p. 284.
13. Cecil, Vol. II, p. 50.
14. M&B, V, p. 286.
15. *Ibid.* p. 351.
16. Russell, G., p. 253.
17. *Ibid.* p. 249.
18. Disraeli, Manchester, p. 4.
19. *Ibid.* p. 6.
20. *Ibid.* p. 18.
21. *Ibid.* p. 19.
22. *Ibid.* pp. 21–2.
23. *Ibid.* pp. 22–3.
24. *Ibid.* p. 25.
25. Cross, p. 25.
26. *The Times*, 24 and 26 January 1874, *passim*.
27. Hansard, Vol. 218, col. 1226.
28. *Ibid.* Vol. 218, col. 1228.
29. *Ibid.* Vol. 218, col. 1231.
30. *Ibid.* Vol. 218, col. 1759.
31. *Ibid.* Vol. 218, col. 1762.
32. *Ibid.* Vol. 218, col. 1771.
33. *Ibid.* Vol. 218, col. 1791.
34. *Ibid.* Vol. 219, col. 1416.
35. *Ibid.* Vol. 219, col. 1421.
36. *Ibid.* Vol. 219, cols 1424–5.
37. *Ibid.* Vol. 219, col. 1426.
38. *Ibid.* Vol. 219, col. 1430.
39. *Ibid.* Vol. 219, col. 1463.
40. *Ibid.* Vol. 219, col. 1467.
41. *Ibid.* Vol. 222, col. 392.
42. *Ibid.* Vol. 224, col. 438.
43. *Ibid.* Vol. 224, col. 440.
44. *Ibid.* Vol. 224, col. 441.
45. BL Add. MS 51272, ff. 81–2.
46. Arnold, *Reports*, p. 125.
47. *Ibid.* p. 126.
48. Hansard, Vol. 224, col. 1565.
49. *Ibid.* Vol. 224, col. 1567.
50. *Ibid.* Vol. 224, col. 1569.
51. *Ibid.* Vol. 224, cols 1580–1.
52. *Ibid.* Vol. 224, cols 1591–2.

53. *Ibid.* Vol. 224, col. 1603.
54. *Ibid.* Vol. 224, col. 1605.
55. *Ibid.* Vol. 229, col. 931.
56. *Ibid.* Vol. 229, col. 933.
57. *Ibid.* Vol. 229, col. 958.
58. *Ibid.* Vol. 229, col. 957.
59. *Ibid.* Vol. 229, col. 1899.
60. *Ibid.* Vol. 229, col. 1904.
61. *Ibid.* Vol. 230, col. 31.
62. *Ibid.* Vol. 230, col. 48.
63. *Ibid.* Vol. 230, col. 1407.
64. *Ibid.* Vol. 231, col. 566.
65. *Ibid.* Vol. 237, col. 1466.
66. *Ibid.* Vol. 237, col. 1469.
67. *Ibid.* Vol. 238, col. 64.
68. *Ibid.* Vol. 238, col. 76.
69. *Ibid.* Vol. 238, cols 880–1.
70. *Ibid.* Vol. 239, cols 261–2.
71. *Ibid.* Vol. 239, col. 947.
72. *Ibid.* Vol. 239, col. 948.
73. Vicnius, p. 77.
74. Hansard, Vol. 225, col. 351.
75. *Ibid.* Vol. 225, col. 352.
76. *Ibid.* Vol. 225, col. 357.
77. *Ibid.* Vol. 225, col. 362.
78. *Ibid.* Vol. 225, col. 368.
79. *Ibid.* Vol. 225, col. 370.
80. *Ibid.* Vol. 225, col. 401.
81. Hansard, Vol. 218, col. 1945.
82. *Ibid.* Vol. 218, col. 1969.
83. *Ibid.* Vol. 222, col. 97.
84. *Ibid.* Vol. 222, col. 98.
85. *Ibid.* Vol. 222, col. 99.
86. *Ibid.* Vol. 222, col. 100.
87. *Ibid.* Vol. 222, cols 101–2.
88. *Ibid.* Vol. 222, col. 104.
89. *Ibid.* Vol. 222, cols 110–11.
90. Cross, p. 34.
91. Garvin, p. 198. Haussmann was rebuilding Paris at around the same time.
92. M&B, Vol. V, p. 491.
93. *Ibid.* p. 492ff.
94. Fulford, *DC*, p. 222.
95. M&B, Vol. V, p. 519.
96. Hansard, Vol. 225, col. 525.
97. M&B, Vol. VI, p. 67.
98. BL Add. MS 45805, f. 131.
99. Gladstone, *Diaries*, Vol. IX, p. 498.
100. *Ibid.* p. 499.
101. *Ibid.* p. 500.
102. BL Add. MS 44349, f. 132.
103. Gladstone, *Diaries*, Vol. IX, (Preface), p. lxv.
104. Cross, p. 65.
105. M&B, Vol. VI, p. 524.
106. *Ibid.* p. 525.
107. *Ibid.* p. 526.
108. *Ibid.* p. 528.
109. *Ibid.* p. 532.
110. *Ibid.* p. 534.
111. *Ibid.* p. 535.
112. Gladstone, *Diaries*, Vol. IX, p. 503.
113. BL Add. MS 44764, f. 43.
114. M&B, Vol. VI, p. 538.
115. BL Add. MS 44764, f. 50.
116. M&B, Vol. VI, p. 539.
117. http://www.oxforddnb.com/view/article/679
118. BL Add. MS 44475, ff. 5–6.
119. BL Add. MS 44438, ff. 137–8.
120. BL Add. MS 44438, f. 207.
121. BL Add. MS 44439, f. 13.
122. BL Add. MS 44766, f. 82.
123. BL Add. MS 44766, f. 175.
124. BL Add. MS 44470, ff. 239–40.

INDEX

PICTURE ACKNOWLEDGEMENTS

Illustrations are reproduced by kind permission of: The Bridgeman Art Library: William Wyld: *Manchester from the Cliff, Higher Broughton* (Manchester Art Gallery); *Peel's Cheap Bread Shop* (Private Collection); Thomas Henry Huxley: Letter to Charles Darwin (Private Collection); Nathan Hughes: *Manhood Suffrage Riots in Hyde Park* (Private Collection); George William Frederick Charles, 2nd Duke of Cambridge, from *The Cabinet Portrait Gallery* (London, 1890–1894) (© Universal History Archive / UIG); Sir George Hayter: *Portrait of the Hon. Mrs Caroline Norton* (© Chatsworth Settlement Trustees); Anna Lea Merritt: *Portrait of Sir Gilbert Scott* (The Heckscher Museum of Art, Huntington). Mary Evans Picture Library: *A Lancashire Cotton-Mill* (Pictorial Gallery of Arts and Sciences); Anthony Ashley-Cooper, 7th Earl of Shaftesbury, sepia photograph by Maull & Co., London; Robert Peel, unattributed portrait (© INTERFOTO / Sammlung Rauch); Chartist demonstration (© Illustrated London News Ltd.); James Anthony Froude, Woodbury photograph; J. C. Armytage: Charles Kingsley; Samuel Wilberforce, sepia photograph by Mowbray, Oxford; Thomas Henry Huxley, unattributed photograph; John Stuart Mill, unattributed photograph (© Everett Collection); William Ewart Gladstone, unattributed photograph; Robert Lowe, unattributed photograph; G. Cook: Richard Assheton, from a photograph by the London Stereoscopic Company; Queen Victoria and Prince Albert, unattributed photograph (© Alinari Archives); James Tissot: *Sir Henry Cole*; Edward Viscount Cardwell, from *Men of Mark: Contemporary Portraits*; William Edward Forster, unattributed photograph; Millicent Garrett Fawcett, photograph by Downey; Newnham College, Cambridge, unattributed photograph (© The Women's Library, London); General William Booth, unattributed photograph (© Illustrated

London News Ltd.); George Edmund Street, unattributed photograph. The National Portrait Gallery: Émile Desmaisons: *Sir James Robert George Graham, 2nd Bt*; Samuel Rowse: *Arthur Hugh Clough*; Samuel Laurence: *John Frederick Denison Maurice*; Sir George Reid: *Samuel Smiles*; Sir James Fitzjames Stephen 1st Bt, photograph by the London Stereoscopic & Photographic Company; Henry Gales: *The Derby Cabinet of 1867*; Elliott & Fry: Matthew Arnold; John Singer Sargent: *Octavia Hill*; Angela Georgina Burdett-Coutts, by an unknown artist. St John's College, University of Cambridge: Samuel Butler: *Family Prayers*; Samuel Butler: *Self-Portrait*.

nexus
obloquy